Microsoft

Microsoft®
Windows® 2000
Server
Administrator's
Companion

PUBLISHED BY
Microsoft Press
A Division of Microsoft Corporation
One Microsoft Way
Redmond, Washington 98052-6399

Library of Congress Cataloging-in-Publication Data
Russel, Charlie.
   Microsoft Windows 2000 Server Administrator's Companion / Charlie Russel, Sharon Crawford.
     p. cm.
   ISBN 1-57231-819-8
     1. Microsoft Windows 2000 server.   2. Operating systems (Computers)   I. Title: Server
administrator's companion.   II. Crawford, Sharon.   III. Title.

QA76.76.O63 R879 2000
005.4'4769--dc21   99-048555

Printed and bound in the United States of America.

4 5 6 7 8 9   WCWC   5 4 3 2 1 0

Distributed in Canada by Penguin Books Canada Limited.

A CIP catalogue record for this book is available from the British Library.

Microsoft Press books are available through booksellers and distributors worldwide. For further
information about international editions, contact your local Microsoft Corporation office, or contact Microsoft Press International directly at fax (425) 936-7329. Visit our Web site at
mspress.microsoft.com.

Acquisitions Editor: David Clark
Project Editor: Barbara Moreland
Technical Editors: Nick Cavalancia, James W. Johnson
Manuscript Editors: Rebecca Pepper, Chrisa Hotchkiss

Dedication

To Kathy Crockett and Pam Truswell, who opened their hearts to us.

"Old friends is always best,
'less you can catch a new one that's fit to make an old one out of."
Sarah Orne Jewett (1849-1909)

Acknowledgments

Two years in the making! A cast of thousands!

Only a little bit of an exaggeration when describing this book, because so many people made contributions both concrete and theoretical to its composition and construction. To begin at the beginning:

Thanks to acquisitions editor David Clark and our agent, David Rogelberg, for their unflagging work and support throughout this project. From the earliest discussions through the last desperate hours, they were there. We are truly grateful. Thanks also to Anne Hamilton, acquisitions manager, who rode to the rescue more than once.

We owe a debt of gratitude to the team at Microsoft Press—especially project editor Barbara Moreland, who has astounding patience and managed to maintain her composure and professionalism even in the midst of the editorial equivalent of the Great Flood. Thanks also to copy editors Rebecca Pepper and Chrisa Hotchkiss and to technical editors Jim Johnson and Nick Cavalancia. It was their task to read and correct nearly 2000 pages of manuscript while retaining both a broad overview and their sanity. They achieved the former, and we can't speak to the latter.

We also appreciate the contributions made by other talented members of the Press production team: Elizabeth Hansford, desktop publisher; Cheryl Penner, senior proofreader/copy editor; Joel Panchot, senior electronic artist; Bill Teel, publishing support specialist; and Julie Kawabata, indexer.

Thanks to all the participants in the Microsoft Windows 2000 beta newsgroups from whom we garnered essential information, tips, and insights. Both beta testers and Microsoft representatives were often extraordinarily helpful, far above and beyond the call of duty.

On a personal level, we'd like to express our appreciation to Madeline Selig of Spear Technologies for being both understanding and flexible in allowing Charlie the time to complete the book.

As always, we thank Dianne King and the late Dr. Rudolph S. Langer, who first placed our feet on the writing road and nudged us along the way.

Contributors

We would like to pretend that we know all there is to know about Microsoft Windows 2000 Server and that, therefore, we could have written every word of this book without a bit of help. But even if there were time enough, the range of subjects and the degree of expertise necessary to do justice to this complex product meant that we needed to bring in some true experts and specialists.

Tom Fronckowiak (LJL Enterprises) contributed two of the chapters on security. His insights and experience were invaluable in helping explain both the concepts and implementation of protective measures in Windows 2000.

L.J. Locher was our expert on performance monitoring and tuning. She wrote about the subject in depth and with admirable clarity.

Mitch Tulloch (MTIT Enterprises, *http://www.mtit.com*) is the expert's expert on Internet services, and we greatly appreciate his professionalism as well as his technical skills.

Paul E. Robichaux (Robichaux & Associates, Inc.) is the computer world's Renaissance man. He is an expert on more subjects than seems fair to the rest of us. In this book, he contributed chapters on Macintosh services, Certificate Services, and managing the registry—subjects that are, for all intents and purposes, totally unrelated—yet he wrote masterfully about all three.

Craig Zacker made enormously valuable contributions on the subjects of Active Directory and Backup. Particularly in the area of Active Directory, his knowledge is unparalleled.

Mickey Souza, whose skill and good humor are exceeded only by her modesty, was our source for information on third-party backup systems.

The companion CD-ROM was organized and designed by Dianne Blake (*http://www.members.home.net/write-it*), who labored long to gather all the software and tips. Our aim was to have a CD that was truly useful and that added real value to the book. We think Dianne met and exceeded that goal.

All these contributors performed well beyond our expectations and made the long process of putting together a very large book much less difficult.

Special Contributor

In the early phases of this project, we wanted to hire someone with basic Windows skills to help us write two or three chapters. An old friend, Stephen Nelson, author of many books, recommended a young and talented newcomer, Jason Gerend.

Jason turned out to be a pearl beyond price—a treasure, in fact. This book would have been much the poorer without his contributions. He didn't just write chapters, he took ownership of them. He made suggestions, pointed out omissions, and did a great deal of research around questions that weren't even his direct responsibility. In addition to being smart, hardworking, and a bundle of energy and initiative, Jason is a splendid human being whom we'd be glad to know, even if he hadn't been such a great collaborator. We've never worked with anyone better—or more fun. We were lucky and delighted to have him as a member of the team.

Contents at a Glance

Part VII
Appendixes

Table of Contents

9 Managing Users and Groups 240

Part III
Network Administration

16   Configuring Storage   538

Part IV
Support Services and Features

24 Managing Software   854

Part V
Internet Servers and Services

Part VI
Tuning, Maintenance, and Repair

Part VII
Appendixes

Introduction

Microsoft Windows 2000 Server is a complex product, and describing it adequately requires significant effort and results in a long, possibly intimidating, book. We've made every effort to make *Microsoft Windows 2000 Server Administrator's Companion* as comprehensive as possible, but, in fact, it's difficult to cover everything in a single volume because so many subjects are worthy of whole books themselves. However, this book should stand any IT implementer—network administrator, systems analyst, help desk professional—in good stead.

The IT implementer can use this book in several ways. It can be read as a

- Guide to deployment
- Ready reference
- Help to making decisions about network organization and operations
- Thorough introduction to the particulars of Windows 2000 Server

We assume a fundamental understanding of networking and the Microsoft Windows family of operating systems, but we don't expect every reader to be an expert on every subject. We've tried to provide background where appropriate, as well as references to additional information.

What's In the Book

We've divided *Microsoft Windows 2000 Server Administrator's Companion* into seven parts, roughly corresponding to each stage in the development of a Windows 2000 network.

- **Part I: Preparing for Installation** Perhaps you've heard Edison's famous quote, "Genius is one percent inspiration and ninety-nine percent perspiration." Modify that slightly and you have a good motto for network building: "A good network is one percent implementation and ninety-nine percent preparation." That's why this book begins with four chapters of planning advice. The first chapter is an overview of Windows 2000, its components, and its features. This is followed by chapters on directory services and namespace planning. The last chapter in this section covers specific issues that need to be addressed when planning your deployment.

- **Part II: Installation and Initial Configuration** This part takes you through the process of installing Windows 2000 and configuring hardware. Also included are chapters on upgrading to Windows 2000 and managing users.

- **Part III: Network Administration** Part III covers day-to-day tasks involved in running a network, including implementing Active Directory, managing storage options, and configuring security.

- **Part IV: Supporting Services and Features** This part addresses the main services that are included with Windows 2000 Server. While few networks will need all of the features Windows 2000 Server offers, all administrators will need to be familiar with messaging and managing software and most will find reading about advanced features useful. You'll find chapters on interoperating with other operating systems plus chapters on Terminal Services, Certificate Services, and Indexing Service.

- **Part V: Internet Servers and Services** In Part V, we cover the components that connect you to the outside world—and, in turn, connect that world to you. Here you'll find chapters on Internet connectivity, Proxy Server, and remote access.

- **Part VI: Tuning, Maintenance, and Repair** This part covers important material on network health. There's a chapter on the performance monitoring tools included with Windows 2000 Server and how to use them. There are also chapters on the important topics of disaster planning and prevention. If, despite your best efforts, the network falters, here's where you'll find a chapter on troubleshooting and recovery. In addition, we include a chapter on the registry—the brains of Windows 2000 Server—and some advice if you're contemplating brain surgery.

- **Part VII: Appendixes and Glossary** At the end of the book, you'll find supplemental material that can prove useful for quick access to important information. The glossary covers terms new to Windows 2000 and familiar terms that take on new meaning. Six appendixes cover the interface changes in Windows 2000 Server, the components that are part of the package, the tools included as part of the software, and other useful information.

Within the chapters themselves, we've tried to make the material as accessible as possible. You'll find descriptive and theoretical information, as well as many step-by-step examples for how to implement or configure a particular feature. These are supplemented with graphics that make it easy to follow the written instructions.

In addition, we've made extensive use of the reader's aids common to all books in the Administrator's Companion series.

Note Notes generally represent alternate ways to perform a task or some information that needs to be highlighted.

Tip Methods of performing tasks more quickly or in a not-so-obvious manner will show up as tips.

More Info References to other books and sources of information are offered throughout the book.

Caution Don't skip over these boxes because they contain important warnings about the subject at hand—often critical information about the safety of your system.

Planning As we stress throughout the book, proper planning is fundamental to the smooth operation of any network. These boxes contain specific and useful hints to make that process go smoothly.

Real World

Everyone benefits from the experiences of others. Real World boxes contain elaboration on a particular theme or background based on the adventures of IT professionals just like you.

We encourage you to take advantage of other books offered by Microsoft Press. In addition to other Windows 2000 titles, the Technical Reference series will provide you with in-depth coverage of specific topics. And the *Windows 2000 Server Resource Kit* is highly recommended for every administrator.

Talk to Us

We've done our best to make this book as accurate and complete as a single-volume reference can be. However, because Windows 2000 Server is such a large and complex product, we're sure that alert readers will find omissions and even errors (though we fervently hope not too many of those). If you have suggestions, corrections, or comments please write and let us know at *W2KServerAdmin@scribes.com*. We genuinely appreciate hearing from you and sincerely hope you find *Microsoft Windows 2000 Server Administrator's Companion* enjoyable and useful.

Part I
Preparing for Installation

Chapter 1
Overview of Windows 2000   2

Chapter 2
Introducing Directory Services   16

Chapter 3
Planning Namespace and Domains   28

Chapter 4
Planning Deployment   42

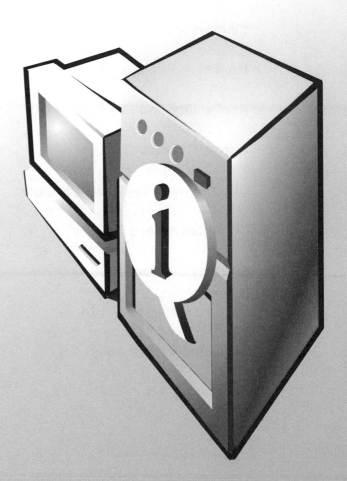

Chapter 1
Overview of Windows 2000

As with any new operating system, there has been a great deal of hype, speculation, criticism, praise, and confusion surrounding Microsoft Windows 2000—and it's undoubtedly worthy of some of each. It's certainly a big advance in the areas of network management, hardware support, Internet access, and more. That's not to say there aren't limitations, however. Windows 2000 has to work in the present as well as the future, and the necessity of backward compatibility results in compromises that are essential but probably not what one would hope for in a perfect world.

However, the positive changes are many. Windows 2000 is certainly more reliable, is easier to manage (once you get used to the changes), and is faster than Microsoft Windows NT. This chapter briefly summarizes Windows 2000, including significant changes to Windows NT Workstation (now called Windows 2000 Professional). *Microsoft Windows 2000 Server,* also called *Microsoft Windows 2000 Server Standard Edition,* is the successor to Microsoft Windows NT 4. Based on Active Directory, it features Kerberos and public-key infrastructure (PKI) security, Terminal Services, COM+, Component Services, Internet Information Services, Indexing Service, and Message Queuing. It also includes up to 4 GB of physical memory and up to 4-way symmetric multiprocessing (SMP).

Microsoft Windows 2000 Advanced Server is the successor to Microsoft Windows NT 4 Enterprise Edition. It has all the features of Windows 2000 Server plus network load balancing, enhanced application failover clustering, up to 8 GB of physical memory, and up to 8-way SMP. *Microsoft Windows Datacenter Server,* which will be released after the two products mentioned above, will have the features of Advanced Server plus up to 32-way SMP, up to 64 GB of physical memory, and even more advanced clustering.

In this book, we make no distinctions among the servers, except that the clustering described is the cluster service released with Windows 2000 Advanced Server. So, except for that limited case, the word *server* applies to all versions of Windows 2000.

Deploying Server and Workstation Functions Together

Even more than in the past, the deployment of Windows 2000 Professional and Windows 2000 Server together will provide exceptional benefits from the zero administration for Windows (ZAW) technologies. These technologies intelligently store user data, applications, system files, and administrative settings from Windows 2000 Professional–based desktops onto servers running Windows 2000 Server.

For example, IntelliMirror is a distributed and highly configurable replication service that allows clients and servers to mirror and share local or distributed file system data. IntelliMirror's Remote Boot Service provides a mechanism for any authorized client computer to download all or part of an installation from a remote server—including a fully configured version of the operating system, applications, and site-specific data.

With ZAW, an application assigned to a user simply appears on the user's Start menu and is installed the first time a user clicks on it. If the application isn't immediately required, the administrator can publish it so that it appears as an option in Add/Remove Programs for the user to install when needed. When an application upgrade becomes available, the upgrade is automatically applied the next time the user launches the application.

User documents and personal settings can be stored, or mirrored, on a server managed by an administrator. This provides

- **Improved access**   Users can log on to any PC on the network; all of their documents and personal settings will appear on any computer they use.

- **Increased availability**   The information mirrored on the server is also resident on the local machine, so it is available even when users aren't connected to the network. When a user reconnects, the information on the server is synchronized with the new local information. Because laptop users' data is synchronized with the server whenever a laptop is connected to the network, network administrators can back up mobile users' data even when the laptops are not connected.

- **Better protection**   All files reside on the server, which can be backed up as part of normal, centralized backup and restore procedures.

While the usual suspects—machines running Windows 95/98, Macintosh, and UNIX—can be connected as clients for Windows 2000 Server, the full range of improvements is available only to the combination of Windows 2000 Server and Windows 2000 Professional installed together. However, a great deal can be gained with gradual, partial upgrades. Benefits can be realized simply by upgrading a single server to Windows 2000 Server.

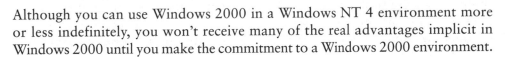

Caution   The primary domain controller (PDC) must be upgraded to Windows 2000 first. If you add a Windows 2000 controller or upgrade any controller other than the PDC on an existing Windows NT domain, you will create a new Windows 2000 domain that looks like the existing domain but is not the same domain.

Although you can use Windows 2000 in a Windows NT 4 environment more or less indefinitely, you won't receive many of the real advantages implicit in Windows 2000 until you make the commitment to a Windows 2000 environment.

Network Management

Admittedly, the network administrator's lot is not always a happy one, particularly when faced with big changes that may have a negative impact on the departmental budget as well as on what some quaintly refer to as a "personal life." There's no question that just about every improvement has its down side. There's the cost (in time) of learning about these new technologies and then putting them in place. Then there's the cost (in cash) of the inevitable hardware and software upgrades needed for deploying Windows 2000 Server and Windows 2000 Professional together in order to reap the technological benefits, not all of which will be immediately apparent (more about that later).

Nevertheless, what Microsoft taketh away with one hand, it often giveth back with the other. In the case of Windows 2000, your efforts will be rewarded with increased reliability, scalability, and security, plus the administrative tools to simplify the management of large and complicated networks.

Planning Even experienced Windows NT administrators (perhaps that should be *especially* experienced Windows NT administrators) should allow plenty of time to learn and practice the new concepts in Windows 2000. The organization of the interface will be unfamiliar, and a dedicated test network is essential for anyone coming to grips with Active Directory for the first time. The companion CD includes tools that can help with deployment.

The Microsoft Management Console

The Microsoft Management Console (MMC) hosts administrative tools displayed as consoles. These tools, composed of one or more applications, are built with modules called snap-ins. This design enables you to customize the tools so that you can delegate specific administrative tasks to users or groups. Saved as MMC files, these custom tools can be sent by e-mail, shared in a network folder, or posted on the Web. Using system policy settings, you can also assign MMC files to users, groups, or computers. A tool can be scaled up or down, integrated seamlessly into the operating system, repackaged, and customized. In fact, you can do everything with these tools short of adding pinstripes and custom upholstery. The details of creating and using Microsoft Management Consoles are covered in Chapter 10, although the use of MMCs is described in many other chapters.

Group Policy

Group Policy is a new management technology introduced in Windows 2000, used to specify options for desktop configurations for groups of computers and users. Group policies are saved as Group Policy objects that in turn are associated with Active Directory objects such as sites, domains, or organizational units (OUs). Group Policies can include security options, software installation and maintenance options, and options for scripts controlling startup and shutdown. Group Policy is covered in Chapter 9.

Zero Administration

The aim of Windows 2000 is to provide "no-touch" clients and servers. In other words, once the clients and servers are set up, hardware, software, and user changes are handled automatically, using rules and profiles to determine what happens. Administrators can control the rules for the entire network from a single central location. Although ZAW is not completely realized in Windows 2000, a good deal of progress has been made in that direction. Table 1-1 summarizes some of the centralized network management tasks in Windows 2000.

Table 1-1. Centralized management tasks in Windows 2000 Server

Task	What Is Done	Technologies Used
Manage user documents	Mirrors user data to the network and caches network data locally on the client	Active Directory, Group Policy, Offline Files, Synchronization Manager, disk quota, and shell enhancements
Manage user settings	Mirrors user settings to the network and applies administrator-set defaults to the user's environment	Active Directory, Group Policy, Offline Files, roaming user profiles, and shell enhancements
Perform remote OS installation	Installs operating system from network servers	Active Directory, Group Policy, Remote Install Server, Remote Installation–capable workstation
Manage user profiles	Allows users to "roam" among computers within the corporate network	Roaming user profiles, Group Policy
Install software	Provides just-in-time software installation (applications and operating system upgrades)	Active Directory, Group Policy, Windows Installer, Software Installation, Add/Remove Programs, Control Panel, and shell enhancements

Terminal Services

Terminal services allows Windows-based applications to run on desktops that can't normally run large Windows applications. All application processing and data storage take place on the server; the client machine needs only to be able to run a "thin client," which requires very small amounts of memory and disk storage space. (Under Windows 2000, a client can simultaneously be a thin client *and* a fat client.) This permits machines that would require hardware upgrades before they were able to run Windows 2000 to have access to applications that would otherwise be unavailable. With the use of a third-party add-on, even DOS, UNIX, and Macintosh machines can be clients.

With Terminal Services, users log on and see only their own session, which is completely independent of any other client session. The application operates on the server, and the entire process is transparent to the user. The setup and use of Terminal Services and Terminal Services clients is covered in Chapter 25.

Interoperability

The typical network in a medium to large enterprise is completely heterogeneous, so interoperability between and among operating systems is imperative. For improved interoperability, Windows 2000

- Communicates natively with UNIX and NetWare systems, using TCP/IP
- Provides services for file and print sharing with UNIX, NetWare, Macintosh, and IBM (this last using SNA Server)
- Supports Open Database Connectivity (ODBC) software, Message Queuing Services, and Component Object Model (COM+) so that new applications can interoperate with existing software and data

In addition, if you deploy Active Directory you can integrate multiple namespaces under various operating systems into one unified and easily manageable directory. Information on interoperating with Novell NetWare is covered in Chapter 20. Specifics about UNIX interoperability are covered in Chapter 21. Chapter 22 describes how to use Macintosh Services on a Windows 2000 network.

System and Network Security

Security is available in Windows 2000 for every configuration, from a simple workgroup to enterprise server systems. The emphasis on security and the fact that security mechanisms permeate every corner of Windows 2000 should not come as a surprise. Security is an increasingly critical issue in virtually every enterprise. Intranets, extranets, and dial-in access, not to mention casual user malfeasance, are all threats to both data and infrastructure. At the same time, an overly complex security apparatus tries the patience of administrators and users alike. Windows 2000 attempts to resolve these conflicting needs with a security system that is genuinely secure yet easy to administer and transparent to the user.

The Security Configuration Manager is a one-stop tool that lets an administrator configure security-sensitive registry settings, access controls on files, and registry keys all in one location. This information can be incorporated into a security template that can then be applied to multiple computers in a single operation.

Windows 2000 Server includes full support for the MIT Kerberos version 5 security protocol, providing a single logon to Windows 2000 Server–based enterprise resources. Kerberos replaces NT LAN Manager (NTLM), which is used in

Windows NT 4 as the primary security protocol. For smooth integration, Windows 2000 supports both methods of authentication—NTLM when either the client or the server is running a previous version of Windows, and Kerberos for Windows 2000 servers and clients. In addition, there is built-in support for Secure Socket Layer/Transport Layer Security (SSL/TLS) for users logging on to a secure Web server.

Other security enhancements include

- An X.509-based public-key certificate server integrated with Active Directory, allowing the use of public-key certificates for authentication.
- Support for tamper-resistant smart cards to store passwords, private keys, account numbers, and other security information.
- Microsoft Internet Protocol Security (IPSec), which governs end-to-end secure communication. Once IPSec is implemented, communications are secured transparently; no user training or interaction is required.

Many of the security functions in Windows 2000 are innate in Active Directory, and full implementation is available only when Active Directory is used. In addition, some security functions cannot be fully realized in a mixed environment of server domains. For example, Windows 2000 includes support for transitive trusts, which means that when a Windows 2000 domain is joined to a Windows 2000 domain forest, a two-way, transitive trust relationship is established automatically. No administrative tasks are required to establish this trust relationship. To set up a trust relationship between a Windows 2000 domain and a Windows NT domain, however, you must explicitly establish it.

Security is so firmly integrated into all aspects of Windows 2000 that it can't really be quarantined into a single section; hence you'll find security material throughout this book. However, basic security concepts are described in Chapter 17. Implementation is delineated in Chapters 18 and 19.

Hardware Support

Windows 2000 includes hundreds of new printer, modem, and other hardware drivers, making hardware installation and setup more efficient. The merger of the Windows NT development and test teams with those of Windows 98 opened up the world of devices supported by Windows 98. Consequently, Windows 2000 supports device types that are difficult to use in Windows NT. A bidirectional parallel port driver lets Windows 2000 communicate with many more scanners, printers, and fax/printer/scanner devices.

Plug and Play (PnP) has finally arrived with Windows 2000, which is especially good news for laptop users. However, many older laptops will need a flash BIOS upgrade or add-on software to take advantage of the power management of Windows 2000.

While adding much new hardware support, Windows 2000 retains compatibility with the Windows NT 4 video drivers. The catch is that using these video drivers will disable the power management functions in Windows 2000, although all other Windows NT 4 drivers should work. Microsoft is encouraging video vendors to write new drivers for Windows 2000, and eventually all of the native Windows NT 4 drivers will be revised.

Availability and Reliability

If you've used Windows NT Server, you no doubt noticed that practically every configuration change requires a reboot. Each time you install a scanner or a network driver or change any of a number of other configuration settings, you have to reboot—and usually right away.

There have been so many complaints about this annoying requirement that an early goal of the Windows 2000 development team was to eliminate as many required reboots as possible. Nearly 50 have been removed, and now a reboot is needed only after installing a service pack, upgrading a domain controller, changing system fonts, changing a default system locale, or adding and removing COM ports (when a change in jumpers is required). As you can see, these changes come up infrequently—a relief to the harried administrator. In addition, new tools to monitor system health can be instrumental in keeping servers up and running a higher percentage of the time.

Windows 2000 Advanced Server (the replacement for Windows NT Enterprise Edition) allows two servers to be connected into a cluster of up to 64 processors, making server resources more available and easier to manage. This cluster monitors the health of standard applications and servers and can automatically recover mission-critical data and applications from many common types of failure—usually in less than a minute. Clustering is covered in Chapter 15.

Active Directory

A directory service is a tool that connects the directories across the network and acts like a big phone book for all users. Using general input (for example, "where are the printers?"), a user can receive a listing of printer resources. The directory services in Windows NT 4 provide important functions in the form of a single logon and a single point of administration and replication. While these are critical, the Windows NT 4 directory services don't scale well enough. Active Directory is the next generation of Microsoft's directory services and offers great advances in scalability, extensibility, and security while providing a hierarchical view of the directory and multimaster replication.

Active Directory combines X.500 naming standards, the Internet's Domain Name System (DNS) as a locating device, and Lightweight Directory Access Protocol (LDAP) as the core protocol. Active Directory allows a single point of administration for all resources, including users, files, peripheral devices, host connections, databases, Web access, services, and network resources. It supports a hierarchical namespace for user, group, and machine account information and can encompass and manage other directories to reduce the administrative burdens and costs associated with maintaining multiple namespaces.

As you can see, there's a lot of good news about Active Directory—including that it paves the way for eliminating the concept of domains. The actual migration to Active Directory is not very difficult, but planning the design of your new directories can be vexatious. Design mistakes can harm the stability and efficiency of the network. Fortunately, you don't need to get rid of your existing domains to take advantage of Active Directory, and migration can be piecemeal. Servers can be upgraded from Windows NT 4 to Windows 2000 without the users being aware of any changes.

Chapters 2 and 3 explore the concepts behind Active Directory—including namespace design. Specific implementation is discussed in Chapters 11 and 12.

Storage and File System Support

Great changes have been made in the area of storage and file system support, including a new version of NTFS—version 5—that allows disk quotas for monitoring and limiting disk space usage on NTFS volumes while drastically improving security. Administrators can establish global disk quotas that prevent users from saving or copying more data to a storage device once they have reached their quota.

Removable Storage

Removable Storage lets you manage your online libraries, such as changers and jukeboxes, and track removable tapes and disks. It presents a common interface to robotic media changers and media libraries, and enables multiple applications to share local libraries and tape or disk drives. It also controls removable media within a single-server system.

Remote Storage

Remote Storage makes it easy to increase disk space on the server without adding more hard disks. It automatically monitors the amount of free space available on local hard disks. When the free space on a managed hard disk goes below a specified level, Remote Storage automatically removes any local data that Removeable Storage has already copied to Remote Storage (while keeping the directory and property information active), providing the free disk space you need. Working with Remote Storage, Hierarchical Storage management moves data to slower, low-cost storage devices until needed. When required, the data is automatically moved back to faster disk drives. Both Remote and Removable Storage are covered in Chapter 16.

Disk Administrator

Using Windows 2000 Server Disk Administrator, system administrators can create, extend, or mirror a volume without shutting down the system or interrupting users. These tasks can be performed remotely. In addition, volume mount points make hundreds of disk volumes accessible without drive letter limitations. The details of disk administration are covered in Chapter 14.

Microsoft Distributed File System

Microsoft Distributed File System (Dfs) identifies files using a common naming scheme, making it easy to browse the network to find the data and files you need. With Dfs, you can create a single directory tree that includes multiple file servers and file shares in a group, division, or enterprise, so you can have logical views of directories and files, regardless of where those files physically reside on the network. Dfs is covered in Chapter 16.

NTFS 5

The new version of NTFS offers many performance enhancements and a host of new features. System administrators have requested many of these features for some time—most notably per-user disk quotas. Also part of the NTFS 5 package is distributed link tracking. With this tracking system, even after a file is moved or has undergone a name change, a shortcut link to the file will still work. Public-key encryption is also included in NTFS 5, enabling you to protect and easily manage sensitive material in a manner that is totally transparent to the user.

The not-so-good news about NTFS 5 is that its new features make dual booting more complex. To dual boot with Windows NT 4 and have an NTFS partition, you must use Windows NT 4 with the latest service pack. The service pack will make the NTFS 5 files readable when the machine is booted into Windows NT. See Chapter 5 for more on issues of dual booting.

Communications

Communication is the lifeblood of businesses—and not just network communications, important as they are. Windows 2000 includes dozens of enhancements to make communicating easier and more reliable. For connections both inside and outside your business, Windows 2000 offers the following tools:

- Through the Internet support built into Windows 2000 Professional, users can send e-mail, chat, and view newsgroups.

- Windows 2000 provides client support for the industry-standard virtual private network (VPN) through two protocols: the Point-To-Point Tunneling Protocol (PPTP) and the Layer Two Tunneling Protocol (L2TP). These protocols allow clients or branch offices to connect to another network (such as their corporate network) over the Internet.

- Microsoft Outlook Express, an Internet standards–based e-mail client, is built into Windows 2000 Professional.

- Users can send, receive, monitor, and administer faxes directly from the desktop. Several easy-to-use utilities are available right from the Start menu.

Internet Services

With Windows 2000, anything that can be done on a corporate network can be done in a Web environment as well. Windows 2000 incorporates a set of services that provide server-side support for the most popular application-level Internet protocols, enabling a Windows 2000 server to function as a Web server, FTP server, SMTP host, or NNTP host.

In the Microsoft Windows NT 4 operating system, these services are provided by an optional component called Internet Information Server. To obtain full support for Internet services in a Windows NT 4 environment, administrators must install Internet Information Server after applying Service Pack 3 or later for Windows NT 4 Server and the Windows NT 4 Option Pack. By contrast, basic Internet services are fully integrated into the Windows 2000 Server and Windows 2000 Advanced Server platforms. These services are now referred to as Internet Information Services 5 instead of Internet Information Server.

Because Internet Information Services are fully integrated with Windows 2000, you can do things like host multiple Web sites on a single Windows 2000 server with only one IP address. In addition, each Web site can have its own user database, which means that multiple independent user domains can coexist on a single server.

Defying Categories

As you can tell from the previous sections, it's difficult to pigeonhole many of the changes in Windows 2000. The NTFS 5 file system affects disk management because it allows the setting of disk quotas for monitoring and limiting disk space usage on NTFS volumes. At the same time, it's an important security component, adding file encryption to its existing security capabilities.

As a result, neat categories aren't always possible. The discussions in this book are organized around particular tasks, thus avoiding a laundry list of tools and their menus.

The Need for Planning

Whether one is designing a new network or making changes to an existing one, planning is the essential, nonglamorous, before-everything-else component. Few enjoy and many actively dislike this task, but it's important to understand that every minute, every hour spent planning will later repay you (or your heirs and assigns) a hundredfold.

Sometimes it's difficult to appreciate the benefits of careful planning—until you've had the misfortune of having to support a poorly considered installation. Windows 2000 is particularly unforgiving of an offhand approach to planning. As has been mentioned before, you can add Windows 2000 Server or Professional to a Windows NT 4 network. However, unless you plan on eventually using Active Directory and other Windows 2000–specific tools, the benefits of just plugging in a couple of Windows 2000 machines will be minimal. And in all cases, designing directories—not to mention applying new concepts such as forests and trees—requires considerable thought and the ability to project current experience into the future. Therefore, the wise systems person takes a longer perspective.

Summary

This chapter has provided only the briefest overview of the Windows 2000 system and a look at just a few of the thousands of changes, large and small, that have been made. Deciding how to implement Windows 2000 on your system will require thought and planning. Although planning and design are important elements in nearly every chapter in this book, the next three chapters are devoted exclusively to the subject. Chapter 2 addresses your use of Active Directory. Chapter 3 covers planning namespace and domains. Finally, Chapter 4 covers the matters to be considered before deploying your first copy of Windows 2000.

Chapter 2
Introducing Directory Services

Everyone uses directories—on or off the computer. After all, if it weren't for the directory of television listings in the newspaper, you'd waste hours just channel surfing, looking for something to watch. (Maybe you do that anyway.)

Another type of directory that most of us find indispensable is the telephone directory. In fact, telephone directories are the source of the analogy for two searching capabilities that are necessary in computer directories. There's the "white pages" search by attribute, in which you know a name or some other fact about the object and you search using that piece of information. The second type of search, called a "yellow pages" search, is done by category. Having both types of searches available means that you don't have to know much about an object in order to locate it.

The lack of coherent, accessible directories is felt acutely on a network of any size. True directory services—a global catalog of network services and resources—are missing from Microsoft Windows NT networks. The directory functions available in version 4 do provide the all-important single logon and single point of administration that corporate environments need, but they have serious deficiencies when large numbers of users are involved. Attempts to organize documents in folders and directories work up to a point, but as the number of objects scales up, management becomes both complex and onerous.

Heretofore, the best-known computer directory service has been Novell Directory Services (NDS), introduced with NetWare 4.0 in 1993. Unfortunately for Novell, NetWare 4.0 had problems of its own that kept it from becoming dominant in the networking arena.

Understanding Directory Services

In a typical Windows NT computing environment, a user can log on to the network with a username, let's say Mperez, and a password. Assuming that permissions are correctly granted, Mperez can click on Network Neighborhood or open a mapped drive and browse for needed files.

All this works very well until the scope of the network changes. The company adds e-mail, and Mperez gains another identity (maryperez@scribes.com). The additional services and databases and administrative tools—each one identifying Mary Perez slightly differently—need to be accessible by the same user. When you consider that this is just one of hundreds or even thousands of users, it isn't hard to see how errors can arise that can be very difficult to solve. As the number of objects in a network grows, directory services—a centralized place for storing administrative data that is used to manage the entire computer system— becomes essential.

Directory services differs from a directory in that it consists of both the directory information source and the services that make the information available to users. Being both a management tool and an end user tool, directory services needs to address these needs:

- Access to all of the servers, applications, and resources through a single logon. (User access is granted or blocked using permissions.)
- Multimaster replication. All information is distributed throughout the system and replicated on multiple servers.
- "White pages" searches based on attributes—for example, by filename or file type.
- "Yellow pages" searches based on classification—for example, all the printers on the third floor or all the servers in the Hartford office.
- The ability to remove dependency on physical locations for purposes of administration. That is, it should be possible to delegate administration of the directory, either partially or completely.

Although Microsoft has occasionally used the term "directory services" in connection with Windows NT (as in the Directory Service Manager for NetWare), Windows NT does not provide a true, hierarchical directory service. In Windows NT, the directory functions are divided among a host of services based on domains. The Domain Name System (DNS) Server provides the translation of names into IP numbers and is integrated with Dynamic Host Configuration Protocol (DHCP) servers used to dynamically allocate TCP/IP addresses. The Windows Internet Naming Service (WINS) is used for NetBIOS name resolution and is required on Windows NT networks for file sharing and some applications. Security is implemented through access control lists (ACLs), the Security Accounts Manager (SAM) database, and other services.

In Microsoft Windows 2000 Server, Active Directory replaces the Windows NT collection of directory functions with an integrated implementation that includes

DNS, DHCP, Lightweight Directory Access Protocol (LDAP), and Kerberos. (You'll learn more about these later in this chapter.)

Real World   Directory Services and X.500

X.500 is a standard for directory services established by the International Telecommunications Union (ITU). The same standard is also published by the International Standards Organization/International Electrotechnical Commission (ISO/IEC). The X.500 standard defines the information model used in directory services. In this model, all information in a directory is stored in entries, each of which belongs to at least one object class. The actual information in an entry is determined by attributes that are contained in that entry.

The original 1988 X.500 standard focused heavily on the protocols to be implemented. Directory Access Protocol (DAP) specifies how user applications access the directory information. Directory Service Protocol (DSP) is used to propagate user directory requests between directory servers when the local directory server cannot satisfy the request.

No extant directory service completely implements the X.500 standard, but all are modeled on the basic specifications of X.500, as is Active Directory. An excellent introduction to directories and X.500 can be found at *http://www.nlc-bnc.ca/pubs/netnotes/notes45.htm.*

Active Directory in Windows 2000

Active Directory has numerous advantages, not the least of which is that it can handle any size of installation, from a single server with a few hundred objects to thousands of servers and millions of objects. Active Directory also greatly simplifies the process of locating resources across a large network. The Active Directory Services Interface (ADSI) allows developers to "directory-enable" their applications, giving users a single point of access to multiple directories, whether those directories are based on LDAP, NDS, or NT Directory Services (NTDS).

In Windows 2000, Active Directory integrates the Internet concept of a namespace with the operating system's directory services. This combination allows the unification of multiple namespaces in, for example, the mixed software and hardware environments of corporate networks—even across operating system boundaries. The ability to subsume individual corporate directories into a general-purpose directory means that Active Directory can greatly reduce the costs of administering multiple namespaces.

Active Directory is not an X.500 directory. Instead, it uses LDAP as the access protocol and supports the X.500 information model without requiring systems to host the entire X.500 overhead. LDAP is based on TCP/IP and is considerably simpler than the X.500 DAP. Like X.500, LDAP bases its directory model on entries, where the distinguished name (see the next section) is used to refer to an entry without ambiguity. But rather than use the highly structured X.500 data encoding, LDAP adopts a simple, string-based approach for representing directory entries. LDAP uses many of the directory-access techniques specified in the X.500 DAP standard but requires fewer client resources, making it more practical for mainstream use over a TCP/IP link.

Active Directory also directly supports Hypertext Transfer Protocol (HTTP). Every object in Active Directory can be displayed as a Hypertext Markup Language (HTML) page in a Web browser. Directory support extensions to the Microsoft Internet Information Service (IIS) translate HTTP requests for directory objects into HTML pages for viewing in any HTML client.

Active Directory allows a single point of administration for all published resources, which can include files, peripheral devices, host connections, databases, Web access, users, other arbitrary objects, services, and so forth. It uses the Internet DNS as its locator service, organizes objects in domains into a hierarchy of organizational units (OUs), and allows multiple domains to be connected into a tree structure. The concepts of primary domain controller (PDC) and backup domain controller (BDC) no longer exist. Active Directory uses domain controllers only, and all domain controllers are peers. An administrator can make changes to any domain controllers, and the updates will be replicated on all other domain controllers.

Terminology and Concepts in Active Directory

Some of the terms used to describe concepts in Active Directory have been around for a while in other contexts, so it's important to understand what they mean when used specifically in reference to Active Directory. This section covers these basic terms and concepts.

Namespace and Name Resolution

"Namespace" is perhaps an unfamiliar term for a very familiar concept. Every directory service is a *namespace*—a circumscribed area in which a name can be resolved. A television listing forms a namespace in which the names of television shows can be resolved to channel numbers. A computer's file system forms a namespace in which the name of a file can be resolved to the file itself.

Active Directory forms a namespace in which the name of an object in the directory can be resolved to the object itself. *Name resolution* is the process of translating a name into some object or information that the name represents.

Attribute

Each piece of information that describes some aspect of an entry is called an *attribute*. An attribute comprises an *attribute type* and one or more *attribute values*. An example of an attribute type might be "telephone number," and an example of a telephone number attribute value might be "345-678-9012."

Object

An *object* is a particular set of attributes that represents something concrete, such as a user, a printer, or an application. The attributes hold data describing the thing that is identified by the directory object. Attributes of a user might include the user's given name, surname, and e-mail address. The classification of the object defines which types of attributes are used. For example, the objects classified as "users" might allow the use of attribute types like "common name," "telephone number," and "e-mail address," while the object class "organization" would allow attribute types like "organization name" and "business category." An attribute can take one or more values, depending on its type.

Object Identity

Every object in Active Directory has a unique *identity*. Objects can be moved or renamed, but their identity never changes. Objects are known internally by their identity, not their current name. An object's identity is a globally unique identifier (GUID), which is assigned by the Directory System Agent (DSA) when the object is created. The GUID is stored in an attribute, *objectGUID*, that is part of every object. The *objectGUID* attribute can't be modified or deleted. When storing a reference to an Active Directory object in an external store (for example, a database), you should use *objectGUID* because, unlike a name, it won't change.

Container

A *container* resembles an object in that it has attributes and is part of the Active Directory namespace. However, unlike an object, a container doesn't represent anything concrete. It is a holder of objects and of other containers.

Tree and Subtree

A *tree* in Active Directory is just an extension of the idea of a directory tree. It's a hierarchy of objects and containers that demonstrates how objects are connected, or the path from one object to another. Endpoints on the tree are usually objects.

A *subtree* is any unbroken path in the tree, including all of the members of any containers in that path. Figure 2-1 shows a tree structure for microsoft.com. Any of the unbroken paths (for example, from nw.sales.seattle.microsoft.com to microsoft.com) is a subtree. Trees and forests are discussed in more detail in Chapter 3.

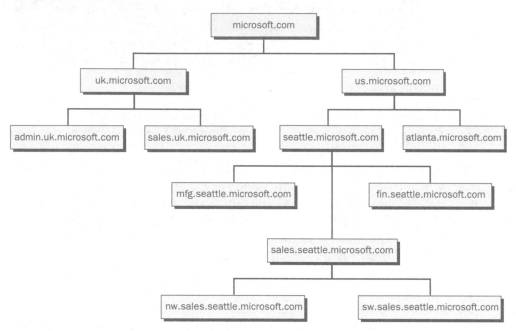

Figure 2-1. *A tree structure with subtrees.*

Distinguished Name

Every object in Active Directory has what's called a *distinguished name* (DN). In this context, "distinguished" means the qualities that make the name distinct. The distinguished name identifies the domain that holds the object as well as the complete path through the container hierarchy used to reach the object. A typical DN might be CN=Mary Perez,OU=Research,DC=scribes,DC=com. This DN identifies the "Mary Perez" user object in the Research organizational unit, in the scribes.com domain.

Note CN translates as common name, OU stands for organizational unit, and DC means domain controller. Some attributes are derived from the X.500 model; an administrator can define others.

Active Directory also uses a *relative distinguished name* (RDN), which is the part of the distinguished name that is an attribute of the object itself. In the previous example, the RDN of the user object is CN=Mary Perez. The RDN of the parent object is OU=Research.

The "DC=" portion of a distinguished name allows X.500 directories to plug in to the DNS namespace, which is also what Active Directory does. The root of the global namespace for Active Directory is the DNS namespace. Thus, DNS domain names merge within the Active Directory naming scheme. For example, scribes.com is a valid DNS domain name and could be the name of an Active Directory domain as well. This DNS integration means that Active Directory fits naturally into Internet and intranet environments. Active Directory servers can be connected directly to the Internet to simplify secure communications and electronic commerce with customers and partners.

Schema

"Schema" is a term commonly used in database work. In the context of Active Directory, the *schema* is all of the pieces that make up your Active Directory: the objects, attributes, containers, and so forth. Active Directory has a default schema that defines the most common object classes, such as users, groups, computers, organizational units, security policies, and domains.

The Active Directory schema can be updated dynamically. That is, an application can extend the schema with new attributes and classes and use the extensions immediately. Schema updates are done by creating or altering the schema objects stored in the directory. ACLs protect schema objects, so that only authorized users can modify the schema.

The Active Directory Architecture

As mentioned previously, Active Directory isn't, strictly speaking, an X.500 directory service, although like all existing directory services, it's derived from that standard. The sections that follow enumerate some of the characteristics of the Active Directory architecture.

The Directory System Agent

The DSA is the process that provides access to the physical store of directory information located on a hard disk. The DSA is part of the Local System Authority (LSA) subsystem in Windows 2000. Clients access the directory information using one of the mechanisms listed on the following page:

- LDAP clients connect to the DSA using the LDAP protocol. Active Directory supports LDAP v3, defined by RFC 2251; and LDAP v2, defined by RFC 1777. Windows 2000 Server clients and Windows 95/98 clients with the Active Directory client components installed use LDAP v3 to connect to the DSA.

- Messaging Applications Programming Interface (MAPI) clients such as Microsoft Exchange connect to the DSA using the MAPI Remote Procedure Call (RPC) interface.

- Windows clients that use Windows NT connect to the DSA using the SAM interface.

- Active Directory DSAs connect to each other to perform replication using a proprietary RPC interface.

Naming Formats

Active Directory supports several name formats to accommodate both users and applications:

- **RFC 822 names,** which are familiar to most users as Internet e-mail addresses, such as maryperez@scribes.com. Active Directory provides a "friendly name" in RFC 822 form for all objects. Thus, a user can use a friendly name both as an e-mail address and as the name used to log on.

- **HTTP URLs,** which are familiar to most users who have Web browsers. A typical URL takes the form *http://domain/path-to-page*, where *domain* refers to a server running Active Directory services and *path-to-page* is the path through the Active Directory hierarchy to the object of interest. The URL for Mary Perez is *http://AServer.scribes.com/Division/Product/Research/MaryPerez*.

- **LDAP names,** which are more complicated than Internet names but are usually hidden within an application. LDAP names use the X.500 attributed naming convention. An LDAP URL specifies the server holding Active Directory services and the attributed name of the object—for example, ldap://AServer.scribes.com/CN=maryperez,OU=Research, OU=Product,OU=Division,O=MegaIntl,C=US.

- **UNC names,** the universal naming convention used in Windows NT Server–based and Windows 2000 Server–based networks to refer to shared volumes, printers, and files. For example, *\\scribes.com\Division.Product.Research.Volume\WordDocs\aprilreport.doc*.

The Data Model

The Active Directory data model is derived from the X.500 data model. The directory holds objects that represent various items, described by attributes. The universe of objects that can be stored in the directory is defined in the schema. For each object class, the schema defines what attributes an instance of the class must have, what additional attributes it may have, and what object class can be a parent of the current object class.

Schema Implementation

The Active Directory schema is implemented as a set of object class instances stored in the directory. This is very different from directories that have a schema but store it as a text file that is read at startup. Storing the schema in the directory has many advantages. For example, user applications can read it to discover what objects and properties are available.

The Security Model

Active Directory is part of the Windows 2000 trusted computing base and is a full participant in the Windows 2000 security infrastructure. The distributed security model is based on the MIT Kerberos authentication protocol (version 5). Kerberos authentication accommodates both public-key and private-key security, using the same ACL support model as the underlying Windows 2000 operating system. ACLs protect all objects in Active Directory. They determine who can see the object, what attributes each user can see, and what actions each user can perform on the object. If a user is not allowed to see an object or an attribute, the fact of its existence is never made known to that user.

An ACL, in turn, is made up of Access Control Entries (ACEs) stored with the object the ACL protects. In Windows NT and Windows 2000, an ACL is stored as a binary value, called a security descriptor. Each ACE contains a security identifier (SID), which identifies the *principal* (user or group) to which the ACE applies and provides information on what type of access the ACE grants or denies.

ACLs on directory objects contain ACEs that apply to the object as a whole and ACEs that apply to the individual attributes of the object. This allows an administrator to control not just which users can see an object, but what properties those users can see. For example, all users might be granted read access to the e-mail and telephone number attributes for all other users, but access to the security properties of users might be denied to all but members of a special security administrators group. Also, individual users might be granted write access to personal attributes such as the telephone and mailing addresses on their own user objects.

Active Directory is the store for the security system, including user accounts, groups, and domains. This store replaces the registry account database and is a trusted component within the LSA.

Delegation and Inheritance

Delegation is one of the most important security features of Active Directory. An administrator can authorize a user to perform a specified set of actions in some identified subtree of the directory. This is called *delegated administration.* Delegated administration allows very fine-grained control over who can do what and enables administrators to delegate authority without granting elevated privileges. This also eliminates the need for domain administrators with broad authority over large segments of the user population.

Administrators grant rights for specific operations on specific object classes by adding ACEs to the container's ACL. For example, to allow user Mary Perez to be an administrator of the Research organizational unit, you would add ACEs to the ACL in Research as follows:

```
"Mary Perez";Grant ;Create, Modify, Delete;Object-Class User
"Mary Perez";Grant ;Create, Modify, Delete;Object-Class Group
"Mary Perez";Grant ;Write;Object-Class User; Attribute Password
```

Now Mary Perez can create new users and groups in Research and set the passwords for existing users, but she can't create other object classes and she can't affect users in other containers (unless, of course, ACEs grant her that access in the other containers).

Inheritance allows a given ACE to be propagated from the container in which it was applied to all children of the container. Inheritance can be combined with delegation to grant administrative rights to a whole subtree of the directory in a single operation.

Naming Contexts and Partitions

Active Directory is made up of one or more naming contexts or partitions. A *naming context* is any contiguous subtree of the directory. Naming contexts are the units of partitioning. A single server always holds at least three naming contexts:

- The schema
- The configuration (replication topology and related data)
- One or more user naming contexts (subtrees containing the actual objects in the directory)

The Global Catalog

The DN of an object includes enough information to locate a replica of the partition that holds the object. Many times, however, the user or application does not know the DN of the target object, or which partition might contain the object. The Global Catalog (GC) allows users and applications to find objects in an Active Directory domain tree, given one or more attributes of the target object.

The Global Catalog contains a partial replica of every naming context in the directory. It contains the schema and configuration naming contexts as well. This means that the GC holds a replica of every object in Active Directory, but with only a small number of their attributes. The attributes in the GC are those most frequently used in search operations (such as a user's first and last names, login name, and so on) and those required to find a full replica of the object. The GC allows users to quickly find objects of interest without knowing what domain holds them and without requiring a contiguous extended namespace in the enterprise.

The Global Catalog is built automatically by the Active Directory replication system. The replication topology for the GC is also generated automatically. The properties replicated into the GC include a base set defined by Microsoft. Administrators can specify additional properties to meet the needs of their installation. Specifics on the administration and deployment of Active Directory can be found in Chapters 11 and 12.

Summary

As you've no doubt gathered, Active Directory is a very powerful tool and, like most powerful tools, it can be the source of great trouble if mishandled. Allow time for careful thought and planning before deploying Active Directory. First to be considered is the design of a logical and efficient directory. A poor tree design can negatively affect the productivity and even the stability of the network. Chapter 3 covers how to plan your namespace and domains for both maximum utility and longevity.

Chapter 3
Planning Namespace and Domains

When you spend time analyzing your organizational structure and needs and determining how best to translate those requirements into your new namespace, you'll be rewarded by reduced support costs, improved flexibility, and less reorganizing later. It's important to understand that planning the namespace of a large or even medium-sized organization or company is an iterative process. You won't get it right the first time, but you need to start somewhere. You should also understand that much of the advice you'll receive will be based on politics and agendas, making the job more difficult than it should be.

Analyzing Naming Convention Needs

To plan what your namespace and domain structure should look like, you need to analyze your organization and attempt to understand its underlying naming needs. This process requires a thorough understanding of the type of organization you have and who the players are, as well as some educated guesses about where the organization will be going in the future.

Trees and Forests

As a first step, you'll need to understand the differences between the two basic types of namespaces—trees and forests—in order to decide how they line up with your organization. You can switch models later, but not without some pain and suffering, and not without having an impact on the overall names used, so take some time here to make sure you understand what your organization really needs. What the organization needs may well be different from what it thinks it wants.

Trees

A tree namespace, like that shown in Figure 3-1, is a single, contiguous namespace, with each name in the namespace directly descended from a single root name. This kind of straightforward naming design is appropriate for an organization that is essentially cohesive and has a single name underlying what may well be many different divisions and diverse businesses. Many small to midsize businesses will fit well within this model. Even very large businesses may be a comfortable fit for a tree structure if the organization is fairly centralized and has a single recognizable name.

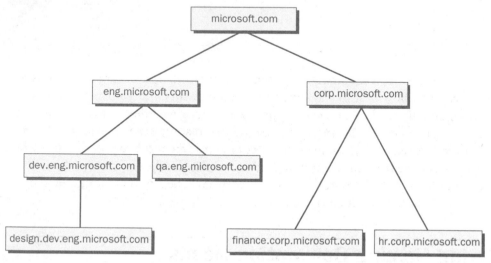

Figure 3-1. *A tree-structured namespace.*

As you can see from the figure, with a tree-structured namespace, each branch of the tree has a name that is directly descended from the root of the tree. This convention makes it easy to find any leaf or branch of the tree by tracing down the structure of its name.

Forests

A forest namespace, like that shown in Figure 3-2, is a collection of essentially equal trees, with no single root to the namespace. The forest namespace is appropriate for an organization that has multiple lines of business, each with its own separate and identifiable name. These will usually be larger businesses, especially those that have grown by acquisition. They typically do not have a single, central information systems group that manages the entire organization, and each of the divisions generally has an essentially separate identity and infrastructure.

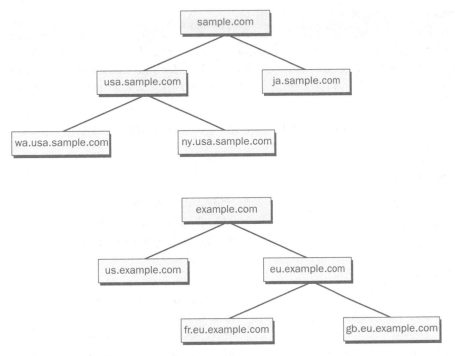

Figure 3-2. *A forest-structured namespace.*

As you can see from the figure, with a forest namespace you essentially have a peer group of trees, each its own contiguous namespace, but the trees do not fit into an overall, contiguous namespace. You can't directly trace the names of all the leaves back up to a single root.

Defining a Naming Convention

Whether you're going to have a single tree or a forest of trees for your overall namespace, you need to make some decisions about what the various branches of the tree will be called. This is easily one of the most delicate and politically sensitive decisions you'll have to make as you lay out your overall naming structure.

There are essentially two types of naming conventions—organizational and geographical. Both have their proponents, and an argument can be made for either choice. Keep in mind that people can get amazingly emotional about what their division or department is called and about its relative weight in the organization. Such political disagreements can be not only bitter but also prolonged beyond any reasonable expectation.

The Organizational Naming Convention

Using an organizational naming convention, you would model your namespace on the way your company or organization is structured. Thus, the root of your tree might be *microsoft.com*, with the first level under that consisting of *admin.microsoft.com*, *finance.microsoft.com*, *mfg.microsoft.com*, *hr.microsoft.com*, and so forth.

The following are advantages and disadvantages of the organizational naming convention.

Advantages

- Reflects company organization
- Is easily understood

- Has a natural growth path
- Permits resources to be organized by type of need

Disadvantages

- Is difficult to adjust when organizational structures and names change
- Can be politically sensitive

- Can be difficult to implement if divisions of the organization have multiple site locations
- Is difficult to support as divisions split and merge

Real World Sites

Sites, a new feature of Windows 2000 provided by the Active Directory, can be used to reduce or eliminate the problem of implementing the organizational naming structure with divisions that have multiple locations. A company can create a site for each island of computers with LAN connectivity. For example, the main office would be a site, and a branch office another site. Any domains that span more than one site automatically adjust their replication parameters to optimize the use of the slow WAN link between the sites. Clients are also automatically directed to local domain controllers for service requests, further decreasing the use of WAN links. For more information on sites and planning your site topology, see Chapter 7.

The Geographical Naming Convention

Using a geographical naming convention, you would model your namespace on the geographical divisions of the organization. For example, with the same root of *microsoft.com*, you might have a first level consisting of *corp.microsoft.com*, *noram.microsoft.com, europe.microsoft.com, africa.microsoft.com,* and so on. Under this first level, you might break each entry down to the individual country or state/province, depending on the size and complexity of your organization.

The following are advantages and disadvantages of the geographical naming convention.

Advantages

- Is apolitical
- Uses names that tend to be persistent
- Offers greater flexibility and granularity

Disadvantages

- Doesn't reflect the nature of the organization
- May require more domains to meet security needs

Tip Sites are useful for optimizing the use of slow WAN links on networks using a geographical naming convention. While usually there aren't any domains that span multiple sites in networks using the geographical naming convention, using sites further optimizes the use of WAN links by tuning inter-domain replication of the Active Directory.

Mixed Naming Conventions

Finally, you may opt to use a mixture of the organizational and geographical naming conventions, especially in a forest namespace where different corporate cultures have grown up and have their own agendas. The catch, of course, is that this can lead to a good deal of confusion and make any support task greater, since there is no consistency in how things are done. In creating your first Active Directory namespaces for Windows 2000, you really should consider making every effort to rationalize the structure, since it will make the overall support job easier in the long run.

Even if you go with a purely geographical naming convention across the whole organization, chances are you'll find it advantageous at the lowest level of the tree to create organizational units or domains because groups working in similar areas or on related projects tend to need access to resources of a similar nature. The needs on the manufacturing plant floor tend to be different from those in accounting, for example. These common needs can identify natural areas of administrative support and control.

Determining Name Resolution

A second decision that you must make is whether you want the namespace you use internally to be the same as the one that you present to the outside world. You might think that the names should be the same, but there can actually be compelling reasons to opt for different internal and external namespaces.

Using the Same Internal and External Namespace

When you have a single namespace, you and your machines have the same names on the internal network as on the Internet. In other words, you get a single name from the appropriate Internet registration authority and you maintain a single DNS namespace, although only a subset of the names will be visible from outside the company. Your network structure will end up looking something like Figure 3-3.

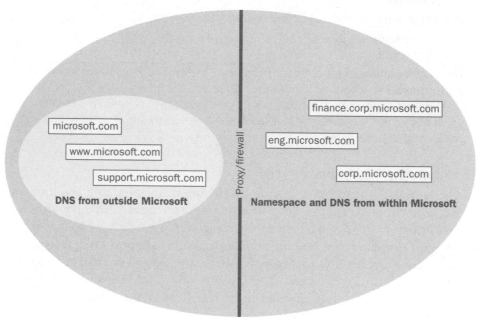

Figure 3-3. *A public/private network with a single namespace.*

When you use the same name for internal and external namespaces, you must ensure that the ability to resolve names from outside your company is limited to machines outside your firewall that are supposed to be externally visible. Make sure that no Active Directory servers reside outside the firewall. However, you'll also need to make sure that your internal machines can resolve names and access resources on both sides of the firewall.

The following are some advantages and disadvantages of using the same internal and external namespace.

Advantages

- Provides consistent naming internally and externally
- Allows single name registration
- Enables users to have a single logon identity and e-mail identity

Disadvantages

- Needs a complex proxy server configuration
- Requires maintenance of different zones that have the same names
- Requires users to work with different views of resources, depending on where they are

Using Different Internal and External Namespaces

If you set up different internal and external namespaces, your public presence might be *microsoft.com,* while internally you would use *msn.com.* All of the resources that reside outside the company network would have names that end in microsoft.com, such as *www.microsoft.com.* Within the company network, however, you'd use a separate namespace that has *msn.com* as its root, as shown in Figure 3-4.

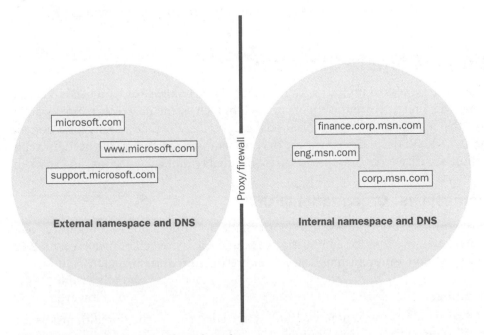

Figure 3-4. *Public/private network with separate namespaces.*

One consideration to remember with this scenario: you'll want to register both the public and private names with the appropriate Internet name registration authority. You might think that you don't need to worry about the internal-only name when you have no intention of exposing it to the Internet. What you're really doing, however, is making sure that no one else uses the same name, since this could cause name resolution problems for your internal clients.

The following are some advantages and disadvantages of using different internal and external namespaces.

Advantages

- Provides a clear distinction between what is internal and what is external
- Offers easier management and proxy configuration
- Makes it easier for users to understand the differences between the internal and external namespaces

Disadvantages

- Requires that two names be registered
- Means that users' logon names are different from their e-mail names

Planning a Domain Structure

Once you've settled on the overall design of your namespace, you need to design your domain structure to support it. Each branch of the namespace breaks down to either a domain or an organizational unit (OU). Whether a branch is a domain or an OU will depend on a variety of considerations, including the need for replication, security policy, resource availability, quality of the connection, and so forth.

Domains vs. Organizational Units

The Windows 2000 network trees are made up of domains and organizational units. Each provides for administrative boundaries between branches on the tree, but they have different implications and resource requirements.

Domains

The core unit of the Windows 2000 Active Directory is the domain, just as it is in Windows NT 3.x and Windows NT 4. All network objects exist as part of a domain, and the security policy is uniform throughout a domain. Unlike

Windows NT, Windows 2000 security is based on Kerberos version 5, and the trust relationships are *transitive*. In transitive relationships, if domain A trusts domain B and domain B trusts domain C, then domain A also trusts domain C.

> **Planning**   One-way Windows NT 4–style trust relationships can still be set up. More important, the relationships between Windows 2000 domains and legacy Windows NT domains are based on the one-way, nontransitive trust relationships inherent in Windows NT. It is essential that you consider these relationships when planning your domain structure.

With Windows 2000, the concepts of primary domain controller and backup domain controller are finally history. Domain controllers (DCs) in Windows 2000 are multiple master and peer based. Each controller of a domain has identical authority over the domain, and if any controller goes down, the others continue to administer and authenticate the domain. Any DC can originate a change to the domain and then propagate the change to the other DCs in the domain.

The domain is also the unit of replication. Changes in the domain are replicated throughout the domain, even when the domain spans multiple sites or locations. This capability allows domain controllers at distant sites to originate changes to the domain and have the changes replicated across the domain.

While access rights are transitive across domain boundaries, administrative rights are, by default, limited to the domain. This allows you to grant administrative rights to a key user in a particular domain without worrying about compromising the overall security of the organization, since the administrative rights stop at the domain boundary unless explicitly granted to other domains.

Organizational Units

The OU concept is new to Windows 2000. It has some of the characteristics of a domain, but without the resource overhead of one. An OU is contained within a domain and acts as a container for directory service objects. It forms a branch of the contiguous namespace, and it can in turn contain other OUs. Thus, the domain *corp.microsoft.com* may contain other domains, such as *finance.corp.microsoft.com,* and it may also contain OUs such as *hr.corp.microsoft.com*. The OU provides a convenient administrative boundary, and rights and privileges for administration can be granted to users in an OU without compromising the rest of the domain. However, an OU does not require a separate domain controller, nor is it involved in replication.

The closest analogy to an OU from the Windows NT domain model is the resource domain, but without the domain controller overhead that was required under

Windows NT. In cases where there is no particular need for a separate security policy for a given administrative container, the OU provides an appropriate and less resource-intensive boundary. Moreover, in case of need, an OU can be easily promoted to a domain.

Designing a Domain Structure

Once you have designed your namespace and everyone involved has signed off on it, you're ready to start designing and implementing your domain structure. The design of your domain structure will closely match the design of your namespace, though you may make a decision that certain namespace boundaries require only OUs, not full domains. Your choice between an organizational unit and a domain should be based on whether you need a separate security policy for the entities within the namespace boundary. If a particular namespace boundary will not require a security policy that is different from that of its parent, you will probably find an OU to be an appropriate division, since it requires fewer resources to implement. As mentioned earlier, you can easily promote an OU to a domain later if that becomes necessary.

Designing a Tree Domain Structure

If you'll be creating a single, contiguous namespace and therefore a pure tree domain structure, you'll want to create the domains in hierarchical order, starting at the top of the tree. The first domain will be your root domain and will, most likely, have either all of the users in it (for smaller, single-domain models) or no users at all (if you use a structural domain as the root domain). For those familiar with the Windows NT 4 domain models, this pattern very roughly corresponds to the "single master" domain model, with one important difference. Users need not (and most often should not) reside in a single master domain, but should reside in their actual appropriate place in the domain structure.

As you branch down the tree of your namespace, you will create domains or organizational units for each branch of the tree. The decision about whether to create an OU or a DC will depend on your overall security model, the quality of the connection to the location, and a variety of other factors, including political considerations from the original namespace planning. If you're in doubt at any point, simply create an OU—it's easy to upgrade the OU to a domain later.

Designing a Forest Domain Structure

The forest of trees structure is most often used to accommodate an existing namespace that is noncontiguous and can't easily be made contiguous. You'll end up with multiple root domains, all on the same level. Below each of these root domains, you'll have a contiguous namespace for that tree. Each branch of the namespace will be either a domain (with its attendant requirement of one or more domain controllers) or an organizational unit. You'll generally create each tree from the top down, and each branch of the tree will automatically have a transitive trust relationship with the other branches of the tree.

The trees in the forest will share the same schema, configuration, and Global Catalog, with transitive Kerberos trust relationships among all members of the forest. The trust hierarchy within each tree will follow the naming hierarchy. The trust hierarchy in the forest as a whole, however, will follow the order in which trees are joined to the forest. This fact is transparent to the users but can be manipulated by the administrator to improve management and referrals.

Domain Security Guidelines

Within each domain, the security requirements, policy, and configuration are consistent. If you need to change the security requirements and policy for a subunit within a domain, you'll need to create that subunit as a domain, not an OU. Keep this limitation in mind as you plan your overall namespace—you'll need to have a separate branch of the namespace in order to have a separate security policy.

What is meant by "security policy"? What sorts of things does it entail? Chapters 17 through 19 deal exclusively with security matters, so for the moment, we'll take a summary view. The security policy includes

- Logon requirements
- Certificates
- Password aging and minimum length requirements
- Smart card or other authentication add-ons
- Machine and time-of-day restrictions

Many of these things will comfortably be the same throughout your organization, but there may well be certain areas that require significantly greater security than that needed in the rest of the organization. If so, plan for areas that require extra care to be in a separate domain so that their more restrictive security won't be imposed on the entire organization.

Creating Organizational Units

In situations where you don't need to create separate domains for security reasons but do want to maintain a separate level in the namespace, you'll create a separate OU. Thus, you might have a domain called *noram.microsoft.com* that you want to divide into business units within the region. You could create separate sales, support, education, human resources, manufacturing, and finance domains under *noram.microsoft.com*. However, the overhead of separate domains (and their required controllers) for each of these units isn't necessary—especially since they all share a single security policy. So simply create OUs for each of them. If you later decide to upgrade one or more of them to a domain, you can do it easily.

Organizational units make useful boundaries for administrative purposes. Various administrative tasks and privileges can be delegated to the administrator for a specific OU, freeing up the domain administrator and giving the OU local control of its own resources.

Planning Multiple Domains

When your organization is complex enough, or simply large enough, that you know you're going to have to create multiple domains, you should spend the extra time up front planning exactly how to implement them. Time spent on the front end will be paid back later ten times over.

Draw out your planned domain structure and compare it to your planned (or existing) namespace. Decide what simply *must* be a domain and what can comfortably be an OU. Identify which servers will be your domain controllers. Keep in mind that the concepts of primary domain controller and backup domain controller from Windows NT are gone. All servers within a domain are of equal weight and importance. Changes made to any domain controller are propagated to all other controllers within the domain. If simultaneous changes are being made against multiple controllers, Active Directory will use update sequence numbers and the timestamps of the changes to resolve any conflicts.

Planning a Contiguous Namespace

When you are planning a contiguous namespace, and thus a single tree structure, you'll initially want to create the root domain for the namespace. In this namespace, you will want to create the primary administrative accounts, but it is best to leave the creation of other accounts until later. User and machine accounts should reside in the leaf of the tree where they are going to do the majority of their work. This is the reverse of Windows NT where, if you were running multiple domains, you often have to create all your user accounts at the highest level of the domain because of the nature of trust relationships.

If you're migrating from an existing Windows NT environment, you may have your users in a single or multiple-master domain. You can continue this arrangement, and it may be the easiest way to migrate from an existing environment. See Chapter 7 for a more thorough discussion on upgrading domains.

Determining the Need for a Forest

If you have an environment where there are already multiple root domains, or where a contiguous namespace doesn't exist, you'll need to create a forest rather than a single tree environment. The first step is to take a long, hard look at your noncontiguous namespaces. Is there any opportunity to consolidate them into fewer contiguous namespaces? Now is definitely the time to do this. It will be much harder to consolidate them later, and you'll have a harder political battle as well.

Creating the Forest

If you've decided that there is simply no way to get down to a single, contiguous namespace, meaning that you'll need to create a forest, you should decide exactly where the root of each tree in the forest will reside. Think about the physical locations of your potential domain controllers, the layout of your network, the bandwidth of various sites, and the current existence of Windows NT 4 domains and controllers. Once you have a good physical and logical map of your network, you're in a position to plan your domain strategy.

You'll want to create your root-level domains first and then start building your trees. This isn't an absolute requirement—if you miss a tree or something changes, you can go back and add another tree to your forest. However, it's generally better to create the roots first, if only for the purpose of getting things lined up and getting your tree-to-tree trust relationships in order.

Caution Once you've created the root of a tree, there is no easy way to rename or delete it, so don't rush into creating your domain structure. Planning it out in detail will save you a huge headache in the long run.

Summary

Planning your namespace and domain is an essential first step to a successful implementation of Windows 2000. It is an iterative process that requires a clear understanding of the political vagaries of the organization. A Windows 2000 namespace can have either a single, contiguous, and hierarchical tree structure or a forest of trees in a noncontiguous namespace. All domain controllers have the same authority over a domain, and there can be multiple organizational units within a domain. We continue our focus on planning in Chapter 4; in Chapter 5, we move from planning to installing.

Chapter 4
Planning Deployment

Deployment involves a good deal more than merely installing an operating system, even a network operating system. The specifics of deployment—installing and configuring applications, file and print services, Active Directory, communications, security, and other functions—are covered in later chapters. This chapter deals with the work that must be done before the first CD-ROM is ever inserted into a drive—planning the hardware and software infrastructure on which your Microsoft Windows 2000 network will be based.

Successful deployment of Windows 2000 depends primarily on planning. Successful planning, in turn, depends on gathering and analyzing data as well as a certain amount of prophesizing. The decisions made at the early stages of deployment will have your fingerprints all over them, for good or ill. Your vision of the future will prevail for years to come in the operation of the organization, and you'll undoubtedly be held accountable if the vision turns out to be a nightmare. Therefore, the more planning you devote to deployment, the better off everyone will be.

Three elements are essential for an effective Information Technology (IT) strategy:

- An analysis of how your business requirements and IT capabilities match up today. Where is your technological structure adequate, and where is it lacking?

- A projection of your business and IT goals. You need one-year, three-year, five-year, and ten-year plans for business needs, and the IT functionality and services to meet those needs.

- A roadmap that provides a path toward achieving the business and IT goals.

This chapter discusses all three of these elements and examines how they are interrelated.

How Information Technology Functions

Most people would agree that the purpose of an Information Technology department is to serve current business needs as well as to advance long-term strategic goals. Unfortunately, this isn't always clear, for a variety of reasons. Sometimes communication is poor. Often no one has ever given much thought to what it takes, technically speaking, to serve business needs. Many networks appear to have sprouted like mushrooms after a rain, without the benefit of anything resembling an overall vision. Changing the situation is complicated by a number of factors:

- Legacy hardware and software
- Incompatible operating systems and applications that were adopted to solve specific divisional or departmental problems
- Rapidly changing technologies and user requirements
- Resistance to change by those who have grown comfortable with older technologies
- Too little staff, time, and money to plan and execute a network upgrade

This last item is virtually universal. However, if these factors plague your organization, it's time to start struggling against the status quo. The situation can't and won't change overnight, but a carefully thought-out plan with clear priorities can do a great deal to move things forward.

Identifying Business Needs

Identifying business needs is a topic of such scope that it can seem overwhelming. A good place to start is with individual departments or areas. For example, consider the needs of your sales, human resources, and marketing departments. What does each area need to do now, and what services will be of benefit in the future?

Consider basic operations (such as accounts payable and inventory) that have to be taken care of daily, as well as less frequent operations (the launching of a new product). What kinds of flexibility need to be built into the IT systems? What sorts of changes must be anticipated to deal with increased Internet activity or increased access for users in remote locations?

The research you perform into the organization's business requirements can also help you overcome resistance—and there's always some resistance—to changes in the infrastructure. As people participate in your research and share your understanding of the organization's current issues and opportunities, more of them will come to have a personal stake in supporting your Windows 2000 deployment.

Getting Specific

Start with a list, ranked in order of importance, of enterprise functions that are necessary to meet your organization's business goals. As part of that list, incorporate the following:

- A total cost of ownership (TCO) analysis identifying potential areas where upgrades to the IT infrastructure can result in cost reductions
- A return on investment (ROI) analysis identifying the financial opportunities that can result from upgrades to the IT infrastructure
- Additional business that can result from the infrastructure upgrade
- Potential risks from not updating the IT infrastructure

Planning You can download the Microsoft Desktop TCO and ROI Calculator at *http://www.microsoft.com/ntworkstation/basics/features/lowesttco/ tcocalculator.asp*.

These are complicated issues with much overlap, so you may have to construct this list more than once. Depending on the size of your operation, this list may have to be subdivided into manageable bites, each one of which constitutes a project of its own.

Planning An estimate of the financial impact that year 2000 and Euro currency conversions will have on your organization should also be incorporated.

Seeing into the Future

To make your network successful, you need to undertake a high-level analysis of what your organization will look like in one, three, five, and even ten years. Will the organization become more centralized or less? Will it expand geographically, or will it contract? Will you have more knowledge workers who require the free flow of information on networks to do their jobs? Will you need to deal with "boundaryless" workers who spend time in the office but who may also telecommute, belong to virtual teams, or even work in their clients' offices? Workers with such needs can make the usual means of information distribution completely inadequate. How will these workers get what they need? How will you balance conflicting demands for access and security?

Computer networks themselves are subject to rapid change because the experience of working on a network changes users' perceptions of what is possible and therefore changes their view of what is needed. Once it's possible to have access to real-time sales figures or inventory counts, the demand for access grows rapidly.

Even modest changes can have a substantial impact on your IT infrastructure. By anticipating changes and planning for them, you ensure that your network can evolve to meet future needs.

Assessing Your Current Setup

It's a rare company that has a complete inventory of its hardware and software. It's an even rarer company that knows the rate at which its hardware and software infrastructure changes. Grand goals for the future can't be met without knowing the facts about the present. After all, even if you're sure you want to go to Chicago, you have little hope of getting there unless you know whether you're currently in Savannah or Seattle. The sections that follow detail the steps for analyzing what you have, so you can determine what you need and how to implement changes.

More Info A useful tool for qualitative analysis of your current infrastructure is Microsoft's IT Advisor, which can be found at *http://www.microsoft.com/enterprise*. It provides a structured way of thinking about your current applications, technology infrastructure, and IT organization, and about how your IT spending is translating into business results.

Documenting the Network

Knowing what hardware and software you have deployed and how that equipment is being used is vital when designing your Windows 2000 network and determining the best way to implement it. After all, you're not tearing out the entire current network and replacing it with brand new, state-of-the-art equipment. (And if you are, that's not as easy as it sounds either.)

Instead, you'll be phasing out legacy hardware and software over a period of weeks or months—perhaps even longer. During this time, the existing hardware and software will still have to be supported. A careful and thorough audit of your existing network can be of great use in determining where potential problems (and opportunities) lie.

The Organizational and Physical Infrastructure

Make a drawing of the physical network, including workstations, servers, routers, wiring closets, and hubs. This picture will clarify where the network can be expanded (and where it cannot), the best traffic routing, and whether servers and other hardware are optimally placed. At the same time, an organizational chart showing all members of the IT staff and the responsibilities assigned to each one can help clarify lines of communication and show where they might be lacking. Make sure that all critical tasks are assigned at every site, organizational unit, or location. You don't want to establish a server at a remote location and have no one there who can manage anything beyond a reboot.

Traffic Patterns

Gather network traffic reports to determine the optimum placement of routers, hubs, and switches; bandwidth requirements for workstations and workgroups; and future needs for network management software. Network analysis utilities are available to help you determine your overhead (or background) network traffic. Traffic patterns are also important in determining appropriate wide area network (WAN) connectivity speeds or the speed to be used on risers connecting floors in a building.

Network Addresses

As you upgrade the network using Active Directory, you'll probably be assigning new network names to most of the nodes on the network. Add the node addresses to the hardware drawing you made earlier so that you can analyze what addresses to assign and what steps will be necessary to make the transition from the old naming system to the new one.

Operating System Connectivity

Many systems already have Windows NT connected to other operating systems such as UNIX and NetWare. You'll need to determine what tools are necessary to maintain the connectivity you want. In addition, hardware placement—routers, switches, and gateways—can all be critical to optimum connectivity.

External Connectivity

Just as most companies don't know what hardware they have, many networks have undocumented external connectivity. Most know about their Internet, WAN, and fax services, but often there are completely undocumented telephone lines used for dial-up networking or remote network management. Document all connections.

Existing Network Operating Systems

Documenting the operating system on each server and workstation on the network is an essential ingredient to a successful operating system upgrade or migration. You'll need to determine what the upgrade or migration must support and what preparatory upgrades are needed.

Existing Applications and Services

You will need an inventory of all of the software running on servers and workstations. Once you have the list, further analysis will be needed to determine what resources the applications require most of the time as well as under extraordinary circumstances. For example, a particular program may generate a modest amount of traffic most of the time except for weekly downloads of 200 MB from a WAN server.

In addition, the inventory of applications and services should be subdivided and classified into categories:

- **Strategic**   Software and services that are essential to business operations and that have the most relevance to current and future goals.

- **Tactical**   Applications and services that are valuable to the business but that are not providing optimal benefit.

- **Legacy**   Software and services that are still used by some groups or departments but that are nearing the end of their useful life. Your plan should call for removing these components before they fall into the obsolete category.

- **Obsolete**   Applications and services that are not only not beneficial to the business but are a hindrance. The goal of IT should be to remove these elements as soon as possible.

Every component belongs in one of these categories, and making the assignments can clarify your thinking and help give shape to your plan.

Making a Roadmap

A recent study commissioned by Microsoft identified six characteristics of successful IT departments. None of the conclusions are startling, but they bear repeating. Companies with successful Information Technology departments will

- **Make IT a business-driven line function, not a technology-driven staff function.**   In other words, the function of the technology people must be firmly connected to business strategies and the everyday work that advances these strategies.

- **Base technology funding decisions on the same considerations as any other corporate expenditure.** Cost/benefit and ROI analyses must be as much a part of every IT investment decision as they would be in the decision to buy a new building.

- **Insist on simplicity and flexibility throughout the technology environment.** Reduce the number of technologies and platforms deployed, and aim for maximum flexibility and ease of implementation.

- **Demand near-term business results from development efforts.** Incremental project rollouts are preferred, as is packaged software over custom software wherever possible. When custom development is necessary, focus on the 20 percent of the functionality that typically adds 80 percent of the value.

- **Drive constant year-to-year operational productivity improvements.** Measure performance against internal and external benchmarks and standards, and strive for constant improvements.

- **Aim for an IT department that is smart about business and a business organization that is smart about IT.** Simply stated, in the better-performing companies the IT and business organizations work together. They speak the same language, talk to each other, and understand each other's capabilities and needs.

These are all grand statements that are difficult to argue with in the abstract but hard to implement in the real world. However, we all have to start somewhere, and keeping these aims in mind and working toward implementing them can only benefit the enterprise overall.

After you've analyzed your present situation as well as the business goals you need to achieve, the next step is to design a roadmap that will take you where you want to go. The roadmap will include a definition of the goals, a risk assessment, and an implementation plan.

Defining Goals

Your deployment goals must be specific, achievable, and measurable. Spell out the problems that have to be solved and how you will address constraints such as end user requirements, costs, schedules, and reliability.

Your plan must then address specifically what you want to accomplish at each stage and how you will measure whether you have done what you set out to do. When deploying Windows 2000 in a particular department, approach the task as a vendor to that department. As a minimum, you'll need to

- Determine who has to agree to the scope of the project and who can sign off at the end of it.

- Determine the scope of the project: what needs to be installed, what needs to be configured, and what the users will be able to do at the end of the project. Involve as many people in the department as possible.

- Get agreement as to what will constitute completion of the project. For example, a project might be considered complete when all workstations are connected to the network with specified software installed, all users can log on, and data can be retrieved under all conditions in n seconds or less. Again, be specific.

- Define a method that will test all areas of the project. Get a sign-off on the method. Allow ample time for testing. Regular, short-loop testing as you go will save much time and aggravation later.

- When the project is complete, get a sign-off that it is in fact complete. Additions and changes that are not in the original scope should be addressed as a new project—a different phase of the deployment. It's very important that every stage have a point of closure.

Some of these steps seem obvious, but it's surprising how often people have no idea whether their upgrade to the system has actually accomplished anything and, if it has, whether the results are what was wanted and needed. All too often the IT people go away dusting their hands and congratulating themselves, while the actual "customers" are far from satisfied.

Assessing Risk

It's not possible to predict everything that can go wrong in a deployment, but you can be sure that something will. Typical problems include sudden changes in business needs or user requirements, costs running higher than expected, and the almost inevitable schedule slippage.

Risks can be managed proactively or reactively. Preventing difficulty is obviously better than reacting to trouble after it pops up, although (just as obviously) this is not always possible. Nevertheless, it's feasible to draw up a risk assessment/risk management plan. Such a plan would include the kinds of problems that might occur, an appropriate response to each problem, and how to minimize the potential loss in case of a problem.

Few things can hurt you more during deployment than a poorly thought-out schedule. At the same time, a schedule that considers risks can go a long way toward minimizing the likelihood of serious problems. The following precautions will help you minimize schedule-related perils:

- **Develop high-risk components first.** Any areas that are already an ongoing tangle—such as messaging or your Web server—should be developed first and independently. New components that haven't been part of your network before should also be tested separately and understood completely before you install them where they can affect critical operations.

- **Include a fudge factor for unforeseen circumstances.** Nothing ever works exactly as you expect. The "five-minute install" turns out to require a change in hardware to work correctly. The quick change of hardware requires an unexpected half-hour of configuration. Estimate how much time each stage of deployment will take, and then double it.

- **Update the project plan and schedule.** When circumstances change and milestones are reached, notify everyone involved in the project by updating and distributing the plan and schedule. If you find yourself two days behind after the first stage of the deployment, don't just plan on working faster to catch up. Instead, update the plan and determine whether the delay is due to a defect in the plan (and therefore likely to multiply over time) or merely a one-time failing. Optimism is a fine quality, but it's more important to be realistic.

Summary

These first chapters have no doubt given you lots to think about—and certainly plenty to do. Nevertheless, no matter how much groundwork you lay, you must eventually put some of your plans into practice—if only to see where they can be improved. Part II starts with the next chapter; there you will begin the process of actually installing and configuring Windows 2000 Server, Windows 2000 Advanced Server, and Windows 2000 Professional.

Part II
Installation and
Initial Configuration

Chapter 5
Getting Started

The first four chapters of the book have dealt with fairly abstract planning. In this chapter, we get down to the matter of actually installing the operating system on a server—but first, yes!—*more* planning. Planning your installation might not reduce the total time it takes to bring your server on line by much, but it will reduce the number of procedures that you have to do, redo, and then do again.

Reviewing System Requirements

Before installing Microsoft Windows 2000 Advanced Server, check that you have the appropriate hardware. This involves both meeting the minimum system requirements (hopefully exceeding them if you want your server to do any real work) and checking the Microsoft Hardware Compatibility List (HCL) to be sure that your computer and peripherals are supported.

Table 5-1 lists the minimum system requirements for Windows 2000 Advanced Server along with some more practical recommendations for the minimum necessary hardware.

> **Note** Planning requirements for Windows 2000 Server are the same as those for Advanced Server, although there is a maximum supported RAM limit of 4 GB. Windows 2000 Professional, however, can be usable on less powerful computers (a Pentium 133 with 32 MB is the minimum hardware recommended by Microsoft), although we recommend increasing the RAM on Windows 2000 Professional systems to at least 96 MB, preferably 128 MB or more, for better performance.

Wallis Simpson was fond of saying that you can never be too rich or too thin (though she was both). However, without a doubt, you can never have too much processing power or too much RAM on a domain controller, or on any server for that matter. The only restriction is economic. Get the most server you can afford.

Table 5-1. Minimum requirements for achieving adequate performance

Minimum	Recommended Minimum
Intel Pentium 166	One or more Intel Pentium II 300 or faster microprocessors (or compatible processors—check the HCL)
64 MB RAM minimum, 128 MB recommended, 8 GB maximum	128 MB RAM minimum, 256 MB or more recommended
VGA monitor	Super VGA monitor capable of at least 800-by-600 resolution
Keyboard and mouse or other pointing device	Keyboard and mouse or other pointing device
850 MB partition with 650 MB free disk space	2 GB free disk space on a 7200 rpm or faster Ultra IDE or (preferably) Ultra Wide SCSI hard disk
Bootable CD-ROM	Bootable 12x or faster CD-ROM or DVD-ROM drive (El Torito–compatible)
1.44 MB floppy	1.44 MB floppy
One or more network adapters	One or more PCI-based Fast Ethernet network adapters

Note Yes, the name of the specification is indeed El Torito. The engineers who developed the standard named it after the restaurant where they had held many, presumably happy, collaborative meetings. Really, we're not kidding.

And before you buy server hardware, check the HCL in the \Support folder on your Windows 2000 installation CD. If you don't see your system listed, check the HCL on the Microsoft Web site (*http://www.microsoft.com/hwtest/hcl/*). If updated drivers are available for your hardware, download and copy them to a floppy disk or available local disk so that you can use them during installation, if necessary.

If a component in your system isn't listed on the HCL, you can visit the manufacturer's Web site or contact the manufacturer of your device to see whether updated drivers are available. In general, though, the rule is this: don't use a server that isn't 100 percent compatible.

Tip While having a fast processor is important for some server applications, older systems can be made to work extremely well by adding more RAM. Even Pentium 100 systems can perform reasonably well as a server if you increase their installed RAM to 256 MB.

Real World   Hardware Compatibility

While it's true that many devices not on the HCL will work most of the time, servers are needed *all* the time. Inevitably, some traceable-to-the-hardware fault will show up, and you'll have no recourse. Microsoft will justifiably point out that you should be using hardware from the HCL. And the manufacturer will shrug and say that they're "working on" drivers. Neither is a good position to be in.

If you have machines that aren't 100 percent compatible, try them out as clients. Often, Windows 2000 Professional will work perfectly well on a machine that's not on the HCL. Certainly, Windows 95 and Windows 98 aren't as fussy and run on almost any machine with an adequate processor and the minimum amount of RAM.

Planning Partitions

Next decide how you want to partition and configure your drives. Microsoft recommends using an NT file system (NTFS) for your entire system, unless you need to remain compatible with an existing operating system on your computer—rather unlikely on a server. NTFS has many advantages, including efficiency, reliability, security, and compression. Also, many Windows 2000 features or services require an NTFS partition. For example, to use your server as a domain controller or Active Directory server, an NTFS partition must be available.

NTFS has always been superior to the file allocation table (FAT) or FAT32 file systems for the reasons previously stated, but it has an unfortunate disability in Windows NT. If, for some reason, your NTFS system drive won't boot up, your only hope for recovery is to perform a parallel installation of Windows NT. Fortunately, Windows 2000 comes equipped with a Safe Mode boot option, ala Windows 95/98, as well as a special Recovery Mode Console that allows you to boot to a command line on a nonbooting system and securely access NTFS partitions. For more information on these features and other ways of recovering nonfunctioning systems, see Chapter 36. Also see the "Dual Boot Considerations" section later in this chapter for more information on parallel installations of Windows 2000.

Real World **Installation and Security**

It is common practice for many users of Windows NT to install the operating system on a FAT partition and then store all data on one or more NTFS partitions. The advantage of using a FAT partition for the operating system installation is that you can use an MS-DOS boot disk to boot and repair your system in case you can't boot Windows 2000. (You'd need a Windows 95 OSR 2 or Windows 98 boot disk to access a FAT32-formatted hard disk if you used this approach with Windows 2000.) However, this approach leaves the system registry and other important information on the system drive open to serious security risk. In addition, when Windows NT or 2000 is installed on a FAT partition, you sacrifice the ability to use the security features built into NTFS to protect your system installation (while also eliminating any hope of achieving C2 security compliance, by the way). Any user can insert a boot disk and access your Windows 2000 system drive (unless you have a BIOS password). The registry and other sensitive security information are also potentially exposed to attack from across a network.

Because of this security risk, we do NOT recommend installing Windows 2000 Advanced Server on a FAT or FAT32 partition. Windows 2000 installed on an NTFS partition has the same recoverability available to a FAT-based Windows NT system, by providing a special Recovery Mode Console that uses the Windows 2000 Setup Boot Disks and CD-ROM to provide command line access to a non-booting NTFS-based system. In addition, Windows 2000 now adds a safe mode boot option, providing even more recoverability than that provided by Windows 95/98, completely eliminating the recoverability advantages FAT-based installations had under Windows NT.

The bottom line is that in any situation where you want security (and it's always needed on a server), install Windows 2000 on an NTFS-formatted partition.

You can create up to four primary partitions on a drive, or you can create up to three primary partitions and one extended partition. To install Windows 2000, in most cases you'll simply use a single, NTFS-formatted, primary partition on your boot drive of around 1or 2 GB. Leave any additional free space on the hard disk as unallocated until after installation, when you can create additional partitions for programs and data in the unallocated space.

Typically, you'll use one or more additional drives for your data, preferably set up with some form of fault tolerance. If you do use a different drive or drives for your data, convert them to dynamic disks and format them with the NTFS file system. This approach will allow you to easily work with your volumes and securely and efficiently store your data. See Chapter 14 for more information on creating dynamic volumes as well as more information on partitions and disks in general.

Gathering Network Information

After determining how you want to partition your drives, locate all the drivers for your hardware. Then record (or create) the following settings:

- **Domain Name System (DNS) name of your computer**   This name can contain both uppercase and lowercase letters, numbers, and the hyphen character. Keep your DNS host name shorter than 15 characters if you want your NetBIOS name to be the same as your DNS name (a good idea for compatibility with non–Windows 2000 clients).

- **Name of domain or workgroup to join (if on a network)**   If you're creating a new Windows 2000 domain, this name should be DNS-compatible: for example, *mydepartment.mycompany.com*.

- **IP address of your computer**   This is required unless your network has a Dynamic Host Configuration Protocol (DHCP) server.

> **Note**   If you don't have a DHCP server and don't assign an IP address to your computer, Windows 2000 will assign your computer a restricted IP address. This IP address will work on a simple network with only one IP subnet, but it won't work on more complex networks, nor will it work as an Internet IP address. For more complex networks, install a DHCP server on the network or assign IP addresses manually. To acquire valid Internet IP addresses, you need to register with your Internet service provider for a scope of IP addresses.

- **Optional Windows 2000 Advanced Server components**   For a full listing of the components available for installation, see Appendix B.

- **Client licensing mode and the concurrent number of clients (if the licensing mode is Per Server)**   Windows 2000 Advanced Server supports Per Server and Per Seat licensing. If you're unsure which licensing mode to use, choose Per Server. You can switch from Per Server to Per Seat once (without additional cost) but not from Per Seat to Per Server.

Real World   Licensing

With Per Seat licensing, each client that accesses your server needs to have its own Client Access License (CAL). Clients with a CAL can connect to any number of servers, making this method the most common licensing method for companies with more than one Windows 2000 server. You would also commonly choose it when using the Windows 2000 Terminal Services, unless you're using the Terminal Services Internet Connector License, in which case you would always use Per Server.

Licensing Per Server requires the server to have a CAL for each concurrent connection. For example, if you choose the Per Server licensing mode with 50 concurrent connections, your server can support a maximum of 50 simultaneous client connections. This licensing mode works well for companies using only a single Windows 2000 server, or for Internet or remote access servers where the client computers might not be licensed as Windows 2000 network clients.

Note   Use License Manager, located in the Administrative Tools folder on the Start menu, to keep track of your license purchases and holdings.

Physical Preparation

Once you've recorded all of these settings, several physical tasks remain:

- Back up any existing data on all the drives for which your server is responsible.

- Disable any disk mirroring for the duration of the setup process.

- Disconnect any connection to an uninterruptible power supply (UPS). UPS equipment can interfere with the setup program's ability to detect devices connected to serial ports.

- Upgrade your System BIOS to the latest version available. This is especially important for ACPI-based systems.

Dual Boot Considerations

Under most circumstances, a server won't have two operating systems, but sometimes such an approach is appropriate. For example, you can use a second, parallel installation of Windows 2000 on the server for fixing your system in case you can't boot your normal installation. In this case, the installations should be not only on separate partitions, but also on physically separate hard disks. This precaution makes sense when you consider that one of the ways a system can become unbootable is through a hard disk crash—if both installations are on the same physical hard disk, you're out of luck.

If a large removable storage device such as an Iomega Jaz drive is available, you can install the parallel installation of Windows 2000 on this disk, which you can then remove for safekeeping. And you can use a second installation of Windows 2000 as a test environment for those inevitable configuration experiments that will have unpredictable outcomes. You might also want to keep an existing installation of Windows NT 4 to minimize server downtime while you transition to Windows 2000. For more information on upgrading your server from Windows NT to Windows 2000, see Chapter 7.

> **Note** Mirroring your system disk provides even more protection against failure than just a parallel installation of Windows 2000. Mirroring your system disk *and* having a second copy of Windows 2000 on your server provides even more flexibility and protection against failure—like wearing both a belt *and* suspenders— probably more than you need. In fact, because of Windows 2000's flexible disaster recovery options, in our opinion adding a dual boot is largely unnecessary on servers. (Workstations are a different issue.)

Multiple Copies of Windows 2000

If you decide to create a parallel installation of Windows 2000, you can choose Windows 2000 Professional rather than the full version of Windows 2000 Advanced Server as your second installation. Use the parallel installation of Windows 2000 only to repair your existing installation, and then use your main installation to fix any additional problems you have.

> **Caution** You must have a different computer name for each operating system installation on a network. A unique security identifier (SID) is generated for each Windows installation on a domain, and each SID is associated with one particular computer name. So, you can boot several operating systems, but in each system your computer is known to the network by a different name.

Dual Boots with Windows NT

Rather than upgrading your server, you can choose to perform a clean install of Windows 2000 Advanced Server. A clean install allows you to preserve your existing installation for use in case you encounter trouble setting up your server with Windows 2000. Performing a clean install is also your only option if your server is running a version of Windows earlier than 3.51 and you don't want to upgrade to 3.51 or 4.0. However, when you perform a clean install, Windows 2000 doesn't migrate your existing programs and settings as it would if you upgraded your server.

The following list shows the issues involved when using a dual boot between Windows NT and Windows 2000 on computers with NTFS drives:

- Only Windows NT 4 with Service Pack 4 or later can access NTFS 5 drives and volumes.

- NTFS 5 features such as disk quotas and encryption don't work in Windows NT 4. (Encrypted files can't be read in Windows NT 4.)

- Windows NT 4 disk utilities such as Chkdsk won't work with NTFS 5 drives. You must use the Windows 2000 versions of these utilities.

- Windows NT 4 emergency repair disks can no longer be used.

- You can't reinstall Windows NT 4 after installing Windows 2000 unless you re-create and reformat the partition on which you installed Windows NT 4.

- Files you save or create in Windows 2000 might not be accessible in Windows NT 4.

- Removable media that is formatted with NTFS is automatically converted to NTFS 5 when inserted or used with Windows 2000.

- Any drives formatted with the FAT32 file system can't be read by Windows NT 4.

Note If you choose to dual boot Windows 2000 with another operating system (or copy of Windows 2000), you must install Windows 2000 on a separate disk partition. Attempts to install two operating systems on a single partition will cause problems—either during installation or shortly thereafter. If, for some reason, you're planning to dual boot Windows 95/98 and Windows 2000, be sure to install Windows 95/98 *first* and then Windows 2000.

Dual Boots with Other Operating Systems

Dual booting Windows 2000 Advanced Server with MS-DOS, Windows 95, Windows 98, or other personal operating systems such as BeOS should be performed on desktop computers and not on your server. Performing a dual boot with UNIX or another server operating system is perhaps more useful, but you should avoid it if possible.

If you do choose to perform a dual boot with another operating system, use the Windows 2000 Backup utility or another Windows 2000 backup program to perform a full backup of your system including system state information. Also, you should create an emergency repair disk by using Windows 2000's Backup utility (just for good measure). When installing or configuring your operating systems, be careful with the master boot record (MBR). Table 5-2 shows a list of additional factors you should consider when working with different operating systems.

Tip If you have the Windows 2000 Resource Kit, you can use the Disksave utility to back up and restore the MBR.

Table 5-2. Dual boot issues with Windows 2000 and other operating systems

Operating System	Issue
Windows 95/98	Install and boot before installing Windows 2000 to keep Windows 95/98 from overwriting the MBR and preventing Windows 2000 from booting.
All operating systems	Programs must be installed separately in each operating system.
All operating systems	Windows 2000 can't be installed on a drive that has been compressed with any program other than the NTFS File Compression utility.
MS-DOS, OS/2	If you install Windows 2000 on a computer that was previously performing dual boots between MS-DOS and OS/2 using the Boot command, at startup you can choose to boot only either Windows 2000 or the operating system you most recently booted.

Installing Windows 2000

How you choose to install Windows 2000 Advanced Server depends on what is already on your server, where your installation files are, and how many installations you have to do. If you already have Windows 95/98 or Windows NT on the machine, run the 32-bit Windows 2000 setup from Windows 95/98 or Windows NT. Otherwise, boot from the Windows 2000 CD-ROM or setup boot disk (or an MS-DOS boot disk with CD-ROM or network drivers), and run the 16-bit Windows 2000 setup program. Both versions of setup can be run from across the network or be automated.

The Phases of Windows 2000 Setup

The Windows 2000 setup process consists of several phases that vary somewhat depending on how you're installing the operating system.

If you install from Windows 95/98 or Windows NT, setup gathers information and copies the files that are necessary for the computer to boot into Windows 2000 text mode, and then reboots into text mode. You then (optionally) select the appropriate partition, after which setup installs Windows 2000 to your hard disk and reboots into the GUI-based Windows 2000 Setup Wizard, which collects more information, configures your devices, and finishes copying files. After this, setup is complete, and your computer reboots into Windows 2000.

If you boot your system from the Windows 2000 setup boot disks, the CD-ROM, or both, you select the partition you want to install on, after which setup installs Windows 2000 to your hard disk and then boots into the GUI-based Windows 2000 Setup Wizard. The Setup Wizard then collects information, configures devices, and finishes installing files to your computer. Setup reboots your computer when it's finished.

If you boot your system with an MS-DOS boot disk, setup copies the necessary files to your hard disk to boot into Windows 2000 text mode and then reboots into Windows 2000 text mode. Setup performs the same process it would perform if you booted from a Windows 2000 CD-ROM or setup boot disk.

Running Setup from Windows

If you already have Windows 95, Windows 98, or Windows NT installed on your server, the easiest way to install Windows 2000 is to run the 32-bit version of setup. To do so, follow these steps:

1. Insert the Windows 2000 CD-ROM, and click Install Windows 2000 if you have CD-ROM AutoPlay (Auto insert notification) enabled, as shown in Figure 5-1. Otherwise, launch winnt32.exe from the \i386 folder on your Windows 2000 CD-ROM.

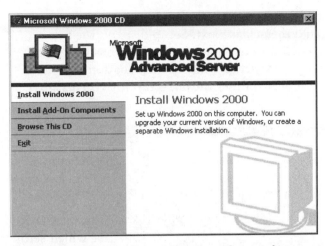

Figure 5-1. *The Windows 2000 AutoPlay window.*

2. To install Windows 2000 Advanced Server from across a network, launch the winnt32.exe program on the network drive containing the Windows 2000 Advanced Server setup files, and then proceed with setup normally.

3. When setup asks whether you want to upgrade your system or install a new copy of Windows 2000 (perform a clean install), as shown in Figure 5-2, choose the Install A New Copy Of Windows 2000 (Clean Install) option, and click Next. Windows 2000 will be installed to a new folder on your hard disk. (For information on upgrading, see Chapter 7.)

Figure 5-2. *The Welcome To The Windows 2000 Setup Wizard window.*

4. Read through the licensing agreement, choose the I Accept This Agreement option button, and then click Next. Setup displays the Select Special Options window, shown in Figure 5-3, used to customize your language options, change how setup will copy installation files, and enable the use of accessibility utilities during setup for visually impaired users.

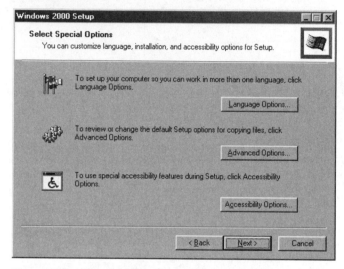

Figure 5-3. *The Select Special Options window.*

5. If you want to set up the Windows 2000 operating system to use character sets from multiple languages, click the Language Options button, choose your primary language from the drop-down list box, select any additional language groups for which you want to install support, and then click OK (Figure 5-4).

Note   You can change the language options after installation by using the Regional Options Control Panel tool.

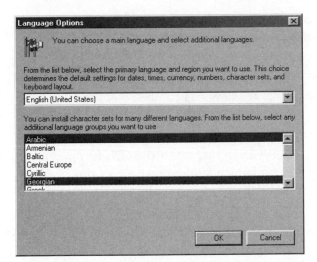

Figure 5-4. *The Language Options window.*

6. To specify the Windows 2000 installation folder and partition, or to tell Windows 2000 setup the location of the installation files, click the Advanced Options button in the Select Special Options window to open the Advanced Options window, as shown in Figure 5-5.

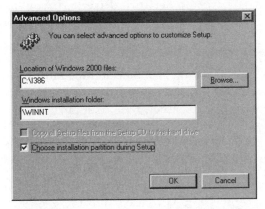

Figure 5-5. *The Advanced Options window.*

7. When you're finished modifying advanced options, click OK.

8. Click Next to copy the installation files to your computer. After setup finishes copying files, it restarts your computer and boots into Windows 2000 text mode for the text-based part of setup. (See the section "Using the Text-Based Phase of Setup" later in this chapter.)

Booting into Setup from Floppies or a CD-ROM

If you don't have Windows 95/98 or Windows NT installed on your server, you need to boot your system with the Windows 2000 CD-ROM or setup boot disk and installation floppies. (You can also boot with an MS-DOS boot disk, but it's much slower.) Because floppy disks are slow and cumbersome, booting from the Windows 2000 CD-ROM is your best bet if your computer supports the El Torito bootable CD-ROM specification.

To boot from the Windows 2000 CD-ROM, insert the CD into the drive and reboot your system. If setup doesn't launch automatically, you may need to configure the BIOS boot order to tell the system to use the CD-ROM drive before the hard disk drive.

If you are unable to boot from the CD-ROM, insert Setup Boot Disk 1 in the floppy drive and reboot the machine. You'll be prompted for the other setup floppies, and then the computer will reboot into the text-based phase of Windows 2000 setup, as described in the next section.

Real World   Installing from a Network Location

To install Windows 2000 from a network location, boot from an MS-DOS or Windows 95/98 boot disk with SmartDrive and network drivers. (If you don't have SmartDrive loaded, setup will literally take hours to copy the necessary files.) Connect to the network drive containing the Windows 2000 Advanced Server setup files, and then run the winnt.exe program. Enter the location of the setup files in the first screen, and press Enter to copy the installation files to your local hard disk. After setup finishes copying the files, remove your boot disk, and press Enter to boot into Windows 2000 for the text-based phase of setup.

Using the Text-Based Phase of Setup

When you boot from the Windows 2000 CD-ROM or floppies, or when you reboot the first time after running setup from MS-DOS, Windows 95/98, or Windows NT, you enter the text-based phase in which the setup program copies the files necessary to boot into Windows 2000 for the GUI-based portion of setup. During the text-based phase of setup, follow these steps:

1. When the Welcome To Windows 2000 setup screen appears, press Enter to continue with setup.

2. Read the licensing agreement for Windows 2000 Advanced Server (unless you ran setup from Windows 95/98 or Windows NT, in which case you already read the agreement). Use the Page Down key to scroll down, and then press F8 to continue.

3. On the next screen, you're asked to choose which disk and partition you want to install Windows 2000 on (unless you launched setup from Windows 95/98 or Windows NT and didn't select the I Want To Choose The Installation Partition During Setup option). All recognized drives and partitions on your system are displayed, organized by SCSI or IDE ID, and bus number. Select a partition or unpartitioned space by using the arrow keys on your keyboard.

Tip If you have a removable drive with a capacity of 829 MB or more, you can install Windows 2000 onto a removable disk. This step is recommended only for parallel installations, not for your primary installation of Windows 2000.

4. To delete the selected partition, press D; to create a new partition, select some unpartitioned free space and press C. If you choose to create a new partition, you will be prompted to format the partition using either the NTFS or FAT file system. If you choose the FAT file system on a partition larger than 2 GB, the partition will be formatted using the FAT32 file system.

Caution Deleting a partition erases all information on the deleted partition. Don't delete a partition unless all data on the partition is reliably backed up.

5. After you finish modifying your partitions, select the partition on which you want to install Windows 2000, and press Enter.

6. Setup confirms your choice of partitions and gives you the option of converting the partition to the NTFS file system. Press Enter when the options on the screen are correct.

7. Setup checks your hard disks for errors and then copies the appropriate files into the newly created Windows 2000 folder (named \WINNT by default). After setup finishes copying files, it prompts you to remove any floppy disks or CD-ROMs, and then it reboots your system and starts the Windows 2000 Setup Wizard.

Using the Windows 2000 Setup Wizard

After the text-based phase of setup is completed, your computer will restart and Windows 2000 will boot up for the first time, loading the Windows 2000 Setup Wizard. To use the Setup Wizard, follow the steps below. At the end of each step, click the Next button or the OK button to continue.

1. The Setup Wizard detects and configures the devices installed on your computer. If setup can't properly detect a device, it will display a Device Configuration dialog box for manual configuration of the device. After the hardware is detected, you are prompted to configure your regional settings. These settings affect such factors as keyboard layout and how dates and currency are displayed.

Tip You can use the Regional Options tool in the Control Panel to change regional settings after you install Windows 2000, so you probably don't need to linger over these dialog boxes.

2. To choose the locale you want to use, to set up the ability to read and write documents in other languages, or to specify how to format numbers, dates, and currencies, click the first Customize button. Otherwise, skip to step 5.

3. From the Your Locale drop-down list box, choose the locale you want to use for numbers, currencies, and date and time settings. To configure your system so that you can read and write documents in other languages, select the check box next to the languages you want to be able to read and write. The other tabs are used to modify how Windows 2000 formats numbers, currencies, dates, and times.

4. To change your keyboard layout, click the second Customize button in the Regional Settings window, and then use the Input Locales options to set up your keyboard for the language you want to use. Click Next.

5. Enter the name of the person the computer will be registered under (if you haven't already) as well as the organization.

6. Choose your licensing mode in the next window (shown in Figure 5-6), either Per Server or Per Seat. If you choose Per Server, specify how

many Client Access Licenses you purchased. See the "Gathering Network Information" section earlier in this chapter for more information on licensing in Windows 2000.

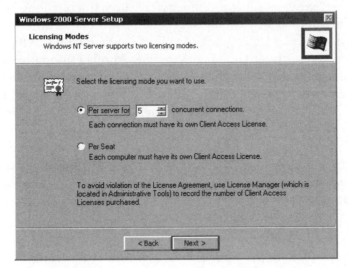

Figure 5-6. *Per Server and Per Seat licensing modes.*

Tip You can use the Licensing Control Panel tool after installing Windows 2000 Advanced Server to modify your licensing options.

7. Enter the name for your computer in the Computer Name text box. Your computer name can contain the numbers zero to nine, uppercase and lowercase letters, and the hyphen character, but no spaces or periods. The name should be DNS-compatible and can be a maximum of 63 characters in length, but for the interest of compatibility with pre–Windows 2000 clients, it should be shorter than 15 characters. See the sidebar "Naming Computers" later in this chapter for advice on naming schemes.

8. After entering your computer name, enter an administrator account password up to 14 characters long in the Administrator Password text box, and type it again in the Confirm Password text box. Click Next.

Real World   Passwords

To make your system as secure as possible, always assign a password to the administrator account, preferably a password at least seven characters long and consisting of mixed letters and characters, uppercase and lowercase. You should also clear the logon history after installing Windows 2000 so that would-be hackers must figure out both the password and the username. Another good precaution after installation is to use the built-in administrator account to make a second account with full administrative privileges. This account can have your name, or you can call it something descriptive. Use it for all your day-to-day administrative work. Assign a special secure password to the built-in administrator account and rename it from the default. Stash the password and name somewhere safe and relegate that account to semi-retirement. Because it's possible to disable *any* administrator account, including the built-in administrator account, it's wise to have a backup account. That way, you'll always have an uncontaminated known-to-be-good administrator account that you can resort to just in case.

9. Use the next window to select the components to install at this time (Figure 5-7). To install an option, select the check box to the left of the option, or select the option and click the Details button to modify the subcomponents that you want installed. (For a list of components and their descriptions, see Appendix B.)

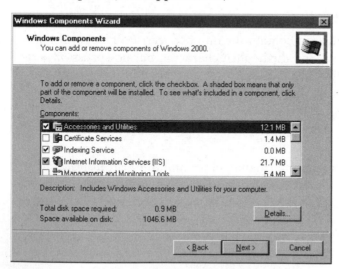

Figure 5-7. *The Windows Components window.*

10. In the Dialing Location window that is displayed if setup detects a modem, select the country, enter the area code of the phone line (if any), enter any codes needed to get an outside line, and then click Next. (You can choose additional locations or modify the current location by using the Phone And Modem Options tool in the Control Panel after you've finished setup.)

11. Review the date, time, and time zone information, make any necessary corrections, and then click Next to configure your network settings.

12. If you checked Windows Terminal Services, choose the mode operation, either Remote Administration Mode, or Application Server Mode. Click Next.

13. Choose the Typical Settings option to install the following commonly used network protocols and services: Client for MS Networks, File and Printer Sharing for MS Networks, and TCP/IP configured to use DHCP (or Automatic Private IP Addressing (APIPA) if no DHCP server is available).

14. To specify your own network settings, choose the Custom option and click Next. Otherwise, click Next and then skip to step 16. Setup displays the default list of networking components, as shown in Figure 5-8, which you can modify to suite your needs.

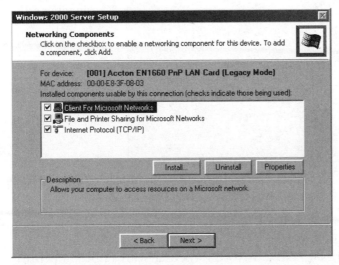

Figure 5-8. *The Networking Components window.*

15. To install additional components, click the Install button, select Client, Service, or Protocol, click Add, select the desired component, and click OK.

16. To turn off an installed component, clear the check box next to the component, or select the component and click Uninstall to remove it from your system.

Note You can perform the same operations found in steps 11 through 15 after setup by right-clicking your network connection in the \Network and Dial-up Connections folder and choosing Properties from the shortcut menu.

---

17. To join a workgroup, choose the first option in the Workgroup Or Computer Domain window shown in Figure 5-9, and type the workgroup name in the Workgroup Or Computer Domain text box.

18. If you are setting up a new domain, choose the first option and clear the Workgroup Or Computer Domain text box so that the box is empty (unless you want to log on to a local workgroup). To join an existing domain, click the second option and enter the domain name you want to join in the Domain Name text box.

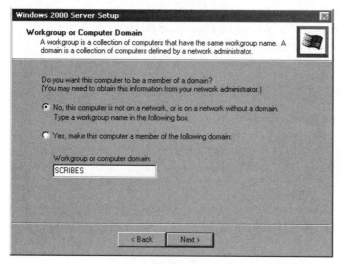

Figure 5-9. *The Workgroup Or Computer Domain window.*

19. Click Next when you're finished configuring your domain or workgroup settings. If you chose to join a domain, a dialog box appears and asks you to enter a username and password for a user with sufficient permissions to create a new computer account for your server. Enter your username and password, and then click OK. Setup then logs on to the domain and configures a computer account for your server. See Chapter 3 for more information on domains and workgroups.

20. Setup then installs the components you specified and configures Windows 2000. After setup finishes this process, it deletes any temporary installation files and then prompts you to remove any CD-ROMs or floppy disks you have in your drives. Click Finish to restart your computer.

21. If any errors occurred during the installation process, setup displays an error message and asks you if you want to view the setuplog.txt log file it created. Click OK to do so. Review the file, and then click Close to restart your system.

22. After setup restarts your computer, you will see the standard Windows 2000 logon screen. Log on and the Configure Your Server Wizard will appear to guide you through configuring additional settings on the server.

Real World   Naming Computers

Take a few moments to think about your naming conventions before you commit yourself. Lots of ways exist to create names on the network, from the cute to the whimsical to the sensible. Sometimes system administrators devise arbitrary schemes based on algorithms known only to them. Or they attempt to insert charm into the process of computer naming. Block those impulses!

It's easy enough for *you* to keep a map of what and where the different clients and servers are on your network, and you won't worry about it that often, anyway. But if you make life hard on users, you pay in the long run. So naming all your domain controllers after Shakespearean characters and naming your client machines after Greek mythology characters might make sense to you. And it does, of course, have a certain poetic grandeur. But it isn't going to help your users figure out that "Cordelia" is the server in Legal, while "Goneril" is the one in Production. On the other hand, using "Legal_Srv" for the server in the Legal department tells everyone immediately which machine it is.

Try to resist the desire to be cute in your machine names. And at all costs, avoid arbitrary names based on some formula that only you know how to crack.

Automating Windows 2000 Advanced Server Installations

Installing Windows 2000 Advanced Server, like installing any operating system, takes a lot of time. Setting up multiple servers can wipe out entire days if you set up each server manually. The time you can save by automating your installations for a large number of similar servers far outweighs the occasional hiccups you might encounter.

Before automating your installations, you should run through a couple of manual installations to get a better feel for the installation process. Review the earlier parts of this chapter and pay attention during your installations. Then progress to using the command-line switches to partially automate setup. Following that, create some scripts that automate parts of the installation process but still allow for user input in other parts. After you get a feel for the process, create and test your fully automated setup scripts.

Tip   If you find yourself spending a lot of time tweaking your setup scripts, don't feel that you must fully automate all setups. Using automated answer files (setup scripts) can provide significant time savings, but it's important to choose the appropriate level of automation for your particular job. Sometimes that will involve creating a single answer file that you'll use to deploy hundreds of servers, and sometimes that will mean using just one or two command-line parameters to speed up the installation of a single server.

Using Setup Command-Line Parameters

You can streamline the setup process on a single machine by launching setup using command-line parameters; you also use command-line parameters to specify an answer file to completely automate setup.

To use a command-line parameter on a computer without Windows 95/98 or Windows NT, boot your computer with an MS-DOS or Windows 95/98 boot disk. (See Table 5-4 for instructions on using command-line parameters in Windows 95/98 or Windows NT.) Then, at the command prompt, type *[path]\winnt.exe[parameter]*, substituting the location of your Windows 2000 setup files for *[path]*. Table 5-3 shows the available parameters for use only with winnt.exe, the 16-bit version of setup.

Table 5-3. Parameters for the WINNT.EXE command

Parameter	Function
/a	Turns on Accessibility features during setup.
/e:[command]	Runs the command following the /e: parameter after the Windows 2000 Setup Wizard completes.
/i:[inf file]	Specifies the filename of the information (.INF) file used for setup (the default is dosnet.inf). Do not include the path to the file.
/r:[folder]	Names an additional folder to be copied into the folder in which you install Windows 2000. The folder remains after setup completes, and additional folders can be copied by using multiple /r: parameters.
/rx:[folder]	Names an additional folder to be copied into the folder in which you install Windows 2000. The folder is deleted after setup completes.
/s:[sourcepath]	Specifies the location of the Windows 2000 setup files. (The default is the current folder.) This must be a full path, X:\path, or \\server\share\path. To specify multiple paths for setup to search for needed files, use multiple /s: parameters.
/t:[drive letter]	Specifies the drive to which you want setup to copy its temporary files. By default, setup uses the partition with the most free space.
/u:[answer file]	Launches setup in unattended mode using the answer file you provide. You must use the /s: switch to specify the location of the answer file.
/udf:[id,UDF file]	Specifies a uniqueness database file (UDF) to be used to modify an answer file. The ID identifies which parameter in the answer file should be replaced with information from the UDF file. For example, /udf:ComputerName,our_company.udf would take the Computer Name from the .UDF file instead of the answer file. If you don't specify a UDF file, you're prompted to insert a disk that contains the $Unique$.udf file.

To use a command-line parameter on a computer with Windows 95/98, Windows NT, or Windows 2000, boot your computer into your operating system and open a command prompt window. Then type *[path]\winnt32.exe[parameter]*, substituting *[path]* with the location of your Windows 2000 setup files as well as replacing *[parameter]* with the appropriate parameter or parameters you want to use. Table 5-4 shows the available parameters and what they do. (These are for use with only winnt32.exe, the 32-bit version of setup.)

Table 5-4. Parameters for the WINNT32.EXE command

Parameter	Function
/checkupgradeonly	Runs a compatibility test on your computer to see whether it has any problems that would interfere with upgrading the OS. Saves a Winnt32.log report in the installation folder for NT upgrades, or an Upgrade.txt report in the Windows folder for Windows 95/98 upgrades.
/cmd:[command]	Runs the command following the /cmd: parameter after the Windows 2000 Setup Wizard completes.
/cmdcons	Enables the use of the Recovery Mode Console at boot time for repairing failed installations. Can only be used after Windows 2000 is installed.
/copydir:[folder name]	Names an additional folder to be copied into the folder in which you install Windows 2000 (\Winnt). The folder remains after setup completes, and additional folders can be copied by using the parameter multiple times. The folder might contain drivers, or other files needed after setup.
/copysource:[folder name]	Names an additional folder to be copied into the folder in which you install Windows 2000. The folder is deleted after setup completes.
/debug[level:filename]	Creates a debug log file with the specified level. The default creates a log file named C:\winnt32.log with the level set to 2 (Warning).
/m:[folder name]	Specifies the location of a folder containing system file replacements. Setup checks this folder first for files to copy and then checks the installation folder.
/makelocalsource	Tells setup to copy all installation files to the local hard disk so the files will be available later during the installation if the Windows 2000 CD-ROM or network share is inaccessible.
/noreboot	Tells setup not to reboot after the initial Windows NT/95/98/2000 file copy phase of setup is complete. This allows you to run additional commands before continuing.
/s:[sourcepath]	Specifies the location of the Windows 2000 setup files. (The default is the current folder.) This must be a full path: for example, X:\path or \\server\share\path. To specify multiple paths where setup should search for needed files, use multiple /s: parameters. (You can also sometimes speed transfers from a server by specifying the same source more than once.) Setup will fail if the first server isn't available.
/syspart:[drive letter]	Specifies a hard disk to which you want to copy the setup startup files. This disk drive is then made active and setup stops, allowing you to remove the disk and insert it in another computer. When you boot the new computer, the next phase of setup will automatically start. You have to use the /tempdrive parameter in addition to the /syspart parameter (both pointing to the same drive).

Table 5-4. *continued*

Parameter	Function
/tempdrive:[drive letter]	Specifies the drive to which you want setup to copy its temporary files and install Windows 2000 on. Setup uses the partition with the most free space by default.
/unattend	Upgrades your previous version of Windows in unattended mode, taking all settings from the previous installation. The unattend switch may not be used by OEMs selling to end users because it explicitly acknowledges understanding and acceptance of the end user license agreement (EULA).
/unattend:[num:answer file]	Launches setup in unattended mode by using the answer file you provide. The *num* parameter specifies the number of seconds to wait after copying files before restarting the computer, and it works only when running setup from Windows 2000. You must use the */s:* switch to specify the location of the answer file.
/udf:[id,UDF file]	Specifies a UDF to be used to modify an answer file. The ID identifies which parameter in the answer file should be replaced with information from the UDF file. For example, /udf:ComputerName,our_company.udf would take the Computer Name from the .UDF file instead of the answer file. If you don't specify a UDF file, you're prompted to insert a disk that contains the $Unique$.udf file.

As you can see, many of these parameters piggyback onto other parameters, and pretty soon you can find yourself typing (and sometimes retyping) in long strings at the command prompt. If you end up doing this a lot, create a batch file (a text file with the .BAT extension) containing the setup command and parameters. Then simply launch the batch file instead of typing all the parameters.

Creating a Distribution Folder

A distribution folder (sometimes called a source directory) is a shared folder on a server that contains the \i386 folder from the CD-ROM and any device drivers or other files that you add to support your specific systems:

If you use the Windows 2000 Resource Kit's Setup Manager tool to create automated setup scripts, you can also have your distribution folder created for you. Or you can create this folder manually. To do so, follow these steps:

1. Connect to the volume where you want to create the distribution folder. Copy the \i386 folder from the Windows 2000 CD-ROM to the volume on which you want to create the distribution folder.

2. Create a subfolder in the \i386 folder for any additional drivers or programs that you want to preinstall on your systems. All files and folders in this folder are copied into the temporary setup folder during installation.

3. Create any additional subfolders, as necessary, for your installations. Table 5-5 describes the special folders that you can create for use by setup.

Tip With Windows 2000, you can apply service packs to distribution folders. This not only eliminates the service pack step of the setup process, but it also ensures that any time a computer needs original Windows 2000 files from the distribution folder, it receives up-to-date files. (So service packs no longer have to be reapplied after changing your system configuration.) To upgrade a distribution folder, run the service pack installation program and point it to the distribution folder.

Table 5-5. Subfolders you can create to store extra files

Folder	Description
\OEM\textmode	The folder in which you place any hardware-dependent files for use while loading Windows 2000 setup and during the text-mode phase of setup. These files include any original equipment manufacturer (OEM) HALs you might use, as well as updated SCSI, keyboard, video, and pointing device drivers.
	Also include the txtsetup.oem file in this folder to control the loading and installation of these files. To create the txtsetup.oem file, create a normal text file and list the filenames of all files in this folder. (Be sure to include this file and all files mentioned in the Unattend.txt file, under the [OEMBootFiles] section.)
\$OEM$\$$	The folder that holds any new system files or files that replace existing system files. These files are copied into the various subdirectories that are created in the Windows 2000 system folder (\winnt).
	This folder must match exactly the structure of the Windows 2000 system subfolders for those folders in which you want to add or replace system files. For example, to copy new or replacement files into the \%windir%\System32 folder, create a \$OEM$\$$\System32 folder.
\$OEM$\$1	The folder in which you place files that you want copied to the drive where Windows 2000 will be installed. Equivalent to the *%systemdrive%* environment variable, and can be used to permit drive letters to be changed without causing problems for applications that point to a hard-coded driver letter. You can also create subfolders here for your files and the entire folder structure will be copied to the system drive.
\OEM\drive_letter	The folder that specifies additional files and folders to be copied into the root folder of the named drive. You will have one entry for each drive having additional files. For example, the files located in the \$OEM$\Cfolder are copied into the root folder of the C: drive during the text-mode phase of setup. Any subfolders of the \$OEM$\C folder are also copied.
	All files must use short (8.3) filenames, but you can rename them after installation by including them in the $$Rename.txt file.

> **Note** The \Display and \Net folders that were used in the \$OEM$ folder in Windows NT 4 are no longer used in Windows 2000. You can also place the \$OEM$ folder outside of the distribution folder if you place the path (file or UNC) to the \$OEM$ folder after the OEMFILESPATH key in your answer file.

Installing Plug and Play Drivers in the Distribution Folder   To configure your distribution folder with additional Plug and Play (PnP) drivers, follow these steps:

1. Create a subfolder in the \$OEM$\$1 folder with a name containing no more than eight characters.

2. Inside the subfolder you created, you can make additional subfolders to categorize the devices; for example, you might have the following directories:

   \$OEM$\$1\Company\Net

   \$OEM$\$1\Company\Video

   \$OEM$\$1\Company\Sound

3. Copy the drivers and .INF files into the appropriate subfolder.

4. If you didn't create additional subfolders and placed all your drivers in the single folder (for example, \$OEM$\$1\Company), add the following line to your answer file: *OEMPnPDriversPath = "Company"*.

   If you created multiple subfolders for your drivers, add them to the answer file in the following format, each folder reference separated by a semicolon: *OEMPnPDriversPath = "Company\net;Company\video;Company\sound"*.

Converting Short Filenames Back to Long Filenames   The Windows 2000 text-mode setup requires the use of MS-DOS 8.3 file formats because the program is based on a 16-bit MS-DOS implementation. Thus, all files that are included in the distribution folder need to have MS-DOS–compliant short names. However, setup will convert them to long names with the use of a renaming file. To create a renaming file, follow these steps:

1. Open NotePad.

2. Using brackets, type in the path to the subfolder containing the files you want to rename (leave blank or use the backslash character (\) for the root folder).

3. Underneath the bracketed heading, enter each short filename you want to rename (not enclosed in quotes) followed by an equal sign and then the long filename in quotes.

4. Repeat step 3 with any additional subfolders in which you have files or folders that need to be renamed. A sample rename file is shown:

```
[media]
filenml.txt = "Your long filename here.txt"
ding.wav = "Really loud and annoying ding.wav"
whiz.drv = "Whizbang Deluxe Video.drv"
[images]
desktp1.bmp = "corporate logo.bmp"
desktp2.bmp = "division logo.bmp"
```

5. Save the file as $$rename.txt in the distribution folder prior to running setup.

A sample $$rename.txt file is also included on the companion CD, in the \Samples\Chapter 5\unattend files folder.

Creating Answer Files by Using the Setup Manager Wizard

When Windows 2000 is installed, the setup program pauses several times along the way, waiting for input from the user. Answer files are simply text files that supply that input to the setup program, thus automating most of the installation process. If you have the Windows 2000 Resource Kit, you have the Windows 2000 Setup Manager Wizard, a handy tool for creating answer files.

Tip In a real labor-saving move, you can set up a typical server or client and then let the Setup Manager Wizard build an answer file that duplicates the configuration of the machine. Then you can use the answer file to set up multiple versions of the typical machine.

To create a new answer file, first install the Windows 2000 Resource Kit support tools. Then choose the Start menu's Run command, type *setupmgr* in the Open text box, and follow these steps:

1. Click Next to begin using the wizard, and then choose the option to create a new answer file (Figure 5-10). The Windows 2000 Setup Manager Wizard walks you through creating or modifying answer files you can use to automate your installations.

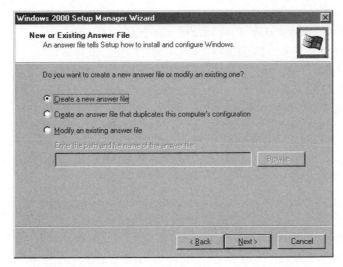

Figure 5-10. *The Windows 2000 Setup Manager Wizard's New Or Existing Answer File window.*

2. Choose the type of installation you want to create an answer file for by choosing the appropriate installation type, as shown in Figure 5-11. Click Next.

3. Select the product you are creating an answer file for.

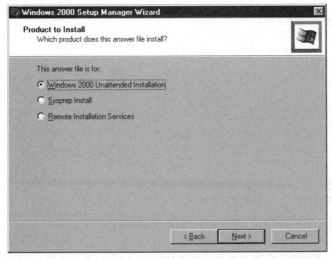

Figure 5-11. *The Setup Manager Wizard's Product To Install window.*

4. Supply the name and organization you want to use, and then click Next. (The dialog box says that if you leave the boxes blank, no name or organization will be specified in the answer file—but for a fully automated answer file, a name and organization are required.)

Real World   Choosing an Interaction Level

When determining the level of user interaction you want to require, you have several choices, and the choice you make determines how much the person running the installation will need to attend to the process. Here's a more detailed explanation of the interaction levels:

- **Provide Defaults**   Uses the information in the answer file as default answers during the Windows 2000 installation. The user still has to confirm the defaults or make changes as the installation progresses.

- **Fully Automated**   Completely automates setup by using the settings you specify in the provided answer file. This option is best for quickly setting up multiple systems with identical configurations.

- **Hide Pages**   Automates the parts of setup that you provide information for, but it requires the user to supply any information you didn't include in the answer file. Use this option to set up a system in a specific way, while still allowing the user some limited customization options. (The user will see only the parts of setup that aren't covered in the answer file.)

- **Read Only**   Hides the parts of setup you provide information for, such as the Hide Pages option. However, if a window with only partial answers is supplied in the answer file (and therefore not hidden from the user), the user can complete only the unanswered portion of the window. Settings provided in the answer file can't be changed during installation.

- **GUI Attended**   Automates the text-based portion of setup. The person running setup will supply answers for the Windows 2000 Setup Wizard. Use this level when you want to automate the text-based portion of setup and allow the person running the installation to provide the settings during the GUI portion.

5. Specify the Licensing mode your servers will use, and, if necessary, how many concurrent connections you have licenses for; then click Next. See the "Using the Windows 2000 Setup Wizard" section earlier in this chapter for more information on Licensing modes or any other setting in the Windows 2000 Setup Manager.

6. Create a list of computer names to use for your systems, as shown in Figure 5-12. Enter a computer name in the Computer Name text box, and then click Add. The Windows 2000 Setup Manager Wizard takes the names (if you have two or more) and creates a UDF that the setup program then queries for computer names, using each name only once. Make sure that your computer names are both DNS-compatible and NetBIOS-compatible if you want to maintain compatibility with pre–Windows 2000 clients.

    Continue entering all the computer names necessary for the number of systems you plan to set up by using this answer file. To remove a name from the list, select the name, and then click Remove. To import a list of names from a text file, click the Import button. You can select Automatically Generate Computer Names Based On Organization Name to have setup do it for you—the names will include a few letters from your organization's name but will be otherwise random and unhelpful. When you have finished, click Next.

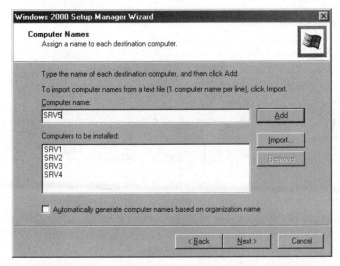

Figure 5-12. *The Setup Manager Wizard's Computer Names window.*

7. Use the next window to specify how administrator account passwords for the systems are to be chosen.

Caution The answer file that the Windows 2000 Setup Manager Wizard creates is an unencrypted text file. If you specify an administrator account password in your answer file, make sure that after installation, you change your administrator account password to something more secure.

8. Select the display settings for your computer to use during setup in the next window. You might want to either leave these at the defaults or use the lowest settings (640 x 480 with 16 colors and 60 Hz display) to ensure compatibility. You can also specify custom settings by clicking the Custom button and specifying the settings you want, but we recommend that you stick with the lowest common denominator settings to reduce problems in installing. You can adjust resolution and colors after installation if necessary. Click Next.

9. Choose the Typical Settings option to install TCP/IP, enable DHCP, and install the Client for Microsoft Networks on your systems, or choose the Custom Settings option to specify how you want to configure the systems' network settings. Click Next.

10. In this window you have the option to join the computer or computers to a domain or a workgroup. If the systems are going to be joining a workgroup, choose the Workgroup option and type in the appropriate workgroup name.

    If the systems are going to be joining a domain, choose the Windows Server Domain option. Type the Windows Server domain name in the text box provided. To create an account for the computer in the domain, click the Create Computer Account In The Domain check box and supply a username and password. The username and password must be for a user account that has sufficient administrative privileges to authorize the creation of a computer account. Click Next to continue.

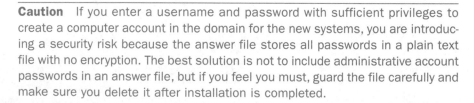

Caution If you enter a username and password with sufficient privileges to create a computer account in the domain for the new systems, you are introducing a security risk because the answer file stores all passwords in a plain text file with no encryption. The best solution is not to include administrative account passwords in an answer file, but if you feel you must, guard the file carefully and make sure you delete it after installation is completed.

11. In the next window, specify the time zone your systems will use. Click Next.

12. At this point, sufficient information has been garnered to create the answer file, but you can specify additional settings as well. If you choose to not edit the additional settings, skip ahead to step 18. Otherwise, select Yes, Edit The Additional Settings and click Next.

13. Choose Regional Settings, where you specify (or decline to specify) the character set for the language and region where the computer will be used. This setting determines default views for times, date, currency, and other characters specific to a region.

14. In the Languages window, select any additional language groups you want to use. Click Next.

15. In the Browser And Shell Settings window, select the customization method for Internet Explorer. You can take the defaults, use a custom autoconfiguration script created with the Internet Explorer Administration Kit, or specify the individual proxy and default home page settings.

16. In the Installation Folder window, choose the folder into which you want to install Windows 2000. Use the default folder and install into a folder named \Winnt unless you have a specific reason to do otherwise.

17. If you choose to create a distribution folder from which the system will install Windows 2000, you'll be asked to specify whether a new folder should be created or an existing one modified (Figure 5-13). If you're going to install Windows 2000 from a CD-ROM, you won't need a distribution folder, so choose No.

18. To install mass storage drivers (typically drivers for newer SCSI adapters or FibreChannel controllers), click the Browse button in the Provide Additional Mass Storage Drivers window. You'll be prompted for the location of the drivers.

19. Specify a replacement HAL if one is needed. Click the Browse button and locate the HAL that the system manufacturer provided.

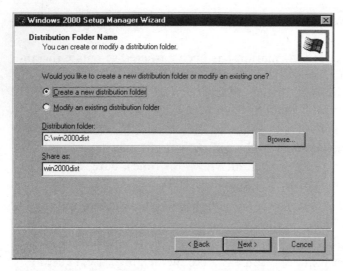

Figure 5-13. *Setup Manager Wizard's Distribution Folder Name window.*

20. Enter any commands to run at the end of setup in the Commands To Run text box, clicking Add after typing each command. Note that you can't run commands that require a user to be logged in. You can remove commands from the list by selecting the command and clicking Remove.

21. To customize the installation, you can include a logo or background to display during setup. A logo bitmap can be specified to run in the corner during the GUI portion of the installation. A background bitmap must be 640 by 480 with 16 colors and will display as the background during installation.

22. In the Copy Additional Files Or Folders window, you can select files or folders that will be automatically copied to the destination computer. The list can be expanded to a variety of folders. Highlight a folder and click Add Files. Then browse for the file or folder to add. Figure 5-14 shows the expanded list after a file has been selected for the \Windows folder on the destination computer.

Tip If you have additional drivers for Plug and Play devices that aren't included with Windows 2000, copy them to the \Plug and Play Drivers folder on the system drive. Windows 2000 setup will search this folder for drivers it couldn't locate.

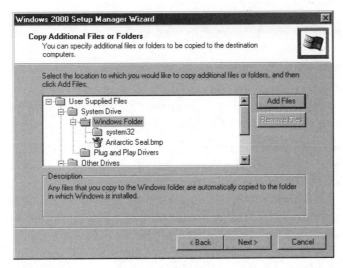

Figure 5-14. *The Setup Manager Wizard's Copy Additional Files Or Folders window.*

23. Type in the name and location for your answer file, and then click Next. Click Finish to end the wizard. The Setup Manager Wizard creates a batch file (with the same name as the answer file) that, when launched, will start setup and use the contents of the answer file. You can use this batch file or launch setup with the appropriate parameters, including the parameter pointing to the answer file. (See Tables 5-3 on page 77 and 5-4 on page 78.)

Note   The batch files that Windows 2000 Setup Manager Wizard creates use the 32-bit version of setup. If you don't have a 32-bit version of Windows on the machine where you're planning to install Windows 2000, modify the batch file to use the 16-bit setup file by deleting the *32* from the third to the last line of the file. Also change the */unattend:* parameter in the second to last line to */u:*.

Using the Answer Files Included with This Book

We've included some sample answer, batch, and UDF files on the companion CD for you to modify. To use the files, copy them from the CD to your hard disk, open them in NotePad, and replace the values you want to change. Or you can use the Setup Manager Wizard and choose the Modify An Existing Answer File option at the opening screen. Save the modified files and begin installation either by launching the batch file or by running setup with the necessary parameters.

Using SysPrep to Clone Your Computer

While creating answer files for running Windows 2000 setup in an automated fashion is very convenient and can save a lot of time for administrators, you can go a step or two further than that under the right circumstances.

One way to further automate the setup process for a new machine is to "clone" an existing system. (One can also use the Remote Installation Service in combination with IntelliMirror to achieve similar results, as discussed in Chapter 24.) Cloning works like this. First, install Windows 2000 and all of the applications you need on a single machine that is identical or very similar to the many machines on which you want to deploy Windows 2000. Then prep this system for cloning by using SysPrep (which is available on the Windows 2000 CD) to clear out the SID and other computer identity information. Clone the configuration using a third-party disk-imaging program, such as PowerQuest's Drive Image or Norton Ghost, which copies and compresses the disk image to a network share. (An evaluation copy of Norton Ghost is included on the companion CD.) You can then boot up a blank system using the floppy disk created by the disk imaging program, copy and uncompress the cloned disk image onto the new system, and be up and running in far less time than would be required to perform even a fully automated operating system and application installation.

However, this solution has some problems. First, your systems need to be fairly similar for the disk images to work on them. The computers don't have to be exactly the same because Windows 2000 leverages Plug and Play to detect changes to most system components. However, the systems do need to have identical mass storage controllers (SCSI controller or IDE chipset), as well as share the same HAL—no mixing ACPI systems with non-ACPI systems or uniprocessor systems with multiprocessor systems. Also, this process doesn't work for domain controllers, unless you script the DCPROMO process into your disk image.

Covering in detail how to use SysPrep and disk imaging tools to mass deploy pre-configured computers is outside the scope of this book, but we can give you a taste of how it works. Please use this section only to whet your appetite. Thoroughly investigate these tools and play with them in a test environment before you begin to install Windows 2000 throughout your organization using this procedure. The following steps summarize how to clone a system.

1. Install and configure Windows 2000 Professional, Server, Advanced Server, or Datacenter Server on your sample system.

2. Install and configure any applications you want to deploy to *all* systems using this drive image.

3. Run the SysPrep program to remove all identity information from your system.

4. Clone the system using a third-party disk-imaging program, and save the disk image to the desired network share. The system you clone will need to be rebooted and run through the mini setup wizard (see step 6) before it can be used again as a normal system. Use a floppy disk to boot the system you want to install your drive image onto and connect to the network share containing your drive image.

5. Use your drive image's client tools to expand the image file onto your new system's hard drive.

6. Reboot the system. A Windows 2000 mini setup wizard will run, detecting any additional Plug and Play devices and hiding any missing devices. The wizard will generate a new SID, and your system will be fully functional. (To force the mini setup wizard to perform a full PnP detection process to eliminate rather than hide any missing devices, run SysPrep with the /pnp switch.)

Tip You can optionally provide an answer file to modify individual machines' system configurations without re-creating the disk image. To do this, create an unattend.txt file as you would normally, rename it to sysprep.inf, place it on a floppy, and insert the floppy right before the mini setup wizard is launched.

Troubleshooting Installations

In most cases, installing Windows 2000 Advanced Server is a relatively painless process; however, when setup fails for some reason or another, life gets more difficult. Fortunately, most installation problems are easily solved. The most common problems are covered here. Additional troubleshooting procedures can be found in Chapter 37.

More Info You can find additional troubleshooting help either in the Windows 2000 Help System's troubleshooters (admittedly not much good unless you have access to a functioning Windows 2000 machine) or in the Microsoft Knowledge Base, available on line through *http://support.microsoft.com*.

Setup Freezes or Locks Up

Sometimes Windows 2000 setup will inexplicably lock up partway through the installation process. If you receive a Stop Error message, write it down and consult either the Stop Errors troubleshooter in Windows 2000 Help or Microsoft technical support.

In general, these failures are intermittent and don't come with anything so helpful as an error message. First reboot your system by pressing Ctrl+Alt+Del. Do this repeatedly, if necessary. If you get no response, press the Reset button on your computer or turn your system off, wait 10 seconds, and then turn it back on. If you see a Boot menu, choose the Windows 2000 Server Setup option to allow Windows 2000 setup to attempt to continue with its installation. If no Boot menu appears, launch setup again. In either case, don't choose to repair your installation, but instead choose to continue with setup.

Setup usually detects that an error occurred with its last attempt to install Windows 2000 and compensates by using a safer method of installation. If setup hangs or stops responding again, repeat this process. Sometimes, setup will hang multiple times before it finishes installing Windows 2000, so be persistent. If installation freezes at a particular part of setup, try choosing simpler setup options, if applicable. For example, leave out optional Windows components.

Other procedures you can use to fix setup problems are as follows:

- Disable your system cache (processor cache) in your BIOS, and then run setup again. Consult your hardware documentation for information on the correct procedure to do this. Once setup is complete, enable your cache again to avoid a significant performance loss.

- Try adding a wait state to your RAM in your system BIOS. This can help with partially faulty RAM chips. (However, if this server is important— and what server isn't?—plan on replacing that iffy RAM before doing any critical work on the machine.)

- Verify that your RAM modules are manufactured by the same company and are of the same speed and type. While this isn't a necessity, it can often eliminate problems.

- Switch the order of your RAM modules, or remove some modules and try installing again.

- Test your RAM modules for faulty RAM chips with a third-party software program. Replace any faulty modules and run setup again.

- Check your computer for an MBR virus by booting it from a floppy disk that has been checked for viruses, and then run a virus checking program and scan your drives for any viruses. If you find any viruses, clean them from your system and run setup again.

Real World   **ACPI BIOS Compatibility Problems**

If setup consistently freezes during the Windows 2000–based Setup Wizard and your system has an ACPI-compatible BIOS, your BIOS may not function in ACPI mode with Windows 2000. The freezes may happen at any time during the Setup Wizard, although they most frequently happen during the device detection phase. If you suspect your BIOS isn't working properly with Windows 2000, download the latest version from your system vendor.

If you still have troubles, or if there is no updated BIOS available, try disabling ACPI during setup by pressing F5 at the beginning of the text-mode phase of Setup, right after setup prompts you to press F6 to install third party storage drivers. If this doesn't solve your setup problems, you don't have a problem with the ACPI support in your BIOS. You can add ACPI support back after finishing setup by opening the Properties dialog box for your standard computer in Device Manager and using the Update Device Driver Wizard to install the ACPI PC driver; however, this might introduce system stability problems and should only be attempted if you like playing the odds.

You can also manually enable or disable ACPI support after the file copy phase of setup completes, right before your computer reboots into the Windows 2000 Setup Wizard. (Sometimes you can do this after your system freezes during the Setup Wizard.) To force Windows 2000 to enable or disable ACPI support, follow these steps:

1. After the text-mode phase of setup completes but before Windows 2000 reboots into the Setup Wizard, go to a command prompt.
2. Type *attrib –r –s –h c:\txtsetup.sif* at the command prompt.
3. Open the c:\txtsetup.sif file using the edit command or another text editor and search for "ACPIEnable=".
4. To force ACPI support to be enabled, which sometimes fixes setup problems, change the "ACPIEnable=" value to 1.
5. To disable ACPI support, change the "ACPIEnable=" value to 0.
6. Save the file and reboot into the Windows 2000 Setup Wizard.

Again, if any of the steps you take reveal questionable hardware, replace the hardware before you rely on the computer to store important data or provide critical functions to users.

Setup Stops During File Copying

If setup locks up while copying files, you might have a problem with IDE drive configuration. Try one of these solutions:

- Reboot the machine using Ctrl+Alt+Del or Reset, and go into your system BIOS. Verify that your IDE controllers are enabled and configured properly. Make sure that any IDE hard disks or CD-ROMs are detected properly. (You might have to reboot your system and watch your display to verify this because often the drives aren't displayed inside the BIOS.)

- Check the physical jumper settings on your drives to make sure that they are properly configured to have one master and a maximum of one slave per IDE channel.

- If your CD-ROM drive is on the same channel as your hard disk, move it to the secondary channel and configure it to master.

- Try lowering the data transfer rate for your drives; for example, configure the drives to use PIO mode 2 instead of Ultra DMA mode or Ultra 66 Transfer mode.

- Check to make sure that your drives are cabled correctly and that the cables aren't faulty.

- Check the hardware settings to make sure that your hard disk controller isn't conflicting with another device. Try removing all cards from your computer except for your display card and SCSI adapter (if you're using a SCSI drive), and run setup again. If setup succeeds, add your cards one by one after installation, and use the Hardware Wizard in Windows 2000 to configure your devices and troubleshoot any hardware conflicts you encounter.

Tip   Windows 2000 provides a variety of tools you can use to boot a system that doesn't want to start, including the Safe Mode and Last Known Good Boot options, as well as the Recovery Mode Console, which allows you command line access to an NTFS or FAT drive that won't boot (see Chapter 36 for more information).

If none of this helps, try the recommendations in the previous section or consult the Windows 2000 Knowledge Base.

Previous OS Will Not Boot

When you install Windows 2000 Advanced Server on a computer that's already using an operating system and you choose not to upgrade, setup creates a dual boot so that you can select which operating system you'd like to use at boot time.

If your computer never displays the Windows 2000 Loader menu that allows you to choose your previous operating system, the problem is most likely one of two issues: either your boot.ini file has a timeout set to 0 (and thus doesn't display the Boot menu), or your MBR was overwritten during setup, preventing you from booting your previous operating system even if you have the proper entry in your boot.ini file.

To restore the ability to boot your other operating system(s), first back up your hard disk with a Windows 2000 backup program that saves the system state information (such as Windows 2000's bundled Backup utility). Create an emergency repair disk, also using Backup, and then follow these steps:

1. Restart your computer, and press the Spacebar after your BIOS screens are displayed and as soon as you see dots displayed at the top of your screen. This displays the Hardware Profile/Configuration Recovery screen.

2. Press F3 to display the Windows 2000 Loader screen with no timeout value.

3. Select your previous operating system, and press Enter to boot into it.

Tip   You can also change the timeout setting by opening the Control Panel's System applet in Windows 2000, clicking the Advanced tab, clicking Startup And Recovery, then selecting the Display List Of Operating Systems For checkbox and setting the number of seconds you want the boot menu displayed.

If this works and you want to display the Windows 2000 Loader automatically, change the *timeout* value in your boot.ini file to a value higher than 0. To do so, follow these steps:

1. At a command prompt either in Windows 2000 (if your boot drive is formatted with NTFS) or in MS-DOS (boot from a floppy disk), type the following command:

   attrib -r –s –h c:\boot.ini

   edit c:\boot.ini

2. Change the timeout value from 0 to the number of seconds that you want your system to display the Windows 2000 Loader screen before automatically booting. (The default is 30 seconds.)

3. Save and exit Edit, and then type the following command:

   attrib +r +s +h c:\boot.ini

4. Reboot your computer normally.

If your computer doesn't have a boot.ini file, you can use or modify one of the boot.ini files included on the companion CD, or create one from scratch. The following is a sample boot.ini file. For an explanation of this file, see Table 5-6.

```
[Boot Loader]
Timeout=30
Default=multi(0)disk(0)rdisk(0)partition(1)\WINNT
[Operating Systems]
multi(0)disk(0)rdisk(0)partition(1)
\WINNT="Windows 2000 Server" /fastdetect
multi(0)disk(1)rdisk(0)partition(1)
\WINNT="Windows 2000 Professional (Parallel Install)" /fastdetect
```

Table 5-6. **The key variables in a boot.ini file**

Variable	What It Describes
Timeout	Number of seconds to display the Windows 2000 Loader menu.
Default	Location of default operating system to boot.
Multi	Hard disk controller number and type being used. Replace with *scsi* parameter for drives connected to a SCSI controller with its BIOS disabled.
Disk	Disk number on which the operating system resides. This value will always be 0 for IDE drives, but will be the SCSI ID of a SCSI drive.
rdisk	Disk number on which the operating system resides. For IDE drives, this will be the ordinal number of the drive, starting at 0. For a SCSI disk, this will always be 0.
Partition	Partition number on which the operating system resides. Numbering begins at 1.
\WINNT	Path to operating system on the specified partition.
"Windows 2000 Server"	Name of operating system displayed in the Windows 2000 Loader Boot menu. Can be anything.

Caution Creating a boot.ini file incorrectly can cause a system not to boot. Don't perform this procedure unless you have a current backup, a working boot disk that can access all necessary resources on your computer (test the disk first!), along with your Windows 2000 Installation CD, setup boot disks, and a newly created Emergency Repair Disk.

When you create your boot.ini file, make sure you use the correct drive and partition number or your system won't boot. Once you've modified or created your boot.ini file, copy it to the root folder of your boot drive and restart your computer. When the Windows 2000 Loader menu appears, select the operating system you want to load and press Enter.

Note Partitions are numbered in the following manner: The first primary partition on each disk is numbered 1. Additional primary partitions are numbered 2 and up. Any logical drives are numbered based on the order in which they appear in Windows 2000.

If the operating system you have trouble booting is Windows NT or Windows 2000, you can use a switch in the [Operating Systems] section of the boot.ini file to aid in your troubleshooting. Table 5-7 describes switches you can use.

Table 5-7. Operating system troubleshooting switches

Switch	Explanation
/basevideo	Boot using the standard VGA driver. Useful if you're having display trouble.
/sos	Display on screen each driver as it loads during kernel load phase. Useful in determining whether a driver is causing your boot failure.
/noserialmice	Turns off the detection of serial mice. Can add =COMX only to eliminate the detection of serial mice on a specific COM port.
/crashdebug	Turns on the Automatic Recovery and Restart feature.
/maxmem:n	Limits amount of memory to "n" megabytes. Useful in troubleshooting memory parity errors.
/scsiordinal:n	Assigns number 0 to the first SCSI controller and 1 to the second.

If you can't boot either operating system properly, you need to eliminate your newly created boot.ini file. Boot your computer using the Recovery Mode Console or a boot disk, type the following lines at a command prompt, and then reboot your system.

attrib –r –s –h c:\boot.ini

del boot.ini

If the operating system doesn't boot properly, you might need to re-create the MBR for the operating system that you had previously installed. This is risky business, so reread the caution on page 97, and make sure that you have the time to reinstall your operating system and restore a backup if you run into trouble. To recreate the MBR for your previous operating system, follow these steps:

1. Boot your computer with a boot disk for the operating system you are unable to boot. (Make sure the disk contains the Sys.com file.)

2. Type the following at the command prompt to transfer your system files from your floppy disk to the hard disk: *A:\sys c:*

Note If this step doesn't work on your operating system, transfer your system files the way your operating system allows, or try using any MBR repair utilities bundled with your operating system.

3. Remove your floppy disk and reboot your computer. Verify that the operating system you wanted to repair boots properly before performing the next step.

4. Boot Windows 2000 by using your Windows 2000 CD-ROM or setup boot disks.

5. When Windows 2000 setup launches, press Enter to begin, and then press "R" to repair an existing installation.

6. Press "R" again, and then press "M" to perform a manual repair.

7. Clear all check boxes except for the Inspect Boot Sector box. Then press Enter.

8. Insert your emergency repair disk when prompted, or press Esc to have setup search for your Windows 2000 installation.

9. When setup is finished repairing your MBR, reboot your computer and choose the appropriate operating system from the Windows 2000 Loader menu.

Summary

To successfully install Windows 2000 Server, it is very important that you assess your system, document it, plan your installation, and then methodically follow through with your plan. When documenting your system configuration, it's crucial that you make sure that your system is powerful enough to run Windows 2000 and that all components are on the HCL. It's also important to thoroughly record all the information you can about the computer, including the network and hardware settings for the system. Also, you can save time as well as a very large headache if you plan ahead by deciding such things as what file format to use on your partitions, whether to perform a dual boot, and whether to automate your installation.

When it comes time to perform your Windows 2000 installation, there are a number of different phases of setup, including the optional Windows-based phase (if you're installing from Windows 95/98/NT), the text-based phase of setup, and the Windows 2000–based Setup Wizard. If you have any trouble during setup or immediately after setup completes (such as not being able to boot into a previous operating system), you can try a number of things to solve your problem, from updating your BIOS to refreshing the Master Boot Record with a previous operating system's boot information. In the next chapter, we move on to configuring the newly installed Windows 2000.

Chapter 6
Configuring New Windows 2000 Server Installations

After installing Microsoft Windows 2000, you need to configure your server with any devices to be added after setup, possibly change your networking protocols and services, and install key server tools such as Dynamic Host Configuration Protocol (DHCP), Domain Name System (DNS) service, and Windows Internet Naming Service (WINS) servers. The goal of this chapter is to help you get your system in basic working order, with information on fine-tuning to come in later chapters. For example, Chapter 12 has more information on the management of DHCP, DNS, and WINS. Also, if you need to configure disks, see Chapter 14 before installing DHCP and DNS.

Configuring Devices

Immediately after finishing an installation of Windows 2000, or any operating system for that matter, check to make sure that devices are recognized and properly configured. While Windows 2000 Setup generally does a good job of detecting and configuring, Setup isn't able to resolve resource conflicts or overcome a lack of drivers. You'll also need to enable devices, such as an uninterruptable power supply (UPS), that were disconnected or disabled before starting the installation.

Windows NT 4 isn't the best operating system for finding and troubleshooting device problems because it lacks Plug and Play (PnP) functions and supports a somewhat limited hardware base. In contrast, Windows 2000 handles these issues well, integrating PnP support along with a more centralized method of managing hardware devices, using Device Manager and the Add/Remove Hardware Wizard, and generally improving device driver support. Check the list of devices in Device Manager for conflicts and for devices that weren't installed during setup, and then use the Add/Remove Hardware Wizard to make the necessary changes. Or you can use Device Manager if you prefer a more hands-on approach.

Using the Add/Remove Hardware Wizard

While you can use Device Manager instead of the Add/Remove Hardware Wizard to handle most of the wizard's functions, you do need to use the Add/Remove Hardware Wizard to add a device that Windows 2000 can't recognize or to unplug or eject a device.

Removing and Adding a Device

To remove a device, select the Uninstall/Unplug A Device option in the Add/Remove Hardware Wizard, and then use the windows that follow either to temporarily unplug a hot-pluggable device or to permanently uninstall a device from your system. You can always add the device back later by using this same wizard or by using autodetection of PnP devices in Windows 2000.

To add a device to your system, make sure the device is physically connected and, if appropriate, turned on. Then double-click the Add/Remove Hardware icon in Control Panel, and when the welcome screen appears, click Next to begin the wizard.

Select the Add/Troubleshoot A Device option, shown in Figure 6-1, and then click Next. Windows 2000 scans your system for PnP hardware, then displays a list of detected hardware. If new PnP hardware is detected, Windows 2000 installs drivers, if it can locate them, and displays a list of devices that it installed. Click Finish to end the installation process.

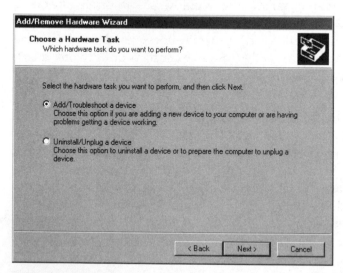

Figure 6-1. *The Choose A Hardware Task screen of the Add/Remove Hardware Wizard.*

Troubleshooting a Device

If, after you add a device, Windows 2000 doesn't detect it or detects it incorrectly, you can troubleshoot the problem by using the Add/Remove Hardware Wizard. When no new devices are found, Windows 2000 displays all the devices on your system—listing any disabled devices or devices with problems first (Figure 6-2).

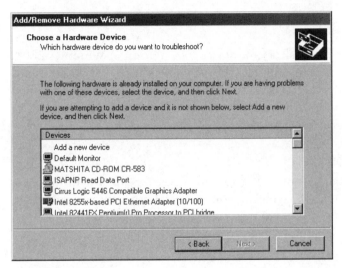

Figure 6-2. *The Choose A Hardware Device screen of the Add/Remove Hardware Wizard.*

When troubleshooting a problem device, select the device from the list, and then click Next to see the status of the device and to start a troubleshooter. To add a device that Windows 2000 couldn't detect, select Add A New Device from the list in the Choose A Hardware Device window, and then follow these steps:

1. Choose whether you want Windows 2000 to search for your hardware or whether you want to select the device manually from a list.

2. Select from the list of devices detected, or select a type of hardware you want to install from the provided list, and click Next.

3. If you chose to select your device manually, select the manufacturer and device, or click Have Disk to supply your own drivers, and then click Next. Windows 2000 installs the drivers for your device and then displays a summary of its actions.

4. Click Finish to complete the wizard.

Tip If you disable something essential—like the mouse and keyboard—you can return to the previous hardware profile by rebooting. When the Loader menu appears, press F8, and choose Last Known Good Configuration. Then choose the version of Windows 2000 you have installed from the Loader menu and press Enter. This action will enable the last good hardware profile.

Using Device Manager

Device Manager is a central repository for device information in Windows 2000. If you've used Device Manager in Windows 95/98, you'll be at home with the new Windows 2000 Device Manager. Use it to view or print the configuration and drivers loaded for any device on your system as well as to disable, uninstall, or change the configuration for a device.

Opening Device Manager

You can access Device Manager in one of several ways. Perhaps the most useful way is to click the Computer Management icon in the Administrative Tools menu on the Start menu. Click the plus sign next to System Tools to expand the tree, and then click Device Manager.

You can also access Device Manager by opening the System tool in Control Panel. Click the Hardware tab and then click the Device Manager button. The Hardware tab also contains the Hardware Wizard and the Driver Signing tool that you can use to specify whether you want to permit the use of unsigned device drivers.

Tip To use the Computer Management snap-in to remotely administer another computer running Windows 2000, select Computer Management in the console tree, and then choose Connect To Another Computer from the Action menu. Select the computer you want to manage, click OK, and you're there.

Working with Device Manager

After opening Device Manager, you'll see a list of all the devices that Windows 2000 has detected on your system (Figure 6-3). Any nonfuntioning devices are displayed with an exclamation point, indicating that a problem exists with the device; disabled devices are displayed with a small red "x" over the icon.

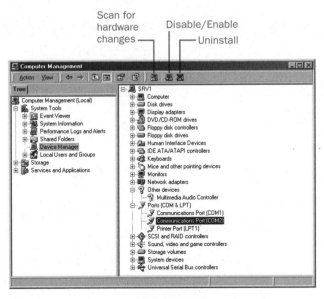

Figure 6-3. *The Device Manager snap-in.*

On the far right side of the toolbar, icons are available according to the device you've highlighted. In Figure 6-3, they are the following buttons (reading from left to right):

- **Scan For Hardware Changes**   Click this button to tell the system to look for changes in hardware. Use this button after adding new PnP devices or after swapping hardware.

- **Disable/Enable**   Highlight a device and click this button to disable it or enable it, depending on its current status. When a device is disabled, its resources are freed and its drivers remain but are not loaded during startup. Take care not to disable something you need to start the machine.

- **Uninstall**   Highlight a device and click this button to uninstall it. This should only be necessary for non-PnP devices. A PnP device can be uninstalled by simply removing it from the computer. Uninstalling a device doesn't remove the device's drivers from the hard disk.

To change the Device Manager display, choose a setting from the View menu. (See Table 6-1.) Use the different view settings for Device Manager to organize your system's devices in a way that makes it easy to find the information you need.

Table 6-1. View settings

Setting	Description
Devices By Type	Shows devices categorized by device type; usually the most useful view (also the default)
Devices By Connection	Shows all devices in relation to how they're connected to other devices
Resources By Type	Shows all system resources, organized by type of resource
Resources By Connection	Shows all system resources, organized and grouped by the device to which they're connected
Show Hidden Devices	Includes devices that are not PnP plus devices that might have been physically removed but still have their drivers installed

Working with Device Properties

To display a device's properties (Figure 6-4), select the device, and then click the Properties toolbar button or double-click the device. In the Device Properties window, there may be several tabs. You can view the status and configuration information, as well as the device manufacturer, device type, and location, in the upper portion of the General tab.

Tip The device name shown in Device Manager is the name of the driver that Windows 2000 is using for the device and can actually be incorrect if the wrong driver is loaded for the device.

The Device Status box in the middle of the General tab displays the status of the device, including any errors. If the device has any problems, the Device Status box will briefly describe the problem, and usually it will also describe the appropriate course of action to correct the problem. Click the Troubleshooter button to use the built-in mechanisms for detecting the nature of the problem.

More Info If you need additional information about a message displayed in the Device status box, check Microsoft support at *http://www.microsoft.com/support/kb.htm*.

Other tabs include the Driver tab, which displays the details of the driver being used. This tab also lets you update or uninstall the driver. The Resources tab displays the hardware resources being used. This tab allows you to see and resolve any conflicts caused by non-PnP devices. Along with these tabs, some devices have additional advanced settings or tabs for device-specific settings.

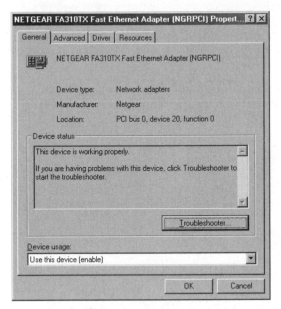

Figure 6-4. *The General tab of the Device Properties window.*

Tip   Device Manager works on remote computers in read-only mode. You can use Device Manager to diagnose problems, but you must make changes locally.

Configuring Networking Settings

While Windows 2000 Setup prompts you for the necessary network settings, you might need to change these settings at some point after completing setup— possibly immediately, if the settings you specified were wrong or incomplete. This section explains how to get your server running properly on your network.

Changing Your Network Identity

Change is sometimes necessary—although with a server, it's better to spend your time planning first than to have to make changes later. However, as Robbie Burns often said while reconfiguring his server, "The best laid schemes o' mice and men gang aft a-gley." So even with careful planning, you can discover that a machine needs to have a different name or needs to be joined to a different domain.

Changing a Stand-Alone Server

To change the identity of a server that isn't a domain controller, log on using an administrator's account and follow these steps:

1. Open the System tool in Control Panel, and then click the Network Identification tab.

2. To change your computer name and domain or workgroup membership, select Properties. Then enter the new name for your computer in the New computer name text box in the Identification Changes dialog box, as shown in Figure 6-5.

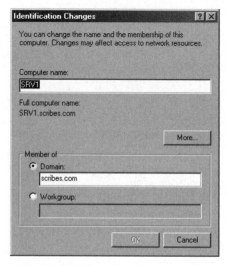

Figure 6-5. *The Identification Changes dialog box.*

3. To change the domain or workgroup you belong to, choose either the Domain option or the Workgroup option, and then type the domain or workgroup name in the text box.

4. Click More to manually specify the domain name for your computer and to preview the NetBIOS name for your system. Click OK when you're finished.

Real World   Naming Computers

It's a good idea to use a computer name that is both DNS-compatible and NetBIOS-compatible so that all types of clients see the same name for your computer. To do this, keep the name shorter than 15 characters long, and don't use asterisks or periods. To obtain the best application compatibility, also try to avoid using spaces, underscores, and hyphens.

> **Note** Changing the identity of a domain controller is a multistep process. First you must demote the domain controller. Then you can change the identity, and finally you can promote the domain controller again. The steps for this process are detailed in Chapter 11.

Configuring Network Components

To add or change the settings for core network components such as clients, services, and protocols, open the Network And Dial-Up Connections folder, right-click the Local Area Connection icon, and choose Properties from the shortcut menu. This procedure opens the Local Area Connection Properties window shown in Figure 6-6, which you can use to view and change your server's networking components.

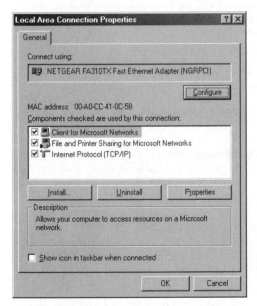

Figure 6-6. *The Local Area Connection Properties window.*

The top of the dialog box shows the network adapter to which you are binding networking services. Beneath that is the media access control (MAC) address for the network interface card, the unique identifier of your network card that is used for communications with other hosts in your subnet.

To install a network component, select Install, choose the type of component you want to install (Client, Service, or Protocol), and then click Add. Select the component from the list presented and click OK. To configure the component (if the component has a configurable option), select the component and click Properties.

Tip If you have a multihomed server (a server with more than one network adapter), give your local area connections a name indicating to which network the adapters are connected.

Configuring TCP/IP

TCP/IP is the most important protocol in today's networks, and it's the backbone for Microsoft's vision of networking in Windows 2000. The protocol is well-suited to enterprise networking, and it's required for accessing the Internet. If you're unfamiliar with TCP/IP, see Chapter 13 for an introduction.

Planning Before installing and configuring protocols on your network, review the checklists in the Windows 2000 Help files. Once you understand the following three areas, you can install all the necessary interlocking pieces.

- TCP/IP concepts such as IP addressing, subnet masks, and gateways
- Whether your network supports DHCP to configure TCP/IP dynamically
- How computers on your network will handle name resolution

Installing TCP/IP

TCP/IP is installed as the default network protocol if a network adapter was detected during installation. If the default was overridden during installation, you can add TCP/IP by following these steps:

1. Click the Start button, select Settings, and then choose Network And Dialup Connections.

2. Right-click the connection for which you want to install TCP/IP, and select Properties.

3. If TCP/IP isn't in the list of components used, as shown in Figure 6-6, click Install.

4. Highlight Protocol, and click Add.

5. In the Select Network Protocol box, highlight Internet Protocol (TCP/IP), and click OK.

6. Verify that the Internet Protocol (TCP/IP) check box is selected, and then click OK.

Using Dynamic Addressing

The easiest and most reliable way to configure machines on a network running the TCP/IP suite is to use a DHCP server to automatically distribute IP addresses. DHCP can also inform clients of the appropriate DNS servers and gateways to use. A DHCP server not only simplifies client configuration, but also saves headaches for the poor soul who would otherwise have to track the use of IP addresses, because it manages the database of available IP addresses dynamically and automatically.

Dynamic addressing using DHCP is the Windows 2000 default setting. If you need to check this or change a statically assigned host to a dynamically configured host, follow these steps:

1. Select the Internet Protocol (TCP/IP) component in your Local Area Connection Properties window, and click Properties (Figure 6-7).

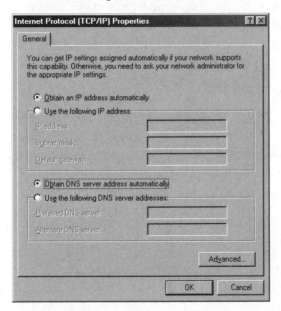

Figure 6-7. *The General tab of the Internet Protocol (TCP/IP) Properties window.*

2. Select the Obtain An IP Address Automatically option. But don't select this option on a machine that is to act as a DHCP server. A DHCP server must have a fixed, static IP address.

3. Select the Obtain DNS Server Address Automatically option if your DHCP server is set up to provide the DNS server addresses to clients; otherwise, select the Use The Following DNS Server Addresses option, and enter the IP addresses for the DNS servers you want to use.

Using Static Addressing

If your network doesn't have a DHCP server or if you're setting up a DHCP server, you need to manually configure TCP/IP to use a static IP address and DNS information. To do this, obtain an IP address from the person who maintains the database of IP addresses that your organization can use. If using DHCP, all DHCP servers also need to be updated to exclude your static IP address. Accomplish this by following these steps:

1. Select the Internet Protocol (TCP/IP) component in the Local Area Connection Properties dialog box, and click Properties.

2. Select the Use The Following IP Address option, enter the address you obtain in the *IP Address* field, and then click Tab to automatically fill in the default subnet mask. Most likely, you'll be able to use the default subnet mask, but if your network is using a specific subnet mask, you need to find the proper mask and enter it in the *Subnet Mask* field.

3. Enter the IP address for your default gateway or router in the *Default Gateway* field. The default gateway forwards, or routes, any traffic destined for hosts outside your local subnet, possibly to another portion of your wide area network (WAN) or to the Internet.

4. Choose the Use The Following DNS Server Addresses option to specify the IP addresses for your DNS servers. Enter the primary and secondary DNS server addresses in the fields provided.

Real World **Assigning IP Addresses for DNS and WINS Servers**

If you're setting up your server to be a DNS or WINS server, you're probably tempted to use a static IP address. While this is an acceptable use of static IPs, a much better method is to take a dynamically assigned address from the DHCP server and then have the DHCP server administrator create an IP reservation for your server with an unlimited lease duration. This step gives you a permanent lease on the IP address you were assigned, making it easy to configure client machines while at the same time allowing the DHCP administrator to take back the address if your server is moved or decommissioned.

Note   The DNS service is critical for resolving hostnames such as *www .microsoft.com* into IP addresses that your computer can access. Without the DNS service, you could access resources only by typing in their IP addresses directly. Or if the resources are on your local network and you have NetBIOS over TCP/IP enabled on the WINS tab of the Advanced TCP/IP Properties dialog box, you could access resources only by broadcasting their names over the network, consuming network bandwidth.

Setting Advanced TCP/IP Options

If you aren't using a DHCP server to configure your server's IP address and associated settings and you need to enter other settings besides just your server's IP address and DNS servers, select Advanced in the TCP/IP Properties window, discussed on page 111. This opens the Advanced TCP/IP Settings dialog box, shown in Figure 6-8, which you use to specify additional settings, including WINS servers, NetBIOS over TCP/IP, and optional TCP/IP parameters. Chapter 13 contains more on configuring TCP/IP.

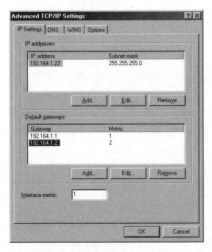

Figure 6-8. *The IP Settings tab of the Advanced TCP/IP Settings dialog box.*

Configuring IP Settings

The Advanced TCP/IP Settings dialog box contains four tabs, the first of which is the IP Settings tab. You use this tab to add the IP address and subnet mask for your network connection as well as the gateways your server should use. To change the options on this tab, follow the steps on the next page.

1. Use the Add, Edit, and Remove buttons under the IP Addresses box to modify your IP address and subnet mask settings. You can use up to five IP addresses and subnet masks for your network connection—either to access different logical IP networks, or to use different IP addresses in a single, logical IP network.

2. To add a default gateway or router, select Add and enter the IP address for the router.

3. Now add the interface metric for the connection. The interface metric assigns a relative cost to using a particular router to access a particular IP address. Assign lower interface metrics with routers connecting to fast networks, such as another section of a local network; assign higher numbers to slower connections, such as an Integrated Services Digital Network (ISDN) or a slow digital subscriber line (DSL) connection to the Internet.

Configuring DNS Settings

Click the DNS tab to access the advanced DNS settings for your network connection, as shown in Figure 6-9. Then use the following procedure to configure your DNS settings:

1. Use the Add, Edit, and Remove buttons beneath the DNS addresses box to add or modify the DNS servers you want to use for this connection. Use the up and down arrows next to the box to change the order in which your server queries the DNS servers.

2. Select the appropriate options for unqualified names.

   - **Append Primary And Connection Specific DNS Suffixes**   Limits the resolution for unqualified names to the domain suffixes and connection-specific suffixes. So if your primary DNS suffix is eng.scribes.com and you type *ping srv4* at a command prompt, DNS will look for srv4.eng.scribes.com. If you also specify a connection-specific name (under DNS Suffix For This Connection), such as dev.scribes.com, DNS will query srv4.eng.scribes.com *and* srv4.dev.scribes.com.

   - **Append Parent Suffixes Of The Primary DNS Suffix**   Includes parent suffixes up to the second-level domain in the resolution of unqualified names. So if the primary DNS suffix is eng.uk.corp.scribes.com and you type *ping srv4* at a command prompt, DNS will query for the following:

     - srv4.eng.uk.corp.scribes.com
     - srv4.uk.corp.scribes.com

- srv4.corp.scribes.com
- srv4.scribes.com
- **Append These DNS Suffixes (In Order)**   Specifies the only domain suffixes to be appended to unqualified domain names during the name resolution process. If you specify domain suffixes here, the primary and connection-specific suffixes are not used.

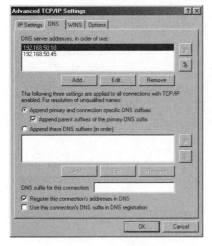

Figure 6-9. *The DNS tab of the Advanced TCP/IP Settings window.*

3. To override the parent DNS domain name specified for your computer on the Network Identification tab of the System Properties Control Panel tool, type the DNS domain name you want to use in the DNS Suffix For This Connection text box.

4. To prevent the full DNS name of your server's IP address from being registered with the DNS server, clear the Register This Connection's Addresses In DNS check box.

5. To register the IP addresses of your network connections in DNS based on the domain name of the connections as well as by the FQDN for your server, select the Register This Connection's DNS Suffix In DNS Registration check box. The domain name of the connection is entered in the DNS Suffix For This Connection text box or assigned by the DHCP server.

Configuring WINS Settings

To configure the WINS settings for your computer, click the WINS tab in the Advanced TCP/IP Settings dialog box (Figure 6-10). If WINS servers are operating on your network, you should add their addresses here. Doing so will give you the best results when communicating with hosts that are running Microsoft pre-Windows 2000 operating systems. As with the other tabs in the Advanced TCP/IP Settings dialog box, use the Add, Edit, and Remove buttons to modify your WINS server list. For a more thorough discussion of when to use WINS servers on your network, see the "Setting Up a WINS Server" section later in this chapter.

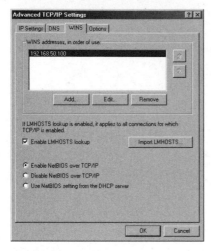

Figure 6-10. *The WINS tab of the Advanced TCP/IP Settings dialog box.*

To enable the use of an LMHOSTS file for resolving NetBIOS names to IP addresses, select the Enable LMHOSTS Lookup check box, and click the Import LMHOSTS button to import an LMHOSTS file. We recommend not using LMHOSTS files unless absolutely necessary because trying to keep them up-to-date can be tricky—the miniscule reduction of network traffic that LMHOSTS files offer isn't worth it.

Tip When you configure a WINS server, use the Ipconfig command at a command prompt to obtain your current IP address, and then enter that address in the WINS *Addresses* field. Don't enter any other WINS server in this field; you don't want your WINS server registering its NetBIOS name with another WINS server if your WINS service hasn't started in time to respond at boot up.

In all likelihood, you'll need to communicate with clients that are running Microsoft operating systems earlier than Windows 2000, so make sure the Enable NetBIOS Over TCP/IP option is selected. Disable this only if you communicate exclusively with other computers running Windows 2000 or computers that rely soley on DNS for name resolution services (for example, UNIX). Also, note that any applications that use NetBIOS won't work if you disable NetBIOS Over TCP/IP.

Configuring TCP/IP Options

If you need to configure any TCP/IP options, click the Options tab in the Advanced TCP/IP Settings dialog box. Select an option you want to configure, and then click Properties. For more information on TCP/IP properties and secure TCP/IP connections, see Chapter 13.

Configuring NWLink IPX/SPX

The NWLink IPX/SPX protocol was designed as an easy-to-use-and-configure, routable protocol that is compatible with NetWare's IPX/SPX protocol. As such, it's a popular protocol in many companies and can be key to maintaining interoperability with different network environments. For detailed information on interoperating with NetWare, see Chapter 20. Fortunately, configuring the NWLink IPX/SPX protocol is easy. Just follow these steps:

1. Install the protocol in the Local Area Connection Properties dialog box, which can be accessed by right-clicking the Local Area Connection icon in the Network and Dial-Up Connections folder and then selecting Properties.

2. Select the protocol and click Properties.

3. To advertise the services running on your server (such as File and Print Services For NetWare or IPX routing) to native NetWare clients, enter a unique eight-digit hexadecimal number to identify your server in the Internal Network Number text box (Figure 6-11).

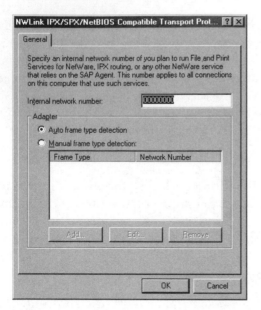

Figure 6-11. *The General tab of the NWLink IPX/SPX NetBIOS–Compatible Transport dialog box.*

4. In most cases, you can also let Windows 2000 handle your frame type detection by selecting the Auto Frame Type Detection option. Windows 2000 then detects the proper frame type by sending out a routing information protocol (RIP) request for all frame types and then waiting for a response back. The frame type for which Windows 2000 received a response then becomes the default. If responses were received for multiple frame types, Windows 2000 sets the default frame types for which the responses were received in this order: Ethernet 802.2, Ethernet 802.3, Ethernet II, SNAP.

5. If you want to specify the frame type manually or add multiple frame types, select the Manual Frame Type Detection option, select Add, and then choose a frame type and enter the network number for that frame type.

Using the Windows 2000 Configure Your Server Tool

The Windows 2000 Configure Your Server tool provides a central location that you can use to install and manage most of the important server tools such as Microsoft Active Directory, DHCP, DNS, and WINS. However, given the some-times bewildering number of administrative tools and Microsoft Management Console (MMC) snap-ins available, having an organized and central location from which to access all of these tools is crucial. You don't actually use the Configure Your Server tool to perform many actions, but it serves as an interface for launching the various MMC snap-ins that you use to accomplish your tasks.

The Windows 2000 Configure Your Server tool appears when you first boot your server after completing setup. If it doesn't appear, set up any additional devices and prepare any additional drives you need for your server programs and data, and then launch the Windows 2000 Configure Your Server tool from the Administrative Tools folder on the Start menu.

In the Configure Your Server tool, use the topics on the left to choose the services you want to configure, and click the hyperlinks and buttons to set up and configure these services. The Configure Your Server tool launches any necessary wizards to walk you through installing the services you selected.

Choosing Whether to Set Up a Domain Controller

The first screen in the Windows 2000 Configure Your Server tool asks whether your server is the only one on your network (Figure 6-12). When you create a new network and this is the first server on the network, choose the This Is The Only Server In My Network option. (See the "Configuring the First Server on Your Network" section later in this chapter for more information.) This selection sets up your server as a domain controller and installs Active Directory, DHCP, and DNS on your server. Otherwise, choose the Are Already One Or More Servers Running In My Network option. Choosing this option allows you to pick exactly which services you want to install on your system. After choosing an option, click Next to continue.

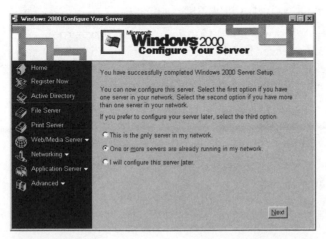

Figure 6-12. *The first screen of the Configure Your Server tool.*

You should be extremely careful about adding a domain controller to an existing Windows NT 4 network. Before you can add any Windows 2000 domain controllers to an existing Windows NT 4 domain, you must upgrade the primary domain controller (PDC) to Windows 2000. This upgrade is required because Windows NT domains are single-master networks where the PDC contains the master records for the domain. Windows 2000 servers use full, multimaster replication, and each domain controller acts as a master repository for domain information. If you add a Windows 2000 server or upgrade any machine other than the PDC on an existing Windows NT domain, you'll create a new Windows 2000 domain that looks like the existing domain but is not the same domain. The Windows 2000 domain controller that will work as the PDC for the network won't have the same security identifier (SID) as the PDC of the NT 4 domain you were trying to upgrade. The result will be a "network" that doesn't work. Therefore, you must upgrade the PDC on a Windows NT domain to Windows 2000 before attempting to install any other iterations of Windows 2000 Server.

Tip When upgrading a PDC to Windows 2000, be sure the server's hardware is capable of handling the upgrade. If there's any doubt as to whether your existing PDC can function with the additional load, you can do a little juggling by promoting a BDC that you're sure of to be the PDC. Then upgrade the new PDC to Windows 2000. See Chapter 7 for more information on upgrading servers.

Configuring the First Server on Your Network

If you're creating a new network or domain and you're setting up the first server in the domain, the Windows 2000 Configure Your Server tool can hold your hand through the configuration process. Just follow these steps:

1. In the first window of the Windows 2000 Configure Your Server tool, choose the This Is The Only Server In My Network option, and click Next (as discussed in the previous section). Choosing this option helps you configure your server as a domain controller running Active Directory, DHCP, and DNS.

2. Click the Show More Details link to view information about how your server's TCP/IP services will be configured, and then click Back.

3. Click Next, and then enter the domain name you want to use in the first text box, as shown in Figure 6-13.

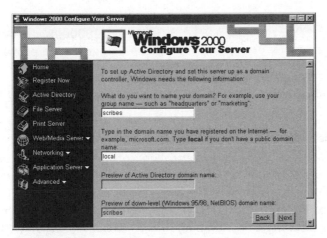

Figure 6-13. *Entering your domain name using the Configure Your Server tool.*

4. To use an Internet-registered domain name (such as scribes.com) as the root for your fully qualified domain name, enter the Internet domain name in the second text box. Or, to specify that your domain is a local domain that isn't a part of an Internet-registered domain, type *local* in the second text box.

5. Verify that the Active Directory and downlevel domain names are correct in the preview boxes at the bottom of the window, and then click Next.

6. Click Next again. Active Directory, DHCP, and DNS are installed in Unattended mode and Windows restarts. Once logged on, Windows displays the Windows 2000 Configure Your Server tool again. (See Chapter 10 for help with any Active Directory installation questions you are asked, or see the sections on installing DHCP and DNS later in this chapter for help with DHCP and DNS questions.)

7. Configure your server to use the static IP address specified in the Windows 2000 Configure Your Server tool. To do this, right-click the Local Area Connection icon in the Network And Dial-Up Connections folder, and choose Properties from the shortcut menu. Select Internet Protocol (TCP/IP), and click Properties. Then enter the proper IP address and subnet mask, and verify that the DNS server addresses include your server's IP address.

8. Open the DHCP Manager and expand the DHCP server.

9. Select the DHCP server and choose All Tasks-Authorize from the Action menu.

10. Reboot your computer, and then use the Windows 2000 Configure Your Server tool to add any additional services you need.

Real World   Special Facts About Windows 2000 Domain Controllers

While it's true that all Windows 2000 domain controllers are equal, some are more equal than others. The first Windows 2000 domain controller is automatically assigned the role of global catalog server. At least one global catalog server is needed on every domain. The global catalog is a database that contains a full replica of all directory objects in its host domain plus a partial replica of all directory objects in every domain in the forest. The global catalog's role is to enable the finding of directory information and to provide universal group membership information during logon. After additional controllers are installed, the role of global catalog server can be reassigned, or more than one machine can be designated as a global catalog server. This process is described in Chapter 11.

The first domain controller is also assigned the operations master roles. A single controller must perform each of these roles because they are functions that can't be executed in different places at the same time. (For example, the creation of security identifiers must be done by a single controller to make sure each identifier is unique.) Under most circumstances, you won't have to change the location for any of the operations master roles, but you should be familiar with each of the roles and what happens in the case of failure. See Chapter 12 for information on operations master roles.

Setting Up a DHCP Server

The DHCP server greatly reduces the administrative task of configuring workstations with an IP address and the appropriate TCP/IP settings for your network. Before installing the DHCP server, determine your IP addressing scheme. (See Chapter 12.) You must also complete these additional steps before installing DHCP:

- Determine the range of unique, free IP addresses that your DHCP server will manage as well as any IP addresses that need to be excluded to support hosts with static IP addresses.

- Make a list of servers that you want to give IP reservations to (such as DNS and WINS servers).

- If your DHCP server will be using Internet-registered IP addresses, register your IP addresses with your ISP.

- Upgrade any Windows NT 4 domain controllers to Windows 2000.

- Determine the hardware and storage requirements for the DHCP server.

- Manually configure the static IP address on the computer where the DHCP service is to be installed.

To install the DHCP service, follow these steps:

1. Open the Configure Your Server tool (if it's not already open) by launching it from the Administrative Tools folder.

2. Click the Networking heading in the column on the left, and then click the DHCP subheading.

3. Click the Start hyperlink (shown in Figure 6-14) to launch the Windows Components Wizard.

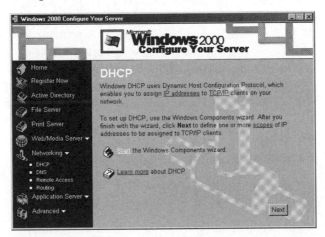

Figure 6-14. *Setting up DHCP using the Configure Your Server tool.*

4. Click Next in the first screen of the Windows Component Wizard.

5. Select Networking Services from the list of components, and then click Details.

6. Select the check box next to the Dynamic Host Configuration Protocol (DHCP) component, and click OK. Click Next to install the service. All the necessary files are copied to your hard disk.

Tip   If you want to install DHCP service on a server that isn't a domain controller, you'll need to tell Active Directory about it. After installation, open DHCP from the Administrative Tools menu. Highlight DHCP in the console tree, and then choose Browse Authorized Servers from the Action menu. Click Add, and then type in the name or IP address of the DHCP server to authorize.

Real World   Using Multiple DHCP Servers

If you plan to use multiple DHCP servers on a subnet for load-balancing and redundancy, configure a superscope on each DHCP server that contains all valid scopes for the subnet as member scopes. Then configure a member scope on each server that has the other servers' addresses excluded so that no addresses appear in both servers' address pools. A good division is to give 80 percent of the addresses to the primary DHCP server and 20 percent to the secondary server.

Creating a New Scope

Now you're ready to launch the DHCP Manager and create a new scope of IP addresses for the DHCP server to manage. But before you can do this, make sure you know which range of IP addresses are approved, which IP addresses need to be excluded for systems with static IP addresses, and which IP addresses need to be reserved for DNS or WINS servers. To open DHCP Manager and create your new scope, follow these steps:

1. Choose DHCP from the Administrative Tools menu.

2. Select the DHCP server in the console tree. Select the Action menu and choose New Scope to launch the New Scope Wizard.

3. Click Next, and enter a name and description for the scope to use for distinguishing this scope from others (Figure 6-15). Click Next.

4. Enter the IP address that your scope begins with in the Start field, and enter the IP address that your scope ends with in the End field, as shown in Figure 6-16.

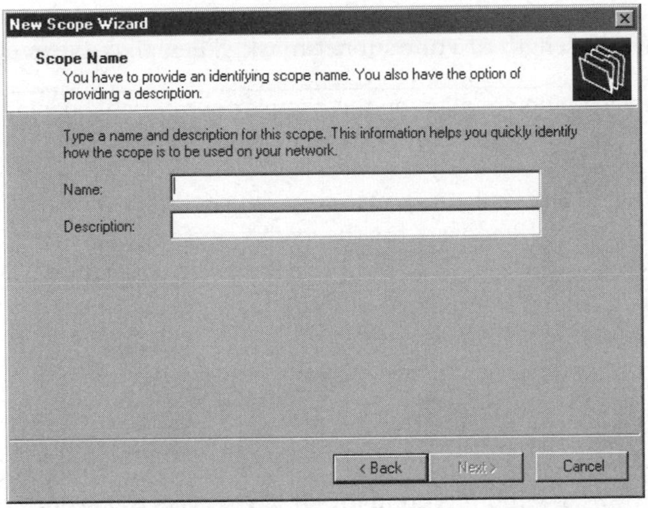

Figure 6-15. *The Scope Name screen of the New Scope Wizard.*

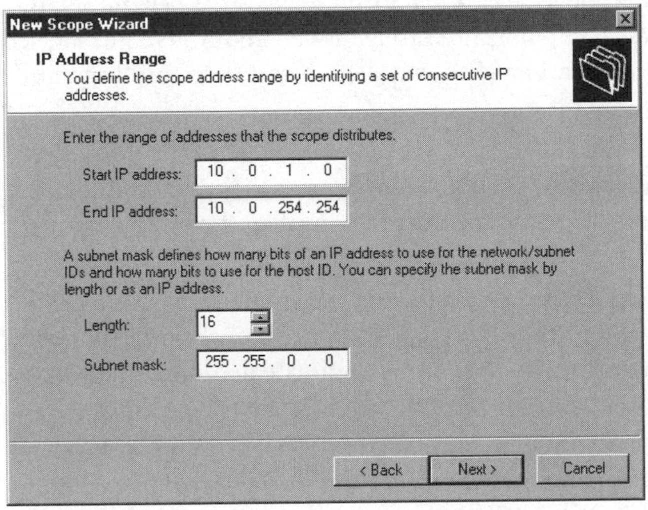

Figure 6-16. *The IP Address Range screen of the New Scope Wizard.*

5. Enter your network's subnet mask in the Subnet Mask box, or use the Length box to adjust the length of your subnet mask. Then click Next.

> **More Info** A good source of information on the complex subject of choosing subnet masks is the book *Microsoft TCP/IP Training* (Microsoft Press, 1997).

6. To exclude a range of addresses from your scope, in the Start IP Address box, enter the start IP address for the exclusion range; in the End IP Address box, enter the end IP address for the exclusion range. Then click Add. Add as many exclusions as needed, and click Next when you're finished.

7. Specify the lease duration for your clients, and then click Next.

Real World Setting Lease Durations

Use longer leases for networks without redundant DHCP servers to permit more time to recover an offline DHCP server before clients lose their leases, or to minimize network traffic at the expense of less frequent address turnover. You can also use longer leases if scope addresses are plentiful (at least 20 percent available), the network is stable, and computers are rarely moved about. In contrast, scopes that support dial-up clients can have shorter leases and therefore function well with fewer addresses.

8. To configure DHCP options, click Yes; otherwise, click No, and then click Next. If you select No, click Finish to complete the setup of your scope.

9. If you chose to specify DHCP options, enter the gateways (routers) you want clients to use in the Gateway Address box, clicking the Add button after entering each one. When you're finished adding gateways, click Next.

10. Enter the domain name of your domain in the Parent Domain box, and add the IP addresses for your DNS servers in the IP Address box, as shown in Figure 6-17, clicking Add after entering each one. Click Next when you're done.

11. In the WINS Server Address box, enter the addresses of any WINS servers you've configured on your network for resolving NetBIOS names into IP addresses for downlevel clients. Click Next.

12. To activate the scope immediately, click Yes; otherwise, click No to activate the scope later. Click Next, and then click Finish to complete your scope configuration.

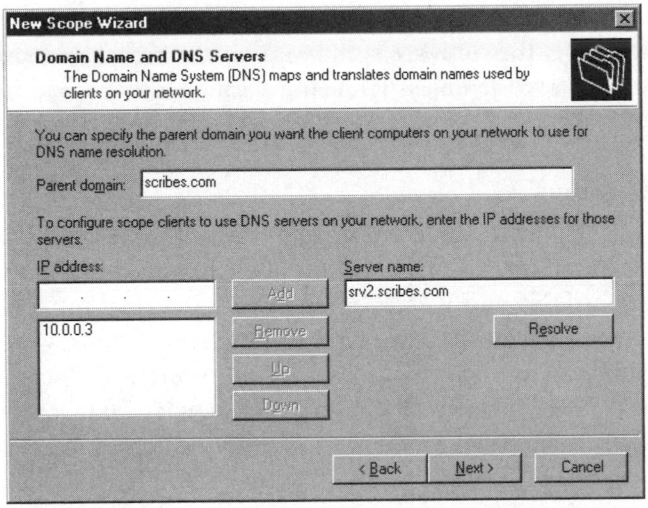

Figure 6-17. *The Domain Name And DNS Servers screen of the New Scope Wizard.*

Authorizing the DHCP Server and Activating Scopes

After you've set up your DHCP server and created the scopes, you need to activate the scopes before any clients can use the server to obtain an IP address. Before scopes can be activated, the server has to be authorized to give leases, unless you installed DHCP on a domain controller, in which case the DHCP server will be authorized automatically the first time you add the server to your DHCP Manager console. Authorizing a DHCP server is an important option that Windows 2000 provides to reduce the ability of hackers to set up rogue DHCP servers—unauthorized servers set up to hand out false IP addresses to clients. To authorize your DHCP server after installing the service, follow these steps:

1. In the DHCP Manager, select DHCP at the root of the console tree.

2. Choose Manage Authorized Servers from the Action menu.

3. Select Authorize in the Manage Authorized Servers dialog box.

4. Enter the name or IP address for your server in the text box provided and click OK.

5. Verify that the information is correct in the dialog box displayed, and then click Yes. Click OK to close the Manage Authorized Servers dialog box.

6. To activate a scope, select the scope from the console tree, and then choose Activate from the Action menu.

Don't activate a scope until you've finished selecting all the options you want. Once you've activated a scope, the Activate command on the menu changes to Deactivate. Don't deactivate a scope unless it's being permanently retired from the network.

Adding Address Reservations

Reservations are handy items that you can use instead of static IP addresses (which require exclusions) for all servers (except DHCP servers) that need to maintain a specific IP address, such as DNS and WINS servers. Using reservations instead of static addresses guarantees that a server will have a consistent IP address while also providing the ability to recover the IP address in the future if the server is decommissioned or moved. You should create the reservation on all DHCP servers that could potentially service the reserved client. To add an address reservation to a scope, follow these steps:

1. Right-click the Reservations folder under the desired scope, and choose New Reservation from the shortcut menu.

2. Enter a name for the reservation in the Reservation Name box.

3. Enter the IP address for the client in the IP Address box, and enter the MAC address for the client in the MAC Address box, as shown in Figure 6-18.

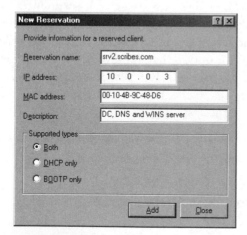

Figure 6-18. *The New Reservation dialog box.*

4. Enter a description for the reservation in the Description box.

5. Determine which type of client you want to allow to use the reservation by selecting DHCP Only, BOOTP Only, or Both. Click Add.

Note   To obtain the MAC address, go to the client computer and type *ipconfig* /all at the command prompt. The MAC address is listed as the physical address.

Enabling Dynamic Updates to a DNS Server

The Windows 2000 DHCP and DNS servers now support dynamic updates to a DNS server—a feature that any administrator who has had to manage a static Windows NT 4 DNS server (or the like) will appreciate. Windows 2000 clients can dynamically update their forward lookup records themselves with the DNS server after obtaining a new IP address from a DHCP server.

In addition, the Windows 2000 DHCP server also supports dynamically updating the DNS records for pre–Windows 2000 clients that can't do it for themselves. This feature currently works only with the Windows 2000 DHCP and DNS servers. The Internet proposal for dynamic updates between DNS servers was in draft form during the creation of Windows 2000, but greater compatibility might be implemented soon after release. To enable a DHCP server to dynamically update the DNS records of its clients, follow these steps:

1. Select the scope or DHCP server on which you want to permit dynamic DNS updates.

2. From the Action menu, choose Properties, and then click the DNS tab.

3. Select the Automatically Update DHCP Client Information In DNS check box, as shown in Figure 6-19.

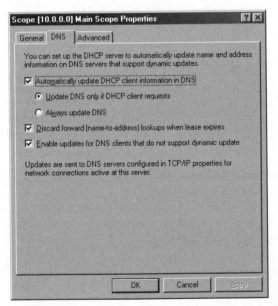

Figure 6-19. *The DNS tab of the Main Scope Properties window.*

4. To update a client's DNS records based on the type of DHCP request the client makes and only when requested, select the Update DNS Only If DHCP Client Requests option.

5. To always update a client's forward and reverse lookup records, select the Always Update DNS option.

6. Select the Discard Forward Lookups When Lease Expires check box to have the DHCP server delete the Host resource record for a client when its DHCP lease expires and isn't renewed.

7. Select the Enable Updates For DNS Clients That Do Not Support Dynamic Update check box to enable the DHCP server to update the forward and reverse lookup records for clients that can't update their own forward lookup records. If you don't select this check box, the DHCP server won't automatically update the DNS records of non–Windows 2000 clients.

> **Tip** If you have static DNS servers such as those in Windows NT 4, these servers can't interact dynamically when DHCP client configurations are changed. This incompatibility can result in failed lookups for DHCP clients. To avoid this problem, upgrade static DNS servers with DNS that supports Dynamic DNS (Windows 2000).

Using Ipconfig to Release, Renew, or Verify a Lease

On a DHCP-enabled computer that's running Windows, you can run a command-line utility to release, renew, or verify the client's address lease. At a command prompt (or in the Run window), use one of the following commands:

- To release a client's lease, type *ipconfig/release*
- To renew a lease, type *ipconfig/renew*
- To verify the client's lease, type *ipconfig/all*

For Windows 95/98 clients, use Winipcfg with the same parameters. The Ipconfig program is useful when troubleshooting problems because it displays every detail of the current TCP/IP configuration. You can find more troubleshooting information in Chapter 38.

Installing and Configuring a DNS Server

DNS servers are an essential part of a TCP/IP-based network as well as an essential part of Active Directory. Microsoft recommends installing DNS on every domain controller when using Active Directory. This arrangement allows the Windows 2000 Dynamic DNS server to use Active Directory to store zone information—thus, full multimaster zone replication using Active Directory is permitted, the task of achieving fault tolerance is simplified, and DNS administration is made less difficult.

If you're using Active Directory–integrated DNS, you can skip the next section. Setting up Active Directory (see Chapter 10) will automatically configure DNS.

Installing DNS

If DNS wasn't installed on the domain controller during the installation of Windows 2000, you can add it easily, although certain configuration steps are necessary. First you must configure the TCP/IP and DNS domain name on the machine where the services are to be installed. Follow these steps:

1. Go to Start and choose Settings, and then select Network And Dial-Up Connections. Right-click the connection you want, and choose Properties.

2. Highlight the Internet Protocol (TCP/IP) entry, and then click Properties. Enter the IP address, subnet mask, and default gateway that you're using. Be sure the Use The Following DNS Server Addresses option is selected. In the Preferred DNS Sever box, enter the computer's assigned IP address.

3. Select Advanced, and then choose the DNS tab. Supply the DNS addresses and names.

4. Right-click the My Computer icon, and choose Properties from the shortcut menu.

5. On the Network Identification tab, select Properties. In the Identification Changes box, select More.

6. In the NetBIOS And DNS Domain Names dialog box, enter the DNS domain name, and click OK. A reboot will be necessary for the changes to take effect.

Once the server is configured correctly, you can install DNS server by following these steps:

1. Open the Configure Your Server tool from the Administrative Tools menu.

2. Select the Networking heading in the column on the left, and then choose the DNS subheading.

3. To install the DNS service, click the Set Up DNS hyperlink.

Configuring the DNS Service

Zones are the brains of DNS; therefore, your DNS server is useless until you set up the zones for your domain. Zones allow you to store portions of the DNS namespace so that a single DNS server can serve a portion of the namespace.

Planning When setting up your domains, start with the top-level domain. Then create subdomains and delegate control of the domains to other DNS servers as necessary.

The two types of zones that you need to be concerned with are forward lookup zones and reverse lookup zones. Forward lookup zones are the types of zones we normally associate with DNS servers; they return an IP address when given a DNS name. Reverse lookups are used less often, yet they are still important. They provide the ability to resolve an IP address into a DNS name, something that Internet Information Server (IIS) uses for its log files and troubleshooting tools such as Nslookup use as well.

Creating a New Forward Lookup Zone

To create a new forward lookup zone on your DNS server so clients can resolve a DNS name to an IP address, follow these steps:

1. Select DNS from the Administrative Tools folder.

2. Select your DNS server from the console tree. Then choose New Zone from the Action menu to start the New Zone Wizard. Click Next to start using the wizard.

3. In the Zone Type window (Figure 6.20) choose one of the following options, and then Click Next to continue:

- **Active Directory-integrated** Use if your domain controllers are all running Windows 2000. This option can also be used on a mixed network if your UNIX servers are compatible with Microsoft DNS.

- **Standard primary** Use if your DNS server is running Windows 2000 Server but is not a domain controller.

- **Standard secondary** Use if your DNS server is hosted on UNIX servers. Use also if this server is to have read-only privileges in the zone with all data obtained from the primary DNS server.

4. Select the Forward Lookup option, and click Next.

Real World **Setting Up Secondary DNS Servers**

Secondary DNS servers play an important role for TCP/IP-based networks. Their primary purpose is to provide redundancy if the primary DNS server doesn't respond to client queries, but secondary servers can also be useful in reducing network traffic if placed in a location where the zone is heavily queried. To provide additional protection from a network link failure, you should place secondary servers on a different subnet with routed LANs or across a WAN link. While we recommend setting up secondary DNS servers for both forward lookup zones and reverse lookup zones, because reverse lookup zones are used so infrequently, fewer secondary servers are required for these zones. They are usually placed outside the network and subnet that the reverse zone serves.

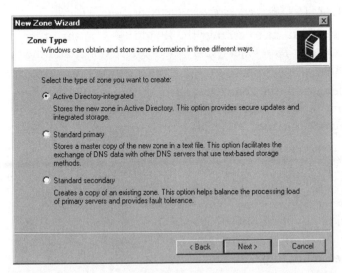

Figure 6-20. *The Zone Type screen of the New Zone Wizard.*

5. Enter the DNS name for the zone in the Name text box, and then click Next.

6. If you chose an Active Directory–integrated zone, it is created now. If you're creating a standard primary zone, skip to step 8. For a standard secondary zone, the Master DNS Servers window opens. Enter the IP addresses of the master servers from which you want to copy the zone data, clicking Add after entering each one (Figure 6-21). Use the Browse button to search for servers.

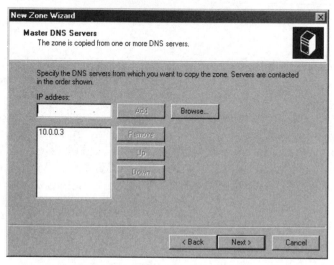

Figure 6-21. *The Master DNS Servers screen of the New Zone Wizard.*

7. Use the Up and Down buttons to arrange the IP addresses in the order that you want to contact them. Click Next when you're done, and then click Finish to complete the configuration of your secondary zone.

8. To create a new file to store the zone date, select the Create A New File With This File Name option and enter the name you want to give the zone file, or use the one provided for you.

9. To use an existing zone file to store your zone data, copy the file to the %SystemRoot%\System32\DNS folder, select the Use This Existing File option, and enter the filename in the box provided.

10. Click Next, review the summary of your zone, and then click Finish to complete the creation of your zone.

Creating a New Reverse Lookup Zone

Reverse lookup zones allow clients to resolve a host's DNS name from an IP address, which is useful for troubleshooting tools such as Nslookup. And performing a reverse lookup with IIS log files allows the recording of a DNS name instead of an IP address. To create a new reverse lookup zone, follow these steps:

1. Launch the DNS Management snap-in from the Administrative Tools folder.

2. Select your DNS server from the console tree, and then choose New Zone from the Action menu to start the New Zone Wizard. Click Next to start using the wizard.

3. In the Zone Type window choose one of the following options, and then click Next to continue:

    - **Active Directory-Integrated**   Use if your domain controllers are all running Windows 2000. This option can also be used on a mixed network if your UNIX servers are compatible with Microsoft DNS.

    - **Standard Primary**   Use if your DNS server is running Windows 2000 Server but is not a Domain Controller.

    - **Standard Secondary**   Use if your DNS server is hosted on UNIX servers. Use also if this server is to have read-only privileges in the zone with all data obtained from the primary DNS server.

4. Select the Reverse Lookup option, and click Next in the Select The Zone Type window.

5. Enter your network address in the Network ID box, shown in Figure 6-22. (See Chapter 13 for more information on network addresses and TCP/IP addressing.)

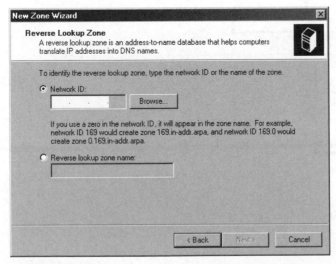

Figure 6-22. *The Reverse Lookup Zone screen of the New Zone Wizard.*

6. To enter the name of the reverse lookup instead of supplying the network ID, select Reverse Lookup Zone Name, and enter the name of the reverse lookup zone. Click Next.

7. If you are creating a lookup zone that is Active Directory–integrated, the zone will now be created. If you are making a standard primary zone, the Zone File window will open.

8. To create a new file to store the zone data, choose the New File option and enter the name you want to give the zone file, or use the name provided for you. To use an existing zone file to store the data, copy the file into the %SystemRoot%\System32\DNS folder, choose the Existing File option, and enter the file name in the box provided.

9. Click Next, review the summary of your zone, and then click Finish to complete the creation of your zone.

Creating Subdomains and Delegating Authority

In most large network environments, you need to create subdomains and delegate their management to other DNS zones that are hosted by other DNS servers. This step eliminates the obviously undesirable situation of having a large namespace hosted in a single zone by a single server. Thus, you might have a zone containing the root domain scribes.com as well as the subdomain marketing.scribes.com; however, you might have the subdomain tech.scribes.com and its subdomains delegated to a separate zone managed by another DNS server, as shown in Figure 6-23.

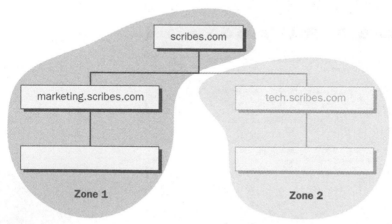

Figure 6-23. *A domain tree with zones identified.*

Caution   Make sure that you have a host record created for your DNS server in the Forward Lookup Zone and a pointer record for your DNS server in the Reverse Lookup Zone. DNS may not automatically create these (especially the pointer record) for you, so double-check them—otherwise your server may not work.

Note that zones must have a contiguous namespace, so it isn't possible to combine subdomains from different branches of your namespace and place them in a single zone—you'd need to create separate zones for each noncontiguous part of the domain. To create a new subdomain in an existing zone and then delegate authority over the domain to another DNS server, perform the following steps:

1. Select the domain in which you want to create a new subdomain, and then choose New Domain from the Action menu.

2. Enter the name of the subdomain in the dialog box that appears, and then click OK. This name should not be fully qualified. For example, if you were creating the subdomain tech.scribes.com under the domain scribes.com, you would type only *tech* in this dialog box.

Note   Subdomains don't have to be delegated to a different DNS server. Subdomains can even be created in new zone files and still be managed by the same server. This ability is useful if you want to host the zones on the same computer, yet manage them differently.

3. To delegate authority over the subdomain, select the parent domain of the subdomain, and then choose New Delegation from the Action menu to start the New Delegation Wizard.

4. Click Next, and then enter the subdomain name for the subdomain you want to delegate. Click Next again.

5. Click Add to open the Create New Resource Record dialog box.

6. Enter the name of the server you want to delegate authority to, or click Browse to locate its resource record in your DNS server's zone files.

7. Enter the IP address or addresses for the server, clicking Add after entering each one. Click OK when you're done.

8. Add any additional DNS servers that will host the delegated subdomain, as shown in Figure 6-24. Click Next to continue.

9. Review the summary window, and click Finish to complete the delegation process.

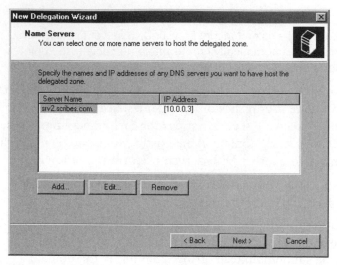

Figure 6-24. *The Name Servers screen of the New Delegation Wizard.*

Adding Host Resource Records

After you create your zones and subdomains, you should add resource records (RRs) for your domain server and any other servers with static IP addresses or IP reservations (DHCP servers, WINS servers, routers, and so on). The steps that follow are for adding new host RRs, but the process to add new pointer RRs, Alias (CNAME) RRs, mail exchangers, or other RRs is quite similar. Note that your DNS server won't work properly without a host record and a pointer record, which may not be created automatically for you.

1. Select the zone and domain or subdomain to which the host belongs, and then choose New Host from the Action menu.
2. Enter the host name, or leave the Name box blank to use the name of the parent domain (Figure 6-25). Enter the host's IP address.
3. Select the Create Associated Pointer (PTR) Record to create an RR for the host in the reverse lookup zone.
4. Click Add Host, and then fill out the fields for any additional host records you want to create, or click Done.

Tip To manually update your zone file, select the zone you want to update, and then choose Update Server Data File from the Action menu.

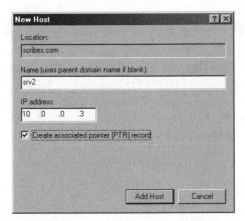

Figure 6-25. *The New Host dialog box.*

Configuring Zone Transfers

Because the DNS service is so important to a modern TCP/IP-based network, and because it's so essential to the operation of Active Directory, we highly recommend that you configure multiple DNS servers in each zone to provide fault tolerance in case one server isn't responding.

Windows 2000 supports several ways of achieving zone transfers between DNS servers managing a zone. If the DNS servers are using Active Directory to store their zone data, Active Directory handles the zone replication, allowing for a full multimaster model with zones transferring only updated records instead of performing full zone transfers.

Windows 2000 also supports Request For Comment (RFC) 1995–compliant incremental zone transfers when using standard zone files. This incremental zone transfer method permits a secondary DNS server to pull only the zone changes that it needs, to synchronize its copy of the zone data with the primary server's. If the serial number of the primary DNS server's zone file matches that of the secondary DNS server's serial number, no changes were made and no zone transfer takes place. Incremental zone transfers occur only if both servers support this feature; when performing zone transfers with Windows NT 4 DNS servers or other DNS servers that don't support this feature, a full zone transfer occurs. In a full zone transfer, the entire contents of the zone file are pulled from the primary DNS server by the secondary server.

If your DNS server is a secondary DNS server on a zone, your server is already configured to perform zone transfers with the master server in the zone. If your server is a primary server in the zone, your server is configured to perform zone transfers with any DNS servers that request them. This situation can be a potential security problem if someone wants to create a rogue DNS server and pull your zone data, so you might want to allow only certain DNS servers to perform zone transfers with your server. To modify the way zone transfers occur on your DNS server, follow these steps:

1. Select the zone in which you want to enable zone transfers, go to the Action menu, and select Properties.

2. Click the Zone Transfers tab, shown in Figure 6-26.

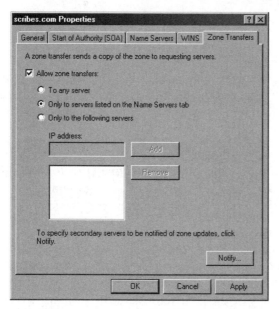

Figure 6-26. *The Zone Transfers tab of the Properties window.*

3. To disable zone transfers entirely on your DNS server, clear the Allow Zone Transfers checkbox.

4. To allow any DNS server to perform zone transfers with your DNS server, select To Any Server.

5. To set up your server to allow only servers that have name server (NS) records in your zone file to perform zone transfers with your server, choose Only To Servers Listed On The Name Servers Tab.

6. To create a list of approved servers with which your DNS server can perform zone transfers, select Only To The Following Servers. Then

enter each server's IP address in the box provided, clicking Add after entering each one.

7. To change whether secondary servers in your zone are notified when your zone file has been updated, click Notify.

8. To disable the notification of secondary servers when changes to your zone file take place, clear the Automatically Notify checkbox, shown in Figure 6-27.

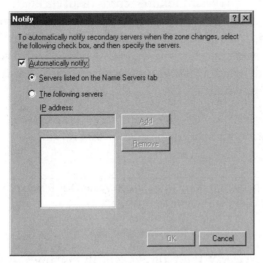

Figure 6-27. *The Notify dialog box.*

9. To notify only DNS servers with name server records in your zone file, select Servers Listed On The Name Servers Tab.

10. To create a list of servers that you want to notify about changes to your zone file, select the The Following Servers option. Then enter each server's IP address in the box provided, clicking Add after entering each one.

Interoperating with Other DNS Servers

By default, the Windows 2000 DNS server performs fast zone transfers with data compression and multiple resource records sent in each message. This zone transfer method works with all Windows DNS servers, and BIND DNS servers versions 4.9.4 or later. If you need to perform zone transfers with BIND servers earlier than version 4.9.4, you'll need to disable this fast zone transfer method. Select your DNS server from the console tree and choose Properties from the Action menu. Then click the Advanced tab, and clear the Bind Secondaries check box.

Enabling Dynamic DNS Updates

In Windows NT 4, the DNS server is a slight management headache because of the lack of dynamic updates. Every time a host is given a new IP address, an administrator has to go in and manually update the DNS zone file with the new IP address. Fortunately, the Windows 2000 DNS server implements RFC 2136–compliant dynamic updates. These dynamic updates allow Windows 2000 clients to update their own forward lookup DNS records, and they allow DHCP and WINS servers to update the forward and reverse lookup records of all clients. They also allow you to scavenge records that haven't been refreshed in a long time, reducing the gradual bloat that happens with DNS databases. (See Chapter 12 for more information on setting up aging and scavenging parameters.) Before you can reap any of the benefits from dynamic DNS, you have to turn it on, so follow these steps to enable dynamic updates:

1. Select the zone in which you want to enable dynamic updates.

2. Choose Properties from the Action menu and select the General tab.

3. In the Allow Dynamic Updates drop-down list box, select Yes.

 Tip For dynamic DNS to work properly, you need to configure your DHCP server to update the DNS server when a client's IP address changes.

Enabling WINS Resolution

The Windows Internet Naming Service (WINS) allows NetBIOS names to be resolved into IP addresses. This capability is important for networks that need to support large numbers of pre–Windows 2000 Microsoft clients. DNS can work together with WINS to search the entire combined DNS and NetBIOS namespace, if necessary, when a client attempts to resolve a hostname.

In Windows NT 4, enabling WINS resolution within DNS is essential to successfully resolving hosts that might have changed their IP addresses recently—the dynamic WINS database provides an up-to-date IP address when the static DNS zone file can't. However, with Windows 2000, dynamic updates to the DNS server eliminate the need to use WINS servers to keep the namespace up-to-date, and WINS will be gradually phased out. To enable WINS resolution in a zone, follow these steps:

1. Select the zone in which you want to enable WINS resolution, and then choose Properties from the Action menu.

2. Choose the WINS tab and select the Use WINS Forward Lookup check box.

3. To prevent the WINS record from being replicated to any secondary servers for compatibility reasons (non-Microsoft DNS servers don't support WINS-R records), select the Do Not Replicate This Record check box.

4. Enter the IP address of each WINS server you want to query, clicking Add after entering each one.

You will find more about setting up WINS in the section "Setting up a WINS Server" later in this chapter.

Setting Up a Forwarder

No name server will be able to answer the queries of all clients; sometimes clients will request a DNS name that isn't in a zone managed by the DNS server. In these instances, you can configure a DNS server to forward the query on to a DNS server that is more likely to have the record in its zone or cache file. This ability is needed most frequently for resolving names external to the network on which the clients reside.

When a client wants to resolve a name outside the internal network, you can configure an internal DNS server to forward the query to a DNS server external to the network, perhaps on the other side of a firewall. This external name server can then perform further queries outside the network as necessary and return the results back to the forwarder DNS server. To configure your DNS server to forward unresolved queries to another DNS server, follow these steps:

Tip For security reasons, a single DNS server will typically forward queries from the internal network to a DNS server on the other side of the firewall. All other internal DNS servers forward their queries to the designated forwarder to be passed on to the external name server (or resolved from the forwarder's cache file).

1. In the console tree, select the DNS server on which you want to enable forwarding, and then choose Properties from the Action menu.

2. Choose the Forwarders tab and select the Enable Forwarders check box.

3. Enter the IP addresses of the DNS server or servers to which you want to forward unresolved queries, clicking the Add button after entering each one.

4. Before moving on to the next server in the list of servers to forward queries to, enter the amount of time you want to spend attempting to contact a DNS server.

5. To configure your DNS server as a slave server—a server that doesn't attempt to resolve any queries from its own zone files or cache—select the Do Not Use Recursion check box.

Setting up a Caching-Only DNS Server

Caching-only servers are DNS servers that don't host any zones and that aren't authoritative for any domains—they simply cache the queries that they perform on behalf of the clients that use the server. Caching-only servers are useful for sites that use a slow WAN link to other DNS servers. By simply caching queries instead of holding its own zone files, a caching-only server reduces network traffic because it never performs any zone transfers. To set up a caching-only server, follow these steps:

1. Install the DNS service, as described earlier in this chapter.
2. Configure the caching server with a static IP address.
3. Launch DNS from the Administrative Tools folder, and choose Connect To Computer from the Action menu.
4. In the Select Target Computer dialog box, select The Following Computer, enter the name of the DNS server from which you want to cache (Figure 6-28), and click OK.

The DNS server will be added to the DNS console on the caching server. The caching server will perform recursive queries on behalf of its clients and over time will accumulate resource records for answering future queries. You can clear the cache on a caching server by right-clicking the server's name in the DNS console and selecting Clear Cache.

Figure 6-28. *The Select Target Computer dialog box.*

Setting Up a WINS Server

WINS is an essential part of any large NetBIOS-based network. It provides the equivalent of a DNS server for the NetBIOS namespace: WINS servers resolve NetBIOS names into IP addresses by using the WINS dynamic database to call up the appropriate name records.

However, WINS and NetBIOS together are on their way out—slowly, perhaps, but inexorably. Because of its proprietary and faulty naure, the WINS server's functions will be replaced by DNS servers as the clients that require NetBIOS support fade away. Although UNIX clients and clients from other operating systems have been relying exclusively on DNS for name resolution for some time, Windows 2000 is Microsoft's first operating system that doesn't need NetBIOS support for networking. Thus, a significant period of transition will occur before you can start scrapping those WINS servers because Windows 95/98, Windows NT, and even MS-DOS/Windows 3.x clients will hang on for some time. So let's get into some of the details about how to tell whether you need WINS, how to install it, and how to set up replication partners.

Determining Whether You Need WINS

If you're asking yourself whether you need WINS at this point, the answer is probably yes. Most large networks will need WINS to provide NetBIOS name resolution for their Windows clients. However, here are some instances in which you don't need WINS servers:

- All clients on the network support name resolution via another method (for example, DNS). Windows 2000 is the first Microsoft operating system that can rely exclusively on DNS for name resolution, so unless all Windows clients are running Windows 2000, you need WINS. If you have a mixed environment with other clients such as UNIX clients, make sure that they're all configured to properly use DNS.

- Your network is small (less than 50 clients) and not subnetted. If your entire network consists of a single network segment, clients that require NetBIOS name resolution can effectively resolve NetBIOS names by broadcast—a technique that doesn't work across routers or on large networks where the NetBIOS broadcasts would generate too much network traffic.

Also, before you implement WINS on your network, you should be aware of the WINS clients that are supported by WINS in Windows 2000. OS/2 with LAN Manager version 2.2c is not supported as a WINS client, but the Windows 2000 WINS server does support the following operating systems as WINS clients:

- Windows 2000
- Windows NT 3.5 or later
- Windows 95 or later
- Windows for Workgroups 3.11 with TCP/IP 32, included on the Windows 2000 CD
- MS-DOS with Microsoft Network Client version 3, included on the Windows 2000 CD
- MS-DOS with LAN Manager version 2.2c, included on the Windows 2000 CD

Non-WINS clients aren't resolvable by WINS unless static entries are added for them. This practice is strongly discouraged; it should not be used unless absolutely necessary because static entries are extremely difficult to eliminate from the WINS database after replication takes place. Instead, clients should be configured to use DNS to resolve names that aren't in the WINS database.

Configuring Your Server to Prepare for WINS

Once you've determined that you need WINS on your network, it's time to configure the server. The most common cause of WINS problems is improper TCP/IP configurationon the server. Follow the steps provided here to properly configure the TCP/IP settings for your WINS server before you install the service:

1. Right-click the Local Area Connection icon in the Network and Dial-Up Connections folder, and choose Properties from the shortcut menu.
2. Select the Internet Protocol (TCP/IP) component, and choose Properties.
3. Configure your server to use a static IP address, or make sure that an address reservation for your server is configured on your DHCP server.
4. Click Advanced, and then click WINS.
5. Select any WINS servers listed on the tab and click Remove, as shown in Figure 6-29. Failing to do this can cause your WINS server to register its own address with another WINS server instead of with itself, which you don't want.
6. Click Add and insert the IP address of the your own server. Then click OK.

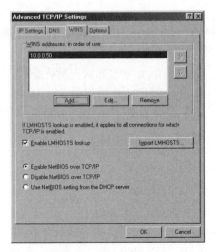

Figure 6-29. *The WINS tab of the Advanced TCP/IP Settings dialog box.*

Installing WINS

After your TCP/IP settings are correct, you're ready to install the WINS component. To do this, you need to use the Windows Component Wizard, accessible either from the Configure Your Server tool or from Add/Remove Programs in the Control Panel. If you installed WINS during Windows 2000 Setup, you can skip this section. Otherwise, use these steps to install WINS.

1. Open the Add/Remove Programs Control Panel applet, and click the Add/Remove Windows Components icon in the frame on the left (the Places bar) to launch the Windows Component Wizard.

2. Click Next, select Networking Services from the list of components, and click Details.

3. Select the Windows Internet Name Service (WINS) component check box, click OK, and then click Next.

> **Tip** Don't install WINS on a multihomed server. You can do it and it will work, but it can cause awful replication problems, especially if the server is on two different subnets. Take our advice, just don't do it!

Adding Replication Partners

WINS servers are extremely easy to set up and require little management, except for replication partners. WINS replication is an important and somewhat delicate issue that should be examined closely before setting up. Deploy as few WINS servers as possible to minimize management migraines. For example, the entire Microsoft corporation uses only twelve WINS servers worldwide. Just about every enterprise can get by with a handful of WINS servers.

Chapter 13 contains a more thorough investigation of WINS deployment and replication planning. You can also refer to the Windows 2000 Resource Kit. To set up a replication partner and configure its settings after planning your WINS deployment, follow these steps:

1. Open WINS from the Administrative Tools folder, and in the console tree expand the WINS server that you want to set up for replication.

2. Select the Replication Partners folder, and then choose New-Replication Partner from the Action menu.

3. Enter the IP address for the WINS server you want to enable replication with, and click OK.

4. To modify the replication parameters for the new replication partner, if necessary, double-click the server in the Replication Partners folder, and then click the Advanced tab.

5. To change the way you replicate with the server, choose an option from the Replication Partner Type drop-down list box (Figure 6-30).

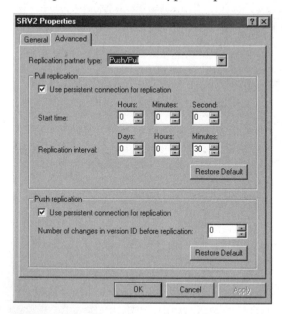

Figure 6-30. *The Advanced tab of the Properties dialog box.*

6. To configure a permanent connection for pull or push replication, select the Use Persistent Connection For Replication check box in either the Pull Replication section, the Push Replication section, or both.

7. In the Start Time fields, enter the time that you want pull replication to begin in hours, minutes, and seconds.

8. In the Replication Interval fields, enter the frequency—days, hours, and minutes—with which you want to replicate with your replication partner.

9. Use the Update Count box to enter the number of changes to the local copy of the WINS database that you will allow before your server should push changes to your replication partner.

Tip   We recommend using push/pull replication on your entire WINS namespace to make troubleshooting replication problems easier. In addition, primary and backup WINS servers *must* use push/pull replication.

Summary

If you put in the planning time recommended in the first part of this book, it's probably paying off around now. Although the configuration of various services and protocols is relatively complex, primarily because of the interdependencies among them, you should have a good idea of which services and protocols will best suit the needs of your network in a Windows 2000 environment. In the next chapter, we address the general topic of upgrading existing systems to Windows 2000 and tying them into the network.

Chapter 7
Upgrading to Windows 2000

Chapters 5 and 6 described how to install and configure Microsoft Windows 2000 Advanced Server on a new or clean system. This chapter moves on to a topic that will probably be more immediately useful: upgrading to Windows 2000.

Because upgrading to a new network environment such as Windows 2000 involves so much more than simply running Setup, this chapter covers many aspects of the process. It discusses the architectural differences between Windows 2000 and prior versions of Windows and how these differences affect the upgrade process, as well as how to plan and prepare for upgrading Windows NT domains. It also covers the actual upgrade process for Windows NT servers and Windows NT–based and Microsoft Windows 95/98–based clients. At the end of the chapter, you'll find information on making the transition from a mixed-mode domain with Windows NT and Windows 2000 domain controllers to a native Windows 2000 domain with only Windows 2000 domain controllers.

Architectural Improvements in Windows 2000

Architectural improvements in Windows 2000 include changes to the types of server roles available and to the type of domain trusts that are used; new support for devices, Plug and Play (PnP), and power management; and, of course, the addition of the Active Directory service. However, all these changes mean that some existing applications and drivers may not work under the new Windows 2000 architecture.

Domain Controllers and Server Roles in Windows 2000

In Windows 2000, the types of server roles are slightly different from those available under Windows NT. Windows NT 4 servers can have one of four roles: primary domain controller (PDC), backup domain controller (BDC), member server, and stand-alone server.

Windows NT domains are single-master based, with the PDC serving as the master repository for a given domain. All changes to the domain must be carried out by the PDC. BDCs serve as working backups to the PDC and also reduce the load on the PDC by serving client requests themselves. BDCs maintain a current copy of the domain by synchronizing periodically with the PDC and can be upgraded to the PDC if that server fails or is taken out of service.

Member servers are simply Windows NT servers that belong to a Windows NT domain and usually perform file sharing or print sharing or run some other type of server software, such as Web, Domain Name System (DNS), or Dynamic Host Configuration Protocol (DHCP) server software.

Stand-alone servers are Windows NT servers that do not belong to a Windows NT domain and are instead part of a workgroup. It is important to understand that although a stand-alone server doesn't belong to a Windows NT domain, it isn't limited in its duties as a server. It can still act as a DNS, DHCP, or other type of server, but by definition it can't be a PDC or BDC.

The member server and stand-alone server roles are the same in Windows 2000 as in Windows NT, but the PDC and BDC roles are replaced with a single domain controller (DC) role. Yes, domains in Windows 2000 are finally multiple-master based, with all Windows 2000 DCs acting as peers to one another. Any DC can make changes to the domain at will. All domain information is stored in Active Directory, which handles replication between all domain controllers. The trade-off is that Windows 2000 DCs cannot exist on a Windows NT domain until the PDC of the domain has been upgraded to Windows 2000. This issue is covered in greater detail later in this chapter, in the section "Planning a Domain Upgrade."

Windows 2000 member servers and stand-alone servers can be promoted to domain controller status, and domain controllers can be demoted to member servers or stand-alone servers without reinstalling the operating system—the only way to demote a BDC under Windows NT. However, as always, it's preferable not to make more role changes than necessary.

Active Directory

Active Directory is probably the most important new feature in the Windows 2000 Server family. It is a scalable, easily administered, and fault-tolerant directory service that is required by Windows 2000 domain controllers and is also recommended for use on Windows 2000 DNS servers. Active Directory is covered in detail in Chapters 10 and 11, so we will address it only briefly in this chapter. It is useful to review a few points before entering into a discussion about upgrading Windows NT domains to Windows 2000.

Active Directory Domains

Although Active Directory doesn't make fundamental changes to the way domains work for end users in Windows 2000, it does introduce some important domain structures that affect the way one should approach domain design. Active Directory, like the directory service in Windows NT, uses domains as the core unit of logical structure. Domains help organize the network structure to match the organization of the company, either politically or geographically. Each domain requires at least one DC (and preferably more) to store the domain information, with each DC being a master of the domain. See Chapter 3 for more on domain planning.

Windows 2000 domains, unlike Windows NT domains, use DNS names for domain names. Like DNS domains, Windows 2000 domains are hierarchically organized. In Active Directory, hierarchically organized groups of domains with a contiguous namespace are called trees, while groupings of trees with noncontiguous namespaces are called forests.

Sites, Structural Domains, and Organizational Units

Active Directory also introduces the concepts of sites, structural domains, and organizational units. A site is defined as a group of one or more Internet Protocol (IP) subnets that share LAN connectivity. Within a site there can be one or more domains, or a single domain can span multiple sites. See "Planning the Site Topology" later in this chapter for further information.

Structural domains are domains that contain no accounts; they simply serve as a root to lower-level child domains. As such, structural domains make it easy to restructure child domains, and they also make replication between domains easier and faster, as all domains simply replicate with the structural domain, which serves as a sort of replication hub. For a further discussion, see the Real World note "Using Structural Domains," later in this chapter.

Organizational units (OUs) are very similar to domains in that they are containers for network objects such as user accounts and resources. Unlike domains, however, they do not mark a security boundary, and they don't require domain controllers. OUs in Active Directory provide an excellent way to provide organization within a domain without the need for additional security policies and domain controllers. They can also easily be converted to domains, and domains can easily be converted to OUs, making them very flexible. You'll find more on the uses and creation of organizational units in Chapter 11.

Trust Relationships in Active Directory

Trust relationships complicate life in an enterprise with multiple Windows NT domains. Windows 2000 takes a big step toward simplification, although, as is often the case with improvements, things may get worse before they get better.

Simply stated, a *trust relationship* is a mechanism by which users in one domain can be authenticated by a domain controller in another domain. Among and between Windows NT domains, all trusts are *nontransitive,* meaning that each trust is a one-way relationship that must be established explicitly. For two domains to trust each other, two separate trust relationships must be established— one for each direction. A nontransitive trust is also strictly limited. For example, suppose that the domain Finance trusts the domain Administration, and the domain Manufacturing trusts the domain Administration. When nontransitive trusts are involved, this statement tells you only that both Finance and Manufacturing allow the domain controller in Administration to authenticate users. It does not tell you anything about the relationship between Finance and Manufacturing. Nor does it indicate whether Administration, in turn, allows either Finance or Manufacturing to authenticate users. Each trust relationship must be established separately and explicitly.

Windows 2000 allows the concept of *transitive* trusts. Transitive trusts are always two-way. In addition, when a Windows 2000 child domain is created, an automatic transitive trust is established between the child domain and the parent domain. However, transitive trusts don't enter the picture until all of the Windows NT controllers are removed from the domain and the domain is explicitly switched to native mode. As long as Windows NT controllers are active, the domain is in the default mixed mode, which is necessary for Windows 2000 DCs to replicate with Windows NT BDCs. The switch from mixed mode to native mode is discussed later in this chapter.

Real World   Whom Do You Trust?

The question of transitive trusts arises in large multidomained enterprises. But even there, it's not an issue until all of the Windows NT domain controllers have been permanently removed from a domain. Although there are advantages to having all domains be Windows 2000 domains, it's not necessary to be in a great rush to reach that point. In the meantime, the existing trusts remain in place during the upgrade process, and the only trusts that are added will be the nontransitive ones that you explicitly and deliberately set. This means that if you are creating a new Windows 2000 domain, you will have to manually create trusts with existing Windows NT domains.

Table 7-1 shows the possible trust relationships between different types of domains.

Table 7-1.   Trust relationships between domains of different types

	Windows NT Domain	Windows 2000 Domain (same forest)	Windows 2000 Domain (different forest)
Windows NT Domain	One-way trust*	One-way trust	One-way trust
Windows 2000 Domain	One-way trust	Two-way transitive trust only	One-way trust

*A one-way trust can be established in both directions.

Hardware Support

Without dispute, Windows NT has always been very particular about hardware. Users of Windows 95 and Windows 98 have long enjoyed broad device driver support, PnP, Power Management, IEEE 1394 (Firewire), and Universal Serial Bus (USB)—the latter in Windows 95 OSR 2.1 and Windows 98. Windows NT users essentially lack all of the above, although they have had other advantages.

Windows 2000 introduces top-of-the-line support for PnP, USB, IEEE 1394 (Firewire), and Advanced Configuration Power Interface (ACPI) device configuration and power management. Device support is also vastly improved, although Windows 2000 still supports fewer devices than Windows 95/98. (There are exceptions, such as printer support. Almost all printers supported under Windows 98 and Windows NT 4 are supported in Windows 2000.) In most cases if the device was supported under Windows NT 4, it will be supported under Windows 2000. However, the same is not always true for Windows 95/98, so check the Hardware Compatibility List (HCL) or contact the device manufacturer to determine whether the device is supported under Windows 2000.

> **Note**   An up-to-date, ACPI-compatible BIOS is required for full use of PnP and Power Management. Legacy Advanced Power Management (APM) and PnP BIOSs are supported, but their features are limited.

Device drivers in Windows 2000 have changed to enhance system stability and to increase the number of devices supported. The Win32 Driver Model (WDM) is now supported, enabling many drivers to work interchangeably with Windows 2000 and Windows 98. Device Driver Signing is also supported, and drivers that haven't been tested and digitally signed by Microsoft trigger an alert when installed. (Administrators can also create policies preventing unsigned drivers from being installed.) Changes have also been made to the driver model to prevent system instability and to facilitate PnP and Power Management, which unfortunately prevents some Windows NT drivers from working in Windows 2000. In addition, power management and PnP aren't available with Windows NT 4 drivers.

Note As in Windows NT 4, device drivers written for Windows 95, 3.x, or MS-DOS will not work in Windows 2000.

Software Support

Software support is an area in which Windows 2000 has some compatibility issues. Like Windows NT 4, Windows 2000 may experience compatibility problems with MS-DOS and Windows 3.x programs (especially any that directly access the hardware). Windows 95/98 applications that don't explicitly support Windows NT or Windows 2000 may also run into problems. Nearly all Windows NT 4 applications run under Windows 2000.

Upgrading an existing Windows 95/98–based system presents additional complexities because vendors often have different versions of their software for Windows 95/98 and Windows NT/2000, or because the same application is installed differently depending on the operating system involved. Consequently, many applications require vendor-provided migration files (upgrade packs) during the operating system upgrade.

Planning a Domain Upgrade

Upgrading a Windows NT domain to a Windows 2000 domain isn't quite the three-click process that you perform when upgrading a single Windows NT 4 workstation. In fact, considerable planning is necessary before you even start Windows 2000 Setup on the first computer. Some computers, such as the PDC and BDCs, must be upgraded in a specific order, with the PDC being upgraded first. Other computers, such as Windows NT member servers and stand-alone servers, as well as client computers, can be upgraded at any time before or after the actual domain is upgraded.

Before you begin upgrading an existing Windows NT domain, it is important to assess the current network and plan the upgrade approach you want to take. This section will help you determine what parts of the existing network you should document, create a recovery plan, plan the first Active Directory tree and the site topology, and come up with a general upgrade strategy.

Documenting the Existing Network

The first step in planning an in-place domain upgrade is to document the current network structure. To do so, you will need to make a note of the existing domain model, the existing trusts, the number and location of the domain controllers, the account and resource domains, the DNS namespaces currently in use, the application servers, and any Windows NT 3.51 servers. The sections that follow describe how to document each of these features.

> **Note**   An *in-place* domain upgrade is a domain upgrade that is performed while leaving the domain intact. Domains can also be upgraded by removing the PDC from the domain, leaving the BDCs to provide services. You upgrade the PDC to Windows 2000, test it, and then bring it back into the production domain.

The Existing Domain Model

The type of domain structure, or model, that the existing Windows NT domains use will determine how you implement the Windows 2000 Active Directory trees and forest. Table 7-2 summarizes the types of domain models that may be in use.

Table 7-2.   Domain models available in Windows NT

Domain Model	Description
Single-domain	A single Windows NT domain
Single-master	One account domain and multiple resource domains
Multiple-master	Multiple account domains with two-way trusts between them and multiple resource domains that trust all master domains
Complete trust	Every domain is a resource domain and an account domain, with each domain trusting every other domain

Existing Trust Relationships

Because the trust relationships will be preserved during the upgrade process, it's wise to check and document what trust relationships actually exist.

Location and Number of Domain Controllers

Determine where the PDCs and all BDCs are located. The PDC must be upgraded first. The BDCs can be upgraded after that and obviously cannot serve their intended function during the actual upgrade.

Account Domains and Resource Domains

Record the current number of account domains and resource domains. Also record how these domains are configured, and give some thought to whether you want to perform a domain restructure before or after you upgrade the network to Windows 2000.

DNS Namespaces

If the company has already deployed any DNS, you should carefully document the namespaces currently in use. Domains cannot be renamed once they've been created, and they must be unique on the network, so it's important to have domain names that aren't already in use in the organization.

Servers

A crucial and sometimes forgotten step in documenting a network is to make an inventory of the application servers. This includes all DNS, DHCP, and WINS servers, as well as application servers such as Exchange servers, SQL servers, proxy servers, and so on. DNS is a required service on a Windows 2000 native domain, so some thought should go into determining whether you want to use existing DNS servers for this purpose, deploy new DNS servers, or use the domain controllers as DNS servers—which is what Microsoft suggests.

Also examine any NetWare servers in the environment and determine whether you want to synchronize Active Directory with Novell Directory Services (NDS). You should also check the release notes included on the Windows 2000 Server CD-ROM for any compatibility issues with the version of NetWare. Chapter 20 discusses interoperating with NetWare.

Application servers such as Exchange, SQL, or media servers should also be evaluated for compatibility with the new Windows 2000 domains. Most servers will have no problems, but this is a good opportunity to double-check, as well as to reevaluate these servers' roles and their effectiveness on the network.

Windows NT 3.51 Servers

Windows NT 3.51 servers exhibit problems in a Windows 2000 domain that make them generally unsuitable for use, so your upgrade strategy must allow for upgrading or decommissioning servers running Windows NT 3.51. The problems include Windows NT 3.51 application servers either denying access to user or group logons, or incorrectly granting access to users or groups that have been denied access. These difficulties occur because of the way in which Windows NT 3.51 generates access tokens when a user logs on to the server.

> **More Info**   For more information on the specific problems that Windows NT 3.51 experiences in Windows 2000 domains, see the *Microsoft Windows 2000 Professional Resource Kit* (Microsoft Press, 1999).

Making a Recovery Plan

After taking stock of the existing network, devise a recovery plan in case something goes wrong during the domain upgrade. If the PDC fails the upgrade to Windows 2000 and you don't have BDCs available, the entire domain can be brought down. For these scenarios as well as others, it is important to have a satisfactory backup plan. This section contains some specific recommendations for ensuring that you're prepared for the worst—just in case.

Make Sure All Domains Have at Least One BDC

You need to be sure that all domains you plan to upgrade have at least one BDC in addition to the PDC to prevent the domain being orphaned if the PDC fails the Windows 2000 upgrade. Also, before you upgrade the PDC, make sure that you synchronize the PDC with all BDCs.

Back Up Each Computer Before Upgrading

It's just common sense to back up the systems before upgrading them. While this is perhaps overly cautious on some Windows NT desktop systems, it really is important on servers, especially domain controllers. Also, make sure that you test the backups; there's nothing more useless than a corrupt backup tape.

Synchronize All BDCs with the PDC

We've already said this, but it's worth repeating: synchronize the PDC with all of its replication partners before upgrading it. If the PDC fails the domain upgrade, you can promote a BDC to the PDC and the domain won't lose any changes.

Take a BDC Offline for Backup

Having freshly synchronized BDCs and new tape backups of the PDC will protect you from most disasters. However, it's good insurance to take a freshly synchronized BDC offline before upgrading the PDC. This provides you with a quickly available, working backup of the domain as it existed before you started the Windows 2000 upgrade process. If the upgraded PDC replicates bad domain information to the BDCs or the domain becomes damaged in some other way, having an offline backup allows you to go back and start over. If you track all changes to the domain after you take the BDC offline, you can even roll back the changes before bringing the BDC back online (if a disaster occurs) and not lose the domain changes.

To prepare a BDC to act as an offline domain backup, synchronize the BDC you want to use with the PDC for your domain, back up this BDC, and then disconnect the network cable to the BDC. If you encounter a major disaster after upgrading your PDC to Windows 2000 and you need to restore your domain to its pre–Windows 2000 state, demote any Windows 2000 DCs you have on your network, reconnect your offline BDC to the network, promote your formerly offline BDC to a PDC, and then synchronize it with the rest of your network. This will return your domain to the state it was in immediately before you took your BDC offline.

Caution All changes to your domain performed after taking your backup BDC offline will be lost if you bring the BDC back online and promote it to a PDC.

Relax

Don't let all of these warnings put you off. If you take precautions and the upgrade goes faultlessly, you won't have to resort to restoring backups or using other recovery mechanisms. That's good news. Just remember that no one ever lost a job because of being too prepared.

Plan the Active Directory Tree

There are several steps you should take in planning the Active Directory tree, including defining the DNS namespace and creating the initial tree structure. This section briefly covers these steps. More detailed information on planning the namespace and the domain structure can be found in Chapter 3.

Define the Namespace

When deciding how to implement a DNS namespace, you usually need to decide whether to use an existing DNS namespace and create the root domain with an existing domain name or to create a new root domain and associated DNS namespace. The decision is crucial because the root domain can't be easily deleted or renamed; you're pretty much stuck with it. (You can change or delete the root domain if you really must, but it involves taking down the entire domain—not a whole lot of fun.) Domain names are also highly political in nature, so if you're fond of your job, don't create the domain structure and namespace without first getting the approval of the powers that be.

That said, the following list summarizes the tasks necessary to define and implement the namespace. (The specifics of some of these tasks are given in the sections that follow.)

- Decide either that you can use an existing domain name for the root domain or that a new one is necessary.

- If you are going to use a new domain name, determine what constraints you have in the name selection process and go through the proper channels to pick the domain name.

- Set up the root domain to form the top level of the namespace, with a couple of domain controllers for redundancy.

- Set up one or more DNS servers for the root domain tree. The DNS server needs to support the service resource record (the DNS resource record for specifying the location of services) and should ideally support dynamic updates as well. Microsoft recommends installing DNS on each domain controller and storing the zone data in Active Directory—not a bad idea.

- Add the other domains as child domains under the root domain. This is an excellent time to perform a domain restructure or to at least consolidate some of the resource domains into OUs.

Create the Initial Tree Structure

Once you've decided on the DNS namespace, you're ready to plan the Active Directory tree in detail. For this chapter, we are going to assume that you have a single-tree forest, with all domains sharing a contiguous namespace. In practice, many companies will need to use a forest with multiple trees, each having its own namespace. However, the process is no different; each tree is constructed and then added to the forest in the same way.

Planning   The first domain that you upgrade to Windows 2000 (or create if you're using a multiple-master-domain model that doesn't lend itself to consolidation under one of the current domains) needs to be the root domain. The root domain stores the configuration and schema for the entire Active Directory forest and cannot be renamed or deleted.

Adapt to Specific Domain Models

Four domain models are available in Windows NT.

Single-Domain Model The single-domain model is easy to upgrade: the single domain under Windows NT becomes the root domain in Active Directory under Windows 2000. You can then use OUs to organize the accounts and resources and to delegate some of the administrative burden.

Single-Master–Domain Model If you have a single-master–domain model, make the former master domain the root of the tree and add the resource domains as child domains of the root. If the company has a centralized network structure, you might want to consider restructuring the domains into a single domain after you've upgraded the domain and switched to native mode. You can use OUs either to mimic the resource domains or to organize them more logically, with the accounts and resources grouped and organized according to the company's structure.

Merging the resource domains back into a single domain offers a number of advantages. Because there are fewer domains to manage, the administrative burden is less. You can use OUs to create a detailed network structure without the necessity of dealing with trusts (although switching to native mode will eliminate most of the hassle of managing trust relationships). In addition, you can delegate administrative authority to the OUs, giving you the flexibility to handle the administrative tasks the way you want. Active Directory queries are also performed faster and more efficiently in a single domain. Finally, since OUs don't require domain controllers, there is the potential to free up some underused computing resources for other tasks. Figure 7-1 shows a single-master Windows NT domain converted to a Windows 2000 Active Directory tree.

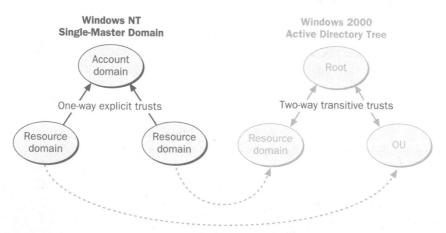

Figure 7-1. *A single-master Windows NT domain converted to a Windows 2000 Active Directory tree, with a resource domain converted to an OU after switching to native mode.*

A company with a more decentralized organization, or one with different business units, may want to stick with multiple domains but convert its resource domains into full-fledged domains, with both resources and user accounts. (With Active Directory, there is no reason to keep distinct resource domains.) This arrangement allows users to be in the same domain as the resources that they use, reducing traffic and making it easier for users to find and access the resources they need. You should wait, however, until the network has been converted to Windows 2000 native mode before moving the accounts because transitive trusts make moving accounts between domains much easier, and this type of trust is available only in a native-mode domain. Alternately, you can establish a two-way trust between the resource domains and the parent domain, but it usually makes more sense to wait until all domains are running in native mode.

Tip   Third-party solutions can provide much of this organizational flexibility in Windows NT 4, with the intent of permitting companies to restructure their domains in a way that works well with Active Directory before they move to Windows 2000. For example, Fastlane Technologies sells a product called DM Manager, which allows companies to upgrade Windows NT 4 domains into a multimaster structure that is very similar to that provided by Active Directory. Using this product allows a company to restructure its domains into a hierarchical domain structure that can be very easily upgraded to a Windows 2000 Active Directory—based network once the company is ready, while benefiting from many of Active Directory's features in the meantime.

Multiple-Master–Domain Model   Because of the flexibility and advantages the single-domain model has to offer, many companies with a multiple-master–domain model choose to consolidate their domains into a single Windows 2000 domain, using OUs to hierarchically structure their network. If you choose to consolidate the domains, you should first perform the domain upgrade just as if you were going to preserve the existing domain structure, and then perform the domain consolidation only after upgrading the network to native mode. After the domains are in native mode, all accounts can be moved into the single domain without the need to reassign permissions on the objects.

If you want to create a single-domain tree (with a contiguous namespace) during the domain upgrade, you can use one of the existing domains for the root of the tree, or you can create a new root domain and add the other master domains as its children, as shown in Figure 7-2. You may want to consider using a structural domain for this root domain. (See the Real World note "Using Structural Domains," later in this chapter.) Upgrade or create the root domain first. Once this domain is up and running with a couple of domain controllers, upgrade the rest of the domains and add them to the tree.

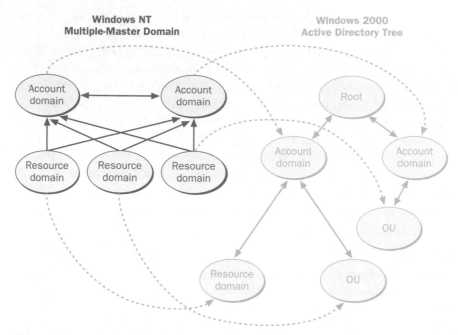

Figure 7-2. *A multiple-master Windows NT domain converted to a Windows 2000 Active Directory tree, with two resource domains converted to OUs after switching to native mode.*

If you want to keep each master domain in an authoritative role, you can create a multiple-tree forest, with each master domain seeded as the root for a new tree in the forest. In this case, it doesn't matter which master domain you upgrade first, but you must upgrade the master domain for each tree before you upgrade the resource domains you plan to add to the tree.

Real World   Multiple-Master Domains and the Case for Domain Consolidation

The Windows NT multiple-master–domain model is widely used in larger organizations for a couple of reasons. First, it allows the network to grow beyond the limitations of the single Security Accounts Manager (SAM) that single domains and single-master domains use. The SAM in Windows NT is stored in the system registry, and once it grows past 40 MB, performance degradation becomes noticeable. This means that the practical limit for a domain is 40,000 objects, with a maximum of 20,000 user accounts. To have more user accounts or objects than this, Microsoft recommends moving to a multiple-master–domain model.

The second reason that companies use multiple-master domains under Windows NT is to allow for physically different network sites that don't possess wide area network (WAN) connections that are fast and reliable enough to allow domain controller replication to take place without consuming an inappropriate amount of the WAN bandwidth. Using a master domain in each site gets around this lack of adequate connectivity, since no replication takes place between master account domains and all of the WAN bandwidth is available for other uses.

The third reason to use a multiple-master Windows NT domain structure is to reflect the company's organization in cases where different parts of the company need to control their own resources and users. Each master account domain can have its own administrator or the administration can be centralized, depending on the desires of the company.

Windows 2000 Active Directory deals with these issues effectively, permitting many companies to move to a single-domain model (or at least to reduce the number of domains) and gain the advantages that that model has to offer. Active Directory stores all domain information in its database (which is external to the registry and free to grow in size), with each domain storing its part of the entire directory instead of one server storing the entire network schema, allowing you to scale the domain to approximately a million objects. No other domain is necessary; all organization can be done with OUs. You can also create multiple physical sites, with a single domain spanning all sites and intersite replication set up to make the best use of slow WAN links.

Complete Trust Model   The Windows NT complete trust model is used most often by very decentralized companies or by companies that implemented domains in a piecemeal fashion and gradually connected the domains. The model provides a lot of autonomy and flexibility for each master domain, but it also entails a large administrative burden.

As with the multiple-master–domain model, many companies, when upgrading a domain that uses the complete trust model to Windows 2000, will try to consolidate their domains into a single tree or even a single domain. However, if you want to maintain the autonomy of the current domain structure of the complete trust model, you can set up each current master domain as a new tree or (if necessary) as a new forest. When you create the Active Directory structure like this, you automatically reduce the amount of administration necessary, as all trusts between domains in an Active Directory tree or forest are automatically transitive.

Note Transitive trusts do not take effect until the domains are converted to Windows 2000 native mode.

When you upgrade the domain, create the root domain first, either by creating a new domain (structural or normal) or by upgrading an existing domain and seeding it as the root of the Active Directory tree. Once you have the root up and running with a couple of domain controllers, you can move on to upgrading the other domains and adding them as children of the root domain or as roots in new trees or forests. If necessary, after upgrading all domains and switching to native-mode operation, you can replace any transitive trusts with Windows NT–style one-way trusts to limit access within a forest or to provide external domains access to specific domains in the tree or forest.

Tip A one-way trust can also be set up to permit a legacy Windows 3.51 or NT 4 domain or a child domain of another forest (such as one belonging to a business partner) to access a specific domain in the tree or forest. When you set up an explicit one-way trust in Windows 2000, it works identically to trusts in Windows NT—that is, the trust is not transitive. If you grant a domain access to a single domain in the tree or forest, the trusted domain cannot access any other domain in the tree, even though the tree is linked with transitive trusts.

Planning the Site Topology

Sites, an important new feature in Windows 2000, define the boundaries of LAN connectivity, making WAN links more efficient. When you set up sites that mark the sections of the network that have high-speed connectivity, Active Directory tunes the way it uses the WAN links by reducing the frequency of replication between sites and by directing clients' service requests (such as client logons or directory searches) to domain controllers that are available locally.

Sites are independent of domains. While domains typically mirror a company's logical organizational structure, sites mirror the physical network structure of a company. A single site may consist of one or more domains, trees, or even forests, and a single domain may span multiple sites. A site may consist of a single IP subnet (often the case because subnets frequently mark physical network boundaries) or multiple IP subnets, but all subnets must share reliable, high-speed connectivity in order to be a part of a single site.

> **Tip** In these days of asynchronous transfer mode (ATM) WAN links, it is becoming increasingly common for a company's WAN link to be as fast (or sometimes faster) than an internal LAN. However, the WAN link charge might be based on usage, or a company might use the link heavily for real-time, bandwidth-intensive tasks such as video, reducing the available bandwidth. In such cases, you may still want to set up a site structure for the Active Directory forest, to avoid burdening the WAN link with excessive replication and service requests.

When planning to upgrade a Windows NT domain to Windows 2000, it is important to plan the site topology so that you can set up the site structure promptly after upgrading. Ask yourself the following questions and make a record of your answers:

- What sites will you need to create in the Active Directory forest?
- What links are available between these sites, and how fast and expensive are they? Are they already heavily utilized, or is an abundance of bandwidth available?
- Are there any planned links between the sites?
- Are there any domains that will span physical sites, and if so, are the links between the sites fast enough to support this?

Two types of connections are available for intersite replication: point-to-point synchronous low-speed RPC and Simple Mail Transfer Protocol (SMTP). Any domains that span multiple sites must have at least a point-to-point synchronous low-speed RPC connection between the sites within the domain. This connection is required because you can't use SMTP for intersite replication between domain controllers in the same domain; you can use SMTP links only for schema, configuration, and Global Catalog information replication. Therefore, if you have multisite domains, double-check the link between the sites to make sure that you have adequate connectivity for this setup.

Real World   Using Structural Domains

Companies that use the multiple-master–domain or complete trust model under Windows NT will usually choose an existing domain to use as the root for their Active Directory tree. However, some organizations may choose to use a structural domain as the root of their tree, with the former master domains as child domains.

A structural domain is simply a domain without user accounts or resources—it exists purely to form the structure of the domain (hence the name) as well as to aid in easy and efficient interdomain replication. Structural domains can be used to provide a domain structure that is well suited to further restructuring in the future. By placing one or more levels of structural domains in the Active Directory tree, you provide an unchanging anchor in the domain tree, under which you can move child domains without altering the higher-level domain structure. At the same time, the structural root domain acts as a shield to the world so that changes in complexity are hidden behind it.

Structural domains are also useful for replication between sites, especially when accessing or replicating the Global Catalog (GC), which is the master catalog for all objects in the host domain's portion of Active Directory and a partial catalog of objects stored in other domains. If you have more than one site, you may choose to create a structural domain at the root that spans all sites and maintains a copy of the GC at each site. (You could also store a copy of the GC in the top-level local domain at each site and just use the structural domain as a link between the sites.) Having an onsite GC permits the local domains at all sites to concentrate on intrasite data processing and replication, with all intersite replication performed by the structural domain.

Using structural domains for replication also makes setting up and maintaining replication links easier. Child domains simply replicate upward to the parent domain, obviating the need to know the name of each domain you need to replicate with.

More Info For more information on structural domains, see *Microsoft Windows 2000 Distributed Systems Guide* (Microsoft Press, 1999).

Developing an Upgrade Strategy

After documenting the existing network infrastructure, making a recovery plan, and designing the Active Directory trees and sites, you're ready to put it all together and create an actual upgrade plan. This section presents some general guidelines that apply to all domain upgrades, as well as some tips for specific domain models.

Make Sure the PDC Is Sufficiently Powerful

Start the domain upgrade by carefully examining the current PDC. Although Windows 2000 uses peer-based, multiple-master domain controllers, the first domain controller retains extra services that in some cases cannot easily be moved to other domain controllers. These services include the Global Catalog server, the Operations Master, and the PDC emulator. (The PDC emulator provides services for Windows NT and Windows 95/98 clients and also performs some tasks in a pure Windows 2000 environment.) In other words, all domain controllers are equal, but the first Windows 2000 domain controller is a little more equal than the others, so you want that machine to be especially fast and powerful.

Create the New Root Domain Before Upgrading the PDC

If you're moving from a multiple-master–domain or complete trust model and want to create a new domain to serve as the root of the domain tree, you need to do this before you upgrade the PDC. By the way, creating this new root domain, whether it's a structural domain or not, involves a brand new system (or at least a clean install) with Windows 2000. Once you have created the new domain and have it running with a couple of domain controllers (as well as any new systems or clean installs), you can upgrade the PDC and join it to this new tree as a child domain.

Upgrade the PDC First

The first server to be upgraded must be the Windows NT PDC in the account domain you want to use as the root of the new Active Directory tree. This is true whether the tree you're creating is the first in the forest or the twentieth in the third forest—you always need to upgrade the PDC first if you want to upgrade the Windows NT domain instead of creating a new domain.

Upgrade the BDCs Right Away

Upgrade all BDCs in the domain as soon as possible after starting the upgrade process. This step will allow you to switch the domain to Windows 2000 native mode and gain the administrative benefits of native mode sooner.

> **Tip**   When you upgrade a BDC to Windows 2000, it will replicate with the first domain controller it can reach. If the former PDC, now Windows 2000, domain controller isn't available, the BDC will try to configure itself as the first Windows 2000 controller in the domain, creating serious problems when the first domain controller comes back online. Make sure that the first Windows 2000 domain controller is visible on the network when upgrading a BDC.

Upgrade Member Servers and Clients Independently

Upgrade member servers and workstations whenever you want—either before or after you upgrade the domain to Windows 2000. Windows 2000 clients and member servers work perfectly well with Windows NT domains; however, the benefits of Active Directory aren't available to them until the domain is upgraded.

Schedule the Domain Upgrade Appropriately

Schedule the domain upgrade at a time that will have the lowest impact on the user population. Although it's probably a forlorn hope, it's best to avoid upgrades during major projects and at the busiest times of year. Even perfect upgrades produce some impact on the users, especially if you perform any domain restructuring or consolidation.

Preparing Domains and Computers for Upgrading

The first step in upgrading to Windows 2000 is to prepare the domains and the computers. This important step will streamline the upgrade process and make it go as smoothly as possible.

Preparing the Domains

To prepare domains for upgrading to Windows 2000, make sure that all servers that you plan to upgrade are running Windows NT 4. It's also a good idea to clean up the directories and user accounts to eliminate old baggage. When you upgrade the domain to Windows 2000, all user accounts are moved into Active Directory—and while Active Directory is extremely scalable, it does take up a decent chunk of hard disk space. There's no point in storing disabled and unused accounts indefinitely, so delete them before you upgrade. Clean out unused directories and uninstall outdated software. Disable trusts that you don't want preserved. Synchronize the PDC with all of the BDCs, and then implement the recovery plan described earlier in the section "Making a Recovery Plan," including taking one of the BDCs offline and disconnecting it from the network.

Preparing the Computers

To prepare the computers for the upgrade, follow these steps for each computer involved:

1. Check the Windows 2000 system requirements to make sure that the computer meets them. Just because the computer fulfills the minimum system requirements doesn't necessarily mean that it's up to the tasks you have planned for it. (For a reminder of Microsoft's minimum system requirements for running Windows 2000 Server, as well as our recommendations for a more realistic set of requirements for a useful system, see Table 5-1 on page 56.)

Real World   **Departing from the HCL**

While it's true that many devices not on the HCL can be made to work most of the time, servers are needed *all* of the time. If you depart from the HCL when configuring a domain controller or other important server, you are taking an unjustifiable risk. Sooner or later, some traceable-to-the-hardware fault will show up, and you'll have no recourse. Microsoft will rightly point out that you should be using hardware from the HCL. And the manufacturer of the hardware will shrug and say that they're "working on" drivers. This is not a good position to be in.

If you have machines that are not 100 percent compatible, try them out as clients. Often, Windows 2000 Professional will work perfectly well with hardware that's not on the HCL. Certainly, Windows 95 and Windows 98 aren't fussy and run on almost any machine with an adequate processor and the minimum amount of RAM.

2. Check the HCL in the Support folder on the Windows 2000 installation CD-ROM. If you don't see the system listed, check the HCL on the Microsoft Web site (*http://www.microsoft.com/hwtest/hcl/*). If updated drivers are available for the hardware, download and copy them to a floppy disk or available local disk so that you can use them during installation, if necessary. If a component in the system is not listed in the Microsoft HCL, you can visit the manufacturer's Web site or contact the manufacturer of the device to see if updated drivers are available. In general, you probably want to replace components that are not listed as 100 percent compatible.

3. Read the Read1st.txt and Relnotes.doc files on the Windows 2000 CD-ROM to check for application or hardware issues.

4. Uninstall any virus protection programs you have installed, unless you know that they work under Windows 2000 without modification.

5. Perform and verify a full system backup.

6. Create or update the emergency repair disk or Windows 95/98 boot disk.

7. Record the hardware configuration of the system for reference in case of a hardware conflict or problem. Items to record include installed devices, IRQs, jumper settings, and the hard disk configurations.

8. Disable disk mirroring if you are using it. (You can enable it after you finish upgrading.)

9. Uncompress the hard disk. (This applies to Windows 95/98 clients only.)

10. Disconnect the serial cable to any serial port uninterruptible power supply (UPS) devices. (USB UPS devices can be left plugged in.)

11. Locate all drivers and get the Windows 2000 CD-ROM or connect to the network share with the Windows 2000 installation files.

Take a deep breath and begin. The remainder of this chapter covers upgrading systems to Windows 2000.

Upgrading to Windows 2000 Professional from Windows 95/98

Although this book concentrates on Windows 2000 server issues, in all likelihood you'll spend more time performing client upgrades than server upgrades. Windows 2000 is the first of the Microsoft network operating systems to provide an upgrade path for the desktop operating systems (Windows 95 and Windows 98) in addition to the workstation operating system (Windows NT Workstation).

Windows 95/98 upgrades are the most difficult upgrade path to Windows 2000, and because of these difficulties, we recommend that you consider performing clean installations instead of upgrades whenever possible. Before deciding whether to upgrade or to perform new installations, read the sections that follow and test out the upgrade on some clients that are representative of the client population. (Chapter 5 covers performing multiple, identical installations of Windows 2000.)

Real World   Why Windows 2000 Professional?

Windows 2000 Professional is by far the best business client that Microsoft sells. However, for some reason Microsoft has not promoted it as the first choice for every business and continues to revise the Windows 95/98 line even though, in general, Windows 95 and Windows 98 are not the best systems for the workplace. Sure, they have functional redirectors for Microsoft networks and can be upgraded to access Active Directory, but they also lack many of the attributes that make a good business operating system. If Windows 2000 will run on the client systems, you're almost always better off using it over Windows 95/98.

Windows 2000 Professional has remarkable system stability, surpassing even that of Windows NT Workstation. System security is customizable; you can make the client's security very loose or extremely tight. (Windows NT 3.51 is qualified for C2-level security, and Windows NT 4 and Windows 2000 are also expected to receive this qualification when they emerge from the somewhat lengthy testing process.) Windows 2000 is also built for speed, with an efficient 32-bit, fully multithreaded, preemptive multitasking and symmetric multiprocessing (SMP) enabled kernel, allowing users to run more applications and to run those applications faster. Users with multiple processors and software written to take advantage of SMP can make use of a second processor—something not available in Windows 95/98. Windows 2000 is actually significantly faster in most applications than Windows 98 on equivalent hardware (assuming that the hardware meets the minimum system requirements for Windows 2000).

Windows 2000 Professional is designed to complement the Windows 2000 Server family, and as such provides the best client services for Windows 2000–based networks, greatly surpassing Windows NT 4 Workstation's excellent network facilities. On a Windows 2000 domain, Windows 2000 Professional clients can be managed remotely, make use of roving desktops, and take advantage of remotely installed applications. (Even the operating system can be installed remotely.)

Difficulties Involved with Windows 95/98 Upgrades

A direct upgrade from Windows 95 or Windows 98 to Windows 2000 is possible, and, to paraphrase Dr. Samuel Johnson, it is not done well, but one is surprised to find it done at all. The difficulty lies in a fundamental difference in architectures: Windows 2000 is based on Windows NT, and Windows 95 and Windows 98 are heir to MS-DOS/Windows 3.x (although obviously all of the later operating systems include huge amounts of new code). To further complicate matters, Windows 95 and 98 don't use the same drivers as Windows 2000 (unless you use WDM drivers in Windows 98), and applications are often coded differently for Windows 95/98 than they are for Windows 2000. These are major obstacles to overcome, although if Windows 2000 drivers are available for the system components, the driver issue can be easily dealt with.

The fact is that some Windows 95/98 applications won't run under Windows 2000 without modification. Thus, when performing an upgrade from Windows 95 or Windows 98, it is important to either uninstall applications that don't run without modification on both Windows 98 and Windows 2000 or to obtain an upgrade pack (also called a migration DLL) from the application vendor.

With that said, you *can* upgrade a Windows 95–based or Windows 98–based system to Windows 2000 Professional, and it can be made to work. However, a prudent person will perform a few upgrades on representative systems before deciding on the upgrade strategy.

Planning Many application packages install different versions of the same program, depending on whether the installation was run under Windows 95/98 or Windows 2000. When this is the case, the Windows 95/98 version usually won't run under Windows 2000. If you are facing this situation, you need to obtain an upgrade pack or a migration DLL from the application vendor. Or you can uninstall the application before the upgrade and then install the Windows 2000–compatible version afterward.

Using a Dual Boot

If you must deal with legacy applications that work only under Windows 95/98, you can set up a Windows 95/98 and Windows 2000 dual boot. Dual booting allows users to select the operating system at boot time, with each operating system installed on a separate partition or disk drive and maintaining its own applications. While using a dual boot allows a lot of flexibility, it isn't something you want to do on a large scale because of the additional administrative work and extra resources required.

If you want to perform a dual boot with Windows 95/98, you should be aware of the following limitations:

- Windows 95/98 cannot access NTFS partitions, although Windows 2000 can access all FAT and FAT32 partitions. Therefore, if you need to be able to access all data on the drive from both operating systems, you need to use FAT or FAT32 to format the partitions. However, using FAT or FAT32 eliminates many of the security advantages Windows 2000 has to offer, so use this solution with caution.

- Each application must be installed separately on each operating system.

- You need a different computer name for each operating system. The computer will appear on the network as *name1* when it's booted into Windows 95 or Windows 98; it will appear as *name2* when it's booted into Windows 2000.

Tip If you are currently using a dual boot between Windows 95/98 and Windows NT, you can upgrade the Windows NT installation to Windows 2000 and then use a dual boot between Windows 95/98 and Windows 2000. However, in this situation, you can't upgrade the Windows 95/98 installation to Windows 2000.

To set up a dual boot, while in Windows 95/98, either launch Setup or, if you have Auto Insert Notification enabled, simply insert the Windows 2000 CD-ROM and click No when prompted to upgrade to Windows 2000. In the first window you see after launching Setup or clicking No, select Install A New Copy Of Windows 2000 to perform a clean install. See "Running Setup from Windows" in Chapter 5 for a complete description of the installation process.

Performing the Upgrade

You can launch Setup either from the Windows 2000 CD-ROM or from a network drive. In either case, first launch Windows 95 or Windows 98, close all programs, and uninstall any virus protection programs you have installed.

To launch Setup from the CD-ROM, insert the Windows 2000 CD-ROM. The Microsoft Windows 2000 CD dialog box appears if you have CD-ROM AutoPlay (Auto Insert Notification) enabled. (If this is not enabled, open the i386 folder on the CD-ROM and double-click winnt32.exe.) This dialog box asks if you want to upgrade the version of Windows, as shown in Figure 7-3. Click Yes to start Setup.

Figure 7-3. *The Microsoft Windows 2000 CD dialog box.*

To upgrade to Windows 2000 Professional from across a network, launch the winnt32.exe program on the network drive containing the Windows 2000 Advanced Server setup files, and then proceed with Setup. Once you've launched Setup, follow these steps to upgrade the computer to Windows 2000 Professional:

1. Select the Upgrade To Windows 2000 option, and then click Next (Figure 7-4). This will upgrade the computer to Windows 2000 Professional while keeping the settings and programs intact.

Figure 7-4. *The first screen of the Windows 2000 Setup Wizard.*

2. Read through the licensing agreement, select the I Accept This Agreement option, and then click Next.

3. Click the hyperlink provided to connect to Microsoft's Web site to look for upgrade files you might need, and then click Next. Setup then scans the system for incompatible software and hardware.

4. If you have upgrade packs (also known as migration DLLs) for any of the programs, select the Yes, I Have Upgrade Packs option, and then click Add to select the folder containing the files. If you don't have upgrade packs, select the second option and click Next.

5. Indicate whether you want to upgrade the drive to NTFS in the next screen, and then click Next. (NTFS is necessary to use the security features of Windows 2000.)

6. If you know that you have hardware for which Windows 2000 doesn't have drivers, click Provide Files to indicate that you will give Setup updated drivers, and then click Next.

7. Setup displays an upgrade report that documents the status of the hardware and software. Read this report carefully to determine whether or not you still want to perform the upgrade. Uninstall programs that Setup reports may cause problems, and then click Next to let Setup upgrade the computer. The Setup program will proceed.

Tip   If you don't provide updated drivers, the devices with outdated drivers won't work until you install newer drivers. You can do this after installing Windows 2000 without causing problems.

Upgrading to Windows 2000 Advanced Server from Windows NT

For existing Windows NT servers or clients, upgrading to Windows 2000 Server or Advanced Server is by far the easiest path. Doing so allows you to preserve all of the settings and, when upgrading the PDC, it allows you to preserve the domain and all of its user accounts and resources. Performing a clean installation (covered extensively in Chapter 5) is also an option, but it is unnecessary unless you are running a server operating system other than Windows NT 3.51 or 4. (Servers running earlier versions of Windows NT are usually better off upgrading to 3.51 or 4 first and then upgrading to Windows 2000, rather than performing a clean install.)

Similarly, setting up a dual boot is not recommended unless you have some need to use the existing Windows NT server or client configuration part of the time. Dual booting between Windows NT 4 and Windows 2000 has a number of limitations; for more information, see "Dual Boot Considerations" in Chapter 5.

To upgrade to Windows 2000 Advanced Server with the Windows 2000 Advanced Server upgrade CD-ROM, you need to be running Windows NT 4 Enterprise Edition. If you have the full version of Windows 2000 Advanced Server, intended for new computers, you can upgrade from any of the following products:

- Windows NT 4 Enterprise Edition
- Windows NT 4 Terminal Server
- Windows NT 4 Server
- Windows NT 3.51 Server

After you've planned the domain upgrade and prepared the computer (as discussed earlier in this chapter), you're ready to begin the upgrade. If you're upgrading a PDC, synchronize with the domain's BDCs one last time before you start the upgrade.

Close all open programs and disable all virus protection programs, and then insert the Windows 2000 CD-ROM. The Microsoft Windows 2000 CD dialog box appears if you have CD-ROM AutoPlay (Auto Insert Notification) enabled. (If this is not enabled, open the i386 folder on the CD-ROM and double-click winnt32.exe.) The dialog box asks if you want to upgrade the version of Windows. Click Yes to start Setup, and then follow these steps to upgrade to Windows 2000:

1. Select the Upgrade To Windows 2000 option, and then click Next. This will upgrade the computer to Windows 2000 while keeping the settings and programs intact.

2. Read through the licensing agreement, select the I Accept This Agreement option, and then click Next.

3. If Setup finds hardware that isn't compatible with Windows 2000, it lists it in the next screen. Select the incompatible hardware and click Have Disk to provide updated Windows 2000 drivers for the device, and then click Next. At this point, Setup reboots, installs Windows 2000, and then reboots into the now upgraded operating system.

4. If you are upgrading a PDC or BDC, the Active Directory Installation Wizard starts. See Chapter 10 for information on how to use this wizard to install Active Directory and a DNS server if you want to deploy both services on the domain controller (a good idea).

Operational Modes in Domains

After you upgrade the PDC to Windows 2000, the domain operates in *mixed mode,* meaning that both Windows 2000 and Windows NT controllers can be present. This is the default setting for Windows 2000 servers. In mixed mode, trusts operate as they do between Windows NT 4 domains.

About Native Mode

To operate in native mode, a Windows 2000 domain must be running only Windows 2000 domain controllers *and* it must be explicitly switched to native mode operation. Since this is a one-way migration, it must be done manually. As soon as you upgrade to native mode, Windows NT 4 controllers can no longer function in the domain. Thus, you shouldn't switch to native mode unless you're sure that you've upgraded all Windows NT BDCs or taken them offline, and that you won't want to use Windows NT domain controllers in the future.

Planning Windows NT 4 member servers work without issues in a Windows 2000 native-mode domain, as do Windows NT 4–based and Windows 95/98–based clients. Native mode refers only to the domain controllers, not to all machines in the domain.

Windows 2000 native-mode domains offer a number of advantages over Windows NT 4 domains, as well as over Windows 2000 mixed-mode domains. Table 7-4 summarizes these advantages. In addition to the advantages listed in the table, switching to native mode allows legacy clients to benefit from the transitive trusts between domains in Active Directory and, once authenticated, to access resources anywhere in the domain tree, provided they have the proper permissions.

Table 7-4.   The differences among Windows NT 4 domains, Windows 2000 mixed-mode domains, and Windows 2000 native-mode domains

Feature	Windows NT 4	Windows 2000 Mixed Mode	Windows 2000 Native Mode
Objects per domain	Fewer than 40,000 (20,000 user accounts) recommended	Fewer than 40,000 (20,000 user accounts) recommended	Up to 1 million
Multimaster replication	No	Yes	Yes
Group types	Global, Local	Global, Local	Universal, Domain Global, Domain Local, Local
Nested groups	No	No	Yes
Cross-domain administration	Limited	Limited	Full
Password filters	Installed manually on each PDC and BDC	Installed manually on each DC	Installed automatically on all DCs
Queries using Desktop Change/ Configuration Management	No	Only on Windows 2000 DCs	Yes
Authentication protocols	NTLM	NTLM, Kerberos	Kerberos

It's important to understand that not all systems in the domain have to be running Windows 2000 in order to operate a native-mode domain. Native mode affects only the operation of the domain controllers. The issue of having non–Windows 2000 systems in the domain is important, however, when it comes to planning WINS server deployment. As long as you have legacy (non–Windows 2000) clients and servers in the domain, you need WINS servers for NetBIOS name resolution (unless you have a small, nonrouted network that can handle NetBIOS name resolution via broadcast). In addition, you shouldn't turn off NetBIOS over TCP/IP for Windows 2000 machines until the network consists entirely of Windows 2000 machines because legacy systems will be unable to communicate with the Windows 2000 systems. (Legacy systems rely on NetBIOS calls for network communication.)

Switching to Native Mode

When all of the Windows NT 4 BDCs have been either upgraded to Windows 2000 or taken offline, you can switch the network to Windows 2000 native mode. To make the switch, log on to a domain controller using an administrator account and follow these steps:

1. Open Active Directory Domains And Trusts from the Administrative Tools folder.

2. Right-click the domain you want to convert to native mode, and choose Properties from the shortcut menu.

3. Click the Change Mode button in the Properties window, shown in Figure 7-5. Notice that the Domain Operation Mode box displays Mixed Mode.

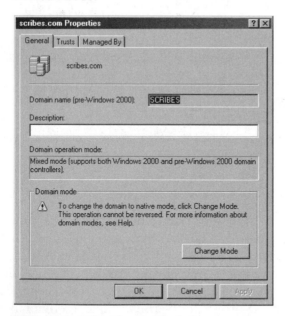

Figure 7-5. *The Change Mode button.*

4. When Windows 2000 asks you to verify the switch, click OK. Click OK in the next dialog box also.

5. Reboot the domain controller you made changes to as well as every DC in the domain *after* the modified DC reports that it is running in native mode.

Caution   Switching to native mode is an irreversible procedure. After switching to native mode, you cannot use Windows NT 4 domain controllers in the domain.

Summary

Upgrading existing servers and clients to Windows 2000 involves even more planning than creating a domain from the ground up, and upgrading machines running Windows 95 and Windows 98 introduces additional complexity. Changing a network's structure before beginning your upgrade can make it function better under Active Directory. As the system administrator, you should recommend new installations on clients and upgraded installations on servers whenever possible. The next chapter moves on to the installation and configuration of printers—after the computers themselves, the most important component of many networks.

Chapter 8
Installing and Managing Printers

Back in the early, heady days of desktop personal computers, people talked a lot about the coming "paperless office." Alas, that day not only hasn't arrived, but in most companies, the paper recycling box is the biggest receptacle in the building!

The cost of basic printers has declined over the years, but increasingly, companies have invested in sophisticated high-speed color printers that enable users to handle jobs that once required an outside print shop. These are expensive both to buy and to use. Therefore, printer sharing remains an important function of enterprise networks. Setting up multiple users to share printers reduces cost and can increase printing output. Routine work can be directed to less expensive printers, long print jobs can be scheduled for off hours, and access to high-end printers can be limited.

Understanding the Basics

This chapter deals with all aspects of printing in Microsoft Windows 2000: understanding the basics, planning printer deployment, installing printers, sharing printers on a network, modifying printer properties, searching for printers, using and managing printers, and troubleshooting printer problems. First we'll review the basics for working effectively with printers in Windows 2000.

Real World   **Printer Terminology**

Printer terminology is a good deal more confusing than it has to be because of the historical use of different names for the same object. In Microsoft Windows NT 4, *print device* is the name for the actual printer, and *printer* designates the software interface. So in other words, *printer* is used to mean the logical entity. In a NetWare or OS/2 networking environment, the term *print queue* is used instead of *printer* (meaning the logical printer), but the net effect is the same.

In Windows 2000, the documentation now uses *printer* to mean the device that does the actual printing and *logical printer* to mean the software interface. In this book, we'll gladly conform to this convention and refer to the print device as the "printer." We'll refer to the software interface as the "logical printer" or, occasionally, the "printer driver."

You can have one logical printer associated with a single printer, or you can have several logical printers associated with a single printer. In this second arrangement, the logical printers can be configured at different priority levels so that one logical printer handles normal printing and another handles jobs to be printed later. For a printer that can use either PostScript or Printer Control Language (PCL), two logical printers will allow users to choose which type of printing to do.

A single logical printer can also be associated with multiple physical printers. If all the print devices use the same printer driver, a single logical printer will allow jobs to be sent to the first available physical printer. This arrangement is called a *printer pool*. The advantage of a printer pool is that an administrator can add or remove physical printers without affecting the users' configurations because the physical printers are interchangeable.

Understanding Network Printers

Network printers are normal printers with additional network hardware such as a network interface card and additional memory, and sometimes a hard disk for spooling large documents. These printers run the appropriate protocol for your network (usually TCP/IP or Internetwork Packet Exchange [IPX] protocol) and have their own unique network address.

Note Network printers are the type most commonly used with print servers, as will be discussed later in this section, but these printers can also function by themselves on a network without a print server.

Network printers are popular in most companies because of their ease of configuration, printing speed, and flexibility in location relative to the print server and clients. No specialized hardware is required on the print server, which isn't always the case with print servers printing to multiple serial or parallel port printers. The direct connection to the network (at either 10 Mb/sec or 100 Mb/sec) also provides a much faster interface than the relatively slow parallel port often used by stand-alone print servers.

Network printers can also be set up without a print server, eliminating the cost of an additional computer. However, since no server is queuing the print jobs from clients, each user sees only his or her own documents in the print queue and can't see where a document is in relation to other documents in line waiting to print. Similarly, because no single print queue exists, the print jobs destined for this printer cannot be centrally managed, and only the user with the currently printing document sees any error messages (such as messages about paper jams). Finally, all preprint processing occurs on the user's computer, increasing the amount of time the computer is partially or completely unavailable for other tasks. For these reasons a print server is desirable with network printers.

One last point about network printers—many of the newer ones support Internet Printing via the Internet Printing Protocol (IPP). Internet Printing is a feature that allows a user with sufficient permissions and Microsoft Internet Explorer 4 or later to print to an Internet Printing–enabled printer from anywhere in the world (or from the user's intranet), not just from the local network.

Understanding Print Servers

Print servers are computers (or sometimes network appliances) that manage the communications between printers and the client computers that want to print to the printers.

> **Note**   Microsoft Windows 2000 Professional as well as the various Windows 2000 Server versions will work as print servers; however, Windows 2000 Professional can support a maximum of only 10 simultaneous users and is unable to support Macintosh or NetWare clients. Windows 2000 Server doesn't have these limitations.

Generally, there are two approaches to print servers. Microsoft's approach in Windows 2000 and Windows NT is to have a print server that is fairly "intelligent," providing clients with appropriate printer drivers and maintaining the printer queue, as well as handling communication between the printers and the client computers.

In contrast, UNIX (and some companies such as Intel and Milan) uses a relatively "dumb" print server. The most popular form of dumb print server is the Line Printer Daemon (LPD). A dumb print server usually acts strictly as an interface between the network and the printer, with each client maintaining its own printer queue. The LPD service runs either on a UNIX server, on a network appliance that provides LPD and network access functionality, or within a printer connected directly to the network. Clients use the Line Printer Remote (LPR) service—an integral part of UNIX and optional in Windows 2000 and Windows NT—to communicate with the LPD service, which then communicates with the printer.

Note   Windows 2000 Server can also be an LPD server for compatibility with UNIX clients and other clients using the LPR service.

Because of the limitations of the LPD service, Windows 2000 and Windows NT print servers are almost always used instead of LPD servers when the network consists mostly of Windows clients. In a mixed UNIX and Windows environment, the LPD service can be installed on a Windows 2000 print server to provide printing services to UNIX clients. A common alternative is for Windows print servers to connect to printers using the LPD service (either on the printer or by connecting to a device running the LPD service), just as if they were normal network printers. In this scenario Windows clients have the benefits of a standard Windows print server while maintaining compatibility with UNIX clients, who interface directly with the LPD service associated with the printer.

Real World   The Line Printer Daemon Service

Printers are often plugged in to a small network device or a UNIX server running the Line Printer Daemon (LPD) service. Devices or computers running LPD are called print servers, although they don't function the same as Windows 2000 or Windows NT print servers.

The LPD service acts as a network gateway for printers to communicate with UNIX clients or other clients using the Line Printer Remote (LPR) service, and many network printers come with the LPD service built in. Printers that lack a network interface can be connected to a device or computer running LPD, which then acts as a network interface card for the printer as well as providing the LPD's usual function of allowing UNIX clients to print to the attached device. Printers using a print server running LPD can be accessed only by clients running the LPR service—an integral part of UNIX and an optional part of Windows and some other operating systems.

Usually if a printer using the LPD service needs to be accessed by Windows clients, a Windows 2000 or Windows NT print server will connect to the LPD and share the printer out as if it were directly attached to the Windows print server instead of through LPD. The Windows print server holds the printer queue and then sends each print job to LPD, which passes the job to the printer. Alternately (or in some cases, additionally), the Windows 2000 server can connect directly to the printer using either a standard TCP/IP printer port or the LPR service, and then run the LPD service to provide print functionality to both Windows and UNIX clients.

Methods of Connecting Printers to Print Servers

Printers can be directly connected to the print server by a network connection to a network printer or with a parallel or serial port connection, although the latter has generally fallen out of favor because of the amount of processing power consumed by managing the ports. USB and IEEE 1394 (Firewire or iLink) printers eliminate some of the disadvantages of connecting printers directly to the print server, but by far the most popular way to connect printers to a print server is via a network connection.

Network printers have built-in network cards and usually additional memory (and sometimes even hard disks). These printers run the appropriate protocol in use on your network (usually TCP/IP or IPX) and have their own unique network addresses.

As was mentioned in the section "Understanding Network Printers," a network connection provides increased bandwidth to a printer. However, more important than the increased bandwidth is the processing power that is conserved by using a network connection compared with a parallel port connection. The high CPU use of parallel and serial port printers causes undue strain on the print server and is one of the primary reasons network printers have become so popular.

Flexibility in locating network printers is another factor that has made network printers successful. While a print server can manage printers in widely separated locations, increasing the number of printers connected to a single computer will inevitably produce cabling inconveniences. It's often easier to plug printers into nearby hubs than it is to run cables (which have length limitations) to all the printers serviced by the print server.

Advantages of Windows 2000 Print Servers

Windows 2000 and Windows NT print servers offer a number of advantages over printers directly connected to the network or connected to the network via a device running the LPD service. All documents are spooled to the print server instead of directly to the printer, allowing client computers to hand off documents to the print server quickly and to continue working while the server queues the documents and handles any additional processing. Since all documents are queued on the print server, all clients can view a centralized queue for the printer, see any error messages, and, if the user possesses the proper permissions, administer the printer or printer queue.

Print servers can also provide a single audit log of all the documents printed by each user as well as any printer management performed. In addition, print servers provide central control over printer driver settings, and they can be set up to provide printer drivers to Windows 2000 and Windows NT clients who download them as needed. Windows clients can also locate printers by browsing the network or searching Active Directory. Do bear in mind that any computer acting as a print server is partially occupied with printing tasks, so any other server applications being run on the same machine might suffer performance degradations. In general, file-sharing services will take precedence, so printing throughput will be reduced before file sharing is slowed.

Understanding the Printing Process

When a Windows application prints a document, the application calls the Windows Graphical Device Interface (GDI), which then calls the printer driver for the appropriate printer. (Other operating systems use different components for this printing stage.) The GDI and the printer driver cooperate to render the document in the printer language of the printer and then pass the rendered document to the client print spooler, as illustrated in Figure 8-1.

The client print spooler gives the print job to the remote print provider (RPP), the RPP sends it to the Windows print server hosting the target printer, and the print server host saves the print job at the end of the print queue for the printer.

> **Note** When using the LPR service to print to a printer via the LPD service, each client maintains an individual print queue. LPR and LPD are the default print services for UNIX computers; Windows operating systems can also use these services for UNIX compatibility, although the services aren't installed by default.

The local print provider on the print server polls the print processor to determine whether the print job needs to be converted to a different data type before printing. When the print job reaches the front of the queue, it moves to the Separator Page Processor (SPP) for the insertion of a separator page, if required. Then the job is despooled to the print monitor, and from there through the appropriate printer port to the printer itself. The printer receives the print job either in its entirety, or gradually as the print monitor feeds the printer at the appropriate rate to keep the printer's buffers full. The printer converts each page to a bitmap format and then prints the document.

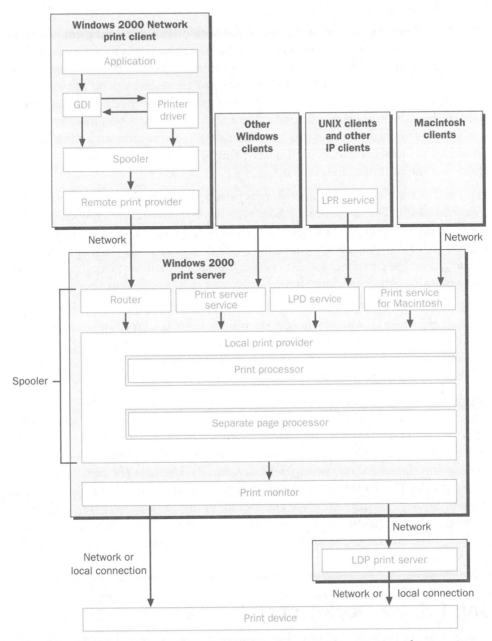

Figure 8-1. *Windows 2000 interaction with various services to print a document.*

Printer Data Types

After a print job reaches the beginning of the print queue, the local print provider polls the print processor to determine whether the print job is in the correct data type for the printer. If the print job is in the incorrect format, the print processor needs to convert it. The data type that is used to represent a print job is important not only because of the need to match the data type supported by the printer, but also because of performance considerations. Therefore, you need to understand the differences between the two main data types supported by the default Windows print processor. (Third-party print processors occasionally—but not often—supply additional data types.)

The most commonly used printer data type supported by Windows is *enhanced metafile* (EMF). This is the default data type for Windows 2000 or Windows NT clients using the popular PCL page description language. The EMF data type is a metafile format that allows better portability, smaller print jobs, and less time consumed on the client workstation preparing a document for printing. EMF files also generally consume somewhat less network bandwidth, but they do require more processing on the print server than do raw print jobs.

The second most commonly used data type is the *raw* data type, which is the default data type for PostScript printers and all clients not running Windows 2000 or Windows NT. Raw print jobs are processed entirely on the client computer and aren't modified at all by the print server.

The Windows 2000 print processor (Winprint) supports three other data types, although they aren't used as often. The data types are *raw (FF appended)*, *raw (FF auto)*, and *text*. *Raw (FF appended)* appends a form-feed character to the print job, which is required by some applications that otherwise don't print the last page when using the *raw* data type with PCL printers. The *raw (FF auto)* data type automatically checks for the presence of a trailing form-feed character and adds one if necessary. The *text* data type encodes the entire print job as plain ANSI text, then adds any additional print specification using the printer's factory default settings. This data type is useful for printers that don't operate properly with other data types.

Planning Printer Deployment

Your company probably already has printers deployed, and hopefully you also have naming conventions and guidelines for putting new printers in place. Even so, you should still review this section—especially if you plan to use the new printer location feature of Windows 2000 and Active Directory, discussed later in this chapter. This feature allows users to more easily locate nearby printers that have the features they need. This section covers establishing naming conventions for your printers, creating location-naming conventions for use with and without Active Directory, and choosing printers and sizing print servers to meet your network's needs.

Establishing Printer Naming Conventions

Effective printer naming methods convey as much relevant information about the printers as possible while keeping the name user friendly and compatible with all relevant clients.

> **Planning** Like planning your network namespace, planning the naming convention you use for your printers is important for maintaining a logical and user-friendly computing environment. For an enterprise, be sure to get management support for the convention. You want to establish a naming scheme that's actually enforceable in your company.

On Windows-based machines, you work with two names: the printer name and the share name. A *printer name* is the name given to a printer at the time of installation, and it can be any length up to 220 characters. A *share name* is the name given to the printer for use on your network, and it can be up to 80 characters long—although it's usually kept to 8 characters or fewer for compatibility with MS-DOS and Windows 3.x–based clients. Printer names show up on the print server and in the comments field when Windows clients browse for a printer. The share name is the name that all clients see when they browse for a printer, use the Add Printer Wizard, or use the Net Use command.

> **Caution** Some legacy applications experience problems with printers whose fully qualified printer name (the computer name and printer share name combined) exceeds 31 characters. This problem can also occur with printers whose names are shorter than 31 characters if the default printer's name exceeds 31 characters. In addition, MS-DOS clients can't access printers with share names longer than 8 characters followed by a 3-character extension.

Usually the printer name used is the actual name of the printer followed by a number if multiple identical printers exist in the same location. Some companies might want to include the location of the printer in the printer name also, so an HP LaserJet 8100 laser printer might be named HP LaserJet 8100-1 or HP LaserJet 8100 Floor 10-1.

The share name needs to be more terse and is often a generic reference to the printer's capabilities. For example, the HP LaserJet 8100 printer just mentioned might use HPLaser1 as its share name. Or if you had a color laser printer, you might use ClrLaser as a share name. You can optionally use a three-letter extension on the share name and still maintain compatibility with MS-DOS clients— some companies use the extension to denote the number of the printer or to refer to its capabilities.

Tip   Avoid using spaces or other special characters in share names unless you maintain an all–Windows 2000 network. Otherwise, some clients, such as UNIX and MS-DOS, won't be able to recognize the names.

Creating Location-Naming Conventions

When you use Windows 2000's Active Directory to store printer information, users can browse or search for printers based on the criteria they want, including printer features and location. In smaller organizations, users can search for printers without using printer location tracking. However, if printer location tracking is to be enabled, the location name becomes more important than the printer name.

Location names are similar in form to domain names and are written in the form *name/name/name/name*. They start with the most general location name and become progressively more specific. For example, a multinational corporation might have the location name structure shown in Figure 8-2.

The Seattle location, for example, could be written NorthAmerica/USA/Seattle. Each part name can be a maximum of 32 characters and can contain any characters except the forward slash (/), which is reserved for use as a delimiter. The entire location name must be no longer than 260 characters, with a maximum of 256 levels (which, for your sake, we really hope is enough!).

If you're not using Active Directory to store your printer information, you can still include location information with printers, although this approach has some limitations. To enter location information, type the location name on the General tab of the printer's Properties window. When you do this, be careful and consistent with your location names. Make sure that all administrators use the same name for a particular location, and keep the names short and easy to remember: users need to know the exact location names when they search for printers if Active Directory's location-browsing capabilities are unavailable. For more on printer location tracking, see "Setting Up Printer Location Tracking" later in this chapter.

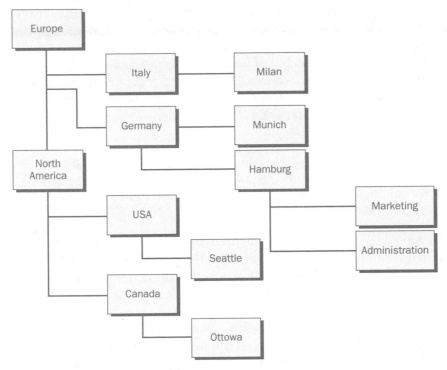

Figure 8-2. *A sample location name structure.*

Choosing Printers and Print Servers

Deploying the right printers and print servers for your company is an important task. While making specific hardware recommendations is impractical, we can give you some advice about how to approach the issue. Even if you already have your network constructed, these tips apply any time you want to add a printer, add a print server, or evaluate how well your current deployment is serving your needs.

Guidelines for Choosing Printers

Before deploying printers for your network, make sure that the printers adequately meet your users' requirements. To begin this process, first determine what kinds of printing services each group of users needs, by considering such factors as print volume, graphics requirements, and features.

Some user populations will require printer features such as collating, double-sided printing, envelope feeders, or large-format printing. Try to match the printer's duty cycle (how many pages the printer is designed to print per month) to the expected print volume. When a printer's duty cycle is consistently exceeded, you risk increased maintenance costs and repairs.

If you have a group of users in relatively close proximity, you can place heavy-duty laser printers in a centralized location for all users. This approach is usually more cost-effective than trying to deploy multiple, lower-cost laser or inkjet printers. It also increases the number of features available to users and simplifies administration and maintenance chores. Even if users are scattered and have a range of needs, using a few high-volume printers is more practical than placing a cheap inkjet on every other user's desk.

Tip In the long term, laser printers are almost always less expensive for black-and-white printing than even the most cost-effective inkjet alternative. This is now usually the case for color printing also. Although inkjet printers are often better suited for printing photos, be aware of their slower speeds and higher consumables costs.

After determining the type of printers you need, check the Windows 2000 Hardware Compatibility List to ascertain whether the printer is supported. Some newer printers might not be listed, so check whether the manufacturer provides Windows 2000 drivers and is in the process of getting the printer certified. If you already have a service contract for a particular manufacturer's printers, you'll probably want to stick to that brand to reduce maintenance headaches. And finally, determine the type of printer interface to use. You'll probably want to get printers with network interfaces built in. To directly connect the printers to a print server, consider printers with USB or IEEE 1394 (Firewire or iLink) interfaces for faster print speeds and easier configuration.

Planning Try to keep your printers on the same network segment as the users of the printer if you expect a high print volume. This approach minimizes the impact to users on other parts of your network. In any case, try to minimize the number of network hops a print job needs to take to get from a user to their default printer.

Guidelines for Choosing Print Servers

Sizing a print server is much like determining the requirements of any other type of server. Collect information and monitor any existing solutions to see where your bottlenecks are, deploy your server, and then monitor and tune the server to make sure that it is achieving your performance requirements.

Unless you need to support a large volume of printing or extremely large or complex documents, print servers generally don't need expensive hardware. Often, computers that have become too slow for their original tasks will do admirably.

A print server must have enough disk space to hold all print jobs while they wait in the printer queue. The amount of space required depends both on the size of the print jobs and on how long the print queue will get. For best performance, use a fast, dedicated drive just for the print spool folder, and don't place any system files—especially the swap file—on this drive. Windows 2000 gives file sharing a higher priority than printer sharing, so if you're using your print server for both services, printing might be slowed somewhat to prevent any file access performance hits.

Real World   Preparing for Print Server Failure

Many companies will have a secondary print server in case the primary print server fails. When the primary print server fails, the administrator has three alternatives. One choice is to send out e-mail instructing users to choose ReserveServer2 for printing. This option is easiest for the administrator—but, inevitably, some users just can't manage the switch.

A second option is for the administrator to switch the users from PrintServer1 to ReserveServer2, which normally has another function but can act as the print server in case the primary server fails. Although this switching process requires some effort by the administrator, it usually takes less time than repairing the primary print server. More importantly, users will be able to print unimpeded while the primary print server is being fixed. (The two network events that you interrupt at your peril are printing and e-mail. When either one isn't working, the complaints are immediate and high volume.)

A third method is the most transparent to the users and works because a print server—in fact, any server—can have more than one name. If your normal PrintServer1 goes off line, you can go to ReserveServer2 and add an alias (PrintServer1); from the point of view of the users and the network, this printer then becomes PrintServer1, and work continues uninterrupted. To give a server a secondary name, you'll need to modify the registry. Go to the registry key *HKEY_LOCAL_MACHINE\System\CurrentControlSet\Services\LanmanServer\Parameters* and add the value OptionalNames REG_SZ String: [*Alias*]. (Replace *Alias* with the server name.)

You'll need to reboot the server to see the change. All the usual warnings apply about not modifying the registry unless you have a saved copy. Also, if you're using WINS, you'll have to add a static IP address for the duration, or WINS won't be able to find the server. When you're ready to bring the original Print Server1 back on line, remove the alias. To monitor the performance of print servers to determine whether they are performing optimally, select the Performance snap-in from the Administrative Tools folder and add counters from the new *Print Queue* object under the Performance category.

Installing Printers

To add a printer to your system in Windows 2000, as in Windows NT 4 and Windows 95/98, you use the Add Printer Wizard. If you've configured printers in any of these operating systems, you'll find that the process is similar in Windows 2000.

Tip To change the default behavior of the Add Printer Wizard for clients, servers, or both, use the Group Policy snap-in, covered in Chapter 9.

After adding a printer by using the Add Printer Wizard, you'll need to set up the appropriate permissions for the printer, set up any installable options with which your printer is equipped, and set your printing defaults. See the "Changing Printer Options" section later in this chapter for more information.

Tip To enable Macintosh clients to print to your print server, use the Windows 2000 Add Component Wizard to install Macintosh print services, and make sure that your server is running the AppleTalk protocol. To allow clients that use the LPR service (such as UNIX clients) to print to your server, install UNIX print services, and make sure that the LPD system service is started if it's not started automatically. You'll find more on UNIX printing in Chapter 21 and more on Macintosh printing in Chapter 22.

Adding Local Printers

Physically connecting printers to the print server isn't popular these days, but sometimes you'll still want to do it. Whether the computer is a print server or simply a workstation, understanding the process of installing a printer under Windows 2000 is helpful. (All versions of Windows 2000 handle adding local printers in the same way.) To use the Add Printer Wizard to set up a local printer that is physically connected to your system, follow these steps:

1. Connect the printer to the appropriate port on your server.

2. Click the Start button, choose Settings, and then click Printers to open the Printers folder.

3. Double-click the Add Printer icon to start the Add Printer Wizard.

4. Click Next in the first screen to begin using the Add Printer Wizard.

5. Select the Local Printer option, select the Automatically Detect My Printer check box (Figure 8-3), and then click Next.

Caution   If you're installing a Plug and Play (PnP) printer, always select the Automatically Detect My Printer check box in the Add Printer Wizard. If you don't select this option, Windows 2000 will detect the printer the next time the system is rebooted and will attempt to install the printer a second time.

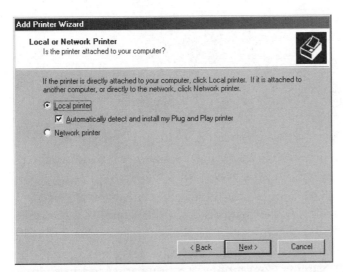

Figure 8-3. *The Local Or Network Printer screen of the Add Printer Wizard.*

6. Click Yes. Windows 2000 displays the New Hardware Found dialog box when it locates the printer. If Windows 2000 has the appropriate drivers for your device, it installs those drivers automatically.

7. If your printer wasn't detected, run the Add Printer Wizard again, but this time clear the Automatically Detect My Printer check box in the Local Or Network Printer screen, and then click Next.

8. In the Select The Printer Port screen, shown in Figure 8-4, choose the port your printer is attached to, and then click Next.

9. Select the manufacturer and model of your printer from the Manufacturers and Printers dialog boxes, and press Next. Or, click the Windows Update button to view a list of updated drivers and click the Have Disk button to provide a driver disk.

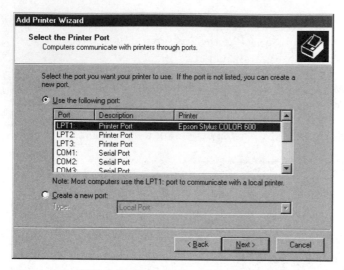

Figure 8-4. *The Select The Printer Port screen of the Add Printer Wizard.*

10. Enter a name for your printer in the Printer Name text box. Enter the share name for the printer on your network.

11. Choose whether to share your printer by selecting either the Do Not Share This Printer option or the Share As option. If Share As is selected, provide a share name for the printer.

12. Enter the location name for your printer in the Location box. (See the "Creating Location-Naming Conventions" section earlier in this chapter for information on choosing a location-naming scheme.) Describe the capabilities of your printer in the Comments box.

13. Print a test page by clicking Yes in the Print Test Page screen, and then click Next to display a summary of your printer installation. To change your installation choices, click Back; otherwise, click Finish to complete your installation.

If you're using a USB or IEEE 1394 connection to the printer, Windows 2000 will automatically detect the printer and install it on your server as soon as you plug the printer into your server (although you might be prompted for drivers). In Windows 2000 Server, the Add Printer Wizard will automatically share the printer and publish it in Active Directory unless you select Do Not Share This Printer on the Printer Sharing screen. In Windows 2000 Professional, the default is to not share the printer unless you select Share As on the Printer Sharing screen—then the printer will be shared and published.

Sharing Printers on a Network

Adding local printers is obviously not the most efficient way to deploy printers. To share printers on a network, you have several options. As the following sections explain, you can add a printer shared by another computer, add TCP/IP printers on a TCP/IP printer port, add printers on an LPR printer port, or add an AppleTalk printing device.

Adding Printers Shared by Another Computer

After using a direct physical connection, the next simplest way to connect to a printer is to use a shared printer on the network. The computer that is sharing the printer might be a print server or simply a workstation with an attached printer. To set up a printer that is already being shared by a server or workstation on your network, follow these steps to use the Add Printer Wizard to connect to the printer:

1. Configure the computer sharing the printer with the proper protocol; make sure that the printer is shared on the network and that you have proper permissions to access it.

2. For a printer connected to a NetWare server, make sure that you have the NWLink IPX/SPX/NetBIOS–Compatible Transport Protocol and Gateway Services for NetWare installed, enabled, and active on your Windows 2000 print server.

Tip   Using Gateway Services for NetWare requires a certain amount of processing power from the print server, decreasing the print server's throughput. Microsoft clients that use a NetWare printer heavily should install the Client Service for NetWare and print directly to the NetWare print server instead of printing through the Windows 2000 server.

3. Click the Start button, choose Settings, and then click Printers to open the Printers folder.

4. Double-click the Add Printer icon to start the Add Printer Wizard.

5. Select the Network Printer option. Enter the printer name in the Name text box, or click Next to browse for the printer. If you choose to browse for a printer, Windows 2000 displays the Browse For Printer screen, shown in Figure 8-5.

Tip   If your printers are published in Active Directory, you can select the Find A Printer In The Directory option button and click Next to search Active Directory by printer location or features.

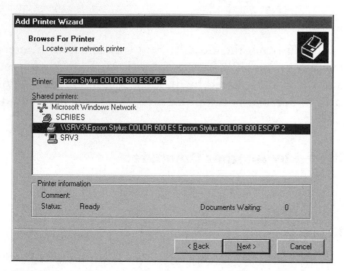

Figure 8-5. *The Browse For Printer screen of the Add Printer Wizard.*

6. Choose the printer from the list of shared printers, and then click Next.

7. If you've already installed one or more printers on your server, choose whether this printer is to be your default printer by clicking the Yes button or the No button and then clicking Next. The Add Printer Wizard then displays a summary of your printer installation.

8. Click Finish, or click Back to make changes to your installation.

Adding TCP/IP Printers on a TCP/IP Printer Port

Most often, you are going to set up a print server to connect to one or more printers already connected directly to the network. One of the most common ways to connect to these network printers is to configure a standard TCP/IP printer port that manages the communications with the TCP/IP-based printers. To set up a network-based printer through a standard TCP/IP printer port—which Windows 2000 treats as a local port—follow these steps:

1. Connect the printer to your network and configure the printer with the proper TCP/IP settings for your network.

2. Click the Start button, choose Settings, and then click Printers to open the Printers folder.

3. Double-click the Add Printer icon to start the Add Printer Wizard.

4. Click Next on the first screen to begin using the Add Printer Wizard.

5. Select the Local Printer option, and clear the Automatically Detect My Printer check box.

6. Select the Create A New Port option button, and then select Standard TCP/IP Port from the drop-down list box. Windows 2000 then launches the Add Standard TCP/IP Printer Port Wizard.

7. Make sure that the printer is connected to the network and turned on, establish a network connection if you haven't already, and then click Next on the first screen of the Add Standard TCP/IP Printer Port Wizard to begin using the wizard.

8. Enter the printer name or IP address in the first text box, as shown in Figure 8-6.

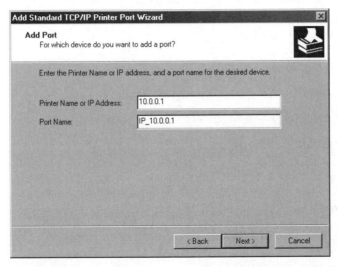

Figure 8-6. *The Add Port screen of the Add Standard TCP/IP Printer Port Wizard.*

9. If necessary, modify the TCP/IP port name that Windows 2000 automatically fills in. Windows 2000 then attempts to connect to the printer.

10. If Windows can't detect the printer, you'll be asked for additional information (Figure 8-7).

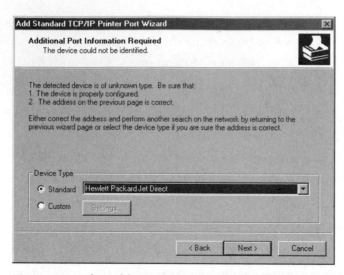

Figure 8-7. *The Additional Port Information Required screen of the Add Standard TCP/IP Printer Port Wizard.*

11. Select your printer from the Standard list box, or select the Custom option button and click the Settings button to display the Configure Standard TCP/IP Port Monitor dialog box, shown in Figure 8-8.

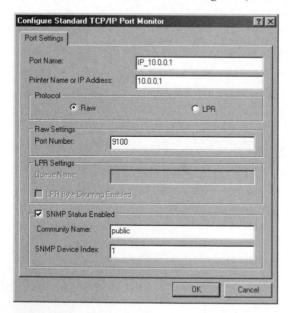

Figure 8-8. *The Configure Standard TCP/IP Port Monitor dialog box of the Add Standard TCP/IP Printer Port Wizard.*

12. Choose the protocol your printer uses, either raw or LPR. (For more information on configuring your server to use an LPR port to communicate with a printer that uses the LPD service, see the next section.)

13. Enter the port number for your printer if you're using the raw protocol. Use the default port number (9100) unless your printer documentation specifies that you must use a different port.

14. To use the LPR protocol, enter the queue name in the box provided.

> **Tip**   Select the LPR Byte Counting check box if you're having problems with incomplete or missing documents. However, be aware that selecting this check box tells your server to count the number of bytes in a document before sending it to the printer, considerably slowing printing.

15. If your printer supports Simple Network Management Protocol (SNMP) as defined in RFC 1759, select the SNMP Status Enabled check box, and enter the Community Name (usually "public") and SNMP Device Index.

16. Click OK when you're finished configuring the TCP/IP port.

17. On the last page of the TCP/IP Port Wizard, click Finish.

18. If Windows doesn't detect the printer, choose the printer model in the next screen, and then click Next.

19. Enter a name for the printer in the Printer Name text box. Click Next.

20. On the Printer Sharing screen, select Do Not Share This Printer if you do not want this printer accessible to users on the network. Select Share As and supply a share name for the printer if you want users on the network to be able to use this printer. Click Next.

21. Enter the location name for your printer in the Location box. (See the "Creating Location-Naming Conventions" section earlier in this chapter for information on choosing a location-naming scheme.) Describe the capabilities of your printer in the Comments box.

22. Print a test page by clicking Yes on the Print Test Page screen. Click Next to display a summary of your printer installation.

Adding Printers on an LPR Printer Port

Another common way to connect to a network printer is to use an LPR port, allowing the print server to communicate with printers using the LPD service—typically used to support UNIX clients. Follow these steps to set up a network-based printer through an LPR port:

1. Connect the printer to your network and configure the printer with the proper TCP/IP and LPD settings.

2. Install UNIX print services by using the Windows Component Wizard. (See Chapter 6 for more information on using the Windows Component Wizard to install system software.)

3. Click the Start button, choose Settings, and then click Printers to open the Printers folder. Double-click the Add Printer icon to start the Add Printer Wizard.

4. Select the Local Printer option, and clear the Automatically Detect My Printer check box.

5. Choose the Create A New Port Type option, select LPR Port from the drop-down list box, and click Next.

6. Enter the name or address of the printer or print server running LPD in the first text box of the Add LPR Compatible Printer dialog box, shown in Figure 8-9.

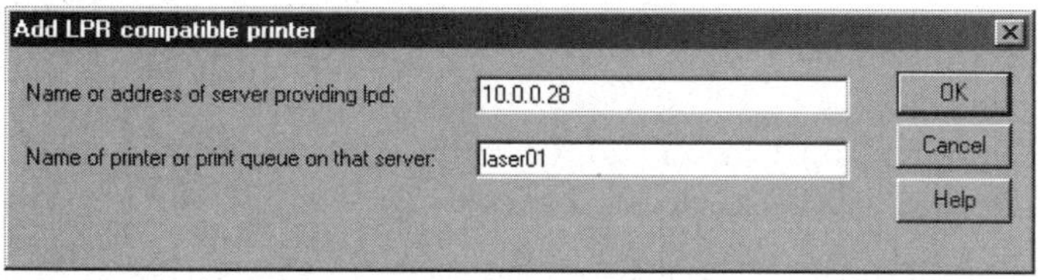

Figure 8-9. *The Add LPR Compatible Printer screen of the Add Printer Wizard.*

7. In the second text box, enter the name of the printer or print queue on the LPD server, and then click OK. Windows adds the port to your list of ports.

8. If Windows doesn't detect your printer, choose your printer model in the next screen, and then click Next.

9. Give your printer a name in the Printer Name text box. Then enter the share name to use for the printer on your network.

10. Enter the location name for your printer in the Location box. Describe your printer's capabilities in the Comments box.

11. To print a test page, click Yes on the Print Test Page screen. Click Next to display a summary of your printer installation.

Adding AppleTalk Printing Devices

In a mixed computing environment with Macintosh clients, you might need to use one or more AppleTalk printing devices. To install an AppleTalk printer, follow these steps:

Note   AppleTalk doesn't support client usernames or passwords, eliminating the ability to set permissions for Macintosh users on the print server. However, you can set permissions for Macintosh users as a group, thus giving all Macintosh clients the same printer permissions. (For information on installing the AppleTalk protocol and AppleTalk networking, see Chapter 22.)

1. Connect and configure the printer.

2. Install Macintosh print services by using the Windows Component Wizard.

3. Open the Printers folder. Double-click the Add Printer icon to start the Add Printer Wizard.

4. Select the Local Printer option, clear the Automatically Detect My Printer check box, and then click Next.

5. Select the Create A New Port option, and then select AppleTalk Printing Device from the drop-down list box and click Next. Windows 2000 searches the network for AppleTalk printers.

6. Choose a printer in the Available AppleTalk Printing Devices dialog box, and click OK to install the printer. When asked if you want to capture the port, click Yes. Windows adds the port to your list of ports.

Note   When you capture the AppleTalk printing port, the printer is exclusively managed by the Windows 2000 print server and can't be simultaneously connected to a Macintosh print server. This limitation gives the administrator of the print server complete control over the printer.

7. Choose your printer model in the next screen if Windows doesn't detect your printer. Enter a name for the printer in the Printer Name text box. Enter the share name to use for the printer.

8. Enter the location name for your printer in the Location box. Describe the capabilities of your printer in the Comments box, and then click Next.

9. Print a test page by clicking Yes in the Print Test Page window. Click Next to display a summary of your printer installation.

Modifying Printer Properties

After you install printers on your print server, you'll need to set security, set various printer options, select the default printer and its options, and select the print server and its options. This section explains how to perform these tasks and more.

Setting Security Options

While some people don't think about security when setting up printers, this can be an important factor to consider. For example, you might not want everyone to print to the five-dollar-a-page dye sublimation printer purchased for the art staff. At a more basic level, you probably don't want most users to modify printer properties or change the priorities of documents in the print queue.

Setting permissions for groups (and occasionally individual users) and auditing the actions users and groups perform is how you handle printer security, just like access to your computer in general. Configure users to belong to groups, and then give the groups the level of permissions appropriate for those users. Turn on auditing for individual users or groups so that you or the person responsible for managing audit logs can track user actions in connection with the printer.

Note You must use an account with Manage Printers permissions to view and change printer security settings.

Printer Permissions Levels

Printers are Windows 2000 resources and thus can be protected like any other resource by the Windows 2000 security features. Printers in Windows 2000 have owners and access control lists (ACLs), which specify the permissions each user or group has. The creator of the printer is automatically made the owner of the printer, and only users with sufficient permissions (Manage Printers) can take the ownership of the printer from the creator. A user or group has three levels of control permissions for a printer: Print, Manage Documents, and Manage Printers.

Caution Macintosh clients assume that if a client can physically send a document to a printer, it implicitly has permission to do so. Therefore, a Macintosh client has no printer security.

Members of the Everyone group are granted the Print permission by default. However, you should remove Print permission from the Everyone group and instead assign it to the built-in Users group. This permits only users with domain accounts to print. Users or groups with Print permissions can do the following: connect to the printer; print documents; and pause, restart, and delete their own documents from the print queue.

The Creator/Owner group is granted the Manage Documents permission level by default. This level grants the Print permissions plus the ability to change the settings for all documents in the print queue and to pause, restart, and delete any documents from the print queue.

The Manage Printers permission level is the Windows 2000 equivalent of Full Control in Windows NT. This level is granted by default to power users, print operators, and server operators on a domain controller and to administrators on a server. In addition to the Printers and Manage Documents permissions, the Manage Printers permission level adds the ability to set printer sharing, modify printer properties, delete printers, change printer permissions, and take ownership of printers.

You should configure a printer according to the same guidelines you would follow for any shared resource. Create a local group with Print permissions, give it a name that matches the printer name, and then add global groups to the local group. If security isn't an issue, give Manage Documents or Manage Printers permission to the local group. For more on groups, see Chapter 9.

Changing Printer Permissions

To change the permissions on a printer, follow these steps:

1. Open the Printers folder located on the Start menu.
2. Right-click the printer to be modified, and then choose Properties from the shortcut menu.
3. Click the Security tab in the printer's Properties window, shown in Figure 8-10.

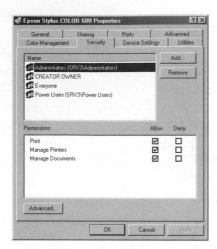

Figure 8-10. *The Security tab of a printer's Properties window.*

4. To change the permissions for a group, select the group from the list, and then select the check boxes in the Permissions section of the window to choose which permissions to give to each group.

5. To add a user or group to the list, click the Add button, select a user or group from the list to add (as shown in Figure 8-11), and then click Add. When you're finished adding users or groups, click OK.

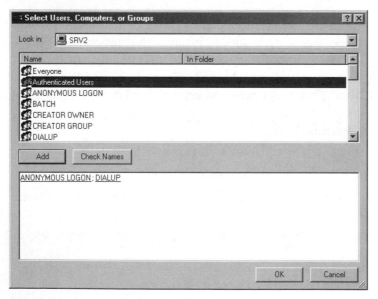

Figure 8-11. *The Select Users, Computers, Or Groups dialog box.*

6. To remove a user or group from the list of users and groups with permission to use the printer, select the user or group, and then click Remove.

7. To view or change more detailed security settings, click the Advanced button.

8. Use the Permissions tab of the Access Control Settings dialog box to view or change all permissions for each user or group. (Additional settings are Read Permissions, Change Permissions, and Take Ownership.)

9. To specify whether the permissions for a particular user or group apply to only the printer, only the documents, or both the printer and documents, select the user or group, click the View/Edit button, and then choose a setting from the Apply Onto drop-down list box. Click OK (Figure 8-12).

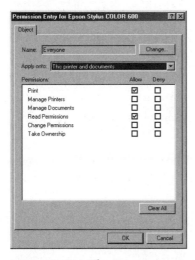

Figure 8-12. *The Permission Entry dialog box.*

Configuring Printer Auditing

To audit actions for your printer (to record the occurrences of successful or unsuccessful printer-related actions by users or groups), follow these steps:

1. In the Printers folder (located on the Start menu), right-click the printer you want to modify, and then choose Properties from the shortcut menu.

2. Click the Security tab in the printer's Properties window, and then click Advanced.

3. Click the Auditing tab. To add an auditing entry, click the Add button.

4. Select a group to audit, and then click OK.

5. In the Auditing Entry dialog box, select the actions that you would like to record, and then click OK.

6. To edit audits you create, select the auditing entry and click the View/Edit button.

You can view the results of the audit settings in the security log. After reviewing the log a few times, you might conclude that you're auditing too many or too few events. If you log too many actions, the log will fill rapidly and events that are more serious can get lost in the long list of relatively trivial ones. If too few events are logged, you might miss a pattern of improper access to printers.

Changing Printer Ownership

The owner of a printer is the person who has control over what level of permission users and groups have on the printer. To change the ownership for your printer, follow these steps:

1. In the Printers folder, right-click the printer you want to modify, and then choose Properties from the shortcut menu.

2. Click the Security tab in the printer's Properties window, and then click Advanced.

3. Click the Owner tab to view the current ownership of the printer.

4. Select the user or group to be the new owner of the printer, and then click OK.

Note Only users or groups with the Manage Printers permission level will appear in the list of users or groups available to take ownership of the printer.

Changing Printer Options

Windows 2000 installs new printers with printer options designed to work for most users, but frequently, you'll need to change them so your printer will work optimally. Some printer modifications to options that you might need to make include changing the default printer, changing print server printer drivers, specifying color profiles, changing printer availability, determining group printing priorities, and setting up printer pools. These features might not be available until you actively enable them. Security settings such as permissions, auditing, and ownership are covered separately in "Setting Security Options" earlier in this chapter.

> **Note** Depending on the printer driver you use, the dialog boxes and printer options that you have will probably be different from those that we show. If you use a printer driver provided by the printer manufacturer, additional tabs and options might be unavailable in the standard Windows 2000 printer drivers.

Changing the Default Printer

Applications on the computer that shares the printer automatically print to the default printer unless a different printer is specified. On a print server, it hardly matters which printer is the default printer, but it is important for clients. After a few users accidentally print out their e-mail on the expensive plotter, you (or maybe just the finance department) begin to see the importance of having the default printer set correctly.

To change the default printer, follow these steps:

1. In the Printers folder, right-click the printer you want to modify.

2. Choose Set As Default Printer from the shortcut menu.

Changing General Options and Printing Test Pages

To change general printer options such as your printer name, or to print a test page, follow these steps:

1. In the Printers folder, right-click the printer you want to modify, and then choose Properties from the shortcut menu.

2. Use the General tab of the Properties window to view or modify the printer name, location name, or comments, as well as to view the printer capabilities.

3. To print a test page, click the Print Test Page button on the General tab.

You can also print a test page by opening Windows NotePad and creating a simple document. In fact, printing in NotePad is an easy troubleshooting technique used to see whether basic printing is working.

Sharing a Printer and Providing Client Drivers

To change the share name your printer uses on a network, to stop sharing your printer, or to install drivers that client machines can use for the printer, follow these steps:

1. In the Printers folder, right-click the printer you want to modify, and then choose Properties from the shortcut menu.

2. Click the Sharing tab. Click the Shared As option, and enter the share name for the printer in the text box provided (Figure 8-13).

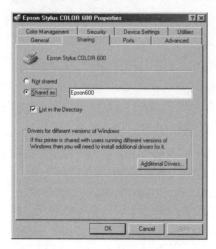

Figure 8-13. *The Sharing tab of a printer's Properties window.*

3. To publish the printer in Active Directory, select the List In The Directory check box, if available. (To change the way printers are published in Active Directory, use the Group Policy snap-in, discussed in detail in Chapter 16.)

4. To add client drivers that are automatically downloaded and installed when a Windows 2000 or Windows NT client connects to the printer, click the Additional Drivers button.

5. In the Additional Drivers dialog box, select the check box next to any client drivers to be installed, and then click OK. To install additional client drivers, you need access to the Windows 2000 installation files, either on CD-ROM or across the network.

When client drivers are installed on a print server, many Windows clients automatically download the drivers when they are initially connected to the printer. Windows 2000 and Windows NT 4 clients automatically check for updated versions of the printer drivers at startup and download newer versions if necessary. Windows NT 3.x clients automatically check and update their drivers when they print to the server. Windows 95 and 98 clients don't automatically check for updated drivers and must be updated manually.

Changing Print Server Printer Drivers

To change the driver that the print server uses for a printer, follow these steps:

1. In the Printers folder, right-click the printer you want to modify and select Properties from the shortcut menu.
2. Click the Advanced tab.
3. Choose a driver from the Driver drop-down list box, or click the New Driver option to start the Update Driver Wizard.

Setting Up Printer Pools and Changing Port Settings

A printer pool is useful for handling a large volume of printing at a location, particularly when there is a mix of large and small documents. For example, someone with a single-page memo doesn't have to be stuck in the queue behind a print job that's the corporate equivalent of the *Encyclopedia Britannica*.

If printers share a single driver, they can appear to clients as one printer. The advantage of using a printer pool is that clients don't need to find which printer is available; they simply print to the single logical printer (print driver) on the print server, which then sends the print job to the first available printer. Administration of the printers is also simplified because all of the printers are consolidated under one driver. If you modify the properties for the single logical printer, all physical printers in the printer pool use the same settings.

Tip   Printers in a printer pool should be located near each other to make finding a completed print job easier.

To set up a printer pool or simply change the port settings for a printer, follow these steps:

1. In the Printers folder, right-click the printer you want to modify and select Properties from the shortcut menu.
2. Click the Ports tab.
3. Select the Enable Printer Pooling check box.
4. To change the transmission retry settings for a port, select the port and click Configure Port.
5. To add additional printers to the printer pool, select the ports to which the additional printers are connected.

Caution   All printers in a printer pool must be identical or must at least be able to use the same printer driver, since they are all configured by one printer driver.

Specifying a Color Profile

Windows 2000 includes the Integrated Color Management (ICM) 2 API for maintaining consistent colors across monitors, color printers, and scanners. When you need to achieve accurate color reproduction, it's useful to set up your printer, as well as your users' monitors and scanners, with an appropriate color profile. To do so, follow these steps:

1. In the Printers folder, right-click the printer you want to modify and select Properties from the shortcut menu.

2. Click the Color Management tab. Select the Automatic option to have Windows 2000 choose the best color profile.

3. To manually select a color profile, choose the Manual option, and then select a profile from the list or click the Add button to install an additional color profile from your device manufacturer. Click OK.

Tip   Color management in Windows has come a long way, but most graphics professionals still use third-party, hardware-based, color-matching solutions when color accuracy is important. However, ICM provides a good way to attain a reasonable measure of accuracy for noncritical work.

Changing Printer Availability

To set up your printer to be available only during certain times—perhaps to discourage after-hours printing—perform the following steps:

1. In the Printers folder, right-click the printer you want to modify and select Properties from the shortcut menu.

2. Click the Advanced tab, and then click the Available From option.

3. Select the earliest and latest times the printer is to be available to users, and then click OK.

Tip   To dedicate a printer to large, high-priority print jobs after normal hours, install a duplicate logical printer (printer driver) for the printer. Make one logical printer available during normal hours to all users. Make the second one available after hours to only particular users or groups.

Determining Group Printer Priorities

Sometimes you might want to make the printer available preferentially to a certain group of users so that they can jump straight to the head of the print queue.

This ability can be extremely useful for users who face time pressures and need to take precedence over other users when printing.

To set up groups to have different priorities on a printer, you need to set up two or more logical printers for the physical printer. Thus, you would have two or more printer drivers set up for a single printer, with each driver possessing a different priority level and a different set of users or groups. To do this, follow these steps:

1. In the Printers folder, click the Add Printer icon to add one or more duplicate logical printers for a physical printer already installed on your print server.

2. Right-click the logical printer you want to change the priority for, and then select Properties from the shortcut menu. Click the Advanced tab.

3. Change the priority to be assigned to the logical printer and the users and groups that use this printer driver by entering a number in the Priority text box. The priority range goes from 1, which is the lowest priority, to 99, which is the highest priority.

4. Click the Security tab and add the users and groups you want to allow to print at this priority level. Remove or deny print permissions to users whose printing should occur at a different priority level. Those users will utilize another printer with its own priority level.

5. Click OK, and repeat the process for all other logical printers created for the printer.

Changing Spool Settings

Print spooling, or storing a print job on disk before printing, affects how clients perceive printing performance as well as the actual printing speed. You can change the way print spooling works to correct printing problems or to hold printed documents in the printer queue in case a user needs to print the document again. Follow these steps to change a printer's spool settings:

1. In the Printers folder, right-click the printer you want to modify and select Properties from the shortcut menu.

2. Click the Advanced tab to display the printer's spool settings, as shown in Figure 8-14.

3. To decrease the time it takes to print a document, select the Spool Print Documents option, and select the Start Printing Immediately option to begin printing as soon as enough data is spooled.

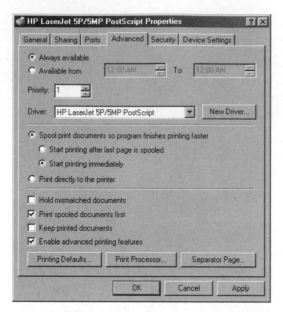

Figure 8-14. *The Advanced tab of a printer's Properties window.*

4. To ensure that the entire document is available to the printer when printing begins, select the Start Printing After Last Page Is Spooled option. This step might correct some printing problems.

5. If you continue to have printing problems, choose the Print Directly To The Printer option to turn off spooling. Enabling this option will cause a performance hit on the server.

6. Select the Hold Mismatched Documents check box to hold documents in the queue that don't match the current printer settings. Other documents in the print queue are unaffected by held documents.

7. Select the Print Spooled Documents First check box to print the highest priority document that is already spooled first, ahead of higher priority documents that are still spooling. This step speeds overall printer throughput by keeping the printer from waiting for documents.

8. Select the Keep Printed Documents check box to keep a copy of print jobs in the printer queue in case users need to print the document again. In this circumstance, the user can resubmit the document directly from the queue rather than printing from his or her application a second time.

9. Clear the Enable Advanced Printing Features check box if you experience printer problems. Doing so turns off metafile spooling, which disables some printer options such as page order, booklet printing, and pages per sheet (if available on your printer).

Changing Print Processor Settings and Specifying a Separator Page

The print processor determines the data format used with documents sent to the printer; generally either *raw* or *EMF*. (See "Understanding the Printing Process" earlier in this chapter for information on these data types and their advantages.) To change the type of print processor your print server uses for a printer, or to specify a separator page to insert between print jobs, follow these steps:

1. In the Printers folder, right-click the printer you want to modify and select Properties from the shortcut menu.

2. Click the Advanced tab. Click the Print Processor button to change the print processor or to specify a data type to use. When you're finished setting options in the Print Processor dialog box, click OK.

3. Click the Separator Page button to select a page to insert between printed documents to help separate the print jobs. Click OK.

Setting Up a Printer to Use Both PostScript and PCL

If you have a printer that supports printing in two printer languages (usually PostScript and PCL), you can set up the printer to simultaneously support both languages. To do this, set up two logical printers (printer drivers) for the printer: one for each data type. Clients with PostScript documents then use the PostScript-enabled logical printer, while users with PCL documents use the PCL logical printer.

Open the Printers folder and click Add Printer to create a logical printer that supports the first data type (either PostScript or PCL). Then use Add Printer a second time to create a logical printer that supports the second data type.

Setting Installable Options and Printer Device Settings

Each printer comes with several configurable device options, such as which paper tray to print from, whether a duplexer is installed, and how to handle downloadable fonts. While the options that are configurable vary with the printer model, you can use the following procedure to change the printer device settings on any printer:

1. In the Printers folder, right-click the printer you want to modify and select Properties from the shortcut menu.

2. Select the Device Settings tab, and then click the underlined words to display a drop-down list box that you can use to configure an option, as shown in Figure 8-15.

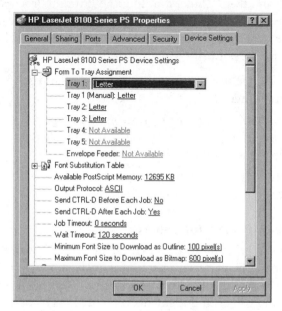

Figure 8-15. *The Device Settings tab of a printer's Properties window.*

Tip If your printer has multiple trays with different forms, match the form to the tray so that documents using the form always print properly. Under the Form To Tray Assignment heading, select each tray and choose the form that the tray holds. If your printer supports Page Protection and has 1 MB or more of available optional memory, go to the Device Settings tab and turn on this option to ensure that complex pages print properly. When you turn this option on, the printer creates each page in memory before beginning to print.

Changing Default Print Settings

After you configure the printer options for your installed printer, you should set the default print settings that are used by clients. When setting the printing defaults that the logical printer uses on the print server, you establish a set of defaults used by all clients that connect to the printer.

This section describes how to set layout options, how to set paper options, and how to set quality defaults for a print server and attached clients.

Setting Layout Defaults

Layout involves such options as the orientation of documents and paper, the order in which pages are printed, and the number of pages per sheet of paper that are printed. To change these settings, follow these steps:

1. In the Printers folder, right-click the printer you want to modify and select Properties from the shortcut menu.

2. Click the General tab, and then click the Printing Preferences button.

3. To change the paper orientation, click the Portrait button, the Landscape button, or the Rotated Landscape button, as shown in Figure 8-16. Note that the preview changes depending on the selection you choose.

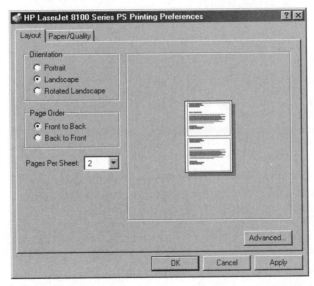

Figure 8-16. *The Layout tab of a printer's Printing Preferences dialog box.*

4. To specify whether the printer should start with the last page of a document or the first page, select either the Front To Back option, which is good for face-down printing, or the Back To Front option, which is better for page-up printers.

5. To print multiple pages per sheet of paper, select the number of pages to print on a sheet from the Pages Per Sheet drop-down list box.

Tip The Rotated Landscape orientation, if available, prints a page in the landscape format, but rotated 90 degrees counterclockwise.

Setting Paper and Quality Defaults

Paper and quality options are important printing defaults because you generally want most users to print on a certain paper size from a particular paper tray and with a certain quality setting. Most users change the default options only if their documents don't print the way they wanted, potentially causing a lot of waste if the defaults are inappropriate and the users don't correct them until after printing a copy (or more). Setting these defaults to a standard size paper (most likely letter size) and at the quality setting most appropriate for your users will save your company a great deal of money over time. To specify paper options and quality settings, follow these steps:

1. In the Printers folder, right-click the printer you want to modify and select Properties from the shortcut menu.

2. Click the Printing Defaults button on the General tab. Click the Paper/Quality tab.

3. Use the Paper Source drop-down list box to select which tray (or other paper source) you want users to print from by default.

4. Select the type of paper your printer is usually stocked with from the Media drop-down list box.

5. If your printer driver has a Quality Settings section, use this part of the dialog box to choose a resolution or quality setting to use on your documents by default. In general, use the lowest quality settings *that are acceptable to your users* to increase printing speed, reduce waste, and lower costs.

6. If you have a color printer, choose whether your users should print black or color by default.

7. If your printer driver doesn't have Quality options on the Quality/Paper tab, click the Advanced button, and use the Advanced Options dialog box to set any layout, quality, or paper options that are available on your printer.

Tip To set duplex printing, staples, and other advanced printer options, use the Advanced Options button—these settings might not be available elsewhere—depending on your printer driver and whether you've enabled these installable options.

Setting Print Server Options

While most printer configuration occurs in the printer driver for a particular printer, you can configure some of the actual print server settings. These settings affect all printers hosted by the print server; they include determining which forms are available to print on and which ports and printer drivers are available to use, as well as some spool settings.

Modifying the Forms Available on the Print Server

Forms are whatever material a printer can transfer ink or laser toner to in the shape of letters, characters, or graphics. Forms can be paper of various sizes, every sort of envelope, or other types of media such as film. Print servers are set up to handle a wide variety of standard forms by default, but occasionally it can be useful to set up additional forms that your printers can use, maybe because you use special company forms. Or perhaps you want to modify or delete an existing form. To do so, follow these steps:

1. In the Printers folder, choose the Server Properties command from the File menu to open the Print Server Properties window, shown in Figure 8-17.

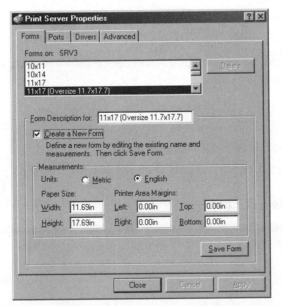

Figure 8-17. *The Forms tab of the Print Server Properties window.*

2. To modify a form, select the form and then use the Measurements boxes to alter it.

3. To create a new form, select the Create A New Form check box, enter a name for the form in the Form Description box, use the Measurements boxes to define the form, then click Save Form.

Configuring Ports and Drivers

You can use the Ports and Drivers tabs in the Print Server Properties window to configure the port and printer drivers that are available on your print server. You can add new ports for your printers or configure the printer drivers you want to make available to clients to download when they connect to your print server. To do so, follow these steps:

1. In the Printers folder, choose Server Properties from the File menu.

2. To view the ports available on your print server, click the Ports tab.

3. Select a port and click Configure Port to modify the port settings, or click Add Port or Delete Port to add or remove a port from your system.

4. Click the Drivers tab to view a list of currently installed drivers on the print server.

5. To view the driver details for a printer driver, select the driver and then click the Properties button to display the Driver Properties window. Use this dialog box to view the properties for each file that makes up the printer driver.

6. To update a printer driver, select the driver and click Update.

7. To add a printer driver that you want to make available to clients to download, click the Add button to launch the Add Printer Driver Wizard, which walks you through the driver installation process.

8. To remove a printer driver, select the driver and click the Remove button.

Configuring Advanced Print Server Settings

The Advanced tab of the Print Server Settings dialog box is extremely useful for configuring your print server for optimal performance and ease of use. You can and should specify where your spool folder is stored, and you can also control how the print server deals with printing events. To configure these settings, follow these steps:

1. In the Printers folder, choose Server Properties from the File menu.

2. Click the Advanced tab. In the Spool Folder text box, enter the location where you want to store your spool folder.

Planning For optimal performance, place the spool folder on a separate drive from Windows 2000, its applications, and especially its swap file. Also make sure that the drive is big enough to hold all documents in the print queue. If you choose to enable the holding of printed documents, the drive needs to be even bigger.

3. Select the check boxes next to the events to be logged.

   To be notified of errors while printing remote documents, select Beep On Errors Of Remote Documents. To send a message to the user when the document finishes printing, select Notify When Remote Documents Are Printed. To display a notification message on the computer the document was printed on (even if the user who printed it is currently logged on elsewhere) select Notify Computer, Not User, When Remote Documents Are Printed.

Tip The Notify When Remote Documents Are Printed feature can be useful on busy print servers when a significant delay might occur between the time that a client sends off a document and the time when the document reaches the head of the queue and actually prints. However, on less busy print servers or for users who need to print frequently, this feature can be annoying. If this situation occurs for your users, you can turn off the option to eliminate the problem.

Searching for Printers

Finding a printer in a large enterprise can be tricky. Windows 2000 and Active Directory provide a useful alternative to wandering the halls: printer location tracking. *Printer location tracking* uses Active Directory to store the printer location, allowing users to search for printers based on their names, locations, and a long list of features (as described in the next section). However, even without printer location tracking, with Windows 2000 you can search for and locate printers easily.

Using Active Directory

To find a printer using Active Directory, point to Search on the Start menu and choose For Printers. With location tracking enabled, when the query form opens the system determines the location of the computer from which the query is being run and fills in the Location box. Click the Browse button to change the location. You can then use the Features tab to specify the particular features needed, or click the Advanced tab to fine-tune the search with a variety of values (Figure 8-18).

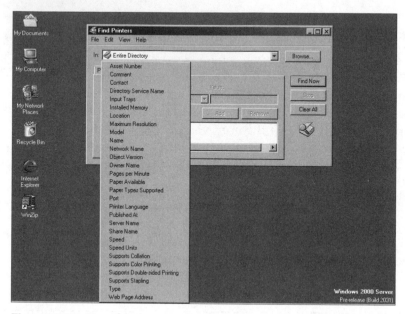

Figure 8-18. *Possible features for designing a printer search.*

Note When location tracking is enabled, you can use the Group Policy snap-in (covered in Chapter 9) to define locations that don't depend on actual geographic locations.

Using Printer Location Tracking

To use printer location tracking, you need to publish your printers in Active Directory with the *Location* field and other relevant fields filled out. Then users can search for printers in Active Directory based on location, color capabilities, and duplexing. This section covers the requirements for using printer location tracking and explains how to enable this feature. (It is turned off by default.)

Meeting the Requirements for Printer Location Tracking

Printer location tracking requires a few conditions to work properly. These conditions are easy for most organizations to meet, but the network infrastructure of some companies will require modification. To use printer location tracking, the following conditions must be in place:

- Active Directory must be installed on the network and must contain more than one site with more than one IP subnet.
- The network must have an IP addressing scheme that matches the network's physical layout reasonably well.
- The client computers must be able to query Active Directory. (They must support LDAP 2 or later.)
- Each site should be on a separate subnet.
- Each subnet that clients need to access should have its own subnet object in Active Directory.

For information on how to install Active Directory and create the appropriate subnets for your enterprise using Active Directory Sites and Services, see Chapter 11.

Note Printer location tracking isn't particularly useful until an enterprise is quite large. However, you should use a compatible naming convention so you can enable printer location tracking at some future time.

Enabling Printer Location Tracking

Once you've prepped your network, follow these steps to set up printer location tracking:

1. Open Active Directory Sites and Services from the Administrative Tools menu.
2. In the Sites folder, right-click the first site and choose Properties from the shortcut menu.
3. Click the Location tab and enter the location name for the site, or click Browse to select the location from the location tree for your enterprise.
4. Click OK and repeat steps 2 and 3 for each site and subnet on your network.
5. Open the Active Directory Users and Computers snap-in, right-click the domain for which you want to enable location tracking, choose Properties from the shortcut menu, and click the Group Policy tab.
6. Select the policy to edit, and then click the Edit button to open the Group Policy snap-in.

7. Open the Computer Configuration folder, open the Administrative Templates folder, and finally, open the Printers folders (Figure 8-19).

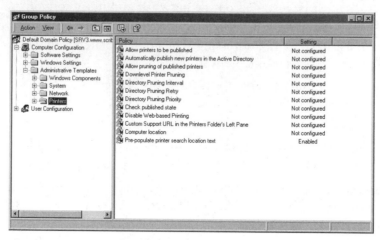

Figure 8-19. *The Group Policy snap-in.*

8. Double-click the Pre-Populate Printer Search Location Text policy, select Enabled, and click OK. Close the Group Policy window, and then close the domain's Properties window.

9. Right-click the first printer in your print server's printer folder, and choose Properties from the shortcut menu.

10. Fill in the location text box, or click Browse to select the location from the location tree for your enterprise.

11. Repeat steps 9 and 10 for all printers on your print server.

12. Test the printer location tracking by searching for client machines to make sure that everything is configured properly.

Real World **Publishing All Printers in the Active Directory**

Most enterprises won't have all their printers hosted by Windows 2000 print servers, yet ideally, all printers that are available to clients should be listed in Active Directory. For this to happen, you'll need to specifically publish printers that are not hosted by a Windows 2000 print server in Active Directory. Open Active Directory Users and Computers (from the Administrative Tools menu), right-click the domain, subnet, or organizational unit in which you want to publish the printer, and choose New Printer from the shortcut menu. Enter the path of the printer to be published in the UNC Path Of Downlevel Print Server To Be Published box, and then click OK.

Managing Printers and Print Servers

Once your printers and print server are configured, it's tempting to consider the job finished, but in reality, managing printers and print servers is an ongoing process. Fortunately, Windows 2000 makes the job of managing printers and print servers fairly easy and flexible. A Windows 2000 print server or hosted printer can be managed by any Windows 2000 machine, or even from any system using a Web browser as long as Internet Information Server (IIS) or Peer Web Services is installed and Web-based printing hasn't been disabled using the Group Policy snap-in.

This section focuses on some common management chores such as connecting to a printer and viewing the print jobs, managing print jobs in the queue, and transferring print jobs from one printer to another—all from either a Windows 2000 machine or a Web browser.

Managing Printers from Windows 2000

You can use any machine running Windows 2000 to manage printers shared by a Windows 2000 or Windows NT print server. In fact, you'll probably administer your printers from a remote machine instead of from the print server. Managing printers in Windows 2000 is similar to the process in Windows NT 4, so if you're familiar with managing printers in NT, you can skip this basic information.

Viewing the Status of a Printer

To view the status of a printer and jobs in the printer's queue, follow these steps:

1. Open the Printers folder on the print server, or perform a search to locate the printer to manage.

2. Double-click the printer to open a monitoring window that you can use to view and manage the printer's queue (Figure 8-20).

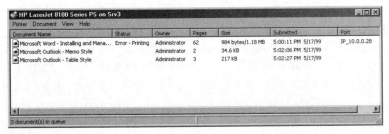

Figure 8-20. *The print queue window.*

Tip You might want to create a folder containing shortcuts to all the print servers you manage. To do this, create a folder wherever it's convenient for you, and then drag the Printers folders for each print server into your newly created folder.

Pausing, Canceling, and Restarting Print Jobs

Use the Print Monitor window to pause, cancel, or restart any or all documents waiting to print, provided you have Manage Printer permissions. (See the "Printer Permissions Levels" section earlier in this chapter for more information on permissions.) To do this, follow these steps:

1. Select the document or documents in the print queue that you want to work with.

2. Right-click the document, and select Pause from the shortcut menu to temporarily stop the document from printing. Right-click the document, and select Resume to continue printing.

3. To cancel a print job, right-click the document and choose Cancel from the shortcut menu. You can also cancel print jobs by selecting them and pressing the Delete key.

4. To restart a print job (force the document to print from the beginning again), right-click the document, and choose Restart from the shortcut menu.

5. To pause the printer, causing all documents to be held, choose Pause Printing from the Printer menu. Select the command again to resume printing.

6. To cancel all print jobs in the print queue, go to the Printer menu and choose Cancel All Documents.

Sometimes a print job will appear stuck in the queue and refuse to be deleted. In that case, you can try turning the printer off and then on again. Or you can stop the Print Spooler service on the print server and restart it.

Modifying a Print Job's Properties

In addition to starting and stopping print jobs in a printer's queue, you can also change the priority and schedule of individual print jobs as well as the person who is notified when the document finishes printing. To do so, follow these steps:

1. Right-click the print job to be modified, and choose Properties from the shortcut menu.

2. To change the person who is notified when the document finishes printing, enter the user's name in the Notify box, shown in Figure 8-21.

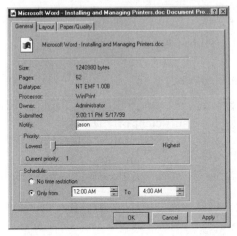

Figure 8-21. *The General tab of a document's Properties window.*

3. Use the Priority slider to adjust the priority of the document, with 1 being the lowest priority and 99 the highest priority.

4. To specify that the document should be printed only during a certain period, select the Only From option and choose the time range to allow the document to print. Click OK.

Tip Use the Schedule feature to set a large document to print only during times when you anticipate the printer to be free.

Moving Documents from One Printer to Another

When a printer makes crackling sounds and zaps anyone who touches it, it's time to call the repair person and move all print jobs to another printer that can use the same driver. To move all documents from one printer (usually because the original printer encountered problems) to another printer, follow these steps:

1. Double-click the printer in the print server's Printers folder from which you want to move documents.

2. Choose Properties from the File menu, and then click the Ports tab.

3. If the printer to which you want to transfer documents is on the same print server, select the port that the second printer is on, and click OK.

4. If the printer is elsewhere on the network, click the Add Port button, and then add the appropriate port for the second printer. (See "Installing Printers" earlier in this chapter for help.)

Managing Printers from a Web Browser

Windows 2000 lets you manage your printers from any browser, provided you have IIS installed on your print server and have sufficient privileges—or Peer Web Services works if you're using Windows 2000 Professional as your print server. (In either case, you might be prompted for your user name and password.) This feature can be extremely useful, providing the ability to manage printers from remote locations.

Tip You can also print across the network or Internet from a Web browser, but to use this feature, you need to use Microsoft Internet Explorer 4 or later. Print to an Internet Printing–enabled printer by opening the printer in your Web browser and then clicking the Connect hyperlink to download and install the appropriate drivers for the printer on your computer. Then use the newly downloaded printer drivers to print your documents. To prevent clients from using Web-based printing, use the Group Policy snap-in, discussed in Chapter 9.

Viewing the Status of a Printer

To view the status of a printer and jobs in the printer's queue, follow these steps:

1. Enter the URL of the print server followed by */printers* in your browser's Address window.

2. To display the printer's queue, click the hyperlink to the printer you want to manage.

Tip You can add print servers or printers to your Favorites folder or add a bookmark just as you can with a Web page.

Pausing, Canceling, and Restarting Print Jobs

You can use the Document List page to pause, cancel, or restart any or all documents waiting to print. To do this, follow these steps:

1. Click a hyperlink under the Printer Actions heading to pause, resume, or cancel the printing of all documents in the print queue.

2. To pause or cancel a specific print job, select the option button to the left of the document, and then click the Pause hyperlink or the Cancel hyperlink under the Document Actions heading, as shown in Figure 8-22.

3. To view the properties for the printer, click the Properties hyperlink under the View heading. Note that you can only view properties in your browser; to change them, you must use a Windows 2000 machine.

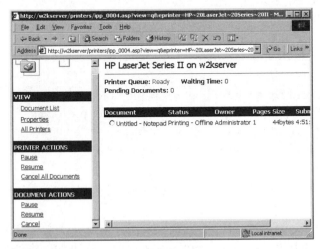

Figure 8-22. *The Document List page for a printer.*

Troubleshooting Printing Problems

The goal in troubleshooting printing problems, as in troubleshooting any type of problem, is first to isolate and identify the problem and then to determine a course of action to fix it. This section will help you diagnose your printer problems, locate the printing subsystem where the error is occurring, and give you some specific tips for solving your problems. The most likely printing problem you'll encounter is a user who can't print, so we present the troubleshooting procedures with this task as the focus.

This section is somewhat condensed, with all client troubleshooting steps presented together and all server steps presented together. In reality, you would often perform basic troubleshooting on the client before you move on to verifying that the print server is working, and you would move on to the most advanced troubleshooting tasks only after you ascertain for sure where the problem is.

Because no set technique exists to identify where a problem lies, the real difficulty in troubleshooting is determining the cause of the problem. To be able to do this, you must understand the various components involved in printing. A little intuition doesn't hurt, either. (For background about the printing process, you might want to reread the "Understanding the Printing Process" section before you continue.)

Printing problems usually fall into the following categories:

- **Physical problems**   Including problems with the printer and the transmission media.

- **Print server problems**   Including problems with printer drivers, permissions levels, and software status.

- **Network connectivity problems**   Including not being able to communicate between the server and the clients because of incorrect protocols, network settings, or hardware failures. (These problems can be handled on either the client or the server, depending on which is experiencing the connectivity problem.)

- **Client problems**   Including problems with printer drivers, permissions, and applications.

Try to determine which category your problem is in before getting into details. A process of elimination usually works. Try printing from a couple of client machines. If only one doesn't work, you've narrowed the problem down to that client machine. If all clients fail, try printing from the print server. If this succeeds, you know that your problem lies either in the print server configuration or in network connectivity. Keep trying alternatives until you've isolated the problem as precisely as possible, and then start applying the most common fixes until you solve the problem.

If you've already partially isolated the problem, jump straight to the heading in this section that applies and continue. If you can't solve the problem by following the guidelines provided here, you should at least be able to isolate the problem to a greater degree.

More Info   If you can't resolve your problems by using the information provided here, check out the Microsoft Knowledge Base. Go to *http://support.microsoft.com*, and click the Search link.

Printing from the Client Machine Experiencing the Problem

Attempting to print from the client machine will allow you to see any error messages generated while printing. These messages often tell you the cause of the problem or at least indicate some possibilities.

If the document prints properly, you probably have a user error, in which case you might need to educate your users as to the proper printing procedure. Otherwise, you might have a problem with a particular program, or the printer driver might be improperly configured for the users.

Note   Many administrators use this step later in their troubleshooting process to minimize the number of times they need to visit client systems. To understand whether the problem affects only the client or clients reporting the problem or whether it's more generalized, they start by checking the print server or printing from another client computer such as the one they're currently using.

Document Prints Incorrectly

When a document prints but appears garbled or has some other defect, a compatibility problem exists between your client, the printer driver, and the printer. Make sure that your client is using the proper client printer driver and that the server is also using the proper printer driver.

You might want to try installing a duplicate logical printer to test whether the printer driver is corrupt. If this isn't the problem, try changing the spool settings on the client driver (or, if multiple clients experience the same problem, the server's printer driver). Specifically try changing the following options on the Advanced tab of the printer's Properties window. (See the "Changing Spool Settings" section earlier in this chapter for a more detailed procedure.)

- To ensure that the entire document is available to the printer when printing begins, select the Start Printing After Last Page Is Spooled option.

- If you continue to have printing problems, choose the Print Directly To The Printer option to turn off spooling. This action will cause a performance hit on the server.

- Clear the Enable Advanced Printing Features check box on the print server to turn off metafile spooling, which disables some printer options such as page order, booklet printing, and pages per sheet (if available on your printer).

Document Fails to Print

If the document doesn't print properly, error messages will frequently appear that might help you identify the problem. Below are some solutions to try.

- If you receive an error stating that the appropriate printer driver wasn't available for download, you need to install the appropriate client drivers on the print server.

- If you receive an error stating that the print device was unavailable, you might have either a network connectivity problem, or the client might lack sufficient permissions.

- If you hear a lot of disk access and the document fails to print, verify that the drive holding the client's spool folder contains enough free disk space to hold the spooled document.

- Determine whether you can see and connect to the print server across the network. Try copying a file to the print server to see whether you can access the print server. (Generally, if you can't access the print server, you can't access any attached printers.)

- Try creating a new local printer with the share name \\<*servername*>\ <*printername*> of the printer as the port name. This will test whether you can copy print files to the print server.

- Print a test document from NotePad. If you can print with NotePad and not with the user's application, the printer drivers are correct and the application is likely the problem.

- If you can't print with NotePad, you can also try printing from the command line by typing the following command: *dir* > [*your printer port name*], substituting the share name of your network printer for *your printer port name*.

Printing from Some Applications Doesn't Work

Some applications experience problems when printing in Windows 2000. Some of the issues you might encounter are listed below.

- **Printing from Microsoft Outlook on a system with multiple languages is slow.**   Occurs if languages are installed on the client that aren't available on the server. To remedy this, copy the fonts to the %*SystemRoot*%\Fonts folder on the print server, and open the Fonts folder (or reboot the server).

- **Access Denied error message occurs when configuring a printer inside an application.**   Occurs when you don't have sufficient privileges to change your printer's configuration. To configure a printer, you need to have Manage Printers permissions.

- **Out-Of-Memory error message occurs on application load on Windows 3.x client.**   Can occur if a default printer isn't selected. Install a printer and configure it as the default printer.

- **MS-DOS program doesn't print on Windows 2000 or Windows NT.** Can occur if you're using an MS-DOS–based program that won't print until it is exited. Try quitting the program. Also, when setting up the printer driver using the Add Printer Wizard, choose Yes when asked whether you print from MS-DOS programs.

More Info   For other issues, consult the printers.txt file on the installation CD for the client operating system if the system is Windows 2000, Windows NT 4, or Windows 95/98. You might also want to check the Microsoft Knowledge Base at *http://support.microsoft.com*.

Checking the Print Server Status

Administrators often check the print server status before actually going to the client machine because they can do it remotely. Here are some matters to check.

- The print monitor might show stalled documents or error messages. If the printer is out of paper or toner or if there's a paper jam, an error message will frequently appear here.

- Check that sufficient free disk space exists on the drive holding the spool folder.

- If documents print garbled, the printer might be using the wrong data type (*EMF* or *raw*). Try using the *raw* data type to see if this corrects the problem. You might also want to clear the Enable Advanced Printing Features check box on the Advanced tab of the printer's Properties window. (See the "Changing Spool Settings" section earlier in this chapter for more information.)

- Check to see whether any documents are printing. If no documents exist in the print queue to observe, print a test page or document from the print server to verify that the print server is printing properly.

- If some documents in the print queue don't print and you can't delete them, the print spooler might be stalled. Restart the Print Spooler service to see whether this corrects the problem. You might also want to add another logical printer (printer driver) for the printer to try to rule out the possibility of a corrupt printer driver.

- Check that the proper services are installed and started for any non-Microsoft clients on your network. For example, if a Macintosh client is having printing problems, check to make sure that the Macintosh print services are installed and running.

Tip To prevent documents with certain languages from printing slowly, install on your print servers the fonts for all languages that your clients will use to print. To do this, copy the fonts to the %*SystemRoot*%\Fonts folder on the print server and open the Fonts folder (or reboot the server).

Printing from Another Client Machine

Attempting to print from another client machine helps determine whether the problem lies on the server or on the original client machine. Print a test document from the client system, and then use these guidelines to address the results of your print attempt.

- **Second client prints** If the second client you attempt to print from prints properly, you need to go back to the original client and perform more in-depth troubleshooting such as reinstalling the printer drivers and testing the printing subsystem.

- **Second client fails to print** If the second client can't print to the specified printer, you most likely have a problem with the print server or printer. If the print server shows no problems, check the printer.

Checking the Printer

If you've ruled out your clients and your server as being the source of the problem but you still can't print any documents on the printer, you need to take a close look at your printer. Pause the print queue, and then go check the actual printer. Are any errors reported on the printer? If you find any paper jams or if the printer is low on toner or needs servicing, the printer will usually report an error message. Make sure that the ready or online light is illuminated and that the printer cable is securely attached, or that the network cable is properly plugged in and the light next to the network port is illuminated (if available).

If you still can't print to the printer, attempt to print a test page directly from the printer. Most printers support this capability. If this works, try configuring a different print server with the printer. If you can print from a different print server, you have a problem with your original print server. If it doesn't work, try pinging the printer to see if you can communicate with it.

Print Spooler Service Is Stalled

If you can't delete documents in the print queue or if documents don't print, the print spooler might be stalled. This will also affect any fax services your server is running. To restart the print spooler service, follow these steps:

1. Open the Computer Management snap-in from the Administrative Tools folder, expand System Tools in the console tree, and then select Services.

2. Double-click the Print Spooler service in the right pane to open the Print Spooler Properties window, shown in Figure 8-23.

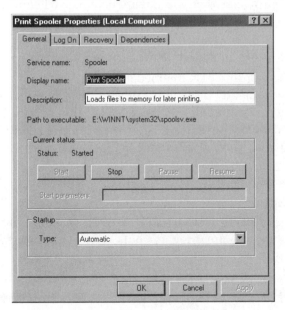

Figure 8-23. *The General tab of the Print Spooler Properties window.*

3. Click the Stop button to stop the service, and then click the Start button to restart the service.

4. To view the services (such as remote procedure call) on which the print spooler depends, click the Dependencies tab. You can also use this tab to view the services that depend on the print spooler to function properly.

5. To configure a recovery process to take place should the print spooler service fail, click the Recovery tab, and then specify whether you want to restart the service, reboot the computer, or run a program after each print spooler failure.

Restarting the service is usually a good option—it will save time. Automatic rebooting of the computer is a last option because of other processes that might be interrupted or stopped by a reboot.

Troubleshooting Printer Location Tracking

Printer location tracking can have its own set of problems, although these are usually related to the way your printers and network are set up. The rest of this section discusses some common problems that you might encounter when using printer location tracking and suggests some courses of action.

Clients Can't Locate Some Printers in Active Directory

This problem usually occurs when a printer isn't named according to the printer location name conventions your company decided to implement. When printer location tracking is enabled, clients by default can locate only printers with location attributes that match the naming convention. To fix the problem, enter the correct location name in the missing printer's *Location* field.

Naming Scheme Needs to Be Changed

If your company changes its organizational structure or if you find that your current location-naming scheme needs to be changed, use the following procedure. (Windows 2000 doesn't ship with any tools for bulk editing of objects in Active Directory.)

Use Active Directory Sites and Services to update the sites and subnet names. Enter the new location names in the *Location* field of each printer that is affected by the location name restructuring. You can also do this with Active Directory Services Interface (ADSI) script.

Summary

As this chapter demonstrates, printing is a much bigger subject than most people imagine. Furthermore, almost all networks need comprehensive and reliable print services. You must plan how to meet present printing needs while also preparing for expansions and changes. Contingency plans are essential because even a brief disruption in printing is not only inconvenient, it's costly. In the next chapter, we'll cover the day-to-day tasks that network administrators perform and how to customize the tools in Windows 2000 Server to make your work easier and more efficient.

Chapter 9
Managing Users and Groups

The central task of a network is to make sure that the customers (the users) have everything they need and nothing they don't. What they need includes access to the files, folders, applications, printers, and Internet connections that they require to do their jobs. What they don't need is any trouble getting at what they *do* need.

The network administrator has additional needs, such as shielding need-to-know material from those who don't need to know and protecting the users from themselves. The key to all of these needs is the configuration of groups, users, and group policies—the topic of this chapter.

Understanding Groups

By definition, groups in Microsoft Windows 2000 are Active Directory directory service or local computer objects that can contain users, contacts, computers, or other groups. In general, though, a group is usually a collection of user accounts. The point of groups is to simplify administration by allowing the network administrator to assign rights and permissions by group rather than to individual users.

Windows 2000 allows two group types: security and distribution. *Security groups* are essentially the only groups used by Windows 2000 because they're the only groups through which permissions can be assigned. Each security group is also assigned a *group scope*, which defines how permissions are assigned to the group's members. Programs that can search Active Directory can use security groups for nonsecurity purposes, such as sending e-mail to a group of users. *Distribution groups* are not security enabled, and no permissions can be assigned to distribution groups.

Later in the chapter, you'll find sections on user rights and how they are defined and assigned to groups. Chapter 10 includes discussion on permissions and how they are assigned.

Assigning Group Scopes

When a group is created, it is assigned a group scope that defines how permissions will be assigned. The three possible group scopes—global, domain local, and universal—are defined in the following sections.

Global Scope

A group with a global scope is truly global in the sense that permissions can be granted for resources located in any domain. However, members can come only from the domain in which the group is created, and in that sense it is not global. Global groups are best used for directory objects that require frequent maintenance, such as user and computer accounts. Global groups can be members of universal and domain local groups in any domain, and they can have the following members:

- Other global groups in the same domain
- Individual accounts from the same domain

Domain Local Scope

A domain local group is the inverse of a global group in that members can come from any domain but the permissions can be only for resources in the domain in which the group is created. The members of a domain local group have a common need to access certain resources in a particular domain. Domain local groups can have one or more of the following members:

- Other domain local groups in the same domain
- Global groups from any domain
- Universal groups from any domain
- Individual accounts from any domain

Note   The nesting rules apply fully only in native mode—that is, when all of the controllers in the domain are Windows 2000 servers. In mixed-mode domains, security groups with global scope can contain only individual accounts, not other groups. Security groups with domain local scope can contain both global groups and accounts. For more on native vs. mixed mode, see Chapter 7.

Universal Scope

A universal security group can have members from any domain and can be assigned permissions to resources in any domain. Although the universal scope sounds like an ideal solution in a multiple-domain enterprise, it's available only in domains that are running in native mode. Universal groups can have the following members:

- Other universal groups
- Global groups
- Individual accounts

Even in native mode, universal groups must be used with discretion because of the negative impact they can have on network performance, as described in the Real World sidebar, "How Groups Affect Network Performance."

Real World   How Groups Affect Network Performance

The importance of planning groups becomes even more apparent when you consider the negative effect that your group organization can have on network performance. When a user logs on to the network, the domain controller determines the user's group memberships and assigns a security token to the user. The token includes the security IDs of all of the groups that the user belongs to, in addition to the user account ID. The more security groups the user belongs to, the longer it will take to assemble the token and the longer it will take the user to log on.

In addition, the security token, once assembled, is sent to every computer the user accesses. The target computer compares all of the security IDs in the token against the permissions for all of the shared resources available at that computer. A large number of users added to a large number of shared resources (including individual folders) can take up a lot of bandwidth and processing time. One solution is to limit membership in security groups. Use distribution groups for categories of users that don't require specific permissions or rights.

Groups with universal scope will have a performance impact of their own because all such groups, along with their members, are listed in the Global Catalog. When there's a change to the membership in a group with universal scope, this fact must be relayed to every Global Catalog server in the domain tree, adding to the replication traffic on the network. Groups with global or domain local scope are also listed in the Global Catalog, but their individual members are not, so the solution is to limit the membership of universal groups primarily to global groups.

Planning a Group Strategy

Looking at your network and the various group types, and then factoring in your specific needs and what you want to accomplish, you might end up feeling as though you're working on a logic puzzle: Mac lives in a blue house, Luisa collects stamps, Sam drives a Toyota, and Ross eats cheese. Which one has red hair?

Nevertheless, as in so many other aspects of network administration, planning is *the* essential step. The domain mode determines the types of groups available to you. A mixed-mode domain can't support groups with universal scope. Thus, as long as you have Microsoft Windows NT backup domain controllers, you are limited to groups with global and domain local scopes. However, with some thought and the use of nesting, these two types of security groups can suffice for almost all purposes.

Determining Group Names

In planning your groups, you should determine a naming scheme that is appropriate for your organization. Two factors should be considered:

- **Group names should be instantly recognizable.**   If they are, administrators searching Active Directory don't have to guess at their meaning.

- **Comparable groups should have similar names.**   In other words, if you have a group for engineers in each domain, give all of the groups parallel names, such as NorAmer Engineers, SoAmer Engineers, and Asia Engineers.

Using Global and Domain Local Groups

You'll need to develop a strategy for using the different groups. For example, users with common job responsibilities belong in a global group. Thus, you'd add user accounts for all graphic artists to a global group called Graphic Artists. Other users with common needs would be assigned to other global groups. Then you must identify resources to which users need access and create a domain local group for that resource. If, for example, you have several color printers and plotters that are used by specific departments, you could make a domain local group called Printers&Plotters.

Next you should decide which global groups need access to the resources you've identified. Continuing the example, you'd add the global group Graphic Artists to the domain local group Printers&Plotters, along with other global groups who need access to the printers and plotters. Permission to use the resources in Printers&Plotters would be assigned to the Printers&Plotters domain local group.

Keep in mind that global groups can complicate administration in multiple-domain situations. Global groups from different domains have to have their permissions set individually. Also, assigning users to domain local groups and granting permissions to the group will not give members access to resources outside the domain.

> **Note**   Remember that the nesting rules apply only in native mode. In mixed-mode domains, security groups with global scope can contain only individual accounts, not other groups. Security groups with domain local scope can contain global groups and accounts.

Using Universal Groups

When you're able to use universal groups (that is, when your domain is running in native mode), keep the following guidelines in mind:

- Avoid adding individual accounts to universal groups, to keep replication traffic down.

- Add global groups from multiple domains to universal groups to give members access to resources in more than one domain.

- Universal groups can be members of domain local groups and other universal groups, but they can't be members of global groups.

Implementing the Group Strategy

Once you've planned your strategy and tested it using a variety of scenarios, you're ready to begin putting the structure into place.

Creating Groups

Use Active Directory Users and Computers to create and delete groups. Groups should be created in the Users container or in an organizational unit (OU) that you've created for the purpose of containing groups. To create a group, follow these steps:

1. Open Active Directory Users and Computers from the Administrative Tools menu.

2. Expand the domain in which the group will be created.

3. Right-click the Users container, point to New, and choose Group from the shortcut menu to open the dialog box shown in Figure 9-1.

4. Fill in the required information:

- The group name must be unique in the domain.

- The group name as it will be seen by pre–Windows 2000 operating systems will be filled in automatically. (In native mode, this field will be Downlevel Name Of New Group but will still be filled in automatically based on the name you provide as the group name.)

- For Group Scope, click Domain Local, Global, or Universal.

- For Group Type, click Security or Distribution.

5. Click OK when you're finished. The new group will appear in the Users container. You might have to wait a few minutes for the group to be replicated to the Global Catalog before adding members.

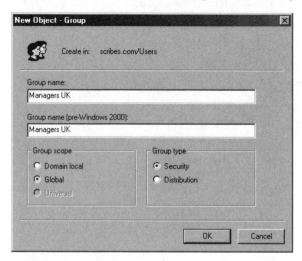

Figure 9-1. *Creating a new group.*

Deleting Groups

When groups are no longer needed, be sure to delete them from the system promptly. Unnecessary groups are a security risk because it is all too easy to grant permissions unintentionally.

Each group, like each user, has a unique security identifier (SID). The SID is used to identify the group and the permissions assigned to the group. When the group is deleted, the SID is deleted and not used again. If you delete a group and decide later to re-create it, you will have to configure the users and permissions as if for a new group.

To delete a group, merely right-click its name in Active Directory Users and Computers and choose Delete from the shortcut menu. Deleting a group deletes only the group and the permissions associated with the group. It has no effect on the accounts of users who are members of the group.

Adding Users to a Group

Once you've created a group, you'll need to add members to it. As was mentioned earlier in the chapter, groups can contain users, contacts, other groups, and computers. To add members to a group, follow these steps:

1. Open Active Directory Users and Computers from the Administrative Tools menu.
2. In the console tree, click the container that includes the group to which you will be adding members.
3. Right-click the group and choose Properties from the shortcut menu.
4. Click the Members tab, and then click the Add button to open the Select Users, Contacts, Or Computers dialog box (Figure 9-2).
5. Highlight the accounts you want to add. (You can use the Shift and Ctrl keys to select multiple accounts.)
6. Click the Add button. This returns you to the group's Properties window with the users added. Click OK.

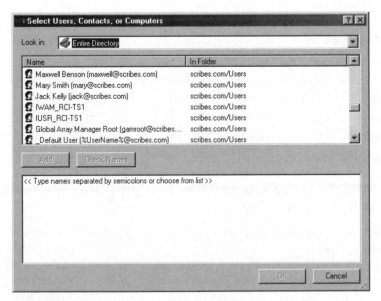

Figure 9-2. *Adding an account to a group.*

> **Note** A contact is an account without security permissions and is typically used to represent external users for the purpose of e-mail. You can't log on to the network as a contact.

Changing the Group Scope

Over time, you might find that you need to change the scope of a particular group. For example, you might need to change a global group to a universal group so that users from another domain can be part of the group. However, the types of changes that can be made to a group scope are quite limited, and you may need to delete the group and create a new one to get the configuration you need.

To change a group scope, right-click the group name in Active Directory Users and Computers and choose Properties from the shortcut menu. Make the necessary changes on the General tab, and click OK when you're finished. The rules for changing a group scope are as follows:

- In mixed mode, a security group cannot have universal scope.
- A global group can be changed to a universal group if the global group is not already a member of another global group.
- A domain local group can be changed to a universal group if the domain local group does not already contain another domain local group.
- A universal group cannot be changed.

Creating Local Groups

A local group is a collection of user accounts on a single computer. The user accounts must be local to the computer, and members of local groups can be assigned permissions for resources only on the computer where the local group was created.

Local groups can be created on any Windows 2000 computer except domain controllers. In general, you don't want to use local groups on a computer that's part of a domain or, at least, you want to do so sparingly. Local groups don't appear in Active Directory, so you must administer local groups separately on each individual computer. To create a local group, follow these steps:

1. Right-click the My Computer icon on the desktop and choose Manage from the shortcut menu.

2. In the console tree, expand System Tools and then Local Users And Groups, as shown in Figure 9-3.

3. Right-click the Groups folder and select New Group from the shortcut menu.

4. In the New Group dialog box, enter the group name. You can include a description if you like.

5. Click the Add button to add members to the group. (You can add members now or later.)

6. Click Create when you're finished, and the new group is added to the list of groups in the details pane.

Figure 9-3. *Creating a local group.*

Managing Built-in Groups and User Rights

Windows 2000 creates four types of built-in groups: local, domain local, global, and system. Each type of built-in group has a predetermined set of user rights. Everyone assigned to the group automatically possesses those rights.

Built-in Local Groups

Member servers, stand-alone servers, and computers running Windows 2000 Professional have built-in local groups that give rights to perform tasks on a single computer. Table 9-1 shows the built-in local groups.

Table 9-1.   Built-in local groups

Local Group	Description
Administrators	Members can perform all administrative tasks on the computer. The built-in Administrator account that's created when the operating system is installed is a member of the group. When a stand-alone server or a computer running Windows 2000 Professional joins a domain, the Domain Admins group is made part of this group.
Backup Operators	Members can log on to the computer, back up and restore the computer's data, and shut down the computer. Members cannot change security settings. There are no default members in the group.
Guests	Members can perform only tasks for which an administrator has granted rights. Members can use only those resources for which an administrator has specifically granted permission.
Power Users	Members can create and modify user accounts and install programs on the local computer but cannot view other users' files.
Replicator	Do not add user accounts of actual users to this group. If necessary, you can add a "dummy" user account to this group to permit you to log on to Replicator services on a domain controller to manage replication of files and directories.
Users	Members of this group can log on to the computer, access the network, save documents, and shut down the computer. Members cannot install programs or make system changes. When a member server or Windows 2000 Professional machine joins a domain, the Domain Users group is added to this group.

Tip If you don't want members of the Domain Users group to have access to a particular workstation or member server, remove Domain Users from that computer's local Users group. Similarly, if you don't want the members of Domain Admins to administer a particular workstation or member server, remove Domain Admins from the local Administrators group.

Built-in Domain Local Groups

The Windows 2000 built-in domain local groups provide users with rights and permissions to perform tasks on domain controllers and in Active Directory. The domain local groups have predefined rights and permissions that are granted to users and global groups that you add as members. Table 9-2 shows the most commonly used of the built-in domain local groups.

Table 9-2.   Commonly used built-in domain local groups

Domain Local Group	Description
Account Operators	Members can create, delete, and manage user accounts and groups. Members cannot modify the Administrators group or any of the Operators groups.
Administrators	Members are automatically granted every right and permission on all domain controllers and the domain itself. The Administrator account, Enterprise Admins group, and Domain Admins group are members.
Backup Operators	Members can back up and restore data on all domain controllers using Windows 2000 Backup.
Guests	Members can perform only tasks for which an administrator has granted rights. Members can use only those resources for which an administrator has specifically granted permission. The Guest User and Domain Guests groups are members by default.
Print Operators	Members can manage all aspects of printer operation and configuration in the domain.
Server Operators	Members can perform most administrative tasks on domain controllers, except the manipulation of security options.
Users	Members can log on to the computer, access the network, save documents, and shut down the computer. Members cannot install programs or make system changes. The Domain Users group is a member by default.

Real World   Just Who Is Everyone?

In Windows NT, all domain users are members of the Everyone group. This group is controlled by the operating system and appears on any network with Windows NT servers. In Windows 2000, the equivalent group is called Authenticated Users. Unlike Everyone, Authenticated Users contains no anonymous users or guests. The Everyone group survives as a *special identity*. You don't see it when you administer groups, and it cannot be placed in a group. When a user logs on to the network, the user is automatically added to Everyone. You can't see or change the membership of the special identities, which also include the Network and Interactive groups.

Built-in Global Groups

Built-in global groups are created to encompass common types of accounts. By default, these groups do not have inherent rights; an administrator must assign all rights to the group. However, some members are added to these groups automatically, and you can add more members based on the rights and permissions you assign to the groups. Rights can be assigned directly to the groups or by adding the built-in global groups to domain local groups. Table 9-3 describes the built-in global groups that are commonly used.

Table 9-3. Commonly used built-in global groups

Global Group	Description
Domain Admins	This group is automatically a member of the domain local Administrators group, so members of Domain Admins can perform administrative tasks on any computer in the domain. The Administrator account is a member of this group by default.
Domain Computers	All controllers and workstations in the domain are members.
Domain Controllers	All domain controllers in the domain are members.
Domain Guests	The Guest account is a member by default. This group is automatically a member of the domain local Guests group.
Domain Users	All domain users and the Administrator account are members. The Domain Users group is automatically a member of the domain local Users group.
Enterprise Admins	This group is for users who are to have administrative rights for the entire network. Enterprise Admins is automatically a member of the domain local Administrators group in the domain in which it is created. You will need to add it to the domain local Administrators group for other domains.
Group Policy Admins	Members can create and modify group policy for the domain.

Tip If you have users who should have fewer rights and/or permissions than the typical user, add these users to Domain Guests and remove them from Domain Users.

Defining User Rights

What users can and cannot do depends on the rights and permissions that have been granted to them. *Rights* generally apply to the system as a whole. The ability to back up files or to log on to a server, for example, is a right that the administrator giveth or taketh away. Rights can be assigned individually, but most often they are characteristics of groups, and a user is assigned to a particular group on the basis of the rights that the user needs.

Permissions indicate the access that a user (or group) has to specific objects such as files, directories, and printers. For example, the question of whether a user can read a particular directory or access a network printer is a permission. Permissions are discussed at length later in this chapter.

Rights, in turn, are divided into two types: privileges and logon rights. *Privileges* include such things as the ability to run security audits or force shutdown from a remote system—obviously not things that are done by most users. *Logon rights* are self-explanatory; they involve the ability to connect to a computer in specific ways. Rights are automatically assigned to the built-in groups in Windows 2000, although they can be assigned to individual users as well as groups. Assignment by group is preferred, so whenever possible, you should assign rights by group membership to keep administration simple. When membership in groups defines rights, rights can be removed from a user by simply removing the user from the group. Tables 9-4 and 9-5 list the logon rights and privileges and the groups to which they are assigned by default.

Table 9-4.   Logon rights assigned to groups by default

Name	Description	Groups Assigned the Right by Default
Access this computer from the network	Permits connection to the computer through the network.	Administrators, Power Users, Everyone
Logon as a batch job	Allows logging on using a batch queue.	Administrators
Logon as a service	Allows logging on as a service using a specific user account and security context.	None
Logon locally	Permits logon at the computer's keyboard.	Administrators, Account Operators, Backup Operators, Print Operators, Server Operators

Table 9-5. **Privileges assigned to groups by default**

Privilege	Description	Groups Assigned the Privilege by Default
Act as part of the operating system	Allows a process to authenticate as any user. A process that requires this privilege should use the LocalSystem account, which already includes this privilege.	None
Add workstations to domain	Allows a user to add new workstations to an existing domain.	Administrators
Backup files and directories	Allows backing up the system; overrides specific file and folder permissions.	Administrators, Backup Operators
Bypass traverse checking	Allows a user to go through directory trees (folder structures) even if the user doesn't have permission to access the directories being passed through.	Everyone
Change the system time	Allows the setting of the computer's internal clock.	Administrators, Power Users
Create a pagefile	Allows the creation and modification of a pagefile.	Administrators
Create a token object	Allows a process to create a token that can be used to access any local resource. A process that requires this privilege should use the LocalSystem account, which already includes this privilege.	None
Create permanent shared objects	Allows a process to create a directory object. Used by kernel-mode components to extend the Windows 2000 object namespace. Components running in kernel mode already have this privilege.	None
Debug programs	Allows the user to attach a debugger to a process.	Administrators
Enable computer and user accounts to be trusted for delegation	Permits a user to set the Trusted for Delegation setting on an object.	Administrators
Force shutdown from a remote system	Allows the shutdown of a computer from a remote location on the network.	Administrators
Generate security audits	Allows a process to make entries in a security log.	None
Increase quotas	Allows a process with write property access to another process to increase the processor quota assigned to that process.	None

continued

Table 9-5. *continued*

Privilege	Description	Groups Assigned the Privilege by Default
Increase scheduling priority	Allows the use of Task Manager to change the scheduling priority of a process.	Administrators, Power Users
Load and unload device drivers	Install and remove device drivers.	Administrators
Lock pages in memory	Allows a process to keep data in physical memory. This is an obsolete privilege that can have a seriously negative effect on system performance. Do not use it.	None
Manage auditing and security log	Allows a user to specify auditing options and to view and clear the security log in Event Viewer. Audit Directory Service Access must be turned on for object access auditing to be performed. (See Chapter 10.) Administrators can always view and clear the security log.	Administrators
Modify firmware environment variables	Allows the configuration of nonvolatile RAM on computers that support such function.	Administrators
Profile a single process	Allows performance sampling on a process.	Administrators, Power Users
Profile system performance	Allows performance sampling of the system.	Administrators
Remove computer from docking station	Allows the removal of a laptop from a docking station using the Windows 2000 interface.	Administrators, Users
Replace a process level token	Allows the replacement of the default token associated with a subprocess.	None
Restore files and directories	Allows restoring files and folders to a system; overrules specific file and folder permissions.	Administrators, Backup Operators
Shut down the system	Shuts down Windows 2000.	Administrators, Backup Operators, Everyone, Power Users, Users
Synchronize directory service data	Allows a user to initiate a synchronization of Active Directory.	Administrators
Take ownership of files or other objects	Allows a user to take ownership of any security object including files and folders, printers, registry keys, and processes. Overrules specified permissions.	Administrators

Assigning User Rights to a Group

Rights are assigned and removed most easily at a domain level using group policy. Suppose you have a group of users whom you want to allow to log on locally to Windows 2000 servers, but you don't want them to be members of any of the groups that have this logon right by default. One way to approach this situation would be to create a group called Logon Rights, add the users to the group, and assign the right to logon locally to the Logon Rights group. To assign a right to a particular group, follow these steps:

1. Open Active Directory Users and Computers from the Administrative Tools menu. Right-click the domain name and select Properties.

2. Click the Group Policy tab, and then click the Edit button. Open Computer Configuration, and then open Windows Settings.

3. Under Security Settings, click Local Properties and then User Rights Assignment (Figure 9-4). In the details pane, double-click Log On Locally.

4. Place a check mark next to Define These Policy Settings and then click Add.

5. Enter the name of the group to be granted this right (or click Browse to search for the group). Click OK twice and close Domain Security Policy.

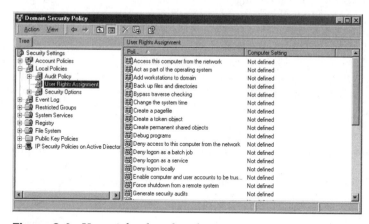

Figure 9-4. *User rights listed under group policy.*

The same process can remove rights, except that you'd click Remove in step 4. Rights can also be assigned to an individual user using this method.

Assigning Rights Locally

Rights can be assigned or removed locally, though you must bear in mind that a defined domain-level policy will override a local policy setting. To assign a policy locally, follow these steps:

1. Open Local Security Policy from the Administrative Tools menu.

2. Under Security Settings, click Local Policies and then User Rights Assignment (Figure 9-5). As you can see, the local settings are shown in addition to the *effective* settings. (Effective policy settings are the policy settings in effect after domain policy settings are applied.)

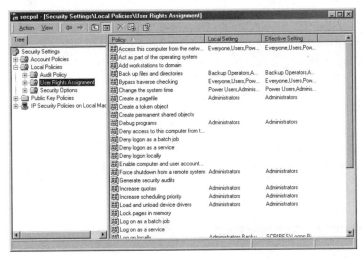

Figure 9-5. *Local policy settings.*

3. In the detail pane, double-click the policy you want to assign to open the Local Security Policy Setting dialog box.

4. Click Add to select a group (or individual) in the Select Users Or Groups dialog box. Highlight the group, click Add, and then click OK.

As you can see in Figure 9-6, the policy setting Deny Logon Locally has been assigned to the Graphic Artists group. The policy is shown as local only—that is, there is no domain policy in effect. The net result is that members of the Graphic Artists group will not be able to log on to this local computer. Their ability to log on or not log on to other computers in the domain is neither specified nor affected.

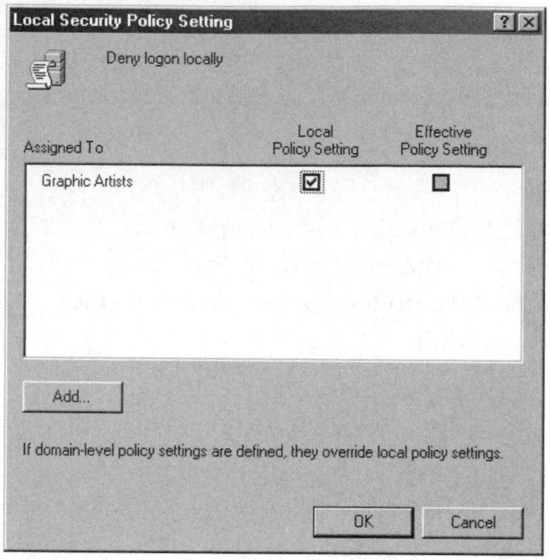

Figure 9-6. *Defining the local policy that denies local logon.*

Figure 9-7 shows another local policy window. In this case, the right to Enable Computer And User Accounts To Be Trusted For Delegation is assigned to Domain Admins through a domain-level policy. A domain-level policy applies whether the local policy is defined or not. Group Policy is covered in more detail later in this chapter.

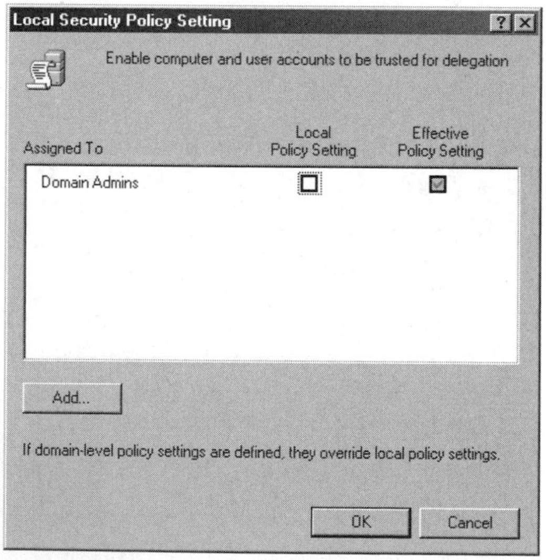

Figure 9-7. *Domain-level policy as the effective policy.*

Creating User Accounts

Every person who will have access to the network requires a user account. A user account makes it possible to

- Authenticate the identity of the person connecting to the network
- Control access to domain resources
- Audit actions performed using the account

Windows 2000 creates only two predefined accounts: the Administrator account, giving the user all rights and permissions, and the Guest account, which has limited rights. All other accounts are created by an administrator and are either domain accounts (valid throughout the domain by default) or local accounts (usable only on the machine where they are created).

Naming User Accounts

In Active Directory, each user account has a *principal name*. The name consists of two parts, the *security principal name* and the *principal name suffix*. For existing Windows NT user accounts, the security principal name is by default the same as the name used to log on to the Windows NT domain. For new Windows 2000 user accounts, an administrator assigns the security principal name. The default principal name suffix is the DNS name of the root domain in the domain tree. So a user identified as EduardoP in a Windows NT domain would have a principal name such as EduardoP@scribes.com.

Account Options

Planning account options for users will simplify the process of creating accounts. The account options to consider include the following:

- **Logon Hours** By default, a user can log on at any hour of the day or night. For security reasons, you might want to restrict access by some or all users to certain times of the day or certain days of the week.
- **Log On To** By default, users can log on to all workstations. For security reasons, you can limit logon access to a particular machine or machines if you have the NetBIOS protocol installed in the domain. Without NetBIOS, Windows 2000 is unable to determine a specific logon location.

- **Account Expiration** You can decide whether you want to set accounts to expire. For obvious reasons, it makes sense to set an expiration date for temporary employees to coincide with the end of their contracts.

Other options—*many* other options—can be set in user accounts and are detailed in the section "Setting User Account Properties." The three options just listed are the most likely to be applied across large numbers of users.

Real World Establishing a Naming Convention

The security principal name should be assigned using a consistent naming convention, so that you and your users can remember user names and find them in lists. Some options for user names include the following:

- **First name plus last initial** Examples are MichaelG and SusanM. In the case of duplicate first names, you can add numbers (MichaelG1 and MichaelG2) or enough letters to provide identification (IngridMat and IngridMur).

- **First name plus a number** Examples are Dave112 and Dave113. This approach can be a problem especially for people with first names that appear frequently in the population. It makes it hard to remember your *own* user name and even harder to identify those of others.

- **First initial plus last name** An example would be MSmith. If you have both a Linda Smith and a Louise Smith, you could use LiSmith and LoSmith or LSmith1 and LSmith2.

- **Last name plus an initial** This convention is useful in a large network. When you have multiple users with the same last name, add a few letters as in SmithLi or SmithLo.

No matter which approach you choose, you must not only accommodate the existing users on your network but you must also be able to integrate future users. Then, even if the company's next hire is U Ti or Chomondely St. J. Montgomery-Glossup, your user-name convention will still be able to handle it.

Passwords

All of your users should have well-chosen passwords and should be required to change them periodically. Passwords should be chosen according to the guidelines in the Real World sidebar "Rules for Good Passwords." Accounts should be set to lockout when invalid passwords are entered. (Allow three attempts, to leave room for typographical errors.)

Real World   Rules for Good Passwords

A good password has the following characteristics:

- It is not a rotation of the characters in a logon name. (How many brain cells would it take to figure this one out?)

- It contains at least two alphabetic characters and one nonalphabetic character.

- It is at least six characters long.

- It isn't the user's name or initials, the initials of his or her children or significant other, or any of these items combined with other commonly available personal data such as a birthdate, telephone number, or license plate number.

Among the best passwords are alphanumeric acronyms of phrases that have a meaning to the user but are not likely to be known to others. This makes the password easy for the user to remember while at the same time making it hard for an outsider to guess.

It pays to educate your users about passwords and password privacy, but most of all, it pays to heed your own advice: make sure that the password you have selected for administration is a good password, and change it frequently. Doing so will help you avoid the consequences of having somebody break into your system and wreak havoc in your very own kingdom. If users will be dialing into the network from home or other remote sites, you might want to include more security than domain-level password authorization.

Administrators should have two accounts on the system: one administrative account and one normal user account. You should use the normal user account unless you are performing administrative tasks. Because of the privileges associated with administrative accounts, they are a prime target for intruders. Chapter 10 includes information on using the secondary logon to keep the administrative account safe.

Creating a Domain User Account

Domain user accounts can be created in the default Users OU, or you can make another OU to hold domain user accounts. To add a domain user account, follow these steps:

1. Open Active Directory Users and Computers from the Administrative Tools menu.

2. Highlight the domain name and, on the Action menu, point to New and then choose User to open the dialog box shown in Figure 9-8.

3. Provide the user's first and last name. The Full Name box is filled in automatically. The full name must be unique in the OU where the user account is created.

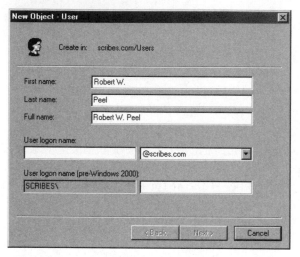

Figure 9-8. *Creating a new domain user account.*

4. Provide the user logon name based on your naming convention. This name must be unique in Active Directory. The pre–Windows 2000 logon name is filled in automatically. This is the name used to log on from computers running Windows operating systems such as Windows NT. Click Next.

5. Provide a password and set password policies. Click Next.

6. A confirmation screen opens, showing the details of the account you are about to create. If the details are correct, click Finish. Otherwise, use the Back button to make corrections.

At this point, the new user account is added to the OU with default settings. It's unlikely that the default settings are exactly what you want, so you'll need to adjust the properties of the new account, as described in the section "Setting User Account Properties."

Creating a Local User Account

A local account cannot access the domain and therefore has access only to the resources on the computer where it's created and used. To create a local user account, follow these steps:

1. Right-click My Computer and choose Manage from the shortcut menu.

2. In the console tree, click Local Users and Groups. Right-click Users and choose New User from the shortcut menu (Figure 9-9).

3. In the New User dialog box, supply the user name, full name, and description.

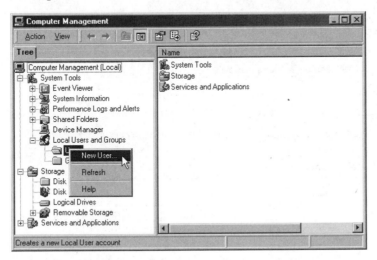

Figure 9-9. *Creating a local user account.*

4. Provide a password and set password policies. Click Create. At this point, the new user account is created with default settings. Local accounts can belong to locally created groups (on the single computer).

Setting User Account Properties

The Properties window for a domain user can have up to a dozen tabs, depending on the domain's setup; Table 9-6 describes these tabs. All of the information entered in the Properties window can be used as the basis for a search in Active Directory. For example, you can find a user's telephone number or department by searching for the user's last name. To set the properties for a domain user account, follow these steps:

1. Open Active Directory Users and Computers from the Administrative Tools menu.

2. Open the OU where the domain user account was created.

3. Right-click the user account and choose Properties from the shortcut menu (Figure 9-10).

4. Click the tab for the properties you want to set. Make the changes and click OK when you're finished.

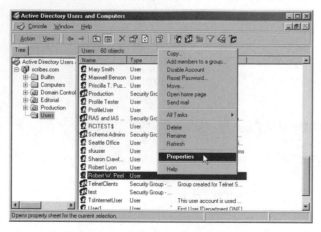

Figure 9-10. *Selecting the properties for a domain user account.*

Table 9-6. Tabs in the Properties window for a domain user account

Tab	Description
General	Documents the user's name, description, office location, telephone number, e-mail address, and Web page address
Address	Documents the user's physical address
Account	Documents the logon name, logon restrictions, password options, and whether the account expires
Profile	Shows the user's profile path, the path of any script that runs at logon, the path to a home folder, and any automatic drive connections
Telephones	Lists additional telephone numbers such as for a pager, cellular phone, or Internet phone
Organization	Documents the user's title, department, company, manager, and direct reports
Member Of	Lists the user's group memberships
Dial-In	Documents the user's dial-in access
Terminal Services, Environment, Sessions, Remote Control	Documents the user's Terminal Services profile

Testing User Accounts

As you develop different types of user accounts, it's advisable to test them. Create a dummy account with the memberships and restrictions you're planning on using. Then log on to a client machine and see whether the account produces the results you expect.

- Test restrictions to logon hours and passwords by attempting to bypass them.

- Test home folders and profiles (discussed in the section "Using Home Folders," later in this chapter) to see whether they are actually created.
- Test roaming profiles by logging on from various machines.
- Test group memberships by performing a task that membership in the group is supposed to allow (or deny), such as logging on to a server.

If unexpected results occur, the time to discover them is before you've deployed a thousand users with the wrong settings.

Managing User Accounts

Especially on a large, busy network, managing user accounts is an ongoing process of additions, deletions, and changes. While these taks aren't difficult, they can be time-consuming and need to be managed carefully.

Disabling and Enabling a User Account

If you need to deactivate a domain user account for some period of time but not delete it permanently, you can disable it. To disable a user account, follow these steps:

1. Open Active Directory Users and Computers from the Administrative Tools menu.
2. Open the container that holds the user account.
3. Right-click the user name and select Disable Account from the shortcut menu (Figure 9-11). An informational box opens telling you that the object has been disabled, and a red circle with an "X" appears over the user account's icon.

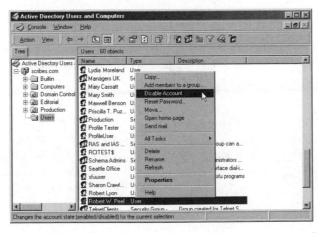

Figure 9-11. *Disabling a user account.*

To enable a previously disabled account, you perform the same steps, choosing Enable Account from the shortcut menu.

Deleting a User Account

Each user account in the domain has an associated security identifier that is unique and never reused, which means that a deleted account is completely deleted. If you delete Jeremy's account and later change your mind, you will have to re-create not only the account but also the permissions, settings, group memberships, and other properties that the original user account possessed. For that reason, if there's any doubt about whether an account might be needed in the future, it's best to disable it and not perform the deletion until you're sure it won't be needed again.

However, accounts do have to be deleted at regular intervals. To delete a domain user account, follow these steps:

1. Open Active Directory Users and Computers from the Administrative Tools menu.
2. Open the container that holds the user account.
3. Right-click the user name and choose Delete from the shortcut menu.
4. An Active Directory dialog box opens, asking you to confirm the deletion. Click Yes and the account is deleted.

Finding a User Account

To search for a particular user account, open Active Directory Users and Computers from the Administrative Tools menu and on the toolbar, click the Find icon, shown here:

This opens the Find Users, Contacts, And Groups dialog box. Don't be misled, though. Open the drop-down list in the Find box and you'll see that you can use this tool to search for computers, printers, shared folders, organizational units, and much more.

To find a specific user, select the scope of your search in the In box. Type in a name, part of a name, or some other descriptive element that's part of the user's profile, and click Find Now. As you can see in Figure 9-12, a search for a portion of a name returns all users with that element in their names.

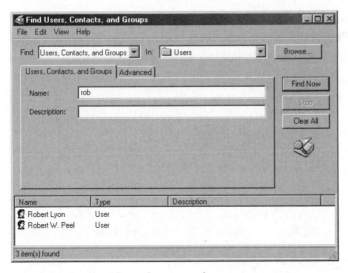

Figure 9-12. *Searching for a user by name.*

The larger the network, the more specific your search will need to be. In a large network environment, you can narrow your search to a specific organizational unit. Open Active Directory Users and Computers from the Administrative Tools menu and select Find from the shortcut menu. Right-click the OU you are interested in.

Moving a User Account

To move a user account from one container to another, follow these steps:

1. Open Active Directory Users and Computers from the Administrative Tools menu.

2. In the console tree, click the OU that contains the user account.

3. Right-click the user account to be moved and choose Move from the shortcut menu.

4. In the Move dialog box, highlight the destination container and click OK.

Renaming a User Account

On occasion, a user account may need to be renamed. For example, if you have an account configured with an assortment of rights, permissions, and group memberships for a particular position and a new person is taking over that position, you can change the first, last, and user logon names for the new person. To rename an existing user account, follow these steps:

1. Open Active Directory Users and Computers from the Administrative Tools menu.

2. In the console tree, click the OU that contains the account.

3. Right-click the user name, and choose Rename from the shortcut menu. (You can also slowly click the user name twice.)

4. Press the Delete key and then the Enter key to open the Rename User dialog box (Figure 9-13).

5. Enter the changes and click OK. The account is renamed, and all permissions and other settings remain intact. Any other personal data in the account's Properties window will have to be changed as well.

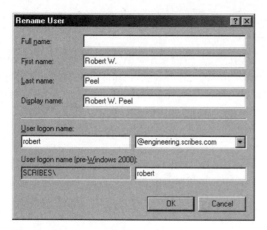

Figure 9-13. *Renaming an existing user account.*

Resetting a User's Password

For passwords to be effective, they must not be obvious or easy to guess. However, when passwords are not obvious or easy to guess, they will inevitably be forgotten. When a user forgets his or her password, you can reset it. The best policy is to reset it to a simple password and require the user to change the password at the next logon to the network.

To reset a password, just open Active Directory Users and Computers from the Administrative Tools menu and find the container for the account whose password you need to reset. Right-click the account name and choose Reset Password from the shortcut menu. In the Reset Password dialog box (Figure 9-14), enter the new password twice, and select the User Must Change Password At Next Logon option.

Figure 9-14. *Resetting a user's password.*

Unlocking a User Account

If a user violates a group policy, such as exceeding the limit for bad logon attempts, Group Policy will lock the account. When an account is locked, it cannot be used to log on to the system. To unlock a user account, follow these steps:

1. Open Active Directory Users and Computers from the Administrative Tools menu.
2. In the console tree, click the OU that contains the locked account.
3. Right-click the user account in the details pane, and choose Properties from the shortcut menu.
4. In the Properties window, click the Account tab.
5. Clear the check box next to Account Is Locked Out. Click OK.

By default, Group Policy does not lock accounts due to failed logon attempts. You should make this setting for security reasons. See the section "Understanding Group Policies," later in this chapter.

Using Home Folders

Home directories or folders are repositories that you can provide on a network server for users' documents. Placing home folders on a network file server has several advantages:

- Backup of user documents is centralized.
- Users can access their home folders from any client computer.

- Home folders can be accessed from clients running any Microsoft operating system (including MS-DOS and all versions of Windows).

The contents of home folders are not part of user profiles, so they don't affect network traffic during logon. (A home folder can also be on a client computer, but that defeats much of its purpose.)

Creating Home Folders on a Server

To create a home folder on a network file server, follow these steps:

1. On the server, create a new folder for the home folders. Right-click the new folder, and choose Properties from the shortcut menu.

2. Click the Sharing tab, and Share This folder (Figure 9-15).

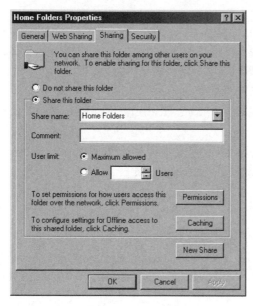

Figure 9-15. *Sharing the new Home Folders folder.*

3. Click the Security tab, and remove the default Full Control from the Everyone group and assign Full Control to the Users group. (This setting will prevent anyone other than domain user accounts from accessing the folder.)

Note Home folders should be stored on a partition formatted with NTFS. Home folders on a FAT partition can be secured only by assigning shared folder permissions on a user-by-user basis.

Providing Home Folders to Users

To provide a user with a home folder, you must add the path for the folder to the user account's properties. Follow these steps to give a user access to a home folder:

1. Open Active Directory Users and Computers from the Administrative Tools menu.

2. Click the OU containing the user account. Right-click the user name, and choose Properties from the shortcut menu.

3. Click the Profile tab.

4. In the Home Folder area, click the Connect option and specify a drive letter to use to connect to the file server.

5. In the To box, specify the UNC name for the connection—for example, *server_name**shared_folder**user_logon_name*. If you use the variable %username%, as shown in Figure 9-16, a home folder will be given the user's logon name.

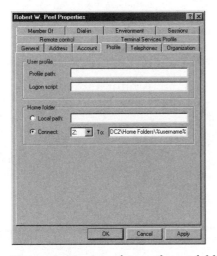

Figure 9-16. *Specifying a home folder.*

Maintaining User Profiles

A *profile* is an environment specifically customized for a user. The profile contains the desktop and program settings for the user. Every user has a profile, whether the administrator configures one or not, because a default profile is automatically created for each user who logs on to a computer. Profiles offer a number of advantages:

- Multiple users can use the same computer, with the settings for each user restored at logon to the same state as when he or she logged off.
- Desktop changes made by one user will not affect any other user.
- If user profiles are stored on a server, they can follow users to any computer on the network running Windows 2000 or Windows NT 4.

From an administrator's standpoint, the information in the profile can be a valuable tool for setting up default user profiles for all users on the network or for customizing default profiles for different departments or job classifications. You can also set up *mandatory* profiles that allow a user to make changes to the desktop while logged on but not to save any of the changes. A mandatory profile always looks exactly the same every time a user logs on. The types of profiles are as follows:

- **Local profiles**   Profiles made on a computer when a user logs on. The profile is specific to a user, local to that computer, and stored on the local computer's hard disk.
- **Roaming profiles**   Profiles created by an administrator and stored on a server. These profiles follow a user to any Windows 2000 or Windows NT 4 machine on the network.
- **Mandatory profiles**   Roaming profiles that can be changed only by an administrator.

Real World   What's Stored in a Profile?

All profiles start out as a copy of the Default User profile that is installed on every computer running Windows 2000. Registry data for Default User is in the Ntuser.dat file contained in the Default User profile. Inside each profile are the following folders:

- **Application Data**   Program-specific settings determined by the program manufacturer plus specific user security settings
- **Cookies**   Messages sent to a Web browser by a Web server and stored locally to track user information and preferences
- **Desktop**   Desktop files, folders, shortcuts, and the desktop appearance
- **Favorites**   Shortcuts to favorite locations, particularly Web sites
- **Local Settings**   Application data, History, and Temporary files
- **My Documents**   User documents and My Pictures, which contains user graphics files
- **NetHood**   Shortcuts to My Network Places
- **PrintHood**   Shortcuts to items in the Printers folder
- **Recent**   Shortcuts to the most recently accessed folders and files
- **SendTo**   Items on the Send To menu
- **Start Menu**   Items on the user's Start menu
- **Templates**   Application templates

By default, only the Cookies, Desktop, Favorites, My Documents, and Start Menu folders are visible in Windows Explorer. The other folders are hidden; to see them you'll need to select Folder Options, click the View tab, and select Show Hidden Files And Folders.

Local Profiles

Local profiles are created on computers when individual users log on. On a computer upgraded from Windows NT 4, the profile is stored in the Profiles folder on the system root partition. On a computer with a new installation of Windows 2000, the user profile is in the Documents And Settings folder (Figure 9-17).

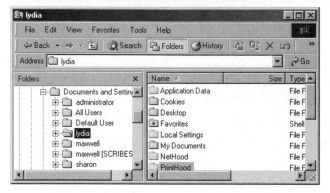

Figure 9-17. *A user's local profile.*

The first time a user logs on to a computer, a profile folder is generated for the user, and the contents of the Default User folder are copied into it. Any changes made to the desktop by the user are saved in that user's profile when he or she logs off.

If a user has a local account on the computer as well as a domain account and logs on at different times using both accounts, the user will have two profile folders on the local computer: one for when the user logs on to the domain using the domain user account and one for when the user logs on locally to the computer. The local profile will be shown with the logon name. The domain profile will also be shown with the logon name but will have the domain name appended to it.

Roaming Profiles

Roaming profiles are a great advantage for users who frequently use more than one computer. A roaming profile is stored on a server and, after the user's logon is authenticated in the directory service, is copied to the local computer. This allows a user to have the same desktop, application configuration, and local settings at any machine running Windows 2000 or Windows NT 4.

Here's how it works. You assign a location on a server for user profiles and create a folder shared with users who are to have roaming profiles. You enter a path to that folder in the user's Properties window. The next time the user logs on to a computer, the profile from the server is downloaded to the local computer. When the user logs off, the profile is saved both locally and in the user profile path location. Specifying the user profile path is all it takes to turn a local profile into a roaming profile, available anywhere in the domain.

When the user logs on again, the profile on the server is compared to the copy on the local computer, and the more recent copy is loaded for the user. If the server isn't available, the local copy is used. If the server isn't available and this is the first time the user has logged on to the computer, a user profile is created locally using the Default User profile. When a profile isn't downloaded to a local computer because of server problems, the roaming profile is not updated when the user logs off.

> **Tip**   Put user profiles on a member server rather than on a domain controller to speed up the process of authentication and to avoid using a domain controller's processing power and bandwidth for the downloading of profiles. In addition, place the profiles on a server that is backed up regularly so that copies of roaming profiles are as recent as possible.

Setting Up Roaming Profiles

Setting up roaming profiles is very easy. Simply assign a location on a server and complete the following steps:

1. Create a shared folder for the profiles on the server.

2. On the Profile tab in the user account Properties window, provide a path to the shared folder, such as *server_name**shared_profile_folder* *%username%*.

Figure 9-18 shows an example of a path for a roaming profile. When you use the variable %username%, Windows 2000 automatically replaces the variable with the user account name.

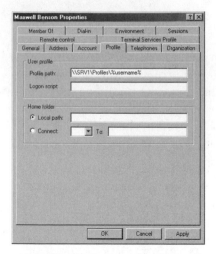

Figure 9-18. *Setting a path for a roaming profile.*

Once you've created a shared profile folder on a server and supplied a profile path in the user account, a roaming profile is enabled. The user's configuration of his or her desktop is copied and stored on the server and will be available to the user from any computer. Most of the time, though, you won't want to send your users off to fend for themselves. Life is easier for them and for you if users are assigned a customized profile that is already set up with appropriate short-cuts, network connections, and Start menu items. For this, you'll need to set up customized profiles.

Creating Customized Roaming Profiles

Creating customized roaming profiles is a simple—albeit multistep—process:

1. Create a user account with a descriptive name such as District Managers or Sales Staff. This is just a "blank" user account that you'll use to create a template for the customized configuration.

2. Log on using the template account and create the desktop settings you want, including applications, shortcuts, appearance, network connec-tions, printers, and so forth.

3. Log off the template account. Windows 2000 creates a user profile on the system root drive in the Documents And Settings folder. Figure 9-19 shows the user account named Editors that has been created to be a template.

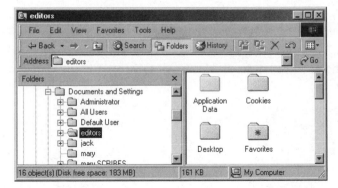

Figure 9-19. *Creating a template for configuring profiles.*

4. Log on using an administrator account. Open Active Directory Users and Computers, and find the account for which you want to assign the customized roaming profile.

5. Right-click the account and choose Properties. Click the Profile tab.

6. In the Profile Path box, enter *server_name\profile_folder\username*. (Figure 9-20 shows an example.) Click OK.

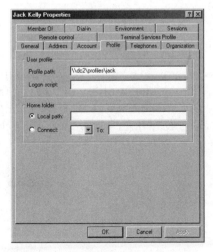

Figure 9-20. *Providing a path to the roaming profiles folder.*

7. In Control Panel, open System.

8. Click the User Profiles tab, and highlight the template profile. Click the Copy To button.

9. In the Copy To dialog box, enter the path of the profiles folder on the server, such as *server_name**shared_folder_name**username*.

10. In the Permitted To Use area, click the Change button to give the user permission to use the profile (Figure 9-21). Click OK to copy the template profile.

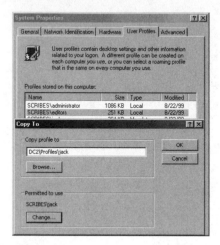

Figure 9-21. *Copying a template profile to a user's profile folder.*

Using Mandatory Profiles

If you're going to all the trouble of assigning customized profiles, you'll undoubtedly want to make the profiles mandatory. A mandatory profile can be assigned to multiple users. When you make a change to a mandatory profile, the change is made to the environments of all of the users to whom you've assigned the mandatory profile. To change a profile into a mandatory profile, you must rename the hidden file Ntuser.dat to Ntuser.man.

Note If you don't see the Ntuser file in the individual's profiles folder, choose Folder Options from the Tools menu and click the View tab. In Advanced Settings, select Show Hidden Files And Folders.

Assigning a Logon Script to a User Profile

Logon scripts can be assigned by profile or through Group Policy. (Group Policy is covered later in this chapter.) To assign a script to a profile, follow these steps:

1. Open Active Directory Users and Computers from the Administrative Tools menu.

2. In the console tree, click Users. Right-click the user account and choose Properties.

3. Click the Profile tab and enter the name of the logon script in the Logon Script box.

4. Click OK when you're finished.

Windows 2000 always looks for logon scripts in the same place—on the authenticating domain controller at the path %SystemRoot%\SYSVOL*sysvol**domain_name*\scripts. Scripts in this folder can be entered in the Logon Script path by name only, as shown in Figure 9-22. If you use folders inside the Scripts folder, you must show that part of the path in the Logon Script path (Figure 9-23). Table 9-7 shows the special variables that can be used when creating logon scripts. Logon scripts can also be created in VBScript and JScript. Replication of logon scripts to all domain controllers is automatic on NTFS volumes on Windows 2000 servers. Other types of files, such as FAT files, must be replicated manually.

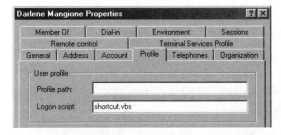

Figure 9-22. *A logon script that's located inside the Scripts folder.*

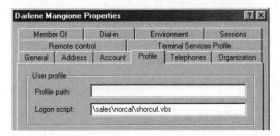

Figure 9-23. *A logon script in subfolders inside the Scripts folder.*

Table 9-7. Logon script variables

Variable	Description
%homedrive%	Letter of the drive containing the user's home directory on the user's local workstation
%homepath%	Full path of the user's home directory
%os%	User's operating system
%processor_architecture%	Processor type on the user's workstation
%processor_level%	Processor level of the user's workstation
%userdomain%	Domain where the user's account is defined
%username%	Account user name

Configuring Shares and Permissions

As has been mentioned before, the whole point of a network is to share resources among the users. However, sharing is also an extension of the security features that begin with user accounts and passwords. Your goal as a system administrator is to make sure that everyone can use the resources they need without compromising the security of files and other resources. Three types of capabilities can be given to users:

- **Rights** Assigned to built-in groups but the administrator can extend rights to groups or individuals. (Rights are covered earlier in this chapter.)

- **Shares** Directories or drives that are shared on the network.

- **Permissions** File system capabilities that can be granted to individuals or to groups.

In the normal course of events, you'll deal with rights only rarely. However, shares and permissions are at the heart of an administrator's responsibilities.

On an NTFS volume, Windows 2000, like Windows NT Server, allows security that's so granular it's practically microscopic. Permissions of various types can be set, including permissions on individual files. This presents quite a temptation to the administrator to micro-manage every resource. Our best advice is to not give in to this temptation. Start with the least restriction possible and add restrictions only when required.

Real World **Differences Between Shares and Permissions**

Shares and permissions, although they sound very much alike, are not at all the same and it's important to understand the differences. Shares apply to drives and directories. Until a drive or folder is shared over the network, users can't see it or gain access to it. Once a folder is shared, everyone on the network has, by default, access to all files in the folder, and to all subfolders of that folder and so on.

On a FAT volume, a drive or folder can be shared and then additional restrictions added in the form of share permissions. These permissions apply only at the drive or folder level—not at the file level—and are limited to allowing or denying Full Control, Read, and Change.

On NTFS volumes, directories have the same share permissions as those on a FAT volume, but another layer of permission is available beyond that. Each folder has a Security Property window that allows more precise restrictions. Each file also has a Security Properties window, allowing access to be granted or denied for individual files. These *folder permissions* and *file permissions* can restrict access both across the network *and* locally. For example, you can leave the share permission for a folder at the default setting, allowing Full Control to Everyone, and use the Security Properties windows to set more restrictive permissions by group or individual—whether for the folder as a whole or file-by-file within the folder.

Share permissions determine the maximum access over the network. This means if you set share permissions to allow Read but deny Change, all users will be restricted to Read only when they access the share over the network. You can, however, grant a user more extensive access through folder or file permissions, and this expanded access will be available when the user logs on *locally*. Or you can block the inheritance of permissions on a subfolder and give a user Full Control of the subfolder over the network—while the parent folder remains Read only.

Shares have no effect on users who can log on locally. For users who will be logging on locally to an NTFS partition, access can be restricted by using permissions.

Using Special Shares

In addition to shares created by a user or administrator, the system creates a number of special shares that shouldn't be modified or deleted. The special share you're most likely to see is the ADMIN$ share which appears as C$, D$, E$, and so on. These shares allow administrators to connect to drives that are otherwise not shared.

Special shares exist as part of the operating system's installation. Depending on the computer's configuration, some or all of the following special shares may be present. None of them should be modified or deleted.

- **ADMIN$** Used during the remote administration of a computer. The path is always the location of the folder in which Windows was installed (that is, the system root). Only Administrators, Backup Operators, and Server Operators can connect to this share.
- *driveletter*$ The root folder of the named drive. Only Administrators, Backup Operators, and Server Operators can connect to these shares on a Windows 2000 server. On a Windows 2000 Professional computer, only Administrators and Backup Operators can connect to these shares.
- **IPC$** Used during remote administration and when viewing shared resources. This share is essential to communication and you do not want to change, modify, or delete it.
- **NETLOGON** Used by the Net Logon service of a server running Windows NT Server while processing domain logons. This resource is provided for servers only, not for Windows NT Workstation.
- **PRINT$** A resource that supports shared printers.
- **REPL$** Created on a server when a fax client is sending a fax.

To connect to an unshared drive on another computer, use the address bar in any window and enter the address (Figure 9-24), using the syntax

```
\\computer_name\[driveletter]$
```

Figure 9-24. *Connecting to an unshared drive on a remote computer.*

To connect to the system root folder (the folder in which Windows is installed) on another computer, use the syntax

`\\`**`computer_name`**`\`admin$

Other special shares such as IPC$ and PRINT$ are created and used solely by the system. NETLOGON is a special share on Windows 2000 and Windows NT servers and is used while processing domain logon requests.

Shares and Permissions on NTFS vs. FAT

On partitions formatted using FAT, you can restrict files only at the folder level, only over the network, and only if the folder is shared. For someone who logs on locally, the shares have no effect.

On an NTFS volume, directories can be shared and also restricted further by means of permissions. On an NTFS volume, you should use folder and file permissions for security control both locally and over the network and allow Full Control access to Everyone on the share.

Sharing a Folder

The easiest way to create shared folders is to use the Configure Your Server tool from the Administrative Tools menu. To do so, follow these steps:

1. Open Configure Your Server and click File Server in the left column.

2. Click the link Start the Shared Folder Wizard to open the Create Shared Folder dialog box.

3. Enter the name and path of the folder and a share name (Figure 9-25).

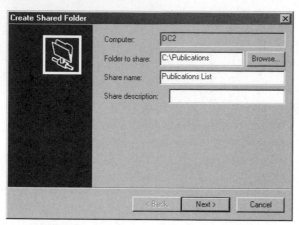

Figure 9-25. *Selecting a folder to be shared.*

4. Select the share permissions you want to assign to the folder (Figure 9-26) bearing in mind that it's almost always better to control access through permissions rather than shares. Click Finish when you're done.

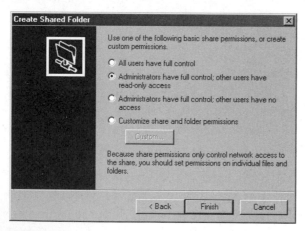

Figure 9-26. *Selecting share permissions.*

You can set shares directly by right-clicking a folder, choosing Properties from the shortcut menu, then clicking the Sharing tab.

Real World   **Share Names and File Names in MS-DOS**

If you have MS-DOS–based machines on your network (that includes Windows versions through 3.11) that will be accessing a shared folder, you must follow the 8.3 naming convention in the *share* name. A share name that doesn't conform to the MS-DOS 8.3 naming standard will not be seen at all by users with MS-DOS or Windows 3.x machines.

The names of files or directories can have up to 255 characters. MS-DOS users connecting to the file or folder over the network will see the name in the 8.3 format. Windows NT will truncate the long names down to a size that a MS-DOS machine can recognize but will not do so for share names. Yes, it's odd. Windows 2000 converts long names to short names using the following rules:

- Spaces are removed.

- Characters not allowed in MS-DOS names are replaced by underscores (_).

- The name is shortened to its first six remaining characters, and then a tilde and a digit are added. For the first file, the digit will be 1. For a second file using the same six characters, the digit will be 2. For example, your file named Budget Figures for March will be shortened to BUDGET~1. A second file, called Budget Figures for the Second Quarter, will be shortened to BUDGET~2.

- If the long name has any periods followed by other characters, the last period and the next three characters are used as the file extension in the short version of the file name. So a file called December.Sales.Presentation will be shortened to DECEMB~1.PRE.

As you can see, long file names when truncated may be quite mysterious. If your network includes MS-DOS computers, you may want to continue using MS-DOS naming conventions for the first six characters. The budget files used above as examples would then be MARBUD~Budget Figures for March.XLS and 2NDQTR~Budget Figures for the Second Quarter.XLS. To the MS-DOS computer, the files would appear as MARBUD~1.XLS and 2NDQTR~1.XLS.

Creating a New Share for a Shared Folder

A single folder might be shared more than once. For example, one share might include Full Control for Administrators and another share for users might be more restricted. To add a new share, follow these steps:

1. Find the shared folder in Windows Explorer, and right-click on it. Choose Sharing from the shortcut menu.

2. In the dialog box that opens, click the New Share button.

3. In the New Share dialog box (Figure 9-27), enter a new Share Name. (Each share must have a unique name.) Set a user limit, if necessary.

4. Click Permissions to restrict access. Again, by default, the shared folder gives Full Control to all users.

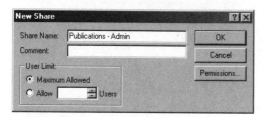

Figure 9-27. *Adding a New Share.*

Stopping Folder Sharing

To remove a folder from being shared, open Computer Management from the Administrative Tools menu. Expand System Tools, then Shared Folders, and then Shares. Right-click the shared folder in the details pane, and choose Stop Sharing from the shortcut menu.

Caution In Windows NT, when users are connected to a folder you are about to stop sharing, you are warned in a dialog box. This doesn't happen in Windows 2000. If you stop sharing a folder that users are connected to, the users are dropped out of the folder without warning and they may lose data.

Share Permissions

Share permissions establish the maximum range of access available. Other permission assignments (on an NTFS volume) can be more restrictive but can't expand beyond the limits established by the share permissions. Table 9-8 summarizes the three types of access, from most restrictive to least restrictive.

Table 9-8.   Types of share permissions

Share Permission	Type of Access
Read	Allows viewing of file and subfolder names, can always view and clear the security log.
Change	Allows the access under Read, plus allows adding files and subdirectories to the shared folder, changing data in files, and deleting files and subdirectories.
Full Control	Allows all the access under Change plus allows changing permissions (NTFS volumes only) and taking ownership (NTFS volumes only).

Setting Share Permissions

To set share permissions for a folder, right-click on the folder and choose Sharing from the shortcut menu. Click the Permissions button to open the dialog box shown in Figure 9-28. The type of access is set by the list at the bottom. Use the Add and Remove buttons to change who has access. Share permissions can be assigned to individual users, to groups, and to the special identities Everyone, System, Interactive, Network, and Authenticated Users.

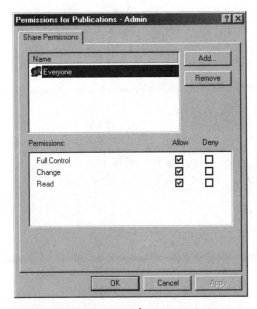

Figure 9-28. *Setting share permissions.*

Mapping Shared Directories and Drives

After traipsing through My Network Place's various windows to find a shared folder, users can simply double-click the folder to open it and access its contents. For easier access, right-click the shared folder and drag it to the desktop. Select Create Shortcut Here after releasing the mouse button.

For frequent use, it's simple to map a folder or drive so that it appears in Windows Explorer (or My Computer) as simply another local drive.

> **Note** A mapped drive is even better than a shortcut in one important respect: if you're using older programs, they're not going to recognize the network places and will not be able to open or save files anywhere other than your own computer. If you map a drive, the program cooperates because the drive on the other computer appears (to the program at least) to be local.

You can set up these connections for users or they can do it for themselves. Here's how it's done:

1. Open My Network Places and find the shared resource you want to map.

2. Right-click the object and choose Map Network Drive from the shortcut menu. The dialog box that appears (Figure 9-29) has three adjustable entries:

   - **Drive** This is the letter that the new folder or drive will be assigned on the local computer.

   - **Connect Using A Different User Name** If the mapping is for anyone other than the current user, click this link and supply the user name and password.

   - **Reconnect At Logon** Select this box to automatically make the connection at logon to the computer where this resource physically resides.

3. Click Finish when you're done.

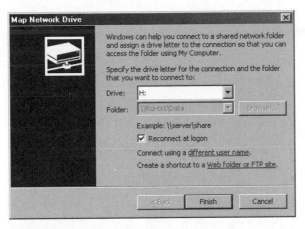

Figure 9-29. *Mapping a network resource.*

Disconnecting from Mapped Resources

To get rid of a mapped drive or folder, you can highlight it and right-click. Choose Disconnect from the shortcut menu (Figure 9-30).

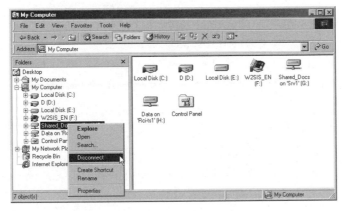

Figure 9-30. *Disconnecting a mapped resource.*

Working with Shared Folders

You can see a list of shares, current sessions, and open files by opening Computer Management from the Administrative Tools menu and then expanding Shared Folders (Figure 9-31).

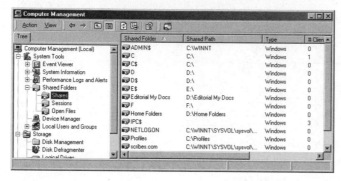

Figure 9-31. *Viewing shared folders.*

Expand Shares to see a list of the shared folders plus the following information about each folder:

- The path to the shared resource
- The type of connection (Windows, Macintosh, NetWare)
- The number of users connected to the share
- A description of the share

Expand Sessions in the console tree to see the following information about the users who are currently connected:

- The user name and the name of the user's computer
- The type of connection (Windows, Macintosh, NetWare)
- The number of files opened by the user on this share
- The time elapsed since the connection was established
- The time since the user last initiated an action
- Whether the user is connected as a guest

Expand Open Files in the console tree for a list of the files currently open. In the details pane, you can see the name of the file, who opened it, the type of connection, the number of locks on the file (if any), and the share permissions that were granted when the file was opened.

For regular viewing of shares, it may be more efficient to make an MMC that contains the Shared Folders snap-in. You can add a Shared Folders snap-in for several servers and switch among them easily (Figure 9-32).

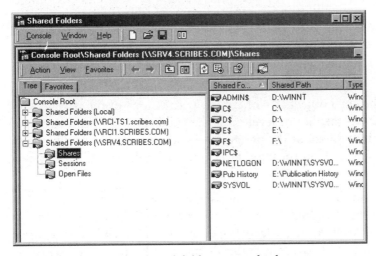

Figure 9-32. *Viewing shared folders on multiple servers.*

Maintaining Folder and File Permissions

On an NTFS volume, you can set permissions down to the file level. This means for any file you can give individual users different types of access. Although you can set such detailed permissions, this way lies madness for all but the most meticulous of control freaks (who are, arguably, already mad).

Always try to operate with the simplest possible permissions. Set as few restrictions as possible. Assign permissions to groups, not individuals. Don't set file-by-file permissions unless it is unavoidable. Managing the minutiae of permissions can easily and quickly soak up all your time and much of your life's blood as well—unless you guard against it.

Considering Inheritance

Just to complicate matters a bit more, there are two types of permissions, explicit and inherited permissions. *Explicit permissions* are the ones you set on folders that you create. *Inherited permissions* are those that flow from a parent object to a child object. By default, when you create a subfolder, it inherits the permissions of the parent folder.

If you don't want the child objects to inherit the permissions of the parent, you can block inheritance at the parent level or at the child level. Where you block inheritance is important. Block at the parent level and no subfolders will inherit permissions. Block selectively at the child level and some folders will inherit permissions and others will not.

To block inheritance at the parent level, choose This Folder Only when assigning special permissions. To block only a certain file or folder from inheriting permissions, right-click the folder, select Properties, and then click the Security tab. Clear the check box for Allow Inheritable Permissions From Parent To Propagate To This Object.

If the check boxes for permissions appear shaded (Figure 9-33), it means the permissions are inherited from a parent object. There are three ways to change this situation:

- Clear the check box for Allow Inheritable Permissions From Parent To Propagate To This Object. Once the check box is cleared, you can make changes to the permissions or change the users or groups in the list.
- Change the permissions of the parent folder.
- Select the opposite permission—Allow or Deny—to override the inherited permission.

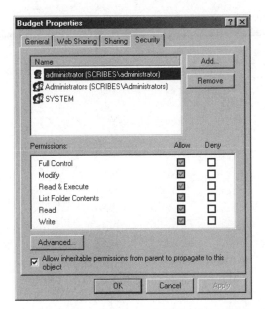

Figure 9-33. *Viewing a folder with inherited permissions.*

Note If neither Allow nor Deny is checked, the users/groups may have acquired the permission through a group membership. Otherwise, failure to explicitly configure Allow or Deny effectively denies the permission.

What the Permissions Mean

Windows 2000 Server has a set of standard permissions that are combinations of specific kinds of access. The individual permissions are Full Control, Modify, Read & Execute, List Folder Contents, Read, and Write. Table 9-9 shows the special permissions and the standard permissions to which they apply.

Table 9-9. **Special permissions for folders**

Special Permission	Full Control	Modify	Read & Execute	List Folder Contents	Read	Write
Traverse Folder/Execute File	Yes	Yes	Yes	Yes	Yes	No
List Folder/Read Data	Yes	Yes	Yes	Yes	Yes	No
Read Attributes	Yes	Yes	Yes	Yes	Yes	No
Read Extended Attributes	Yes	Yes	Yes	Yes	Yes	No
Create Files/Write Data	Yes	Yes	No	No	No	Yes
Create Folders/Append Data	Yes	Yes	No	No	No	Yes
Write Attributes	Yes	Yes	No	No	No	Yes
Write Extended Attributes	Yes	Yes	No	No	No	Yes
Delete Subfolders and Files	Yes	No	No	No	No	No
Delete	Yes	Yes	No	No	No	No
Read Permissions	Yes	Yes	Yes	Yes	Yes	Yes
Change Permissions	Yes	No	No	No	No	No
Take Ownership	Yes	No	No	No	No	No

File permissions include Full Control, Modify, Read & Execute, Read, and Write. As with folders, each of these permissions controls a group of special permissions. Table 9-10 shows the special permissions associated with each standard permission.

Table 9-10. **Special permissions associated with standard permissions**

Special Permission	Full Control	Modify	Read & Execute	Read	Write
Traverse Folder/Execute File	Yes	Yes	Yes	No	No
List Folder/Read Data	Yes	Yes	Yes	Yes	No
Read Attributes	Yes	Yes	Yes	Yes	No
Read Extended Attributes	Yes	Yes	Yes	Yes	No
Create Files/Write Data	Yes	Yes	No	No	Yes
Create Folders/Append Data	Yes	Yes	No	No	Yes
Write Attributes	Yes	Yes	No	No	Yes
Write Extended Attributes	Yes	Yes	No	No	Yes
Delete Subfolders and Files	Yes	No	No	No	No
Delete	Yes	Yes	No	No	No
Read Permissions	Yes	Yes	Yes	Yes	Yes
Change Permissions	Yes	No	No	No	No
Take Ownership	Yes	No	No	No	No

Tip Any user or group assigned Full Control on a folder can delete files and subfolders no matter what the permissions are on the individual files or subfolders.

How Permissions Work

If you take no action at all, the files and folders inside a shared folder will have the same permissions as the share. Permissions for both directories and files can be assigned to

- Domain local groups, global groups, universal groups, and individual users.
- Global groups, universal groups, and individual users from domains that this domain trusts.
- Special identities such as Everyone and Authenticated Users.

The important rules for permissions can be summarized as follows:

- By default, a folder inherits permissions from its parent folder. Files inherit their permissions from the folder in which they reside.
- Users can access a folder or file only if they've been granted permission to do so or they belong to a group that has been granted permission.
- Permissions are cumulative, but the Deny permission trumps all others. For example, if the Technical Writers group has Read access to a folder and the Project group has Modify permission for the same folder, and Alex is a member of both groups, Alex will have the higher level of permission, which is Modify. However, if the Technical Writers group permission is changed to explicitly Deny, Alex will be unable to use the folder, despite his membership—and ostensibly higher level of access— in the Project group.
- The user who creates a file or folder owns that object and can set permissions to control access.
- An administrator can take ownership of any file or folder but cannot pass ownership along to anyone else.

Configuring Folder Permissions

Before sharing a folder on an NTFS volume, set all the permissions on the folder. When you set folder permissions, you're also setting permissions on all the files and subfolders in the folder.

To assign permissions to a folder, right-click the folder in Explorer and choose Properties. Then click the Security tab and select Permissions.

To remove an individual or group from the list, just highlight the name and click Remove.

To add to the list of those with permissions, click the Add button. This opens the Select Users, Computers, Or Groups dialog box (Figure 9-34).

Click OK when you're done and the Folder Permissions box opens with the new names.

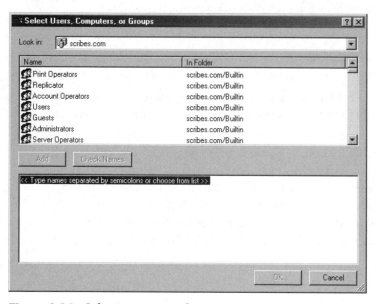

Figure 9-34. *Selecting users and groups.*

Assigning Permissions to Files

Permissions for individual files are assigned in the same way as folders. There are, however, some special considerations:

- Remember to grant permissions to groups, rather than individuals.
- Create groups and assign file permissions to them rather than assign permissions directly to local groups.

Configuring Special Permissions

In some circumstances, you may find it necessary to set, change, or remove special permissions on either a file or folder. (Special permissions on a folder affect only the folder). To access special permissions, follow these steps:

1. In Explorer, right-click the file or folder and choose Properties from the shortcut menu.
2. Click the Security tab, and then click the Advanced button.
   - To add a user or group, click the Add button. Double-click the user or group name to open the Permission Entry dialog box.
   - To view or modify existing special permissions, highlight the name of the user or group and click the View/Edit button.
   - To remove special permissions, highlight the name of the user or group and click Remove. If the Remove button is dimmed, clear the check box for Allow Inheritable Permissions From Parent To Propagate To This Object, and skip to step 6.
3. In the Permission Entry dialog box (Figure 9-35), select where you want the permissions applied in the Apply Onto box. (See Table 9-11 and Table 9-12 for explanations of the choices in this drop-down box.) Apply Onto is available for folders only.
4. In Permissions, click Allow or Deny for each permission.

5. To prevent subfolders and files from inheriting these permissions, select Apply These Permissions To Objects And/Or Containers Within This Container Only.

6. Click OK to close the dialog boxes.

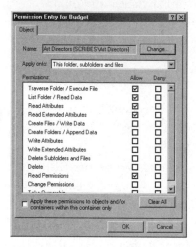

Figure 9-35. *Setting special permissions for a folder.*

In the Permission Entry dialog box for folders, you can choose how and where the special permissions are applied. Tables 9-11 and 9-12 demonstrate the application of the special permissions depending on whether Apply These Permissions To Objects And/Or Containers Within This Container Only is selected.

Table 9-11. Application of special permissions when Apply These Permissions To Objects And/Or Containers Within This Container Only is selected

Selected in Apply Onto	Applies to current folder?	Applies to subfolders in current folder?	Applies to files in current folder?	Applies to subsequent subfolders?	Applies to files in subsequent subfolders?
This folder only	Yes	No	No	No	No
This folder, subfolders, and files	Yes	Yes	Yes	No	No
This folder and subfolders	Yes	Yes	No	No	No
This folder and files	Yes	No	Yes	No	No
Subfolders and files only	No	Yes	Yes	No	No
Subfolders only	No	Yes	No	No	No
Files only	No	No	Yes	No	No

Table 9-12. Application of special permissions when Apply These Permissions To Objects And/Or Containers Within This Container Only is not selected

Selected in Apply Onto	Applies to current folder?	Applies to subfolders in current folder?	Applies to files in current folder?	Applies to subsequent subfolders?	Applies to files in subsequent subfolders?
This folder only	Yes	No	No	No	No
This folder, subfolders, and files	Yes	Yes	Yes	Yes	Yes
This folder and subfolders	Yes	Yes	No	Yes	No
This folder and files	Yes	No	Yes	No	Yes
Subfolders and files only	No	Yes	Yes	Yes	Yes
Subfolders only	No	Yes	No	Yes	No
Files only	No	No	Yes	No	Yes

Ownership and How It Works

As you've seen, Administrators and members of a few other select groups are the only ones who can grant and change permissions. The exception is when a user is the owner of the folder or file in question. Every object on an NTFS partition has an owner and the owner is the person who created the file or folder. The owner controls access to the file or folder and can keep out anyone he or she chooses.

Figure 9-36 shows an example of a folder called Max's Private Stuff made by the user Maxwell (Figure 9-36).

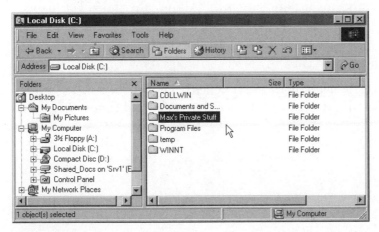

Figure 9-36. *A user's new folder.*

To see who has permission to access his new folder, Maxwell right-clicks the folder and chooses Properties and then clicks Security. When he clicks the Permissions button, the dialog box shown in Figure 9-37 opens.

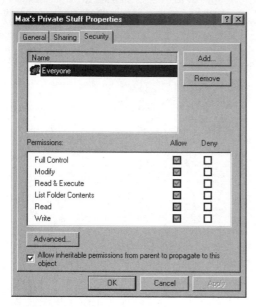

Figure 9-37. *Viewing the permissions for a new folder.*

Much to his surprise, it appears that everyone on the network has access to his "private" stuff. But since Maxwell is the owner of the folder, he can change the permissions so that he has the folder all to himself. To do so, he explicitly adds his name to the permissions list and clears the Allow Inheritable Permissions option.

After this is done, even the administrator will see an Access Denied message when trying to open the folder.

Of course, nothing on the network can be completely beyond the reach of administrators, so the administrator can right-click the folder and choose Properties from the shortcut menu. When he or she clicks the Security tab, the information box shown in Figure 9-38 opens.

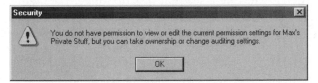

Figure 9-38. *The administrator tries to view permissions for a folder owned by a user.*

In the Security Properties window, no changes can be made. However, if the administrator clicks the Advanced button and then the Owner tab (Figure 9-39), he or she can change the owner of the folder to an administrator.

Figure 9-39. *Changing the ownership of a folder.*

No matter what the status of the folder, the administrator can take ownership. When Maxwell logs on the next time, he'll still have access to Max's Private Stuff, but if he clicks Advanced and then Owner, he'll see that he's no longer the owner of the folder. Thus, even though administrators can go into all areas without an invitation, they can't do so without leaving evidence of their presence.

Note The owner of a file or folder can also grant the Take Ownership special permission to others, allowing those users to take ownership at any time.

Understanding Group Policies

For many small to medium-sized networks, the groups built into Windows 2000 Server can, with perhaps a little tweaking, provide perfectly adequate security. In larger settings and settings with special needs, however, the security settings may be too strict for some groups and too lax for others. For these situations, group policies can give administrators a degree of control that is as granular as one could wish for. In addition, group policies can reduce the amount of lost productivity when users accidentally delete system configuration files, "lose" vital folders, or introduce a virus to the network.

Group Policy is the successor to the System Policy Editor in Windows NT. There is, however, one important difference: you can make group policies without having a Ph.D. in computer mysteries. They can be complex and extremely detailed, but they do work. Group policies can control all aspects of the environment, both large and small, and they are usually set at the site and domain level. With the Group Policy snap-in, you can specify settings for registry-based policy settings, security settings, software installation, scripts, and folder redirection.

Third parties can extend Group Policy to host other policy settings. All of the data generated by Group Policy is stored in a Group Policy object (GPO), which is replicated in all domain controllers within a single domain.

Real World   Windows NT 4 Policies and Windows 2000

System policies set in Windows NT 4 do not migrate to Windows 2000. A Windows NT client upgraded to Windows 2000 will have only Active Directory–based group policies; no Windows NT 4 policies will survive the upgrade. The primary difference between Windows NT system policies and Windows 2000 group policies lies in where the policies are written. Windows 2000 uses only the following four trees of the registry:

HKEY_LOCAL_MACHINE\Software\Policies

HKEY_CURRENT_USER\Software\Policies

HKEY_LOCAL_MACHINE\Software\Microsoft\Windows\CurrentVersion\Policies

HKEY_CURRENT_USER\Software\Microsoft\Windows\CurrentVersion\Policies

The first two are preferred. When a group policy changes, these trees are essentially deleted and their contents rewritten. Although none of the templates that come with Windows 2000 include values that write to other places in the registry, it is possible to do so. (Windows NT 4 policies can write to any part of the registry.) However, it is inadvisable to employ Windows NT–style policies that write to other parts of the registry for the following reasons:

- Only the four trees just listed are secure. Applications, the operating system, or users can modify other parts of the registry.

- Once a policy is set in another part of the registry, it will persist until the registry is edited or the policy is specifically reversed.

- Sticking with the Active Directory Group Policy gives you considerably more control over when and how policies will change.

Windows NT 4 Workstation and Server clients do not have Active Directory, so you will have to continue to use System Policy Editor (Poledit.exe) to set policy for those clients. Group policies will not apply to them. Similarly, run Poledit.exe on Windows 95 and Windows 98 clients and copy the resulting Config.pol file to the SYSVOL folder of the Windows 2000 domain controller.

Components of Group Policy

Group Policy consists of several configurable components. The first is administrative templates, which set registry-based policy. Five administrative templates are included with Windows 2000. Two of these are installed by default:

- **System.adm** System policies for Windows 2000 clients
- **Inetres.adm** Internet Explorer policies for Windows 2000 clients

These templates use the four areas in the registry reserved for Group Policy settings. Three additional administrative templates (Common.adm, Windows.adm, and Winnt.adm) are for setting policy for Windows NT, Windows 95, and Windows 98 clients. They are used with the System Policy Editor (Poledit.exe) on the clients themselves and should not be loaded into Group Policy.

The other components of Group Policy are as follows:

- **Security Settings** Configures security for users, computers, and domains
- **Scripts** Specifies scripts for computer startup and shutdown as well as for user logon and logoff
- **Folder Redirection** Places special folders such as My Documents or specified application folders on the network
- **Software** Assigns applications to users (See Chapter 24 for more on publishing software on the network.)

All components of Group Policy can be edited using the Group Policy Editor.

Group Policy Objects

Group Policy settings are stored in a Group Policy object (GPO). One or more GPOs can apply to a site, domain, or OU (SDOU), just as multiple SDOUs can be associated with a single GPO. GPOs store information in two locations: in a folder structure called a Group Policy template (GPT) and in a Group Policy container (GPC) in Active Directory.

The GPT can be found in the SYSVOL folder of all domain controllers. It contains information about software policy, file and application deployments, scripts, and security settings. A GPC contains GPO properties, including the Active Directory class information related to application deployment. The information stored in a GPC changes infrequently.

Note   A GPO that applies locally will be stored in the local computer's %SystemRoot%\system32\grouppolicy folder. A computer can have only one local group policy.

Group Policy Templates   When you create a GPO, the corresponding GPT folder structure is created automatically. The actual name of the folder for the GPT will be the globally unique identifier (GUID) for the GPO—a number that is useful to the computer but otherwise incomprehensible. However, to see the policy folder, look in %SystemRoot%\SYSVOL*sysvol**domain_name*\policies.

Group Policy Containers   Nonlocal Group Policy objects will also have an Active Directory component called a GPC that includes subcontainers with version information, status information, and a list of which Group Policy extensions are employed in the GPO. GPCs have no direct relevance to administration.

Access to Group Policy

Group policies are created and modified in a number of different ways, depending on the type of group policy you want to implement. Table 9-13 describes how to apply Group Policy in various ways.

Table 9-13.   Applying Group Policy

To Apply Group Policy To	Follow These Steps
The local computer	For security policy only, select Local Security Policy from the Administrative Tools menu. On a Windows 2000 Professional machine, open Control Panel, click Administrative Tools, and select Local Security Policy.
Another computer	Open MMC* and add the Group Policy snap-in. In the Select Group Policy Object dialog box, browse to find the Group Policy object you want.
A domain	Open Active Directory Users and Computers. In the console tree, right-click the domain and choose Properties from the shortcut menu. Click the Group Policy tab.
An organizational unit	Open Active Directory Users and Computers. In the console tree, right-click the OU and choose Properties from the shortcut menu. Click the Group Policy tab.
A site	Open Active Directory Sites and Services. In the console tree, right-click the site and choose Group Policy from the shortcut menu. Click the Group Policy tab.

*Details about using the Microsoft Management Console (MMC) can be found in Chapter 10.

Managing Group Policies

Group policies are inherited and cumulative. When you associate a GPO with an Active Directory container, the group policy is applied to all computer and user accounts in the container.

> **Note** The Users and Computers folders in Active Directory Users and Computers are not organizational units and therefore cannot have group policies applied to them. The Domain Controllers folder is, however, an OU and can have a specific GPO.

Order of Inheritance

As a rule, Group Policy settings are passed from parent containers down to child containers. This practice means that a policy that is applied to a parent container will apply to all of the containers—including users and computers—that are below the parent container in the Active Directory tree hierarchy. However, if you specifically assign a group policy for a child container that contradicts the parent container policy, the child container's policy will override the parent group policy.

If policies are not contradictory, both can be implemented. For example, if a parent container policy calls for an application shortcut to be on a user's desktop, while the child container policy calls for another application shortcut, both will appear. Policy settings that are disabled are inherited as disabled. Policy settings that are not configured in the parent container are not inherited.

Overriding Inheritance

Two options are available in Windows 2000 for changing how inheritance is processed. One option is No Override. When this option is set, child containers cannot override any GPO set in a higher level. This option is not set by default and must be turned on in each GPO where it's desired. To set the No Override option, follow these steps:

1. Open the GPO you want to administer. (Refer back to Table 9-13.)
2. Right-click the GPO and choose No Override from the shortcut menu (Figure 9-40). A check mark appears next to the GPO under No Override.
3. Click OK.

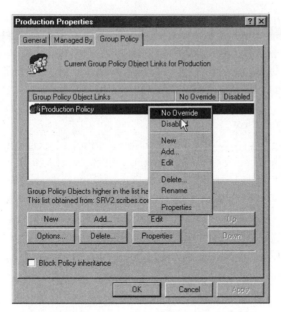

Figure 9-40. *Preventing an override to the GPO's inheritance policy.*

A second option is Block Policy Inheritance. This option is available in a check box in the GPO's Properties window. (The check box can be seen in Figure 9-40.) When you select this option, the child container will not inherit any policies from parent containers. If there is a conflict between these two options, the No Override option always takes precedence.

Order of Implementation

Group policies are processed in the following order:

- Windows NT 4 system policy (if any)
- Local group policy
- Site
- Domain
- Organizational unit
- Child OU

As you can see, local policy is processed first, and the OU of which the user or computer is a member is processed last. There are two exceptions to this. The Block Policy Inheritance option can be set for an SDOU, meaning that policy from above will not be applied. However, an SDOU group policy set to No Override is *always* applied, with the highest policy in the tree taking precedence.

Implementation and Effective Policy

Because policy can be set at several levels, when you click on a policy object, you'll see both local policy and the policy in effect on the system. These may not be the same if the computer is inheriting settings from domain-level policies. If you make a policy setting and it isn't reflected in effective policy, it's likely that a policy from the domain is overriding your setting.

It's also possible that the policy change hasn't been refreshed since you made the change. To force a policy refresh for the local computer, open a command window and type in:

```
secedit /refreshpolicy machine_policy
```

To change the interval between automatic updates, see "Refreshing Group Policy" on page 313.

Setting the Scope of the GPO

A Group Policy object applies to all of the users and computers in the SDOU with which the GPO is associated. Inevitably, there will be users and computers in the SDOU that should not have a particular GPO applied. In addition, policies for a particular GPO apply only to users who have Read permission for that GPO. To filter the application of a GPO, you can create security groups and assign Read permission only to the groups to which the GPO applies.

Filtering the scope of a GPO involves using the Access Control List (ACL) Editor to allow or deny access to the GPO for particular groups. To set access, follow these steps:

1. Open the GPO you want to administer. (Refer back to Table 9-13.)

2. On the Group Policy tab, highlight the GPO and click Properties.

3. Click the Security tab. At the bottom of the Security tab, click the Advanced button to open the ACL Editor (Figure 9-41).

4. Add or remove groups, or edit the settings. Click OK several times when you're done to close all of the open windows.

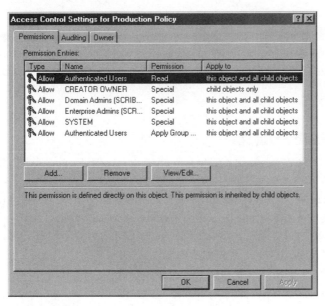

Figure 9-41. *Setting the scope of a GPO.*

Table 9-14 shows the settings to use to have a GPO apply or not apply to a security group. The location of the security group doesn't matter when making the settings. What matters is the location of the users or computers who are members of the security group. If a user or computer is not a member of the SDOU that the GPO is associated with (either directly, through a link, or by inheritance), no combination of permissions or membership in a security group can force the GPO to apply to that user or computer.

Table 9-14. Setting policies for security groups

Intended Result	Permissions Needed	Outcome
This group policy will be applied to the members of this group.	Apply Group Policy: Allow Read: Allow	Group policy will be applied to all members except members who belong to another group with Apply Group Policy or Read set to Deny.
This group policy will not be applied to members of this group.	Apply Group Policy: Deny Read: Deny	Group policy will not be applied to any members of this group, no matter what other groups they belong to.
Membership in this group should not be a relevant factor in whether this group policy is applied.	Apply Group Policy: No setting Read: No setting	Application of this group policy to members of this group will depend on whether members belong to other security groups with Allow or Deny settings.

> **Tip** Bear in mind that just because something can be done doesn't mean that it should be done. Proceed carefully when it comes to setting permissions. Users who are in favor of security in the abstract become annoyed when they receive unnecessary "access denied" messages. Apply restrictions cautiously and only after you're sure you understand the implications of a particular policy, especially in the area of inheritability.

Creating a Group Policy Object

When you create an Active Directory domain, a default domain policy is also created. You can see it by right-clicking the domain in Active Directory Users and Computers, choosing Properties, and clicking the Group Policy tab. With some judicious adjustments to meet the needs of your own situation, you might never need anything else. Nevertheless, the time may come when you need to set up a GPO of your own. To do so, follow these steps:

1. Open Active Directory Users and Computers (for domain or OU GPOs) or Active Directory Sites and Services (for site GPOs).

2. Right-click the object for which you want to create a GPO, and choose Properties from the shortcut menu.

3. Click the Group Policy tab, and then click the New button.

4. Type in a name for the new GPO, and choose one of the following buttons:
   * **Add** To add a link to the new policy.
   * **Edit** To open the new GPO in the Group Policy Editor.
   * **Options** To set No Override or to disable the GPO.
   * **Delete** To remove the GPO permanently or remove it from the list. If you choose Remove The Link From The List, the GPO remains in Active Directory but is no longer applied to the particular SDOU.
   * **Properties** To set filtering for the GPO through security groups.

5. Click OK when you're finished.

Using the Group Policy Editor

You can edit Group Policy settings by accessing a GPO through the methods described in Table 9-13. For frequently accessed GPOs, create a Microsoft Management Console (MMC) that includes the Group Policy snap-in, and then save the console in a convenient location so that you can open it quickly when you need it. For example, to make an MMC that is focused on the default domain policy, follow these steps:

1. Click the Start button and choose Run.

2. Type in *mmc* and click OK.

3. From the Console menu, choose Add/Remove Snap-in.

4. Click the Add button and select Group Policy from the list of available snap-ins.

5. Click Add. This opens the Select Group Policy Object dialog box. Click the Browse button.

6. In the Browse For A Group Policy Object dialog box (Figure 9-42), select Default Domain Policy, and click OK.

7. Click Finish in the Select Group Policy Object dialog box. Close the open dialog boxes.

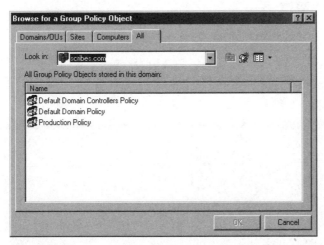

Figure 9-42. *Finding an existing Group Policy object.*

Inside the Group Policy Editor

If you click Default Domain Policy in the Group Policy console tree, you'll see that the Group Policy Editor (GPE) displays two nodes: Computer Configuration and User Configuration. When you click these nodes, you'll find that each displays extensions for Software Settings, Windows Settings, and Administrative Templates.

Use the Computer Configuration folders to customize policies for computers on the network. These policies go into effect when the computer is turned on and the operating system starts. Settings in these folders apply to any user who logs on to the computer. For example, if you have machines in a training room for which you want to enforce a strict environment, the Computer Configuration node is where you'd make those settings.

The User Configuration node contains settings for customizing environments or setting policies for users on the network. User Configuration policies come into play when a specific user logs on to the network.

Disabling a Branch of a GPO   If a GPO has an entire node under User Configuration or Computer Configuration that is not configured, disable the node to avoid processing those settings. This speeds startup and logon for all users subject to that GPO. To disable a node, follow these steps:

1. Right-click Group Policy Object, either in a console or in the Group Policy Properties window.

2. Choose Properties from the shortcut menu.

3. On the General tab, select the option to disable the User Configuration or Computer Configuration settings for this GPO (Figure 9-43).

4. Click OK when you're finished. The disabled settings will no longer affect any SDOU linked to this GPO.

Figure 9-43. *Disabling unused parts of a GPO.*

Finding Group Policy Links

With numerous GPOs on a network, it's important to keep track of links between GPOs and SDOUs. To find out what SDOU uses a particular GPO, right-click Group Policy Object, either in a console or in the Group Policy Properties window. Choose Properties and then click the Links tab. Click the Find Now button, and a list of SDOUs that use the Group Policy object is returned.

Refreshing Group Policy

Policy changes are immediate, but they are not propagated to clients automatically. Client computers request policy when

- The computer starts
- A user logs on
- An application requests a refresh
- A user requests a refresh
- A Group Policy refresh interval is enabled and the interval has elapsed

To set a Group Policy refresh interval, follow these steps:

1. Open the GPO.
2. In the console tree, select Computer Configuration, then Administrative Templates, System, and finally Group Policy.
3. In the details pane, double-click Group Policy Refresh Interval For Computers.
4. Enable the refresh interval. Click OK.

Don't make the interval very short because of the large amount of network traffic generated by each refresh. The refresh interval for domain controllers is set separately.

Using Group Policy for Folder Redirection

Folder Redirection is an extension to Group Policy that allows you to place designated folders on the network. In particular, you may want to redirect users' My Documents folders or other folders that may become quite large over time. With redirected folders the following conditions apply:

- A user can log on to different computers and still have the folders available.

- When employing roaming profiles, only the network path to the redirected folders is part of the profile, not the folders themselves. This makes logging on and off much faster.

- Folders on a network server can be backed up as part of routine maintenance with no action on the part of the user.

Folders can be redirected to one location for everyone in the SDOU affected by the Group Policy object. They can also be redirected to different locations according to security group membership.

Redirecting to One Location

By far the most common form of redirection is to send everyone's My Documents folder to a single location on a network server. The following steps show how to do this. You can substitute other Windows special folders in the steps to redirect them as well.

1. Create a shared folder on the server.
2. Open the Group Policy object linked to the SDOU containing the users whose folders are to be redirected.
3. In the console tree, click User Configuration, then Windows Settings, and finally Folder Redirection (Figure 9-44).

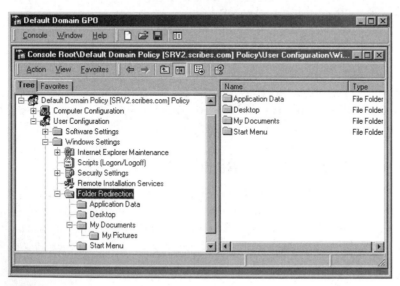

Figure 9-44. *Locating the Folder Redirection node in the GPO.*

4. Right-click My Documents and choose Properties from the shortcut menu.

5. In the drop-down list, select Basic - Redirect Everyone's Folder To The Same Location. Enter the path for the shared folder on the server. Use a UNC path with the %username% variable, as shown in Figure 9-45.

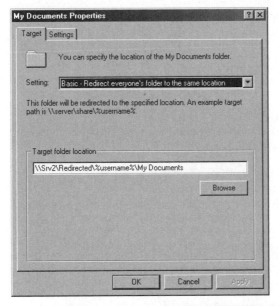

Figure 9-45. *Setting a path for the redirection of My Documents folders.*

6. Click the Settings tab. The following settings are enabled by default:

- **Grant The User Exclusive Rights To My Documents**   The user and the local system have exclusive rights to the folder. No administrative rights are enabled. If this setting is disabled, the permissions that exist on the folder in its present position will remain.

- **Move The Contents Of My Documents To The New Location**

- **Policy Removal**   The default is to leave the folder in the new location when the policy is removed. If you choose to redirect the folder back to the local user, see the section "Removing Redirection," later in this chapter.

- **My Pictures Preference**   My Pictures will follow My Documents as a subfolder.

7. Click OK when you're finished.

Redirecting by Group Membership

Special folders can also be redirected to various locations based on the user's membership in security groups. To do so, follow these steps:

1. Create the shared folders at the locations to which the folders will be redirected.

2. Open the Group Policy object linked to the SDOU containing the users whose folders are to be redirected.

3. In the console tree, click User Configuration, then Windows Settings, and finally Folder Redirection.

4. Right-click the special folder (in this case My Documents), and choose Properties from the shortcut menu.

5. In the drop-down list, select Advanced - Specific Locations For Various User Groups, and then click the Add button.

6. In the Specify Group And Location box, enter the security group and the location for the redirected folders (Figure 9-46). Always use a UNC path, even if the folders are to be on the local computer, so that roaming users will be able to see their folders.

Figure 9-46. *Setting folder redirection for an entire group.*

7. Click OK. Add more groups and locations as needed.

8. Click the Settings tab. The following settings are enabled by default:

   - **Grant The User Exclusive Rights To My Documents** The user and the local system have exclusive rights to the folder. No administrative rights are enabled. If this setting is disabled, the permissions that exist on the folder in its present position will remain.

- **Move The Contents Of My Documents To The New Location**
- **Policy Removal**   The default is to leave the folder in the new location when the policy is removed. If you choose to redirect the folder back to the local user, see the next section, "Removing Redirection."
- **My Pictures Preference**   My Pictures will follow My Documents as a subfolder.

9. Click OK when you're finished.

Removing Redirection

When folders have been redirected and later the policy changes, the effect on the folders depends on the combination of choices made on the Settings tab in the special folder's Properties window. Table 9-15 shows the various combinations of settings and the outcome when the policy is changed. (Software policy settings are covered in Chapter 24.)

Table 9-15.   Settings and their outcome when redirection is removed

Policy Removal Option	Move Contents Of Folder To New Location	Outcome When When Policy Is Removed
Redirect the folder back to the local user profile location when policy is removed	Enabled	The folder returns to its user profile location; the contents of the folder are copied back to the original location; the contents are not deleted from the redirected location.
Redirect the folder back to the local user profile location when policy is removed	Disabled	The folder returns to its user profile location; the contents of the folder are not moved or copied back to the original location. Warning: this means that the user cannot see the folder contents.
Leave the folder in the new location when policy is removed	Enabled or Disabled	The folder and its contents remain at the redirected location; the user has access to the contents at the redirected location.

Summary

The success of a network operation is measured by both the availability of some information and resources and the restriction and protection of others. Windows 2000 offers the network administrator the tools and functionality to meet the information needs of users, while protecting sensitive information stored on or passed through the network. This chapter has explored the options available to the administrator for configuring groups, users, group scope, permissions, and group policy through Windows 2000. Proper management of built-in and customized groups provides accessibility and security for any network—from the simplest to the most complex. The next chapter covers day-to-day administrative tasks, including using the secondary logon and Microsoft Management Console.

Part III
Network Administration

Chapter 10
Managing Day-to-Day Operations

If it's true, as Mies van der Rohe said, that "God is in the details," then a network is a very holy place indeed. A network administrator's job consists of masses of details, and if you're to cope, you must find ways of handling and tracking them. Microsoft Windows 2000 supplies plenty of tools for this, including ones that allow you to delegate tasks to other users or groups, use scripts to automate tasks, and schedule tasks to run periodically. Nevertheless, administering a network is still largely a process of planning and organization, and in that area there's no substitute for brainpower. This chapter discusses some of the tools that can help in the daily business of network management.

Using the Secondary Logon

Recommended administrative practice dictates that an administrator be logged on to a privileged account (one with administrative rights) only while doing chores that require privileges. For ordinary work, the administrator is supposed to log off from the privileged account and then log on again to an ordinary account. Of course, it's not unusual that ten minutes later a situation arises requiring use of the privileged account. So then it's necessary to log off from the ordinary account and log back on to the administrator account, with the process reversed again a few minutes later.

After a few days of this, even the most security-conscious person begins to toy with the idea of logging on to the administrator account and staying there. And in time, most administrators succumb to the temptation and stay in the privileged account most of the time.

This practice makes Microsoft Windows NT systems highly susceptible to "Trojan horse" attacks. Just running Microsoft Internet Explorer and accessing a nontrusted Web site can be very risky if done from an administrator account. A Web page with Trojan code can be downloaded to the system and executed. The execution, done in the context of administrative privileges, will be able to do considerable mischief, including such things as reformatting a hard disk, deleting all files, or creating a new user with administrative access. When you think about it, it's like handing the keys to your network to a complete (and malicious) stranger.

This problem is finally addressed in Windows 2000 with the RunAs service. This service enables you to work in a normal, nonprivileged account and still access administrative functions without logging off and then logging back on again. To set up the RunAs service, follow these steps:

1. While logged on with administrative rights, choose Services from the Administrative Tools menu.

2. In the list of services, double-click RunAs Service.

3. Verify that Startup Type is set to Automatic and that Current Status is set to Started. (If it isn't, click the Start button.) Click OK to close the dialog box.

After performing these steps, create an ordinary user account for your own use (if you don't have one already). Make sure that the user account has the right to log on locally at the machine you want to use.

Note Windows 2000 views all domain controllers as special cases. On a domain controller, for example, all management of users and groups must be done through the Active Directory Users and Computers snap-in. Also, by default, users can't log on locally to a domain controller. Chapter 9 has more on creating user accounts and granting rights.

Starting a Command-Line Window for Administration

With the RunAs service started, you can log on with your regular user account and then open a command shell for performing administrative tasks, as follows:

1. After logging on as a regular user, open a command window and enter the command *runas /user:<domain\username> cmd*. In this case, *username* is the account with administrative privileges. If you are logged on as a local user, the command is *runas /user:<machinename\username> cmd*.

2. A command-line window opens, and you're prompted for the password for the administrative account.

3. After you enter the password, a second window opens. As shown in Figure 10-1, the title bar of the window clearly indicates that it is running as the account selected.

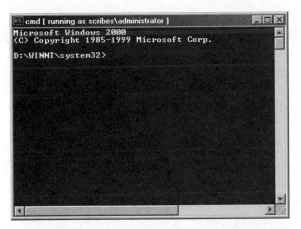

Figure 10-1. *A command-line window for an administrator account.*

You can perform any command-line tasks you want from this window. Of course, there are some administrative tasks that can't be done from the command line or that can be done only with great difficulty. Some applications, such as Control Panel and the Printers folder, are launched from the shell at the time of logon, so if you're logged on as an ordinary user, the Control Panel functions stay in that context.

To stop the shell and start it again as an administrator so that you can use functions like Control Panel, follow these steps:

1. Right-click the taskbar and choose Task Manager from the menu.

2. Click the Processes tab. Highlight Explorer.exe, and click End Process. A warning message appears. Click Yes. The entire desktop, except for Windows Task Manager and any active applications, disappears.

3. Select the Applications tab in Windows Task Manager, and then click New Task.

4. In the Create New Task box, enter *runas /user:<domain\username> explorer.exe*. As before, *username* is the account with administrative privileges. If you're logged on locally, use the command *runas /user: <machinename\username> explorer.exe*.

5. Enter the password for the user name. The desktop, along with the taskbar, returns. This desktop is in the security context of the user name you specified in the command.

To return to the ordinary user's desktop, use Task Manager again to shut down Explorer.exe. Then start a new instance by typing ***explorer.exe*** (without *runas*, so that Internet Explorer is restarted in the original security context) in the Create New Task dialog box.

Caution Don't close Task Manager while you're working in the desktop's administrative context—just minimize it to the taskbar. Closing Task Manager can produce unpredictable results and is likely to cost you more time than you can possibly save by using RunAs.

Administration Tools

Most of the tools you'll need for managing a Windows 2000 network come as part of the Windows 2000 Server and Windows 2000 Advanced Server packages, but only a few of them are automatically installed along with the operating system. Table 10-1 gives the complete list of Administration Tools.

Table 10-1. Administration Tools for Windows 2000

Tool Name	Description
Active Directory Domains and Trusts	Administers domain trusts, changes the domain mode, adds and changes user principal name suffixes
Active Directory Sites and Services	Establishes and administers sites, replication, and security services
Active Directory Users and Computers	Manages users, computers, and groups within a domain
Certification Authority	Manages Certificate Services, which issues certificates for public key security
Cluster Administrator (Advanced Server only)	Handles the configuration of clusters and nodes
Component Services	Configures and administers Component Object Model (COM) components and applications
Computer Management	Administers disks, shares, users, groups, and services on the local computer
Configure Your Server	Sets up and configures Windows services
Connection Manager Administration Kit	Manages and customizes local and remote connections
Data Sources	Adds, removes, and configures Open Database Connectivity (ODBC) databases and drivers
DHCP	Manages Dynamic Host Configuration Protocol (DHCP) services
Distributed file system	Manages Distributed file system (Dfs) installation, topology, and replication
DNS	Manages DNS services

Table 10-1. *continued*

Tool Name	Description
Event Viewer	Displays application, security, and system notification logs
Internet Authentication Service	Configures security and authentication for dial-in users
Internet Services Manager	Manages Internet Information Services (IIS)
Licensing	Manages client licenses
Local Security Policy	Views and configures user rights, audit policy, and other security settings for the local computer
Network Monitor	Captures frames of network data for detection and analysis of network problems
Performance	Views system performance graphs; configures performance logs and alerts
QoS (Quality of Service) Admission Control	Assigns network bandwidth by subnet
Remote Storage	Manages the storage of infrequently accessed files
Routing and Remote Access	Administers dial-up, virtual private networking, and internetwork connections
Server Extensions Administrator	Manages Front Page server extensions
Services	Starts, stops, and configures services
Telephony	Manages telephony clients and servers
Telenet Server Administration	Starts, stops, and returns information about Telnet Server
Terminal Services Client Creator	Makes floppy disks for installing Terminal Services client software
Terminal Services Configuration	Configures new connections for Terminal Services; modifies and deletes existing connections
Terminal Services Manager	Displays terminal servers in trusted domains
WINS	Administers WINS

Installing Administration Tools Locally

To install the full set of Administration Tools locally, open the i386 folder on the Windows 2000 Server or Windows 2000 Advanced Server CD-ROM, and then double-click the Adminpak.msi file. This starts the Administration Tools Setup Wizard (Figure 10-2), which will install the tools (and later remove them and reinstall them, if you wish). Click Next and the installation proceeds.

Figure 10-2. *The first screen of the Administration Tools Setup Wizard.*

Making Administration Tools Available Remotely

To make the Administration Tools available to others on your network, you can assign the tools to other computers or publish them in Active Directory. Chapter 24 covers the process of assigning and publishing to other users.

Support Tools

The Windows 2000 Support Tools are immensely valuable because they provide functionality not otherwise available in the operating system. You'll probably never use some of the tools, but a few will prove to be worth their weight in Microsoft stock options. This section discusses a few of these utilities. You can see a complete list by choosing Tools Help from the Windows 2000 Support Tools menu.

If you don't see the Support Tools on your Programs menu, you'll need to install them. To install the Windows 2000 Support Tools, insert the Windows 2000 CD-ROM. Open the Support folder and then the Tools folder. Double-click Setup.

Note The tools provided on the Windows 2000 CD-ROM are a subset of the tools you can get by purchasing the full *Microsoft Windows 2000 Server Resource Kit*. The *Resource Kit* is a separate product with its own companion CD, available from Microsoft Press.

Network Connectivity Tester

Network connections can fail in a spectacular number of ways—at any number of servers and in a variety of client configurations. Determining the source of a problem can be a daunting process. Netdiag.exe can report on an equally spectacular number of functions, running tests on the DNS server, the WINS server, Kerberos, the bindings, the WAN, trust relationships, the IP configuration, the routing table, IPX, NetWare, DHCP, the default gateway, and more. Netdiag.exe can be run on Windows NT and Windows 95/98 as well as Windows 2000, so you can use this excellent troubleshooting tool on servers and clients alike.

Windows 2000 Domain Manager

With Netdom.exe, most forms of domain management can be handled from the command line. Machine accounts can be added, removed, renamed, or moved to another domain. Netdom.exe also retrieves information about trusts and lets you establish trusts, synchronize the time, and verify secure channel passwords. The syntax for Netdom.exe is simple, but the range of possible parameters is extensive.

More Info   Command syntax and examples are available in the Support Tools Help files. To find the syntax for a specific tool, open a command window and enter *tool_name /?*.

Active Directory Replication Monitor

Rather than merely monitoring low-level replication among servers, the Active Directory Replication Monitor (Replmon.exe) reports on a wide range of Active Directory functions. It displays the site topology while reporting on the server's properties, indicating whether it is a Global Catalog server, and listing its replication partners, its replication history, and the attributes replicated.

The units of replication among domain controllers are directory partitions that must contain the most current information about objects in the domain. If a server is down or the network is disrupted, the information may not be completely up-to-date. The Replication Monitor can synchronize a monitored server with a specific replication partner to get everything back in order. It also generates status reports for servers throughout a forest for troubleshooting replication errors.

Disk Probe

Disk Probe (Dskprobe.exe) is indispensable when a critical hard disk goes bad. It is a sector editor that you can use to repair damaged partition tables, replace the master boot record, and repair or replace partition boot sectors. Even better, Disk Probe will save master boot records and partition boot sectors as files that can be used to restore the sectors if they become damaged in the future. This can be a great benefit because these data structures aren't part of the file system and are not backed up by any backup program. Table 10-2 briefly describes some of the Windows 2000 Support Tools. For a complete list, See Appendix F.

Table 10-2.   Additional Windows 2000 Support Tools

Tool	Filename	Format	Description
ADSI Edit	Adsiedit.msc	GUI	Low-level editor for Active Directory; enables adding, moving, and deleting objects within Active Directory.
Dependency Walker	Depends.exe	GUI	Scans any Win32 module and reports all dependent modules. Used to find the minimum set of files needed to load an application and to find what functions a module uses or exports.
Distributed file system Utility	Dfsutil.exe	Cmd	Queries and troubleshoots Dfs.
DNS Trouble-shooting Tool	Dnscmd.exe	Cmd	Allows you to view and modify DNS servers, zones, and resources.
Global Flags Editor	Gflags.exe	GUI	Edits global registry settings or flags in use by the kernel.
Memory Profiling Tool	Memsnap.exe	Cmd	Takes a snapshot of all of the memory resources being used by all processes and reports the information to a log file.
Registry Console Tool	Reg.exe	Cmd	Modifies the registry database from the command line. Used to query, add, delete, copy, save, and restore entries.
Remote Command Line	Remote.exe	Cmd	Runs command-line programs on remote computers using named pipes only.
Security Administration Tools	Sidwalk.exe Showaccs.exe Sidwalk.msc	Cmd/Cmd/GUI	Manage access control lists.
SNMP Query Utility	Snmputilg.exe	GUI	Graphical version of Snmputil.exe used to troubleshoot Simple Network Management Protocol (SNMP).

Microsoft Management Console Basics

The Microsoft Management Console (MMC) is a powerful addition to the system administrator's arsenal. The MMC works as a packager of system tools, enabling the system administrator to create specialized tools that can then be used to delegate specific administrative tasks to users or groups. Saved as MMC (.MSC) files, these custom tools can be sent by e-mail, shared in a network folder, or posted on the Web. With system policy settings, they can also be assigned to users, groups, or computers. The tools are flexible enough to be modified, scaled up or down, and generally shaped for any use to which you might want to put them.

To build a custom tool, you can either start with an existing console and modify it or start from scratch. In a mature network, you'll most likely use the former method, taking predefined consoles and adding or subtracting snap-ins.

Creating an MMC-Based Console with Snap-ins

Building your own tools with the MMC's standard user interface is a straightforward process. The next few sections walk you through the creation of a new console and describe how to arrange its administrative components into separate windows.

1. Click the Start button and select Run. In the Open text box, type *MMC* and then click OK. An empty MMC window opens, as shown in Figure 10-3, ready for you to add snap-ins.

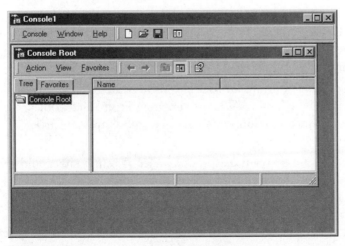

Figure 10-3. *An empty MMC window.*

2. From the Console menu, select Add/Remove Snap-in. (The menu commands on the menu bar at the top of the MMC window apply to the entire console.) The Add/Remove Snap-in dialog box opens. Here you can choose which snap-ins are in the console file as well as enable extensions. In the Snap-ins Added To box, accept the default, Console Root.

3. Click the Add button. This opens a dialog box listing the snaps-ins installed on your computer (Figure 10-4).

Figure 10-4. *The Add Standalone Snap-in dialog box.*

4. Highlight a snap-in to see a description of its function. Double-click a snap-in to add it to the console. For this example, we'll add Computer Management. The Computer Management dialog box asks you to select the computer to manage (Figure 10-5).

5. Select the Local Computer option, and select the check box Allow The Selected Computer To Be Changed When Launching From The Command Line. These options are common to many of the snap-ins. Click Finish.

6. From the Add Standalone Snap-in dialog box, select Event Viewer and click Add. As before, select the Local Computer option and select the check box. Click Finish, then close the list of available snap-ins. The Add/Remove Snap-in dialog box lists two snap-ins: Computer Management (Local) and Event Viewer (Local).

7. Click the Extensions tab. By default, the box labeled Add All Extensions is checked, which means that when this console is opened on a

particular machine, all extensions that are locally installed on that machine will be used. If this box isn't checked, only extensions that are selected on the list of available extensions will be loaded.

8. Click OK to close the Add/Remove Snap-in dialog box. The Console Root window now has two snap-ins, rooted at the Console Root folder.

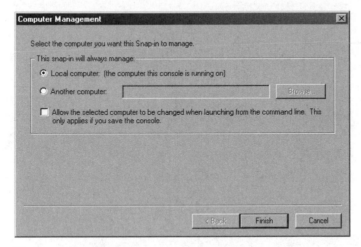

Figure 10-5. *The Computer Management dialog box.*

Save the console by choosing Save from the Console menu. You will be prompted for a name—be as descriptive as possible. The file is saved in the Administrative Tools folder by default. This folder is part of your profile, so an added benefit is that if you use roaming profiles, any tools you create will go with you. See Chapter 9 for information on creating roaming profiles.

Customizing the Layout of a Console

Once you've added the snap-ins, you can provide different administrative views in the console by adding windows. To create one window for each of the snap-ins, follow these steps:

1. In the left pane of the console window, right-click the Computer Management folder and select New Window From Here. This opens a new Computer Management window rooted at the Computer Management snap-in.

2. In the Console Root window, right-click the Event Viewer folder and select New Window From Here. Click the Show/Hide Console Tree toolbar button in each window to hide the console tree (Figure 10-6).

Figure 10-6. *The Show/Hide Console Tree Favorites button.*

3. Close the original Console Root window. From the Window menu, choose Tile Horizontally. The console window should now look like Figure 10-7.

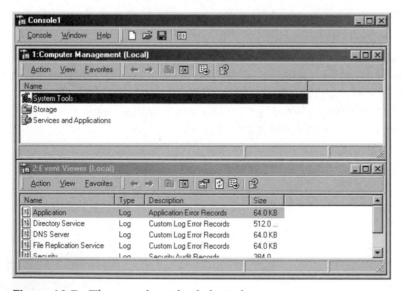

Figure 10-7. *The console with tiled windows.*

Note that the buttons and menus in each window apply only to that window. Remember to save your console file after completing the changes.

Setting Options for a Console File

When creating consoles for workgroup managers or other users, you may want to restrict how the console is used. Console options can be set so that users can access only the tools that the administrator allows. To set console file options, follow these steps:

1. With the console file open, click the Console menu and choose Options. This opens the Options dialog box.
2. Click the Console tab. Choose the console mode:
   - **Author Mode**   No restrictions. The user can access all parts of the console tree as well as change this console file at will.
   - **User Mode—Full Access**   The user can access all parts of the console tree but cannot make changes that affect functionality. Cosmetic changes, such as the arrangement of windows, are saved automatically.
   - **User Mode—Limited Access, Multiple Window**   The user can access only the parts of the console that were visible at the time the console file was saved.
   - **User Mode—Limited Access, Single Window**   The same as the previous mode, except that only one window is visible.
3. In all but Author mode, you can also select the Do Not Save Changes To This Console option, so that the console always opens in the same view.
4. Click OK and save the console file.

Modifying Console Files

After you've saved a console file in any mode other than Author mode, the Console menu is no longer visible, even to administrators. This prevents the user from changing the options. To modify a console file, open a command-prompt window and type *mmc /a*. The /a switch sets Author mode, overriding any User mode setting, and opens the console window, from which you can open any console file and make changes.

> **Note**   The system administrator can set user profiles to disallow the use of the /a switch, and should do so to ensure that inappropriate modifications can't be made.

Distributing and Using Consoles

As mentioned earlier, the default location for saved console files is the Administrative Tools folder. Console files can be distributed in a variety of ways. You can copy a console file to a shared folder on the network, or you can mail it to another person by right-clicking the file, pointing to Send To, and selecting Mail Recipient. When you assign a console to be used by a particular person, be sure that the person's user profile includes permission to access the tools and services in the console. The user will also have to have any administrative permissions necessary to use the system components administered by the console.

If you know the location of a console, you can open it from Windows Explorer by clicking it as you would any other file. You can also open it from the command line. For example, to open the Fax Service console (which resides in a system folder) from the command line, type *mmc %systemroot%\system32\faxserv.msc*.

Using MMC for Remote Administration

MMC-based tools are admirably suited for remote administration. You can easily construct a console to administer a number of computers or a single machine. This section describes how to create a console that can be used to remotely administer a domain controller. The console will include the Services snap-in, which manages system services, and the Event Viewer snap-in, which allows access to the various event logs. To make this remote administration console, follow these steps:

1. Click the Start button, and then select Run. In the Open text box, type *MMC* and then click OK. An empty MMC window opens.

2. From the Console menu, select Add/Remove Snap-in. The Add/Remove Snap-in dialog box opens.

3. Click Add to open the Add Standalone Snap-in dialog box.

4. Select Services, and then click Add.

5. In the This Snap-in Will Always Manage area, select Another Computer and then click Browse. This will open another Select Computer dialog box.

6. Highlight the computer you want this snap-in to manage, and then click OK. Click Finish.

7. Repeat steps 4 through 6, except choose the Event Viewer snap-in. Close the Add Standalone Snap-in dialog box. Click OK in the Add/Remove Snap-in dialog box.

8. At this point, the console will look like the one in Figure 10-8. Save it under a descriptive name. You can use this console to view events on the remote machine and to start and stop services.

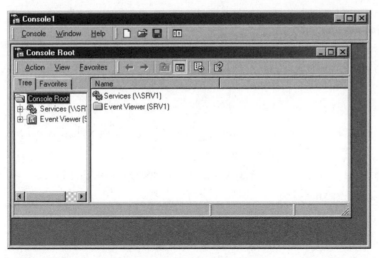

Figure 10-8. *A console for remote administration.*

As you can see, consoles can be configured in dozens, if not hundreds, of different ways and then distributed. Snap-ins for every imaginable function will increasingly be available from Microsoft as well as third-party suppliers.

> **Note**   Because consoles are excellent tools for organizing and delegating administrative chores, examples of their use can be found in many other chapters of this book.

Automating Chores with Scripts

Of necessity, most network administrators quickly acquire scripting skills. There aren't enough hours in the day to do everything manually, even if that were desirable. In addition, good scripts are like any program: once the information is entered correctly, there's no need to worry about it until something external changes.

Through ActiveX, Windows 2000 enables scripting options using Visual Basic, Scripting Edition (VBScript); JScript; or Perl. Previously, the only native scripting language supported by Windows was the MS-DOS command language, and many administrators will undoubtedly continue to use MS-DOS scripts because they're very small and very fast. Why use anything else if an MS-DOS script will do the job? The answer is that you shouldn't. However, in a large enterprise or for more complicated scripts, a more sophisticated scripting language is in order.

The Windows Scripting Host (WSH) is built into Windows 2000 and Windows 98. In addition, Windows 95 and Windows NT can run WSH, so scripts are portable across the Windows spectrum. Scripts run under WSH using Wscript.exe and Cscript.exe. Wscript.exe runs in the background, and Cscript.exe runs at the command prompt. To run a script from the command line, the syntax is

```
Cscript <scriptname.extension> [options] [arguments]
```

To view the entire list of host options, enter *Cscript //?* at a command prompt. The most important options are listed below.

- **//B**   Specifies batch mode; script errors and prompts are not displayed
- **//D**   Enables active debugging
- **//T:*nn***   Indicates the maximum time in seconds that the script is permitted to run

Real World   Uses for WSH

WSH is useful for logon and logoff scripts that can be assigned to users—individually or as a group—or to computers. The other important use for WSH is the creation of user accounts, a tedious process at best and, in a large enterprise, quite impossible without scripts. Chapter 9 covers Group Policy objects and the creation of user accounts.

Auditing Events

Auditing certain computers, users, and operating system events is a necessary part of network administration. You choose what's to be audited and then, by reviewing the event logs, track usage patterns, security problems, and network traffic trends. Beware of the impulse to audit everything, however. The more events you audit, the bigger the logs. Reviewing huge event logs is a painful chore, and eventually no one looks at them anymore. Therefore, it's critical to decide on an auditing policy that protects your network without creating a large administrative burden. Also bear in mind that every audited event results in a small increase in performance overhead.

By default, all auditing categories are turned off when Windows 2000 is installed. Table 10-3 lists the categories of events that can be audited.

Table 10-3. Auditing categories

Event Category	Description
Account logon events	Activated when a domain controller receives a logon request
Account management	Activated when a user account or group is created or changed
Directory service access	Activated when an Active Directory object is accessed
Logon events	Activated when a user logs on or logs off
Object access	Activated when an object is accessed
Policy change	Activated when a policy affecting security, user rights, or auditing is modified
Privilege use	Activated when a user right is used to perform an action
Process tracking	Activated when an application executes an action that is being tracked
System events	Activated when a computer is rebooted or shut down or another event occurs that affects security

Every audited event tells you something, but it's not always something you need to know. For example, auditing successful logons and logoffs may reveal the use of a stolen password, or it may just produce endless pages showing that your duly authorized users are logging on and off as expected. Auditing logon failures, however, will definitely be rewarding if someone is trying a random password hack.

Before you can audit access to Active Directory objects (described in the next section), you must turn on the Audit Policy setting, using Group Policy. To do so, as well as to enable auditing of any of the other categories in Table 10-3, follow these steps:

1. Choose Active Directory Users and Computers from the Administrative Tools menu.
2. Right-click the domain name in the console tree, and choose Properties from the shortcut menu.
3. Click the Group Policy tab and then the Edit button.
4. In the left pane of the Group Policy console, click your way through Computer Configuration, Windows Settings, Security Settings, and Local Policies to reach Audit Policy (Figure 10-9).

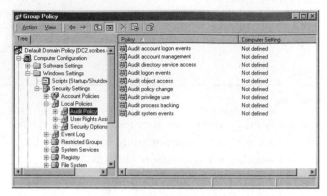

Figure 10-9. *Choosing categories of events to audit.*

5. Right-click the event category you want to audit, and choose Security.

6. In the dialog box that opens, select the check box to define the setting and select the option to audit successful and/or failed attempts.

Audit Settings for Objects

Assuming that you've turned on a policy setting for auditing an Active Directory object, you create audit settings by following these steps:

1. Right-click the object you want to audit, and choose Properties from the shortcut menu. Click the Security tab.

2. Click the Advanced button, and then click the Auditing tab (Figure 10-10).

3. Click Add to set up auditing for a new group or user. Make your selection and click OK.

4. In the Auditing Entry For Collwin dialog box (Figure 10-11), select the objects you want to audit from the Apply Onto drop-down list. Then, in the Access window, select each type of access that you want audited. (Table 10-4 describes each event.) Click OK when you're finished.

Note By default, audit settings are inherited by child objects. On the Auditing tab of the Access Control Settings For Collwin box (shown in Figure 10-10) is a check box for allowing inheritable auditing entries. Clear this box and the audit settings for this object will remain constant, even if the parent object's audit settings are changed. In addition, clearing the box will remove any audit settings that have already been inherited. The second check box on this tab resets existing auditing and allows audit entries to be inherited from the parent object once again.

Real World   Auditing Cautions

Windows 2000 allows such granularity that it's possible—no, *easy*—to create a real morass when selecting audit settings. So many items can show up in the event log that really important issues may be lost in the crowd. Be very careful when deciding what events need to be audited. Audit as few as is reasonable. You can always add events later as circumstances dictate.

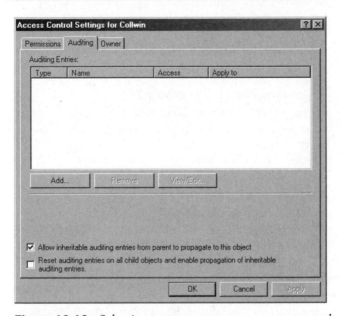

Figure 10-10. *Selecting a group or user or computer to be audited in connection with an object.*

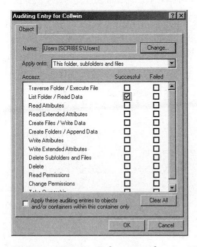

Figure 10-11. *Selecting the specific events you want audited.*

Table 10-4. File system events that can be audited

Event	Activated When
Traverse Folder/Execute File	A folder is traversed (that is, someone passes through the folder on the way to a parent folder or a child folder) or an application is run
List Folder/Read Data	A folder is opened or data is viewed in files
Read Attributes	The attributes of a file or folder are viewed
Read Extended Attributes	Extended attributes (defined and created by programs) of a file or folder are viewed
Create Files/Write Data	A file is created inside a folder or a file is changed, overwriting existing information in the file
Create Folders/Append Data	A folder is created inside the folder being audited or information is added to an existing file
Write Attributes	A file or folder attribute is changed
Write Extended Attributes	Extended attributes (defined and created by programs) of a file or folder are changed
Delete Subfolders and Files	A file or subfolder is deleted
Delete	A specific file is deleted
Read Permissions	Permissions for a file or folder are viewed
Change Permissions	Permissions for a file or folder are modified
Take Ownership	Ownership of a file or folder changes

Viewing Event Logs

Event logs must be viewed with regularity for auditing to have any effect. To view the security log, open Event Viewer from the Administrative Tools menu and then click Security Log. Double-click any entry to see more information about it. The security entries in Figure 10-12 are the result of *one* event. The folder was set to audit successful List Folder/Read Data events. One user opening the folder one time generated all the entries you see. Of course, you'll generally learn more from auditing failed events than from auditing successful ones, but this does demonstrate the need to choose one's auditing battles carefully.

Searching Event Logs

No matter how selective you are, the event logs will mix all sorts of information together, making searches for specific information difficult. To search for a specific type of event, highlight the log in Event Viewer, and choose Find from the View menu. In the Find dialog box (Figure 10-13), select the type or types of events you want returned. Table 10-5 describes the other options in the Find dialog box.

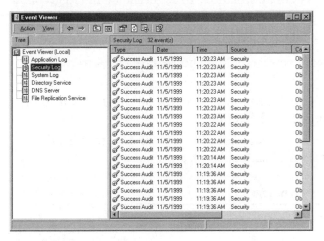

Figure 10-12. *Viewing the security log.*

Figure 10-13. *Searching for specific events in a log.*

Filtering Event Logs

If you don't have enough specific information to locate what you need, you can filter an event log for certain types of information. To use event log filtering, follow these steps:

1. Choose Event Viewer from the Administrative Tools menu.
2. Right-click the log you want to search, and choose Properties from the shortcut menu.
3. Click the Filter tab. Table 10-5 describes the fields on this tab. Click OK when you're ready to start the filtering.
4. The log appears, filtered as you requested. To view the full, unfiltered log again, return to the Filter tab and click Clear.

Table 10-5. Options for filtering event logs

Option	Use to Search or Filter For
Information	Notification that some major operation has been performed successfully.
Warning	Notification of some problem or potential problem. Warnings may or may not be significant. For example, replication performed after repeated tries will generate a warning.
Error	Notification of an important event. Errors signify a loss of data or a loss of function. For example, failure of a service to start during boot up will generate an error.
Success Audit	Events audited for success.
Failure Audit	Events audited for failure.
Event Source	A source for an event, such as a system component or a program.
Category	Events by category, such as logon/logoff, policy change, or process tracking.
Event ID	The specific ID number assigned to each logged event.
User	A specific user.
Computer	A specific computer.
From	Events after a specific date. The default is the first date in the log. You can click the drop-down box to select events on a specific date.
To	Events before a specific date. The default is the last date in the file.

Setting the Size of Event Logs

When an event log is full, a dialog box will pop up to notify you. If this happens often, you may want to reduce the number of items being reported or increase the size of the log. To set event log options, follow these steps:

1. Choose Event Viewer from the Administrative Tools menu.
2. Right-click the log you want to configure and choose Properties.
3. On the General tab, set the options you want. Under When Maximum Log Size Is Reached, there are three options.
   - If you don't archive this log, choose Overwrite Events As Needed.
   - If you archive this log at regular intervals, you can select the Overwrite Events Older Than option. Fill in the appropriate number of days.
   - Do Not Overwrite Events, the last option, means that the log must be cleared manually. When the maximum log size is reached, new events will simply not be recorded.
4. Click OK when you're finished.

Real World   **Calling a Halt When the Log Is Full**

Maybe you are so security-conscious that none of the event log options are acceptable. If you absolutely, positively mustn't lose a single security event, you can set the computer to halt when the security log is full. A registry change is necessary to make this happen. First, set Event Log Wrapping to either Do Not Overwrite Events or Overwrite Events Older Than *n* Days. Then start RegEdit.exe and proceed to HKEY_LOCAL_MACHINE\SYSTEM\CurentControlSet\Control\Lsa\CrashOnAuditFail, and change the value to *1*.

This setting will take effect after a reboot and then, when the log is full, the system will simply stop. After restarting, only administrators will be able to log on until the security log is cleared. This is a drastic measure, but it is necessary in some cases.

Archiving Event Logs

If you will be using event logs to track system usage trends, you must save them. To archive an event log, open Event Viewer from the Administrative Tools menu, and click the log you want to archive. Then, from the Action menu, choose Save Log As. If you save the file in the event log format (.EVT), it can be reopened in Event Viewer, and all the binary data for each event will be retained. You can also save logs as .TXT files or in comma-delimited format (.CSV), but in those cases the binary data isn't saved. Chapter 32 has details on using Event Viewer and the logs that are generated to learn more about the network and tune its performance.

Delegating Control

Obviously, one of the simplest ways to minimize your administrative chores is to delegate them. In a Windows NT network, the usual way to grant broad administrative rights is to make users members of the Domain Admins group. Or you can parcel out administrative rights through some combination of other groups such as Print Operators or Server Operators.

These groups are still available, but Windows 2000 makes delegation even simpler: it allows you to assign responsibility for management of some portion of the namespace to another user or group. The recipient of the delegated authority can have complete administrative control within the area chosen but not the sweeping administrative rights inherent in being a member of the Domain Admins group.

Assign control by organizational unit (OU) whenever possible, because assigning permissions at the object level quickly becomes too complicated to be worthwhile. Records of security assignments are critical, so keep track of all delegations. To delegate control, use the Delegation of Control Wizard, which always assigns permissions at the OU level. (Detailed descriptions of permissions are provided in Chapter 9. For more on the planning and deployment of security policies, see Chapters 17 and 18.) To use the wizard, follow these steps:

1. Open Active Directory Users and Computers from the Administrative Tools menu.

2. Double-click the domain node, and then right-click the container whose control you want to delegate and choose Delegate Control from the shortcut menu. This starts the Delegation of Control Wizard. Click Next.

3. Click the Add button to select the user or group to be granted control. Make your selection from the Select Users, Computers, or Groups screen (Figure 10-14).

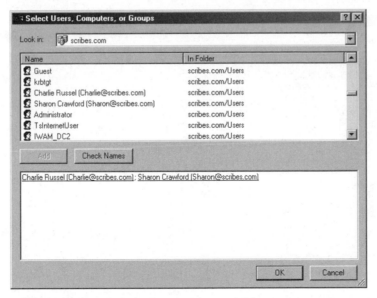

Figure 10-14. *Selecting the recipients of delegated control.*

4. In the Tasks to Delegate screen, select the tasks that you want to delegate. Select predefined tasks or click Create a Custom Task. Click Next.

5. If you selected a predefined task, you're essentially finished. Review the summary and click Finished.

   If you selected Create a Custom Task, you're presented with more specific choices as to what objects you're delegating control on· and the specific permissions to be granted. When those choices are made, you'll see a summary of the delegation. Click Finished.

Using Task Scheduler

While it's true that you could—and still can—schedule tasks using the AT command, as described later in this chapter, Task Scheduler provides a graphical interface and is much easier to use. Tasks can be scheduled during off-hours and to run repeatedly. The Task Scheduler service is started at boot up and runs in the background. To use Task Scheduler, open Control Panel, double-click the Scheduled Tasks folder, and then follow these steps:

1. In the Scheduled Tasks window, double-click the Add Scheduled Task entry. This starts the Scheduled Task Wizard. Click Next.

2. Select a program from the screen (Figure 10-15), or click the Browse button to locate another program. Click Next.

3. Supply a name for the task, and then indicate how often you want it performed. Click Next.

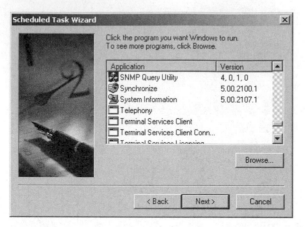

Figure 10-15. *Selecting the program to be scheduled.*

4. Select the time of day you want the task performed. Depending on the timing you've selected, you'll also need to specify one of the following:

   • **Daily Task**   Every day, every *n* days, or weekdays only.

   • **Weekly Task**   Every *n* weeks; supply the day of the week.

   • **Monthly Task**   Select the day of the month, and select which months.

5. Supply the user name and password for the user who will be scheduling tasks. Click Next. Note that the account you specify must have the privileges necessary to run the task. For example, if you're scheduling a backup program, the user must have backup rights.

6. If you need to specify parameters for the task being scheduled, select the check box next to Open Advanced Properties and then click Next.

7. Make the necessary changes and click OK.

Tip   For tasks to run as expected, it's important that the computer's date and time be set correctly.

Many programs will start to run in Task Scheduler and then pause, waiting for input that never comes—or that comes much later, when someone looks at the machine to see what's going on. To make sure you have all of the parameters for a task to be able to run successfully, open a command prompt and type *program_name* /?. Then right-click the task in the Scheduled Tasks window and choose Properties. Enter the necessary parameters in the Run text box and click OK.

You might want to schedule a task to run right away so you can test its performance. If a task is scheduled by a user and that user isn't logged on at the scheduled time, the task still runs but is in the background and not visible.

Changing a Schedule

Even the best schedule can run up against reality now and again, so you need to be able to adjust your planned events.

- To run a task immediately, right-click the task's icon in the Scheduled Tasks window and choose Run from the shortcut menu.

- To stop a task that's running, right-click the task's icon in the Scheduled Tasks window and choose End Task. If the scheduled task has been set up to start another task, the End Task command will halt only the original scheduled task.

- To temporarily halt all Task Scheduler actions, open the Advanced menu in the Scheduled Tasks window and choose Pause Task Scheduler. Any tasks that do not start because Task Scheduler is paused will run again only at their next scheduled time. To start Task Scheduler up again, click the same menu and choose Continue Task Scheduler.

- To stop using Task Scheduler, open the Advanced menu in the Scheduled Tasks window and choose Stop Using Task Scheduler. No scheduled tasks will run, and the Task Scheduler service will no longer start automatically when the system is rebooted.

Tracking Task Scheduler

The system maintains a detailed log of Task Scheduler's activities. To view the log, double-click Scheduled Tasks in Control Panel. From the Advanced menu, choose View Log. This opens a log like the one shown in Figure 10-16, with the most recent entry at the bottom of the window. The Details view in the Scheduled Tasks window displays information about each task (Figure 10-17).

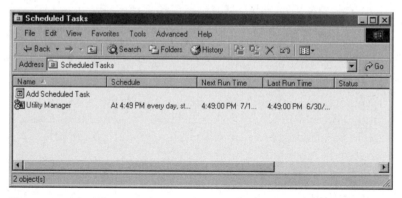

```
SchedLgU.Txt - Notepad
File  Edit  Format  Help
        Started at 5/31/99 12:22:23 PM
"Task Scheduler Service"
        Exited at 5/31/99 2:08:25 PM
"Task Scheduler Service"
        Started at 5/31/99 2:12:26 PM
"Task Scheduler Service"
        Started at 6/12/99 1:50:59 PM
"Task Scheduler Service"
        Exited at 6/15/99 11:22:14 AM
"Task Scheduler Service"
        Started at 6/15/99 11:25:59 AM
"Synchronize.job" (mobsync.exe)
        Started 6/30/99 12:53:00 PM
"Synchronize.job" (mobsync.exe)
        Finished 6/30/99 12:54:01 PM
        Result: The task completed with an exit code of (0).
"Disk Cleanup.job" (cleanmgr.exe)
        Started 6/30/99 1:04:38 PM
"Disk Cleanup.job" (cleanmgr.exe)
        Finished 6/30/99 1:04:45 PM
        Result: The task completed with an exit code of (1).
[ ***** Most recent entry is above this line ***** ]
```

Figure 10-16. *The Task Scheduler log.*

Figure 10-17. *The Details view for scheduled tasks.*

If a scheduled task doesn't execute as expected, right-click the task in the Task Scheduler window and choose Properties from the shortcut menu. Verify that the task is in fact enabled. (The Enabled check box in the Task Properties window should be selected.)

Viewing Tasks on a Remote Computer

If you are an administrator of a remote computer running Windows NT or Windows 2000, you can view and edit the Task Scheduler settings on that computer. Find the computer in the My Network Places window (in Windows 2000) or in the Network Neighborhood window (in Windows NT), and then double-click the Scheduled Tasks folder.

To view and edit scheduled tasks on computers running Windows 95 or later, the remote computer must

- Have remote administration enabled
- Specify your user account as having remote administrative access
- Share the hard disk on which the Scheduled Tasks folder resides

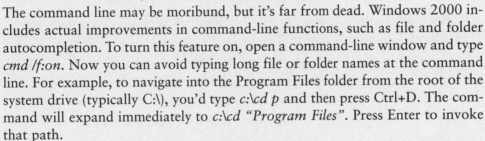

Real World   Autocompletion on the Command Line

The command line may be moribund, but it's far from dead. Windows 2000 includes actual improvements in command-line functions, such as file and folder autocompletion. To turn this feature on, open a command-line window and type *cmd /f:on*. Now you can avoid typing long file or folder names at the command line. For example, to navigate into the Program Files folder from the root of the system drive (typically C:\), you'd type *c:\cd p* and then press Ctrl+D. The command will expand immediately to *c:\cd "Program Files"*. Press Enter to invoke that path.

The feature will also work with files. Let's say you're in C:\Program Files\Windows Media Player and you would like to execute Mplayer.exe. At the command line, type *mp* and then press Ctrl+F. The path will expand to include Mplayer.exe. Press Enter to actually execute the file.

For the full documentation, open a command window and type *help cmd*.

Using the AT Command

You can also use the AT command to schedule tasks. By default, the AT command is run using the LocalSystem account, which requires administrative privileges. To specify another account as the user of the AT command, follow these steps:

1. Open Control Panel and double-click Scheduled Tasks.
2. In the Scheduled Tasks window, open the Advanced menu and then choose AT Service Account.

3. Click This Account and specify a particular user and password. Click OK.

AT Command Syntax

The command structure for the AT command is as follows:

```
AT [\\computername] [id] [[/delete]|/delete [/yes]]
AT [\\computername] time [/interactive] [/every:date[,…] |
/next:date[,…]] command
```

The following parameters can be used with the AT command. Used without parameters, the AT command returns a list of scheduled commands.

- **\\computername**   Specifies a remote computer. Without this parameter, the local computer is assumed.

- *id*   Indicates the identification number, if one is assigned.

- **/delete**   Cancels a scheduled command. If no identification number is specified, all scheduled commands on the computer will be canceled.

- **/yes** Forces a yes answer to all system queries when canceling all commands.

- *time*   Specifies when the command is to run, expressed as *hours:minutes* in 24-hour notation.

- **/interactive**   Allows the task to interact with the desktop of the user logged on at the time the job is run.

- **/every:***date*[,...]   Runs the command on the date specified. The date can be specified as one or more days of the week (M, T, W, Th, F, S, Su) or as one or more days of the month (numbers 1 through 31). Separate multiple dates with commas. If this parameter is omitted, the current day of the month is assumed.

- **/next:***date*[,...]   Runs the command on the next occurrence of the specified day. If this parameter is omitted, the current day of the month is assumed.

- *command*   Indicates the program, batch file, or command to be run. If a path is required, use the Uniform Naming Convention (UNC) path.

Here are some important facts to keep in mind about the AT command:

- The AT command doesn't automatically load Cmd, the command interpreter, so if the command parameter doesn't point to an executable file, you must explicitly specify Cmd, followed by the /c switch, at the beginning of the command.

- Commands scheduled using AT run as background processes, so there is no displayed output. To redirect output to a file, use the redirection symbol (>). The redirection symbol must be preceded by the escape symbol (^), so a sample command would be *at retrieve.bat ^>c:\daylog.txt.*

- If you have to use a drive letter to connect to a shared directory, include an AT command to disconnect the drive when the task is completed. Otherwise, the assigned drive letter will be neither available nor seen at the command prompt.

Note   You can switch back and forth between the AT command and Task Scheduler, although there are some limitations. For example, if you schedule a task using AT and later modify that same task using Task Scheduler, the task is then "owned" by Task Scheduler and you can no longer access it using AT.

Summary

Windows 2000 supplies plenty of tools to help in the management of daily operations, including ones that handle delegation, scripts, and task scheduling. However, it's still up to the humans to do the planning and decide which tools are appropriate for which chores. Every network has its own quirks and needs, and only experience can show you the optimal path. The next chapter covers the basics of installing and using Active Directory.

Chapter 11
Installing and Configuring Active Directory

Managing Microsoft Active Directory directory service is an important part of the Microsoft Windows 2000 administration process, and familiarity with the various tools provided for this purpose is essential. Nearly all the tools use Microsoft Management Console (MMC) snap-ins to provide the user interface. The Administrative Tools program group on the Start menu includes some snap-ins, but you must add others manually by using the MMC's Add Snap-in function.

You'll find that some of the Active Directory management tools are programs that you run every day, while others are needed only during Active Directory installation or occasionally thereafter. The MMC snap-ins that provide Active Directory management functions are as follows:

- **Active Directory Installation Wizard**   Creates domain controllers, new domains, trees, and forests
- **Active Directory Domains and Trusts**   Changes the domain mode, manages domain trust relationships, and configures user principle name (UPN) suffixes
- **Active Directory Users and Computers**   Creates, manages, and configures Active Directory objects
- **Active Directory Sites and Services**   Creates and configures domain sites and manages the domain controller replication process
- **Active Directory Schema**   Modifies the schema that defines Active Directory objects and properties

In addition to the MMC snap-ins, Microsoft Windows 2000 Server includes separate utilities for importing data to and exporting it from Active Directory. This chapter examines the tasks that Active Directory administrators typically perform by using the Active Directory Installation Wizard, the Active Directory Domains and Trusts snap-in, and the Active Directory Users and Computers snap-in. The next chapter examines the Active Directory Sites and Services snap-in and the Active Directory Schema Administrator snap-in.

Using the Active Directory Installation Wizard

Unlike Microsoft Windows NT Server version 4 and earlier, Windows 2000 Server doesn't allow you to designate a system as a domain controller during the operating system installation. Every Windows 2000 server installs as a stand-alone system or a member of a domain. After the installation is complete, you can promote the server to domain controller status by using the Windows 2000 Active Directory Installation Wizard. This tool provides a great deal of additional flexibility to Active Directory administrators because servers can be promoted or demoted at any time, while Windows NT 4 servers are irrevocably designated as domain controllers during the installation process.

Also gone is the distinction between primary and backup domain controllers. Windows 2000 domain controllers are all peers in a *multiple-master replication system*. This means that administrators can modify the contents of the Active Directory tree on any server functioning as a domain controller, and the system will replicate the changes to all the other controllers on the domain. This is a major advance from the Windows NT 4 *single-master replication system,* in which an administrator can change only the primary domain controller (PDC), after which the changes are replicated to all the backup domain controllers (BDCs).

Another advantage of Windows 2000 is that you can use the Active Directory Installation Wizard to demote a domain controller back to a stand-alone or member server. In Windows NT 4, once you install a server as a domain controller, you can demote it from a PDC to a BDC, but you can't remove its domain controller status completely, except by reinstalling the operating system.

The basic function of the Active Directory Installation Wizard is to configure a server to function as a domain controller, but depending on the current state of Active Directory on your network, this task can take several forms. If you're installing the first Windows 2000 Server on your network, then promoting the system to a domain controller creates an entirely new Active Directory with that computer hosting the first domain in the first tree in the first forest.

> **Note**   Be sure to read Chapter 3 before launching into Active Directory. Unless you have an independent test network where you can make mistakes without serious consequences, it's essential that you know where you're going before you get on the train.

Preparing for Installation

To promote Windows 2000 Server to a domain controller, you first complete the entire operating system installation process. After the final reboot, you then log on to the machine by using an administrator account.

NTFS 5

To host Active Directory, the server must have an NTFS 5 partition. NTFS 5 is an updated version of the file system introduced in the first release of Windows NT. When you create new NTFS partitions during a Windows 2000 installation or upgrade existing NTFS partitions created with prior Windows NT versions, the system uses NTFS 5. If you choose to install Windows 2000 on a system with only FAT partitions, you must convert at least one partition to NTFS before you can use the Active Directory Installation Wizard. You can do this by using the Convert.exe utility from the command prompt or the Disk Management screen in the Computer Management snap-in for the MMC.

> **Note**   Converting the Windows 2000 boot partition (the partition on which Windows 2000 is installed) requires a reboot of the system. Because the conversion can't actually occur while the Windows 2000 GUI is loaded, a registry flag is used to schedule the conversion to take place the next time the machine restarts. You can then reload the Active Directory Installation Wizard and begin the installation sequence again.

DNS Server

The last requirement for installing Active Directory is that the server must have access to a DNS server. Active Directory uses DNS to store information about the domain controllers on the network. Client systems locate a domain controller for authentication by sending a query to the DNS server identified in their TCP/IP client configurations. The DNS server that Active Directory uses need not be running on the computer being converted to a domain controller, nor does it have to run the Microsoft DNS service. However, the DNS server you use must support the Service Location resource record defined in the RFC 2052 document and the Dynamic Update protocol defined in RFC 2136.

> **More Info** RFCs (requests for comments) are the TCP/IP specification documents published by the Internet Engineering Task Force (IETF). All the documents are in the public domain and available for viewing at *http://www.rfc-editor.org*.

A DNS server is essentially a database composed of individual elements called *resource records* that contain information about the computers on a TCP/IP network. Various types of resource records are defined in the DNS specifications, and Active Directory requires a new type of resource record—the SRV (the DNS resource record for specifying the location of services)—to store information about Active Directory domain controllers. In addition, a DNS server used by Active Directory requires the ability to dynamically update its records, based on the availability of the domain controllers on the network. More information on DNS and dynamic DNS can be found in Chapter 13.

Until recently, network administrators have configured DNS servers by manually creating the resource records that identify the computers on the network. Each time a system was added or taken out of service, the administrator had to add, remove, or modify the resource record associated with it. A Windows 2000 network running Active Directory uses multiple domain controllers to provide fault tolerance and load balancing. If a domain controller should fail or become unavailable to clients for any reason, another domain controller takes over its duties automatically.

Unfortunately, traditional DNS servers have no such automatic self-configuration capabilities. A network administrator has to manually modify the appropriate SRV resource record every time a domain controller goes offline and another takes its place. The Dynamic Update protocol defined in RFC 2136, on the other hand, enables DNS servers to receive messages from domain controllers containing their availability status. The server modifies its own resource records based on the contents of these messages, thus ensuring that all the domain controllers identified in the resource records are available and that all the available domain controllers are listed in the DNS server.

The Microsoft DNS Server version included with the Windows 2000 Server products supports both new specifications, as does the UNIX-based DNS Server BIND version 8.1.2. If you already have a DNS server supporting these features on your network, you should specify its IP address in the new server's TCP/IP configuration before you begin the Active Directory installation process. You need not install a DNS server on your new domain controller in this case because the Active Directory Installation Wizard will locate the specified server and create the appropriate SRV resource records in it.

However, if a DNS server supporting the new features isn't available on the network, the wizard will offer to install and configure Microsoft DNS Server on the system automatically. You can refuse the offer and install a DNS server on another system, but your new server must be able to access that DNS server in order to install Active Directory and promote the system to a domain controller.

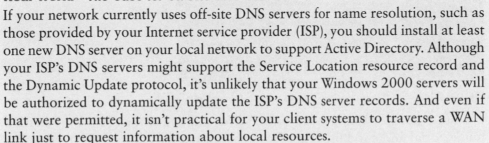

Real World   The Case for On-Site DNS Servers
If your network currently uses off-site DNS servers for name resolution, such as those provided by your Internet service provider (ISP), you should install at least one new DNS server on your local network to support Active Directory. Although your ISP's DNS servers might support the Service Location resource record and the Dynamic Update protocol, it's unlikely that your Windows 2000 servers will be authorized to dynamically update the ISP's DNS server records. And even if that were permitted, it isn't practical for your client systems to traverse a WAN link just to request information about local resources.

Promoting Your First Server to a Domain Controller

Assuming you've already designed the Active Directory hierarchy that you're going to use on your network (as discussed in Chapter 3), the process of actually installing Active Directory and promoting a server to a domain controller is quite simple. The following sections examine the process of installing Active Directory on the first server of a Windows 2000 network. In the "Choosing Installation Options" section later in this chapter, we'll cover the various Active Directory installation options you can use when installing subsequent servers.

Launching the Active Directory Installation Wizard

Following the standard wizard pattern, installing Active Directory on a server is a matter of responding to prompts in a sequence of screens. Windows 2000 incorporates links to the wizard onto the Active Directory page of the Windows 2000 Configure Your Server home page. This page is displayed in the Microsoft Internet Explorer browser automatically after the OS installation, as shown in Figure 11-1. This local Web page is designed to walk you through all the processes needed to configure a new server by asking questions in wizard fashion and linking to the appropriate tools for each task.

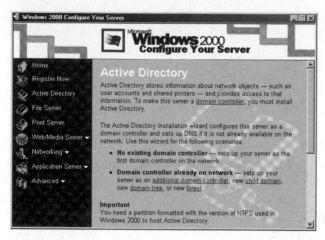

Figure 11-1. *The Windows 2000 Configure Your Server home page.*

For users new to Windows 2000, this Web page functions as a combination minitutorial and checklist of server configuration procedures. More advanced users can bypass the configuration Web page and launch the wizard directly by running the executable file Dcpromo.exe from the Run dialog box. Or users can run the file from the command prompt after logging on using the local administrator account. Dcpromo.exe is located in the \%*systemroot*%\System32 folder, making it possible to execute it from any folder without specifying a path.

Note   When you upgrade a Windows NT 4 primary domain controller to Windows 2000 Server, the system launches the Active Directory Installation Wizard automatically after the operating system installation finishes.

After a welcome screen, the Installation Wizard prompts you for the action you want to perform, based on the system's current Active Directory status. If the server is already a domain controller, the wizard provides the option to only demote the system back to a stand-alone or member server. (Domain controllers are covered in Chapter 7.) On a computer that isn't yet a domain controller, the wizard displays the Domain Controller Type screen shown in Figure 11-2, which prompts you to select one of the following options:

- **Domain Controller For A New Domain**   Installs Active Directory on the server and designates it as the first domain controller in a new domain
- **Additional Domain Controller For An Existing Domain**   Installs Active Directory on the server and replicates the directory information from an existing domain (Creating replicas is covered later in this chapter.)

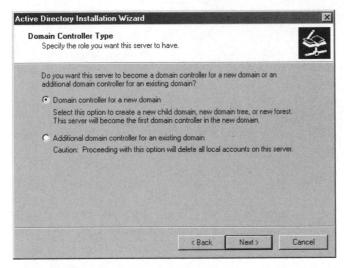

Figure 11-2. *The Domain Controller Type screen of the Active Directory Installation Wizard.*

Creating a New Domain

When you install the first Active Directory server on your network, you select the Domain Controller For A New Domain option in the Domain Controller Type screen. This instructs the wizard to install the Active Directory support files, create the new domain, and register it in the DNS. The new domain is further configured in one of two ways, as shown in the Create Tree Or Child Domain screen (Figure 11-3).

- **Create A New Domain Tree**   Configures the new domain controller to host the first domain in a new tree
- **Create A New Child Domain In An Existing Domain Tree**   Configures the new domain controller to host a child of a domain in an already existing tree

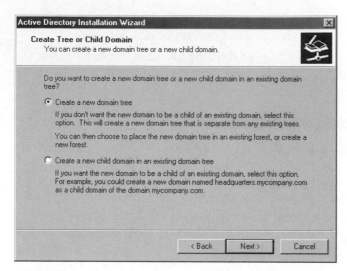

Figure 11-3. *The Create Tree Or Child Domain screen of the Active Directory Installation Wizard.*

Because this is to be the first Active Directory server on the network, you should select Create A New Domain Tree. The wizard then displays the Create Or Join Forest screen, shown in Figure 11-4, which enables you to specify one of the following options:

- **Create A New Forest Of Domain Trees**   Configures the domain controller to be the root domain in a new forest of trees
- **Place This Domain Tree In An Existing Forest**   Configures the domain controller to host the first domain of a new tree in a forest already containing one or more trees

Select Create A New Forest Of Domain Trees in this instance, because the first Windows 2000 domain controller on your network will always be a new domain, in a new tree, in a new forest. As you install additional domain controllers, you can use these same options to create other new forests or to populate the existing forest with additional trees and domains.

Specifying Domain Names

To identify the domain controller on the network, you must specify a valid DNS name in the New Domain Name screen (Figure 11-5) for the domain you're creating.

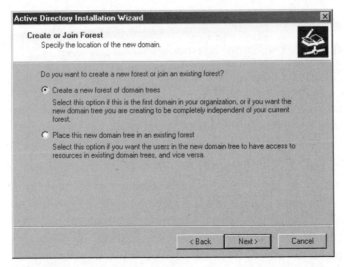

Figure 11-4. *The Create Or Join Forest screen of the Active Directory Installation Wizard.*

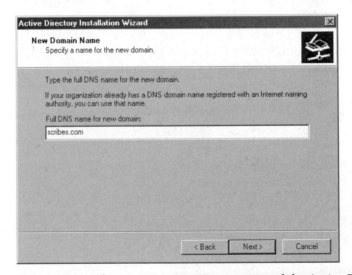

Figure 11-5. *The New Domain Name screen of the Active Directory Installation Wizard.*

This name doesn't have to be the same as the domain your organization uses for its Internet presence (although it can be). Nor does the name have to be one registered with the Internet Network Information Center (InterNIC)—the organization responsible for maintaining the registry of DNS names in the *com, net, org,* and *edu* top-level domains. However, using a registered domain name is a good idea if your network users will be accessing Internet resources at the same time as local network resources, or if users outside the organization will be accessing your local network resources via the Internet.

When users access Internet resources at the same time as Windows 2000 network resources, the possibility exists for your unregistered domain name to conflict with a registered Internet domain using the same name. When Internet users are permitted to access resources on your network using standard application-layer protocols like HTTP and FTP, confusion can arise if internal and external users must use different domain names.

After you enter a DNS name for the domain, the system prompts you for a NetBIOS equivalent to the domain name for use by clients that don't support Active Directory. Windows 2000 systems still use the NetBIOS namespace for their computer names, but Active Directory uses DNS naming for domains. Windows NT 4 and Microsoft Windows 9x systems use NetBIOS names for all network resources, including domains.

If you have any downlevel clients on your network (that is, Windows NT 4, Windows 9x, Microsoft Windows for Workgroups, or Microsoft Network Client for MS-DOS systems), they'll only be able to see the new domain using the NetBIOS name. The NetBIOS Domain Name screen (Figure 11-6) will contain a suggested name that you can use, based on the DNS name you specified, or you can replace it with a name of your own selection that is 15 characters or fewer.

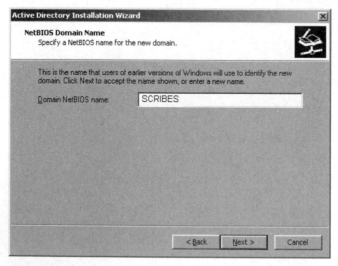

Figure 11-6. *The NetBIOS Domain Name screen of the Active Directory Installation Wizard.*

Locating Active Directory Files

After you specify domain names, the wizard prompts you for the locations of the Active Directory database, log files, and the system volume. The Active Directory database will contain the actual Active Directory objects and their properties, while the log files track the activities of the directory service. You specify the directories for these files in the Database And Log Locations screen, shown in Figure 11-7. The default location for both the database and the logs is the *%systemroot%*\Ntds folder on the system volume, but you can modify these locations as needed—in fact, you probably should, so as not to have all your directory eggs in one basket.

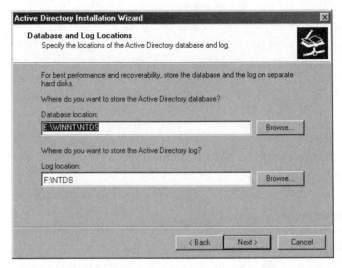

Figure 11-7. *The Database And Log Locations screen of the Active Directory Installation Wizard.*

The Shared System Volume screen enables you to specify the location of what will become the Sysvol share on the domain controller. The *system volume* is a share containing domain information that is replicated to all the other domain controllers on the network. By default, the system creates this share in the *%systemroot%*\Sysvol folder on the system drive.

The Active Directory database, logs, and system volume must all be located on volumes using the NTFS 5 file system. If the wizard detects that any of the volumes you've chosen don't use NTFS 5, you must either convert them or select other volumes before you can complete the Active Directory installation process.

Real World Storing the Active Directory Database and Logs

Because Active Directory often writes to the database and the logs at the same time, Microsoft recommends not to store them on the same hard disk. This isn't a major issue on a single domain controller or other small network, but on an enterprise network with frequent directory service updates and many domain controllers replicating their databases, the data storage burden can be significant, so using separate disks is strongly recommended.

The recommendation for the placement of the database and log files calls for the use of separate hard disks, not separate volumes on the same disk drive. This is because the physical constraints of the disk's head traveling mechanism can be responsible for a reduction in disk performance. The heads on a single disk drive can't be in two positions at the same time, so the device must perform writes to the database and the logs consecutively. When the files are stored on separate disks, the writes can occur simultaneously. It is also preferable to use SCSI drives for this purpose rather than EIDE, since SCSI is better suited to executing simultaneous commands on multiple devices.

Using Automatic DNS Configuration

At this point, the Active Directory Installation Wizard has all the configuration information it needs to install Active Directory and promote the server to a domain controller. The system checks to see that the domain names you supplied are not already in use by your DNS server or any other computers on your network. If, for example, the NetBIOS name you selected is already being used by a Windows NT 4 domain on the network, the wizard prompts you to select another name.

The wizard also checks to determine whether the DNS server hosting your domain supports the Dynamic Update protocol. If the system can't contact the DNS server specified in the computer's TCP/IP client configuration, or if the specified DNS server is incapable of supporting a Windows 2000 domain, the wizard offers to install Microsoft DNS Server and configure it to function as the authoritative server for the domain. The Configure DNS screen enables you to specify whether you want to install the DNS server or configure one yourself. If you elect to use another machine for the DNS server, you must install and configure it before you can complete Active Directory installation.

Finishing Active Directory Installation

After the wizard contacts the DNS server that will provide the locator service for the new domain, it completes the installation and configuration of Active Directory without further user input. The wizard logs all the activities that occur during the installation process in two files called Dcpromo.log and Dcpromoui.log, located in the %*systemroot*%\debug folder. Installation can take several minutes, after which you must reboot the system for the changes to take effect. The wizard creates an administrator account for the new domain using the same password as the local administrator account with which you logged on before starting Active Directory installation.

The procedure for installing additional domain controllers on your network is similar to that for the installation of the first domain controller. The following sections examine the other options provided by the Active Directory Installation Wizard and how you use them to build a Windows 2000 network with Active Directory.

Choosing Installation Options

Planning an effective directory service strategy is an essential element of an Active Directory deployment. As stated earlier, before running the Installation Wizard on any Windows 2000 Server, you should have a directory structure in mind that outlines which domains, trees, or forests you intend to create in Active Directory and how they should be configured. As you create additional domain controllers on the network, you can use the Installation Wizard to specify any of the Active Directory installation options.

Creating a Replica Domain Controller

Replicas provide fault tolerance for an Active Directory domain, and they can reduce internetwork traffic by enabling network clients to authenticate using a domain controller on the local segment. When a domain controller malfunctions or is unavailable for any reason, its replicas automatically assume their functions. Even a small domain needs at least two domain controllers to maintain this fault tolerance.

To create a replica of an existing domain, you run the Active Directory Installation Wizard on a newly installed Windows 2000 Server after joining the domain you intend to replicate. For the computer to join the domain, you can either join the domain for the first time and supply the administrative credentials that enable the system to create a computer object in the domain, or create the computer object manually using Active Directory Users and Computers. After joining the domain, log on to the system using the local administrator account and launch the wizard from the Configure Server page or by running Dcpromo.exe from the Run dialog box.

When the Domain Controller Type screen appears in the wizard, select Additional Domain Controller For An Existing Domain and specify the DNS name of the domain to be replicated. You must then supply the user name, password, and domain name of an account with administrative privileges in the domain.

The rest of the process is exactly like the creation of the first domain, as outlined in "Promoting Your First Server to a Domain Controller" earlier in this chapter. The wizard installs Active Directory on the server, creates the database, logs, and the system volume in the locations you specify, registers the domain controller with your DNS server, and replicates the data from an existing domain controller for that domain.

Once the replica of the domain controller is up and running, it is indistinguishable from the existing domain controller, as far as client functionality is concerned. The replicas function as peers, unlike Windows NT servers, which are designated as primary and backup domain controllers. Administrators can modify Active Directory contents (either objects or schema) from any domain controller, and the changes will be replicated to all of the other controllers for that domain.

When creating a replica, the Active Directory Installation Wizard automatically configures the replication process between the domain controllers. You can customize the replication process using Active Directory Sites and Services included with Windows 2000 Server. (See "Using Active Directory Sites and Services" in Chapter 12.)

Creating a Child Domain in an Existing Tree

When you create the first Windows 2000 domain on your network, you're also creating the first tree in a forest. You can populate the tree as you create additional domains by making them children of existing domains. A *child domain* is one that uses the same namespace as a parent domain. This namespace is established by the DNS name of the parent domain, to which the child adds a preceding name for the new domain.

For example, if you create a domain called Mycorp.com, a child of that domain would be called something like Research.mycorp.com. Typically, child domains reflect the geographical, departmental, or political divisions of an organization, but you can use any tree design principle you want. A parent domain can have any number of children, and the tree structure can extend through any number of generations, which enables you to use a single namespace to create a domain tree that reflects the structure of your entire organization.

To install Active Directory and create a child domain, you must first join your Windows 2000 Server to the parent domain by joining that domain and supplying administrative credentials or by manually creating a computer object in the domain using Active Directory Users and Computers. Then log on to the system using the local administrator account and launch the Active Directory Installation Wizard from the Configure Server page or by running Dcpromo.exe from the Run dialog box.

A child domain is not a replica; it is a completely separate domain located in the same tree. Therefore, when the wizard displays the Domain Controller Type screen, you must select Domain Controller For A New Domain. In the Create Tree Or Child Domain dialog box, you select Create A New Child Domain In An Existing Domain Tree. The wizard then prompts you for the DNS name of the domain that is to be the parent of the child. After supplying this, you specify the short name for the child domain. The short name is the name that will be added to the parent domain's DNS name to form the full name of the child domain. For example, to create a child domain called Research.mycorp.com, you specify Mycorp.com as the parent domain name and Research as the short name of the child.

As with the creation of the first domain in the tree, you must supply a NetBIOS name for the new domain of no more than 15 characters (Figure 11-6). In the above example, the domain would be called Research. You must also supply credentials for an account that has administrative privileges in the parent domain. The wizard then completes the Active Directory installation and prompts you for a system reboot.

Creating a New Tree in an Existing Forest

In addition to creating child domains in an Active Directory tree, you can also create entirely new trees, thus forming a forest. Each tree in a forest has its own separate namespace, but the trees all share the same schema and configuration.

If, for example, you modify the schema to add customized attributes to a particular object in one tree, those attributes will be present in the same object type in all of the other trees in the forest.

Before you create a new tree in an existing forest, your new Windows 2000 Server must join the root domain of that forest. The root domain is the first domain created in the forest, and you join the system to that domain by logging on to it and specifying credentials for an administrative account in the domain or manually creating a computer object in the domain using Active Directory Users and Computers.

Once the computer has an account in the forest's root domain, you can launch the Active Directory Installation Wizard from the Configure Server screen or run Dcpromo.exe from the Run dialog box. When the Domain Controller Type dialog box appears, select Domain Controller For A New Domain. Then select Create A New Domain Tree in the Create Tree Or Child Domain dialog box, and select Place This New Domain Tree In An Existing Forest in the Create Or Join Forest dialog box.

To create the new tree, you must first specify the DNS name of the root domain in the forest and then the DNS name that you want to assign to the first domain in the new tree. This second DNS name must not be a part of any existing namespace in the forest. That is, if a tree already uses Mycorp.com as the DNS name of its root domain, you can't use the name Research.mycorp.com for the root domain in your new tree, even if that exact domain name doesn't exist in the Mycorp.com tree.

After supplying the DNS names, you furnish a NetBIOS equivalent in the usual manner, and you provide credentials for an administrative account in the forest's root domain. The wizard then completes the installation process and prompts you to reboot the system.

Creating a New Forest

The fundamental difference between creating a new tree and creating a new forest is that forests each have their own individual schema and configuration. The most obvious scenario in which a network would have multiple forests is when two organizations with existing Active Directory installations merge, and sufficient schema and configuration differences exist between the two to make joining them into one forest impractical.

The procedure for creating a new forest is the same as that for creating the first domain on the network, as described in "Promoting Your First Server to a Domain Controller" earlier in this chapter. Once you complete this or any of the other Active Directory installation processes described in the preceding sections, you can log on to the domain and proceed to perform the activities outlined in the rest of this chapter and in the next chapter.

Upgrading Windows NT 4 Domain Controllers

Windows 2000 simplifies the process of converting the domains from a Windows NT 4 network to Windows 2000 Active Directory domains by enabling you to upgrade the servers gradually. Windows NT domain controllers can co-exist on the same network as Windows 2000 domain controllers and can even function in the same domain. The only special rule for the upgrade process is that you must upgrade the PDC of a Windows NT 4 network before any of the BDCs.

When you install the Windows 2000 operating system on the PDC, the Active Directory Installation Wizard launches automatically after the final reboot and begins the promotion process. After the server is promoted to a domain controller, the system can host your existing domain, using the NT 4 BDCs as replicas. You can then upgrade the BDCs at your own pace.

When all the domain controllers are running Windows 2000, you can then use the Active Directory Domains and Trusts snap-in to convert the domain from mixed mode to native mode, enabling you to take full advantage of Active Directory's grouping capabilities. See "Changing the Domain Mode" later in this chapter for more information on switching the domain operational mode.

Demoting a Domain Controller

A major difference between Windows 2000 domain controllers and Windows NT domain controllers is that you can demote a Windows 2000 domain controller to a stand-alone or member server. When you launch the Active Directory Installation Wizard, the program ascertains that the system is already functioning as a domain controller and only provides the option to demote the server, as shown in Figure 11-8.

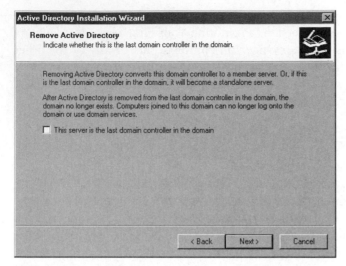

Figure 11-8. *The Remove Active Directory screen of the Active Directory Installation Wizard.*

The Configure Your Server screen also detects the status of the system and provides only a single option (Figure 11-9).

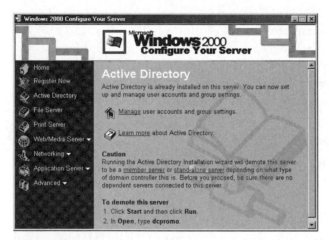

Figure 11-9. *The Windows 2000 Configure Your Server screen.*

Demoting a domain controller erases the Active Directory database from the machine, removes all references to it from the DNS server, and returns the system's security accounts to a state identical to that of a newly installed Windows 2000 server. If the domain to which the system belongs has replica domain controllers on the network, the server remains a member of that domain after the demotion.

If the server is the sole domain controller for a particular domain, the demotion causes that domain to be erased completely from Active Directory, and the system becomes a stand-alone server until you join it to another domain. If the server is the only controller of a forest's root domain, you must destroy all the other domains in the forest before you can proceed with the demotion of the root domain controller. To demote the controller, follow these steps.

1. Open the Active Directory Installation Wizard by running Dcpromo.exe. If you see a message box like the one in Figure 11-10, don't proceed with the demotion of the server until you're sure at least one other Global Catalog server exists in the domain. (See "Setting a Global Catalog Server" later in this chapter.)

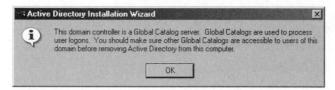

Figure 11-10. *A warning message when demoting a Global Catalog server.*

2. You'll see the screen shown in Figure 11-8. Click Next.

3. Provide a password for the server administrator account. You'll then see a summary showing what you've selected and what the result will be if you proceed (Figure 11-11).

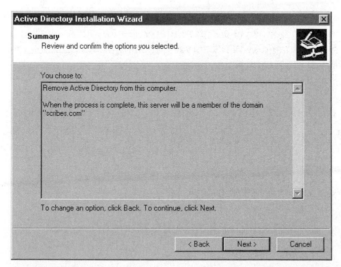

Figure 11-11. *The Summary screen of the Active Directory Installation Wizard.*

The Configuring Active Directory screen will open and provide a running description of the processes being performed (Figure 11-12). This will take at least a few minutes, and sometimes considerably longer, depending on the machine. When the configuration is complete, the server will no longer be a domain controller and you'll be prompted to click Finish and then Restart Now.

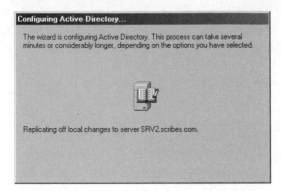

Figure 11-12. *The Configuring Active Directory screen.*

Changing a Domain Controller Identification

Changing a domain controller's network identity requires demoting the server from its status as a domain controller, changing the identity, and then promoting the machine again.

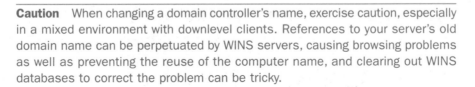

> **Caution** When changing a domain controller's name, exercise caution, especially in a mixed environment with downlevel clients. References to your server's old domain name can be perpetuated by WINS servers, causing browsing problems as well as preventing the reuse of the computer name, and clearing out WINS databases to correct the problem can be tricky.

First open Run from the Start menu, type in *dcpromo*, and click OK. Follow the steps in the previous section, "Demoting a Domain Controller." Once the domain controller is demoted, follow these steps to change the computer's network identity:

1. Open the System tool in Control Panel and click the Network Identification tab.

2. Click the Advanced button to open the Identification Changes dialog box.

3. Enter the new name for your computer (Figure 11-13), or make changes to the domain or workgroup to which the computer belongs.

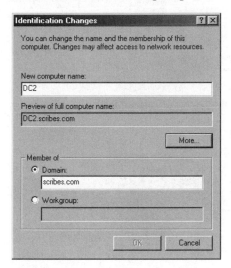

Figure 11-13. *The Identification Changes dialog box.*

4. Click the More button to manually specify the DNS domain name for the computer and to preview the NetBIOS name. Click OK when you're finished.

Note   Try to use a computer name that is both DNS and NetBIOS–compatible so that all types of clients see the same name for your computer. To do this, keep the name shorter than 15 characters in length and don't use asterisks or periods. It's also preferable to avoid using spaces, underscores, and hyphens for the best application compatibility.

Once you've made the change to the computer's network identity, you can promote it once more to a domain controller by following these steps:

1. Open Run from the Start menu and enter *dcpromo* to start the Active Directory Installation Wizard.

2. Select the type of domain controller you want—an additional controller for an existing domain or a controller for a new domain.

3. Supply a user name and password, being sure to use an account with sufficient privileges to perform the operation (Figure 11-14).

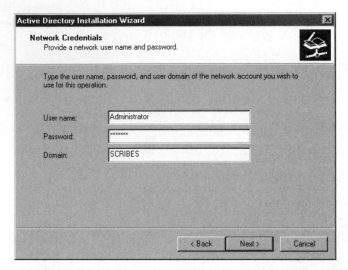

Figure 11-14. *The Network Credentials screen of the Active Directory Installation Wizard.*

4. Supply the full DNS name of the domain, the locations for the Active Directory database, the Active Directory log, and the Sysvol folder.

5. The Summary page will again show you which options you've selected. Click the Back button to make any changes; otherwise, click Next.

6. Active Directory will be configured (Figure 11-15). The process takes several minutes, even on a relatively fast system.

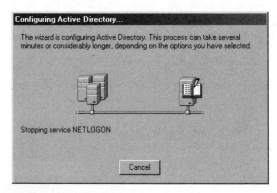

Figure 11-15. *The Configuring Active Directory screen.*

At the end of the process, the Active Directory Installation Wizard informs you that Active Directory is installed and to which domain and site. A reboot is required before the installation of Active Directory is complete.

Setting a Global Catalog Server

The first Windows 2000 domain controller in a forest is automatically a Global Catalog server. The Global Catalog (GC) contains a full replica of all directory objects in its host domain plus a partial replica of all directory objects in every domain in the forest. The point of a GC is to provide authentication for logons. In addition, because a GC contains information about all objects in all the domains in the forest, finding information in the directory doesn't require unnecessary queries across domains. A single query to the GC produces the information about where you can find the object.

> **Tip**   As long as your enterprise has any Windows NT domain controllers, each domain must have at least one Global Catalog server.

By default, there will be one GC, but any domain controller can be configured as a Global Catalog server. If you need additional logon and search services, you can have multiple Global Catalog servers in the domain.

To make a domain controller into a Global Catalog server, follow these steps:

1. Choose Active Directory Sites and Services from the Administrative Tools menu.
2. Open Sites and select the applicable site.
3. Open Servers and then select the domain controller you want to make into a Global Catalog server.
4. Select NTDS Settings from the righthand pane and choose Properties from the Action menu.
5. On the General tab, select the Global Catalog Server check box.

As long as your enterprise is operating in *mixed mode* (that is, you have domain controllers other than Windows 2000 domain controllers), you must have at least one Global Catalog server per domain. Once you've upgraded every domain controller to Windows 2000, you can switch the domain to native mode, described in "Changing the Domain Mode" later in this chapter.

Using Active Directory Domains and Trusts

Windows 2000 Active Directory Domains and Trusts is an MMC snap-in that you can use to view a tree display containing all the domains in your forest. With this snap-in, you can manage the trust relationships between the domains, change the domain mode, and configure the user principal name (UPN) suffixes for the forest. Active Directory Domains and Trusts also provides access to Active Directory Users and Computers for each domain that you use to view and modify the properties of individual objects.

Launching Active Directory Domains and Trusts

Windows 2000 Server adds the Active Directory Domains and Trusts Manager snap-in to the Start menu by default, so after logging on using an account with administrative privileges, you can run the utility by selecting Active Directory Domains and Trusts from Administrative Tools in the Start menu's Programs group. The MMC snap-in file is called Domain.msc, so you can also launch the manager from the Run dialog box by executing that filename.

When Active Directory Domains and Trusts Manager loads, the console tree (on the left) displays all the domains in the forest in expandable tree fashion, stemming from a root labeled Active Directory Domains and Trusts, as shown in Figure 11-16. The result pane (on the right) displays the children of the currently selected domain, or if you select the root, the root domains of all the trees in the forest. The functions provided by Active Directory Domains and Trusts are all accessible from the Action menus produced by clicking a domain name or the root object, as well as within the Properties window for a domain.

Figure 11-16. *The Active Directory Domains and Trusts snap-in.*

Changing the Domain Mode

When you open the Properties window for a domain, the General tab (Figure 11-17) displays the NetBIOS name by which the domain is known to downlevel clients and enables you to specify a description for that domain. This tab also displays the domain's current operational mode and allows you to change it.

Figure 11-17. *The General tab of the Properties window for a domain.*

By default, newly installed domain controllers operate in mixed mode, which means that you can use Windows NT BDCs as domain controllers in a Windows 2000 domain. Thus, you can upgrade an existing Windows NT domain to Windows 2000 gradually by first upgrading the Windows NT PDC to Windows 2000. You can then use Active Directory to store information about your domain and modify the directory using the Active Directory snap-ins included with Windows 2000 Server.

When Windows 2000 Server is operating in mixed mode, the Windows NT BDCs are fully functional domain controllers in the Active Directory domain, capable of multiple-master replication just like Windows 2000 domain controllers. The only drawback to using mixed mode is that you can't take advantage of the Windows 2000 advanced grouping features, such as the ability to nest groups and create groups with members in different domains.

Once you've completed upgrading all the Windows NT BDCs in your domain to Windows 2000, you can switch the computer to native mode, which enables these grouping capabilities. However, once you switch the operational mode for the domain from mixed to native, you can't switch it back without reinstalling Active Directory. Be sure that you'll have no further need for Windows NT domain controllers on your network before making this modification.

> **Note** Mixed mode refers to the domain controllers only in a particular domain. After switching to native mode, you can still use Windows NT domain controllers in the same tree, as long as they are located in different domains.

Managing Domain Trust Relationships

The trust relationship between domains is managed on the Trusts tab of a domain's Properties window (Figure 11-18). When you establish a trust relationship between two domains, users in one domain can access resources located in another trusted domain. An Active Directory domain tree is a collection of domains that share not only the same schema, configuration, and namespace, but are also connected by trust relationships.

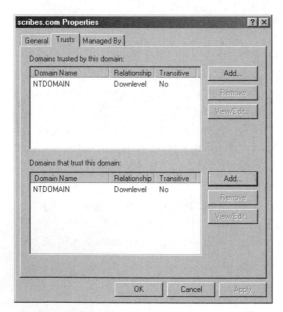

Figure 11-18. *The Trusts tab of the Properties window for a domain.*

Windows 2000 supports two types of trust relationships: the explicit, one-way trusts used by Windows NT, and the transitive, hierarchical trusts provided in Active Directory domains by the Kerberos security protocol. Windows NT trust relationships function in only one direction. For example, when domain A trusts the users in domain B, it doesn't automatically follow that B trusts the users in A. An administrator must explicitly create the trusts in both directions to achieve a mutual relationship between the domains.

Active Directory automatically creates Kerberos trust relationships in all the domains in a tree; they run in both directions, and they are transitive. A *transitive trust relationship* is one that is propagated throughout a tree hierarchy. For instance, when domain A trusts domain B and domain B trusts domain C, then domain A trusts domain C. The creation of each new domain in a tree includes the establishment of the trust relationships with all the other domains in the tree, enabling users to access resources in any one of the tree's domains (assuming they have the appropriate permissions) without manual configuration by an administrator.

To provide domain access to users in another tree or to grant the users in your domain access to another tree, you can manually establish trust relationships by clicking one of the Add buttons on the Trusts tab and specifying the name of a domain. These are one-way relationships; you must establish a trust for each domain in order to create a bidirectional trust. Depending on the nature of the domain to trust or be trusted, the relationship might or might not be transitive. You can establish a transitive trust relationship with Windows 2000 domains in another tree, but relationships with Windows NT domains can't be transitive.

To establish a trust relationship with another domain, you specify the name of the domain in the Add Trusted Domain dialog box and supply a password. To complete the process, an administrator of the other domain must specify the name of your domain in the Add Trusting Domain dialog box and furnish the same password. Both domains must approve before the systems can establish the trust relationship.

Specifying the Domain Manager

The third tab in a domain's Properties window, shown in Figure 11-19, identifies the individual who is the designated manager for the domain. This tab provides contact information about the manager derived from the associated user account in Active Directory. You can change the manager by clicking the Change button and selecting another user account from the Active Directory display shown.

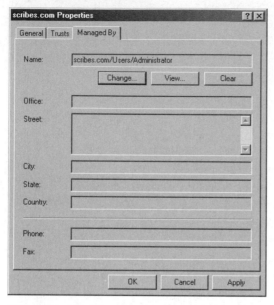

Figure 11-19. *The Managed By tab of a domain's Properties window.*

Configuring User Principle Name Suffixes for a Forest

A UPN is a simplified name that users can supply when logging on to Active Directory. The name uses the standard e-mail address format consisting of a user-name prefix and a domain-name suffix, separated by an at sign (@), as defined in RFC 822 (for example, *user@domain.com*). UPNs provide network users with a unified logon name format that insulates them from the Active Directory domain hierarchy and the need to specify the complex LDAP name for their user objects when logging on.

By default, the suffix of the UPN for users in a particular forest is the name of the first domain created in the first tree of that forest, also called the *forest DNS name*. Using Active Directory Domains and Trusts Manager, you can specify additional UPN suffixes that users can employ in place of the forest DNS name when logging on. To do this, you select the root object in the console tree of the main Active Directory Domains and Trusts display (that is, the object labeled *Active Directory Domains and Trusts*), and choose Properties from the Action menu. On the UPN Suffixes tab, click the Add button to specify additional suffixes. These suffixes apply to the entire forest and are available to any user in any domain of any tree in that forest.

Managing Domains

The Active Directory Domains and Trusts snap-in also provides access to the Active Directory Users and Computers snap-in that you use to view and modify the objects in a domain and their properties. When you select a domain in the console tree of the main display and choose Manage from the Action menu, the MMC opens the Active Directory Users and Computers snap-in with the focus on the selected domain.

Using Active Directory Users and Computers

The Active Directory Users and Computers snap-in is the primary tool for Active Directory administrators, and it's the tool that you will use most often for day-to-day directory maintenance. Active Directory Users and Computers displays all the objects in a domain by using a Windows Explorer–style expandable tree display. Dialog boxes for each object provide access to the object's properties, which you can modify to update user information and account restrictions.

You also use Active Directory Users and Computers to create new objects and model the tree hierarchy by creating and populating container objects like organizational units (OUs). The following sections examine the most common tasks that administrators perform using Active Directory Users and Computers.

Launching Active Directory Users and Computers

Active Directory Users and Computers, like most of the Active Directory administration tools, is a snap-in for the MMC. The snap-in file is called Dsa.msc, and you can launch the manager in any one of three ways.

- Select Active Directory Users and Computers from the Administrative Tools group in the Start menu's Programs group.
- Highlight a domain in the console tree of the Active Directory Domains and Trusts snap-in, and choose Manage from the Action menu. This opens a new MMC dialog box called Active Directory Users and Computers, leaving the existing Domains And Trusts window intact.
- Open the Run dialog box from the Start menu and execute the Dsa.msc snap-in file.

To perform many of the functions provided by the Active Directory Users and Computers snap-in, you must be logged on to the domain using an account that has administrative privileges. You can use the Delegation of Control Wizard to delegate administration tasks for specific objects to other users without giving them full administrative access to the domain, as discussed in "Delegating Object Control" later in this chapter.

Viewing Active Directory Objects

The main Active Directory Users and Computers dialog box (Figure 11-20) contains many of the standard MMC display elements. The console tree (on the left) lists an Active Directory domain and the container objects within it in an expandable display. The result pane (on the right) displays the objects within the highlighted container. The manager includes a specialized toolbar providing quick access to commonly used functions and a description bar that provides information about the manager's status or the currently highlighted object. The program displays the actions that you can perform on each object in the Action menu once you have clicked the objects.

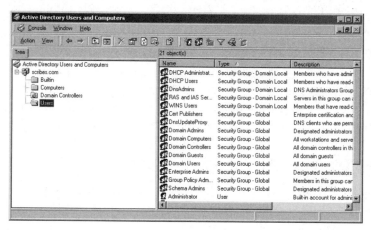

Figure 11-20. *The main Active Directory Users and Computers screen.*

Active Directory Object Types

The objects in the Active Directory Users and Computers screen represent both physical entities, such as computers and users, and logical ones, such as groups and organizational units. The default object types in a newly created Active Directory domain are listed in Table 11-1.

Table 11-1.   Object types created in a new Active Directory domain

Object Type	Icon	Function
Domain		Root object of Active Directory Users and Computers display; identifies the domain currently being administered by the manager.
Organizational Unit		Container object used to create logical groupings of computer, user, and group objects.
User		Represents a network user and functions as a repository for identification and authentication data.
Computer		Represents a computer on the network and provides the machine account needed for the system to log on to the domain.
Contact		Represents a user external to the domain for specific purposes such as e-mail delivery; doesn't provide the credentials needed to log on to the domain.
Group		Container object representing a logical grouping of users, computers, or other groups (or all three) that is independent of the Active Directory tree structure. Groups can contain objects from different organizational units and domains.
Shared Folder		Provides Active Directory–based network access to a shared folder on a Windows 2000 system.
Shared Printer		Provides Active Directory–based network access to a shared printer on a Windows 2000 system.

By modifying the schema that control the directory service structure, you can create new object types in Active Directory and modify the attributes of existing types. For more information, see "Using Active Directory Schema Manager" in Chapter 12.

Normal Mode vs. Advanced Mode

By default, the Active Directory Users and Computers display operates in normal mode. Normal mode displays only the objects that administrators are most likely to access during a typical Active Directory maintenance session. This includes the organizational units containing the built-in users and groups created during Active Directory installation and all the objects created by administrators after the installation. Normal mode also hides certain tabs in an object's Properties window from view, including the Object tab and the Security tab that you use to set permissions for the object.

When you choose Advanced Features from the manager's View menu, however, the display changes to include all the system objects in Active Directory, which represent policies, DNS records, and other directory service elements, as well as the LostAndFound container, shown in Figure 11-21.

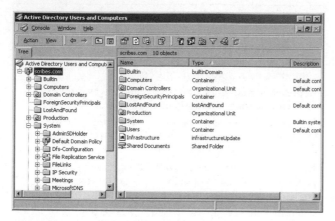

Figure 11-21. *The Active Directory Users and Computers Advanced Features mode displaying all of the system objects in the selected domain.*

From this interface, you can view information about the system objects and control access to them by modifying the associated permissions. Because access to these objects isn't required as frequently, you can suppress their appearance by leaving the manager in normal mode. However, when you want to modify the permissions for standard objects like organizational units, users, and groups, you must enable Advanced Features to see the Security tab in an object's Properties window.

Changing the Domain

You can use the Active Directory Users and Computers snap-in to administer any domain on the network. To change the currently displayed domain in the manager, highlight the root or domain object in the console tree and choose Connect To Domain from the Action menu. This displays the Connect To Domain dialog box, where you can enter the name of the domain or browse to another domain.

From the Action menu, you can also choose Connect To Domain Controller to access the selected domain by using a specific domain controller on the network. Unless your domain controllers are out of sync, the information should be the same on all of the replicas, but sometimes you might want to select a domain controller at a different location to avoid a slow or expensive WAN connection.

Using Filters to Simplify the Display

When you begin to populate Active Directory with new objects, it can rapidly grow to an unwieldy size. The sheer number of objects in the display can make locating the specific object you need difficult. To temporarily suppress the display of objects you don't need to see, you can apply a filter to the Active Directory Users and Computers snap-in based on object types or based on the contents of specific object attributes.

When you choose Filter Options from the View menu, the Filtering Options dialog box appears, as shown in Figure 11-22. Here you can opt to display all object types, select specific object types to display, or build a custom filter based on object attributes.

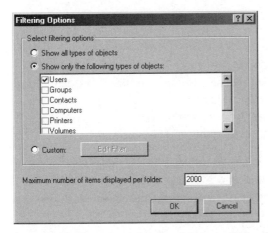

Figure 11-22. *The Filtering Options dialog box of Active Directory Users and Computers.*

When you select the Custom option and click the Edit Filter button, you see a Find Custom Search dialog box like the one shown in Figure 11-23. In this dialog box, you can select an object type, choose an attribute of that object, and specify a full or partial value for that attribute.

For example, you can display only the user objects that have the value *Sales* in the *Department* attribute (as shown in the figure), or you can choose to display only the users that have a particular area code in the *Telephone Number* attribute. This enables you to quickly zero in on the objects you need to use without scrolling through an unnecessarily cluttered display.

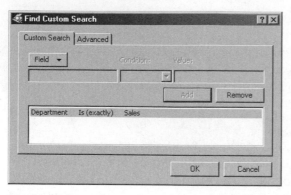

Figure 11-23. *The Find Custom Search dialog box of Active Directory Users and Computers.*

Finding Objects

You can also search for specific objects in the entire Active Directory without modifying the manager's display. By selecting the domain object and choosing Find from the Action menu, you display the Find Users, Contacts, And Groups dialog box (Figure 11-24), in which you can specify the type of object you want to locate, a specific domain, or the entire directory, and the name and description of the object.

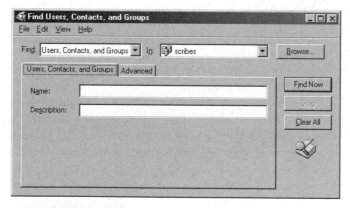

Figure 11-24. *The Find Users, Contacts, And Groups dialog box of Active Directory Users and Computers.*

The program then searches the GC that is automatically created on the first controller in a domain to locate the desired object. The GC is a subset of the entire Active Directory, containing only the most commonly used attributes, which makes it easier to search for a specific object. Without the GC, the task of searching an Active Directory installation that includes domain controllers in remote locations could require extensive WAN traffic that is both slow and expensive.

> **Note** Although Active Directory always creates the GC on the first domain controller for a domain, you can change its default location by modifying the NTDS settings in the Active Directory Sites and Services snap-in. You can also specify additional attributes that are to be stored in the GC by using the Active Directory Schema snap-in.

The Advanced tab in the Find Users, Contacts, and Groups dialog box uses the same interface as the Custom Filter feature discussed in the previous section. In the same way, you can search for objects based on any of their attributes. If an attribute you select isn't part of the GC, the search will proceed by looking through the actual contents of the domain controllers on your network. In some cases, this can slow down the search process considerably.

> **Tip** Much of the same Active Directory object searching functionality found in the Active Directory Users and Computers snap-in is also available from the Start menu's Search feature.

Default Active Directory Objects

A newly created Active Directory domain contains organizational unit, computer, user, and group objects that the Active Directory Installation Wizard creates by default. These objects provide access to the system at several levels and include groups that enable administrators to delegate specific network maintenance tasks to others. Even if you don't expect to use these objects in the future, you must use them to create other objects with the appropriate permissions for your network.

If, for example, you don't want to have any single user with the full control granted to the administrator account, you must still log on as administrator in order to create new user objects with the rights and permissions you want. With Active Directory, you can "orphan" parts of the directory structure if you modify, delete, or disable the administrator account without first creating other user objects and granting them equivalent permissions to the various parts of the directory.

The default objects created in an Active Directory domain, along with their functions and their locations in the domain hierarchy, are listed in Table 11-2.

Table 11-2. Objects created by default in an Active Directory domain

Object Name	Object Type	Location	Function
Builtin	Builtin Domain	Domain root	Default container for groups providing access to server administration functions.
Computers	Container	Domain root	Default container for upgraded computer accounts.
Users	Container	Domain root	Default container for upgraded user accounts.
Domain Controllers	Organizational Unit	Domain root	Default container for new Windows 2000 domain controllers.
Account Operators	Security Group—Builtin Local	Builtin	Members can administer domain user and group accounts.
Administrators	Security Group—Builtin Local	Builtin	Members can fully administer the computer/domain.
Backup Operators	Security Group—Builtin Local	Builtin	Members can bypass file security to back up files.
Guests	Security Group—Builtin Local	Builtin	Users are granted guest access to the computer/domain.
Print Operators	Security Group—Builtin Local	Builtin	Members can administer domain printers.
Replicator	Security Group—Builtin Local	Builtin	Supports file replication in a domain.
Server Operators	Security Group—Builtin Local	Builtin	Members can administer domain servers.
Users	Security Group—Builtin Local	Builtin	Ordinary users.
DHCP Users	Security Group—Domain Local	Users container	Members who have read-only access to DHCP Server.
DnsAdmins	Security Group—Domain Local	Users container	DNS administrators.
RAS and IAS Servers	Security Group—Domain Local	Users container	RAS and IAS Servers.
WINS Users	Security Group—Domain Local	Users container	Members that have read-only access to WINS.
Cert Publishers	Security Group—Global	Users container	Enterprise certification and renewal agents.

Table 11-2. *continued*

Object Name	Object Type	Location	Function
DnsUpdateProxy	Security Group—Global	Users container	DNS clients that are permitted to perform dynamic updates on behalf of some other clients (such as DHCP servers).
Domain Admins	Security Group—Global	Users container	Designated administrators of the domain.
Domain Computers	Security Group—Global	Users container	All workstations and servers joined to the domain.
Domain Controllers	Security Group—Global	Users container	All domain controllers in the domain.
Domain Guests	Security Group—Global	Users container	All domain guests.
Domain Users	Security Group—Global	Users container	All domain users.
Enterprise Admins	Security Group—Global	Users container	Designated administrators of the enterprise.
Schema Admins	Security Group—Global	Users container	Designated administrators of the schema.
Administrator	User	Users container	Built-in account for administering the computer/domain.
Guest	User	Users container	Built-in account for guest access to the computer/domain.
IUSR_xxx	User	Users container	Built-in account for anonymous access to Internet Information Services (IIS).
IWAM_xxx	User	Users container	Built-in account for anonymous access to IIS out-of-process applications.
Krbtgt	User	Users container	Key Distribution Center Service Account.

The next sections examine the procedures for creating new objects in a domain and modifying their attributes.

Creating an Organizational Unit

The directory service schema dictate which objects you can create in an Active Directory domain, where they can be located, and which attributes they are permitted to have. Active Directory Users and Computers lets you create objects only in locations appropriate to the object type. For example, you can't create an organizational unit (OU) object that is subordinate to a user object, but a user object can be subordinate to an OU object.

OUs can be subordinate to each other, however, and the number of OU layers you can create in your Active Directory domain is unlimited. To create an OU, you click the domain object or another OU in the Active Directory Users and Computers scope or result pane, and choose New from the Action menu and select Organizational Unit. You can also click the Create New Organizational Unit button on the Active Directory Users and Computers toolbar to achieve the same effect. After you specify a name for the new object in the Create New Object dialog box, the manager creates an icon with the appropriate name and inserts it into the Active Directory Users and Computers display.

Once you've created an OU, you can populate it with other objects, such as users, computers, groups, and other OUs, or you can modify its attributes by opening the Properties window from the Action menu.

Configuring OU Objects

The Properties window for an OU consists of three tabs. The General tab and the Managed By tab enable you to specify information about the OU such as a descriptive phrase and an address for the location of the object, as well as the identity of the person responsible for managing the OU. The information that you include on these tabs (if any) depends on the criteria you use to design your Active Directory. An OU can be associated with a particular department within an organization, a physical location such as a room, a floor, or a building, or even a branch office in a particular city or country.

The Group Policy tab is where you create and manage the links to group policy objects in Active Directory. Group policy objects are collections of system settings that control the appearance and functionality of network clients. When you apply group policies to OUs, domains, and sites, the system settings are inherited by all the objects contained in those entities. You can link OUs to multiple group policy objects on this tab, and you can control the priorities with which the policies are applied. When you use the Edit button on the Group Policy tab to modify a group policy object, Active Directory Users and Computers launches the Group

Policy snap-in for the MMC. (For more on setting group policy and using the Group Policy snap-in, see Chapter 9.)

When you enable Advanced Features in the Active Directory Users and Computers View menu, the OU's Properties window also displays the Object tab (Figure 11-25) and the Security tab (Figure 11-26). The Object tab displays the full path to the object in the domain hierarchy, the dates and times of its creation and last modification, and the update sequence numbers from when it was created and last modified.

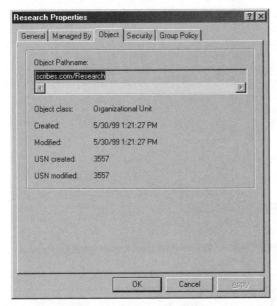

Figure 11-25. *The Object tab of the Research Properties window.*

The Security tab enables you to control access to the object by assigning permissions to users and groups. With the Allow Inheritable Permissions check box, you can also control whether the object inherits permissions that have been assigned to its parent object.

The Advanced button on the Security tab provides access to the Access Control Settings dialog box, shown in Figure 11-27, from which you can control access to the object in much greater detail. In the Security dialog box, you can specify whether specific users and groups are permitted to create and delete child objects in the OU, but this screen enables you to specify which object types they can create and delete.

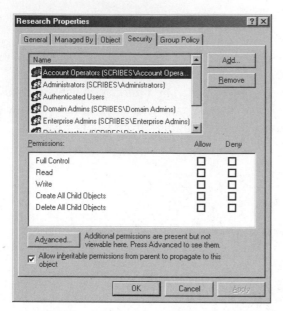

Figure 11-26. *The Security tab of the Research Properties window.*

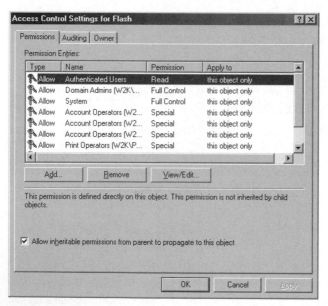

Figure 11-27. *The Access Control Settings dialog box.*

Delegating Object Control

Active Directory is designed to support much larger enterprise networks than Windows NT domains, and larger networks naturally require more attention and maintenance from administrators. Active Directory makes it possible for administrators to delegate control over specific container objects to other users without giving them full access to the domain. To do this, launch the Delegation of Control Wizard by choosing Delegate Control from the Action menu for a domain or organizational unit.

The wizard first prompts you to specify the container object over which you want to delegate control and the users, groups (or both) to whom you want to delegate control. Once you've done this, the wizard displays the Active Directory Object Type screen (Figure 11-28) that you use to specify which types of objects in the container the selected users/groups should be able to control. You can, for example, grant a specific user or group control over the user objects in only the container, enabling them to update user information but preventing them from modifying other types of objects.

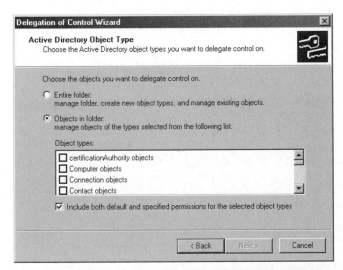

Figure 11-28. *The Active Directory Object Type screen of the Delegation of Control Wizard.*

In the Permissions dialog box, you specify the degree of control you want the selected users/groups to have over the objects you selected. The Filter Options box enables you to select whether you want to work with general permissions that concern the entire object, or property permissions that control access to the object's individual attributes. With this type of permission, you can grant users the ability to modify some of an object's properties while protecting others. This way, you can conceivably allow department managers to perform simple modifications on user objects, such as changing addresses and phone numbers, without endangering any other properties of the object.

Once you've supplied the wizard with the appropriate information, it configures the selected object with the appropriate permissions. If you check out the Security tab in the object's Properties window (which is visible only when Advanced Features is enabled in the Active Directory Users and Computers View menu), you can see the permissions that the wizard has assigned to the users or groups you selected.

Creating a User Object

A typical Active Directory installation usually consists of more user objects than any other type, and the creation and management of user objects accounts for much of the Active Directory administration burden. The task of manually creating a user object is just like that of creating an organizational unit or any other object. After selecting the container in which the user object will reside (usually an OU), you select the container and choose New from the Action menu and select User or click the Create New User button on the Active Directory Users and Computers toolbar, producing the dialog box shown in Figure 11-29.

Figure 11-29. *The Create New Object dialog box.*

In the Create New Object dialog box, you specify the first and last name of the user and the logon name that the user will supply when connecting to the network. The downlevel logon name for the user (that is, the name with which the user will log on at Windows NT or Windows 9.x workstations) then appears automatically. The next dialog box provides a field for the user object's password and enables you to set basic password and account options for the user, as follows:

- User must change password at next logon
- User cannot change password
- Password never expires
- Account disabled

After a summary screen confirming your input, Active Directory Users and Computers creates the user object in the container you selected.

Configuring User Objects

Once you've created a user object, you can proceed to the configuration process, in which you add information about the user to the Active Directory database and define the user's access to the network. The Action menu that Active Directory Users and Computers generates when you click a user object contains several of the commands most commonly used by administrators, as well as access to the Properties window for the user. These commands are as follows:

- **Add Members To A Group** Generates a dialog box from which you can select the groups to which the user will belong
- **Name Mappings** (visible only when Advanced Features is enabled) Enables administrators to map X.509 certificates and Kerberos names to the user object
- **Disable Account** Prevents the user from logging on to the network using the account until it is manually enabled by an administrator
- **Reset Password** Generates a dialog box with which you can modify the user account's logon password
- **Move** Enables administrators to move the user object to another container object (that is, domain or organizational unit) in Active Directory
- **Open Home Page** Opens the default browser on the system and displays the URL listed in the *Home Page* field on the General tab of the user object's Properties window

- **Send Mail** Opens the default e-mail client on the system and addresses a message using the e-mail address listed in the *E-Mail* field on the General tab of the user object's Properties window.

While Active Directory Users and Computers provides these functions on the Action menu for the sake of convenience, you can also access most of them through the user object's Properties window, which provides a complete interface to the object's attributes. The following sections examine the 11 tabs in this window and the functions located on each one.

Note The attributes appearing on the tabs of the Properties window are those included in the default schema used by Active Directory. You can modify the schema to create additional attributes or change existing ones by using the MMC Active Directory Schema Manager snap-in. See Chapter 12 for more information on using this tool.

The General Tab

The General tab contains basic information about the user, including the first and last names you specified when creating the object. This tab also has fields for a descriptive phrase about the user, office location, and the user's telephone number, e-mail address, and home page URL. Apart from the *name* fields, the information on this tab is optional and is used solely for reference purposes. Users can search Active Directory using the values of the attributes on this (and other) tabs and automatically insert the user's e-mail address and home page URL into the appropriate client applications, but these fields don't affect the user's access to the network in any palpable way.

The Address Tab

On the Address tab, you find fields where you can insert mailing address information for the user. As on the General tab, these are reference fields that don't play a major role in the object's configuration.

The Account Tab

The Account tab (Figure 11-30) contains the user logon name you specified during the creation of the object as well as its downlevel user name.

The Logon Hours button and the Logon To button provide access to dialog boxes that enable you to restrict the hours and days of the week that the user is permitted to log on to the network (Figure 11-31) and the workstations from which the user can log on to the network.

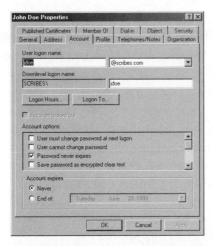

Figure 11-30. *The Account tab of the Properties window.*

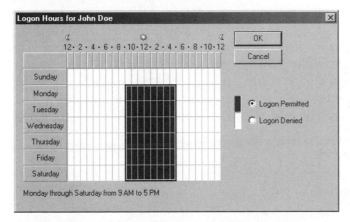

Figure 11-31. *The Logon Hours dialog box.*

The Account Locked Out check box is selected whenever the user account has been disabled, either deliberately by an administrator, or because of repeated logon failures. Clearing this check box releases the account and permits the user to log on again. The Account Options area contains numerous password and account options (some of which are duplicated in the Create New Object dialog box). When creating new user accounts, the following must be selected or cleared:

- **User Must Change Password At Next Logon**   Presents the user with a dialog box during the next logon requiring a new password
- **User Cannot Change Password**   Prevents the user from changing his or her own password

- **Password Never Expires**   Prevents the user account from being subject to expiration policies defined in the Account Expires box
- **Account Disabled**   Prevents the user from logging on using this account until it is cleared by an administrator

The Profile Tab

On the Profile tab, you can specify the location of the user profile associated with the object. By default, every user who logs on to a Windows 2000 system has a profile directory created in the Documents And Settings folder on the system drive. When you specify a profile path on this tab, the system stores a copy of the profile in the specified directory. If this directory is located on a shared network drive, the user can access the profile from any system on the network. The *Logon Script* field specifies the name of the script that the workstation should execute when the user logs on to the network.

From the Home Directory box, you can create a personal directory on a network drive over which the user has full control. Storing data files on a network drive makes it easier to protect them from tampering and accidental erasure. You can configure the workstation to map a drive to the shared drive automatically during the logon process by specifying a drive letter and the UNC name of a network share in the *Connect* fields. In the *Shared Documents Folder* field, you can specify a location where users who require access to the same documents can store files.

The Telephones/Notes Tab

The Telephones/Notes tab contains fields for all the various phone numbers associated with a user, including pager, mobile, fax, and IP phone numbers. A multiline *Comments* field provides a general-purpose area for notes.

The Organization Tab

The Organization tab provides fields in which you can specify the user's title, department, and company. In the Manager box, you can identify the user's superior by selecting another user object from Active Directory. A multiline *Direct Report* field can store a supervisor's notes on the user.

The Member Of Tab

The Member Of tab is where you specify the groups of which the user should be a member. Clicking the Add button displays an object listing from which you can select the appropriate groups. The Set Primary Group button is enabled only for

Macintosh users. The Windows Services for Macintosh recognizes a single group affiliation—usually the group with which the Macintosh user shares documents on a server.

Note   You can also add a user to a group from the Members tab of the group object's Properties window.

The Dial-In Tab

On the Dial-In tab, you control whether the user should be permitted access to the network through a dial-in Remote Access Service (RAS) connection. With the Allow Access option, you can select whether the user object should require callback or caller ID for security verification, and you can specify a static IP address and static routes for the connection.

The Published Certificates Tab

The Published Certificates tab, which is visible only when you enable the Active Directory Users and Computers Advanced Features display option, lets you manage the X.509 certificates linked to the user object. From this page, you can view the certificates published for the user account, add new certificates, remove certificates, and export certificates to files.

The Object Tab

The Object tab (visible only when Advanced Features is enabled) displays the full pathname of the user object, the dates it was created and last modified, and the update sequence numbers (USNs) from when it was created and last modified.

The Security Tab

The Security tab (also visible only when Advanced Features is enabled) lets you assign permissions that control access to the user object. The tab is virtually identical to the same tab in the Properties windows for other object types. Chapter 9 has more information on the creation and configuration of user accounts.

Creating a Group

Group objects make it possible to assign permissions and other object attributes to multiple users in a single operation, as well as to distribute e-mail to large number of addresses (when Microsoft Exchange Server is installed). When you assign permissions to an Active Directory object (or to an NTFS file or directory), you can add groups to the object's access control list (ACL), which causes the permissions to be propagated to all of the group's members. You create group objects in Active Directory Users and Computers just as you would any other object type, and then you select the objects that you want to be members of the group.

Group objects can exist in organizational units, in other groups (when the domain is operating in native mode), or directly beneath the domain root. When you select one of these container objects in Active Directory Users and Computers and choose New from the Action menu and select Group, you see the Create New Object dialog box shown in Figure 11-32.

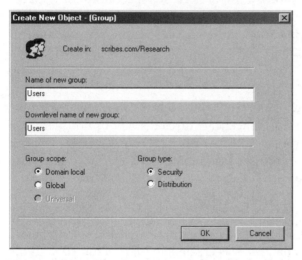

Figure 11-32. *The Create New Object dialog box.*

As with other objects, you must first specify a name (up to 64 characters long) for the new group and a downlevel NetBIOS name equivalent (up to 15 characters long). Then with the Group Scope options, you select one of the following options:

- **Domain Local**   A Domain Local group can contain user objects, other Domain Local groups in the same domain, Global groups from any domain in the forest, and Universal groups. You can insert Domain Local groups into the ACL for any object in that domain but not objects in other domains. Domain Local groups don't appear in the GC.

- **Global**   A Global group can contain user objects and other Global groups from the same domain. Unlike Domain Local groups, you can insert Global groups into the ACL for any object in the forest. Global groups are included in the GC, but their members are not; Global group memberships are replicated only within their domain.

- **Universal**   The most comprehensive group scope, a Universal group can contain other Universal groups, Global groups, and users from any domain in the forest. Like Global groups, you can insert Universal groups into the ACL for any object in the forest. Universal groups appear in the GC with their members; using Global groups as members of the Universal group lessens the update traffic to the GC because changes to the Global group memberships (which aren't included in the catalog) are far more frequent than changes to the Universal group memberships.

> **Note**   Group nesting (that is, the storage of groups within other groups) is an Active Directory feature that is available only when the domain is running in native mode. To operate in native mode, all of the domain's controllers must be running Windows 2000 Server. For more information on switching from mixed mode to native mode, see "Changing the Domain Mode" in this chapter.

After selecting the group scope, you select one of the following group types.

- **Security**   Security groups are intended for inclusion in the ACLs of network resources such as files and printers. They can also serve as distribution lists for e-mail.

- **Distribution**   Distribution groups are intended solely for use as e-mail distribution lists.

When you click OK, the manager creates the group object in the container you selected.

Configuring Group Objects

The Properties window for a group object contains up to six tabs (depending on whether Advanced Features is enabled).

The General Tab

The General tab provides fields where you can insert a description of the group object, specifies the group's type and scope, and includes a multiline field for comments.

The Members Tab

The Members tab is where you specify the objects that are to be the members of the group. Clicking the Add button produces a dialog box in which you can browse Active Directory and select the desired objects.

The Member Of Tab

When operating in native mode, Active Directory group objects can be members of other objects. On the Member Of tab, you can select the groups of which the new group is to be a member.

The Managed By Tab

The Managed By tab enables you to specify information about the person responsible for administering the group object.

The Object Tab

The Object tab (which appears only when Advanced Features is enabled in Active Directory Users and Computers) displays the full pathname of the group object, the dates of its creation and last modification, and its USNs at its creation and last modification.

The Security Tab

The Security tab (which appears only when Advanced Features is enabled in Active Directory Users and Computers) enables you to set the permissions that specify which objects will have access to the group object and how much access they will have.

Creating a Computer Object

In addition to container objects, group objects, and user objects, Active Directory also has objects representing computers. To log on to a domain, a Windows 2000 computer must have an object representing it in the Active Directory hierarchy. When you promote a system to a domain controller or log on to a domain for the first time, Windows 2000 automatically creates a computer object. (In the case of a first-time logon, the system prompts for the user name and password of an account with sufficient privileges to create new objects. However, you can also create computer objects manually, just as you would create any other object.)

Selecting a container, choosing New from the Action menu and selecting Computer produces a Create New Object dialog box in which you supply the name for the new computer object (which can be the computer's NetBIOS or DNS name). You can also specify the particular user or group that is authorized to join the computer to the domain.

> **Tip** The Active Directory Users and Computers snap-in creates objects one at a time, but sometimes administrators have to create a great many objects, and this tool becomes impractical. For more information on creating objects en masse, see "Batch Importing and Exporting" in Chapter 12.

Configuring Computer Objects

Once Active Directory Users and Computers creates the computer object, you can configure its attributes using the following seven properties: General, Operating System, Member Of, Location, Managed By, Object, and Security. Almost all of the tabs have the same purpose as those in other objects. The two that are unique to the Computer object are Operating System and Location.

The Operating System tab identifies the operating system running on the computer, the version, and the currently installed service pack. These fields are not editable; they are blank when you manually create a computer object and are filled in when the computer joins a domain. The Location tab enables you to specify which locations are served by the site in the directory setup.

Using Remote Computer Management

Active Directory Users and Computers provides administrative access to remote computers represented by objects in Active Directory. When you click a computer object and choose Manage from the Action menu, the manager opens the MMC Computer Management snap-in with that computer as its focus. With this capability, you can read the remote system's event logs, manipulate its services, and perform many of the other tasks provided by the Computer Management snap-in.

Publishing a Shared Folder

Shared folder objects enable you to publish shared network directories in Active Directory, enabling users to access them directly by browsing in the Network Neighborhood for the object. This eliminates the need for users to know the exact location of the shared folder. Creating a shared folder object doesn't actually create the share; you must do this manually on the Sharing tab of the drive or folder's Properties window in the Windows Explorer window or the My Computer window. You can also create shared folder objects from Distributed file system (Dfs) folders.

To create a shared folder object, click a container object in Active Directory Users and Computers and choose New from the Action menu and select Shared Folder. In the Create New Object dialog box, specify a name for the new object and enter the UNC pathname to the share. After the manager creates the object, you can configure it using the tabs in the object's Properties window (described on pages 51-52).

> **Note**   The permissions that you set on the Security tab of the shared folder's Properties window don't control access to the shared folder itself, only to the shared folder object. To access the folder by using Active Directory, a user must have permission to access both the share and the object. The same is true for a printer object.

Publishing a Printer

Creating a printer object enables users to access the printer through Active Directory in much the same way that they can access shared folders. You create a printer object just as you do a shared folder object, by selecting a container and choosing New\Printer from the Action menu and specifying the UNC path to the shared printer. The manager then creates the object, combining the name of the host system and the share to form the object name.

Moving, Renaming, and Deleting Objects

Once you've created objects in Active Directory, you can use Active Directory Users and Computers to remodel your tree at any time by moving objects to different containers, renaming them, and deleting them. The Action menu for nearly every Active Directory object contains a Move command that opens a dialog box in which you can browse for a container where you want to place the object. You can also select several objects by holding down the Ctrl key while clicking them and move them all to the same container.

Moving a container object to a new location automatically moves all of the objects within the container at the same time and also modifies the references to that object in all other Active Directory objects. If, for example, User X is a member of Group Y and you move the organizational unit containing X's user object to a new location, X remains a member of Y, and Group Y's member list is automatically updated to show X in its new location. In the same way, when you rename an object using the Rename command on the Action menu or by clicking the object once, all the references to that object throughout Active Directory change to reflect the new name. When you delete a container object, all of the objects in the container are deleted as well.

Summary

This chapter has covered the basic tools and techniques for administering Active Directory in Windows 2000 Server. Active Directory Users and Computers, in particular, is a tool that administrators use frequently to perform day-to-day maintenance tasks. The next chapter covers Active Directory tools that you'll use far less often.

Chapter 12
Managing Active Directory

Tasks like promoting domain controllers and creating and configuring objects are required in every Active Directory installation, but many administrators of smaller networks never have to deal with the more advanced features of Active Directory. This chapter discusses Active Directory management tools that administrators use only once in a great while, and some administrators never use at all. Tasks like modifying the Active Directory schema and dividing a large network into sites are not to be taken lightly. You should fully understand the ramifications of your actions before you even load tools like Active Directory Sites and Services or Active Directory Schema snap-ins.

Using Active Directory Sites and Services

Active Directory Sites and Services is a snap-in for the Microsoft Management Console (MMC) that administrators use to create and manage the sites that make up a Microsoft Windows 2000 network as well as to establish links between sites. A *site*, in Active Directory terminology, is defined as a group of computers on one or more Internet Protocol subnets that are well connected. A *subnet* is network that is a component of a larger network. For more information on subnets, see Chapter 13.

Well connected means that the systems share a network transport that provides low-cost, high-speed communications between the machines and typically refers to systems in a single location that are connected by LANs. Systems that aren't well connected are those that use relatively slow, expensive communications. Active Directory consists of one or more sites, but sites aren't part of the name-spaces you deal with when you create the Active Directory hierarchy.

When designing trees and forests for Active Directory installation, the boundaries between forests, trees, domains, and organizational units (OUs) are often politically motivated. For example, Active Directory for a large corporation might consist of separate trees corresponding to corporate divisions, domains for individual departments, and OUs for workgroups. Sites, on the other hand, are always based on geographical locations and the types of connections between those locations.

As an example, suppose this imaginary corporation has two divisions, each of which has its own Fast Ethernet LAN running at 100 Mbps. If the two divisions are located in separate buildings on the same campus, they might have a high-speed fiber-optic connection between the two LANs, also running at 100 Mbps. In this case, because all of the computers in the two divisions are equally well connected, they can be said to form a single site. If, on the other hand, the two divisions are located in separate cities and are connected by a T-1 operating at only 1.544 Mbps, the divisions would form two separate sites because all of the computers on the network aren't equally well connected.

Sites don't appear as objects in the Active Directory namespace; they're completely separate from the hierarchy of forests, trees, and domains. A site can contain objects from different domains, and a domain's objects can be split among different sites. The basic reasons for dividing an enterprise network into sites is to take advantage of the efficient communications between well-connected systems while regulating the traffic over slower, costlier connections. Specifically, Active Directory uses sites during *authentication* and *replication*.

- **Authentication**   When a user logs on to the network from a workstation, the system authenticates the user with a domain controller at the same site whenever possible. This speeds up the authentication process and helps to reduce WAN traffic.

- **Replication**   Domain controller replication activities that must cross site boundaries are subject to special conditions because of the need to use WAN connections.

Sites in Active Directory are associated with particular IP subnets used by your network. During the authentication process, the workstation transmits information about the subnet on which it resides. Domain controllers use this information to locate an Active Directory server on the same subnet as the workstation.

The use of sites during replication is more complex. When two domain controllers are located at the same site, replication takes place at full LAN speed: usually from 10 to 100 Mbps. Two domain controllers located in different buildings or cities, on the other hand, are likely to be connected using WAN technology that is far slower and also far more expensive than LAN technology. Therefore, maximizing the efficiency of the communications between sites is typically a matter of when and how often replications that use WAN links occur.

Defining Site Objects

When you create the first Windows 2000 domain controller on your network, the Active Directory Installation Wizard creates your first site, names it Default-First-Site-Name (yes, that's actually the name), and associates it with the server you've just promoted. You can supply a more descriptive name for this site if you want or leave it as is. If all the Active Directory servers on your network will be located near enough to each other to communicate by using LAN connections, you don't need any other sites or the Sites and Services snap-in. As you promote each server on the network to a domain controller, Active Directory will add it to the site and automatically configure the replication topology between the servers.

If you will have servers at remote locations, however, you can create additional sites by using Sites and Services. By creating subnet objects and associating them with specific sites, you give Active Directory the information it needs to automatically add each server that is subsequently promoted to a domain controller to the appropriate site, based on the subnet where the machine is located. If you move a server to new location at a different site, however, you must also manually move the server object to the new site object. Thus, if you plan to install and configure a domain controller at the home office and then ship it to a remote location, you'll have to use Sites and Services to move the server object to the appropriate site.

To move a server to a new site, follow these steps:

1. Open Active Directory Sites and Services.
2. Click the plus sign (+) next to Sites to open the list of available sites.
3. To open the list of servers, click the site where the server currently is.
4. Right-click the server you want to move and choose Move from the shortcut menu (Figure 12-1).
5. In the Move Server window, select the new site for the server and click OK.

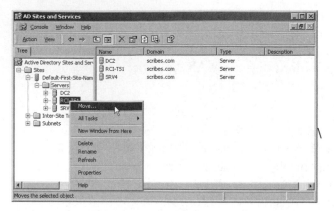

Figure 12-1. *Moving a server from one site to another.*

Subnet Objects

Active Directory uses subnet objects to define the boundaries of a site. Subnet objects each consist of a network address and a subnet mask used by some or all of the computers in a site. You can associate a site with multiple subnet objects so that if your network has multiple subnets in a single location, you can include all of them in a single site. On a network with two or more sites, subnet objects are needed for the Active Directory Installation Wizard to place the server objects for newly promoted domain controllers into the correct sites. Without subnet objects, the wizard is likely to create the server object in the wrong place. If this occurs, you can manually move the server object to the proper site by using the method described in the previous section.

Server Objects

Server objects are always children of site objects and are created by the Installation Wizard whenever it promotes a Windows 2000 server to a domain controller. Don't confuse an Active Directory server object with the computer object that the wizard also creates during the promotion process. The two, although linked, are completely separate objects with different purposes. You can manually create server objects in the Sites and Services snap-in, but this shouldn't be necessary.

When Active Directory installation includes two or more sites, the Installation Wizard uses the subnets associated with the site objects to determine which site is appropriate for the server object. If no site is associated with the subnet used by a new domain controller, the wizard still creates the server object. Afterward, you'll have to create the site where the server belongs and move the server to it. Or you'll need to create a new subnet object and associate it with an existing site.

Understanding Domain Replication

Replication is the process of copying Active Directory data between domain controllers to ensure that all of them possess the same information. The Windows 2000 *multiplemaster replication* capabilities make the entire replication process more complex than it is in Microsoft Windows NT. On a Windows NT network, servers write all domain directory changes to the primary domain controller first, which then propagates the information to the backup domain controllers. This process is *single-master replication*. In Windows 2000, administrators can modify Active Directory by writing to any domain controller. All of the domain controllers execute periodic replication events that copy their modifications to all the other domain controllers. The schedule and topology for these replication events differ depending on whether the domain controllers are at the same or different sites. The following sections examine these two different replication scenarios.

Intrasite Replication

Replication between domain controllers in the same site is known as *intrasite replication* and is completely automatic and self-regulating. A module called the knowledge consistency checker (KCC) creates connections between the domain controllers in the site and triggers replication events whenever anyone modifies the directory information on a domain controller. Because all of the domain controllers in the site are assumed to be well connected, the replication process is designed to keep *latency* (that is, the delay between directory writes and their propagation to the other domain controllers) to a minimum, even at the expense of network bandwidth.

The KCC dynamically creates connection objects in Active Directory; when communication between domain controllers in the same site is disrupted, the KCC immediately creates new connections to ensure timely contact between the systems. *Timely contact* within a site means that no domain controller is more than three connections (or *hops*) away from any other domain controller. Administrators can create additional connection objects, which can improve communication between controllers and reduce latency further by decreasing the maximum number of hops allowed, but this approach also increases the system resources used by the replication process, including processor cycles, disk accesses, and network bandwidth. As a general rule, the replication topology within a site requires no administrative maintenance.

Intersite Replication

When you create multiple sites in Active Directory, the domain controllers assume that the network connections between the sites are slower than those within a site, more expensive, or both. As a result, the domain controllers use *intersite replication* to attempt to minimize the replication traffic between sites and also to provide administrators with a much more flexible replication topology.

When you have domain controllers in multiple sites, Active Directory still creates a default replication topology automatically during the installation process. However, distinct differences exist between the default replication patterns for intrasite and intersite topologies. These differences include the following:

- **Number of connections** The KCC still automatically creates connections between domain controllers in different sites, but it creates fewer of them. The three-hop-maximum rule isn't observed between sites, in the interests of minimizing the bandwidth used.

- **Replication schedule** Replication activities within a site are triggered by changes to the Active Directory database on a domain controller. Replication between sites takes place at scheduled times and intervals. Administrators can customize the schedule to take advantage of time periods when traffic is low and bandwidth is less expensive.

- **Compression** Domain controllers transmit replication data uncompressed within a site, thus saving the processor cycles needed to decompress the data at the destination. Traffic between sites is always transmitted in compressed form, to conserve bandwidth.

One of the primary functions of the Sites and Services snap-in is to configure the replication pattern between sites. To do this, you create site link and site link bridge objects that specify how and when replication data should be transmitted between sites. The following sections examine the functions of Sites and Services and how you use it to create a customized domain controller replication topology for your network.

Launching Sites and Services

The Sites and Services tool is a standard snap-in for the MMC application, which you launch by selecting Active Directory Sites and Services from Administrative Tools in the Start menu's Programs group. The snap-in module is called Dssite.msc; you can also launch Sites and Services by executing that filename from the command line or the Run dialog box.

Viewing Replication Objects

The Sites and Services interface uses the same console tree and results panes as many of the other Active Directory administration tools. The Sites container in the console tree contains the *Default-First-Site-Name* object automatically created by the Active Directory installation, and two other containers called the Inter-Site Transports container and the Subnets container. When you create additional sites, they appear as separate objects in the Sites container. Administrator-created objects appear in the containers under Sites, subnet objects in the Subnets container, and site link and site link bridge objects in the Inter-Site Transports container.

Creating Site Objects

Creating additional site objects in Active Directory is simply a matter of right-clicking the Sites container and choosing New Site from the context menu. When the New Object - Site dialog box appears (Figure 12-2), you supply a name for the site object and select a site link that it should use to define the transport mechanism for the site. The Active Directory Installation Wizard creates the *Defaultipsitelink* object during the installation process, so this object is always available if you haven't yet created any other site links. After the site object is created, you can move server objects into it and associate them with the subnets on which they're located.

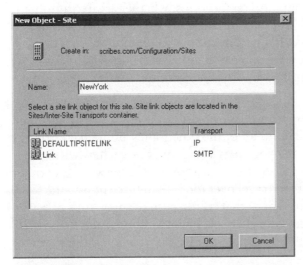

Figure 12-2. *The New Object - Site dialog box.*

Examining Site Object Properties   Each site object in Active Directory has a Servers container holding objects representing the servers in the site, a *Licensing Site Settings* object, and an *NTDS Settings* object. The site object's Properties window enables you to specify a description for the site and its location, as well as containing the standard Object, Security, and Group Policy tabs found in the windows for so many other Active Directory objects.

The *Licensing Site Settings* object specifies the computer and domain licensing the site. In the Properties window for the *NTDS Settings* object, you can disable the KCC's automatic generation of a replication topology either within the site, between this site and other sites, or both. If you want to manually configure the replication behavior for a site, you can enable these options, but this is usually unnecessary. You can create additional connections to supplement those created by the KCC and configure the site's replication behavior in other ways without disabling its core functionality.

Creating Server and Connection Objects

Server objects are created during the installation of Active Directory on each domain controller, in the site associated with the subnet on which the server is located. Each server object contains an *NTDS Settings* object, which in turn contains the objects that represent that server's connections to other domain controllers on the network. These connections must exist for domain controllers to replicate their Active Directory data. All connections, whether created automatically by the KCC or manually by an administrator, appear as objects associated with a server. A connection object is a unidirectional conduit to another domain controller on the network, either in the same or another site. For replication traffic to travel in both directions, separate connection objects must exist for each of the two servers.

The KCC automatically creates connection objects that ensure the continued replication of Active Directory data to all of the functioning domain controllers in each domain. When the status of your network changes—such as when a domain controller goes down and forces the replication traffic between any other two domain controllers in the site to travel over more than three hops—the KCC creates new connection objects to reduce that traffic path to three hops or fewer. When the nonfunctioning domain controller becomes operational again, the KCC can remove connection objects to bring the replication traffic back to its recommended topology.

Normally, the only reason you'd manually create connection objects is to customize your network's replication topology. If, for example, you want replication activities to occur only at specific times, you can create a connection object and configure its schedule. You can also create connection objects to decrease the number of hops between specific domain controllers.

The major difference between manually created connection objects and those created by the KCC is that the manual objects remain in place until you remove them manually; the KCC doesn't remove them no matter how the replication topology changes. Connection objects created by the KCC, however, are removed automatically as the replication topology changes. To create a connection object, follow these steps:

1. Right-click a server's *NTDS Settings* object in the Sites and Services' console tree and choose New Active Directory Connection from the shortcut menu. This displays the Find Domain Controllers dialog box.

2. Select the domain controller you want to create a connection to and click OK to open the New Object Connection dialog box.

3. Supply a name for the new connection and click OK. The program adds a connection object to the details pane.

The Properties window for a connection object contains the familiar Object tab and Security tab as well as an Active Directory Connection tab, shown in Figure 12-3. On this tab, you can supply a descriptive phrase for the connection, select the mode of transport for the replication messages (IP, RPC, or SMTP), and schedule the replication events.

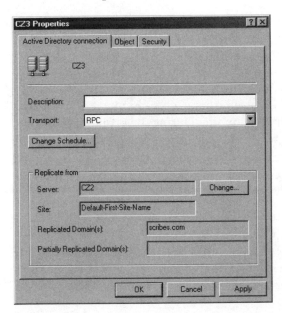

Figure 12-3. *The Active Directory Connection tab of the Properties window.*

The dialog box displayed when you click the Change Schedule button (Figure 12-4) enables you to specify the hours of the day during which replication should occur and the interval between replication events (either once, twice, or four times an hour). Keep in mind that this connection controls only the replication messages traveling from the server under which the object appears to the server you selected as the destination when creating the object. Traffic going in the other direction is controlled by the other server's connection object (if it exists).

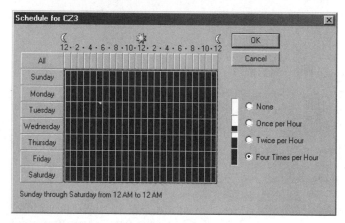

Figure 12-4. *The Schedule dialog box.*

Creating Subnet Objects

The Subnets container is where administrators create objects representing the IP subnets on the network and associate them with specific site objects. When you promote the first server to a domain controller, the Active Directory Installation Wizard creates a site and places the server object in that site. If you create additional sites, subnet objects are used to ensure that each subsequent domain controller you install is placed in the appropriate site. During the promotion process, the wizard identifies the subnet on which the server resides and searches Active Directory for a corresponding subnet object. When the wizard finds the subnet object, it reads its properties to determine the site with which that subnet is associated, and it creates the new server object in that site.

Subnet objects aren't essential to Active Directory's replication topology. You can create sites and move the server objects into them manually. However, if you'll be installing a lot of servers, subnet objects automate the construction of the replication topology and make the entire site deployment process more manageable. To create a subnet object, follow these steps:

1. Right-click the Subnets container in the console tree of the Sites and Services snap-in and choose New Subnet from the shortcut menu.
2. In the New Object - Subnet dialog box (Figure 12-5), type the name for the object, which must be the subnet's network address and mask.
3. Select the site with which that subnet is to be associated and click OK.

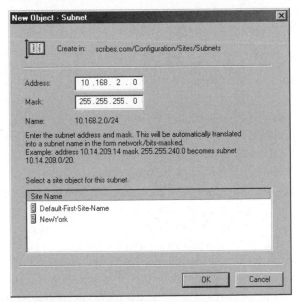

Figure 12-5. *The New Object - Subnet dialog box.*

Any servers on that subnet that you promote to domain controllers will be automatically added to this site. You can associate multiple subnets with a single site to support a network of almost any size.

Note The network address is the portion of the IP address that identifies the network on which a computer resides. The number of bits masked refers to how many of each IP address's 32 bits the system uses to identify the network. The design of the network and the IP addresses you use for workstations determine the value for this number. For example, if your organization has a class B network address (which uses 16 bits to identify the network) and uses a further 8 bits to identify subnets, the result is a total of 24 out of 32 bits that are devoted to the network address. The value for the subnet object's name field would therefore be something like 10.168.2.0/24.

Creating Site Link Objects

The Inter-Site Transports container is where you create the site link and site link bridge objects that dictate how replication traffic is to be transmitted between sites. Two containers within Inter-Site Transports represent the two transport protocols supported by Active Directory: IP and Simple Mail Transport Protocol (SMTP).

A site link object represents the WAN mechanism used to transmit data between two sites, such as a leased T-1 connection or an Asynchronous Transfer Mode (ATM) backbone, in the case of IP, or any means by which systems send e-mail using SMTP. Active Directory creates a default site link object called *Defaultipsitelink* when it creates the network's first site during the promotion of the first server to a domain controller. If all your sites are linked using technologies with exactly the same speed, you don't need to create additional site links. When you have different technologies connecting sites, however, you create multiple site link objects in order to have different replication schedules for each one.

When creating a site link object, you select two or more sites that are connected by the transport mechanism and specify a cost value for the link. The cost value enables you to assign priorities to the various WAN connections, based on their relative speeds. A higher cost value indicates that a connection is more expensive to use, and the KCC schedules less frequent replications on its connections between those two sites as a result. Each increment in the cost value represents 15 minutes in the replication schedule. A cost value of 3, for example, would cause replication to occur every 45 minutes.

To create a site link object, follow these steps:

1. Right-click either the IP or SMTP transport in the console tree of Sites and Services and choose New Site Link from the shortcut menu.

2. In the New Object - Site Link dialog box, specify a name for the object and select the sites that the link connects. If the link is to represent a point-to-point connection like a T-1, you select only two sites. For a technology like an ATM backbone, which can connect several sites, you would select more than two site objects. When the site link object connects more than two site objects, you can assume that any one of the chosen sites can transmit to any other chosen site.

3. Click the OK button, and the manager creates the link object.

> **Note** Site link objects can't route replication traffic. This means that if a site link connects site A to site B and another link connects site B to site C, site A can't transmit to site C. For this to occur, you must create a site link bridge, as explained in "Creating Site Link Bridge Objects."

Configuring Site Links   Right-click the new link object and select Properties to configure its properties. The Site Link Properties window for a site link object (Figure 12-6) contains the standard Object tab and Security tab, as well as a General tab on which you can provide a description of the object and specify the sites connected by the link. You can add new sites to the link as needed after creating the object.

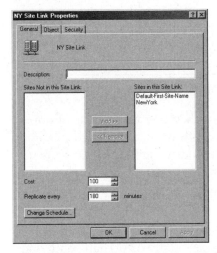

Figure 12-6. *The General tab of the Site Link Properties window.*

The General tab also contains fields with which to specify the cost for the link (from 1 to 32,767) and the interval between replication events (from 15 to 10,080 minutes). Clicking the Change Schedule button enables you to specify time periods during which replication is or is not permitted. If you want to limit replication activities to nonpeak traffic hours, for example, you can specify that replication events not occur between the hours of 9 A.M. and 5 P.M. The KCC observes the site link object's scheduling limitations when it dynamically creates connections between domain controllers.

Tip   Although the cost value determines the interval between replication events, you can adjust the frequency of replication by using the Replicate Every selector on the General tab of the Site Link Properties window. If clients are consistently receiving incorrect directory information from domain controllers, increase the frequency of replication.

Creating Site Link Bridge Objects

Site link bridge objects function much like site links, except that instead of grouping sites, they group site links. A site link bridge object typically represents a router in the network infrastructure. You create a site link bridge object to enable route replication traffic between linked sites. When you create a site link bridge containing two links that connect site A to site B and site B to site C, the bridge makes it possible for site A to transmit replication data to site C through site B.

The procedure for creating a site link bridge object is virtually identical to that of creating a site link object, except that you select two or more site links instead of sites. You don't need to specify a routing cost for a site link bridge because Active Directory automatically computes it by adding up the routing costs of all of the bridge's sites. Thus, a site link bridge object containing two sites with routing costs of 3 and 4 would have a routing cost of 7.

Using Active Directory Schema

The *schema* is the blueprint of Active Directory, dictating what kinds of objects can exist in the database and what the attributes of those objects are. To customize Active Directory for use on a network, you can modify the schema to create new object types, add new attributes to existing object types, and modify the type of information installed on an attribute. To do this, use the MMC snap-in called Active Directory Schema.

Modifying the schema is a task that the average administrator will never have to perform. At most, you'll change the schema occasionally or perhaps only once. Modifying the schema is subject to the same cautions as modifying a Windows 2000 system's registry, except on a larger scale. Just as improper registry modifications can adversely affect a single system, improper schema modifications can have a devastating effect on the entire network.

Examining Schema Security

Because modifying the Active Directory schema isn't something you should do casually, Windows 2000 uses several safety mechanisms to prevent the schema from being modified accidentally or injudiciously. You can modify the schema only when the requirements of all three safety mechanisms have been satisfied.

Schema Administrator Permissions

To modify the schema, you must be logged on to a Windows 2000 server or workstation using an account that is a member of the Schema Administrators group. This is a built-in group created during Active Directory installation that grants its members permission to write to the schema object. The administrator account is automatically made a member of the Schema Administrators group.

Users who aren't members of this group can also modify the schema if an administrator has granted them the appropriate permissions to the schema object.

Schema Floating Single-Master Operations

Active Directory uses a multiple-master replication system for modifications of the database contents, but for schema modifications, it uses a single-master system. This means that only one domain controller can modify the schema at once. Unlike most single-master replication models, which require all modifications to be written to one designated system and subsequently copied to the other replicas, administrators can modify the Active Directory schema from any domain controller. The mechanism that makes this possible is called Schema Floating Single-Master Operations. While an administrator is modifying the schema on one domain controller, write access requests to the schema on all of the other domain controllers will be denied.

Read-Only Schema Access

Finally, all domain controllers are configured by default during Active Directory installation to permit read-only access to the schema. To enable write access, you must create a new entry in the registry. Using one of the Windows 2000 registry editors (Regedit.exe or Regedt32.exe), browse to this key:

```
HKEY_LOCAL_MACHINE\System\Current Control Set\Services\NTDS\Parameters
```

Create a new DWORD entry called *Schema Update Allowed*. Assign the entry a value of *1* to enable write access to the schema. Change the value to *0* to disable write access again after the modifications are complete.

Launching Active Directory Schema

Because of its infrequent use and potential dangers, the Schema Manager is two removes from the Administrative Tools menu. To view or change the schema, you must first install the Administrative Tools (as described in Chapter 10). Then you run the Active Directory Schema Snap-in in an MMC console by following these steps:

1. Click the Start button and select Run. Type *mmc* and press Enter.

2. Select Add/Remove Snap-in from the Console menu.

3. Click the Add button and select Active Directory Schema from the list of snap-ins provided. Once the snap-in is loaded, you can save the console screen to a file to provide easy access to the snap-in in the future. When

the view pane opens, you see two containers in the console tree, which hold the object classes and the attributes that make up those classes, shown in Figure 12-7. Highlighting either of these two containers displays Active Directory's classes or attributes in the results pane.

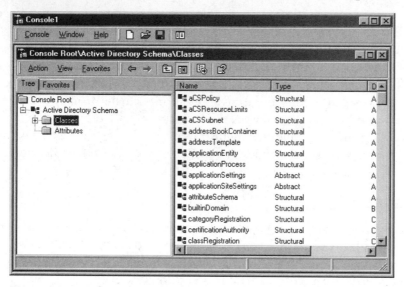

Figure 12-7. *Schema Manager object classes and attributes stored in Active Directory.*

However, before changing the schema, be sure that the schema snap-in is accessing the Active Directory database on the domain controller that is currently functioning as the master (that is, the one domain controller to which write access is permitted). To determine which domain controller you are currently accessing, follow these steps:

1. Select Active Directory Schema and choose Change Domain Controller from the shortcut menu. In the Change Domain Controller dialog box (Figure 12-8), you'll see the current domain controller and be able to choose to change the focus to any other domain controller, or you can specify a particular controller.

2. Right-click the Active Directory Schema object in the console tree and choose Operations Master from the shortcut menu.

3. In the Change Operations Master dialog box, you'll see which domain controller is the operations master and specify whether the schema can

be modified on that system. To change the schema, either change the master replica to the domain controller you're currently using or change the replica you're using to the master.

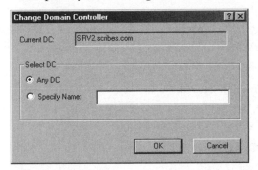

Figure 12-8. *The Change Domain Controller dialog box.*

Modifying the Schema

The process of modifying the Active Directory schema involves creating or modifying the classes and attribute object types displayed in Schema Manager. *Classes* are essentially collections of attributes that either form an Active Directory object type by themselves or contribute certain attributes to another object type. The latter instance is known as an *auxiliary class*. To add attributes to an existing object type, the best method is to create a new class containing the new attributes and add it to the object type as an auxiliary. This method is more manageable and less dangerous than modifying the class representing the object type itself.

Third-party software products might supply their own schema modifications that create entirely new object types, but adding attributes to an existing object type is the most common form of schema modification manually performed by administrators—for example, adding attributes to the user object type that enable you to store additional information about the user in Active Directory. This relatively easy process consists of the steps below, which will be examined in more detail in the following sections.

- Creating new attribute objects corresponding to the information fields you want to add to the object
- Creating a new class object to be used as an auxiliary to the existing object type
- Adding the newly created attributes to the new auxiliary class
- Adding the auxiliary class to the existing object class

Creating Attributes

Creating an attribute is a matter of supplying a name by which the attribute will be identified and specifying the type of data that will be stored there. The data can be text or numerical, and you can apply constraints that limit the data to a particular length or value type. For example, to add an attribute to hold the user's social security number, you would specify that the attribute's data should be in integer form and limited to nine digits. To create an attribute object, follow these steps:

1. Right-click the Attributes container in Schema Manager's console tree and choose New Attribute from the context menu. This produces the Create New Attribute dialog box shown in Figure 12-9.

Figure 12-9. *The Create New Attribute dialog box.*

2. In the Identification box, specify the name for the new object. The *Common Name* field should contain the name by which the attribute will be listed in standard dialog boxes, and the *LDAP Display Name* field should contain the name by which it is known in the LDAP directory hierarchy. (LDAP stands for Lightweight Directory Access Protocol.) Often, these two names will be the same. The *Unique X500 Object ID* field must contain a numerical string that uniquely identifies the attribute object in the X.500 namespace. Standards bodies like the International Telecommunications Union issue Object IDs (OIDs) to ensure that they have unique values.

3. In the Syntax And Range box, define the nature of the data to be stored in the attribute. The *Syntax* field provides over a dozen options that define the types of information that can be stored in an attribute. The

Minimum field and *Maximum* field enable you to define a range of possible values. You can also specify whether the attribute should be able to have multiple values.

4. Click the OK button, and the manager creates the new attribute object.

Caution   Don't be tempted to make up your own OIDs. Even if you're running Active Directory on an isolated network, it's all too easy to supply an OID for a new attribute or class that duplicates one of the hundreds of other OIDs already assigned to Active Directory objects.

Configure the new (or any other) attribute object by opening the Properties window from its context menu, shown in Figure 12-10. From this window, you can specify a description for the object, modify its range of possible values, and enable any of the following options:

- Show objects of this class while browsing.
- Deactivate this attribute.
- Index this attribute in Active Directory.
- Ambiguous Name Resolution (ANR).
- Replicate this attribute to the Global Catalog (GC).
- Attribute is copied when duplicating a user.

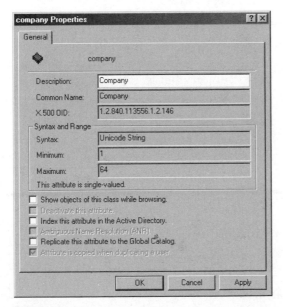

Figure 12-10. *The Properties window of an attribute object.*

Creating Object Classes

Attribute objects by themselves are useless until they belong to an object class. You can add the attribute objects you've created to an existing class, but creating a new class object for them is generally more practical. To create a class object, right-click the Classes container in the schema snap-in and choose Create Class from the shortcut menu. This displays the Create New Schema Class dialog box shown in Figure 12-11.

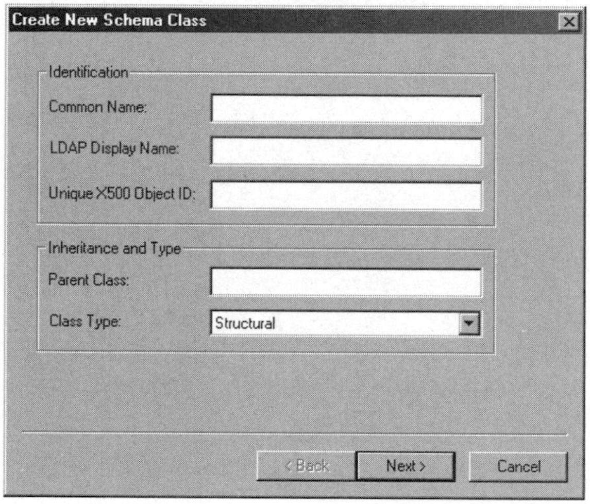

Figure 12-11. *The Create New Schema Class dialog box.*

As with an attribute object, you must first specify a common name, an LDAP display name, and a unique X.500 object ID. Then in the Inheritance And Type box, specify the parent class for the new object (that is, the class from which the new object should be derived), and choose one of the following three class types:

- **Structural class** The typical directory objects that you work with in programs like Active Directory Manager. A structural class object can have either an abstract class or another structural class as its parent object.

- **Abstract class** Objects from which structural class objects are derived. You can also specify an existing abstract class as the parent of a new abstract class object.

- **Auxiliary class** Collections of attributes that you can add to either an abstract or structural class object to augment its capabilities. New auxiliary class objects can be derived only from abstract classes.

To hold your new attributes, you should create an auxiliary class type.

Adding Attributes to a Class

Once you've created the attribute objects and the class object that will contain them, you must add the attributes to the class. You do this by opening the Properties window for the newly created class object. The window for a class object has four tabs, including the standard Security tab. On the General tab, supply a description for the object and specify whether the object class should show while browsing. You can also disable the object by selecting the Deactivate This Class check box.

On the Attributes tab (Figure 12-12), add your newly created attribute objects to the class by clicking the Add button for either the Mandatory or Optional list and selecting the objects by name. When an attribute is mandatory, you must supply a value for the attribute when creating a new object of that class. If, for example, you create a *social security number* attribute, add it to your auxiliary class as a mandatory attribute, and then add the auxiliary class to the user class; the next time a new user object is created, a social security number will be required for the user. Values for optional attributes aren't required.

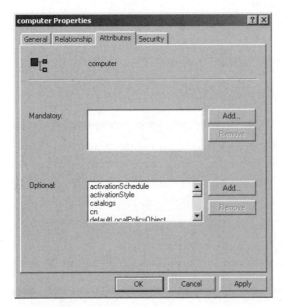

Figure 12-12. *The Attributes tab of the Properties window.*

Adding an Auxiliary Class to a Structural Class

An auxiliary class object can't store attribute information until you add the auxiliary class object to a structural class object, like a user or computer. To do this, open the structural class object's Properties window and select the Relationship tab (Figure 12-13).

Figure 12-13. *The Relationship tab of the Properties window.*

On this tab, click the Add button for the Auxiliary Classes list, and select the class object you just created. This causes Active Directory to add the attributes in the auxiliary class to the structural class. In the Possible Superior list, specify which other object classes can contain the current object class. For example, the user object class has the organizational unit object class in its Possible Superior list, which enables the creation of new users in OUs. The opposite is not true, however; you can't create an OU beneath a user, so the user object isn't a possible superior of the OU object.

Modifying Display Specifiers

Once you've added new attributes to a class, the attributes exist in the Active Directory database, but you can't see them in utilities like Active Directory Users and Computers. To view, add, or modify the values of the new attributes, you must first alter the display specifiers that control how attributes appear in applications. *Display specifiers* are Active Directory objects that define the labels for the attributes that appear in a dialog box and control the contents of the context menu that appears when you right-click an object of a modified class.

For example, you might create a new attribute intended to store users' social security numbers and name it *SocialSecurityNumber*. You probably don't want the attribute name to appear this way in Active Directory Users and Computers, so you create the display name *Social Security Number* and make it the equivalent of *SocialSecurityNumber*. To modify the display specifier objects, you can use a Microsoft Visual Basic script and execute it from the Windows 2000 command prompt.

The following script assumes that two new attributes, called *SalaryLevel* and *SocialSecurityNumber*, have been created and added to an auxiliary class called *HumanResources*, which has, in turn, been added to the user object class. The first section connects to the display specifiers container in Active Directory.

```
Dim oRoot
Dim oDisp
Dim oCont
Dim aMenu
Dim iCount
Dim sNewMenu
Dim oFileSystem
Dim sOutFile
Dim sSystemFolder
Set oFileSystem = WScript.CreateObject("Scripting.FileSystemObject")
sSystemFolder = oFileSystem.GetSpecialFolder(1)
Set oRoot = Getobject("LDAP://RootDSE")
Set oCont = GetObject("LDAP://" & "CN=409, CN=DisplaySpecifiers," & _
    oRoot.get("configurationNamingContext"))
Set oDisp = oCont.GetObject("displaySpecifier","cn=user-Display")
MsgBox "Display Specifier: " & oDisp.Name
```

The following routine assigns display names to the two new attributes. These names will appear in all dialog boxes providing access to these attributes.

```
oDisp.PutEx 3,"attributeDisplayNames" , _
    Array("SalaryLevel,Annual Salary", _
    "SocialSecurityNumber,Social Security Number")
oDisp.SetInfo
```

The next routine creates a new entry, called *HR Info*, on the context menu that appears when you right-click a user object in the My Network Places window. When you access this context menu item, the program executes another Visual Basic script called Hrshell.vbs that enables users to view the values for the new attributes.

```
MsgBox "Adding Shell Context Menu item"
iCount = 0
If Not IsEmpty(oDisp.shellContextMenu) Then
    aMenu = oDisp.GetEx("shellContextMenu")
    For iCount = LBound(aMenu) to UBound(aMenu)
        MsgBox "Existing Menu item: " & aMenu(iCount)
```

(continued)

```
    Next
    iCount = iCount + 1
End If
sNewMenu = CStr(iCount) & ",&HR Info...,hrshell.vbs"
oDisp.PutEx 3,"shellContextMenu" , Array(sNewMenu)
oDisp.SetInfo
```

This next routine creates the Hrshell.vbs script.

```
MsgBox "Adding Shell Context Menu Program"
Set sOutFile = oFileSystem.CreateTextFile(sSystemFolder & _
    "\hrshell.vbs",True)
sOutFile.WriteLine "Dim Args"
sOutFile.WriteLine "Dim oUser"
sOutFile.WriteLine "Set Args = Wscript.Arguments"
sOutFile.WriteLine "MsgBox " & Chr(34) & "LDAP Path: " & Chr(34) & _
    " & Args(0)"
sOutFile.WriteLine "MsgBox " & Chr(34) & "Object Class: " & _
    Chr(34) & " & Args(1)"
sOutFile.WriteLine "Set oUser = GetObject(Args(0))"
sOutFile.WriteLine "MsgBox " & Chr(34) & "HR Info" & Chr(34) & _
    " & vbCRLF & " & _ Chr(34) & "Salary: " & Chr(34) & _
    " & oUser.SalaryLevel & vbCRLF & " & Chr(34) & "Soc Sec No: " & _
    Chr(34) & " & oUser.SocialSecurityNumber"
sOutFile.WriteLine "Set oUser = Nothing"
sOutFile.WriteLine "WScript.Quit"
sOutFile.Close
```

The following routine adds a similar entry to the user context menu in Active Directory Users and Computers, causing the application to execute the Hradmin.vbs script. This script creates a dialog box in which administrators can modify the values for the new attributes.

```
MsgBox "Adding Admin Context Menu item"
iCount = 0
If Not IsEmpty(oDisp.adminContextMenu) Then
    aMenu = oDisp.GetEx("adminContextMenu")
    For iCount = LBound(aMenu) to UBound(aMenu)
        MsgBox "Existing Menu item: " & aMenu(iCount)
    Next
    iCount = iCount + 1
End If
sNewMenu = CStr(iCount) & ",&HR Admin...,hradmin.vbs"
oDisp.PutEx 3,"adminContextMenu" , Array(sNewMenu)
oDisp.SetInfo
```

The next section creates the Hradmin.vbs script and terminates the script.

```
MsgBox "Adding Admin Context Menu Program"
Set sOutFile = oFileSystem.CreateTextFile(sSystemFolder & _
    "\hradmin.vbs",True)
sOutFile.WriteLine "Dim Args"
sOutFile.WriteLine "Dim oUser"
sOutFile.WriteLine "Dim temp"
sOutFile.WriteLine "Set Args = Wscript.Arguments"
sOutFile.WriteLine "MsgBox " & Chr(34) & "LDAP Path: " & Chr(34) & _
    " & Args(0)"
sOutFile.WriteLine "MsgBox " & Chr(34) & "Object Class: " & _
    Chr(34) & " & Args(1)"
sOutFile.WriteLine "Set oUser = GetObject(Args(0))"
sOutFile.WriteLine "temp = InputBox(" & Chr(34) & "Old Salary: " & _
    Chr(34) & " & oUser.SalaryLevel & vbCRLF & " & Chr(34) & _
    "New Salary" & Chr(34) & ")"
sOutFile.WriteLine "if temp <> " & Chr(34) & Chr(34) & _
    " then oUser.Put " & Chr(34) & "SalaryLevel" & Chr(34) & ",temp"
sOutFile.WriteLine "temp = InputBox(" & Chr(34) & _
    "Soc Sec Number: " & Chr(34) & " & oUser.SocialSecurityNumber & _
    vbCRLF & " & Chr(34) & "New Number" & Chr(34) & ")"
sOutFile.WriteLine "if temp <> " & Chr(34) & Chr(34) & _
    " then oUser.Put " & Chr(34) & "SocialSecurityNumber" & _
    Chr(34) & ",temp"
sOutFile.WriteLine "oUser.SetInfo"
sOutFile.WriteLine "Set oUser = Nothing"
sOutFile.WriteLine "WScript.Quit"
sOutFile.Close
MsgBox "Quit..."
Set oDisp = Nothing
Set oCont = Nothing
Set oRoot = Nothing
Set oFileSystem = Nothing
WScript.Quit
```

When you save this script to a text file with a .VBS extension and execute it from the command prompt, Windows 2000 adds the context menus to the My Network Places window and the Active Directory Users and Computers snap-in and creates the scripts that selecting those context menus executes. This part of the schema modification process is obviously the most complex. After you create your own scripts, carefully test and debug them on a nonproduction network before executing them on live domain controllers.

Performing Batch Importing and Exporting

While MMC snap-ins like Active Directory Users and Computers make it easy to create and configure new objects in Active Directory, deploying the directory service on a large scale might require the creation of thousands of objects. In cases like these, manually creating individual objects is impractical at best. Anticipating the need for the mass creation of Active Directory objects, and particularly user objects, Windows 2000 includes tools that enable administrators to perform batch imports and exports of Active Directory objects. Among these tools is Ldifde.exe, a command-line utility for importing, exporting, and modifying Active Directory objects using the LDAP Data Interchange Format (LDIF).

Using the Ldifde.exe Utility

Active Directory uses LDAP to define its namespace and supports LDIF. LDIF is a standardized format for saving directory service information in text files. If you're running another directory service that also supports LDIF on the network, you can import its data into Active Directory by using the Ldifde.exe utility. You can also use Ldifde.exe to export Active Directory objects to LDIF files and modify existing objects.

The syntax for using the Ldifde.exe utility is as follows.

```
Ldifde [-a username password] [-b username domainname password]
    [-c FromDN ToDN] [-d RootDN] [-f filename] [-g] [-i] [-j] [-k]
    [-l attributes] [-m] [-n] [-o attributes] [-p scope] [-r filter]
    [-s servername] [-t] [-v] [-?]
[-a username password] - specifies the username and password for
    simple authentication to the LDAP directory.
[-b username domainname password] - specifies the user name, domain
    name, and password for the SSPI bind method (by default, the
    utility logs in to the LDAP directory as the current user, with
    the SSPI bind method).
[-c FromDN ToDN] - replaces all occurrences of FromDN with ToDN.
[-d RootDN] - specifies the root object where the utility should
    commence its search (default = current naming context).
[-f filename] - specifies the name of the LDIF file that the utility
    will import data from or export data to.
[-g] - disables paged search.
[-i] - causes the utility to operate in import mode (default = export
    mode).
[-j] - specifies the location of the utility's log file.
[-k] - causes the program to ignore "constraint violation" and
    "object already exists" errors.
[-l attributes] - specifies the attributes that the utility should
    look for during a search of a LDAP directory.
```

[-m] - enables Windows NT's Service Account Manager (SAM) logic
    during export operations.
[-n] - prevents the utility from exporting binary values.
[-o *attributes*] - specifies the attributes that the utility should
    omit from inputting.
[-p *scope*] - specifies the search scope (Base, OneLevel, or Subtree).
[-r *filter*] - specifies the objects for which the utility will search
    (default = "(objectClass=*)").
[-s *servername*] - specifies the name of the server to which the
    utility will bind (default = domain controller of the currently
    logged on domain).
[-t] - specifies a port number to use when communicating with the
    LDAP service (default = 389).
[-v] - causes the program to operate in verbose mode.
[-?] - displays help information for the program.

Exporting Objects   To export Active Directory information to an LDIF file,
execute a command like the following:

```
ldifde -f research.ldif -s cz2 -d "ou=Research,dc=scribes,dc=com"
    -p subtree -r (objectCategory=CN=Person,CN=Schema,CN=
    Configuration,DC=scribes,DC=com)"
```

The *–f* parameter specifies the name of the LDIF file that the utility will create.
The *–s* and *–d* parameters identify the server that the utility should use to access
Active Directory and the OU where the export process should begin. The *–p*
parameter specifies that the utility should export the entire subtree below the
Research OU, and *–r* specifies that the program should export only person (that
is, user) objects. When you execute the command, Ldifde.exe searches Active
Directory, starting in the Research OU and traveling down the subtree to the bottom, writing the information about each user object it finds to the Research.ldif
file. A typical LDIF entry for a user object (in this case the *Administrator* object)
appears as follows:

```
dn: CN=Administrator,CN=Users,DC=scribes,DC=com
changetype: add
accountExpires: 9223372036854775807
badPasswordTime: 0
badPwdCount: 0
codePage: 0
cn: Administrator
countryCode: 0
description: Built-in account for administering the computer/domain
instanceType: 4
isCriticalSystemObject: TRUE
```

(continued)

```
memberOf: CN=Domain Admins,CN=Users,DC=scribes,DC=com
memberOf: CN=Enterprise Admins,CN=Users,DC=scribes,DC=com
memberOf: CN=Schema Admins,CN=Users,DC=scribes,DC=com
memberOf: CN=Administrators,CN=Builtin,DC=scribes,DC=com
lastLogoff: 0
lastLogon: 125652212356113520
logonCount: 7
distinguishedName: CN=Administrator,CN=Users,DC=scribes,DC=com
objectCategory: CN=Person,CN=Schema,CN=Configuration,DC=scribes,DC=com
objectClass: user
objectGUID:: RedjUwbB0hGJSwBgl7B3yg==
objectSid:: AQUAAAAAAUVAAAAiqcyP/CUyF8WwOoy9AEAAA==
primaryGroupID: 513
pwdLastSet: 125631016521025648
name: Administrator
sAMAccountName: Administrator
sAMAccountType: 805306368
userAccountControl: 66048
uSNChanged: 2113
uSNCreated: 2113
whenChanged: 19990210163330.0Z
whenCreated: 19990210163330.0Z
```

Importing Objects   To import users or other objects from another LDAP directory service, you must first export the information using whatever tools the other product provides, and then import the LDIF file into Active Directory using a command like the following:

```
Ldifde -i -f newusers.ldif
```

In this example, the *–i* parameter puts the program into import mode, and the *–f* parameter specifies the name of the LDIF file you created from the other directory service.

Modifying Objects   You can also use Ldifde.exe to modify the information stored in Active Directory objects, albeit in a roundabout way. After exporting Active Directory object information to an LDIF file, modify the attribute values in the file using any text editor, and then import it back into Active Directory. The new information will overwrite the old, effectively modifying the Active Directory object information. If faced with a situation where you have to make a great many similar changes to the directory, such as a company move requiring new mail addresses for all users, use Ldifde.exe and a text editor with search and replace capabilities to quickly modify thousands of objects in the Active Directory database.

Understanding Operations Master Roles

Domain controllers must handle five operations master roles in every Active Directory forest. Some of the operations master roles are critical to your network, and if the machine providing them fails, you'll know about it at once. Others can be unavailable for a long time without you or your users being any the wiser. The roles are as follows:

- **Primary domain controller (PDC) emulator**   Acts as a Windows NT primary domain controller in domains that have Windows NT backup domain controllers or that have computers without Windows 2000 client software
- **Schema master**   Controls all updates and modifications to the schema
- **Domain naming master**   Controls the addition or removal of domains
- **Relative identifier (RID) master**   Allocates relative IDs to each domain controller
- **Infrastructure master**   Updates changes to group-to-user references when memberships in groups are changed

Normally, you have no reason to interfere with the operations master roles. Transferring of roles is relatively trivial. You make a transfer when the original role holder is available. In serious circumstances when the controller holding the role is unavailable, you can seize a role, but it's a drastic measure and you should not take it lightly. In all cases, except with the PDC emulator, when an operations master role is seized (rather than transferred), you must not bring the original holder of the seized role back online without completely reformatting the boot disk and reinstalling Windows 2000. The next several sections explain the operations master roles in more detail.

Primary Domain Controller Emulator

When upgrading a Windows NT domain, only one domain controller can create users, groups, and computer accounts—the basics of security. This Windows 2000 domain controller is configured as the PDC operations master and emulates a Windows NT primary domain controller. The PDC emulator supports the Kerberos and NTLM protocols, allowing Windows NT domain controllers to synchronize with a Windows 2000 environment running in mixed mode.

Every domain must have a domain controller that acts as a PDC emulator as long as the domain contains either clients without Windows 2000 client software or Windows NT backup domain controllers. If the controller acting as the PDC emulator isn't available, it will affect users because the network itself will be disrupted. So if you know that the controller acting as the PDC emulator will be unavailable, transfer this role.

Transferring the PDC Emulator   To transfer the role of PDC emulator, follow these steps:

1. Choose Active Directory Users and Computers from the Administrative Tools menu.
2. Right-click the domain node and choose Connect To Domain Controller from the shortcut menu.
3. Select the domain controller that you want to give the role of PDC emulator. Click OK.
4. Right-click the domain node and choose Operations Masters from the shortcut menu. Click the PDC tab to see the current focus (the controller that will become the PDC emulator) and the controller that is the current operations master.
5. Click Change and then OK.

Seizing the PDC Emulator   If the PDC emulator becomes unavailable unexpectedly and it can't be returned to service quickly, you'll need to seize the role of the PDC emulator and force it to another domain controller. To seize the PDC emulator, follow these steps:

1. Choose Run from the Start menu (or open a command window), type *ntdsutil*, and press Enter.
2. At each prompt, supply the following information and then press Enter:
   - At ntdsutil, type *roles*
   - At fsmo maintenance, type *connections*
   - At server connections, type *connect to server* followed by the fully qualified domain name of the controller that is to be the new PDC emulator (Figure 12-14)
   - At server connections, type *quit*
   - At fsmo maintenance, type *seize PDC*
   - At ntdsutil, type *quit*

When the original PDC emulator becomes available again, you can use the same procedure to return the PDC emulator role.

Figure 12-14. *Using ntdsutil to seize and move the PDC emulator role to a new server.*

Schema Master

Not surprisingly, the schema master handles all updates to the schema. Only one schema master will exist in an entire forest. The schema master role is assigned to the first domain controller in a domain and will remain there unless you change it. Because modifications of the schema are uncommon, the schema master can be nonfunctional for an extended period without affecting users.

Transferring the Schema Master   To transfer the schema master role, follow these steps:

1. Open the Active Directory Schema snap-in.
2. Right-click Active Directory Schema in the console window and choose Change Domain Controller. Change the focus to the controller that will assume the schema master role.
3. Right-click Active Directory Schema in the console window and choose Operations Master from the shortcut menu. Click the Change button and then click OK.

Seizing the Schema Master   Don't seize the schema master unless there's no hope of returning the original controller to service. Before seizing the schema master role, the original schema master must be disconnected from the network. To seize the schema master role, follow these steps:

1. Choose Run from the Start menu (or open a command window), type *ntdsutil*, and press Enter.
2. At each prompt, supply the following information and then press Enter:
   - At ntdsutil, type *roles*
   - At fsmo maintenance, type *connections*

- At server connections, type *connect to server* followed by the fully qualified domain name of the controller that is to be the new schema master
- At server connections, type *quit*
- At fsmo maintenance, type *seize schema master*
- At ntdsutil, type *quit*

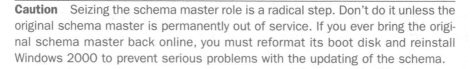

Caution   Seizing the schema master role is a radical step. Don't do it unless the original schema master is permanently out of service. If you ever bring the original schema master back online, you must reformat its boot disk and reinstall Windows 2000 to prevent serious problems with the updating of the schema.

Domain Naming Master

Only one server in the enterprise performs the role of domain naming so that the domain naming master is created in the first domain and the role remains there no matter how large the forest. The domain naming master can be unavailable for some time, and the network will be unaffected until there's a need to establish a new domain. Therefore, unless the controller playing this role is to be permanently removed from the network, you usually won't need to either transfer or seize this role.

Transferring the Domain Naming Master   If you need to transfer this role to another controller, follow these steps:

1. Choose Active Directory Domains and Trusts from the Administrative Tools menu.
2. Right-click Active Directory Domains and Trusts and choose Connect To Domain Controller from the shortcut menu.
3. Select the domain controller that you want to give the role of domain naming master. Click OK.
4. Right click Active Directory Domains and Trusts again and select Operations Master from the shortcut menu. A dialog box will open showing the current domain naming master and the computer that will become the domain naming master.
5. Click Change and then OK.

Seizing the Domain Naming Master   If the domain naming master must be unexpectedly and permanently removed from the network, you can seize the domain mastering role and reassign it to another domain controller. To seize the role, follow these steps:

1. Choose Run from the Start menu (or open a command window), type *ntdsutil*, and press Enter.

2. At each prompt, supply the following information and then press Enter:
   - At ntdsutil, type *roles*
   - At fsmo maintenance, type *connections*
   - At server connections, type *connect to server* followed by the fully qualified domain name of the controller that is to be the new master
   - At server connections, type *quit*
   - At fsmo maintenance, type *seize domain naming master*
   - At ntdsutil, type *quit*

Caution   Before seizing the domain naming master, the controller holding the domain naming master role must be disconnected completely from the network. Seizing the domain naming master role is a radical step, and you should not do it unless the original domain naming master is permanently out of service. If you ever bring the original domain naming master back online, you must first reformat its boot disk and reinstall Windows 2000.

Relative Identifier Master

When a domain controller creates a security object—a user, a group, or a computer account—it assigns a unique security identifier (SID) to the object. The SID is made up of two parts: the domain security ID that is common to all security objects in the domain, and the relative ID that is unique to each object. The RID master is the controller in each domain that allocates and tracks the sequences of relative IDs.

Users won't notice temporary loss of the RID master. Administrators are also unlikely to notice unless they're creating security objects and the domain runs out of relative ID numbers. So transferring the RID master role isn't usually necessary unless the RID master is to be removed permanently from the network.

Transferring the RID Master If you need to transfer this role to another controller, follow these steps:

1. Choose Active Directory Users and Computers from the Administrative Tools menu.

2. Right-click the domain node and choose Connect To Domain Controller from the shortcut menu.

3. Select the domain controller that you want to give the role of RID master. Click OK.

5. Right-click the domain node and choose Operations Masters from the shortcut menu. A dialog box will open. On the RID tab, the current focus (the controller that will become the RID master) will be shown as well as the current operations master (Figure 12-15).

6. Click Change and then OK.

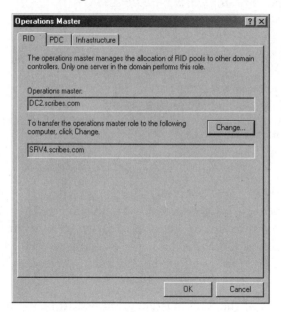

Figure 12-15. *The RID tab of the Operations Master dialog box.*

Seizing the RID Master If the RID master must be unexpectedly and permanently removed from the network, you can seize the RID mastering role and reassign it to another domain controller. To seize the role, follow these steps:

1. Choose Run from the Start menu (or open a command window), type *ntdsutil*, and press Enter.

2. At each prompt, supply the following information and then press Enter:
   - At ntdsutil, type *roles*
   - At fsmo maintenance, type *connections*
   - At server connections, type *connect to server* followed by the fully qualified domain name of the controller that is to be the new master
   - At server connections, type *quit*
   - At fsmo maintenance, type *seize RID master*
   - At ntdsutil, type *quit*

Caution   Before proceeding with the seizure, the controller holding the RID master role must be disconnected completely from the network. Seizing the RID master role is a radical step. Don't do it unless the original RID master is permanently out of service. If you ever bring the original RID master back online, you must first reformat its boot disk and reinstall Windows 2000.

Infrastructure Master

The infrastructure master is responsible for keeping up with the changes in group membership and distributing updates to other domains. One infrastructure master exists in each domain. If the controller holding the infrastructure master role becomes unavailable, it won't affect users. Even administrators won't notice until a number of user account changes don't show up in other domain controllers. Therefore, it's best not to transfer the infrastructure master role unless the controller is going to be unavailable for a considerable period.

Real World   **Placing the Infrastructure Master Role**

Unless the domain has only one domain controller, don't assign the infrastructure master role to the controller hosting the GC. To find out whether changes need to be distributed to other domains, the infrastructure master looks to a GC and updates itself using the GC information. If the GC and the infrastructure master are on the same controller, the infrastructure master will never find any outdated data, so nothing is replicated to other domains. See Chapter 10 for more on the GC.

Transferring the Infrastructure Master   To transfer the infrastructure master role to another controller, follow these steps:

1. Choose Active Directory Users and Computers from the Administrative Tools menu.

2. Right-click the domain node and choose Connect To Domain Controller from the shortcut menu.

3. Select the domain controller that you want to give the role of infrastructure master. Click OK.

4. Right-click the domain node and choose Operations Masters from the shortcut menu. Click the Infrastructure tab to see the current focus (the controller that will become the infrastructure master) as well as the controller that is the current operations master.

5. Click Change and then OK.

Seizing the Infrastructure Master   If the infrastructure master is unexpectedly and permanently removed from the network, you can seize the infrastructure mastering role and reassign it to another domain controller. To seize the role, follow these steps:

1. Choose Run from the Start menu (or open a command window), type *ntdsutil*, and press Enter.

2. At each prompt, supply the following information and then press Enter:

   - At ntdsutil, type *roles*

   - At fsmo maintenance, type *connections*

   - At server connections, type *connect to server* followed by the fully qualified domain name of the controller that is to be the new master

   - At server connections, type *quit*

   - At fsmo maintenance, type *seize infrastructure master*

   - At ntdsutil, type *quit*

Caution   Before proceeding with the seizure, the controller holding the infrastructure master must be disconnected completely from the network. Seizing the infrastructure master role is a drastic step. Don't do it unless the original infrastructure master is permanently out of service. If you ever bring the original infrastructure master back online, you must first reformat its boot disk and reinstall Windows 2000.

Summary

Active Directory is a major part of the Windows 2000 enterprise network infrastructure, and planning, deploying, and maintaining it is a major part of the network administrator's burden. Learning to use the Active Directory tools included with Windows 2000 makes it possible to create and maintain a directory service infrastructure that is efficient and largely self-regulating. With Active Directory solidly in place, you can move on to other administrative responsibilities, which are discussed in following chapters. Chapter 13 covers network addresses and Internet protocols.

Chapter 13
Understanding Network Addresses

Although the basics of setting up addressing on a server are covered in Chapter 6, you'll need to know more to deal with even a slightly more complex network environment. This chapter covers some of the theory behind Transmission Control Protocol/Internet Protocol (TCP/IP) and the tools you'll use to handle IP addresses on your network.

The TCP/IP Protocol Suite

Whole books have been written about TCP/IP, and justifiably so. Although most administrators don't need to know every detail of programming a TCP connection or what to expect as a return value from a *gethostbyname()* call, they do need to understand enough to configure the protocol and make it work properly.

The important thing to remember about TCP/IP is that it isn't a single entity. TCP/IP is short for Transmission Control Protocol/Internet Protocol, but these are only two of the protocols included in the TCP/IP suite. There are a variety of other protocols, each with its own specialized area of importance and use.

Another important fact about TCP/IP is that it's everywhere; it isn't controlled by any one company or vendor. Both Internetwork Packet Exchange/Sequenced Packet Exchange (IPX/SPX) and NetBIOS Enhanced User Interface (NetBEUI) are proprietary protocols, each developed and ultimately controlled by an individual vendor. TCP/IP, on the other hand, is an open standard controlled by the Internet Engineering Task Force (IETF) and by the users of the Internet itself in the form of RFCs (requests for comments). Anyone can submit an RFC for consideration and inclusion into the written definitions of the protocols and policies of the Internet and TCP/IP.

Virtually every kind of computer and operating system in use today has TCP/IP available and supports it as a networking protocol. A particular type of computer may use some other, proprietary protocol as well, but when it comes to connecting multiple computers running multiple operating systems across diverse network-ing hardware and topology, there's really only one way to get there—TCP/IP.

Internet Protocol

IP is the core protocol of the TCP/IP suite. To quote from RFC 791, "The Inter-net Protocol is designed for use in interconnected systems of packet-switched computer communication networks." IP performs only one basic function: to deliver a packet of bits (called a *datagram*) from point A to point B over any network "wire" it happens to encounter along the way.

> **Note** The term "wire" is used very loosely here and elsewhere to indicate the actual—usually physical—network connection between two points. In fact, that wire could just as easily be a piece of optical fiber or even a radio or infrared wave. But in all cases it functions as the transmission medium through which the pack-ets travel.

IP doesn't in and of itself know anything about the information in the datagram it carries, nor does it have any provision beyond a simple checksum to ensure that the data is intact or that it has reached its destination. That is left to the other protocols in the TCP/IP suite.

Transmission Control Protocol

According to RFC 793 (the defining RFC for the protocol), TCP is "a connection-oriented, end-to-end reliable protocol designed to fit into a layered hierarchy of protocols which support multi-network applications." Let's elaborate on some of those terms.

- **Connection-oriented** TCP provides for the communication of packets between two points, sending the datagram specifically from one com-puter or device to another.

- **End-to-end** Each TCP packet designates a specific endpoint as its desti-nation. Packets are passed along the wire and ignored except by the ac-tual endpoint of the packet and any device that needs to direct it.

- **Reliable** This is the key point of TCP. When a program such as FTP uses TCP for its protocol, the TCP/IP suite takes responsibility for the reliability of the communications. The protocol itself provides for inter-process communication to ensure that packets that are sent out not only get there, but also that they get there in the order in which they were sent. If a packet is missed, the protocol will communicate with the send-ing device to ensure a resend of the packet.

Because TCP has to create a reliable connection between two devices or processes, each packet involves substantially more overhead than is needed with other, less reliable protocols within the suite. But by the same token, the programmer writing the application that uses TCP doesn't have to include lots of error checking and handshaking in the application itself.

User Datagram Protocol

The User Datagram Protocol (UDP), another protocol in the TCP/IP suite, is a connectionless, transaction-oriented protocol designed to send packets with a minimum of protocol overhead. It provides no guarantee that its intended recipient received the packet, or that packets were received in the order they were sent. UDP is frequently used in broadcast messages where there is no specific intended recipient, such as Boot Protocol (BOOTP) and Dynamic Host Configuration Protocol (DHCP) requests, but it can also be used by applications that prefer to ensure reliable delivery internally rather than in an underlying protocol. It is defined by RFC 768.

Windows Sockets

Windows Sockets (commonly referred to as Winsock) provides a standard way for application programs to communicate with a TCP/IP stack without having to consider any underlying variations in the TCP/IP stack implementation.

In the past there were many different vendors of TCP/IP protocol and applications suites for MS-DOS–based computers, each slightly different from the others. This situation made it extremely difficult to write an application that required TCP/IP and yet would work with all of the TCP/IP implementations that existed. Winsock was designed to get around this problem by providing a uniform set of application programming interface (API) calls that would be the same regardless of the underlying differences in the actual implementation of TCP/IP.

The original Winsock version 1 had a fair number of difficulties, and version 1.1 was released soon after its initial implementation. The current version of Winsock supported by Windows 2000 Server is version 2, which provides for full backward compatibility with earlier versions while offering improved functionality and support for additional features and expandability. Note that Winsock 2 has been around since Microsoft Windows NT 4, so applications are now widely available that use this API, something that will become more important as IP version 6 (discussed later in the chapter) is rolled out.

Requests for Comments

Requests for comments (RFCs) come in many guises, but all of them have the same intent and a somewhat similar format. They are designed to provide a way for an extremely diverse group—the users of the Internet—to communicate and agree on the architecture and functionality of the Internet. Some RFCs are official documents of the IETF, defining the standards of TCP/IP and the Internet; others are simply proposals trying to become standards; and others fall somewhere in between. Some are tutorial in nature, while others are quite technical. But all are a way for the Internet, an essentially anarchic entity, to organize and communicate.

There's no need to list all the RFCs here, and you certainly don't need to read them all, but you should know where to find them and be aware of the most important ones. You can find listings of RFCs in a number of places; an excellent site is *http://www.cis.ohio-state.edu/hypertext/information/rfc.html*. The RFCs at this location are organized and linked logically to make it easy to find the information you're looking for. This site, however, isn't nearly as up-to-date as the official RFC editor site, *http://www.rfc-editor.org/*. If you want to be sure you've got the

Table 13-1.   Some key RFCs and what they cover

RFC Number	Subject
RFC 768	User Datagram Protocol (UDP)
RFC 791	Internet Protocol (IP)
RFC 792	Internet Control Message Protocol (ICMP)
RFC 793	Transmission Control Protocol (TCP)
RFC 821	Simple Mail Transfer Protocol (SMTP)
RFC 822	Standard for the Format of ARPA Internet Text Messages
RFC 854	Telnet Protocol
RFC 959	File Transfer Protocol (FTP)
RFC 1011	Official Internet Protocols
RFC 1034	DNS Concepts and Facilities
RFC 1035	DNS Implementation and Specification
RFC 1166	Internet Numbers
RFC 1542	Clarifications and Extensions for the Bootstrap Protocol
RFC 1886	DNS Extensions to Support IP version 6
RFC 1918	Address Allocation for Private Internets
RFC 2052	A DNS Resource Record (RR) for Specifying the Location of Services (DNS SRV)
RFC 2131	Dynamic Host Configuration Protocol (DHCP)
RFC 2136	Dynamic Updates in the DNS System (Dynamic DNS)
RFC 2460	Internet Protocol version 6 (IPv6) Specification

most current information, you should use the latter site. Table 13-1 shows some of the most important RFCs and their subject matter.

IP Addresses and What They Mean

Your IP address is to the Internet (or to the other computers on your local network) much the same as your street address is to your mail carrier. It uniquely identifies your computer using a simple, 32-bit addressing scheme. This scheme, which originated in the late 1960s and early 1970s, uses four octets separated by dots, in the form *w.x.y.z*, to describe both the network's address and the local machine's address on that network.

In terms of IP addresses, all networks fall into one of three classes: A, B, or C. These different classes describe networks (sometimes referred to as licenses) of very different sizes and complexities. The licenses to use a range of IP addresses are controlled by Network Solutions, successor to InterNIC (Internet Network Information Center).

Class A Networks

A class A network has an address that begins with a number from 0 through 126 for the first octet—the "w" portion of the address. This octet describes the network itself, and the remainder of the address is the actual local device's address on that network. A class A network with the network address of 10 (the "w" portion), would contain all IP addresses from 10.0.0.0 to 10.255.255.255.

The class A address 127 has a special meaning and isn't available for use. This means that there are a total of 127 possible class A addresses in the world (from 0 through 126), and that each class A network can contain more than 16 million unique network devices. The class A addresses were spoken for long ago and are assigned to such entities as the Department of Defense, Stanford University, and Hewlett-Packard.

Real World   127: The Loopback Address

All IP addresses that begin with the network number 127 are special. Your network card interprets them as "loopback" addresses. Any packet sent to an address beginning with 127 is treated as if it had gotten to its intended address, and that address is the local device. So packets addressed to 127.0.0.1 are treated the same as packets to 127.37.90.17; both are actually addressed to your current machine, as are all the other 16 million addresses in the 127 class A network. (You too can have your very own class A network. Of course, you can talk only to yourself, but who cares?)

Class B Networks

A class B network uses the first two octets, "w" and "x," to describe the network itself, and the remainder of the address is the actual local device's address on that network. The first octet in a class B network must begin with a number from 128 through 191, resulting in approximately 16,000 class B networks, each of which can have approximately 64,000 unique addresses. This is still a pretty large network, and most of the class B networks were assigned long ago to large organizations or companies such as Rutgers University and Toyota Motor Corporation.

Many of the addresses in the class B address space have been broken up into smaller groups of addresses and reassigned. Large Internet service providers (ISPs), for example, use this technique to more efficiently use the available address space.

Class C Networks

A class C network has an address that begins with a number from 192 through 223 for the "w" octet of the address and uses the first three octets (*w.x.y*) to describe the network itself. The last octet, "z," describes the actual local device's address on that network. This arrangement makes for roughly 2 million class C networks, each of which can have a maximum of 254 devices on the network. That's enough for a small business or a department, but not for a major corporation.

Class D and Class E Addresses

An IP address with a number from 224 through 239 for the "w" octet of the address is known as a class D address, which is used for multicast addresses. The IP address space that uses the numbers from 240 through 247 for the "w" octet is referred to as a class E address. This space is reserved for future use.

Real World   IP Addresses for Networks That Will Never, Ever Be Connected to the Internet

Suppose you know that your internal, private network will never be directly connected to the Internet? This is becoming increasingly common as companies are moving toward sheltering their entire network behind proxy servers and firewalls. Should you use any old numbers then? No, you really shouldn't. There is a special set of network addresses reserved for just such uses. These addresses are defined in RFC 1918, and by using these addresses you can comfortably employ a substantially larger address space than you would otherwise be able to access.

Using these special network addresses also protects the integrity of the Internet. There have already been instances where networks using addresses that were already assigned to other organizations were connected to the Internet, causing substantial problems. Since these special addresses are officially only for private networks, they are automatically filtered at routers, protecting the Internet.

The special addresses are as follows:

- 10.0.0.0 through 10.255.255.255 (a class A network)
- 172.16.0.0 through 172.31.255.255 (16 contiguous class B networks)
- 192.168.0.0 through 192.168.255.255 (256 contiguous class C networks)

If you need to create a test network, for example, or have some other reason to be sure you won't ever be connecting to the Internet, but you need to use TCP/IP for your network protocol, you should use addresses from this special set of addresses. You should also use these addresses for your internal network when you connect to the Internet only through a proxy server or firewall that shields your actual IP address from being seen. Microsoft Proxy Server 2 is such a proxy server. When you use a firewall or proxy server, you require "real" IP addresses only for machines that sit outside your firewall and are visible to the Internet as a whole, saving on IP address space.

Routing and Subnets

If every computer on the Internet had to know the location of every other computer on the Internet and how to get from here to there, the entire Internet would have come to a grinding halt long ago. Early on, it became apparent that a method was needed to filter and route packets so that you could easily not only print to your network printer but also reach any other computer on the Internet without having to know a whole lot about how to get there. Enter subnets, routers, and gateways.

What Is a Subnet?

A *subnet* is simply a portion of the network that operates as a separate network, without regard to what happens outside and without affecting the rest of the network. A subnet will usually be a separate physical "wire" that has only a single point of contact with other areas of the network, through a router or bridge.

Setting up a subnet involves using what is known as a *subnet mask* to allow computers in a subnet to see and directly communicate only with other computers in the same subnet. A subnet mask is an address, again in *w.x.y.z* form, that masks or blocks areas outside the subnet from sight. The mask works by letting you see only those portions of the IP address space that aren't masked by a 1. (Remember that each octet is actually an 8-bit binary value. To "mask by 1" means to ensure that the appropriate bit has been set to a value of 1.) For example, if you have a class C address of 192.168.222.17, and your subnet mask is 255.255.255.0 (a typical class C subnet), as shown in Figure 13-1, you can see only addresses in the last octet of the address (the "z" portion).

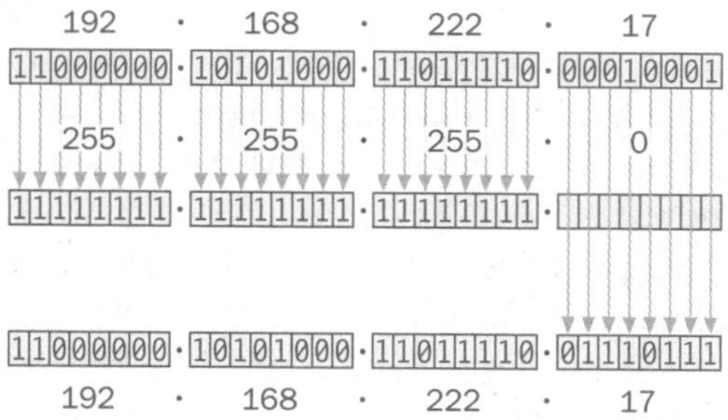

Figure 13-1. *Subnet masking.*

So if your IP address is 192.168.222.17, the address at 192.168.223.25 will be hidden from you by your subnet mask of 255.255.255.0, and you can send a packet to that address only by first passing that packet to a gateway or router that knows both where you are and either where the other network is or how to find it. If, on the other hand, you send a packet to a printer with the IP address 192.168.222.129 or to a computer at 192.168.222.50, you will have no problem. The system can see that address, and the packet goes directly to its destination.

If you can assign an entire class of addresses to a subnet, it's pretty easy to figure out what your mask is, but if you can assign only a portion of a class, you'll need to sit down with your binary-to-decimal conversion tables and determine exactly what the correct subnet mask should be. (Remember that this is all done in binary.) If you understand how it works, you can customize your subnet mask or work out what the one you have is actually doing.

Note If you don't want to bother tweaking your subnet mask, we recommend using the default subnet mask for your network class. For a class A network, this is 255.0.0.0; for a class B network, it's 255.255.0.0; and for a class C network, use 255.255.255.0.

All of the subnet masks on a single portion of your network must be the same. If they aren't, you're going to have all sorts of problems. One machine may be able to send a packet to another, but the other might not be able to send the packet back.

Gateways

A gateway can have different functions on a network, but for the moment we're going to focus on the subnet and routing functions. As we mentioned, if you've got a subnet mask of 255.255.255.0 and the "y" octet of your IP address is 222, you can't see an IP address on the network with a "y" octet of 223.

How, then, do you get to an IP address on another subnet? The answer is a *gateway*. This is a physical device—usually a router, but sometimes just a computer with more than one network card—that's physically connected to both portions of the network. It takes your packets from the 222 subnet and sends them over to the 223 address. Thus, it acts as a gatekeeper between the two separate portions of the network, keeping the traffic with 222 addresses in the 222 subnet and letting only traffic with 223 addresses cross over to the 223 segment.

Routers

A *router* is a device that connects to more than one physical segment of the network and sends packets between those segments as required. If it doesn't know where the packet goes, it knows who to ask for directions—another router. It constantly updates its routing tables with information from other routers about the best way to get to various parts of the network. If your network is part of the Internet, that router has to be able to handle a huge number of possible routes between locations and decide instantaneously on the best way to get from point to point.

Routing Protocols

Detailed information about how routing protocols work and the algorithms involved in routing and address resolution are beyond the scope of this book, but it's useful to know what some of the protocols are, if only to recognize acronyms when they're thrown about. In that spirit, the most common TCP/IP address resolution protocols are as follows:

- **ARP (Address Resolution Protocol)**   Maps the IP address to the physical hardware address (the media access control, or MAC, address) of that IP address, permitting you to send something to an IP address without having to know what physical device it is.

- **RARP (Reverse Address Resolution Protocol)** Maps the physical hardware address (the MAC address) to the IP address, permitting you to determine the IP address when you know only the physical hardware address.

- **Proxy ARP (Proxy Address Resolution Protocol)** Provides a method for implementing subnets on older versions of TCP/IP that don't support subnetting. Described in RFC 1027.

Real World Routing Flaps

The Internet has grown exponentially in the last few years, stretching the technology for resolving addresses to the limit, and sometimes past the limit. When a major router on the Internet goes down—even momentarily—all the other routers on the Internet have to tell one another about it and recalculate new routes that bypass that router. This adjustment results in large numbers of packets passing back and forth, with the result that the traffic becomes so heavy that the routing updates can't occur properly, since the information doesn't make it through the traffic. Such a situation is called a *routing flap*, and it can cause a large portion of the Internet to come to a virtual halt.

Routing flaps don't happen very often, but they are becoming more and more of a problem. In addition, the current router technology is reaching the limit of its ability to calculate the best route from all the possible routes when major changes are caused by the failure of a key router.

Although various people who should know better have been predicting the imminent collapse of the Internet for several years, we don't think things are quite that dire. While there are grounds for concern, a good deal of both money and energy are being invested in finding solutions. The next generation of TCP/IP (known as IPng or IP version 6, discussed later in this chapter) will help, as will new algorithms for how the routing calculations are performed.

Name Resolution

As useful as the 12-decimal-digit IP numbers are when it comes to computers recognizing other computers, they're not the sort of information that human minds process very well. Not only is there a limit to how many 12-digit numbers one can memorize, but numbers can easily change. IP version 6 addresses are 128 bits expressed in strings that may have as many as 32 hexadecimal characters, though they're often shorter. (Actually, IP version 6 addresses could even be written as 128 ones and zeroes, but that's not likely to catch on.) Obviously, easy-to-remember names are preferable to strings of numbers or strings of characters and numbers. This section looks at how names are handled in the TCP/IP and Internet world.

The Domain Name System

The Domain Name System (DNS) was designed in the early 1980s, and in 1984 it became the official method for mapping IP addresses to names. With Windows 2000, DNS has also become the method clients use to locate domain controllers using Active Directory. (The Lightweight Directory Access Protocol, or LDAP, is used by clients to actually access the data stored in the Active Directory database.) While there have been modifications to the overall structure of DNS, the overall result is still remarkably like the original design.

> **More Info**   See RFC 1591 for an overall description of DNS, and RFC 1034 and RFC 1035 for the actual specification. RFC 2136 provides the specification for dynamic updates (Dynamic DNS), with which Windows 2000 complies.

The Domain Namespace

The domain namespace describes the tree-shaped structure of all the domains from the root ("." or "dot") domain down to the lowest level leaf of the structure. It is a hierarchical structure in which each level is separated from those above and below with a dot, so that you always know where you are in the tree.

Before the Internet moved to DNS, a single master file (Hosts.txt) had to be sent via FTP to everyone who needed to convert from numbers to names. Every addition or change required the Hosts file to be propagated to every system. This, obviously, created an enormous overhead even when the Internet was still quite small. DNS is a distributed database that is extensible to add information as needed. It permits local administration of local names while maintaining overall integrity and conformance to standards.

Root Domains

The root domains are the first level of the tree below the root. They describe the kinds of networks that are within their domain in two or three letters, such as ".com" for commercial domains and ".edu" for educational domains. The original root domains were functionally based and had a decidedly U.S. slant. That's not surprising, given that most of the namespace was originally set up and administered by the Department of Defense. As the Internet grew, however, this approach made less and less sense, especially with a distributed database like DNS that allowed for local administration and control. Geographical root domains were added to the functionally based ones, such as ".it" for Italian ones, and so on. See Chapter 3 for information on planning your namespace and domains.

How Names Are Resolved into Addresses

When you click a link to *http://www.microsoft.com* and your browser attempts to connect to that site, what actually happens? How does it find *www.microsoft.com*? The short answer is that it asks the primary DNS server listed in the TCP/IP Properties window on your workstation. But how does that DNS server know where the site is?

Real World   **Where Domain Names Come From and How You Get One**

These days virtually every business (and many individuals) wants its own domain. The keeper and distributor of domain names used to be Network Solutions, formerly called InterNIC. Recently this task was opened up to competition, and there are now a myriad of companies that will register your domain name for you. The list is too big and volatile to include here—for a complete listing visit the Internet Corporation for Assigned Names and Numbers (ICANN) Web site at *http://www.icann.org*. You can link to any of the accredited registrars from this site and perform a search to find out if your chosen name is taken.

You should have alternative names in mind as well; you'll probably need them. After you've researched existing names and chosen one that isn't taken, simply register the name with your chosen registrar. Pay roughly $70(US) or you'll lose the name. That fee is good for two years; then you'll be billed at about $35(US) per year.

Finally, you must create the necessary DNS records on your DNS server, or have your ISP do it. If you're connecting to the Internet through an ISP that is going to be maintaining your DNS records, by all means let the ISP do the work and set everything up, once you've done the name research.

Long ago, domain names were free and forever, but those days are gone. If you don't pay your bill from your chosen registrar, your domain name will be up for grabs, and chances are that someone else will claim it before you're able to re-register it. The available short names are disappearing at a rapid rate, and many people are finding that they need to think up longer versions to find something that isn't taken.

When a TCP/IP application wants to communicate with or connect to another location, it needs the address of that location. But it usually knows only the name it's looking for, so the first step is to resolve that name into an IP address. The first place it looks for the name is in the locally cached set of names and their IP addresses that it has resolved recently. After all, if you asked about *www.microsoft.com* just a few minutes ago, why should it go through all the trouble of looking that name up again? It's not likely that the IP address will have changed in that time.

Suppose, however, that you haven't been on the Internet for a couple of days, and your DNS server doesn't have any recent information about *www.microsoft.com*. In that case the TCP/IP application asks around to see if anyone else knows the IP address. This can happen in a couple ways. The default method is to use recursion, in which the DNS server queries the root server of the domain, which passes back the location of the DNS server that is authoritative regarding the next level down in the domain, which the original DNS server then queries. This process recurs until it reaches a DNS server that contains the IP address of the desired host in its zone data.

> **Tip**   You may want to disable the use of recursion on your DNS server if your server is in use on an internal network and you want your clients to failover to a secondary DNS server that handles name resolution for hosts outside your local network.

If you disable recursion on the DNS server, or if the client doesn't request the use of recursion, the DNS entry for the desired host is found by iteration. When using iteration, the DNS server checks its zone and cache data, and when it finds that it cannot complete the request, it sends to the client a list of DNS servers that are more likely to have the host name in their zones. The client then contacts those servers, which may in turn respond with their own list, possibly even to the point that the client may query the Internet root servers looking for the appropriate DNS server.

> **Tip**   You may want to enable the use of Windows Internet Name Service (WINS) lookup to search the WINS database for any names not located in the DNS zone data, providing for a complete search of both the DNS and NetBIOS namespaces.

Reverse Lookups

In most cases, you have a host name for which you need to locate the IP address, but in some instances you may have only an IP address for which you need to look up the host name. Reverse lookup was added to the DNS specification for this reason. The only problem with creating reverse lookups is the difference between the way the DNS namespace is organized and the way in which IP addresses are assigned. DNS names go from specific to general, beginning with the host name and ending with the root of the domain (the period at the end of a fully qualified domain name). IP addresses work in reverse fashion. So to facilitate the lookup of a host name from an IP address, a special domain, the in-addr.arpa domain, was created.

In the in-addr.arpa domain, the octets of an IP address are reversed, with in-addr.arpa appended to the address. For example, the IP address 10.230.231.232 would be queried as 232.231.230.10.in-addr.arpa. This query locates the new resource record (RR) type PTR (pointer), which is used to map an address in the reverse lookup zone to the A record (address) of the desired host. Once the A record is found, the associated DNS name is then returned to the client.

Dynamic DNS and Active Directory Integration

Dynamic DNS, new to Windows 2000 Server, makes DNS more flexible by permitting clients to update their DNS records dynamically. This capability eliminates the need to update DNS entries manually when clients change IP addresses. Unfortunately, the standard dynamic DNS service described in RFC 2136 allows for only a single-master model, in which a single primary DNS server maintains the master database of zone data (the addresses and host names for a particular domain). This database can be replicated with secondary DNS servers, but only the primary server can manage dynamic updates to the zone. If the primary server goes down, client updates to the zone aren't processed.

The dynamic DNS server in Windows 2000 Server can overcome the limitations of a single-master model and use Active Directory to store its zone data, permitting a multiple-master model. Since the Active Directory database is fully replicated to all Active Directory–enabled domain controllers, any domain controller in the domain can update DNS zone data. Using Active Directory to store the zone data also allows for added security features and simplified planning and management, as well as faster directory replication than is possible using a single-master model, because Active Directory replicates only relevant changes to the zone.

Zone Storage and Active Directory

A DNS server is required to support the use of Active Directory, so if a DNS server can't be found on the network when a server is being promoted to domain controller, the DNS service will be installed by default on the domain controller.

Once Active Directory is installed, the storage and replication of your zones can be done in one of two ways:

- **Standard zone storage using a text-based file** With this method, zones are stored in .DNS text files located in the %SystemRoot%\System32\ DNS folder. The filename will be the same as the zone name you chose when creating the zone. Figure 13-2 shows part of a text DNS zone file.

- **Directory-integrated zone storage** Zones are stores in a *dnsZone* container object located in the Active Directory tree, shown in Figure 13-3.

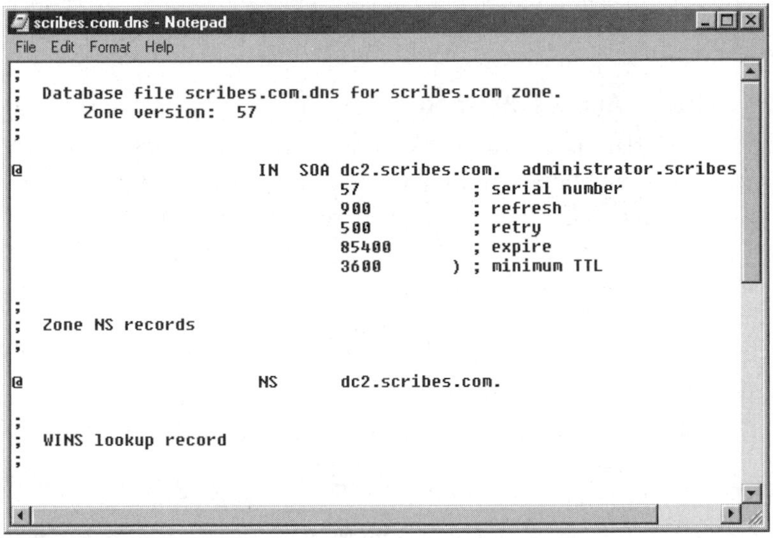

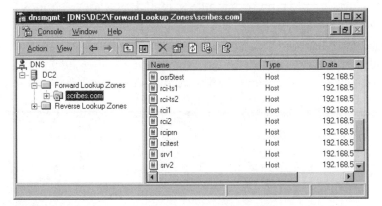

Figure 13-2. *Zone storage in a text file.*

Figure 13-3. *DNS zone stores in an Active Directory tree.*

The second method is much preferred, not only because integrated zones are automatically replicated and synchronized whenever a new domain controller comes online, but also for reasons of administrative simplicity. Keeping a DNS namespace separate from the Active Directory namespace doubles your work (and your chances for error) when testing replication or modifying your domain, for example.

> **More Info**   DNS is one of the (many) subjects in this book that is a book-length topic in its own right. For more information on the configuration of DNS, consult the *Microsoft Windows 2000 Server Resource Kit* (Microsoft Press). For in-depth coverage of the subject, see *DNS and BIND* by Paul Albitz and Cricket Liu (O'Reilly & Associates).

Lightweight Directory Access Protocol

LDAP is used to access data in the Active Directory database. Once again, DNS is used to locate domain controllers, and LDAP is used to access the Active Directory data. LDAP runs on top of TCP/IP, and Active Directory supports both versions 2 and 3 of LDAP. Any LDAP product complying with these specifications can be used to access data in Active Directory. For more information on Active Directory and LDAP, see Chapter 2.

Dynamic Host Configuration Protocol

One of the problems facing organizations using TCP/IP these days is deciding how to manage internal IP addresses. This is a special concern for companies that hand out addresses that are Internet-valid. However, even if your company uses a private network, the chore of managing all of the IP addresses can quickly become an administrator's nightmare, especially if you deal with intermittently connected computers such as laptops and remote computers. DHCP provides a simpler way to handle addresses for computers that are connected irregularly.

DHCP allows the administrator to assign the available IP addresses only as required. A mobile user can connect a laptop to the network when necessary and be assigned an appropriate address automatically. Likewise, a dial-in user doesn't need a permanent IP address; one can be assigned when the connection is made to the network, and when the connection is broken the address is made available for someone else's use. With DHCP, a modest pool of IP addresses can serve a much larger pool of users.

How DHCP Works

To receive an IP address, the client computer sends out a DHCP discover broadcast, which a DHCP server picks up and responds to by offering the client an IP address that the client can use. The client responds to the first offer it receives and sends back to the DHCP server a request for the IP address offered. The DHCP server sends an acknowledgment telling the client that it succeeded in leasing the IP address for the amount of time specified by the DHCP server.

DHCP clients attempt to renew their leases at bootup, as well as after 50 percent of the lease time has passed. In this renewal process, the discover stage is skipped and the client simply begins with a request. If the renewal of the lease fails at the 50 percent mark, the client waits until 87.5 percent of the lease has passed and then attempts to acquire a new IP address by sending out a DHCP discover broadcast and starting the IP lease process again.

Using Multiple DHCP Servers

Because DHCP uses UDP broadcasts, your DHCP servers won't see (and thus won't respond to) client requests on a different subnet unless the router between the two is configured to forward broadcasts. In most large establishments, this means separate DHCP servers for each subnet because broadcast traffic is an unnecessary burden on your routing capacity. In addition, you may well want a second DHCP server configured (if not activated) for each subnet to provide for redundancy and to give your network a way to issue addresses should the main DHCP server fail.

If you do opt to allow your routers to pass along broadcasts, they must support RFC 1542 (BOOTP) as well as be configured to forward broadcasts. Check the documentation for your router for configuration information; most new routers (and newer versions of router software) support this. If your router doesn't support RFC 1542 and you have clients that do not have access to a local DHCP server, you must configure a DHCP relay agent to forward client broadcasts to a DCHP server on another network segment.

Tip   Although you can use DHCP remotely with supported routers, it's best to situate your DHCP servers on-site. WAN failures do occur, and even a brief one can keep clients from being able to acquire or maintain an IP address. Letting a WAN be in a position to put your LAN out of business is a poor gamble.

Windows 2000 Server supports integration of DHCP with dynamic DNS to facilitate the updating of a client's DNS record when the client receives a new IP address from a DHCP server. This feature fixes an incompatibility between DHCP and DNS that has existed until this point. Unfortunately, the IETF did not finish the final specifications for dynamic updates between DNS servers before Windows 2000 was completed, so it is likely that this DHCP–dynamic DNS integration will work only with Windows 2000 DNS servers.

If you're still using static DNS servers on your network, you need to enable WINS lookup for DHCP clients that use NetBIOS to help avoid failed DNS lookups for DHCP clients. Whenever you can, however, you should replace or upgrade existing static DNS servers with dynamic DNS servers such as the one provided with Windows 2000.

Typically, you need one DHCP server for every 10,000 clients, though this number can be higher if you have large disk capacity and a fast CPU, or lower if your IP address class or network layout prevents this kind of server utilization. DHCP is very disk intensive, so make sure that if your server will be handling a significant number of clients you have sufficient hardware, such as a large and fast redundant array of independent disks (RAID), adequate memory, and one or more fast CPUs. For information on evaluating the performance of your current system, see Chapter 32.

Real World   DHCP and Availability

DHCP itself does not support synchronization with other DHCP servers. If your network demands increased reliability, have a backup DHCP server offline with the same scope as the primary server, so if the primary server goes down you can bring the backup online immediately.

You may also want to split the address space between two DHCP servers, with the primary server handling 80 percent of the address space and the secondary server handling 20 percent. If the primary server fails, the secondary server handles all client leases from its 20 percent of the address space until the primary server is brought back online. If both servers are down, clients maintain their IP addresses until their leases run out.

If server reliability is a problem on your network, consider increasing the lease time to allow more time to bring servers back online before clients lose their addresses.

Windows Internet Name Service

NetBIOS is an interface originally developed to allow applications to access network resources in Microsoft's MS-DOS operating system. NetBIOS host names are up to 15 characters long and part of a flat namespace, so that all names must be unique on a network. Normally, host names are resolved by broadcast—not the most efficient means in terms of either time or network bandwidth. Routers also usually do not forward NetBIOS broadcasts, eliminating the ability to resolve host names on a different subnet.

The Windows Internet Name Service (WINS) provides a solution to this problem by maintaining a dynamic database of IP addresses and their associated NetBIOS names. However, WINS is still limited in many ways by the underlying architecture of NetBIOS and is now an optional service in a Windows 2000 network. While many of us may be eager to do away with WINS, it will be around for quite some time to provide compatibility with downlevel (legacy) Microsoft operating systems such as Microsoft Windows 95/98 and Windows NT. When deploying WINS servers on your network, deploy only the minimum number necessary to provide adequate service to your clients. WINS servers can be a pain to replicate, so keeping the number of servers down can be a big plus. (Microsoft itself, for example, uses no more than about 12 WINS servers worldwide.)

> **Tip** Don't install WINS on a multihomed server. WINS has enough replication problems without complicating the situation by placing the server on two subnets.

To make WINS and Browsing work correctly when you are in an enterprise environment with subnets and multiple domains, you should keep a few tricks in mind. There are three possible scenarios listed here, and each will be discussed in the sections that follow.

- Single domain across a subnet boundary
- Multiple domains within a subnet boundary
- Multiple domains across a subnet boundary

Single Domain Across a Subnet Boundary

To see the resources of a single domain across a subnet boundary, with only TCP/IP as your protocol, you'll need to set up WINS servers on both sides of the router or mess around with Lmhosts files. Avoid Lmhosts files like the plague: They're a pain to get right in the first place and have to be manually edited every time there is a change anywhere. And they don't deal well with DHCP, under which IP addresses are subject to change. However, if you're setting up a virtual private network with Internet-connected clients, you may not be able to avoid Lmhosts, since these clients won't have an available WINS server.

In general, it's a good idea to have a domain on each side of your router. The alternative is much more traffic across the router than you really want, since every authentication request would have to cross over. The obvious choice is to put a WINS server in each domain. No special requirements need to be met for this to work, since Browsing doesn't need to be told about another domain.

Real World   Browsing vs. browsing

A source of possible confusion in any discussion about Microsoft networking is the subtle distinction between the common meaning of the word "browsing" and the very specific meaning that the word has in Microsoft networking. Many texts use "browsing" to mean looking for or at the resources available, which is a reasonable use of the word. However, "Browsing" in the Microsoft networking sense refers to the Computer Browser service used by Windows-based computers to maintain browse lists of all shared resources on the network. It's easy to get confused, and we'll try to avoid that here by always capitalizing "Browsing" when using it in the Microsoft networking sense.

Multiple Domains Within a Subnet Boundary

If you're running a forest within a single subnet, you'll probably want a WINS server in each domain, but you don't need to do anything special with Browsing. You can set up and explicitly add the other domains to browse, but this step isn't required.

Multiple Domains Across a Subnet Boundary

Now we get to the tricky one. For everything to work in multiple domains across a subnet boundary, you'll need to set everything up very carefully. Since the Browsing packets won't cross the subnet boundary unless they know where they're going, you'll need to explicitly set the Computer Browsing service to browse the domain on the far side of the router. Each domain in the forest or tree will need to be configured to browse any domains on the far side of the router.

For the technical details of WINS and Browsing, see the *Microsoft Windows 2000 Server Resource Kit*. Once you've gotten to a pure Windows 2000 network, with no downlevel clients, you can happily turn off WINS and make your life a lot easier.

IP Version 6

As was pointed out earlier, the explosive growth of the Internet has pushed it to the very limits of the original design. The number of IP addresses has grown almost exponentially in recent years, leading to the fear that there will soon not be enough addresses to connect all the devices and computers that people want to connect. This fear has been assuaged for large corporations, which have been placing their networks almost entirely behind firewalls and proxy servers and using their own internal networks, where each corporation is free to use its own class A network address. However, there will come a time in the near future when IP version 4 will impede the growth and management of the Internet, requiring a solution.

To find a solution to the limitations of the 32-bit address space and the limits to the routing protocols in the current structure of TCP/IP, the IETF and others began working on a new version of IP several years ago. Different working groups originally proposed different solutions, but over time these groups have arrived at a consensus on the next generation of IP, known as IPng or more correctly as IP version 6 (often shortened to IPv6). It was formally accepted by the IETF in December 1994, and the current specification is in RFC 2460. IPv6 defines a 128-bit IP address space compatible with the current implementation of TCP/IP (version 4, or IPv4). The specifications call for packets to include additional information for improved routing and handling of mobile devices. IPv6 will not only enlarge the address space available, but will also improve network performance, ease configuration issues, and provide enhanced security.

Despite the benefits, many are not looking forward to the deployment of IPv6. After all, most companies try to minimize the number of protocols they need to support. Supporting yet another protocol is regarded with less enthusiasm than

Real World   **Unreal Numbers of Addresses**

IPv6 addresses have four times the number of bits that IPv4 addresses do (128 vs. 32), but what does that actually mean? The 32-bit address structure can enumerate more than 4 billion hosts on as many as 16.7 million networks, but the number of potential IPv6 addresses totals 2^{96} times the size of the IPv4 address space (4 billion x 2^{96}). This works out to 340,282,366,920,938,463,463,374,607,431,768,211,456 possible addresses. Of course, given routing and hierarchical requirements, this theoretical address space is diminished greatly when making practical estimates. The mathematically minded should consult RFC 1715, in which Christian Huitema analyzes other addressing schemes (including the French and U.S. telephone systems) and concludes that 128-bit addressing will suffice for another 25 years of Internet growth.

Friday afternoon performance audits. The transition will be gradual, however, and there is an incredible amount of work in progress to ensure that it is painless as well.

IPv4 and IPv6 will exist side by side for an extended period, and most vendors are working to see that future products support both versions of IP seamlessly. For example, Microsoft is currently developing an IPv6 stack for Windows 2000 that will operate side by side with the IPv4 stack currently in use, which means that existing functionality won't be altered, and all applications written for the Winsock 2 (Windows Sockets) interface will automatically be IPv6 compatible once an IPv6 stack is installed.

Note Windows 2000 does not ship with an IPv6 stack. While some operating systems, such as Linux kernels version 2.2 and later do ship with IPv6 support, IPv6 is still in the experimental stage, and supporting it is something you needn't worry about right away. However, if you want to be prepared, you can start by reading *IPv6 Clearly Explained* by Pete Loshin (Morgan Kaufman Publishers).

Using the Administration Tools for TCP/IP

Windows 2000 Server provides several useful MMC snap-ins, including tools for setting up and managing a DNS server, a WINS server, and a DHCP server. Although the way you launch these tools may vary slightly depending on whether you're using Active Directory, once you have the tools loaded they act the same.

The DNS Snap-in

The DNS snap-in allows you to easily set up and manage a DNS server to locally resolve names to IP addresses and maintain authoritative records for your own domains. For more information on setting up and configuring a DNS server, see Chapter 6.

Connecting to Another Server

To add a server to the list of DNS servers that you administer, follow these steps:

1. Choose DNS from the Administrative Tools folder to open the DNS snap-in.

2. Right-click DNS at the top of the console tree and choose Connect To Computer from the shortcut menu. This opens the Select Target Computer dialog box.

3. Select The Following Computer option, type in the name or IP address of the remote DNS server to add (Figure 13-4), and click OK.

Windows 2000 Server's DNS snap-in will attempt to connect to the server. If it is successful, it will display the statistics for that server, as well as the types of records and zones maintained by the server.

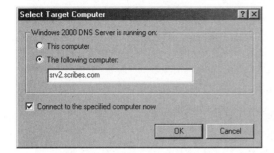

Figure 13-4. *The DNS snap-in.*

Note   Unfortunately, the Windows 2000 Server DNS snap-in supports only those DNS servers running on Windows 2000 and Windows NT, so it can't administer any other DNS servers you may be running.

DNS Functions

When you highlight a server in the DNS snap-in, the Action menu lists the following functions:

- **Configure The Server**   Opens the Configure DNS Server Wizard, which walks you through setting up your DNS Server.

- **New Zone**   Opens the New Zone Wizard, which steps you through the creation of a new primary or secondary DNS zone.

- **Set Aging/Scavenging For All Zones**   Configures when records are refreshed and when unused records are scavenged or deleted.

- **Scavenge Stale Resource Records**   Tells server to delete (scavenge) unused (stale) records.

- **Update Server Data Files**   Increments the serial number and updates the database. Forces other DNS servers to update their stored information.

- **Clear Cache**   Removes the records for any hosts not in this server's DNS zone, forcing the server to perform additional queries the next time those hosts are queried.

- **All Tasks** Displays a submenu with some frequently used commands:
  - *Start* starts a DNS server that has been stopped.
  - *Stop* stops the DNS server so you can work on it.
  - *Pause* briefly takes the zone offline without stopping the actual server service.
  - *Resume* resumes the operation of a paused DNS server.
  - *Restart* stops the DNS server and then restarts it.
- **New Window From Here** Opens a new MMC window with the currently selected item at the root of the console tree.
- **Delete** Removes the selected item.
- **Refresh** Refreshes the DNS snap-in display to show any changes that have been made.
- **Export List** Exports the information shown in the DNS snap-in to a text file.
- **Properties** Shows detailed properties for the selected item.
- **Help** Displays the DNS Help system.

Real World   Changing DNS Records

When you make a change to the DNS records, make sure you select Update Server Data Files. This option will increment the serial number, letting other DNS servers know that you've made a change and that they need to update their information. If you're using conventional DNS zones, do this only from the primary DNS server for a zone. If you're using Active Directory–integrated DNS, you can make the changes to any Active Directory–based DNS and it will propagate correctly to the other Active Directory DNS servers as well as notify secondary servers that there are updated records.

Supported DNS Record Types

Windows 2000 Server DNS supports a wide variety of DNS record types, including many that will become increasingly important as the world moves to IPv6. The supported record types are shown in Table 13-2.

Table 13-2.   Supported DNS record types

Record Type	Common Name	Function	RFC
A	Address record	Maps a fully qualified domain name (FQDN) to a 32-bit IPv4 address	1035
AAAA	IPv6 address record	Maps an FQDN to a 128-bit IPv6 address	1886
AFSDB	Andrews file system (AFS) or DCE record	Maps a DNS domain name to a server subtype that is either an AFS version 3 volume or an authenticated name server using distributed computing environment (DCE) or network computing architecture (NCA)	1183
CNAME	Canonical name or alias record	Maps a virtual domain name (alias) to a real domain name	1035
HINFO	Host information record	Specifies the CPU and operating system type for the host	1700
ISDN	ISDN information record	Maps an FQDN to an ISDN telephone number	1183
MB	Mailbox name record	Maps a domain mail server name to the actual host name of the mail server	1035
MG	Mail group record	Maps a domain mailing group to the actual mailbox (MB) resource records of its members	1035
MINFO	Mailbox information record	Specifies a mailbox for the person who maintains the mailbox or list, and can also specify a mailbox for related errors	1035
MR	Mailbox renamed record	Maps an old mailbox name to a new mailbox name for forwarding purposes	1035
MX	Mail exchange record	Provides routing information to reach a given mailbox	974
NS	Name server record	Specifies that the name server listed has a zone starting with the owner name	1035
PTR	Pointer resource record	Points to another DNS resource record, most often used in reverse lookup to point to the A record	1035
RP	Responsible person information record	Provides information about the person responsible for a server	1183

(continued)

Table 13-2. *continued*

Record Type	Common Name	Function	RFC
RT	Route-through record	Provides routing information for hosts lacking a direct WAN address	1183
SRV	Service locator record	Provides a way of locating multiple servers providing similar TCP/IP services	2052
TXT	Text record	Maps a DNS name to a string of descriptive text	1035
WKS	Well-known services record	Describes the most popular TCP/IP services supported by a protocol on a specific IP address	1035
X25	X.25 information record	Maps a DNS address to a public switched data network (PSDN) address number	1183

More Info For more information on each of these record types and what they mean, refer to the related RFC or see the *Microsoft Windows 2000 Server Resource Kit* (1999), available from Microsoft Press.

The WINS Snap-in

The WINS snap-in for MMC allows you to set up and manage a WINS server to resolve IP addresses into the NetBIOS names needed to browse your network. If you've installed the WINS server, WINS will be listed on the Start menu's Administrative Tools menu. For additional information on setting up and configuring a WINS server, see Chapter 6.

Tip In the TCP/IP Properties window for your WINS server's network connection, make sure the primary and secondary WINS servers are set to the WINS server you're working on. If a WINS server lists another WINS server in the TCP/IP Properties window, you may end up with some serious replication problems if the WINS service isn't available quickly enough at boot time.

Adding a Server

To add a WINS server to those managed by the WINS snap-in, follow these steps:

1. Choose WINS from the Administrative Tools folder.
2. Highlight WINS at the top of the console tree. On the Action menu choose Add Server. The Add Server dialog box opens.

3. You can add the server either by name or by IP address. Click OK when you're done.

By default, you'll see the primary and secondary WINS servers for the local machine in the left pane of the WINS window. The right pane of the WINS window highlights the current statistics for the selected WINS server.

WINS Functions

The WINS snap-in lets you manage all of the functionality of the Windows Internet Name Service on multiple servers from the same application. The following are some functions you can perform with the WINS snap-in:

- To view the status of your WINS servers, click Server Status in the console tree. The status of your servers appears in the pane on the right.
- To view records in the WINS database, right-click the Active Registrations folder in the console tree under the desired server. Choose either Find By Name to search for a particular name or Find By Owner to display the Find By Owner dialog box, which shows all of the records in the WINS database. When viewing records, you can use the Record Types tab of the Find By Owner dialog box to filter the type of records displayed.
- To add a static entry to the database, right-click the Active Registrations folder and choose New Static Mapping from the shortcut menu.

Caution   Add static entries only for computers that do not support WINS and only if absolutely necessary. Static entries are notoriously difficult to eliminate after replication and can be deleted only by the owner.

- To initiate scavenging, which purges the WINS database and does general cleanup on it, select the WINS server you want to scavenge and choose Scavenge Database from the Action menu. When initiating scavenging, don't attempt to alter the scavenging parameters for WINS. These parameters have been extensively tested and optimized by Microsoft. Any change you make will be for the worse.
- To modify the properties for your WINS server, select the server you want to work on, and then choose Properties from the Actions menu. This displays the Properties window shown in Figure 13-5, which you can use to modify the path to the backup copy of the WINS database, change the length of name leases, and modify logging and other options.

All of these functions can be performed on multiple WINS servers, not just the one you are running the application from.

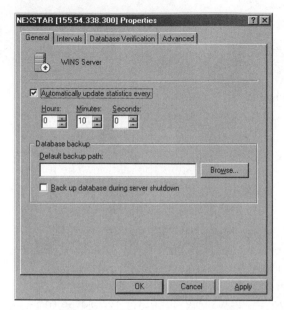

Figure 13-5. *The Properties window for a WINS server.*

More Info For more information on WINS, see the *Microsoft Windows 2000 Server Resource Kit* (1999), available from Microsoft Press. Another good source is the *Microsoft TCP/IP Training Kit* (1997), also available from Microsoft Press.

Replicating with Other WINS Servers

If your network is large, you may need to install multiple WINS servers and set up replication among them. The WINS snap-in makes this task fairly easy, but be careful when setting up replication partners because replication problems can be troublesome with WINS servers.

Planning It is generally preferable to set up replication between WINS servers in a hub or star pattern, as shown in Figure 13-6, with a single-master WINS server in the center and all other WINS servers replicating only with this server, using the push/pull method. While using a double hub, also shown in the figure, can provide additional redundancy, the replication problems that can arise generally outweigh the added reliability.

To view the replication partners for a WINS server, click the Replication Partners folder under the desired server. You can add replication partners by going to the Action menu, choosing New, and then choosing Replication Partner. To delete a replication partner, select the partner and choose Delete from the Action menu. To modify the replication properties, select the replication partner and choose Properties from the Action menu.

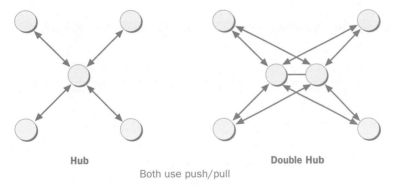

Hub   Double Hub

Both use push/pull

Figure 13-6. *Hub and double-hub architectures.*

Tip   When configuring replication partners, use push/pull replication for all WINS servers to simplify replication troubleshooting.

The DHCP Snap-in

The DHCP snap-in is used to set up and manage a DHCP server, which in turn assigns and manages IP addresses and their properties for DHCP clients on the network. If you've installed the DHCP server, DHCP will be listed on the Administrative Tools menu. For detailed information on setting up and configuring DHCP, see Chapter 6.

DHCP Functions

The DHCP snap-in, shown in Figure 13-7, provides a single point from which to administer all of the properties and functionality of your DHCP servers. The following are some functions you can perform with the DHCP snap-in:

- To add a DHCP server to the list of managed servers, select DHCP in the console tree and choose Add Server from the Action menu.

- To browse a list of authorized DHCP servers, select DHCP in the console tree and choose Manage Authorized Servers from the Action menu.

- To remove a server from the list of managed servers, select the server, click Action, and choose Delete.

- To create a new scope of IP numbers, select the server you want to create the scope for, click Action, then choose New Scope, New Superscope, or New Multicast Scope, depending on the type of scope you want to create.

- To modify a scope's properties, highlight the scope in the console tree, click Action, and choose Properties. This will display the Scope Properties window shown in Figure 13-8.

- To temporarily deactivate a scope on the server, select the scope, go to the Action menu and choose Deactivate. To return the scope to use, go to the Action menu and choose Activate.

- To delete a scope, select the scope, go to the Action menu, and choose Delete.

- To view the address pool, leases, reservations, or options in use for a scope, select the appropriate subfolder of the scope.

- To exclude a range of IP addresses from a scope, right-click the Address Pool folder under the appropriate scope and choose New Exclusion Range. Enter the range of addresses you want to exclude and then click Add.

- To add reserved addresses to the scope for particular clients, right-click the Reservations folder under the desired scope and choose New Reservation. Enter the IP address and MAC address for the client, enter a name and comment for the reservation, select whether to allow only DHCP or BOOTP or both types of clients to use the reservation, and then click Add.

Tip Use reservations instead of static IP addresses (which require exclusions) for all servers that need to maintain a specific IP address, such as DNS and WINS servers. This guarantees the server a consistent IP address while also providing the ability to recover the IP address in the future if the server is decommissioned or moved.

- To configure the DHCP options for a scope, right-click the Scope Options folder under the desired scope and then choose Configure Options. To configure the DHCP options for a server, right-click the Server Options folder under the desired server and choose Configure Options.

Real World   Scopes, Superscopes, and Multicast Scopes

A scope is simply the range of possible IP addresses on a network. If you find that you need to add more clients to a network and the scope is exhausted, you can add an additional scope. A superscope is a collection of scopes grouped together into a single administrative whole. Grouping scopes together into a superscope makes it possible to have more than one logical subnet on a physical subnet. A multicast scope lets you use ranges of class D addresses—addresses that are then shared by many computers (members of the multicast group).

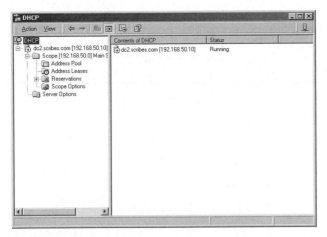

Figure 13-7. *The DHCP snap-in.*

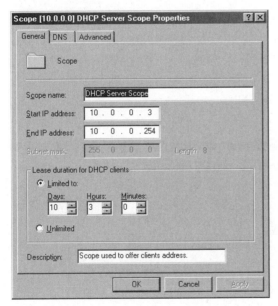

Figure 13-8. *The General tab of Properties window for a DHCP scope.*

The DHCP server lets you preconfigure many of the options that would normally need to be set manually for a standard, fixed-address, TCP/IP device. With the DHCP snap-in you can set many of the options either globally or individually for each scope. Individual clients can override these default settings, of course, but in most cases this will be neither necessary nor desirable if you've set up your DHCP options correctly. The options you can configure on a per scope or global basis are as follows:

- Time Offset
- Router
- Time Server
- Name Servers
- DNS Servers
- Log Servers
- Cookie Servers
- LPR Servers
- Impress Servers
- Resource Location Servers
- Host Name
- Boot File Size
- Merit Dump File
- DNS Domain Name
- Swap Server
- Root Path
- Extensions Path
- IP Layer Forwarding
- Nonlocal Source Routing
- Policy Filter Masks
- Max DG Reassembly Size
- Default IP Time-to-Live
- Path MTU Aging Timeout
- Path MTU Plateau Table
- MTU Option
- All Subnets are Local
- Broadcast Address
- Perform Mask Discovery
- Mask Supplier Option
- Perform Router Discovery
- Router Solicitation Address
- Static Route Option

- Trailer Encapsulation
- ARP Cache Timeout
- Ethernet Encapsulation
- TCP Default Time-to-Live
- Keepalive Interval
- Keepalive Garbage
- NIS Domain Name
- NIS Servers
- NTP Servers
- Vendor Specific Info
- WINS/NBNS Servers
- NetBIOS Over TCP/IP NBDD
- WINS/NBT Node Type
- NetBIOS Scope ID
- XWindow System Font
- XWindow System Display
- NIS+ Domain Name
- NIS+ Servers
- Boot Server Host Name
- Bootfile Name
- Mobile IP Home Agents
- Simple Mail Transport Protocol (SMTP) Servers
- Post Office Protocol (POP3) Servers
- Network News Transport Protocol (NNTP) Servers
- World Wide Web (WWW) Servers
- Finger Servers
- Internet Relay Chat (IRC) Servers
- StreetTalk Servers
- StreetTalk Directory Assistance (STDA) Servers

As you can see, there are numerous options that you can configure for individual clients or DHCP scopes. Our recommendation is to set only the options you know you need to set. Leave alone anything you're uncertain about.

Summary

Although it's not necessary to become an expert on TCP/IP to run a network, some basic knowledge is required. Likewise, although Windows 2000 Server provides tools for administering DNS, WINS, and DHCP servers, there's no substitute for an understanding of how all these functions come together. TCP/IP and DNS in particular are worth studying in some depth because so many network difficulties can be traced to the misconfiguration of one or the other. The next chapter covers the configuration of hard disks for maximum efficiency and security.

Chapter 14
Implementing Disk Management

Under normal circumstances, this would be a combined chapter on disk management and storage. However, with Microsoft Windows 2000 the subject of computer and network storage has become more complex for the administrator while at the same time it has become simpler for the user. Windows 2000 Server provides for both local and remote storage and for storage on removable media—all in a way that is completely transparent to the user. After all, the user doesn't really care whether a program or file is stored on disk, on tape, or somewhere on the intranet, as long as it's available when needed. This chapter covers the more traditional disk management tasks that are possible under Windows 2000, and the next chapter takes a look at some of the less traditional methods of storage that are now possible.

Understanding Disk Terminology

Before going into the details of managing disks and storage, let's review some definitions.

- **Physical drive**   The actual hard disk itself, including case, electronics, platters, and all that stuff. Not terribly important to the disk administrator.

- **Partition**   A portion of the hard disk. In many cases, this will be the entire hard disk space, but it needn't be.

- **Allocation unit**   The smallest unit of managed disk space on a hard disk or logical volume. Also called a cluster.

- **Primary partition**   A portion of the hard disk that's been marked as a potentially bootable logical drive by an operating system. MS-DOS can support only a single primary partition, but Microsoft Windows NT and Windows 2000 can support multiple ones. There can be only four primary partitions on any hard disk.

- **Extended partition**   A nonbootable portion of the hard disk that can be subdivided into logical drives. There can be only a single extended partition per hard disk, but it can be divided into multiple logical drives.

- **Extended volume**   Similar to, and sometimes synonymous with, a spanned volume, this is any dynamic volume that has been extended to make it larger than its original size. When it uses portions of more than one physical disk, it is more properly referred to as a spanned volume.

- **Logical drive**   A section or partition of a hard disk that acts as a single unit. An extended partition can be divided, for example, into multiple logical drives.

- **Logical volume**   Another name for a logical drive.

- **Basic disk**   A traditional disk drive that is divided into one or more partitions, with a logical drive in the primary partition, if present, and one or more logical drives in any extended partitions. Basic disks do not support the more advanced functions of Disk Management, but they can be converted to dynamic disks in many cases.

- **Dynamic disk**   A Disk Management–managed hard disk that can be used to create various volumes.

- **Volume**   A unit of disk space composed of one or more sections of one or more dynamic disks.

- **Simple volume**   The Disk Management equivalent of a partition. A portion of a single dynamic disk, it can be assigned either a single drive letter or no drive letter and can be attached (mounted) on zero or more mount points.

- **RAID (redundant array of independent [formerly "inexpensive"] disks)** The use of multiple hard disks in an array to provide for larger volume size, fault tolerance, and increased performance. RAID comes in different levels, such as RAID-0, RAID-1, RAID-5, and so forth. Higher numbers don't indicate greater performance or fault tolerance, just different methods of doing the job.

- **Spanned volume**   A collection of portions of hard disks combined into a single addressable unit. A spanned volume is formatted like a single drive and can have a drive letter assigned to it, but it will span multiple physical drives. A spanned volume—occasionally referred to as an extended volume—provides no fault tolerance and increases your exposure to failure but does permit you to make more efficient use of the available hard disk space.

- **Striped volume**   Like a spanned volume, a striped volume combines multiple hard disk portions into a single entity. A striped volume uses special formatting, however, to write to each of the portions equally in a stripe to increase performance. A striped volume provides no fault tolerance and actually increases your exposure to failure, but it is faster than either a spanned volume or a single drive. A stripe set is often referred to as RAID-0, although this is a misnomer because plain striping includes no redundancy.

- **Mirror volume**   A pair of dynamic volumes that contain identical data and appear to the world as a single entity. Disk mirroring can use two drives on the same hard disk controller or use separate controllers, in which case it is sometimes referred to as *duplexing*. In case of failure on the part of either drive, the other hard disk can be split off so that it continues to provide complete access to the data stored on the drive, providing a high degree of fault tolerance. This technique is called RAID-1.

- **RAID-5 volume**   Like a striped volume, this combines portions of multiple hard disks into a single entity with data written across all portions equally. However, it also writes parity information for each stripe onto a different portion, providing the ability to recover in the case of a single drive failure. A RAID-5 volume provides excellent throughput for read operations but is substantially slower than all other available options for write operations.

- **SLED (single large expensive disk)**   Now rarely used, this strategy is the opposite of the RAID strategy. Rather than using several inexpensive hard disks and providing fault tolerance through redundancy, you buy the best hard disk you can and bet your entire network on it. If this doesn't sound like a good idea to you, you're right. It's not.

Overview of Disk Management

Hard disk storage has been the usual long-term storage method for modern computers, from the mainframe to the desktop, and that's not likely to change, even considering the richer storage options that have been added to Windows 2000. This section looks at each of the new facilities.

RAID

RAID (redundant array of independent disks) is a term used to describe a technique that has gone from an esoteric high-end solution to a normal assumption on most servers. Seven or eight years ago, RAID was mostly unheard of, although the original paper defining RAID was written in 1988. Until recently, most server systems relied on expensive, higher-quality hard disks—backed up frequently. Backups are still crucial, but now you can use one form or another of RAID to provide substantial protection from hard disk failure. Moreover, this protection costs much less than those big server drives did.

RAID can be implemented at a software or hardware level. When it is implemented at the hardware level, the hardware vendor provides an interface to administer the arrays and the drivers to support the various operating systems it may need to work with. Although there are advantages to using a hardware RAID solution, it's not cheap.

Windows 2000 includes an excellent and flexible implementation of RAID levels 0, 1, and 5 in software. It doesn't cover all of the possibilities by any means, but it is certainly sufficient for many purposes.

Disk Administration Enhancements

The task of disk management in Windows 2000 brings not only a brand new interface, based on the Microsoft Management Console (MMC), but also a whole new set of capabilities (Figure 14-1). Anyone who has spent much time with Windows NT will probably not miss the old Disk Administrator at all.

The MMC's Disk Management snap-in for managing your physical disks is divided into two panes. By default, the top pane shows the drive letters (volumes) associated with the local disks and gives their properties and status, while the bottom pane has a graphical representation organized by physical drive. It can be used as a stand-alone snap-in or as part of the Computer Management console, shown in Figure 14-2.

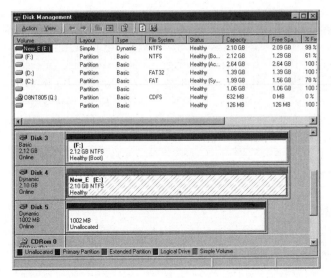

Figure 14-1. *Disk Management with an MMC interface.*

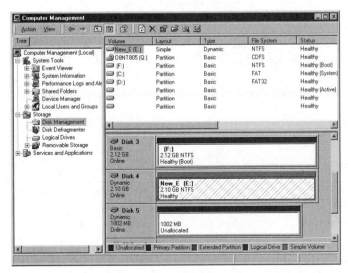

Figure 14-2. *The Computer Management console and the Disk Management snap-in.*

Hardware RAID

While Disk Management provides an excellent software RAID solution, hardware RAID is also now widely available, from either the original server vendor or from third parties, and it provides substantial advantages over software RAID. Hardware RAID solutions range from a simple RAID controller to fully integrated, stand-alone subsystems. Their features vary, as does their cost, but all claim to provide superior performance and reliability over a simple software RAID solution such as that included in Windows 2000. In general, they do. Some of the advantages that they can offer include the following:

- Hot-swap and hot-spare drives, allowing for virtually instantaneous replacement of failed drives

- Integrated disk caching for improved disk performance

- A separate, dedicated system that handles all processing, for improved overall performance

- Increased flexibility and additional RAID levels, such as RAID-10 (also called RAID 0+1), a combination of striping (RAID-0) and mirroring (RAID-1) that provides for fast read and write disk access with full redundancy

Not all hardware RAID systems provide all of these features, but all have the potential to improve the overall reliability and performance of your hard disk subsystem. As such, they should definitely be considered for any mission-critical server.

Remote Management

The new Disk Management snap-in in Windows 2000 Server lets you manage not only the local hard disks but also drives on other computers running Windows 2000, enabling the administrator to manage disk tasks and space allocations from a workstation without having to sit at the machine that is being administered. This capability is a boon for remote site management and—using the MMC—makes it easy to delegate authority and administrative responsibilities for a group of computers to others without having to give them full administrative privileges.

Dynamic Disks

The other major feature that Disk Management adds in Windows 2000 is the concept of dynamic disks. By converting a disk to a dynamic disk, you give Disk Management the ability to manage it in new ways, *without requiring a reboot* in most cases. You can extend a disk volume, span a volume across multiple physical disks, stripe the volume for improved performance, mirror it, or add it to a RAID-5 array—all from the MMC and all without a reboot, once the disk is converted to a dynamic disk. The initial creation or conversion of the first of your basic disks to a dynamic disk will require a reboot, unfortunately, but once you've gotten over that hurdle, you'll breeze through the remaining tasks. When combined with the new remote management functionality, dynamic disks give the system administrator powerful tools for managing the type and configuration of hard disk storage across the enterprise.

Disk Management Tasks

Like all MMC snap-ins, the Disk Management snap-in can be opened in a number of ways. One of the most direct ways is to right-click the My Computer icon in the upper left corner of your desktop and choose Manage from the menu. This opens a local version of the Computer Management snap-in, containing the System Tools, Storage, and Services and Applications snap-ins. Click Storage to access the Removable Storage (if you have removable storage drives installed), Disk Defragmenter, Logical Drives, and Disk Management snap-ins, and then click Disk Management to open the Disk Management window. To open the Disk Management snap-in only, double-click the file Diskmgmt.msc in the %WinDir%\System32 directory. Note that the .MSC extension will likely be hidden unless you've changed the default options in Windows Explorer.

When you open the Computer Management snap-in, you have the ability to manage not only the resources of the local computer but also those of remote computers. This makes it easy to manage the disks on a remote computer. If you run the Disk Management snap-in only, you'll be limited to managing disks on your local computer, unless you create a custom MMC. See Chapter 10 for information on creating and customizing MMCs.

Adding a Partition or Volume

Adding a new drive or partition to a Windows 2000 server is straightforward. First, obviously, you need to physically install and connect the drive. If you have a hot-swappable backplane and array, you don't even have to shut the system down to accomplish this task. If you're using conventional drives, however, you'll need to shut down and power off the system.

Once the drive is installed and the system is powered up again, Windows 2000 will automatically recognize the new hardware and make it available. If the disk is already partitioned and formatted, you'll be able to use it immediately. If it's a brand new disk, you'll need to prepare it first. Even if it is a disk that has been used and formatted but doesn't contain any critical data, we strongly recommend that you upgrade it to a dynamic disk.

Adding a New Disk Using the Write Signature And Upgrade Disk Wizard

To use the Write Signature And Upgrade Disk Wizard to add a new disk once the logon is complete, follow these steps:

1. Open the Computer Management console by right-clicking the My Computer icon on your desktop and choosing Manage from the shortcut menu.

2. On the Storage menu, choose Disk Management. If the disk is new, you'll see the first screen of the Write Signature And Upgrade Disk Wizard, shown in Figure 14-3. This wizard allows you to upgrade the new disk to a dynamic disk. Click Next.

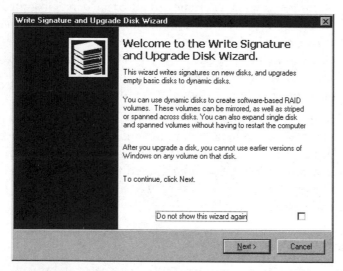

Figure 14-3. *The first screen of the Write Signature And Upgrade Disk Wizard.*

3. You'll see a confirmation of the disk (or disks, if you've added more than one) that can be selected for upgrading, shown in Figure 14-4.

4. Make sure that there is a check mark to the left of the disk or disks to be upgraded and then click Next again. You'll get a confirmation message. If all the options are correct, click Finish and the disk will be upgraded to a dynamic disk.

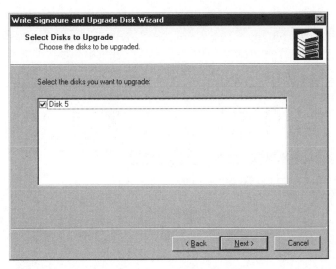

Figure 14-4. *The Select Disks To Upgrade screen of the Write Signature And Upgrade Disk Wizard.*

5. Once the wizard finishes, you'll be at the main Disk Management console, shown in Figure 14-5. Notice that the disk is still not formatted or allocated and is highlighted in black (if you haven't changed the default color settings for the Disk Management console).

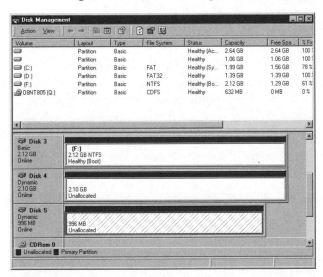

Figure 14-5. *The main Disk Management console, showing the new disk (Disk 5).*

Creating a Volume

To create a new volume (the dynamic disk equivalent of a partition), complete these steps:

1. In the Disk Management console, right-click the unallocated disk and choose Create Volume from the shortcut menu. The Create Volume Wizard opens to guide you through the process of creating the new volume on the dynamic disk (Figure 14-6). Click Next.

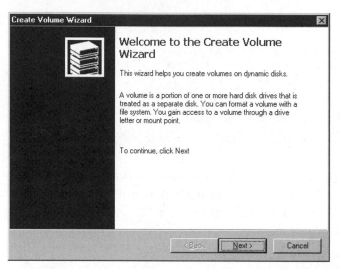

Figure 14-6. *The first screen of the Create Volume Wizard.*

2. Select the type of volume you'll be creating (Figure 14-7). Depending on the number of available unallocated volumes, you'll see one or more options for the type of volume. These options include Simple, Spanned (the Windows NT 4 Volume Set), Striped (RAID-0), Mirrored (RAID-1), and RAID-5. Click Next.

3. Select the dynamic disks to use for the new volume. The choices available and the selections you'll need to make will depend on the type of volume you're creating and the number of available unallocated disks. Figure 14-8 shows a RAID-5 volume being created.

4. On the same screen, adjust the size of the new volume. By default, the new volume will use the maximum available space from each of the selected disks. For spanned volumes, this will be the sum of the free space on the selected disks; for other types of volumes, it will be the number of disks times the available space on the smallest of the selected disks. Click Next.

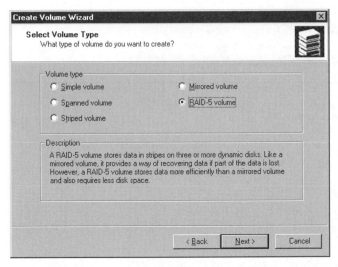

Figure 14-7. *Select the type of dynamic volume you want to create.*

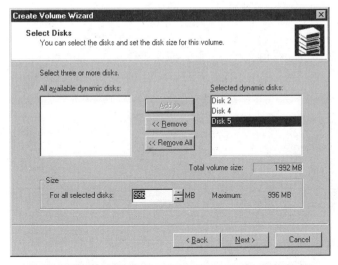

Figure 14-8. *Select the dynamic disks that will be part of this volume.*

5. Select either a drive letter or a mount point for the new volume (Figure 14-9), or opt not to assign a drive letter or path at this time. With Windows 2000, you can "mount" a volume on an empty subdirectory, minimizing the number of drive letters and reducing the complexity of the storage that is displayed to the user. If you want to take advantage of this feature, use the Browse button to locate the directory where

you will mount the new volume. See the Real World "Mounting a Partition or Volume" for more on this subject. Click Next.

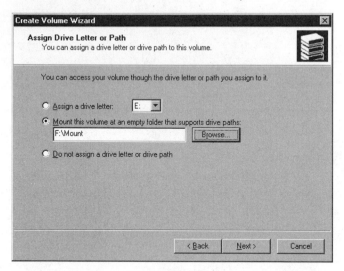

Figure 14-9. *Select a drive letter or mount point for the new volume.*

6. Select the formatting options you want (Figure 14-10). Even when mounting the volume rather than creating a new drive, you can choose your format type without regard to the underlying format of the mount point. Click Next.

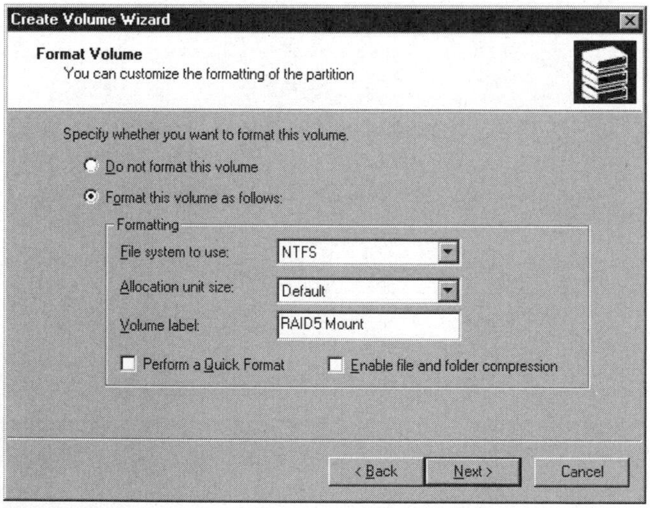

Figure 14-10. *Set the formatting options for the new volume.*

7. You'll see a confirmation screen. If all of the options are correct, click Finish to create and format the volume. You return to the Disk Management console, where you'll see the new volume (Figure 14-11).

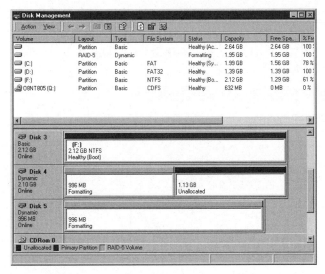

Figure 14-11. *The new RAID volume being generated and formatted.*

Real World   Mounted Volumes

Windows 2000 borrows a concept from the UNIX world by adding the ability to mount a volume or partition on a subfolder of an existing drive letter. A mounted volume may also have a drive letter associated with it, although it does not need to, and it can be mounted at more than one point, giving multiple entry points into the same storage.

A volume must be mounted on an empty subfolder of an existing NTFS volume or drive. FAT and FAT32 drives do not support mounted volumes. You can, however, mount a FAT or FAT32 volume at any mount point. You can mount only a single volume at a given mount point, but you can then mount further volumes on top of an existing mounted volume, with the same rules and restrictions as any other mount. The properties of a drive will not show all of the available disk space for that drive, since they will not reflect any volumes mounted on the drive.

Mounted volumes can be used to provide a mix of redundant and nonredundant storage in a logical structure that meets the business needs of the enterprise while hiding the complexities of the physical structure from the users.

Creating a Partition

You can create partitions only on basic disks, not on dynamic disks. To create a new partition, follow these steps:

1. In the Disk Management console, right-click the unallocated basic disk and select Create Partition. The Create Partition Wizard, shown in Figure 14-12, opens to guide you through the process of creating the new partition on the basic disk. Click Next.

Figure 14-12. *The first screen of the Create Partition Wizard.*

2. Select the type of partition you'll be creating (Figure 14-13). If this is a removable drive, you'll see only an option for a primary partition, but with a nonremovable disk you'll be able to choose either a primary or an extended partition. A basic disk can hold up to four primary partitions or three primary partitions and one extended partition. Click Next.

3. Specify how much of the available space on the disk you want to use for this partition (Figure 14-14). Click Next.

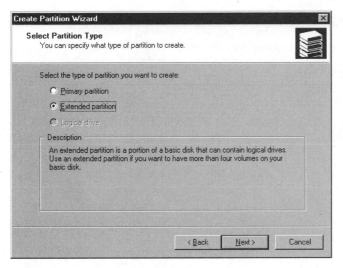

Figure 14-13. *Select the type of partition you want to create.*

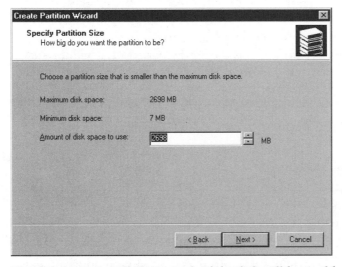

Figure 14-14. *Specify how much of the disk will be used by this partition.*

4. If you're creating an extended partition, continue with step 6. If you're creating a primary partition, select either a drive letter, as shown in Figure 14-15, or a mount point for the new partition. You can also choose to defer giving the new partition a mount point or drive letter. However, it will be unavailable to your users until you do. Click Next.

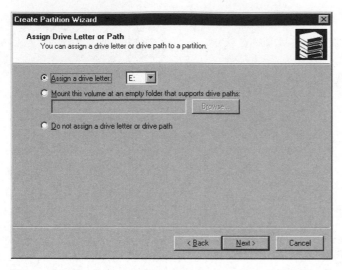

Figure 14-15. *Select a drive letter or a mount point for the new partition.*

5. Select the formatting options you want, or opt to defer formatting until later. Click Next.

6. You'll see a confirmation screen. If all the options are correct, click Finish to create the partition. If it is a primary partition, it will be formatted and the drive letter or mount point assigned. If it is an extended partition, you'll need to format it and choose the drive letters and mount points for it, as discussed in the next section, "Creating Logical Drives in an Extended Partition."

Real World   Formatting Options

Windows 2000 supports three different file system formats: FAT, FAT32, and NTFS. Before any disk or volume can be used, it must be formatted. For disks larger than 510 MB, you will probably find that FAT32 or NTFS use space most efficiently. However, only NTFS supports the more advanced features of Windows 2000.

You can choose to quick-format a drive to make it available more quickly, but this option simply removes the file entries from the disk and does no checking for bad sectors. You should select this choice only when recycling a disk that has already been formatted and when you are confident that it hasn't been damaged.

On an NTFS volume or partition, you can specify the allocation unit size. This option lets you tune the disk for a particular purpose, depending on the disk's size and intended function. A database storage volume that will contain large database files that are managed by the database program may lend itself to large allocation units (also called clusters), while a disk that must hold many small files is a candidate for smaller clusters. However, the default sizes are an excellent compromise for most situations and should be modified only with caution and with a clear understanding of the consequences for your environment.

You can also choose to enable disk and folder compression on NTFS volumes and partitions. This causes all files and folders on the volume to be compressed, as opposed to individual files or folders that you select. Compression can minimize the amount of hard disk space used by files but can have a negative impact on performance.

Creating Logical Drives in an Extended Partition

If you've created a new extended partition, the next step is to create logical drives in the partition. You can assign one or more logical drives in an extended partition, and each of those logical drives can be assigned a drive letter and/or one or more mount points. Each of the logical drives can be formatted with any of the supported file systems, regardless of the format of other logical drives. To create a logical drive, follow these steps:

1. In the Disk Management console, right-click on the Free Space portion of the extended partition and select Create Logical Drive from the menu to open the Create Partition Wizard (shown earlier in Figure 14-12). Click Next.

2. You'll see the Select Partition Type screen, shown in Figure 14-16, with the Logical Drive option selected and the only choice active. Click Next and specify the size of the logical drive you'll be creating, as shown in Figure 14-17. You can specify the entire partition for a single drive, or you can divide the partition into multiple logical drives. Click Next.

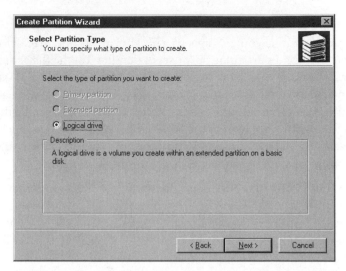

Figure 14-16. *The Select Partition Type screen of the Create Partition Wizard.*

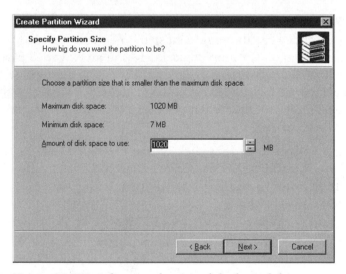

Figure 14-17. *Adjusting the size of the logical drive.*

3. Select the drive letter or mount point for the new logical drive, as shown in Figure 14-18. You can also choose not to assign a letter or mount point at this time. Click Next.

4. Select the formatting options you want. Click Next again, and you'll see the final confirmation screen. If all of the options are correct, click Finish to create and format the new logical drive. If you need to create additional logical drives on the partition, you can repeat these steps as many times as required to create the number of logical drives desired.

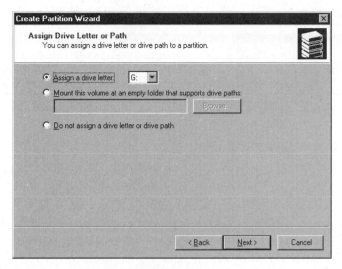

Figure 14-18. *Assigning a drive letter or mount point for the logical drive.*

Deleting a Partition, Volume, or Logical Drive

Deleting a partition, deleting a logical drive, and deleting a volume are essentially the same task, with one important exception. When you delete a logical drive, you end up with free space on the partition, but other logical drives on the partition are untouched. When you delete a partition or volume, the entire volume or partition is deleted. You cannot, however, delete an extended partition until all of the logical drives in the partition have first been deleted. You can directly delete a primary partition or a volume.

In all cases, when you delete a volume, logical drive, or partition, you'll end up with free or unallocated space and no data on the volume, drive, or partition when you're done, so make sure you've got a good backup if there's a chance you might later need any of the data. To delete a partition, logical drive, or volume, follow these steps:

1. Right-click the partition, logical drive, or volume and choose Delete Partition, Delete Logical Drive, or Delete Volume.

2. If you're deleting a volume or partition, you'll see a warning message similar to the one shown in Figure 14-19. Deleting an extended partition involves extra steps, since you must first delete the logical drives in the partition before you can delete the partition itself.

Once the volume or partition has been completely deleted, the space it occupied will be unallocated. Space that is unallocated on dynamic disks can be used to create mirrors, extend an existing volume, create a RAID array, or otherwise manage the storage on your server. Space that is unallocated on basic disks can be partitioned.

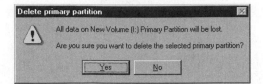

Figure 14-19. *Confirmation message for deleting a volume.*

Converting a Disk to a Dynamic Disk

The advantages of dynamic disks are substantial. Even if you use hardware RAID controllers and hot-swappable disks to manage your hard disks, you'll probably find it a good idea to use dynamic disks. There is a caveat, however. Since you can't boot from or even see a dynamic disk from another operating system, you may want to consider leaving at least your boot drive as a basic drive, since doing so will make working with it somewhat easier. If you need to provide for redundancy on that drive, and if hardware RAID is an option, use RAID level 1 to make recovery from a failed hard disk or other disaster as painless as possible. To convert a basic disk to a dynamic disk, follow these steps.

1. Right-click the disk's icon on the left side of the Disk Management console, and choose Upgrade To Dynamic Disk from the shortcut menu.

2. You'll see a dialog box like the one shown in Figure 14-20, listing the available basic disks on your machine. The disk you clicked will be checked, and you can select other disks to upgrade at the same time. Click OK to continue with the upgrade.

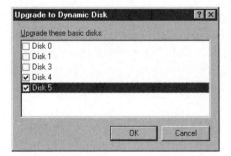

Figure 14-20. *You can select more than one disk to upgrade.*

3. You'll get a warning message stating that no other version of Windows can use these disks. Click Next.

4. If there are no file systems on the disks you've chosen to upgrade, that's all there is to it. However, if there are file systems on any of the disks, you'll get a warning message stating that the file systems will be force dismounted. Click Yes and the upgrade will proceed. You can now

manage the disks dynamically, and they can be part of mirrors, RAID-5 arrays, or other enhanced disk configurations that aren't supported by basic disks.

Caution   If there are any open files on the disk to be upgraded, you may experience data loss. You should only perform disk upgrades during quiet times when no users are logged onto or using the server.

Extending a Volume

You can add space to a volume without having to back up, reboot, and restore your files if the volume is on a dynamic disk and if it is a simple volume or a spanned volume. You do this by converting the volume to a spanned or extended volume that incorporates unallocated space on any dynamic disk. Unfortunately, you can't increase the size of a RAID-5 or RAID-0 (striped) volume simply by adding disks to the array, unless you're using a version of hardware RAID that supports this functionality. To extend a volume, follow these steps:

1. In the Disk Management console, right-click on the volume you want to extend. Choose Extend Volume from the menu to open the Extend Volume Wizard. Click Next.

2. Highlight one or more disks from the list of dynamic disks that are available and have unallocated space. Click Add to add the selected disk or disks, and indicate the amount of space you want to add (Figure 14-21). Click Next.

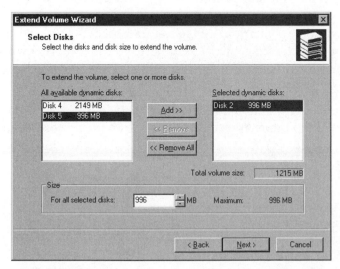

Figure 14-21. *Selecting the disks to use to extend the volume.*

3. The Extend Volume Wizard displays a final confirmation screen before extending the volume. Click Finish to extend the volume, or click Cancel if you change your mind.

Caution It's important to remember that a spanned (extended) volume is actually less reliable than a simple disk. Unlike a mirror or RAID-5 volume, in which there is built-in redundancy, a spanned or striped volume will be lost if any disk in the volume fails.

Real World **Extending—Administrator's Friend or Foe?**

Most administrators have wished at some point that they could simply increase the users' home directory space on the fly without having to bring the system offline for several hours while the entire volume is backed up and reformatted to add the additional hard disks, the backup is restored, and the share points are re-created. Fun? Hardly. Risky? Certainly. And definitely a job that means coming in on the weekend or staying late at night—in other words, something to be avoided if at all possible.

All this makes Windows 2000's ability to create additional space on a volume without the need to back up the volume, reformat the disks, and re-create the volume a seductive feature. However, if you're using conventional hard disks without hardware RAID, you may want to think twice before you decide to take advantage of this capability. To be able to extend a volume on the fly, you need to use only simple or spanned volumes. Neither is redundant, exposing your users to the risks of a failed drive. Yes, you have a backup, but even under the best of circumstances, you'll lose some data if you need to restore a backup. Further, using spanned volumes actually increases your risk of a hard disk failure. If any disk used as part of the spanned volume fails, the entire volume is toast and will need to be restored from backup.

Why, then, would anyone use spanning? Because they have hardware RAID to provide the redundancy. This combination offers the best of both worlds—redundancy provided by the hardware RAID controller and flexibility to expand volumes as needed, using Windows 2000's disk management.

Note Windows 2000 uses the terms "extended" and "spanned" nearly interchangeably when describing volumes. Technically, however, a spanned volume must include more than one physical disk, while an extended volume may also refer to a volume that has had additional space added to the original simple volume on the same disk.

Adding a Mirror

When your data is mission-critical and you want to make sure that no matter what happens to one of your hard disks the data is protected and always available, you should consider mirroring the data onto a second drive. Windows 2000 can mirror a dynamic disk onto a second dynamic disk so that the failure of either disk will not result in loss of data. To mirror a volume, you can either select a mirrored volume when you create the volume (see "Creating a Volume," earlier in this chapter) or you can add a mirror to an existing volume. To add a mirror to an existing volume, follow these steps:

1. In the Disk Management console, right-click the volume you want to mirror. If a potential mirror is available, the shortcut menu will list the Add Mirror command.

2. Choose Add Mirror to display the Add Mirror dialog box, shown in Figure 14-22, where you can select the disk to be used for the mirror.

Figure 14-22. *The Add Mirror dialog box.*

3. Highlight the disk that will be the mirror, and click Add Mirror. The mirror will be created immediately and will start duplicating the data from the original disk to the second half of the mirror, as shown in Figure 14-23. This process is called *regeneration*. (The process of regeneration is also used to distribute data across the disks when a RAID-5 volume is created.)

Note   Regeneration is both CPU- and disk-intensive. When possible, you will want to create mirrors during slack times or during normally scheduled downtime. This goal should be balanced, however, by the equally important goal of providing redundancy and failure protection as expeditiously as possible.

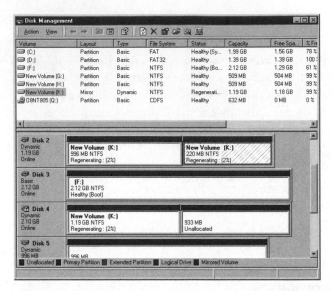

Figure 14-23. *A newly created mirrored disk in the process of regeneration.*

Tip To improve your overall data security and reliability, you should mirror your volumes onto disks that use separate controllers whenever possible. This process is known as *duplexing,* and it eliminates the disk controller as a single point of failure for the mirror while actually speeding up both reading and writing to the mirror, since the controller and bus are no longer potential bottlenecks.

Drive Failure in a Mirrored Volume

If one of the disks in a mirrored volume fails, you'll continue to have full access to all of your data without loss. Windows 2000 will send an alert to the console (Figure 14-24), mark the failed disk as missing, and take it offline, but it will continue to read and write from the other half of the mirrored volume as though nothing had happened. Be warned, however. You no longer have any fault tolerance on that volume, and any additional failure will result in catastrophic data loss.

Figure 14-24. *The warning message that displays when a disk that's part of a mirrored volume fails.*

Once you've replaced the failed disk or corrected the problem and reactivated it, the mirror will automatically start regenerating. If the problem can be solved without powering down the system, you can regenerate the mirror on the fly. To reactivate the failed disk, follow these steps:

1. Right-click the icon for the failed disk on the left of the Disk Management console, shown in Figure 14-25.

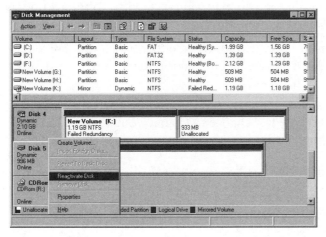

Figure 14-25. *Reactivating a failed disk that's part of a mirrored volume.*

2. Choose Reactivate Disk, and Windows 2000 brings the disk back online and starts regenerating the failed mirror, as shown in Figure 14-26. Once the mirror has been regenerated, the disk status changes from Regenerating to Healthy.

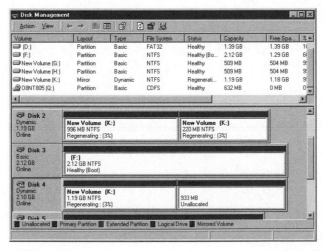

Figure 14-26. *Data being regenerated on a reactivated mirrored disk.*

Removing a Mirror

If you need to make additional disk space available on your system and you have no additional disks available, you can remove the mirror from a mirrored volume. When you remove a mirror, the data on one of the disks is untouched, but the other disk becomes unallocated space. Of course, you will have lost all redundancy and protection for the data, so you'll need to take steps to restore the mirror as soon as possible, and until then you may want to modify your backup schedule for the remaining disk. To remove a mirror, follow these steps:

1. In the Disk Management console, right-click either half of the mirror. Choose Remove Mirror from the menu, and the Remove Mirror dialog box opens, shown in Figure 14-27.

2. Highlight the disk that you want to remove from the mirror. Click Remove Mirror. You'll get one last chance to change your mind. Click OK and the disk you highlighted becomes unallocated space.

Figure 14-27. *The Remove Mirror dialog box.*

Breaking a Mirror

If a disk fails and you can't replace it with an identical one, you should break the mirror until a replacement becomes available. Breaking a mirror severs the connection between the two disks, allowing the remaining disk to continue to function normally until a replacement disk becomes available. You may also find it useful to break a mirror even when both disks are still functioning, since you then end up with two identical copies of the same data. One of the halves of the broken mirror continues to have the same drive letter and/or mount point, while the second half of the broken mirror is assigned the next available drive letter. To break a mirror, follow these steps:

1. In the Disk Management console, right-click either disk of the mirrored volume.

2. Choose Break Mirror from the shortcut menu. You'll be asked to confirm that you really want to break it.

3. Click Yes, and the mirror is broken. You'll have two disks. One will retain the drive letter or mount point of the original mirror, and the other will be assigned the next available drive letter. They will both contain exact duplicates of the data at the instant of the break but will immediately start to diverge as they are modified.

Real World   Backing Up Active Files

One of the most difficult tasks faced by the system administrator is to get a reliable, sure backup of a file that is in constant active use, such as a data file for a database such as SQL Server or Oracle. The Break Mirror command can be used to get around this problem. You can momentarily stop the database, break the mirror, and restart the database. Now you have a copy of the data file that is no longer in active use and can be safely and effectively backed up. Once the backup has completed, you can delete the broken volume and re-create the mirror.

Converting a Volume or Partition from FAT to NTFS

You can convert a volume or partition from the FAT or FAT32 file system to the NTFS file system without losing data or interrupting the availability of the rest of the server. However, Windows 2000 offers no graphical way to do this—you'll have to run a command-line utility. To convert a volume or partition, open a command window and type

convert <volumename | mountpoint | driveletter:> /fs:ntfs [/v].

This command converts the volume or drive from either FAT or FAT32 to NTFS. If you use the /v command-line switch, the conversion will be fairly noisy, listing the name of each file and directory that's converted. If someone has a file open on the volume and the program cannot gain exclusive access to it, you will be offered the opportunity to schedule the conversion for the next time you reboot. This option is alright if you have a planned maintenance reboot coming anyway, but otherwise you probably shouldn't schedule the conversion, since it may end up taking a fairly long time if the drive is large and contains a lot of files.

Real World NTFS Conversion Planning

If you schedule a conversion to NTFS for the next reboot before you're actually ready to reboot the server and your server needs to be rebooted unexpectedly, you will simply have to wait while the conversion happens. There is no way to bypass the conversion once you've committed to it. This can turn a minor downtime into a major headache if it happens in the middle of the production day. Don't commit to a conversion unless you are sure you can afford the downtime if Windows 2000 decides it needs to reboot.

Formatting a Partition or Volume

Before a partition, logical drive, or volume can be used, it must be formatted. Formatting lays down the necessary structure to support the file system you choose for the volume. You must format a volume or drive when it is first created, and at any later point if you want to clear it off. You can also use Format to change the type of file system on a drive, partition, or volume, but all data on the target will be deleted during the formatting. (The command-line *convert* command—which allows conversion of FAT and FAT32 targets to the NTFS format only—preserves any data on the target.) The file systems that are supported by Windows 2000 are FAT, FAT32, and NTFS.

In general, we recommend that you use NTFS unless you have a compelling reason not to. One case in which you would not use NTFS is when log files will reside on the volume or partition. A FAT or FAT32 volume tends to be faster and more appropriate for large files that grow constantly in small increments, as log files do. However, even with log files, you should use the FAT or FAT32 file system only when security or quotas are not an issue, since these file systems do not support quotas or the security features of NTFS.

Another reason to use FAT or FAT32 is to allow the computer to support dual booting into other operating systems. NTFS is not visible or accessible from other operating systems, while FAT can be used by a variety of operating systems and FAT32 can be used by Microsoft Windows 95 and by Microsoft Windows 98. To format a logical drive, partition, or volume, follow these steps:

1. In the Disk Management console, right-click the logical drive, partition, or volume you want to format, and choose Format from the menu. You'll see the dialog box shown in Figure 14-28. Select the file system you want to use: FAT, FAT32, or NTFS.

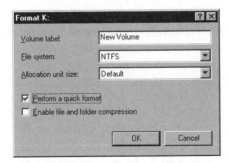

Figure 14-28. *The Format dialog box.*

2. Select the allocation unit size (also called the cluster size). Normally, you'll simply accept the default here. See "Optimum Cluster Size" for a discussion of this issue.

3. Type in a name for the volume, logical drive, or partition. The default name is New Volume.

Real World   Assigning Volume Names

The name you assign to a volume, partition, or drive should tell you something about it rather than simply mimicking the drive letter. A volume name like "Big50GBSCSI" tells you pretty conclusively that it's that big new SCSI drive you just bought, unless, of course, you already have half a dozen of them on your server, in which case you're going to need to come up with a more effective name. On the other hand, a volume name of C_DRIVE is just about useless, since the drive letter is available from anywhere that the volume name is.

4. Check the Perform A Quick Format box if you want to format the drive quickly. We recommend, however, that you not do this unless you have a strong need to make the volume available immediately. The full, long version of the format checks the entire drive for defects. It can take a while on a large drive, and the overall system performance will tend to suffer while the format is going on, but the greater sense of confidence in the volume should be worth the wait.

5. If the entire drive will be compressed, check Enable File And Folder Compression. Note, however, that you can choose to compress individual folders and even individual files regardless of whether you check this option now. And with the size and cost of drives these days, we think this option is much less useful than it once was.

6. Click OK and the formatting begins. Windows 2000 can handle only one format at a time, so you'll be unable to format any other partition or volume until this one finishes.

Real World   Optimum Cluster Size

A discussion of the best cluster size for a particular application or need is beyond the scope of this chapter and can be fairly heated, with an enormous amount of unsubstantiated and generally false statements being bandied about. Suffice it to say that the defaults are good for almost all situations and that decisions to choose something other than the default allocation size should be made only when there is a specific, clearly understood reason and a compelling need to do so. You can choose cluster sizes from 512 bytes up to 256 KB. You will not be able to enable file and folder compression on NTFS if you go beyond 4 KB for your allocation unit size.

If you seriously think you need to change the cluster size for a particular volume, we suggest you first make the change in a controlled lab environment and perform confidence and performance tests to ensure that the change meets your needs and doesn't cause unintended side effects.

Changing a Drive Letter

You can change the drive letter of a volume or partition at any time, and you can even have multiple paths to a given drive. In addition, unlike Windows NT, Windows 2000 allows you to change the drive letter of a removable drive, such as a Jaz or Zip drive. To change a drive letter, follow these steps:

1. Right-click on the drive in the Disk Management console, and choose Change Drive Letter And Path.

2. A dialog box displaying the current drive letter and any mount-point paths for the disk appears, as shown in Figure 14-29. Highlight the drive letter shown and click Edit. Select the new drive letter from the drop-down list. Click OK.

3. You see a confirmation message warning that the change could affect the ability of some programs to run. Click Yes and the drive letter change will take place immediately, unless there are open files on the drive. If there are open files on the drive, the drive will temporarily have two drive letters, the old one and the new one. You'll see the warning shown in Figure 14-30. Click Yes to confirm the change.

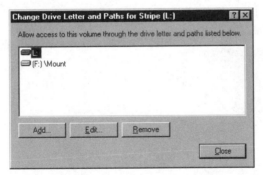

Figure 14-29. *Changing the drive letter and path of a logical drive.*

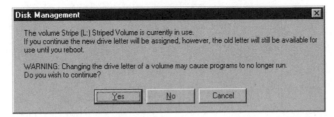

Figure 14-30. *Message warning that a drive has a dual identity.*

Mounting a Volume

Windows 2000 adds a new feature to the disk and storage management process. You can mount a dynamic volume—or any partition or logical drive in an extended partition—on any empty directory that resides on a drive that is both NTFS formatted and nonremovable. The mounted volume can be formatted as FAT, FAT32, or NTFS and appears to users as a simple directory. This feature makes it possible to create larger file systems that use multiple hard disks without the inherent risks of using spanned volumes, since the failure of any one of the mounted volumes affects only the directories that were part of that volume. You can also easily support multiple formats from a single drive letter. To mount a volume, follow these steps:

1. From the Disk Management console, right-click on a volume or partition. Choose Change Drive Letter And Path from the menu. The Change Drive Letter And Path dialog box, shown previously in Figure 14-29, opens.

2. Click the Add button; the Add New Drive Letter Or Path dialog box opens, shown in Figure 14-31.

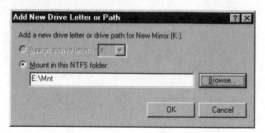

Figure 14-31. *The Add New Drive Letter Or Path dialog box, used to mount a volume.*

3. You can type in the mount point or use the Browse button to select or create a mount point. Any empty directory that resides on a nonremovable NTFS volume or drive can be the mount point.

4. Once you've selected or typed in the mount point, click OK, and the volume or partition is mounted.

Caution   It's actually easy to get yourself into trouble with this new feature. Disk Management will let you make multiple levels of mounted volumes, including ones that are recursive. We think you're well advised to mount volumes *only* at the root level of a drive. Trying to mount below that point can lead to confusion and make management and documentation difficult.

NTFS Version 5

The NTFS file system format has been around, essentially unchanged, since the original version of Windows NT. With Windows 2000, Microsoft has made substantial changes to NTFS to support the new features that administrators and users have been asking for. These new features include disk quotas—finally—and the ability to encrypt files and whole file systems at the physical disk level.

Note   The new version of NTFS, known as NTFS version 5, is a logical extension of the original NTFS but is not completely compatible with it. If you're going to use NTFS in a dual-boot configuration with Windows NT 4 on the same machine as Windows 2000, you must install Windows NT 4 Service Pack 4 or later to permit your Windows 2000 NTFS partitions to be seen when booted into Windows NT 4. Also keep in mind that the quotas and encryption available in NTFS version 5 are not supported under Windows NT 4 and will not be enforced or available in it.

Disk Quotas

Probably the most annoying missing piece of the disk management equation for most Windows NT administrators has been the inability to manage and limit the disk resources of their users without buying an add-on product. Windows 2000 finally addresses this rather glaring omission and provides for either advisory or absolute quotas on disk usage by user or group. However, each volume or partition is treated as a separate entity—there's no way to limit a user or group of users to a total amount of disk usage across the entire server or enterprise. (Sounds like an opportunity for a third-party solution, doesn't it?)

Enabling Disk Quotas

By default, disk quotas are turned off for all partitions and volumes. You must enable them for each volume on which you want a quota. Quotas are available only for volumes that are assigned a drive letter. You can set different quotas for individual users or for groups of users, or you can set them the same for all users. Follow these steps to enable quotas on each volume where you want them:

1. Right-click the drive letter in Windows Explorer, and choose Properties.
2. Click the Quota tab to display the dialog box shown in Figure 14-32.

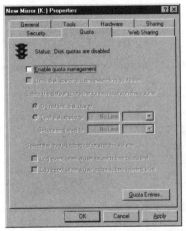

Figure 14-32. *The Quota tab of the Properties window for a logical drive.*

3. Select the Enable Quota Management option.
4. Define the limits on disk usage for this drive letter. The available choices are:
   - **Deny Disk Space To Users Exceeding Quota Limit**   When this option is selected, the quotas are enforced on all disk usage. When it is cleared, the limits are advisory only.

- **Limit Disk Space To**   Here you can specify the limits of disk space usage for new users on the volume.

- **Set Warning Level To**   This option indicates the limit at which users will receive a warning message.

- **Logging options**   You can choose to log when users exceed their warning limit or their usage limit, or you can leave these options blank if you don't want logging.

5. You'll see a confirmation message. If everything is correct, click OK to scan the drive and enable quotas.

Setting Quota Entries for Users

There's one catch with quotas enabled as described in the previous procedure: They apply only to users. Administrators slip by without having quotas enforced unless you explicitly set them in a separate quota entry. To set quotas on administrators, or to tweak the quotas for individual users, you need to perform these additional steps:

1. In Windows Explorer, right-click the drive you want to set quota entries for and choose Properties. Click the Quota tab to display the dialog box shown previously in Figure 14-32.

2. Click the Quota Entries button to display the quota entries for the volume. You'll see the window shown in Figure 14-33. This window contains entries for everyone who has ever stored files on the volume, unless you have explicitly removed the entries for users who no longer store files there.

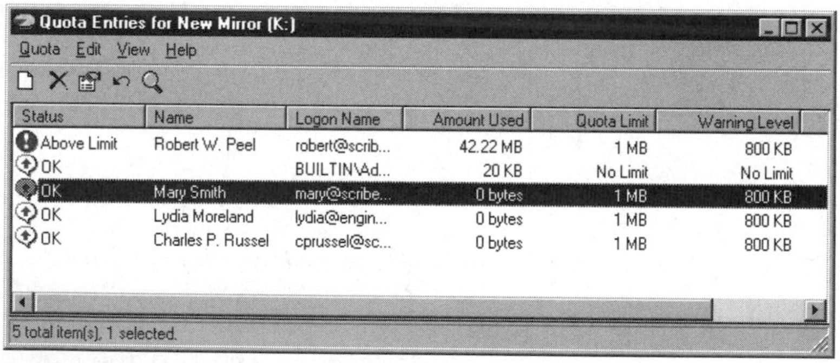

Figure 14-33. *The Quota Entries window.*

3. You can change the properties for any entry by double-clicking the entry, which displays the dialog box shown in Figure 14-34. The figure shows a user whose quota has been lowered so that he is now exceeding his disk space limit. He will be unable to store any additional data on the volume until he is below the limit.

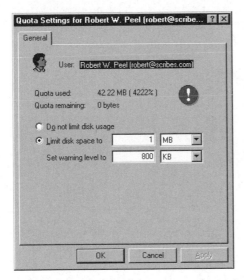

Figure 14-34. *Quota settings and status for a user.*

The Quota Entries window lets you sort by any of the columns to make it easy to quickly identify problem areas or to locate an individual entry. You can also use the Find function to locate a specific entry.

Real World Avoid Individual Quotas

Resist the temptation to fine-tune a disk's quotas for each individual. Giving in will lead to an administrative nightmare, especially since you then cannot manage quotas for the all-users audience, only for individual users. Make changes to the quotas for an individual only when there is a compelling reason to do so, and then keep careful records so that all administrators have ready access to the information.

Exporting and Importing Quotas

If you have a complicated quota system set up so that some users get more space than others do, implementing that system on a new volume can be a pain. But Windows 2000 lets you export the quotas from one volume to another. If there isn't an entry for a user on the new volume yet, one will be created. If a user already has a quota entry, you'll be asked if you want to overwrite it with the imported quota entry for that user (Figure 14-35). Avoid importing quota settings onto an existing drive unless you're changing your overall quotas across the entire server. Any customizations you've made on the current drive could be lost, and having to acknowledge each change that affects an existing user lends itself to mistakes. In addition, any special limits set for specific users on the source volume will be applied to the target volume.

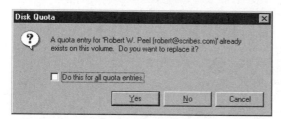

Figure 14-35. *Confirmation message for overwriting a quota entry with an imported entry.*

There are two ways to import quotas from one volume to another. You can open the Quota Entries window for the source volume, click Quota and choose Export to save the entry to a file, and then open the Quota Entries window for the target volume and choose Import from the Quota menu. Or you can simply open both Quota Entries windows and drag the entries you want to import from the source window to the target one.

Creating Quota Reports

You can use the Quota Entries window to create reports on disk usage. Select the accounts you want to include in the report and drag them into the reporting tool you'll be using. The supported formats include Rich Text Format, Comma Separated Value, CF_UNICODETEXT, and CF_TEXT. If you drag the entries into Microsoft Excel, for example, you'll get not only the entries but the column headings as well. This makes whipping out a disk usage report pretty trivial.

Encrypting on the File System Level

Version 5 of NTFS adds the ability to encrypt individual files or entire subdirectories in a totally transparent way. To their creator, encrypted files look exactly like regular files—no changes to applications are required to use them. However, to anyone except the creator/encryptor, the files are unavailable, and even if someone did manage to gain access to them, they would be gibberish, since they're stored in encrypted form.

Encryption is simply an advanced attribute of the file, as compression is. However, a file cannot be both compressed and encrypted at the same time—the attributes are mutually exclusive. Encrypted files are available only to the encryptor, but they can be recovered by the domain or machine recovery agent if necessary. Encrypted files can be backed up by normal backup procedures if the backup program is Windows 2000–aware. Files remain encrypted when backed up, and restored files retain their encryption.

Under normal circumstances, no user except the actual creator of an encrypted file has access to the file. Even a change of ownership will not remove the encryption. This prevents sensitive data, such as payroll, annual reviews, and so on, from being accessed by the wrong users, even ones with administrative rights.

Caution   Encryption is available only on the NTFS version 5 file system. If you copy the file to a floppy disk or to any file system other than NTFS version 5, the file will no longer be encrypted. This is true even of NTFS file systems on earlier versions of Windows NT.

When you encrypt a folder, all new files created in that folder are encrypted from that point forward. You can also elect to encrypt the current contents when you perform the encryption. Be warned, however: If you choose to encrypt the contents of a folder when it already contains files or subfolders, those files and subfolders will be encrypted *for the user performing the encryption only*. This means that even files that are owned by another user will be encrypted, and available for your use only.

When new files are created in an encrypted folder, the files are encrypted for use by the creator of the file, not the user who first enabled encryption on the folder. Unencrypted files in an encrypted folder can be used by all users who have security rights to use files in that folder, and the encryption status of the file will not change unless the filename itself is changed. Users can read, modify, and save the file without converting it to an encrypted file, but any change in the name of the file will trigger an encryption, and the encryption will make the file available only to the person that triggers the encryption. To encrypt a file or folder, follow these steps:

1. In Windows Explorer, right-click the folder or files you want to encrypt, and choose Properties from the pop-up menu.
2. Click the Advanced button of the General tab to open the Advanced Attributes dialog box shown in Figure 14-36.

Figure 14-36. *The Advanced Attributes dialog box.*

3. Select the Encrypt Contents To Secure Data option, and click OK to return to the main Properties window for the folder or file. Click OK or Apply to enable the encryption. If any files or subfolders are already in the folder, you're presented with the dialog box shown in Figure 14-37.

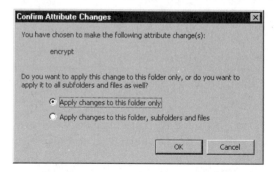

Figure 14-37. *Choosing whether to encrypt the files already in a folder or just new files.*

4. If you choose Apply Changes To This Folder Only, all of the current files and subfolders in the folder will remain unencrypted, but any new files and folders will be encrypted by the creator as they are created. If you choose Apply Changes To This Folder, Subfolders And Files, all of the files and folders below this folder will be encrypted so that only you can use them, regardless of the original creator or owner of the file.

5. Click OK and the encryption occurs.

Summary

Windows 2000 Server provides the system administrator with a much richer set of disk management tools than any previous version of Windows. The addition of dynamic volumes has materially reduced the number of reboots required to manage disk resources. The administrator can now reconfigure arrays on the fly, adding disks and extending volumes to manage disk space without having to reboot for every change. When combined with hardware RAID controllers and hot-swap drives, these tools finally give the administrator the ability to manage a 24-hour-7-day operation.

The features introduced in the new version of NTFS, including quotas and file system encryption, give the administrator additional flexibility and options to control file system abuse and to protect sensitive data so that even administrators don't have inappropriate access to confidential information. And it is all done in a way that is transparent to the user.

The next chapter looks at clustering, a way to use more than one machine to improve the scalability and fault tolerance of your critical applications and services. Windows 2000 supports two distinct types of clustering—network load balancing and server clustering.

Chapter 15
Using Clusters

Microsoft Windows 2000 supports two clustering technologies: Network Load Balancing clusters and server clusters. These technologies can be combined to provide a highly available and highly scalable cluster. This chapter describes the two types of clustering supported by Windows 2000, their place in the enterprise, and their configuration and requirements.

What Is a Cluster?

A *cluster* is a group of two or more computers functioning together to provide a common set of applications or services with a single apparent identity to clients. The computers are physically connected by hardware in the form of either a network or shared storage. The clustering software provides a common interface externally while managing the resources and load internally.

Windows Clustering provides the following benefits:

- **High availability**   When a clustered application or service fails or a computer in the cluster fails, the cluster responds by restarting the application or service on another member of the cluster or by distributing the load from the failed server to the rest of the cluster.

- **Scalability**   For cluster-aware applications, adding more machines to the cluster adds additional capabilities.

- **Manageability**   Administrators can move applications, services, and data from computer to computer within the cluster, allowing them to manually balance loads and to offload machines scheduled for maintenance.

Network Load Balancing Clusters

Network Load Balancing (NLB)—known as the Windows Load Balancing Service in Microsoft Windows NT 4—gives TCP/IP-based services and applications high availability and scalability by combining up to 32 servers running Windows 2000 Advanced Server in a single cluster. Client requests for applications and services provided by the cluster are distributed across the available servers in the cluster in a way that is transparent to the client.

If a server fails or is taken offline, the cluster is automatically reconfigured and the client connections redistributed across the remaining servers. If additional servers are added to the cluster, they are automatically recognized and the load is reconfigured and distributed.

Server Clusters

Server clusters distribute the workload among the servers in a cluster, with each server running its own workload. Like other types of clusters, server clusters are scalable and highly available. In the event of a failure, applications and services that can be restarted, such as print queues and file services, are restarted transparently. Ownership of shared resources passes to the remaining servers. When the failed server becomes available again, the workload is automatically rebalanced.

Server clusters use shared disk drives to provide transparent access. They require specially certified hardware, but when properly set up and configured, they provide for extremely high availability with no single point of failure.

Cluster Scenarios

In deciding whether and how to implement clustering, you first need to understand what problem is being solved and how best to solve it using the available technologies. Then you can make a business case for the particular solution or combination of solutions that best solves the particular problem. This section describes various scenarios and the type of clustering appropriate for each.

Intranet or Internet Functionality

An intranet or Internet server is a prime candidate for an NLB cluster. By enabling an NLB cluster across multiple servers, you provide your site with both redundancy and increased capacity. If a server should fail, the load is distributed transparently among the remaining servers.

Each Web server in the cluster runs its own Web server and accesses only local Web pages. This version is "shared nothing" clustering—there are no shared disks and no shared applications or data, with the possible exception of a common back-end database. NLB clusters are an appropriate and relatively inexpensive way to achieve both redundancy and high availability for your Web site, whether internal or external. Clients that need access to the Web pages are distributed among the servers in the cluster according to the load at each server. What makes this work is that most Web pages change fairly infrequently, allowing manual updates of all Web servers with the same information when you need to make changes.

Mission-Critical Availability

If your business absolutely, positively can't be run without a certain application, you need a highly reliable server to make sure that the application is always available. A server cluster is a good solution in this scenario, providing both high availability and scalability. With a server cluster, you group your critical applications into two groups, one group to a server. All the resources for each group are self-contained on the server, but if either server in the cluster fails, the other picks up the services and applications from the failed server, allowing for continuous availability of critical services and applications.

Server clusters require a substantially greater investment in hardware than NLB clusters. In addition, they aren't suitable for "shared nothing" clustering, since they use a shared disk array to keep resources in sync. When a server fails, the other server picks up the applications that had been running on the failed server. Since the disks are shared, the remaining server has access to the same set of data as the failed server, and thus there's no loss of functionality.

Integrated Windows Clustering

As you can see from the previous example, Windows 2000's clustering model lends itself well to an integrated approach that can help maximize your investment in hardware and resources. An NLB cluster can distribute the load of an essentially static Web or other TCP/IP load, passing specific applications to another cluster, which in turn uses the resources of the server cluster that runs the mission-critical messaging and database servers.

Requirements and Planning

Before you attempt to implement any form of clustering, you need to clearly understand the business reason for doing so. You also need to be aware of the costs and benefits of the implementation as well as the resource requirements for a successful implementation. Treat the implementation of a Windows 2000 cluster as you would any other major project. Clearly state the business case for the cluster, and get a commitment from all levels before you expend substantial resources on the project.

Identifying and Addressing Goals

The first step in planning your cluster is to identify your goals for the implementation and the needs that using clusters will meet. This sounds obvious, but it is actually the part of the process that is most often overlooked. The implementation of any technology should always be first and foremost a business decision, not a technology decision. Creating and maintaining clusters is not a trivial task, and it requires both technological and financial resources. You'll have a hard time selling your project if you haven't clearly identified one or more needs that it will meet.

In identifying the needs to be met and the goals of your project, you need to be as objective as possible. Always keep in mind that what you might view as "cool" technology can look remarkably like scary, unproven gobbledygook to those in the organization who are less technically savvy than you are. This doesn't mean that those individuals won't support your project, but it does mean that you need to make the case for the project on a level that they can understand and identify with.

Start by clearly identifying the business goals that you're trying to accomplish. State the general goals, but provide enough detail to make the success of the project clearly measurable. Identify the specific gains you expect and how those gains will be measured. Be sure to clearly indicate how the needs you've identified are currently being met. This step is critical because it lets you point out both the costs of your suggested method and the risks associated with it.

Identifying a Solution

Once you know the business needs you're trying to meet, you can identify some solutions. If you've clearly laid out your goals and objectives for the project, the technology that achieves those goals will be driven by those needs, not the other way around. This is also the time to use your best political judgment. You need to identify not only the best way to meet the business needs, but also how much you can realistically sell and implement in a single shot. If you think that ultimately you will need a fully integrated, three-tiered, multiple-cluster solution, you may want to build your plan around a phased approach that allows you to distribute the risks and costs over a broader period.

In addition, if you're proposing a clustering solution to the problem, spend some time and energy identifying methodologies that might be considered alternatives to clustering and clearly laying out the strengths and weaknesses of those alternatives. This effort will short-circuit objections and diversions as you build support for your project.

Identifying and Addressing Risks

As you plan your schedule, be sure to identify the risks at each step of the process and to plan solid fallback positions if problems arise. Selling the project is also much easier if it's clear that you've actually thought about the risks. For example, if your goal is to replace an existing manual methodology, have you left yourself a way to fall back to it if there are problems? Or are the two mutually incompatible? If you're replacing an existing client/server application with a clustered, Web-based, distributed, *n*-tiered application, have you made a clear road map for how you will make the transition from one to the other? What are the risks for that transition?

Spend some time identifying failure points in your project. If you're building a server cluster to provide 24-hour-7-day access to your Microsoft Exchange messaging, have you identified redundant network connections to the cluster? It does little good to create a highly available server if the network connection to it is questionable.

Making Checklists

Take the time to identify all the possible pieces of your cluster implementation ahead of time. Use this to build a checklist of steps that you need to take and the dependencies at each point. At each major step, identify the hardware, software, knowledge, and resources that will be required, and create a checklist of the prerequisites for that step. The time you spend planning your clustering implementation will easily be saved in the actual installation and implementation, while greatly reducing your risks of failure.

Network Load Balancing Clusters

NLB provides a highly available and scalable solution for TCP/IP-based network applications such as a Web server or FTP server. By combining the resources of two or more servers into a single cluster, NLB can provide for redundancy of information and resources while servicing far more clients than a single server alone could handle.

NLB Concepts

NLB is a Windows 2000 Networking driver. It acts independently of the TCP/IP networking stack and is transparent to that stack. The NLB driver sits between the TCP/IP stack and the network card drivers, with the Windows Load Balancing Service (WLBS.exe)—the necessary NLB control program—running on top, alongside the actual server application (Figure 15-1).

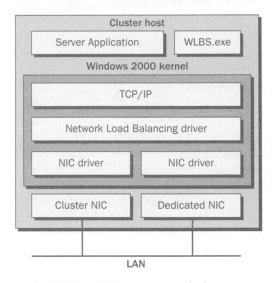

Figure 15-1. *NLB as a network driver.*

Optimally, each server participating in an NLB cluster should have two network interface cards (NICs), although this is not an absolute requirement. Communications and management are materially improved with two NICs, however, especially in unicast mode. (Unicast mode, as opposed to multicast mode, allows each NIC to present only a single address to the network.) Overall network throughput is also improved, since the second network adapter is used to handle host-to-host traffic within the cluster.

NLB supports up to 32 computers per cluster. Each server application can be balanced across the entire cluster or can be primarily hosted by a single computer in the cluster, with another computer in the cluster providing directed failover redundancy. For fully distributed applications, the failure of any single host causes the load currently being serviced by that host to be transferred to the remaining hosts. When the failed server comes back online, the load among the other hosts will be redistributed to include the restored server.

Note NLB is supported only by Windows 2000 Advanced Server and requires that TCP/IP be installed. It works over Fiber Distributed Data Interface–based or Ethernet-based networks from 10 megabits per second (Mbps) to 1 gigabit per second (Gbps). It uses from 250 KB to 4 MB of RAM and roughly a megabyte of disk space.

Choosing an NLB Cluster Model

A host in an NLB cluster can use one of four models, each with its own merits and drawbacks. These models are

1. Single network adapter in unicast mode
2. Single network adapter in multicast mode
3. Multiple network adapters in unicast mode
4. Multiple network adapters in multicast mode

The choice of model for a given host and cluster will vary depending on the circumstances, requirements, and limitations imposed on the design of the cluster. The sections that follow provide details on each of the models.

Note   NLB in Windows 2000 does not support a mixed unicast mode and multicast mode environment. All hosts in the cluster must be either multicast or unicast. Some hosts, however, may have a single adapter while others have multiple adapters. In addition, NetBIOS cannot be supported in a single-adapter-only configuration.

Single Network Adapter in Unicast Mode

A single network adapter running in unicast mode is in some ways the easiest type of host to set up, and with only a single adapter, is cheaper than one with multiple network adapters. It does, however, impose significant limitations:

- Overall network performance is reduced.
- Ordinary communications among cluster hosts are disabled.
- NetBIOS support is not available within the cluster.

Single Network Adapter in Multicast Mode

Using multicast mode in clusters in which one or more hosts have a single network adapter means that normal communications are possible between hosts within the cluster. This capability overcomes one of the most awkward of the limitations of single adapter/unicast mode. However, there are still significant disadvantages:

- Overall network performance is reduced.
- Some routers do not support multicast MAC addresses.
- NetBIOS support is not available within the cluster.

Multiple Network Adapters in Unicast Mode

Using multiple network adapters in unicast mode is generally the preferred configuration. It does impose the cost of a second network adapter per host, but given the relatively low cost of network adapters, including the per port cost of hubs, this is a relatively minor price to pay for the resulting advantages:

- No limitations are imposed on ordinary network communications among cluster hosts.
- Ordinary NetBIOS support is available via the first configured adapter.
- No bottlenecks occur due to a single network adapter.
- The model works with all routers.

Multiple Network Adapters in Multicast Mode

If you are forced by circumstances to use some hosts within a cluster that have only a single network adapter and you must be able to maintain normal network communications among the hosts in the cluster, you will need to run all of the hosts in multicast mode, even those with multiple adapters, since you can't run some hosts in unicast mode and some in multicast mode. This limitation may cause a problem with some routers, but otherwise it is a viable solution.

Planning the Capacity of an NLB Cluster

In general, an NLB cluster should contain as many hosts as are needed to handle the client load for the applications being run in the cluster. The exception to this would be cases in which the sole function of the cluster is to provide failover tolerance for a critical TCP/IP application—that is, when a single server can handle the load and the second server is there simply for fault tolerance.

The maximum number of hosts in a given cluster is 32. If your application will require more than 32 hosts, you can set up multiple clusters, using round-robin DNS to distribute the load among the clusters. The effective limitation, however, is likely to be the network saturation point. If you do run multiple clusters in a subnet, you should host each on its own network switch to minimize the network bottleneck.

Although fewer and more powerful servers may look cost-effective for a given application, you should consider how the failure of a server will affect the application and the remaining servers. If the remaining servers can't handle the resulting load, you may have a cascading failure, bringing down the entire application. Always provide sufficient server capacity within the cluster to handle the expected load when a single server is down. Also consider ways to limit the load to the application when there has been a failure.

When determining the expected cluster capacity, you also need to consider the application being clustered and the type of load it imposes on the cluster. Plan your servers according to where the limitation and stress will be greatest. File serving applications are I/O intensive, e-mail applications such as Microsoft Exchange are very CPU intensive, and database applications tend to be RAM hogs as well as a drain on the disk I/O subsystem.

Providing Fault Tolerance

While NLB clusters provide overall fault tolerance for your TCP/IP application, they are not a complete solution for all possible failures. Because they are "shared nothing" clusters, there is always some data lag between servers. For fully fault-tolerant, high-availability clustering that can run any application, you probably want to use server clustering. This provides the greatest level of fault tolerance.

One thing you can do to improve the overall fault tolerance of the cluster is to make the hard drives fault tolerant. Both hardware and software RAID solutions are viable options for improving the fault tolerance of an NLB cluster. For more on RAID and fault tolerance in general, see Chapters 14 and 35.

Optimizing an NLB Cluster

Optimizing an NLB cluster calls for clearly understanding where the bottleneck in your clustered application is likely to be. An application that is essentially a file and print server, for example, tends to be a heavy user of both disk I/O and network bandwidth. Microsoft Exchange, on the other hand, puts a heavy load on the CPU, and to a somewhat lesser extent, on RAM. Focus your optimization efforts on the bottleneck and you'll get the most gain for your effort.

One area that can be a problem is running an NLB cluster in a switched environment without planning your network load carefully. If each of the servers in your cluster is connected to a different switched port, you can easily end up flooding your switched ports, since every client request to the cluster will pass through all switched ports to which a member of the cluster is attached. Running in multicast mode can exacerbate the problem. If you're running in a switched environment, we suggest that you follow these guidelines:

1. Use a top-quality hub to connect the servers in the cluster to one another, and uplink the hub to a single switched port.

2. Use unicast mode. If you enabled multicast mode during setup, change it. (You'll need to change this on all servers in the cluster.)

3. Edit the registry on each of the hosts in the cluster, changing the following key from the default parameter of 1 to 0:

```
HKEY_LOCAL_MACHINE\System\CurrentControlSet\Services\WLBS
    \Parameters\MaskSourceMAC
```

This change allows the switch to tell which MAC address is really the source of traffic, helping it to do its switching job properly. You'll need to restart the servers after making this change.

Server Clusters

A server cluster is a group of independent nodes that work together as a single system. They share a common cluster database that enables recovery in the event of the failure of any node. A server cluster uses a jointly connected resource, generally a disk array on a shared SCSI bus, which is available to all nodes in the cluster. Each Windows 2000 Advanced Server node in the cluster must have access to the array, and each node in the cluster must be able to communicate at all times with the other nodes in the cluster.

Windows 2000 supports server clusters only on machines running Advanced Server. Additionally, as shipped, it supports only two-node clusters using a shared disk resource, via either Fibre Channel or a shared SCSI bus. Both nodes of the cluster must be running TCP/IP for networking and should have at least one dedicated network interconnect available. To avoid a single point of failure, a second network interconnect is highly recommended.

Server Cluster Concepts

To understand and implement server clusters, it is important to understand several new concepts and their ramifications, as well as specialized meanings for certain terms.

Networks (Interconnects)

A cluster has two distinct types of networks: the *private network* that's used to maintain communications between nodes in the cluster and the *public network* that clients of the cluster use to connect to the services of the cluster. Each of these networks can share the same network card and physical network cabling, but it is a good practice to keep them separate. Having them separate gives you an alternate path for interconnection between the nodes of the cluster. Since the interconnect between the nodes of a cluster is a potential single point of failure, it should always be redundant. The cluster service will use all available networks, both private and public, to maintain communications between nodes.

In the event of a failure of communications between nodes of the cluster, the nodes are partitioned and each node attempts to gain control of the quorum resource (discussed later under "Types of Resources") and thus the shared disk. One node will shut down, while the other will attempt to maintain the processes of the cluster. However, since there is no guarantee that the node with a working network card will be the one that gains control, it is possible that all services from the cluster will be unavailable.

Nodes

A *node* is a member of a server cluster. It must be running Windows 2000 Advanced Server and Windows Clustering. It must also be running TCP/IP, must be connected to the shared cluster storage device, and must have at least one network interconnect to the other nodes in the cluster.

Groups

Groups are the units of failover. Each group contains one or more resources. Should any of the resources within the group fail, all will fail over together according to the failover policy defined for the group. A group can be owned by only one node at a time. All resources within the group run on the same node. If a resource within the group fails and must be moved to an alternate node, all other resources in that group must be moved as well. When the cause of failure on the originating node is resolved, the group will fall back to its original location, based on the failback policy for the group.

Resources

Any physical or logical entity that can be brought online or offline can be a server cluster resource. It must be able to be owned by only one node at a time and will be managed as part of the cluster. The *quorum resource* is a special resource. It is the repository of the configuration data of the cluster and the recovery logs that allow recovery of the cluster in the event of a failure. The quorum resource must be able to be controlled by a single node, it must provide physical storage for the recovery logs and cluster database, and it must use the NTFS file system. The only resource type supported for a quorum resource is the Physical Disk resource as shipped with Windows 2000 (this and other resource types are described in the next section), but it is possible that other quorum resource types will be developed and certified by third parties.

Types of Resources

Windows 2000 Advanced Server includes several different resource types; the sections that follow examine each of these resource types and the role they play in a server cluster. The available cluster resource types are

- Physical Disk
- DHCP
- WINS
- Print Spooler
- File Share
- Internet Protocol
- Network Name
- Generic Application
- Generic Service

Physical Disk

The Physical Disk resource type is the central resource type required as a minimum for all server clusters. It is used for the quorum resource that controls what node in the cluster is in control of all other resources. The Physical Disk resource type is used to manage a shared cluster storage device. It has the same drive letter on all cluster servers.

DHCP and WINS

The DHCP service provides IP addresses and various other TCP/IP settings to clients, while the WINS service provides dynamic resolution of NetBIOS names to IP addresses. Both can be run as a resource of the cluster, providing for high availability of these critical services to network clients. In order for failover to work correctly, the DHCP and WINS databases must reside on the shared cluster storage.

Print Spooler

The Print Spooler resource type lets you cluster print services, making them fault tolerant and saving a tremendous number of help desk calls when the print server fails. It will also avoid the problem of people simply clicking the Print button over and over when there's a problem, resulting in a very long and repetitious print queue.

In order to be clustered, a printer must be connected to the server via the network. Obviously, you can't connect the printer to a local port such as a parallel or USB port directly attached to one of the nodes of the cluster. The client can address the printer either by name or by IP address, just as it would a nonclustered printer on the network.

In the event of a failover, all jobs that are currently spooled to the printer are restarted. Jobs that are in the process of spooling from the client are discarded.

File Share

You can use a server cluster to provide a high-availability file server using the File Share resource type. The File Share resource type lets you manage your shared file systems in three different ways:

- As a standard file share with only the top-level folder visible as a share name.

- As shared subfolders, where the top-level folder and each of its immediate subfolders are shared with separate names. This makes it extremely easy to manage users' home directories, for example.

- As a stand-alone Distributed file system (Dfs) root. You cannot, however, use a cluster server File Share resource as part of a fault-tolerant Dfs root.

Internet Protocol and Network Name

The Internet Protocol resource type is used to manage the IP addresses of the cluster. When an Internet Protocol resource is combined with a Network Name resource and one or more applications, you can create a *virtual server*. Virtual servers allow clients to continue to use the same name to access the cluster even after a failover has occurred. No client-side management is required, since to the client the virtual server is unchanged.

Generic Application

The Generic Application resource type allows you to manage regular, cluster-unaware applications in the cluster. A cluster-unaware application that is to be used in a cluster must, as a minimum,

- Be able to store its data in a configurable location
- Use TCP/IP to connect to clients
- Have clients that can reconnect in the event of an intermittent network failure

When you install a generic, cluster-unaware application, you have two choices: you can install it onto the shared cluster storage, or you can install it individually on each node of the cluster. The first method is certainly easier, since you install the application only once for the whole cluster. However, if you use this method you won't be able to perform a rolling upgrade of the application, since it appears only once. (A rolling upgrade is an upgrade of the application in which the workload is moved to one server while the application on the other server is upgraded and then the roles are reversed to upgrade the first server.)

To give yourself the ability to perform rolling upgrades on the application, you need to install a copy onto each node of the cluster. You will need to place it in the same folder and path on each node. This method uses more disk space than installing onto the shared cluster storage, but it permits you to perform rolling upgrades, upgrading each node of the cluster separately.

Generic Service

Finally, server clusters support one additional type of resource—the Generic Service resource. This is the most basic resource type, but it does allow you to manage your Windows 2000 services as a cluster resource.

Defining Failover and Failback

Windows 2000 server clusters allow you to define the failover and failback policies for each group or virtual server. This ability enables you to tune the exact behavior of each application or group of applications to balance the need for high availability against the overall resources available to the cluster in a failure situation. Also, when the failed node becomes available again, your failback policy will determine whether the failed resource is immediately returned to the restored node, is maintained at the failed-over node, or migrates back to the restored node at some predetermined point in the future. These options allow you to plan for the disruption caused when a shift in node ownership occurs, limiting the impact by timing it for off-hours.

Configuring a Server Cluster

When planning your server cluster, you'll need to think ahead to what your goal is for the cluster and what you can reasonably expect from it. Server clusters provide for extremely high availability and resource load balancing, but you need to make sure your hardware, applications, and policies are appropriate.

High Availability with Load Balancing

You can configure your cluster with static load balancing, in which some applications run on one node while others run on another node. If one node fails, the applications or resources on the failed node will fail over to run on the other node, providing high availability of your resources while balancing the load across the cluster. In the event of failure, you will have a reduced load capacity, and you should implement procedures either to limit the load by reducing performance or availability, or to not provide some less-critical services during a failure.

Maximum Availability Without Load Balancing

By configuring one node as a "hot spare," you can provide maximum availability for critical applications. This scenario requires that your server nodes be sufficiently powerful to run the entire load of the cluster by themselves, and it certainly has the greatest hardware cost. But if one node fails, the other node takes over all processing for the cluster, and there is no reduced capacity for the applications.

Partial Failover (Load Shedding)

You can configure your cluster so that critical applications are protected in a failure situation but noncritical ones simply run as though they were on a stand-alone server. If the server on which they are running fails, the noncritical applications or resources are unavailable until the node is recovered. The critical applications on the node, however, are set to fail over to the other node of the cluster. You may even have applications on the remaining node that are set to shut down if the other node fails, allowing you to maintain a high level of performance and availability of your most critical applications while shedding the load from less critical applications and services when necessary. This strategy can be very effective when you must, for example, service certain critical applications or users under any and all circumstances but can allow other applications and users with a lower priority to temporarily fail.

Virtual Server Only

You can create a server cluster that has only a single node, which allows you to take advantage of the virtual server concept to simplify the management and look of the resources on your network. Having a single node doesn't give you any additional protection against failure or any additional load balancing over that provided by simply running a single stand-alone server, but it allows you to easily manage groups of resources as a virtual server.

This scenario is an effective way to stage an implementation. You create the initial virtual server, putting your most important resources on it in a limited fashion. Then, when you're ready, you add an additional node to the server cluster and define your failover and failback policies, giving you a high-availability environment with minimal disruption to your user community. In this scenario, you can space hardware purchases over a longer period while providing services in a controlled test environment.

Planning the Capacity of a Server Cluster

Capacity planning for a server cluster can be a complicated process. You need to thoroughly understand the applications that will be running on your cluster and make some hard decisions about exactly which applications you can live without and which ones must be maintained under all circumstances. You'll also need a clear understanding of the interdependencies of the resources and applications you'll be supporting.

The first step is to quantify your groups or virtual servers. Make a comprehensive list of all applications in your environment, and then determine which ones will need to fail over and which ones can be allowed to fail but still should be run on a virtual server.

Next determine the dependencies of these applications and what resources they need in order to function. This information allows you to group dependent applications and resources in the same group or virtual server. Keep in mind that a resource can't span groups, so if multiple applications depend on a resource, such as a Web server, they must all reside in the same group or on the same virtual server as the Web server and thus will share the same failover and failback policies.

A useful mechanism for getting a handle on your dependencies is to list all your applications and resources and draw a dependency tree for each major application or resource. This will help you visualize not only the resources that your application is directly dependent on, but also the second-hand and third-hand dependencies that might not be obvious at first glance. For example, a cluster that is used as a high-availability file server uses the File Share resource. And it makes perfect sense that this File Share resource is dependent on the Physical Disk resource. It's also dependent on the Network Name resource. However, the Network Name resource is dependent on the IP resource. Thus, although the File Share resource isn't directly dependent on the IP resource, when you draw the dependency tree you will see that they all need to reside in the same group or on the same virtual server. Figure 15-2 illustrates this dependency tree.

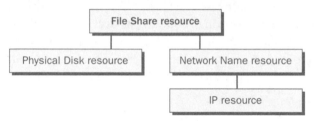

Figure 15-2. *The dependency tree for a File Share resource.*

Finally, as you're determining your cluster capacity, you need to plan for the effect of a failover. Each server must have sufficient capacity to handle the additional load imposed on it when a node fails and it is required to run the applications or resources that were owned by the failed node.

The disk capacity for the shared cluster storage must be sufficient to handle all the applications that will be running in the cluster as well as to provide the storage that the cluster itself requires for the quorum resource. Be sure to provide enough RAM and CPU capacity on each node of the cluster so that the failure of one node won't overload the other node to the point that it too fails. This possibility can also be managed to some extent by determining your real service requirements for different applications and user communities and reducing the performance or capacity of those that are less essential during a failure. However, such planned load shedding may not be sufficient and frequently takes a significant amount of time to be accomplished, so give yourself some margin to handle that initial surge during failover.

Summary

Windows 2000 Advanced Server provides two clustering models: Network Load Balancing clusters (formerly known as the Windows Load Balancing Service) and server clusters. Clusters provide a highly available and scalable environment. Network Load Balancing clusters use standard hardware to distribute TCP/IP applications across a cluster. Server clusters use specialized shared disk resources to provide failover and static load balancing for a variety of applications. The next chapter covers configuring your storage as well as planning for fault tolerance and flexibility in managing your storage needs.

Chapter 16
Configuring Storage

This chapter covers the following advanced Microsoft Windows 2000 storage tools: the Distributed file system, Removable Storage, and Remote Storage. The chapter also explains how to set up shared folders on a corporate network or on the Internet. While many books combine file sharing and removable storage with the discussion of local storage management, Windows 2000 provides enough new functionality to warrant a whole chapter to cover these subjects separately.

In Windows 2000, both file sharing and removable storage have become simpler for the end user. And while the associated administrative chores have been streamlined, file sharing and removable storage are now more complex to administer because the capabilities of once-simple technologies have grown.

The Distributed File System

One of the problems with file sharing and networks is that users often have difficulty finding the files on the network that they need to access. If you have a single file server on your network, this problem might be inconsequential. However, when you start adding multiple file servers in multiple locations, helping users find the appropriate shares can become a full-time job.

The Distributed file system (Dfs) was designed to help alleviate this dilemma while also providing such benefits as load balancing, additional fault tolerance, and conservation of intrasite network bandwidth. Dfs achieves these goals by hiding the underlying structure of file shares inside a virtual folder structure such that users will see a single contiguous folder structure, which in reality might consist of folders residing on a dozen different servers scattered across your organization. To help you make the most of Dfs, the following sections explain its advantages, define its concepts, outline its structure, and then show you how to set up Dfs and administer it.

Note You can download Dfs version 4.x to use in Microsoft Windows NT 4. However, this version is considered beta software. Dfs version 5, which is included with Windows 2000, works much better and has considerably more functionality than earlier versions.

Advantages

The principal advantage of Dfs is its single point of access to all network shares. Another benefit is that it allows you to organize file shares and to manage increased availability and fault tolerance as well as load-balancing functionality. In addition, security is easy with Dfs. The next sections elaborate on these advantages and why you might want to use Dfs on your network.

One Point of Access for All Network Files

Dfs makes it easier for users to find and access the file shares they need. Without Dfs, users often must connect to a number of different shares on multiple file servers to obtain the files they need. Unless the users know which servers and file shares to look in, they might not find the files at all. Dfs permits the creation of a virtual, hierarchically organized collection of file shares so that users can simply connect to a single server (the host server for the Dfs structure). All the folders that the users need appear as if they're stored on that server even though the folders are actually stored on multiple servers, as shown in Figure 16-1.

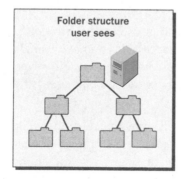
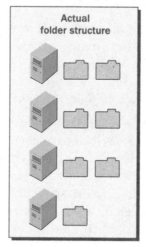

Figure 16-1. *The folder structure a user sees when using Dfs, and the actual folder structure.*

Note Unfortunately, the current implementation of Dfs in Windows 2000 doesn't provide enough flexibility when creating a virtual folder hierarchy because *midlevel junctions*—Dfs links from a folder other than the Dfs root—are unsupported. See the "Structure and Topology" section for more information on this limitation.

High Availability and Better Performance

Availability and performance improvements are the poster children of Dfs that never seem to make it onto the poster. Dfs supports setting up shared folder topology in a way that maximizes availability, increases fault tolerance, and allows administrators to set up load balancing for heavily used file shares. When redundant file shares are combined with Windows 2000 domains that use sites to delineate areas of high connectivity, Dfs also increases network link performance by linking users to the shared folder nearest them.

To reach this high availability, Dfs shields the actual file shares from users. Users navigate the Dfs folder structure, oblivious of where the files they access are coming from. You can take advantage of this abstraction in any number of ways. For example, you can increase availability by permitting server upgrades and maintenance without taking the folder share offline. To do so, simply change the Dfs link to point to another server with a copy of the folder share. This ability to stay online can be especially useful for Web sites. Simply create a Web site in a shared folder, create a Dfs link to the shared folder, and configure Internet Information Server (IIS) to use the Dfs link to the folder for the Web site. If you need to take down the server that is storing the shared folder, just change the Dfs link to point to a copy of the shared folder on another server—no hyperlinks are broken by doing this.

When using Dfs in a Windows 2000 domain, the Dfs topology is published in Active Directory and automatically replicated to all domain controllers in the domain, which ensures that users will always have access to the Dfs tree, even if one or more servers are down. You can also set up a Dfs root or shared folder on one server to replicate with a duplicate shared folder on another server, providing fault tolerance in the event that one of the servers fails.

Replication between Dfs shared folders also allows for easy network load balancing. By configuring a Dfs link to point to a number of different servers, each with identical shared folders that are replicated to stay identical, popular file shares can gain a performance benefit: having multiple servers hosting the folders while still appearing to end users as being hosted on a single machine, as shown in Figure 16-2.

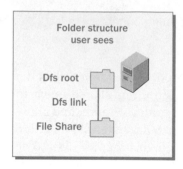
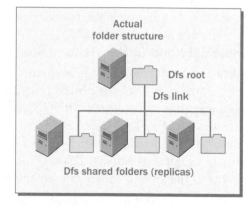

Figure 16-2. *The folder structure a user sees when using Dfs and load balancing, and the actual folder structure.*

Security

Another advantage is that Dfs security is easy. You set the permissions for the Dfs root—who can access and modify the Dfs structure—but all other security is handled by the file system, NTFS. This arrangement makes sense since Dfs provides only a virtual structure to the existing set of file shares. The same security settings that apply to accessing file shares directly apply to accessing the file shares via the Dfs tree.

Concepts and Terminology

Because Dfs is such a new technology to Windows, a brief primer on the most important concepts and terms is in order. The next sections cover the Dfs client and server components and talk about Dfs on stand-alone servers as well as servers belonging to a Windows 2000 domain. Then you'll learn how a Dfs structure is created and what components make up the Dfs topology.

Dfs Clients

To access the Dfs folder structure, you need a Dfs client. Table 16-1 shows the type of Dfs client support that is provided by various operating systems. Note that if you don't have a Dfs client, you can't access the Dfs tree and gain the benefits of Dfs; however, you *can* access the file shares just as you would if Dfs weren't set up on your network. If you're running an operating system that doesn't include "Microsoft" in the title, you're out of luck for now. Perhaps when more and better Active Directory clients come out for other operating systems, this situation will change.

Table 16-1.   Operating system support for Dfs access

Operating System	DFS Client Support
non-Microsoft, Macintosh, UNIX, OS/2	None
MS-DOS	None
Windows 3.x	None
Windows 95	Downloadable client for Dfs 4.x and 5
Windows 98/98 Second Edition	Dfs 4.x and 5 stand-alone client included, Dfs 5 domain-based client downloadable
Windows NT 4 with Service Pack 3 or later	Dfs 4.x and 5 stand-alone client included
Windows 2000	Full support built in

Dfs Servers

The server-side component for Dfs is built into Windows 2000 Server and can't be removed. Windows NT 4 with Service Pack 3 or later can also host Dfs roots. However, Dfs roots can be hosted only on stand-alone Windows NT servers, not on servers that belong to a domain, because domain-based Dfs relies heavily on Active Directory, which Windows NT has only limited capabilities to interact with.

To use the folder synchronization feature of Dfs to keep two file shares identical, you need to host the file shares on Windows 2000 NTFS partitions. This requirement should be obvious because using FAT partitions for file shares is kind of like climbing flagpoles during thunderstorms—worse than pointless.

Finally, you can't set up a Dfs server on a NetWare or UNIX box. Dfs is currently one of those Microsoft-only features, both on the client and the server, although hopefully, this will change soon. However, you can include file shares in the Dfs tree from any operating system that can be resolved by a UNC path, including Microsoft Windows 95, Windows 98, and NetWare.

Dfs In and Out of Domains

Dfs comes in two flavors: stand alone and domain based. Those astute readers who figured out that these two flavors depend on whether the server hosting the Dfs root is a stand-alone server or a server belonging to a Windows domain can take a free coffee break.

Stand-alone Dfs, or a Dfs structure with its Dfs root hosted on a server not belonging to a Windows 2000 domain, has a couple of limitations when compared with its more virile, domain-enhanced sibling. The first of these limitations is that stand-alone Dfs can't use Active Directory. This limitation is obvious, since Windows 2000 domains are based on Active Directory. The most important result of this shortcoming is that stand-alone Dfs can't perform automatic replication of shared folders in a replica set, nor can it replicate the Dfs root in any way.

The second limitation of stand-alone Dfs is that it can have only a single layer of Dfs links. This is actually currently a limitation of domain-based Dfs also, as midlevel junctions have yet to be implemented. Consequently, both stand-alone and domain-based Dfs topologies are limited to a single layer of Dfs links. To achieve deeper folder trees, the file shares need to either have subfolders or you need to create a Dfs link to another Dfs root on another server.

Domain-based Dfs topologies differ from stand-alone Dfs in a couple of ways. Domain-based Dfs must be hosted on a member server or domain controller of a Windows 2000 domain. Hosting Dfs on a server in a Windows 2000 domain automatically publishes the Dfs topology in Active Directory, providing fault tolerance and network-performance optimization by directing clients to the nearest Dfs shared folder in a replica set, as discussed in the next section.

Active Directory also allows domain-based Dfs to automatically synchronize shared folders in a replica set, as well as copies of the Dfs root. And, while domain-based Dfs can currently create only one level of Dfs links per Dfs root (just like stand-alone Dfs), in future versions of Windows, domain-based Dfs will support a largely unlimited number of nested Dfs links.

Structure and Topology

The structure of a Dfs tree begins with a Dfs root. The *Dfs root* is a normal shared folder that serves as the root folder for a particular Dfs tree. Since Dfs is only a virtual file system, the folder used as the Dfs root functions the same as any other shared folder and can contain normal files and subfolders. The server that stores the Dfs root is called the *host server*.

> **Note**   Windows NT supports only one Dfs root per server, while Windows 2000 has no architectural limitations on the number of Dfs roots that can be supported on a single server. However, Windows 2000 currently possesses the same one-Dfs-root-per-server limitation as Windows NT.

By itself, a Dfs root is nothing more than just another file share. However, you can use the Distributed File System MMC snap-in to add Dfs links to other file shares in your organization. A Dfs link works almost identically to a hyperlink on a Web page. Dfs links that you create transparently link the Dfs root folder to any other shared folder on the network. When a user opens the Dfs root, all linked folders appear as if they were subfolders of the Dfs root. Then, when users open a subfolder, they seamlessly open the linked file share. Whether it's on a different drive on the same server or on a server in an entirely different department, users are never aware that the folder they opened is anything but a normal subfolder of the folder they were previously in (the Dfs root).

Dfs links have a really cool feature: they don't have to link to just one folder. Instead, a Dfs link can link to up to 32 identical folders, called *Dfs shared folders*, or *replicas*, with the end user seeing only a single, ordinary folder. You can create replicas for normal file shares as well as for the Dfs root, and you can set them up to automatically synchronize with all other replicas in the replica set (if you're using domain-based Dfs).

Using *replica sets*—a group of identical replicas—creates a level of fault tolerance and load balancing, increasing both the total uptime of the file shares as well as the responsiveness of the file share. Dfs clients automatically choose a replica in their site, if available, reducing intrasite network utilization. If more than one replica is available on the client's site, each client randomly chooses a replica, allowing the load to be spread evenly across all available servers.

You can also create Dfs links to other Dfs roots hosted on other servers. These links are called *inter-dfs links* (Figure 16-3), and currently they are the only way of creating Dfs trees deeper than a single level. Inter-dfs links are also the way to link different DNS namespaces, since all normal Dfs links must be to file shares within the same DNS namespace. To achieve the flexibility to create a deeply nested, hierarchical tree, Dfs needs to support *midlevel junctions*: Dfs links from a folder other than the Dfs root. Unfortunately, midlevel junctions aren't supported by Windows 2000 yet but hopefully that will change with the next revision of Dfs.

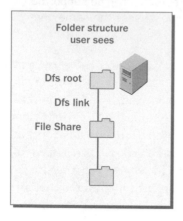
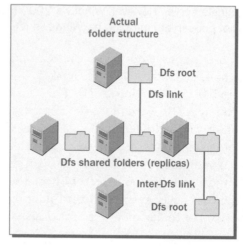

Figure 16-3. *The various components of a Dfs tree.*

Real World   Hierarchical Dfs Without Midlevel Junctions

Dfs version 5, which ships with Windows 2000, lacks a key feature: midlevel junctions. Midlevel junctions allow you to create a hierarchically organized Dfs tree within a single Dfs root. Until this feature is released in a later version of Dfs, the best way to create a hierarchical tree structure in Dfs is by using inter-dfs links. Inter-dfs links allow one Dfs root to link to another Dfs root, which in turn can have its own Dfs links, and also link to other Dfs roots. This allows multiple levels of depth in the Dfs topology, with each Dfs root permitting the tree to go an additional level deeper. To create an inter-dfs link, create a normal Dfs link but choose a Dfs root as the target folder instead of a normal file share.

Setup

Setting up Dfs is simple. Just create or open a Dfs root and then add Dfs links to any file shares you want to appear in the Dfs root. Of course, before doing this, check with your users and compile a list of network shares that they need access to. Dfs is useless if the right network shares aren't part of the Dfs tree.

Creating or Opening a Dfs Root

The first step in working with Dfs is to create a Dfs root (or open one to work with an existing root). To do so, follow these steps:

1. Launch the Distributed File System MMC snap-in from the Administrative tools folder.

2. If a Dfs root exists, open it by choosing Display An Existing Dfs Root from the Action menu. Use the Display An Existing Dfs Root dialog box to enter the host server's name or browse to the Dfs root.

    If no Dfs root exists, create one by choosing New Dfs Root from the Action menu and then clicking Next. The New Dfs Root Wizard opens, as shown in Figure 16-4.

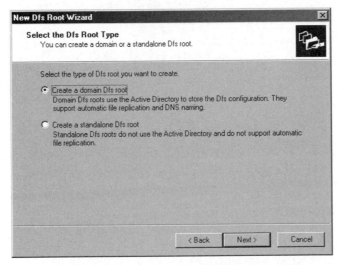

Figure 16-4. *The New Dfs Root Wizard.*

3. If your server belongs to a Windows 2000 domain, select the Create A Domain Dfs Root option and click Next; otherwise, select the Create A Standalone Dfs Root option and click Next, and skip to step 5.

4. Select the host domain to use for the Dfs root on the next screen, and then click Next.

5. Enter the DNS name of the server to host the Dfs root on the next screen, or click Browse to search the network for the appropriate host. Click Next.

6. Choose an existing file share to use as the Dfs root, or create a new share to host the Dfs root by entering the path to the folder and the share name to use for the folder (Figure 16-5). Then click Next.

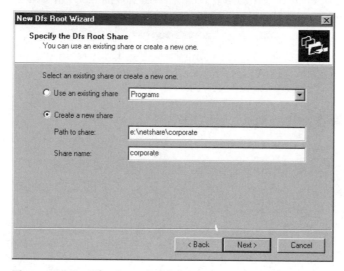

Figure 16-5. *The Specify The Dfs Root Share screen of the New Dfs Root Wizard.*

7. Enter a name for the Dfs root into the Dfs Root Name box, which Dfs users will see when they open the Dfs root, enter any comments into the Comments box, and then click Next.

8. Review the settings and then click Finish to create the Dfs root.

Tip If you frequently administer multiple Dfs roots, open a blank MMC, open the Distributed File System snap-in, open all the roots you want to use, and then save the console file. Then, when you need to access all the Dfs roots, launch the saved console file instead of the standard snap-in.

Adding Dfs Links

Dfs links are what make a Dfs root special. Without Dfs links, it's just another file share. Dfs links allow users to navigate from the Dfs root to other file shares on the network without leaving the Dfs structure. To create a Dfs link, follow these steps:

1. From the tree pane on the left, select the Dfs root to add Dfs links to.

2. Choose the Action menu's New Dfs Link command. This displays the Create A New Dfs Link dialog box, shown in Figure 16-6.

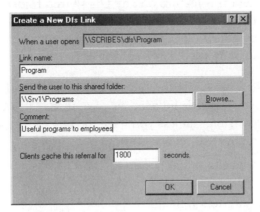

Figure 16-6. *The Create A New Dfs Link dialog box.*

3. In the Link Name box, enter the name users will see for the shared folder you're linking to.

4. Enter the shared folder's UNC or DNS path into the second text box, or click Browse to browse to the shared folder to link to.

5. Enter any comments you want users to see into the Comment text box.

6. Use the Clients Cache This Referral For text box to enter the length of time for clients to cache the referral before checking to see whether the referral is still accurate. Setting a longer time reduces network traffic, but it can lead to inaccurate referrals or interruption of service in the event that the Dfs link is changed—during a failover from one member of a replica set to another, or manually to prepare for maintenance for the server hosting the file share.

7. Click OK when you're finished.

Note Just as the text in a Web page hyperlink doesn't necessarily reflect the filename of the Web page that it's linking to, a Dfs link name can be completely different from the actual name of the shared folder to which it links.

Configuring Replication

One of the key features of Dfs is the ability to set up a shared folder in the Dfs tree to automatically (or manually) replicate itself with an identical shared folder also in the Dfs tree. You can implement this feature on any Dfs shared folder or on the Dfs root itself. If you want to set up a new replica for the Dfs root, see the next section; if you want to set up a new replica for another shared folder in the Dfs tree, skip to the "Replicating Shared Folders" section.

Replicating the Dfs Root   The Dfs root is the most important part of the Dfs tree to replicate because it hosts most of the Dfs links in the tree. If the Dfs root server goes down, the Dfs tree is inaccessible—unless you have the Dfs root replicated. To set up the Dfs root to be replicated, follow these steps:

1. Launch the Distributed File System snap-in and display the Dfs root you want to replicate.

2. Choose New Root Replica from the Action menu.

3. The New Dfs Root Wizard appears. Enter the DNS name of the server you want to use to host the Dfs root replica, or click Browse to search the network for the appropriate host. Click Next.

4. Choose an existing file share to use as the Dfs root replica, or create a new share to host the Dfs root replica by entering the path to the folder and the share name you want to use for the folder. Click Finish.

5. Repeat steps 2–4 for any other shared folders you want to use as a replica for this Dfs root, and then proceed to step 6.

6. Choose the Action menu's Replication Policy command to display the Replication Policy dialog box, shown in Figure 16-7.

7. Select the shared folder you'd like to make the initial master for the replica set, and then click Enable.

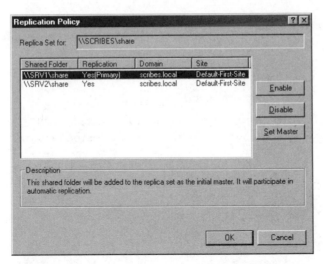

Figure 16-7. *The Replication Policy dialog box.*

8. Select each shared folder you want to participate in replication, and click Enable after selecting each one.

9. If you want to change the initial master for the replica set, select the shared folder and click Set Master.

10. Click OK when you're finished.

Note Domain-based Dfs leverages Active Directory for full, multimaster file replication; however, when you first create a replica set, you need to specify an initial master that will be used as the initial source folder for the other replicas to synchronize with.

Replicating Shared Folders An easy-to-use, fault-tolerant, and high-performance file system isn't worth much if the data you want to access is unavailable. Therefore, Dfs has shared folder replication. You can set up any shared folder to have up to 32 replicas of itself such that even after the most profound disaster, at least one server will still be available with the data your users need. (This isn't a challenge, though; if you knocked out power to the entire network, you would make all of the servers inaccessible.)

While replicating shared folders is basically the same as setting up the Dfs root to be replicated, a slight difference exists, so follow these steps for a complete walk-through:

1. Select the Dfs link in the Dfs tree for which you want to add replicas.

2. Choose New Replica from the Action menu.

3. Enter the UNC path to the network share you want to use as a replica into the box provided, or click Browse to locate the share on the network (Figure 16-8).

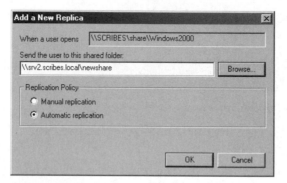

Figure 16-8. *The Add A New Replica dialog box.*

4. Choose whether you want the shared folder to be replicated automatically (by default, every 15 minutes) or manually. Click OK.

Caution Don't set some shared folders in a replica set to replicate automatically and others to be replicated manually. You'll cause the shared folders to synchronize poorly.

5. Repeat steps 2–4 for any other shared folders you want to add to the replica set, and then proceed to step 6.

6. Choose Replication Policy from the Action menu to display the Replication Policy dialog box.

7. Select the shared folder you would like to make the initial master for the replica set, and then click Enable.

8. Select each shared folder you would like to participate in replication, and click Enable after selecting each one.

9. If you want to change the initial master for the replica set, select the shared folder and click Set Master.

10. Click OK when you're finished.

Note Domain-based Dfs leverages Active Directory for full, multimaster file replication; however, when you first create a replica set, you need to specify an initial master that will be used as the initial source folder for the other replicas to synchronize with.

Removable Storage

The new Windows 2000 Removable Storage MMC snap-in is the hub for all interactions between programs and any removable storage devices you have installed on the system. It is both a tool that you can use to manage the devices and media and an API that programs can take advantage of to obviate the need to directly manage devices and media.

The Removable Storage MMC snap-in is an important tool that you will most likely need to use if you want to use a Removable Storage–compatible program with the removable devices. You use the tool to manage and allocate the devices and media and to prepare them for use with Windows 2000 Removable Storage–compatible programs. As such, you use Removable Storage for almost every task except manipulating data on your media—a task that is reserved for applications, such as a backup program or hierarchical storage management program like bundled Remote Storage.

This section covers some of the history behind Microsoft's decision to include the Removable Storage MMC snap-in in Windows 2000, briefs you on its potentially new terminology and conventions, and shows you step by step how to use it to manage your media and devices.

Benefits and Requirements

One of the primary advantages that Windows (all versions) has over MS-DOS is that programs no longer need their own device drivers. Instead, peripheral and system manufacturers write a single driver for the operating system and all Windows applications automatically gain access to the device. Unfortunately, while Windows has created a much-improved foundation for device support in the past, however, programs still needed to be hard coded with device drivers in order to use some device types—just as with MS-DOS.

Perhaps the most important types of devices that have historically fallen outside the Windows built-in device driver support are removable storage devices. While Windows 95/98 and Windows NT support some types of removable drives directly in the file system—notably floppy or hard disk–based devices such as Iomega Zip and Jaz drives and competitors—most removable storage devices remain unsupported or only partially supported by the operating system. This inconsistency requires backup programs (and other programs that need access to removable storage devices) to directly support all devices the program wants access to, still leaving device support limited and varied from program to program—not a particularly desirable effect.

To remedy this situation, Windows 2000 introduces the Removable Storage API and the Removable Storage MMC snap-in. Hardware vendors can now write a single Windows 2000 driver with Removable Storage support, and all Windows 2000 applications that are Removable Storage–aware can use any device that Removable Storage recognizes.

> **Note** Windows *does* have built-in support for removable devices such as tape drives that use the Win32 tape/disk API. However, the support isn't as functional as it could be, and the Removable Storage API supplements this API with a more robust API that provides a media database as well as other features that were previously left up to individual programs to implement. Note that devices with drivers not written to explicitly support the Removable Storage API might not be recognized in Removable Storage. Devices using Windows NT drivers won't be available for use in Removable Storage.

In addition to the behind-the-scenes improvements, Removable Storage handles almost all aspects of maintaining removable storage, except the actual handling of data. Your programs handle the data writing. (Removable Storage also doesn't support volume management such as media siding or striping.) Removable Storage makes it easy to keep track of and handle your media, whether in a stand-alone drive or in a robotic library, and it also allows you to easily perform any other media-related and drive-related tasks.

So, what are the requirements for using Removable Storage? The first requirement, not surprisingly, is a removable storage device. (And, yes, you should make sure that it's in the Hardware Compatibility List.) Devices with Windows NT 4 drivers probably won't do here. If you don't have a Windows 2000 driver for the device, Removable Storage probably won't recognize it, even if some other programs do. (All programs that use the Removable Storage API require that Removable Storage recognize and configure a device before the program can use it.)

If you plan to use a robotic media library with Removable Storage and want the library to be automatically configured (trust us, you do), make sure that all drives in the library are connected to the same SCSI bus as the drives' associated media changer, and that no other devices reside on this SCSI bus. Also make sure that the library supports drive-element address reporting. (Check with the device manufacturer on this.)

Tip While it's not required, you should try to keep the number of media to under 1000 so that Removable Storage's database doesn't start to slow down.

Concepts and Terminology

Removable Storage has its own language relative to removable devices, their associated tapes or disks, collections of tapes or disks, and the states a removable device can be in. You might already know some of this terminology, but some of it might be new and strange. In the interest of speaking the same language, here's a quick discussion of how Removable Storage handles its tasks, as well the terminology it uses.

Removable Devices and Libraries

Removable Storage collectively refers to removable storage devices and their associated media (tapes or disks) as libraries. While this term is more applicable to robotic optical or tape libraries, the term is also applied to stand-alone drives such as Zip, CD-ROM, and tape drives that hold only a single tape or disk.

Before you purchase a removable storage library to use with Removable Storage, check the Hardware Compatibility List (HCL) to make sure that Windows 2000 fully supports the device. Also check to make sure that the program you plan to use the device with supports the class of device. Some programs such as Remote

Storage support only a subset of the devices in the HCL, mainly for functionality reasons instead of compatibility.

Media Pools

Media pools are perhaps the most important Removable Storage concept to understand. All removable media belong to a *media pool*, which is basically just a group of media that all have the same properties (more on this later), and media are available for use by applications only if they belong to the appropriate media pool. This fact is important, and you might miss it (as we did) if you just blindly throw a piece of media in the library and start the backup program—and find that no media is available for the application.

Two types of media pools exist: system pools and application pools. All media that aren't reserved for use by an application reside in one of the three system media pools. See Table 16-2 for a description of the three system media pools.

Table 16-2. The three system media pools and their purposes

System Media Pool	Purpose
Free	To hold empty (blank but formatted) media available to all applications.
Import	To hold newly added media to the system that has a recognizable format but has never been used in the system before. You can move the media to the free media pool if you want to erase the media or to an application pool to use in a particular application.
Unrecognized	To hold unrecognized media until they can be moved into the free pool or an application pool by a user or an application.

 Tip The *free media pool* is where applications look when they need media and no media exists with space available in the application's pool. Therefore, you should try to keep some media in the free media pool so that applications can draw from it as necessary.

An *application media pool* is any media pool that applications create to hold their own media. For example, the Windows 2000 Backup program creates its own media pool, as does Remote Storage. Applications can create multiple media pools, or multiple applications can share the same media pool, although most require media to be in their own application pool.

Removable Storage Media Identification

Removable Storage keeps track of all media that you insert into the removable storage libraries. Removable Storage accomplishes this in one of two ways: by using on-media identifiers or by using barcodes.

On-media identifiers are small data stamps that Removable Storage imprints on the media the first time you insert them into a removable storage library connected to the system. The identifier has two parts: a label type and a label ID. The label type identifies the format used on the media, while the label ID uniquely identifies the tape or disk. Removable Storage uses these two identifiers to determine which media pool to place new media in and to keep track of all the media in the system. Table 16-3 shows how Removable Storage deals with recognized and unrecognized labels.

Table 16-3. Removable Storage and media identifiers

	Label Type Recognized	Label Type Unrecognized
Label ID Recognized	Media placed in appropriate media pool and database updated to show media is online	NA
Label ID Unrecognized	Media placed in import media pool	Media placed in unrecognized media pool

If you have a robotic library that has a barcode reader, you can use it to quickly keep track of all media that goes with the library. Removable Storage can use either the on-media identifier or the barcode to identify the media, although using the barcode is often much faster than using on-media identifiers because you don't have to mount each piece of media in order to keep track of it.

Removable Storage handles media that have file systems on them (such as CD-ROMs and Zip disks) a little differently than other types of media. The label type for these media is usually the format type (NTFS, FAT, or CDFS), and the label ID is the volume serial number. Additionally, in the case of CD and DVD media,

Removable Storage permits multiple media with the same label ID (such as a CD-ROM tower with multiple copies of the same disc), since the media can function interchangeably.

Media States

Removable Storage uses *media states* to figure out the current status of a piece of media, both in terms of the physical state of the media—whether it is being used or sitting idle; and in terms of the media's availability for additional data—for example, whether the media is full, formatted incorrectly, or reserved by a single program. Removable Storage refers to these two types of media states as Physical states and Side states, and they are displayed in the Removable Storage MMC snap-in when you view the removable storage libraries.

Note Libraries and drives also have their own states, but they are fairly self-explanatory and less important than media states.

Physical States Physical states describe the actual physical availability of the media—is the media in the drive, and if so, is it ready to be used? Removable Storage recognizes the following five Physical states:

- **Idle** The media is in the library or shelved offline in a changer.
- **In-use** The media is currently in the process of being mounted.
- **Loaded** The media is mounted and available for read/write operations.
- **Mounted** The media is mounted but not yet available for read/write operations.
- **Unloaded** The media has been dismounted and can be removed from the drive.

Side States A *side* is where information is actually stored on a tape or disk, and yes, it does refer to which physical side of the tape or disk information is stored on. (Most media these days are single sided.) Side states in Removable Storage indicate media use instead of the location of media that Physical states report.

Side states are used in part to determine which media pool to place the media into, and as such, Removable Storage examines not only the formatting information for the media, but also the on-media identification labels (discussed earlier in this chapter) to determine whether the media belongs in one of the system media pools or in an application media pool. Media pools can hold media sides that contain media only in the same state as the pool—for example, the import pool can contain sides that are currently in only the Imported state, the unrecognized pool can contain sides only in the Unrecognized state, and so on. The nine side states that Removable Storage uses are as follows:

- **Allocated** The side is reserved by an application.
- **Available** The side is currently available for use by applications.
- **Completed** The side is in use but full, so it's unavailable for further write operations.
- **Decommissioned** The side is no longer available for use because it's reached its allocation maximum.
- **Imported** The side label type is recognized, but the label ID hasn't yet been cataloged into a media pool by this computer's Removable Storage tool.
- **Incompatible** The formatting of the side is incompatible with the library. The media should be removed.
- **Reserved** The side is unavailable to all applications except the application that allocated the opposite side. Applies only to dual-sided media where one side has already been allocated.
- **Unprepared** The side has been placed in the free media pool but doesn't yet have a free media label. This state is temporary and will change to the available side state barring a problem.
- **Unrecognized** Removable Storage can't recognize the side's label type and ID.

Use and Management

Removable Storage is a tool that helps you manage the removable storage devices and media, and thus, you'll find that most of the tasks involve managing something.

Opening the Removable Storage Snap-in

The Removable Storage MMC snap-in isn't listed by itself in the Administrative Tools folder like many of the server management consoles are; instead, you'll have to either load it directly from a blank MMC window, use the Run dialog box, or access it from the Computer Management snap-in.

To access Removable Storage from the Computer Management snap-in, launch the Computer Management snap-in from the Administrative Tools folder on the Start menu, and then expand the storage root in the console tree and select Removable Storage from the tree, as shown in Figure 16-9.

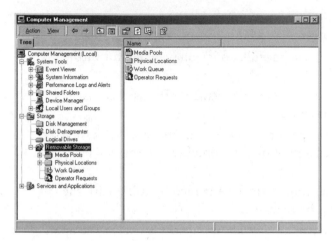

Figure 16-9. *Removable Storage displayed in the Computer Management console.*

To open the Removable Storage snap-in directly, choose Run from the Start menu and either type *%SystemRoot%\System32\Ntmsmgr.msc* into the text box provided to open the snap-in directly, or type *mmc* to open a blank MMC and then open the Ntmsmgr snap-in from the %SystemRoot%\System32 folder.

Managing Libraries

Because libraries are the actual physical drives or robotic changers that hold the removable media, the tasks involved with managing libraries are all physically oriented: configuring libraries added to the system, enabling and disabling libraries, changing the available media types, working with robotic libraries, and cleaning libraries. Use the following sections to help you with these and other chores.

Configuring Libraries   When you first connect a removable storage device to the system, Windows 2000 tries to recognize and configure it. When you launch Removable Storage, it performs its own device configuration and attempts to configure all removable storage devices connected to the system. All compatible stand-alone removable drives are automatically configured, although some robotic libraries aren't. For a robotic library to be automatically configured, all drives in the library must be connected to the same SCSI bus as the drives' associated media changer. The library must also support drive-element address reporting. (You're going to need to check with the device manufacturer on this one; we can't help you here.)

Note As mentioned in the "Benefits and Requirements" section earlier in this chapter, Removable Storage recognizes devices somewhat independently of Windows 2000, and a device that is recognized by Windows 2000 won't necessarily be recognized by and compatible with Removable Storage. As usual, check the HCL to make sure that your device is supported.

If the robotic library isn't automatically configured, you *can* configure the device manually. However, it's a rather tricky process involving manually editing the system registry, among other tasks. If you want to do this, consult the Windows 2000 Resource Kit; otherwise, get a different drive, or pay someone to configure the device for you.

Enabling and Disabling Libraries   To enable or disable a removable storage library (making the library unavailable for use by applications), open Removable Storage and then follow these steps:

1. Open the Physical Locations folder in the console tree.
2. Right-click the library you want to enable or disable, and then choose Properties from the shortcut menu.
3. Select or clear the Enable Library check box at the bottom of the General tab, and then click OK.

Inventorying Libraries   Removable Storage automatically creates an inventory of the media as you insert them into the library (actually, each time a library door is accessed). However, you might want to change the way Removable Storage updates the media inventory, or you might want to force Removable Storage to recheck the inventory.

Note This topic really applies only to robotic storage libraries. Stand-alone drive libraries don't need any special attention to keep their inventories up-to-date.

To accomplish these tasks, follow these steps:

1. To inventory the robotic storage library, right-click the library in the Physical Locations folder of Removable Storage and choose Inventory from the shortcut menu. Removable Storage inventories the library according to the default method specified for the library.

2. To change the default method of inventorying for a library, right-click the library in the Physical Locations folder of Removable Storage and choose Properties from the shortcut menu. Then choose an option from the Inventory Method drop-down list box, described in Table 16-4.

3. Clear the Perform Full Inventory On Mount Failure check box if you don't want Removable Storage to conduct a full inventory every time the library fails to mount a tape or disk (Figure 16-10).

Table 16-4. Library inventory methods and their descriptions

Inventory Method	Description
None	No automatic inventory is performed.
Fast	Performs a quick inventory using a barcode reader if available; otherwise, by checking which slots have had media swapped.
Full	Mounts each media in the library and reads the media's on-media identifier. Can be slow on libraries with a lot of media.

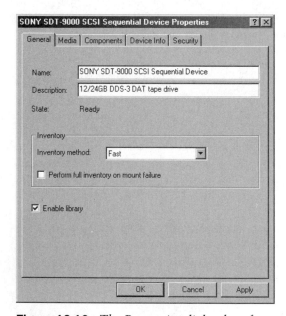

Figure 16-10. *The Properties dialog box for a storage library.*

Changing Available Media Types   If the storage library supports more than one type of media, you might need or want to change the media that Removable Storage will support in the library. To do so, follow these steps:

1. Open the Physical Locations folder in the console tree of the Removable Storage snap-in.

2. Right-click the library you want to configure, and then choose Properties from the shortcut menu.

3. Click the Media tab, and then click the Change button to add or remove media support for the library.

4. To disable the support for a certain media, select a supported media from the Selected Types list on the left and click Remove.

5. To add a media to the list of media the library supports, choose a media type from the list on the right and then click Add. Note that the storage library must be able to physically accept the media as well as to recognize and perform the desired operations on the media.

Setting Door and Inject/Eject Port Timeouts   All libraries have at least one inject/eject port that is used for inserting and removing media from the library, and robotic libraries also often have a door that can be opened to directly access media in a particular drive. To set the amount of time allowed before Removable Storage times out the port or door, thereby preventing further operations with it, follow these steps:

1. Open the Physical Locations folder in the console tree of the Removable Storage snap-in.

2. Right-click the library you want to configure, and then choose Properties from the shortcut menu.

3. Click the Components tab, and then enter a timeout period in minutes for the library door (if available) and inject/eject ports.

Tip   To open a library door, right-click the library in the Physical Locations folder and then choose Door Access from the shortcut menu. When prompted, you can open the door and access the media until the door timeout period expires. However, whenever you open the library door, Removable Storage needs to perform a full inventory unless you use a barcode reader. Therefore, it's preferable to use the inject/eject port in most circumstances.

Enabling and Disabling Individual Drives in a Library   If you have a storage library with multiple drives, you can disable or enable individual drives as needed. To do this, follow these steps:

1. Open the Physical Locations folder in the console tree of the Removable Storage MMC snap-in.
2. Select the library containing the drive you want to configure, and then double-click Drives.
3. Right-click the drive you want to enable or disable, and then choose Properties from the shortcut menu.
4. Clear the Enable Drive check box on the General tab to disable the drive.

Cleaning Libraries   Most removable storage libraries need to be cleaned—depending on the use and drives—maybe once a week or more. Because of this ongoing need, Removable Storage makes it easy to clean the drives and keep track of when you last cleaned them.

To clean a robotic library, right-click the library you want to clean and choose Cleaner Management from the shortcut menu. Then use the Cleaner Management Wizard to clean the drive.

To clean a stand-alone library, manually insert the cleaning tape and clean the drive as instructed by the drive manufacturer or the tape manufacturer. When you're finished, open the Physical Locations folder in the console tree, expand the appropriate library, and then right-click the drive you cleaned in the pane on the right and choose Mark As Clean from the shortcut menu.

Managing Media Pools

Handling media pools is the most important task that you perform with Removable Storage. Applications draw from either the free media pool or one or more application media pools when they require media. The following sections cover all of the media pool management tasks you'll need to perform, including creating and deleting media pools as well as configuring application media pools to automatically move media to and from the free media pool as necessary.

Tip   To move a piece of media from one media pool to another, drag the media from its current location to the media pool in which you want to store it.

Creating Media Pools   Most of the time Removable Storage and your applications create all of the media pools you'll need, but there may be times when you might want or need additional pools. To create additional media pools, follow these steps:

1. Double-click Media Pools in the console tree, and select the Media Pools folder to create a new root media pool, or select a media pool that can contain other media pools if you want to create a child media pool.

2. Choose Create Media Pool from the Action menu.

3. In the Create A New Media Pool Properties dialog box shown in Figure 16-11, enter a name for the media pool into the Name box.

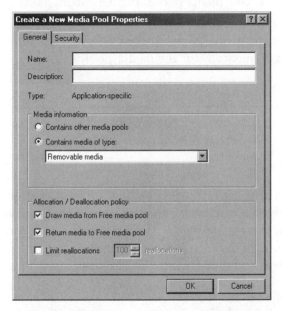

Figure 16-11.   *The Create A New Media Pool Properties dialog box.*

4. Enter a description of the purpose of the media pool into the Description box.

5. To make the media pool hold other media pools, select the Contains Other Media Pools option.

6. To configure the media pool to actually hold media, select the Contains Media Of Type option and choose the media type you want to store in the media pool from the drop-down list box.

7. Select the Draw Media From Free Media Pool check box if you want the media pool to take media from the free media pool when no media are available in this media pool. Selecting this option is generally prudent, as it reduces the need to manually manage the media.

8. Select the Return Media To Free Media Pool check box if you want the media pool to return media to the free media pool when the media is no longer needed. This is also usually a good idea.

9. To limit the number of times the media pool draws media from the free media pool, select the Limit Reallocations check box and enter the number of reallocations you want to allow. You might want to do this in order to leave some media in the free media pool for other media pools to draw from should they have no available media in their own pool.

10. To change the permissions for the media pool, click the Security tab and assign the appropriate access permissions for the media pool.

Tip   You can create a media pool to hold different types of media—perhaps for a backup program that needs access to the tape drive as well as a magneto optical (MO) drive. To do this, create a media pool that stores other media pools, and then open the new media pool and create a child media pool for each media type you want to use.

Deleting Media Pools   When an application media pool is no longer required—either you've uninstalled it or you no longer use the application for which the media pool was created—you might want to delete the media pool. To do so, move all media in the media pool you want to delete into another media pool, select the media pool you want to delete, and then click the Delete toolbar button.

Configuring Media Pools   To change the way the media pool works—perhaps to change whether or not the media pool draws media from the free media pool when necessary or to change the media type for the media pool—follow these steps:

1. Right-click the media pool you want to configure and then choose Properties from the shortcut menu.

2. In the Media Pool Properties dialog box, modify the name for the media pool in the Name box, if necessary.

3. Change the description of the purpose of the media pool in the Description box.

4. To make the media pool hold other media pools, select the Contains Other Media Pools option.

5. To configure the media pool to actually hold media, select the Contains Media Of Type option and choose the media type you want to store in the media pool from the drop-down list box.

6. Select the Draw Media From Free Media Pool check box if you want the media pool to take media from the free media pool when no media are available in this media pool. This is generally a smart move, as it reduces the need to manually manage the media.

7. Select the Return Media To Free Media Pool check box if you want the media pool to return media to the free media pool when the media is no longer needed. This is also usually a good idea.

8. To limit the number of times the media pool draws media from the free media pool, select the Limit Reallocations check box and enter the number of reallocations you want to allow.

9. To change the permissions for the media pool, click the Security tab and assign the appropriate access permissions for the media pool.

Managing Physical Media

Physical media—tapes or disks—are the reason storage libraries and media pools exist. Actually dealing with the physical media is pretty easy, and the kind of tasks involved include inserting and ejecting media, mounting and dismounting media, enabling and disabling media, and moving media between media pools. Simple stuff, but we'll quickly walk you through it anyway.

Injecting and Ejecting Media   Injecting (inserting) and ejecting media in stand-alone drives is pretty simple: to inject, place the media in the drive; to eject, press the eject button. You don't really require any help with that. However, robotic storage libraries can be a little more complex, and you should normally use Removable Storage to handle injecting and ejecting media into these libraries rather than using only the device's physical buttons or ports. To inject or eject media from a storage library, follow these steps:

1. To inject a tape or disk into the storage library, right-click the library and choose Inject from the shortcut menu. Follow the instructions presented by the Media Inject Wizard.

2. To eject a tape or disk from the storage library, expand the Physical Locations folder and then open the storage library containing the media you want to eject.

3. Double-click the media icon in the console tree to display all media inserted in the library.

4. Right-click the media you want to eject, and then choose Eject from the shortcut menu.

5. Follow the instructions in the Media Eject Wizard to eject the media.

Mounting and Dismounting Media When you insert a piece of media in a library, the media is in the Idle state and can't be immediately accessed by an application. To be used, the media must first be mounted, after which it will be in the Loaded state. Most applications will automatically mount the media you request; however, you can also mount the media yourself. To do so, right-click the media you want to mount and choose Mount from the shortcut menu.

To eject a piece of media, first the media must be idle. Normally if an application is finished accessing the media, the media will return to the Idle state; however, if the media is currently in the Loaded state and you need to eject the media immediately, you need to manually dismount the media before you eject it. To dismount the media, right-click the media you want to dismount and then choose Dismount from the shortcut menu.

Disabling Media If you want to make a particular piece of media unavailable for use, you might consider ejecting it and storing it somewhere. However, if you want to keep the media in the library but disable it, use the following steps:

1. Right-click the media in Removable Storage and choose Properties from the shortcut menu.

2. Clear the Enable Media check box on the General tab. Click OK.

Using the Work Queue

The work queue is a list of all activities that have been performed in Removable Storage and acts in much the same way as the Windows 2000 event log does, although you can actually have some control by using the work queue, in the case of events that are still pending.

To view the work queue or the operator requests list, select the appropriate list from the console tree in the Removable Storage MMC snap-in. The work queue lists all actions performed or pending in Removable Storage, along with any other information about the action. To perform a task using the work queue, follow these steps:

1. To view any additional information about an action, such as additional error messages on failed actions, right-click the action and choose Properties from the shortcut menu.

2. To cancel a pending action, right-click the action and choose Cancel Action from the shortcut menu.

3. To adjust the priority of a pending action, right-click the pending action and choose Reorder. Removable Storage displays the Change Mount Order dialog box, shown in Figure 16-12.

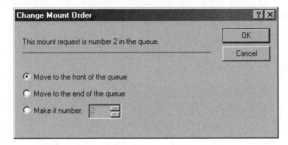

Figure 16-12. *The Change Mount Order dialog box.*

4. To move the request to the beginning of the queue, select the Move To The Front Of The Queue option.

5. To move the request to the end of the queue, select the Move To The End Of The Queue option.

6. To specify exactly which place in the queue the request should be, select the Make It Number option and select the number in the queue that you want the request to be.

Working with Operator Requests

Operator requests occur when an action requires direct operator interventions, such as the insertion of offline media or the need for a new cleaning cartridge.

Usually when an operator request occurs, the system displays a message indicating that a specific action is required. Perform the action and click OK to resolve the request. If you want to refuse the request or manually mark the request as completed, follow these steps:

1. Select Operator Requests in the Removable Storage console tree.

2. Right-click the pending operation, and choose Refuse from the shortcut menu to cancel the request, or choose Complete from the shortcut menu after fulfilling the request, as shown in Figure 16-13.

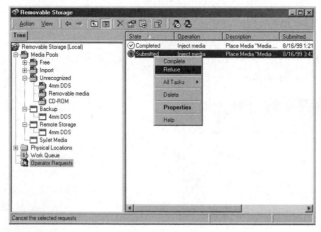

Figure 16-13. *The operator requests list in the Removable Storage snap-in.*

3. To modify how long Removable Storage keeps old operator requests, right-click Operator Requests in the console tree, choose Properties from the shortcut menu, and then use the Operator Requests Properties dialog box to change these settings.

4. To change how Removable Storage notifies you when an operator request is due, right-click the Removable Storage root in the console tree, choose Properties from the shortcut menu, and then set the values for the Send Operator Requests To Messenger Service and the Tray Icon For Pending Operator Requests check boxes as desired.

Remote Storage

While hard disk prices have dropped dramatically and capacities have improved tremendously, you can never have too much hard disk space. Because of this insatiable need for disk space, Windows 2000 includes a hierarchical storage management utility from Seagate Software that lets servers capitalize on a resource several times cheaper than hard disk space: tapes. This utility, called Remote Storage, takes advantage of the Windows 2000 built-in from-the-ground-up support for hierarchical storage utilities and enables Windows 2000 to extend an NTFS volume almost infinitely. Remote Storage does this by transparently migrating infrequently used files to tape while keeping them easily accessible.

Users see migrated files as if they were still stored on the disk instead of on tape. Even when users access migrated files, the only noticeable differences are a small dialog box informing them that the file is being recalled from tape and a somewhat longer file load time. In addition, except for the setup and configuration of Remote Storage, this feature comes with little or no burden to administrators. Remote Storage performs all migration and recovery from tape automatically (unless the required media is offline, in which case Removable Storage will place a request for an operator).

To help you capitalize on this new lease on a hard disk's life, the following sections examine key concepts and requirements of Remote Storage, its setup and configuration, and its data recovery and protection.

Concepts and System Requirements

You probably have some questions about the purpose of Remote Storage: How does it interact with other programs such as the backup program and antivirus program? And what kind of hardware and software do you need to make it work? We had the same questions when we first encountered Remote Storage, so we provide you with some background here that you can use to answer those nagging questions.

Purpose

Remote Storage is also known as Hierarchical Storage Management because it allows for two tiers of data storage. The first tier, local storage, is the standard hard disk or removable disk drive hosting an NTFS volume (such as an Iomega Jaz drive). The second tier, provided by Remote Storage and aptly referred to as the remote storage tier, is the tape drive or robotic tape library. Data is initially stored in local storage, and once the data has *settled down* (has not been accessed within a specified period of time), it is copied or migrated to remote storage but also left intact, or cached, in local storage for quick access. (Note that Remote Storage only manages files physically on a volume—it doesn't follow Dfs links.) Finally, as local storage fills up and it becomes necessary to free up space for additional data, the files that have settled down and been migrated to remote storage are converted to placeholders or links, freeing up the space they used to consume.

> **Note** Remote Storage will probably be renamed Hierarchical Storage, which just adds confusion to the alphabet soup that also includes Removable Storage. To try to clear this up, remember that Remote Storage *is* the hierarchical storage manager; Microsoft just decided to call it Remote Storage. Also, Remote Storage uses Removable Storage to handle media. Don't fret too much about this— Microsoft gets them mixed up too.

Files that have been moved to remote storage and are no longer cached locally still appear to be resident in local storage (Figure 16-14). These placeholders look and act the same as normal locally stored files, except for a couple small differences.

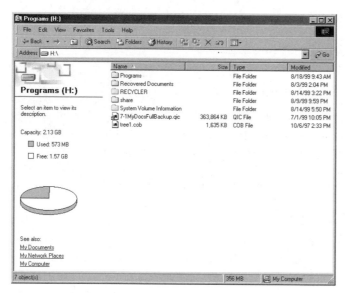

Figure 16-14. *Windows Explorer in Details view.*

The first difference is that the icon for the file that was moved to remote storage has a small clock face on it to indicate that to open the file, a user will have to wait while Windows 2000 retrieves the file from remote storage (Figure 16-15).

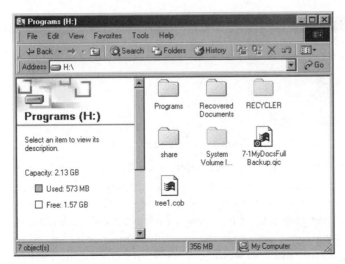

Figure 16-15. *Windows Explorer in Large Icon view displaying a remote storage placeholder.*

The second difference is that, although Windows Explorer shows remote files using the same amount of disk space as when the files were stored locally, and it doesn't change how disk quotas work (remote files count against a disk quota the same as local files do), Windows Explorer does subtract remote files from the total space used on a disk estimate. In other words, Windows 2000 treats remote files exactly the same as local files except when calculating the amount of free space on a disk, at which point Windows 2000 recognizes that remotely stored files take up no local disk space. Windows Explorer also adds a Remote Storage tab to the Properties dialog box of managed volumes, allowing administrators to view and change the settings on managed volumes directly from within Windows Explorer.

When a user accesses a remotely stored file, the Recalling From Remote Storage dialog box appears, explaining that Windows is recalling the file from Remote Storage (Figure 16-16). If a user doesn't want to wait for the file, he or she can click Cancel and leave the file in remote storage. Otherwise, the file is restored into local storage and its last-accessed-date timestamp is reset, preventing it from migrating to remote storage until the file has settled down.

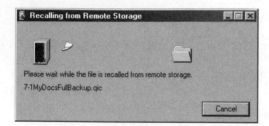

Figure 16-16. *The Recalling From Remote Storage dialog box.*

Copy and move operations performed on placeholders act a little differently than normal file copy and move operations. Placeholders that are renamed or moved to a different location on the same volume don't need to be recalled from remote storage. However, when a user copies the file, Remote Storage recalls the file and then copies it to the new location. (Note that the new file is in no way linked to the old file in remote storage, just like you would expect from a copied file.) When a user moves a placeholder to a different volume, Remote Storage recalls the file, copies it to its new location, and then deletes the original file.

Program Compatibility

Compatibility with Windows 2000 programs is an important Remote Storage issue. While Remote Storage is thoroughly integrated into the operating system, some programs might not behave optimally unless they are specifically made aware of Remote Storage. Two examples are backup programs and antivirus programs.

Backup programs that aren't Remote Storage aware can back up all locally stored data and data links, but they have no way of backing up data that has been moved to remote storage (except by restoring the remotely stored files, rendering Remote Storage useless). If a backup program is Remote Storage aware (such as the Windows 2000 Backup program), you might have the option to retrieve files from remote storage and back them up along with all locally stored data, and then return the files to remote storage when finished.

Many antivirus, backup, search, and indexing programs that aren't Remote Storage aware have a nasty tendency to access every file they check, thereby resetting Remote Storage usage data, as well as pulling files from remote storage in order to check them for viruses. Remote Storage–aware programs don't have this liability.

Real World **Find Fast**

Microsoft Office 97 causes all Word documents, PowerPoint documents, and HTML files in remote storage to be recalled at the end of Office 97 installation. You can stop this by terminating the Findfast.exe process. You should turn FindFast off by using the FindFast Control Panel tool and by making sure that the Findfast.exe shortcut isn't in the Startup folder on the Start menu. Office 95 and Office 97 might also recall files from remote storage when you use the Edit menu's Find command.

Fortunately, Remote Storage has a workaround for programs that aren't Remote Storage aware. Remote Storage minimizes the effects of programs that aren't Remote Storage compatible by limiting the number of successive recalls from remote storage that it allows. If a program recalls a file from remote storage and requests that another file be recalled within 10 seconds of the last file being recalled, Remote Storage counts this. When the count reaches a configurable limit (the default is 60), Remote Storage prohibits further recalls during that session. Setting a limit doesn't usually bother normal users but can prevent an antivirus program that isn't Remote Storage aware from restoring all remote storage files.

Data Safety

You're probably wondering how to ensure that your data is adequately backed up when working with Remote Storage. If a file has been moved to tape, what happens if the tape gets damaged or lost? And what happens if the link to the file in local storage is lost? You can assuage your fears of data loss in several ways. The first way you're already familiar with—frequent and thorough backups.

Most companies will combine making regular backups of the local storage systems with creating copies of Remote Storage's media, the second way of protecting data. Thus, every time you back up the local storage, you make a copy of the Remote Storage media and keep that with the local storage backup. This step ensures that the entire storage system is backed up: both the local storage tier and the remote storage tier. You can also protect the data by using a Remote Storage–compatible backup program to back up data in remote storage along with the local storage backup. The recovery process is the same as any other type of backup.

To summarize, if you want to thoroughly protect the data and you have the ability to copy the Remote Storage media, use a strategy similar to the following one. (For more specific information, see the "Data Recovery and Protection" section later in this chapter.)

- Back up the local data regularly.
- Every time you perform a full backup, create a copy of the associated Remote Storage media and keep that copy with the full backup.
- Make more than one copy (up to three) of the Remote Storage media master, and regularly synchronize these copies with the media master.
- Consider backing up data in remote storage at the same time as you back up local storage. It might take longer and use more media, but it offers greater data protection and flexibility in case of a disaster.

System Requirements

Remote Storage isn't particularly resource intensive, and as such, it works well on almost any system that meets the recommended system configuration for Windows 2000 Server. Note that you can't run Remote Storage on a Windows 2000 Professional machine, and Remote Storage can manage volumes formatted only with NTFS 5.

However, Remote Storage is somewhat fussy about the removable storage subsystem you use. The drive needs to be recognized by Removable Storage; you should use hardware only in the Hardware Compatibility List. Additionally, at shipping, Remote Storage supports only SCSI 4 mm, 8 mm, and DLT tape libraries that Removable Storage recognizes. Remote Storage doesn't support optical drives, QIC tape libraries, or any type of removable disk drive (Jaz, Zip, and so on). Some of these restrictions might change as more drivers are released for Windows 2000, but some devices such as QIC tapes and Jaz drives just aren't meant for Remote Storage, so forget about them. If you're thinking about QIC tapes, you probably don't need Remote Storage—you need another hard disk.

Caution Microsoft recommends that you avoid using Remote Storage with Exabyte 8200 tape libraries.

Client systems using Windows File Manager can't access files managed by Remote Storage, which precludes Windows 3.x clients from accessing these files. Also, Windows 95 users should refrain from using File Manager if they want to access Remote Storage files.

Setup and Configuration

The following sections explain how to set up Remote Storage on the system, as well as how to configure it optimally for your needs and make sure that your data is appropriately protected from disaster.

> **Note**   If you launch Remote Storage and walk through the Remote Storage Setup Wizard before you configure the system with a supported storage library, you will need to uninstall and reinstall Remote Storage in order to use it, since Remote Storage won't detect added devices after installation.

Setting Up Remote Storage

Remote Storage is easy to set up. Just make sure that the storage library you want to use with Remote Storage is connected and configured, and then follow these steps:

1. Open the Add/Remove Programs tool from the Control Panel.
2. Click Add/Remove Windows Components in the left pane.
3. Select the Remote Storage check box, if it isn't already selected, and click Next.
4. Restart the computer.
5. Launch Remote Storage from the Administrative Tools folder on the Start menu. The Remote Storage Setup Wizard appears. Click Next. The wizard detects any compatible storage devices and checks the security settings.
6. On the next screen, shown in Figure 16-17, select the volumes with which you want to use Remote Storage (only NTFS volumes appear), and then click Next.
7. In the Desired Free Space box, enter the minimum amount of free space you want available on the managed volumes, as shown in Figure 16-18.
8. In the Larger Than box, enter the size of the smallest files you want Remote Storage to migrate to tape if more disk space is needed.

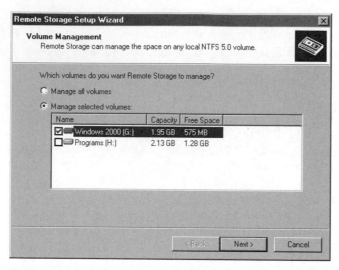

Figure 16-17. *The Volume Management screen of the Remote Storage Setup Wizard.*

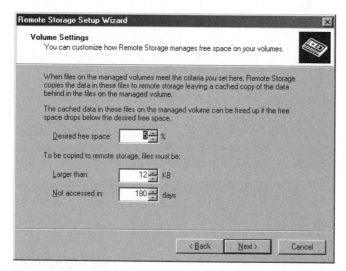

Figure 16-18. *The Volume Settings screen of the Remote Storage Setup Wizard.*

9. In the Not Accessed In box, enter the number of days that need to have passed since the file was last accessed in order for the file to be eligible for migration to tape. Then click Next.

10. Select the media you want Remote Storage to use from the Media Types drop-down list box (only detected, supported media are listed). Click Next.

11. Click Change Schedule to change when Remote Storage copies files to tape, or click Next to continue.

12. Review the settings you entered, and then click Finish to complete Remote Storage setup.

Setting Up Additional Volumes with Remote Storage

If you want to set up additional storage volumes on the system for use with Remote Storage after you've already completed the initial setup, you can use the Add Volume Management Wizard. To do so, follow these steps:

1. Launch the Remote Storage MMC snap-in from the Administrative Tools folder on the Start menu, or enter *%SystemRoot%\System32\ RsAdmin.msc* into the Run dialog box or at a command prompt.

2. Select the Managed Volumes folder in the console tree.

3. Click the New Managed Volume(s) toolbar button to launch the Add Volume Management Wizard, and then click Next on the first screen.

4. Select the check box next to the NTFS 5 volume you want, or choose the Manage All Volumes option to instruct Remote Storage to manage all eligible volumes (Figure 16-19). Then click Next.

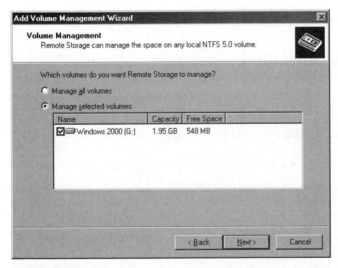

Figure 16-19. *The Volume Management screen of the Add Volume Management Wizard.*

5. In the Desired Free Space box, enter the amount of free space you want to have on the volume, as a percentage of total space.

6. Enter the minimum file size you want Remote Storage to migrate to tape in the Larger Than box. Note that migrating files smaller than 12 KB generally doesn't make sense since they don't take up much room, but you can change this setting as needed.

7. In the Not Accessed In box, enter the number of days that must elapse since a file was last accessed before the file is eligible for migration to remote storage. Then click Next. Keep in mind that setting this number too high will limit the amount of disk space that Remote Storage can free up, but setting it too low will cause an unnecessary amount of recall from tape.

8. Review the settings on the final wizard screen, and then click Finish.

Changing Volume Settings

Remote Storage uses a set of rules to govern which files are eligible for migration to remote storage. You set these rules initially when you set up a storage volume on the computer for Remote Storage to manage, using either the Remote Storage Setup Wizard or the Add Volume Management Wizard. However, you might want to change these settings later or add exclusions such that certain file types never get migrated to tape. To do this, follow these steps:

1. Launch the Remote Storage MMC snap-in from the Administrative Tools folder on the Start menu.

2. Select the Managed Volumes folder in the console tree, right-click the volume you want to configure, and choose Settings from the shortcut menu.

3. In the Desired Free Space box, enter the amount of free space you want to have on the volume, as a percentage of total space.

 Tip You can also change a managed volume's settings by right-clicking the volume in Windows Explorer, choosing Properties from the shortcut menu, and then clicking the Remote Storage tab. However, you can't change inclusion and exclusion rules from here.

4. Enter the minimum file size you want Remote Storage to migrate to tape in the Larger Than box. Most users will find that if anything, they'll want to increase this file size, although if you have a lot of seldom-accessed smaller files, you could consider lowering this setting also.

5. In the Not Accessed In box, enter the number of days that must elapse since a file was last accessed before the file is eligible for migration to remote storage. Keep in mind that setting this number too high will limit the amount of disk space that Remote Storage can free up, but setting it too low will cause an unnecessary amount of recall from tape.

6. Click the Include/Exclude Rules tab to create or modify rules that specify file types to exclude from Remote Storage, as shown in Figure 16-20.

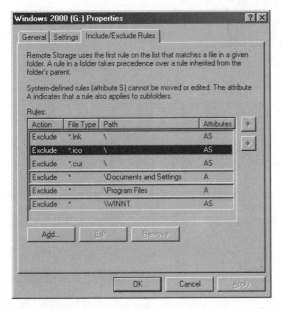

Figure 16-20. *The Include/Exclude Rules tab of a managed volume's Properties dialog box.*

7. Select a rule that you want to modify (some rules can't be changed), and then click Edit to modify the rule or Remove to delete it.

8. To add a new rule, click Add to display the Edit Include/Exclude Rule dialog box, shown in Figure 16-21.

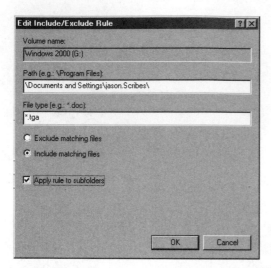

Figure 16-21. *The Edit Include/Exclude Rule dialog box.*

9. Enter the folder path you want to apply the rule to in the Path box, or enter a backslash to apply the rule to the entire volume.

10. In the File Type box, enter the type of file that you want to include or exclude from Remote Storage.

11. Select Exclude Matching Files if you want to exclude files matching the criteria from Remote Storage.

12. Select Include Matching Files if you want to explicitly allow Remote Storage to manage files matching the criteria. This is useful if you want to make an exception to an exclude rule for only a certain folder.

13. Select the Apply Rule To Subfolders check box if you want Remote Storage to apply the rule to all subfolders of the folder listed in the Path box.

Turning Off Remote Storage for a Managed Volume

If you plan to uninstall Remote Storage, you should discontinue managing all of the volumes first so that you can recall the files in remote storage. This step is important because if you don't, you might lose the ability to access files stored in remote storage.

You might also want to do this if you plan to perform a complete (clean) reinstallation of Windows 2000. Recalling the data allows you to either leave the data intact on the drive while you reinstall Windows, or back up the data using a backup program that isn't Remote Storage–aware. (If you want to reformat the drive, you can back up the data and then restore it once you're finished.) If you don't recall the data or back up all data (including data in remote storage) before doing a clean reinstall of Windows 2000, you're left performing a somewhat complicated Remote Storage recovery procedure. See the "Data Recovery and Protection" section later in this chapter for more information.

Another case in which you might choose to discontinue Remote Storage's management of a volume is when the media you're using for the volume fills up and you don't want the remote storage database to span multiple tapes. In this instance, you can discontinue Remote Storage's management of the volume, which tells Remote Storage to stop adding files to remote storage but to not recall the files already in remote storage.

Whatever the reason for ending Remote Storage's management of a volume on the system, you can use the Remove Volume Management Wizard to remove a managed volume from Remote Storage:

1. Launch the Remote Storage MMC snap-in from the Administrative Tools folder on the Start menu.

2. Click Managed Volumes in the console tree.

3. Right-click the volume you want to remove from Remote Storage and then choose Remove from the shortcut menu. Click Next when the Remove Volume Management Wizard opens.

4. To recall all files from remote storage and place them back on the managed volume so that Remote Storage is no longer used at all on this volume, select the Recall Copied Files From Remote Storage option, shown in Figure 16-22. Note that the managed volume needs to have enough free disk space to hold all recalled files.

5. To stop Remote Storage from adding additional files to remote storage while letting it continue to manage the files currently in remote storage, select the Maintain Copied Files In Remote Storage option, and then click Next.

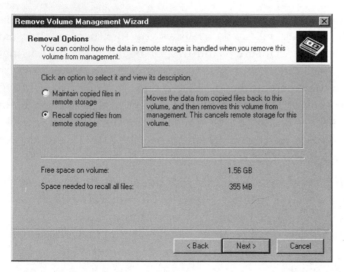

Figure 16-22. *The Removal Options screen of the Remove Volume Management Wizard.*

6. Click Yes in the dialog box that opens.

7. Review the settings and then click Finish to implement them.

Performing Tasks Manually

Remote Storage is configured to perform almost all operations automatically, using the Windows 2000 Scheduled Tasks folder. However, sometimes you might need to immediately copy all eligible files to remote storage, create additional free space on a managed volume, or validate all placeholders. To perform these tasks, follow these steps:

1. Launch the Remote Storage MMC snap-in from the Administrative Tools folder on the Start menu.

2. Click Managed Volumes in the console tree.

3. Right-click the volume you want to perform a task on, choose All Tasks from the shortcut menu, and then choose the appropriate task from the submenu. See Table 16-5 for a description of the tasks you can perform.

4. Click OK in the dialog box that opens.

Table 16-5.   Tasks that you can perform manually

Task	Description
Copy files to remote storage	Immediately copies all eligible files on the managed volume to remote storage.
Validate files	Verifies that all placeholders and locally cached files are still linked to valid data in remote storage, and updates volume statistics.
Create free space	Removes all cached data from files that have already been migrated to remote storage. This creates free space only if there is data cached locally.

Viewing Remote Storage Tasks

Remote Storage places all tasks in the Scheduled Tasks folder—both tasks that Remote Storage performs automatically as well as tasks that you perform manually. To view the tasks or modify when (or whether) they are performed, follow these steps:

1. Open the Scheduled Tasks folder by opening the Start menu and choosing Programs, Accessories, System Tools (Figure 16-23).

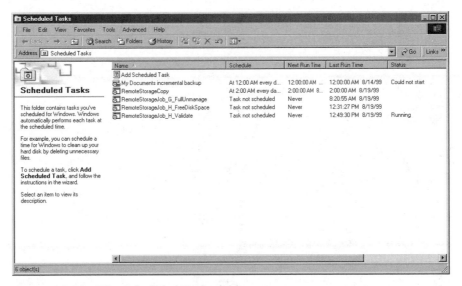

Figure 16-23. *The Scheduled Tasks folder.*

2. To perform a scheduled task immediately, right-click the task and choose Run from the shortcut menu.

3. To cancel a currently running task, right-click the task and choose End Task from the shortcut menu.

4. To view the properties of the task (perhaps to change the schedule), right-click the task and choose Properties from the shortcut menu.

Changing Task Schedules

To change the schedule Remote Storage uses to copy files to remote storage, or to validate placeholders and cached files or create free disk space, follow these steps:

1. To change the Remote Storage file copy schedule, right-click the Remote Storage root in the Remote Storage console tree and choose Change Schedule from the shortcut menu.

2. Click the Change Schedule button.

3. Use the dialog box provided to set up the schedule, shown in Figure 16-24.

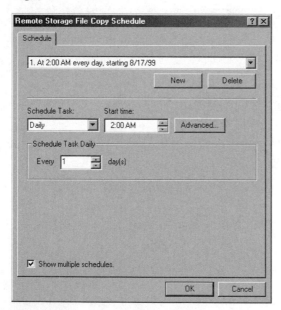

Figure 16-24. *The Remote Storage File Copy Schedule dialog box.*

4. To make multiple schedules, select the Show Multiple Schedules check box and use the New and Delete buttons to add or remove schedules.

5. To modify advanced scheduling information, click the Advanced button.

6. To modify the schedules for other Remote Storage tasks, open the Scheduled Tasks folder by opening the Start menu and choosing Programs, Accessories, and then System Tools.

7. Right-click the task and choose Properties from the shortcut menu.

8. Click the Schedule tab and then modify the scheduling information as described in steps 4 and 5.

Setting Recall Limits

As described in the "Program Compatibility" section earlier in this chapter, the Remote Storage recall limit feature can come in handy. Remember, you should use the recall limit feature because programs that aren't Remote Storage compatible such as backup, antivirus, and search programs have an annoying knack for pulling all the data out of remote storage, making Remote Storage fairly useless. When you set a recall limit, also known as a runaway recall limit because it limits only recalls that take place within 10 seconds of the last recall, you prevent these automatic assaults on the remote storage by stopping runaway recalls from remote storage. This usually doesn't affect end users because most users aren't that fast, unless they're performing a mass copy operation. To configure the recall limit, follow these steps:

1. Right-click the Remote Storage root in the Remote Storage console tree and choose Properties from the shortcut menu.

2. Click the Recall Limit tab, shown in Figure 16-25.

3. In the box provided, enter the number of successive recalls that take place within 10 seconds of the last recall that you want to allow before preventing further recalls. If the users frequently perform mass copy operations and you use Remote Storage–aware applications, you might want to set this limit higher; otherwise, leave it alone or reduce it as needed.

4. If you want to exempt users with administrative privileges from this limit, select the Exempt Administrators From This Limit check box.

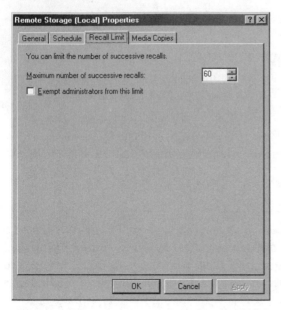

Figure 16-25. *The Recall Limit tab of the Remote Storage (Local) Properties dialog box.*

Caution Selecting the Exempt Administrators From This Limit check box will allow noncompatible applications run by an administrator to potentially recall all files from remote storage if the administrator doesn't explicitly kill the process recalling the data.

Data Recovery and Protection

You might think that because data stored remotely is on tape, it's safe. Perhaps in some ways it is safer than when it's located on a local hard disk, but data protection is even more important for remotely stored data because of the inability of tape devices to have fault tolerance such as mirrored drives. Also, because the technology is new, an administrator is more likely to make an error that prevents data recovery from remote storage. Therefore, you must learn about and implement a good data protection plan.

Since even the best data protection plans can't always prevent a disaster, you must also know how to recover data if a problem occurs. The following sections will teach you how to protect and recover data with Remote Storage.

Understanding Data Protection Strategies

The strategy you use to protect the remotely stored data will vary somewhat depending on your ability to create copies of the Remote Storage media. (You need two drives of the same media type in order to do this.)

> **Tip** Most of you don't need to be told to back up Windows 2000 itself—you know that backing up your operating system is as important as backing up your data. However, if you're one of those rare administrators who doesn't already do this, you should know that the entire Remote Storage database is stored in only two places: the %SystemRoot%\System32\RemoteStorage folder and on each media master tape. If the local folder is deleted, you're stuck restoring from your Remote Storage tapes—a complicated procedure (described in Knowledge Base article Q235469). We highly recommend that you back up your entire system on all essential servers.

Single Drive Strategies   If you're using only a single tape drive with Remote Storage, we recommend that you back up the local files according to your preexisting backup plan. For example, you might perform an incremental backup every night and a full backup every weekend. For full backups, make sure that you instruct the backup program to back up migrated Remote Storage data, or else you won't have any backup of data in remote storage. Note that this almost certainly means backing up to a different drive than the one holding the Remote Storage media. If you don't have another backup device, consider purchasing a duplicate of the Remote Storage device and follow the advice in the next section, "Multiple Drive Strategies"—you'll be better off in the end.

You probably don't need to back up migrated files on the differential or incremental backup schedule because files that are added to remote storage probably haven't changed since the last full backup. You can restore these files to local storage from the last full backup. If the files have changed since the last full backup *and* have been migrated to remote storage and had their local cache removed (if you have a long backup schedule or a short migration schedule and a full volume), you can restore the files from a recent differential or incremental backup. Keep in mind, of course, that the longer you go between full backups, the more incremental patches you'll have to apply if you need to restore from backup (a good reason to use differential backups instead), or the more data that is lost if you don't frequently perform incremental backups. See Chapter 34, "Using Backup," for more information on using the Windows 2000 built-in backup utility.

Tip The backup schedule that is best varies from situation to situation. Always closely evaluate the importance of the data. The more important the data, the more stringent the backup strategy and fault tolerance plans need to be.

In addition to the regular backup schedule, we recommend that you frequently verify the remote storage placeholders and cached files to make sure that they are still linked to valid data in remote storage. Note that Remote Storage automatically creates an appropriate validation schedule when you install it.

Multiple Drive Strategies If you have multiple drives of the same media type that you can use to make copies of the Remote Storage media, you have a little more flexibility for data protection than you would with a single drive. Although the backbone of the data protection plan will still rest on a good backup plan, you can supplement this by creating copies of the remote storage media and frequently synchronizing the copies.

Back up the local files according to your preexisting backup plan. For full backups, you can choose to instruct the backup program to back up migrated Remote Storage data. This provides some extra insurance by eliminating the need to deal with Remote Storage when recovering; instead, you simply restore all data to local storage and don't even worry about Remote Storage. This is a good idea if you have the facilities (and time) to do it. Otherwise, back up only local storage, according to the normal backup schedule.

Caution You can't restore Remote Storage files to another computer. If you want to be able to restore data to another computer, you must use backups that also backed up migrated remote storage files.

In addition to your backup schedule, you should make one to three copies of the *media master* (the media that holds the remote storage data), and routinely synchronize them. If the media master fails, you can recreate it from one of the copies. If you don't back up the migrated remote storage files during the full backups, make sure that you synchronize a media copy and keep it with your full backup. This ensures that the full backup has all data backed up.

In addition to the regular backup schedule, you should frequently verify the remote storage placeholders and cached files to make sure that they are still linked to valid data in remote storage. Remote Storage automatically creates a validation schedule when you install it, and this is usually fine for most purposes. Just make sure that it covers all the volumes Remote Storage manages.

Working with Media Copies

Since you can't create fault-tolerant arrays of remote storage devices, Microsoft provides the ability to create copies of Remote Storage media so that some level of redundancy exists for remotely stored data. The next several sections show you how to work with media copies: how to specify the number you want, how to delete them, how to synchronize them, and how to recreate a failed media master from a media copy.

Tip Place new media in the free media pool instead of manually in the Remote Storage pool. Remote Storage will automatically take and appropriately format media from the free media pool when necessary.

Changing the Number of Media Copies You don't explicitly create media copies for Remote Storage; instead, you specify how many you want and Remote Storage automatically goes about creating them. When one copy is finished, Remote Storage will begin creating the next copy, provided enough media is available in the Remote Storage application pool or free media pool. Each group of media copies is called a *media copy set* and includes one copy of each of the media masters. (It's possible to have more than one media master when the amount of data in remote storage is too big to fit on one tape.) To specify the number of media copy sets you want, follow these steps:

1. Right-click the Remote Storage root in the Remote Storage console tree and choose Properties from the shortcut menu.

2. Click the Media Copies tab, and then specify the number of media copy sets you want to create for each media master set (up to three maximum).

Tip If you decide that you don't need as many media copy sets as you originally thought, you can decrease the number of sets that Remote Storage will display and access, as just described. However, note that doing so does *not* deallocate any media. If you want to free up media, you need to delete the media copies, as described in the next section.

Deleting and Checking the Status of Media Copies If you no longer need a media copy or want to check to see whether the media copy is functioning well (that is, to see if you have a bad tape), you should delete or check the media copies. Don't just reduce the number of copies Remote Storage supports. To delete or check on the status of a media copy, follow these steps:

1. Select the Media folder in the Remote Storage console tree.

2. Right-click the media master that is associated with the media copy you want to delete or check, and then choose Media Copies from the shortcut menu.

3. View the status information of the media copies, and then click the appropriate Delete Copy button for any media copies you want to delete.

Synchronizing Media Copies   Synchronizing media copies is so easy it's ridiculous. Just open the Remote Storage MMC snap-in, right-click Media in the console tree, and then choose Synchronize Media Copies from the shortcut menu. The Media Synchronization Wizard appears and walks you through the rest of the process. Piece of cake.

> **Planning**   You can't recall or copy data to remote storage while synchronizing media copies. Therefore, you might want to synchronize the media copies after hours.

Recreating a Media Master in Case of Disaster   If the media master is damaged or lost, you can recreate it from a recently synchronized media copy. Note that you'll lose all data that has been migrated to remote storage since the last time you synchronized the media copy unless the data's local cache hasn't been erased yet. So follow these steps only if you're experiencing errors:

1. Make sure that you have sufficient media available in the remote storage pool or free media pool, and then open the Media folder in the Remote Storage console tree.

2. Right-click the most recently synchronized media copy for the media master that you want to recreate, and then choose Media Copies from the shortcut menu.

3. Click the Recovery tab and click Re-create Master.

Recovering from Disaster   Disasters happen. Servers go down. Drives fail. The cable goes out during the Super Bowl. These are facts. However, if you're prepared ahead of time, you can reduce the negative impact of disaster when it strikes.

A few different types of disaster can occur with Remote Storage, and a few ways exist to recover from them. If the hard disk fails, restore locally stored files from the religiously kept backups, but be careful not to perform a Remote Storage validation operation until all incremental or differential backups are restored. As long as the Remote Storage database stored in the %SystemRoot%\System32\ RemoteStorage folder isn't affected, you don't need to do anything else other than perform a validation operation to clean up any invalid placeholders.

If the hard disk storing Windows 2000 fails, restore the system from backup. The system should function normally; however, you might see the following error when recalling a file from remote storage:

Path\filename.doc. The file can not be accessed by the system.

If you experience this error, see Knowledge Base article Q235469 and perform the Restore A Damaged RSS Database procedure.

If you need to perform a clean reinstall of Windows 2000, the best approach is to first recall all data from remote storage. (Refer back to the "Turning Off Remote Storage for a Managed Volume" section earlier in this chapter.) However, if a disaster occurs that precludes you from recalling the data and you can't restore the system from backup, you need to perform a special procedure to restore the Remote Storage database from the Remote Storage media after reinstalling Windows 2000. To see how to perform this procedure, refer to Knowledge Base article Q235469. If you see any of the following error messages when accessing Removable Storage, refer to Knowledge Base article Q235032:

- Backup can't connect to Removable Storage. This service is required for use of tape drives and other backup devices.
- REMOVABLE STORAGE: Server execution failed.
- The removable storage database failed to load. Check the event log.

Shared Folders

After examining the Distributed file system, Removable Storage, and Remote Storage, discussing sharing folders on the network or the Internet sounds a bit commonplace. Nevertheless, sharing folders is important and we're going to tell you how to do it anyway. So there.

Using the Shared Folders Snap-in

You can administer shared folders in Windows 2000 in two ways. You can right-click a shared folder in Windows Explorer and choose Sharing from the shortcut menu, or you can use the Shared Folders MMC snap-in. The Shared Folders MMC snap-in provides a way of viewing all of the file shares at once, along with the current connections and open files. Windows Explorer doesn't. Therefore, we're going to talk about the Shared Folders MMC snap-in now, and we'll talk about Windows Explorer later, in the "Configuring Web Shares" section.

To use the superior Shared Folders tool, follow these steps:

1. Open the Computer Management MMC snap-in from the Administrative Tools folder on the Start menu, or enter *%SystemRoot%\System32\ Compmgmt.msc* in the Run dialog box or at a command prompt.

2. Expand the Shared Folders folder in the console tree (Figure 16-26).

3. Use the Shares, Sessions, and Open Files folders to view the current file shares on the system you're managing and to see how much activity the shares are getting.

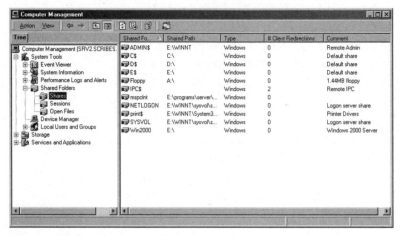

Figure 16-26. *The Shared Folders tool in the Computer Management console.*

Setting Up Shared Folders

Windows 2000 makes it easy to share a folder or volume on the system with other users on the corporate network. Just follow these steps:

1. In the Computer Management console, open the Shared Folders folder in the console tree.

2. Right-click the Shares folder and choose New File Share from the shortcut menu.

3. In the Create Shared Folder dialog box shown in Figure 16-27, click the Browse button to locate or create the folder you want to share.

4. Enter the name you want to give the file share. This name should ideally be DNS and NetBIOS compatible for the best interoperability with downlevel and non-Microsoft clients.

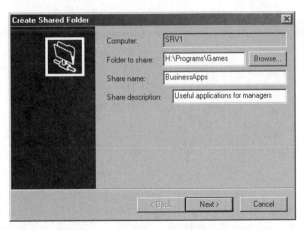

Figure 16-27. *The Create Shared Folder dialog box.*

5. Enter a description for the shared folder in the Share Description box, and then click Next.

6. Optionally, specify the Share Level permissions for the folder, and then click Finish.

Real World   Setting Permissions

We strongly recommend that you implement NTFS file-level permissions *instead* of share-level permissions. Using share-level permissions alone isn't secure enough in most instances, and using both introduces an unacceptable level of complexity.

However, there are some exceptions to this rule; for example, you might want to permit all users to access a volume in a certain subfolder but allow only a certain group to access the root directory. (Administrators can always access the root folder for a drive by connecting to the drive's hidden administrative share, for example, C$.) In this instance, you could create two file shares: one at the subfolder level with no share-level security and one at the root-folder level with share-level security to allow only the specified group access.

Somewhat more useful is the ability to hide file shares by adding the dollar sign ($) character to the end of the share name. This notation allows any user to connect to the share—provided he or she knows the share name. Once users connect, they're still bound by NTFS security permissions, but this can be handy for storing useful power tools that an administrator might want to be able to access from a user's system and user account. File security isn't really an issue—you just don't want users mucking around with the files.

Ending Folder Sharing

To stop sharing a folder on the network, follow these steps:

1. In the Computer Management console, open the Shared Folders folder in the console tree and then open the Shares subfolder.

2. Right-click the shared folder you want to stop sharing and choose Stop Sharing from the shortcut menu.

3. Click OK.

Disconnecting Users

If you need to disconnect users from the server for some reason—say to close off the server while you update the files—follow these steps:

> **Caution** Be kind to your users and warn them before disconnecting them. Disconnecting a user who is working on a file can cause data loss and resultant ill feelings.

1. Open Shared Folders in the Computer Management console, and then open the Sessions subfolder.

2. Right-click the user you want to disconnect, and choose Close Session from the shortcut menu.

3. To disconnect all sessions, right-click the Sessions folder and choose Disconnect All Sessions from the shortcut menu.

4. To close an open file, click the Open Files folder, right-click the file you want to close, and then choose Close Open File from the shortcut menu.

5. To close all open files, right-click the Open Files folder and choose Disconnect All Open Files from the shortcut menu.

Limiting Simultaneous Connections

You can limit the number of simultaneous user connections you want to allow to a shared folder so that a given shared folder doesn't overburden the server with user connections. To do so, follow these steps:

1. Open Shared Folders in the Computer Management console, and then open the Shares subfolder.

2. Right-click the shared folder you want to limit access to, and then choose Properties from the shortcut menu.

3. To place no limit on the number of connections you allow to the shared folder (other than that set by the number of licenses you have), select the Maximum Allowed option on the General tab, as shown in Figure 16-28.

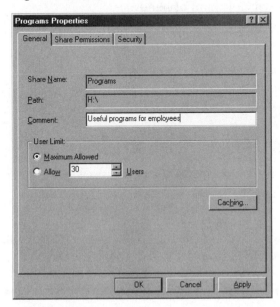

Figure 16-28. *The General tab of a shared folder's Properties dialog box.*

4. To manually limit the number of connections you want to allow to the shared folder, enter the number of connections you want to allow into the Allow box, and then click OK.

Note Windows 2000 Professional supports a maximum of 10 simultaneous users.

Setting Permissions

As mentioned previously, you really shouldn't use share-level permissions in most instances unless you're not using NTFS file-level security. Share-level permissions allow or deny access to a shared folder depending on the user's group membership and the security settings of the file share. File-level security, on the other hand, has a much more granular level of control, providing the ability to grant or deny users and groups the ability to perform a wide range of actions on both folders *and* individual files. Since you would normally use NTFS permissions in a situation where security is important, we generally don't recommend setting share-level permissions. You *can* do it, however, so here's how. (You can also change NTFS permission using this procedure, which is kind of handy.)

1. Open Shared Folders in the Computer Management console, and then open the Shares subfolder.

2. Right-click the shared folder you want to set permissions for, and then choose Properties from the shortcut menu.

3. Click the Share Permissions tab to set share-level permissions for the folder.

4. Click the Security tab to set NTFS file-level permissions for the folder.

See Chapter 9 for more information on setting NTFS permissions.

Configuring Web Shares

If you have IIS installed on the system, you have the ability to share any folder on the system with all Web users on the intranet that can access the server. Typically, Web shares are set up with IIS, but you can also do it quickly using Windows Explorer. Follow these steps:

1. Open Windows Explorer, right-click the folder or drive you want to share on the Web, and choose Properties from the shortcut menu.

2. Click the Web Sharing tab.

3. Choose the Web site you want to share the folder on from the Share On drop-down list box.

4. Select the Share This Folder option, and then in the Edit Alias dialog box that appears (Figure 16-29), enter the folder name you want to use for the share. Note that the alias you enter is appended to the Web site's name: *http://myserver.mycompany.com/alias.*

5. Set the access permissions for the folder by selecting check boxes in the Access Permissions section of the dialog box. (It *is* important to set these access permissions, especially if the server is visible on the Internet.)

6. Use the Application Permissions options to choose which level of permissions you want to grant to applications in this folder, and then click OK.

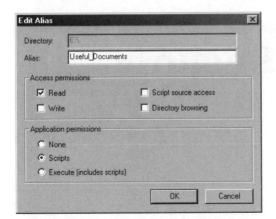

Figure 16-29. *The Edit Alias dialog box.*

Tip For more thorough control over the Web shares, launch the Internet Services console from the Administrative Tools folder on the Start menu. See Chapter 27 for more information.

Summary

Shared Folders provides an easy way to administer and create file shares on the network, intranet, or Internet, while the Distributed file system provides a way of taking all of the disparate file shares and bringing them together into one hierarchical folder structure. Removable Storage provides a much-needed level of abstraction and management for removable storage devices of all types, allowing applications to focus on their core purpose: working with data, not devices and media. Remote Storage builds on this foundation by making it easier for companies to build and maintain immense libraries of archived data, while at the same time making it vastly easier to retrieve archived data as necessary.

Together these technologies make Windows 2000 a more powerful server operating system, although a sometimes complex one to administer. However, this complexity comes from the breadth of features Windows 2000 provides, and Windows 2000 uses these features well by empowering users with simpler and more powerful access to the files they need. Such a complex system requires sophisticated security capabilities. The next chapter covers how to plan a secure operating environment with Windows 2000.

Chapter 17
Planning for Security

Security, in definition and practice, has changed tremendously within just the past few years. Stretching technology to increase the scope and latitude of what we're able to accomplish exposes new and often venomous danger points. Amidst the legions of hackers, spies, terrorists, corporate raiders, professional criminals, and vandals, unprotected networks can fall prey to attack. Today's system administrator has real security threats to address and needs to implement a solution that is both safe and unobtrusive.

Microsoft Windows 2000 includes a bevy of configurable security features and options ranging from an entire public-key infrastructure to a protocol that protects individual packets as they cross the network. But before we dive into implementing the security features of Windows 2000 in Chapters 18 and 19, let's review some of the basic security considerations.

In this chapter, we'll introduce cryptographic smart cards, revisit some of the security components that are integral to earlier Microsoft products, and explore the new security features added to Windows 2000. We'll review the common denominators of security such as authentication, data protection, and access control. We'll tour the Windows 2000 public-key infrastructure and take a detailed look at some of the security-enabled protocols the server uses. We'll introduce virtual private networks (VPNs). Finally, we'll cover the underlying cryptographic application interface in Windows 2000, Microsoft Cryptographic Application Programming Interface (Cryptographic API, or CryptoAPI).

Smart Cards

New to the Windows 2000 authentication suite is the support of cryptographic smart cards. A *smart card* is a tamper-resistant, credit card–like hardware token that can be used to add additional protection to security-enabled protocols and applications. Unlike credit cards, which have magnetic strips on the back, smart cards use metallic contacts as the hardware interface and require a card reader—Plug and Play readers are recommended for use with Windows 2000. Manufacturers typically provide a software application interface, such as Crypto Service Provider, for use with Microsoft CryptoAPI, or they use a PKCS #11 module. Support for Gemplus, GemSAFE, and Schlumberger Cryptoflex smart cards is included with the Windows 2000 installation.

Smart cards provide the strongest form of user authentication in Windows 2000. Either a PIN or a password is required to access the card, which protects the user's credentials from both rogue parties and applications. In addition to storing public-key certificates and private keys, smart cards can also provide on-card functionality, such as digital signing, to ensure that a user's private key is never exposed.

Unlike software private keys, smart cards can also be moved from computer to computer with ease, providing a high portability level of a user's credentials. Included in the list of security features is the ability to block a smart card from the system after a certain number of unsuccessful logon attempts, making dictionary attacks impractical. (A *dictionary attack* is a password attack in which a malicious user sends hundreds or thousands of credentials by using a list of passwords based on common words or phrases.)

Security Basics

The term *security* covers a lot of ground, and Windows 2000 uses a wide range of methods and mechanisms to implement security. But before you can evaluate those mechanisms, you need to know what a good security system is designed to accomplish. For all the protocols, passwords, and secret keys, security revolves around three basic concepts:

- **Authentication**   Confirming the identity of a person or entity before allowing accesses to a resource
- **Data protection**   Ensuring the privacy and integrity of transmitted or stored data
- **Access control**   Restricting the access of data and resources to privileged users

In addition to these three security mainstays, two other security features are discussed in this section: auditing and nonrepudiation.

Authentication

Authentication describes the process in which a person or entity identifies itself to a second party. In general terms, this can mean showing a driver's license to a bank teller or inserting a bank card into an ATM and entering a PIN. In computer language, authentication is a bit more deductive. Unlike the bank teller, who has the luxury of personal contact, nearly all computer-related authentication scenarios are virtual. In a Windows 2000 environment, authentication involves two distinct processes: interactive logon and network authentication.

Interactive logon means logging on to either a domain account or a local computer. Previous versions of Windows were password-based only; Windows 2000 logon now allows smart card authentication. Once the user is logged on to the domain account, network authentication is required to identify the user to each network resource he or she requires.

Proof of Identity

Typically, *proof of identity* comes in the form of a shared secret between the requestor and the authenticator: a password, a PIN, or an encryption key. The principle word here is "secret." The fulcrum of the entire authentication process is the authenticator's belief that the requestor—and only the requestor—possesses that secret. Once this fails to be true, the system, to some degree or another, is compromised.

Depending on the protocol being used, the shared secret is communicated to the authenticator, who then either grants or denies access. Secure protocols protect the secret in transit; more elaborate schemes don't send the secret at all. Public-key technology uses a *pair* of encryption keys—a private key that is never exposed and a public key that can be disseminated. The next section explores the types of protocols Windows 2000 uses to prove possession of identification credentials.

Authentication Protocols

Clearly, the effectiveness of an authentication process and the safety of your secret depend on the protocol being used. Countless books before this one have guided users through installations that require choosing a unique password and then warned them against the hazards of losing the password. Yet how many of our passwords leave our fingertips and slip unprotected through a network? Table 17-1 shows the Windows 2000 protocols that are designed purposely to thwart would-be attackers and that authenticate both internal and external users. Active Directory maintains user accounts that hold security credentials for authentication purposes, such as passwords and public-key certificates, and it can store multiple security credentials for each of these protocols.

Table 17-1.   Authentication protocols

Protocol	Used For
Kerberos version 5	Network authentication. Provides mutual authentication between user and resource.
Secure Socket Layer/Transport Layer Security (SSL/TLS)	Network authentication. Based on X.509 public-key certificates.
Windows NT LAN Manager (NTLM)	Network authentication. Used for Windows NT 4 compatibility.
Microsoft Challenge Handshake Authentication Protocol version 2 (MS-CHAP v2)	Network and dial-up authentication. Uses separate encryption keys for sending and receiving.
Extensible Authentication Protocol (EAP)	Network and dial-up authentication. Provides support for additional authentication schemes, including smart cards.
Password Authentication Protocol (PAP)	Network and dial-up authentication. Sends passwords in clear text.

Hardware-Enabled Authentication

Hardware is used for authentication purposes to make it more difficult for someone to impersonate a requestor. By storing encryption keys on a smart card, a PC card, or any other cryptographic token, the logon becomes a more secure process. It requires an extra level of possession that a mere password does not. It requires something you *know*—a PIN or password to access the smart card—and something you *have*—the smart card itself. An attacker might somehow obtain your PIN, but without the smart card, the PIN or password is useless. To decrease the vulnerability of secret keys, well-designed cryptographic tokens generate encryption keys directly on the token and prohibit extraction of encryption keys, except possibly in encrypted form.

We're also beginning to hear much about the use of *biometrics* to facilitate authentication: fingerprint identification, face recognition, and hand geometry verification. Biometrics extend the logon requirements considerably, from something you know or have, to something you *are*.

More Info   Federal Information Processing Standards Publication number 140-1 (FIPS 140-1) is a standard published by the National Institute of Standards and Technology (NIST) that specifies security requirements for cryptographic modules. The standard identifies four levels of security: Levels 1–4, with Level 1 representing the lowest level of security and Level 4 representing the highest. You can find this standard at *http://csrc.nist.gov/fips/fips1401.htm*.

Mutual Authentication

Authentication isn't necessarily a one-way street. Many times a requester will want proof of identity from the authenticating host. For instance, when creating a secure link to a restricted directory over which confidential data is to be exchanged, the identity of both the client and the server is important. Protocols like SSL/TLS allow mutual authentication between client and server.

Single Sign-on

One of the additional Windows 2000 security features is the ability to authenticate to any computer or resource on the network by logging on to a single domain account. Through single sign-on, the user can log on to a domain account once, with a single password or smart card. The user's single sign-on security credentials are stored in Active Directory, and each time a domain resource is required, a network authentication occurs transparently.

The advantages of single sign-on, as opposed to authenticating to each network resource when it's needed, are quite obvious. Users have fewer passwords to remember and fewer authentication screens to endure; administrators find it easier to manage only one account per user.

Data Protection

The authentication schemes that protect passwords as they cross an unsecured network are critical to maintaining a secure system; equally important is the data you send once you're logged on. Whether it's a company's proprietary information or a personal credit card, the concern is the same: keeping network information from being read by unauthorized persons and preventing it from being modified.

Of course, sensitive information doesn't need to be on its way somewhere to be vulnerable. While tools like network sniffers can weed out data packets, attacks can also occur on files sitting on a hard disk. In addition to network security, Windows 2000 provides security for your stored data.

Data Confidentiality

The privacy of data, whether it's an e-mail message, input to a Web page, or distinct IP packets, is jeopardized once the information is transmitted over nonsecure communication lines, such as the Internet. Using encryption algorithms and keys, data privacy can be protected. Without the appropriate decryption keys, unintended recipients intercepting the transmission will receive nothing but encrypted garbage.

Note Cryptographic operations use both an algorithm and a key. The *algorithm* is the specific mathematical process that performs the operation. The *key* is the input to the algorithm.

The strength of the encryption also depends on the algorithm used and the length of the key. With enough computing power, any encryption key can be broken. Windows 2000 supports a range of key lengths, from 40-bit encryption for export internationally, to 128-bit encryption for use within North America.

Typically, the bulk of data is encrypted using a cipher block algorithm (also known as a symmetric algorithm) and a key. The strength of this method lies in the cipher block chaining (CBC). Encrypting a block at a time, the output of one block is used as the input of the next. In this way, repeated patterns of data won't produce the same encrypted data. The input to the first block is a random number called an initialization vector (IV). The IV assures that each time a message is encrypted, a unique result is produced.

For confidentiality of transmitted data at the network level, Windows 2000 employs Internet Protocol security (IPSec). IPSec encrypts TCP/IP packets before transmission and decrypts them upon receipt.

Confidentiality of stored data is also a concern. Although access to stored files can be restricted for certain users through file permissions, intruders who gain unauthorized access to your hard disk can modify those permissions. To combat this problem, Windows 2000 uses a transparent encryption scheme called Encrypting File System (EFS). Files on NTFS volumes can be encrypted and decrypted with users' EFS public/private-key information. Users need only select the files to be encrypted. The actual encryption occurs behind the scenes. This system, however, allows only self-encrypting—files can't be encrypted and then shared with other users.

Data Integrity

While encryption can guarantee the confidentiality of a file, it can't guarantee the file's *data integrity*—that is, that the file has not been modified or tampered with. Fortunately, Windows 2000 also supports digital signing. *Digital signing* of a file, module, or other software component is somewhat like signing a contract on paper. The signer is responsible for what he or she signs. Whoever subsequently views the document and signature can tell who signed it.

However, digital signatures offer a great deal of security beyond that. A *digital signature* is generated by hashing the document and encrypting it with the signer's private encryption key. This procedure produces a signature that is cryptographically tied to both the signer and the content of the document. Changing the content breaks the signature.

Upon verification, the digital signature is decrypted with the signer's public key. The resulting hash is compared against a newly computed hash of the message. This process proves undeniably that the signer signed the message, because his or her key was used to verify the signature; in addition, it verifies that the contents of the document haven't changed because the encrypted hash matched the newly computed hash.

In Windows 2000, digital signing has two meaningful purposes. First, it guarantees the integrity of data stored locally or being passed over a network. Second, it authenticates modules or other software components that are obtained from untrusted sources, such as the Internet. Validating the signature of a module verifies that the software hasn't been tampered with and that it was signed by a trusted software publisher.

The two most common digital signature algorithms are RSA and Digital Signature Algorithm (DSA). DSA signatures are 40 bytes long, while the length of RSA signatures depends on the key size. A key pair, consisting of a public key and a private key, with a 128-byte public key typically produces a 128-byte signature.

Access Control

As explained earlier, authentication is the first layer of security in the protection of network objects and resources. The second layer is *access control*—that is, controlling which resources can be accessed, by whom, and with which permissions. An authenticated user doesn't necessarily have authorization to access all files, printers, and registry keys. Access control is enforced by the manager for each object type, but it's up to the object owner to determine which access control restrictions to impose.

Access is controlled by assigning rights to users and by setting permissions for objects. Permissions specify which users can access a specific object and which type of access is allowed. For example, the owner of a quarterly finance spreadsheet might set permissions that allow read/write access to the head of finance, allow read-only access to everyone in finance, and deny access to everyone else.

Groups of users have their own rights, and those can be specified when granting object permissions. In the previous example, establishing read-only permissions for everyone in finance probably means setting a group's rights, not setting users' rights individually.

Permissions can be explicitly set for an object, or for ease of administration, they can be inherited from parent objects. However, the granularity of access control doesn't stop at objects. Permissions can even be set for attributes of an object, allowing access to some fields, such as the e-mail address of a user account, but denying access to other fields, such as the user's telephone number. Standard object permissions include the following:

- Reading an object
- Modifying an object
- Deleting an object
- Reading an object's permissions
- Modifying an object's permissions
- Changing an object's owner

Auditing

Another Windows 2000 security feature is *auditing*, which allows an administrator to keep tabs on events that might possibly compromise the system. Events such as logons and logoffs, access to files, and user-account management can all be audited. The administrator can choose which objects to audit, which events on that object to audit, and which users or groups using that object to audit. Both successful and unsuccessful access attempts can be audited.

> **Tip**   Viruses can leave trails of inappropriate writing of executables and DLLs. Auditing successful and failed write access to these files and monitoring the security log for unexpected occurrences will give you a head start at detecting viruses on your system.

In addition to auditing users' security-related events, Windows 2000 provides a means of tracking security management events because an audit trail will reflect any changes in security policies. For instance, if an administrator changes the permissions of a particular object to deny access to a specific group, this change in permissions will appear on the audit trail. Chapter 18 shows how to manage the security log that Windows 2000 generates.

Nonrepudiation

Finally, let's take a look at nonrepudiation, another Windows 2000 security feature. *Nonrepudiation* is undeniable proof that a correspondence was sent or received and usually refers to security-enhanced e-mail messages. Proof that a message was sent is a property exhibited by digital signatures. For undeniable proof of receipt, the recipient of a signed or encrypted message responds to the sender with a signed receipt.

> **Caution** Some e-mail packages allow for receipts of signed messages, but this doesn't necessarily demonstrate nonrepudiation. A *signed receipt* is undeniable proof that a message was received only if it is cryptographically tied to both the recipient and the original message.

Public-Key Infrastructures

Now that we've looked at more basic security concepts, let's examine some of the security-enabled protocols. In recent years, public-key infrastructures (PKIs) have gained momentum in both commercial and government sectors. Based on public-key technology, a PKI describes a system of public-key certificate generation and management, including distribution and revocation. The important elements of this infrastructure are certificate authorities (CAs) that issue certificates, clients that use certificates, and directories that store certificates. Many PKIs use a registration authority that assures user identity and authorization before certificates are granted. Figure 17-1 shows a typical Microsoft Windows 2000 PKI.

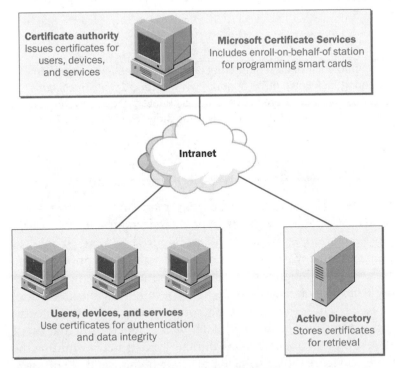

Figure 17-1. *A typical public-key infrastructure.*

One of the distinct advantages of using public-key certificates for authentication is that servers no longer need to store and maintain a password list for their individual users. Because identification is based on a trust relationship with the CAs, the servers need to trust only the authority that issued the requester's certificate. Once the chain of trust is determined and the certificate is verified, authentication can be established.

RSA Laboratories maintains a list of public-key cryptography standards (PKCS) that define public-key-related formats. Table 17-2 contains four notable standards.

Table 17-2. Important public-key cryptography standards

Standard	Subject
PKCS #7	Cryptographic Message Syntax Standard, the basis for Secure Multipurpose Internet Mail Extensions (S/MIME). Defines the format of signed and encrypted messages. The degenerate case allows the exchange of public-key certificates and certificate revocation lists (CRLs).
PKCS #10	Certification Requests. Used by clients to request certificates from CAs.
PKCS #11	Cryptographic Token Interface. Analogous to Microsoft's CryptoAPI.
PKCS #12	Personal Information Exchange (PFX). Enables the encrypted transfer of private keys and associated certificates from one computer to another.

More Info   You can find a list of current Internet-draft categories associated with the Internet Engineering Task Force (IETF) at *http://www.ietf.org/1id-abstracts.html*. A number of categories listed there are relevant to this chapter: IP Security (IPSec), Public-Key Infrastructure (X.509) (PKI), S/MIME Mail Security (S/MIME), and Transport Layer Security (TLS).

Public-Key Encryption vs. Symmetric-Key Encryption

While PKIs depend heavily on public-key technology, many of the functions performed by PKI entities combine public-key encryption and symmetric-key encryption. *Symmetric-key encryption* has been around for hundreds of years. It involves the use of a single encryption key for both the encryption and decryption of data. Encrypting data this way is analogous to placing a document in a safe and locking it with a key. When the document needs to be retrieved, the same key is used to unlock the safe. Relatively speaking, this method is secure and fast. Unfortunately, this type of encryption doesn't lend itself well to encrypting data to a person. Since the key must remain private, the difficulty exists in transmitting the key. After all, if there's a secure means to send the key, why not send the message via that route to begin with?

Public-key encryption, also known as asymmetric encryption, emerged from the necessity to share encrypted data with people, where no secure path existed to pass an encryption key. Public-key encryption uses a pair of keys: a public key that is distributed, and a private key that remains secret. To encrypt a message to someone, the encryption algorithm uses the recipient's public key. The resulting encrypted message can be decrypted only by the recipient's private key. This method is analogous to a safe with an entry slot. Anyone can slip a document in, but only the person with the correct private key can retrieve it. This scheme works for self-encryption of files as well. The Windows 2000 EFS, for instance, protects data with the user's public key. To decrypt, the user's private key is accessed and used.

Unfortunately, public-key encryption algorithms are slow and are rarely used to encrypt large amounts of data. Instead, public keys are used to protect symmetric keys that encrypt large chunks of data. For example, suppose Rosemary wants to encrypt a portfolio to Harold. Rosemary will encrypt the portfolio using a symmetric-key algorithm like the Data Encryption Standard (DES). She will then encrypt the symmetric key with Harold's public key, producing an encrypted symmetric key. Harold, upon receiving the encrypted portfolio and key, will decrypt the encrypted symmetric key with his private key and use the resulting symmetric key to decrypt the message.

Public-key encryption extends to digital signatures as well. Digital signature algorithms actually reverse the encryption process. Encrypting the hash of a message with a user's private key generates a digital signature. The signature can be verified later by decrypting the hash with the user's public key.

Public-Key Certificates and Private Keys

Most public-key infrastructures, including Windows 2000 PKI, revolve around the use of X.509 public-key certificates. We know that PKI users have a private key and a circulated public key. A public-key certificate cryptographically binds a public key to the user who holds the corresponding private key. Certificates are issued and digitally signed by a CA. Table 17-3 lists the fields of an X.509 certificate.

When a certificate is used, it is validated by verifying the signature with the issuing authority's public key. As long as the issuing CA is trusted (or is within a trusted path), you can be certain that the user or entity named in the certificate holds the corresponding private key.

Table 17-3. Public-key certificate fields

Certificate Field	Description
X.509 version	Windows 2000 supports X.509 version 3 certificates.
Serial number	Unique number that the CA assigns to a certificate.
Signature algorithm	ID of the algorithm that the CA uses to digitally sign the certificate.
Issuer	Name of the CA that issues the certificate.
Validity period	A pair of dates indicating when certificate validation begins and when it ends.
Subject	Name of the certificate user.
Public key	Public key that, with the corresponding private key, makes up a user's key pair.
Extensions	Additional information that a CA can include in the certificate. Examples of extensions are alternate names, such as the user's e-mail address; key usage, which indicates which operations a public key can be used for; and basic constraints, which show whether the certificate is a CA certificate.
Signature	Digital signature generated by the issuer.

Of course, certificates aren't issued solely to users. CAs have their own certificates. CAs can also issue certificates to services and devices that need to be accessed on the network. A Web server that accepts Secure Socket Layer–encrypted transmissions and a directory that provides two-way authentication are both good examples of entities that use certificates.

Even though certificates belong to users and other entities, that doesn't mean that a user or entity is limited to one certificate—or, for that matter, that a user can be a member of only one root hierarchy. Certificates are issued for many different purposes: server authentication, file encryption, and code signing, to name a few. A user holds any number of certificates and private keys under different CAs or under the same CA; each might differ in usage, privilege, key size, and algorithm. For example, a security model might need multiple levels of access with separate CAs handling each level. On the other hand, a single user might hold Level 2 and Level 4 certificates; another might hold Level 1 and Level 3 certificates.

Having certificates under different root certificate authorities (root CAs) is common too. Consider Celine, a human resources director who has both an enterprise certificate, which allows her to access her company's human resources server, and a certificate from a commercial CA, which allows her to browse the company's 401(k) stock portfolio over the Internet.

At the very least, the functions of encryption and digital signatures should be split into separate certificates. Private keys used for encryption can be archived so that encrypted data of a lost key can be recovered. Since the integrity of digital signatures depends on sole possession of the private key, digital signature private keys should not be archived.

Certificate Authorities

Certificate authorities exist to issue certificates for entities—including users, services, devices, subordinate authorities, or the CA itself—which meet the policy set forth for the CA. The CA accepts and fulfills certificate requests and revocation requests and might also manage the policy-directed registration process that a user completes to get his or her certificate. For information on how to install a CA using Microsoft Certificate Services, see Chapter 19.

Root and Subordinate Certificate Authorities

While CAs can issue and revoke certificates for a host of users, larger companies might be too big to administer with a single CA. In addition, enterprises might want to delegate authority of certain certificate types, or they might have divisions that manage their own resources and need to enforce separate certificate-issuing policies. Production, for instance, might want to issue certificates to anyone whose e-mail address is within the company domain. Engineering might require a picture ID for registration. On the other hand, by using autonomous CAs, users between the two divisions are cryptographically isolated. A digitally signed message sent from a user in production to a user in engineering will have no common basis of trust.

To solve this dilemma, CAs can be stacked hierarchically. Root CAs preside over domains, using a certificate they issue to themselves (a self-signed certificate). They also issue certificates to subordinated authorities and in general do *not* issue user certificates. Subordinate authorities issue certificates to users and other end entities and might also issue certificates to other subordinate CAs. Root CAs are implicitly trusted—subordinate CAs and clients derive trust from the root.

Figure 17-2 shows an example of a CA hierarchy. By stacking CAs hierarchically, an enterprise can manage the certification system from a single authority while delegating control of policy decisions to discrete authorities.

Windows 2000 also distinguishes between enterprise CAs and stand-alone CAs. The primary difference is that the enterprise CA uses Active Directory for user information and policy decisions and can publish certificates and CRLs to Active Directory. The stand-alone CA requires the certificate requestor to supply all user-identifying information.

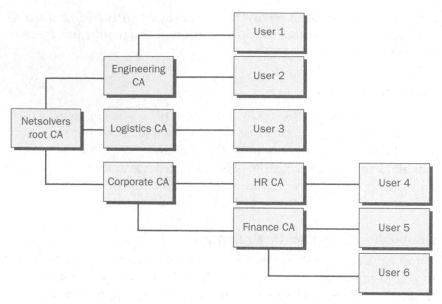

Figure 17-2. *A certificate authority hierarchy.*

Chain Verification and Trust

Before a received digital signature can be verified, the signer's certificate must be validated. This is true of any application, whether it's a service, device, or user performing the verification. Without a hierarchical chain back to a trusted root CA, the identity of the user in the certificate can't be confirmed.

Chain verification is a two-step process. The first step is to build the certificate chain from the signer's certificate to a trusted root CA. Consider the CA hierarchy in Figure 17-2. Suppose User 1 in engineering is trying to verify a signature from User 5 in finance. User 1 will build the certificate chain for User 5 back to the root CA, Netsolvers root CA, which is in User 1's trusted store. The certificate chain, built bottom up, would be User 5: Finance CA: Corporate CA: Netsolvers root CA. The verifying entity obtains these certificates from the transmission protocol if they're included or from an accessible certificate store. The root CA certificate, since it's the pivotal trust component, should always come from a protected, trusted certificate store such as Active Directory.

The second step of chain verification is to verify the certificate chain top down. The verifying entity checks each certificate for validity, starting with the trusted root. Validity checking includes verifying the certificate's digital signature, checking the certificate's validity period, and ensuring that the certificate hasn't been revoked. Depending on policy, applications might also check any certificate extensions that the certificate contains.

> **Note** Currently, typical PKI implementations include two-tier or three-tier hier-
> archies. As the popularity of the public-key infrastructure spreads, CA vendors
> will make more attempts to unite and centralize certificate authorities and root
> certificate authorities, which will result in longer certificate chains.

Cross-Root Certification

Even with a central root CA and a multitiered CA hierarchy that spans the breadth
of a company, users might need to verify digital signatures under different root
CAs. This verification is especially important when integrating commercial CAs,
such as Verisign, to perform code signing, among other tasks. Using cross-root
certification, root CAs can be connected so that validation paths of certificates
under different roots extend back to the user's root CA.

Certificate Registration

Before being able to use his or her generated public/private key pair for encryption or digital signatures, a user must first obtain a certificate from a CA. A user
does this by sending a certificate request—which includes his or her name and
public key—to a CA. A number of registration models can exist depending on
the registration policy a CA wants to uphold. Many commercial CAs handle
PKCS #10 certificate requests and also allow Web-based certificate generation.

For more secure needs, a registration authority can act as a certificate-requesting
agent to ensure proper proof-of-identity procedures and to forward certificate
requests to the CA. Microsoft Certificate Services includes an enroll-on-behalf-
of station where administrators, using enrollment agent certificates, can program smart cards for users. Figure 17-3 shows two examples of certificate request
scenarios.

In the first example, a client requests a certificate from an enterprise CA, perhaps
using the Certificates snap-in Certificate Request Wizard. User information and certificate rights are obtained from Active Directory. The Certificate Request Wizard
generates a public/private key pair for the user. The public key is included in the
certificate request and sent to the CA. The private key is saved on the user's computer. Upon receipt of the certificate request, the CA issues and signs the certificate
and pushes it to a directory where other users and entities can retrieve it.

The second example shows an administrator programming a smart card through
the enroll-on-behalf-of station. In this case, the private key is written directly to
the card. In neither scenario is the private key exposed to the CA or anyone else.
Again, once the certificate is issued, it's written to a directory for public availability. The smart card is returned to the user and is ready for authentication.

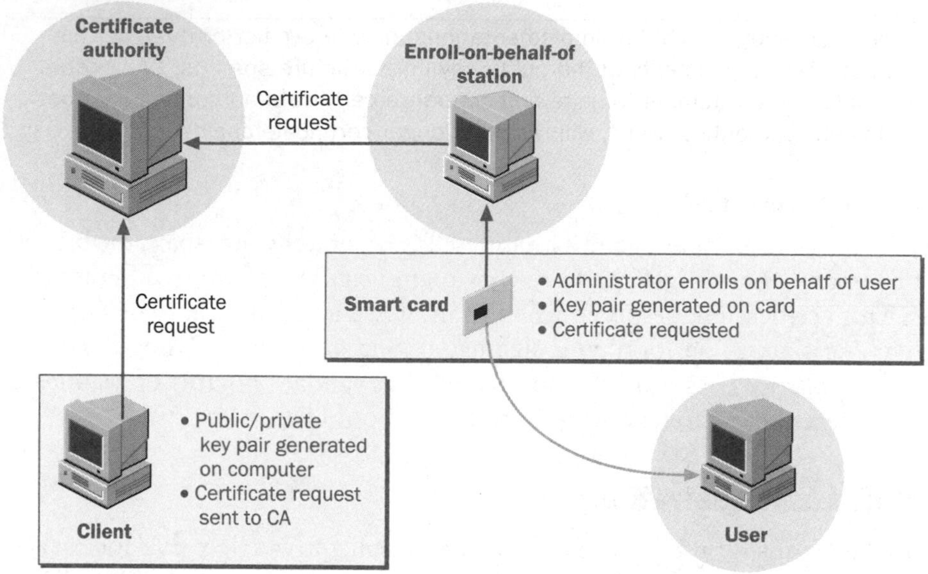

Certificate
authority

Certificate
request

Enroll-on-behalf-of
station

Certificate
request

Smart card

- Administrator enrolls on behalf of user
- Key pair generated on card
- Certificate requested

- Public/private
  key pair generated
  on computer
- Certificate request
  sent to CA

Client

User

Figure 17-3. *Two certificate request scenarios.*

Certificate Directories

An important piece of the PKI is the directory in which certificates are stored and from which they can be retrieved. To encrypt data to a user, the user's public-key certificate is needed. Similarly, when verifying a digitally signed message, the certificate chain back to the verifier's root must be established.

In a Windows 2000 environment, Active Directory acts as a repository for certificates; any user or computer with appropriate rights can retrieve them. In addition, external users' certificates can be mapped to Active Directory user accounts.

Tip Typically, once a client application retrieves a given certificate, it will cache the certificate locally to save the overhead of another retrieval. Use the Certificates snap-in to view stored certificates by purpose or by storage category, such as personal or trusted roots.

Certificate Revocation

In addition to issuing and signing certificates, CAs are responsible for maintaining a list of certificates that are no longer valid. This list, called a certificate revocation list (CRL), is digitally signed by the issuing authority.

Such a list is a necessary requirement for a public-key infrastructure. Consider Julio, a laptop user who dials in to his company's network to access a server that contains finance accounts. He uses his certificate and corresponding private key to authenticate himself to the finance server. Now suppose Julio's laptop is stolen. In the past, a compromised password might have resulted in the administrator changing the user's password.

In a public-key infrastructure, however, verification is based on possession of a private key. The finance server has no knowledge of a specific user, only the CAs that it trusts. By using the CRL as a revoking mechanism, the finance server can retrieve a current list of revoked certificates. Once the stolen certificate has been placed on the CRL and the CRL has been published and retrieved, verification of the certificate results in a failure and access is denied.

Like user certificates, a CRL is digitally signed by the issuing CA and can be verified with the CA's certificate. Table 17-4 describes the fields of an X.509 CRL.

Table 17-4. Certificate revocation list fields

CRL Field	Description
X.509 version	X.509 CRLs version. The current CRL version is X.509 version 2.
Signature algorithm	ID of the algorithm that the CA uses to digitally sign the CRL.
Issuer	Name of the CA that issues the CRL.
Last update	Date and time that the current CRL is issued.
Next update	Date and time that the next CRL will be issued.
List of revoked certificates	Each entry in the list includes the certificate serial number and the date when the certificate was revoked. Optional extensions can be added, such as a reason flag.
Extensions	Optional information that the CA can include in the CRL.
Signature	Digital signature that the issuer generates.

Just as with the certificate registration and issuing procedures, policies are established for CAs that dictate certificate revocation. These policies should include such procedural decisions as how often CAs refresh their CRLs, which mandatory and discretional extensions CAs can include in their CRLs, and under what circumstances certificates get revoked. Under one policy, for instance, certificates of employees who leave the company are subject to revocation. Under another, a user merely being denied certain privileges is grounds for revoking his or her certificate.

Because certificates have a validity period, CRLs need contain only revoked certificates that aren't yet expired. Once a certificate expires (in other words, the Valid To date has passed), verifying entities will refuse the certificate and it can be removed from the CRL.

We should also consider CRL dispersal. The rate at which CRLs are issued, or "refreshed," is a policy decision made by the CA and can be as frequent as once a day. For highly secure domains, the refresh rate can be even more frequent. To be current, verifying entities need to obtain the latest CRL. Microsoft Certificate Services allows CRLs to be published to Active Directory, to a URL for HTTP access, or to a CRL file.

Certificate Renewal

Another set of certificate policy decisions relates to the certificate renewal procedure—specifically, *whether* certificates are allowed to be renewed, *when* certificates are renewed, and *how* certificates are renewed. Renewing certificates with the same key allows a user to extend the life of a public/private-key pair. In contrast, renewing a certificate with a different public key once a user's certificate expires could make it difficult to read previously encrypted messages.

Security-Enabled Protocols

Security in Windows 2000 exists at different levels—from the protection of entire messages at the application level, to secure channels, to the protection of data packets within IP. The security protocols residing at these different layers provide mechanisms not available at other layers.

S/MIME, for example, provides public-key-based encryption, integrity, and authentication of e-mail messages at the application level. SSL resides beneath the application layer, adding security to application protocols. IPSec, on the other hand, provides application-independent data protection at the IP layer. The following sections examine Windows 2000 security protocols.

Secure Multipurpose Internet Mail Extensions

S/MIME is included with Microsoft Outlook and Outlook Express. It uses private-key certificates to secure e-mail messages and files in accordance with the PKCS #7 standard. It supports both encryption and digital signatures. By nesting single S/MIME contents, messages can also be signed and then encrypted, or signed multiple times.

Signed Messages

A PKCS #7 digitally signed message includes the message signature, the signature algorithm, and information about the signer. Optionally, the signer's certificate or certificate chain can be added as well as any CRLs that the verifier might need. Authenticated attributes, which are protected by the digital signature, and unauthenticated attributes can also be added to the PKCS #7 content. The time at which a message is signed is an example of an authenticated attribute.

The content that is signed might or might not be included in the PKCS #7 message. If the content isn't included, the verifier needs both the PKCS #7 content and the original file that was signed to complete the verification. If the original file is easily available, this method saves the overhead of having redundant data.

Encrypted Messages

The current PKCS #7 standard requires the use of two algorithms for message encryption. Since public-key algorithms are slow, the message is first encrypted with a symmetric-key algorithm, such as DES. The small symmetric key is then encrypted to the recipient, using a public-key algorithm, such as RSA. In this way, a message can be encrypted to multiple recipients while the actual content has to be encrypted only once.

The PKCS #7 message includes the encrypted content and symmetric-key algorithm along with information for each recipient. This information contains the symmetric key encrypted to that specific recipient. Upon receipt, an application searches the list of recipients for one that matches the current user's certificate. It then decrypts the symmetric key with the user's private key and subsequently decrypts the message.

Other Content Types

The degenerate case of the PKCS #7 message allows for the absence of the content and any signature information. This format provides a transport for certificates and CRLs. Table 17-5 shows the typical file extensions for different PKCS #7 files.

Table 17-5. Common PKCS #7 file extensions

Extension	Description
.P7M	PKCS #7 encrypted file or signed file with content added
.P7B	PKCS #7 file extension
.P7S	PKCS #7 signature file (signed file without the content)
.P7C	PKCS #7 certificate or CRL-only file

Kerberos Version 5

Kerberos is another authentication security protocol used by Windows 2000. It is used over a nonsecure network to mutually identify the requestor (user) and authenticator (network resource). Once identified, the user and network resource can encrypt transmissions to ensure privacy.

Kerberos works by issuing tickets to users for accessing resources on the network. Before exploring the high-level details of Kerberos, you need to understand some objects and services.

- **Ticket** A packet of data that allows a client to access a resource. It includes an encrypted piece of client information that, when decrypted, confirms identity.

- **Ticket-granting ticket (TGT)** A special ticket that allows the client to obtain temporary tickets from the ticket-granting service for each authentication.

- **Key distribution center (KDC)** A service that runs as part of Active Directory and administers TGTs.

- **Ticket-granting service (TGS)** A service that is accessed by a client with a TGT and that administers tickets for network resources.

The use of a ticket-granting service keeps the user from having to log on for each resource request. Figure 17-4 shows the details of a client using Kerberos to authenticate to a server. The steps are enumerated below.

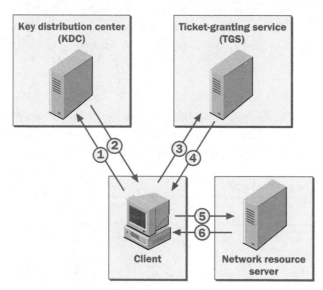

Figure 17-4. *A client using Kerberos to authenticate to a server.*

1. A client authenticates once to the key distribution center by using a password or smart card.

2. The KDC issues a TGT to the client, for access to the TGS.

3. When the client wants to access a network resource, such as the corporate finance server, he or she requests a service ticket from the TGS, sending the TGT as proof of identity.

4. The TGS replies with a service ticket for use at the requested network resource server.

5. The client sends the service ticket to the network resource server for access.

6. To mutually authenticate, the network resource server replies with a packet that the client can decrypt.

Once a client completes the first two steps, steps 3–6 can be repeated each time a user needs to access another resource.

Note The advantage of this mechanism is that all Kerberos authentication occurs behind the scenes. The user needs to enter a password only once into the KDC—authentication to all other resources happens transparently.

Windows NT LAN Manager

Windows NT LAN Manager (NTLM) is the primary authentication mechanism for Windows NT 4. In Windows 2000, it is replaced by Kerberos as the default authentication protocol. NTLM is included as part of Windows 2000 for configurations that involve authentication between Windows NT and Windows 2000 machines.

Secure Socket Layer

Another Windows 2000 security protocol, Secure Socket Layer (SSL), uses public-key technology to provide a secure channel for applications communicating over an nonsecure network. A Web browser and Web server, for instance, could use SSL to communicate securely over the Internet. Before sending encrypted data, the client and server must engage in a security handshake to authenticate the parties involved and establish security levels. The handshake is a multipart process:

1. The client initiates connection with a request for a secure channel.

2. The server responds with its public-key certificate and can optionally request the client's certificate for mutual authentication.

3. The client verifies the server's certificate. If the server requested the client's certificate, the client sends it and the server verifies it.

4. The client generates and encrypts a session key with the server's public key found in its certificate.

5. All communication between the server and client is symmetrically encrypted and decrypted using the session key.

Figure 17-5 illustrates the SSL handshake process. In addition to authentication, the SSL handshake allows the two parties to agree on security parameters. Because of SSL's positioning, it can add security to application protocols such as HTTP, Telnet, FTP, Gopher, and NNTP.

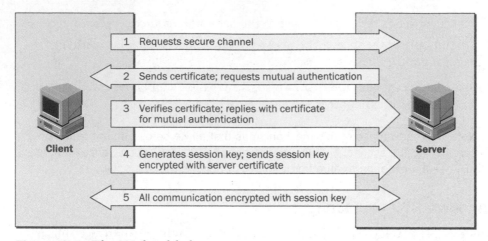

Figure 17-5. *The SSL handshake process.*

Internet Protocol Security

Finally, the Windows 2000 IPSec security protocol provides end-to-end security of network data using encryption, digital signature, and hashing algorithms. The IPSec driver protects individual packets before they reach the network and unwraps the protection once they're received. Because the IPSec driver resides at the IP transport layer, individual applications don't need to handle the specifics of data security during transmission. Data passed though the network from security-ignorant applications can still be protected. Because IPSec protects the packets of data—not the actual link—IPSec can provide security for networkwide transmissions, and only the two computers engaging in communications need to know about it. IPSec provides a number of security features:

- **Authentication** Use of a digital signature verifies identity of sender.
- **Integrity** Use of hash algorithms ensures that data hasn't been altered.
- **Privacy** Use of encryption protects data from being read.
- **Anti-replay** Prevents packets from being re-sent by an attacker to gain unauthorized access.
- **Nonrepudiation** Use of public-key digital signatures proves message origin.
- **Dynamic rekeying** Ability to generate keys during communication so that parts of transmissions are protected with different keys.
- **Key generation** Diffie-Hellman key agreement algorithm allows two computers to agree on a key without ever exposing it.
- **Key lengths** Provides configurable key lengths for export restrictions or highly sensitive transmissions.

IPSec Policy Management

An important component of IPSec is the policy agent. The policy agent begins during system startup and is responsible for retrieving IPSec policy information from either Active Directory or the registry and feeding it to the IPSec driver. For domain computers, the domain policy information is acquired from Active Directory at startup and at policy-defined retrieval intervals. For stand-alone systems or systems that are offline, the policy agent retrieves policies from the registry. When an offline machine reconnects, the retrieved domain policy overrides the local policy.

Figure 17-6 shows how policy information is transferred from Active Directory to the IPSec driver. The IPSec policy agent retrieves security policies and feeds them to the IPSec driver.

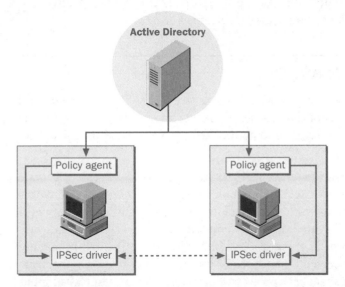

Figure 17-6. *How policy information is transferred from Active Directory to the IPSec driver.*

Chapter 18 describes how you can use IPSec Policy Management to define and manage IPSec policies for single computers or entire domains. Windows 2000 also provides predefined policies that can be customized to specific needs.

How IPSec Works

Before data can be protected and transmitted between two IPSec-enabled machines, a negotiation must take place to agree on which keys, mechanisms, and security policies to use to protect the data. This negotiation produces a security association (SA).

For IPSec communications, an initial SA called Internet Security Association and Key Management Protocol (ISAKMP) is established between the two computers to provide a method of key exchange. Using the ISAKMP for protection, a second negotiation takes place to produce a pair of IPSec SAs and keys, one for inbound and one for outbound communications. Specifically, these SAs include an agreed algorithm for encryption and integrity and the agreed IPSec protocol to use. The two IPSec protocols are:

- **Authentication Header (AH)**   Provides data authentication, integrity, and anti-replay to IP packets
- **Encapsulating Security Payload (ESP)**   Provides confidentiality along with data authentication, integrity, and anti-replay to IP packets

The IPSec SAs and keys are loaded into the IPSec driver on their respective machines and are used to protect data during transmission.

Virtual Private Networks

Before we start discussing virtual private networks (VPNs), what they mean, and why they're useful, take a second to consider that acronym, VPN: "Virtual," as in simulated. "Private," as in secret and confidential. "Network," as in a collection of computers.

Logically, a VPN is simply an extension of a private network. In reality, private networks are geographically isolated from remote users and other private networks by nonsecure communication lines such as the Internet. By using a secure, network-level protocol like IPSec, a private link can be emulated between two separate networks. What is actually the wrapping of data before it passes through nonsecure extranets or intranets is perceived by both requestor and authenticator as a private dedicated line. Since data packets are protected by encryption, any in transit interception results in unreadable data.

Unlike using IPSec for peer-to-peer transmissions, VPNs use a dedicated server that is tied to the private network. By accepting connections from only VPN-authorized clients, the VPN server allows private traffic within the physical enclave to proceed normally without requiring additional internal security.

Before you can establish a VPN connection, VPN authorization must be confirmed for the client. Authorization is based on the remote access policies set by the network administrator and on the dial-in properties of the client requesting the connection. Once a user is determined to be authorized and one-way or mutual authentication occurs, the VPN can be established. Windows 2000 includes two protocols that are used to encapsulate data over the virtual private network:

- **Point-to-Point Tunneling Protocol (PPTP)**   Provides data encryption using Microsoft Point-to-Point Encryption
- **Layer Two Tunneling Protocol (L2TP)**   Provides data encryption, authentication, and integrity using IPSec

Remote Access VPNs

An authorized but isolated user can access the protected resources of a private or hidden network by authenticating to the network's VPN server and establishing a VPN connection. The remote user can be at home or on the road needing to connect through an ISP and the Internet, or the remote user can be part of the same intranet but detached from the secure or hidden network.

For example, suppose engineering has a hidden enclave within an enterprisewide network, complete with secret documents and alpha-version software. They want to grant access to the hidden network to the VP of Engineering but don't want to compromise the confidentiality of the information as it crosses the company's intranet. By providing a VPN server that blocks unauthorized users but allows the vice president to authenticate and establish a VPN connection, engineering's secret network is extended to one more user.

Note   Simply because you have a VPN connection to a private network does not mean that you have full access. You still need the correct permissions to access specific resources.

Once the client establishes a VPN connection with the VPN server, the user appears to be accessing the private network directly. Figure 17-7 shows remote access for an Internet-based VPN.

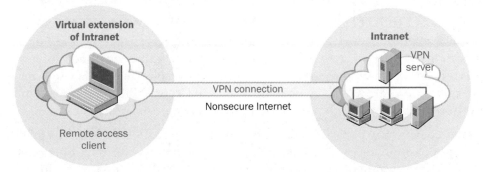

Figure 17-7. *Remote access for an Internet-based VPN.*

Router-to-Router VPNs

A VPN connection can also be established for two mutually exclusive private networks. In this case, both the VPN client and VPN server are routers. Like remote access VPNs, router-to-router VPNs can involve enclaves that are part of the same intranet, or they can involve private networks that require the Internet infrastructure for communication. Figure 17-8 shows a router-to-router connection for an intranet-based VPN.

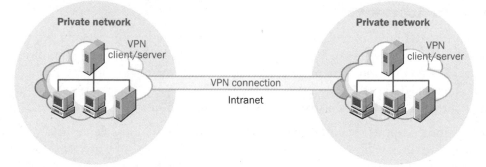

Figure 17-8. *A router-to-router VPN connection.*

Here the VPN client authenticates itself to the VPN server, and a secure VPN connection is negotiated. Again, the logical appearance in both cases is that the private networks are physically connected. You'll find more on VPNs in Chapter 31.

Security Modules

This chapter would be incomplete without a brief glance at the underlying interface that supports Windows cryptographic-enabled applications, such as Microsoft Certificate Services and Microsoft Internet Explorer.

Cryptographic Application Programming Interface

Microsoft's CryptoAPI provides a standardized set of cryptographic functions, such as CryptGenKey, CryptVerifySignature, and CryptEncrypt, that allow applications to offer security without having to maintain their own cache of keys or certificates or know the particulars of the cryptographic device they're using. Since private keys are handled within the bounds of CryptoAPI, applications don't need to fumble around with unprotected private-key information.

When used, CryptoAPI passes each of its cryptographic calls off to one of a number of cryptographic service providers (CSPs) that actually perform the operation. Figure 17-9 shows the relationship between the API and the service providers.

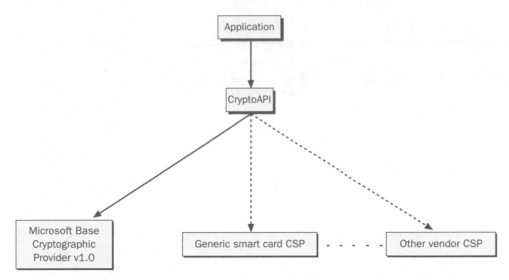

Figure 17-9. *Cryptographic service providers "plugged in" to CryptoAPI.*

Cryptographic Service Providers

Cryptographic service providers vary according to the algorithms they use, the key lengths they support, and the cryptographic tokens with which they interface. A vendor introducing a new type of smart card, for instance, writes a CSP for its smart card that "plugs in" to the CryptoAPI. Being able to plug in allows applications to use a myriad of new and existing services without having to particularize their cryptographic calls to any one vendor-defined interface.

By displaying a list of available CSPs and allowing the user to choose, applications can take advantage of emerging technologies with little, if any, modification to their source code. Because CSPs provide the specific interface to the cryptographic device, whether it's software based or hardware based, they are responsible for any initialization required, such as PIN or password validation.

Summary

This chapter covered basic security concepts as well as the major security components of Windows 2000. The next two chapters continue with Windows 2000 security. Chapter 18 describes how to implement the concepts and components described in this chapter; Chapter 19 explains how to install and configure Certificate Services.

Chapter 18
Implementing Security

In the realm of computer security, one of the most common and critical mistakes administrators make is to confuse the presence of security features with a secure system. It's not enough to piece protocols, methods, and algorithms together into a collage of security. In such environments, the weakest link usually goes unnoticed until it's too late. To be effective, system security must be applied as a whole, and it needs be well designed, complete, and easy to maintain.

Well-designed systems are accompanied by policies that dictate how, when, and at what level security is applied. Complete systems provide multilevel security that is both sound and as transparent to the user as possible. Easily maintained systems allow administrators to centrally manage security and keep track of critical events.

With features like security templates, public-key cryptography, Internet Protocol Security (IPSec), and comprehensive auditing procedures, Microsoft Windows 2000 makes it easy to apply security policies to individual computers or to scale them to domains or entire enterprises.

Using Templates to Implement Security Policies

Windows 2000, as you now know or are quickly learning, has a rich and diverse range of security features. With these features, however, comes a multitude of security policies and attribute settings that need to be configured. Configuring a system with policies consistent with your company's security needs is, in itself, no small task. Multiply that by all of the computers at your site or in your organization, and you've got yourself quite a chore. And that doesn't include the maintenance time required whenever company policies need to be reevaluated.

Enter security templates. A *security template,* quite simply, is a configuration file for all of the security attributes of a system. Security templates are powerful and help ease the strain of administration. Using a single interface, an administrator can generate a security template that reflects the company's security needs and then apply it to a local computer or import it into a Group Policy object in Active Directory. When you incorporate the template into a Group Policy object, all computers affected by that object will receive the template settings.

Running the Security Templates Snap-in

Security templates can be created and modified with the Security Templates snap-in of the Microsoft Management Console (MMC). To add the snap-in to the MMC, run *mmc.exe* from the Run dialog box, which is accessed from the Start menu. From the Console menu, choose Add/Remove Snap-In. Click the Add button on the Stand-alone tab and select Security Templates from the list of snap-ins provided. Click Add in the Add Stand-alone Snap-In dialog box to add the Security Templates entry to the Add/Remove Snap-In dialog box and then click Close. Click OK in the Add/Remove Snap-In dialog box, and the Security Templates snap-in will be added to Console Root in the console tree.

In the console tree, expand Security Templates and the Security\Templates folder to display an initial list of templates. These are predefined templates that can be tweaked for a company's specific needs. When a new template is created or an existing one is copied, it's added to this list. Select any one of these preloaded policies, and the right pane of the console displays all of the security areas available for configuration (Figure 18-1).

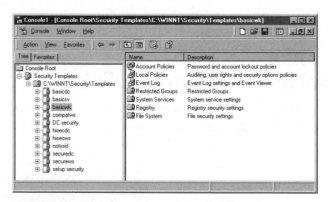

Figure 18-1. *Predefined security templates.*

Essentially, each template in the list represents a single readable .INF file. The snap-in is merely an interface for modifying these security template files. The files can be found in the system root folder under %SystemRoot%\Security\Templates.

The following is a small excerpt from the securews template (Securews.inf), showing the Account Policies area:

```
[System Access]
;------------------------------------------------
;Account Policies - Password Policy
;------------------------------------------------
MinimumPasswordAge = 2
MaximumPasswordAge = 42
MinimumPasswordLength = 8
PasswordComplexity = 1
PasswordHistorySize = 6
RequireLogonToChangePassword = 0
ClearTextPassword = 0
```

Examining Template Policies

Each template contains attribute settings for the seven areas of security configurable in Windows 2000. Double-click a security area in the right pane of the console or expand the console tree in the left pane to display the specific sections.

Account Policies

The Account Policies area includes policies pertaining to user accounts. It contains Password Policy, Account Lockout Policy, and Kerberos Policy.

Local Policies

The Local Policies area includes policies pertaining to who has local or network access to the computer and how events are audited. This area contains Audit Policy, User Rights Assignment, and Security Options.

Event Log

The Event Log area contains attributes that determine how the application, security, and system event logs behave. Log attributes include maximum size and access restriction. Event logs can be viewed in Event Viewer.

Restricted Groups

The Restricted Groups security setting is for adding members to built-in user groups, which have predefined capabilities, or to other administrator-defined groups that might be privileged. Built-in user groups include Administrators, Power Users, and Backup Operators.

System Services

The System Services area includes security attributes of all system services on the local computer. System services include file services, print services, network services, and telephone services.

Registry

The Registry area contains security attributes for existing registry keys, including auditing information and the access permissions.

File System

The File System area allows the configuration of access permissions and auditing of specific directories and files on the local system.

Using Predefined Templates

The predefined templates supplied by Windows 2000 can be used as is, or they can be customized to conform to a more rigorous security requirement. These templates span a range of security levels and represent typical security scenarios for the different types of computers found in a system—namely workstations, servers, and domain controllers. Table 18-1 shows some of the predefined security templates, categorized by security level.

Table 18-1. Some predefined security templates

Security Level	Template Name	Description
Default	basicwk	Default workstation template
	basicsv	Default server template
	basicdc	Default domain controller template
Secure	securews	Secure workstation or server template
	securedc	Secure domain controller template
Highly secure	hisecws	Highly secure workstation or server template
	hisecdc	Highly secure domain controller template
Compatible	compatws	Compatible workstation or server template
Out of the box	Setup security	Out-of-the-box default settings template
	DC security	Out-of-the-box domain controller settings template

Default Security Templates

The basic security templates for workstations, servers, and domain controllers contain Windows 2000 default settings for account and local policies, as well as typical values for event log maintenance and basic permissions for system services. In addition, these basic templates include default access permissions for system files, directories, and registry keys that, when applied, overwrite the existing security settings of these objects and their children. These basic templates, however, intentionally omit user rights assignments so as not to overwrite any assignments made by application setup programs. This omission means that the basic security templates can be applied to a machine to reset the security configuration of that system.

A closer look at the three basic templates reveals minor differences among them. While the basic workstation template includes default configurations for necessary system services, the basic server template adds default configurations for automatic startup of server-only services, such as Microsoft SMTP Service and License Logging. The basic domain controller template omits system services configuration all together. The basic domain controller template is more suited for a domain controller that services users.

Secure Security Templates

Two secure templates are provided: one for the domain controller and a combined template for the workstation and server. With stricter password and lockout policies and with audit logs that restrict guest access and hold up to five times the audit information of the basic templates (ten times for the domain controller), the secure templates provide a medium layer of security.

The secure templates also enable more of the auditing features than the basic templates do. Unsuccessful login events and privilege use, as well as successful and unsuccessful account management and policy changes, are configured for auditing. In addition, the secure domain controller template provides auditing for object and directory service access. Account and local policies also appear in the secure domain controller template, though they are absent from the basic domain controller template. Since the permissions of files, folders, and registry keys are configured securely by default, these security areas are omitted in this template type.

Highly Secure Security Templates

The highly secure templates are actually quite lean and concentrate on the security of communications in native-mode (Windows 2000) environments. In short, security attributes are set for digitally signing client-side and server-side communications and for signing and encrypting secure channel data. Since maximum protocol protection is set, however, systems to which these templates are applied will not be able to communicate with machines running Microsoft Windows 95, Microsoft Windows 98, or Microsoft Windows NT. Aside from there being no Authenticated Users in the Power Users restricted group in the highly secure workstation/ server (hisecws) template, the highly secure workstation/server and domain controller templates are essentially the same.

Compatible Security Template

In the basic workstation template, Authenticated Users are, by default, Power Users. The secure and highly secure workstation templates remove Authenticated Users from the Power Users group. Since the goal of the compatible security template is to allow most applications to run successfully, but not at the cost of compromising the security levels of Power Users, this template also removes Authenticated Users from the Power Users group. With the Authenticated Users group downgraded, the template facilitates compatibility by lowering security on the folders, files, and registry keys typically accessed by applications.

Out-of-the-Box Security Templates

The setup security template contains out-of-the-box security settings for workstations and servers. The domain controller security template builds on the setup security template, adding default security settings for domain controllers.

Modifying a Predefined Template

You can use a predefined template as a starting point for your own security scheme. First make a copy of it by right-clicking the template name and choosing Save As. Next specify a filename, being sure to retain the .INF extension. You can modify the attributes in any of the security areas of your new template by fully expanding the template tree to that area. For attributes, right-click an attribute name and choose Security from the shortcut menu to open the Template Security Policy Setting dialog box. For the Restricted Group, Registry, and File System folders, right-click the folder and choose Add Group, Add Key, or Add File, respectively.

Defining New Templates

You may also choose to generate a security template entirely from scratch. In the console tree of the Security Templates snap-in, right-click the parent default template folder (%SystemRoot%\Security\Templates) and choose New Template. In the dialog box that appears, type a template name and a description of the template's purpose. The new template is saved as an .INF file in the Templates folder and is added to the list of available templates.

At this point, the new template file is empty, except for some version and description info. Viewing any of the policy attributes in the new template will list attributes as Not Defined. The Restricted Groups, Registry, and File System folders will simply contain no entries.

For each security area, you can configure any or all of the security attributes or you can choose to leave that area unconfigured. To modify an attribute's settings, right-click the attribute in the right pane and choose Security. The Template Security Policy settings dialog box appears. Select the Define These Policy Settings In The Template check box to enable the settings and set the attribute. Figure 18-2 shows the dialog box for the Retention Method For Security Log attribute. The stored settings in the various attributes represent a range of data types, including Boolean (enable, disable), integers (maximum file size), and dates and times.

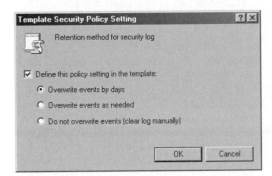

Figure 18-2. *The dialog box for the Retention Method For Security Log attribute.*

It's just as easy to configure those security areas that contain a list of items instead of individual attributes. Right-click Restricted Groups, Registry, or File System, and select Add Group, Add Key, or Add File, respectively. You can then browse for the object to add and choose access permissions, ownership, and auditing information in the Access Control dialog box.

Once the security template is complete, save it by right-clicking the template name and choosing Save. It's then ready to be applied to the local computer or to a Group Policy object.

Planning When creating new security templates for your system architecture, remember that security can be applied through the layering of templates. The configuration database allows templates to be imported one after another, so that the security policies in the different templates have a masking effect. Conflicts of specific attributes are resolved by giving highest priority to the most recently loaded template. This means that templates with varying degrees of security do not need to contain redundant data. Instead, basic security attributes can be applied with a standard security template that you load first. Higher-level security templates then need to contain only security differences between the two levels.

Applying Templates

A security template containing system security settings can be either applied to a local computer or pushed to a group of computers by importing it into a Group Policy object. Applying the template to a local computer is done through the Security Configuration and Analysis snap-in. See the section "Importing and Exporting Templates," later in this chapter, for detailed instructions.

To import the security template into a Group Policy object, choose the target Group Policy object in the MMC. Expand the object, and then expand Computer Configuration and Windows Settings to display Security Settings. Right-click Security Settings and choose Import Policy. A list of security templates appears, each templete being an .INF file. Choose the desired template.

Tip Reduce the administrative hassle of configuring large arrays of security attributes by modifying predefined templates whenever possible.

Using Security Configuration and Analysis

Security Configuration and Analysis is an MMC snap-in that allows an administrator to check the state of a system's security against one or more security templates and make appropriate modifications. Useful as both a setup tool and a maintenance tool, the snap-in lets you import predefined or modified security templates, analyze every security area against those templates with a single command, and view concise results. You can then synchronize system security to the template at once or resolve discrepancies on an attribute-by-attribute basis.

This tool, along with an appropriate security template, is invaluable for setting up the initial security configuration of a machine on which many security attributes and file, folder, and registry-key permissions have to be defined. A company or division's entire computer security policy can be translated into a single template and imported to quickly configure one or more machines. In addition, the snap-in is useful for maintaining the security level of a system. Invariably, in the course of resolving temporary network or administrative problems, security attributes become disabled and permissions of objects are set to full access. Periodically analyzing a system's security against its defining template allows you to locate and easily fix security flaws.

Finally, the tool permits you to export security templates that have been modified during the configuration of a machine or to reevaluate such templates in the Security Templates snap-in. If more than one template has been imported, you can save a single composite template that is the sum of all of the template settings.

Opening a Security Database

Like any other MMC snap-in, Security Configuration and Analysis is added to the MMC by choosing Add/Remove Snap-In from the Console menu. Click the Add button and select Security Configuration And Analysis from the list of snap-ins provided.

Security templates are imported into a database, which is used to perform the analysis and configuration. Security database files use an .SDB extension. To create a new database or open an existing one, right-click Security Configuration And Analysis and choose Open Database. In the Open Database dialog box, select an .SDB file to open or type a new filename to create a database. When you type a new filename, a second dialog box appears allowing the import of a base security template. Choose a predefined template or a template modified with the Security Templates snap-in. The list of predefined templates is in the %SystemRoot%\Security\Templates folder. See the section "Using Predefined Templates," earlier in this chapter, for an explanation of these security templates.

Importing and Exporting Templates

Once you have opened a security database, you can import additional security templates into it. To do so, right-click Security Configuration And Analysis and choose Import Template. Select the .INF template file that you want to import. This template supplements the current database template or templates; it does not replace them.

In the process of analyzing and configuring a system's security with a database template, you may find it necessary to define a more precise policy and thereby modify the template. This modification is *not* saved to the original imported template; instead, it is saved as a database copy. To use the modified template on another machine, you'll need to export it. You can also combine multiple imported templates into a single composite template that you then export. To export a template, right-click Security Configuration And Analysis and choose Export Template. In the ensuing dialog box, choose a filename for the template, using the .INF extension.

Analyzing Security and Viewing the Results

Once you have imported the necessary templates into the database, you can analyze the system. To analyze system security, right-click Security Configuration And Analysis and choose Analyze System Now. In the Perform Analysis dialog box, select the target path and filename of the analysis results. Click OK, and the Analyzing System Security progress window appears, as shown in Figure 18-3.

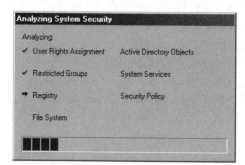

Figure 18-3. *The Analyzing System Security progress window.*

The analysis generates two types of results. First, the success and failure of each analyzed component is written to an error log. Second, the security areas listed under Security Configuration And Analysis in the console tree are populated. Each area gives the analysis results in an attribute-by-attribute comparison. When the analysis is complete, view the error log by right-clicking Security Configuration And Analysis and choosing View Log File. The log appears in the right pane with a date and time stamp; it reports on the completion of each analyzed area. The following code is a small excerpt from a typical log file:

```
View Log File
---------------------------------------------
07/03/1999 18:49:00
----Analysis engine is initialized successfully.----

----Reading Configuration info...

...

----Analyze Security Policy...
Analyze password information.
Analyze account lockout information.
Analyze other policy settings.

System Access analysis completed successfully.
Analyze log settings.
Analyze event audit settings.

Audit/Log analysis completed successfully.

Registry values analysis completed successfully.
```

This log file does not show discrepancies in individual attributes but rather integral errors in the analysis. To view the actual analysis results, expand Security Configuration And Analysis in the console tree. The familiar seven areas of system security appear: Account Policies, Local Policies, Event Log, Restricted Groups, System Services, Registry, and File System.

To view analysis results for any of these areas, expand the area and highlight a subcategory. Restricted Groups and System Services are not hierarchical and need only to be highlighted. Figure 18-4 shows sample results for Security Options under Local Policies.

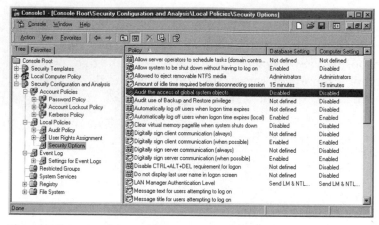

Figure 18-4. *Analysis results for Security Options.*

In the right pane of the console, each attribute is followed by two settings: the stored template (database) setting and the analyzed system (computer) setting. The icon for the attribute in which settings agree contains a green check mark. If the database and computer settings differ, a red "X" punctuates the attribute icon. Attributes that are not configured in the template are not analyzed, and no marking appears in the icon.

In the figure, all attribute settings agree except Allow System To Be Shutdown Without Having To Log On. This setting is enabled in the template but disabled on the system. Seven other attributes are not configured (defined) in the template and thus are not analyzed.

Configuring Security

After you've successfully analyzed the system and found discrepancies between database and computer settings, you have a few alternatives. Depending on your evaluation of the results, you may decide that the current security template is not appropriate for this computer. A more stringent or relaxed template may be required, or perhaps vital attributes were left unconfigured and additional security areas need to be addressed. The solution is to import a template that is better suited to your particular security requirements. Templates can be added in increasing order of importance. New templates that are merged into the database override any conflicting attributes or permissions.

On the other hand, you may decide that the correct template was indeed used but that the computer settings are actually inappropriate. In this case, you'll want to change the database template so that further analysis won't show any discrepancies. To do so, right-click the offending attribute and choose Security to display a dialog box in which you can change the database template. For example, right-clicking the attribute showing a conflict in Figure 18-4 displays the dialog box shown in Figure 18-5. You can change the template setting to match the computer setting, or you can clear the Define This Policy In The Database check box to specify that the setting should no longer be considered during analysis.

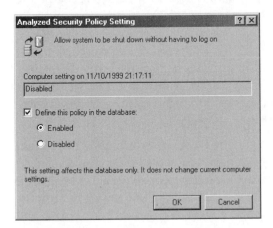

Figure 18-5. *Reconciling a conflict between a system security setting and a template setting.*

Finally, you may determine that the security template is right on and that the system is in violation of your security policy and needs to be aligned. Once you've weeded out all of the template mismatches and only valid discrepancies remain, you'll want to configure the system. Do this by right-clicking Security Configuration And Analysis and choosing Configure Computer Now.

Enabling Authentication

Among its many other tasks, the domain controller authenticates users to a network, using security policies and user authentication information stored in the Active Directory directory service. During an *interactive logon,* a user logs on to a domain account with a password or smart card. The domain controller confirms the user's identity with the information stored in Active Directory. Once an interactive logon to a domain controller has taken place, *network authentication* is performed for the user without any further effort on the user's part. The user can access resources on the network without having to reenter a password or smart card personal identification number (PIN). An interactive logon can also authenticate a user to a local computer rather than a domain account. With a local interactive logon, network authentication requires the reentry of a password any time the user needs to access a network resource.

The Kerberos version 5 authentication protocol is used for interactive logon and is also the default protocol for network authentication. Each domain controller includes Kerberos version 5. Both the key distribution center and the ticket-granting service are components of Kerberos and become integral parts of the domain controller. The key distribution center runs as part of Active Directory, which stores passwords and user account information for authentication. A Kerberos client is installed on all Windows 2000 workstations and servers. See Chapter 17 for more information on Kerberos authentication.

Remote access clients, in addition to logging on to the network, must be authenticated by the remote access server before they can access the network. Smart cards and certificates, as well as password-based protocols, are used for dial-up networking. The next section explains how to obtain and use cryptographic tokens for network authentication, as well as how to configure remote clients and servers.

Obtaining Smart Cards and Certificates

Smart cards combine the security of public-key cryptography with the portability of passwords. Before a smart card can be used for authentication, a logon certificate needs to be programmed onto the card. This is done by an administrator, who requests a smart card certificate from a certificate authority (CA) through an enroll-on-behalf-of station. See Chapter 19 for information on preparing a CA to issue smart card certificates.

More Info   Visit the PC/SC Workgroup Web site at *http://www.smartcardsys.com/* for information on emerging smart card technologies and smart card vendors.

Setting Up an Enrollment Agent

To request smart card certificates from a CA, the administrator needs a special certificate to sign the request. This certificate, known as an *enrollment agent certificate,* must be requested by a logged-on domain administrator from the dedicated machine that will be used to program smart cards. An enrollment agent certificate is a software-based certificate and private key that can be requested through the Certificates MMC snap-in. (See the section "Requesting Certificates," later in this chapter.) Be sure to use the enrollment agent certificate template, as this is what authorizes the administrator to make smart card certificate requests.

Caution   It's possible, though highly inadvisable, to allow users to program their own smart cards by giving them access rights to the enrollment agent certificate template. Administrative programming and distribution of smart cards provides more accountability.

Programming Smart Cards

Once the administrator has installed a smart card reader on a system and has obtained the enrollment agent certificate, the system is ready to program smart cards. Smart card installation adds a cryptographic service provider (CSP) to the system that will be selected during the smart card programming process. (See the section "Cryptographic Application Programming Interface" in Chapter 17 for more information.)

The Web-based request process first generates a public/private-key pair on your smart card. Using the public key and the user's name, the certificate authority issues and signs a certificate. Finally the certificate is added to the smart card. To program a smart card, follow these steps:

1. With the domain administrator as the current user, open Microsoft Internet Explorer and specify the certificate server URL. The URL will be the name of the server followed by *Certsrv*.

2. Select Request A Certificate and then click Next.

3. Select Advanced Request and then click Next.

4. Choose the option Request A Certificate For A Smart Card On Behalf Of Another User Using The Smart Card Enrollment Station. Click Next.

5. The Smart Card Enrollment Station Web page appears. Set the fields to the values shown in Table 18-2.

6. Click Submit Certificate Request.

7. After the request has been fulfilled by the certificate authority, you are prompted to insert the card and enter the smart card's PIN. This loads the certificate onto the card.

Table 18-2. Values for fields on the Smart Card Enrollment Station Web page

Field	Value
Certification Template	Smart card login
Certificate Authority	CA to issue certificate
Cryptographic Service Provider	The smart card manufacturer's CSP
Administrator Signing Certificate	The enrollment agent certificate (see the previous section)
User To Enroll	The name of the end user of the smart card

Note Smart card certificates for users requiring different functionality (such as encryption) can be programmed similarly by specifying a different certification template.

Obtaining Software-Based Certificates

Authentication can also be accomplished with private keys and certificates residing on a local computer. See the section "Requesting Certificates," later in this chapter, for information on how to obtain a certificate through the Certificates snap-in.

Logging On with Smart Cards

Once a smart card reader has been installed on the target system and the user has obtained a properly programmed smart card from the administrator, the user can use the smart card to log on to the computer. To do so, the user simply inserts the smart card into the reader and enters a PIN when prompted to do so. This process takes the place of pressing Ctrl+Alt+Del and entering a user name and password.

Caution To keep thieves from accessing the system by using a stolen card, the system tallies incorrect login attempts. After three consecutive failures, the card is locked out of the system.

Enabling Remote Certificate or Smart Card Authentication

As was mentioned earlier, a user's public-key certificate, used for authentication, can be either programmed onto a smart card or stored locally on the computer. Follow the steps in the next two sections to enable dial-in authentication for each scenario.

Authentication with Certificate on Smart Card

1. From the Start menu on the remote machine, open Control Panel and double-click Network And Dial-up Connections.

2. Right-click the network or dial-up connection for which you want to enable authentication and choose Properties. In the Properties window for the dial-up connection, click the Security tab (Figure 18-6).

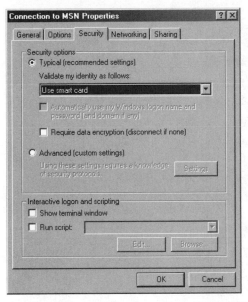

Figure 18-6. *The Properties window for the dial-up connection.*

3. Ensure that Typical is selected and that the Validate My Identity As Follows list box is set to Use Smart Card, as shown in Figure 18-6. The Require Data Encryption check box can be selected for additional security.

Authentication with Certificate Stored on Local Computer

1. From the Start menu on the remote machine, open Control Panel and double-click Network And Dial-up Connections.

2. Right-click the network or dial-up connection for which you want to enable authentication and choose Properties. In the Properties window for the dial-up connection, click the Security tab (Figure 18-6).

3. Select the Advanced option in the dial-up connection's Properties window and click the Settings button. In the Advanced Security Settings dialog box, shown in Figure 18-7, select Use Extensible Authentication Protocol (EAP) and make sure that the list box shows Smart Card Or Other Certificate (Encryption Enabled).

4. Click the Properties button to display the Smart Card Or Other Certificate Properties window, as shown in Figure 18-8. To configure authentication for certificates residing in the local certificate store, select Use A Certificate On This Computer.

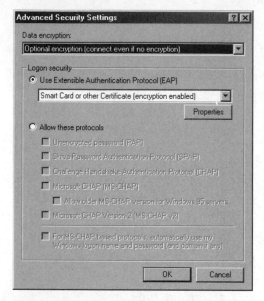

Figure 18-7. *The Advanced Security Settings dialog box.*

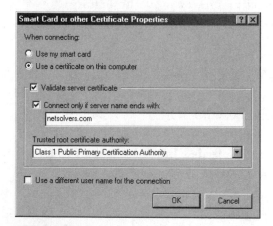

Figure 18-8. *Setting properties for smart card or certificate authentication.*

> **Note** The Advanced Security Settings dialog box is also used to set alternate password authentication protocols for a connection. These protocols, listed under Allow These Protocols, range from the unencrypted Password Authentication Protocol (PAP) to version 2 of the Microsoft Challenge Handshake Authentication Protocol (MS-CHAP v2). One or more of these allowable protocols can be selected.

5. Two other certificate-specific options appear in this window. First you can restrict connections to specific servers. To do this, select the Validate Server Certificate option and activate one or both of the validation methods:

   - **Connect Only If Server Name Ends With** This option requires servers to be in a certain domain. For instance, enter *netsolvers.com* in this box to connect only to servers in the Netsolver domain.

   - **Trusted Root Certificate Authority** This option lets you choose which certificate hierarchy the server belongs to. See the section "Importing Certificates," later in this chapter, for information on how to add a certificate as a root certificate authority.

   The second option, Use A Different User Name For The Connection, keeps the authentication process from automatically using the certificate subject as the user name. This allows you to specify an alternate name.

6. Click OK to close the window.

> **Planning** Whether you're using smart card–based authentication, password-based authentication, or a mix of the two, ensure that your remote access clients and remote access servers support at least one common authentication method.

Configuring Authentication for a Remote Access Server

In addition to configuring the remote access client, you'll also need to set up the remote access server to allow smart card–based and certificate-based logins. Follow these steps to do so:

1. Choose Routing And Remote Access from the Administrative Tools folder on the Programs menu.

2. Right-click the name of the remote access server and choose Properties. On the Security tab, click Authentication Methods, ensure that the Extensible Authentication Protocol (EAP) check box is selected, and then click OK twice.

3. Back in the Routing And Remote Access dialog box, expand the remote access server and click Remote Access Policies. Right-click the policy that will be used when the smart card clients log on and choose Properties. Click the Edit Profile button, and in the Edit Dial-In Profile dialog box, click the Authentication tab. Select the Extensible Authentication Protocol check box. This will also enable the EAP type; make sure that Smart Card Or Other Certificate is selected. Click the Configure button and select the machine certificate to use for authentication.

Note If clicking the Configure button returns an error stating that no certificate could be found, a machine certificate needs to be installed. This can be accomplished by ensuring that your enterprise CA is configured for auto-enrollment, which automatically allocates computer certificates for members of the domain. With this configured, run *secedit /refreshpolicy machine_policy* from a Windows 2000 command prompt on your remote access server to create a computer certificate.

Implementing Access Control

In the real world, authorization is dictated by policy. When it comes to using resources, reading documents, or accessing rooms, different people have different access rights. The implementation of this policy can be locked safes or badge-access rooms. In the Windows 2000 environment, authorization is also based on policy. Different people or groups of people have different access rights. Policy here is implemented through access control. Quite simply, access control determines which users can access which resources. Resources in Windows 2000 are

- Files and folders, which can be accessed through Windows Explorer
- Shared volumes, folders, and files, which are allowed permissions on both NTFS and FAT file systems
- Active Directory objects, which are managed with the Active Directory Users and Computers snap-in
- Registry keys, which are managed with the Registry Editor
- Services, which are managed with the Security Configuration Tool Set
- Printers, which are configured through Settings on the Start menu

Each resource has a security descriptor associated with it that defines the object's owner, the object's access permissions, and the object's auditing information. Auditing of the object is discussed in the section "Auditing," later in this chapter.

For Active Directory objects, administrative responsibility can be delegated to group administrators. Delegating allows object permissions to be managed in one organizational unit of the domain, without requiring multiple administrators for the entire domain. For more information, see the section "Delegating Object Control" in Chapter 10.

Establishing Ownership

The owner of an object controls who can access the object by setting object permissions. By default, the object's owner is its creator. Typically, administrators create most network objects and are responsible for setting the object permissions.

One of the standard permissions associated with all objects is the Take Ownership permission. By granting this permission, the owner allows a user (or member of a group) to assume ownership of the object. Taking ownership can be done through the tool that manages the specific type of object. For example, printers are managed through the interface found under Settings on the Start menu. The Security tab on the Properties window for the printer shows the groups and users for which permissions are set. Clicking the Advanced button opens the Access Control Settings dialog box. With the correct permissions, ownership can be modified on the Owner tab. Administrators can assume control of any object under their administrative jurisdiction, regardless of the setting of the Take Ownership permission for the object.

Assigning Permissions

Object permissions are broken down into specific actions that can be performed on that particular object. For registry keys, this includes the ability to create subkeys and set values. For Active Directory objects, permissions include the ability to create and delete children.

Permissions are set for the specific users or groups who perform actions on a particular object. For a given folder, one group may be granted permissions to create and delete files within that folder. Another group may be allowed only to list the folder's contents. Figure 18-9 shows printer permissions granted to Everyone.

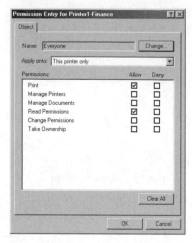

Figure 18-9. *Printer permissions for the group Everyone.*

To display permissions for a user or group, choose an entry in the Access Control Settings dialog box, and click the View/Edit button. The owner of the object, or a user or group granted Change Permissions permission, can use this dialog box to modify permissions for the user or group. To add a user or group to the access control list (Figure 18-10), click the Add button and select the user or group to add. Remember to set the appropriate permissions.

Tip The burden of administering a domain of user rights and permissions can be eased by following a few guidelines. First, delegate administration to local authorities whenever closer management of users and services makes sense. Second, assign permissions on a group basis, rather than on a user basis. Third, set permissions at common node points in Active Directory and let them propagate down the tree to lower nodes.

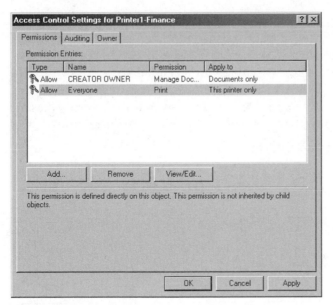

Figure 18-10. *The Access Control Settings dialog box.*

Managing Certificates

Public-key certificates serve as the security medium for many of the Windows 2000 protocols and mechanisms. Network authentication, IPSec, Encrypting File System (EFS), Secure Socket Layer (SSL), and Secure Multipurpose Internet Mail Extensions (S/MIME) all use certificates. MMC provides the Certificates snap-in for the single purpose of managing user, computer, and service certificates.

To add the Certificates snap-in to MMC, run *mmc.exe* from the Start menu. From the Console menu, select Add/Remove Snap-In. Click the Add button and select Certificates from the list of snap-ins provided. You'll be given a choice of which account to manage certificates for: My User Account, Service Account, or Computer Account. For the service and computer accounts, you can select which computer the snap-in will manage. For the service account, you'll also need to specify which service to manage.

Note Users can manage only their personal certificates. Certificates for computers and services are managed by administrators.

The certificate store is made up of five categories: Personal, Trusted Root Certification Authorities, Enterprise Trust, Intermediate Certification Authorities, and Active Directory User Object. Trusted Root and Intermediate CA certificates are preloaded. To view the details of any certificate, double-click the certificate. Figure 18-11 shows the public key of a VeriSign root certificate.

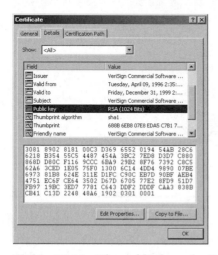

Figure 18-11. *The public key of a VeriSign root certificate.*

Exporting Certificates and Private Keys

The Export command in the Certificates snap-in really provides two distinct functions. First, it allows a certificate or certificate chain to be exported for the purpose of sharing it with users or computers that are not privy to a certificate directory. Second, it allows the export of a certificate or certificate chain *along with the associated private key* for cryptographic use on another machine.

Note By default, only private keys for basic EFS and EFS recovery agents are marked as available for export. This keeps all other private keys from being unnecessarily exposed. Certificates and keys that are purposely meant to be exported can be marked during certificate request.

You can export any type of certificate, including those in root CAs. Naturally, only certificates with available private keys (that is, personal certificates) that are marked as exported can be exported together. To export a certificate, follow these steps:

1. Find the certificate in the Certificates snap-in and right-click the entry.

2. Point to All Tasks and choose Export. You'll be welcomed to the Certificate Export Wizard.

3. Make your way through the wizard, choosing whether to export the private key (if available).

4. Choose the format for storing the certificate. DER Encoded Binary and Base 64 Encoded are single-certificate formats. With the PKCS #7 format, you can include the full certificate chain. Private-key combinations are stored in a PKCS #12 file and are password protected; you'll need to specify a password for the file.

5. Enter a target path and filename for the exported certificate.

Tip With a highly populated certificate database, finding a particular certificate for exporting or enabling may be difficult. Use the Find Certificate command, found by right-clicking the Certificates snap-in, to locate certificates by issuer (Issued By), subject (Issued To), fingerprint (SHA1 Hash or MD5 Hash), or serial number.

Importing Certificates

Users can import certificates into any one of the certificate categories found in the certificate store. In the Certificates snap-in, right-click the certificate category to which you want to import the certificate, point to All Tasks, and choose Import. Enter the certificate filename, which should have a standard certificate format extension (.PFX, .P12, .CER, .CRT, .P7B, .STL, .SPC, .CRL, or .SST). For PKCS #12 files, which contain private keys as well as certificates, you'll need to enter the password used to protect the file.

Caution Root certificates are the basis of trust for certificate verification. Be extremely careful when importing a root certificate. Ensure that the certificate was received from a trusted source and that the certificate thumbprint matches a trusted publication.

Requesting Certificates

Before using any application that relies on the public-key infrastructure, you'll need a certificate. Chapter 19 covers how to configure and install Microsoft

Certificate Services. Certificate servers configured to be enterprise CAs can request certificates by using the Certificates snap-in.

> **Tip** Using Internet Explorer version 3 or later, you can request certificates from Microsoft Certificate Services, running in either Standalone or Enterprise mode, through the Web interface.

The certificate request process involves first generating a key pair consisting of a public key and a private key. The private key is stored and protected on the local computer. The public key, along with information identifying the user, is sent to the CA as a certificate request. If the CA determines that the user, device, or service is authorized for the certificate being requested, the CA generates and signs the certificate. The certificate can then be retrieved with the Certificates snap-in and placed in the local certificate store.

To request a certificate, right-click the Certificates folder under the Personal certificate store. Point to All Tasks, choose Request New Certificate, and follow the instructions in the Certificate Request Wizard. You'll need to choose a certificate type (the purpose for which the certificate will be used), a friendly name for the certificate, and the CA that will issue the certificate, if more than one is available. To allow you to download the certificate once the CA has issued it, the Certificate Request Wizard provides the Install Certificate option.

> **Caution** The advanced options of the Certificate Request Wizard will allow private keys to be exported. Be extremely judicious when selecting this option. Exported private keys can allow other users to read your encrypted data.

Enabling Certificates for Specific Purposes

Certificates can be issued for specific types of uses. These uses are programmed directly into the certificate, using a certificate extension field. For example, the Key Usage certificate extension tells whether a certificate can be used for data signing, certificate signing, nonrepudiation, or other functions. The Enhanced Key Usage extension extends this property to other uses, such as time stamping or file recovery.

Certificates can also be enabled for certain purposes on an account basis. That is, a user or administrator can decide which certificates to allow or disallow for specific uses. While the actual certificate can't be modified, the attributes in the certificate store can be configured. For example, a certain certificate may have no internal key usage restriction. However, a user may want to enable that certificate only for code signing and secure e-mail.

To set certificate purposes, right-click the certificate and choose Properties. The three choices for enabling certificate purposes, as shown in Figure 18-12, are Enable All Purposes For This Certificate, Disable All Purposes For This Certificate, and Enable Only The Following Purposes. Choose the third option and select the purposes you want that certificate used for. Remember that only purposes allowed by the actual certificate or certificate path will appear in the list.

Figure 18-12. *Options for enabling certificate purposes.*

Using Internet Protocol Security Policies

IPSec provides end-to-end security for network communications—in the form of confidentiality, integrity, and authentication—using public-key technology to protect individual IP packets. Chapter 17 provides a description of this protocol. This section covers the MMC snap-in for IPSec configuration, IP Security Policy Management.

To add the IP Security Policy Management snap-in to the MMC, select Add/Remove Snap-In from the Console menu. Click Add and select IP Security Policy Management from the list of available snap-ins. The dialog box that appears allows you to select the range of management: the local computer, the local computer's domain, another domain, or another computer.

Defining IPSec Policies

An IPSec policy is passed from the policy agent to the IPSec driver and defines proper procedures for all facets of the protocol, from when and how to secure data to what security methods to use. Policies can get a bit involved. Before jumping into the actual configuration, let's go over some terminology by defining the components of an IPSec policy.

- **IP filter**   A subset of network traffic based on IP address, port, and transport protocol. It tells the IPSec driver what outbound and inbound traffic should be secured.

- **IP filter list**   The concatenation of one or more IP filters, defining a range of network traffic.

- **Filter action**   How the IPSec driver should secure network traffic.

- **Security method**   Security algorithms and types used for authentication and key exchange.

- **Tunnel setting**   The IP address or DNS name of the tunnel endpoint (if using IPSec tunneling to protect the packet destination).

- **Connection type**   The type of connection affected by the IPSec policy: remote access, LAN, or all network connections.

- **Rule**   A composite of the components: an IP filter, a filter action, the security methods, a tunnel setting, and a connection type. An IPSec policy may have multiple rules to protect each subset of network traffic differently.

Using Predefined IPSec Policies

Three basic predefined policies are available for immediate use or as a starting point for more involved IPSec policies. Figure 18-13 shows the predefined policies.

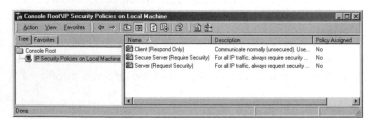

Figure 18-13. *The three predefined IPSec policies.*

The Client (Respond Only) policy should be used on computers that normally do not send secured data. This policy will not initiate secure communications. If security is requested by a server, the client will respond, securing only the requested protocol and port traffic with that server.

The Server (Request Security) policy can be used on any computer—client or server—that needs to initiate secure communications. Unlike the Client policy, the Server policy attempts to protect all outbound transmissions. Unsecured inbound transmissions will be accepted but not resolved until IPSec requests security from the sender for all subsequent transmissions. The strictest of the predefined policies, the Secure Server (Require Security) policy will neither send nor accept unsecured transmissions. Clients attempting to communicate with a secure server must use at least the Server predefined policy or an equivalent.

The section that follows demonstrates how to generate an IPSec policy from scratch. Let's first peruse one of the predefined policies to get our feet wet. Notice in Figure 18-13 that the Secure Server policy is selected . Right-clicking this policy and choosing Properties brings up the Secure Server (Require Security) Properties window, with the Rules tab in the foreground, as shown in Figure 18-14.

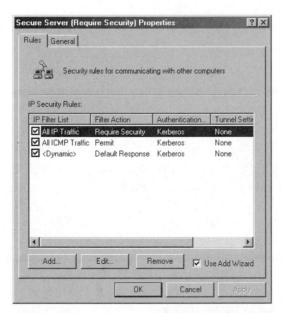

Figure 18-14. *The Secure Server (Require Security) Properties window.*

This policy has three rules, all activated, as indicated by the check marks. The first rule has an IP filter of All IP Traffic, a filter action of Require Security, an authentication method of Kerberos, a tunnel setting of None, and a connection type of All. A rule can be added or removed from this list with the appropriate buttons. Clicking the Edit button brings up an Edit Rule Properties dialog box with five tabs, one for configuring each field of the rule (Figure 18-15).

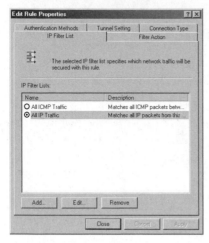

Figure 18-15. *The Edit Rule Properties dialog box.*

We'll explore these configurations in the next section. Back in the Secure Server (Require Security) Properties window (Figure 18-14), you can view the general properties of the policy—including a policy description and minute intervals at which to check for policy change—by clicking the General tab.

Clicking the Advanced button on the General tab displays a Key Exchange Settings dialog box, shown in Figure 18-16. This dialog box allows you to specify the life of a key in minutes or sessions. Using a short key lifetime makes transmission more secure by increasing the number of keys that an attacker would have to break, but it adds overhead to transmission time. Selecting the Master Key Perfect Forward Secrecy check box ensures that existing keys cannot be reused to generate additional keys. This option should be used with caution, as it adds significant overhead. Clicking the Methods button allows you to select security methods and preference order. A security method includes an encryption and integrity algorithm, along with a Diffie-Hellman group, which affects key generation.

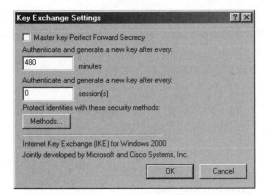

Figure 18-16. *The Key Exchange Settings dialog box.*

Creating an IPSec Policy

In addition to using a predefined IPSec policy as a template, an administrator can generate policies from the ground up with the IP Security Policies item in the MMC. A custom policy can be restrictive or permissive, simple or powerful, depending on the function of the machine, the environment in which it operates, and the types of systems it communicates with.

To add an IPSec policy, right-click the IP Security Policies item in the MMC and select Create IP Security Policy. You're presented with the IP Security Policy Wizard. The following steps guide you through this wizard:

1. Click Next at the welcome screen.

2. On the next screen, enter a meaningful policy name and description and click Next.

3. Select or clear the Activate The Default Response Rule check box, based on whether the policy should allow negotiation with computers that request IPSec. Clearing this check box will add an inactivated response rule to the policy. Click Next.

4. If you selected the Activate The Default Response Rule check box in the previous step, you see the dialog box shown in Figure 18-17, in which you choose the authentication method. Kerberos version 5 is the Windows 2000 default protocol but is allowed only on machines that are members of a domain. The second choice, Use A Certificate

From This Certificate Authority (CA), promotes public-key authentication. You'll need to choose a certificate authority that is appropriate for the certificate to be used. The third and final option allows you to type a preshared key that will be used for key exchange. This string must also be known by the requesting computer for successful exchange. Click Next when you've made your choice.

5. Select the Edit Properties check box if you want to display the policy's Properties window. You can also display this window by right-clicking the policy once it's listed and choosing Properties.

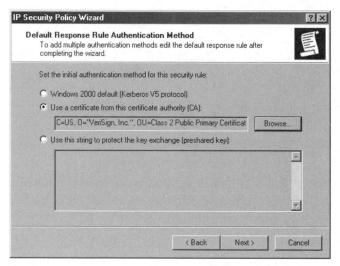

Figure 18-17. *Choosing an authentication method for the Default Response rule.*

Editing an IPSec Policy

The previous section showed how to create an IPSec policy, but in order to really add functionality to your policy, you'll need to edit it. (To do so, right-click the policy and choose Properties.) Figure 18-14 in the previous section shows the Properties window for an IPSec policy. A newly created policy will contain only one default response rule, which will be activated—or not activated—depending on the choices you made in the wizard during policy creation.

You add functionality to an IPSec policy by creating rules that govern when and how security should be supplied. Each combination of a filter list, filter action, authentication method, tunnel setting, and connection type is a separate rule.

Rules can be added manually or with the Add Wizard; both accomplish the same thing, but the wizard is a bit friendlier. We'll turn off the Add Wizard by clearing the Use Add Wizard check box in the lower right corner of the Properties window for the policy. Doing so will allow us to explore each aspect of a rule in its native dialog box. Editing rules after they're created will be done through this interface as well.

With the Add Wizard turned off, click the Add button. You're presented with the New Rule Properties dialog box, which, except for the title, is the same as the Edit Rule Properties dialog box shown in Figure 18-15. The dialog box has five tabs, one for each element of a rule. We'll look at each of the tabs in turn.

IP Filter List   The IP filter list is made up of one or more filters that specify which network traffic to act on. As shown in Figure 18-18, the All IP Traffic and the All ICMP Traffic filter lists are added by default but are not activated. In the figure, a third filter list has been added and activated by clicking its option button.

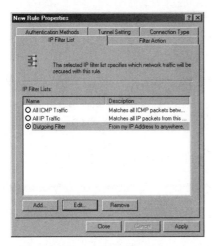

Figure 18-18. *The IP Filter List tab of the New Rule Properties dialog box.*

Clicking the Add button brings up the IP Filter List dialog box, which allows you to specify filters to include in a customized filter list. Figure 18-19 shows a filter list under construction. Here, if you click the Add button with the Use Add Wizard option turned on, the IP Filter Wizard will start, which allows you to construct a new filter based on the following categories:

- **Addressing**   Filters the source and destination addresses specified by IP address (My IP Address, Any IP Address, Specific IP Address, or Specific IP Subnet) or a specific DNS name.

- **Protocol**   Filters by protocol type, such as TCP, and source and destination ports.

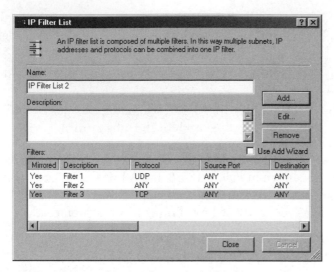

Figure 18-19. *The IP Filter List dialog box.*

Filter Action   The filter action determines how the IPSec driver responds to those computers represented by entries in the filter list and what security methods to use. You can choose one of the supplied actions shown in Figure 18-20 by selecting it, or you can add your own action.

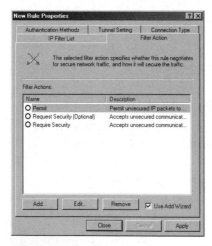

Figure 18-20. *The Filter Action tab of the New Rule Properties dialog box.*

The Request Security action causes the driver to attempt to establish secure communications with the client, but if this is unsuccessful it will communicate without security. The Require Security action requires clients to establish trust and security methods. The Permit action allows unsecured IP packets to pass through.

Adding an action involves choosing a filter name, a description, and general behavior that either permits communications, blocks communications, or negotiates security. If you choose to negotiate security, you'll need to configure two other areas. Under Handling Non-IPSec Clients, you choose either not to communicate with computers that don't support IPSec or to allow unsecured communication.

You also select a Security Method: high (encrypted, authenticated, and unmodified), medium (authenticated and unmodified), or custom. For the custom security method, you'll choose encryption and integrity algorithms and specify session key settings such as how often to generate new keys.

Authentication Methods   The authentication method specifies how trust will be established with the remote computer. You can specify one or more methods to use when requesting secure communications or when being requested for secure communications. Figure 18-21 shows three allowable authentication methods, listed in order of preference. Change the priority of a method with the Move Up and Move Down buttons. The Add button provides you with three choices for a new method. These choices are

- **Windows 2000 Default (Kerberos V5 Protocol)**
- **Use A Certificate**   This option uses public-key certificates for authentication. You'll need to specify the certificate authority of users or entities to authenticate. To allow authentication for users under separate CAs, add a separate authentication method for each.
- **Use This String To Protect The Key Exchange**   This option uses a preshared key that you specify in the box provided. You can use multiple preshared keys by adding additional authentication methods.

Tunnel Setting   The Tunnel Setting tab allows you to specify a tunneling endpoint if you choose to invoke IPSec tunneling. The endpoint can be specified as a DNS name if you're running DNS service on your network, or it can be in the form of an IP address.

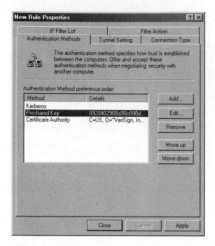

Figure 18-21. *The Authentication Methods tab of the New Rule Properties dialog box.*

Connection Type Finally, the Connection Type tab allows you to further refine a rule based on connection type. The All Network Connections option is set as the default; you can instead select either Local Area Network or Remote Access to create a stricter rule.

Assigning IPSec Policies

Once an IPSec policy has been established in the IP Security Policies item in MMC, it can be applied to a single machine or to a set of computers governed by a Group Policy object. To assign an IPSec policy to a local machine, right-click the policy name and choose Assign. The active policy's icon will include a green dot. If another policy has already been assigned, this action will reset that policy for this computer. Assign IPSec policies to groups by selecting the target Group Policy object in the MMC. Under this object, expand Computer Configuration, Windows Settings, and then Security Settings. Select IP Security Policies, right-click the desired policy, and choose Assign.

Tip IPSec policies can be transferred using the Import Policies and Export Policies commands on the Action menu under All Tasks.

Securing Local Data

Encryption of stored files in Windows 2000 is accomplished through the use of the Encrypting File System (EFS). Using public-key encryption, EFS allows files and directories stored on NTFS partitions to be encrypted and decrypted transparently. EFS accesses the user's EFS public and private keys to perform self-encryption. Therefore, files encrypted with EFS can't be shared with (that is, encrypted to) other users. Another encryption method, such as S/MIME, must be used to securely share files with other users. In addition, if files encrypted with EFS are saved to another machine, the user's key information must be imported to that machine for decryption to occur.

Files are automatically encrypted to a third party, called a recovery agent. In the event of key loss, the recovery agent can decrypt the files. EFS encrypts the bulk of the file with a single symmetric key. The symmetric key is then encrypted twice: once with the user's EFS public key to allow decryption, and once with the recovery agent's public key to allow data recovery. See the section "Public-Key Cryptography vs. Symmetric-Key Cryptography" in Chapter 17 for more information on data encryption.

Encrypting Files and Folders

Encrypting files with EFS is as easy as setting any other file attribute, such as Hidden or Read-Only. To encrypt a file in Windows Explorer, follow these steps:

1. Right-click the file and choose Properties.
2. On the General tab, click Advanced.
3. Select the Encrypt Contents To Secure Data check box and then click OK twice.
4. In the dialog box that appears, decide whether you want to encrypt the parent folder. If you do encrypt this folder, files subsequently added to this folder and its subfolders will be encrypted.

Note Remember that system files, compressed files, and files on partitions other than NTFS can't be encrypted using EFS. Further, a drive's root folder cannot be encrypted using EFS.

Like normal files, encrypted files can be moved and copied via the Edit menu commands Cut, Copy, and Paste. Files moved or copied using drag-and-drop will not necessarily retain their encryption. You can also rename encrypted files as you would any other file.

Caution Encrypted files and directories are not immune from deletion. Any user with appropriate rights can delete an encrypted file.

To encrypt a folder, right-click the folder and choose Properties. On the General tab of the folder's Properties window, click Advanced and select Encrypt Contents To Secure Data. Click OK twice and you'll be asked if you want all files and subfolders in the target folder to be encrypted as well. It's important to mention that the folder itself is not encrypted, merely the files within the folder. The folder is simply marked as having encrypted files within it.

Tip To ensure the security of temporary files that have been created by applications, mark your system's Temp folder for encryption.

Decrypting Files and Folders

EFS allows a user to reverse the encryption process. However, describing this as a mere decryption operation is a bit misleading. Indeed, removing data encryption from a file does cause the file to be decrypted, but any encrypted file is also decrypted every time a user or application accesses it. What we're talking about is permanent decryption so that files can be easily shared with other users.

To indicate that a file should no longer be encrypted or that a folder should no longer encrypt its files, follow these steps:

1. Right-click the file or folder in Windows Explorer and choose Properties.

2. Select the General tab and click Advanced.

3. Clear the Encrypt Contents To Secure Data check box.

More Info For a description of the specifics of cryptography, including symmetric-key and public-key methods, visit the security page of the Microsoft Web site at *http://www.microsoft.com/security*.

Recovering Files

Naturally, when you encrypt files to protect them from prying eyes, you run the risk of protecting them from yourself and ultimately losing the data. EFS requires the user's private key (associated with the user's EFS public-key certificate) to decrypt a file. As long as this key is available, EFS-protected files can be accessed. In the event of key loss, a secondary means of retrieving the data is necessary. Consider, too, that a key may be lost due to the voluntary or involuntary departure of a user; for example, a user who encrypts company files may leave the company.

The ability to recover files starts when an individual user backs up his or her EFS public-key certificate and associated private key. To back up this information, the user must export the certificate and key through the Certificates snap-in in the MMC. (See the section "Exporting Certificates and Private Keys," earlier in this chapter.) If the private key is ever lost, the user can import the saved EFS private key and certificate and salvage the data.

> **Note**   Exported keys and certificates are stored in a standard PKCS #12 (also known as Personal Information Exchange or PFX) format. This format is understood by a number of security-enhanced applications, allowing exchange of keys between independent computers or applications.

If a user is unable to decrypt lost data, an administrator can salvage the data by using a recovery agent certificate. In addition to obtaining a recovery agent certificate (see the section "Requesting Certificates," earlier in this chapter), the administrator will need to add that certificate to a recovery policy in Active Directory by using the Add Recovery Agent Wizard from the Group Policy snap-in.

Real World   Protecting Recovery Agent Certificates

Recovery agent certificates should be squirreled away in a secured storage facility to prevent possible data compromise. Upon receiving the recovery agent certificate, the recovery agent should export it to a diskette or other device that can be protected and delete it from the machine. When data needs to be recovered, the certificate and associated private key can be imported. Once the data has been recovered, the certificate should again be deleted. For information on exporting certificates, see the section "Exporting Certificates and Private Keys," earlier in this chapter.

Auditing

Both a proactive and reactive security tool, auditing informs administrators of events that might be potentially dangerous and leaves a trail of accountability if a security infraction does occur. Auditing failed login attempts, for instance, can warn of rogue users attempting to gain unauthorized access to the system. In addition to auditing normal system events, you can audit policy modification to keep a trail of when a specific event audit was disabled and by whom.

By default, auditing of all security categories is turned off. The administrator establishes an audit policy by determining which types of security events to audit. Based on the security needs of the organization, the administrator may also choose to audit access to individual objects.

Establishing an Audit Policy

The first step in establishing an audit policy is to determine which event categories should be audited. The following event categories are available for audit:

- Account logon events
- Account management
- Directory service access
- Logon events
- Object access
- Policy change
- Privilege use
- Process tracking
- System events

To select the event categories to audit, you must first determine whether the computer is a domain controller. If it is not, choose Computer Management from the Administrative Tools folder. In the Computer Management console tree, expand System Tools, Group Policy, Computer Configuration, Windows Settings, Security Settings, and Local Policies to reach Audit Policy.

If the computer is a domain controller, open the Active Directory Users And Computers snap-in, expand the domain's entry, click Action, and then click Properties. On the Group Policy tab, select the policy and click Edit. Then expand

Computer Configuration, Windows Settings, Security Settings, and Local Policies, and then select Audit Policy.

Using either technique, selecting Audit Policy displays the auditable event categories in the right pane. To modify the policy for an event category, right-click that event and choose Security. Select the check box for auditing successful events and/or auditing failed attempts.

Auditing Access to Objects

Once the Audit Object Access category is enabled in the Audit Policy item, members of the Administrators group can specify audit criteria for files, folders, network printers, and other objects. The audit criteria for an object include

- Who is audited for this object
- Whether accessing this object succeeded or failed
- What type of object access is audited

Tip Auditing of local files and folders is limited to NTFS partitions.

Examples of access types include viewing a folder's permissions, executing a file, and deleting an object. Follow these steps to select an object for auditing:

1. Right-click the object in Windows Explorer and choose Properties.
2. On the Security tab, click Advanced.
3. On the Auditing tab, click Add.
4. In the Name box, enter the user or group to audit, or select one from the Name list.
5. Click OK to display the Auditing Entry dialog box. Use the Access list to select whether successful access, failed access, or both types of access are audited.
6. For folders, use the Apply Onto drop-down list to indicate where the auditing should take place.
7. Select or clear the Apply These Auditing Entries To Objects And/Or Containers Within This Container Only check box to invoke or prevent inheritance, respectively.

You'll find more detailed descriptions of auditing in Chapter 10.

Viewing the Security Log

The security log details audit information of events specified in your audit policy. Each time an auditable event occurs, it's added to the log file, where it can filtered, sorted, searched for, or exported. The security log, along with the application and system logs, is located in Event Viewer and can be found in the Computer Management console tree by expanding System Tools, Event Viewer, and Security.

Each entry in the log contains critical information about the audited event, including whether the attempt failed or was successful, the date and time of the event, the event category and ID, and the audited user and computer. Additional information can be obtained for each entry by right-clicking the entry and choosing Properties.

Manipulating the Security Log

The security log can be sorted by any of the fields listed in the display, such as user or date of event. Simply clicking a field header at the top of the pane will cause the log events to be arranged in ascending order by that field. Clicking the field header again will sort in descending order. For even more efficiency, you can filter the log to show only those events you're interested in—for example, failed audits only. On the View menu, click Filter. On the Filter tab of the Security Properties window that appears, select which event criteria to view and click OK.

Tip   Choose Find from the View menu to search through the displayed lists for specific events, such as all events with a certain event ID.

Security Log Maintenance

The security log has a defined maximum size. To set the size, right-click Security in Event Viewer and choose Properties. Edit the Maximum Log Size field specifying the size in kilobytes. The options beneath this field specify how events are overwritten:

- Overwrite as needed.
- Overwrite events older than X days.
- Do not overwrite events.

Tip   Presumably, all event categories specified in the event policy are relevant. Be careful that automatic event wrapping does not overwrite events more frequently than either log archival or manual log interrogation.

To archive the security log, right-click Security in Event Viewer and choose Save Log File As. Choose the path and filename for the file. If you save it as an event log file (with the extension .EVT), the file can be opened in Event Viewer at a later time.

More information on the settings for the Security Log as well as on other components in Event Viewer can be found in Chapter 10.

Summary

As this chapter has shown, security issues extend to nearly every corner of Windows 2000. Learning to use the security-related snap-ins in Microsoft Management Console will help you manage the rich features this operating system has to offer and will help prevent security weaknesses in your system.

Part IV of the book, which discusses supporting services and features of Windows 2000, begins with the next chapter. Chapters 17 and 18 covered security in broad terms by discussing planning and implementation. Chapter 19 brings security into sharper focus by covering a particular security feature of Windows 2000, Microsoft Certificate Services.

Part IV
Supporting Services and Features

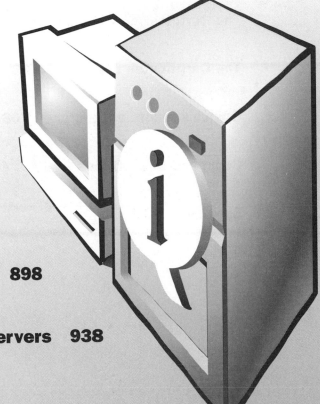

Chapter 19
Using Microsoft Certificate Services

In Chapters 17 and 18, you learned about the security protocols and tools that Microsoft Windows 2000 supports. Some of these protocols, like Kerberos and Internet Protocol security (IPSec), are primarily used to protect network traffic from intrusion; others, like Secure Multipurpose Internet Mail Extensions (S/MIME) and Encrypting File System (EFS), protect messages and files from compromise. Even components that don't have anything to do with security directly, like the Active Directory Simple Mail Transport Protocol (SMTP) site connector, can use these services to gain enhanced security.

The Windows 2000 public-key infrastructure (PKI) provides a way to issue, revoke, and track digital certificates. Microsoft Certificate Services, included as an optional component in Windows 2000 Server, allows you to issue new certificates, certify them as valid, and revoke certificates that you no longer want to use. In this chapter, you'll learn how to install, configure, and manage Certificate Services to provide security for individual computers, domains, and your entire enterprise, both on the Internet and on your intranets. (If you need to know how to manage certificates on a machine, see the section "Managing Certificates" in Chapter 18.)

Tip A terminology note: Certificate Services is the actual software; *certificate authority* (CA) refers to any entity, such as Certificate Services, that issues certificates. This chapter uses the two terms interchangeably.

More Vocabulary

Chapters 17 and 18 exposed you to most of the security vocabulary you'll need to work with Certificate Services, but you need to learn some additional terms, as defined in the following sections.

Policy Modules

A *policy module* is a set of instructions that tells the CA what to do with incoming certificate requests. A policy module can automatically approve or reject a request, based on any criteria coded into the module; it can also mark a request as pending and leave it for a human administrator to handle. Policy modules can also modify the content of a certificate by adding or removing extensions; the standard policy module supplied with Windows 2000 does the following:

- Approves incoming requests or marks them as pending, depending on the CA type and the setting you specify
- Adds an optional extension to the certificate that specifies where the issuing CA's certificate can be obtained
- Adds an optional extension that specifies where certificate revocation lists (CRLs) for the issuing CA can be obtained

Other applications, notably Microsoft Exchange Server, can implement their own policy modules, which can replace or augment the standard policy behavior. Microsoft offers tools that allow you to develop your own policy module if you need to change the policy behavior to match your organization's security standards.

Exit Modules

An *exit module* allows the CA to take some action after a certificate is generated. For example, an exit module might publish new certificates by putting them in the Active Directory directory service or mailing them to the original requestor. The standard Windows 2000 exit module performs two tasks: if the requestor specifies a file path, an Active Directory location, or both, the exit module publishes the new certificate to one or both locations; and it publishes CRLs for the CA to the location you specify.

Certificate Publishers

A *certificate publisher* serves the same function as any other kind of publisher: it makes desirable information available to clients who want it. Specifically, certificate publishers make certificate and CRL information available to clients, using whatever mechanism they want. The default certificate publisher in Windows 2000 is Active Directory, although you're free to export certificates or store them in another type of directory or publishing system.

Certificate Templates

A *certificate template* defines a cookie-cutter set of attributes and extensions that a newly issued certificate will have. For example, the Administrator certificate template specifies different attributes from a Domain Controller certificate. The idea behind certificate templates is that the person requesting a certificate can just pick a template that embodies the attributes and extensions he or she needs the new certificate to have, instead of being required to pick and choose from dozens (or even hundreds) of arcane attribute names.

Windows 2000 supports 19 certificate templates, listed in Table 19-1. When you request a certificate using a particular template, the CA knows which attributes and extensions to populate the new certificate with; as an administrator, you can control which templates individual users and groups can use when requesting new certificates. (In fact, you can also control whether they can request certificates at all!)

Each template defines the content of the certificate, using some combination of the nine template features listed in Table 19-2. You can't control the content of templates, so you must work with the attribute combinations hard coded into them by Microsoft.

Table 19-1. Certificate templates

Template	Purpose	Recipient
Administrator	Signs code; signs certificate trust lists (CTLs); secures e-mail and EFS file systems; authenticates clients	People acting in an administrative role in the domain
Authenticated Session	Allows signature-only operations for client authentication	Network clients
Basic EFS	Encrypts EFS intermediate keys and files	People who have access to EFS volumes
Code Signing	Signs executable code to assert its trustworthiness	People who are authorized to sign executables and controls
Computer	Authenticates computers to servers and vice versa	Computers within a domain
Domain Controller	Authenticates clients to servers; authenticates servers to clients	Computers that act as Active Directory controllers
EFS Recovery Agent	Recovers encrypted files when the original key material is unavailable	People who have EFS recovery privileges
Enrollment Agent	Requests certificates for users or computers	People who have certificate request authority
Exchange Enrollment Agent (offline request)	Generates offline certificate requests for Exchange mailbox owners	Enrollment agents who can request new certificates for Exchange users
Exchange Signature Only	Generates signature-only certificates for Exchange users	People who you want to allow to send signed messages with Exchange Server
Exchange User	Generates signature- and encryption-capable certificates	People who you want to allow to send signed or encrypted messages
IPSec	Allows the use of IPSec encryption and authentication	Computers that use IPSec security
IPSec (offline request)	Allows computers that are not currently .attached to the network to use IPSec when connected	Computers that use IPSec security
Router (offline request)	Authenticates clients to a server	Computers or routers that are managed as part of a domain
Smart Card Logon	Authenticates a client to a logon server	Smart card holders who use smart cards to log on; can't be used for secure e-mail or EFS security

Table 19-1.   *continued*

Template	Purpose	Recipient
Smart Card User	Authenticates a client; provides e-mail security	Smart card holders who have permission to use their smart cards to log on and secure e-mail
Subordinate Certification Authority	Issues and revokes certificates while acting as a subordinate CA	Subordinate CA computers
Trust List Signing	Signs the CTL	Administrators who have authorization to change the CTL's contents
User	Authenticates client-to-server messages; signs and encrypts e-mail; encrypts EFS data	Individual users with no other special privileges
User Signature Only	Signs e-mail; signs client-to-server authentication messages	Individual users who don't have encryption capability
Web Server	Authenticates server to clients	Web servers

Table 19-2.   Certificate template features

Attribute Type	Specifications
Basic constraints	Specifies whether this certificate can be used to sign other certificates and, if so, how many levels of nesting the resulting hierarchy can contain.
Default CSP list	Provides a list of cryptographic service providers (CSPs) that can be used with this certificate type. For example, EFS requires certificates generated with the Microsoft RSA CSP.
Display name	Displays the name when someone views the certificate's information; this is a "friendly" name that's less complex than the certificate's distinguished name (DN).
E-mail name	Specifies the e-mail address associated with the holder of this certificate.
Extended key usage	Specifies a list of extended functions (including signing a CTL, encrypting e-mail, and establishing secure network connections) for which this certificate can be used. The extended key usage information coexists with, and doesn't override, the standard key usage fields.
Key usage	Specifies what combination of basic operations (digital signatures, encryption, and key exchange) this certificate can be used for.
Machine certificate template	Specifies whether certificates that use this template are intended for use by people or by computers.
Security permissions	Specifies who can request a particular kind of certificate. For example, the default permissions for the Administrator template allow only users with administrative access to request administrator-level certificates.

Certificate Authority Types

Computers running Certificate Services can act as one of two distinct types of CAs: enterprise or stand-alone. Which type of CA you install determines who you can issue a certificate to and what it can be used for, so the distinctions between them are important. The only real difference between the two is which policy module is installed, but the operational differences between them are significant.

Enterprise CA

The enterprise CA is designed to act as part of an enterprise security infrastructure. In that job, it can issue and revoke certificates for end users and subordinate CAs, according to the active policy modules and security settings you apply to the CA. As befits anything saddled with the "enterprise" label, enterprise CAs require Active Directory access. Several key features distinguish the enterprise CA from the stand-alone CA:

- An enterprise CA is always trusted by all users and computers in its domain because the CA certificate appears in the Trusted Root Certification Authorities trust list in Active Directory.

- Certificates issued by an enterprise CA can be used to log on to Windows 2000 domains with smart cards (as discussed in Chapters 17 and 18).

- An enterprise CA publishes certificates and CRL information to Active Directory.

Another important difference between enterprise CAs and stand-alone CAs is that enterprise CAs use certificate types and templates to construct the content of newly issued certificates. This capability leads to some useful features. First, because they use templates, enterprise CAs can stuff the newly formed certificate with the proper set of attributes. In addition, enterprise CAs automatically fill in the subject name for newly issued certificates. Enterprise CAs have the unique property that they will always either reject or approve a certificate request—they will never mark one as pending. Enterprise CAs make this go/no-go decision based on the security permissions set on the requested template type, as well as on the account's permissions and group memberships in Active Directory.

Stand-Alone CA

The stand-alone CA doesn't require Active Directory—it's designed to be a separate box that can issue certificates for extranet or Internet use. As such, its purpose is to issue certificates for people to use who aren't part of your core organization and who won't have Active Directory access. The basic mechanics of certificate issuance for a stand-alone CA are similar to those for an enterprise CA, with a few exceptions:

- Requests sent to a stand-alone CA are automatically marked as pending because the CA has no way to use templates and Active Directory information to verify them. This lack of directory information also means that requestors must completely fill out all the information in their request, since the CA has no way to look it up.

- Certificates issued by a stand-alone CA can't be used for smart card–based logons, although you can store such certificates on a smart card.

- Certificates and CRLs generated by the stand-alone CA aren't published anywhere—you must manually distribute them.

You *can* install a stand-alone CA on a server that participates in an Active Directory organization. If you do, the CA will be able to publish certificate information if its server is a member of the Certificate Publishers group.

Preinstallation

Before you can successfully and securely install the CA, you must understand some concepts and be able to answer some questions that you'll be asked during the installation and setup process.

Understanding Certificate Authority Roles

In general, a CA can function in four separate roles. These roles determine what the CA's certificates are used for, which in turn determines what your users and computers will be able to do.

Enterprise Root CA

A root CA sits at the top of a certificate chain, as described in the section "Public-Key Infrastructure" in Chapter 17. An *enterprise root CA,* then, serves as the root CA for an entire enterprise—it occupies the topmost position in the certificate trust chain for all certificates issued by any component of the organization. The enterprise root CA can issue certificates for subordinate CAs, users, and computers, but as a practical matter, it will normally issue only subordinate CA certificates. Those subordinates are then responsible for issuing certificates to users and computers in the organization. Splitting certificate issuance that way allows you to delegate authority to issue certificates to the lowest possible level in your organization, while still maintaining robust control over the content, format, and use of those certificates.The enterprise root CA self-signs its certificate, asserting that it is the root by that signature. This allows it to issue certificates for individual users, computers, and subordinate CAs. Once the enterprise root CA is installed, it functions as an enterprise CA (as discussed earlier in the chapter).

Enterprise Subordinate CA

The *enterprise subordinate* CA requires a CA certificate issued by a root CA, so it forms a link in the certificate hierarchy. It acts as an enterprise CA, so it requires Active Directory access; it can issue certificates to subordinate CAs or directly to end users and computers.

Stand-Alone Root CA

The *stand-alone root* CA behaves as a stand-alone server—it doesn't have to participate in Active Directory, but it can. This independence is an advantage. You can easily disconnect a stand-alone CA from your network so that it remains secure from network-borne attack attempts. Many organizations use stand-alone root CAs for issuing their most valuable certificates, including subordinate CA certificates, because of the extra security gained by keeping the CA computer network free.

Stand-Alone Subordinate CA

Like its root counterpart, a *stand-alone subordinate* CA can use Active Directory but isn't required to. It issues certificates only to end users (typically people, since without Active Directory there's no reason to issue certificates to computers).

Real World   Protecting the Jewels

Since CAs can issue certificates, and since certificates form the backbone of the Windows 2000 access control and security features, you need to take special measures to protect your CAs from compromise or loss. It's tempting to think of a CA as just another server, but remember that it's more valuable than the average server. At a minimum, Microsoft recommends that you complete the following tasks to secure your CAs:

- Protect them against physical damage or tampering. Lock your CAs in a secure area with good physical access control and fire suppression. Keep tight control over who has access to the machines, and make sure you take advantage of whatever security features your server vendor has included.

- Protect them against data loss. You need to diligently back up your CAs, since losing the CA's private key will prevent you from recovering user certificates *and* will force you to reissue *every* certificate the CA has issued in the past.

- Protect your server against hardware failures and viruses. If you lose access to the CA's database you won't be able to recover certificates.

- Protect your CAs' private keys. It's easy to store the CA keys in an encrypted file; in fact, Microsoft makes this the default. However, the big stand-alone CA providers like Thawte, GTE CyberTrust, and VeriSign all use special-purpose hardware devices to store the keys. These devices, which range from PC cards to the titanium-encased SafeKeyper, let you store your keys in a tamperproof hardware enclosure that makes the keys available only to authorized applications.

To get the most bang for your security dollar, you need to apply these three measures appropriately to each CA, along with the Windows 2000 access control and auditing features. Depending on how your certificate hierarchy is organized, you might need to do more to protect a higher-value asset (like your enterprise root CA) than a lower-value one, but that doesn't mean you should ignore subordinate CAs.

Preparing for Installation

You need to perform several tasks before you can install Certificate Services. As part of the installation process, your CA will either issue and sign its own root CA certificate or request a certificate from another CA; to avoid having to repeat this process, it's best to have all the needed information available before you start the installation.

First determine what kind of CA you want. If you want to use an enterprise CA, you'll need to have Active Directory installed; you can install stand-alone CAs with or without Active Directory. Also consider whether you'll want to use advanced options. Certificate Services uses a set of programming interfaces that Microsoft calls CryptoAPI. Each set of cryptographic routines on a Windows 2000 system has to be packaged as a CryptoAPI CSP. By installing and removing CSPs, you can customize the set of cryptographic algorithms that your servers use. In fact, that's just what Microsoft's High Encryption Pack for Windows 2000 does—it installs CSPs with stronger algorithms than the default versions included on the Windows 2000 CD. Normally, a Certificate Services installation will use whatever CSPs it finds on your server. However, you can instruct it to use, or not use, specific CSPs if you want to.

Installation and Configuration

Once you've made the decisions necessary to set up a new CA, you're ready to install the software and configure it to meet your needs.

Installing Certificate Services

You install Certificate Services using the Windows Components Wizard. You can install the CA, the Web enrollment component, or both from the wizard. To complete the installation, follow these steps:

1. Launch the Windows Components Wizard by opening Add/Remove Programs in Control Panel and clicking Add/Remove Windows Components.

2. When the wizard opens, select Certificate Services from the component list. The installer will warn you that once the CA software is installed, you can't change the name of the server or move it into or out of an Active Directory domain. If you have a server that you want to use as

an enterprise CA, make sure you've used *dcpromo* to make it Active Directory–capable before continuing with the installation.

3. If you want to install only one of the components (for example, if you want to set up a CA with no Web-enrollment capacity), click the Details button and clear any component you don't want installed.

4. The Certification Authority Type Selection screen appears (Figure 19-1). Select the option that corresponds to the CA type you want: enterprise root, enterprise subordinate, stand-alone root, or stand-alone subordinate. If you want to change the CSP list for this CA, make sure to select the Advanced Options check box. (See "CAs Linked into a Hierarchy" later in the chapter for more details.)

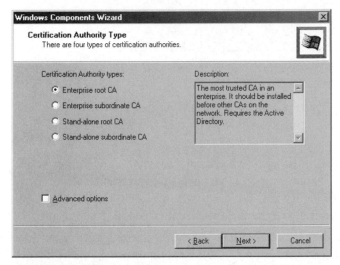

Figure 19-1. *The Certification Authority Type Selection screen of the Windows Components Wizard.*

5. If you selected the Advanced Options check box, you'll see the Public And Private Key Pair Selection screen shown in Figure 19-2. Use this screen to select the CSP you want your CA to use (bearing in mind that some CSPs might not be supported for generating certificates from some templates). The Microsoft Base Cryptographic Provider 1.0 CSP is the default choice; other CSPs will be available, depending on the software you have installed and whether you have any smart cards or special-purpose cryptographic tokens available.

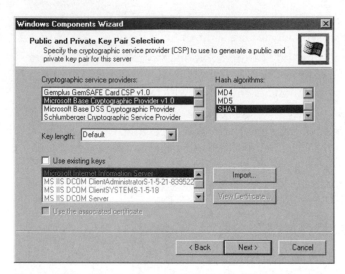

Figure 19-2. *The Public And Private Key Pair Selection screen of the Windows Components Wizard.*

6. On the Public And Private Key Pair Selection screen, choose among its various options to configure Certificate Services the way you want it and click Next.

- The Hash Algorithms box allows you to choose the hash algorithm you want to use for signatures. Don't use MD4; if possible, don't use MD5 either. Both algorithms have known (albeit mostly theoretical) weaknesses. Instead, leave the default setting of SHA-1 alone.

- The Key Length drop-down list lets you select a key length if you're generating a key pair. You can leave the default value of 1024 bits, or you can go all the way up to 4096 bits if you need to. However, some non-Microsoft PKI components can't handle sizes above 1024 bits.

- The Use Existing Keys check box allows you to recycle an existing key pair, provided that it was generated with algorithms compatible with your selected CSP. As you choose different CSPs, you'll see that this check box (and the contents of the list below it) changes to reflect whether any keys exist that you could potentially use.

- The Import button lets you import certificates from a PFX/PKCS #12 file, and the View Certificate button will show you the properties for the selected certificate.

- The Use The Associated Certificate check box lets you use an existing certificate if the key pair you've selected has one associated with it *and* if it's compatible with your chosen CSP.

7. The CA Identifying Information screen will appear, shown in Figure 19-3. Enter identifying information for this particular CA, including a unique name for it and the organization, organizational unit, locality, state/province, and country where the CA is located. You can also enter an e-mail address for the CA and a comment. By default, newly generated CA certificates are valid for two years; you can adjust that period with the Validity Duration controls. Click Next.

Caution If you enter an organization name that includes special characters (like & * [ ] and so on), the CA will have to encode them in Unicode to remain compliant with the X.509 standard. This might prevent some applications from decoding and verifying your CA certificate, so the installer will warn you and give you a chance to remove the special characters before proceeding.

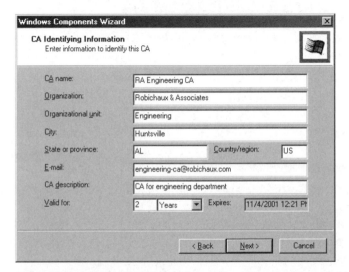

Figure 19-3. *The CA Identifying Information screen of the Windows Components Wizard.*

8. On the Data Storage Location screen (Figure 19-4), specify where the CA's certificate database and log files will be stored. Note that the location you specify *isn't* where issued certificates and CRLs are stored; it's actually where the CA's own certificates are stored. Make sure you specify a location that is regularly backed up!

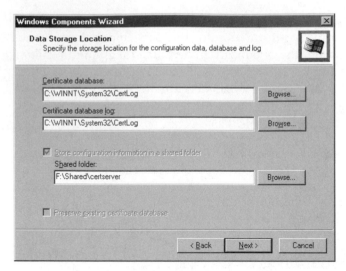

Figure 19-4. *The Data Storage Location screen of the Windows Components Wizard.*

9. On the Data Storage Location screen, also consider these options:

- If you're going to be interoperating with clients that aren't using Active Directory, or if you're not using it, you can specify that you want the CA to maintain a shared folder to store newly created certificates in—just select the Store Configuration Information In A Shared Folder check box, and then supply the name of an existing folder.

- If you're reinstalling Certificate Services on a machine that's already been acting as a CA, selecting Preserve Existing Certificate Database will force the installer not to overwrite the existing certificates, meaning that you will still be able to use old certificates after the installation finishes.

10. If you're installing a subordinate CA, you'll have to request a certificate for this subordinate CA from whatever root CA you're using. The section "CAs Linked into a Hierarchy" later in the chapter details how this process works and covers the specifics; if you're installing a subordinate CA now, jump ahead and see what you need to do before proceeding with the wizard. Click Next.

11. If you're running the IIS WWW service, the installer will tell you that it must stop the service to complete the installation.

12. When the wizard finishes the installation, you'll be prompted to restart your server. After rebooting, notice that the CA service starts automatically.

Installing the Certification Authority Snap-in

You might have already installed the Certificates snap-in, as described in Chapter 18. Before you can manage any CAs, however, you'll need the Certification Authority snap-in. You can add it to an MMC console by following these steps:

1. Open MMC with whatever console you want the CA to be managed from.

2. Choose Add/Remove Snap-In from the Console menu to open the Add/Remove Snap-In dialog box. Click the Add button.

3. The Add Stand-Alone Snap-In dialog box will appear. Choose the Certification Authority item in the list of snap-ins and then click the Add button.

4. The Certification Authority dialog box shown in Figure 19-5 will appear. Use the controls in the This Snap-In Will Always Manage group to determine which CA you want this snap-in to configure. By selecting a particular CA, you can limit what the console user is permitted to do. The Allow The Selected Computer To Be Changed When Launching From The Command Line check box gives you added flexibility by letting you change the snap-in's target at any time.

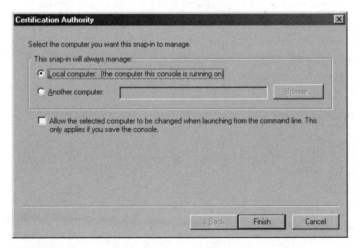

Figure 19-5. *The Certification Authority dialog box.*

5. Click Finish to close the Certification Authority dialog box. Click Close to close the Add Stand-Alone Snap-In dialog box, and then click OK to close the Add/Remove Snap-In dialog box.

The Certification Authority Snap-in

Once you have the Certification Authority snap-in installed, notice that it includes one subordinate item for each CA on the target server. Each CA, in turn, has five folders shown below it. Each folder displays some sort of list, so you can customize the list columns and fields using the View submenu on the context menu. Right-click the folder, and then use the Choose Columns and Customize commands until you've configured the list the way you want it. The five folders you can view under each CA are as follows:

- **Revoked Certificates**   Lists all the certificates that have currently been revoked. Right-clicking this folder, pointing to All Tasks, and choosing Publish allows you to publish a new CRL (although you'll get a warning message if your existing CRL is still valid).

- **Issued Certificates**   Lists the certificates that this CA has issued. You can right-click individual certificates and use the Revoke command.

- **Pending Requests**   Shows the requests that are stuck at the CA waiting for you to approve or disapprove them. Remember, for enterprise CAs, this list will always be empty; for stand-alone CAs, it might contain zero or more requests at any given time.

- **Failed Requests**   Lists requests that failed or were rejected, including the common name, e-mail address, and submission date of the failed request.

- **Policy Settings**   Lists the certificate templates that are available on this server. You can add templates to the list by right-clicking the Policy Settings folder, pointing to New, and choosing Certificate To Issue, or you can remove templates by right-clicking the target item and choosing Delete. You can view the specifics of individual templates by double-clicking them, but there's no way to modify the contents of a template item.

Managing the Certification Authority Service

The Certification Authority service actually runs as a standard Windows 2000 service, so you can manage it in two separate ways. First, you can use the Services item in the Computer Management snap-in to start and stop the service, set recovery options, change the security context it runs in, and so on. (See Chapter 10 for more on using the Services item.) More interestingly, right-clicking the Certification Authority item, or one of the CAs beneath it, gives you access to some useful commands.

First is the Retarget Certification Authority command, which appears when you right-click the Certification Authority item. You use this command to change the CA server that you're managing. By default, the snap-in will attach to the local server unless you specified another one when you installed it. This command lets you pick another CA server in your domain and administer it instead. The remaining commands appear when you right-click an individual CA and choose the All Tasks submenu; they're discussed in the following sections.

Starting and Stopping the CA

You can stop and restart the CA with the Start Service and Stop Service commands. When you stop the CA, it simply stops—you don't get a chance to confirm your command or change your mind. The same is true for starting the service. Note that you have to stop the service before restoring the CA database, although the snap-in will offer to do that for you when you try to do a backup.

Backing Up the CA

Backing up and restoring the CA data is critical because if you lose the CA, you'll lose the ability to issue, revoke, or renew certificates for the CA's assigned domain. You can (and should) use the Windows 2000 Backup utility to back up the certificate database; you can also use the Certification Authority Backup Wizard, which is slightly easier to use for the task at hand. All the wizard does is copy the current state of the CA's data to a folder you specify; you can back up or archive those files easily without stopping the CA.

Selecting the Backup CA command starts the wizard, the first screen of which is just an introduction telling you what the wizard does. If the CA service isn't running, you'll be prompted to start it, since it must be active for the wizard to work. The second screen of the wizard, shown in Figure 19-6, is where you specify what you want backed up.

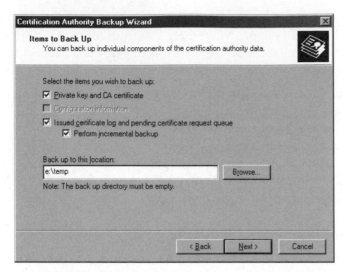

Figure 19-6. *The Date Types screen of the Certification Authority Backup Wizard.*

This wizard screen provides the following options:

- The Private Key And CA Certificate check box forces the Backup wizard to back up the private key and associated certificate that the CA uses. If you choose this option, the wizard will ask you for a password that it uses to encrypt the private key and certificate data.

- The Configuration Information check box is normally enabled for stand-alone CA servers; for servers that are using Active Directory, the configuration information is kept there instead. If you're using a stand-alone CA without Active Directory and want its configuration recorded, select this box.

- The Issued Certificate Log And Pending Certificate Request Queue check box causes the Backup wizard to copy the log file showing which certificates have been issued and the queue of pending requests. Failure to back this up could lead to a loss of queued requests if you have to do a restore, so you should leave it selected.

- The Perform Incremental Backup check box allows you to avoid the overhead of backing up the entire log and queue each time. When it's checked, the Backup wizard will back up only the entries that have been changed since the last backup. However, you must perform at least one full backup (with this check box cleared) before you perform your first incremental backup.

- Use the Backup Location controls to specify which directory you want the backup material stored in. The backup folder is supposed to be empty; the wizard will warn you if it isn't. You have to put each backup in a different location; for example, if you do one full and two incremental backups each week, you'll need three separate folders to store the backed-up files.

Once you complete the Backup wizard process, you'll have a set of files in the specified folder. The file <caName>.p12 contains the private key material for the CA, while the Database folder contains the log files. Use your preferred backup tool to make a good copy of these files and you'll be able to restore the CA when you need to.

Restoring the CA

The Restore CA command runs the Certification Authority Restore Wizard, which in every way is the mirror image of the Backup wizard. It requires that the CA service be stopped, and it lets you restore the data you backed up using the Backup wizard. You can selectively restore any combination of the private key and CA certificate, the configuration data, and the issued certificate log and pending request queue. Select the appropriate check boxes, tell the wizard where your backup files are, confirm that you want the data restored, and restart the CA when you're done.

One caveat: if you want to restore a series of incremental backups, you must first restore the corresponding full backup and then repeat the process for each incremental backup—in the right order! This argues in favor of giving your backup folders descriptive names like *Certserver backup\1999-0815*.

Renewing the CA Certificate

Occasionally, you might need to renew your CA certificate. How often you do this depends on the lifetime you set for your CA certificate when you generate it, as well as on whether the CA's key has been compromised and how big your current CRL is. The Microsoft CA allows you to reissue a CA certificate with the existing key material or to generate a new key pair and use it in the new certificate. The former option is useful when you just want a new certificate (for example, because your current certificate is about to expire), while the latter is what you use when you need new key material (as in the case of a compromise.)

When you right-click the CA and choose the Renew CA Certificate command, the snap-in will first warn you that the CA service must be stopped to generate the renewal. If you choose to proceed, a dialog box will explain why you might need a new certificate and ask you whether you want to generate a new key pair. Whichever option you choose, the snap-in will do its work quietly, issue the new certificate, and restart the CA service.

Configuring the CA's Properties

Each CA has a set of properties that you can define, including properties for its policy and exit modules. You change these properties in the CA Properties window, which appears when you right-click a CA object and choose Properties from the context menu.

The General tab of the Properties window shows you the name and description for the CA; it also identifies the CSP and hash algorithm that the CA is using. You're stuck with all of these values—you can't modify them after the CA is created. You can also use the View Certificate button to see a certificate's details.

> **Note** Remember that you can selectively enable and disable certificate capabilities (like code signing, client authentication, and so on) by opening the individual certificate's Properties window and selecting the purposes for which you want to use the certificate. However, you can't add or remove purposes not specified in the original template used to issue the certificate.

The Policy Module Tab

The Policy Module tab shows you which policy module is currently active on your CA. In almost all cases, this will be the Enterprise and Stand-Alone Policy module that Microsoft provides with Windows 2000. If you want to use an alternate module, you can use the Select button on the tab to select another one.

More interesting is the Configure button, which opens the two-tabbed policy module Properties window. The Default Action tab lets you control what happens to incoming requests. For an enterprise CA, the Always Issue The Certificate option is permanently selected; stand-alone CAs can also use the Set The Certificate Request Status To Pending button, which is selected by default.

The X.509 Extensions tab (Figure 19-7) allows you to customize two sets of locations: where CRLs are published and where end users can obtain the CA's certificate. Both of these sets of locations are encoded as X.509 extensions in the certificate—hence, the tab's name. You can enable, disable, add, and remove publication points and access points by using the controls in this dialog box. Table 19-3 lists the variables you can use to insert the server name, CA name, and other useful variables into the URLs you use to specify these points. Note that the URLs you provide are encoded into the certificate, but you must still make sure the CRLs and certificates are available at those places.

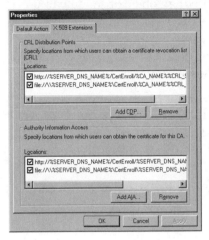

Figure 19-7. *The X.509 Extensions tab and the Default Action tab of the Properties window.*

Table 19-3. **Variables used to specify distribution points and authority access points**

Variable Name	Value It Is Replaced With
%1	Full DNS name of the CA server
%2	NetBIOS name of the CA server
%3	Name of the CA
%4	Renewal extension period (e.g., how long a certificate's expiration date is extended upon renewal) for the CA
%5	Location of the domain root in Active Directory
%6	Location of the configuration container in Active Directory
%7	The 32-character "clean" version of the CA name, with punctuation stripped out and a hash of the name
%8	CRL suffix; used to identify the CRL after the CA certificate has been renewed

Note If you change any of the X.509 extension values, you'll have to stop and restart the CA before the changes will take effect. This requirement holds true for most changes to the CA.

The Exit Module Tab

The Exit Module tab looks and works much like the Policy Module tab—it shows which exit modules your CA is configured to use. Unlike policy modules, which are strictly one to a customer, you can have more than one exit module in use at once; each is executed in sequence. Since Microsoft provides only one exit module, though, this point is moot unless you're using a third-party module. The Configure button on the Exit Module tab opens the exit module Properties dialog box, which has only one tab: Certificate Publication.

The Microsoft exit module automatically publishes certificates into Active Directory (if present) or to the location that the certificate request specified. By using the Certificate Publication tab of the exit module's Properties window (click the Configure button on the Exit Module tab to see this window), you can turn publication on and off in two ways:

- Select the Allow Certificates To Be Published In The Active Directory check box to allow the exit module to load certificates into Active Directory, when present.
- Select the Allow Certificates To Be Published To The File System check box to allow publication to the shared folder you defined at CA setup time.

By default, the CA always publishes CRLs to the *%SystemRoot%\system32\certserv\certenroll* folder; each CRL is given a name starting with the letter *c* and containing the date it was generated, in YY/MM/DD format. If more than one CRL is generated on the same day, a suffix number is added. For example, *c991031.crl* is the only CRL published on October 31, 1999, while *c9912252.crl* is the second CRL published on December 25, 1999. You can take these files and publish them via HTTP, FTP, or other means, including manually or automatically loading them onto smart cards.

The Storage Tab

The Storage tab, shown in Figure 19-8, shows you where configuration and certificate data are stored. You can't change any of these values once the CA is set up, but having a way to double-check the file locations in case you need them can be useful.

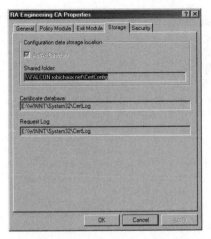

Figure 19-8. *The Storage tab of the Properties window.*

The Security Tab

The Security tab gives you control over which users and groups can do what with your CA. You can apply up to 10 permission settings to the CA, shown in Table 19-4. By default, four groups have access control lists (ACLs) that give them some combination of these permissions:

- The Administrators group has the allow flag turned on for the Manage, Enroll, and Read Configuration permissions. Even though the Manage permission enables the other permissions, you can turn it off if you want to allow administrators to enroll users without managing the CA.

- The Authenticated Users group has Enroll and Read Configuration permission.

- The Domain Admins group has Manage, Enroll, and Read Configuration permissions.

- The Enterprise Admins group has Manage, Enroll, and Read Configuration permissions.

Table 19-4. CA-related permissions

Permission	Allows
Approve Certificate	Approves or rejects a certificate request whose status is pending.
Enroll	Requests new certificates for users or computers.
Manage	Makes administrative and configuration changes to the CA. Granting or denying this permission does the same for all the other ones, too.
Modify Owner	Changes ownership of the CA objects.
Modify Permissions	Changes ACLs and access control entries (ACEs) on the CA.
Read Configuration	Reads configuration data from the local disk or Active Directory; this implies Read Control permission too.
Read Control	Reads control information for the CA.
Read Database	Reads certificate information from the CA database.
Revoke Certificate	Revokes a user, computer, or CA certificate.
Write Configuration	Saves configuration changes to Active Directory or the local disk.

Working with Certificate Templates

Certificate templates give you an easy way to stamp out cookie-cutter certificates that you can use for well-defined purposes. Unfortunately, you can't edit the templates yourself, but with 19 different types, you should be able to find *something* to use for any role to which you need to issue certificates. When someone requests a certificate using your CA's Web enrollment pages (as described in the section "Obtaining Smart Cards and Certificates" in Chapter 18), they can choose any of the templates that are available. You determine which templates they can use by adjusting the security permissions on the templates.

Setting Security Permissions and Delegate Access

Before you can adjust security permissions on a template, you must install the Active Directory Sites and Services snap-in. Then right-click the Sites node, point to View, and choose Show Services Node. When the Services node appears, expand the Services, Public Key Services, and Certificate Templates nodes.

At that point, you can right-click an individual template from the list in the MMC window, and then choose Properties to see that template's individual properties. When the Properties window appears, switch to the Security tab (Figure 19-9). Adjust the properties to reflect the access you want individual users or domain groups to have; for example, if you don't want anyone to issue enrollment agent certificates, just deny full control to all users, and that's that.

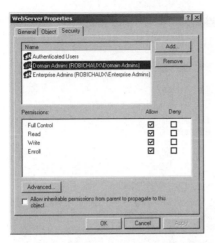

Figure 19-9. *The Security tab of the Properties window.*

Enabling Automatic Enrollment

You can use a Group Policy setting to allow automatic issuance of certificates for computers. This allows you to automatically generate, issue, and store a new certificate for each computer that joins your domain. As long as you have administrative privileges on the Group Policy object (GPO) for your domain, you can make this change by using the Automatic Certificate Request Setup Wizard. Here's what to do:

1. Open the GPO you want to edit by using the Group Policy snap-in. (See Chapter 9 if you need a refresher on GPOs.)

2. Expand the GPO's Computer Configuration node, and then expand the Windows Settings, Security Settings, and Public Key Policies nodes.

3. Right-click the Automatic Certificate Request Settings folder, point to New, and then choose Automatic Certificate Request. The Automatic Certificate Request Setup Wizard appears. Click Next.

4. The second screen of the wizard appears (Figure 19-10). Choose the template that matches the type of certificate you want issued to newly enrolled computers, and then click Next.

5. The third screen of the wizard lists available CAs in the domain; choose the one you want to issue automatically generated certificates, and then click Next.

6. Double-check the information on the completion page of the wizard, and then click Finish to create a new automatic request.

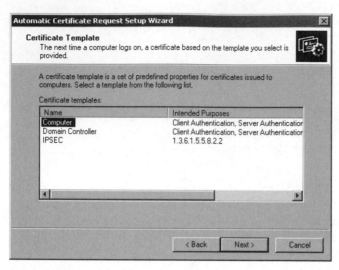

Figure 19-10. *The Certificate Template screen of the Automatic Certificate Request Setup Wizard.*

Managing Revocation and Trust

Certificates provide you with a way to securely verify the identity of principles on your network. However, just having a big bag of certificates doesn't help you with security—you must also make decisions about which certificates you trust, and you need a mechanism to "untrust" certificates if they're compromised or if, for some reason, the holder no longer needs (or should no longer have) them.

In the Windows 2000 public-key infrastructure (PKI), you codify decisions about trust by specifying which root CAs go on your CTL. You can specify CTLs for individual users and groups; you can also specify a default CTL as part of a GPO so that new users, computers, and groups inherit a default CTL that you specify. Likewise, you render certificates untrusted either by removing their issuing CA's certificate from the CTL or by revoking the certificate itself, depending on whether or not you issued it. (You can revoke only certificates that your CA issued in the first place.)

Revoking certificates is simple: open the CA snap-in, switch to the Issued Certificates node, right-click the target certificate, point to All Tasks, and choose Revoke Certificate. The command lets you choose a revocation reason. (The default is Unspecified, but you can also mark a certificate revoked for a particular reason, such as key compromise or a change in the user's affiliation.) As soon as you choose a reason, whomp! The certificate is revoked. There's no appeal; you can't "unrevoke" a certificate, but clients might not notice that the certificate has been revoked until they get the next CRL update.

Publishing CRLs

When you revoke a certificate, Windows 2000 adds it to the CRL immediately, but the CRL isn't published right then—the server will automatically update the CRL and publish it at the interval you specify. You can manually publish the CRL at any time by right-clicking the Revoked Certificates item in the CA snap-in, pointing to All Tasks, and choosing Publish. After asking you to confirm that you want to supersede the existing CRL, the snap-in will force the CA to publish the current CRL to the CRL distribution points you previously specified.

Windows 2000 can also publish CRLs on a schedule you set. The Properties window for the Revoked Certificates item in the CA snap-in, as shown in Figure 19-11, lets you control the interval at which CRLs are published. By default, CRLs are updated weekly, but you can specify an interval ranging from one hour to 9999 years. You can also turn off scheduled CRL publication completely; you might want to do this if you want to control the circumstances and timing under which new CRLs are issued.

Figure 19-11. *The CRL Publishing Parameters tab of the Revoked Certificates Properties window.*

Changing CRL Distribution Points

The CA honors any certificate publication information it finds in the incoming certificate request. However, it depends on you to specify where CRLs should be published and where the certificates should point for users who want a copy of the CA's certificate. You supply these locations on the X.509 Extensions tab of the Policy Module Properties window (Figure 19-7). By default, CRLs and root certificates are distributed via HTTP, LDAP, and a shared folder, but you can turn off these distribution points and add your own at any time.

Controlling Which Trusted Certificates Are Distributed

You can change the set of trusted root certificates that is distributed as part of a GPO. This enables you to build and deliver a certificate set containing only the CAs you want users in particular groups to be able to trust. Let's say you use a third-party root CA (like VeriSign) with your own enterprise subordinate CA. You could set up one GPO for each department and then tweak the list of CAs for that department so that the legal department, for example, doesn't trust any of your internal CAs.

You can make three basic changes to the root list in a GPO: you can import root certificates and add them to the list, you can remove an existing root certificate from the list, or you can change the root certificate's allowed roles. All of these possibilities require that you open the GPO whose trusted certificate list you want to modify and then expand it so you can see the Trusted Root Certification Authorities item. (You will need to expand the Computer Configuration, Windows Settings, Security Settings, and Public Key Policies nodes.) At that point, you can do the following:

- To import a new certificate and begin trusting it, right-click the Trusted Root Certification Authorities item, point to All Tasks, and choose Import. Tell the Import Wizard where the certificate you want to import lives; it will load the certificate into the list of trusted roots and display it.

- To remove a root certificate from the list, right-click it and choose the Delete command. You'll see a confirmation dialog box that warns you of the consequences of removing the certificate.

- To edit the list of approved uses for a root certificate, right-click the root certificate name and choose Properties. A dialog box like the one shown in Figure 19-12 will appear. Use the options in the Certificate Purposes group to specify what you trust this certificate to do. When the Enable Only The Following Purposes check box is selected, you can enable or disable specific purposes by selecting or clearing them in the list.

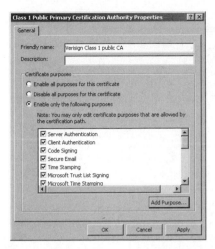

Figure 19-12. *The General tab of the Certification Authority Properties window.*

This list of root certificates is distributed as part of the group policy; that means it will be available to all members of the group. Don't confuse this list with the CTL—more on that in a minute.

Managing Certificate Trust Lists for a Group Policy Object

The CA list you manage in the Trusted Root Certification Authorities item is nothing more than a bag of CA certificates—there's no implication that your enterprise trusts them (or not). To use certificates issued by other CAs, you have to put them on the CTL; your CA signs the CTL and distributes it to indicate that you've designated the CAs on the CTL as trusted. You can import a CTL that you've generated on another Windows 2000 machine, or you can create a new one. Both actions occur in the Enterprise Trust node under the Public-Key Policies component of a GPO, and both are available as commands when you right-click the Enterprise Trust folder.

To create a new CTL, point to New on the shortcut menu and choose Certificate Trust List to open the Certificate Trust List Wizard. Once the wizard opens, you'll have to complete several steps to successfully create a new CTL:

1. On the Certificate Trust List Purpose screen of the wizard (Figure 19-13), specify the prefix used to name the CTL, how long you want the CTL to remain valid, and for what purposes you trust CAs on the CTL. Click Next.

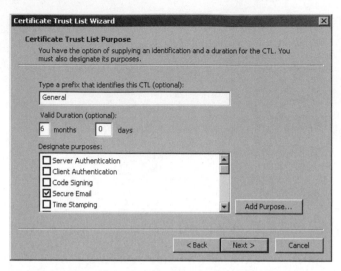

Figure 19-13. *The Certificate Trust List Purpose screen of the Certificate Trust List Wizard.*

2. On the Certificates In The CTL screen of the wizard, add CA certificates to the CTL (Figure 19-14). You can add CA certificates from the certificate store or from a file using the corresponding buttons. Click Next.

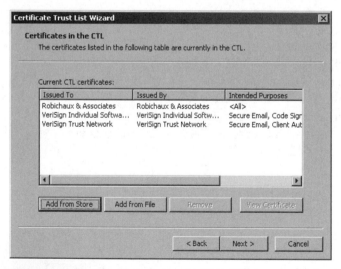

Figure 19-14. *The Certificates In The CTL screen of the Certificate Trust List Wizard.*

3. Designate a certificate to use for the CTL signature. The certificate you select here will be used to sign the CTL, so be sure to choose a certificate that you have good control over. (That way, no one can steal it and spoof your CTL.)

4. Once you've chosen a signer for the CTL, you can choose to add a secure timestamp, which guarantees the date and time recorded in the CTL. However, you must have access to a secure timestamp service.

5. Provide a name and description for the CTL; these items are displayed in the MMC whenever the CTL is shown in a list.

6. Click Finish and the CTL will be created. Once it is available, you can remove it or edit it (using the wizard interface) by right-clicking it and using the appropriate commands.

Managing Stand-Alone CAs

You already understand the differences between an enterprise CA and a stand-alone CA, but some subtle functional differences exist too—two management tasks are unnecessary for enterprise CAs but mandatory for stand-alone CAs.

Setting the Default Action for New Requests

By default, a stand-alone CA is set to mark all incoming certificate requests as pending. This forces the requests into a queue of pending requests (shown in the Pending Requests item under the CA node), where they sit until a human operator either approves or rejects them. You can change this setting by opening the CA Properties window, clicking the Policy Module tab, clicking Configure, and using the two options on the Default Action tab to change the default action from Set As Pending to Always Issue (or vice versa). Once this action takes effect, all incoming requests will be treated as you specify, but this change won't affect any pending requests.

Changing Certificate Request Status

Let's say that you have some pending requests in your queue. How can you approve or reject them? The answer lies in the same place as it does for most other "How do I . . . ?" questions involving the MMC: the right mouse button. Right-clicking a request in the Pending Requests list allows you to approve or reject it.

The Certificates Snap-in

The Certification Authority snap-in is for managing CAs, not the certificates they issue. A corresponding snap-in is intended just for managing certificates—the Certificates snap-in. Clients on your network can manage their own certificates by using the Certificates button on the Content tab of Microsoft Internet Explorer's Internet Options dialog box; it does most of what the snap-in can do without requiring that you give your users access to the snap-in.

The basic functions of the Certificates snap-in (along with its installation requirements) are discussed in the section "Managing Certificates" in Chapter 18. However, the behavior and functionality of the Certificates snap-in change slightly when you use it in a domain that has an enterprise or stand-alone CA—you'll notice two new items in the Certificates store: Other People and REQUEST. The Other People store allows you to manage certificates issued to people who aren't in your Active Directory; for example, you can use it as a repository for certificates issued to business partners by an outside CA. The REQUEST store holds certificate requests that are awaiting your approval decision.

CAs Linked into a Hierarchy

Your network design may call for connecting several CAs so that you have separate root and subordinate CAs. Splitting up CAs like this is considered good security by most experts because it allows you to have a root CA that issues certificates only to subordinate CAs, so it can be better protected than the subordinate CA servers. To accomplish this with Certificate Services, first install and configure a root CA as described earlier in this chapter. In particular, you must indicate that you want the newly installed CA to be an enterprise root or a stand-alone root server.

Once you've installed and configured the root CA, your next task is to install and configure each subordinate CA. The installation process is largely identical to the process required to install a root CA, except that you must perform an additional step after you specify the storage location you want to use for your certificates: you must request a certificate for the new CA. You do this with the CA Certificate Request screen, shown in Figure 19-15. What you *do* with this screen will depend on whether the root CA that "owns" this subordinate CA is available on your network or not. The next two sections describe each scenario.

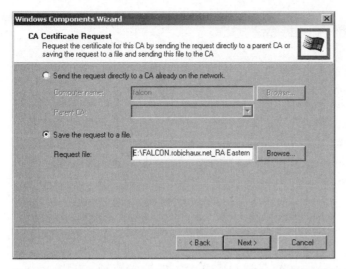

Figure 19-15. *The CA Certificate Request screen of the Windows Components Wizard.*

Requesting a Certificate If Your Root CA Is On Line

If you're using an all–Windows 2000 PKI, and if your root (or parent) CA is available on the network, you're in luck—all you have to do is select Send The Request Directly To A CA Already On The Network, specify the computer name of the parent CA server, and then choose the parent CA instance on that computer from the Parent CA list box. (Remember, a single CA server computer can host multiple CAs.)

Requesting a Certificate If Your Root CA Is Off Line

If your root CA isn't available on your network, you'll need to select Save The Request To A File. That forces the wizard to generate a PKCS #10 format certificate request and store it in a disk file. You can then e-mail that file to the root CA, put it on a floppy or smart card, paste it into a Web page, or do whatever else your root CA requires. If you want to submit a certificate request to a Windows 2000 Certificate Services server, you can do so with the following steps:

1. Open Internet Explorer and connect to *http://caServerName/certserv*, where *caServerName* is the DNS name of your root CA.

2. When the Web CA Request screen appears, click the Request A Certificate option, and then click Next. On the following screen, click the Advanced Request button and click Next.

3. Click the Submit A Certificate Request Using A Base-64-Encoded PKCS#10 File Or A Renewal Request Using a PKCS#7 File button, and then click Next.

4. Submit the actual subordinate CA request by opening it in Notepad, copying its text, and pasting it into the Saved Request text box. As an alternative, you can use the Browse button to locate the .P10 file on disk and upload it, but this may require that you modify your Internet Explorer settings so that your root CA is a trusted site.

5. Click Submit. Depending on how you have configured your root CA, you'll get either a message saying that the certificate request is pending or one indicating that it was approved. If it was approved, use the Download Certificate button to retrieve the certificate and store it on your local disk.

Note If you're *not* using a Windows 2000 CA, the exact procedure you use to send the request to your CA will vary; consult your CA vendor or documentation for details.

A subtlety is involved in using a third-party CA: The Windows 2000 CA Service expects to be able to build a full certificate path when it starts. If your root CA includes CA certificates for all CAs in the certificate path (the Windows 2000 CA does), you don't have to do anything extra. If not, you'll have to manually add the CA certificates of any parent CAs to the Intermediate Certification Authorities certificate store, as well as adding the root CA certificate to the Trusted Root Certification Authorities store. You can do these in any order; the key is to make sure that you've added certificates for the root CA and all subordinate CAs that are parents of the CA you're installing before you try to install the new subordinate CA's certificate and start the CA service.

Once you've loaded any needed certificates from the certificate path and have requested and received a certificate for your new subordinate CA, you still have to load it into the certificate store. You do this from the Certification Authority snap-in. Select the newly installed subordinate CA, and then click Actions, point to All Tasks, and choose Install CA Certificate. Until you do so, your new subordinate CA won't be able to process any requests.

Command-Line Utilities

Certificate Services includes three command-line tools that you can use for various administrative tasks. While none of these tools are necessary for ordinary operation of your CAs, sometimes they will come in handy.

The Certsrv Tool

Certsrv.exe is the actual executable that implements the Certificate Services code. Normally, you'll start and stop the server using the Services snap-in; however, you can manually start it from the command line. This allows you to start the server only when you need to issue a new certificate; many sites choose to run their root CAs in this on-demand mode because it helps reduce the risk of an accidental or malicious issuance of an unwanted certificate.

As an extra bonus, if you run Certsrv.exe with the -z command switch, it will display a log of its activities in the console window you used to start it. This is invaluable for debugging or just for gaining a better understanding of how the server accomplishes its tasks.

The Certreq Tool

Most of the time you'll request certificates through the Web interface (see "Requesting Certificates" in Chapter 18) or through a program that's been written to take advantage of Certificate Services. However, sometimes manually requesting a certificate is useful. For example, you typically need to manually request certificates for subordinate stand-alone CAs, and requesting test certificates from a new server is often useful so you can verify that it's working properly. The Certreq tool (Certreq.exe) allows you to request a new certificate from a CA in your domain or retrieve any certificate previously issued by that CA—you can even retrieve revoked or expired certificates.

The Certreq tool has two slightly different forms; the one that you use to request certificates looks like this:

```
certreq[-rpc] [-binary] [-config configString]
    [-attrib attribString]
[requestFile [certFile | chainFile] ]
```

- The -rpc switch forces the Certreq tool to contact the CA with a standard Windows remote procedure call (RPC) request instead of a Distributed COM request.
- The -binary flag specifies that you want the certificate or CRL to be stored as a binary file instead of in base-64 encoding. You normally use

this option when you want to take the object returned from the server and import it into a program that uses certificates directly.

- Use the *-config* switch to specify which CA you want to send your request to; you have to specify both the server and CA names. For example, to request a certificate from a CA named Netsolvers Purchasing on a server named HQ4, you'd write

```
certreq -config HQ4\"Netsolvers Purchasing"
```

You can also use a single hyphen in place of a server/CA name if you want to request a certificate from the default CA for your domain.

- If you want to specify additional attributes in the certificate request, use the *-attrib* switch, along with the attribute names and values you want to use. Each name-value pair must be separated with a newline character, like this:

```
attrib "Hair color:blond\nEye color:blue"
```

- If you want to submit a request generated by another program, you can do so by specifying the request's file name. That's what the *requestFile* parameter is for. The Certreq tool can forward requests in three formats: PKCS #10 (used to request new certificates), PKCS #7 (used to request renewal of an existing certificate), or KeyGen (used to request a new certificate). The request file can be either raw binary or base-64 encoded, as long as it's in one of the supported formats.

- If you're using Active Directory, the CA will publish newly generated certificates for you. If not, or if you need to get the certificate back as a file so you can do something with it, specify a filename in place of the *certFile* parameter and Certreq will put a copy of the new certificate in the specified file—provided that the CA approves the request, of course. In the same vein, supplying a filename in place of the *chainFile* parameter will cause Certreq to provide you with a copy of the entire certificate chain for the new certificate, starting at the root CA and including all subordinate CA certificates.

The Certutil Tool

The Certutil tool is practically a Swiss Army knife—you know, the really big ones you see at camping stores. It has a total of 40 different modes; these modes perform tasks ranging from stopping the CA service to creating a backup of the CA's private keys to scanning a certificate file for particular ASCII characters that can confuse older certificate service implementations.

Summary

This chapter explained the fundamentals of planning for and deploying the public-key infrastructure services that Microsoft includes with Windows 2000. You learned how to install and manage Microsoft Certificate Services and how to set policies that govern what users can do with it. In the next chapter, you'll learn how to make Windows 2000 Server interoperate with Novell NetWare servers and clients.

Chapter 20
Interoperating with Novell NetWare

Many enterprise networks are a mixture of operating systems, old and new hardware, and a variety of software. Fortunately, Microsoft Windows 2000 Server provides a number of services that allow Novell NetWare servers and clients to interoperate with Windows computers of every description. These services include the following:

- **NWLinkIPX/SPX/NetBIOS Compatible Transport protocol (NWLink)**   The Windows 2000 implementation of the IPX/SPX protocol—the legacy NetWare communication protocol. NWLink supports connectivity between computers running Windows 2000 and computers running NetWare and compatible systems.

- **Gateway Service for NetWare (GSNW)**   Enables a computer running Windows 2000 Server to connect to NetWare servers, including NetWare 4.x servers or later running either Novell Directory Services (NDS) or bindery emulation. Support for login scripts is also included. You can use GSNW to create gateways to NetWare resources. Creating a gateway enables computers running only Microsoft client software to access NetWare resources.

- **File and Print Services for NetWare (FPNW)**   Enables a computer running Windows 2000 Server to provide file and print services directly to NetWare and compatible client computers. The server appears to the NetWare clients to be just like any other NetWare server, and the clients can access volumes, files, and printers on the server.

Installing NetWare Services for Windows 2000

Both Novell and Microsoft provide a number of ways for clients to access NetWare and Windows 2000 Server resources. Novell provides client software for MS-DOS, Microsoft Windows 3.x, Microsoft Windows 95/98, Microsoft Windows NT 4 Workstation, and Microsoft Windows 2000 Professional. Microsoft has NetWare client software for Windows 95/98, Windows NT 4 Workstation, and Windows 2000 Professional. With the installation of any of these clients, a computer can be a client of Windows 2000 Server and NetWare simultaneously. Windows 2000 also provides the ability to access NetWare resources without the need to install any client software through the use of GSNW.

Novell Clients

Novell client software for Windows 3.x, Windows 95/98, Windows NT 4 Workstation, and Windows 2000 Professional provides full compatibility with NetWare, its utilities, and third-party applications written using the NetWare application programming interface (API). Unlike earlier versions of NetWare clients for Windows-based environments, Novell currently provides full 32-bit client support.

Microsoft Clients

Microsoft provides its own clients for NetWare access. Windows 95 and Windows NT 4 Workstation supply a NetWare client that can be used to access legacy NetWare 3.x bindery-based servers. Microsoft Windows 2000 Professional, Windows NT 4 Workstation, Windows 95, and Windows 98 provide software to allow clients to log on to an NDS-based server (such as NetWare 4.x and 5.x). These clients provide better integration with Windows-based networking, they require less memory overhead (due to shared libraries), and they are full 32-bit applications. The Microsoft-based NetWare clients provide almost complete support of the NetWare APIs, although not all third-party applications will work if they use older or uncommon NetWare API calls.

Using Gateway Service for NetWare

Installing and configuring each computer with a NetWare client can be very time-consuming in a large enterprise. Fortunately, there is a way to provide NetWare server connectivity without the need to install new software on each client. With GSNW, you can create a gateway through which Microsoft client computers—without Novell NetWare client software—can use NetWare file and print resources. You can make gateways for resources located in NDS trees as well as for resources on servers running NetWare 2.x or later with bindery security. These resources include volumes, directories, directory map objects, printers, and print queues.

GSNW depends on another NetWare compatibility feature of Windows Server: the IPX/SPX/NetBIOS Compatible Transport Protocol (NWLink for short). NWLink is an implementation of the Internetwork Packet Exchange (IPX), Sequenced Packet Exchange (SPX), and NetBIOS transport protocols used by a NetWare network. The Microsoft implementations of these protocols can seamlessly coexist with other protocols on the same network adapter.

The primary drawback of using GSNW is that it's harder to customize security on a user-by-user basis for NetWare resources. Each user profile must use a separate share on the gateway and, consequently, a separate drive letter, which limits the number of shares that can be created. Also, since the Windows 2000 Server must translate each server message block (SMB) call into NetWare Core Protocol (NCP) and back again, using GSNW can actually be slower than having software installed for each client.

Note   The translation overhead is greatly reduced when communicating with a NetWare 5–based server using TCP/IP.

Installing and Configuring the NWLink Protocol

To install the NWLink protocol, follow these steps:

1. Right-click My Network Places and choose Properties. The Network And Dial-up Connections window opens, shown in Figure 20-1.

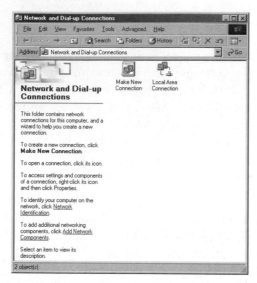

Figure 20-1. *The Network And Dial-up Connections window.*

2. Right-click the Local Area Connection icon, and choose Properties from the shortcut menu to display the Local Area Connection Properties window, shown in Figure 20-2.

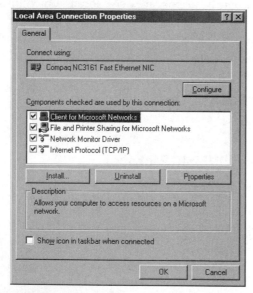

Figure 20-2. *The Local Area Connection Properties window.*

3. Click Install to display the Select Network Component Type dialog box, shown in Figure 20-3.

Figure 20-3. *The Select Network Component Type dialog box.*

4. Highlight Protocol in the network component list box, and click Add to open the Select Network Protocol dialog box (Figure 20-4).

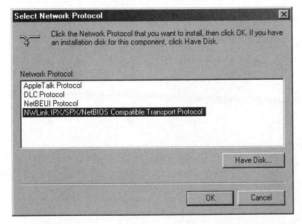

Figure 20-4. *The Select Network Protocol dialog box.*

5. Highlight NWLink IPX/SPX/NetBIOS Compatible Transport Protocol and click OK to add the protocol to your system. You may need to insert your Windows 2000 Server CD-ROM to complete the installation process.

6. Click OK to save the new network configuration.

Once you have installed the NWLink protocol, your Windows 2000 server will be able to communicate with your NetWare server. You can proceed to the next step, which is installing and configuring GSNW.

> **Note** Although early versions of Novell NetWare supported TCP/IP, the Microsoft and Novell implementations of the protocol were not compatible until NetWare 5. As a result, Windows 2000 Server requires NWLink to communicate with NetWare 4.x and earlier servers. If you are communicating with a NetWare 5 server, you don't need to install the NWLink protocol before installing GSNW.

Installing GSNW

To install and configure GSNW, follow these steps:

1. Right-click My Network Places and choose Properties.
2. Right-click the Local Area Connection icon and choose Properties from the shortcut menu. The Local Area Connection Properties window opens.
3. Click Install to display the Select Network Component Type dialog box.
4. Highlight Client in the network component list box and click Add. The Select Network Client dialog box opens, shown in Figure 20-5.

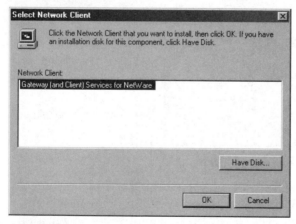

Figure 20-5. *The Select Network Client dialog box.*

5. Highlight Gateway (And Client) Services For NetWare and click OK. You may need to insert your Windows 2000 Server CD-ROM to complete the installation process.

6. The Select NetWare Logon dialog box appears, shown in Figure 20-6. Specify the user name, tree, and context that the gateway will use when logging on to the NetWare server.

   • If the gateway will be logging on to a bindery-based NetWare server, select the Preferred Server option and then select the appropriate server from the Preferred Server list box.

   • If the gateway will be logging on to an NDS-based directory tree, select the Default Tree And Context option and then provide the tree and context names to use when logging on.

   • To run the NetWare login script when the gateway first attaches to the NetWare server, click the Run Login Script check box.

7. Click OK to save the logon information.

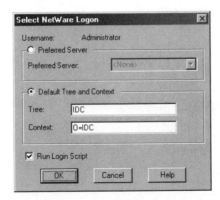

Figure 20-6. *The Select NetWare Logon dialog box.*

Configuring GSNW

Once you have installed GSNW, you can modify its configuration by clicking the GSNW icon in Control Panel to display the Gateway Service For NetWare dialog box, shown in Figure 20-7. In this dialog box you can set the following options:

- When logging on to a bindery-based NetWare server, select the Preferred Server option and then choose the appropriate server from the Select Preferred Server list box.

- To log on to an NDS-based directory tree, select the Default Tree And Context option and then provide the tree and context names needed to log on to the NetWare server.

- In the Print Options group, select the print options you want to use when printing to NetWare-based printers.

- To run the NetWare logon script when the gateway first attaches to the NetWare server, select the Run Logon Script check box.

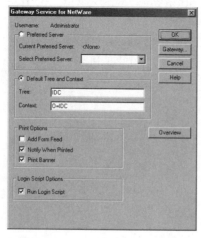

Figure 20-7. *The Gateway Service For NetWare dialog box.*

Enabling the Gateway

To enable the gateway, click Gateway in the Gateway Service For NetWare dialog box to display the Configure Gateway dialog box (Figure 20-8). Select the Enable Gateway check box and specify the user name and password required by GSNW to connect to the NetWare server.

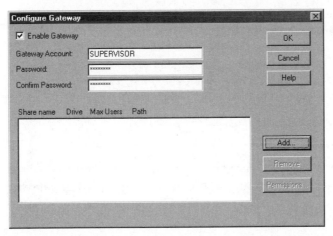

Figure 20-8. *The Configure Gateway dialog box.*

Note   NetWare IDs are typically limited to eight characters or fewer.

You can also establish one or more shares on the NetWare server for use by your Windows 2000 clients. Click Add in the Configure Gateway dialog box to display the New Share dialog box, shown in Figure 20-9.

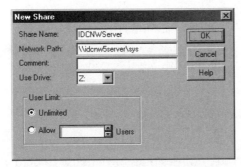

Figure 20-9. *The New Share dialog box.*

Once the new share has been created, click the Permissions button to specify which Windows 2000 Server users and groups have access to the resource and what their rights for the resource are. These same rights need to be established with any Windows 2000 Server share.

Tip   Everyone with rights to GSNW has access to any share you define, and each share takes up one of the 26 available drive letters. You might need to reorganize the NetWare server directory structure to minimize the number of shares required.

Configuring NetWare Server

To finish configuring GSNW, the NetWare system administrator must place the user account specified in the GSNW configuration in a group called Ntgateway and must grant that user account access to the NetWare resources you want to share on the Windows 2000 server.

First create a group called Ntgateway on the NetWare server. Make sure that the user specified by GSNW is created on the NetWare server and is part of the Ntgateway group. Then create a share for the NetWare resource and grant the Windows 2000 user access to the share resource.

Running NetWare Utilities

With Windows 2000 Server and GSNW, you can run many of the standard NetWare utilities as well as many NetWare-aware applications from the command prompt. GSNW does not support utilities for NetWare 4.x and earlier. Also, for some administrative functions, you must use Windows 2000 Server–based management tools.

Note   To run NDS administrative utilities on Windows 2000 Professional, you must use the NetWare client software.

Windows 2000 Server supports many NetWare utilities that you can use to manage the NetWare network from a computer running Windows 2000 Workstation or Windows 2000 Server. (Some utilities may require additional files that are supplied either with Windows 2000 Server or with NetWare, as discussed in the next section.)

The following MS-DOS–based utilities are known to work with Windows 2000:

Chkvol	Help	Rconsole	Settts
Colorpal	Listdir	Remove	Slist
Dspace	Map	Revoke	Syscon
Fconsole	Ncopy	Rights	Tlist
Filer	Ndir	Security	Userlist
Flag	Pconsole	Send	Volinfo
Flagdir	Psc	Session	Whoami
Grant	Pstat	Setpass	

The Windows 2000 Server Net Use command or Microsoft Windows Explorer perform the same functions as the NetWare Attach, Login, and Logout commands. The Net Use command is also similar to the Capture command for printing when MS-DOS–based and Windows-based applications must print to a specific port. In addition, you can use the Add Printer Wizard to connect to NetWare print queues. The Net Use command can also be used to connect to volumes and printers in NDS trees as well as on NetWare bindery-based servers. The Windows 2000 Server Net View command performs the same function as the NetWare Slist utility.

Using NetWare-Aware Applications

Many NetWare-aware applications will run on Windows 2000 Server through GSNW just as if they were running on a NetWare client computer. However, not all NetWare-aware applications are supported. Many applications require special files that are supplied either with NetWare or with Windows 2000 Server.

Nwipxspx.dll

Many older 16-bit NetWare-aware applications require the Nwipxspx.dll file supplied by Novell. The file is part of the standard Novell client installation. Find it and copy it to the \SystemRoot\System32 folder on the machine where you'll be using the NetWare applications.

Netware.drv, Nwnetapi.dll, and Nwcalls.dll

NetWare-aware applications that use the NetWare API to send and receive NetWare Core Protocol (NCP) packets may require Netware.drv and either Nwnetapi.dll or, for more recent versions of NetWare, Nwcalls.dll. Netware.drv should be installed in the \SystemRoot\System32 folder when you install GSNW. If you copy any of these files to your computer running Windows 2000 Server or modify your search path during the current Windows 2000 Server work session, you must log off and then log on for the changes to take effect.

Real World   Obtaining Current NetWare Software Files

To get the NetWare files you need, check with your NetWare network administrator or your local Novell representative to see if the latest client files are available locally. Or you can get the files over the Internet from *ftp.novell.com*. Novell also posts revisions of NetWare client software and drivers on CompuServe at *http://www.compuserve.com/computing/subs/Novelldown.asp*

Sharing Windows 2000 Resources with NetWare Clients

Now that you've learned all about accessing Novell NetWare resources from a Windows 2000–based environment and network, you need to know the other side of the story—how to access Windows 2000 Server resources from NetWare clients and servers. Microsoft provides a separate add-on package called Microsoft Services for NetWare, which consists of File and Print Services for NetWare (FPNW) and Directory Service Manager for NetWare (DSMN).

FPNW allows administrators of NetWare 4.x and earlier (in bindery emulation mode only) to integrate Windows 2000 Server into their NetWare network. It emulates a NetWare server, enabling a Windows 2000 server running this service to integrate into an existing NetWare-based network with no changes to the NetWare clients. NetWare clients do not know that they are accessing an FPNW-enabled Windows 2000 server.

Administrators working with networks through the NetWare bindery (version 4.x and earlier) can have a difficult time because they have to manage each server and its users separately from the rest of their servers. But using Windows 2000 and DSMN, they can manage multiple environments while maintaining only a single user account and associated password for each end user on the network.

Administrators simplify the task of controlling their mixed Windows 2000 and NetWare environments by using Windows 2000 Active Directory. DSMN copies the NetWare user accounts to Active Directory and then propagates any changes back to the NetWare server, all without the need to install any software on the NetWare servers.

More Info   More information on Microsoft Services for NetWare can be found on the Microsoft Web site at *http://www.microsoft.com/windows/server/*.

Selecting the Right Client Services

Once Windows 2000 Server and the network are configured to access NetWare-based resources, the most important decision is the choice of client services. You can choose to install client services for each network client, or you can simplify things by installing GSNW. Tables 20-1 and 20-2 list some conditions that may exist on your network and the best choice for service or client in each case. The reality is that you'll undoubtedly have to opt for a less-than-perfect choice, but these tables can provide a starting point.

Table 20-1.   Choosing between client services and gateway services

Scenario	Gateway Service	Client Service
Users' home directories are located on the NetWare server.	X	
Users' home directories are located on the Windows 2000 server.		X
Applications are located on the Windows 2000 server.		X
Applications are located on a NetWare server, and they are used by all users.		X
Applications are located on a NetWare server, but their access is restricted to certain groups.	X	
Users need access only to NetWare-based printers.		X
Users need access to files on a NetWare server that are shared among large numbers of users.		X
Users need access to files on a NetWare server that are restricted to a user or group.	X	
Users are more comfortable using utilities and commands of NetWare than those of Windows 2000 Server.	X	
Users are more familiar with utilities and commands of Windows 2000 Server than with those of NetWare.		X

Table 20-2. Choosing between Novell and Microsoft clients

Scenario	Novell Client	Microsoft Client
The client is running on a non-Intel (i.e., alpha) platform.		X
Legacy NetWare-based applications are required.	X	
Windows 95/98 peer-to-peer sharing services are used on your network.		X
Microsoft FPNW is used on your network.		X
The client has limited resources (i.e., hard disk space and memory).		X

Understanding Permissions and Security Concepts

When using GSNW, NetWare file attributes are not exactly the same as those for Windows 2000 Server. Table 20-3 shows the file rights mapping between Windows 2000 Server and NetWare for files opened through GSNW.

Table 20-3. Comparing Windows and NetWare file attributes

Windows File Attributes	NetWare File Attributes
A (Archive)	A
S (System)	Sy
H (Hidden)	H
R (Read-only)	Ro, Di (Delete inhibit), Ri (Rename inhibit)

GSNW does not support the following NetWare file attributes:

- Rw (Read/write)
- S (Shareable)
- T (Transactional)
- P (Purge)
- Ra (Read audit)
- Wa (Write audit)
- Ci (Copy inhibit)

When you copy a file from a Microsoft networking client to the NetWare file server by means of GSNW, the Ro, A, Sy, and H file attributes are preserved.

When you use a Windows 2000 server running GSNW to directly access NetWare servers, you can use NetWare utilities, such as Filer and Rights, to set attributes that are not supported by GSNW.

Summary

Windows 2000 Server provides many ways of working with Novell NetWare. Whether you want your NetWare clients to access files on a Windows 2000 server or your Windows 2000 clients to access files on a NetWare server, the tools are available. As usual, thorough planning is important for a minimal performance impact and a smooth transition. Interface between Windows 2000 and another system, UNIX, is discussed in the next chapter.

Chapter 21
Interoperating with UNIX

Enterprise computing inevitably means being able to work with and interconnect to a variety of environments and operating systems. One of the most prevalent alternative operating systems that Microsoft Windows 2000 users work with is UNIX—in all of its various forms. On its own Windows 2000 has basic connectivity tools that enable it to function on the same network with UNIX servers. Additional add-ons from Microsoft and third parties help UNIX and Windows 2000 work nearly seamlessly together, so the system administrators of both environments can provide their users with full access to the resources of the other environment almost transparently.

This chapter looks at that basic interoperability and explores some of the add-ons that can extend the functionality and interoperability for both systems. It starts by examining permissions and security issues because they are related to many of the other subjects in this chapter. Next it covers connectivity and file systems, followed by a look at the new Microsoft Windows NT Services for UNIX (SFU) package released in early 1999. Finally it examines the differences between Windows 2000 and UNIX shells.

Permissions and Security Concepts

One of the most important and pervasive differences between Windows 2000 and UNIX is the manner in which they handle permissions and security. These differences are subtle and frequently lead the unwary to make false assumptions. Because Chapters 17 and 18 already explain in great detail how Windows 2000 handles security, we'll spare you here, but if you're going to coexist with UNIX servers, you need to understand how UNIX handles security to avoid problems. Let's take a look at a UNIX file listing first, then examine symbolic links, privilege levels, and permissions.

A UNIX File Listing

A UNIX file listing might look like this:

```
-rwxr-x--x  2 charlie    dba          2579 Aug 30 15:49 resize
```

This listing tells us virtually all we need to know about the security and permissions of the file we're looking at. Let's start at the left of the line and work our way across to see what we've got and what it means—and how it compares to Windows 2000.

The first dash (-) tells us that this listing is *not* a directory. If it were a directory, a "d" would be there instead. UNIX treats a directory as simply another file, although a special one, and the permissions have a slightly different meaning when referring to a directory as opposed to a file. We'll cover directory permissions in a bit, but let's stay with regular files for now.

The next three characters correspond to the permissions of the file owner—who may be someone other than the original creator since UNIX allows a user to "give" a file to another user. The "r" indicates that the owner has the right to read the file; the "w" means that she or he can write to it, delete it, or otherwise modify it; and the "x" allows the owner to execute the program.

Real World   UNIX-Executable Programs

In Windows 2000, the operating system decides whether a program is executable based on the filename. If the filename has an extension of .COM, .EXE, .BAT, or .CMD, it can be executed, assuming the user has the appropriate permissions. In UNIX, no association exists between the extension and whether the file is executable. (In fact, most UNIX files have no extension at all.) The only determinant of whether a file is executable is the permission of the file. So, while it might be the convention on a particular system to always name shell scripts (the UNIX equivalent of a batch file) with a name that ends in .sh or .ksh, this has no actual meaning. The file must be given the execute permission before it can be executed.

The fifth, sixth, and seventh characters correspond to the permissions of members of the same group as the owner of the file. The "r" indicates that members of the group can read the file (or perform actions that leave it unchanged, such as copying it); the dash indicates that they do *not* have permission to write to it, delete it, or otherwise modify it; the "x" gives them the ability to execute the program.

Finally, the last three characters of the first group correspond to the permissions of the rest of the world. The initial dash indicates that these users don't have the right to read the file, or in any way look at the contents, nor do they have permission to copy the file. The second dash indicates that they don't have permission to change, modify, or delete the file, and finally, the last "x" indicates that they can execute the file, if executing doesn't actually require a read.

Real World   Permissions

UNIX has only three basic permissions: Read, Write, and Execute.

Read   The right to read a file or list its contents. The right to make a copy of the file. For directories, the right to list the contents of the directory.

Write   The right to alter the contents of a file. For a directory, the right to create files and subdirectories. If you have Write permission on a directory, you have the right to delete files in the directory even if you don't have Write permission on the file—if you also have either Read or Execute permission on the directory.

Execute   The right to execute the file. Even the owner of a file needs this permission to execute it. For a directory, the right to change into the directory or to execute files within the directory. Having this right on a directory does not, however, give you permission to list the contents of the directory, so you might be able to execute a file without being able to see that it is there.

The next character, the number "2," indicates that there are two hard links to the file. A *hard link* gives the exact same file another name. There is still only a single actual file stored on the hard disk, but there are two directory entries pointing to the file. There are no practical limits to the number of hard links that can exist to a single file, but all links to the file must exist on the same file system.

The next two groups in the listing are the owner of the file, "charlie," and the group for the file, "dba." While these will normally be user and group names, they could also be a number if either the owner or group of the file doesn't actually have an account on the system.

Next we have the size of the file (2579 bytes in this case), the date and time the file was created or last updated, and the name of the file—actually, the directory entry for the file that corresponds to this hard link to the file. Note that no link has any preference over any other. There is nothing significant about which name comes first; they are all treated equally. And deleting one link does not delete the file—just that reference to it. Any other versions of the file remain.

Symbolic Links

UNIX supports both hard links and symbolic links. *Symbolic links* are analogous to Windows 2000 shortcuts but with several differences. The most important difference is that in UNIX when you access the symbolic link, you actually access the file it points to, not the link itself. For example, if you edit a symbolic link to a text file, you're actually editing the original text file. With a Windows 2000 shortcut, you can use the shortcut only to start an executable file or to open a folder.

A symbolic link differs from a hard link in that the actual file has precedence over any of the symbolic links to it. In fact, the listing for a link to our resize file makes it immediately clear that this is a symbolic link, not a hard link:

```
lrwxrwxrwx  1 charlie    dba   2579 Aug 30 15:49 resize -> /u/cpr/
resize
```

As you can see, the listing not only begins with the letter "l" in the first position, but it actually shows where the link is pointing to. You'll notice that the two filenames are identical. While this isn't a requirement, it is the most common use of symbolic links—to make a file appear as if it were in one place when it actually resides elsewhere.

Another feature of a symbolic link that distinguishes it from a hard link is that it can cross file systems and even machines. You can have a symbolic link that points to a file that resides on a completely different computer.

Caution If you copy a file on top of a symbolic link, the link will be broken. Your new file will actually replace the link with the file. The original file will still exist, however, making the duplication of files confusing at best.

Privilege Levels

Traditionally, UNIX divides the world up into only three types of users: the owner of a file, a member of the same group as the owner, and all the rest of the world. These three privilege levels are known as owner, group, and other. So far, so good. This sounds a lot like Windows 2000, right? Well, not really. The biggest difference is in that second privilege level: group.

On UNIX systems with traditional security, a user is active only in a single group at a time. When that user creates a file, it is created with permissions for the group based strictly on the current group of the file creator. This situation can have interesting and subtle complications when compared to the Windows 2000 methodology. If a user's primary logon is to one of the standard groups, things will generally behave as you would expect. However, when a user belongs to a specialized group with limited membership and creates files while that group is the active group, the ability of users outside the group to access the file may be constrained.

A user who isn't an active member of the group that owns a file and who isn't the actual owner of the file is in the other privilege level. This arrangement is essentially the same as the Windows 2000 group called Everyone. A user in the other category has no permission to access the file except what every other user has.

Real World **The UNIX Super User**

In discussions of UNIX security, keep in mind one overriding principle: the *root user* (sometimes called the *super user*) has access to everything. In the Windows 2000 world, you can easily set a file or directory so that even those users with administrative privileges don't have access without changing the ownership of the file, but in the UNIX world, that restriction doesn't exist. Not only that, but the super user can even change identities to have the same identity as you.

Basic Connectivity

Now that you understand the differences between the security models of Windows 2000 and UNIX, let's look at how they are compatible. For one thing, with no additional add-ons, Windows 2000 coexists reasonably well with UNIX servers. The default networking protocol for both operating systems is now the same—TCP/IP. They can easily share DNS, DHCP, and other services. And simple connectivity between Windows 2000 and UNIX can be handled by FTP and telnet clients on the Windows 2000 machines.

File Transfer Protocol

All versions of Windows 2000 include a simple FTP command-line client and can handle FTP from within Microsoft Windows Explorer to a limited extent. The character-mode client provides no frills but should feel quite comfortable to the UNIX user—and it works without quirks. Those who want a more graphical and friendly FTP client have a variety to choose from, including some that are pure freeware or shareware. Our personal favorite is WS_FTP Pro from Ipswitch (*http://www.ipswitch.com*). Windows 2000 also includes a full-featured FTP server as part of the Internet Information Services (IIS) suite. With both an FTP server and a client natively available, you can easily copy files between the UNIX and Windows 2000 machines on your network.

Telnet

All versions of Windows 2000 come with the new character-mode telnet client that debuted in SFU. The frankly horrible semigraphical telnet client that had been around since Microsoft Windows 3 is finally gone. The new client is faster, has better terminal emulations, and is actually quite decent for most uses. It supports American National Standards Institute (ANSI)—including color, VT52, VT100 and VTNT, a special emulation that can be useful when running character-mode Windows 2000 applications such as Edit. If your need for terminal emulation isn't met by one of these modes, there are excellent third-party commercial telnet clients available.

Windows 2000 Server even has a built-in telnet daemon, or server. This server is the excellent one shipped as part of SFU, but it's limited to two simultaneous connections.

File Systems

Windows 2000 network file sharing is based on the traditional Microsoft networking mechanism of server message blocks (SMBs). UNIX systems, on the other hand, use the Network File System (NFS)—originally developed by Sun Microsystems—to share file systems across the network.

Until the release of SFU, only third-party NFS solutions were available for Windows systems that needed to be able to share file resources with UNIX systems. Most of these third-party solutions were expensive and problematic. The biggest issue was their inability to keep up with Windows NT service packs, which seemed to break these NFS solutions more often than not. In addition, these solutions often had significant performance problems.

However, several powerful SMB-based UNIX solutions address the problem of sharing file resources between Windows NT and UNIX. These SMB solutions vary in cost from free to expensive and support native Windows networking at either the workgroup or domain level. With the release of Windows 2000, only time will tell how well these solutions will manage to keep up with the changes in the Windows 2000 security model as compared to the Windows NT model.

The Network File System

When it was created, NFS was designed to run as a broadcast protocol using User Datagram Protocol (UDP). This protocol created substantial performance and network traffic issues for those intending to implement large amounts of NFS networking and made it difficult to share file systems across routed boundaries. Eventually, the NFS standard was changed to support TCP for NFS networking, and many modern clients and servers support this mechanism. However, many older NFS implementations still out there don't support TCP, so the default mechanism for SFU and other NFS implementations in Windows 2000 is UDP.

Overall, performance of NFS file transfers to and from a Windows 2000 server is substantially inferior compared to most SMB implementations. For environments in which large files must be routinely copied back and forth between Windows 2000 and UNIX systems, NFS is likely to be an unsatisfactory solution. However, if your needs are more for transparent access to UNIX resources residing on UNIX servers, NFS is the way to go. It provides a fully integrated environment to the Windows 2000 user. (If you install SFU as it's presented later in this chapter, keep these considerations in mind.)

The Server Message Block

The biggest issue that the SMB-on-UNIX crowd has to deal with is the changing Windows 2000 security model. Two mechanisms are used for handling security with the SMB-on-UNIX solutions—workgroup-level security and Windows NT 4 domain-level security.

Workgroup security suffers all the same problems as workgroups in the enterprise environment: it becomes more difficult to manage as the number of users and machines involved increases, and it has limited options for actually managing security. However, workgroup security has a definite place in the smaller environment, where it's easy to understand and simple to set up. Plus, there's a nice cost advantage—a widely available and well-implemented freeware SMB server called Samba is available on virtually all UNIX platforms. Other commercial workgroup SMB servers are also available that run on a variety of platforms. They tend to be more Windows-like and easier to setup and administer than Samba, which shows its open source heritage.

Windows NT 4 domain SMB servers are also available from a number of UNIX vendors. All of these are based on AT&T's initial port to UNIX of Microsoft's advanced server technology. Each is limited to running on the platform for which it was designed, and each has slight differences because the port from AT&T required tweaking in most cases. All SMB servers can be either a primary domain controller or a backup domain controller in a Windows NT domain, but all will have problems dealing with the new security model in Windows 2000. These servers, being based on the Windows NT 4 security model, will force you to stay in mixed mode, unfortunately.

The SMB domain servers do have one important advantage over the SMB workgroup servers: to the users and administrators of the Windows network, they all look and feel exactly like a native Windows NT 4 server. The familiar Windows NT Server administration tools are used to manage them, and servers and shares look exactly like a Windows NT server to your users, eliminating training and user-interface issues. Also, all of the SMB servers have one advantage over the NFS solutions: they tend to be significantly faster at file transfers, especially when handling large files.

Services for UNIX Overview

To simplify connecting to and working with UNIX systems, Microsoft released the SFU package, which contains all the basics needed for interoperating between Windows 2000 and UNIX. These products include NFS, telnet, the UNIX Korn shell and utilities, and a password synchronization daemon. Before installing SFU, you need a little background on password synchronization. Then we'll look at the other SFU products in more detail.

Understanding Password Synchronization

Password synchronization is a one-way synchronization utility that allows you to manage your users' passwords for both Windows 2000 and UNIX from the Windows 2000 Server. SFU includes precompiled password synchronization daemons (known in UNIX as single sign-on daemons, or SSOD) for three major versions of UNIX: HP-UX, Sun OS, and Digital UNIX. It also includes source code that theoretically allows you to compile on any other UNIX system you might need to support. Realistically, however, if you don't have one of the three provided ports of the secure daemon, you're likely to find that your only viable option is the nonsecure method of password synchronization using rlogin.

Obviously, the use of rlogin has inherent security concerns because it involves the passing of clear text passwords across the network, but it's relatively easy to set up and may be perfectly sufficient in a smaller network that is adequately secured from external influences. It also requires no additional software or configuration and is essentially platform independent.

Managing a UNIX Pod

UNIX hosts are organized into pods, with the password synchronization method being managed on a per-pod basis. You can create a new pod, add a host to an existing pod, or change the synchronization method for a pod by using the Password Synchronization Service Administrator (psadmin.exe).

When you create a new pod, you're prompted for the member hosts of the pod and the password synchronization methodology that will be used for the pod. You can change this later. You also have an option to turn on verbose logging. By default, only failures are logged, but with verbose logging enabled, all synchronization actions are logged to Event Viewer.

Using rlogin to Synchronize Passwords

While some UNIX environments don't permit the use of rlogin, where it's a viable option, it provides a simple and easily configured mechanism. Where the network is completely isolated from the outside world by a highly secure firewall (or there's no connection to the outside world at all), you can use rlogin to manage the synchronization between your Windows 2000 and UNIX machines. This option has the virtue of requiring no additional software on the UNIX host because most versions of UNIX support rlogin.

To set up rlogin password synchronization, you first need to configure the remote UNIX hosts to correctly support rlogin for the root account. This requires creating a .rhosts file on the server. This .rhosts file *must* have permissions such that *only* root (or the account authorized to change passwords) can write to the file, and it must be owned by root (or that alternate account) and reside in the home directory of the root or alternate account. It should contain a listing for the machine where the password change will be made—generally a domain controller. The listing should have only the short name for the machine, not the fully qualified domain name.

The default configuration for rlogin synchronization uses the root account, expects a prompt of "#", and expects that the password-changing command is passwd. If your environment is different from this, you can modify these defaults by using the Password Synchronization Service Administrator.

Real World Account Names

Unlike Windows 2000 and Windows NT accounts, which are case insensitive, the user accounts on UNIX systems are fully case sensitive. If you already have mixed-case Windows 2000 accounts, you'll likely find it takes more time and grief to align the accounts than you save in the long run. But if you're just adding Windows 2000 into an existing UNIX environment, you can make password and account synchronization easy and straightforward by creating the corresponding Windows 2000 accounts as lowercase only from the very beginning. The display names associated with the accounts can remain mixed case; only the underlying account name needs to be all lowercase.

Using Secure Password Synchronization

SFU provides for secure password synchronization using precompiled binaries that run as daemons on the UNIX server, allowing the UNIX server to receive encrypted passwords sent by Windows 2000 and then modify the UNIX password for the same account. However, the caveats about case sensitivity relative to rlogin synchronization apply equally to secure synchronization.

Installing the Password Synchronization Daemon on UNIX

To install the password synchronization daemon, copy the SSOD and ssod.config files for your version of the secure daemon to the UNIX machine that will be the target for password synchronization. A typical target location for these files would be /usr/local/etc, but this will vary from system to system and isn't critical. If you use FTP to copy the files, make sure you use a binary transfer to prevent corruption of the files.

Once you've copied the files to the UNIX machine, use the appropriate mechanism to install them. This will vary depending on your platform but can include pkgadd or other installation mechanisms. Edit the provided ssod.config file to reflect both the locations of files on your system and the type of synchronization appropriate. Both Network Information Service (NIS) and /etc/passwd are supported, as is password shadowing.

The ssod.config file must reside in the same directory as the daemon. Once the daemon is configured, you can start it manually or add it to the appropriate startup file. Startup mechanisms vary from platform to platform but can include /etc/rc.local and shell wrappers in an /etc/rc2.d directory.

When you create the UNIX pod and select Use Encryption, the Secure Propagation Settings dialog box will open. Enter the port number you've configured on the UNIX side and the secret encryption key that you chose in the ssod.config file. This key will be used to encrypt the password before it is passed over the network.

Note All hosts in a UNIX pod must use the same encryption key, but different pods can use different keys.

Installing Services for UNIX

Now you're ready to install SFU. To do so, follow this procedure:

1. Insert the SFU CD-ROM into the drive, and the first screen of the Services for UNIX Add-On Pack Setup Wizard will appear, as shown in Figure 21-1.

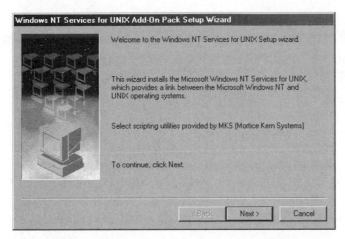

Figure 21-1. *Initial screen of the Windows NT Services for UNIX Add-On Pack Setup Wizard.*

2. Click Next, accept the license agreement, and click Next again.

3. Enter the 25 characters of the new license mechanism, as shown in Figure 21-2. The good news is that these characters are not case sensitive. The bad news is that it's extremely easy to mistype the string, and you can't cut and paste them from another source. Click Next.

Figure 21-2. *Entering the license key for your copy of SFU.*

4. Select the type of installation. As always, we recommend choosing a custom installation—if only so you know what you're actually getting. Figure 21-3 shows the defaults for a custom installation on Windows 2000 Server.

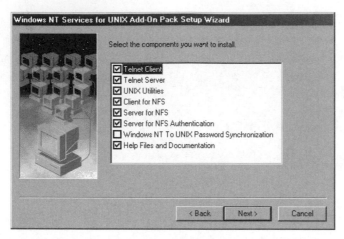

Figure 21-3. *The defaults for installation of SFU on Windows 2000 Server.*

5. Select the Server For NFS option only if you're going to share your Windows 2000 file systems back to UNIX. (See the section "The Network File System" earlier in this chapter for more specifics about when it's appropriate to select Server For NFS.)

6. The Windows NT To UNIX Password Synchronization option isn't selected by default. Generally, you should select this feature only in large environments under these conditions:

   • Large numbers of users are working on both Windows 2000 and UNIX regularly.

   • You're running NIS for all your UNIX systems.

   • Your NIS server is one of the supported and supplied SSOD platforms (Sun OS, HP-UX, and Digital UNIX).

   Alternately, if you have only a few UNIX systems and no security concerns, you can use the nonsecure method of password synchronization discussed earlier—rlogin. It has the virtue of being simple and easy to manage, but it does allow the unscrupulous person with physical access to your network to read clear text passwords on the network.

7. Once you've made your selections, click Next and Finish, and the installation will begin. In most cases, you'll need to reboot at the end, depending on the options you chose.

Services for UNIX Configuration

Now that you've installed SFU, let's look at its configuration. SFU originated as several different products from various sources, which have been pulled together into a single package. Each product has a different interface and configuration mechanism, and as a result they don't have a cohesive look and feel. Even so, the functionality is all there and not, generally, dependent on the other pieces. The basic pieces of the product (most of which we've already covered briefly) fall into the following three categories:

- **Connectivity services**   Includes both a telnet server and an improved, text-based (character-mode) telnet client, along with a password synchronization daemon. The telnet client was such a major improvement that Microsoft included it as part of the standard Windows 2000 product.

- **File services**   Includes NFS client and server support.

- **Usability services**   Provides a set of UNIX utilities and a Korn shell.

The telnet client and server, NFS client and server, and UNIX utilities are discussed in more detail in the following sections. The Korn shell is explained later, toward the end of this chapter. Let's begin with connectivity services.

Connectivity Services

The telnet client and server provide an excellent method for communicating between Windows 2000 machines and UNIX machines. But the telnet services can also offer substantial benefits in daily administration of the Windows 2000 machines themselves. By adding a telnet service to your Windows 2000 servers, you provide a simple, low-overhead command-line interface to the servers that will let you easily manage a variety of administrative tasks from a single desktop and even over a slow dial-up line.

The Telnet Server

As installed, the telnet server works optimally for most installations. It provides access from any server or workstation that has a telnet client installed, offering improved interoperability in the enterprise and improved manageability even in a pure Windows 2000 environment. It will accept logins from a variety of clients, including the graphical telnet client shipped with Windows NT and Microsoft Windows 95/98 and a variety of character-mode terminal clients from virtually any operating system. Additionally, it can meet specific site requirements to improve security, simplify logins, and so on.

The NT LAN Manager   The SFU telnet server supports NT LAN Manager (NTLM) for authentication of client logins. NTLM automatically authenticates the user based on his or her Windows 2000 logon, giving a transparent connection to the host while ensuring that clear text passwords don't pass over the network. NTLM must be supported on both the client and server side, however, making this option viable only between Windows machines, not directly to or from UNIX machines.

When using NTLM logon, users are restricted to local drives on the machine they are logged on to. If they need to map network resources, they can do so by explicitly mapping with full credentials. For example,

net use g:\\server\share\user:domain\username

Administration   The telnet server is administered by using the tlntdmn.exe program, which is installed by default in <SFU Root>\telnet and provides a simple text menu that will run from virtually any character-mode window, including a remote telnet login. With the tlntadmn.exe program, you can list the current users, terminate a user or users, display (and modify) the registry settings for the server, and start and stop the service. The registry settings you can change include the following:

- **The allowing of logins from a trusted domain**   The default is on.
- **The default mapping that simulates the Alt key from a telnet session**
- **The default login domain, initially set to "."**   By changing this setting, you can make it easier for users to log in. Set this to your normal Windows 2000 domain name, and the system won't require a login of the DOMAIN\username format, but it will accept a simple user name.
- **The default shell**   The user will receive this command shell when logging in. By default, it is %SystemRoot%\system32\cmd.exe/q/k. Leave the default alone. Users can easily change their shell once they have logged in, and sticking to the default will reduce confusion and problems.
- **The login script that is executed when the user logs in**   The default value is <SFU Root>\Telnet\login.cmd. Use this script to customize the settings for your users and make any drive mappings that you'll need to be made automatically. The default Windows 2000 logon script will *not* automatically execute for telnet sessions.

- **The maximum number of connections allowed to the server** The default (and maximum) is 63. However, the actual number may be less if fewer licensed connections are available for the Windows 2000 machine.

- **The maximum number of failed logins permitted before the session returns a failure** The default is 3, a reasonable number.

- **The option to use NTLM for authentication** The allowable values are as follows:

  - **0** No NTLM is used.

  - **1** NTLM is used if available; otherwise a login prompt is presented.

  - **2** NTLM only is permitted. No login prompt is presented.

  - **The default TCP/IP port number used for telnet** The default is 23.

Note Using a value of 2 (NTLM only) in a mixed UNIX and Windows 2000 environment would effectively lock out UNIX users from the Windows 2000 servers because they wouldn't have a client that supports NTLM authentication. Forcing NTLM does, however, eliminate the passing of clear text passwords over the network.

Registry Settings You can use the provided telnet administration program to edit the registry settings for the telnet server, or you can edit them manually by using regedit or regedt32. The subkey for the telnet server is HKEY_LOCAL_MACHINE\SOFTWARE\Microsoft\TelnetServer\1.0. The keys and their types, which correspond to the tlntadmn.exe settings explained in the previous section, are listed in Table 21-1.

Table 21-1. Registry settings for the telnet server

Registry Key	Type	Default Value
AllowTrustedDomain	REG_DWORD	0x00000001
AltKeyMapping	REG_EXPAND_SZ	
DefaultDomain	REG_EXPAND_SZ	
DefaultShell	REG_EXPAND_SZ	%SystemRoot%\system32\cmd.exe/q/k
LoginScript	REG_EXPAND_SZ	%SystemRoot%\system32\login.cmd
MaxConnections	REG_DWORD	0x0000003f (63)
MaxFailedLogins	REG_DWORD	0x00000003
NTLM	REG_DWORD	0x00000002 (NTLM only)
TelnetPort	REG_DWORD	0x00000017 (23)
Termcap	REG_DWORD	%SystemRoot%\system32\termcap

In addition, a specific subkey exists for performance tuning: HKEY_LOCAL_
MACHINE\SOFTWARE\MICROSOFT\TelnetServer\1.0\Performance
\NumThreadsPerProcessor. The minimum value for this setting is 2, and the default is 10 (0x0000000a). For most environments, the default value will optimize performance.

Caution   Use extreme care when editing the registry because changes can result in a computer that won't boot. Be sure to back up your registry before making any changes.

The Telnet Client

While Windows 2000 comes with a familiar graphical-mode telnet client,
Windows 2000 includes the new SFU character-mode telnet client that provides
greatly improved scroll bars and the ability to authenticate use of encrypted passwords when connecting to telnet servers that support NTLM authentication. It
is both faster and better behaved than the graphical-mode client it has replaced.

Furthermore, the telnet client provides terminal emulations, including an ANSI
emulation that supports colors correctly when connecting to servers that support
it, such as those running the Santa Cruz Operation (SCO) variant of UNIX. There
is also a new VTNT emulation that supports enhanced features when connecting between Windows NT and Windows 2000 machines—including the ability
to run complex character-mode applications such as edit.exe that won't work with
standard terminal emulations.

The telnet configuration is done from within a telnet session by "escaping" to the
telnet prompt. Press Ctrl+right bracket (]) to bring up the telnet prompt once
you've started a telnet session. From here, you can use the following:

- **?**   To get help
- **close**   To close the current connection
- **display**   To show the current operating parameters
- **open** *<machinename>*   To open a connection to a machine (You can
  use an IP address here as well.)
- **quit**   To exit the telnet client completely
- **set**   To set an operating parameter The choices are
  - **set ?**   Displays help on other set options
  - **set NTLM**   Turns on NTLM authentication
  - **set LOCAL_ECHO**
  - **set TERM** *<value>*   Sets the requested terminal emulation (Choices
    are ANSI, VT52, VT100, and VTNT.)

- **status** To print the current status
- **unset** To clear the options selected with the Set command

Real World **Terminal Emulation Choices**

If you connect primarily to UNIX systems, set TERM to ANSI and set NTLM off, but if you connect frequently to both Windows NT and UNIX systems or primarily to Windows NT systems, you'll find the VTNT emulation a better choice, and you'll still fall back to ANSI when connecting to a system that doesn't support VTNT.

File Services

SFU provides additional file service connectivity beyond the native FTP client and server in Windows 2000. The addition of NFS client and server allows native connectivity in a way that looks and feels natural to both UNIX and Windows 2000 users.

By using the seamlessly integrated NFS client, you can map exported file systems from your UNIX servers just as if they were native Windows 2000 shares, using either the UNIX server:/export format or the Windows \\server\share format. And the NFS server allows you to share the file resources with your UNIX systems or with other NFS clients, including Windows 2000 clients. Let's look at NFS client first.

The NFS Client

When you install the NFS client, it adds an applet to the Control Panel for administering NFS client settings. Open Control Panel and double-click Client For NFS to open the Client For NFS Properties window shown in Figure 21-4. The following sections detail the options you can select to administer the NFS client settings.

Authentication Set your authentication options according to the type of UNIX system and environment you'll be connecting to. The following are options on the Authentication tab:

- **NIS** Appropriate in a large enterprise where NIS is already installed.
- **PCNFSD** Appropriate for all other environments. The PC NFS daemon server can be either on one of the UNIX servers or on a Windows 2000 NFS server.

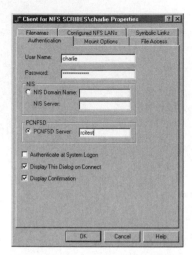

Figure 21-4. *The Authentication tab of the Client For NFS Properties window.*

The following additional settings are available:

- **Authenticate At System Logon**   Automatically verify password and user name for NFS connections at initial logon. Off by default, this option can slow the logon if connectivity problems occur but presents users with a more transparent environment.

- **Display This Dialog On Connect**   When selected, users will be prompted for logon credentials to connect to an NFS server. They will be prompted for each connection, giving them the option to select alternate authentication. A nuisance, normally, but a useful setting if your default authenticator is down.

- **Display Confirmation**   Each connection displays a confirmation dialog box before actually connecting. Usually a nuisance except when debugging a problem.

Mount Options   The Client For NFS Properties window, shown in Figure 21-5, allows you to specify the size of read and write buffers (the default is 64 K), initial timeout, number of retries, and whether to use hard or soft mounts. Unless you have a compelling reason to change these settings, you should leave them alone. They are optimal for connections that will support them and will automatically fall back if necessary.

There are three additional mount settings in the Client For NFS Properties window:

- **Enable Version 3 Remote Write Caching**   When selected, write requests will be written to the remote server's cache rather than forcing a file

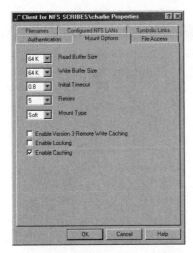

Figure 21-5. *The Mount Options tab of the Client For NFS Properties window.*

system to write immediately. This can speed up performance substantially but carries the usual caveats and should be enabled only where the server supports it and is suitably protected by an uninterruptible power supply (UPS).

- **Enable Locking**   When selected, and when supported by the remote server, files opened by the client will be locked until you close them.

- **Enable Caching**   When selected, read requests are cached locally, reducing the number of calls to the remote hard disk.

File Access Permissions   The default file access permissions for the NFS client are Read, Write, and Execute for the user (owner) of the file, but only Read and Execute for the Owner group and for other users (equivalent to a umask of 022).

Filename Mapping   You can map how new filenames are created and how existing filenames are mapped between the remote NFS server and your NFS client, as shown in Figure 21-6. The choices for filenames you create from the client are as follows:

- **Preserve Case (No Conversion)**   Appropriate only if you use NFS primarily as a network storage resource but won't have to use the files created from the UNIX environment, where mixed-case filenames can be a nuisance.

- **Convert To Lower Case**   The preferred choice when you'll be using files from both Windows 2000 clients and UNIX clients.

- **Convert To Upper Case** The preferred choice when your remote NFS server is on an operating system that prefers or requires uppercase filenames.

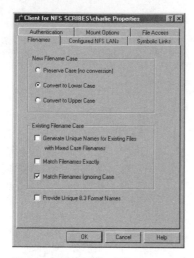

Figure 21-6. *The Filenames tab of the Client For NFS Properties window.*

The choices for mapping to existing filenames are the following:

- **Generate Unique Names For Existing Files With Mixed Case Filenames** Appropriate when there may be mixed-case filenames stored on the server. UNIX is fully case sensitive.

- **Match Filenames Exactly** Search for filenames preserving case sensitivity. Appropriate when mixed-case filenames may exist and when different files with identical names except for the case may exist.

- **Match Filenames Ignoring Case** Search for filenames ignoring case sensitivity. Appropriate and useful when the file may have been created with a mixed case, or when the program looking for it may expect a particular case.

- **Provide Unique 8.3 Format Names** Useful when you may need to access the files from an older 16-bit application that doesn't understand long filenames. Applies to both new and existing files.

Note In a mixed environment where users will be accessing files from both Windows and UNIX, you'll find that setting filename mapping to convert automatically to lowercase but to match by ignoring case will provide the least disruption to both communities of users.

Configuring NFS LANs Before your NFS client can effectively browse the network for exported (shared) file systems, you need to configure your NFS LAN. You have two choices for configuring NFS LANs: FavoriteLAN and named broadcast LANs. You should use broadcast LANs to divide your network into logical segments to limit the broadcasts to only a specific portion of your network and cut down network traffic.

You can create a single FavoriteLAN that has the NFS servers you connect to most frequently. You enter these servers by name or IP address, regardless of which segment they are on. By using a FavoriteLAN, you limit the amount of network broadcast traffic and speed up connecting to your preferred resources. To create a FavoriteLAN and add a server to it, follow these steps:

1. Open the Client for NFS window and click the Configured NFS LANs tab to display it, as shown in Figure 21-7.

Figure 21-7. *The Configured NFS LANs tab of the Client For NFS Properties window.*

2. Click the Add button to open the Add LAN dialog box, shown in Figure 21-8.

Figure 21-8. *The Add LAN dialog box.*

3. Click the Add Server To Favorite LAN option button, and then click OK to open the NFS Hosts dialog box, shown in Figure 21-9.

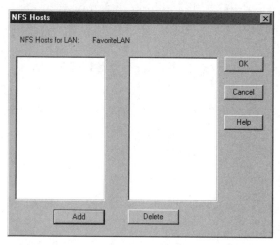

Figure 21-9. *The NFS Hosts dialog box.*

4. Click the Add button to open the Add Host dialog box, shown in Figure 21-10. This will let you enter an NFS host either by name or by IP address.

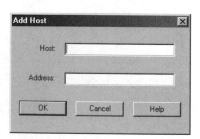

Figure 21-10. *The Add Host dialog box.*

5. Type in either the name or the IP address. The other will be returned automatically.

6. Click OK to return to the NFS Hosts dialog box shown in Figure 21-9. You can add additional hosts at this time or click OK a few times to add the NFS host and log on to it.

If the logon is successful and you have confirmation dialog boxes enabled, you'll see a message similar to that shown in Figure 21-11. If your name and password weren't authenticated, you'll see the message in Figure 21-12. You can try again or accept the anonymous logon. If you accept the anonymous logon, you'll still have access to the NFS host but only whatever access has been allowed for anonymous users.

Figure 21-11. *The NFS Login Successful dialog box.*

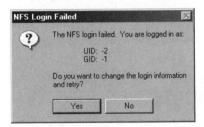

Figure 21-12. *The NFS Login Failed dialog box.*

Creating and using a named broadcast LAN is much the same process as using a FavoriteLAN, except that you must know something about the network segment on which the broadcast LAN resides. To create a broadcast LAN, follow these steps:

1. Open the Client For NFS window and click the Configured NFS LANs tab to display it, as shown in Figure 21-7. Click the Add button to open the Add LAN dialog box, shown in Figure 21-8.

2. Type a name for the LAN segment you're adding and select the Specify LAN To Browse option button to open the Broadcasting dialog box shown in Figure 21-13.

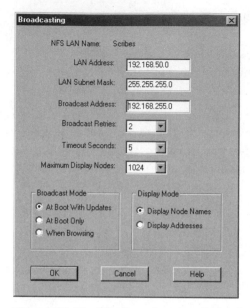

Figure 21-13. *The Broadcasting dialog box.*

3. Specify the LAN address and subnet mask, or type in the broadcast address directly. The LAN Address and LAN Subnet Mask boxes will clear once the Broadcast Address box has been filled in. This is normal.

4. Select the broadcast parameters, timeouts, and so on. The defaults are a good starting point, and you should modify them only if you know why you are modifying them and what the consequences are.

Tip To speed up the boot process, change the Broadcast Mode to When Browsing. However, this will slow down your initial browsing for NFS hosts, especially on large networks.

5. Once you've set your options, click OK and the LAN segment will be added to your NFS LANs.

6. Set the refresh interval to an appropriate figure for your environment. The default value is five minutes, which is reasonable on a large network where the available hosts might change frequently. On smaller, or static, networks, you may find it advantageous to lengthen this interval substantially to reduce broadcast traffic on the network.

7. Once you've added all the LAN segments you want, click OK. You might get a success or failure logon message, as shown in Figures 21-11

and 21-12, and then you'll be prompted for a reboot. Save up your changes to do them all at once, because you're going to have to reboot before they'll take effect.

> **More Info** See the *Microsoft Windows 2000 Resource Kit* (Microsoft Press, 1999) for more information on broadcast addresses, subnets, and TCP/IP masks.

Symbolic Links *Symbolic links* are a way for a file or directory to exist in one physical location but to be seen as existing in another location or locations. When a symbolic link references a file or directory that's local to the machine where the link is located, Client for NFS doesn't need to do any special manipulation to follow the link. But you can also create symbolic links on an NFS server that point to files or directories that actually reside on a remote machine.

To resolve these links, Client for NFS must have a mapping file that identifies the actual machine to which the link points. This mapping file can reside on the local client machine, or it can be located centrally on the network for easier administration. The mapping file is an ASCII text file and has this format:

```
# Lines beginning with a # sign are comments and are ignored
mnt     \machine\export
```

Use the Symbolic Links tab to set your options.

> **Caution** By default, Client for NFS doesn't resolve or display unresolved links. It also won't allow a rename or a delete on a symbolic link. You should enable the Rename or Delete options of symbolic links only if you fully understand the consequences and know what mechanism or program will be doing the renaming or deleting. If you delete a symbolic link and replace it with a file of the same name, it will no longer be a symbolic link. Two files will now exist on the NFS server: the original file in its original location, and the replacement file in the link location.

Connecting to an NFS Export Connecting to an NFS export is the same as connecting to any shared file system resource on the network. Using Microsoft Windows Explorer, you'll find an NFS Network in addition to the Microsoft Windows Network and any other networks you have configured under My Network Places, as shown in Figure 21-14.

When you want to connect to an exported NFS file system, you can use standard Windows syntax (\\server\share) or standard UNIX syntax (server:/share). Using standard UNIX syntax is somewhat faster since it immediately resolves to the

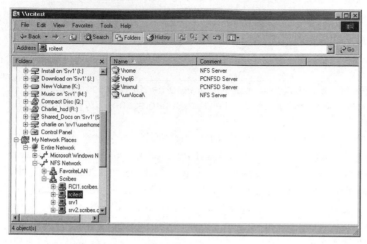

Figure 21-14. *An integrated NFS client.*

native NFS syntax and bypasses the need to look for a conventional Windows share of the same name.

You can also use the command-line Net Use commands to connect to a particular resource directly if you know where it is. For example, to map the next available drive letter to the exported /home file system on server1 of NFS server, you could use either of the following commands:

```
net use * server1:/home
net use * \\server1\home
```

The NFS Server

You can use the robust SFU NFS server to provide resources from your Windows 2000 machines to any machine on your network that supports NFS. You could even use it to export file systems to other Windows 2000 machines running SFU NFS client, although we'd generally recommend that you stick to native Windows 2000 networking for that. The following sections describe the options available for NFS configuration.

Shares   Shares are created using the Control Panel's Server For NFS Configuration shown in Figure 21-15. You can share either individual directories or an entire drive. You can't share a subdirectory of an already shared resource, since NFS doesn't support this, so you'll want to plan your shares to make sure you share from as far up the tree as necessary. Each drive letter is shared as the top of a file system.

In the UNIX environment, all file systems are viewed as being subdirectories of the root file system. Because Windows 2000 doesn't have this concept of a single

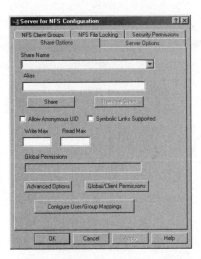

Figure 21-15. *Server For NFS Configuration.*

root file system, each disk drive letter is shared as a separate file system. Driveletters in the form "D:" are converted to the syntax "/D/". So the share of your F:\UserHome folder would be visible to NFS clients on the network as: /F/ UserHome. To create an NFS share, follow this procedure:

1. Open Server For NFS Configuration from Control Panel. The dialog box shown in Figure 21-15 will display.

2. Type in the drive and folder you want to share (*export*, in NFS-speak), as shown in Figure 21-16—where we're adding a share of the D: drive. You can't add an alias for it until the share is successfully created.

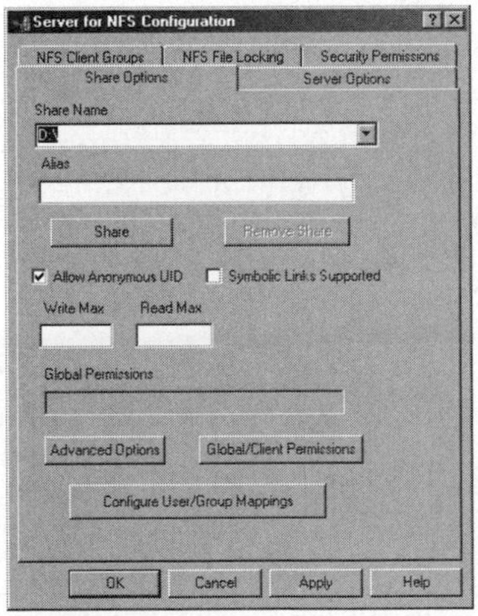

Figure 21-16. *Adding a share name.*

3. Select the Allow Anonymous UID option if you want to support anonymous mounts of this share. Don't select Symbolic Links Supported unless you really need this support—it imposes a significant performance penalty.

4. Click Share, and you'll be prompted for the permissions on the share, as shown in Figure 21-17.

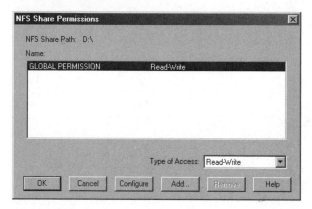

Figure 21-17. *The default permissions on an NFS share—global Read-Write.*

5. Accept the default permissions unless you know you need to limit access to this share point. Generally, we recommend using the underlying file system permissions to manage security, leaving share permissions wide open.

6. Click OK to return to the Share Options tab. Make any additional setting changes you need to here.

7. Click Advanced Options to see available advanced options. The defaults are correct for almost all situations. If you know you need to set certain settings explicitly for your environment and you know what all the settings mean, you can change them; otherwise, leave well enough alone. Click OK to close the Advanced Export Options dialog box.

8. Click OK to create the share and make it available to other systems.

NFS Share Aliases   You can create an alias for an NFS share to make your Windows 2000 NFS shares look more like what a UNIX user would expect to see. Keep in mind that NFS aliases require a reboot to take effect, so you should first create all your share points and then add all the aliases after the fact to reduce the number of reboots required. To create an alias, follow these steps:

1. Open Server For NFS Configuration from Control Panel. The dialog box shown in Figure 21-15 will display.

2. Select the share for which you want to create an alias from the Share Name drop-down list.

3. Type an alias into the Alias text box. Don't use a leading slash (/)—it will be added automatically when the alias is made available.

4. Click the Server Options tab and make sure the Return Alias Name box is selected. This ensures that broadcast queries for available exports to the NFS server will return the alias name, not the full share name.

5. Click Apply and the alias will be created. You'll get a warning message that reminds you that a reboot is required before it will take effect. If you have other aliases to create, click OK on the message box and continue. If you're done making aliases, click OK on the message box, then click OK on the dialog box to exit Server For NFS Configuration.

Client Groups   Server for NFS provides a mechanism for managing permissions and shares by groups of computers, known as Client groups. By creating Client groups, you can export (share) file system resources to specific groups of computers without having to specify each individual computer each time. This ability also improves management and administration by letting you manage a group's members from one location.

Changes to group membership (and thus permissions) are automatically changed for each shared NFS resource that references that client group. To create Client groups, follow this procedure:

1. Open Server For NFS Configuration. Click the NFS Client Groups tab to display it, as shown in Figure 21-18.

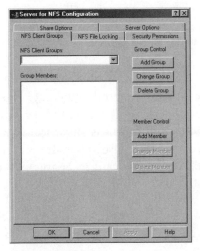

Figure 21-18. *The NFS Client Groups tab of the Server For NSF Configuration dialog box.*

2. Click the Add Group button to add a new group. This will open the New Group dialog box, shown in Figure 21-19. Type in a name for the group that describes the group of computers and click OK.

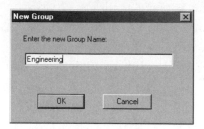

Figure 21-19. *The New Group dialog box.*

3. Add members to the group by clicking the Add Member button to open the New Member dialog box, shown in Figure 21-20. Type in either the IP address or the name of the client computer that will be added to the group and click OK.

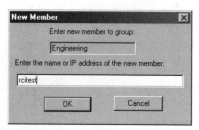

Figure 21-20. *The New Member dialog box.*

4. Continue adding members to the group until you're finished. Then click Apply to make this group immediately available and to continue working in Server For NFS Configuration, or click OK to make the group available.

File Locking　You can enable file locking for NFS clients, and you can enable it on a system-wide basis, being propagated both locally and across the network. The NFS File Locking tab of Server For NFS Configuration is shown in Figure 21-21. By default, locking is turned off, but if you expect to use applications across the NFS mount that require file locking, you'll probably want to enable it. Any changes to file locking require a reboot, so plan accordingly.

Security　Server For NFS Configuration uses access control entries to simulate the permissions that are typical in the UNIX and NFS world. You can, however, inhibit certain behaviors that are normally possible in the UNIX permission set but not generally done in Windows 2000 or Windows NT. Specifically, you can inhibit the ability of an NFS client to deny access to the owner and group of a file. You can also set permissions for objects to more closely match the way Windows 2000 manages them by selecting the Implicit Permissions option and by selecting FULL Control (Group) and FULL Control (World), as shown in Figure 21-22.

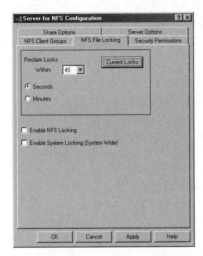

Figure 21-21. *The NFS File Locking tab.*

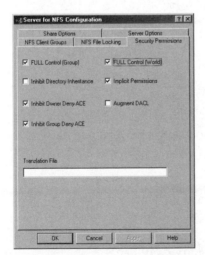

Figure 21-22. *The Security Permissions tab.*

> **Caution** The UNIX and Windows 2000 security models have inherently different permissions sets. Any attempt to align them is merely an approximation.

Usability Services

UNIX users expect a bevy of command-line utilities that don't exist in the Windows 2000 world. However, SFU includes only a limited subset of the more common UNIX utilities based on the Mortice Kern Systems (MKS) Toolkit, including the MKS Korn shell to facilitate sharing scripts. If you require a full set of UNIX utilities, an MKS add-on (MKS Toolkit Services for UNIX Update Edition) provides the rest of the MKS Toolkit and more than 200 UNIX utilities.

The SFU utilities break down into four basic categories: file and directory utilities, text utilities, programming utilities, and security-related utilities. In each case, the most critical ones are available, but if you expect to use scripts from the UNIX world in Windows 2000, you'll likely find this list insufficient to meet your needs unless you're careful in crafting the script or you take advantage of the included Perl programming utility to jump beyond the limits of the Korn shell.

File and Directory Utilities The file system utilities included in SFU are as follows:

- **mkdir** Creates a directory. With the *–p* switch, will create missing directories if necessary to create the target directory.
- **mv** Moves files and directories.
- **cp** Copies files and directories.
- **rm** Removes (deletes) files and directories.
- **rmdir** Removes directories if they are empty.
- **ls** Lists files and directories.
- **touch** Changes various dates and times associated with a file or files.
- **ln** Creates a link to a file or files.
- **find** The full UNIX find command.
- **tee** Pipes a copy of the standard output of a program to one or more files.

Text Utilities The text utilities included in SFU are as follows:

- **vi** Provides a full emulation of the standard UNIX file editing utility.

- **wc (word count)**   Counts the number of words, bytes, characters, or lines in a file or standard input.

- **sort**   Sorts and merges files or standard input according to a rich set of criteria.

- **tail**   Displays the last *n* lines of a file (10 lines by default).

- **head**   Displays the first *n* lines of a file (10 lines by default). Reverse of tail.

- **more**   Displays a file page by page. (This is actually closer to the UNIX "less" utility, supporting bidirectional movement.)

- **sed**   The streams editor.

- **cat**   Concatenates.

- **grep**   Gets regular expression. The SFU implementation supports egrep (extended grep) and fgrep (fast grep) as well.

Programming Utilities   The programming utilities included in SFU are as follows:

- **sh**   The Korn shell.

- **Perl**   Practical Extraction and Reporting Language. Version 5.004_04 of Perl.

Security-Related Utilities   The security utilities included in SFU are as follows:

- **chmod**   Changes the access permissions of the specified files or directories. Change mode.

- **chown**   Changes the owner (and, optionally, the group) of the specified files or directories. Change owner.

Real World   Utilities in Other Implementations

Both the full MKS Toolkit and the Interix subsystem include a far greater group of utilities than those that come natively with SFU. Interix also includes its own implementation of telnet (which is licensed per user, unfortunately, adding substantially to the cost). The MKS Toolkit includes several graphical utilities, including a rather good graphical version of vi and a number of other utilities that lend themselves well to a graphical implementation. Both MKS and Interix include versions of tar that will write to tape or floppy disk much as a UNIX administrator would expect.

Shells and POSIX

No discussion of Windows and UNIX interoperability would be complete without a discussion of the differences between their shells. Interestingly, no one has ported an emulation of the Windows NT/2000 cmd.exe shell to UNIX yet. But there have been a variety of emulations and ports of UNIX shells to Windows 2000, which is good because the average UNIX user wouldn't be willing to give up the full-featured Korn or POSIX shell to work within the limitations of the Windows command shell.

The Korn Shell

As you already know, SFU provides an excellent implementation of the UNIX Korn shell in Windows 2000. It's based on the MKS Korn shell implementation with the quirks that are native to that implementation.

The MKS Korn shell, either in SFU or directly from MKS, makes the maximum accommodation to the Windows 2000 world. It isn't case sensitive and will completely ignore case when matching filenames, although it will, like NTFS, preserve case. It also doesn't convert the Windows 2000 drive letter syntax into a more UNIX-like single root file system. This makes it feel quite comfortable for Windows 2000 users who sometimes also spend time in the UNIX environment, but somewhat less so for UNIX users who have to occasionally spend time at the Windows 2000 command prompt.

Scripts written for UNIX can be ported to an MKS Korn shell fairly easily. Functions are supported, and even double bracket compares ([[]]) work as expected. The biggest problem is handling drive letters and the resulting confusion of syntax. PATH entries are separated by semicolons rather than colons to accommodate the requirement to use colons after the drive letter; consequently, scripts that expect to parse the PATH statement using the colon as a field separator must be rewritten. And scripts that must work on both UNIX and Windows 2000 systems will have to be written with this consideration in mind—not hard, just not something the average UNIX user expects to have to deal with.

Another problem that scripts will have to address is the lack of a common root file system. This is best masked by using fully qualified filenames and paths in variables and then referencing paths relative to the variables rather than the explicit path. This isn't a big problem, and it will tend to support good programming practices in any case.

POSIX Shells and Subsystems

While the SFU (and MKS) Korn shell is simply another shell running on top of the native Windows 2000 kernel, some full POSIX subsystems also support UNIX at the kernel level. The best of these is undoubtedly the Interix POSIX implementation from Softway Systems, a fully POSIX-compliant subsystem that integrates directly into the Windows 2000 kernel.

The Interix POSIX shell takes the opposite approach from that taken by the MKS/SFU Korn shell—it makes virtually no concessions to the Windows 2000 world and instead implements a fully case-sensitive, rooted file system in Windows 2000. Consequently, scripts written for UNIX run exactly as you would expect them to run without additional changes, or at least that's the theory. However, the absolute case sensitivity causes no end of problems, and the lack of concession to Windows 2000 syntax means you need to remember that native Windows 2000 programs have names like notepad.exe, not notepad.

You can find ways around the problems, including using a set of utilities whose sole function is to convert Windows 2000 paths and case to POSIX and back. However, the issues with using UNIX scripts in both environments parallel those with the MKS/SFU implementation: you'll need to remember the differences and write your scripts to handle them.

Summary

Windows 2000 shares the same underlying networking protocol as UNIX systems, making coexistence and even full interoperability possible. The SFU package provides all the basic tools to share file system resources with UNIX hosts, either as a server or as a client, and third-party SMB tools also provide this functionality from the UNIX side. Using SFU to add a UNIX Korn shell to Windows 2000 provides a familiar environment for UNIX users and administrators, and the built-in Windows 2000 telnet client and server lets users from either system log on to the other. The next chapter will extend the interoperability story to cover Apple Macintosh computers.

Chapter 22
Using Macintosh Services

Despite continual reports of its demise, the Apple Macintosh remains popular in many environments, especially ones where users are doing high-end graphics, page layout, Web design, or video production. However, the Macintosh has never caught on as a file server, especially given the attractive price/performance ratio of Intel-based servers running Microsoft Windows NT and Microsoft Windows 2000.

Anticipating that Windows NT and Windows 2000 would be widely adopted for department and workgroup servers, Microsoft included in them two services that allow Macintosh users to share files and printers with Windows, OS/2, and even MS-DOS users. The File Server for Macintosh (FSM) service handles the publishing of shared files, and the Print Server for Macintosh (PSM) service allows Macintosh and Windows users to share each others' printers. In addition, Windows 2000 includes an implementation of the AppleTalk network protocol. The mechanism these services use is simple: you share folders and files and then enable Macintosh file sharing on the share. Windows clients can use the share normally, while Macintosh clients use Apple's file-sharing software to connect to the Windows 2000 server and get the files.

In this chapter, you'll learn how to install, configure, and administer both FSM and PSM. Along the way, you'll gain a basic understanding of Macintosh networking, as well as some of the implications of sharing files among users on different platforms.

Talking the Talk

It's an old chestnut in the computer world that different systems have different terms to describe the same thing. Like most old chestnuts, this one has some basis in fact, particularly when comparing Windows and Mac OS. This section goes over the Macintosh terminology you'll need to know in order to understand and work with FSM and PSM.

Macintosh-Accessible Volumes

When you configure a folder for shared access, Microsoft software calls it a *share*. If you configure the same folder for access by Macintosh clients, it's called a *Macintosh-accessible volume* (MAV). That's because Mac OS supports the mounting of volumes; if you share one folder on a Mac OS computer, that folder appears on client desktops as an entire volume. In other words, even though a MAV appears to Mac OS clients as a volume, it may actually be only a single folder that you've shared from your Windows 2000 server.

Forks, Streams, and Codes

Windows uses file extensions to determine the type of data stored in a file. If you take an .EXE file and rename it with a .ZIP extension, presto! The Windows 2000 shell thinks the file is a compressed archive and will treat it accordingly. By changing the application associated with a particular extension, you can control which program the shell will launch to handle a particular file type. The system that Mac OS uses is a bit more sophisticated: Each file has a *type code* and a *creator code*. These codes, which are 4 bytes apiece, allow Mac OS to link documents with their applications no matter what the document's name is. It also allows the user, or the OS, to intelligently substitute one application for another.

Let's say that you have a Dreamweaver file. Although it contains HTML, it will have a type code of *TEXT* and a creator code of *DmWr*. Any application that understands plain text files will be able to see this document and open it, regardless of what the file's actual name is, and the embedded creator code means that Mac OS will automatically launch Dreamweaver when you double-click the file.

NTFS, used in Windows, can support multiple data areas within a single file. These areas are called *streams*. For example, a file for your payroll application might contain one stream with employees' personal information, another with a list of project codes, one for vacation hours for each employee, and so on. Mac OS supports two streams in each file, but it calls them *forks*: a data fork and a resource fork. The *data fork* contains the file's data, while the *resource fork* holds other elements (such as icons, sounds, fonts, or QuickTime movie information) that are not part of the file's content. Some Macintosh applications use both forks; others use the data fork only. (In general, the Macintosh versions of cross-platform applications like Microsoft Office and Adobe Acrobat use the data fork only.) However, Mac OS itself uses the resource fork to store some information about the file, including the type and creator codes and the file's custom icon (if it has one).

When a Macintosh client stores a file on a MAV, FSM creates two separate NTFS streams: one for the resource fork and one for the data fork. If a Windows user comes along and opens the file, FSM will deliver the data fork only, so the Windows application doesn't get confused by the contents of the resource fork. If a Macintosh user opens a file that doesn't have a resource fork, FSM will create one on the fly and store it for future use. The net result is that Macintosh users see what looks and acts like a normal Macintosh volume, and Windows clients see something that looks and behaves like an ordinary Windows folder.

A Brief Digression Concerning AppleTalk

Each OS vendor has its own proprietary networking protocol: Novell has IPX/SPX, Microsoft has NetBEUI and SMB, and Apple has AppleTalk. Windows 2000 includes an AppleTalk protocol stack that allows you to use Windows 2000 machines as AppleTalk routers; in addition, the AppleTalk protocol is required to install and use FSM and PSM.

AppleTalk and Media Types

In an additional terminology twist that may be confusing, Apple software uses different names for the AppleTalk protocol, depending on the type of physical network on which it is running. AppleTalk over Ethernet is EtherTalk, while AppleTalk over Apple's proprietary LocalTalk cabling system is called LocalTalk. (AppleTalk can also be run over token ring and Fiber Distributed Data Interface [FDDI] networks, but those instances are relatively rare.) Most Mac OS computers built since 1995 or so have Ethernet built in, but older machines that don't will be networked with either plug-in Ethernet cards or built-in LocalTalk hardware. By adding a LocalTalk adapter to your Windows 2000 server, you can use the Windows 2000 AppleTalk router to route traffic between clients on LocalTalk and Ethernet networks. (See the section "AppleTalk Routing" later in this chapter for more details on how the AppleTalk router works.)

AppleTalk Networking Demystified

Each physical AppleTalk network has a number, ranging from 0 to 65534. You can assign the network numbers yourself, or you can allow the first device on the network to choose its own network number. All devices on the same physical subnet will share the same network number; apart from that you can use any number for any network as long as you don't duplicate any numbers. This scheme is necessary because most AppleTalk installations are actually internets—they consist of many small networks interconnected by routers, just like the Internet.

> **Note** AppleTalk comes in two flavors: Phase 1 and Phase 2. Since Windows 2000 supports only AppleTalk Phase 2, the rest of this section pertains only to Phase 2 networks. If you're still using Phase 1, you won't be able to use FSM or PSM, but you can use Apple's AppleShare products.

Every device on an AppleTalk network is called a *node*. Printers, servers, routers, and client computers are all nodes, and AppleTalk doesn't keep track of node types, as NetBIOS does. Each node has both a node name (assigned by the device owner) and a node number. (Each node can choose its own number at random, or the device owner can assign one as long as it doesn't conflict with another device on the same network.) A single network can contain up to 253 nodes.

Nodes can be logically grouped into *zones* to collect related resources together in one container. Typically, you create zones when your Macintosh users are spread out. For example, you might define a separate zone for each floor of a large building or set up one zone per field office. This allows users to browse for items that are "near" them in some sense. Any node can belong to any one zone on a network, and each network can have multiple zones. Zones can also span physical networks. Overall, zones are very similar to Windows 2000 domains—at least for resource browsing; zones don't offer any kind of authentication or security.

AppleTalk Routing

Since AppleTalk networks are usually internets, routers are critical. An AppleTalk router joins two or more networks, transferring packets among them according to their destinations. This is actually no different from a TCP/IP or IPX/SPX router, although the exact list of data kept by the routers is different. AppleTalk routers keep a list of the network number (or the network range) assigned to each physical network and a list of zones available on the internet. Clients display the zone list to the user, while the network range list is used by the actual routing process.

One interesting difference between AppleTalk routing and IPX or IP routing is that some AppleTalk routers are seed routers. In addition to its regular duties of routing packets from one network to another, a *seed router* distributes routing information to nonseed routers. It also broadcasts initialization data (including network numbers and zone lists) so that nodes on a seeded network can initialize themselves using that data. The Windows 2000 AppleTalk router can act as either a seed router or a nonseed router. Each AppleTalk network must have at least one seed router; you can have multiple seed routers on a network, but they have to seed the same information.

Planning   If you're using Windows 2000 as a seed router, the AppleTalk stack on that machine must be installed, configured, and started before any other routers are brought up—those routers will look for a seed router as soon as they're started.

Understanding Macintosh Services

Each of the three components that together provide Macintosh support in Windows 2000 has its own set of responsibilities.

- The AppleTalk stack handles network communications with Macintosh clients, as well as AppleTalk routing. You can install and use the AppleTalk protocol without the file or print services; doing so lets you route AppleTalk traffic or accept calls via Remote Access Service (RAS) from remote Macintosh users.

- FSM handles the publishing of files from a MAV to Macintosh clients. As part of that duty, it converts Macintosh file forks to and from NTFS streams on the fly; it also manages the creator, type, and icon data needed by Mac OS Finder. When Windows clients use files on a MAV's underlying share, they access files through the standard server service, which FSM is layered on top of.

- PSM allows you to offer your Macintosh clients the same set of shared printers that you offer to your Windows clients. It converts PostScript output from Macintosh clients into device-independent bitmap (DIB) files that Windows 2000 printer drivers can handle. In addition, PSM lets you create printer pools and prioritize print jobs—two features missing from Mac OS. However, this requires you to *capture* the printers you want to use. Captured printers can't be used directly by AppleTalk clients; instead, they must send their print requests to the Windows 2000 Server, which in turn will forward them to the printer itself. If you leave the printer uncaptured, AppleTalk clients can print to it but you can't audit, control, or prioritize the printing from your Windows 2000 Server—that's the inherent trade-off. As an extra bonus, PSM allows Windows users to print to printers on the AppleTalk network.

Installing and Configuring AppleTalk

The first step in making your Windows 2000 Server available to your Macintosh users is to install the AppleTalk network stack. Installing FSM or PSM before AppleTalk will cause AppleTalk to be installed, but it's easier to troubleshoot Macintosh-related problems if you're sure that the underlying protocol stack works before you install the service components.

Installing AppleTalk

Since AppleTalk is a network protocol, you install it from the Network and Dial-Up Connections dialog box. Before attempting to install AppleTalk, make sure you have access to a Windows 2000 CD-ROM or network install point. To install AppleTalk, follow these steps:

1. From the Start menu, point to Settings and choose Network And Dial-Up Connections.

2. Right-click Local Area Connection. The Local Area Connection Properties window appears, shown in Figure 22-1.

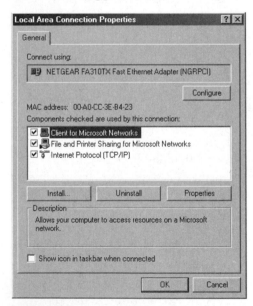

Figure 22-1. *The Local Area Connection Properties window.*

3. Click the Install button. When the Select Network Component Type dialog box appears, select the Protocol icon and click Add.

4. In the Select Network Protocol dialog box, select AppleTalk Protocol from the list and click OK. If prompted, provide the location of your Windows 2000 distribution.

Tip These steps will install and bind AppleTalk to all network interface cards (NICs) on your computer. If you want to remove AppleTalk from specific NICs, open each NIC's Properties window and clear the AppleTalk check box.

Configuring AppleTalk Routing

Before you configure the AppleTalk protocol itself, you need to configure AppleTalk routing if you plan to use it. This ensures that your Windows 2000 machine has a current zone list and network information before the AppleTalk configuration process requires it. AppleTalk routing is handled from the Routing and Remote Access console. To turn on and configure routing, follow these steps:

1. From the Start menu, point to Programs and then to Administrative Tools and choose Routing And Remote Access.

2. Double-click the server you want to configure. The icon expands to list the routing protocols installed on that server. At a minimum, you'll see AppleTalk; depending on how Routing and Remote Access is configured, you may also see other items.

3. Right-click AppleTalk Routing and choose Enable AppleTalk Routing (Figure 22-2).

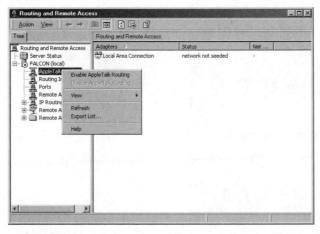

Figure 22-2. *Enabling AppleTalk routing.*

4. In the right pane of the console, the adapters to which AppleTalk is bound will change to show a status of Routing (Default), indicating that the router has started and is available for traffic routing on those interfaces, but that it's not seeding the network. If you want your Windows 2000 Server to act as an ordinary router, that's all you have to do.

Establishing a Seed Router

Microsoft notes that it's much more efficient to use a hardware AppleTalk seed router than it is to use a Windows 2000 computer. If you don't have any hardware routers, though, you can use Windows 2000 as a seed router for your AppleTalk network. Once you've installed the AppleTalk stack as described earlier, follow these few additional steps:

1. In the Routing And Remote Access console, expand the server you're configuring and select AppleTalk Routing.

2. Right-click Local Area Connection in the console window and choose Properties. The Local Area Connection Properties window shown in Figure 22-3 appears.

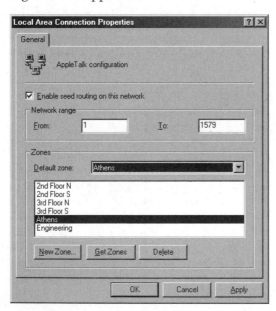

Figure 22-3. *The Local Area Connection Properties window for AppleTalk.*

3. Select the Enable Seed Routing On This Network check box. This activates the controls in the Network Range and Zones areas.

4. Choose the range of network numbers that you want this router to seed by filling in the From and To boxes in the Network Range area. You can choose arbitrary network numbers, but they cannot overlap and they must be unique. Each network can support 253 nodes, so assign a range that's big enough for the number of nodes on that network. AppleTalk networks usually group more than one network into a zone, which is why you can specify a range of networks to seed instead of just one.

5. Build the list of zones you want seeded to the network by doing the following:

   - Start by clicking the Get Zones button; this causes Windows 2000 to query the network for available zones just as a client would. The results appear in the zone list.

   - Use the New Zone button to add any new zones you want to make available. Zone names can contain any printable ASCII character except * : = @, and they must have fewer than 32 characters. (Note that there's no way to rename a zone after it's created; you have to delete and re-create it.) Remove unwanted zones with the Delete button.

   - Specify a default zone for network nodes in the Default Zone box. The default zone contains any node whose owner hasn't assigned it to another zone; the router automatically assigns unzoned devices to the default zone, so that's where Macintosh users will see them.

Be sure to configure your seed routers before setting up (or starting) other routers on your network.

Configuring the AppleTalk Protocol

AppleTalk was designed to be a low-overhead, low-maintenance protocol, so configuring it is pretty easy. In fact, there's virtually no configuration to it—you simply indicate whether your adapter will accept inbound AppleTalk connections and what AppleTalk zone your server will appear in. Here's how to configure these parameters:

1. From the Start menu, point to Settings and choose Network And Dial-Up Connections. Right-click on the adapter you want to configure. (Use

the Local Area Connection item if you have only one NIC.) The corresponding Properties window appears.

2. Select the AppleTalk Protocol item and then click Properties.

3. The AppleTalk Protocol Properties window appears (Figure 22-4). If you're configuring the only network adapter on your system, the Accept Inbound Connections On This Adapter check box will be selected and dimmed, since you must accept inbound connections on at least one adapter.

   The This System Will Appear In Zone box lets you control which zone the server appears in; you can use the default zone or explicitly assign it to a particular zone.

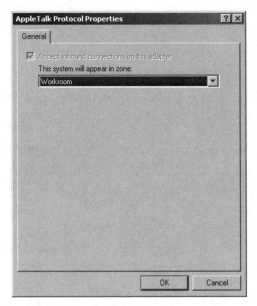

Figure 22-4. *The AppleTalk Protocol Properties window.*

4. Click OK, and then click OK again in the adapter's Properties window.

Note The AppleTalk performance object encapsulates about two dozen protocol-specific parameters (including counters that record the total amount of inbound and outbound AppleTalk traffic and the number of routed packets).

Setting Up File and Print Services

Once you've installed and configured the AppleTalk protocol, you're ready to install and configure the Macintosh services themselves. Even though FSM and PSM are two separate packages, we've grouped them together in this section because their respective installation processes are very similar. You can install the components in any order.

Prerequisites for Installing Macintosh Services

Before installing the Macintosh service components, you must meet a few prerequisites. First if you're going to install FSM you must have at least one NTFS partition on your server. This is because you can create MAVs only on NTFS or CD-ROM File System (CDFS) partitions—and even if you want to create MAVs only on CDFS partitions, you need an NTFS partition or FSM won't install.

Second you should already have installed and configured the network adapters you plan to connect to your AppleTalk networks and verified that they work. Finally you should have installed and configured AppleTalk and tested your installation to make sure that your existing network clients can see your new server as an AppleTalk node. You may need a tool like EtherPeek or Dartmouth's InterNetMapper to do this.

Note If you want your Macintosh users to have access to files that are on ordinary shares (not MAVs), you can use a third-party utility like Thursby Software's (*http://www.thursby.com*) DAVE, which allows Macintosh computers to log on to Windows NT or Windows 2000 domains and use shared files and printers using Microsoft's native network protocols.

Real World   Beware the Magic FSM Numbers

Although installing and managing FSM is pretty straightforward, there are some magic numbers that you need to be aware of. These numbers (or, more accurately, limits) curb some of the things you can do with FSM:

- Macintosh volumes can support filenames of only 31 characters maximum, while NTFS supports 256-character filenames. Macintosh files appear with their correct names on Windows systems that support long filenames, but they'll have truncated 8.3 names on systems that don't. FSM will truncate NTFS filenames that exceed the 31-character limit, so Macintosh clients will see only the first 31 characters.

- NTFS allows a maximum path length of 255 characters, and so does Mac OS. However, under some circumstances FSM may not send the Macintosh folder or file information for items whose combined path lengths exceed 260 characters.

- Like NTFS, Macintosh file systems are case-insensitive. If you have the POSIX subsystem enabled, don't use POSIX filenames, or the Macintosh clients will get confused.

- MAV volume names can be up to 27 characters long, but the FSM tools can create only 12-character names (although you can use the Macfile utility to work around this).

- AppleTalk requires that all share names served by a single machine fit into a single announcement packet. This packet cannot exceed 4760 bytes in size, meaning that there is an upper limit of about 175 MAV names (at 27 characters each) per server.

Creating Accounts for Macintosh Users

FSM and PSM get account information from Microsoft Windows 2000 Active Directory directory service. This means that Macintosh clients can't log on to your FSM or PSM servers unless they have a valid account in your directory or unless you allow guest access to your servers. It's a good idea to set up the accounts you'll need for your Macintosh users as part of installing and configuring Macintosh support on your server; that way, as soon as you get the MAVs and shared printers created, your users can start connecting to the server.

Tip Mac OS users can supply a domain name along with their user name when they log on. Suppose that you have accounts in two domains: Engineering\Paulr and Ra\Paul. If you want to log on to an FSM server that's part of the Engineering domain as Engineering\Paulr, you can leave off the domain name; if you want to use your master account (Ra\Paul), you can, but you must add the domain prefix.

PSM must be supplied with a set of user account credentials so that it can send print jobs to the standard Windows 2000 Print Manager. It uses the system account by default, but for security purposes it's a better idea to create a separate account to be used only with PSM.

Installing the Components

To install both PSM and FSM, you use the Windows Components Wizard. The actual process is very simple:

1. From the Start menu, point to Settings and then to Control Panel and choose Add/Remove Programs. When the Add/Remove Programs window appears, click the Add/Remove Windows Components icon to start the wizard.

2. At the first screen of the wizard, click Next. The Windows Components screen appears; scroll through the component list to find Other Network File And Print Services. Select it and click Details.

3. The Other Network File And Print Services dialog box appears (Figure 22-5). Select the Macintosh services you want to install and then click OK. When you return to the wizard, click Next.

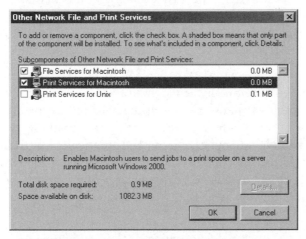

Figure 22-5. *The Other Network File And Print Services dialog box.*

4. Click Finish to finalize the installation.

Once you've installed the FSM and PSM components, you must configure them before they'll do anything useful. The only MAV that a newly installed FSM server will offer to clients is the one containing Microsoft's plug-in authentication module.

Installing Microsoft's
Authentication Module on the Macintosh

When a Mac OS client connects to a Windows 2000 FSM server, the client has to send its user name and password credentials as clear text with no encryption. This is nonsecure because an attacker with a network analyzer can easily grab the credentials from the network and use them to log on to the Windows 2000 Server directly.

Mac OS supports encrypted authentication when talking to AppleShare servers, but to add that same level of security to Mac OS–FSM connections you must choose one of two options. One is to configure your server to accept Apple-encrypted authentication, and the other is to install an additional user authentication module (UAM) on the Macintosh side. The Microsoft UAM allows the Mac OS client to encrypt its credentials using the same scheme that Windows clients use when talking to a Windows 2000 Server. It also offers two other useful benefits: it allows you to use longer passwords (14 characters instead of the 7-character limit imposed by AppleShare), and it lets your clients know when their Windows 2000 password has expired.

The Microsoft UAM is stored in a special MAV called Microsoft UAM Volume. This MAV is always available to Macintosh clients on an FSM server; there's no way to remove or rename it, and it's available as soon as the FSM service is started. The UAM volume contains four items: a text file (Readme.uam) explaining what the UAM does and how to install it, an application that automatically installs the appropriate UAM for a given Mac OS configuration, and versions of the UAM for AppleShare versions 3.8 (present on Mac OS 7.5 and later) and 3.6 (for older Mac OS versions). To install the Microsoft UAM on a Mac OS client, follow these steps:

1. On the Macintosh computer, open the Chooser from the Apple menu.

2. Select the AppleShare icon in the Chooser. If you have multiple AppleTalk zones on your network, select the zone your FSM server is in from the AppleTalk Zones list.

3. Select the FSM server to which you want to connect. The Chooser will look similar to Figure 22-6. Click OK to attempt the connection.

4. The AppleShare logon dialog box appears. Log on to the FSM server, either as a guest (click the Guest button) or as a user with credentials on the server (click the Registered User button and then enter the user name and password). Click OK when you're done.

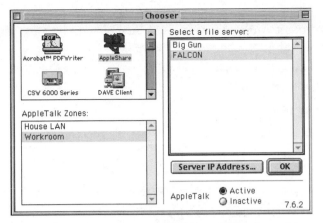

Figure 22-6. *The Chooser with the FSM server and its zone selected.*

5. The Microsoft UAM Volume icon appears on the Macintosh desktop. Open it and launch the MS UAM Installer application; it will install the UAM version that is appropriate for this particular client.

If you want to install the UAM on multiple machines, it may be easier to copy the appropriate UAM to the destination machines instead of logging on from every workstation. This process is a little different from the one just outlined:

1. Find out what version of the AppleShare client the target machine has. Open the System folder, go to the Extensions subfolder, select the AppleShare extension, and choose Get Info from the File menu in the Finder to get its version.

2. Find the matching folder on the Microsoft UAM Volume: either MS UAM for AppleShare 3.8 or MS UAM for AppleShare 3.6. Open it and you'll find a subfolder named AppleShare Folder.

3. Look in the System folder of the target machine. If no AppleShare folder is there, drag the AppleShare folder you found in the Microsoft UAM Volume in step 2 into the System folder. If the folder is there, open the AppleShare folder from the Microsoft UAM Volume and drag the MS UAM 5.0 extension into the target system's AppleShare folder.

Once you've installed the Microsoft UAM, the logon process for Mac OS clients will be a bit different from what they're accustomed to. The ordinary process works like this: the user picks a zone and server in the Chooser, clicks OK, and fills out the AppleShare logon dialog box. When multiple UAMs are installed— as will be the case after you complete the preceding steps—clicking OK in the

Chooser produces a dialog box listing the available UAMs. You'll need to train your users to use the Microsoft Authentication 5.0 UAM. After choosing that UAM, they'll see the logon dialog box shown in Figure 22-7.

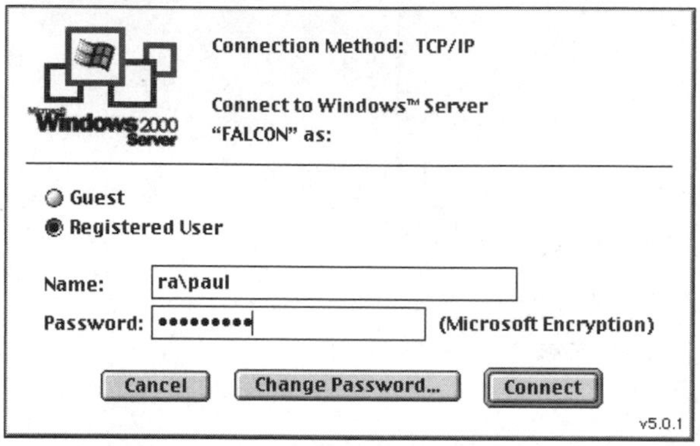

Figure 22-7. *The Microsoft UAM logon dialog box.*

Configuring FSM Options

Apart from its obvious uses, the Shared Folders snap-in also allows you to configure some helpful FSM parameters, including the message that users see when they log on, the kinds of authentication your server will accept, and the number of users that can connect at once. To get to these options, open the Shared Folders snap-in, right-click Shared Folders, and choose Configure File Server For Macintosh. You see the Configuration tab of the File Server For Macintosh Properties window, shown in Figure 22-8. You can perform four useful tasks with this tab:

- Change the name that the FSM server presents to AppleTalk clients by providing a name in the Server Name For AppleTalk Workstations field. This has no effect on how the computer appears in Active Directory, but it can present a friendly name to Macintosh users if you're using machine-generated names.

- Provide a logon message that appears to Macintosh users when they log on. This might be a warning notice, an announcement about upcoming maintenance, or whatever you want to put in front of your users' faces.

- Control some security aspects of how clients talk to your server:

  - The Allow Workstations To Save Password check box governs whether users can tell their computers to save their account credentials on their computers. Allowing this makes things easier for end users but less secure.

- The Enable Authentication box lets you choose the authentication types you want your server to accept. The default is to allow Apple clear text or Microsoft encrypted authentication; you can also choose to accept only Microsoft authentication, only Apple clear text or Apple encrypted authentication, or only Apple and Microsoft encrypted authentication. The last choice is recommended because it allows modern Mac OS clients to securely log on whether or not they're using the Microsoft UAM.

- Regulate how many users can connect concurrently to your FSM server. Normally, FSM allows an unlimited number of AppleTalk connections to your MAVs, but you can throttle that number back by selecting Limited To and entering a connection limit in the box.

Tip   The contents of the Limited To box are stored in HKLM\System\ CurrentControlSet\Services\MacFile\Parameters\MaxSessions. A value of 0xFFFFFFFF means "unlimited"; otherwise, FSM interprets this number as the session limit.

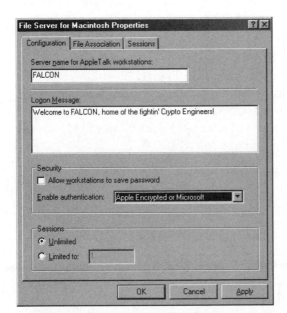

Figure 22-8. *The File Server For Macintosh Properties window.*

The File Association and Sessions tabs of the File Server For Macintosh Properties window are covered under "Managing Type and Creator Codes" and "Sending Messages to Users," respectively, later in this chapter.

Sharing Files with FSM

Once you have FSM installed and configured, you'll find that you can't do anything with it until you create some MAVs. The general process to follow looks like this:

- Create the MAVs to which you want your users to have access.
- Give the MAVs and the items they contain appropriate permissions (bearing in mind that Macintosh and Windows 2000 permissions are very different).
- Each of these steps is covered in the sections that follow.

Creating MAVs

Windows 2000 offers two slightly different ways to create new MAVs. The first way is already familiar: you can use the Create Shared Folder Wizard to create a new Windows share, making it visible to Macintosh (or NetWare) clients when you create it. Alternatively, you can create a MAV for an existing Windows share by using the wizard to create a new Macintosh-only share pointing to the same item.

To launch the Create Shared Folder Wizard, open the Shared Folders snap-in, right-click Shares in the Shared Folders tree, and choose New File Share. The Create Shared Folder Wizard appears as shown in Figure 22-9. Note that the Apple Macintosh check box is no longer dimmed; to create a new MAV on top of the new share, all you have to do is select that box. Optionally, you can edit the Macintosh-visible share name in the Macintosh Share Name field, but the wizard will supply a reasonable default name for you.

There's one caveat to this process. You cannot create a MAV inside another MAV. For example, let's say that you create a share and a MAV at the root of an NTFS volume on drive F. You can create a Windows share on F:\Downloads, but you can't create a MAV there, since you can't nest them. For this reason, Microsoft recommends not creating MAVs at the root level of your drives; instead, create them on the bottom-most enclosing folder of the items you actually want accessed.

When you click Next in the wizard, you'll see the standard share permissions selection window. The default permissions on new shares are pretty scary: if you create a combined MAV/Windows share, the Everyone group gets Full Control on it, and if you create a MAV-only share, all Mac OS users get the Macintosh equivalent. You'll usually want to restrict things a bit more than that.

Figure 22-9. *The Create Shared Folder Wizard.*

Assigning Security and Permissions

The most important thing to understand about FSM's permission handling is this: the Mac OS supports access controls only on folders, *not on files*. FSM does a good job overall of translating between Windows 2000 and Mac OS permissions, but it can't do anything to overcome this limitation. As a workaround, FSM automatically applies the permissions of the parent folder to its child files and subfolders.

Windows users can assign permissions on each file in a folder, but Mac OS won't honor them. This defeats the whole purpose of file-level security, so FSM implements an inelegant, subtle, but useful workaround. File-level permissions apply only if they're more restrictive than permissions on the file's enclosing folder. For example, let's say that you assign the Everyone group Full Control rights on a MAV named Contracts. You then change the permissions on one file, Big-deal.doc, so that Everyone has Deny:Write and Allow:Read permissions on that file. A Macintosh user who attaches to that MAV will be able to open the folder and the file. As far as Mac OS is concerned, the user will have full access to the file, but the server won't honor any write requests: if you open the file, edit it in Microsoft Word, and try to save it, you'll get an error—the server won't allow you to have write access to the file.

The next thing to understand is who gets access by default. As was mentioned earlier, when you create a new MAV the default is to give the Everyone group Full Control permission on the entire MAV. Members of the Administrators and Server Operators groups can manage the FSM service itself, and users with Administrator privileges on the server always have Full Control over all files in the MAVs on that server.

Macintosh vs. NTFS Permissions

Apple's permission scheme groups user data into three categories: private data (only the owner can use it), group data (only members of a single group can use it), and public data (everyone can use it). While this is conceptually easier to understand than the Windows 2000 permissions scheme, it's also a lot less flexible. In Mac OS you can assign permissions on objects using only these three categories; there's no way to do things like give multiple workgroups access to a single file inside a folder. One nice feature of this approach is that the owner doesn't have to be a member of the group that has permissions on the folder.

Another difference is that Windows 2000 automatically assigns permissions by inheritance (at least when the Allow Inheritable Permissions From Parent to Propagate To This Object check box is selected, which is the default); Mac OS allows folders to inherit permissions or not, as the folder owner sees fit. Each folder in a hierarchy can have different permissions. For example, it's common to give users Read-Only access to the root of a shared disk and then give them Read/Write permission to folders they need to access.

The third, and perhaps most critical, major difference between the two systems is the way the Everyone group behaves. In Windows 2000, permissions given to the Everyone group don't trump permissions assigned to specific individual or groups, but in Mac OS they do. This means that you need to be careful about assigning Everyone permissions on the Mac OS side, since they may not behave as you expect.

The Macintosh permissions themselves are also quite a bit different from Windows 2000 permissions. Mac OS users can assign a total of five permissions to folders they own:

- Can't Rename, Move, Or Delete This Item applies to individual folders; when this permission is in effect users can't take those actions on the folder, although they may be able to modify files or subfolders within it.

- None keeps users from doing anything with a folder.

- Read/Write gives users the equivalent of Windows 2000's Full Control permissions; they can rename, move, delete, create, or open items in the folder.

- Read Only allows users to see and open folders and files in the folder, but they can't make changes.

- Write Only allows users to create new items in a folder but doesn't allow them to open the folder or items contained inside it. Apple also calls this "drop box" permission.

How do these permissions map to Windows 2000 permissions? The Windows 2000 Read permission equates to the See Files permission and the See Folders permission on the Macintosh side. The Windows 2000 Write and Delete permissions each equal the Make Changes permission on the Macintosh side. These mappings are two-way; if a Macintosh user grants Everyone the See Files and See Folders permissions on a MAV, that's the equivalent of giving the Windows 2000 Everyone group Read permission.

Primary Groups

You can give permission to an arbitrary number of groups in Windows 2000—any object can have a virtually unlimited number of different permissions assigned to it. On the Macintosh side, however, each object can have only one set of groups assigned to it. FSM bridges this conceptual gap by designating one Windows 2000 group as the *primary group* for an object. While other groups may have permissions that they can use from Windows clients, only the primary group gets access rights on the Macintosh side, using the User/Group permission slot that Mac OS uses. You set the primary group by setting the group that has permissions on the folder on your Windows 2000 Server.

Allowing Guest Access to Your Server

Although anonymous access is the norm for Web servers, it's not always desirable for file, print, or application servers. Strictly speaking, the Guest account isn't anonymous, but as a practical matter it doesn't give you the same ties between a known account name and a person that regular accounts usually do.

If you want to allow guests to access your FSM volumes, you can do so in one of two ways: you can force Mac OS clients to use the Windows 2000 Guest account, or you can force them to use the Mac OS Guest account, which uses the Windows 2000 Guest account on the server. (See "Allowing Mac OS Guests" later in this chapter for more details on this approach.) Which approach is best? The Mac OS Guest feature lets users click a Guest button in the Chooser and log on without providing a user name or password, while the Windows 2000 account requires you to disseminate the password for your Guest account. Since you probably don't want anyone other than Mac OS users to use your Windows 2000 Guest account, the Mac OS Guest account is the better solution for most applications. No matter which approach you take, be sure to set appropriate permissions on your MAVs so that guests can only see, and modify, what you want them to.

Regardless of whether you choose the Macintosh or Windows 2000 Guest account, you need to perform some preliminary steps to make guest access work:

1. Set appropriate permissions on the files and folders in the MAV. In particular, be sure to deny access by the Windows 2000 Guest account to any file or folder that you don't want guests to get at. We recommend doing this first so that you can verify that the permissions are correct before you open your server to your users.

2. Enable the Windows 2000 Guest account. The account that you enable will depend on which guests you want to give access to; you can enable a domain guest account, or you can use the built-in account on the FSM server itself if it's not a domain controller. We recommend enabling the server's built-in guest account and limiting its access to other resources on the system with a snap-in.

   If you're using the Mac OS Guest account, open the Properties window for the MAV you want guests to access and make sure the Guests Can Use This Volume check box is selected. This setting has no effect if you're requiring users to log on with your Windows 2000 Guest account.

Tip If you pause or stop the FSM service before enabling the Windows 2000 Guest account, you can use the Guest account, once enabled, on another Windows machine to connect to the share and double-check that your permission settings are as you expect them.

Real World Using Private Volumes

You can create a volume that no one except its owner can see. This is a good way to allow users to set up shares so that they can get to their files from Macintosh or Windows machines without allowing access by anyone else. It's particularly handy for administrators, since you can use this feature to set up a share of useful tools or reference material that's accessible—to you—from anywhere on your network.

To create a private volume, set the Macintosh permissions so that only the owner has access; set the User/Group and Everyone permissions to None. Users will see the MAV in the list of available shares after they log on to the server, but the private volume will be dimmed, and users won't be able to mount it unless they get the owner's name and password.

Controlling Mac OS–Only Security Features

The AppleShare protocol provides some additional security features that you can set on a per-share basis. You access all of these features through the Properties window of an individual MAV. To display this window, shown in Figure 22-10, right-click the MAV of interest in the Shared Folders snap-in and then choose Properties. The interesting area is the SFM Volume Security area (SFM stands for Services for Macintosh), which isn't present in the Properties window of a Windows-format share.

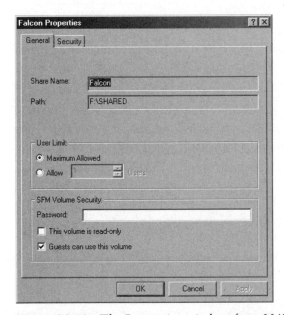

Figure 22-10. *The Properties window for a MAV.*

Volume Passwords   The Password field in the SFM Volume Security area allows you to assign a case-sensitive password to individual volumes. Mac OS users have to provide that password *and* have access permissions for the items they want to use; Windows users don't need the volume password. The volume password provides an additional level of security because users who don't have the password can't connect to the volume at all. Without a volume password in place, users can connect to the server and see items for which they have See Folders and See Files permissions, even if they can't open or change them.

Note Some older versions of Mac OS don't allow users to save volume passwords so that volumes can be mounted automatically; however, all versions of Mac OS since version 8 (circa 1996) do allow it, so don't count on volume passwords to add much security for those users that save them.

Read-Only Volumes When you mount a standard CD-ROM on your system, it remains Read-Only no matter what permissions you might have assigned the files and folders on it. FSM gives you a similar option: by selecting the This Volume Is Read-Only check box in the SFM Volume Security area, you can mark a volume as Read-Only. This setting overrides any permissions a Mac OS user has. When this setting's in effect, Mac OS essentially treats the entire volume as though it were locked.

Allowing Macintosh OS Guests As was mentioned earlier, the Mac OS Guest account and the built-in Windows 2000 Guest account are very different beasts. Regardless of what permissions (if any) you grant to the Windows 2000 Guest account, you can still choose to make your MAVs available to Mac OS guests by selecting the Guests Can Use This Volume check box in the SFM Volume Security area of the MAV's Properties window. However, if you disable the Windows 2000 Guest account, selecting this check box has no effect, because when a Mac OS user chooses to log on as a Mac OS guest, FSM maps that request to the Windows 2000 Guest account. Since the Guest account is disabled by default in Windows 2000 Server, Advanced Server, and Datacenter Server, Mac OS guests can't mount MAVs unless you take action to reenable the Guest account.

Managing Type and Creator Codes

As was discussed earlier in the chapter, FSM takes care of translating between Windows 2000–style extensions and Mac OS type and creator codes. It does this using a set of registry values (stored in HKLM\System\CurrentControlSet\ Services\MacFile\Parameters\Type_Creators) that contains the type and creator codes you've defined and a separate list (under HKLM\System\CurrentControlSet\ Services\MacFile\Parameters\Extensions)that ties an extension to an entry in the type/creator list. FSM uses these mappings to establish a type and creator code for a file so that Mac OS clients see the appropriate icon, and get the expected behavior, when they work with files on a MAV. Files with extensions that don't map to a type/creator pair in these databases get a generic icon and creator that tells Mac OS that they're plain text files. This probably isn't what you want for most files.

FSM includes an extensive set of mappings, but there are three circumstances under which you may need to modify them. The first is that some of the mappings are ancient—Microsoft includes mappings for programs like Symantec's MORE and Lotus 1-2-3 that haven't been sold for the Macintosh in five years or so—and you may need to update them. You might also find that you don't like the default mapping for a particular file type. As an example, StuffIt (the Mac OS equivalent of WinZip) has two versions, a full version and a decompress-only version called StuffIt Expander. The default FSM mapping binds StuffIt files to the full version, which most users won't have, so it makes more sense to tie that extension to StuffIt Expander instead. The final situation in which you might need to edit these mappings is when you need to add a file type that FSM doesn't know about. Since the version as shipped isn't aware of a number of very common extensions (including .BMP, .GIF, .JPG, .PNG, .HTM, and .JS), this is probably the most common problem you'll encounter.

To edit these associations, you use the File Association tab of the File Server For Macintosh Properties window (Figure 22-11). The layout of this tab is a little confusing until you understand how it works. The top portion of the tab (including the Files With MS-DOS Extension box and the Associate button) is where you choose the extension for which you want to create an association. The With Macintosh Document Creator And Type area lets you see, and edit, the Mac OS types and creators that are available to make associations with.

The overall process is simple, but there are some variations along the way, depending on why you're editing the associations. The first step is to add a new type and creator pair; you need to do this when you're adding a new extension or mapping or revising an existing one (since there's no way to edit a type and creator pair once it's in the database). To add a new pair, click the Add button and then supply the creator, file type, and description you want it to use. You can select an existing creator or file type or enter a new one. If you need to look up the type or creator for a file, you'll have to do it on the Macintosh side, using a utility like ResEdit or More File Info. After you've entered the information, the new type and creator pair will appear in the list.

Once you've added the new type and creator pair, you can attach it to an existing extension or add a new extension and attach the Mac OS information to it. To link an existing extension with a type and creator pair, select the type and creator pair in its list and then select the matching extension from the Files With MS-DOS Extension list and click the Associate button. To add a new extension, type it into the Files With MS-DOS Extension box and then click Associate to create it and tie it to the selected type and creator combination.

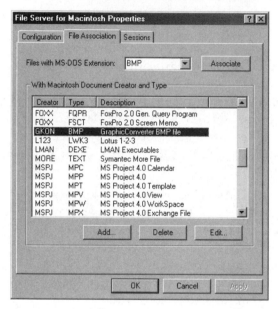

Figure 22-11. *The File Association tab of the File Server For Macintosh Properties window.*

Tip Mac OS users who are connected to a MAV won't see the updated association information until they log off and remount the volume.

To delete an association, select the type and creator item in the list and then click the Delete button. FSM will ask you to confirm your command, since removing a type and creator pair will remove it *and* any associated extensions from the registry.

Sending Messages to Users

Occasionally you need to send a message to your users to tell them something important—so important that you don't want to wait for it to go out in e-mail. You might be notifying them that something is (or is going to be) down for maintenance, that the building is on fire, or that Michael Jordan is coming back from retirement. In Windows 2000, you use the Server Manager to send messages to users who are connected to a server; for Mac OS clients, you use the Sessions tab of the File Server For Macintosh Properties window (Figure 22-12). Sending a message is trivial—you type it into the Message box and click the Send button. All Mac OS users who are logged on to your server when you send the message will see a pop-up window with your message in it.

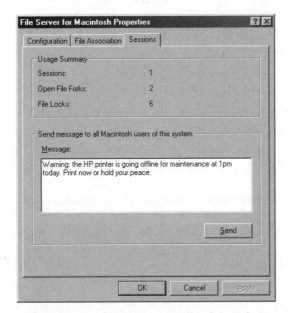

Figure 22-12. *The Sessions tab of the File Services For Macintosh Properties window.*

As a bonus, the Sessions tab shows you how many users (listed as Sessions) are logged on to your server, how many file forks are open, and how many files are locked because they're open. While this is occasionally interesting, it's no substitute for the Macfile Server performance object, which you can monitor using the performance monitoring tools discussed in Chapter 32.

Using the Macfile Utility

If you prefer to use a command-line utility to manage your servers, you're in luck—Windows 2000 includes an updated version of the Macfile utility included with Windows NT 4. Macfile provides a command-line interface that lets you manage FSM servers, MAVs, users, and files from a Windows 2000 command shell. Like the venerable Net User command, Macfile grows on you once you get used to it, because it makes short work of many common administrative tasks. Macfile actually has four separate functions:

- Macfile Server lets you manage server-related settings, including the number of sessions your server will support, whether guests are allowed to log on or not, and what message is displayed to users at logon.

- Macfile Volume allows you to create and remove MAVs and to set properties on the MAVs already on your server.

- Macfile Directory allows you to set owner, user, and group permissions on a MAV, using Macintosh-like specifiers.

- Macfile Forkize is the odd man out—it's used for manipulating the data and resource forks of a Macintosh file on a MAV. It also has some additional switches that let you change the type and creator of a file or group of files.

Using Macfile Server

The Macfile Server command lets you work with the same settings as the Configuration tab of the File Server For Macintosh Properties window you saw earlier in Figure 22-8. Here's the full version of the command:

```
MACFILE SERVER
        [/SERVER:\\computername]
        [/MAXSESSIONS:number | UNLIMITED]
        [/LOGINMESSAGE:message]
        [/GUESTSALLOWED: TRUE | FALSE]
```

- The /SERVER flag lets you specify which server your changes apply to. If you leave it off, FSM assumes that you're modifying options on the local server.

- The *MAXSESSIONS* switch lets you specify a limit on the number of current sessions you want your server to support.

- The *LOGINMESSAGE* switch lets you change the logon message displayed to users. Enclose your message in double quotes and keep it to fewer than 255 characters.

- The *GUESTSALLOWED* switch lets you specify whether your server will accept guest connections or not, subject to the limitations and caveats presented earlier in the chapter.

Using Macfile Volume

If you want to add, remove, or reconfigure a MAV, the Macfile Volume command is the tool to use. This command actually has three separate modes, each triggered by its own command switch.

The Macfile Volume /Remove Command

The least complex variant of Macfile Volume is the one that lets you remove existing MAVs. This isn't surprising, since removing a volume requires only that you specify the MAV you want removed (and, optionally, the server that hosts it). Here's what the command looks like:

```
MACFILE VOLUME /REMOVE
        [/SERVER:\\computername]
        /NAME:volumename
```

- The *SERVER* switch lets you supply the name of the FSM server that hosts the volume you want to remove. If you don't specify a name, the command assumes you're removing a MAV from the local server.

- The *NAME* switch is how you specify the MAV to remove. To remove a MAV whose name contains embedded punctuation or spaces, enclose the name in double quotes.

The Macfile Volume /Add Command

Adding a volume is pretty easy. When you create a new MAV using the Shared Folder Wizard, you provide settings as described earlier in this chapter. The only required settings are the name you want the MAV to have and the path to the folder the MAV sits on—and so it is with Macfile Volume /Add. The full version of the command is shown below. (Note that the /SERVER and /NAME switches work the same as they do with Macfile Volume /Remove.)

```
MACFILE VOLUME /ADD
        [/SERVER:\\computername]
        /NAME:volumename
        /PATH:filepath
        [/READONLY:TRUE|FALSE]
        [/GUESTSALLOWED:TRUE|FALSE]
        [/PASSWORD:password]
        [/MAXUSERS:number|UNLIMTED]
```

- */PATH* specifies the full path, including the drive letter, of the folder you want to share as a MAV. This folder cannot be inside a folder or volume that's already shared as a MAV.

- */READONLY* controls whether FSM treats this volume as read-only or not. This has the same effect as the This Volume Is Read-Only check box in the MAV Properties window; as with that check box, the default setting for this switch is *FALSE*.

- */GUESTSALLOWED* controls whether guests may log on to this MAV or not. It's identical to the Guests Can Use This Volume check box; the default value is *TRUE*.

- */PASSWORD* specifies a volume password, as described in the section "Volume Passwords" earlier in this chapter. By default, no password is assigned when you create a volume.

- */MAXUSERS* governs the maximum number of concurrent users allowed to use this MAV. The default setting doesn't impose a limit (like the Maximum Allowed option in the MAV Properties window), but you can specify a numeric limit here.

The Macfile Volume /Set Command

The Macfile Volume /Set command lets you change the settings supplied when you created the MAV; you can toggle its read-only status, specify whether guests may use it or not, set the volume password, and indicate how many users can use the MAV. The syntax is very similar to that needed for the /Add switch:

```
MACFILE VOLUME /SET
        [/SERVER:\\computername]
        /NAME:volumename
        [/READONLY:TRUE|FALSE]
        [/GUESTSALLOWED:TRUE|FALSE]
        [/PASSWORD:password]
        [/MAXUSERS:number|UNLIMITED]
```

Using Macfile Directory

The name Macfile Directory is a little misleading; Macfile Permissions might have been a better choice, since you use the command to assign permissions to a directory within a MAV (or to the directory that contains the MAV). You can individually assign an owner, assign a group, or set permissions for the owner or group. The command is shown below. (The *SERVER* and *PATH* switches work as previously discussed.)

```
MACFILE DIRECTORY
        [/SERVER:\\computername]
        /PATH:directorypath
        [/OWNER:ownername]
        [/GROUP:groupname]
        [/PERMISSIONS:permsmask]
```

- The *OWNER* switch specifies what Windows 2000 account owns the MAV. This change applies to the actual directory for the MAV, and it's also reflected in the Sharing section of the Mac OS Info window for the MAV—both the Mac OS client and the FSM server see the change in ownership.

- The *GROUP* switch changes the primary group that has Mac OS permissions for the MAV. Since Mac OS clients can resolve permissions for only one group entry, you have to choose which of the Windows 2000 group permissions is primary. *Groupname* can be the name of any valid Windows 2000 group, whether it's local or stored in the domain directory.

- The *PERMISSIONS* switch accepts as its argument an 11-digit bit mask that specifies, bit by bit, which permissions you want to apply to the MAV in question. Table 22-1 shows what the bits in the mask mean; for each position in the mask, a value of 1 means the permission is turned on, and a value of 0 means it's off.

Table 22-1. What the bits in the /*PERMISSIONS* mask field mean

Bit Position	Meaning
1 (leftmost)	OwnerSeeFiles: 1 = the owner can see files in the folder; 0 = the owner can't see the files.
2	OwnerSeeFolders: 1 = the owner can see enclosed folders; 0 = the owner can't see the folders.
3	OwnerMakeChanges: 1 = the owner can make changes to the files and folders; 0 = the owner can't make changes.
4	GroupSeeFiles: 1 = members of the primary group can see files in the folder; 0 = members of the primary group can't see the files.
5	GroupSeeFolders: 1 = members of the primary group can see enclosed subfolders; 0 = members of the primary group can't see the subfolders.
6	GroupMakeChanges: 1 = members of the primary group can make changes to the files and folders; 0 = members of the primary group can't make changes.
7	WorldSeeFiles: 1 = everyone can see files in the folder; 0 = everyone can't see the files.
8	WorldSeeFolders: 1 = everyone can see enclosed subfolders; 0 = everyone can't see the subfolders.
9	WorldMakeChanges: 1 = everyone can make changes to the files and folders; 0 = everyone can't make changes.
10	Cannot Rename, Move, or Delete: Setting this bit to 1 is the same as locking the folder on the Mac OS side.
11 (rightmost)	Apply Changes Recursively: When this bit is set, the rest of the permissions mask you specify will be applied to all subfolders of the target folder. This is the equivalent of the standard Windows 2000 permission inheritance behavior.

Note You must specify either the /*OWNER,* /*GROUP,* or /*PERMISSIONS* switches when you use Macfile Directory.

With one exception (when you turn on bit 11 in the mask for the /*PERMISSIONS* switch), none of these changes are applied recursively.

Using Macfile Forkize

The remaining command, Macfile Forkize, is much like a Swiss Army knife—it has several useful functions that aren't needed often but that are occasionally really handy. You use Macfile Forkize to do two things: change the type or creator code for a file or combine the resource and data forks of a file. Here's the command syntax:

```
MACFILE FORKIZE
        /TARGETFILE:filepath
        [/SERVER:\\computername]
        [/TYPE:typecode]
        [/CREATOR:creatorcode]
        [/DATAFORK:filepath]
        [/RESOURCEFORK:filePath]
```

- The /TARGETFILE switch designates the full path to the file you want to forkize. If you're combining a data and resource fork, /TARGETFILE specifies where the resulting file goes. If you're changing a type or creator, it specifies where the file to be modified is currently located. As always, paths that contain special characters or spaces must be enclosed in double quotes.

- The /TYPE and /CREATOR switches let you specify the four-character type and creator codes for a particular file. For example, to change a single file so that its type is TEXT and its creator code matches the code for Macromedia's Dreamweaver, you'd use this command:

```
macfile forkize /targetfile:f:\shared\html\welcome.htm /
type:TEXT /creator:DmWr
```

This is a quick way to fix up types and creators of existing files after you change the associations using the methods described earlier in this chapter (except that you can't use wildcards with the /TARGETFILE switch, so you'll need another way to process multiple files, like a short Windows Scripting Host [WSH] script).

- The /DATAFORK and /RESOURCEFORK switches specify the locations of the files whose forks you want to join. FSM doesn't do any checking as to whether your request makes sense or not, so there's nothing stopping you from welding the resource fork of Microsoft Word 98 for the Macintosh onto the data fork of a document (for example).

Sharing Printers with PSM

PSM works in two different but related ways. First of all, it allows Mac OS users to print to any printer shared by your Windows 2000 PSM server. As far as the Macintosh users are concerned, any printer (regardless of its native capabilities) shared from your PSM server appears to be a 300 dots-per-inch PostScript level 1 printer. Handily, the PSM service also works in the reverse way: it allows you to capture an AppleTalk network printer so that Windows users can print to a queue on the Windows 2000 Server and have their jobs go to the AppleTalk printer—without putting AppleTalk on the clients themselves.

Before You Install PSM

As was mentioned earlier, in the section "Setting Up File and Print Services," the best way to install PSM is to first install, configure, and test the AppleTalk protocol. Once you're confident that it's working properly, the next step is to create a user account for the PSM service. FSM doesn't need its own account, since permissions are already set on the files and folders it makes available to Macintosh users. However, to control printing you'll need to have a separate account to which you can assign permissions. Use the tools discussed in Chapter 9 to create a new user to be used exclusively with PSM and then follow these steps to configure the PSM service to use this account instead of the default LocalSystem credentials.

1. Open the Computer Management snap-in from an MMC console.
2. Switch to the Services view.
3. Find the Print Server for Macintosh service, right-click it, and choose Properties.
4. In the PSM Properties window, click the Log On tab and then click the This Account option. The account and password controls become active. Select the PSM account you created, enter its password in the appropriate fields, and then click OK.

Sharing a Printer for Macintosh Users

The first step in creating a printer to which Mac OS users can print is to create a shared printer, either by creating a new printer from scratch using the Add Printer Wizard (discussed in Chapter 8) or by sharing an existing printer.

If you want to share an existing printer that's already attached to your Windows 2000 Server, just switch to the Sharing tab of its Properties window, select the Shared As option, and give the shared printer a name. If you're creating a new printer, the process is slightly more complicated.

1. Start the Add Printer Wizard by double-clicking the Add Printer icon in the Printers folder. When the wizard appears, click Next to move on to the next page.

2. On the next screen of the wizard, select the Local Printer option and, if appropriate, select the Plug And Play Detection check box. Click Next.

3. On the Select The Printer Port screen of the wizard (Figure 22-13), select the Create A New Port option and then choose AppleTalk Printing Devices from the Type list. Click Next.

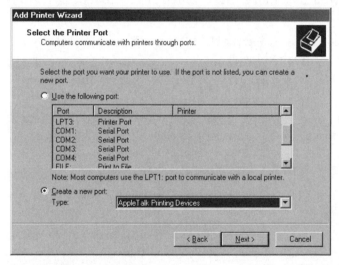

Figure 22-13. *The Select The Printer Port screen of the Add Printer Wizard.*

4. The wizard pops up an AppleTalk browser that works much like the standard My Computer browser you're already accustomed to. Search through the AppleTalk zones on your network until you find the printer you want to use, select it, and click OK in the browser.

5. Complete the Add Printer Wizard by naming your new printer (using a name that's less than 32 characters long) and being sure to share the printer when prompted.

Tip As part of the configuration process, you can set restrictions on who can use the printer (with the Security tab of the printer's Properties window) or on when and how it can be used (with the Advanced tab).

Once you've taken these steps, the newly created shared printer will be available to Macintosh users as soon as the PSM service is stopped and restarted.

Capturing Existing AppleTalk Printers

Capturing an AppleTalk printer has two side effects. The first is that Mac OS users can no longer print directly to the captured device—that's what capturing does. The second is that any user, Mac OS or Windows, of the PSM server *will* be able to print to the captured device, providing you've shared it. To capture an existing AppleTalk printer, you must first create a shared printer to represent it on the Windows 2000 Server by doing the following:

1. Create a new shared printer using the Add Printer Wizard. Tell the wizard that the printer is attached locally.

2. Switch to the Ports tab of the printer's Properties window and click the Add Port button.

3. When the Printer Ports dialog box appears, choose AppleTalk Printing Devices from the Create A New Port list and then click the New Port button.

4. The AppleTalk Printing Devices browser appears. Choose the AppleTalk zone that contains the printer you want to capture and then click OK.

If you want to release a captured printer or recapture one that's been released, you can do so with the Ports tab of the printer's Properties window. Follow these steps to do so:

1. Select the target printer, open its Properties window, and then switch to the Ports tab.

2. On the Ports tab, click the Configure Port button.

3. Select or clear the Capture This AppleTalk Printing Device check box.

4. Stop and restart the PSM service.

Remember, a captured device is available to Windows and Mac OS users who print only to the corresponding queue on Windows 2000 PSM Server; an uncaptured or released AppleTalk printer is available only to clients that speak AppleTalk.

Summary

The continuing popularity of Macintosh computers means that they are a part of many enterprise networks. Windows 2000 includes services that allow Macintosh users to share files and printers with Windows, OS/2, and even MS-DOS users. In addition, Windows 2000 includes an implementation of the AppleTalk network protocol. With these tools, Macintosh users can be integrated into a Windows 2000 network with very little difficulty. The next chapter moves to another area of supporting services, the messaging and faxing capabilities of Windows 2000.

Chapter 23
Configuring Mail Services

Every company needs some kind of messaging service. Most commonly, employees need e-mail access, and perhaps they need newsgroup access, intracompany e-mail as provided by Microsoft Exchange Server or Lotus cc:Notes, or fax services. This chapter discusses two popular and frequently used messaging programs, Microsoft Outlook 2000 and Microsoft Outlook Express 5; it also covers the Microsoft Windows 2000 built-in fax services.

Microsoft Outlook 2000 is one of the most popular and powerful messaging programs available today. It is relatively easy to use, has many handy messaging and calendar features, works well with Microsoft Exchange Server and other services that interface with Messaging Application Programming Interface (MAPI), and has excellent support for standards-based Internet e-mail. It comes with Microsoft Office 2000, making it a simple installation for many companies. Let's see how to set it up.

Tip Even though this chapter covers Outlook 2000, Outlook 98 is quite similar, and many procedures described here work for both versions of Outlook. If Outlook 97 is still deployed in your organization, we strongly recommend upgrading because Outlook 98 and Outlook 2000 are much faster and more flexible. Outlook 98 is also a free upgrade from Outlook 97.

Setting Up Outlook 2000

Most companies include Outlook as a part of their Office 2000 installation (by default). You can also acquire and install the program separately.

The first time you run Outlook, you'll need to configure it for the current user. You'll need to supply a user name and e-mail address, provide mail servers (if you haven't already set up e-mail on the computer), and specify whether to set up Outlook with the Internet Only configuration, the Corporate Or Workgroup configuration, or the No E-Mail configuration. Table 23-1 summarizes some key features of each type of Outlook configuration.

> **Tip** Use the Corporate Or Workgroup configuration only if you need Exchange Server or other mail service support. The Internet Only configuration is highly optimized for Internet E-Mail and, in general, performs much faster for Internet-based e-mail than the Corporate Or Workgroup configuration does.

To configure Outlook 2000 for a new user in your company, follow these steps:

1. Launch Outlook 2000 from the Programs folder of the Start menu.

2. If a previous version of Outlook is installed on the computer, specify whether Outlook is used for e-mail. Clicking Yes will retain all settings from the older Outlook version and finish the configuration process.

3. If other e-mail programs are on the computer, such as Outlook Express, Eudora, or Netscape Messenger, Outlook lets you use settings from any of these programs. Select the program from which to import settings, or select None Of The Above, and click Next.

4. Select which configuration of Outlook 2000 to use, as shown in Figure 23-1.

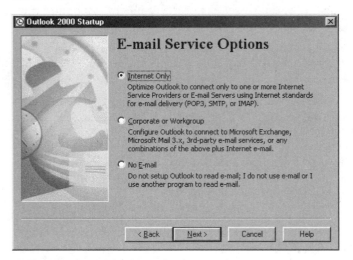

Figure 23-1. *Outlook configuration choices.*

5. If you haven't set up an e-mail account on the system yet, the e-mail part of the Internet Connection Wizard is displayed, walking you through e-mail account setup. Provide the user name, Post Office Protocol (POP) or Internet Message Access Protocol (IMAP) server settings, and any other information it requests.

Tip   You can change your Outlook configuration at any time after Setup completes by choosing Options from the Tools menu, clicking the Mail Services or Mail Delivery tab, and then clicking the Reconfigure Mail Support button. You won't have to reboot, but you may have to exit Outlook using Exit And Log Off from the File menu and restart Outlook. You will also need access to the Office 2000 installation files.

Table 23-1.   Differences between Outlook 2000 configurations

Feature	Internet Only	Corporate or Workgroup	No E-Mail
Calendar and Contacts	Yes	Yes	Yes
Internet e-mail (POP3/SMTP)	Yes	Yes	No
IMAP4 folders	Yes	No	No
LDAP directory support	Yes	Yes	No
Send/receive faxes	With WinFax Starter Edition	With Windows 2000's Fax Service	No
Exchange Server support	Via POP/SMTP (Exchange 5 or later) and IMAP4 (Exchange 5.5+)	Yes	No
Exchange Server public folder support	No	Yes	No
Exchange Server Global Address List	Via LDAP (Exchange 5 or later)	Yes	No
Voting, message recall	No	Via Exchange Server	No
Read receipts	Via Message Disposition Notifications standard	Via Exchange Server and Message Disposition Notifications standard	No
Delivery receipts	No	Via Exchange Server	No
Autodial for e-mail	Yes	No	No
Send and receive meeting requests	Yes	Yes	No
Send iCalendar meeting requests	Yes	Yes	No
Read iCalendar Free/Busy info	Yes	Yes	Yes
See Free/Busy details	No	Via Exchange Server	No
Direct booking of resources	No	Via Exchange Server	No
Newsgroup support	Via Outlook Express (installed)	Via Outlook Express (installed)	Via Outlook Express

Adding and Modifying Accounts and Services

Once you've configured Outlook 2000, you'll want to set up multiple mail accounts so that a user can send and receive mail on several different e-mail accounts or message services. When you install Outlook, the Setup program helps you establish your primary message account, but you can easily establish additional accounts any time after Setup completes.

The first point to remember about establishing additional Outlook 2000 mail accounts or services is that some differences exist between the Internet Only and the Corporate Or Workgroup configurations. Both are easy to set up, but just to simplify matters, we'll look at each configuration separately.

Tip If you chose to import settings from another e-mail program or a previous version of Outlook that had multiple mail accounts configured, Outlook 2000 preserves these mail settings, probably obviating the need to configure additional accounts.

Adding Accounts to the Internet Only Configuration

The Outlook 2000 Internet Only configuration is optimized for sending and receiving standards-based Internet e-mail, and you can set up Outlook to send mail using Simple Mail Transport Protocol (SMTP), to receive mail using both POP3 and IMAP4, and also to search LDAP directories. To set up additional accounts like this, follow these steps:

1. Choose Accounts from the Tools menu. Outlook displays the Internet Accounts dialog box, shown in Figure 23-2.

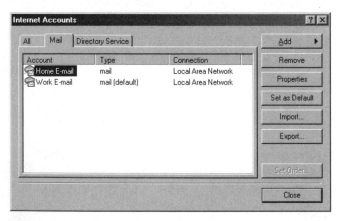

Figure 23-2. *The Mail tab of the Internet Accounts dialog box.*

2. To add an e-mail account, click the Add button, choose Mail from the shortcut menu, and use the Internet Connection Wizard screens to configure the account's POP or IMAP server information, e-mail address, and other settings.

3. To add an LDAP directory service account, click the Add button and then choose Directory Service from the shortcut menu. Use the screens provided to enter the LDAP server name for the account, to enter the user's account name and password, and to specify whether this LDAP server should be used to check names when sending e-mail.

Adding Services to the Corporate Or Workgroup Configuration

Outlook 2000's Corporate Or Workgroup configuration supports a wide variety of messaging services, such as Internet E-Mail, Exchange Server, Microsoft Mail, Lotus cc:Mail, Fax, and LDAP directories. To use these services you need to add them to your Outlook profile, which is based on the Windows Messaging/Exchange client. (You can view your profile or set up additional profiles by using the Control Panel tool labeled Mail or Mail and Fax.) To set up these services, follow these steps:

1. Choose Services from the Tools menu. The Services dialog box appears, shown in Figure 23-3.

2. To add a service, click the Add button, select the service to add from the Add Service To Profile dialog box, and click OK. Use the dialog boxes presented to enter the necessary information about the service you're adding.

Figure 23-3. *The Services tab of the Services dialog box.*

Changing Where Your Outlook Data Is Stored

By default, Outlook stores all of its local data in a single file with a .PST file extension called a personal folders file. This file is stored in the following hidden folder: \Documents and Settings*username*\Local Settings\Application Data\ Microsoft\Outlook\outlook.pst.

However, you might find it more convenient to relocate this file or to specify an existing file if a user already has a personal folders file. Outlook's Internet Only configuration is somewhat limited in the methods of changing the location of the default personal folders file, while the Corporate Or Workgroup configuration provides a little more flexibility. Use the appropriate method depending on which Outlook configuration you're setting up.

Changing Locations in an Internet Only Configuration

Unfortunately, the Internet Only configuration doesn't provide a simple way to change the location of the default personal folders file, where all Outlook items are stored. The reason for this is somewhat mysterious, but regardless of the Microsoft Office development team's decisions, you can circumvent this limitation in a couple of ways. The following two sections explain how.

Tip   To find out where the personal folders file is currently stored, right-click Outlook Today on the Outlook Bar and choose Properties. Then click Advanced and take note of the path listed in the Path box.

Opening a Different Folder   If you're using the Internet Only configuration, the easiest way to move your personal folders file is to open the personal folders file you want to use, have Outlook deliver your e-mail to this personal folders file, and then close the old personal folders file. To do this, follow these steps:

1. To create a new personal folders file to use as your default personal folders file, choose New from the File menu, and then choose Personal Folders File from the submenu. Enter a name and location for the file, and then click Create.

2. To use an existing personal folders file for the Outlook folder store, choose Open from the File menu, and then choose Personal Folders File from the submenu. Locate the file, and click Open.

3. Display the folder list by choosing Folder List from the View menu.

4. Right-click the root of the personal folders file in the folder list you want to use, and then choose Properties from the shortcut menu.

5. Select the Deliver POP Mail To This Personal Folders File check box, as shown in Figure 23-4, and then click OK.

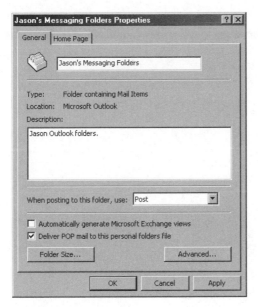

Figure 23-4. *The General tab of the Properties window for a personal folders file.*

6. Click OK in the next dialog box and restart Outlook. When Outlook asks if you'd like to re-create the Outlook Bar, click Yes.

7. You can transfer any data from your old personal folders file into your new one, and then close the old folder store by right-clicking the root of the folder store and choosing Close from the shortcut menu.

Trashing a File   The second way to change the location of your personal folders file is to find it and move it. If you haven't used Outlook yet and therefore have no data in your Outlook folders, we suggest moving this empty folder file to the Recycle Bin. Note that this method doesn't work well with Outlook 98. (It's prone to throwing tantrums and refusing to work; if you have Outlook 98, we recommend using the approach described earlier.) Once you're rid of this unwanted file, follow these steps to open an existing personal folders file or to create a new file in the location of your choice:

1. Launch Outlook and then click OK in the dialog box telling you that your personal folders file can't be located.

2. In the Create/Open Personal Folders File dialog box, choose an existing personal folders file and click Open, or go to the folder in which you'd like to create a new personal folders file, enter a filename, and click Open.

3. If you chose to create a new personal folders file, enter the name of the file into the Name text box of the Create Microsoft Personal Folders dialog box, shown in Figure 23-5.

Figure 23-5. *The Create Microsoft Personal Folders dialog box.*

4. Choose the type of encryption to use on the file. (This is supplementary to any NTFS file encryption you might be using.)

5. Optionally, specify a password and then click OK. Outlook asks whether to re-create the Outlook Bar shortcuts. Click Yes to do so; otherwise, click No. (This will break all the standard Outlook Bar shortcuts.)

Changing Locations in a Corporate Or Workgroup Configuration

The technique for changing the location of your personal folders file (the container of all Outlook items) in the Corporate Or Workgroup configuration is a lot more sensible than that for changing it in the Internet Only configuration. While you can still simply delete your old personal folders file and then create a new one in the location of your choice, Outlook also provides an interface for managing different personal folders files and specifying which one to use for receiving e-mail as well as which Contacts folders to use as address books. (The Internet Only configuration has a limited ability to maintain multiple address books.)

To change the default personal folders file location, use the following steps; to learn how to manage different address books, see the next section, "Managing Address Books."

1. Choose Services from the Tools menu.

2. Click Add, choose Personal Folders, and click OK to add a new or existing personal folders file to your Outlook configuration; otherwise, skip to step 7.

3. Name your new file or specify the location of your existing file and then click Open.

4. If you chose to create a new personal folders file, enter the name of the file into the Name text box of the Create Microsoft Personal Folders dialog box, shown previously in Figure 23-5.

5. Choose the type of encryption to use on the file. (This is supplementary to any NTFS file encryption you might be using.)

6. Optionally, specify a password and then click OK. Outlook asks whether you want the Outlook Bar shortcuts re-created. Click Yes to do so; otherwise, click No. (This will break all of the standard Outlook Bar shortcuts.)

7. Click the Delivery tab of the Services dialog box and, in the drop-down list box, choose the personal folders file to which you want your POP e-mail delivered, as shown in Figure 23-6.

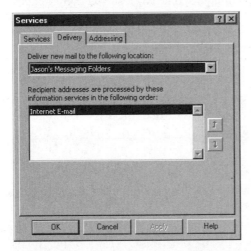

Figure 23-6. *The Delivery tab of the Services dialog box.*

8. To remove the old personal folders file from your Outlook configuration, click the Services tab, select the file from the list, and click Remove.

9. When you next start Outlook, it asks whether you want the Outlook Bar shortcuts re-created. Click Yes to do so; otherwise, click No. (This will leave all of the standard Outlook Bar shortcuts pointing to your old personal folders file.)

Managing Address Books

The Outlook 2000 Corporate Or Workgroup configuration has a couple different address books that are available to users depending on the services they have installed. If the address books aren't set up optimally for users or if the users don't understand the differences between the address books, this can cause problems.

To help you deal with this issue, this section explains the different address books available in the Corporate Or Workgroup configuration. Then in the two sections that follow, you'll learn how to create a new Contacts folder and set it up as an address book, and you'll learn how to change the way Outlook handles these address books.

> **Note**   The Internet Only configuration doesn't have the same ability to manage different address books as the Corporate Or Workgroup configuration does. You can set up multiple folders to store contacts and configure them as address lists just like the Corporate Or Workgroup configuration; however, you can't specify which Contacts folder should be checked first, and LDAP directories that you set up to function like an address book don't show up in the Address Book window (only in the address book available when sending messages).

The default address book in Outlook 2000 and the address book that we recommend you use to store all of your address information is the Contacts folder. This folder can contain just about any type of address information you'd like to store: e-mail, Exchange mailbox, X500, postal, telephone numbers, Web page addresses, and so on. It's also customizable and integrated extremely well into Outlook.

If you're connected to an Exchange server, you also have the Global Address List, a directory of mail accounts kept on the Exchange server. (You can also access this list by using the Internet Only configuration if your Exchange server is configured as an LDAP server.) This address list is read-only, but you can add addresses from the Global Address List to your personal address book (PAB) or Contacts folder (whichever one you have set up to store your personal addresses) by right-clicking the address and choosing Add To Personal Address Book from the shortcut menu.

The Corporate Or Workgroup configuration also allows you to use a .PAB file to store addresses. This feature was mainly retained for backward compatibility with old Exchange and Windows Messaging clients, which use the PAB as the default address book. We generally don't recommend using a .PAB file unless you need to maintain compatibility with one of these programs.

Configuring a Folder as an Address Book

Outlook 2000 can use any folder containing contacts as an address book—you're not limited to just one Contacts folder. To create a new folder in which to store contacts, and to make this folder available as an address book, follow these steps:

1. Choose New from the File menu, and then choose Folder from the submenu.

2. Enter a name for the folder in the Name text box, as shown in Figure 23-7.

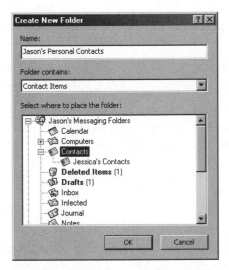

Figure 23-7. *The Create New Folder dialog box.*

3. Select Contact Items from the Folder Contains drop-down list box.

4. Choose the folder in your personal folders file or an Exchange Server mailbox in which to create your new Contacts folder, and then click OK. If Outlook asks if you'd like to create a shortcut to the folder on the Outlook Bar, click OK.

5. Display the folder list by choosing Folder List from the View menu.

6. Right-click the Contacts folder you created, and choose Properties from the shortcut menu.

7. Click the Outlook Address Book tab.

8. Select the Show This Folder As An E-Mail Address Book check box, and then click OK, as shown in Figure 23-8.

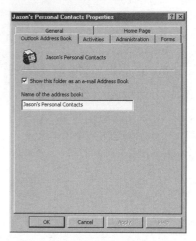

Figure 23-8. *The Outlook Address Book tab of the Properties window.*

Tip This procedure works in the Internet Only configuration as well as in the Corporate Or Workgroup configuration; however, with the Internet Only configuration, the Contacts folder can't become your default address book. In addition, you need to use the View menu's Folders And Groups command in the address book in order to see other Contacts folders you've created.

Configuring Address Book Handling

Outlook lets you easily configure which address book to store your personal addresses in, which address book to display when addressing messages, and the order in which Outlook checks your address books when searching for an addressee, if you're using the Corporate Or Workgroup configuration. To configure these options, follow these steps:

1. Choose Services from the Tools menu.

2. Click the Addressing tab, shown in Figure 23-9.

3. From the first drop-down list, choose the address book to be displayed first when you call up the address book.

4. From the second drop-down list, choose the address book in which to store all new addresses.

5. Use the Add button and the Remove button to change which address books are selected, and use the up and down arrows to adjust the order in which the address books are selected.

6. Click OK when you're finished.

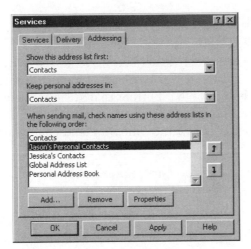

Figure 23-9. *The Addressing tab of the Services dialog box.*

Customizing Outlook

Now that you've handled the basic setup, you might want to change a number of Outlook settings for particular users. The following sections explain how to customize some key Outlook features such as the toolbars and personalized menus, and even how to eliminate the overly perky Office Assistant.

Eliminating Clippit

Just in case you have a pathological employee who hates that cute, animated paperclip (Clippit) that all of us Outlook users have come to know and love, here's how to make Office Assistants go away—for good. (You can turn it back on if you want, but it won't appear unless you choose the Show Office Assistant command from the Help menu to specifically request it.)

1. Go to the Help menu and choose Show Office Assistant if the Office Assistant isn't visible.

2. Right-click the Office Assistant and then choose Options from the shortcut menu.

3. Clear the Use The Office Assistant check box and click OK.

Tip The Office Assistant settings are shared among all Office 2000 applications, so if you turn off the Office Assistant in one program, you turn it off in all programs.

Customizing Toolbars and Toggling Personalized Menus

Outlook 2000 lets you customize your toolbars and also turn off the Personalized Menus and Toolbars feature if a user doesn't like it. (The Personalized Menus and Toolbars feature of Office 2000, like the Personalized Menus feature of Windows 2000, hides menu commands and toolbar buttons that are infrequently used.) To do so, right-click the toolbar you want to customize and choose Customize from the shortcut menu. Then do any of the following and click Close when you're finished.

- To turn off the Personalized Menus and Toolbars feature, clear the Menus Show Recently Used Commands First check box.

- To create a new toolbar, click the Toolbars tab, click New, enter a name for the toolbar, and then click OK. A small, floating toolbar appears onscreen.

- To add commands to a toolbar, click the Commands tab, select a menu category, and then drag a command to the toolbar of your choice.

- To modify the appearance of a toolbar button, right-click the button and use the shortcut menu to modify its appearance.

- To remove a toolbar button, drag it off the toolbar.

Tip You can change any toolbar button to point to a Web page by right-clicking it while in the Customize mode, choosing Assign Hyperlink from the shortcut menu, choosing Open from the submenu, and then using the Assign Hyperlink dialog box to locate the Web page to link to.

Changing the Default Mail Program

When you install Outlook, the program automatically becomes your default e-mail and newsreader program. To change the default e-mail program you use on your system to another program, follow these steps:

1. Open the Internet Options Control Panel tool.

2. Click the Programs tab, shown in Figure 23-10.

3. Select the program you want to use to edit and create Web pages (HTML documents) from the HTML Editor drop-down list box.

4. Select the program you want to use by default to send and receive e-mail from the E-Mail drop-down list box.

5. Choose the default newsreader you want to use for reading Internet newsgroups by selecting a program from the Newsgroups drop-down list

box. This newsreader will automatically be launched when you choose the View menu in Outlook's Go To command and then click News.

6. Choose the program you want to use to handle Internet voice calls from the Internet Call drop-down list box.

7. Choose the program you want to use to manage your calendar from the Calendar drop-down list box.

8. Choose the program you want to use to manage your address book from the Contact List drop-down list box.

9. Click OK when you're finished.

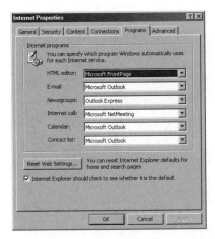

Figure 23-10. *The Programs tab of the Properties window.*

Note If you change the default e-mail program from Outlook to another program, the next time you launch Outlook, you'll be asked whether you want to use Outlook as your default e-mail program. Click No.

Creating Custom Forms

Outlook uses forms for just about every bit of information you enter into the program. E-mail messages, calendar items, contacts, and notes are all forms— whenever you enter information in Outlook (other than in a settings dialog box), you're entering it into a form. In most cases, Outlook's default forms work the best, but you might want to customize these forms for your company's own uses.

Customizing Outlook forms is fairly easy, but you can get caught up in a lot of complexity if you feel like it. This section doesn't teach you all the details of Outlook 2000 form design, but it's enough to get you started.

More Info For more information on designing your own Outlook forms, we suggest you pick up a good Outlook book such as *Building Applications with Microsoft Outlook 2000 Technical Reference* (Microsoft Press, 1999).

To create a basic custom form, follow these steps:

1. Choose Forms from the Tools menu and then choose Design Form from the submenu.

2. Choose the form on which you want to base your custom form and then click Open. Outlook displays the selected form in Design mode, as shown in Figure 23-11.

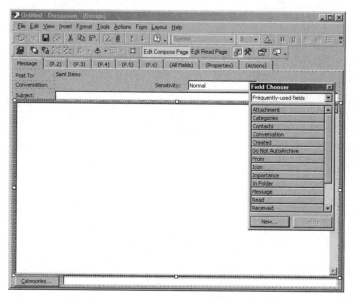

Figure 23-11. *The Design mode view.*

3. To add a field to your form, drag the field from the Field Chooser onto your form.

Tip Tabs with parentheses around their names are hidden to users. The tabs become visible to users when you add fields to them.

4. To reposition a field, click it and then drag it to a new location.

5. To delete a field, select it and then press Delete.

6. If you are customizing a post-based form or a message-based form, click the Edit Read Page toolbar button to display the Read page, which is used to display information once it has been entered (for example, a posted post or sent e-mail).

7. To add a display for a field you added to the Compose page, create a new field by clicking the New button in the Field Chooser, and then use the New Field dialog box to name the field and choose the field type and format.

8. Drag the new field onto the Read page.

9. Right-click your field and then choose Properties from the shortcut menu.

10. Use the Display tab to change how the field appears on your form.

11. Click the Value tab (Figure 23-12). Then click the Choose Field button, choose the appropriate field to display from the All Mail Fields submenu, and click OK.

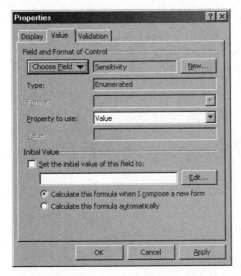

Figure 23-12. *The Value tab of the Properties window.*

12. When you're finished designing your custom form, click the Publish Form toolbar button.

13. Choose the location in which to store the form. (See the "Storing and Publishing Forms" Real World sidebar for more information on storing forms.)

14. Enter a name for the form and click Publish.

Real World   Storing and Publishing Forms

You can save a custom form in Outlook 2000 in a variety of ways. For instance, you can save the form as a template by using the Save As command. This creates a file that you can use in another program or attach to an e-mail message to send to someone else. Or you can save the form in a folder in your message store, which is good if you plan to simply attach the form to an e-mail or you don't plan to share the form with others.

You can also publish a form to a public folder (or private folder), making it available to all users only while they're in the folder to which you saved the form. This is perfect for forms that you've customized for use with a particular public folder and really aren't applicable elsewhere, such as a form customized for bug reports. Finally, you can publish the form in one of the two Outlook forms libraries. The forms libraries are as follows:

- **Personal forms library**   This library is stored in the mailbox in which you receive mail, and forms published to this library are available only to you. It's handy for storing forms intended only for personal use.

- **Organizational forms library**   This library is stored on your Exchange server, and forms stored in it are available to all users with access to your Exchange server. This is the best place to store a form that you want all users in your organization to have access to.

Using Outlook with Exchange Server

Now that you've configured Outlook 2000 and customized it the way you want it, the next several sections will help you integrate it with your company's Exchange Server infrastructure. Outlook 2000 is the best Exchange Server client on the market, and most companies that use Exchange Server for their intracompany e-mail will probably find themselves upgrading to Outlook 2000 at some point.

Note   Explicit Exchange Server support is available only in Outlook's Corporate Or Workgroup configuration, although some features can be emulated by enabling support on the Exchange server.

Setting Up Offline Folder Access

One way to change how Outlook works with Exchange is to set up Outlook to cache a copy of your Exchange folders locally, for offline use. You would usually do this for laptop users, but you could also do it for users with a slow or unreliable connection to their Exchange server (or for users with a fast connection to a slow and unreliable Exchange server). To set up your folders for offline access, follow these steps:

1. Choose Services from the Tools menu.

2. Select the Microsoft Exchange Server service from the list of installed services, and then click Properties.

3. Click the Advanced tab and click the Offline Folder Settings button.

4. Enter the filename and path for the file to use as your offline folder store, choose an encryption method, and click OK.

5. Select the Enable Offline Use check box and click OK.

6. Display the Outlook folder list, right-click a folder you want to make available for offline viewing, and then choose Properties from the shortcut menu.

7. Click the Synchronization tab, select the When Offline Or Online option, and click OK.

Tip You don't need to set up your Inbox, Outbox, Deleted Items, Sent Items, Calendar, Contacts, Tasks, Journal, Notes, or Drafts folders for offline access—Outlook does that automatically.

Synchronizing Offline Folders

After you've set up your Exchange folders for offline access, you need to synchronize with your Exchange server before going offline. If you only go offline infrequently and you know ahead of time that you'll be going offline (such as taking your laptop home for the weekend), you can probably get away with manually synchronizing just before you go offline. However, if you frequently or unpredictably go offline, you should set up a synchronization schedule to have reliable offline access to your Exchange folders. To synchronize your offline folders, follow these steps:

1. Choose Synchronize from the Tools menu, and then choose the command from the submenu that corresponds to the folders to synchronize.

2. To modify your synchronization settings, choose Options from the Tools menu, and then click the Mail Services tab, shown in Figure 23-13.

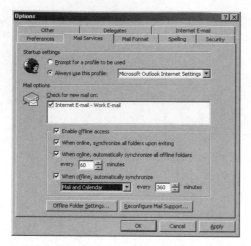

Figure 23-13. *The Mail Services tab of the Options dialog box.*

3. Select the When Online, Synchronize All Folders Upon Exiting check box to synchronize every time you quit Outlook while online.

4. To routinely synchronize your folders while online, select the When Online, Automatically Synchronize All Offline Folders Every check box and specify how frequently to synchronize.

5. To routinely connect and synchronize your folders while offline, select the When Offline, Automatically Synchronize check box and specify how frequently to synchronize.

6. Click the Offline Folder Settings button, and then select the check boxes next to the folders that you want to make available offline, as shown in Figure 23-14.

7. To be able to access the Global Address List while offline, select the Download Offline Address Book check box, and optionally click the Settings button to specify further details.

8. Select the Synchronize Forms check box to download updated copies of any forms posted in Exchange folders to which you have access.

9. Select the Synchronize Folder Home Pages check box to keep the home pages for any Exchange folders up-to-date in your offline folder store.

10. Click the Download Options button and use the Download Options dialog box to modify the 50-KB message size download limit or to specify exceptions to this rule.

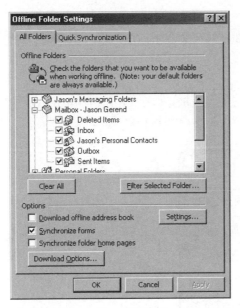

Figure 23-14. *The All Folders tab of the Offline Folder Settings dialog box.*

11. Use the Quick Synchronization tab to create a subset of commonly used folders that you can synchronize at times instead of performing a full synchronization.

12. Click OK when you're finished.

Assigning Delegates

Outlook makes it easy to delegate the chore of managing e-mail, which is nice for those fortunate enough to have hapless underlings to delegate tasks to. Outlook lets you achieve this wondrous state of e-mail nirvana by allowing you to name one or more users as delegates with permission to access your Exchange folders and to send and receive messages on your behalf.

To set this capability up, you obviously need to have a mailbox on an Exchange server and the Exchange services set up on your system; however, you get the most bang for your delegated buck if you also set up your mail to be delivered to your Exchange mailbox instead of your personal folders file. Doing this gives you more granular control over which folders your delegate can access, and what kind of permissions your delegate has to each folder. To assign control over your Outlook folders, follow these steps:

1. Choose Options from the Tools menu, click the Delegates tab, and then click Add.

Tip If the Delegates tab is unavailable, click the Other tab, click Advanced Options, click Add-In Manager, and make sure that the Delegate Access add-in is selected.

2. From the Global Address List, select the people you want to make delegates for your Outlook folders and then click OK. Outlook displays the Delegate Permissions dialog box, shown in Figure 23-15.

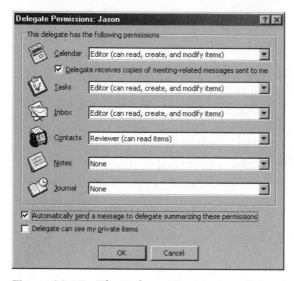

Figure 23-15. *The Delegate Permissions dialog box.*

3. For each of your Outlook folders, choose the permission levels that you want to give to the delegate and then click OK.

Real World Sorting Incoming Mail by Mail Account

Wouldn't it be nice if you could set up Outlook to deliver mail from different accounts to different locations—for example, to deliver your Exchange mail and your work Internet mail to your Exchange mailbox and to deliver your personal mail to your personal folders file? Well, you can't. However, you can get the same results by creating message rules to move messages sent to certain mail accounts to whatever folder you want. (See the section "Creating Message Rules to Automatically Process Mail" later in this chapter for more information.) Note that this cool feature is limited in Outlook Express, just in case you were wondering.

Modifying Permissions on Exchange Folders

Exchange folders, like folders on an NTFS volume in Windows 2000, have their own permissions settings that you can use to maintain tighter security on your network. You can set a number of different permissions levels, listed in Table 23-2. To change the permissions settings for a folder, follow these steps:

1. Display Outlook's folder list. Then right-click the folder on which to set permissions and choose Properties from the shortcut menu.

2. Click the Permissions tab and then click Add to add any users or groups for which you want to specify permissions (Figure 23-16).

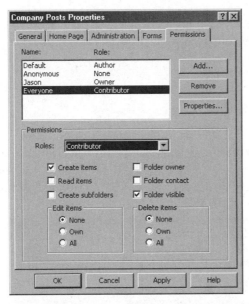

Figure 23-16. *The Permissions tab of the Properties window.*

3. Select a preset permissions level for the selected user or group from the Roles drop-down list box. (See Table 23-2 for a listing of the pre-set roles.)

4. If necessary for your system, create a custom permissions level by using the check boxes and option buttons in the bottom section of the dialog box.

5. Click OK when you're finished.

Table 23-2. Exchange permissions roles

Role	Permissions
Owner	Can read, modify, and delete all items and files and create items and subfolders. Owners can change others' permissions for the folder.
Publishing Editor	Can read, modify, and delete all items and files and create items and subfolders.
Editor	Can read, modify, and delete all items and files.
Publishing Author	Can create and read items and files, create subfolders, and modify and delete items and files they created.
Author	Can create and read items and files and modify and delete items and files they created.
Reviewer	Can have read-only access to items and files.
Contributor	Can create only items and files. All items not created by the user are hidden.
None	Cannot access the folder.

Customizing Your Public Folders

You can use the Corporate Or Workgroup configuration in conjunction with Exchange Server public folders to create some remarkably easy-to-use and flexible workgroup messaging solutions. You can modify the default views for your folders, configure rules to apply to new posts, create moderated folders, and use custom forms for posting to the folders.

To customize your Exchange public folders, log on using an account which has administrative privileges to the Exchange folders and then follow the steps outlined in the next few sections to customize the details of your public folders.

Changing the Default View

While the default view is often the most appropriate view to use in your public folders, sometimes a little change is in order. Although you can't create custom views and use them as the default view for all users of a public folder, you can group messages in several ways, kind of like a newsgroup, by following these steps:

1. Right-click the folder for which you want to change the default view and choose Properties from the shortcut menu.

2. Click the Administration tab and then select the view to use from the Initial View On Folder drop-down list box.

Changing the Default Form for a Folder

If Outlook's default form just doesn't fit the purpose of your Exchange public folders, you can change it to another form that's a better match. This is easy to do, but coming up with a customized form that works in your folder and suits your needs is a little more difficult.

> **More Info**   For some in-depth information on creating custom solutions with Outlook, see *Programming Microsoft Outlook and Microsoft Exchange* (Microsoft Press, 1999).

To change the default form for your folder or to allow additional forms to be used in the folder, follow these steps:

1. Right-click the folder for which you want to change the default form and choose Properties from the shortcut menu.

2. Click the Forms tab and verify that the form to use is published in the folder. If the form is listed, skip to step 5. If the form isn't listed, click the Manage button.

3. Click Set, choose the forms library where the form is published, and click OK.

4. Select the form you want to use, click Copy to store it in your public folder (Figure 23-17), and click Close.

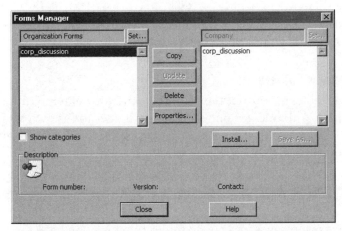

Figure 23-17. *The Forms Manager makes forms available in your folder.*

5. Select the Only Forms Listed Above option to add forms to your folder and specify which forms users are permitted to use, as shown in Figure 23-18.

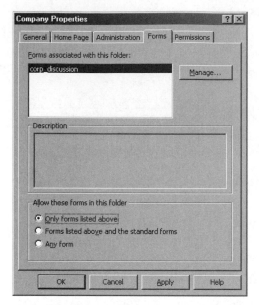

Figure 23-18. *The Forms tab of the Properties window.*

6. Select the Forms Listed Above And The Standard Forms option or the Any Form option to allow users more latitude with the forms they can use in the folder.

7. Click the General tab and then, from the When Posting To This Folder, Use drop-down list box, select the form to use as the default form for the folder. Click OK when you're finished.

Applying Rules to Public Folders

Outlook 2000's customizable rules are extremely useful, and fortunately, Outlook provides similar rule-making abilities for public folders as it does for its own folder store. (See the section "Creating Message Rules to Automatically Process Mail" later in this chapter for information about rules for your mail folders.)

Unlike the Outlook rules you apply to your local folder store, rules you create for public folders are processed on the Exchange server and apply to all users—an attribute that makes them particularly useful for keeping public folders tidy. To create a rule to manage messages in a public folder to which you have Owner privileges, follow these steps:

1. Right-click the folder for which you want to create a message-handling rule, and choose Properties from the shortcut menu.

2. Click the Administration tab, and then click the Folder Assistant button.

3. Click Add Rule to create a new rule to apply to the folder.

4. Use the options in the Edit Rule dialog box to apply the properties you specify to all messages posted to the folder, as shown in Figure 23-19.

5. You can specify multiple phrases or words to use as selection criteria in the Subject or Message Body boxes by separating them with semicolons.

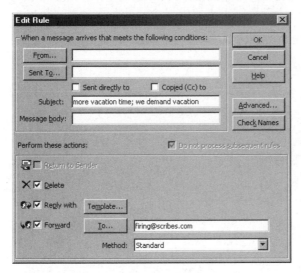

Figure 23-19. *The Edit Rule dialog box.*

6. Click the Advanced button to provide additional selection criteria such as size or date or to have the rule apply only to items that don't match these criteria.

7. Click OK when you're finished, create any additional rules, and then click OK.

Configuring Moderated Folders

Moderated folders are an excellent way to make sure that only "approved" communications appear in a public folder that you maintain or set up. Moderated folders work by forwarding all incoming posts to another public folder or to one or more moderators for review, after which the moderators place the approved posts into the moderated folder.

There are many reasons to set up a moderated folder, but it usually just boils down to improving the quality of the folder's content. Of course, someone's got to personally monitor and approve all posts to the folder, which can be a lot of work, so usually you want to set up a moderated folder only when a free-for-all public folder starts to decay into chaos.

To change an Exchange Server public folder over which you have Owner privileges into a moderated folder, follow these steps:

1. Right-click the folder you want to turn into a moderated folder and choose Properties from the shortcut menu.

2. Click the Administration tab, and then click the Moderated Folder button to display the Moderated Folder dialog box, shown in Figure 23-20.

Figure 23-20. *The Moderated Folder dialog box.*

3. Select the Set Folder Up As A Moderated Folder check box.

4. Enter the name of the person who should receive all new posts, or click the To button to select the person from one of your address lists.

5. Select the Reply To New Items With check box to notify users who post messages that their messages are being reviewed.

6. To create your own reply message, choose the Custom Response option, click Template, and create your message.

Note The standard message that Outlook sends to users who post to a moderated folder is as follows: "Thank you for your submission. Please note that submissions to some folders or discussion groups are reviewed to determine whether they should be made publicly available. In these cases, there will be a delay before approved submissions can be viewed by others."

7. Use the Add button and the Remove button to create a list of people authorized to moderate the folder (to add and delete messages from the folder). Click OK when you're finished.

Scheduling with Outlook

Scheduling is Outlook's other forte after messaging. Outlook 2000 has a useful and full-featured calendar, and it also has some additional features such as the ability to send meeting requests, plan meetings for optimal times, and publish calendars to a Web page. This section briefly covers some of these features.

> **More Info** For more in-depth information about Outlook 2000's scheduling features, pick up a copy of *Running Microsoft Outlook 2000* (Microsoft Press, 1999).

Sending Meeting Requests

You can use Outlook's Meeting Request feature to send special e-mail messages to people with a form allowing them to easily accept or reject the meeting request. They can also save the meeting time to their calendars, provided that they use a scheduling program compatible with the meeting request format you send.

> **Note** By default, Outlook sends meeting requests in a format that is readable only to other Outlook users; however, you can choose to send the request in the iCalendar format, which is readable by Lotus Organizer 5.1 and any other program that supports the iCalendar standard.

To send a meeting request, follow these steps:

1. Display your Calendar in Outlook.
2. Choose New Meeting Request from the Actions menu. Outlook displays a new Meeting form, shown in Figure 23-21.
3. Use the To button and the text box next to it to list the people with whom you want to request a meeting.
4. Fill in the subject, location, and time information for the meeting.
5. To schedule an online meeting, select the This Is An Online Meeting Using check box and select the software you want to use to conduct the meeting from the drop-down list box.
6. If the attendees have free/busy information from their calendars published in Exchange or on the Internet in the form of an iCalendar file, click the Attendee Availability tab to see if the time you specified is available for everyone to attend.

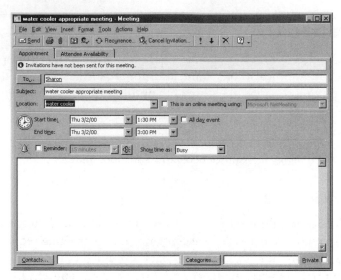

Figure 23-21. *A new meeting request message.*

7. To send the meeting request using the iCalendar format, choose Send As iCalendar from the Tools menu.

8. Click the Send toolbar button to send the meeting request. Everyone you send the meeting request to will receive an e-mail message with Accept, Decline, and Tentative buttons that they can use to quickly respond to your meeting request, and they can add the meeting to their calendar, if appropriate.

> **Tip** To use free/busy information that a person or resource has published on the Internet, the URL of the contact's iCalendar file needs to be recorded in the Internet Free/Busy Address box on the Details tab of his or her Contact item.

Planning a Meeting for the Optimal Time

Outlook 2000 includes the Plan A Meeting tool, a handy tool that is also available in meeting requests on the Attendee Availability tab. This tool allows you to easily find a time when all required attendees and resources are available by checking their free/busy information in Exchange or on the Internet in an iCalendar file. To use the tool to plan a meeting, follow these steps:

1. Display your calendar in Outlook.

2. Choose Plan A Meeting from the Actions menu. Outlook displays the Plan A Meeting tool, shown in Figure 23-22.

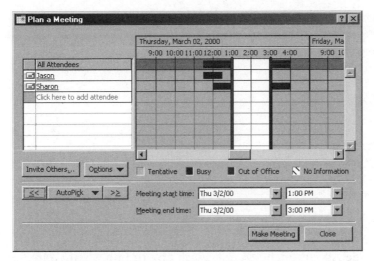

Figure 23-22. *The Plan A Meeting tool.*

3. Click the Invite Others button to specify the people to attend your meeting and to select any resources you need, such as a meeting room.

4. Enter a tentative start time and end time in the Meeting Start Time and Meeting End Time boxes. Don't worry if the time isn't available.

5. Click the AutoPick button and then choose the requirements for the meeting to take place from the shortcut menu. Outlook automatically finds the next available timeslot that matches your criteria.

6. Click the double chevron (>>) to the right of the Autopick button to look for another timeslot in the future, or click the double chevron (<<) to the left of the Autopick button to find a timeslot closer to the present.

7. When you've found your time, click the Make Meeting button and use the new meeting request form to send out invitations to all attendees.

Saving a Calendar as a Web Page

Outlook 2000 includes the nifty ability to save your calendar as a Web page—one of the quickest ways to publish a user's or group's schedule to an intranet or to the Internet. To save your calendar as a Web page, follow these steps:

1. Display your calendar in Outlook.

2. Go to the File menu and choose Save As Web Page. Outlook displays the Save As Web Page dialog box, shown in Figure 23-23.

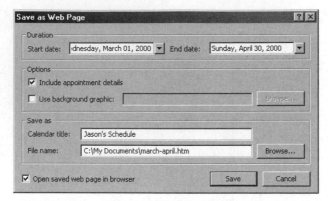

Figure 23-23. *The Save As Web Page dialog box.*

3. Choose the starting and ending dates for your Web page.

4. Select the Include Appointment Details check box to publish any information you included in the *Notes* field of your calendar items.

5. Select the Use Background Graphic check box and click Browse to specify a background image for your Web pages.

6. Enter a title for your calendar in the Calendar Title box.

7. Enter a filename in the File Name box and use the Browse button to find the folder or Web site to which you want to publish your page.

8. Click the Save button when you're finished. If you chose a location on a Web server, the Web Publishing Wizard will start and walk you through publishing the page to the specified Web site.

Tip Before this feature will work, you need to have the Web Publishing Wizard installed, even if you already have Internet Information Services (IIS) installed locally or on the network. Additionally, you might need to tweak IIS to support posts from the Web Publishing Wizard.

Customizing the Way Outlook Handles E-Mail

Another Outlook 2000 benefit is that it makes dealing with your e-mail easier and more secure. You can set up rules to automatically process your messages, create filters to handle junk mail and adult-content messages, and provide encrypted message support and digitally sign your messages. Outlook can simplify your e-mail life in many other ways, but because this book isn't about Outlook, we can only briefly touch on its virtues.

Turning on Junk Mail and Adult-Content Rules

If you post messages on Internet newsgroups using a real e-mail name, perhaps you know the joy of receiving lots of junk mail and so-called adult messages. Fortunately, Outlook can help you deal with this—and not by abandoning your e-mail address, picking a new one, and keeping it a secret (although this is a sure-fire way to reduce the hassle).

Outlook has configurable filters for junk mail and adult messages that allow you to color—or move to another folder—messages that contain certain keywords. To turn on these filters, follow these steps:

1. Display your Inbox and then click the Organize toolbar button.

2. Click the Junk E-Mail tab, shown in Figure 23-24.

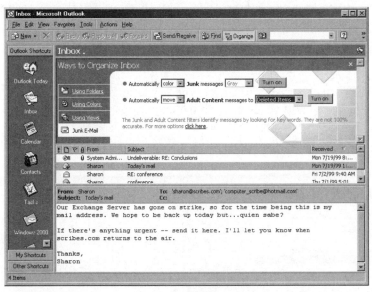

Figure 23-24. *Using junk e-mail filters and adult-content filters.*

3. To color junk or adult e-mails a different color, choose Color from the first drop-down list box and then select the color to use from the second.

4. To move junk or adult e-mails to a different folder, such as the Deleted Items folder, choose Move from the first drop-down list box and then select the folder to move the messages to from the second box.

5. Click Turn On to apply the rule.

Caution Junk e-mail filters and adult-content filters work by looking for messages with certain keywords in them. Sometimes they might snag legitimate messages. Therefore, you might not want to set up the rules to move messages to the Deleted Items folder. You might also want to use the Rules Wizard to copy the rule, and then modify it by adding a list of exceptions to the rule so that key messages aren't accidentally deleted.

Creating Message Rules to Automatically Process Mail

Outlook 2000 contains an extremely useful tool called the Rules Wizard that allows you to create client-side rules or server-side rules (when used with an Exchange server) that will process your e-mail for you. If you're using Outlook with an Exchange server, you can also use the Out Of Office Assistant command on the Tools menu to create a special server-side rule that can handle and respond to mail received while you're out of the office. To use this feature, follow these steps:

1. In the Inbox, choose the Rules Wizard from the Tools menu.

2. Click New to create a new rule.

3. Use the Rules Wizard's screens to supply the conditions to which the rule should be applied and to determine which actions should be performed. Click Finish when you're done.

4. To disable a rule in the Rules Wizard screen shown in Figure 23-25, clear the check box next to it.

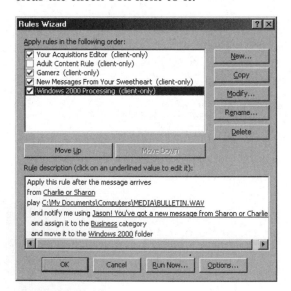

Figure 23-25. *Using the Rules Wizard to create and manage rules for processing your e-mail.*

5. To run a rule now on the messages you currently have, select the message and click the Run Now button.

6. To import or export message rules, click the Options button.

7. When you're finished creating rules, click OK.

Setting Up Security

Outlook allows you to increase the security of your e-mail messages by using a digital ID to digitally sign and optionally encrypt your e-mail messages. Digitally signing your e-mail allows the recipients of your messages to verify that you were the sender of the message and not someone trying to impersonate you. Encryption allows you to encode your messages such that your e-mail can't be read by anyone other than the intended recipient, even if the message is intercepted.

To use secure e-mail in Outlook, you need to obtain a digital ID from a certificate authority such as VeriSign or from the Key Management Server on your Exchange Server network. To obtain a digital ID, choose Options from the Tools menu, click the Security tab, and then click the Get A Digital ID button. Once you have a digital ID, follow the steps below to set up Outlook for secure e-mail.

Tip To strengthen the security of Outlook's message encryption, you can download a 128-bit encryption version of Outlook 2000 from Microsoft's Office 2000 Web site at *http://officeupdate.microsoft.com*.

1. After obtaining and installing your digital ID in Microsoft Internet Explorer, as directed by the certificate authority you obtained your digital ID from, choose Options from the Tools menu.

2. Click the Security tab and click the Setup Secure E-Mail button. Outlook displays the Change Security Settings dialog box, shown in Figure 23-26.

3. Enter a name for your security settings in the Security Settings Name box.

4. Select S/MIME from the Secure Message Format drop-down list box to specify the settings for Internet e-mail, or select Exchange Server Security to specify the settings for use with Exchange Server mail.

5. Select the Default Security Setting For This Secure Message Format check box to use these settings for all secure e-mail in this message format (S/MIME-based Internet e-mail or Exchange Server mail).

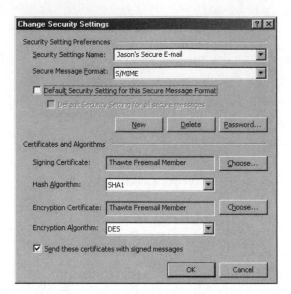

Figure 23-26. *The Change Security Settings dialog box.*

6. Select the Default Security Setting For All Secure Messages check box to use these security settings for all secure messages, both Internet E-Mail and Exchange Server mail.

Caution Don't use Exchange Server security for all secure messages unless your Exchange Server ID is S/MIME-compatible, because secure e-mail to Internet-mail-based recipients might not be readable (if encrypted) or the signature might be unrecognizable (if signed).

7. If your digital ID isn't already displayed, click the Choose button next to the Signing Certificate box to select the digital ID to use. Note that the e-mail address on the certificate must match the e-mail address you use to send mail.

8. To be able to receive encrypted replies from your recipients, select the Send These Certificates With Signed Messages check box.

9. Click OK and then select the Encrypt Contents And Attachments For Outgoing Messages check box at the top of the Security tab to automatically encrypt all messages you send.

10. Select the Add Digital Signature To Outgoing Messages check box to automatically sign all messages you send.

11. Select the Send Clear Text Signed Message option to allow recipients whose e-mail programs don't support signatures (such as most programs you access through Telnet) to be able to read your messages.

Using Outlook with Newsgroups

Outlook doesn't explicitly support Internet-based Network News Transfer Protocol (NNTP) newsgroups. Instead, it does something slightly confusing: it takes the version of Outlook Express you have installed on your system—or the version that was installed when you installed Outlook 2000—disables all mail support in the program, and calls it Microsoft Outlook Newsreader in some places and Outlook Express in others. This is confusing to many, and we personally disable this Outlook Newsreader and use Outlook Express by default. It works exactly the same as Outlook Newsreader, except that if you have any additional mail accounts that you like to use in Outlook Express (such as a Hotmail account), they aren't hidden when you access your newsgroups from Outlook.

Microsoft might decide to integrate Outlook Express's Newsreader directly into a future version of Outlook. Until then, we recommend that you stick to the full-blown version of Outlook Express, unless you or your users access e-mail only in Outlook, in which case the Outlook Newsreader might be just the ticket for you to eliminate the confusion of having two different Inboxes. You make the call.

Configuring Outlook Express

Outlook Express is the free, fully featured e-mail and newsgroups client that is installed by default in all currently shipping Microsoft operating systems, making it a cinch to support. Clients are also available for the Apple Macintosh, several flavors of UNIX, and Windows 3.1, although these clients differ a little from the Windows versions, most notably the Macintosh client.

Both the Macintosh client and the UNIX client have additional support for Exchange Server, a feature not available in the Windows 3.1 clients. However, the fullest support for Exchange Server is found in Outlook 2000. Again, because this book isn't about Internet Explorer and Outlook Express, we'll only briefly cover some topics relevant to system administrators.

More Info   For further information on end-user features, refer to the *Microsoft Internet Explorer 5 Resource Kit* or *Microsoft Pocket Guide to Microsoft Internet Explorer 5* (both Microsoft Press, 1999).

Note   The Windows 3.1, 95/98, NT, and 2000 versions of Outlook Express *do* support Exchange Server via POP3 or IMAP folders, available in Exchange 5 and 5.5, respectively. However, public folder support and other Exchange Server features aren't available in the Windows Outlook Express clients.

Setting Up Accounts

Outlook Express is installed by default in Windows 2000 and with all installations of Internet Explorer, so let's jump straight into setting up accounts in Outlook Express. If you set up your e-mail account when you ran the Internet Connection Wizard, you don't even need to configure your mail account unless you have additional accounts you'd like to set up. However, you will need to configure your news servers for access to newsgroups, so read this section anyway. To set up accounts, follow this procedure:

1. Launch Outlook Express and then choose Accounts from the Tools menu.

2. Click the Add button. Select Mail to add a new e-mail account, select News to add a new news server, or select Directory Service to set up an LDAP directory server. Figure 23-27 shows these options.

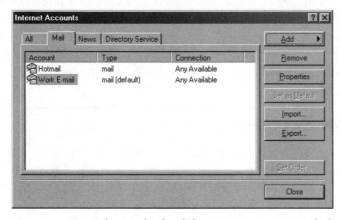

Figure 23-27. *The Mail tab of the Internet Accounts dialog box.*

3. Use the Internet Connection Wizard to set up your account and click Finish when you're done.

Real World   Outlook Express

When you join a Windows 2000–based domain, Outlook Express automatically configures itself with support for Active Directory. You can then use the Find People feature of Outlook Express to search Active Directory, along with any other LDAP directories and your address book.

Outlook Express now includes the ability to access Web-based e-mail, specifically the Hotmail service. When you set up a Hotmail account in Outlook Express, you can access your Hotmail folders just as if they were IMAP4-based instead of Web-based. Other services might be supported—check with your e-mail provider to see if they support Outlook Express.

Changing Where Your Mail Is Stored

Your message store is where Outlook Express stores all of your local folders, including both local e-mail folders and all downloaded newsgroup information. The message store is stored by default in \Documents and Settings*user-account*\Local Settings\Application Data\Identities\{84B06BA3-9B42-4256-A39B-765E5CB06C82}\Microsoft\Outlook Express.

Note The long, cryptic string in the middle of the above path is different on every machine—this is what it looks like on one of our client machines.

This place isn't bad for storing your Outlook Express folders, but you might want to place the message store somewhere easier to access if you like to poke around in the folder manually or back up only your Outlook Express folders (perhaps so you can perform a clean install of the operating system). To move your Outlook Express message store, follow these steps:

1. Go to the Tools menu and choose Options.

2. Click the Maintenance tab and then click the Store Folder button.

3. Click Change, browse to the folder in which you want to store your Outlook data, and click OK.

Sharing Address Books with Outlook

By default, Outlook Express is set up to share its address book with Outlook's default Contacts folder. This is really handy if you use both Outlook and Outlook Express and would like to have a single address book shared across both applications. (You might do this so that you can access your Hotmail account via Outlook Express or use Outlook Express's newsreader function.)

However, sharing an address book can also be a pain if you want to keep separate address books or if you have a tendency to forget that the address book is shared and not simply imported. (It's hard to understand why anyone would be foolish enough to think that the contacts are simply imported, and therefore delete the entire contacts list, but it has happened—or so we've been told.)

To toggle the sharing of your contacts list between Outlook and Outlook Express, perform the following procedure:

1. Click the Addresses toolbar button to display the address book in Outlook Express.

2. Choose the Options command from the Tools menu.

3. Select the first option, shown in Figure 23-28, to store all of your addresses in Outlook's Contacts folder.

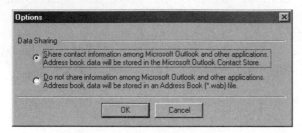

Figure 23-28. *The Options dialog box.*

4. Select the second option to store your addresses in the Windows Address Book (.WAB)—a holdover from the days Outlook Express was called Internet Mail and News.

5. Click OK when you're done.

Customizing Outlook Express's Appearance

You can customize Outlook Express's appearance to better suit you or your users or even to look like Outlook (sort of). While Outlook Express's interface can't be customized, as the Outlook 2000 interface can, and the program doesn't yet support personalized menus and toolbars, as Outlook 2000 and Windows 2000 do, you can still tweak it by using the following procedure:

1. From the View menu, choose Layout. To make Outlook Express look more like Outlook, select the Outlook Bar check box and clear the Folder List check box, as shown in Figure 23-29. Figure 23-30 shows the results.

2. To display your contacts list under the folder list (if displayed), select the Contacts check box.

3. Use the Preview Pane check boxes to toggle the preview pane and preview pane header on or off, as well as to control where the pane is placed onscreen.

4. To add or remove buttons from a toolbar, click the Customize Toolbar button. When you're finished customizing your toolbar in the Customize Toolbar dialog box, click Close.

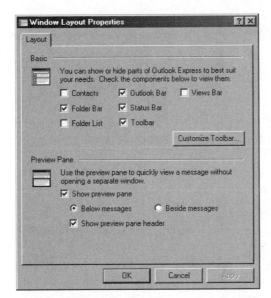

Figure 23-29. *The Window Layout Properties dialog box.*

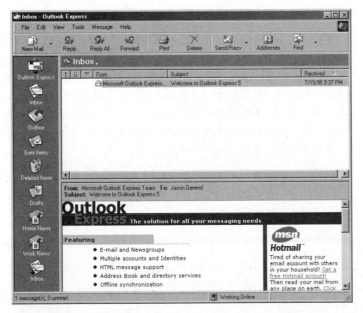

Figure 23-30. *Outlook Express's appearance made to look similar to Outlook's appearance.*

> **Tip** You can add shortcuts to the Outlook Bar in Outlook Express just as you can in Outlook 2000: display the folder list and drag the folder onto the Outlook Bar.

Setting Up Outlook Express Identities

Outlook Express has a relatively new feature called identities that you're going to think is kind of pointless. *Identities* are a nonsecure way of setting up Outlook Express for multiple users (or for a single user with multiple personalities, if you prefer)—all in a single user account. When you set up a new identity, a new folder is created—with the long string of gibberish being your unique, new identity—called something like \Documents and Settings*useraccount*\Local Settings\ Application Data\Identities\{84B06BA3-9B42-4256-A39B-765E5CB06C82}\.

The folder store isn't in a different user account, just a different folder in the same user account. It's not really a feature that was created with Windows NT or Windows 2000 in mind, but is instead intended for users of Windows 95/98 who don't set up separate profiles. If multiple users want to share a computer, we recommend that they set up multiple user accounts, which adds file security that identities don't provide (assuming that you use an NTFS volume to store your user settings).

However, the identities feature is occasionally handy for keeping your personal folder store moderately separate from your business folder store, although it usually makes more sense to set up separate folders in your single Outlook Express folder store and use message rules to move messages received from different accounts to different folders. (For more information, see "Creating Message Rules to Automatically Process Mail and News" later in this chapter.) If you *still* want to set up and use multiple identities after reading this, you've probably found a good reason, so without further ado, here's how to do it:

1. From the File menu, choose Identities, and then choose Add New Identity from the submenu.

2. Enter your name and then select the Require A Password check box to provide a minimal amount of security to your identity. Click OK when you're finished.

3. In the Manage Identities dialog box shown in Figure 23-31, select the identity to use as the default identity when starting Outlook Express and then click Close to be done with identities.

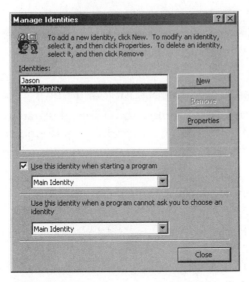

Figure 23-31. *The Manage Identities dialog box.*

Changing the Default Mail Program

When you install Outlook Express, the program automatically becomes your default e-mail and newsreader program. To change the default e-mail program you use on your system to another program, follow these steps:

1. Open the Internet Options Control Panel tool.

2. Click the Programs tab and then select the programs to use for each type of Internet activity, as shown in Figure 23-32.

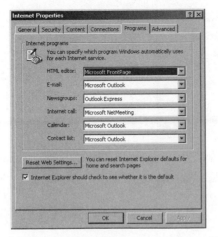

Figure 23-32. *The Programs tab of the Internet Properties window.*

> **Note** If you change the default e-mail program from Outlook Express to another program, the next time you launch Outlook Express, you'll be asked whether you want to use Outlook as your default e-mail program. Click No.

Creating Message Rules to Automatically Process Mail and News

Outlook Express, like Outlook 2000, has the ability to create rules that will automatically process your e-mail and newsgroup messages for you. (Remember message rules don't work for IMAP4 or HTTP mail accounts, only for POP3 accounts.) To use this feature, follow these steps:

1. In the Inbox, choose Message Rules from the Tools menu, and then either select Mail to create a new rule that processes e-mail, or select News to create a new rule that processes posts in newsgroups that you read.

2. In the Select The Conditions For Your Rule box (Figure 23-33), select the rule conditions.

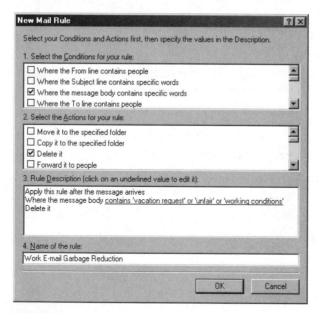

Figure 23-33. *The New Mail Rule dialog box.*

3. In the Select The Actions For Your Rule box, select the actions to perform when your specified conditions are met.

4. Click the underlined words in the Rule Description box to fill in necessary information.

5. Enter a name for the rule in the text box at the bottom of the dialog box and then click OK.

6. To disable a rule in the Message Rules dialog box shown in Figure 23-34, clear the check box next to it.

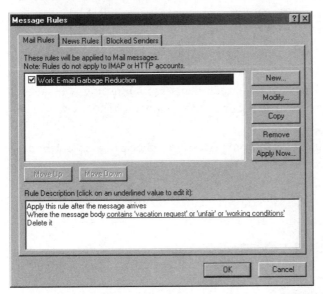

Figure 23-34. *The Mail Rules tab of the Message Rules dialog box.*

7. To run a rule now on the messages you currently have, select the message and click the Apply Now button.

8. To add people to a list of blocked senders from whom messages are deleted (for e-mail messages) or hidden (for news messages), click the Blocked Senders tab, click Add, and then enter the sender's e-mail address in the text box provided.

Configuring Secure E-Mail

Outlook Express allows you to increase the security of your e-mail messages by using a digital ID to digitally sign and optionally encrypt them. Digitally signing your e-mail allows the recipients of your messages to verify that you were the sender of the message and not someone trying to impersonate you. Encryption allows you to encode your messages such that your e-mail can't be read by anyone other than the intended recipient, even if the message is intercepted.

To use secure e-mail in Outlook Express, you need to obtain a digital ID from a certificate authority such as Verisign, Inc. For more information on obtaining a digital ID, choose Options from the Tools menu, click the Security tab, and then click the Get A Digital ID button. Once you have a digital ID, follow these steps to set up Outlook for secure e-mail:

1. After obtaining and installing your digital ID in Internet Explorer as directed by the certificate authority you obtained your digital ID from, go to the Tools menu and choose Options.

2. Click the Security tab, and click the Digital IDs button to verify that your certificate is installed correctly.

3. Select the Encrypt Contents And Attachments For Outgoing Messages check box at the bottom of the Security tab to automatically encrypt all messages you send.

4. Select the Digitally Sign All Outgoing Messages check box to automatically sign all messages you send.

5. To be able to receive encrypted replies from your recipients, click Advanced and then select the Include My Digital ID When Sending Signed Messages check box, as shown in Figure 23-35.

Figure 23-35. *The Advanced Security Settings dialog box.*

6. Select the Encode Messages Before Signing option to prevent the message from being tampered with. Note that recipients whose e-mail programs don't support S/MIME signatures (such as most programs you access through Telnet) won't be able to read your messages.

7. Select the Add Senders' Certificates To My Address Book option to automatically save other users' certificates to your address book when you

receive digitally signed messages, allowing you to send encrypted messages back to the sender.

8. Select the Only When Online option to check digitally signed messages
you receive to see if the certificates are valid or select Never to disable
this check.

Tip   To strengthen the security of Outlook Express's message encryption, you
can download a 128-bit encryption version of Internet Explorer from the Windows
Update site.

Using Fax Services

Finally, Windows 2000 includes basic fax capabilities for use with a fax/modem
if you have one. While the services are limited (for example, they can't be shared
over a network), they are still useful in the absence of a more powerful faxing program such as WinFax Pro. Nonetheless, in the interest of thoroughness, we briefly
cover administering fax services and using them to send faxes from your system.

Note   The Outlook 2000 Corporate Or Workgroup configuration uses the
Windows 2000 Fax Services when you install the Fax Mail Transport in Outlook.
The Internet Only configuration of Outlook uses its own WinFax Lite faxing services.

Using the Fax Service Management Tool

As you already know, Windows 2000 includes a set of basic fax facilities that you
can use to send and receive faxes, provided you have a fax modem installed locally on your computer. To administer this service, follow these steps:

1. Open the Fax Service Management tool located in the
   Accessories\Communications\Fax folder on the Start menu.

2. Right-click Fax Service On Local Computer (or Remote Computer if
   you're remotely administering the service) and choose Properties from
   the shortcut menu.

3. Use the Retry Characteristics boxes to specify how persistent to be in
   retrying failed fax transmissions, as shown in Figure 23-36.

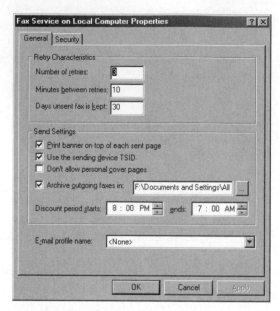

Figure 23-36. *The General tab of the Fax Service On Local Computer Properties window.*

4. Use the Send Settings boxes to set the different options you'd like to use when sending faxes.

5. Click the Security tab and set the permissions to use for the fax service so that only the users and groups you select will have access to fax services on your computer. Click OK when you're finished.

6. Select the Devices category in the console tree to view a list of fax modems installed on your system and their attributes, as shown in Figure 23-37.

7. To change the attributes for a device, right-click the device and choose Properties from the shortcut menu. Windows displays the Properties window for the selected device.

8. Select the Enable Send check box and the Enable Receive check box to allow the device to send or receive faxes.

9. If you chose to enable the reception of faxes, choose how many rings to allow before the fax modem answers the line and attempts to receive the fax.

10. Enter the transmitting station identifier (TSID) in the first text box to identify the sender of your faxes.

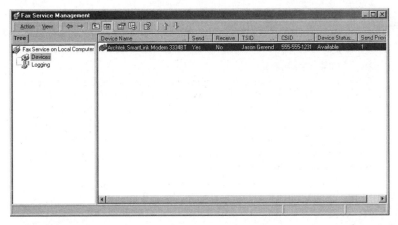

Figure 23-37. *The Fax Service Management console with the available fax devices displayed.*

11. Enter the called station identifier (CSID) that you want to use to name the recipient of faxes you receive in the second text box.

12. Click the Received Faxes tab.

13. To automatically print received faxes, select the Print On check box and select your printer from the drop-down list box provided.

14. To save the faxes to a folder (which we recommend), select the Save In Folder check box and enter the folder name in the box provided.

15. To forward received faxes to your local Inbox, select the Send To Local E-Mail Inbox check box and choose the profile to use. Click OK when you're done.

16. Select Logging from the console tree and then set the appropriate level of detail to log for each category that is logged. (See Tables 23-3 and 23-4 for details.)

Table 23-3.   Categories of events to be logged by the Fax Service

Category	Description
Inbound	Events generated while receiving faxes
Initialization/termination	Events generated while starting or stopping the Fax Service
Outbound	Events generated while sending faxes
Unknown	Fax-related events generated for unknown reasons

Table 23-4. Levels of detail available when logging Fax Service events

Level of Detail	Description
None	No events are logged.
Minimum	Only severe error events are logged. For example, a fax attempt that failed repeatedly or a fax that was received but could not be delivered to the appropriate storage location would be logged at this level.
Medium	In addition to the events logged at the minimum level of detail, warnings and some informational events are also logged. For example, a fax that was sent or received successfully or a fax transmission that was retried would be logged at this level.
Maximum	All events are logged. For example, a fax that was received and delivered to the appropriate location would be logged at this level.

Using the Fax Service to Send a Fax

If you bought this book, you probably don't need us holding your hand while you send a fax in Windows 2000. However, you might appreciate a nudge in the right direction, so here's a brief overview of using the Windows 2000 built-in Fax Service to send a fax.

1. To send a fax from an application, choose the application's Print command and print to the fax printer. This launches the Windows 2000 Send Fax Wizard.

2. To send a simple coversheet-based fax, choose Send Cover Page Fax from the Accessories\Communications\Fax folder on the Start menu. This launches the Send Fax Wizard.

3. The first time you run the Send Fax Wizard, you'll be asked to edit your current user setup or keep the current settings. Make a decision and move on.

4. Enter the recipient's name or use the Address Book button to find it in your Outlook Contacts folder.

5. Enter or verify the recipient's fax number and then click Add to include it in the list of people to send the fax to.

6. If you live somewhere with multiple area codes for local numbers, select the Use Dialing Rules check box and click the Dialing Rules button to set up a list of area codes that can be dialed without incurring long-distance charges. You can also use the Dialing Rules button to change your location information, set up calling cards, and view your modem properties.

7. In the next window, select a cover page template, enter a subject, and type your note.

8. Use the following window to schedule the fax transmission, click Next, review your fax summary, and then click Finish to add the fax to your queue.

Tip The fax queue can be accessed like a normal printer queue from the Printers folder.

Summary

All companies need messaging solutions, and some of the most popular messaging programs and services to run in Windows 2000 are Outlook 2000 and the built-in Outlook Express and Fax Services. To understand how to perform routine, day-to-day tasks with these programs, you need to buy another book or just play around with the programs. However, a beginner's book probably won't explain how to configure and customize these programs for you and your users, as this chapter does. The tasks described in this chapter—configuring the programs, data storage locations, setting up new accounts, creating message rules in Outlook and Outlook Express, working with an Exchange server, and setting up secure e-mail—will help you with configuration and customization. The next chapter dives deeper into the software sea by covering server-based software management and installation, tasks that can make getting applications to your users almost effortless. OK, at least *easier*.

Chapter 24
Managing Software

Among an administrator's most tedious tasks is the management of software on client systems. Users don't have certain necessary software. Client systems need to be upgraded. Microsoft Windows 2000 clients must be deployed. All of this requires a great deal of time if you must physically go to each client system and perform each installation and configuration.

Windows 2000 addresses this problem by giving administrators the ability to deploy applications and operating systems automatically to users and computers that need them. This ability can be combined with other IntelliMirror technologies such as User Data Management and User Settings Management to allow the transparent deployment of systems that are ready to use, complete with Windows 2000 and the users' system settings and data.

Although this chapter discusses User Data Management and User Settings Management only briefly, it covers Software Installation and Maintenance as well as Remote Installation Services in detail, so read on. (A more thorough discussion of folder redirection is available in Chapter 9.)

Tip Since both Software Installation and Maintenance and Remote Installation Services are based on Group Policy and use the Group Policy snap-in extensively, we recommend that you have a good understanding of Group Policy before using these tools. Chapter 9 provides an introduction to Group Policy.

IntelliMirror and Systems Management Server

IntelliMirror is a set of technologies that allow users' data, settings, and applications to follow them to other computers on the network—or even off the network, in the case of laptops. The technologies that provide this ability are really just outgrowths of Group Policy. Briefly, these technologies are as follows:

- User Data Management is just a buzzword created to embody two technologies—folder redirection and offline folders. These technologies allow users to access their files from any computer on the network or from their laptops while disconnected from the network. Folder redirection is covered in Chapter 9, while offline folders is a fairly simple technology that you probably don't need much help with. (Consult the Help system or the Windows 2000 Resource Kit for additional information on offline folders.)

- User Settings Management is more simply known as roaming profiles; it allows users to log on to any computer on the network and have all of their settings follow them.

- Software Installation and Maintenance allows administrators to assign applications to users or computers so that they will always have certain applications available. Assigned applications are automatically installed from the network and can be uninstalled remotely by the administrator. Administrators can also publish applications in the Active Directory directory service, allowing users to install them when needed.

- Remote Installation Services (RIS) is closely related to the IntelliMirror technologies. RIS allows administrators to deploy Windows 2000 Professional to clients across the network. All the clients need to do is boot up from the network (using a network boot-compliant computer) and select the operating system (OS) to be installed. The rest is performed automatically.

Initially, there was a lot of confusion about how IntelliMirror relates to Microsoft's older Systems Management Server 2 (SMS). IntelliMirror and SMS each offer somewhat overlapping features, with each possessing several features the other lacks. This isn't really a problem, however, as the two technologies are designed to complement each other, with IntelliMirror providing easy and effective services for high-speed networks running Windows 2000 on the client machines and SMS providing advanced capabilities with all Windows clients and in complex networks with varying speed interconnections.

When choosing whether to use IntelliMirror or SMS (or, more likely, both), it is important to look at the features and implementation of both technologies (as well as of RIS, which is closely related to IntelliMirror). The following list describes each technology, highlighting their differences. Table 24-1 summarizes the best mix of services for your type of network.

- **RIS**   Permits remote installation of Windows 2000 Professional on computers across the network, even if the computer is blank or nonbooting. Its functionality is similar to that provided by using unattended answer files and SysPrep, without the need to have local access to the Windows 2000 setup files or image.

- **IntelliMirror**   Allows user data, settings, and applications to be available on any computer on the network as well as on roaming laptops that periodically synchronize with the network. IntelliMirror distributes data, software, and settings using a *pull* approach, meaning that the client requests data from Active Directory as needed. This approach works best when connectivity between the client and the nearest domain controller or software distribution server is at LAN speeds.

- **Systems Management Server**   Manages the deployment of software over multiple sites, controlling the schedule and providing inventorying capabilities as well as providing planning and diagnostic tools. SMS can push software to clients using almost any version of Windows and to distribution points where users can then pull the software onto their computers or use IntelliMirror to do so.

Table 24-1.   Technologies to use based on network type and client environment

Client Type	Simple LAN with High-Speed Interconnections	Complex LAN or Multiple Sites
Windows 2000	IntelliMirror RIS	SMS IntelliMirror RIS
Mixed Windows environment with some Windows 2000 clients	SMS IntelliMirror	SMS IntelliMirror
Legacy Windows clients (Microsoft Windows 3.x, Microsoft Windows 95/98, Microsoft Windows NT)	SMS	SMS

Understanding Software Installation and Maintenance

The Software Installation and Maintenance component of the IntelliMirror technologies is an extremely useful tool for administrators. It can be used to make applications available for installation from across the network (that is, to publish applications), to assign applications to certain groups or computers, or to uninstall applications installed using the tool.

Software Installation and Maintenance leverages Windows 2000's Group Policy and Windows Installer features to permit the easy deployment and management of applications in the enterprise. Here's how it works: To deploy an application, you edit the appropriate group policy and add the application's native Windows Installer package to the Software Installation and Maintenance user or computer policy, depending on whether you want it to apply to users or computers. (This process is described in more detail later in this chapter.) Group Policy then makes the application available to the appropriate group of users or computers. The next time a user logs on or a computer is rebooted, the policy is applied to the user or computer and the application either is automatically installed, is added to a list of installable programs in Add/Remove Programs, or is installed on first use from the Start menu. The new Windows Installer handles the automatic installation or uninstallation of all programs, as well as any upgrades or repairs.

Choosing an Installation Package Format

Before deploying an application using IntelliMirror, you need to decide whether to use a native Windows Installer package (if one is available for your application), to repackage the application, or to use a zero administration for Windows applications package (a .ZAP file).

If the application comes with a native Windows Installer package (one with an .MSI file extension), you can in many cases simply copy the package to the applications file share and add the package to the group policy. If you don't have a Windows Installer package for the application, the next best choice is to author your own installation package, using a commercial authoring package from InstallShield or WISE Solutions, or to repackage the application into a Windows

Installer package. You can repackage applications with Seagate Software's WinInstall program, a light version of which is included with Windows 2000 Server. WinInstall is discussed later in this chapter.

> **Tip** The Microsoft Office 2000 Server Resource Kit (available from Microsoft Press) includes an Installation Customization tool that allows you to create custom Windows Installer packages that you can deploy using IntelliMirror.

The last option for applications not natively authored for Windows Installer is to create a .ZAP file for the application—basically a special text file that points to the setup program for the application. This approach has some limitations. Because legacy applications that aren't repackaged can't take advantage of the Windows Installer service, .ZAP files are not able to do the following:

- Assign applications to users or computers. You can, however, publish applications with a .ZAP file, as described later.
- Install applications with elevated permissions. (Windows Installer gives higher permissions to installation programs to eliminate the need to always use an administrator account to install software.)
- Install applications automatically on first use.
- Perform a complete rollback of an unsuccessful installation or permit applications to repair themselves. (The application must be Windows Installer–aware to take advantage of the last feature.)

Deciding Whether to Publish or Assign

Another important decision to make when deploying applications is whether to publish them in Active Directory or assign them to users or computers. When you publish an application in Active Directory, it becomes available from Add/Remove Programs for those users to whom the group policy applies. Assigning an application to a user or computer makes the application available without any special action on the user's part. (Assigned applications appear on the Start menu and are installed on first use.) Table 24-2 summarizes the differences between publishing and assigning applications.

Table 24-2. Differences between publishing and assigning deployed applications

	Published Applications	Applications Assigned to Users	Applications Assigned to Computers
When after deployment is the software available for installation?	After the next logon.	After the next logon.	After the next reboot.
How is the software installed?	Via Add/Remove Programs in Control Panel.	On first use. (Icons are present on the Start menu and/or the desktop.)	The software is already installed.
Is the software installed when a file associated with the application is opened?	Yes.	Yes.	The software is already installed.
Can the user remove the software?	Yes, via Add/Remove Programs. (Reinstallation is also supported.)	Yes, although the software will become available again after the next logon.	No, although software repairs are permitted. Local administrators can uninstall software.
What package types are supported?	Windows Installer packages and .ZAP files.	Windows Installer packages.	Windows Installer packages.

Setting Up Software Installation and Maintenance

Software Installation and Maintenance is actually fairly simple to set up and configure. Basically, you create a network share, copy the applications into it, and then add the installation packages to the appropriate group policy. The sections that follow tell all.

Creating a Software Distribution Point

To deploy applications on a large scale, first create a file share on the server you want to use as a software distribution point, as follows:

1. Log on to the server you want to use as the application server, using an administrator account.

2. Create a file share for the applications, giving it the following permissions:

   - Everyone (or Authenticated Users) = Read
   - Administrators = Full Control, Change, Read

3. Create any additional folders for the application categories and applications, and then copy the Windows Installer packages, .ZAP files, and application files into the appropriate folders.

Tip   Consider using the Distributed file system (Dfs) of Windows 2000 to manage the software distribution point. Dfs allows you to use load balancing, fault tolerance, and file replication on these folders, increasing the availability of your applications for users.

Opening the Software Installation Snap-in

Before you can add or administer deployed applications, you need to open the Software Installation snap-in. Follow these steps:

1. Open the Active Directory Users and Computers snap-in or the Active Directory Sites and Services snap-in, depending on whether you want to apply policy to groups or computers.

2. Right-click the site, domain, or organizational unit (OU) that you want to create a group policy for, and choose Properties from the shortcut menu.

3. Click the Group Policy tab, select the Group Policy object you want to modify, and click Edit, as shown in Figure 24-1.

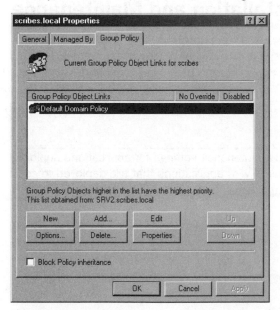

Figure 24-1. *The Group Policy tab of a domain's Properties window.*

4. Double-click the Software Settings folder under either the Computer Configuration or User Configuration heading (depending on whether you want to assign or publish applications to users or to computers), and then expand the Software Installation icon underneath it, as shown in Figure 24-2.

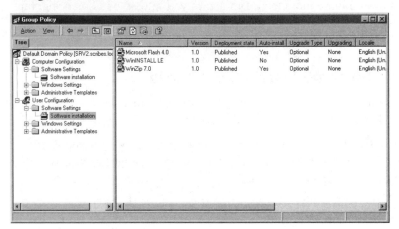

Figure 24-2. *The Group Policy console.*

Configuring Software Installation and Maintenance

You can configure a number of options that control how software packages are deployed and managed. These options determine how packages are added to the group policy, the amount of control users have over an installation, and the default application for a given file extension, as well as which categories you can use for grouping applications. The following sections cover these options in greater detail.

Note Software Installation and Maintenance settings for applications deployed to users and groups are not shared with applications that are deployed to computers. Each type of deployment maintains its own set of applications and settings.

Setting Software Installation Options

To change the default location for installation packages, specify how new packages should be added, change the level of control users have over installations, or specify that applications should be automatically uninstalled when appropriate, follow these steps:

1. In the Group Policy snap-in, double-click the Software Settings folder under either User Configuration or Computer Configuration, right-click the Software Installation icon underneath it, and choose Properties from the shortcut menu to display the Software Installation Properties window (Figure 24-3).

2. Under Default Package Location, enter the path of the file share where you want to have applications stored by default (most likely the root of your software distribution point).

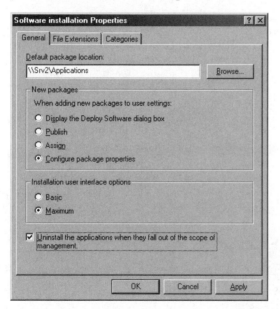

Figure 24-3. *The General tab of the Software Installation Properties window.*

3. In the New Packages area, select the default action you want to perform on new packages. See Table 24-3 for more information on these options.

4. In the Installation User Interface Options area, select Basic to show users only a limited amount of information about the installation progress, or select Maximum to display all screens and messages to the user.

5. If you want to have applications uninstalled automatically when the group policy no longer applies to the user or computer, select the Uninstall The Applications When They Fall Out Of The Scope Of Management check box.

Table 24-3. Options for default behavior when adding new packages

Option	What It Does
Display The Deploy Software Dialog Box	Displays a dialog box asking whether you want to publish (User Configuration only) or assign the application, or whether you want to customize the publish or assign configuration.
Publish (User Configuration only)	Automatically publishes the application, using the default settings.
Assign	Automatically assigns the application, using the default settings.
Configure Package Properties	Displays the application's advanced properties, allowing you to customize the publish or assign configuration.

Setting Defaults for File Extensions

If you deploy more than one application that is capable of handling a given file format, you may want to change the application used by default to open files in that format. To do so, follow these steps:

1. In the Group Policy snap-in, double-click the Software Settings folder under either User Configuration or Computer Configuration, right-click the Software Installation icon underneath it, and choose Properties from the shortcut menu.

2. Click the File Extensions tab (Figure 24-4).

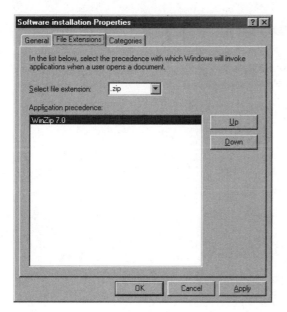

Figure 24-4. *The File Extensions tab of the Software Installation Properties window.*

3. Select a file extension from the Select File Extension list box to see the applications associated with it.

4. If more than one application is associated with a given extension, select the application you want to have as the default application for the extension, and click the Up button to move it to the top of the list.

Creating Application Categories

Application categories are extremely useful when you have a large number of applications deployed in a given group policy. When applications are organized by category, persons who use the Add/Remove programs tool can choose to view only the applications in the desired category, instead of seeing an unsorted list of applications. Before you can assign an application to a category (which will be discussed later in this chapter), you need to set up a list of categories. To do so, follow these steps:

1. In the Group Policy snap-in, double-click the Software Settings folder under either User Configuration or Computer Configuration, right-click the Software Installation icon underneath it, and choose Properties from the shortcut menu.

2. Click the Categories tab (Figure 24-5).

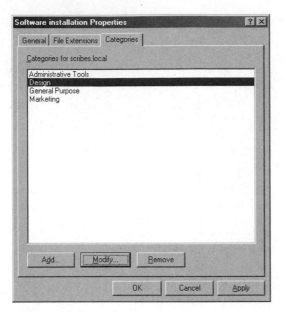

Figure 24-5. *The Categories tab of the Software Installation Properties window.*

3. To add a category, click the Add button and type in the category name. To remove a category, select the category and click Remove. To rename a category, select the category and click Modify.

Working with Packages

Of course, software packages are what the Software Installation and Maintenance part of IntelliMirror is all about. Once you've set up the group policy and configured the general software installation options, you're ready to start adding software packages and working with them. The following sections help you add packages to the group policy, change their properties, upgrade and modify packages, and remove obsolete packages.

Adding a Package to a Group Policy

Before users can easily access applications that you copy to the software distribution point discussed earlier in this chapter, you need to add the installation packages to the group policy. To do this, follow these steps:

> **Tip** If you want to apply any modifications (transforms) to your package, you must do so when adding the package to your group policy. Transforms cannot be added to currently deployed packages.

1. In the Group Policy snap-in, double-click the Software Settings folder under either User Configuration or Computer Configuration, choose the Action menu's New command, and then choose Package from the submenu.

2. Select either Windows Installer Package or ZAW Down-Level Application Packages (.ZAP) from the Files Of Type list box, depending on the type of application you want to deploy. (Note that you can only deploy .ZAP files to users and groups, not computers.)

3. Select the package for the application you want to deploy and click Open. Note that for best results you should use the My Network Places icon to navigate to your package, ensuring that Group Policy learns the network path instead of a local file path.

4. Select Published in the Deploy Software dialog box to publish the application in Active Directory (Figure 24-6). (If Published is already selected, see the section "Managing General Settings" earlier in this chapter.)

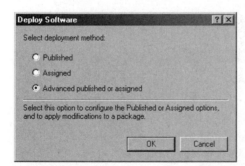

Figure 24-6. *The Deploy Software dialog box.*

5. To assign the application with the default properties, select Assigned, and click OK. To modify how the application is deployed, select Advanced Published Or Assigned, and click OK. (The next section describes the deployment options.)

Note You will see the Deploy Software dialog box only if you selected the Display The Deploy Software Dialog Box option in the Software Installation Properties window, as described earlier in the section "Setting Software Installation Options." Otherwise, the package you selected will be automatically published or assigned, or you will see the package's Properties window, discussed in the next section.

Changing Application Properties

Once you've added a software package to a group policy, you may want to change the package's properties, perhaps changing the application's category, deployment type (assign or publish), or security settings. Use the following steps to change these and other settings:

1. In the Group Policy snap-in, double-click the Software Settings folder under either User Configuration or Computer Configuration.

2. Double-click the software package you want to modify.

3. Change the name or view the package information on the General tab of the Properties window.

4. Click the Deployment tab to change how the application is deployed (Figure 24-7).

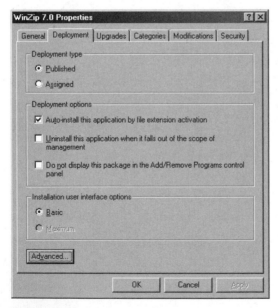

Figure 24-7. *The Deployment tab of a software package's Properties window.*

5. In the Deployment Type area, choose whether you want to assign the application or publish it.

6. Select the Auto-Install This Application By File Extension Activation check box to automatically install the application when a user opens a file associated with the program.

7. Select the Uninstall This Application When It Falls Out Of The Scope Of Management check box to automatically remove the application when the group policy no longer applies to the user or computer.

8. To prevent users from installing or uninstalling the application from Add/Remove Programs, select the Do Not Display This Package In The Add/Remove Programs Control Panel check box.

9. In the Installation User Interface Options section, select Basic to show users only a limited amount of information about the installation progress or select Maximum to display all screens and messages to the user.

10. Click the Advanced button to specify whether previous installations of the product should be uninstalled prior to installation of this product via Group Policy or to force Group Policy to ignore language settings when deploying the package.

11. To assign the application to a category, click the Categories tab, select a category, and click Select. You can assign an application to more than one category.

12. Click the Security tab to assign permissions for the application.

Applying Package Upgrades

Upgrading applications can be a pain for administrators. The new version of Microsoft Office is released and suddenly everyone wants it. In the past, this has often led to version management nightmares when some users couldn't read files created by other users, and managing applications in general was a headache. Fortunately, Microsoft (to name only one vendor) has worked to make this situation better. (For instance, they now change their file formats only when necessary.) Using IntelliMirror's Software Installation and Maintenance features helps a lot, because administrators can better manage the upgrade process. Of course, users of SMS have always had these features available.

When you get a new version of an application, you can start by publishing it (as an upgrade and a full installation) so that users can upgrade to it if they want to. After a period of time, you can assign the application to users, requiring them to either upgrade or install the new version in parallel with the old version. At this time you can also prevent new installations of the old version. Once all users have had a chance to get accustomed to the new version, you can remove the old software package and force it to be uninstalled from users' systems, completing the transition. Use the following procedure to install upgrades. See the section "Removing and Redeploying Packages" later in this chapter for information on how to complete the process and remove obsolete packages.

Tip You may find it useful to apply a transform to the upgrade package—for example, to allow Microsoft Word 97 users simply to upgrade to Microsoft Word 2000 without installing the rest of Office 2000. To do this, see the next section, "Applying Package Modifications."

1. In the Group Policy snap-in, double-click the Software Settings folder under either User Configuration or Computer Configuration.

2. Select the package containing the upgrade, *not* the package containing the previous version. (You'll need to add the upgrade package to the group policy first.)

3. Right-click the upgrade package and choose Properties from the shortcut menu.

4. Click the Upgrades tab and then click Add.

5. In the Add Upgrade Package dialog box (Figure 24-8) indicate whether you want to choose a package to upgrade from the current Group Policy object (GPO) (most likely) or from another GPO.

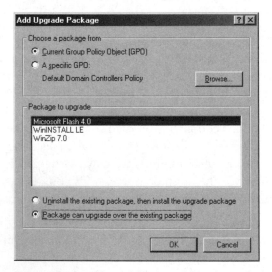

Figure 24-8. *The Add Upgrade Package dialog box.*

6. Select the package you want to upgrade from the list of packages provided.

7. Select the Uninstall The Existing Package, Then Install The Upgrade Package option if you want to completely remove the old application before installing the new version, thus discarding all of the users' settings. (See the Tip that follows these steps for more information on this option.)

   Select the Package Can Upgrade Over The Existing Package option to use the new package to upgrade the older package, preserving the users' settings. Click OK when you're done.

8. On the Upgrades tab (Figure 24-9), use the Add and Remove buttons to add or remove packages that you want the new package to upgrade.

Figure 24-9. *The Properties window for an upgrade package.*

9. Select the Required Upgrade For Existing Packages check box if you want to require users to upgrade to the new package, and click OK when you're finished. The upgrade package is then applied or made available to users and computers at the next logon (for users) or the next reboot (for computers).

Tip Use the Uninstall The Existing Package, Then Install The Upgrade Package option when an upgrade either isn't possible (in the case of upgrading to a different application) or isn't desirable (when the upgrade process works poorly).

Applying Package Modifications

Package modifications, also called transforms, allow you to customize an installation package without completely reauthoring it. For example, instead of offering Office 2000 only in its complete configuration, you may want to offer users the choice to install a subset of the programs installed by default. Without using transforms, you would have to create a completely separate package, consuming an excessive amount of disk space. Instead you can create a transform to simply modify an existing package to your needs, saving disk space and time. Thus, rather than adding two different packages to your group policy for two different configurations of an application, you can add your complete package and then add the complete package a second time with a transform to modify the original package to your specifications. Instead of storing two full-sized packages, your complete package is stored once, with the small transform piggybacking off of it.

Since transforms are merely an easy and efficient way to modify a package for deployment, not a mechanism for allowing a single package to present multiple options to users and administrators, you still need to add the package to your group policy multiple times—once for each configuration you want available to users. Additionally, transforms must be applied at the time you add the package to Group Policy; they cannot be added to currently deployed packages. To create a transform, follow these steps:

1. In the Group Policy snap-in, double-click the Software Settings folder under either User Configuration or Computer Configuration. On the Action menu, point to New and then choose Package from the submenu.

2. Select the package for the application you want to deploy, and click Open. Note that for best results you should use the My Network Places icon to navigate to your package, ensuring that Group Policy learns the network path instead of a local file path.

3. Choose the Advanced Published Or Assigned option from the Deploy Software dialog box, and then click OK.

Tip To see the Deploy Software dialog box in step 4, you must have selected the Display The Deploy Software Dialog Box option in the Software Installation Properties window, as described earlier in the section "Setting Software Installation Options."

4. Click the Modifications tab and then click Add.

5. Use the Open dialog box to select the Windows Installer transform package you want to add.

> **Caution**   Do not click OK in the Properties window until you have configured all settings the way you want them. As soon as you click OK, the package is assigned or published in Active Directory and is immediately deployed, potentially affecting a lot of users. If, after clicking OK, you realize you made a mistake, you can fix it either by upgrading the incorrectly configured package with a correct one or by removing the package from Active Directory and all users.

6. On the Modifications tab, add or remove any additional transforms and place them in the proper order, using the Move Up and Move Down buttons, as shown in Figure 24-10. Transforms at the bottom of the list are applied last and therefore take precedence over earlier transforms because they can overwrite files written by earlier transforms.

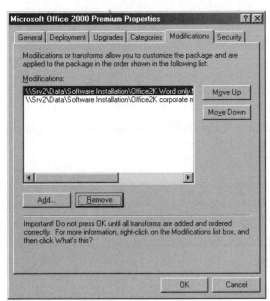

Figure 24-10. *Placing transforms in the correct order.*

7. If necessary, use the Upgrades tab to configure any upgrades, as described earlier in the section "Applying Package Upgrades."

8. Review all tabs of the Properties window to ensure that the settings are correct, and then click OK when you're finished.

Removing and Redeploying Packages

When an application has outlived its usefulness in your company, it's time to remove it from your systems—or at least to stop deploying it on new systems. There are also times when you may want to redeploy an application so that it is reinstalled on all clients. Use the following steps to accomplish these tasks:

1. In the Group Policy snap-in, double-click the Software Settings folder under either User Configuration or Computer Configuration.

2. Right-click the application you want to remove or redeploy, and choose All Tasks from the shortcut menu.

3. To redeploy the application, choose Redeploy Application from the submenu and then click Yes in the next dialog box. To remove the application, choose Remove from the submenu.

4. In the Remove Software dialog box, shown in Figure 24-11, choose the first option if you want to remove the software immediately from all computers in the group policy. Choose the second option to prevent new installations of the software while allowing users who are currently using the software to continue using it and to perform repairs. Click OK.

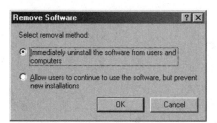

Figure 24-11. *The Remove Software dialog box.*

Repackaging Applications

If you want to deploy an application that doesn't have a native Windows Installer package, you'll probably want to either repackage the application or create your own installation program. Several third-party tools exist that permit you to author your own setup program. This section describes how to repackage applications using Seagate Software's WinInstall LE software package, which is included with Windows 2000 Server. Repackaging applications provides the benefits of the Windows Installer, discussed in the section "Choosing an Installation Package Format" earlier in this chapter.

Real World **Best Practices for Installation**

You can take a number of precautions to minimize problems with the installation package you are creating. If you follow these recommendations, the applications should deploy properly on a wide range of hardware:

- Always create installation packages on a clean computer—that is, on a computer with no software on it except the operating system and operating system service packs. (The computer on which you create an installation package is known as the reference computer.)

- Don't install the Seagate Software Console on the reference computer. By definition, this makes the system "unclean."

- Don't map any drives on the reference computer.

- Roll the computer back to a clean state after every installation by uninstalling the program and using a program such as Reg.exe to restore a clean registry.

- Consider setting up multiple reference computers so that you can be creating an installation package on one while rolling the other back. These computers don't need to be fast or have much hard disk space, so just about any system can be pressed into service for this role.

- If you have to use an unclean computer as a reference computer, make sure that none of the files installed by the programs you're repackaging are already present on the computer—especially .DLL files.

- Close any antivirus programs, and uninstall programs such as CleanSweep (or any other programs that may write data during the repackaging).

- Close all e-mail, word processing, and other programs, and disable any screen saver or other memory-resident programs.

- Don't delete files or drag files to the Recycle Bin during the repackaging process.

Creating the "Before" Snapshot and Installing the Application

The first step in repackaging an application is to take a snapshot of the system state before you install the program. To do this, follow these steps:

1. On the clean reference computer, connect to the server hosting WinInstall LE and launch the Discover (Discoz.exe) program in the \Seagate Software\Wininstall folder, which is placed by default in the %SystemRoot%\Program Files folder.

2. Click Next in the first screen of the WinInstall Discover Wizard.

3. In the first box of the next screen, enter a useful, descriptive name for the application you are installing, as shown in Figure 24-12. Note that this is the name that will be published in Active Directory for users to see.

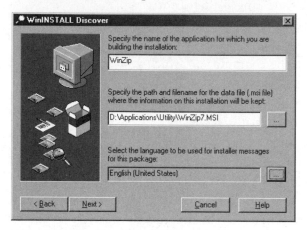

Figure 24-12. *Specifying the application name and path.*

4. In the second box, enter the path and filename where you want to store the package.

5. Click the button next to the third box if you want to change the language that Windows Installer uses for messages to the user, and then click Next.

6. In the next screen, select the drive you want WinInstall to use for temporary files, and then click Next. Note that this drive should have at least 250 MB of free space available and should be a local drive for optimal Discover process speed.

7. For each drive that you expect the program to make changes on, select the drive and click the Add button to add it to the list of drives that Discover will monitor for changes. Click Next when you're done. Since it takes added time to scan each drive, don't add drives that you know will not be modified.

8. In the next window, shown in Figure 24-13, specify any folders that you want to exclude from scanning by selecting them and clicking Add. To exclude specific files or a range of files from the scanning process, click the Files & Wildcard Entries button.

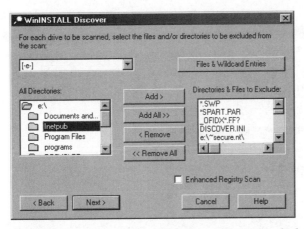

Figure 24-13. *Specifying folders and files to exclude from the scan.*

9. Select the Enhanced Registry Scan check box to be sure that the scanning process picks up all changed registry keys.

Note   For the most reliable packaging results, we recommend not altering the exclusions much or at all. Additionally, we recommend that you always select the Enhanced Registry Scan check box.

10. Click Next when you're finished to start the actual Discover process. WinInstall scans the system in preparation for the program installation.

11. When the Discover process is finished, you see a dialog box asking if you want to run the setup program now. Click OK, locate the setup program, and click Open.

12. Install the program exactly as you want your users to install it. When you're finished, restart the computer.

13. Make any modifications you want to the program, and then continue with the next section to finish repackaging the application.

Creating the "After" Snapshot

After you've created the initial system snapshot and installed the program, you're ready to create the "after" snapshot, which will complete the repackaging process. To do so, follow these steps:

1. Connect to the server hosting WinInstall LE, and launch the Discover (Discoz.exe) program again. You see the screen shown in Figure 24-14.

2. To create the "after" snapshot, select the Perform The 'After' Snapshot Now option and click Next. Discover then compares the system to the "before" snapshot and creates the Windows Installer package.

To abort the repackaging process, select the Abandon The 'Before' Snapshot And Start Over option. This step will allow you to start over and create a new "before" snapshot.

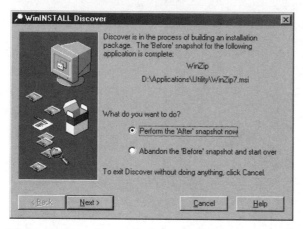

Figure 24-14. *Creating the "after" snapshot.*

3. In the dialog box that shows the results of the repackaging process, click OK, and then click OK in the next dialog box to finish repackaging the application.

Setting Up Remote Installation Services

RIS is a cool new feature of Windows 2000 Server that allows administrators to install Windows 2000 Professional on client computers without ever touching the computer. You can also use RIS with the IntelliMirror technologies (User Settings Management, User Data Management, and Software Installation and Maintenance) to install Windows 2000 Professional remotely and then automatically add a user's personalized work environment—complete with the user's computer settings, software applications, and data.

It's not hard to see the advantages RIS offers to an administrator who is short of both time and money. The sections that follow describe how RIS works, help you

determine whether your network meets the requirements for RIS, and explain how
to install, configure, and use RIS to set up client systems.

> **Note**   If the system doesn't support Preboot Execution Environment (PXE) network
> booting, you may have to insert a RIS boot disk in the system, but otherwise you
> don't have to touch it unless you want to.

How RIS Works

RIS is a combination of technologies that provides the nifty ability to easily boot
a system and install an operating system from a remote server—all without needing any data on the system beforehand.

The first technology that facilitates the ability to install an operating system remotely
is Preboot Execution Environment (PXE). PXE allows a user of a computer with
a PXE-compliant network interface card (NIC) to boot directly from the network
by pressing F12 at bootup.

When the client boots to the network using a PXE-compliant NIC (or a network
boot disk and a NIC that is supported by the disk), it requests an IP address from
a Dynamic Host Configuration Protocol (DHCP) server, which also supplies the
IP address of the nearest RIS server.

When a prestaged client contacts the RIS server, the RIS server queries Active
Directory for the unique GUID for the client and then transmits the name of any
operating system images the client is permitted to install automatically. If the client
isn't prestaged, it must log on to Active Directory and use the Client Installation
Wizard to select an operating system image. (RIS uses Group Policy to determine
which images the user has access to, and it displays only those images.)

RIS Requirements and System Recommendations

RIS servers need to meet the minimum system requirements for Windows 2000
Server and in addition must have a separate 2-GB hard disk or partition for the
operating system images. (You can get by with less if you deploy only a couple

of images.) As was mentioned in Chapter 5, however, you shouldn't be using a system that meets only the minimum system requirements, especially when it comes to RAM. Don't deploy a server with less than 128 MB of RAM, and if you're going to combine services such as Active Directory, DHCP, DNS, and RIS, get 256 MB of RAM or more; the extra cost is small and the performance gain is large. In addition, RIS must be installed on an NTFS 5 formatted partition that is separate from the system partition. RIS doesn't support Dfs links or Encrypting File System (EFS) files.

> **Tip** Operating system images stored on a RIS server can be synchronized with operating system images on other RIS servers via the use of Dfs. However, RIS cannot follow Dfs links, so all needed data and images must be stored locally.

RIS clients also need to meet or preferably exceed the minimum system requirements for Windows 2000 Professional, and in addition should have a 10 Mbps or preferably 100 Mbps NIC that supports PXE remote boot or is explicitly supported by the remote boot disk. (See the section "Creating a Remote Boot Disk" later in this chapter for more information.)

Installing RIS

Before you can use RIS on the network, you need to install it, of course. Once you've chosen the server you want to use as a RIS server, use the following procedure to install the service and run the initial setup wizard:

1. Open Add/Remove Programs from Control Panel, and then click the Add/Remove Windows Components button in the left pane to launch the Windows Components Wizard.

2. Select the Remote Installation Services check box, and then click Next to install it. If Windows prompts you to reboot, reboot the server.

3. Launch Add/Remove Programs again from Control Panel, and click the Configure button next to Configure Remote Installation Services (Figure 24-15).

4. Click Next in the first screen, enter the folder path you want to use as the root for the RIS operating systems, and click Next. Note that the path you enter cannot be on the system partition, and it must be an NTFS 5 formatted partition with enough free disk space for all of the installations. You cannot use a Dfs share either.

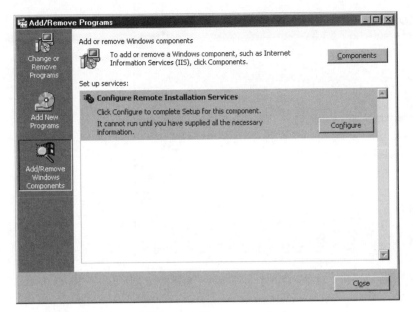

Figure 24-15. *The Add/Remove Programs window.*

5. Select the Respond To Client Computers Requesting Service check box if you want to turn on RIS immediately. Otherwise, select the Do Not Respond To Unknown Client Computers check box to prevent computers not already having a computer account in Active Directory from receiving an operating system installation. (This precaution avoids the potential security risk described in the Real World sidebar "Reasons for Ignoring Unknown Clients" later in this chapter.) Click Next.

6. In the next screen, enter the path to the Windows 2000 Professional installation files, and then click Next.

7. Enter a name for the folder that will store this operating system image, and then click Next.

8. Enter a user-friendly name for the operating system image in the Friendly Description box of the next screen (Figure 24-16). This is the description users will see listed as an operating system choice when they boot their system from the network.

9. Enter a more detailed description of the operating system image in the Help Text box, and click Next. This will supplement the friendly description in helping a user decide which operating system image to install.

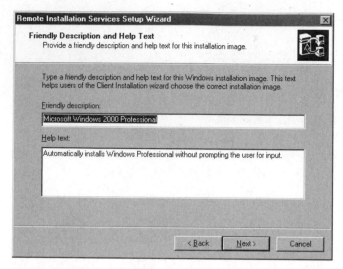

Figure 24-16. *Specifying a friendly description and help text for an operating system image.*

10. Review the settings in the next screen, and then click Finish to set up the server. RIS configures a number of settings and copies the necessary files, and then the service starts, if you chose to enable it, allowing the server to begin serving client requests.

11. If the RIS server isn't already an authorized DHCP server, open the DHCP snap-in.

12. Right-click the DHCP root in the console tree, and choose Manage Authorized Servers from the shortcut menu.

13. Click the Authorize button, enter the IP address for the RIS server in the dialog box, and then click OK.

Configuring and Administering RIS

The Remote Installation Services Setup Wizard does an adequate job of setting up the server with all of the default settings, but sooner or later you're going to need to tweak these settings. The next several sections tell you how.

Tip You can administer most functions of a RIS server from a Windows 2000 Professional system by installing the Windows 2000 Administration Tools (Adminpak.msi) from the i386 folder of the Windows 2000 Server CD-ROM. This tool also allows you to administer most other server services from a Windows 2000 Professional machine.

If all client computers that use RIS to install an operating system are to contain the same settings, all RIS servers need to be configured in exactly the same way. Windows 2000 doesn't support replication of operating system images or RIS configuration settings between RIS servers. You can, however, use the replication capabilities of SMS for image replication between RIS servers.

Enabling or Disabling RIS

To enable the RIS server to respond to client requests or to disable the RIS server from serving client requests, follow these steps:

1. Open the Active Directory Users and Computers console.
2. In the applicable domain and OU, right-click the server hosting RIS and choose Properties from the shortcut menu.
3. Click the Remote Install tab (Figure 24-17).
4. Select the Respond To Client Computers Requesting Service check box if you want to turn on RIS, or clear it if you want to disable RIS.

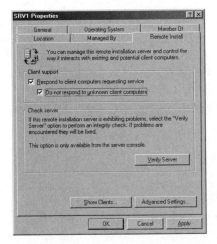

Figure 24-17. *The Remote Install tab of a RIS server's Properties window.*

5. Select the Do Not Respond To Unknown Client Computers check box if you want to prevent computers not already having a computer account in Active Directory from receiving an OS installation.

Real World Reasons for Ignoring Unknown Clients

Selecting the Do Not Respond To Unknown Client Computers check box adds one extra step (creating a computer account for a client) to the process of deploying Windows 2000 Professional, but it does so for a couple of good reasons. The first reason for the added step is security. If this check box isn't selected, anyone who can reach the server can receive an operating system installation, provided that the user has adequate permissions.

The second reason is compatibility with existing remote-boot applications. If you don't select this check box and you are using another company's remote boot/ installation program on the network, clients may not be able to reach the other program. When you clear this check box, you ensure that only prestaged clients with registered computer accounts will use RIS. See the section "Prestaging a Client" later in this chapter for more details.

Verifying Server Functionality

The most reliable way to determine whether a RIS server is working is to attempt an operating system installation from it. However, this is predictably inconvenient, and it's often handy to be able to check on basic functionality directly from whatever computer you're using to manage the server. Microsoft has provided the Check Server Wizard for just this purpose. To use it, follow these steps:

1. Open the Active Directory Users and Computers console.
2. In the applicable domain and OU, right-click the server hosting RIS and choose Properties from the shortcut menu.
3. Click the Remote Install tab.
4. Click the Verify Server button to start the Check Server Wizard.
5. Click Next in the first window, and the wizard checks the server. Read the summary of the test results and click Finish.

Note The Check Server Wizard checks only that the RIS server is properly set up. It doesn't check the integrity of any operating system images on the server or the ability of clients to properly reach the server across the network. If you experience any problems, check the server's event log and check the functionality of the DHCP, DNS, and Active Directory services.

Viewing Clients

You may want to view a list of clients that have used the server to install Windows 2000 Professional or that are prestaged to install Windows 2000 from the server. To do so, follow these steps:

1. Open the Active Directory Users and Computers console.
2. In the applicable domain and OU, right-click the server hosting RIS and choose Properties from the shortcut menu.
3. Click the Remote Install tab.
4. Click the Show Clients button to see a list of clients that have been serviced or that are ready to be serviced by the server.

Changing How Clients Are Configured

You might want to change how RIS configures clients, especially if your company has its own computer naming convention. By default, the computer name is created by appending a number to the user name used to log on to Active Directory during the client installation. This can be changed to another scheme if desired.

The Active Directory location in which the new client computer account is created can also be changed. The default location is in the Computers container in the same domain as the RIS server, but you can change this to the same container as the user's user account (probably the Users container) or to any other location in Active Directory. Note that if an end user will be setting up the computer, the user's account needs to have sufficient permissions to create a new computer account in the specified location, unless the system is prestaged, as described in the section "Prestaging a Client" later in this chapter. To change the way in which RIS configures new clients, use the following procedure:

1. Open the Active Directory Users and Computers console.
2. In the applicable domain and OU, right-click the server hosting RIS and choose Properties from the shortcut menu.
3. Click the Remote Install tab.
4. Click the Advanced Settings button.
5. Select the field you want to use to generate client computer names from the list box, as shown in Figure 24-18, or click the Customize button to create your own computer name format, as shown in Figure 24-19.

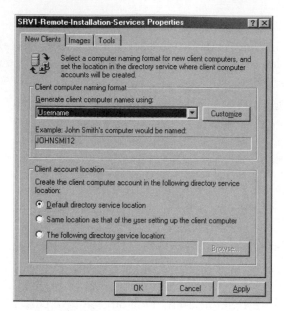

Figure 24-18. *Selecting a predefined computer naming format.*

Tip You can combine several fields when defining a computer naming format. For example, the string %1First%10Last%# would yield computer names using the first letter of a user's first name and then 10 characters from the user's last name, followed by a number, such as JGEREND11.

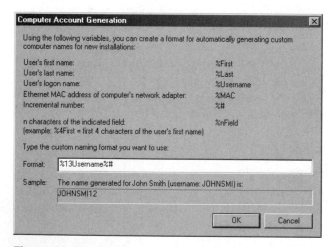

Figure 24-19. *Defining a customized computer naming format.*

6. To create the clients' computer accounts in the default location in Active Directory (the Computers container in the RIS server's domain), select the Default Directory Service Location option on the New Clients tab.

   To create the computer accounts in the same place in Active Directory as the user's user account (probably the Users container), select the Same Location As That Of The User Setting Up The Client Computer option.

   To manually specify a location in Active Directory for the computer accounts, select The Following Directory Service Location, and then click Browse and locate the appropriate container (possibly a RIS Clients container). Click OK when you're done.

Managing Operating System Images

Despite the fact that RIS is able to deploy only Windows 2000 Professional (support for Windows 2000 Server may be added at some point), it is often useful to maintain several different images on the RIS server. You may want to add a completely new image derived from an existing system—applications and all—or you may want to apply an answer file to an existing image to modify how the operating system is set up. (See the section "Using Remote Installation Preparation" later in this chapter for information about creating images of computers, complete with installed applications and other settings.) To manage the images, use the following procedure:

1. Open the Active Directory Users and Computers console.

2. In the applicable domain and OU, right-click the server hosting RIS, choose Properties from the shortcut menu, and then click the Remote Install tab.

3. Click the Advanced Settings button, and then click the Images tab (Figure 24-20).

4. To view or change the friendly description and help text associated with an image, select the image and click Properties. You can also see whether the image is CD-based (flat) or RIPrep-based here.

5. To remove an unattended answer file associated with an operating system image, select the image you want to remove and click Remove.

6. To add an image, click Add. The Add Wizard starts. Note that the Add button doesn't work for RIPrep images and answer files.

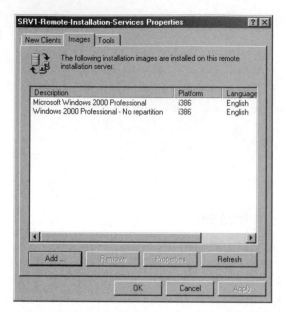

Figure 24-20. *The Images tab of the RIS Properties window.*

7. In the first screen of the wizard, you can specify a new answer file for an existing image by selecting Associate A New Answer File To An Existing Image. This saves the time and space required to make and store a new image. Click Next.

8. To create a new image from the Windows 2000 Professional CD, select the Add A New Installation Image option, and then click Next. Use the Add Installation Image Wizard to create the image and associated answer file, and click Finish when you're done to complete the process.

9. Choose whether you want to use a sample answer file provided by Windows, an answer file from another RIS server, or an answer file you created already in another location. Click Next.

10. If you chose to use an answer file from another server or location, specify the server or location, and then click Next.

11. Select the operating system image to which you want to apply the answer file (Figure 24-21), and then click Next.

Note Back up the answer files before removing them from RIS. To remove an image, not just the associated answer file, open Microsoft Windows Explorer and actually delete the physical folder containing the image.

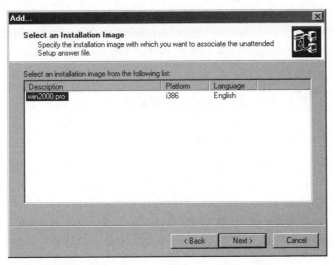

Figure 24-21. *The Select An Installation Image screen of the Add Wizard.*

12. If you chose to use a sample answer file, select the answer file you want to use, and then click Next.

13. Enter a filename for the answer file and then click Next.

14. Enter a user-friendly name for the operating system image in the Friendly Description box of the next screen. This is what users will see as an operating system choice when they boot their system from the network.

15. Enter a more detailed description of the operating system image in the Help Text box. Click Next, review the settings you chose, and click Finish.

Note   RIS doesn't support unattended installs on computers containing ISA or non–Plug and Play devices.

Adding RIS Tools

RIS allows independent software vendors (ISVs) and original equipment manufacturers (OEMs) to add tools that are available to users and administrators for use prior to the installation of the operating system. Since client systems may have blank hard disks before Windows 2000 is installed via RIS, the maintenance and troubleshooting tools provided by some ISVs and OEMs can be extremely useful. These tools can also provide administrators with a handy way to update such things as the client's system BIOS.

RIS doesn't ship with any tools installed, and there is no built-in mechanism for adding tools; instead, you must use the external setup program supplied with the tools to install them. You can then use the Tools tab of the Remote Installation Services dialog box (the previous section described how to display this dialog box) to view the properties for the tools or remove the tools' associated template files (files with the extension .SIF), making the tools unavailable to clients.

Using Remote Installation Preparation

The other way to create an operating system image for deployment with RIS is to use the Remote Installation Preparation (RIPrep) Wizard. RIPrep allows you to create a Windows 2000 Professional installation (complete with applications and settings), image it, and then deploy it using RIS.

Although this technique is very similar to using the System Preparation (SysPrep) tool included with the Windows 2000 Resource Kit in combination with a third-party disk-imaging program, using RIPrep has a couple of advantages. First, the hardware on the client systems can be completely different from that on the reference system, since RIS uses Windows 2000's Plug and Play functionality to perform a complete device scan. SysPrep performs only a partial device scan and still requires systems to have identical mass storage controllers. (See Chapter 5 for more information.)

Second, there is no need to copy the system image to the client's hard disk, since all information is pulled from the RIS server after performing a network boot. In addition, the installation process can be automated to such a degree as to obviate the need for trained supervision of the installation—even most untrained users will have no trouble starting a RIS installation.

Caution   The operating system and all applications and files must be installed in a single boot partition on the C: drive of the reference computer in order for RIPrep to function properly.

To create an operating system image using RIPrep, follow these steps:

1. Install Windows 2000 Professional via RIS on the reference system, using the standard Windows 2000 Professional image.

2. Install any applications that don't use Windows Installer. (Windows Installer applications are better deployed using the Software Installation and Maintenance feature of IntelliMirror.)

3. Configure the system the way you want to deploy it—for example, by changing the color scheme or uninstalling games.

4. Close all applications and stop all services running on the system.

5. Run Riprep.exe from the RIS server's RemoteInstall\Admin\i386 folder. Click Next in the first screen of the Remote Installation Preparation Wizard.

6. Enter the name of the RIS server on which you want to store the image, and then click Next.

7. Enter a name for the folder that will store this operating system image, and then click Next.

8. Enter a user-friendly name for the operating system image in the Friendly Description box of the next screen (Figure 24-22). This is the name users will see listed as an operating system choice when they boot their system from the network.

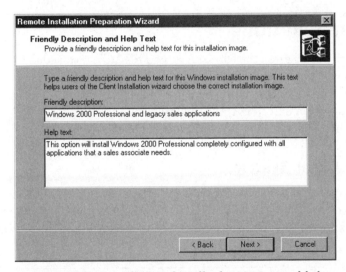

Figure 24-22. *Specifying a friendly description and help text for an installation image.*

9. Enter a more detailed description of the operating system image in the Help Text box. This will provide information to help users decide which operating system image to install. Click Next.

10. In the last screen, review the settings you chose and then click Next.

11. Review the information presented after the image is created, and click Next to copy the image to the RIS server. When this process is complete, the system will shut down. Upon reboot, a mini-setup program will run, preparing the system to create another RIPrep image, if desired.

Real World   Remote Installation Cautions

Make sure that the BIOS on both the reference system and the RIS clients has up-to-date Advanced Configuration Power Interface (ACPI) support with a date of January 1, 1999, or later. RIPrep doesn't support mixing ACPI and non-ACPI systems, and we don't recommend it. Additionally, certain desktop shortcuts may not work properly on RIS clients made from RIPrep images. For example, Microsoft Outlook 2000's desktop shortcut will not work after a RIPrep RIS installation. To fix this, disable 8.3 name creation on the reference computer before running RIPrep. For information on how to do this, consult the Microsoft Knowledge Base. You cannot include encrypted files in a RIPrep image.

Performing User Installations

Once you've installed and configured the RIS servers, you're ready to start deploying systems. While this is in many cases an easy, end-user job, you may need to do a little preparation beforehand, and you must ensure that client systems meet certain prerequisites. This section describes these preparations and, finally, walks you through a sample OS installation, just so you know what to expect.

Prerequisites for Client Systems

A system that is to be used as a RIS client needs to meet the minimum system requirements for Windows 2000 Professional and in addition must have a network card that either supports PXE remote booting or is supported by the remote boot disk.

Note   When installing clients from a RIPrep image, the hard disk is formatted by default into one large partition on the first disk. If you prefer, you can have it create a partition on the first disk that is exactly the same size as the image partition and leave the rest of the disk unpartitioned. To do this, set the UseWholeDisk key in the Riprep.sif file from Yes to No.

Preparing for a Remote Installation

If the RIS client computer has a PXE-compliant network card, you don't have to do anything to prepare for an operating system installation using RIS. If the system doesn't have a PXE-compliant card, you must create a remote boot disk before using RIS. In either case, you can choose to prestage the system by creating a computer account for the system in Active Directory before the installation, allowing the installation to proceed completely automatically, if desired. (Someone will still have to press F12 to boot the computer from the network, but other than that the installation can be automatic.)

Prestaging a Client

You can prestage clients that you plan to set up using RIS by creating managed computer accounts for them in Active Directory. These computer accounts are associated with the client systems' globally unique identifiers (GUIDs) and thus are not prone to theft by rogue clients. Prestaging clients further streamlines the installation process and increases security by eliminating the need for a user to create the computer account for the system via the Client Setup Wizard. To prestage a client, follow these steps:

1. Open the Active Directory Users and Computers console.

2. Open the domain or OU in which you want to create the new computer account.

3. Right-click the container you want to use to store the computer account, point to New on the shortcut menu, and then choose Computer from the submenu.

4. In the New Object - Computer dialog box (Figure 24-23), enter the name you want to assign to the computer in the Computer Name box.

5. Change the computer name used for clients using earlier versions of Windows, if necessary, in the Computer Name (Pre-Windows 2000) box, and then click Next.

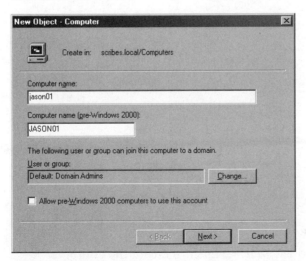

Figure 24-23. *Assigning a name to a new computer.*

6. Select the This Is A Managed Computer check box, and then enter the GUID for the computer in the Computer's Unique ID box, as shown in Figure 24-24. Click Next.

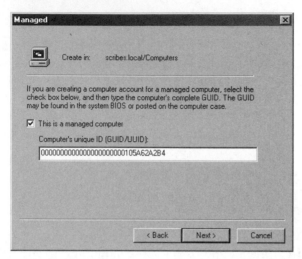

Figure 24-24. *Entering a GUID for a new computer.*

7. In the next screen, choose whether you want the client to be serviced by the RIS server that is nearest and fastest to respond or by a specific RIS server, as shown in Figure 24-25. Click Next.

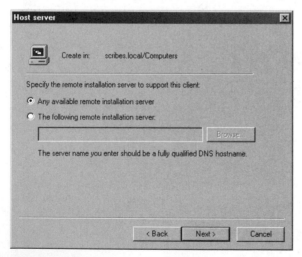

Figure 24-25. *Specifying a RIS server for the client.*

8. Review your settings and then click Finish to create the computer account.

Real World   Working with GUIDs

RIS uses a computer's GUID to keep track of client computers. The GUID comes from the PXE ROM on PXE-enabled network cards or from the network card's MAC address when you boot with the Remote Boot Disk. (In this case it is the MAC address with 24 zeros appended to the beginning of the address.) The computer manufacturer often writes the GUID on a sticker located on or inside the computer's case. It can also be located inside the system BIOS.

If you have trouble finding the GUID, there are a couple ways you can locate it for prestaging clients. The first way is using a network sniffer such as netmon while the client performs a network boot. (RIS clients send their GUID when looking for a RIS server.) A much easier way to deal with this dilemma is to set up a RIS server configured to answer all RIS client requests on a private subnet. (See the "Enabling or Disabling RIS" section earlier in this chapter.) Then connect any clients you want to prestage and have them perform a network boot, login, and select an OS image. Just before the client performs the Windows 2000 installation, a summary screen is shown that displays the GUID, among other things. At this point the client is prestaged in Active Directory (as long as the RIS server you used is part of your Active Directory). You should write down the GUID for future reference.

Creating a Remote Boot Disk

If the client you are configuring doesn't have a NIC that is PXE remote-boot compatible, you need to create a remote boot disk in order to use RIS to install Windows 2000 Professional on the system. To do so, follow these steps:

1. Place a blank, 1.44-MB floppy disk in the computer's floppy drive.

2. Connect to the RIS server and launch Rbfg.exe from the server's \RemoteInstall\Admin\i386 folder.

3. In the Windows 2000 Remote Boot Disk Generator dialog box, select the floppy drive you will use, as shown in Figure 24-26.

4. To view a list of network cards supported by the remote boot disk, click the Adapter List button.

5. Click the Create Disk button to create the disk.

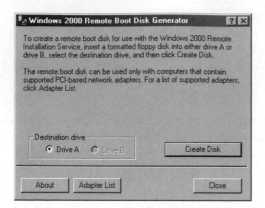

Figure 24-26. *The Windows 2000 Remote Boot Disk Generator dialog box.*

Performing a Remote Operating System Installation

The actual process of installing an operating system remotely is fairly easy, and you may choose to have users do it themselves. We'll walk you through the procedure here, just to cover all bases. To perform a remote OS installation, go to the client system and follow these steps:

1. If you're using a boot disk, place it in the floppy drive, and press F12 when prompted to boot from the network.

2. Press Enter in the first screen to begin the Client Installation Wizard.

3. Enter a valid user name for the domain you're joining in the first box, and then press Tab. If the computer isn't prestaged, make sure that the user account has sufficient privileges to create a new computer account.

4. Enter the password for the account and then press Tab.

5. Enter the DNS name of the domain and then press Enter.

6. Choose either Setup, Custom Setup, Restart a Previous Setup Attempt, or Maintenance and Troubleshooting Tools, and then press Enter. (Some or all of these options may not be available depending on your Group Policy settings, as described in the Tip on the next page.)

7. If you choose to perform a custom setup, enter the computer name and directory service path you want to use for the computer account, and then press Enter.

8. In the next screen, choose the image you want to use and then press Enter.

9. Verify that the settings are correct and then press Enter. Windows 2000 Professional is then installed on the client system.

Tip You can control whether or not clients can perform automated installations or custom setups, gain access to RIS tools, or restart setup in case of a problem by using User Configuration–Windows Settings–Remote Installation Services–Choice Options in Group Policy.

Summary

Windows 2000 provides two important new tools for managing and deploying software on a network: RIS and the Software Installation and Maintenance component of IntelliMirror. RIS allows client systems to boot from across the network and automatically receive and install Windows 2000 Professional, providing a quick, easy, and powerful way to deploy basic or fully configured systems (especially when used in combination with IntelliMirror). Software Installation and Maintenance enhances the Group Policy functionality of Windows 2000 to make it easy to assign or publish applications with native Windows Installer packages or repackaged legacy applications. This allows users to move from computer to computer on the company network and have their applications installed automatically on each computer they use. The next chapter describes how to deploy another type of software management tool—Terminal Services.

Chapter 25
Deploying Terminal Services

Windows Terminal Services was introduced for Microsoft Windows NT 4 Server with the separate Terminal Server Edition, but in Microsoft Windows 2000, it is a fully integrated part of *all* Windows 2000 servers—simply another installable service. You can use Windows Terminal Services as a mechanism to manage and control your servers from anywhere in your enterprise, or you can take advantage of its application server ability to vastly simplify deployment and maintenance of a wide range of applications to a diverse user population.

This chapter covers Windows Terminal Services concepts, requirements, and installation procedures. It also covers three main applications that are used to administer your Terminal Services servers and clients: Terminal Services Manager, Terminal Services Configuration, and Terminal Services Client Creator.

Concepts

Windows Terminal Services is a new concept for many system administrators who expect systems to be essentially single user. It brings true multiuser capability to Windows. UNIX systems have traditionally been primarily multiuser, with a single large server that serves many terminals.

Each user who connects to a Windows 2000 server using Windows Terminal Services is actually using the resources of the server itself, not the particular workstation at which he or she is seated. The user doesn't depend on the speed of the workstation, but rather is actually sharing the processor, RAM, and hard disks of the server itself.

Each user gets his or her own Windows Terminal Services session, and each session is completely isolated from other sessions on the same server. An errant program in one session can cause that session's user to have a problem, but other users are unaffected.

Each user who connects to a Windows 2000 server using Windows Terminal Services is actually functioning as a terminal on that server. Windows Terminal Services supports a wide variety of machines as terminals—from diskless display stations running Microsoft Windows CE entirely in memory, to Microsoft Windows 95/98 workstations, to Windows 2000 servers. The terminal is responsible solely for the console functions: that is, the keyboard, the mouse, and the actual display. All else resides on and is part of the server.

Remote Access

Terminal Services provides an ideal solution for the mobile user who needs to be able to run network-intensive or processor-intensive applications even over a dial-up connection. Because the local machine is responsible only for the actual console, the responsiveness and bandwidth requirements are substantially better compared to trying to run applications across a dial-up line.

Central Management

Because all applications in a Windows Terminal Services session are running on the server, management of sessions and applications is greatly simplified. Any changes to applications or settings need only be made once, on the server, and these changes are seen by all Windows Terminal Services sessions.

In addition, Windows Terminal Services allows an administrator to view what is happening in a user's session, or even to directly control it. Help desk personnel can actually see exactly what the user is seeing without leaving their desks. If the user is configured accordingly, the help desk person can share control of the session, walking the user through a difficult problem.

When configured in remote administration mode, Windows Terminal Services can also be used as a management tool. When enabled in this mode, administrators can log on directly to the machine from their desktops to perform normal system maintenance without having to sit at the server console. This is a powerful addition to the administrator's repertoire, enabling direct control of all servers without having to leave the desktop. Every system administrator will probably enable the remote administration mode of all of their servers. The overhead on the server is minimal compared to the benefits.

Requirements

Windows Terminal Services can be installed on any machine that supports Windows 2000 Server. It requires approximately 14 MB of additional hard disk space to host the client installation files, but otherwise no additional space for the operating system. However, the real requirements are substantially higher for a machine that will be used with Windows Terminal Services in application server mode. Since each user will be executing his or her programs on the server itself, you need to determine exactly how your users work and what their real requirements are. Each installation will be different, but we can provide some guidelines to help you size your server appropriately.

RAM

Each session on the Windows Terminal Services server will use a minimum of approximately 20 MB of RAM for that session just to log on. Add to this any RAM required to run the programs that each session launches. A typical user running Microsoft Outlook, Microsoft Word, and Microsoft Excel while connecting to the Internet will use approximately 40 MB of RAM, or approximately 20 MB beyond what the session itself requires. However, a power user can easily use twice that amount, while developers or other extreme users can go even farther.

CPU

Predicting exactly how much CPU power will be required per user is difficult, since each user has a different mix of applications. But a Pentium II processor running at 400 MHz should be able to support between 15 and 30 users depending on the type of user and assuming sufficient RAM is available to prevent excessive swapping.

Network Utilization

Typical network utilization depends on the type of client and the level of graphics being transmitted (an 800-by-600 connection takes a lot less bandwidth to support than a 1280-by-1024 connection), but the average bandwidth per user should work out to somewhere between 2 and 6 Kbps.

Capacity Planning

The figures just mentioned should give you some starting points to plan your Terminal Services implementation, but the ultimate capacity your implementation will require depends on *your* situation and scenario. Use these figures only as a starting point for your own planning. You should create a test environment that mimics your ultimate implementation on a smaller scale with real users and real applications to gather your own data. Some of the factors that play a major role in the requirements of your terminal services implementation are as follows:

- Which applications do your users run? Do they use a single dedicated application or a wide variety of essentially standard applications?

- Are your users primarily performing a single, routine task, or are they knowledge workers using the computer as their primary tool?

- Are your users all connected via a LAN, or are they a mix of WAN, LAN, and mobile users?

Installation

Installing Windows Terminal Services is simply a matter of selecting the Terminal Services option in the Windows 2000 Server Setup dialog box during the initial installation of Windows 2000 Server or adding the service after the installation of Windows 2000 Server is complete, using the Windows Components Wizard. If you elect to add Terminal Services after the initial installation, however, you should do it before you install any applications on the server if you expect to use the server as an application server. If you're installing Terminal Services only in administrative mode, the timing is less important, but it's still best to add Terminal Services as soon as possible after the initial installation.

Installation of Terminal Services at Windows 2000 Install

To install Windows Terminal Services during the initial installation of Windows 2000 Server, you need to do a nonupgrade install, unless you're upgrading from a Windows NT 4 Terminal Server Edition installation. If you do a fresh install, you will have an opportunity to change the Windows components that are installed just after you give the machine a name and initial Administrator password. Select Terminal Services from the list of components. If the machine you'll be installing Terminal Services on is also going to be a domain controller, you can install Terminal Services Licensing as well.

Real World **Installing the Minimum**

Many system administrators prefer to initially install only the bare minimum operating system on any machine. This practice limits your risk, improves the likelihood that you'll have a successful install, and lets you isolate problem-causing portions of the operating system as they are installed. If you're installing Terminal Services on a machine and you like to use this technique for your installations, you can delay the addition of Terminal Services until after the base operating system has been installed. But you should install Terminal Services as soon after you have the machine up and running as is practical.

The Terminal Services component of Windows 2000 Server requires approximately 14 MB of hard disk space, but this is strictly for the client installation-creator files. Terminal Services itself requires essentially no additional space for the operating system. However, each user who connects using Terminal Services will require a minimum of about 400 KB of disk space for his or her profile (and many users will require a lot more space) and whatever storage space he or she uses on the server.

Installation of Terminal Services After Initial Installation

You can add Windows Terminal Services after the initial installation of Windows 2000 Server. You can use the Configure Your Server Wizard if you want or simply open Add/Remove Programs in the Control Panel. In either case, you should install Windows Terminal Services as soon after installing Windows 2000 as is practical. To install Terminal Services using Control Panel:

1. Open Add/Remove Programs from Control Panel.
2. Click Add/Remove Windows Components in the left pane of the dialog box to open the Windows Components Wizard.
3. Select Terminal Services from the list of Windows components available, shown in Figure 25-1. Don't make any changes to other settings in this wizard unless you are adding or removing other components.

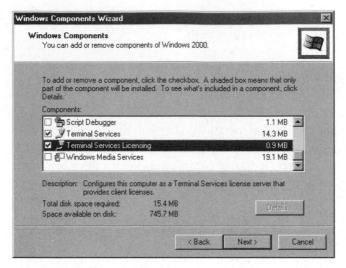

Figure 25-1. *The Windows Components screen of the Windows Components Wizard.*

4. You can also select Terminal Services Licensing if this machine is destined to be a domain controller. When you've made your selections, click Next to select the appropriate mode for Terminal Services, either Remote Administration Mode or Application Server Mode, shown in Figure 25-2. (If you opted to install Terminal Services Licensing, click Next to display the Terminal Services Licensing Setup screen; make any necessary changes.) Click Next and Windows 2000 will start the configuration process.

Real World   Adding and Removing Multiple Components

The temptation to install more than one application or add multiple components to Windows 2000 at a single pass is great. Knowing that you may have to reboot the machine for each of the applications, wouldn't it be easier to simply add everything at once, stacking up your reboots and saving time? Unless this is a very familiar software and machine configuration that you've done repeatedly, *resist the temptation*. Yes, you'll save some time if everything goes right, but it's much harder to troubleshoot a problem if you've changed multiple components at once, and it's a lot tougher to recover to a known stable state.

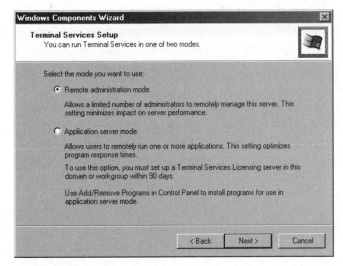

Figure 25-2. *The Terminal Services Setup screen of the Windows Components Wizard.*

5. You will be prompted to insert your original Windows 2000 Server CD-ROM. If the necessary files are found in a different location, go ahead and click OK anyway. You'll get an opportunity to choose a different location from the default.

6. Click the Finish button once the additional files are loaded. Then you'll be prompted for a reboot. The changes you've made won't become effective until after that reboot.

Installing Programs

Installing programs on a Windows 2000 server with Terminal Services installed in remote administration mode is no different from installing on a server without Terminal Services. No special steps are required, and no changes to the installation process or special compatibility scripts to support applications are required. If the application will install and run under Windows 2000 Server, it should install and run with Terminal Services installed in remote administration mode.

On the other hand, installing programs on a Windows 2000 server with Terminal Services installed in application server mode is a different kettle of fish. When you activate the application server mode, Windows 2000 knows it must be pre-pared to deal with multiple users accessing the same application running simul-taneously in separate memory spaces without interference or crossover. You must carefully follow the steps required to ensure that the application is installed cor-rectly and that it will function correctly as a multiuser application.

Not all applications will install successfully, and of those applications that are supported and that will install successfully, some will require special steps or they may have special compatibility scripts that need to be run. Consult the documen-tation for the given application. You may want to look at the site that VeriTest maintains at *http://www.veritest.com*, which lists applications that have been tested for use in a Terminal Services environment.

Install Mode vs. Execute Mode

Windows 2000 Server, when configured as a Terminal Services Application Ser-ver, has two separate and distinct modes of operation—install mode and execute mode. To install an application on a server, you must be in install mode or it will not be installed correctly.

Windows 2000 is usually smart enough to recognize when you are running an installation program and will refuse to allow you to install it while the server is in execute mode. If, for example, you double-click an application's setup program, you'll get a message box like that shown in Figure 25-3.

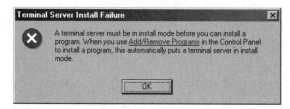

Figure 25-3. *The Terminal Server Install Failure dialog box.*

Unfortunately, this protection mechanism does *not* always work when you sim-ply insert a CD into your CD-ROM drive; often, the installation program auto-matically starts. Allowing a CD to autoplay will sometimes bypass the recognition algorithm and attempt to actually install the program, usually for those CDs that have front-end menus that are called something other than Setup.exe.

You can change to install mode in either of two ways: by using the Change command on the command line or by using Add/Remove Programs in Control Panel. In general, it's best to use Add/Remove Programs, but when you need to script an installation, you'll need to use the command-line version.

Using Add/Remove Programs to Install Applications   Generally, installing new applications from the server's console is best, although this isn't absolutely required for most applications. Wherever you run the installation from, however, you should make sure that all users are logged off the terminal server before beginning installation. To install a program using Add/Remove Programs, follow these steps:

1. Open Add/Remove Programs from Control Panel.

2. Click Add New Programs and then click CD Or Floppy to display the Install Program From Floppy Disk Or CD-ROM dialog box shown in Figure 25-4. Click Next.

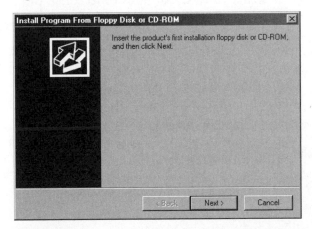

Figure 25-4. *The Install Program From Floppy Disk Or CD-ROM dialog box.*

3. The Run Installation Program dialog box shown in Figure 25-5 opens. If Windows 2000 is able to find the setup program, you'll see it already highlighted in the Open box. But if you're installing from a network drive or Windows 2000 can't locate it for some other reason, use the Browse button to locate the installation program for the application you're installing.

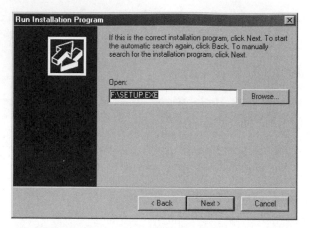

Figure 25-5. *The Run Installation Program dialog box.*

4. When you have highlighted the correct setup program in the box, click Next to begin the installation. While the installation is proceeding, the After Installation dialog box will remain open in the background.

5. Once the installation has completed, whether successfully or not, do *not* accept an immediate reboot if you have a choice and the application requires one. Finish the installation and then return to the After Installation dialog box. Click Next to get to the final dialog box shown in Figure 25-6 and then click Finish. If your application requires a reboot, you can do it now.

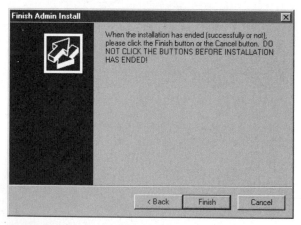

Figure 25-6. *The Finish Admin Install window.*

The Change Command

The Change command was introduced in Windows NT 4 Terminal Server Edition and is available in Windows 2000 Server only when you have Terminal Services installed. The Change command allows you to change between user modes (install and execute), reassign port mappings for Terminal Services sessions, and enable or disable logons to Terminal Services. The three basic commands, and their options for the Change command, are as follows:

1. **Change User**   Initiates change between install or execute mode when running as an application server. Options are:
   - **Install**   Installs new applications on the server for multiuser access
   - **Execute**   Allows programs to be executed in multiuser mode (the default value on startup)
   - **Query**   Displays the current user mode

2. **Change Port**   Changes the port assignments of COM port mappings for MS-DOS compatibility. Options are:
   - **portx=porty**   Maps port X to port Y
   - **/D portx**   Deletes the current mapping for port X
   - **Query**   Displays the current port mappings

3. **Change Logon**   Enables or disables logon sessions. Options are:
   - **Enable**   Allows users to log on from Terminal Services sessions
   - **Disable**   Prohibits users from initiating logon sessions (Current sessions aren't disconnected or terminated.)
   - **Query**   Displays the current logon status

Using the Change Command to Install an Application   You can also install new applications into Windows Terminal Services using the Change command. This is especially useful for scripting installations that will be installed on multiple terminal servers in an identical configuration. To install a new application using the Change command, follow these steps:

1. Disable new logons to the server by typing *change logon /disable*.

2. Find out which users are currently logged on to the server and what their session IDs are by typing *query session*.

3. Warn the users that they will need to log off their current session by typing *net send * "message"*.

4. Reset sessions of users that are currently logged on to the server with the command *reset session <sessionID>*.

5. Change to install mode with the command *change user /install*.

6. Run the application's setup or installation program.

7. Change back to execute mode by typing *change user /execute*.

8. Reenable logons to the server with *change logon /enable*.

As you can see, using the Change command, along with other command-line utilities included with Windows 2000, enables you to easily script the installation of a program to Windows Terminal Services. In large organizations where multiple terminal servers are being used to support large user populations, using command-line utilities easily ensures that applications are installed uniformly across the enterprise, simplifying support and training.

Installing Office 2000

Installing Microsoft Office 2000 on a Windows 2000 server that is running in application server mode requires special considerations. Like many applications that are essentially designed as single-user applications, you need to adjust settings to prevent corruption of user-specific data when the application is run in a multiuser environment.

You need a portion of the Office 2000 Resource Kit to install Office 2000 for use on a Windows 2000 Terminal Services server. You need to install the core tools portion of the kit, which you can download from *http://www.microsoft.com/office/ork/2000/appndx/toolbox.htm*. Once installed, run Add/Remove Programs to install Office 2000 as follows:

1. Log on to the server console with an account that has administrative privileges. The installation won't run from within a Terminal Services session.

2. Open Add/Remove Programs from Control Panel. Click Add New Programs and then click the CD Or Floppy button.

3. If the setup program for Office 2000 isn't found automatically, use the Browse button to locate it. Once the setup program is shown, a dialog box will appear similar to that shown in Figure 25-7.

4. Modify the command line shown to add TRANSFORMS="<PATH>\termsrvr.mst" at the end. Replace the <PATH> portion with the path of the Terminal Services Tools installation from the Office 2000 Resource

Kit. The default location of this file is C:\Program Files\ORKTools\ToolBox\Tools\Terminal Server Tools\termsrvr.mst, but feel free to move the file to an easier-to-type location. Click Next to begin the installation.

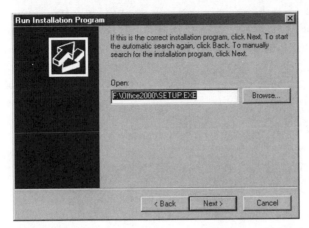

Figure 25-7. *The Run Installation Program dialog box.*

5. When the installation has completed, close the After Installation dialog box by clicking Next and then Finish.

The special Office 2000 installation is one example of the compatibility scripts that many applications require to run correctly in Terminal Services.

Administration

Windows Terminal Services can be centrally administered and configured across your domain from a single console. Four main applications are used to administer your Terminal Services servers and clients:

- **Terminal Services Manager** Monitors and controls the connections to all of the Terminal Services servers on your network
- **Terminal Services Configuration** Runs only locally on each terminal server; a Microsoft Management Console (MMC) snap-in that lets you modify the configuration of the local Terminal Services server.
- **Terminal Services Client Creator** Makes Terminal Services Client disks
- **Terminal Services Licensing** Manages Client Access Licenses for Terminal Services across the domain or workgroup

Terminal Services Manager

Terminal Services Manager (Tsadmin.exe) is the main mechanism for managing the various connections to your servers. A typical Terminal Services Manager window is shown in Figure 25-8. From here you can see not only the available terminal servers on your network, but also who is connected to them, which sessions are active, which protocols are being used, and so on.

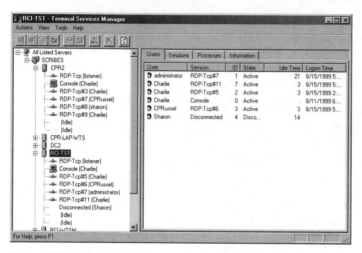

Figure 25-8. *A typical Terminal Services Manager window.*

Overview

Terminal Services Manager shows all of the servers in your domain. By default, it connects to only a single server at a time, although you can opt to connect to all of the available servers at once. The icons for the current active connection, server, and domain are shown in a different color (green, by default). With Terminal Services Manager, you can view and manage the users, sessions, and processes by network, domain, server, or connection, giving you a comprehensive look at the critical information for your Terminal Services deployment.

Finding Servers

You can use Terminal Services Manager to identify all of the servers in your network that are currently active or all of the servers in a particular domain. To find all the servers in a domain, right-click the domain name in the left pane of Terminal Services Manager and select Find Servers In Domain. To find all the servers on your network, right-click All Listed Servers and choose Find Servers In All Domains, shown in Figure 25-9.

Caution   Using either of the Find Servers commands causes a domain-wide or network-wide series of broadcast messages. Use this command with caution.

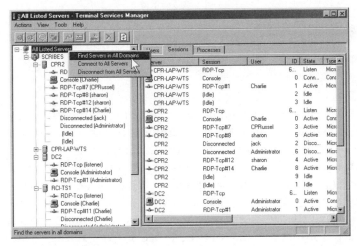

Figure 25-9. *The shortcut menu for All Listed Servers in the Terminal Services Manager window.*

Making Connections

To manage the processes, sessions, and users connected to a given server, you need to first connect to that server using Terminal Services Manager. To connect to a server, right-click the server's icon in the left pane of Terminal Services Manager and choose Connect. To connect to all the servers in a domain, right-click the domain name in the left pane of Terminal Services Manager, shown in Figure 25-10, and choose Connect To All Servers In Domain. To connect to all the servers on your network, right-click the All Listed Servers icon and choose Connect To All Servers.

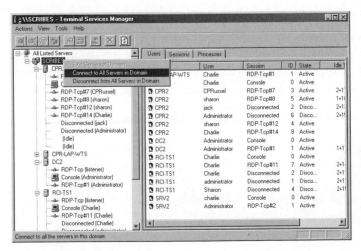

Figure 25-10. *Connecting to all servers in a domain.*

Caution Connecting to all the servers in a domain or network is a network-intensive process and can seriously deteriorate network performance. Under normal circumstances, you should connect only to an individual server.

Managing Connections

Terminal Services Manager lets you view and manage each of the connections to your terminal servers, including locally logged on connections that show as a console session. From any nonconsole session that has sufficient permissions, you can forcibly disconnect a session, reset a session entirely, log off a session, view the status of the connection, manage users' sessions, send a message to the display of a connection, use remote control to take control of a session on the connection, and connect to any other session. You can also use Terminal Services Manager to see a variety of information about the processes and status of the connections to a server and even to kill a hung process.

Note Within a console session, the only feature available is Send Message. This makes managing your servers from one of their consoles difficult. If your normal workstation is, in fact, the console of one of your servers, open a terminal session to your own server and work from that—you'll have full capability to manage and control your Terminal Services environment from there.

Disconnecting Sessions   When a session is disconnected, all the programs of that session continue to run but the input and output from the session are no longer transmitted to the remote terminal. Disconnecting a session leaves user programs and data in their normal state, protecting them from loss of data. Disconnecting a session doesn't release memory or other resources from the server, and the session continues to be counted as a licensed session.

Any user can disconnect his or her own session, or an administrator with the Full Control privilege can disconnect a session. To disconnect a session using Terminal Services Manager, right-click the session in either pane of Terminal Services Manager and choose Disconnect from the shortcut menu. You'll be prompted for confirmation, as shown in Figure 25-11. Click OK and the session will be disconnected.

Figure 25-11. *Confirming disconnection of a session.*

You can disconnect multiple sessions on multiple servers as well. Simply highlight the sessions in the right pane of Terminal Services Manager and right-click. Choose Disconnect from the menu, click OK in the prompt shown in Figure 25-11, and the sessions will be disconnected. The console where the sessions are being displayed will receive a message like that shown in Figure 25-12. When you click Close in the message, the message box will disappear.

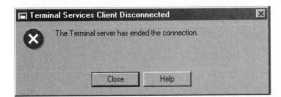

Figure 25-12. *The Terminal Services Client Disconnected message box.*

Real World   Using Disconnect to Manage Your Sessions from Multiple Locations

Disconnecting from a Terminal Services session has a lot of advantages for the mobile user who may need to connect from a different location or who wants to be able to work in relatively short bursts as time permits. When you disconnect from a session, everything continues to run, just as if you were connected. So when you reconnect to the same server, the session is restored exactly as you left it. Then you can easily return to a project or document exactly where you left off.

Resetting Sessions   You can reset a session if the session is your own or if you have the Full Control privilege for sessions. When you reset a session, all work in that session is lost, programs stop running, and memory is freed. To reset a session, right-click the session and choose Reset from the menu. You'll get a warning message. Click OK and the session will be reset.

You can reset multiple sessions by highlighting them in the right pane of Terminal Services Manager, right-clicking them, and selecting Reset. You must have the Full Control privilege for each of these sessions, or they must be your own.

Caution   Resetting a session can result in data loss for the user of that session. You should reset a session only when the session has stopped responding or has otherwise malfunctioned.

Logging Off a Session You can log off your own session or log off a user's session if you have the Full Control privilege. Right-click the session in the right pane of Terminal Services Manager and select Log Off from the shortcut menu, shown in Figure 25-13. You'll get a warning that the user's session will be logged off. If you click OK, the session will be logged off. Logging off a session will free up any resources used by that session, returning them for use by other connections.

Caution Logging off a session can result in data loss for users of that session. You should always warn users by sending them a message before logging off their session.

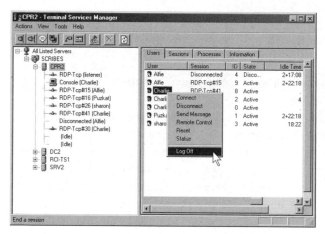

Figure 25-13. *The shortcut menu for the Users tab of Terminal Services Manager.*

Viewing Processes and Other Information About a Session You can view the active processes in a session and a variety of other information about the session, including which client the session is coming from, the security level, the session resolution, and so forth. To view the active processes in a session, highlight the session in the left pane of Terminal Services Manager and click the Processes tab in the right pane, as shown in Figure 25-14. To view information about the same session, click the Information tab in the right pane, as shown in Figure 25-15.

You can also use Terminal Services Manager to show all the processes, users, and sessions on a given server, for the whole domain, or for the entire network. The Processes tab is shown in Figure 25-16 for the entire Scribes domain. You can sort the processes by user, session, or server. If you have the Full Control privilege, you can even kill a process from here, although the usual caveats about killing processes apply.

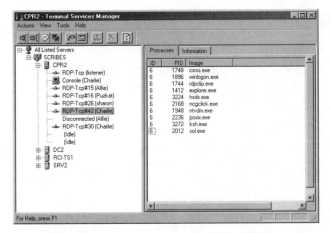

Figure 25-14. *The Processes tab of Terminal Services Manager.*

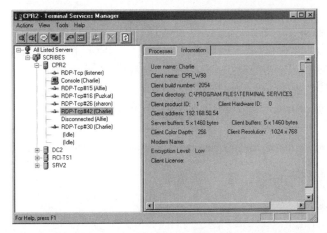

Figure 25-15. *The Information tab of Terminal Services Manager.*

Managing User Sessions   You can use Terminal Services Manager to view and manage the user sessions on a particular server or across the entire domain or network. To view all of the users across your entire domain, highlight the domain name in the left pane of Terminal Services Manager and click the Users tab in the right pane. In the left pane, you'll see a list of all the servers in the domain, and the connected users appear in the right pane. You can select any entry in the right pane and send a message to the user's session, disconnect the session, or take control of the user's session for troubleshooting or training.

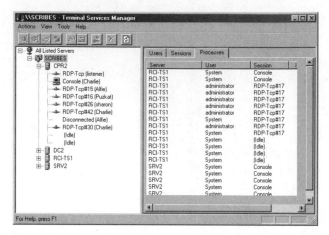

Figure 25-16. *The Processes tab for the entire Scribes domain in Terminal Services Manager.*

Sending a Message to a Session   You can use Terminal Services Manager to send a message to a particular session. To send a message to all of the sessions on a particular server, however, you need to use the command-line Msg program. To send a message to a particular session or user, follow these steps:

1. Right-click the session or user in the right pane of Terminal Services Manager.

2. Choose Send Message to open the dialog box shown in Figure 25-17.

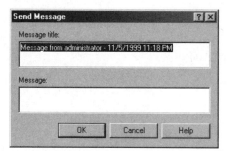

Figure 25-17. *The Send Message dialog box of Terminal Services Manager.*

3. Type in the message you want to send. Press Ctrl+Enter to start a new line.

4. Click OK to send the message.

You can also use the command-line Msg command to send a message to a particular session or to all the users on a particular server. The Msg command has additional options and functionality over the graphical Terminal Services Manager messaging. The syntax for the Msg command is as follows:

```
msg {username|sessionname|sessionid|@filename|*}
[/SERVER:servername] [/TIME:seconds] [/V] [/W] [message text]
```

The options for the Msg command are as follows:

- *username*   Sends the message to a particular user on the server.
- *sessionname*   Sends a message to a particular session, identified by the session name.
- *sessionid*   Sends a message to a particular session identified by session ID.
- *@filename*   Sends a message to a list of usernames, sessionnames, or sessionids contained in the file.
- *   Sends a message to all users connected to the server.
- **/SERVER:***servername*   Specifies the server to which the session or user is connected. The default is the current server.
- **/TIME:***seconds*   Specifies the number of seconds to wait for the recipients to acknowledge the message. If the message isn't acknowledged in the time specified, it will go away. The default time is 60 seconds if no /TIME option overrides the default.
- **/V**   Displays information back to your command line about the actions being performed on the server.
- **/W**   Waits for a response from the user before returning control to the command line. If no response is received before the message times out, control is returned when it times out.
- *message text*   Specifies the message to send. If none is specified, the text is accepted from STDIN or you will be prompted for the text.

Controlling a Session   If you have appropriate permission (Full Control), you can connect to another user's session and remotely control it. The keyboard, mouse, and display will be the same for both your session and the user's session. This gives you the ability to easily troubleshoot a user's session or train the user by walking him or her through the steps of a particular task. Input for the session comes equally from your session and the user's. If the user or protocol settings are set to view only the session, not directly control it, you will see only what the user does on his or her screen, but you won't be able to interact with it using your mouse or keyboard.

By default, when you connect to a user's session using remote control, the user will be notified that you are connecting and asked to confirm the permission. This notification can be turned off on a per-user basis by modifying the user's account in Active Directory. (See Chapter 9 for more on user accounts.) You can also configure this notification on a per-protocol basis for a given server using Terminal Services Configuration (explained shortly).To take control of a user's session, follow these steps:

1. Right-click the session or user in the right pane of Terminal Services Manager.

2. Choose Remote Control to open the dialog box shown in Figure 25-18. Select an appropriate hot key that will terminate the remote session. The default is Ctrl+*, where the asterisk symbol (*) is from the numeric keypad.

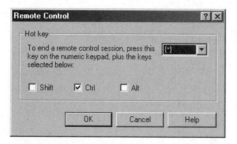

Figure 25-18. *The Remote Control dialog box.*

3. The dialog box shown in Figure 25-19 will appear to the user, requesting permission to allow you to connect, while a dialog box opens on your session advising you that your session is waiting to establish control. If permission isn't required for this protocol or user, the user won't get a message at all.

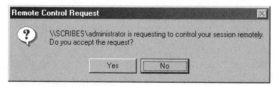

Figure 25-19. *The Remote Control Request dialog box.*

Until the user confirms permission to connect to his or her session, your session will appear to freeze.

You can also use the Shadow command to take control of a user's session. The Shadow command has the following syntax:

```
shadow {sessionname|sessionid} [/SERVER:servername] [/V]
```

where *sessionname* and *sessionid* identify the particular session you want to take control of, and the server defaults to the current server if /SERVER isn't specified. The /V (verbose) option gives additional information about the actions being performed.

Connecting to a Session   You can connect to another session on the server you are on if you have the appropriate permission and the other session is either in an active or a disconnected state. You can always connect to a session that is logged on with the same user account as your current logon, or you can connect to another user's session if you have Full Control or User Access permission. You will be prompted for the user's password.

This ability to connect to another session can be a useful tool for both administrators and users. Get home and realize you forgot to finish off that important memo? Log on remotely and connect to your working session at the office and pick up right where you left off. To connect to a session, follow these steps:

1. Right-click the session or user in the right pane of Terminal Services Manager.
2. Choose Connect to connect to the session. If the session is that of a different user than your current user, you'll be prompted for the target session user's password, as shown in Figure 25-20. If the session is one of your own, you'll be switched to that session and your current session will be disconnected.

Figure 25-20. *The Connect Password Required dialog box.*

Note   You can connect to another session only from a Terminal Services session. You can't connect to or from a console session.

Terminal Services Configuration

Use the Terminal Services Configuration MMC to change the settings for all connections to a particular server (Figure 25-21). From here, you can change any of the settings listed below.

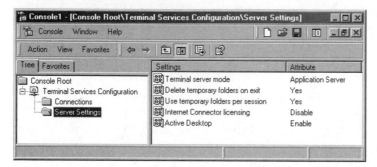

Figure 25-21. *The Terminal Services Configuration MMC.*

- **Terminal Server Mode**   Displays whether Terminal Services is running in application server mode or remote administration mode. Changes to the Terminal Services modes aren't made from here, but from Add/ Remove Programs in Control Panel. (This can be a bit disconcerting at first. To display the Terminal Services Setup window, you must click Add/Remove Windows Components. Then, in the Windows Components dialog box, make no selections and click Next. Now you can select the desired Windows Terminal Services mode.)

- **Delete Temporary Folders On Exit**   When enabled, automatically deletes any temporary folders created on the server when the user logs off. Default is true (Yes).

- **Use Temporary Folders Per Session**   When enabled, each session gets its own set of temporary folders. Default is true (Yes).

- **Internet Connector Licensing**   When enabled, Internet Connector allows up to 200 anonymous concurrent connections over the Internet. All users connecting via Internet Connector must be nonemployees.

This setting is available only when running in application server mode. The default is false (Disable). Note that a separately purchased Internet Connector License must be installed before this option can be enabled.

- **Active Desktop**   When enabled, user connections are permitted to use Active Desktop. Set this option to disabled to reduce the amount of resources and bandwidth required for Terminal Services sessions.

Connection Properties

You can change the properties of the connections from Terminal Services Configuration. By default, the only connection protocol installed is Microsoft Remote Data Protocol (RDP) 5. Other protocols are available from third parties, including the Independent Computing Architecture (ICA) protocol used by Citrix MetaFrame. All protocols can be configured from this point.

RDP allows you to configure a wide variety of settings for each server (listed in Table 25-1). Most of these settings are normally controlled by the client, or you can set the server to override the client settings. To set properties for the RDP connections, double-click the RDP-Tcp entry under Connection to open the dialog box shown in Figure 25-22.

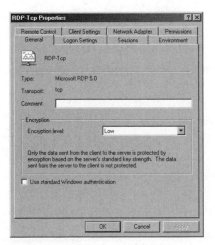

Figure 25-22. *The RDP-Tcp Properties window.*

Table 25-1. **Terminal Services Configuration settings for RDP**

Tab	Property	Setting	Meaning
General	Encryption Level	Low	Data from client to server is encrypted using the standard encryption key.
		Medium	Data is encrypted using the standard key in both directions.
		High	Data is encrypted in both directions using the maximum key length supported.
	Use Standard Windows Authentication	False	Uses alternate authentication package if installed.
Logon Settings	Use Client-Provided Logon Information	True	Client determines the logon security user.
	Always Use The Following Logon Information	False	Logon information for all clients uses this same logon information.
	Always Prompt For Password	False	Client can use embedded password.
Sessions	Override User Settings: (disconnected, active, and idle sessions)	False	User settings control termination of disconnected sessions, active session limit, and idle session limit.
		True	Session limits are controlled by the server.
	Override User Settings: (session limit action)	False	User settings control session limit behavior.
		True	Server settings control session limit behavior—disconnect or end the session.
	Override User Settings (reconnection)	False	User settings control reconnection.
		True	Server settings control reconnection.
Environment	Initial Program	False	Client specifies initial program.
		True	All clients are forced to run the program specified.

Table 25-1.   *continued*

Tab	Property	Setting	Meaning
	Client Wallpaper	Disable	Disallows wallpaper on user desktop.
		Enable	User can display wallpaper on his or her desktop.
Remote Control	Use Remote Control With Default User Settings	True	Settings for remote control are set as part of the user's account data.
	Do Not Allow Remote Control	False	All remote control to sessions on the server is disabled.
	Use Remote Control With The Following Settings	False	When true, you will override remote control settings for all users connecting to the server.
Client Settings	Use Connection Settings From User Settings	True	Printer and drive connections are specified as part of the user's account settings.
	Drive Mapping	Selected	Users aren't permitted to map drives. (Requires ICA protocol.)
	Windows Printer Mapping	Not selected	Clients can map Windows printers, and mappings are remembered.
	LPT Port Mapping	Selected	Automatic mapping of client LPT ports is disabled.
	COM Port Mapping	Selected	Clients can't map printers to COM ports.
	Clipboard Mapping	Not selected	Clients can map clipboard.
	Audio Mapping	Selected	Clients can't map audio. (Requires ICA protocol.)
Network Adapter	Network Adapter	All	All available network adapters are configured for use with this protocol.
	Connections	Unlimited	There is no limit to the number of connections permitted.
		Maximum	The maximum number of connections permitted via this adapter.
Permissions	Full Control	Administrators/ SYSTEM	Administrators and SYSTEM have Full Control privilege.
	User Access	Users	Query, Logon, Message, and Connect privileges.
	Guest Access	Guests	Logon privileges only.

Terminal Services Client Creator

You can create client disks for Windows 2000, Windows NT (x86 and Alpha), Windows 95/98, or Microsoft Windows for Workgroups 3.11. Other clients will require the ICA protocol and you'll need to have Citrix MetaFrame to create client disks for them.

The 32-bit clients require two 3.5 inch 1.44 MB floppy disks, while the Windows for Workgroups clients require four floppy disks. You can use already formatted floppy disks, or the client creator program can format them for you. To create Windows Terminal Services Client floppy disks, follow these steps:

1. Choose the Terminal Services Client Creator program from the Administrative Tools folder on the Programs menu. This will open the Create Installation Disk(s) dialog box shown in Figure 25-23.

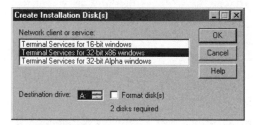

Figure 25-23. *The Create Installation Disk(s) dialog box.*

2. Select the type of disk you'll be making and the destination drive. If you want the disks to be formatted as part of the creation process, select the Format Disk(s) box. Click OK and you'll be prompted to insert the disks into the designated drive, as shown in Figure 25-24.

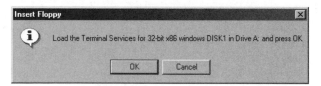

Figure 25-24. *The Insert Floppy information box.*

3. If you opt to format, you'll get the usual confirmation message warning you that everything will be erased. If you don't opt to format the disks and the disk you insert isn't empty, you'll get an error and be prompted to insert a blank, formatted floppy.

Terminal Services Client

You can install and run Terminal Services Client on any computer running Windows 2000, Windows NT 4, Windows 95/98, or Windows for Workgroups 3.11. Special clients are also available for other operating systems, including Windows CE and MS-DOS, as well as any client that can run Java. Some of these clients, however, require the use of the Citrix MetaFrame ICA protocol. Special Windows CE–based thin clients are available from a number of manufacturers that allow you to connect to a Windows 2000 Terminal Services server with no hard disk at all—the base operating system and Terminal Services Client are loaded in ROM.

Installing Terminal Services Client

To be able to install Terminal Services Client on a workstation, you'll need to have either a floppy drive available or a network connection to run the installation over the network. In either case, the steps are essentially the same. To install Terminal Services Client using floppy disks, follow these steps:

1. Insert client installation disk #1 into your floppy drive and run Setup from the floppy disk. You'll be prompted to read the license agreement, and you'll be reminded to close open programs. Click Continue.

2. Fill in the registration information, click OK, and then click OK again to confirm it. The information will be written to the floppy disk. You'll be prompted to consent to the license agreement, as shown in Figure 25-25.

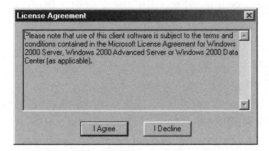

Figure 25-25. *Agreeing to the license agreement.*

3. Click the I Agree button to continue to the installation program, shown in Figure 25-26.

4. You can change the installation location by clicking the Change Folder button. When the location is correct, click the large button to begin setup.

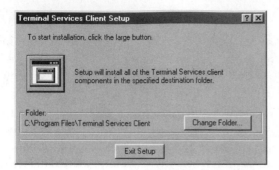

Figure 25-26. *The Terminal Services Client Setup window.*

5. Choose the program group you want your Terminal Services Client programs to go into and then click Continue. The default program group is Terminal Services Client. You'll be prompted for the additional disks as necessary.

6. When the installation is complete, you'll get a final prompt. Click OK. No reboot is required.

Client Connection Manager

Client Connection Manager allows you to create connections to your Windows Terminal Services servers and save the properties of those connections.

Creating a Connection To create a connection using the Client Connection Manager, follow these steps:

1. On the client machine, open the Programs submenu on the Start menu. Point to Terminal Services Client and then choose Client Connection Manager to open the Client Connection Manager window.

2. Choose New Connection from the File menu to open the Client Connection Manager Wizard shown in Figure 25-27.

3. Click Next to open the Create A Connection screen in Figure 25-28.

4. Type in a name for the connection. Then either type in a name or IP address for the server or use the Browse button to locate one. Click Next to display the Automatic Logon screen shown in Figure 25-29.

Figure 25-27. *The Client Connection Manager Wizard.*

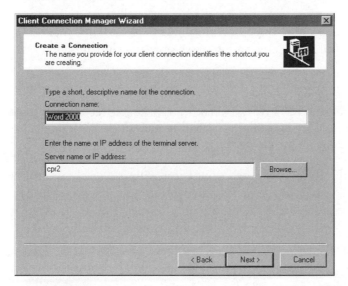

Figure 25-28. *The Create A Connection screen of the Client Connection Manager Wizard.*

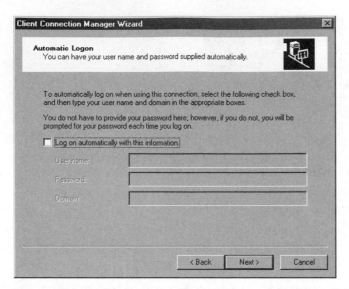

Figure 25-29. *The Automatic Logon screen of the Client Connection Manager Wizard.*

5. If you want the connection to automatically log on to the remote server as a particular user, select the Log On Automatically With This Information check box and fill in the user name, password, and domain name. Click Next.

Note Automatic logons may seem like a good idea, but if you have password aging enabled on your network, it can be a major nuisance. We recommend that you leave this option disabled unless you don't require users to periodically change their passwords.

6. Select the screen resolution that the connection will use, as shown in Figure 25-30. The choices available here depend on your video card. By default, the connection will use a window on your desktop. If you want the connection to be displayed on a full screen, select the Full Screen check box. Click Next.

7. Set the properties of the connection (Figure 25-31). The choices are:

   • **Enable Data Compression** When selected, data is compressed before being passed to the client and must be expanded by the client before being displayed. When using a low speed connection, such as over a modem or slow WAN, this can improve performance.

   • **Cache Bitmaps** When selected, commonly used bitmaps are cached to a file on your local disk, speeding up displays. Click Next.

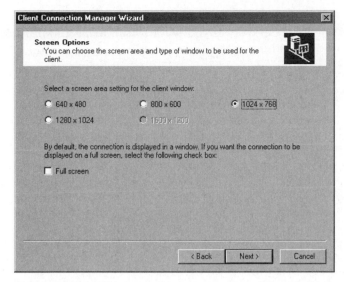

Figure 25-30. *The Screen Options screen of the Client Connection Manager Wizard.*

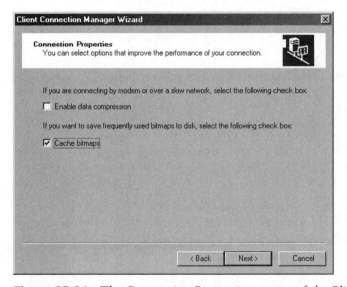

Figure 25-31. *The Connection Properties screen of the Client Connection Manager Wizard.*

8. Specify the program you want to run in this connection. The default is to simply start the Windows desktop. If you want to run a specific program, select the Start The Following Program check box and fill in the details for the program, as shown in Figure 25-32. Click Next.

Figure 25-32. *The Starting A Program screen of the Client Connection Manager Wizard.*

9. Choose an icon for the connection. The choices are rather limited, but you can use any other source of icons. You can also choose the program group for this connection, as shown in Figure 25-33. The default will be the same program group as the Client Connection Manager. Click Next.

10. If everything is correct, click Finish in the final confirmation screen to create the connection. Or click Back to make any necessary changes. Clicking Cancel will abort the process.

Configuring a Connection   The only way you can modify an existing connection is to use the Client Connection Manager. To modify a connection, follow these steps:

1. Open the Client Connection Manager and right-click the connection you want to modify, as shown in Figure 25-34.

Figure 25-33. *The Icon And Program Group screen of the Client Connection Manager Wizard.*

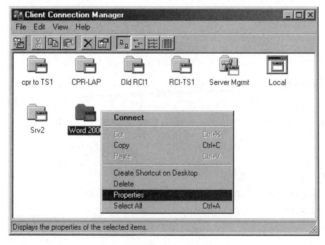

Figure 25-34. *Modifying the properties of an existing Client Connection Manager connection.*

2. Select Properties to open the dialog box shown in Figure 25-35.

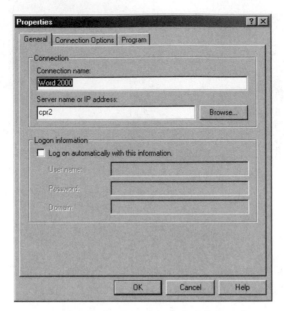

Figure 25-35. *The Properties dialog box for a connection in Client Connection Manager.*

On the General tab, you can change the following settings:

- **Connection Name** Change the name used to refer to the connection.
- **Server Name Or IP Address** Change the server the client connects to.
- **Logon Information** Change the embedded password if your password has changed or if you want to change from automatic logon to manual.

On the Connection Options tab, you can change these settings:

- **Screen Area** Change the resolution used for the connection.
- **Connection Startup** Change whether to use the entire screen for the connection or run the connection in a window.
- **Network** Enable or disable data compression.
- **Bitmap Caching** Enable or disable local storage of common bitmaps.

On the Program tab, you can change these settings:

- **Start The Following Program** If enabled, you can specify the program that will be run once you're logged on, and you can specify the starting directory. If disabled, the Windows desktop will be started.

- **Program Icon**   Change the icon for the program.
- **Program Group**   Change the group in the Start menu where the program can be started from.

Exporting and Importing Connections   The connections you create in Client Connection Manager are not, by default, available as a text file, but are stored in each client machine's registry at HKEY_CURRENT_USER\Software\Microsoft\ Terminal Server Client*<connection name>*. You can export the settings you created for a particular connection, or for all your connections, to a text file that will let you move it to another user or even another machine. This can vastly simplify the deployment of Terminal Services in a large organization. Unfortunately, there isn't a command-line way to do it, so you'll still have to touch each machine. But at least you will be sure to use a consistent setup across all clients. To export a single connection, follow these steps:

1. Highlight the connection you want to export in the Client Connection Manager and choose Export from the File menu.
2. Select the location and filename to export the file to, using the Export As dialog box. Files are given the .CNS extension. If the connection includes full logon information, you'll be prompted to confirm that you want to save the password with the export.

Caution   When you export the password as part of exporting a connection, the password is encrypted in the .CNS file, but anyone with access to the file could create a connection with your account. If you export the password, take appropriate precautions against physical access to the file.

To export all of the connections in Client Connection Manager, follow these steps:

1. Choose Export All from the File menu of Client Connection Manager.
2. Select the location and filename to export the connections to, using the Export As dialog box. All of the connections will be saved to a single .CNS file. If any of the connections include full logon information, you'll be prompted to confirm that you want to save the password as part of the export.

To import a connection or connections into Client Connection Manager, use this procedure:

1. Choose Import from the File menu of Client Connection Manager.
2. Locate the file to import, using the Import From dialog box.

If you have ever created a connection using Client Connection Manager, you'll be prompted to allow overwriting of the default connection. If you click Yes, you'll be prompted to allow automatic replacement of all connections that are duplicates. If you click No, you'll be prompted to preserve existing connections that are duplicates. If you don't allow the automatic replacement, you'll be prompted for each connection.

Connecting with Terminal Services Client

The Client Connection Manager is a useful tool for creating permanent connections to one or more servers, but if you just want to quickly connect to a server but have no need to preserve the information in a permanent connection to it, you can use Terminal Services Client (Mstsc.exe). To use Terminal Services Client, follow these steps:

1. Select Terminal Services Client from the Terminal Services Client program group to open the Terminal Services Client dialog box, shown in Figure 25-36.

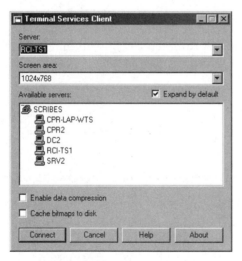

Figure 25-36. *The Terminal Services Client dialog box.*

2. Set the properties for this connection and click Connect. The properties you can set here are as follows:

   • **Server** Contains a list of your most recent connections. You can type in the name or IP address of an unlisted Terminal Services server.

   • **Screen Area** Lists the supported resolutions for your current display.

- **Available Servers**   Lists all of the available servers on your network.
- **Expand By Default**   Expands the domains to show all available servers in each domain.
- **Enable Data Compression**   Compresses video information before being passed to the client.
- **Cache Bitmaps To Disk**   Locally caches frequently used bitmaps to improve performance.

When you use Terminal Services Client, you will always be prompted to log on to the server to which you are connecting. You will also always log on to the Windows desktop. If you want to create a permanent connection, or one that will run only a particular program, you must use Client Connection Manager to create the connection.

Summary

Windows 2000 Terminal Services is an important addition to *all* versions of Windows 2000 Server. It provides a way to centralize management and application deployment across your entire enterprise. Terminal Services Manager lets you control the connections to your servers across the entire enterprise, while Client Connection Manager lets you create and deploy preconfigured connections to clients. You must specially install applications that will be used by Terminal Services Client to be able to properly handle the multiuser environment. You can run all Windows 2000 servers in remote management mode to give the system administrator the ability to easily connect to all of the servers in his or her network. The next chapter covers additional servers that come with Windows 2000, including Indexing Service and Message Queuing.

Chapter 26
Understanding Other Services

In addition to the services discussed in other chapters of this book, Microsoft Windows 2000 Server includes the Indexing Service and Microsoft Message Queuing. This chapter covers the basic concepts and tasks involved in using these services in various environments. Neither of these services is essential, and most networks can function perfectly well without them. However, when deployed correctly, these services offer benefits that can enhance almost any network.

Understanding the Indexing Service

The Indexing Service provides Web-type indexing and querying to corporate intranets, Internet sites, and more conventional networks without reformatting documents. With the click of a button, end users can index and query the contents of intranet or Internet sites on Windows 2000 Server with Internet Information Services (IIS). The Indexing Service does more than just index documents, however. It provides a system for publishing information on your intranet or on the Web. Because the Indexing Service indexes both the content and properties of formatted documents, you don't need to convert existing documents to HTML to make them available to your users. Instead, documents in a variety of formats, such as Microsoft Word or Microsoft Excel, are directly available.

Even though its primary function is the indexing of Web servers, the Indexing Service is useful on any network where searches for documents are common, and it is essential on any network with frequent searches through large numbers of files.

The Indexing Service functions much as one would expect—it catalogs a set of documents, enabling dynamic full-text searches using either the search function, a query form, or Microsoft Internet Explorer. Just as an index in a book maps an important word to a page inside the book, content indexing on a computer takes a word within a document and maps it back to that document. Documents to be indexed can be specified in catalogs and can include document properties as well as the actual text in the document. Once the Indexing Service is set up, it needs no ongoing maintenance, and administration is required only if you need to change a basic configuration. If you didn't include the Indexing Service in your original installation of Windows 2000, you can add it through Add/Remove Programs in Control Panel.

Defining Terms

When administering the Indexing Service, you'll encounter a number of terms that have a special meaning when used in the Indexing Service context. Here are some of the most common ones, with their definitions:

- **Corpus**   The entire collection of HTML pages and other documents indexed by the Indexing Service.

- **Virtual root**   An alias to a physical location on disk. For example, in IIS, the virtual root /maildocs points to the physical disk location %SystemRoot%\help\mail.

- **Scope**   The range of documents to be searched when executing a query. Physical paths or virtual roots can specify scopes.

- **Scan**   The process by which files and directories are checked for modifications. Scanning is performed against virtual roots that have been selected for indexing.

- **Catalog**   A directory where all temporary (word lists) and persistent (shadow and master) indexes and cached properties are stored for a particular scope.

- **CiDaemon**   A child process created by the Indexing Service. CiDaemon works in the background, filtering documents for the Indexing Service.

- **Filter**   Part of a dynamic link library (DLL) of filters, each designed to extract textual information and properties from a specific type of formatted document.

- **Query**   A request to search files for specific data.

- **Word list**   When a document is indexed, the index information goes first to a small temporary index, called a word list. Word lists are maintained in memory until the Indexing Service combines them into the existing indexes.

- **Persistent index**   Data for an index that is stored on disk. Unlike word lists, which exist only in memory, a persistent index survives shutdowns and restarts. Persistent-index data is stored in a highly compressed format. There are two types of persistent indexes: shadow indexes (also referred to as saved indexes and as temporary indexes) and master indexes.

- **Shadow index**   A persistent index created by merging word lists and occasionally other shadow indexes into a single index. A catalog can have multiple shadow indexes.

- **Shadow merge**   The process by which word lists and shadow indexes are combined into a single shadow index. A shadow merge is performed to free up memory used by word lists and also to make the filtered data persistent.

- **Master index**   A persistent index that contains the indexed data for a large number of documents. This is usually the largest persistent data structure. In an ideal state, this is the only index present because all of the indexed data is stored in the master index and there are no shadow indexes or word lists. A master index is created through a master merge.

- **Master merge**   The process by which shadow indexes are combined with the current master index into a single master index. Unlike shadow merges, this is usually a fairly long process.

How Indexing Works

The Indexing Service uses filters that can read certain types of documents, extract the text and properties, and send that information to the indexing engine. The filters included with Windows 2000 will index the following kinds of documents: text, HTML, Microsoft Office 95 and later, and Internet Mail and News (provided IIS is installed). The Indexing Service can use other filters made available by software vendors. The vendor that supplies the filter will also supply installation instructions.

After extracting the text and properties, the Indexing Service determines the language the document is written in and removes words that are on the language's exception list. The exception list contains prepositions, pronouns, articles, and so forth and is appropriately named Noise.*xxx*, where *xxx* represents the language. Figure 26-1 shows a portion of the Noise.eng file, which contains the exception list for American English. You can add words to or remove words from the exception list using any text editor, such as Notepad.

After words from the exception list are removed, the remaining words are stored first in a word list in memory. At least once a day, the word lists are combined to form temporary saved indexes, and later the Indexing Service consolidates the temporary indexes into a single master index. All this is done automatically, although under certain circumstances you may need to intervene by initiating a merge manually, as described later in this chapter.

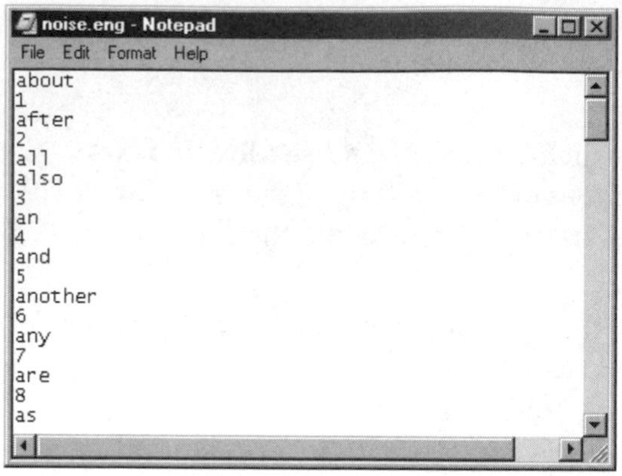

Figure 26-1. *A portion of the exception list for American English.*

Planning Your Indexing Service

When designing an indexing site, the first question that arises is how much storage space will be needed. The minimum disk space allocated should be at least 30 percent of the size of your corpus, and 40 percent is better. During a master merge, the Indexing Service may temporarily need up to 45 percent of the corpus size.

Depending on the filters used to index a group of documents, the actual size of the indexes may be less than the standard 30 percent. For example, if you write a filter for indexing large documents (such as large image files), you can limit indexing to the first few hundred bytes (about all you'd need to get the header information), thus reducing the amount of space needed for the index.

Note   Because most Indexing Service operations are read requests (searching the indexes, returning the results, and then accessing the actual documents), disk striping is a good way to reduce disk-bound I/O operations. Disk striping is covered in detail in Chapter 14.

Planning for future site growth is essential. Moving documents to larger disks to overcome space limitations can cause query errors until you are able to run a complete reindex, which can take many hours. Another critical part of planning an Indexing Service site is to make sure that plenty of memory is available on the indexing machine. Table 26-1 shows the minimum memory required versus the recommended amount for different quantities of documents . As usual, the more memory you have available, the better. With large numbers of documents, a faster CPU will also speed up indexing and searches.

Table 26-1.   Memory requirements by number of documents indexed

Number of Documents	Minimum Memory	Recommended Memory
Fewer than 100,000	64 MB	64 MB
100,000 to 250,000	64 MB	64 MB to 128 MB
250,000 to 500,000	64 MB	128 MB to 256 MB
500,000 or more	128 MB	256 MB or more

Merging Indexes

The Indexing Service automatically combines memory-resident word lists into disk-resident temporary lists and, once a day, merges all temporary indexes into a master index. Depending on the number of temporary lists, merging can be a long process that uses much of the CPU's resources. Queries will be slower during a merge, and other processes on the computer will be slower still.

By default, merges are done at midnight local time. If this is unsuitable for your system, you can change when the master merge is performed. You can also initiate a merge manually when a large number of documents in a catalog are changed. This section describes how to perform these two tasks.

Setting the Time to Start a Master Merge

To change the operation's schedule from the default time, follow these steps:

1. Run Regedt32.exe or Regedit.exe.

2. Navigate to HKEY_LOCAL_MACHINE\SYSTEM\CurrentControlSet\Control\ContentIndex.

3. In the right-hand pane of the Registry Editor window, double-click the value MasterMergeTime (Figure 26-2).

4. The DWORD Editor dialog box opens. In the Data box, type the number of minutes after midnight when a master merge should be initiated. Be sure to select Decimal from the Radix options.

5. Click OK and close the Registry Editor.

Note   MasterMergeTime has a valid range of values from 0 to 1439 minutes, though no error is reported if you enter a larger value. The default is 0. When the specified number of minutes after midnight have passed, the Indexing Service initiates a master merge.

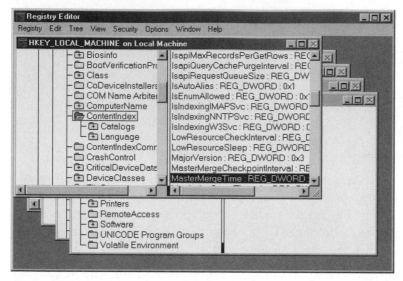

Figure 26-2. *Locating the setting for the master merge time.*

Manually Merging Indexes

If a large number of documents change in a short period, you may want to perform a merge of the temporary indexes without waiting for the scheduled master merge. To initiate a merge, follow these steps:

1. Open the Indexing Service MMC.

2. Right-click the appropriate catalog, point to All Tasks on the shortcut menu, and choose Merge (Figure 26-3).

3. You'll be asked to confirm that you want to merge the catalog. Click Yes.

Tip When indexing a large number of documents, you'll get the best results on a powerful computer with sufficient RAM. If you have 48 MB or more of RAM and the MaxFreshCount is 5000 or less, try increasing the MaxFreshCount to 10,000 or 15,000. If a lot of disk thrashing occurs, it may help to add more RAM. MaxFreshCount is also located in the registry at HKEY_LOCAL_MACHINE\SYSTEM\ CurrentControlSet\Control\ContentIndex, and it is discussed further in Table 26-3.

Setting Up an Indexing Console

For easy and frequent access, you should ideally set up a Microsoft Management Console (MMC) with Indexing Service. To do so, follow these steps:

1. Choose Run from the Start menu. Type *mmc* and press Enter.

2. Choose Add/Remove Snap-in from the Console menu. Click the Add button.

3. In the Add Standalone Snap-In box, select Indexing Service and click Add. Click Close.

4. Click OK and you see an Indexing Service MMC like the one shown in Figure 26-4.

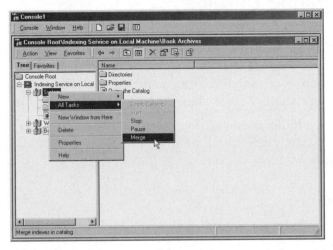

Figure 26-3. *Initiating a merge of temporary indexes.*

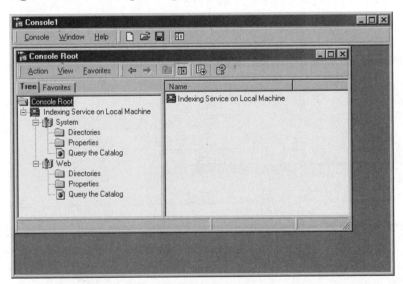

Figure 26-4. *The Indexing Service in the MMC.*

You can also administer the Indexing Service by opening Computer Management from the Administrative Tools menu. In the console tree, the Indexing Service is under the Services and Applications node. The illustrations and examples shown in the following sections use the Indexing Service in the MMC, but you can also perform these tasks just as well through Computer Management.

Creating and Configuring Catalogs

A catalog contains all of the index information for a particular set of file directories. During installation the Indexing Service creates a default catalog called System. This catalog lists the contents of all permanently attached disk drives and, by default, all of the directories and subdirectories on the drives. If IIS is installed, the Indexing Service also creates a Web catalog that contains all the IIS files.

You can create catalogs, adding and removing them as needed. You can also configure catalogs, setting what directories are to be included or excluded and specifying what properties are to be stored.

Creating a Catalog

To create a catalog for the Indexing Service, open the MMC with the Indexing Service snap-in and follow these steps:

1. Highlight Indexing Service in the console tree.

2. On the Action menu, choose New, then choose Catalog.

3. In the Add Catalog dialog box, supply a name for the catalog and a path to the folder in which you want the catalog placed (Figure 26-5). Click OK.

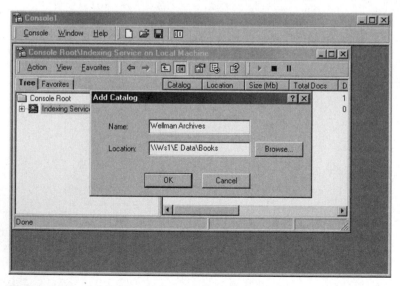

Figure 26-5. *Adding a catalog to the index.*

4. You must stop and restart the Indexing Service before the new catalog will be found and indexed. To do so, right-click Indexing Service and choose Stop from the shortcut menu. Then, to restart the Indexing Service, right-click Indexing Service again and choose Start from the shortcut menu.

Tip Catalogs can't be added to a remote computer if the default administrative shares have been removed.

Configuring a Catalog

Once you've created a catalog, you need to configure it so that it works as you expect. To do so, open the Indexing Service console and locate the catalog. Right-click the catalog and choose Properties to do the following:

- **Indexing a Web server**   Click the Tracking tab and, in the WWW Server box, select the Web server you want to index. If IIS isn't installed, this option won't be available.

- **Indexing files with unknown extensions**   Click the Generation tab. Ordinarily this setting is inherited from the overall Indexing Service properties and is inactive by default. If you want all of the files in this catalog to be indexed, including those without installed filters, clear the Inherit Above Settings From Service check box. Select the box next to Index Files With Unknown Extensions.

- **Generating abstracts**   Click the Generation tab. The Generate Abstracts setting is inherited from the overall Indexing Service properties and is inactive by default. To select this option, you must first clear the Inherit Settings From Service check box. If Generate Abstracts is selected, the Indexing Service will produce abstracts in the list of query results. This slows the query process, so it's best not to increase the default size of abstracts.

- **Adding a network share alias automatically**   Click the Tracking tab. By default, this setting is inherited from the Indexing Service, where it is enabled.

With the exception of Generate Abstracts, all of the changes listed above take effect only after you stop and restart the catalog. To do so, right-click the catalog, point to All Tasks on the shortcut menu, and choose Stop. Then right-click again, point to All Tasks, and choose Start. If you change the Generate Abstracts setting, you'll need to stop and restart the Indexing Service for the change to be recognized.

Including or Excluding a Directory

By default, the System catalog includes everything on the local drives, excluding only temporary Internet files and history files. When you create a new catalog, you have to add the directories that are to be included as well as specifically exclude directories that are not to be part of the index. To add a directory to a catalog, follow these steps:

1. Open the Indexing Service console. Under the new catalog, right-click Directories, point to New on the shortcut menu, and choose Directory.

2. In the Add Directory dialog box, supply the path to the directory and the Uniform Naming Convention (UNC) path, if necessary.

3. If the directory is on another computer, supply a name and password for a user with permission to access the remote share, as shown in Figure 26-6. Be sure to include the domain name (or the machine name for a local user account).

4. Click OK, and the directory becomes part of the catalog.

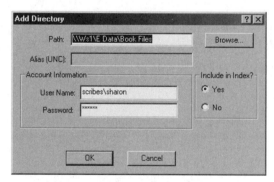

Figure 26-6. *Adding a directory on a remote computer to the catalog.*

To change settings for a directory, double-click the directory in the details pane of the Indexing Service console to open the Add Directory dialog box.

To exclude a particular directory, you must specify it. For example, the Wellman Archives catalog shown in Figure 26-7 includes a directory called Book Files. In that directory is a subdirectory called Correspondence that we want to exclude from indexing. To exclude a directory, follow these steps:

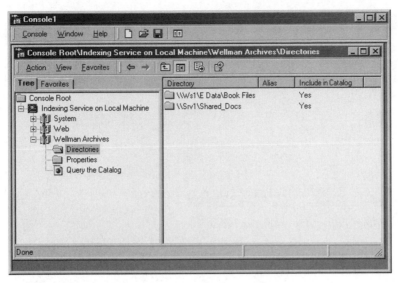

Figure 26-7. *A catalog that includes directories from two remote computers.*

1. Open the Indexing Service console. Under the appropriate catalog, right-click Directories, point to New in the shortcut menu, and choose Directory.

2. In the Add Directory dialog box, supply the path to the directory you want to exclude and the UNC path, if necessary. Again, if the directory is on another computer, supply a name and password for a user with permission to access the remote share.

3. In the Include In Index area, select No. Click OK.

The directory will appear in the directory list, but under Include In Catalog, the entry will be No. For example, Figure 26-8 shows that the Correspondence sub-directory has been excluded from the index.

Tip   Although you can include a directory and then specifically exclude a portion of it, this process does not work in reverse. If you exclude a directory, you cannot then include some portion of it, even if you specify the directory and set it to be included in the index. If you attempt to do this, the directory will be in the catalog's directories and will be listed as being included in the catalog, but it will not be indexed.

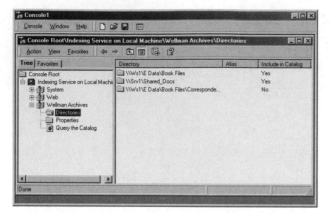

Figure 26-8. *Excluding a directory from the index.*

Real World   Indexing and Security

The Indexing Service is fully compatible with NTFS security. If the catalog is on an NTFS volume, users will not see documents in the results list unless they have permission to do so. However, if you index a UNC share, the results list will show the documents on that share whether or not the user has permission to access the documents.

Users will also be able to see a catalog on a FAT drive whether they have permissions or not. If the remote FAT volume isn't hosted by Microsoft Windows NT or Windows 2000, the system will be forced to scan the volume periodically for changes.

Remote Novell NetWare and UNIX shares can be indexed; however, there is no security checking. Novell NetWare volumes must be periodically rescanned to detect changes.

Encrypted documents are not indexed. If a document in the index is later encrypted, it is removed from the index.

Configuring the Property Cache

The Indexing Service saves certain file properties in a two-level cache in each catalog. The primary level contains a small number of values that are accessed frequently. The secondary level contains values that are used less often. Table 26-2 shows the properties that are stored in each catalog by default.

Table 26-2.   Property values stored in a catalog by default

Friendly Name	Function	Value	Storage Level
DocTitle	Document title	0x2	Secondary
	Unique identifier for NTFS volumes	0x5	Primary
	Work ID of the parent directory	0x6	Primary
	Secondary storage ID, used internally by the Indexing Service	0x7	Primary
File Index	Unique identifier of a document in an NTFS partition	0x8	Primary
Path	Document path	0xb	Secondary
Size	Document size	0xc	Secondary
Attrib	Document attributes	0xd	Primary
Write	Date and time the document was last written to	0xe	Secondary

In general, you should approach changing these properties with caution, always bearing in mind the following facts:

- Adding property values to either level—but particularly to the primary level—will have a negative effect on the performance of the Indexing Service.

- Adding variable-length properties to the primary level will increase the size of the cache exponentially.

- After you add a property value to either level and then restart indexing, you can't change the level for that property.

You should not assume that changing the property cache is always a poor idea. For example, you may want to be able to include in the index such information as when files were created or when they were last accessed.

Adding a Property to the Property Cache

To add a property to the properties saved in the property cache, follow these steps:

1. Open the Indexing Service console. Under the appropriate catalog, click Properties.

2. In the details pane, highlight the property you want to add.

3. On the Action menu, choose Properties to open the property's Properties window.

4. To include this property in the property cache, select the Cached check box (Figure 26-9). You can see and change the datatype and the size of the property. (Only properties with variable sizes can be adjusted.) The storage level can also be assigned, but it cannot be changed. In all cases, however, it's advisable to accept the default settings. Click OK when you're done.

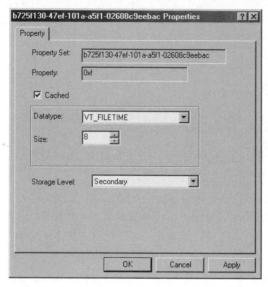

Figure 26-9. *Adding a property to the property cache.*

Changes take effect after the Indexing Service is stopped and restarted, but these newly added properties will be included in the property cache only for new documents. To update the entire index with the newly included properties, perform a full scan of the index, as described in the next section. If you later decide to remove a property or alter its settings, you can do so by clearing the Cached check box in the property's Properties window. Again, a full scan is required to update the entire index.

Running a Scan of the Index

A full scan of the index consists of a complete inventory of all of the documents in the catalog. The Indexing Service automatically performs a full scan when it is first installed, when a directory is added to a catalog, and as a part of recovery if an error occurs. Incremental scans are done automatically when the Indexing Service restarts to detect documents that were changed while it was inactive. You can perform a full or incremental scan at any time by following these steps:

1. Open the Indexing Service console. In the console tree, click the appropriate catalog and then click Directories.

2. In the details pane, highlight the directory to be scanned.

3. On the Action menu, point to All Tasks and then choose Rescan (Full) or Rescan (Incremental), depending on the type of scan you want to perform. You'll be asked to confirm your choice. Click Yes and the scan will proceed.

Registry Entries for the Indexing Service

The Indexing Service is controlled by entries in the registry. These entries can be edited using Regedit.exe or Regedt32.exe, although the usual caveats apply because a misstep in the registry can cause problems not only in the Indexing Service but elsewhere in Windows 2000 as well. Edit only those entries that you must. If the Indexing Service console has a method for making changes, use that instead. Always back up the registry before editing it.

Entries for the Indexing Service can be found in the registry at HKEY_ LOCAL_MACHINE\SYSTEM\CurrentControlSet\Control\ContentIndex. Figure 26-10 shows the registry entries for the Indexing Service. (Remember, the values displayed by Regedt32 are in hexadecimal. An entry of 0x7530 is actually 30,000 in decimal.) Table 26-3 lists some of the critical operational parameters for the Indexing Service that are accessible through the registry.

Figure 26-10. *The Indexing Service entries in the registry.*

Table 26-3. Selected registry entries for the Indexing Service

Registry Entry	Function
DaemonResponseTimeout	Sets the period (in seconds) after which the CiDaemon process should have responded appropriately. Used to determine whether the CiDaemon process is looping because of a corrupt file.
EventLogFlags	Controls the generation of event log messages.
FilterContents	Indicates whether the contents of a file will be filtered or whether only the properties of the file will be filtered. A value of 0 specifies that the contents will not be filtered. With any other value, the file will be filtered.
FilterDirectories	When set to a value of 0, directories will not be filtered for system properties or displayed in query results. With any other value, the directories will be filtered.
FilterFilesWithUnknownExtensions	Indicates whether files with nonregistered extensions will be filtered. When set to a value of 0, only registered file types will be filtered.
FilterRetries	Indicates the maximum number of times a file will be retried for filtering after a failure.
GenerateCharacterization	Controls the automatic generation of file abstracts.
IsapiMaxEntriesInQueryCache	Shows the maximum number of cached queries.
IsapiMaxRecordsInResultSet	Indicates the maximum number of rows to return for a single query.
IsapiMaxRecordsPerGetRows	Indicates the maximum number of rows to fetch when getting data to display on an HTML page.
IsapiRequestQueueSize	Controls the maximum number of Web query requests to queue when the server is busy with other requests.
MasterMergeTime	Indicates the time at which a master merge will occur. This value is stored as the number of minutes after midnight.
MaxCharacterization	Shows the maximum number of characters in abstracts generated automatically.
MaxFilesizeFiltered	Controls the maximum size of a single file to be filtered using the default filter. If the size of a file exceeds this value, only file properties will be filtered. This limit does not apply for registered file types.
MaxFreshCount	Specifies the maximum number of files whose latest indexed data is not in the master index. If this number is exceeded, a master merge will be performed.

Table 26-3.   *continued*

Registry Entry	Function
MaxIndexes	Sets the maximum number of persistent indexes in the catalog. If this number is exceeded, a shadow merge will be performed to bring the total below this number.
MaxPendingDocuments	Sets the maximum number of pending documents to be filtered before considering the content index out of date for property queries.
MaxQueryExecutionTime	Identifies the maximum execution time (in seconds) for a query. If the CPU time for a query takes longer than this value, processing will stop and an error message will be returned.
MaxShadowFreeForceMerge	A master merge is forced when free space on the catalog hard disk has fallen below the MinDisk-FreeForceMerge value *and* the disk space occupied by the shadow indexes exceeds this value.
MaxShadowIndexSize	A master merge is started when the disk space occupied by the shadow indexes exceeds this percentage of the catalog drive.
MaxWordLists	Sets the maximum number of word lists that can exist at a time.
MinDiskFreeForceMerge	A master merge is forced when the free space on the catalog drive has fallen below the percentage set here *and* the disk space occupied by the shadow indexes exceeds the value of MaxShadowFreeForceMerge.
MinSizeMergeWordLists	Sets the minimum combined size of word lists that will force a shadow merge.

Querying the Index

The simplest way to query the index is to use the Search operation on the Start menu. Point to Search, choose For Files And Folders, and enter a filename or a single word from the text or some other known property. Depending on the number of documents to be searched, the use of the Indexing Service can make a remarkable difference in search times. Even in small- to medium-sized databases, a search that takes 10 seconds without indexing appears instantaneous with indexing.

Queries can also be performed using the Indexing Service query form, which enables wide-range searches. Clicking the Query The Catalog directory in the Indexing Service console opens the query form (Figure 26-11).

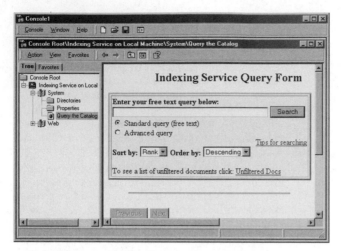

Figure 26-11. *The built-in Indexing Service Query Form.*

With the query form, you can do the following:

- Search for words and phrases.

- Search for words or phrases that are in proximity to other words or phrases.

- Search for words or phrases within textual properties. For example, you can search for a word that appears in a document's abstract or summary.

- Search for words or phrases in specific document formats, such as within an Excel spreadsheet or a Microsoft PowerPoint presentation.

- Use the relational operators <, <=, =, =>, >, and != against a constant, such as a date or file size.

- Use the Boolean operators AND, OR, AND NOT, and NEAR. (Note that the Boolean operators are available only in the English language.)

- Use wildcard characters such as * and ? and regular expressions for "fuzzy" queries.

- Rank results by the quality of the match.

The Indexing Service uses three types of files—very similar to those implemented by IIS—to allow the development of custom query forms, formatted results pages, and administrative scripts. These file types are

- Internet data query files

- HTML extension files

- Index data administration files

Creating Query Forms

With a query form, you can conveniently search for a word or phrase anywhere in a set of documents. The user simply enters a word or phrase, and all documents containing the word or phrase are returned in a list.

With the Indexing Service, the administrator of a Web server can create customized forms to help employees and other clients find specific information from a set of documents. For example, a form can be tailored to search for a word or phrase (such as "systems management") or for properties (such as the author or subject). You create a query form in standard HTML format, just as you would create any Web page. If you know how to create pages in HTML format, you can quickly put together a simple query form such as the following:

```
<FORM ACTION="/scripts/querydemo.idq?" METHOD="POST">
So what's your question?:
<INPUT TYPE="TEXT" NAME="CiRestriction" SIZE="60" MAXLENGTH="100" VALUE=" ">
<INPUT TYPE="SUBMIT" VALUE="Start Search">
<INPUT TYPE="RESET" VALUE="Clear">
</FORM>
```

The *<FORM ACTION>* line shows the location of the .IDQ (Internet data query) file, which defines query parameters such as the scope of your search, any restrictions, and query result sets. A basic .IDQ file looks something like this:

```
[Query]
CiColumns=filename,size,rank,characterization, vpath,DocTitle,write
CiFlags=DEEP
CiRestriction=%CiRestriction%
CiMaxRecordsInResultSet=100
CiMaxRecordsPerPage=25
CiScope=/
CiTemplate=/scripts/bdq.htx
CiSort=rank[d]
CiCatalog=d:\
```

The following list explains each line of the sample .IDQ file:

```
[Query]
```

Identifies the information that follows as a query specification.

```
CiColumns=filename,size,rank,characterization,vpath,DocTitle,write
```

Indicates the kind of information to return in the result set.

```
CiFlags=DEEP
```

Tells the query to search all subdirectories within the scope.

`CiRestriction=%CiRestriction%`

Indicates the query terms to search for.

`CiMaxRecordsInResultSet=100`

Sets the maximum number of results to be returned, 100 in this example.

`CiMaxRecordsPerPage=25`

Determines how many results are shown on each Web page returned, 25 in this example.

`CiScope=/`

Tells where to start the query. In this example, the query starts at the root of the storage space.

`CiTemplate=/scripts/bdq.htx`

Indicates what file to use to format the results; in this case, it's Bdq.htx.

`CiSort=rank[d]`

Tells how to sort the results. In this example, the results will be listed by rank—by how well the document matches the query—and *[d]* indicates that the results will be listed in descending order.

`CiCatalog=d:\`

Points to the index to use. In this example, the index stored on d:\ is to be used.

The combination of the sample HTML file and the sample .IDQ file produces the query form shown in Figure 26-12. Both of these files are in the \Samples\ Chapter 26 folder on the companion CD.

Figure 26-12. *Creating a simple query form.*

Real World   "File Not Found" Errors

When you issue a query in the Indexing Service, the result set may include links to documents that were recently deleted from the server. Clicking on these links will return "file not found" errors. This problem occurs when you index and then delete files that contain long filenames. When these files are created, Windows 2000 creates an 8.3 short filename so that older applications can access the document. When the Indexing Service catalogs these files, it stores the information for both the long and short filenames. However, when the file is deleted, the Indexing Service removes only the information on the short filename from the catalog. Queries that match the document still return hits to the entry for the long filename.

This long filename entry is usually removed when a master merge occurs, but it may not happen soon enough to prevent users from becoming annoyed. If this becomes a problem, you can edit the registry to prevent Windows 2000 from creating short filenames for older applications. To do this, open the Registry Editor (Regedt32.exe), and navigate to HKEY_LOCAL_MACHINE\SYSTEM\CurrentControlSet\Control\FileSystem. Set the NtfsDisable8dot3NameCreation value to 1. The usual warnings apply regarding backing up the registry before messing with it.

More Info   For more on writing custom query forms and other aspects of the Indexing Service and IIS, see *Running Microsoft Internet Information Server 4.0* by Leonid Braginski and Matt Powell (Microsoft Press, 1998).

Indexing a New Site

When you create a new Web site, the site is not automatically marked as indexed when you create a catalog for it. To correctly index a new Web site, follow these steps:

1. Open the Indexing Service console, and create a new catalog.

2. Right-click the new catalog and choose Properties from the shortcut menu.

3 Click the Tracking tab and select the Web site that you want to index. Click OK.

4. Open the Internet Information Services console. Right-click the appropriate Web site and choose Properties from the shortcut menu.

5. Click the Home Directory tab (Figure 26-13), select the Index This Resource check box, and click OK.

6. Stop the Indexing Service and then restart it. The new catalog should come on line and begin indexing the new Web site.

Figure 26-13. *Setting up indexing on a new Web site.*

Examining Performance

The performance of the Indexing Service depends, obviously, on the number and size of the documents being indexed and the resources available to the Indexing Service. When the number of documents being indexed is fewer than 100,000, no special hardware or tuning is likely to be needed. The Indexing Service will work in the background and without attention. As the number of documents grows, however, performance will begin to lag unless sufficient memory is available.

Modifying the Indexing Service's Performance

You can adjust the performance of the Indexing Service based on how you use the service. It's not always necessary to perform hardware upgrades. Instead, you can reduce the amount of resources needed for indexing by reducing the demand that indexing places on the system. Alternatively, you can give the Indexing Service a high priority on a given system when many documents need to be processed. To adjust the Indexing Service's performance, follow these steps:

1. Open the Indexing Service console. In the console tree, right-click Indexing Service and choose Stop from the shortcut menu.

2. On the Action menu, point to All Tasks and choose Tune Performance.

3. In the Indexing Service Usage dialog box, you can select the option that best describes how this computer uses indexing.

   If you select the Customize option and then click the Customize button, the dialog box shown in Figure 26-14 opens.

Move the Indexing slider to Instant for immediate indexing of all new and modified documents. Move the slider to Lazy for indexing to take place when the system isn't busy with other tasks and for indexing that will not affect overall system performance.

Move the Querying slider to High Load for processing many queries at a time. Move the slider to Low Load if few queries are expected at a time.

4. Click OK twice when you're finished.

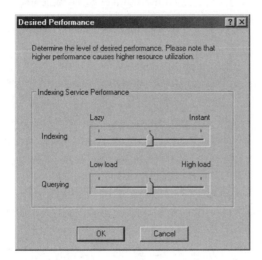

Figure 26-14. *Customizing indexing performance.*

Changes to the Indexing Service's performance are unlikely to have noticeable results except in an environment where indexing needs are either very high or very low. In most environments, the Indexing Service works unobtrusively in the background without fine-tuning.

Using Performance Monitor

Chapter 32 describes how to use the data from Performance Monitor to target processes and components that need to be optimized, monitor the results of tuning and configuration efforts, and understand and observe the trends in workloads and the corresponding effect they have on resource usage. Among the many performance counters available in Windows 2000 are several that can assist in monitoring the Indexing Service and the Indexing Service Filter. Table 26-4 lists the relevant counters and what they measure. See Chapter 32 for details on analyzing performance data to determine acceptable values for counters and for information on solving any performance problems that are found.

Table 26-4. Performance Monitor counters related to the Indexing Service

Performance Object	Counter	Description
Indexing Service	# documents indexed	Number of documents indexed in the current indexing session
	Deferred for indexing	Number of documents in use that need to be indexed
	Documents to be indexed	Smallest number of documents known to need indexing
	Index size (MB)	Total size, in megabytes, of all saved indexes
	Merge progress	Percentage of merge completed
	Running queries	Number of queries currently being processed
	Saved indexes	Number of saved indexes
	Total # of documents	Number of documents known to the Indexing Service
	Total # of queries	Total number of queries in the current indexing session
	Unique keys	Number of unique keys (words, properties) in the index
	Word lists	Total number of word lists
Indexing Service Filter	Binding time (msec)	Average time in milliseconds to bind to a filter
	Indexing speed (MBph)	Speed of indexing document contents in megabytes per hour
	Total indexing speed (MBph)	Speed of indexing document contents and properties, in megabytes per hour

Troubleshooting the Indexing Service

This section lists common error messages and possible solutions. Some of the most common problems with the Indexing Service can be fixed quite easily. For more complex issues, search the Microsoft Knowledge Base on line at *http://support.microsoft.com/search/* for solutions.

No Documents Matched the Query

- Instead of receiving a list of matching documents when you perform a query using the Indexing Service, you may receive the error message "No Documents Matched the Query." This common error means that the catalog is responding correctly but that there is an incorrect setting somewhere. To find the incorrect setting, try each of the following procedures in turn, testing after each one.

- Try the samples in the \inetpub\issamples\sdk directory. You may need to change the pointer to the catalog if you are not using the default catalog. In an .IDQ file, you should see a line like the following:

```
CiCatalog=d:\inetpub\wwwroot\tmjs_index
```

Make sure that the path is pointing to the directory that contains the catalog's Catalog.wci directory. In an Active Server Pages (ASP) file, you will need to add the Q.Catalog line in the code segment below:

```
set Q = Server.CreateObject("ixsso.Query")
        set util = Server.CreateObject("ixsso.Util")
    Q.Catalog="<catalog_name>"
    Q.Query = CompSearch
    Q.SortBy = "rank[d]"
    Q.Columns = "DocTitle, vpath, filename, size, write, characterization, rank"
    Q.MaxRecords = 300
```

Replace *<catalog_name>* with the name of your catalog as it appears in the Indexing Service console. (Include the quotation marks.)

- In the code of your page, make sure that one of the following is true:

In an .IDQ:

```
CiScope=/
CiRestriction=%CiRestriction%
CiCatalog=<path to the directory holding the Catalog.wci directory>
```

In an ASP:

```
FormScope=/
Q.Query=compsearch
Q.Catalog="<catalog_name>"
```

Replace *<catalog_name>* with the name of the catalog as it appears in the Indexing Services console. This will ensure that you are running the widest possible search with the most chances of returning results against the correct catalog, with nothing on the query line to prevent results from appearing.

- Open Internet Services Manager from the Administrative Tools folder on the Programs menu. Right-click the root of your Web site and choose Properties. On the Home Directory tab, make sure that the Index This Resource check box is selected. Then try your query again.

- The Indexing Service does its indexing as the System account. If the System account does not have at least Read permissions on the files that are to be cataloged, the files will not be indexed. Also, make sure that the System account has Full Access permissions on the root of the drive that physically contains the catalog and on the Catalog.wci directory.

- Users are allowed to view only results that they have permissions to see. If you are accessing the query page as an anonymous user, make sure that the anonymous user has at least Read permissions on the document you are trying to find.

- Authenticate coming into the query page as an administrator if possible. Try setting the directory that the query page is located in to Basic/Clear Text authentication only, so that you receive a prompt when you attempt to connect to that page. If you get results, you have a permissions issue. If you log on as an administrator and still receive a "No Documents Matched the Query" message, you probably do not have a permissions issue.

- If you are querying on a specific page and it is returning in a #*filename* query, but it is not being filtered (the abstract is not populated), and it is an HTM, HTML, or ASP page, make sure you do not have a ROBOTS=NOINDEX metatag in the header of the document. This will not prevent indexing, but it will prevent filtering.

.PDF Files Aren't Indexed

Adobe makes a filter to enable the indexing of .PDF (Portable Document Format) files. After you install the filter, you may notice that .PDF files are no longer indexed after the Indexing Service is restarted or the computer is restarted.

The problem is caused when the Indexing Service restarts and reregisters all of the filter .DLL files. One of these .DLL files has a default association with the .PDF extension and therefore registers itself as the filter for these files. To fix this problem, ensure that the list of filter .DLL files includes the PDF filter by following these steps:

1. Start the Registry Editor (Regedt32.exe).

2. Locate the following key in the registry:

   HKEY_LOCAL_MACHINE\SYSTEM\CurrentControlSet\Control\ ContentIndex

3. Add the path to the Pdffilt.dll to the DLLsToRegister key. The path to the .PDF filter should be added as the last entry in this key.

4. Close the Registry Editor.

Query Produces Inconsistent Results

When you use the Indexing Service to run a query and you set the sort method to anything other than Rank Descending, you do not receive the top matching records and you may get a different set of files on subsequent queries. Sorting on Rank Descending is the only way to get the top matching records from the catalog when the maximum number of returns is limited. Sorting on anything other than Rank Descending returns a subset of the total matching documents.

Catalog Is Reportedly Corrupted

If the Indexing Service reports that the catalog is corrupted after the indexing process is completed, it means that a file can't be filtered and that Filter Retries is set to a number greater than 4. This can occur as soon as the indexing process has completed or several minutes later.

When this happens, the information that the filter process sends to the Indexing Service causes a report that the catalog information is corrupted even though the data on the drive is fine. To fix this, start the Registry Editor (Regedt32.exe) and navigate to HKEY_LOCAL_MACHINE\SYSTEM\CurrentControlSet\Control\ContentIndex\FilterRetries. Change the value of this key to 4 or less, close Registry Editor, and restart the Indexing Service.

Indexing Is Slow and Some Documents Aren't Indexed

On occasion, it may take an extremely long time to index documents, and some documents may appear not to get indexed at all. In addition, the abstract for documents may be blank or contain incorrect information. This is usually caused by third-party software that places a lock on the Web content that you are attempting to index. Antivirus software programs and any other software that monitors or scans your Web content for extended periods of time can cause this problem. To work around this problem, disable any software that may be monitoring the Web content.

Understanding Microsoft Message Queuing

As more and more business operations become dependent on computers, networks, and online databases to function, limitations on how conventional software works are increasingly apparent. For example, physicians in remote areas transmitting information to a medical center need to send and receive extremely crucial information over reliable communications channels. A mortgage broker-age needs to receive loan applications through the Internet, process them into a database, and automatically request credit reports and other information that will come from different sources at different times.

Overall, customer service requirements are forcing companies to look at integrating several existing applications in order to present a single, near-real-time view of the customer and his or her relationship to the company, often through the Web. Many events have to go on at once, and all events have to be secure and reliable while traveling over channels whose performance may be inconsistent. To fulfill these needs, a solution must meet the following three technical requirements:

- Applications must not need to know about each other's communication protocols, implementation details, or data organization in order to communicate.

- Sending applications may run at different times and thus must be able to send data asynchronously and move on to other work without waiting to connect to some receiving application.

- Data must not be lost, garbled, duplicated, or exposed to security risks even when transported over networks that do not provide these protections inherently.

In addition to integration, which takes the form of back-and-forth communication between applications, many companies want to make applications that are aware of each other's business events. A *business event* is an event in an application, such as a change of address, that may be of interest to another application but that doesn't require an answer from that application. Of course, in addition to technology requirements, the usual needs for solutions to be cost-effective, simple to use, and easy to integrate into existing systems must be met.

Microsoft Message Queuing, included as part of Windows 2000 Server, is an important technology in the construction of these solutions. Message Queuing is a developer's environment and, as such, is beyond the scope of this book. However, information on the uses of Message Queuing may help you decide what purposes it might serve in your particular enterprise.

What the Message Queue Does

Most distributed applications are built using *synchronous* communication technologies, such as remote procedure calls and remote data access. Synchronous communication works like a telephone call. You place a call to someone, he or she answers, and you can have a quick and usually efficient exchange of information. The problem arises when the person at the other end of the call doesn't answer. You must keep redialing at regular intervals until you get an answer—not quick and not efficient.

If the person at the other end of the phone line has voice mail, the communication becomes *asynchronous*. You can leave your message with some assurance that the other party will eventually retrieve the message and take appropriate action. In the meantime, you can get on with other tasks without having to interrupt them to repeatedly redial the phone.

Message Queuing implements asynchronous communications by enabling applications to exchange messages whether the applications are running at the same time or at different times. The applications can be on the same machine or on different machines on a network. The messages can contain data in any format that's understood by the sender and the receiver. When an application receives a request message, it reads the contents of the message and acts accordingly. The receiving application can send a response to the requesting application if that's desirable.

While the messages are in transit between senders and receivers, they are kept in waiting areas called *queues,* which is where the technology got its name. The queues protect messages from being lost and provide a central place for receivers to look for messages when they are ready. Applications make requests by sending messages to queues associated with the intended receiver. If a response is expected, the sender includes the name of a *response queue* (that the sender creates in advance) in the requests made to the receiver.

Planning a Message Queuing Network

Before developing (or purchasing) queuing applications, you should review the factors that will influence how well Message Queuing will work in your environment. Table 26-5 describes the essential points.

Table 26-5.   Factors in planning a Message Queuing network

Site Factor	Consideration
Communication channel	The channel between sites must be permanent.
Bandwidth	The available bandwidth must be sufficient to support the message traffic.
Performance	The number of Message Queuing servers must be balanced against performance needs. The more servers, the more traffic. Too much server redundancy and the Active Directory replication traffic will cause a big performance hit.
Organization	Users should be grouped in the same site to keep traffic down.

Hardware Issues Involved in Message Queuing

Assuming that you don't have the luxury of building a queuing operation with all new hardware, you can do several things to make sure that the machines assigned to be Message Queuing servers can handle the load:

- Increase the amount of system RAM. (Whatever it is, it's never too much.)
- Upgrade the processor or add additional processors.
- Increase the speed and size of the hard disks.
- Use disk striping. The best performance is achieved with five separate disks used for message files, message log files, transaction log files, application data files, and Windows 2000 virtual memory paging files. At a minimum, the message files, message log files, and transaction log files should be on separate disks.
- Reduce or eliminate the other services running on the server.
- Minimize the number of dependent clients supported by each server. (Dependent clients require continuous connection to a Message Queuing server in order to perform message queuing operations.)

More Info For the nuts and bolts of building applications with Microsoft Message Queuing, consult *Programming Distributed Applications with COM and Microsoft Visual Basic 6.0* by Ted Pattison (Microsoft Press, 1998).

Summary

The Indexing Service offers administrators of Web sites or networks with large numbers of documents a way to locate and access documents quickly and easily. Queries can be delimited by document contents and properties. Microsoft Message Queuing is a set of technologies that developers can use to build applications for the integration of systems and to bolster the reliability of communications. The next chapter begins the portion of the book devoted to Internet servers and services with a discussion of the basics of Internet Information Services.

Part V
Internet Servers and Services

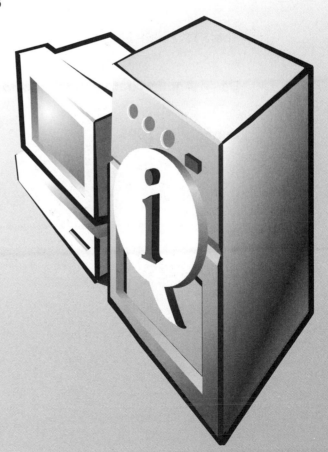

Chapter 27
Basics of Internet Information Services

Microsoft Windows 2000 incorporates a set of services that provide server-side support for the most popular application-level Internet protocols, enabling a Windows 2000 server to function as a Web server, a File Transfer Protocol (FTP) server, a Simple Mail Transport Protocol (SMTP) host, or a Network News Transfer Protocol (NNTP) host.

In the Microsoft Windows NT 4 operating system, these services are provided by an optional component called Internet Information Server (IIS). To obtain full support for Internet services, administrators have to install Internet Information Server 4, found in the Windows NT 4 Option Pack, on the computer running Windows NT 4 Server after applying Service Pack 3 or later.

In contrast, basic Internet services are fully integrated into all the Windows 2000 Server platforms. These services are now referred to as Internet Information *Services* 5 (IIS 5) instead of Internet Information *Server* 5 to emphasize their integration with the underlying operating system. This chapter examines the protocols that IIS 5 supports, along with the other tools that you can use to manage Internet services on Windows 2000 Server platforms. Chapter 28 takes a more detailed look at how to configure the services described in this chapter.

Protocols Supported

In Chapter 12, the discussion of the TCP/IP suite focused mainly on the network-layer protocols (such as IP) and transport-layer protocols (such as TCP and UDP) and how they work. The only application-layer protocols considered were the rather specialized ones called DHCP and DNS, which provide addressing and name resolution functions on TCP/IP internetworks like the Internet.

In addition, TCP/IP includes a whole series of application-layer protocols whose function is to allow users to interface with client/server applications and distributed applications on an internetwork. Examples of these protocols include Telnet, HTTP, FTP, Gopher, SMTP, NNTP, and so on. Other protocols, such as Simple

Network Management Protocol (SNMP) and remote network monitoring, provide network management functions to simplify management of hosts on an internetwork. And because TCP/IP is constantly evolving, protocols are being enhanced and newer ones are emerging as older ones become obsolete.

As outlined in the next four sections, Microsoft has chosen to implement four of these application-layer protocols within the framework of IIS 5 on Windows 2000.

HTTP

As you probably already know, HTTP is the application-layer protocol of TCP/IP that makes the World Wide Web (the Web) possible. This protocol handles the publishing of static and dynamic Web content on Windows 2000 Server. This publishing occurs when you create Web sites, as you'll learn later in this chapter.

The name of the underlying Windows 2000 service that supports HTTP is World Wide Web Publishing Service (WWW Publishing Service), which uses the associated executable System32\inetsrv\Inetinfo.exe. In Event Viewer, the service goes by the short name W3SVC.

Note   You can display and configure Windows 2000 services by using the Computer Management snap-in, one of the default shortcuts in the Administrative Tools program group. When you open the Computer Management console, expand the Services And Applications node and select the desired service underneath it to display the various entries. Then double-click an item in the right pane to open its configuration dialog box and display or configure its various settings.

HTTP defines a client/server protocol that describes how communications occur between HTTP servers (called Web servers) and HTTP clients (called Web browsers). The following is a typical HTTP session between a Windows 2000 Server running IIS 5 (a Web server) and a client machine running Microsoft Internet Explorer 5 (a Web browser). An HTTP session is essentially made up of a connection, a request, and a response.

1. The client machine uses TCP to establish a connection to the server, typically using port 80, which is the default or well-known port number for HTTP connections. You can specify other port numbers on the server if you want, but the client then needs to know the port number in order to connect to the server. The connection is formed using a standard TCP three-way handshake.

2. Once connected to the server, the client machine requests a Web page or some other file from the server. The page could be specified by entering

its URL into the Address box in Microsoft Internet Explorer, or the user might simply click a hyperlink on another page to request the new one. Either way, the client sends a packet to the server containing an HTTP Get Request message. A typical client's Get Request message might look like the following:

```
GET /samples/sampsite/sampsite.htm HTTP/1.1
Accept: image/gif, image/x-xbitmap, image/jpeg, image/pjpeg, */*
Accept-Language: en-us
Accept-Encoding: gzip, deflate
User-Agent: Mozilla/4.0 (Compatible; MSIE 5.0; Windows NT 5.0)
Host: ws1
Connection: Keep-Alive
```

The various lines of this request are called headers, and these headers allow the client to communicate information to the server such as this:

- The particular Web page or other file that is being requested (in this example, the Web page sampsite.htm)

- The fact that the client supports version 1.1 of HTTP

- The Multipurpose Internet Mail Extensions (MIME) types, languages, and encoding methods that the client understands

- The type of client being used, which here is Internet Explorer 5

- The Web server from which the page is requested (in this example, the Windows 2000 server called WS1)

- Various other information, such as the fact that HTTP Keep-Alives are enabled on the client

3. The server responds to the request by sending a series of packets containing the Web page or other file requested by the client. The first of these returned packets contains header information, which the server communicates to the client. For example, in response to the Get Request message sent by the client in step 2, the first packet sent by server WS1 starts with the following information:

```
HTTP/1.1 200 OK
Server: Microsoft-IIS/5.0
Date: Mon, 26 Jul 1999 20:09:59 GMT
Content-Type: text/html
Accept-Ranges: bytes
Last-Modified: Mon, 14 Oct 1996 01:38:00 GMT
ETag: "08c375570b9bb1:968"
Content-Length: 1066
```

(continued)

```
<HTML>
<HEAD>
<TITLE>Sample Web Site</TITLE>
</HEAD>
<BODY BGCOLOR="FFFFFF">
<BODY BACKGROUND="/samples/images/
backgrnd.gif" BGCOLOR="FFFFFF">
etc...
```

The first few lines here are headers, and what the server is basically saying to the client is this:

- HTTP 1.1 requests are acceptable to the server.

- Error code 200 means the server accepts the client's request as valid and is returning the page that the client requested.

- The type of server, date and time, and various other information follows.

After the headers comes the beginning of the actual Web page requested by the client, showing the HTML that formats the information for the client so that it can be displayed as a Web page.

4. At this point, if HTTP Keep-Alives are enabled, the TCP connection between the client and server stays open in case the client wants to request additional files from the server. If Keep-Alives are disabled, the TCP connection is terminated after the page is downloaded, and a new TCP connection must be established to download the next file (an embedded image within the page, for example). Establishing this connection can be a real pain if, for example, the Web page you are downloading has 33 embedded images, three Java applets, one ShockWave animation, and other neat stuff in it. Without Keep-Alives, the additional overhead of establishing and tearing down TCP connections for each file downloaded slows the process down a bit, so it's usually smart to leave Keep-Alives enabled (as explained in the next chapter).

That's basically all there is to HTTP. It's a simple client/server application-layer protocol based on the underlying TCP transport-layer protocol. HTTP is by far the most important of the four Internet protocols supported by IIS, and it is the basis of the Web.

 More Info Version 1.1 of Hypertext Transfer Protocol is defined in RFC 2068.

Real World   Troubleshooting HTTP Sessions

Unless Internet communications are specifically encrypted using the Secure Sockets Layer (SSL) protocol, HTTP sessions are transmitted in clear (unencrypted) text, which allows you to view the header information in HTTP packets using a tool such as Network Monitor. You can optionally install Network Monitor on Windows 2000 Server by using Add/Remove Programs in Control Panel and selecting Add/Remove Windows Components; select the Management And Monitoring Tools component, and click the Details button to access the Network Monitor option. This tool is often useful when trying to troubleshoot HTTP session problems.

Another useful tool for troubleshooting HTTP session problems is the telnet client program that is started from the command line. By starting telnet and opening a connection to the server using the HTTP port 80 instead of the usual telnet port 20, you can manually enter HTTP Get Request headers and view the results. Note that after typing your headers, you enter a single blank line (CR/LF) to transmit the request to the server. Make sure you have Local Echo enabled on your telnet client and that you have set a large buffer size as well, to receive the response from the server.

FTP

FTP is an older TCP/IP application-layer protocol that enables users to transfer files over an internetwork like the Internet. The name of the underlying Windows 2000 service that supports FTP is called the FTP Publishing Service, and it has the same associated executable as the WWW Publishing Service: System32\inetsrv\Inetinfo.exe. In Event Viewer, the service goes by the short name MSFTPSVC.

More Info   The File Transfer Protocol is defined in RFC 959.

FTP defines a client/server protocol that describes how communications take place between FTP servers and FTP clients. Specifically, FTP enables clients to upload files to or download files from an FTP server over an internetwork. A typical FTP session is essentially made up of a connection, a request, and a response, as the following example shows.

1. The client forms a TCP connection with port 21 on the server. Port 21 is the standard TCP port that an FTP server continually "listens" to for FTP clients' connection attempts. Once a connection is formed, a randomly assigned port number above 1023 is given to the client. This initial TCP connection is used for transmission of FTP control information—that is, for commands sent from the client to the server—and for response codes returned from the server to the client.

2. The client then issues an FTP command to port 21 on the server using the first TCP connection established in step 1. These commands are all issued as clear (unencrypted) text over the Internet connection, which means you can use the same tools (Network Monitor and telnet) to monitor and troubleshoot FTP sessions that you can for HTTP. Typical FTP commands include Get (download a file), Put (upload a file), Binary (switch to binary mode), Cd (change to a different directory on the server), and so on.

3. If the command issued by the client initiates a data transfer (upload or download) with the server, the server opens a second TCP connection with the client for performing the transfer. This second TCP connection uses port 20 on the server and a randomly assigned port number greater than 1023 on the client. (The first TCP connection—to port 21 on the server—is used only to send control information between the client and server, not for data transfer.)

4. Once the data transfer is complete, the second TCP connection goes into a TIME_WAIT state until either another data transfer takes place or the connection times out.

 Tip You can use the Netstat utility from the command line to view information about TCP connections that FTP uses. Just open a command-prompt window on the client or server and type *Netstat -p tcp* to see the TCP connections.

SMTP

SMTP is a popular TCP/IP application-layer protocol that forms the basis of the Internet's e-mail system. The console name of the underlying Windows 2000 service that supports SMTP is Simple Mail Transport Protocol, and it has the same associated executable as the WWW Publishing Service: System32\inetsrv\inetinfo.exe. In Event Viewer, the service is referred to as SMTPSVC.

SMTP is both a client/server and server/server protocol, and it is used essentially for transferring e-mail from one SMTP host to another over an internetwork. A typical SMTP session begins with a connection followed by a series of commands. For example, consider the following scenario, in which the local (initiating) SMTP host wants to transfer e-mail to the remote (responding) SMTP host:

1. An SMTP client connects to a local SMTP host to send an e-mail message addressed to a user residing in the domain of a remote SMTP host. The local host is responsible for transferring the message to the remote host so the intended recipient will be able to receive it.

2. The local SMTP host forms a TCP connection on port 25 with the remote SMTP host using a standard TCP three-way handshake. Once the connection has been established, the remote host returns a Ready response to the local host, indicating that it's ready to initiate an SMTP session.

3. The local host issues a Helo command, to which the remote host responds with OK. An SMTP session is now established.

4. The local host issues a Mail From command indicating the name of the user who sent the e-mail. The remote host responds with OK.

5. The local host issues a Rcpt To command indicating the name of the user to whom the e-mail is directed. The remote host responds with OK.

6. The local host issues a Data command indicating that the body of the message will now be transferred. The remote host responds with OK.

7. The message body is then transferred as a data stream of 7-bit ASCII characters. (8-bit binary data must be encoded into 7-bit ASCII data using the MIME protocol, since SMTP only understands ASCII.) The local host indicates the end of the data stream with a period (.), which is on a line by itself.

8. If the intended recipient is running the SMTP client and is connected to the remote host, the recipient will then receive the message that the sender addressed to him or her (but see the Real World sidebar "SMTP Limitations").

9. Further messages are then transferred. The local host terminates the SMTP session by issuing a Quit command, after which the TCP connection between the hosts is terminated.

More Info   The Simple Mail Transfer Protocol was originally defined in RFC 821, but various extensions to this protocol are further defined in RFCs 974, 1869, and 1870.

Real World   SMTP Limitations

The SMTP protocol is designed mainly for moving e-mail from one SMTP host to another and has no facility to store messages in folders for users so that the messages can be retrieved and read later. SMTP clients must therefore be continually connected to an SMTP host in order to retrieve and read their e-mail; otherwise, the e-mail will bounce. As a result, other Internet e-mail protocols have been developed to enable e-mail to be temporarily stored until users can connect to retrieve their messages.

The most popular of these protocols are Post Office Protocol version 3 (POP3) and Internet Message Access Protocol version 4 (IMAP4). However, IIS 5 in Windows 2000 supports neither of these protocols because the SMTP Service is primarily intended to provide e-mail–sending capability to Active Server Pages (ASP) applications running on IIS—it's not designed to function as a corporate e-mail server. If you want the full Internet capabilities of a corporate SMTP/POP3/IMAP4 e-mail server, you can use Microsoft Exchange Server for this purpose.

NNTP

NNTP is a TCP/IP application-layer protocol that forms the basis of the USENET system of newsgroups used on the Internet. The console label of the underlying Windows 2000 service that supports NNTP is Network News Transport Protocol, and it has the same associated executable as the WWW Publishing Service: System32\inetsrv\Inetinfo.exe. In Event Viewer, the service is called NNTPSVC.

NNTP is both a client/server protocol and a server/server protocol that provides the following functionality:

- Allows an NNTP client (newsreader) to connect to an NNTP server (host) to download a list of available newsgroups on the server, read individual messages in the newsgroups, and reply to existing messages or post new ones to the server.

- Allows one NNTP host to replicate its list of newsgroups and their messages with another host on an internetwork. This replication between hosts is performed by using newsfeeds (or simply feeds), which can either be pushed or pulled between hosts.

Some of the commands that a newsreader can use during a session with a host include the following:

- **List**   Retrieves a list of newsgroups available on the host.
- **Group**   Selects a particular newsgroup from which to retrieve messages
- **Article**   Retrieves a specific message from a newsgroup

---

More Info   The Network News Transfer Protocol is defined in RFC 977.

The commands used for communications between hosts (called NNTP control messages) include these:

- **Newgroup**   Indicates that a new newsgroup has been created
- **Rmgroup**   Indicates that a newsgroup should be deleted
- **Cancel**   Indicates that a specific message in a newsgroup should be deleted

---

More Info   A full discussion of an NNTP session is beyond the scope of this book, but you can learn more about NNTP control messages in RFC 1036.

Other Protocols

Although IIS 5 supports only the four application-layer Internet protocols just described, it does support other complementary Internet protocols that provide enhanced functionality to HTTP, FTP, SMTP, and NNTP. These additional protocols include the following:

- **Secure Sockets Layer (SSL) 3**   Used to encrypt authentication and data transmission for HTTP and NNTP transmission using public-key cryptography.
- **Transport Layer Security (TLS)**   Used for encrypting SMTP transmissions only. A variant of SSL.
- **Lightweight Directory Access Protocol (LDAP)**   Used by the SMTP Service for accessing information in a directory service.
- **Multipurpose Internet Mail Extensions (MIME)**   Used by the HTTP service for communicating acceptable file formats to HTTP clients.

More Info   A full discussion of these four Internet protocols is beyond the scope of this book, but you can find information about them in the following RFCs:

SSL/TLS: RFCs 2246, 2487, and 2595

LDAP version 3: RFC 2251

MIME: RFCs 2045, 2046, 2047, 2048, and 2049

Administration Tools

Windows 2000 Server contains a variety of tools for administering the four core IIS 5 services just discussed. The next several sections describe the tools for administering these services.

Internet Information Services

Internet Information Services, a stand-alone snap-in for the Microsoft Management Console (MMC), is the primary tool used for administering IIS 5 on Windows 2000–based networks; therefore, it's the primary tool we'll use for IIS 5 administration in this chapter and the next. Note that the actual snap-in is called Internet Information Services, whereas the shortcut created in the Administrative Tools folder for the default console within which this snap-in is installed is called Internet Services Manager.

By default, when you install Windows 2000 Server, it supports only the WWW, FTP, and SMTP Publishing Services, so you can use the Internet Information Services console to create and manage Web sites, FTP sites, and SMTP sites (Figure 27-1). You can install the NNTP Publishing Service later by opening Control Panel's Add/Remove Programs utility and selecting the Add/Remove Windows Components option. Select the Internet Information Services component and click Details to locate this service.

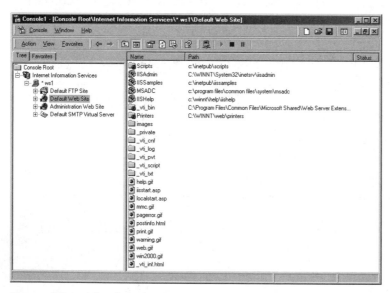

Figure 27-1. *The default Internet Information Services console window.*

Internet Services Manager (HTML)

The Internet Services Manager (HTML) tool, usually shortened to ISM (HTML), is really an ASP application running on IIS 5. It allows administrators to remotely manage many aspects of IIS 5 by using a standard Web browser like Internet Explorer 5. ISM (HTML) is installed on Windows 2000 Server by default. Chapter 28 covers the ISM (HTML) tool in more detail.

Administration Scripts

For the programmatically minded, you can use the Windows Scripting Host (WSH) to run administration scripts on Windows 2000 Server to perform common administrative tasks like creating new Web sites, configuring Web site security, creating virtual directories, stopping and starting Web sites, and so on. You can write these scripts in Visual Basic Scripting Edition (VBScript), or JavaScript. You'll find sample administration scripts in the \Inetpub\AdminScripts folder.

The WWW Publishing Service

Now let's take a look at some basic concepts and tasks associated with the WWW Publishing Service. We'll begin by examining the Default Web Site that is included as an example when you install Windows 2000 Server on a machine. Then we'll look at common tasks such as creating new Web sites and virtual directories and using Web sharing.

> **Note** Whether IIS was installed on your Windows 2000 Server during setup depends on how the installation was done. For example, if you upgraded a Windows NT 4 server that had a previous version of IIS installed on it, then Setup automatically upgrades these services to IIS 5. Otherwise, a default installation of Windows 2000 Server installs IIS 5 and creates the Default Web Site, Default FTP Site, Administration Web Site, and Default SMTP Virtual Server, but not the Default NNTP Virtual Server.

The Default Web Site

In Figure 27-1 you saw an administrator's view of the Default Web Site—a series of sample configuration files whose default location on the server's local file system is C:\Inetpub\wwwroot, the root WWW publishing directory. The \Inetpub directory actually contains several important subdirectories, which are summarized in Table 27-1.

Note that some of these subdirectories will be present only if their related Windows 2000 optional components are installed on the server. Note also that you don't necessarily need to store Web site content in any of these directories— content can be located in any directory on the server, or on a network share located on some other server, as you'll soon see.

Table 27-1.   IIS-related subdirectories located within the default C:\Inetpub directory

Subdirectory	Description
AdminScripts	Sample IIS administration scripts for the Windows Scripting Host.
ftproot	Root directory of Default FTP Site.
iissamples	Miscellaneous sample material.
Mail	Remote administrator for the SMTP service, using a Web browser.
mailroot	Various folders used by the SMTP service.
News	Remote administrator for the NNTP service, using a Web browser.
nntpfile	Various folders used by the NNTP service.
scripts	Default location for application scripts used by the Default Web Site. Includes samples and tools.
wwwroot	Root directory of the Default Web Site.

Connecting to a Web Site

On the server, you can access the home page of the Default Web Site (Figure 27-2) in various ways by using a Web browser. Try out these methods:

- From the local console, click Start, point to Run, enter *http://127.0.0.1*, and click OK. This will open Internet Explorer and access the home page by using the TCP/IP loopback address.
- From the local console, start Internet Explorer, enter *localhost* in the Address bar, and press Enter.
- From the Internet Information Services console, select the Default Web Site node and *either*
  - Right-click and choose Browse from the shortcut menu, *or*
  - Click the Action button on the toolbar and select Browse from the drop-down menu.

When you attempt access from a remote machine on the connected network, you will see an "under construction" message, but that message actually tells you that the site is active and accessible. To connect, start Internet Explorer, press Ctrl+O to open the Open dialog box, enter any of the following, and then click OK:

- The IP address of the Web server (for example, 172.16.11.202)

- The NetBIOS name of the Web server (for example, WS1)
- The DNS name of the Web server (for example, ws1.scribes.com), provided either a name server is accessible or the Hosts file is configured on the client

Figure 27-2. *The home page of the Default Web Site.*

Other Web Sites

The Default Web Site is only one small example of how you can use the IIS 5 WWW Publishing Service. In fact, you can create as many different Web sites as you want using IIS 5, and you can host the content (pages, images, and other files) for these sites in a variety of locations. Each Web site acts as a separate entity, or *virtual server*; that is, it acts as if it were running on its own Windows 2000 server and using the full resources available to it on that server. To illustrate this, let's create a new Web site on the server WS1, create a simple home page for it, and then test it by connecting to it from another machine on the network.

Using the Web Site Creation Wizard

Before using the Web Site Creation Wizard to create a new Web site, you must decide how to name this site on the network. As you saw previously, when you use a Web browser like Internet Explorer to connect to a Web site and view its home page, you can specify the URL of the site in a variety of ways, including using the site's IP address, NetBIOS name, or fully qualified DNS name.

For this example, you'll bind a second IP address to the network interface card (NIC) on the Windows 2000 server WS1 and establish a mapping between the new Web site you'll create and the new IP address you'll add. (Other ways to distinguish different Web sites on the same server are discussed in the section "Web Site Identification" in Chapter 28.) To add a second IP address, follow these steps:

1. Right-click the My Network Places icon on the desktop and choose Properties from the shortcut menu (or start the Network And Dial-Up Connections utility in Control Panel).

2. In the Network And Dial-Up Connections window, right-click the Local Area Connection icon and choose Properties from the shortcut menu (or double-click the icon and click the Properties button).

3. In the Local Area Connection Properties window, double-click Internet Protocol (TCP/IP).

4. In the Internet Protocol (TCP/IP) Properties window, click the Advanced button.

5. In the IP Addresses box in the Advanced TCP/IP Settings dialog box (Figure 27-3), click Add, specify an additional IP address and subnet mask, and click Add.

6. Click OK until all dialog boxes have been closed.

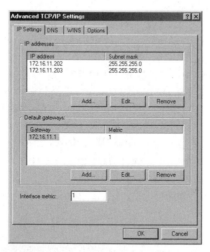

Figure 27-3. *Adding additional IP addresses for Web site identities.*

Two more steps are required prior to creating the site. First, establish a new directory, C:\scribesweb, on the local server, which will store the content for the new site. Then create a simple home page called Default.htm within this site, using basic HTML. If you aren't familiar with HTML, enter the following text into NotePad and save the file in the \scribesweb directory as Default.htm, ensuring that your editor does not add a.TXT extension:

```
<HTML>
<HEAD><TITLE>Scribes Ltd.</TITLE></HEAD>
<BODY>
<H1>Welcome to Scribes Ltd.</H1>
<HR>
This site is under construction!
</BODY>
</HTML>
```

Now create a new Web site called Scribes Ltd. (named after the domain name Scribes.com) by following these steps:

1. Start the Internet Information Services console on server WS1 (or start it on a different server or workstation and connect to computer WS1 by clicking the Action button on the toolbar and selecting Connect from the drop-down menu) and select the server's name in the console tree.

2. Click the Action button on the toolbar, point to New, and choose Web Site from the drop-down menu (or right-click the WS1 node in the console, point to New, and choose Web Site from the shortcut menu). The first screen of the Web Site Creation Wizard appears (Figure 27-4). Click Next.

Figure 27-4. *The first screen of the Web Site Creation Wizard.*

3. Type *Scribes Ltd.* as the description for the site. This name is displayed in the Internet Information Services console window and identifies the new site for the administrator. Click Next.

4. Specify your second IP address as the one to be mapped to the site, leaving the remaining settings as they are (Figure 27-5). Click Next.

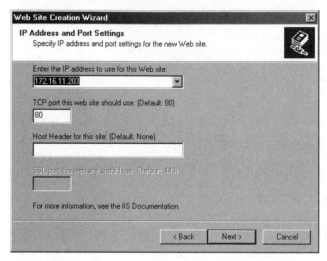

Figure 27-5. *The IP Address And Port Settings screen of the Web Site Creation Wizard.*

5. Specify the path to the home directory for the Web site as C:\scribesweb. (Using the Browse button is easiest.) Note that the home directory for your site can be either a local directory or a network share. Leave the check box selected to allow anonymous access to the Web site. (Because this is a public Web site, you want anyone to be able to access it.) Click Next.

6. Leave the access permissions set at their default settings. (We'll consider these permissions in more detail in Chapter 28.)

7. Click Next and then click Finish to complete the Wizard. The new Scribes Ltd. Web site should appear as a node under server WS1 in the Internet Information Services console window, showing its single Web page Default.htm (Figure 27-6).

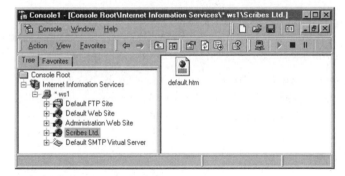

Figure 27-6. *The new Scribes Ltd. Web site.*

Testing the New Web Site

To test the IP *address mapping* (Web site identity) for the new Web site, go to a different machine on the network, start Internet Explorer, and open the URL *http://172.16.11.203*, which specifies the new Web site using its associated IP address. The page Default.htm should load in the browser window (Figure 27-7). Note that if a name server mapped this IP address to a DNS name like *www.scribes.com*, you could access the Web site by using *http://www.scribes.com* instead of by using the IP address.

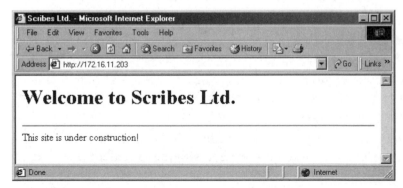

Figure 27-7. *Testing the new Scribes Ltd. Web site from a remote machine.*

As a further test, try opening the following URLs from the same machine:

- *http://172.16.11.202*
- *http://ws1*
- *http://ws1.scribes.com* (only if DNS is enabled)

Each of these URLs specifies an identity for the Default Web Site on the server WS1 and should open the "under construction" home page for this site. We'll look more at Web site identities in Chapter 28.

Virtual Directories

In the previous example you created a new Web site called Scribes Ltd. whose content was located in the home directory C:\scribesweb on server WS1. To access content in this directory, you can use either of the following URLs:

- *http://<IP_Address>,* where *<IP_Address>* represents the IP address bound to the server's NIC that is mapped to that particular Web site
- *http://<DNS_Name>,* where *<DNS_Name>* is the fully qualified DNS name (such as *ws1.scribes.com*) that is associated on the name server with the IP address mapped to that particular Web site

Taking the first URL, you can associate or map a particular URL with the Web content stored in the site's home directory as represented here:

C:\scribesweb ↔ *http://172.16.11.203.*

But what if you want to locate content for this Web site in a variety of locations and not just in the \scribesweb directory on the server? You can do this by using something called a virtual directory. A *virtual directory* is a way of mapping an alias (a portion of a URL) to a physical directory containing additional Web site content not located in the home directory for the site.

For example, let's say we want to store additional content in the directory C:\salesstuff on the local server and associate it with the virtual directory /sales. Note that the virtual directory uses a forward slash (/) instead of a backslash (\). The URL-to-directory mapping would be

C:\salesstuff ↔ *http://172.16.11.203/sales*

Note that from the point of view of the client using the Web browser, the /sales content appears as a subdirectory of the home directory for the Scribes Ltd. Web site. In other words, the content *virtually* appears as a subdirectory of the home directory *http://172.16.11.203*. But in fact, the content is *physically* located in an entirely separate part of the directory tree on the server's file system (instead of being located in \scribesweb\sales, as you might expect from the URL). Virtual directories thus enable a kind of virtual file system specified by URLs that bears no direct relationship to the actual location of Web content for the site.

Local Virtual Directories vs. Remote Virtual Directories

The content that is mapped to the alias representing a virtual directory can be located in one of two places, resulting in two different kinds of virtual directories:

- **Local virtual directory**   The content is located on the local Windows 2000 server. This solution might be the simplest because all content for the Web site is located on the local server and can be backed up in a single operation. Content for different departments of a company can be located in different directories on the server for security and integrity reasons.

- **Remote virtual directory**   The content is located on a remote file server on the network. This solution is often the best when publishing legacy content that is already stored on network file servers. Security is enhanced because a user account is required to access the remote share and suitable permissions can be assigned to this account. This remote placement of content also increases security by allowing content developers access only to file servers instead of to the Web servers themselves, and it reduces the processing load on the Web server. The only disadvantage is that the performance is slightly slower for content hosted on remote file servers, but this can be minimized by physically locating file servers close to the Web server on the network.

The Virtual Directory Creation Wizard

Now let's use the Virtual Directory Creation Wizard to create a remote virtual directory for the new Scribes Ltd. Web site. Before running the wizard, you must perform two tasks:

- Create a new user account in the domain to control access to shares mapped to remote virtual directories. You can give this user account any name you want, but for now, use the name RVD, which stands for remote virtual directory. Create this account by using the Active Directory Users And Computers console on a domain controller, and give it a secure password that never expires.

- Create the content directory and populate it with a Default.htm page. To do this, first create the content directory C:\salesstuff on file server SRV1. Share this directory using the default share name Salesstuff, and assign Read permission to the RVD account that you just created. Create a new Default.htm page for this directory or copy the previous one.

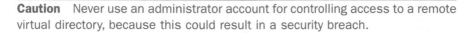

Caution Never use an administrator account for controlling access to a remote virtual directory, because this could result in a security breach.

Now create a new remote virtual directory called /sales within the Scribes Ltd. Web site, by following these steps:

1. Start the Internet Information Services console on server WS1 (or start it on a different server or workstation and connect to computer WS1 by clicking the Action button on the toolbar and choosing Connect from the drop-down menu).

2. Select the Scribes Ltd. Web site in the console tree, click the Action button on the toolbar, point to New, and choose Virtual Directory from the drop-down menu (or right-click the Scribes Ltd. node in the console, point to New, and choose Virtual Directory from the shortcut menu). The Virtual Directory Creation Wizard starts. Click Next.

3. Specify *sales* as the alias for the virtual directory. Note that you don't include the forward slash here. Click Next.

4. Specify the UNC path \\SRV1\salesstuff as the path to the share that will be associated with the new remote virtual directory (Figure 27-8). You can also use the Browse button to locate the share on the connected network. Click Next.

5. Use the Browse button to select the RVD user account. (This step enters the account in the form *<Domain>\<Account>* into the User Name text box, which is required.)

6. Specify the password you assigned to this account, click Next, and confirm the password.

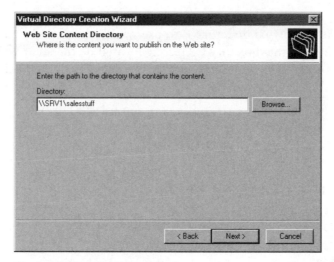

Figure 27-8. *The Web Site Content Directory screen of the Virtual Directory Creation Wizard.*

7. Click OK and leave the access permissions settings at their default.

8. Click Next and then click Finish to complete the wizard.

If you now examine the Scribes Ltd. node in the Internet Information Services console tree, you'll notice a new node beneath it representing the new virtual directory (Figure 27-9). Try viewing the Default.htm page in this virtual directory by accessing the URL *http://172.16.11.203/sales* from a Web browser on a remote machine.

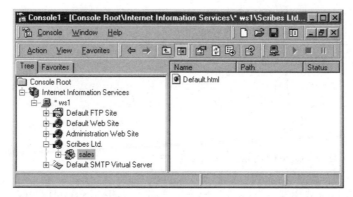

Figure 27-9. *The /sales virtual directory within the Scribes Ltd. Web site.*

Web Sharing

Another way to create a new virtual directory is to use what's called Web sharing. For example, say you have the directory C:\Testing located on the local Web server WS1 and you want to share this directory as a virtual directory of the Default Web Site. To do this, follow these steps:

1. Right-click the \Testing directory in My Computer and select Sharing from the shortcut menu.

2. In the Testing Properties window, click the Web Sharing tab.

3. Select the Default Web Site from the Share On drop-down box. This will create a new local virtual directory mapped to the \Testing directory for its content.

4. To open the Edit Alias dialog box (Figure 27-10), select the Share This Folder option. You can specify an alias that is different from the name of the folder if you like.

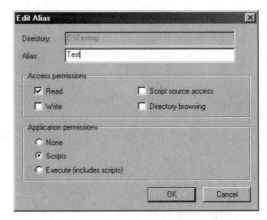

Figure 27-10. *The Edit Alias dialog box.*

5. Click OK twice and the virtual directory is created. Try accessing this directory by using the URL *http://WS1/test*. (Place a Default.htm page in the \Testing directory first.)

Virtual Directories, Physical Directories, and Icons

Virtual directories can be confusing for a couple of reasons. First, there are two different icons you can use for nodes representing virtual directories in the IIS console. Second, physical directories can behave like virtual directories if they're physically located as subfolders of the home directory or another virtual directory. Take a look at Figure 27-11 as an example. Looking at the various subnodes under the Scribes Ltd. node in the console tree, notice that

- The /sales virtual directory has an icon that looks like an open package or box with something green in it. This is the default appearance of a virtual directory icon and means that the virtual directory is configured as an application root, that is, the starting directory for a Web application, typically one developed by using ASP.

- The /support virtual directory has an icon that looks like a folder with a globe attached to it. This is a virtual directory that isn't configured as an application root. (You'll see how to configure and remove application roots in the next chapter.) Note also that the /support virtual directory has an /MIS virtual directory beneath it, which you would access by using the URL *http://<Web_Site_Identity>/support/MIS.*

- The /management virtual directory is currently unavailable for some reason (perhaps its associated content physical directory has been moved or deleted), and as a result it appears in the console tree as a red stop sign saying "Error".

- Finally, the /marketing directory isn't a virtual directory at all, but rather a subdirectory of the C:\scribesweb physical directory on the local server WS1. As a result, it appears with an ordinary folder icon in the console tree. However, users can connect to it as if it were a physical directory by using the URL *http://<Web_Site_Identity>/marketing.*

Figure 27-11. *Confusion between virtual and physical directories.*

The FTP Publishing Service

Now let's look at concepts and tasks associated with the FTP Publishing Service (the FTP service). We'll begin by examining the Default FTP Site included as an example when you install Windows 2000 Server. Then we'll look at common tasks such as creating new FTP sites and virtual directories. We can move fairly quickly here because these tasks are similar to ones you just learned for the WWW Publishing Service.

The Default FTP Site

Like the WWW service, installing the FTP service on a Windows 2000 server creates a new default site called the Default FTP Site. (The WWW service and the FTP service are both installed by default whenever you install the core Internet Information Services on Windows 2000 Server, but you can remove either of them by using Add/Remove Programs in Control Panel.) Unlike the Default Web Site, with its sample pages and numerous directories, however, the Default FTP Site is completely empty. This is singularly uninteresting, so let's move on!

Other FTP Sites

As with the WWW service, you can create as many different FTP sites as you want using IIS 5, and you can host the content (pages, images, and other files) for these sites in either local directories or network shares. Each FTP site acts as a separate entity, or virtual server, and acts as if it were running on its own Windows 2000 server using the full resources available to it on that server. To illustrate this, we'll create a new FTP site on the server WS1, place a test file in its home directory, and then download the test file from another machine on the network.

Using the FTP Site Creation Wizard

As with Web sites, you can specify FTP sites on an internetwork in a variety of ways, including using the site's IP address, NetBIOS name, or fully qualified DNS name. For the present example, use the extra IP address that was bound to the network card on the server WS1 in the previous section. You must also create a home directory for the new FTP site, so you'll create the directory C:\ftphome on the local server. Then you'll copy a bitmap file like \Winnt\Greenstone.bmp to the C:\ftphome directory so you'll have something to download from the client. Follow these steps to create the new FTP site:

1. Start the Internet Information Services console on server WS1 (or start it on a different server or workstation and connect to server WS1 by clicking the Action button on the toolbar and choosing Connect from the drop-down menu) and select the server's name in the console tree.

2. Click Action on the toolbar, point to New, and choose FTP Site from the drop-down menu (or right-click the WS1 node in the console, point to New, and choose FTP Site from the shortcut menu). This starts the FTP Site Creation Wizard. Click Next.

3. Type *Scribes FTP Site* as the name for the site. This name is displayed in the Internet Information Services console window and identifies the new site for the administrator. Click Next.

4. Specify your second IP address as the one to be mapped to the site, leaving the port number at its default setting. Click Next.

5. Specify the path to the home directory for the new FTP site as C:\ftphome. (Using the Browse button is easiest.) Note that the home directory for your site can be a local directory or a network share. Click Next.

6. Make sure that both Read permissions and Write permissions are selected. This will allow you to both download files from and upload files to your new FTP site.

7. Click Next and then click Finish to complete the Wizard. The new Scribes FTP Site should appear as a node under server WS1 in the Internet Information Services console window (Figure 27-12). Note that the Greenstone.bmp file within the home directory doesn't appear in the right pane of the console window. This is different from Web sites, where files in home directories and virtual directories are displayed in the console window.

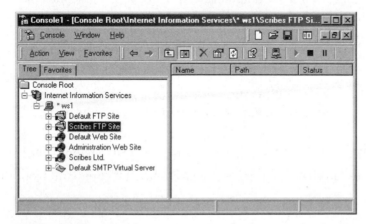

Figure 27-12. *The new Scribes FTP Site shown in the Internet Information Services console window.*

Testing the New FTP Site

To test the new FTP site, go to a different machine on the network, start Internet Explorer 5, and open the URL *ftp://172.16.11.203*, which specifies the new FTP site using its associated IP address. The file Greenstone.bmp should be displayed in the browser window, along with the IP address you're connecting to and the user name Anonymous (Figure 27-13).

Figure 27-13. *Connecting to the new Scribes FTP Site using Internet Explorer 5.*

Once you've connected to the FTP site, you can perform various actions in Internet Explorer, including the following:

- Download the file to your machine by right-clicking its icon, choosing Copy To Folder, and specifying the destination folder on your machine (or anywhere else accessible on the network).

- Drag and drop files from My Computer on your local machine into the browser window to upload them to the FTP site.

- Right-click the file icon and choose Properties to display the type, location, size, and date modified of the original copy of the file on the FTP site.

- Log on to the FTP site as a different user (if access is controlled by user names) by choosing the Login As command from the browser's File menu.

- View the FTP welcome message (if there is one) using the Help menu.

Now isn't that more fun than using the old text-based FTP command from the command prompt?

Virtual Directories

You can create virtual directories for FTP sites the same as you can for Web sites. Let's look at this briefly now.

Using the Virtual Directory Creation Wizard

You've already seen the Virtual Directory Creation Wizard. It doesn't matter whether you create the virtual directory within a Web site or within an FTP site—the same wizard creates them. But just for variety, since you created a remote virtual directory for the Scribes Ltd. Web site last time, this time, create a local virtual directory for the Scribes FTP Site. (The following steps are compressed since you're already familiar with the wizard.)

1. Create the directory C:\uploads on the server WS1. This directory will be used as an FTP drop box—a directory where users can upload files but can't view the contents of the directory or download files from it.

2. Right-click the Scribes FTP Site node in the console tree of Internet Information Services, point to New, and choose Virtual Directory from the shortcut menu. Click Next.

3. Type *drop* as the alias for the virtual directory. Click Next.

4. Specify the path C:\uploads for the location of the content directory that maps to the virtual directory being created. Click Next.

5. Change the access permissions to enable write access and disable read access on the directory.

6. Click Next and then click Finish to complete the wizard.

The new local virtual directory /drop is now visible as the node underneath the Scribes FTP Site node in the console tree (Figure 27-14). Note that the icon used to represent FTP virtual directories is different from the ones used to represent Web virtual directories.

Testing the New Virtual Directory

Try accessing the new virtual directory from a remote machine by opening the URL *http://172.16.11.203/drop* virtual directory on the Scribes FTP Site using Internet Explorer. A message should appear in a dialog box saying, "An error occurred opening that folder on the FTP Server. Make sure you have permission to access that folder." Click OK to close the error message.

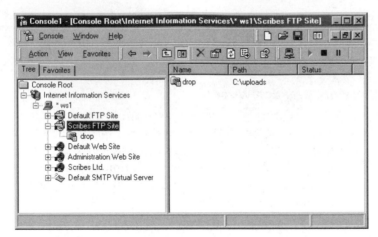

Figure 27-14. *The /drop virtual directory within the Scribes FTP Site.*

Now try dragging a file from My Computer into the browser window. Verify on the server WS1 that the file was indeed uploaded to the \uploads directory on the server. Now try refreshing the browser window. The same error message will appear as before. Click OK to close the error message, and the browser window—which is still open to the /drop virtual directory—should appear empty. This verifies that anonymous users can upload files to the virtual directory but can't view or download files from it.

Basic Administrative Tasks

This chapter concludes with a look at some of the basic administrative tasks you can perform on Web sites and FTP sites by using the Internet Information Services console. The next chapter takes a more detailed look at the various settings that you can configure for these sites. For now, the focus is on basic tasks like configuring permissions, stopping and starting services, and enabling Microsoft FrontPage extensions on the server.

Configuring Permissions

Understanding permissions and how they are configured and applied on IIS 5 is a part of the larger picture of understanding IIS security in general. This section covers the various levels of security that you can use to control access to content in Windows 2000 Server Web sites and FTP sites—and looks at the order in which these layers are applied. You'll also learn a fast and easy way to secure your Web sites and FTP sites: by using the IIS 5 Permissions Wizard. (More detailed information on configuring individual aspects of IIS 5 security is covered in the next chapter.)

Understanding IIS 5 Security

Administrators can control access to content on Web sites and FTP sites hosted on IIS 5 in four different ways. These methods are applied in order each time a user tries to access a Web or FTP resource (an HTML or other file) on the server. The four-stage access control model is presented below, and only when all four of these rules have been applied and passed is the user granted access to the requested resource.

1. Is the user's IP address or domain name allowed access to the resource?

   If not, access is denied and no further rules are applied. You can configure IP address and domain name restrictions using the Directory Security tab of the Properties window for the Web site, FTP site, or virtual or physical directory, or on the File Security tab of the Properties window for a file. Note that the Properties windows referred to here and in the next two steps apply to those accessed from the Internet Information Services console window. (See the next chapter for more information on these Properties windows.)

2. Has the user been properly authenticated for accessing the resource?

   If not, access is denied and no further rules are applied. You can configure authentication security settings on the Directory Security tab of the Properties window for a Web site or virtual or physical directory, on the File Security tab of the Properties window for a file, or on the Security Accounts tab of the Properties window for an FTP site. Note that you can't configure this level of security on virtual directories that are located within FTP sites, only on those within Web sites.

3. Are the IIS access and application permissions configured to allow users access to the resource?

   If not, access is denied and no further rules are applied. You can configure IIS access and application permissions on the Home Directory tab of the Properties window for a Web site or FTP site; on the Virtual

Directory tab of the Properties window for a virtual directory; on the Directory tab of the Properties window for a physical directory; or on the File tab of the Properties window for a file.

4. Do NTFS permissions on the resource allow the user to access the resource?

   If not, access to the resource is denied to the user. NTFS permissions are configured in the usual way by using the Security tab of the Properties window for the resource in My Computer.

> **Note** In the four-stage access control model, steps 2 and 4 are user-specific, while steps 1 and 3 apply regardless of the user's identity. In other words, IP address/domain name restrictions and IIS access/application permissions are global settings that apply uniformly for all users.

Using the Permissions Wizard

An easy way to configure permissions on Web sites and FTP sites, virtual and physical directories, and files in Internet Information Services is to use the Permissions Wizard. To see how the wizard works, follow these steps to configure permissions on the /sales virtual directory created earlier within the Scribes Ltd. Web site.

1. Right-click the /sales node under the Scribes Ltd. node in the console tree of Internet Information Services, point to All Tasks, and choose Permissions Wizard from the shortcut menu. This starts the Permissions Wizard.

2. Click Next to move to the Security Settings screen of the wizard. You'll be asked if you want security settings for the selected node to be inherited from the parent node or whether new settings should be specified. Select the first option, Inherit All Security Settings, and click Next.

3. Click Next once more. The Security Summary screen appears, indicating what security settings will be applied from the parent node—which in this case is the Scribes Ltd. Web site (Figure 27-15). Note that the four types of security settings that are listed on this screen agree with the four rules for access control discussed previously—except that they aren't listed in order here!

4. Click Back twice to return to the previous Security Settings screen, and this time select the second option, Select New Security Settings From A Template. Click Next to move to the Site Scenario screen of the wizard (Figure 27-16).

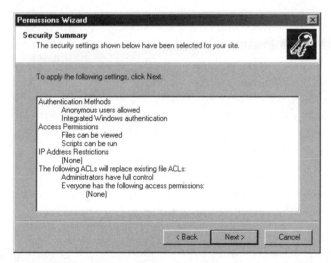

Figure 27-15. *The Security Summary screen of the Permissions Wizard.*

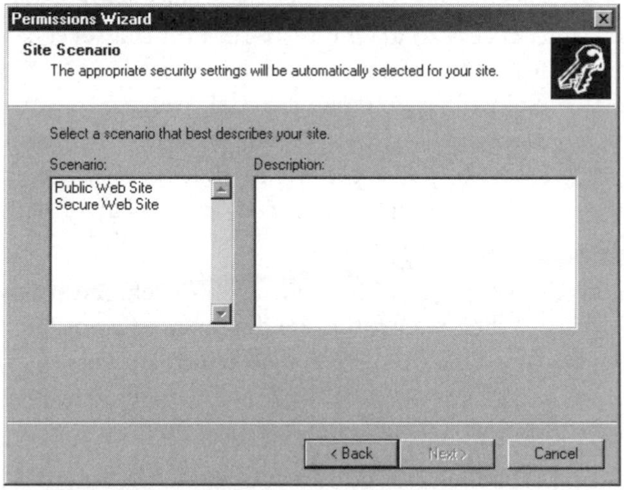

Figure 27-16. *The Site Scenario screen of the Permissions Wizard.*

This screen provides two different basic security templates that you can apply to the selected site or virtual directory. The two options here are

- **Public Web Site**   This template allows all users to browse static and dynamic content on the selected site or directory. Use this setting to configure security for public Internet sites.

- **Secure Web Site**   This template allows only users with a valid Windows 2000 account to view static and dynamic content on the selected site or directory. Use this setting to configure security for private intranet sites.

5. Select the first option, Public Web Site, and click Next twice to display the Security Summary screen for this choice. Note that the only authentication method that will be configured is Anonymous Users Allowed.

6. Click Back to return to the Site Scenario screen. Select the second option, Secure Web Site, and click Next twice to display the Security Summary screen for this choice. Note the variety of authentication methods allowed (discussed in the next chapter). Click Next and then click Finish to complete the wizard.

Obviously, the Permissions Wizard allows you to perform only a general configuration of IIS 5 security settings. For more granular security, you have to use the Internet Information Services Properties windows, discussed in the next chapter.

Stopping, Starting, and Pausing IIS Services

Remember that individual Web sites and FTP sites that are created on IIS 5 are actually virtual servers; that is, they act and behave as if they were separate Windows 2000 servers and had access to all the resources on the server. This allows Web sites for many different companies to be hosted on a single Windows 2000 Server machine. Sometimes you might need to stop, start, or pause IIS services on these machines, however. For example, when files are being modified on a Web site, it's usually smart to pause the site so that no new user connections can be established with the site and to allow users who are currently connected a grace period before they're disconnected.

Another example is when you're testing a Web application developed by using ASP—you might need to stop and then restart the site during the testing process if the application hangs or becomes unresponsive. The trouble is, if you have multiple sites running on your server, you don't want to bring them all down just to deal with the problems of a particular site.

To solve this problem, Windows 2000 Server allows you to use the Internet Services Manager to stop individual Web sites and FTP sites without having to stop the WWW and FTP Publishing Services for all sites on the server. To pause, stop, or start a site, simply select the node in the console tree that represents the site and do one of the following:

- Click the appropriate control button on the toolbar.
- Right-click the node and make the appropriate choice from the short-cut menu.
- Click the Action button and select the appropriate choice from the drop-down menu.

Alternately, you can start, stop, or restart all Web and FTP sites on your server by selecting the node representing the server in the console tree of Internet Services Manager; simply click the Action button on the toolbar and select Restart IIS from the drop-down menu. You might expect that you could stop all Web sites running on a machine by stopping the WWW Publishing Service using the Services node under System Tools in Computer Management. Don't do it this way. IIS is implemented differently from other Windows 2000 services and should not be stopped or started in this fashion. Finally, if you want to restart IIS from the command line, you can type *iisreset<Computer_Name>*. You can also use this command in a batch file.

Using FrontPage Server Extensions

IIS 5 uses a set of proprietary server-side DLLs called FrontPage extensions to support many of the advanced FrontPage features, such as its ability to create navigation bars, search tools, discussion Webs, and so on. Finally, let's look at installing FrontPage server extensions. In IIS 5, this is a basic Web server administration task for networks where developers use the popular Web content creation tool, FrontPage. We won't get into content development at all but will simply examine how to enable the server to operate with FrontPage.

Enabling FrontPage Extensions on a Web Site

Even though the necessary software to support FrontPage is preinstalled, you still need to enable these extensions on the specific Web sites that your FrontPage content developers will be using. To illustrate, use the Scribes Ltd. Web site and follow these steps:

1. Right-click the Scribes Ltd. node in the Internet Service Manager console tree, point to All Tasks, and choose Configure Server Extensions from the shortcut menu. This opens the Server Extensions Configuration Wizard (Figure 27-17). Note that this wizard can't create a new Web site; it can configure a Web site only for FrontPage users.

Figure 27-17. *The Server Extensions Configuration Wizard.*

2. Click Next to create local Windows groups that can be used to identify which users are FrontPage administrators, authors, and browsers for the selected Web site. These three groups can be described as follows:

   • **Administrators**   Can create new FrontPage Webs, change settings on the Web site, control the site authoring process, author new content, and browse existing content in the site.

   • **Authors**   Can author new content and browse existing content in the site.

   • **Browsers**   Can browse only existing content in the site.

3. Click Next to specify a Windows group or user account that will be the Web administrator for the selected site.

4. Click Next to specify SMTP e-mail settings for the site (if necessary).

5. Click Finish to enable and configure FrontPage extensions on the site.

6. Click the Action button on the Internet Information Services toolbar
   and choose Refresh from the drop-down menu to refresh the window
   view. Suddenly your selected Web site has been populated with a whole
   series of virtual and physical subdirectories with their associated server
   extension files (Figure 27-18).

Caution Don't delete any of these FrontPage files or directories, or the server
extensions might fail to work properly!

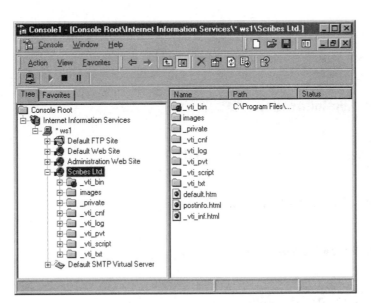

Figure 27-18. *Directories created by enabling FrontPage server extensions on
the site.*

Summary

IIS 5 is an integral part of Windows 2000 Server. No additional software is needed
to manage multiple Web sites—even on the same server. Wizards are supplied to
guide the administrator through all the basic configuration processes including
creating Web sites and virtual directories and setting permissions. Setting up an
Internet server has never been simpler. Keeping it running reliably and safely can
be a more difficult process. The next chapter covers the more complex administrative tasks of Web site and FTP site management.

Chapter 28
Advanced Internet Information Services

The previous chapter examined some basic administration tasks associated with Internet Information Services (IIS) on the Microsoft Windows 2000 Server platforms. This chapter explains how to configure the basic WWW and FTP Publishing Services in more detail. It also examines the NNTP and SMTP Services and how to configure them. Finally, it briefly covers remote administration of IIS using Internet Services Manager (HTML).

IIS settings can be configured and its servers, directories, and files can be administered at four different levels. The four levels of administration apply to the WWW, FTP, SMTP, and NNTP services discussed later in this chapter. Those levels are

- **Server-level administration**   The configuration of those settings that apply globally to all virtual servers on a Windows 2000 server with IIS installed. Server-level settings are inherited by all virtual servers and their virtual and physical directories and files.

- **Site-level administration**   The configuration of those settings that apply to a particular virtual server on the IIS machine—that is, to a particular Web, FTP, SMTP, or NNTP site on the machine. While server-level settings apply globally to those virtual servers that support Web sites and FTP sites on the machine, each of these virtual servers can also have its settings separately configured at the site level.

- **Directory-level administration**   The configuration of those settings that apply to a particular virtual (or physical) directory located within a virtual server. While site-level settings apply globally to all virtual (or physical) directories located within a particular Web, FTP, SMTP, or NNTP site, each directory can also have its settings separately configured at the directory level.

- **File-level administration**   The configuration of those settings that apply to a particular file located within a virtual (or physical) directory. While directory-level settings apply globally to all files located within a particular directory, each file can also have its settings separately configured at the file level. These file-level settings override those configured at the directory level and are a subset of the directory-level settings.

Rudimentary configuration tasks can be performed by the various wizards examined in the previous chapter, such as the Web Site Creation Wizard, the Virtual Directory Creation Wizard, the Permissions Wizard, and so on. To fully configure the various aspects of IIS on a Windows 2000 server, you need to use the various Properties windows for IIS objects. These objects include physical and virtual servers, physical and virtual directories, and files. Each of these types of objects is represented by a node in the console tree of the Microsoft Management Console (MMC), which—with the Internet Information Services snap-in installed on it—is the main tool for managing and configuring these objects.

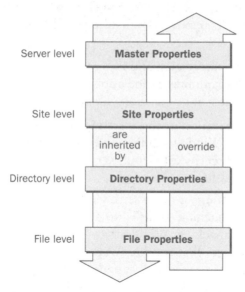

Figure 28-1. *The four levels of IIS administration.*

Figure 28-1 illustrates the four levels of IIS administration and how settings on Properties windows are inherited and overridden between these levels. We'll look at these settings later in the chapter, but first, let's take a look at the four administration levels in more detail. For all four levels, we'll focus specifically on the WWW Publishing Service because it has the broadest range of configuration options.

Real World   Inheritance of Settings

Settings configured for an object (physical or virtual server, physical or virtual directory, or file) are automatically inherited by objects at lower levels. For example, if you configure an IIS setting at the server level, this setting will be inherited (if applicable) by all virtual servers, virtual directories, physical directories, and files relating to IIS. You can override these inherited settings at any particular level, however. For example, you could override the settings for a particular virtual server (Web or FTP site) and all its directories and files, for a particular virtual or physical directory and the files it contains, or for a particular file. Note that once you have manually modified an inherited setting at some level, subsequently changing the setting at a higher level doesn't cause your modification to be automatically overwritten. Instead, you are prompted to decide whether you want to override the modified setting or not.

Server-Level Administration

Server-level administration involves the following tasks:

- Connecting to a machine running IIS to administer that machine
- Backing up and restoring the configuration of the machine
- Enabling global bandwidth throttling for all Web and FTP sites on the machine
- Configuring various master properties that apply globally to all Web and FTP sites created on the machine.
- Compressing files by using HTTP compression
- Configuring the global Multipurpose Internet Mail Extensions (MIME) map
- Setting server extensions (if you have Microsoft FrontPage 2000 server extensions installed)

Let's begin with the general administration tasks and global settings that you can configure for IIS running on a Windows 2000 server. You can perform some common server-level administration tasks using the IIS console introduced in Chapter 27.

Connecting to an IIS Server

You can administer multiple Windows 2000 servers running IIS from a single IIS console window. To administer a server, you need to connect to it first. To do so, follow these steps:

1. Select the root node (called Internet Information Services) in the IIS console tree.

2. Click the Action button on the toolbar and choose Connect from the drop-down menu, or right-click the root node and choose Connect from the shortcut menu. (Remember that in a console window, the drop-down Action menu provides the same options as the shortcut menu that displays when you right-click any selected node.)

3. In the Connect To Computer dialog box, type the name for the IIS machine to which you want to connect in the text box, and click OK. You can specify the name of the machine as any of the following:

    - NetBIOS name (for instance, ws1)
    - IP address (for instance, 172.16.11.210)
    - Fully qualified DNS name (for instance, ws1.scribes.com)

4. To disconnect from a server, select the node in the console tree that represents the server, click the Action button, and choose Disconnect.

Creating Configuration Backups

You can save the configuration setting for an IIS machine and all of its Web and FTP sites to a configuration backup file. Each backup file is stamped with a version number and its time and date of creation. You can create any number of backup files and restore these files if you want to restore your previous settings. This feature is quite useful—it allows you to take a snapshot of your IIS configuration before you start modifying permissions and other settings for the virtual servers, directories, and files on your machine.

Note Configuration backup files restore only the IIS settings on your machine's Web and FTP sites and their virtual and physical directories and files. They don't back up the actual content files themselves—that is, the HTML, image, and scripts within a Web site. Use the Windows 2000 Backup Wizard and the Recovery Wizard to back up the content files for your sites.

Backing Up a Server Configuration

To back up the configuration of your IIS machine, follow these steps:

1. Select the node in the console tree that represents your server.

2. Click the Action button and choose Backup/Restore Configuration from the drop-down menu.

3. As Figure 28-2 shows, the Configuration Backup/Restore dialog box that appears displays the various backup files you have created, their version numbers, and time/date of creation. Version numbers start with zero and increase sequentially.

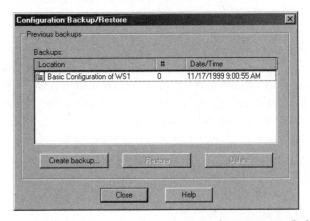

Figure 28-2. *The Configuration Backup/Restore dialog box.*

4. To create a new backup file, click the Create Backup button and give the file a friendly name. The backup file will be saved in the System32\ inetsrv\MetaBack directory. The information is stored in binary format and is specific to the machine on which it has been created. If you reinstall Windows 2000 on the machine, you'll be unable to use previously created backup files to recreate your IIS configuration.

Restoring a Server Configuration

To restore the configuration of your server to a previous version, open the Configuration Backup/Restore dialog box, select the backup file you want to restore to, and click Restore. Note that IIS must stop its services in order to perform a restore, so a restore takes longer than a backup.

Tip You can export the contents of the right-hand pane of the console window by selecting a particular node in the left-hand pane, clicking the Action button, and choosing Export List. You can save the information as an ASCII or Unicode text file in either tab-delimited format or comma-delimited format. This is a great way to document home directories for the various virtual directories you create within a Web site.

Configuring Server Properties

By far, the most time-consuming part of server-level IIS administration is configuring settings that are global to all virtual servers created on your machine. To access these settings, select a particular server node in the console tree, click the Action button, and choose Properties from the drop-down menu. (Or you can select the particular server node and click the Properties button on the toolbar.) The Properties window for the specified server opens (ws1, in the example in Figure 28-3). The server name that's displayed for that server in the console tree can be either the NetBIOS name, the IP address, or the DNS name of the server. In this window you'll configure master properties, enable bandwidth throttling, configure MIME types, and possibly even configure FrontPage server extensions.

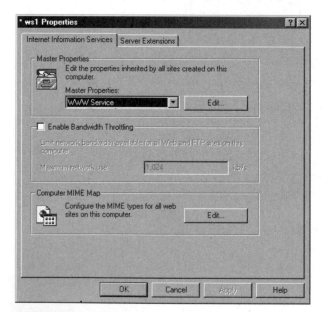

Figure 28-3. *The Properties window for the IIS server named ws1.*

Master Properties

In the Properties window, the Master Properties section allows you to open the master properties window for either the WWW or FTP service running on your machine. For example, selecting WWW Service and clicking Edit opens the WWW Service Master Properties window for the server ws1 (Figure 28-4). You use the 10 tabs in this Properties window to configure the global default settings for existing Web sites that all the new Web sites you create will inherit. Note that some of the settings at this level are unavailable, as they can't be applied to all Web sites but only to specific Web sites. For example, the IP Address setting on the Web Site tab can't be globally configured because it is specific to each Web site.

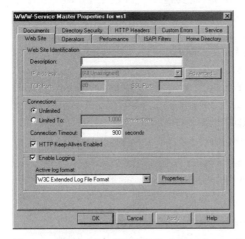

Figure 28-4. *The WWW Service Master Properties window for the IIS server named ws1.*

Most of these tabs are covered later in this chapter in the "Site-Level Administration" section; they're identical, and all settings can be configured at that level. The Service tab is the only tab we'll look at here because it's unique to server-level administration. This tab allows you to specify a single Web site on your IIS 5 machine that can be managed using the earlier version of Internet Services Manager (ISM) that is included in Microsoft Windows NT. It also allows you to configure HTTP compression, which is explained in the next section.

> **Note** The settings you configure on the various IIS tabs are stored in a special hierarchical database structure called the *metabase*. The metabase allows more granularity in storing information than the registry, although some information is still stored in the registry for initiating IIS; for managing global functions like caching, threads, and concurrency; and for backward compatibility with previous versions of IIS (if you upgraded your machine from Windows NT to Windows 2000, for example). The metabase is stored as the file Metabase.bin in the System32\Inetsrv folder.

HTTP Compression

The Master Properties window lets you take advantage of *HTTP compression,* a new feature that allows IIS 5 to compress files before sending them to clients (Web browsers) that request them. HTTP compression works only if the client supports this feature, and it can speed transfer of information between servers and clients considerably during an HTTP session. HTTP compression works with static Web content, where it caches information that has been requested and compressed for future use, and with dynamic content by performing compression on demand. HTTP compression adds extra processing overhead to the server (especially for dynamic files) and should be monitored accordingly.

HTTP compression is enabled or disabled at the server level, meaning that it must be globally turned on or off, for all Web sites on the server. To enable HTTP compression, follow these steps:

1. Open the Master Properties window for the particular server on which you want to enable this feature, select WWW Service, and click Edit.
2. Click the Service tab on the WWW Service Master Properties window for your server.
3. Specify whether you want to compress static files, application files, or both types of files.
4. For static files, specify the path to a temporary folder on a local drive where compressed files will be cached. This folder should be on an NTFS partition and shouldn't be shared.

5. For static files, specify the maximum amount of content that can be cached in the temporary folder, or select Unlimited. (You'd better have a lot of disk space in that case!)

Bandwidth Throttling

Referring back to Figure 28-3, another server-level setting that you can configure is bandwidth throttling. By specifying a value in Kbps, you can limit the amount of network bandwidth used by all aspects of IIS on your particular machine. This ability is useful primarily if your machine takes on several roles in your network, such as a Web server, file and print server, application server, or domain controller. When you learn about site-level administration later in this chapter, you'll see that you can also apply bandwidth throttling to particular sites (virtual servers) hosted on the server (machine or physical server). Note that bandwidth throttling applies only to static content, not to dynamically generated content.

MIME Map

In the Properties window for the server (refer to Figure 28-3), you can also configure the MIME mappings for that server. These mappings are used in HTTP headers sent by your IIS server to client browsers and indicate to the client which file types are registered and their associated MIME content types. For example, the file extension .HTM is mapped to the content type text/html.

You can create, modify, or remove these mappings, but it's seldom necessary. You can also configure MIME mappings at the site level, directory level, and file level, but you should normally configure them at the server level because changes you make at other levels will be overwritten if the server-level mappings are modified.

Server Extensions

By default, the installation of Windows 2000 Server will also install the IIS FrontPage server extensions on your machine. Therefore, the Properties window shown in Figure 28-3 will also include the Server Extensions tab, new to IIS 5 (Figure 28-5).

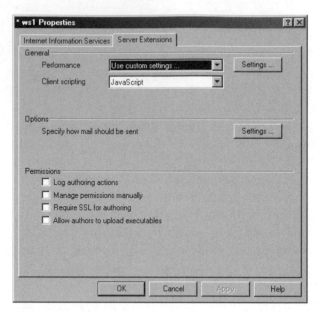

Figure 28-5. *The Server Extensions tab for the IIS server named ws1.*

You can use this tab to perform the following tasks:

- Configure cache settings to match the size of your FrontPage Web site in order to optimize performance
- Specify the client scripting language (Microsoft VBScript or JavaScript) that will be used to generate client-side script by those FrontPage extensions involved in scripting
- Configure SMTP e-mail settings for FrontPage extensions that are used as form handlers
- Enable logging of author actions in the Author.log file located in the _vti_log folder of the root FrontPage Web site
- Specify how FrontPage security settings are managed for the machine
- Require a Secure Socket Layer (SSL) connection for FrontPage clients that are authoring content
- Allow FrontPage authors to upload executables like CGI scripts and Active Server Pages (ASP) content to the server
- Set various other features, depending on what additional software is installed on the server (such as Microsoft Office 2000)

A full discussion of integration between FrontPage 2000 and IIS is more complex than we can cover in this book, but we must mention two more points here. First, a Server Extensions tab will also appear at the site level. The settings at the site level are similar to those shown in Figure 28-5, although several new options appear, including the ability to enable or disable authoring on the particular FrontPage Web site or subweb, and the ability to specify how version control will be maintained for authoring. Second, the FrontPage Administrator tool of earlier FrontPage versions is now integrated as an MMC snap-in named FrontPage Server Extensions, and is also accessible through the shortcut called Server Extensions Administrator in the Administrative Tools folder.

Site-Level Administration

Site-level administration of IIS differs considerably in its tasks depending on which of the four IIS services you are dealing with: WWW, FTP, SMTP, or NNTP. As a result we will defer a detailed discussion of the various tasks involved in administering different kinds of sites (virtual servers) until later in this chapter. (In other words, to learn how to administer WWW sites, go to the section "Managing WWW Sites.") Nevertheless, there are a few general points concerning site-level administration that can be made here:

- The site-level properties for a particular Web or FTP site on IIS are almost identical to those at the server level (compare Figures 28-4 and 28-8). So virtually any administrative action you can perform on the WWW or FTP service at the server level can also be performed at the site level. Actions on the SMTP and NNTP services can be performed only at the site level, not the server level.

- Furthermore, site-level settings for a newly created Web or FTP site are inherited from the server-level master properties previously specified. You can, however, modify settings at the site level and have those settings override the settings configured at the server level.

- Another important point to consider is that site-level settings are inherited by all virtual and physical directories and files within the site (that is, within the virtual server). This is true whether you are considering WWW, FTP, SMTP, or NNTP sites.

Directory-Level Administration

Directory-level settings are inherited by all files within the directory. They also override those configured at the site and server levels. Directory-level settings apply to both virtual and physical directories within a particular Web or FTP site.

Directory-level properties are simply a subset of site-level properties. In fact, the WWW Service master properties for a particular IIS machine are configured through a Master Properties window that has 10 tabs: Web Site, Operators, Performance, ISAPI Filters, Home Directory, Documents, Directory Security, HTTP Headers, Custom Errors, and Service. Also, the Properties window for a particular Web site, such as the Default Web Site, has a set of tabs comparable to the set in the server's Master Properties window, replacing the Service tab with a Server Extensions tab.

Similarly, as Figure 28-6 shows, the Properties window for a particular virtual (or physical) directory within a Web site has a subset of the tabs in the Web site's Properties window: Virtual Directory (vs. Home Directory), Documents, Directory Security, HTTP Headers, and Custom Errors . The following list summarizes the kinds of settings you can configure at the directory level:

- Location of content for the directory (local directory, network share, or redirection to a URL)
- Access permissions (script source access, read, write, directory browsing, log visits, and index this resource)
- Application settings (application name, starting point, execute permissions, and so on)
- Default documents and document footers
- Anonymous access and authentication control
- IP address and domain name restrictions
- Secure communications using SSL
- Content expiration
- Custom HTTP headers
- Content rating
- MIME mappings
- Custom HTTP errors

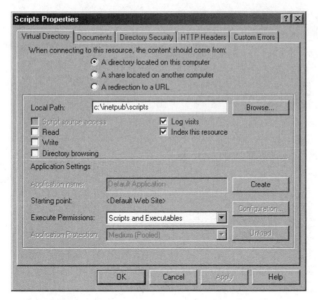

Figure 28-6. *The Properties window for the Scripts virtual directory within the Default Web Site.*

Note Remember that directory-level settings for a newly created Web site are inherited from the server-level and site-level settings previously specified. Modifying the settings at the directory level overrides similar settings configured at higher levels.

File-Level Administration

File-level administration is the last of the four levels of IIS administration. At this level you configure the properties of individual files within a Web or FTP site's home directory or other directories. For example, while a WWW service directory-level Properties window has five tabs, the Properties window for an individual Web page or other file has only four tabs: File, File Security, HTTP Headers, and Custom Errors (Figure 28-7).

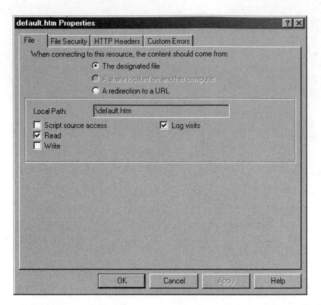

Figure 28-7. *The Properties window for the file Default.htm located within the home directory of the Default Web Site.*

Configuring file-level properties is basically the same as configuring directory-level properties, except that a single file can't have a default document specified for it as a directory can and you can't configure the following options at the file level: Directory Browsing, Index This Resource, and Enable Document Footer. Also, the location of the file can be either specified or redirected to a URL.

Managing WWW Sites

Let's now look in detail at the various site-level administrative tasks we can perform on IIS. We'll begin by looking at how to manage Web sites or virtual servers created using the WWW service. Then we'll consider FTP sites and SMTP and NNTP virtual servers in the following sections.

We've already briefly considered the Master Properties dialog box for the WWW service in Figure 28-4 and seen that there are ten tabs that contain various settings we can configure. Nine of these ten tabs are also used at the site level for administering individual Web sites, and in this section we'll look at these various tabs and their settings in detail. For our choice of a Web site to configure in this section, we have selected the Default Web Site.

Note A Server Extensions tab will also be present if FrontPage extensions are configured on the Web site, as discussed earlier in this chapter.

The Web Site Tab

The Web Site tab of the Properties window (Figure 28-8) allows you to specify Web site identities, configure a limit for the maximum number of concurrent TCP connections with the server for HTTP sessions, enable or disable HTTP Keep-Alives, and enable IIS logging on your server. Let's examine how to assign identities to Web sites first.

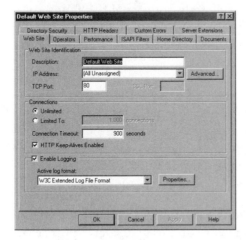

Figure 28-8. *The Web Site tab for the Default Web Site.*

Web Site Identification   Each Web site hosted on an IIS machine must have a unique identity so browser clients can connect to it to download its content. Web sites are defined using three different parameters: IP address, TCP port number, and host header name.

The identity for a Web site is specified on the Web Site tab of the Properties window for the particular Web site under consideration. For Web sites on the same machine to have unique identities, they must differ from each other in at least one of the three parameters just mentioned. Let's look at some different ways of specifying Web site identities by considering how to host several different Web sites on the same server.

Configuring Multiple IP Addresses on the Server's Network Card   You can configure multiple IP addresses on the server's network card or install multiple network cards, each with a different IP address. Select a different IP address for each Web site. Leave each site's TCP port set to 80 (the default TCP port for HTTP), and don't configure host header names. The advantage here is that clients can connect easily to each site by using the site's IP address in the URL they request (or by using a fully qualified DNS name if a unique host name has been configured on the DNS server for each of the IIS machine's IP addresses).

The disadvantage is that if many sites must be hosted on the machine, then many IP addresses must be obtained and assigned to it. This isn't a problem on a private internetwork when using one of the private IP address blocks like 10.y.z.w, 172.16-31.z.w, or 192.168.z.w. On servers directly connected to the Internet, however, you must obtain a sufficient number of IP addresses from your Internet service provider. Nevertheless, this method of specifying Web site identities is the preferred and commonly used one.

Configuring Only One IP Address for the Server's Network Card   Specify a different TCP port (above 1023) for each Web site hosted on the machine. The main disadvantage here is that clients must know the port number of the Web site to which they want to connect. For example, if the DNS name of the server is ws1.scribes.com and a Web site on the server is assigned port 8023, the client will have to use the URL *http://ws1.scribes.com:8023* to access the site.

Configuring One IP Address and Leaving the TCP Port Set to Default   Configure only one IP address for the server's network card and leave the TCP port set to the default value of 80 for each site. Configure a unique host header name for each site, using the Advanced button. Host header names are a feature of HTTP 1.1, which is supported by IIS 5. The host header name associated with each site is typically the fully qualified DNS name that is assigned to the site in the database of an available DNS server (or in the local Hosts file on the clients).

Note   When you open the Properties window for the Default Web Site and select the Web Site tab, the IP address is specified as (All Unassigned). This means that this Web site will respond to any IP addresses that aren't specifically assigned to other Web sites on the machine. That's actually what makes this site the Default one, and only one Web site on an IIS machine can have its IP address specified this way.

When the client requests a URL like *http://sales.scribes.com*, the client passes the host header name sales.scribes.com in the HTTP request headers that it sends to the server. (See Chapter 27 for more information on HTTP headers.) The server parses the host header name, identifies which Web site the client is requesting, and returns the appropriate files. One disadvantage is that the client must also support host header names—that is, the ability to pass the DNS name of the site in its HTTP request headers. Host header names are supported by Microsoft

Internet Explorer 3 or later and by Netscape Navigator 2 or later. Another disadvantage is that host header names don't work with SSL connections because the HTTP session is encrypted.

If you're working with older browsers that don't support host header names, you can implement a cookie-based mechanism to enable the browsers to distinguish between Web sites having the same IP address and TCP port number. See the online documentation for more information on how to do this.

> **Tip** Unlike the previous version (IIS 4 for Windows NT), when you change the TCP port number for a Web site in IIS 5, you don't need to reboot your server for the change to take effect.

Connections The Web Site tab also allows you to configure a limit for the maximum number of concurrent TCP connections with the server for HTTP sessions. You can also enable or disable HTTP Keep-Alives and specify a connection timeout value. HTTP Keep-Alives are a feature of HTTP 1.1 that enables a client to keep a TCP connection open with a server after downloading a file, in case other files need to be immediately downloaded from the server. If clients start complaining about the server being sluggish or that they're frequently receiving HTTP 500: Busy errors, try decreasing the connection timeout value so that unused TCP connections will time out more quickly.

> **Note** Connection timeouts specified on the Web Site tab are for active TCP sessions. TCP has its own settings for automatically terminating half-open TCP connections, such as those created during a Denial of Service (DoS) attack that tries to bring down a Web server by flooding its network connection with TCP SYN packets.

IIS Logging The Web Site tab also allows you to enable IIS logging on your server. This feature is enabled by default and allows administrators to monitor access to the site by client browsers. Logging information can be saved in a variety of formats, including the following:

- **NCSA Common Log File Format** Creates a space-delimited ASCII file with a predetermined set of fields
- **ODBC Logging** Logs IIS traffic to any ODBC-compliant database using the specified data source name (DSN) for the database

- **W3C Extended Log File Format**   (the default) Creates a space-delimited ASCII file with a group of fields that the administrator can specify

New IIS logs can be created on an hourly, daily, weekly, or monthly basis, or when the existing log file grows to a specified size. Logs are stored by default in the \%WinDir%\System32\LogFiles folder, but you can use the Properties button to modify this setting. Note that the older Microsoft IIS Log File Format (supported under IIS 4) is no longer available here.

> **Tip**   Enabling IIS logging on the Web Site tab doesn't actually mean that visits to all parts of your site will be logged. In the Web site's dialog box, you can use the Home Directory tab's Log Visits check box to enable or disable the logging of access to content located in the site's home directory. On other tabs, you can similarly track visits to other directories or even individual files.

The Operators Tab

A *Web site operator* is a user account that can perform common administrative tasks that relate only to that site. Operators are like site administrators, as opposed to members of the Administrators group who can administer all aspects of all sites on a machine. Operators have the necessary rights to configure the following options and characteristics for the Web sites on which they are defined:

- Access permissions
- Logging
- Content expiration
- Content ratings
- Default documents
- Footers

However, operators cannot perform tasks that would modify the basic nature of the site itself, such as configuring the IP address, the TCP port number, bandwidth throttling, and application settings. Operators also can't create or delete virtual directories.

The Performance Tab

You can tune performance for individual Web sites using the Performance tab of the site's Properties window, shown in Figure 28-9. On this tab you can configure the following settings:

- **Expected number of hits per day**   The slider basically adjusts the settings for the IIS cache. For best performance, set the slider so that it is slightly higher than the actual number of hits per day you are receiving. If you set it too high, you're wasting system resources (memory).

- **Bandwidth throttling**   You can use the Master Properties window for the server (at the server level) to globally limit the amount of network bandwidth that all IIS functions use for your machine. You can also specify a bandwidth limit for an individual Web site (at the site level). This restriction might be necessary, for example, if you're hosting multiple sites on your server and one of these sites is extremely popular. Limiting bandwidth for the popular site gives users better access to the remaining sites. Note that setting this value higher than the setting previously configured in the Master Properties window will override the Master Properties setting.

- **Process throttling**   This option is useful when running ASP applications out-of-process on IIS, which is more CPU-intensive than running them in-process. Selecting this option will limit the CPU use for such applications in this site, but it doesn't actually produce any consequences unless Enforce Limits is also selected. (The consequences depend on the amount by which the limit is exceeded.) Leaving the Enforce Limits setting cleared results in an event being written to the application log whenever the limit is exceeded.

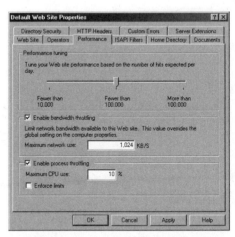

Figure 28-9. *The Performance tab for the Default Web Site.*

The ISAPI Filters Tab

Internet Server Application Programming Interface (ISAPI) filters are optional DLLs that perform specific actions when IIS processes an HTTP request from a client. You can use the ISAPI Filters tab to install a series of these filters and specify the order in which IIS processes them. Filters installed here at the site level are used only by the selected site; filters installed at the server level apply to all sites on the server.

ISAPI filters perform their action before the server actually responds to the HTTP request itself. For example, you could design an ISAPI filter to perform custom authentication, encrypt data, write traffic information to a custom log file, or perform some other action. Implementing ISAPI filters is beyond the scope of this book.

The Home Directory Tab

The Home Directory tab (Figure 28-10) allows you to specify the location of the content that is mapped to a Web site's home directory, to specify various access permissions and other settings for the directory, and to specify application settings relating to any Web application you have implemented in this directory.

Figure 28-10. *The Home Directory tab for the Default Web Site.*

Home Directory   The home directory for a site determines the location of any content that is accessed using a URL such as *http://Site_Name/File_Name*, where *Site_Name* represents the NetBIOS name, IP address, or DNS name of the site, and *File_Name* represents the name of any particular HTML page, image file, script, or other file in the site's home directory. You can specify the home directory for a site in three different ways:

- As a directory located on a local drive of the machine.
- As a uniform naming convention (UNC) path to a network share located on a file server. (You need to specify credentials for connecting to the share.)
- As a redirection to a URL that instructs the client to connect to a different Web server (not even necessarily an IIS one) in order to access the content mapped to the home directory. This redirection can be either temporary or permanent.

Real World   Redirecting Access

Being able to redirect the home directory (or any virtual directory) to a URL is useful when Web sites are being developed or are down for maintenance or upgrade. IIS gives you the option of redirecting a request for any file in the home directory to the same URL (such as a We're Down for Maintenance page) or to a similar file in the remote directory (for example, to redirect the client to a temporary mirror site). You can also redirect access to a subdirectory of the current home directory if your maintenance page or mirror content is located on the same server.

Specify a permanent redirection only if you really plan to move the site's content to another server, as some browsers that receive an HTTP 301 Permanent Redirect message might actually modify a favorite or bookmark linked to the site automatically. The result is that when redirection is turned off, the client continues to access the alternate site instead of the original one.

Access Permissions If you specify the location of the home directory as either a local directory or a network share, you have the option on the Home Directory tab of specifying various access permissions and other settings for the directory (Figure 28-10). These settings aren't available if you specify redirection to a URL for the home directory location. You can specify the following settings:

- **Script Source Access** Select this check box if you want users to be able to access the actual source code of scripts, such as ASP files. Note that this does nothing unless you also select either Read or Write. (Selecting Read then lets users read the source file for the script, while selecting Write allows them to modify the script.) This option is used primarily on development servers where content is created. It is disabled by default.

- **Read** Selecting this check box allows users to view the contents of a directory or file and its associated properties, such as creation time and file size. This setting is enabled by default.

- **Write** Selecting this check box allows users to modify the contents of a directory or file. Only browsers that support the PUT feature of HTTP 1.1—such as Internet Explorer 4 or later—can write files to the server. This setting is disabled by default.

- **Directory Browsing** Selecting this check box allows users to view the contents of the home directory when no default home page is present in the directory. This setting should generally be disabled (and is by default) in order to hide the directory structure of your content directories from accidental viewing by users who might use this to snoop in places you don't want them to go.

- **Log Visits** Selecting this check box causes an entry to be added to the IIS log files whenever any file in the home directory is accessed by a client. Note that Enable Logging must first be selected on the Web Site tab before this feature will work. Logging of the home directory is enabled by default.

- **Index This Resource** Select this check box if you want the Indexing Service to add the contents of the home directory to its master index. By default, the Indexing Service is installed when you install Windows 2000 Server.

Note Although Read access is enabled by default on the Default Web Site, whether you can access a particular Web site and its contents depends on a number of conditions. See the section "Understanding IIS 5 Security" in Chapter 27 for more information on securing access to IIS Web sites.

Application Settings If you have selected a local directory or network share for your home directory, you also have the option on the Home Directory tab to specify application settings relating to any Web application you have implemented in this directory. An example of a Web application might be a collection of ASPs working together to provide some programmatic functionality to the user who visits the site. Developing Web applications is not the subject of this book, but the settings that can be configured here include these:

- **Application Name** Use this field to give your application a unique friendly name.

- **Starting Point** Applications can consist of a tree of directories and their contents. The top of this tree is the application starting point.

- **Configuration** This button opens the Application Configuration dialog box, which allows you to configure numerous options for mapping applications to their interpreting script engines or programs, caching ISAPI applications for faster performance, specifying session timeout values, choosing a default ASP script language, and debugging settings.

- **Execute Permissions** This option allows you to specify which types of applications are allowed to run in the home directory. Choices include None, Scripts Only, or Scripts And Executables.

- **Application Protection** This option allows you to specify whether your application should run within the core IIS process (low protection), in a separate application thread pool together with other applications (medium protection), or in its own isolated thread pool as a separate process (high protection). The idea here is to protect other applications running on the server in case this one crashes. Selecting high protection means that the failure of your application won't affect any other applications running on the server, and you can restart your application without having to reboot the server. The more applications that run at medium or high protection levels, however, the greater the demand on the server's processing power.

Caution If you specify Write access for the directory along with Scripts And Executables, your security might be threatened: an untrusted user might be allowed to upload a hostile executable program file to the server and cause damage.

The Documents Tab

The Documents tab of the Properties window for a Web site allows you to specify possible filenames for default documents for the home directory and specify the order in which a browser attempts to access them. The three types specified by default are (in order) Default.htm, Default.asp, and Iisstart.asp.

For example, if a browser tries to connect to the Default Web Site on the server ws1.scribes.com by using the URL *http://ws1.scribes.com*, the server will first check to see whether a file named Default.htm resides in the home directory. If such a file is there, it will be returned to the client. If not, the server will check for a file named Default.asp. The process continues until either a file is returned or the list of default documents is exhausted. You can specify additional default document names, such as Index.htm, or delete existing ones if you like. You can also disable default documents entirely, in which case, clients must know and type in the actual name of the file they want to access on the server—for example, by using the URL *http://ws1.scribes.com/default.htm*.

This tab also lets you specify the name of a footer file (written in HTML) that is appended to the bottom of every file retrieved from the site by a client. You could use this, for example, to add a copyright statement or disclaimer to the bottom of each page. If you're using FrontPage to develop your content, you can create complex footers that display information like the date when the file was last modified, a hit counter, and so on.

The Directory Security Tab

The Directory Security tab allows you to specify whether anonymous users are allowed to access content in your site, to restrict access to a Web site, and to enable secure HTTP communication. Let's take a look.

Anonymous Access and Authentication Control To specify whether anonymous users are allowed to access content in your site or whether some form of authentication will be required, open the Authentication Methods dialog box, shown in Figure 28-11, by clicking the Edit button within the Anonymous Access And

Authentication Control field on the Directory Security tab. Use the dialog box to configure these settings:

- **Anonymous Access** This option specifies whether anonymous access is allowed and which Windows 2000 user account is used to provide this kind of access. The default anonymous user account, created during installation of IIS on the server, is named IUSR_*servername*, where *servername* is the NetBIOS name of the server. Anonymous access means users can access content in the site using their Web browsers without needing to have their credentials authenticated in any way, and it's the typical authentication method used for public Web sites on the Internet. The other forms of authentication discussed next authenticate the user's credentials in some fashion and are used primarily for intranets, extranets, and secure Internet sites.

- **Basic Authentication** This option specifies whether basic authentication is allowed. If used, the client will be presented with a dialog box requesting credentials and those credentials are then passed over the network connection in unencrypted form. Basic authentication is defined in the original HTTP 1 specification and is supported by virtually all types of Web browsers, including the oldest ones. If users accessing your site are using older browsers that can't be authenticated using other forms of authenticated access, you might need to enable basic authentication on your site, but be aware that it is intrinsically insecure.

- **Digest Authentication For Windows Domain Servers** This new authentication method is defined in the HTTP 1.1 specification. It's supported by IIS 5 and can work across firewalls and proxy servers. A hash or message digest is passed across the connection instead of the user's actual credentials. The information is transmitted in clear text but is hashed, so it's essentially undecodable and secure. The domain controller for which the authentication request is made requires a plain-text copy of the user's password, however, so special precautions must be taken to secure the domain controller.

- **Integrated Windows Authentication** This is a new name for the option that was formerly called Windows NT Challenge/Response Authentication (and before that, NTLM—or NT LAN Manager—Authentication). A cryptographic exchange is used to securely authenticate the user without actually passing credentials across the connection. The user isn't prompted for credentials; instead, his or her currently logged on credentials are used. Integrated Windows authentication can also use Kerberos authentication if the server has Active Directory installed on it and if the client browser supports it.

Figure 28-11. *The Authentication Methods dialog box.*

 Tip Integrated Windows authentication is designed to be used primarily on intranets and other internal networks because it won't work through an HTTP proxy connection.

 Real World Combining Different Authentication Methods

Consider the consequences of selecting more than one method in the Authentication Methods dialog box. If you select Anonymous Access together with some form of authenticated access like Basic Authentication, anonymous access is attempted first. If this fails, authenticated access is tried. Anonymous access could fail if the NTFS permissions on the resource explicitly deny access to the anonymous user account, for example.

If you select two or more forms of authenticated access, the most secure forms are attempted first. For example, integrated Windows authentication would be tried before attempting basic authentication. For information on how authentication fits into the general scheme of IIS security, see Chapter 27.

IP Address and DNS Restrictions The Directory Security tab also allows you to restrict access to a Web site by giving clients a particular IP address or DNS domain name. Figure 28-12 shows the IP Address And Domain Name Restrictions dialog box that you can access from this tab.

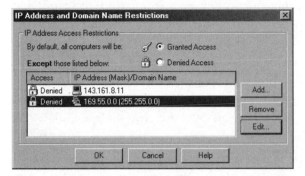

Figure 28-12. *The IP Address And Domain Name Restrictions dialog box.*

Use this dialog box either to allow all clients access to the site except for those whose IP addresses or domain names are specified here, or to deny all clients access to the site except for those whose IP addresses or domain names are specified here. You can place restrictions on clients in three ways:

- Specify the IP address of a particular client.
- Specify a network ID and subnet mask representing a range of IP addresses.
- Specify the DNS name of a particular domain.

Note that selecting the last option can significantly affect server performance because reverse DNS lookups must be performed on all clients prior to granting them access. For information on how IP address and domain name restrictions fit into the general scheme of IIS security, see Chapter 27.

Secure Communications The Directory Security tab also allows you to enable secure HTTP communications by implementing the SSL 3 protocol, which you can use to encrypt Web traffic between client and server. SSL is essential if you plan to use your server for running Web applications that involve financial transactions or hosting sensitive information. Web browsers access a secure server using SSL by using URLs that are prefixed by *https://* instead of the usual *http://* prefix.

SSL is based on public-key cryptography, in which digital certificates are used to establish the identity and trustworthiness of servers (and of clients), while a public/private key pair is used for encrypting and decrypting transmissions to ensure that the information being transmitted is secure and has integrity (in other words, that it's from who it says it's from). Public-key cryptography and its associated concepts are covered in Chapter 17.

Before attempting to implement secure communications, you must establish access to a certificate authority (CA) that can grant the IIS server the necessary server certificate and public/private key pair. For this purpose, you have a choice:

- Use a trusted public CA like VeriSign, Inc. to obtain the certificate and key pair. This solution is good if you want to enable secure communications for a public Internet site you are hosting on your server.

- Install Certificate Services on one or more Windows 2000 servers in your enterprise and be your own CA. This solution is best if you want to enable secure communications to a private intranet site you are hosting on your server. See Chapter 19 for information on how to install and configure Certificate Services.

To enable SSL, you first need to generate a certificate request file and submit this to a CA in order to receive a server certificate from the CA. The server certificate contains the associated public key and is used for verifying the identity of the server and establishing secure connections.

To obtain a server certificate, follow the steps outlined below. For our example, the server certificate is being requested for the Default Web Site on server ws1.scribes.com, while the server running Certificate Services is the domain controller dc1.scribes.com. The name of the CA for our scribes.com enterprise is Scribes.

1. Click the Server Certificate button on the Directory Security tab of the Default Web Site Properties window. This starts the Web Server Certificate Wizard (Figure 28-13). Click Next.

Figure 28-13. *The Web Server Certificate Wizard.*

2. Select Create A New Certificate. Click Next.

3. Select Prepare The Request Now But Send It Later if you plan to submit a security request file to a public CA. (Later, you'll need to install or bind the certificate you receive from the CA to your server.) Or select Send The Request Immediately To An Online Certification Authority if you want to request, obtain, and bind the certificate in one shot by submitting your request directly to a certificate server in your enterprise. (We'll follow the second option here.) Click Next.

4. Specify a friendly name for the certificate (the name Default Web Site is suggested here by default) and a bit length to indicate the strength of the encryption key (512 or 1024 bits). Click Next.

5. Specify organization and organizational unit names for your certificate. Click Next.

6. Specify a common name for your site. Use the fully qualified DNS name for the site if your site is a public one on the Internet. In this example, we'll use ws1.scribes.com as the common name for the Default Web Site. Click Next.

7. Specify the city, state, and country. Use official names and not abbreviations (except for two-letter country codes). Click Next.

8. Select the CA you want to submit your request to (the server in your enterprise running Certificate Services). Click Next.

9. Confirm your information, and click Next.

10. A certificate request file is generated and submitted to the server running Certificate Services, which will return the requested server certificate and public/private key pair. The wizard will automatically install the certificate on the server at this point and prompt you to click Finish when it's done.

Once a server certificate is installed on your Web site, you can view the certificate information by clicking the View Certificate button on the Directory Security tab. Figure 28-14 shows a certificate installed on the server ws1.scribes.com, which was obtained from the server dc1.scribes.com, the Windows 2000 server running Certificate Services.

Figure 28-14. *Server certificate for ws1.scribes.com issued by the CA known as Scribes.*

Now finish enabling SSL for the Default Web Site on ws1.scribes.com by following these steps:

1. Switch to the Web Site tab of the Default Web Site Properties window and verify that the SSL port is specified as 443, the default SSL port. (You can use the Advanced button to configure other SSL identities for the site if you want.)

2. Switch back to the Directory Security tab and click the Edit button in the Secure Communications section of the tab. The Secure Communications dialog box opens (Figure 28-15).

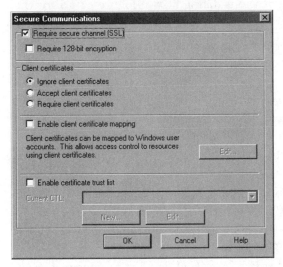

Figure 28-15. *Enabling SSL using the Secure Communications dialog box.*

3. Select the check box Require Secure Channel (SSL) and click OK to finish configuring SSL for the Default Web Site. (The other options in this dialog box are discussed in the sidebar "Secure Communications Options.") Click OK again to apply the changes to your site and effect the settings.

4. Now test secure communications by using Internet Explorer to open the URL *http://ws1.scribes.com*. Select the Default Web Site node in the console tree of IIS, click the Action button, and select Browse from the drop-down menu.

5. Internet Explorer starts and tries to access the default home page of *http://ws1.scribes.com*. The result should be a message displayed that says "This page must be viewed over a secure channel." Choose Open from the File menu and enter the revised URL *https://ws1.scribes.com*.

6. A dialog box might appear indicating that you are about to view pages over a secure connection; if it does, click OK. The home page Default.htm should display.

Real World **Secure Communications Options**

Besides enabling SSL using the server certificate installed on the IIS system, you can also use the Secure Communications dialog box in Figure 28-15 for the following purposes:

- To specify that SSL connections will use strong 128-bit encryption. (This is available only in the United States and Canada under current U.S. encryption laws.)

- To specify how to handle client certificates. Client certificates verify the identity of clients and are typically used when remote users need to securely access a corporate intranet over a nonsecure Internet connection. You can specify either to ignore, accept, or require client certificates during SSL communications.

- To enable client certificate mapping. This feature enables administrators to create mappings between Windows 2000 user accounts and client certificates so that users who have the appropriate client certificate can automatically be authenticated and logged on to the network.

- To enable a certificate trust list (CTL). A CTL is a list of approved CAs for the Web site that are considered trusted by the Web site. CTLs are created using the CTL Wizard by selecting the New button at the bottom of the Secure Communications dialog box.

The HTTP Headers Tab

You can use the HTTP Headers tab of the Properties window for a Web site to enable content expiration on the site, to specify custom HTTP headers that are returned by the server to requesting HTTP clients, to enable and specify Recreational Software Advisory Council (RSAC) content ratings on the server, and to specify additional MIME mappings for a particular Web site.

Content Expiration When you enable content expiration on the site, the result is that when a client browser requests a file from the site, the HTTP headers returned by the server include information regarding the expiration date of the site's contents. The client can then decide whether it needs to download a newer version of the file or use an existing copy in the client browser cache.

Tip If your site contains information that changes frequently (like sports scores), you can force clients to always retrieve fresh copies of files from the server (and never use cached versions of these files) by selecting the Expire Immediately option.

Custom HTTP Headers   This rather esoteric feature allows you to specify custom HTTP headers that are returned by the server to requesting HTTP clients. You might use this option in certain situations involving firewalls or proxy servers to enable or disable specific features during HTTP sessions.

Content Rating   This option is used to enable and specify RSAC content ratings on the server. These settings rate the site's violence, sex, nudity, and language content and are typically enabled on sites hosting content unsuitable for viewing by minors.

More Info   For more information about the RSAC, see *http://www.rsac.org*.

MIME Map   The global MIME mappings for an IIS server were discussed in the previous section on server-level administration. For site-level administration, you can specify additional MIME mappings for a particular Web site.

The Custom Errors Tab

The Custom Errors tab allows you to specify how your server will generate HTTP error messages when users attempt to access the selected Web site (Figure 28-16).

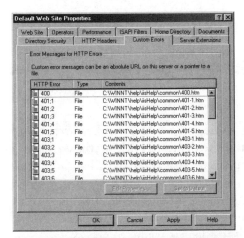

Figure 28-16. *Specifying custom HTTP error messages.*

The HTTP specification defines that the first header line returned by a Web server in response to a request by a client will contain a number and associated message indicating the status of the request. These three-digit numbers are called *HTTP status codes,* and they fall within various ranges:

- **200 through 299**   A successful HTTP transaction has occurred. (The most common status code is 200 OK.)

- **300 through 399**   Redirection to another URL has occurred.

- **400 through 499**   An error has occurred. Examples include the following:

  - **400 Bad Request**   The server couldn't understand the syntax of the request.

  - **401 Unauthorized**   The user's credentials won't allow him or her to log on to the server.

  - **403 Forbidden**   Access is denied for some reason other than user credentials, such as the client having a restricted IP address or needing to use SSL to access the server.

  - **404 File Not Found**   The file you're trying to access doesn't exist (or is misplaced or misnamed) on the server.

- **500 through 599**   A server error has occurred or the requested feature isn't implemented.

Instead of returning bare HTTP status codes and their brief messages for the error codes (400 through 499), however, IIS is configured by default to use predefined HTML pages that contain somewhat more information than the status codes and messages. These "error files" are located in the \%WinDir%\help\iishelp\common folder on the server, and you can modify them if you want.

Alternatively, by selecting one of these error files on the Custom Errors tab and clicking Edit Properties, you can specify that the default HTTP status codes and messages will be returned by the server when that error occurs, or that any specified file located in either a local folder or a network share will be returned when that error occurs. Companies commonly use this feature to create error pages that contain elements like the company logo, the e-mail address of customer support, or even a search tool for finding the page the client is trying to access.

Note   IIS uses more detailed error messages than are included in the original HTTP specification. For example, the HTTP error code 401—which in HTTP simply means unauthorized—is represented in IIS by a group of codes spanning from 401.1 through 401.5, representing various reasons why a server might deny a user's credentials.

Managing FTP Sites

The four levels of IIS administration that apply to the WWW Publishing Service also apply to the second core service of IIS, the FTP Publishing Service. Because administering servers, sites, directories, and files is similar between the two services, this section is condensed to avoid repetition.

FTP Service Master Properties

In addition to the general server-level tasks of connecting to an IIS server to administer its services, backing up and restoring a server configuration, and throttling total bandwidth used by all IIS operations on the machine, IIS also lets you globally configure the master properties for all existing FTP sites on your server and for all new ones you might create in the future.

To configure the FTP service master properties for a particular server, simply select the node in the IIS console tree that represents the server, click the Action button on the toolbar, and choose Properties from the drop-down menu to open the Properties window for that server. (See Figure 28-3 in the "Server-Level Administration" section earlier in this chapter. We'll continue to use server ws1 as an example.) From this window, select FTP Service from the Master Properties section and click Edit to open the FTP Service Master Properties window for server ws1 (Figure 28-17).

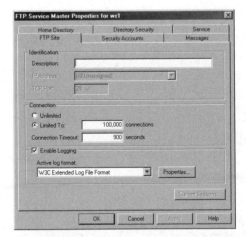

Figure 28-17. *The FTP Service Master Properties window for server ws1.*

This Properties window has six tabs used for configuring the default global settings for existing FTP sites. All new FTP sites you create on the machine will inherit these settings. Note that some of the settings at this level are unavailable because they can't be applied to all FTP sites but only to specific FTP sites. For example, the *IP Address* field on the FTP Site tab can't be globally configured, since it is specific to each FTP site.

Of the six tabs in this window, only the Service tab is unique to the server-level FTP properties. This Service tab performs a function similar to the Service tab of the WWW Service Master Properties window: it allows you to specify a single FTP site on your IIS 5 machine that can be managed using the ISM included in IIS 3 on Windows NT. The other five tabs are common to site-level FTP properties and are discussed next.

Configuring FTP Site Properties

The site-level properties for a particular FTP site are almost identical to those at the server level (Figure 28-17) except that the Service tab is absent. This section covers the various settings that you can configure using the Properties window for a particular FTP site. Remember that site-level settings for a newly created FTP site are inherited from the server-level master properties previously specified, while modifying settings at the site level overrides similar settings configured at the server level. We'll use the properties of the Default FTP Site for this discussion.

The FTP Site Tab

Like the Web site properties used in site-level administration, the FTP site properties allow you to specify FTP site identities, configure connections, and enable logging. The connections and logging settings work the same way as those for Web site properties, so we won't say anything more about them here. But we'll look at identification and current sessions.

Identification   Like Web sites, each FTP site hosted on an IIS machine must have a unique identity so FTP clients can connect to it to upload or download files. Unlike Web sites, however, FTP uses two (not three) parameters to define an FTP site: IP address and TCP port number.

The identity for an FTP site is specified on the FTP Site tab of the Properties window for the particular FTP site under consideration. For FTP sites on the same machine to have unique identities, they must differ from each other in at least one of the two parameters. In other words, to host several different FTP sites on the same server, you could use one of the following methods:

- Configure multiple IP addresses on the server's network card and select a different IP address for each FTP site, leaving each site's TCP port set to 21 (the default TCP port for FTP). Clients can then connect to a specific site by using either the site's IP address or its associated fully qualified DNS name (if either a DNS server is available on the network or a local hosts file is configured on the client). This method is preferred for public FTP sites, since it is the easiest way for users to connect.

- Configure only one IP address for the server's network card and use this IP address for every FTP site while assigning a different TCP port (above 1023) to each FTP site hosted on the machine. In this case, the user must know the TCP port of each site in order to connect to it. This method is sometimes used to hide private FTP sites from view (although FTP is inherently nonsecure anyway, as you shall soon see).

Current Sessions   The Current Sessions button on the FTP Site tab opens the FTP User Sessions dialog box for that site, which displays all users who are currently connected to the site, the IP addresses of their clients (or of your proxy server if they're behind your firewall), and the time elapsed since they connected (Figure 28-18). You can select any user to disconnect him or her from your site, or you can click Disconnect All to terminate all sessions on your site.

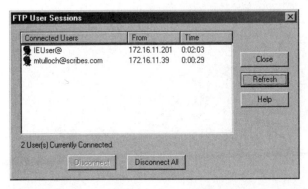

Figure 28-18. *Displaying the current connections to the Default FTP Site on server ws1.*

Note Figure 28-18 displays two anonymous users who are connected to the Default FTP Site, which is configured to allow anonymous access. The user IEUser@ accessed the site by opening the URL *ftp://ftp.scribes.com* in Internet Explorer 5, while the user mtulloch@scribes.com used the Windows command-line FTP utility and logged on with user name *anonymous* together with the voluntary (but optional) password equal to the user's e-mail address *mtulloch@scribes.com*. On the other hand, if users log on using basic authentication (described next), the FTP User Sessions dialog box will show their user names in the Connected Users column. (If they connect using Internet Explorer, this user name will appear twice for some strange reason.)

The Security Accounts Tab

The Security Accounts tab of an FTP site's Properties window functions similarly to the Directory Security tab of a Web site's Properties window. FTP site operators have limited administration rights on the site, similar to those granted to Web site operators discussed previously. However, authentication control is much simpler for the FTP service (Figure 28-19). While the WWW service supports four levels of authentication (anonymous, basic, digest, and integrated) plus the option of enabling SSL for encrypted transmission, FTP supports only the anonymous access and the basic authentication methods.

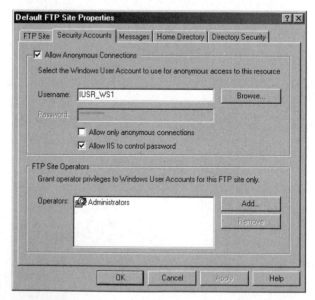

Figure 28-19. *The Security Accounts tab for the Default FTP Site on server ws1.*

Because you already know about anonymous access and basic authentication, now you just need to learn how to configure FTP authentication settings using the Security Accounts tab, which at first glance appears a bit confusing. Two check boxes account for this confusion:

- Allow Anonymous Connections
- Allow Only Anonymous Connections

Table 28-1 shows how combinations of selecting and deselecting these two check boxes produce different combinations of anonymous access and basic authentication. If you enable anonymous access, IIS needs a user account to make this work. By default, the IUSR_*servername* account is specified, but you can select another one if you like. (Make sure it has the right to log on locally to the server console, because this is necessary for basic authentication to work.) You can then either specify the password manually or allow IIS to synchronize the password with those set in Windows.

Table 28-1. Combinations of anonymous and basic authentication for FTP

Allow Anonymous Connections	Allow Only Anonymous Connections	Result
Yes	Yes	Only anonymous access is enabled.
Yes	No	Both anonymous access and basic authentication are enabled, with anonymous access being attempted first.
No	N/A	Only basic authentication is enabled.

Note If you must enable basic authentication on your FTP site, only users who have the right to log on locally to the IIS server hosting the FTP site will be able to be authenticated and connect to the site. Make sure you physically secure the server from misuse by these users if they are working in your organization.

Real World FTP Security

FTP is viewed as less secure than HTTP because FTP supports only anonymous access and basic authentication. For instance, if you're running an internal FTP site within a company and are using basic authentication, any person with a network sniffer could potentially obtain a trace of an FTP session and determine a user's password. Furthermore, if you connect to an FTP site using Internet Explorer and are authenticated using basic authentication (after entering your credentials into the Login As box), your user name appears in the URL as something like *ftp://mtulloch@ftp.scribes.com*. So if you leave your machine, lock your console or people will know who logged on to the FTP site.

The Messages Tab

FTP sites typically have a welcome, exit, and maximum connections message that the server provides for users as appropriate. Specify the text of these messages on the Messages tab of an FTP site's Properties window.

The Home Directory Tab

FTP has two possible choices for the location of the home directory mapped to the virtual root of the site. One is a local directory on one of the server's disks; the other is a UNC path to a network share located on a file server somewhere else on the network. (Credentials must be supplied to access this share.) Specify either of these on the Home Directory tab shown in Figure 28-20. Note that FTP sites can't be redirected to a URL like Web sites can (Figure 28-10).

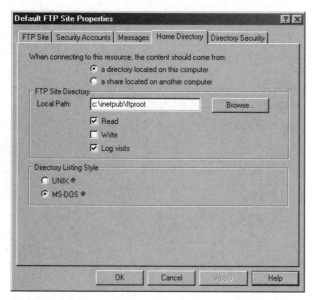

Figure 28-20. *The Home Directory tab for the Default FTP Site on server ws1.*

Access Permissions   FTP permissions are simpler than WWW permissions:

- **Read**   Selecting this check box allows users to read or download files stored in the home directory and allows users to list the contents of the directory.

- **Write**   Selecting this check box allows users to upload files to the home directory.

- **Log Visits** Selecting this check box causes an entry to be added to the IIS log files whenever any file is downloaded from or uploaded to the home directory by a client. Note that Enable Logging must first be selected on the FTP Site tab before this feature will work. Logging of the home directory is enabled by default.

Directory Listing Style When a Web browser like Microsoft Internet Explorer accesses an FTP site, provided that Read access is enabled for the home directory, the user is presented with a directory listing showing the contents of the directory. This directory listing can be presented in either the original FTP style (UNIX style) or in standard Windows style (MS-DOS style). The same information is presented either way; it's just displayed differently.

Tip If you're hosting a public FTP site on the Internet, select UNIX style for maximum compatibility with users running older FTP client software. Some clients might be unable to interpret MS-DOS style correctly.

The Directory Security Tab

Like Web sites, you can also control access to FTP sites according to the IP address or DNS domain name to which the remote user belongs (discussed for Web sites earlier in the chapter).

Configuring FTP Directory Properties

In FTP directory-level administration (that is, in the administration of FTP virtual directories), Properties windows of virtual directories created within FTP sites have only the following two tabs:

- **Virtual Directory** You can configure the location of the content for the virtual directory and specify the access permissions.

- **Directory Security** You can specify IP address and domain name restrictions for the virtual directory.

Note that unlike Web sites, *physical* directories within an FTP site aren't displayed within the IIS console window. The FTP service in IIS requires no file-level administration because individual files within an FTP site aren't displayed in the console window either.

Managing NNTP Virtual Servers

The third core IIS facility on Windows 2000 Server is the Network News Transfer Protocol Service (NNTP Service). NNTP is the application-layer protocol that underlies the worldwide USENET system of news servers on the Internet. IIS includes an NNTP Service that can be used to create news sites, which are also implemented as virtual servers like Web and FTP sites. Use Add/Remove Programs in Control Panel to install the NNTP Service subcomponent of IIS if you need to.

What NNTP Service Does

NNTP Service on IIS fully supports both the client/server and server/server portions of NNTP and can be administered either through the IIS snap-in for the MMC or by a Web browser using NNTP Service Manager (HTML). Like other core IIS facilities, NNTP Service is fully integrated with Windows 2000 event and performance monitoring, and it integrates with the Indexing Service for full-text indexing of newsgroup content.

NNTP Service can be used to implement private news servers for hosting departmental discussion groups within your company or to implement public news servers that provide customer support resources to Internet users. It isn't designed to pull feeds from USENET hosts on the Internet, however. For that purpose, you should obtain Microsoft Exchange Server 5.5 and implement the Internet News Service on it to give it NNTP capability. You can use Microsoft Outlook Express to connect to NTTP service on an IIS machine in order to download a list of newsgroups, read existing messages, reply to messages, and post new messages.

When you install NNTP Service on IIS, it automatically creates the Default NNTP Virtual Server (Figure 28-21). We'll configure this virtual server in a moment, but first you should know that you can host multiple NNTP virtual servers on a single machine. In this way, several departments in your company can run separate news servers on a single IIS machine, just as they can run separate Web or FTP servers. We'll look at how to do this next and then consider other aspects of managing NNTP virtual servers. Notice that NNTP Service is managed with a combination of Properties windows and wizards, just like the other IIS core services.

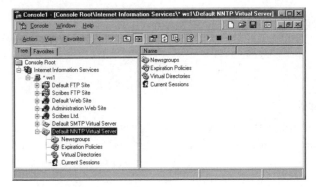

Figure 28-21. *The IIS console tree showing the Default NNTP Virtual Server on the IIS server ws1.*

NNTP Service Wizards

You can run the following wizards from the IIS console to configure and manage various aspects of NNTP virtual servers:

- New NNTP Virtual Server Wizard
- New Virtual Directory Wizard
- New Expiration Policy Wizard
- New Newsgroup Wizard

New NNTP Virtual Server Wizard

To create a new NNTP virtual server, just select the server's node in the IIS console tree, click the Action button, point to New, and choose NNTP Virtual Server from the drop-down menu. This starts the New NNTP Virtual Server Wizard, which takes you through the following steps:

1. Specify a display name for the new NNTP virtual server that will be used in the IIS console tree.

2. Specify an IP address and port number for the server. (The standard TCP port for NNTP is 119.) The identity of the virtual server you are creating must be different from that of any existing virtual servers on the machine.

3. Specify locations for the internal server files and news content files. These can be local directories or network shares.

4. Click Finish, and a new NNTP virtual server is created on your IIS machine.

New Virtual Directory Wizard

NNTP Service allows you to create virtual directories within your NNTP virtual server. You can use these virtual directories to store portions of the news server's content. To see how this works, follow this procedure to create a new virtual directory within the Default NNTP Virtual Server:

1. To start the wizard, select the Virtual Directories node under Default NNTP Virtual Server in the console tree, click the Action button, point to New, and choose Virtual Directory from the drop-down menu.

2. In the opening screen of the wizard (Figure 28-22), specify the newsgroup subtree whose content you want to store in the directory. For example, if you wanted to store messages for the newsgroups scribes.support.pc, scribes.support.mac, and scribes.support.unix, you could specify scribes.support in this text box. We'll actually do this now and create the three newsgroups later. Click Next.

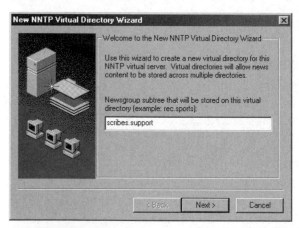

Figure 28-22. *Creating a new NNTP virtual directory within the Default NNTP Virtual Server on ws1.*

3. Choose File System or Remote Share, and then click Next to specify a path to the local directory or network share where the content will be located. (If you choose a network share, you must enter appropriate credentials.) Choose File System and specify C:\support as your path. Click Finish.

4. The Virtual Directories node under the Default NNTP Virtual Server node in the console tree now shows the new virtual directory listed there, along with its associated newsgroup subtree. You can double-click the new virtual directory to open a Properties window where you can reconfigure its settings or configure additional settings.

New Expiration Policy Wizard

In the New Expiration Policy Wizard, you can create an expiration policy that specifies how long articles will remain in newsgroups before they expire (are deleted). Articles can expire if they surpass a specified age. Follow these steps to create an expiration policy for the scribes.support.* newsgroups:

1. Start the New Expiration Policy Wizard.

2. Specify a descriptive name for the expiration policy, like *Expiration Policy for scribes.support.* groups*. Click Next.

3. Specify that you want the policy to apply to only a selection of newsgroups on the selected virtual server. Click Next.

4. Click Add, enter *scribes.support* as the pattern that groups need to match in order to have this expiration policy, and then click OK. You can add several patterns if you want, to apply your expiration policy to several disjointed newsgroup subtrees. Click Next.

5. Specify the time in hours that articles are allowed to remain in the group before expiring. (The default is 168 hours, or 7 days.) Click Finish.

6. Select the Expiration Policies node under the Default NNTP Virtual Server node in the console tree to see the new expiration policy displayed. You can double-click the expiration policy to open its Properties window and reconfigure it manually if you want.

New Newsgroup Wizard

To add a new newsgroup, select the Newsgroup node in the console tree, click the Action button, point to New, and choose Newsgroup from the drop-down menu. Specify a display name for the new newsgroup and click Next. Or you can provide a description and prettyname. Click Finish. It's just that simple.

Configuring the Default NNTP Virtual Server

To configure an NNTP virtual server, use the various tabs in its Properties window. For simplicity, we'll continue to use the Default NNTP Virtual Server as our example. You'll notice some similarities between configuring NNTP virtual servers and Web/FTP sites discussed previously. Along the way we'll also create the three scribes.support.* newsgroups mentioned earlier.

The General Tab

Figure 28-23 shows the General tab of the Default NNTP Virtual Server Properties window on the Windows 2000 server called ws1.scribes.com. On this tab, you can specify the following options:

- **Name** This is the friendly name of the NNTP virtual server in the console tree.

- **Path Header** Whatever you enter here appears in the Path line of the NNTP headers attached to messages posted to this virtual server. Typically, you might enter the fully qualified DNS name of the virtual server here, but this is optional.

- **IP Address** Like FTP sites discussed earlier in this chapter, NNTP virtual servers are uniquely identified by a combination of IP address and TCP port, and each NNTP virtual server hosted on the same IIS machine must differ in at least one of these parameters. Although you already know the advantages and disadvantages of the different ways of configuring this, note that the Advanced button allows you to configure additional identities (combinations of IP address, TCP port number, and SSL port number) for an NNTP virtual server, if you want to.

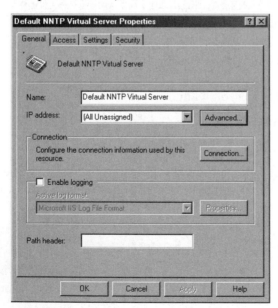

Figure 28-23. *The General tab of the Properties window for the Default NNTP Virtual Server.*

Connections and logging on this tab are similar to that for Web and FTP sites discussed earlier in this chapter. You can enable logging here, but you can also enable/disable it on a directory-by-directory basis, just as you can with Web and FTP sites.

The Settings Tab

The Settings tab contains a variety of settings related to how NNTP functions for the selected virtual server. Specifically, you can set the following options:

- Enable or disable posting to the virtual server by NNTP clients. For example, you might disable posting when you are performing maintenance on the server.

- Limit the maximum size of a message that can be posted. This is usually a good idea.

- Limit the maximum amount of data that can be posted by a user during a single connection. This is also a good idea.

- Allow other NNTP servers to pull newsfeeds from this virtual server. This option does not enable pulling from other IIS servers because the NNTP Service on IIS doesn't support this—rather, this option applies to USENET hosts and Exchange Servers running the Internet News Service.

- Allow newsfeeds to post articles to this NNTP virtual server.

- Allow control messages. This allows clients and servers to issue special commands to the virtual server for performing tasks like creating new newsgroups or deleting existing ones.

- Specify the DNS name of an SMTP mail server to be used for moderated newsgroups hosted on the virtual server.

- Specify the fully qualified DNS name to which the moderator belongs.

- Specify the e-mail address for the administrator of the virtual server so that this person can receive any error messages generated by the NNTP Service when messages posted to a moderated newsgroup can't be delivered to the specified SMTP mail server.

Managing Newsgroups

To view the list of existing newsgroups on the virtual server, to modify the properties of a group, to create new groups, or to delete existing ones, use the NNTP server's Newsgroups node. Note that a number of default newsgroups already exist within the Default NNTP Virtual Server. Let's create the three newsgroups described earlier. Follow these steps to create the group scribes.support.pc:

1. Select the Newsgroups node, click the Action button, select New, and then select Newsgroup on the drop-down menu. This opens the New Newsgroup Wizard, shown in Figure 28-24.

Figure 28-24. *The New Newsgroup Wizard.*

2. Enter *scribes.support.pc* for the name of the newsgroup. Click Next.
3. Enter a description, if you want.
4. Enter a newsgroup prettyname. (Some clients support this feature.)
5. Click Finish, and the new newsgroup should appear in the right pane of the console.

Repeat these steps to create the scribes.support.mac and scribes.support.unix groups. We'll test these groups in a moment.

Tip If you have hundreds (or thousands) of newsgroups defined on your virtual server, you can use the Limit Enumeration option on the Newsgroups shortcut menu to locate newsgroups whose properties you want to modify. In the Find Newsgroups dialog box, just specify a portion of the newsgroup name and the maximum number of results you want returned.

The Security Tab

On the Security tab you can specify an NNTP operator who can perform limited administrative tasks on the virtual server, just like for Web and FTP sites discussed earlier.

The Access Tab

The Access tab allows you to specify which authentication methods can be used when users try to connect to the virtual server. Do this by clicking the Authentication button under Access Control, which opens the Authentication Methods dialog box. These methods are similar to those for Web sites as discussed earlier in this chapter, although the way this dialog box presents them is slightly different.

Connection Control is the same as IP Address And Domain Name Restrictions for Web and FTP sites, which were discussed earlier. Secure Communication is also similar. Click the Certificate button to start the somewhat misnamed Web Server Certificate Wizard described earlier in this chapter.

Connecting to the Default NNTP Virtual Server

Once you've configured your NNTP virtual server properties, you can test it by trying to access your newsgroups using an NNTP client like Outlook Express. Follow these steps:

1. Start Outlook Express and cancel out of the wizard that tries to help you configure an SMTP mail account (if this wizard appears).
2. Choose Accounts from the Tools menu to open the Internet Accounts dialog box.
3. Click Add and choose News to create a new NNTP account. Specify your name, e-mail address, and the fully qualified DNS name of the news server (or its IP address if you prefer). If the NNTP virtual server doesn't have anonymous access enabled, select the check box My News Server Requires Me To Log On and specify your credentials accordingly.
4. Click Next and then click Finish.
5. Close the Internet Accounts dialog box. You'll be prompted to download newsgroups from the news account you just added. Click Yes.
6. The Newsgroup Subscriptions dialog box appears, showing you all the newsgroups available on the NNTP virtual server you connected to and allowing you to subscribe to groups of your choice. Double-click a group to subscribe to it.
7. Click OK to return to the main Outlook Express window.
8. To test the newsgroups, simply browse through them on your virtual server, post messages, read messages, and so on (Figure 28-25).

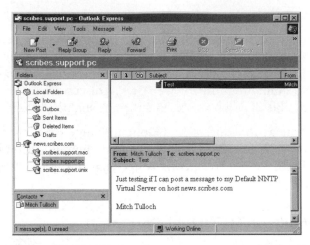

Figure 28-25. *Testing the new newsgroups by posting to them using Outlook Express.*

Displaying NNTP Sessions

After you make some test postings, switch to the IIS console on your IIS server and select the Current Sessions node under the Default NNTP Virtual Server node in the console tree. This will display information regarding the users who are currently logged on to the virtual server. You can select any user, click Action, and choose either to terminate that user's connection or terminate all connections to the NNTP virtual server.

Rebuilding an NNTP Virtual Server

You can perform one important maintenance task on an NNTP virtual server: rebuilding the indexes and hash tables that the virtual server employs to keep track of the articles that have been posted to it. Circumstances that warrant rebuilding the server include manually deleting files from the NNTP directories where newsgroup content is stored, experiencing a disk failure and losing some newsgroup content, or having trouble accessing articles.

To rebuild the Default NNTP Virtual Server, for example, follow these steps:

1. To stop the Default NNTP Virtual Server, select the Virtual Server in the console tree and then click the Stop button on the console toolbar

(or click the Action button or right-click the Virtual Server node and then choose the Stop command).

2. With the Default NNTP Virtual Server node still selected, click Action, point to All Tasks, and choose Rebuild Server from the drop-down menu.

3. Select a standard or thorough rebuild (thorough is slower), and click Start.

Managing SMTP Virtual Servers

The fourth and last core service that is included as part of IIS on Windows 2000 Server is the Simple Mail Transfer Protocol Service (SMTP Service). SMTP is the application-layer protocol that underlies the worldwide system of SMTP hosts (mail servers) on the Internet. If it's not already installed on IIS, use the Add/Remove Programs utility in Control Panel.

What SMTP Service Does

You can administer SMTP Service on IIS 5 either by using the IIS snap-in for the MMC or via a Web browser using SMTP Service Manager (HTML). Like other core IIS facilities, it is fully integrated with Windows 2000 event and performance monitoring. IIS includes SMTP Service primarily for use by mail-enabled Web applications. A simple example is an HTML form that a user fills out and submits, upon which the form handler (the script or program that takes the information entered by the client and actually does something with it) composes an e-mail message and sends it using SMTP Service.

Note that SMTP Service included with IIS isn't intended to replace a company mail server—IIS has no facility for creating individual user mailboxes. SMTP Service is intended mainly for mail forwarding by mail-enabled Web applications, although it can both send and receive mail and relay mail from other SMTP hosts. If you need a full-featured mail server for your company, try Exchange Server 5.5 and implement the Internet Mail Service on it to give it SMTP capability.

When you install SMTP Service on IIS, it automatically creates a Default SMTP Virtual Server, as shown in Figure 28-26. You can host multiple SMTP virtual servers on a single machine, but this is rarely needed because the Default SMTP

Virtual Server can be configured to forward mail for multiple SMTP domains. Like other IIS core services, SMTP Service is managed by a combination of Properties windows and wizards.

Figure 28-26. *The Default SMTP Virtual Server shown in the IIS console window.*

SMTP Directories

Important to the operation of an SMTP virtual server are a series of directories that are used for processing mail. For the Default SMTP Virtual Server, these directories are all located within the \inetpub\mailroot directory on the server. Some of the more important directories include the following:

- **Drop**   If SMTP Service receives incoming messages that are addressed to recipients belonging to SMTP domains managed by the SMTP virtual server, they are dropped here. Web applications can then be written to collect incoming mail delivered to this directory and process it accordingly.

- **Pickup**   If SMTP Service picks up outgoing messages, they are placed in the Pickup folder and delivered to their destination SMTP host once a connection is made with that host (or with an intermediate host that can relay mail).

- **Queue**   If a message that a Web application places in the Pickup folder can't be delivered immediately (for example, if the remote SMTP host is temporarily down), it is moved to the Queue folder to await further attempts at delivery.

- **Badmail**   If message delivery repeatedly fails, outgoing mail is classed as undeliverable, and if it can't be returned to sender, it winds up here.

Configuring the Default SMTP Virtual Server

To configure an SMTP virtual server, use the various tabs in its Properties window. For this example, we'll use the Default SMTP Virtual Server for simplicity. Configuring an SMTP virtual server is similar to configuring Web and FTP sites and NNTP virtual servers (all discussed previously).

The General Tab

The virtual server identity is configured on the General tab of the Properties window for the virtual server. IIS logging is implemented the same as for the other IIS core services. Note, however, that logging is disabled by default.

Identification   An SMTP virtual server has a two-part identity similar to that of an NNTP virtual server. The two parameters that uniquely specify an SMTP virtual server are IP address and TCP port number. (The default TCP port number is 25.) By clicking the Advanced button on this tab, you can assign multiple identities (IP address and TCP port number) to your server, but each identity must differ by at least one of these parameters. The usual procedure is to leave the TCP port set to 25 and use one IP address for the virtual server, with a mapping from this address to a fully qualified DNS name in a DNS server or Hosts file.

Connections   Clicking the Connection button in the Connection section of the General tab opens the Connections dialog box (Figure 28-27). Here you configure connection limits separately for incoming and outgoing messages. You can either specify the number of connections allowed numerically or set them as unlimited by clearing the check boxes. You can set a timeout value also for outgoing connection attempts. You can also limit connections on a per-domain basis if multiple SMTP domains are configured for the virtual server. Note that you can specify the outgoing TCP port here, while you specify the incoming TCP port as part of the virtual server's identity settings. (See the previous section.)

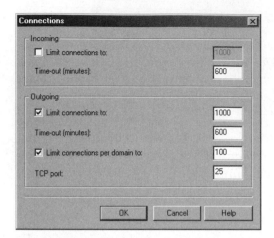

Figure 28-27. *Configuring connection settings for the Default SMTP Virtual Server.*

IIS Logging   IIS logging is implemented the same as for the other IIS core services. Note, however, that logging is disabled by default.

The Access Tab

On the Access tab, you can choose the type of access and control you want.

Anonymous Access and Authentication Control   SMTP Service supports anonymous access, basic authentication, and Windows Security Package (Windows integrated security) for inbound connection attempts. Basic authentication security uses a user name and password, while Windows Security Package includes the Windows 2000 domain name as well. Clicking the Authentication button on the Access tab opens the Authentication dialog box where you configure these settings. Note that by default an SMTP virtual server is configured to try to authenticate inbound connection attempts using all three authentication methods, if necessary.

The Transport Layer Security (TLS) option is essentially a variant of SSL encryption, and you can enable it here for inbound connection attempts. You must first obtain a server certificate from a CA and install it on the SMTP virtual server before TLS can be properly enabled. (See the next section.) For more information on IIS authentication methods, see the earlier coverage of Web sites, FTP sites, and NNTP virtual servers, all in this chapter.

> **Note** The settings configured here specify how your SMTP virtual server authenticates remote SMTP hosts that are trying to connect to it to deliver mail—that is, for inbound connection attempts. To specify authentication methods for outbound connection attempts, select Outbound Security on the Delivery tab.

Secure Communications As expected, if you click the Certificate button, the Web Server Certificate Wizard (still a misnomer) starts. Click the Communication button to require that access take place on a secure channel, once the certificate has been installed on the virtual server. If you choose Require Select Channel, you must also enable TLS in the Authentication dialog box. Requesting, obtaining, and installing server certificates is discussed earlier in this chapter.

Connection Control IP address and domain name restrictions function in the same way for SMTP Service as it does for the other three IIS core services.

Relay Restrictions Click the Relay button in the Relay Restrictions field on the Access tab to open the Relay Restrictions dialog box (Figure 28-28). This setting is important because allowing untrusted SMTP hosts to relay mail through your SMTP virtual server is an invitation for sending spam. You should generally deny relay privileges to all hosts and grant them to only known hosts that you trust or those that can properly authenticate with your server.

Figure 28-28. *Configuring relay restrictions for the Default SMTP Virtual Server.*

The Messages Tab

You can use the Messages tab to limit messages in three ways:

- Limit the maximum message and session sizes in kilobytes for this virtual server. (Session size refers to all the messages delivered by a single SMTP connection.)

- Limit the maximum number of outbound messages that can be sent in one connection. If more messages need to be sent, additional connections will be opened between the hosts.

- Limit the maximum number of recipients for a message.

In addition, you can change the directory where nondelivery reports (NDRs) are sent and also send copies of NDRs to an e-mail address that you specify.

Tip Make sure the maximum session size is greater than the maximum message size. Don't choose a maximum session size that's too low, or a remote SMTP host might continually resubmit a message for delivery. On the other hand, if you regularly send a lot of messages to a few domains, set the maximum number of outbound messages per connection low enough so that SMTP Service opens multiple connections to the remote host, resulting in faster and more efficient transfer of messages.

The Delivery Tab

The Delivery tab allows you to specify the following different settings related to mail delivery:

- **Outbound** Allows you to specify how your virtual server responds when it tries to connect to a remote SMTP host to deliver mail but can't connect. For outbound mail, you can specify a series of retry intervals, a delay notification value, and an expiration timeout value.

- **Local** For local delivery, you can specify only delay notification and expiration timeout values.

- **Outbound Security** Allows you to specify the authentication method (No Authentication, Basic Authentication, or Windows Security Package, any of which can run with or without TLS) when attempting an outbound connection with a remote SMTP host. If you specify either form of authenticated access, you need to specify credentials as well.

Note that you can configure only one outbound authentication method for an SMTP virtual server, and anonymous access is selected by default because this is most commonly used on the Internet.

- **Advanced** Clicking this button opens the Advanced Delivery dialog box, on which you can configure:

  - **Maximum Hop Count** Allows you to specify the maximum number of hops between SMTP hosts that is allowed before the message is determined to be nondeliverable. The value you specify here is included in the header fields of each message sent. Be sure to specify a value here to prevent messages from endlessly looping when they can't be delivered directly to the remote host.

  - **Masquerade Domain** Allows you to specify the DNS domain name, which replaces the local domain name in the Mail From header field of each message sent. This feature is optional.

  - **Fully Qualified Domain Name** Allows you to specify the full DNS name of the SMTP virtual server. The value displayed here is the one found on the Network Identification tab of the Control Panel's System Properties window, but you can change this if your server has multiple roles and DNS names.

  - **Smart Host** Allows you to route all outgoing messages to a specific SMTP host instead of trying to connect to the host responsible for the recipient's DNS domain. You can enter either a fully qualified domain name or an IP address. (Place square brackets around the IP address if you use one.) This feature is optional.

  - **Attempt Direct Delivery Before Sending To Smart Host** This option can be enabled only when a smart host has been specified. Its use is self-explanatory.

  - **Perform Reverse DNS Lookup On Incoming Messages** Should be left disabled because it causes a significant hit on server performance.

The LDAP Routing Tab

If you want your SMTP virtual server to be able to access an LDAP-compliant directory service to obtain information like the addresses of senders and recipients, you can enable this feature and specify the name, schema type, binding type, account, password, and naming context for connecting to the directory server. If you enable LDAP Routing, the default entries in the fields allow the SMTP virtual server to connect to and use the Windows 2000 Active Directory. Supported directory services include

- Microsoft Exchange Server directory
- Microsoft Windows 2000 Active Directory
- Microsoft Site Server 3 Membership Directory
- Microsoft Commercial Internet System 2 LDAP service
- Custom directory service, such as an Internet service like Four11 or Bigfoot

The Security Tab

SMTP operators have limited administration privileges for the virtual server, similar to the way operators function in Web sites, FTP sites, and NNTP virtual servers.

SMTP Domains

Each SMTP virtual server that is created manages at least one SMTP domain. This domain is specified automatically as the default local domain, and you can view it by selecting the Domains node under the SMTP virtual server node in the console tree. This is the DNS domain that is being serviced by the virtual server, and any incoming messages addressed to recipients within this domain will either be dropped in the Drop folder or returned to sender with an NDR.

You can have only one default local domain on the virtual server, and this domain is stamped on the message headers of all outgoing messages. However, you can create additional alias domains so that your virtual server can manage more than one SMTP domain. Alias domains use the same settings as the default domain and deliver incoming messages to the same Drop folder.

You can also create remote domains and specify delivery requirements for each one differently, which is useful if some remote SMTP hosts that you need to connect to use TLS but others don't. Global TLS configuration isn't enough in this case. In addition, for remote domains you can specify a predefined delivery route and even use wildcards to include subdomains. Use remote domains for connecting to remote SMTP hosts to which you frequently need to send mail.

Note   Like NNTP Service, an SMTP virtual server node has a Current Sessions node under it in the console tree that you can use to view current connections to the server and terminate any or all of those connections.

The New Domain Wizard

Use the New Domain Wizard to create either alias domains or remote domains. We'll only look at how to create alias domains here. (See the online documentation for information about creating remote domains.) To create an alias domain for the Default SMTP Virtual Server, follow these steps:

1. Select the virtual server node in the console tree, click the Action button, point to New, and choose Domain from the drop-down menu. This starts the New SMTP Domain Wizard.

2. Select the Alias domain type button, which will create an alias domain for the default local domain. Click Next.

3. Specify the DNS name for the new alias domain, netsolvers.com. Click Finish.

4. View the domains for the Default SMTP Virtual Server by selecting the Domains node in the console tree. Any incoming messages that are addressed to recipients in the netsolvers.com domain will be dropped in the Drop folder and stamped with the default domain name, scribes.com.

Tip   By opening the Properties window for the default local domain, you can change the location of the folder where mail is dropped from Mailroot\Drop to some other local folder on your server. Alias domains always use the same Drop folder as the default local domain, however.

Remote Administration

Our final topic for the chapter is using a standard Web browser like Microsoft Internet Explorer for remote administration of IIS sites, servers, and services. Until now we've used only the IIS console for IIS administration. However, IIS requires a remote procedure call (RPC)–based connection and is thus intended primarily for administration on the internal network of a company. By using ISM (HTML), however, administrators can manage most (but not all) aspects of IIS from remote locations, even over a nonsecure connection on the Internet and through a proxy server or firewall (if configured properly). This section looks briefly at ISM (HTML) and how to use it.

The Administration Web Site

ISM (HTML) is an optional component of IIS that is installed by default when you install Windows 2000 Server. Once this component is installed, a new Web site appears in the console tree of the IIS console window. This new Web site is called the Administration Web Site and is basically an ASP application that allows administrators to manage IIS using any Web browser that supports JavaScript.

Enabling Remote Administration

To be able to use ISM (HTML), administrators need only to be able to connect to the Administration Web Site. To make this possible, you need to perform this procedure first:

1. Open the Properties window for the Administration Web Site in the IIS console.

2. On the Web Site tab, find the TCP port number assigned to this site and write it down. (A random port number between 2000 and 9999 is assigned to the site during installation of the component, and you need to know this number to be able to connect to the site using a Web browser.)

3. Switch to the Directory Security tab and open the IP Address And Domain Name Restrictions dialog box. By default, only the local host computer (127.0.0.1) is allowed access to the Administration Web Site; all other IP addresses are denied.

4. Add to the Granted list the IP address of any machines from which you want to be able to remotely administer the server. (Remote clients need to have static IP addresses.)

5. Apply the changes by closing the Properties window for the Administration Web Site. You're ready to go.

Testing Remote Administration

To test your configuration of the Administration Web Site, start Internet Explorer on the machine whose IP address you have granted access and open the URL *http://Server_Name:Admin_Port*, where *Server_Name* is the IP address or DNS name of the IIS server, and *Admin_Port* is the TCP port number you noted for remote administration.

A dialog box appears requesting your credentials (user name, password, and Windows 2000 domain), after which you will be informed that you are using a nonsecure connection for performing remote administration. (You can configure SSL on the Administration Web Site just as on any other Web site if you prefer more security.)

At this point (if you've done everything correctly), ISM (HTML) should be functional and you should be connected to the Administration Web Site with your browser (Figure 28-29). You can perform most administration tasks using ISM (HTML), but not all. For example, you can't configure certificate mapping using ISM (HTML) because to do so requires coordination with other Windows 2000 services that aren't accessible from a Web browser.

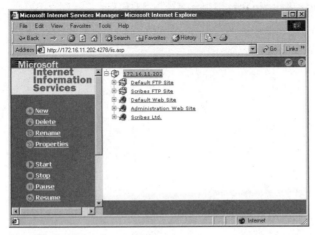

Figure 28-29. *The opening page of ISM (HTML) as seen in Internet Explorer 5.*

Summary

This chapter demonstrated the common administration tasks of configuring the settings of the four IIS core services: WWW, FTP, NNTP, and SMTP. You can configure these services at up to four different levels: server, site, directory, and file. And you configure them by using a combination of Properties windows and wizards. The next chapter addresses Microsoft Internet Explorer and its role in the enterprise.

Chapter 29
Internet and Intranet

This chapter focuses on administering Microsoft Internet Explorer 5 in the corporate Microsoft Windows 2000 enterprise. Microsoft Internet Explorer 5 is a suite of Internet tools that includes the Microsoft Internet Explorer 5 Web browser, Microsoft Outlook Express mail and news client, Microsoft NetMeeting and Microsoft Chat collaboration tools, and a variety of other tools, components, and supporting files. Using tools like the Microsoft Connection Manager Components (included with Windows 2000 Server) and the Microsoft Internet Explorer Administration Kit (available separately from Microsoft), corporate network administrators can easily deploy and manage Internet Explorer 5 and its components onto 32-bit, 16-bit, and UNIX platform client desktops.

Note This chapter focuses on the deployment and administration of Internet Explorer 5 and client connections for users. For information on using Internet Explorer 5 from a user's perspective, consult one of the books from Microsoft Press, such as *Running Microsoft Internet Explorer 5* by Bryan Pfaffenberger (1999).

Internet Explorer Administration Kit

Let's begin by considering how you can deploy and install Internet Explorer 5 and its associated components within your corporate enterprise. (Managing client connections will be covered later in this chapter.) The installation of Internet Explorer 5 itself is, of course, not an issue if your desktop machines all have Microsoft Windows 2000 Professional installed on them, since Internet Explorer 5 is included with the Windows 2000 Professional operating system, but configuring and managing these machines is an important aspect of network administration in a Microsoft Windows–based network.

Fortunately, Microsoft provides a set of tools—called the Internet Explorer Administration Kit (IEAK)—that makes it easy to deploy, install, customize, and manage Internet Explorer 5 on the desktop. The IEAK contains tools that can be used to customize the configuration of Internet Explorer 5 to match your organization's needs. For example, administrators can specify a home page, a Favorites list, a Links bar, and so on. This customization can be done prior to installing Internet Explorer 5 on desktop machines, and the Setup program that installs it can itself be configured to require minimal user intervention during installation.

In addition, administrators can prevent users from modifying specified configuration settings such as security and connection settings. This reduces the support costs of maintaining and troubleshooting Internet Explorer 5 deployments and facilitates adherence to corporate standards and policies with regard to Internet access. The tools and programs that make up the IEAK include the following:

- **Internet Explorer Customization Wizard** This wizard provides administrators with an easy way of configuring and building customized installation packages for Internet Explorer 5 and its associated components. Administrators can use the wizard to create special packages for mobile users with limited hard disk space on their machines; create packages that can be installed from network shares, CD-ROMS, or over the Internet; create packages with different security settings for different groups of users; and so on.

- **IEAK Profile Manager** This tool can be used by administrators to manage users' settings automatically after Internet Explorer 5 has been installed on their machines.

- **IEAK Toolkit** This is a miscellaneous collection of programs and files that helps administrators configure and manage various aspects of Internet Explorer 5 and its associated components. The Toolkit contents are located in the Toolkit folder of the IEAK program folder.

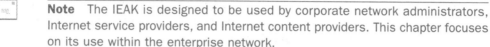

Note The IEAK is designed to be used by corporate network administrators, Internet service providers, and Internet content providers. This chapter focuses on its use within the enterprise network.

Another component of the IEAK is the Connection Manager Administration Kit (CMAK). This kit provides administrators with an easy way of configuring and building customized Microsoft Connection Manager dialers that can be installed on users' machines to configure their Internet connection. Windows 2000 Server includes a newer version of this component than the one included with IEAK 5; it can be used to create customized Connection Manager service profiles for client machines running Windows 2000 Professional. The version of CMAK included with the IEAK can create service profiles only for earlier versions of Microsoft Windows. The CMAK for Windows 2000 is discussed later in this chapter.

Obtaining the IEAK

The IEAK is included in the *Microsoft Internet Explorer 5 Resource Kit,* available from Microsoft Press. You can also download the IEAK from Microsoft's IEAK Web site at *http://www.microsoft.com/windows/ieak/en/default.asp*.

Regardless of how you obtain the IEAK, you need to go to Microsoft's IEAK Web site afterward and register your copy to obtain the necessary customization code to run it. This involves creating a personal profile for yourself and choosing a licensing agreement. (You must specify whether you will be using the IEAK to distribute Internet Explorer 5 to either corporate intranet users or external Internet users.) Once you've completed the profile and accepted the agreement, the customization code is e-mailed to you immediately.

Installing the IEAK

Installing the IEAK is straightforward and is done from the main menu of the Microsoft Internet Explorer Administration Kit 5 CD (or the CD that accompanies the *Microsoft Internet Explorer 5 Resource Kit*). By default, the application is installed in the folder C:\Program Files\IEAK.

Planning Your Internet Explorer 5 Deployment

The IEAK gives administrators a great deal of control over most aspects of Internet Explorer 5 and its associated components, including the ability to lock down program settings to prevent users from changing them. Before actually creating your installation packages, you need to carefully plan how you want to customize them. In doing so, ask yourself questions like these:

- Which groups of users need their own specially tailored Internet Explorer 5 installation packages?

- What platforms (32-bit Windows, 16-bit Windows, UNIX) will you need to create packages for?

- What Internet Explorer 5 components will each group of users need?

- What settings need to be preconfigured for users?

- Which settings should users be able to modify and which should be controlled by administrators?

- What media (CD-ROM, floppy disks, network share, Web directory) will be used for storing your installation packages?

- What third-party software do you want to include in your installation packages?

- What additional desktop and user settings do you want to configure?

In addition, you will need to think about these questions:

- What machine will you use for building your installation packages? This machine must be running a 32-bit Windows operating system and must have sufficient hard disk space to store the packages you create.

- Have you created any custom bitmaps, Favorites lists, digital certificates, or other items required for creating your installation packages? You can import Internet Explorer 5 settings from a machine that is already appropriately configured.

- What connection profile will you use? Have you already established one, or will you need to create a new one as part of the process of creating an installation package?

Creating an Installation Package

The Microsoft Internet Explorer Customization Wizard is used to create custom Windows Update Setup packages for installing Internet Explorer 5 and its associated components. These packages can then be distributed to users in various ways, such as on CD-ROMs or floppy disks, as e-mail attachments, or as downloads available from a shared folder on the network or from a Web page. The wizard also lets you create different packages for different groups of users. Packages can be created either from scratch or with settings imported from an existing Internet settings (.INS) file (also called an IEAK profile) on a machine that is already configured. An IEAK installation package contains the following:

- The Internet Explorer 5 Setup file (Ie5Setup.exe) and its associated .INF file

- Various program files

- The branding cabinet file (Branding.cab) containing .INS, .INF, and other customization files

- The component information cabinet file (Iecif.cab) containing additional components and their customization files

To run the Customization Wizard on the build computer on which the IEAK is installed, click Start, point to Programs, point to Microsoft IEAK, and choose Internet Explorer Customization Wizard. This opens the initial screen of the wizard (Figure 29-1).

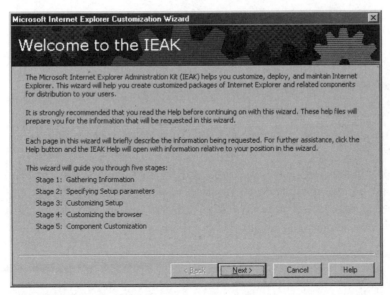

Figure 29-1. *The opening screen of the Microsoft Internet Explorer Customization Wizard.*

The Customization Wizard runs in five stages, using a series of step-by-step screens. The screens that are presented during each stage depend to an extent upon the various choices you make along the way, so we can present here only a general outline of the steps that might be involved in a typical customization session. For a more detailed explanation of how to use the IEAK, see either the online Help file for the product or the *Microsoft Internet Explorer 5 Resource Kit*.

Stage 1: Gathering Information

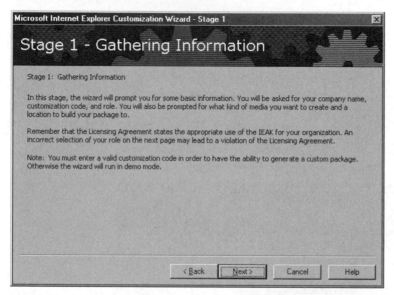

Figure 29-2. *The screen that introduces Stage 1 of the Microsoft Internet Explorer Customization Wizard.*

Stage 1 of the Customization Wizard, the first screen of which is shown in Figure 29-2, prompts the user for basic information such as the company name, customization code, role, target media, and so on. You must provide a valid customization code or the wizard will run only in demo mode. The wizard leads you through the following screens:

1. **Company Name And Customization Code** You must obtain a valid customization code or the IEAK will run only in demo mode. Specify also which title best describes your role in the company: corporate administrator, service provider, or content provider. You must be licensed for your particular role.

2. **Platform Options** Specify the platform for which you want to build your customized Internet Explorer 5 deployment package. Choices include 32-bit Windows (Windows 9x/NT 4.0), 16-bit Windows (Windows 3.11/WFW/NT 3.51), and UNIX. Note that different platforms support different features.

3. **File Locations** Specify a folder on the build server in which the finished package will be stored. By default, this folder is called C:\builds*mmddyyyy*, where *mm* is the current month, *dd* is the current date, and *yyyy* is the current year.

4. **Advanced Options** By default, Automatic Version Synchronization (AVS) is turned on. This feature provides version information for the various Internet Explorer 5 components you have available so that you can determine whether you have the most recent version of these components. To use AVS, you must be connected to the Internet. If you downloaded the IEAK from the Internet, you must run AVS at least once when you create your first package. You also specify here the folder in which AVS will store its downloaded Internet Explorer 5 components. You can optionally specify an existing .INS file (an IEAK profile) to use as a starting point for your custom package. Settings in the .INS file are imported into the wizard and used as defaults, but you can modify them as desired.

5. **Language Selection** Specify the localized language to which your customized package will be directed. A package can be customized for only a single language, so if you need pages for several different languages you must run the wizard several times.

6. **Media Selection** Specify the target medium for your package. This can be any of the following. (Not all options are available under all licensing schemes.)

   • Download From A Web Site On The Internet (Or On An Intranet). For example, users could click on a link to start the installation.

   • CD-ROM Distribution (Uses Autorun).

   • Flat. Select this option (which refers to a flat file system) if you want users to download the package from a shared folder on the network. The installation files are all written to the same folder.

   • Multiple Floppy Disks. Service providers can distribute their complete package on a set of distribution floppies, but CD-ROM is generally preferable.

- Single Floppy Disk. Service providers can distribute a single floppy disk that will connect users to a distribution Web site so that they can download the rest of their package.

- Single-Disk Branding. This produces a single floppy disk that can be used to brand an already existing Internet Explorer 5 installation with a corporate logo bitmap, Favorites list, and so on.

7. **Feature Selection**   Use this screen of the wizard to specify which features of Internet Explorer 5 and its components you want to customize in succeeding stages of the wizard. (This walkthrough will assume that all options are selected.)

Stage 2: Specifying Setup Parameters

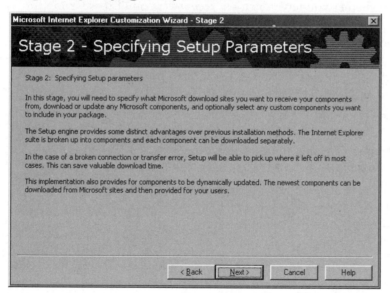

Figure 29-3. *The screen that introduces Stage 2 of the Microsoft Internet Explorer Customization Wizard.*

Stage 2 of the wizard, the first screen of which is shown in Figure 29-3, lets you specify which Microsoft download sites you want to receive your Internet Explorer 5 components from and, optionally, to specify any custom software components you want to include in your package. The Setup engine is designed to be able to resume after a broken connection and continue downloading at the point at which it was interrupted, which saves time when performing long downloads over unreliable Internet connections. This stage of the wizard takes you through the following screens:

8. **Download Locations** If you left AVS enabled in the previous stage, you need to specify which Microsoft site you will use for downloading the latest versions of your Internet Explorer 5 components. Choose a location that is close to your geographical region.

9. **Automatic Version Synchronization** Shows the status of each of the Internet Explorer 5 components you currently have available for installation. The first time you run the wizard, all components are displayed with a yellow exclamation point icon, which indicates that you have an older version of this component. After you run AVS, some of your components will show up with a green check mark icon, indicating that you have the most recent version of the component, while new components available on the Microsoft site you are connected to will show up with a red X icon, indicating that you have not yet downloaded those components. You can select a specific component that you want to update and click Synchronize to download it from the Microsoft site, or you can just click Synchronize All.

10. **Add Custom Components** Allows you to package up to 10 third-party components into your Internet Explorer 5 package. You can include scripts and self-extracting executable programs that you want to distribute to your users. You can compress custom components into .CAB files for distribution as well. Applications that will be distributed with Internet Explorer 5 over the Internet should be digitally signed to verify their authenticity to users downloading them.

Stage 3: Customizing Setup

Stage 3 of the wizard, the first screen of which is shown in Figure 29-4, lets you customize the Setup title bar, bitmap, custom component install title, installation options, user install sites, and other information. This stage of the wizard takes you through several screens.

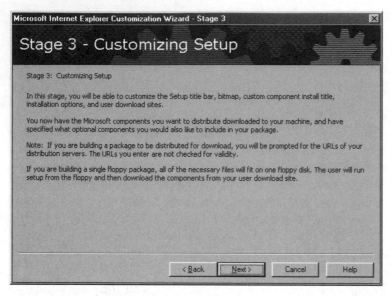

Figure 29-4. *The screen that introduces Stage 3 of the Microsoft Internet Explorer Customization Wizard.*

11. **CD-ROM Autorun Customization** If you specified CD-ROM as your distribution medium, you can specify an Autorun splash screen and a Readme file.

12. **Customize Setup** Lets you customize how the Windows Update Setup program will appear to users installing the package. You can specify the title bar and bitmap graphic for the Setup screen, as well as other information.

13. **Silent Install** If you have selected the corporate (intranet) licensing option, you can specify the degree to which users interact with the computer during the installation. The three choices are

- Interactive Install. Users will be prompted to make decisions and enter information during the installation.

- Hands-Free Install. Users are not prompted during the install, but message screens will inform users of the progress of the installation and any errors that occur will be displayed.

- Completely Silent Install. Users will not even know that the installation is taking place, as no prompts, messages, or errors will be displayed.

14. **Installation Options**   Specify which components are included in the installation and provide up to ten setup options for users to select or deselect components. You can create custom installation options or use the standard ones, which are Minimal, Typical, and Full.

15. **Component Download Sites**   Specify up to ten different Web or FTP sites from which users can download your package. These can be either corporate intranet or public Internet sites, depending on your licensing scheme. (This option assumes that you indicated that users will perform their installation from a Web site in Stage 2 of the wizard.) For silent installations you can specify only one site.

16. **Component Download**   Customize the URL that is pointed to by the Windows Update option of the Tools menu in Internet Explorer 5.

17. **Installation Directory**   Specify the folder on users' machines where the package will be installed (or leave this decision to users).

18. **Corporate Install Options**   If you selected a corporate installation during Stage 1 of the wizard, this screen provides a number of options. You can disable the Custom Installation option so that users cannot choose which components to install, disable the saving of uninstall information that allows users to revert to their previous version of Internet Explorer, and specify whether Internet Explorer will be the users' default browser (or leave the choice up to them).

19. **Advanced Installation Options**   Allows you to further customize installation by indicating which components will be displayed in the Customize Component Options screen during setup.

20. **Components On Media**   Specify whether components not selected for installation should nevertheless still be installed on the medium to make them available for automatic install later if desired.

21. **Connection Manager Customization**   The CMAK, which is included with the IEAK, is designed to allow administrators to customize and manage Internet connections for users. You can either start the CMAK Wizard at this point to customize a connection or use an existing custom connection profile created earlier with the CMAK. The CMAK is discussed later in this chapter.

22. **Windows Desktop Update**   This option is for corporate administrators only; it allows you to specify whether to include the Windows Desktop Update in your package. You do not need to include this component for users who are currently running Microsoft Windows 98 or later.

23. **Digital Signatures**   Specify whether to digitally sign your package. By using the Certificates snap-in for Windows 2000 Server, you can generate digital certificates and public/private key pairs, acting as your own certificate authority (CA).

Stage 4: Customizing the Browser

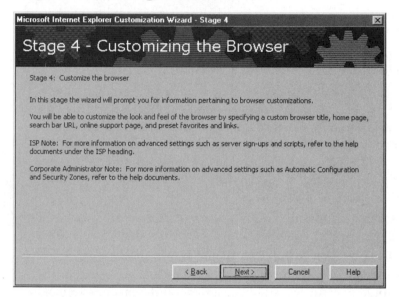

Figure 29-5. *The screen that introduces Stage 4 of the Microsoft Internet Explorer Customization Wizard.*

Stage 4 of the wizard, the first screen of which is shown in Figure 29-5, asks you to provide information concerning browser customization by specifying a browser title, default home page, search bar URL, online support page, preset list of favorites and links, and other information. This stage of the wizard takes you through the following screens:

24. **Browser Title**   Specify the text that will appear in the title bar of Internet Explorer 5 once the package is installed. For example, if you specify the title bar text as *Scribes.com*, that text will be displayed in

the title bar of users' copies of Internet Explorer 5 as "Microsoft Internet Explorer provided by Scribes.com." You can specify a toolbar background bitmap image here as well.

25. **Browser Toolbar Buttons**   Specify additional custom toolbar buttons that you want to appear on users' browser screens once installed. You can add these additional buttons to existing ones or delete the existing ones first and then add your own buttons. Developers can create new buttons for the toolbar and attach them to scripts and executables. (See MSDN Online for details.)

26. **Animated Logo**   If you don't like the rotating Internet Explorer logo in the top right corner of the browser window, you can replace it with your own animated corporate logo. Specify the path to the bitmap here.

27. **Static Logo**   Here you can specify a static logo to replace the Internet Explorer logo.

28. **Important URLs**   Specify the home page, search bar, and online support page URLs for your customized browser.

29. **Favorites And Links**   This is one of the most useful IEAK options. At this screen you can preconfigure the Favorites folder and Links bar on your customized browser. You can specify individual URLs one by one here, or you can import them from the \Windows\Favorites folder (or some other folder) of any machine that is accessible on the network. Note that, unfortunately, you can import a maximum of only 255 URLs in this way. You can also test each URL prior to creating your package.

30. **Channels**   Specify which custom channels or channel categories you want to include in your package. You need a Channel Definition Format (.CDF) file for each channel. Corporate administrators may want to delete all existing channels for the package if this feature is not used internally on the network.

31. **Welcome Page**   Specify a custom welcome page that is displayed when Internet Explorer 5 is started for the first time, use the default Internet Explorer 5 welcome page, or go directly to the user's home page. Custom welcome pages are specified by entering their URL.

32. **User-Agent String**   This advanced feature allows you to append a custom string to the user-agent string for Internet Explorer. User-agent strings are part of HTTP and can be used for tracking site visits and other things.

33. **Connection Settings** Lets you import connection settings for your package and modify those settings. You can also delete existing settings if any are present.

34. **Automatic Configuration** Specify a pointer to a configured file on a server that can be used to globally change configuration settings on all stations where you have deployed your package, instead of having to modify these settings on each user's computer. This useful feature reduces the administrative overhead and support costs of managing Internet Explorer on users' desktops. Changes to users' configurations are performed using the IEAK Profile Manager, which is discussed later in this chapter.

    Most settings are specified using an IEAK profile (an .INS file), but special advanced proxy settings can be specified using JavaScript files in .JS, .JVS, or .PAC format. Select the Enable Automatic Configuration option, specify the URL to the .INS file and script files, and specify a time interval in minutes to indicate how often the browser will check for a newer version of the configuration files. If you select the Automatically Detect Configuration Settings option and are using DNS and DHCP on your network, Internet Explorer will automatically be customized the first time users start it on their machines. This allows administrators to create Internet Explorer 5 packages that are not fully customized and then have users' copies of Internet Explorer 5 further customized when the users first start the program on their desktops.

35. **Proxy Settings** Proxy servers are used with firewalls to protect corporate networks over their Internet connections. They can also be used to cache frequently requested Web content and help balance network traffic. Specify your proxy settings for individual Internet protocols like HTTP, Secure HTTP, FTP, Gopher, and Socks Proxy.

36. **Security** Lets you import CAs and customize Microsoft Authenticode security to allow Internet Explorer 5 security settings to function properly. An additional screen called Security Settings lets you customize different security settings for each zone and customize content ratings.

37. **Sign-Up Screens** These screens appear only when the service provider licensing option is specified; they allow service providers to specify how their users will sign up for their services and connect to their Internet sites. We won't discuss these options further, since this chapter focuses on corporate deployment of Internet Explorer 5.

Stage 5: Customizing Components

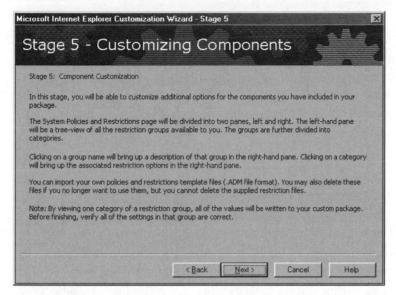

Figure 29-6. *The screen that introduces Stage 5 of the Microsoft Internet Explorer Customization Wizard.*

Stage 5 of the wizard, the first screen of which is shown in Figure 29-6, lets you customize additional options for the components you have included in your installation package. You do this by using the System Policies And Restrictions screen, a two-pane view in which the left pane displays a tree view of the various groups and categories of restrictions you can configure, while the right pane shows the options you can configure for the restriction you have selected. The IEAK includes support for importing your own system policy template (.ADM) files for customizing what is displayed here. This stage of the wizard takes you through the following screens:

38. **Programs**   Lets you import current default program settings to specify which Windows program is used for which Internet service. You can specify the programs to use for each of the following:

    - HTML Web page editor (no default)
    - SMTP e-mail client (Outlook Express is the default.)
    - NNTP news client (Outlook Express is the default.)

- Internet call client (Microsoft NetMeeting is the default.)
- Calendar client (no default)
- Contact list (Windows address book is the default.)

39. **Outlook Express Accounts** Specify the Internet hosts (servers) to which Outlook Express will connect for mail and news services. You can supply a host for each of the following:

- Incoming mail (POP3/IMAP4) server
- Outgoing mail (SMTP) server
- Internet news (NNTP) server

You can also specify that the applications must log on to any of these servers using Secure Password Authentication, which requires a Security Service Provider Interface (SSPI) provider such as Microsoft NT Lan Manager (NTLM), which is Windows 2000's authentication protocol for Windows NT 4 servers and clients. You can lock down these settings so that users can't change them or modify their Internet accounts.

40. **Outlook Express customization screens** Specify a custom welcome message that will appear when users first start the program on their desktops. You can also specify Outlook Express as the default mail and news client, indicate newsgroups that will automatically be subscribed to, turn on junk mail filtering, choose which view elements of the program will be enabled by default, specify the signature that will be appended to messages, indicate whether plain text or HTML will be used for sending messages, and other options.

41. **Address Book Directory Service** Specify additional options for directory services to be used by the Windows address book. Any LDAP-compliant directory service can be specified here, such as Four11 or Bigfoot on the Internet or Windows 2000 Active Directory on a corporate network.

42. **System Policies And Restrictions** This screen is a powerful tool that allows administrators to configure and lock down various desktop, shell, and security options for all users in their organization. You can also import policy files to customize the settings you can configure here.

Deploying IEAK Packages

Once you've completed the wizard, click Finish to generate and compress the custom installation package files and create the customized version of Internet Explorer 5. The final result will be stored in the appropriate subfolder of the \builds folder on the build computer. You can then do the following:

- Digitally sign your package (for 32-bit Windows platforms only).

- Prepare your distribution Web site or virtual directory (or network share or some other medium) and create a link to the Ie5setup.exe file that users will download and use to install Internet Explorer 5. See Chapter 27 for information on creating Web sites and virtual directories.

- Copy the language version folder and its contents to the appropriate virtual directory on the Web site. For example, if your package is an English language version, you need to copy the contents of the \Builds*mmddyyyy*\Download\Win32\En folder on the build machine (assuming a 32-bit package was created) to the appropriate virtual directory on the Web server.

- Copy the Ie5sites.dat file, which points to the download sites you specified during the wizard. This file is typically found in the IEAK profile folder for that package on your build machine—for example, \Builds*mmddyyyy*\Ins\Win32\En.

- Notify your users of the Web page (or other medium) they need to visit so that they can install the package by clicking on a specified link to the Ie5setup.exe file.

- If you want to later manage users' Internet Explorer 5 configurations automatically, using the IEAK Profile Manager, you need to copy the IEAK profile (the .INS file) for your build to the URL you specified during the wizard.

IEAK Profile Manager

The IEAK Profile Manager is a tool for modifying and maintaining the IEAK profile associated with a particular package. The profile specifies the configuration settings for the package, and the Profile Manager lets you modify any aspect of that profile. Furthermore, if you didn't enable automatic configuration when you created the package with the Internet Explorer Customization Wizard, you can enable it later using the Profile Manager.

The Profile Manager works by allowing you to open a selected .INS file (an IEAK profile), make changes to it, and save the result. The Profile Manager also maintains the companion files to the .INS file, which are stored in the same folder as the .INS file for that package. Two basic types of settings can be configured using the Profile Manager:

- **Wizard settings** Administrators can modify any settings that were specified during stages 2 through 5 of the Internet Explorer Customization Wizard.

- **Policies and restrictions** These settings refer to users' desktop, shell, and security settings (system policy settings), which were specified on the System Policies And Restrictions screen of the Internet Explorer Customization Wizard (step 42 under "Stage 5: Customizing Components" earlier in this chapter.

Using Profile Manager

To start the IEAK Profile Manager on the build computer, click Start, point to Programs, point to Microsoft IEAK, and choose IEAK Profile Manager. This opens the IEAK Profile Manager main window. You can either import an existing .INS file or create a new one. Figure 29-7 shows a file that has been imported from a package located on the build computer.

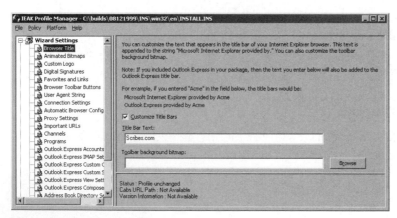

Figure 29-7. *The IEAK Profile Manager.*

> **Note** The IEAK Profile Manager window cannot be resized and should be displayed on screens with a resolution of 800 by 600 or higher.

Using the Profile Manager is straightforward: Simply select the type of wizard or policy settings you want to modify in the left pane of the window and make the appropriate modifications in the right pane. Save the results when finished (or use Save As to keep the existing .INS file while creating a new one with your new settings). Be sure to test your new configuration on a test machine before deploying it on your production site, where users' machines can be updated using autoconfiguration.

Connection Manager Administration Kit

The CMAK included with Windows 2000 Server (and the earlier version included with IEAK 5) is used to customize Connection Manager service profiles for the installation packages you create. Using the CMAK, you can create and manage custom Connection Manager service profiles that enable your Internet Explorer 5 users to connect to your Internet or intranet services. Microsoft Connection Manager is the client dialer and connection software tool that uses the service profiles created with the CMAK. In other words, the service provider or corporate network administrator creates a service profile, packages it with Connection Manager, and deploys it onto users' client desktop machines—enabling users to connect to the corporate intranet or to the service provider's Internet Web site and access its services.

In particular, the CMAK can be used to do the following:

- Create and manage dial-up and virtual private network (VPN) Connection Manager service profiles for connecting to ISPs and corporate networks
- Configure custom programs to run automatically when a user connects to your service
- Import existing connection settings and modify them
- Configure system policies and restrictions for connections
- Enable users to use the Internet Connection Wizard on their machines to sign up for your service

Like the IEAK, the CMAK is implemented as a wizard that takes you through a series of steps to create a new Connection Manager service profile. Preliminary planning is important here, just as it is for the IEAK; you need to ensure that you have any branded graphics, access numbers, scripts, or other items ready before running the wizard. The online CMAK Guide states that creating a new Connection Manager service profile involves six different phases. We will cover these phases only briefly here and only in regard to corporate deployments of installation packages.

More Info For more information on using the CMAK, refer to the online CMAK Guide or see the *Microsoft Internet Explorer 5 Resource Kit* (Microsoft Press, 1999).

For a corporate deployment of Internet Explorer 5, the six phases of the process look like this:

- **Phase 1: Planning** Create phone book and region files for your service providers and decide what type of connection you want and how you want it to be customized. The online CMAK Guide includes a planning worksheet that is very helpful for this task.

- **Phase 2: Developing custom elements** Create any custom graphics or other items needed for your profile.

- **Phase 3: Running the CMAK Wizard** The wizard creates a new service profile for the connection; this wizard is discussed later.

- **Phase 4: Preparing for delivery** You can deliver the connection to users either as part of an IEAK installation package or as a separate package.

- **Phase 5: Testing** Test your deliverables before letting users download them.

- **Phase 6: Providing support** Develop a strategy for supporting your users after the service profile has been delivered.

Installing CMAK

As mentioned earlier in this chapter, the version of CMAK included with the IEAK does not support the Windows 2000 platform but only legacy Microsoft Windows platforms. If you plan to deploy Connection Manager connections to client machines running Windows 2000 Professional, you need to use the version of CMAK included with Windows 2000 Server. To install the CMAK and Phone Book Services (PBS) on Windows 2000 Server, open Add/Remove Programs in Control Panel and select Add/Remove Windows Components. Then select Management and Monitoring Tools, click Details, and select Connection Manager Components.

Using the CMAK Wizard

Figure 29-8. *The first screen of the Connection Manager Administration Kit Wizard.*

Once installed, the CMAK Wizard (Figure 29-8) can be started either from within the IEAK Wizard (see step 21 in "Stage 3: Customizing Setup" earlier in this chapter) or directly from the Start menu by selecting Connection Manager Administration Kit from the Administrative Tools folder on the Programs menu of Windows 2000 Server. To create a new Connection Manager service profile for a typical corporate networking scenario, start the CMAK Wizard and follow these steps:

1. **Service Profile Source**   Specify whether you want to create a new service profile or edit an existing one.

2. **Service And File Names**   Specify a name for your service (for example, Scribes Connection Services) and a filename to be used for your service profile folder and files.

3. **Merged Service Profile**   Lets you merge the settings of a number of existing service profiles into the one you are creating or editing.

4. **Support Information**   Lets you specify a line of support information for your profile. For example, you could enter *Call 1-800-SCRIBES for customer support* or something similar.

5. **Realm Name**   Lets you specify a realm if one is needed. The realm is automatically appended to the user name during connection establishment, using a separator character that you specify. Microsoft Internet Authentication Service Commercial Edition, available in Microsoft Commercial Internet System, supports the use of realm names for remote authentication purposes.

6. **Dial-Up Networking Entries**   Specify the dial-up networking entries associated with the phone numbers in the address book. You can either specify DNS and/or WINS addresses or let the server assign these IP addresses to the client during connection establishment.

7. **VPN Support**   Allows you to enable a virtual private networking connection for this service profile. If you enable this feature, you can either specify DNS and/or WINS addresses or let the server assign these IP addresses to the client during connection establishment.

8. **Connection Actions**   Specify actions that will occur before connection establishment, after connection establishment, or before connection termination. In succeeding screens of the wizard, you specify the actual programs or scripts to be run and any parameters needed by them. For example, after connection establishment you might want to automatically download any phone book updates.

9. **Auto Applications**   Specify additional programs or scripts that will run during a communications session. For example, you might want to open your e-mail client program automatically once a connection is established.

10. **Logon Bitmap**   Specify the bitmap to be displayed in the logon dialog box. For example, you might use your corporate logo here.

11. **Phone Book Bitmap**   Specify the bitmap to be displayed in the Phone Book dialog box.

12. **Phone Book**   Specify whether you want to include a phone book in this service profile.

13. **Phone Book Updates**   Specify how your clients will receive updates to their phone books, typically by connecting to a Connection Point Services server that is specified by a URL. If you do not include a phone book in your service profile, you must specify one here that can be downloaded later by clients.

14. **Icons** Specify icons to be used to represent Connection Manager on the client machines. Use a corporate logo icon if desired.

15. **Status Area Icon Menu** Lets you customize the shortcut menu that appears when users right-click the status area icon.

16. **Help File** Specify a Help file to be used by your users. You can either use the default one or specify a custom one that you have created for your users.

17. **Connection Manager Software** Your users must have Connection Manager 1.2 installed on their machines in order to use the service profile you are creating. If they don't have it, you can indicate here that the Connection Manager software itself is to be included with your service profile. Users can then download the package, install Connection Manager, and have it configured by the profile you have created for them.

18. **License Agreement** Specify a text file containing the license agreement you want your users to accept (if desired).

19. **Additional Files** Specify other programs and files to be included in the service profile you are creating that are not specified elsewhere in the wizard.

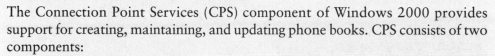

Real World **Connection Point Services**

The Connection Point Services (CPS) component of Windows 2000 provides support for creating, maintaining, and updating phone books. CPS consists of two components:

- **Phone Book Services (PBS)** This extension to Internet Information Services (IIS) 5 enables users to connect to a server and download updates to the Connection Manager profiles on their client machines. Queries from Connection Manager are handled by the WWW Publishing Service on IIS 5.

- **Phone Book Administrator (PBA)** This tool lets you create and edit multiple phone books, specify service types for points of presence (POPs), and publish new phone book information to the PBS, using the FTP service on IIS 5.

Deploying CMAK Packages

When you are done with the CMAK Wizard, click Finish to build your customized Connection Manager service profile. Makecab.exe will run within a command-prompt window to generate and compress the connection package. A final screen will display the location of the self-installing executable service profile, which by default is located in C:\Program Files\Cmak\Profiles*Service_ Directory\Service_Profile,* where *Service_Directory* and *Service_File* are the directory and file, respectively, specified in step 2 of the CMAK Wizard.

If you started the CMAK Wizard from within the IEAK Wizard, you can then continue with the IEAK Wizard, and your Connection Manager service profile will be packaged together with the Internet Explorer 5 installation package you are creating. If you started the CMAK Wizard from the Administrative Tools folder, you can copy your service profile package files to a Web site or network share and deploy the package as you would an Internet Explorer 5 package, or you can select it later from the IEAK Wizard when creating an Internet Explorer 5 package. If users on the Internet will download the service profile package separately, it should be signed with Microsoft Authenticode technology.

To install the new connection, users simply click on the link of the appropriate Web page, where they can choose either to download the self-extracting file and run it later or to open it from its remote location, which installs it immediately on their machines. At the end of installation, users can optionally add a shortcut to their desktops for the new connection. The connection will also appear in the Network And Dial-up Connections folder, accessed from Control Panel. Figure 29-9 shows the dialog box for a new connection, which is opened by double-clicking on the connection shortcut.

Figure 29-9. *A new Connection Manager connection created using the CMAK Wizard.*

Summary

This chapter has looked at how corporate network administrators can deploy and manage Internet Explorer 5 and Connection Manager connections using tools like the Internet Explorer Administration Kit and the Connection Manager Administration Kit. Deploying and managing Internet tools and client connections is an important task for today's network administrator, and Windows 2000 makes this task easy.

Once you have deployed Internet Explorer, you may choose to utilize a server to act as a proxy between your internal network and the Internet. The next chapter covers the installation and configuration of Proxy Server, as well as other proxy-related concepts.

Chapter 30
Proxy Server

Microsoft Proxy Server 2 is an important part of the Microsoft BackOffice suite—one that most, if not all, Microsoft Windows 2000 administrators will consider to be an important addition to their environments. It provides an excellent gateway separating your internal network from the Internet. It is also a highly effective tool for hiding the internal details and IP addresses of your network while increasing your overall Internet-access speed and reducing your overall bandwidth requirements.

Concepts

The purpose of Proxy Server is fairly simple: to isolate your internal, private network from the outside, public Internet while still providing full access and functionality to your users who need to connect to the Internet. Sort of like a one-way glass mirror that lets you see out but doesn't let anyone see in.

Proxy Server maintains control of connectivity and isolates your internal network by having two (or more) completely separate physical connections—one to the Internet and one to your internal network. Each network is connected to a different network card on the proxy server, and all packets must pass through the Proxy Server software to get from one connection to the other.

The mechanisms that Proxy Server uses to achieve these aims are fairly straightforward. The following three basic techniques are used:

- Network address translation
- Packet filtering
- Caching

Let's briefly look at each technique and then learn how to install and implement Proxy Server in a Windows 2000 environment.

Network Address Translation

Network address translation (NAT) hides your actual IP address from machines beyond the device doing the translation. Using Proxy Server isn't the only possible way to perform NAT. Windows 2000 Server also performs basic NAT, as do many routers or other network devices. If all you need is address translation, you might do fine with the ability already built into Windows 2000 Server, but Proxy Server provides a full package that goes beyond simple translation. When you run Proxy Server or use another method to perform NAT, the IP addresses assigned to your internal workstations and servers don't need to be "real," official IP addresses but can be any IP addresses you want.

Real World **IP Address for Internal Networks**

While in theory you could use any internal IP addresses you want to, you definitely should *not* use ones that belong to someone else. So how can you take advantage of NAT so that you don't need to have official IP addresses for every machine on your network? Simple—use the addresses specially assigned for this purpose.

Way back when folks were first deciding how to parcel out IP addresses (and long before anyone figured out how to do NAT), they decided that there would be a need for addresses that could be used for test networks or other situations that didn't require using the official addresses. So they created a special set of IP addresses called *private network addresses,* defined in RFC 1918, to provide class A, class B, and class C networks for test or other networks that will not be physically connected to the Internet.

These private network addresses allow you to have a much larger address space than would be possible if you had to stick to officially assigned addresses, while at the same time protecting the integrity of the Internet. If a machine with one of these addresses were to inadvertently connect to the Internet, it wouldn't cause a conflict with another machine on the Internet because these addresses are automatically filtered by routers.

The following addresses are designated for private networks that won't be directly connected to the Internet. They can, of course, be connected to the Internet via Proxy Server or another method that performs NAT.

```
10.0.0.0 through 10.255.255.255 (a single Class A network)
172.16.0.0 through 172.31.255.255 (16 contiguous Class B networks)
192.168.0.0 through 192.168.255.255 (256 contiguous Class C networks)
```

Proxy Server automatically includes these addresses in its local address table (LAT) when you initially install the program.

Another byproduct of using Proxy Server for address translation is that all the machines on your network *appear* to have the same single address to the outside world: the outside address of the proxy server itself. This is the only address that needs to have an official public IP address assigned to it, except for your router if that's how your connection is managed.

Packet Filtering

Since every packet that passes to or from the Internet and your internal network must first pass through the proxy server, Proxy Server is in a perfect position to act as a gatekeeper. With Proxy Server 2, Microsoft added the ability to filter packets, giving you many of the capabilities of a firewall. This packet filtering works by inspecting each packet to see which protocol is being used and whether it's a permitted connection.

When packet filtering is enabled, you can also restrict access to specific external sites or enable only certain external sites to be seen. In addition, some third-party Proxy Server plug-ins can add additional controls and functionality.

Caching

Every organization has certain sites that virtually everyone seems to go to regularly. Even sites that are fairly dynamic have a lot of information (like HTML documents, graphics files, and so on) on them that doesn't change often. Proxy Server can cache information from frequently accessed sites so that when users on the network connect to the site, much of the information is actually being delivered from the proxy server, not from the remote site. Caching improves the apparent speed of your connection to the Internet significantly, since it provides the information locally for some of the more popular sites, and—by reducing the traffic required to the Internet for those sites—it increases the available bandwidth for all other sites that users visit.

Proxy Server can use the slack times when few users are connected to the Internet to check frequently accessed sites to make sure that the information it has stored for that site is current. This monitoring helps to balance and smooth out the demand through your Internet connection, reducing costs and providing improved throughput during busier times because fewer pages and images will need to be downloaded.

Installation

To install Proxy Server, you'll need at least two network interface cards (NICs), one for internal connections to the proxy server and one for external connections. The external NIC should be directly connected to your Internet gateway. In addition to the roughly 12 MB of hard disk space that Proxy Server requires, you'll also need sufficient hard disk space to support the local caching of Web pages. For a small network, this could be on the order of 100 MB to 200 MB, but larger and more active networks will require substantially more—at least ten times more.

For security reasons, your internal NIC should be on a separate physical segment of the network from the external NIC. You need to ensure that all traffic stays only on the segment on which it belongs and that everything passes through the proxy server. Your external NIC should have a valid, official IP address registered to your domain. The internal NIC and all your internal machines can have either valid, registered IP addresses, or they can use IP addresses from the RFC 1918 range of privatized addresses. Normal routing rules apply on the internal segment, with the proxy server's internal IP address being the final gateway.

To install Proxy Server 2 on a Windows 2000 server, you need to use Msp2wizi.exe, the Microsoft Proxy Server Setup Wizard available on the Microsoft Web site at *http://www.microsoft.com/proxy*. This wizard will patch Microsoft Proxy Server 2 during the installation to allow it to work with Windows 2000. If you're running a later version of Proxy Server, you won't need this wizard. To install Proxy Server 2 on Windows 2000, follow these steps:

1. Close all Microsoft Management Console (MMC) applications before proceeding.
2. Locate the Microsoft Proxy Server Setup Wizard (Msp2wizi.exe) and start it to open the standard Microsoft license agreement screen, shown in Figure 30-1.

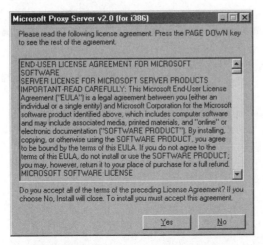

Figure 30-1. *The standard license agreement screen of the Microsoft Proxy Server 2.0 Setup Wizard.*

3. Read the license carefully and then click Yes to agree to it. (If you click No, the setup will terminate.) Once you've clicked Yes, the main wizard screen will open, as shown in Figure 30-2.

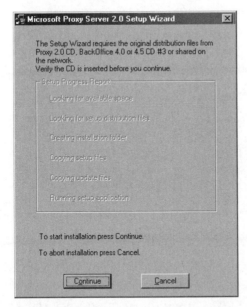

Figure 30-2. *The Microsoft Proxy Server 2.0 Setup Wizard.*

4. Insert your Microsoft Proxy Server CD or the BackOffice 4.5 CD #3 into your CD drive, and click Continue to start the actual Microsoft Proxy Server installation program shown in Figure 30-3. If you don't have the CD inserted in the drive, a standard Browse dialog box will prompt you to locate the source folder. Click Continue.

Figure 30-3. *The Microsoft Proxy Server Setup Wizard's welcome screen.*

5. Type in the product license key that came with your copy of Proxy Server, and click OK to continue. Your product ID will be displayed. Click OK again to open the installation location dialog box shown in Figure 30-4.

Figure 30-4. *The Microsoft Proxy Server installation location dialog box.*

6. At this dialog box, you can change the installation location by clicking the Change Folder button. When you've chosen the location, click the large button to begin installation, and set your installation options, as shown in Figure 30-5.

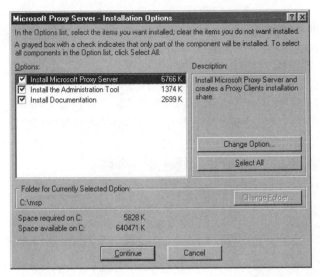

Figure 30-5. *The Microsoft Proxy Server - Installation Options dialog box.*

7. Select the options you want to install for Proxy Server. The default is to install all options, requiring approximately 12 MB of free disk space. When you've made your selections, click Continue.

8. The installation program will stop your Web services to install Proxy Server. When the services stop, you'll be prompted to enable caching and to choose the size and location of the cache, as shown in Figure 30-6.

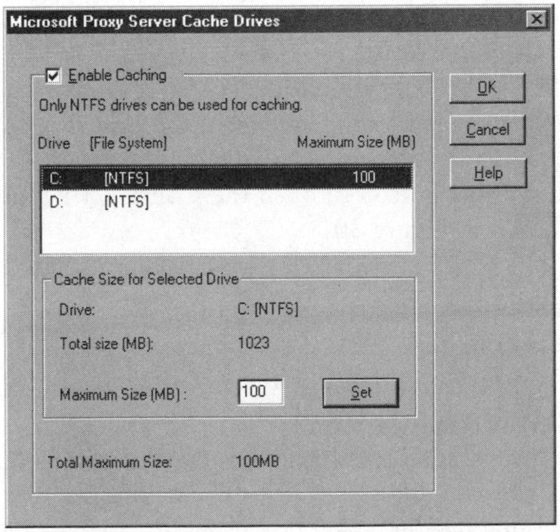

Figure 30-6. *The Microsoft Proxy Server Cache Drives dialog box.*

9. Set the size and location of your local Web cache. The default is a single 100-MB cache, but this size probably won't be optimal for larger installations. You can place your cache on any NTFS drive, and you should distribute it across your available NTFS volumes. Click OK.

10. The Local Address Table Configuration dialog box appears, shown in Figure 30-7. Here you can build your local address table. This table tells the proxy server which addresses are local and which addresses to expect to be outside the proxy server.

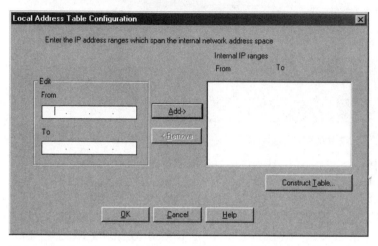

Figure 30-7. *The Local Address Table Configuration dialog box.*

11. In the Edit box, type the range of addresses on your local network. You don't need to add any RFC 1918 privatized addresses—they'll be added automatically when you click the Construct Table button.

12. Click the Add button to move a range of addresses from the Edit box to the Internal IP Ranges box. When you've added all your internal IP addresses, click the Construct Table button to open the Construct Local Address Table dialog box shown in Figure 30-8.

13. To add the private IP addresses automatically, select the Add The Private Ranges To The Table check box. If you want to allow Windows 2000 to use the internal IP routing table, specify the network cards from which it should read to prevent adding addresses from the external interface. When you've made your selections, click OK.

14. A setup message will appear, warning you that the automatically constructed LAT might include external addresses. Click OK again to return to the Local Address Table Configuration dialog box in Figure 30-7.

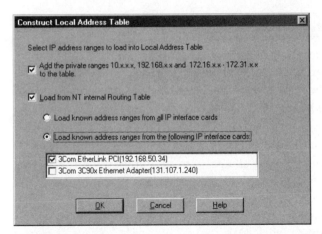

Figure 30-8. *The Construct Local Address Table dialog box.*

15. Now you'll see the automatically configured LAT as Proxy Server is about to construct it. Edit it to remove any external addresses from the table or any other errors you encounter. If any local addresses aren't showing, add them in. When the table is correct, click OK to open the Client Installation/Configuration dialog box shown in Figure 30-9.

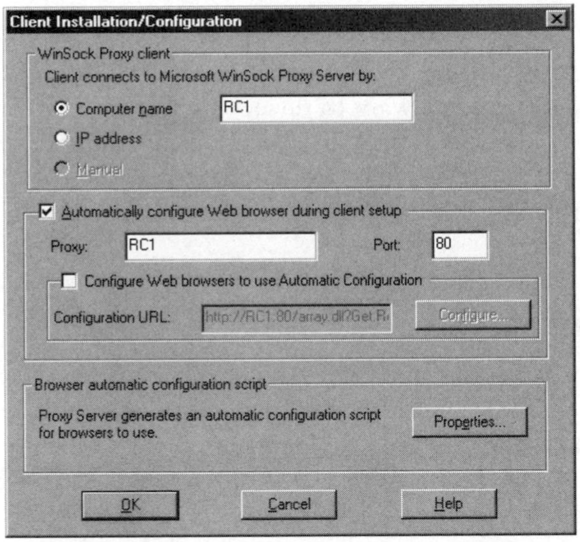

Figure 30-9. *The Client Installation/Configuration dialog box.*

16. In the Client Installation/Configuration dialog box, set the options that control how clients connect to Proxy Server. The defaults use the computer's NetBIOS name and automatic configuration of the client during initial client setup. Generally, the defaults are fine, but if you have specific needs, you can modify these settings. When you've completed the settings, click OK to open the Access Control dialog box.

17. If you enable access control on the WinSock and Web Proxy services (the default), only those clients that have been explicitly assigned permission to use them will be allowed access to the Internet via this proxy server. No clients will have access to the Internet until you configure the proxy server. If you clear the boxes, all clients will have access. You can change this setting from the proxy administrator later. When you've finished making your settings, click OK.

18. A message appears stating that packet filtering can be enabled later. Click OK and Proxy Server will finish installing. When it completes and restarts the Web services, click Finish and you're done. Note that you'll need to reboot your server for all your settings to take effect.

Configuration

After you finish installing Proxy Server, most of your settings will already be configured, although you will most likely want to review your configuration or set up additional options not available from the Proxy Server installation program. The following sections deal with all aspects of configuring and administering Proxy Server in Windows 2000 except security, which is covered separately later in the chapter.

Administering Proxy Server

The primary way to administer Proxy Server is by using the Internet Services Manager MMC snap-in, although you can also administer proxy servers from a command prompt. Note that if you're remotely administering the proxy server, the computer you're administering the server from needs to use the same proxy client version number as your proxy server's version number. To use the Internet Services Manager MMC snap-in to manage your proxy server, follow these steps:

1. Launch the Internet Services Manager snap-in from the Administrative Tools folder on the Programs menu.

2. Select Internet Information Services in the console tree, and then choose Connect from the File menu.

3. Enter the name of the proxy server you want to connect to (unless you're logged on to the proxy server locally, in which case click Cancel and skip to the next step).

4. To configure Web Proxy, WinSock Proxy, or Socks Proxy, right-click the appropriate item in the console tree (Figure 30-10) and choose Properties from the shortcut menu.

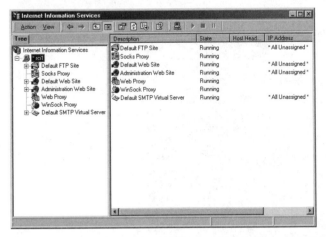

Figure 30-10. *The Internet Information Services window.*

Real World **Using the Command Line and Scripts**

If you often perform the same task on multiple proxy servers on your network, you may want to use the command-line interface, create scripts to automate the administrative chores, or both. A full discussion of scripting Proxy Server is outside the scope of this book. (Consult Proxy Server's Help system for more information on using the command line.) However, a small primer is in order. Proxy Server installs two command-line utilities: the RemoteMsp and the WspProto tools. The RemoteMsp tool allows you to remotely configure a proxy server from a command line or script, while the WspProto tool allows you to add, edit, and delete WinSock Proxy service definitions, also via the command-line interface.

Joining Arrays

To distribute the load of large networks with high-bandwidth connections to the Internet and to provide for fault tolerance, you can create an array of proxy servers. If you have only a single proxy server, you won't have an array, obviously, but when you create a second proxy server, you won't automatically have a proxy array until you explicitly join the servers into one. To join or create a proxy server array, from the console of one of the proxy servers follow these steps:

1. Open the Internet Information Services MMC snap-in and right-click Web Proxy. Choose Properties from the shortcut menu to open the Web Proxy Service Properties window for that server, shown in Figure 30-11.

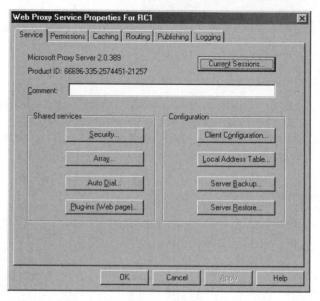

Figure 30-11. *The Web Proxy Service Properties window.*

2. Click the Array button and then click Join Array. Type in the name of another proxy server that you want to join into an array with, and click OK.

3. If the other server isn't already part of an array, you'll be prompted to give the new array a name, as shown in Figure 30-12.

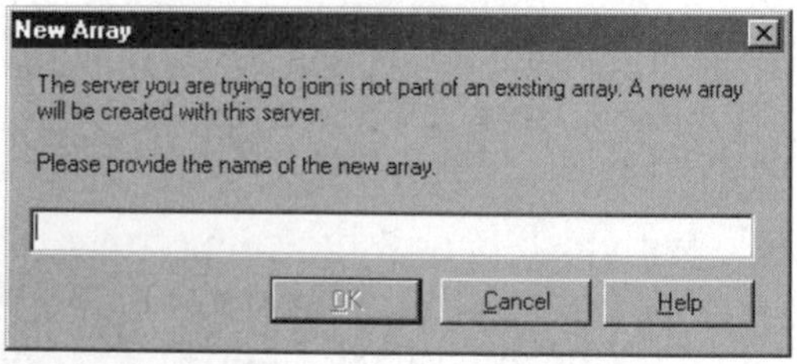

Figure 30-12. *The New Array dialog box.*

4. Type in a name for the new array and click OK. Click OK again to return to the main Properties window. Click Apply to effect the changes.

Setting the Client Configuration

You can set the client configuration for clients connecting to your proxy server by opening the Web Proxy Properties window. Here you can decide whether clients use the IP address or the computer name to connect to the server, and whether the Web browser is automatically configured during client setup. You can also modify the automatic browser configuration script. To set the client configuration, follow these steps:

1. Open the Internet Information Services MMC snap-in and right-click Web Proxy. Choose Properties from the shortcut menu to open the Web Proxy Service Properties window for that server, shown in Figure 30-11 earlier.

2. Click Client Configuration to open the Client Installation/Configuration dialog box shown in Figure 30-13.

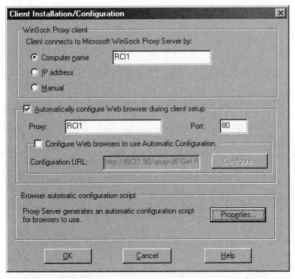

Figure 30-13. *The Client Installation/Configuration dialog box.*

3. By default, clients will connect to the server using its name. If necessary, you can change this to connect using the IP address. If you're using arrays, you can use a DNS name that resolves to all of the members of the array, improving fault tolerance and availability. Select the Manual option to allow the Mspclnt.ini file on each client to control connectivity.

This can be useful if you're manually performing load balancing through several different IP addresses.

4. By default, any Web browsers found on client machines are automatically configured when the proxy server client is installed. Clear the Automatically Configure Web Browser During Client Setup check box if you want to require manual configuration of Web browsers.

5. Click the Properties button in the Browser Automatic Configuration Script box to change the default configuration options that are set by the automatic Web browser configuration.

6. Click OK to finalize your changes, and then click OK again to apply them and close the Web Proxy Service Properties window.

Configuring Local Addresses

Your local addresses are maintained in the LAT that was created during initial installation. You can change this LAT at any point, using the Internet Information Services MMC snap-in. To configure Proxy Server's local addresses:

1. Open the Internet Information Services MMC snap-in and right-click Web Proxy. Choose Properties from the shortcut menu to open the Web Proxy Service Properties window for that server, shown in Figure 30-11 earlier.

2. Click Local Address Table to open the Local Address Table Configuration dialog box shown in Figure 30-14.

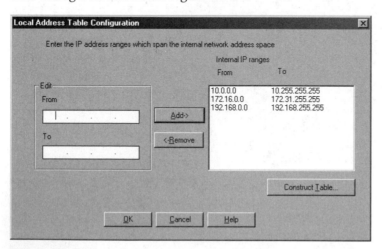

Figure 30-14. *The Local Address Table Configuration dialog box.*

3. You can add address ranges here manually by typing them into the Edit box and clicking Add, or you can use the Construct Table button to allow Proxy Server to automatically configure what it can. Click Construct Table to open the Construct Local Address Table dialog box shown in Figure 30-15.

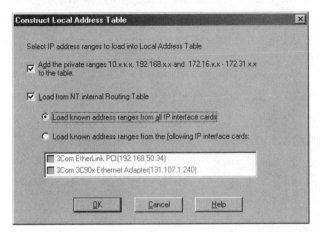

Figure 30-15. *The Construct Local Address Table dialog box.*

4. By default, the private address ranges are automatically added to the LAT, as well as all addresses recognized from the internal IP routing table. If you elect to allow Proxy Server to use the internal IP routing table, you should specify the network cards it should read from to prevent adding addresses from the external interface. Once you've made your selections, click OK.

5. A setup message will appear, warning you that the automatically constructed LAT might include external addresses. Click OK to return to the Local Address Table Configuration dialog box shown in Figure 30-14.

6. The automatically configured LAT that Proxy Server is about to construct appears. Edit this LAT to remove any external addresses from the table or any other errors you encounter. If any local addresses aren't showing, add them in.

7. Click OK to accept the changes to the LAT, and then click OK again to apply the changes and close the Web Proxy Service Properties window.

Configuring Auto Dial

On smaller networks that connect to the Internet with a dial-up connection, you can decide whether you want the proxy server to use autodialing and how it should occur. This might also be important where you use modems or a modem bank as a backup route to the Internet. To configure autodialing, follow these steps:

1. Open the Internet Information Services MMC snap-in and right-click Web Proxy. Select Properties from the shortcut menu to open the Web Proxy Service Properties window for that server, shown in Figure 30-11 earlier.

2. Click the Auto Dial button to open the Microsoft Proxy Auto Dial dialog box shown in Figure 30-16.

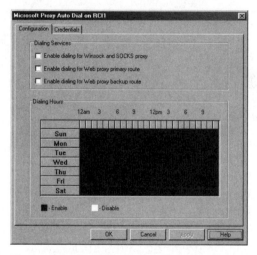

Figure 30-16. *The Microsoft Proxy Auto Dial dialog box.*

3. By default, autodialing is disabled. You can enable dialing for WinSock Proxy and Socks Proxy, Web Proxy, or both. For Web Proxy, you can set autodialing as the default route to the Internet or use it as a backup route.

4. Change the hours when autodialing is permitted by highlighting the hours during which you want to disable dialing. Highlighting acts as a toggle based on the status of the first square being highlighted. If the hour in the first square is enabled, the highlighted area will be disabled, and if the hour in the first square is disabled, the highlighted area will be disabled.

5. Click the Credentials tab to choose the RRAS phone book entry to use for the connection. For more on RRAS and phone book entries, see Chapter 31.

6. When you've completed your autodial configuration, click OK to return to the Web Proxy Service Properties window. Click OK again to accept the changes and close the window.

Backing Up and Restoring a Proxy Server Configuration

You can (and *should*) back up your Proxy Server configuration. This will allow you to restore all of your configuration changes should you have to reinstall Proxy Server or recreate the settings on another machine. Restores can be full restores or partial restores that include everything except machine-specific settings.

To back up your Proxy Server configuration, follow these steps:

1. Open the Internet Information Services MMC snap-in and right-click Web Proxy. Choose Properties from the shortcut menu to open the Web Proxy Service Properties window for that server, shown in Figure 30-11 earlier.

2. Click the Server Backup button and type the name of the folder to save the configuration to. The default is *<msproot>*\config. The filename will be in the form Msp*<date>*.mpc.

3. Click OK to save the configuration, and then click OK to close the Web Proxy Service Properties window.

To restore an earlier Proxy Server configuration, follow these steps:

1. Open the Internet Information Services MMC snap-in and right-click Web Proxy. Choose Properties from the shortcut menu to open the Web Proxy Service Properties window for that server, shown earlier in Figure 30-11.

2. Click the Server Restore button to open the dialog box shown in Figure 30-17.

3. Select a full or partial restore. A partial restore will restore all configuration settings except those that are computer specific.

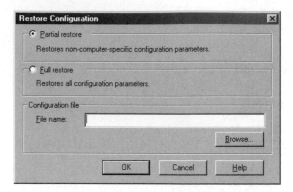

Figure 30-17. *The Restore Configuration dialog box.*

4. Type in the filename to restore, or use the Browse button to locate a saved configuration. The default extension for a saved configuration is .MPC.

5. Click OK, and the configuration is restored without further confirmation. Click OK again to close the Web Proxy Service Properties window.

Configuring Web Proxy

In addition to the general, shared, service-related parameters that you can configure for Proxy Server, you can also configure specific parameters for Web Proxy, including caching, routing, Web publishing, and logging, the subjects of the next several sections.

Web Proxy Caching

Proxy Server can cache remote pages that are frequently accessed to reduce bandwidth demand on the Internet connection and improve the perceived speed to the client. By default, caching is enabled. To configure caching, follow these steps:

1. Open the Internet Information Services MMC snap-in and right-click Web Proxy. Choose Properties from the shortcut menu to open the Web Proxy Service Properties window for that server.

2. Click the Caching tab.

3. Select your configurations and click OK to accept the changes and close the window, or simply apply the changes and leave the window open for further configuration changes.

The available caching options are as follows:

- **Enable Caching**   Enabled by default. You can control the behavior of the caching as well. Choices are

  - **Updates Are More Important**   Checks are done for updates more frequently.

  - **Equal Importance**   Balanced behavior.

  - **Fewer Network Accesses Are More Important**   Proxy Server will keep cached items alive longer, increasing the number of cache hits.

- **Enable Active Caching**   Enabled by default. You can control the behavior as well. Choices are

  - **Faster User Response Is More Important**   More prefetching of expected pages is performed.

  - **Equal Importance**   Balanced behavior.

  - **Fewer Network Accesses Are More Important**   Proxy Server will be less inclined to proactively prefetch pages to reduce the amount of network bandwidth used.

- **Cache Size**   You can use any *local* NTFS drive for caching. Click this button to change the size and location of proxy server cache files.

- **Advanced**   Gives you the ability to fine-tune the specific settings of the proxy server. If you think you need to fiddle with this—and you think you know why you're doing it—have fun.

Routing

Web Proxy can be directly connected to the Internet, or it can route Internet requests to another proxy server or an array of proxy servers, providing an additional layer of isolation and management. To configure routing on Web Proxy, follow these steps:

1. Open the Internet Information Services MMC snap-in and right-click Web Proxy. Choose Properties from the shortcut menu to open the Web Proxy Service Properties window for that server.

2. Click the Routing tab, shown in Figure 30-18.

3. Make your configurations and click OK to accept the changes and close the window, or simply apply the changes and leave the window open for further configuration changes.

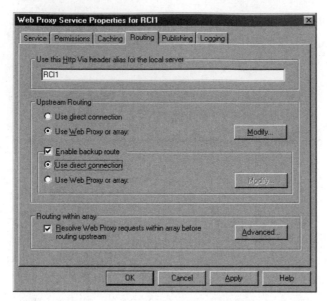

Figure 30-18. *The Routing tab of the Web Proxy Service Properties window.*

The available settings on the Routing tab are as follows:

- **Use This Http Via Header Alias For The Local Server** Enabled by default. The name of the server. This name is appended to the Http Via header for all proxied requests.

- **Upstream Routing** Select either a direct connection to the Internet (the default) or choose to use another Web Proxy or array.

- **Enable Backup Route** Possible only when the Use Web Proxy Or Array option is selected for Upstream Routing. This designates an alternate route to the Internet should the primary Web Proxy or proxy array be unavailable.

- **Routing Within Array** Available only when this proxy server is part of an array. Enabled by default when part of an array. Client requests are routed within the array for cached objects. Or when a member is unavailable, other array members can service the request, distributing the load and caching across the array.

Web Publishing

Proxy Server allows servers downstream from the proxy server to publish to the Internet, using either reverse proxying or reverse hosting. Any computer on the internal network can be allowed to publish to the Internet with all incoming and outgoing requests being filtered by Proxy Server. Requests can be redirected to specific internal servers (reverse proxying), or Proxy Server can maintain a list of internal servers that are permitted to publish to the Internet, listen to requests for those servers, and respond for them. To enable Web publishing, follow these steps:

1. Open the Internet Information Services MMC snap-in and right-click Web Proxy. Choose Properties from the shortcut menu to open the Web Proxy Service Properties window for that server.

2. Click the Publishing tab, shown in Figure 30-19.

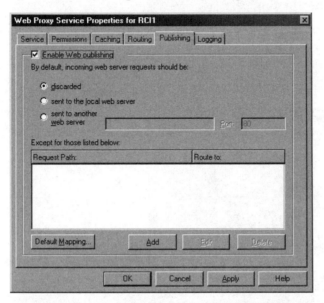

Figure 30-19. *The Publishing tab of the Web Proxy Service Properties window.*

3. Make your configuration selections and click OK to accept the changes and close the window, or simply apply the changes and leave the window open for further configuration changes.

By default, Web publishing is disabled. But when it is enabled, the following incoming Web server requests can be used:

- **Discarded**   Unless mapped, incoming requests go to the bit bucket.
- **Sent To The Local Web Server**   Unless mapped, incoming requests go to the Web server on the local machine.
- **Sent To Another Web Server**   Unless mapped, incoming requests go to the specified Web server.

- **Except For Those Listed Below** Allows you to set up explicit mappings to different servers and route requests for the requested server to its mapped server.

Logging

By default, Proxy Server logs a variety of information about the use of Web Proxy. You can configure the logging to use standard files or to go to a database for more detailed analysis, as well as configure the level of detail stored. To configure logging for Web Proxy, follow these steps:

1. Open the Internet Information Services MMC snap-in and right-click Web Proxy. Choose Properties from the shortcut menu to open the Web Proxy Service Properties window for that server.

2. Click the Logging tab, shown in Figure 30-20.

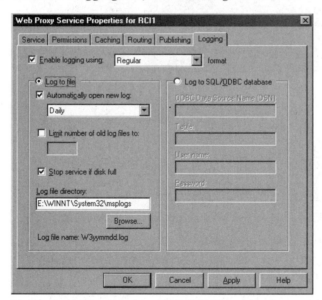

Figure 30-20. *The Logging tab of the Web Proxy Service Properties window.*

3. Make your configuration selections and click OK to accept the changes and close the window, or click Apply to simply apply the changes and leave the window open for further configuration changes. The available settings are as follows:

- **Enable Logging Using**   Regular or verbose format. Controls how much detail is logged.
- **Log To File**   Change the settings for file logging. Options are
  - **Automatically Open New Log**   Daily, weekly, or monthly.
  - **Limit Number Of Old Log Files To**   Set the number of log files to save.
  - **Stop Service If Disk Is Full**   Stop the proxy service if the disk becomes full and you can't continue logging.
  - **Log File Directory**   Location of log files.
- **Log To SQL/ODBC Database**   Allows connection to any SQL or ODBC data source. Options are
  - **ODBC Data Source Name (DSN)**   The ODBC connection name.
  - **Table**   The table in the data source to store the log information.
  - **User Name**   The user name used to connect to the data source.
  - **Password**   The password to use to connect to the data source.

Configuring WinSock Proxy

In addition to the general, shared, service-related parameters that you can configure for Proxy Server, you can also configure specific parameters for WinSock Proxy, including adding or editing the protocols that WinSock supports. You can also configure logging for WinSock Proxy and enable access control.

Configuring Protocols

Proxy Server comes with a variety of preconfigured protocols that are supported through the WinSock service. These include some 31 different protocols, including AOL, Finger, FTP, IMAP4, POP3, and RealAudio. You can edit the existing definitions, add additional ones, or remove ones you don't want to support on your network. To configure the protocols, follow these steps:

1. Open the Internet Information Services MMC snap-in and right-click WinSock Proxy. Choose Properties from the shortcut menu to open the WinSock Proxy Service Properties window for that server.
2. Click the Protocols tab, shown in Figure 30-21.

Figure 30-21. *The Protocols tab of the WinSock Proxy Service Properties window.*

3. To add a protocol, click the Add button to open the dialog box shown in Figure 30-22. Here you can define the settings for your new protocol, including the port, type of connection (TCP or UDP), the direction (Inbound or Outbound), and the range of ports that the protocol can spawn off to (port ranges for subsequent connections). When you have selected all your settings, click OK to return to the main WinSock Proxy Service Properties window.

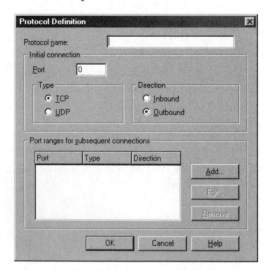

Figure 30-22. *The Protocol Definition dialog box.*

4. To edit a protocol, highlight it and click Edit. A dialog box similar to Figure 30-22 opens, but now you'll see the existing settings as defined for the protocol. Make the necessary changes, and then click OK to return to the main WinSock Proxy Service Properties window.

Caution Do not edit any of the well-defined protocols that are shipped with Proxy Server unless you know a great deal about TCP/IP *and* you know why you're changing any given protocol.

5. To remove a protocol that you don't want to support on your network through the proxy server, highlight the protocol and click Remove.

6. To load a previously saved list of protocols and their settings, click the Load button. Select the .WPC file that contains your protocol settings. The file is a pure ASCII file and can be viewed or edited with NotePad or another pure ASCII editor. Loading a .WPC file will replace your current list of protocols.

7. To save your current protocol settings, click the Save button and then name the file. The current list of protocols will be saved with a .WPC extension. This file is a pure ASCII file and can be edited with NotePad or another ASCII editor.

8. Once you've completed your protocol settings, click the Apply button to effect the changes and continue modifying the WinSock Proxy settings, or click OK to implement the changes and close the window.

Logging

By default, Proxy Server logs a variety of information about the use of WinSock Proxy. You can configure the logging to use standard files or to go to a database for more detailed analysis, as well as configure the level of detail stored. Configuring logging for the WinSock Proxy service is very similar to configuring logging for the Web Proxy. To configure logging for the WinSock Proxy service, follow these steps:

1. Open the Internet Information Services MMC snap-in and right-click WinSock Proxy. Choose Properties from the shortcut menu to open the WinSock Proxy Service Properties window for that server. Click the Logging tab, shown in Figure 30-23.

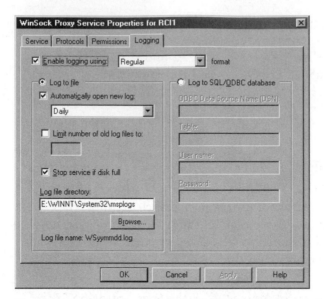

Figure 30-23. *The Logging tab of the WinSock Proxy Service Properties window.*

2. Make your configuration selections and click OK to accept the changes and close the window, or click Apply to simply apply the changes and leave the window open for further configuration changes.

The following settings are available:

- **Enable Logging Using** Regular or verbose format. Controls how much detail is logged.

- **Log To File** Change the settings for file logging. Options include

  - **Automatically Open New Log** Daily, weekly, or monthly.

  - **Limit Number Of Old Log Files To** Set the number of log files to save.

  - **Stop Service If Disk Full** Stop the proxy service if the disk becomes full and you can't continue logging.

  - **Log File Directory** Location of log files.

- **Log To SQL/ODBC Database** Allows connection to any SQL or ODBC data source. Options include

  - **ODBC Data Source Name (DSN)** The ODBC connection name.

  - **Table** The table in the data source to store the log information.

  - **User Name** The user name used to connect to the data source.

  - **Password** The password used to connect to the data source.

Real World   Performance Monitoring

When you install Proxy Server on your Windows 2000 Server, it installs a preconfigured performance monitoring chart for use with the System Monitor MMC snap-in, as shown in Figure 30-24. You can use this chart to monitor the overall health and success of Proxy Server. For more on performance monitoring, see Chapter 32, "Monitoring and Tuning."

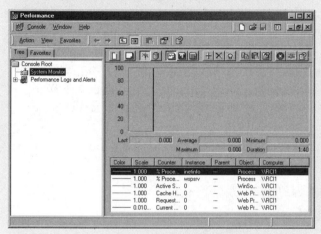

Figure 30-24. *The Proxy Server Performance window.*

Security

Proxy Server supports a number of features to improve your network's security and to let you manage which users are allowed to connect to which sites. You can filter packets at the external interface, preventing inappropriate packet traffic from entering or leaving your network, and you can control access to the various proxy services by user and group access control lists. This filtering can be particularly helpful in a large network where certain users or areas shouldn't be permitted access outside the internal network, or even outside a particular segment of the network. A good example is a training room where you want users to be able to see only the servers and services that they should see.

A detailed discussion of Proxy Server security is beyond the scope of this chapter, but we can at least delineate where and what the options are. They include

- Packet filtering
- Access control

- Domain filters
- Alerting
- Logging

Packet Filtering

Proxy Server comes with a set of predefined packet filters that you can enable. In addition, you can create your own packet filters that minutely control which kinds of packets you will allow into your network. To enable and configure packet filtering, follow these steps:

1. Open the Internet Information Services MMC snap-in and right-click Web Proxy. Choose Properties from the shortcut menu to open the Web Proxy Service Properties window for that server, as shown earlier in Figure 30-11.

2. Click the Security button to open the Security dialog box shown in Figure 30-25.

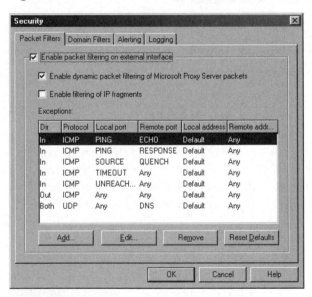

Figure 30-25. *The Packet Filters tab of the Security dialog box.*

3. Select Enable Packet Filtering On External Interface.

4. The predefined packet filters are shown. You can add additional custom packet filters by clicking the Add button to open the Packet Filter Properties window shown in Figure 30-26.

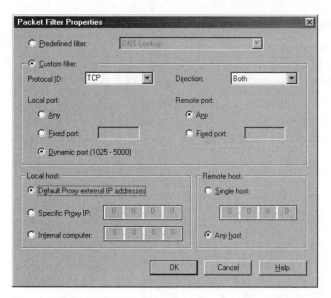

Figure 30-26. *The Packet Filters Properties window.*

The options for custom filters are as follows:

- **Protocol ID**   TCP, UDP, or ICMP.
- **Direction**   Incoming, outgoing, or both.
- **Local Port**   Any port, a fixed port, or dynamic ports.
- **Remote Port**   Any port or a fixed port.
- **Local Host**   The computer that exchanges packets with the remote host, usually the proxy server itself.
- **Specific Proxy IP**   A specific external interface of the proxy server can exchange packets for this custom filter.
- **Internal Computer**   A specific computer normally hidden behind the proxy server can exchange this type of packet with the remote host.
- **Remote Host**   The remote host that can exchange this type of packet with the local host. Can be a specific host or any host.

5. Once you've configured any custom packet filters and made any other changes to existing filters, click OK to accept the changes and return to the main Web Proxy Service Properties window.

6. Make your configuration selections and click OK to accept the changes and close the window, or click Apply to apply the changes and leave the window open for further configuration changes.

Enabling Access Control

You can enable access control permissions on the various protocols, permitting or disallowing use of the protocols by user or by group. This option can be useful for controlling access from areas of the network or particular groups of users that have no business reason to be accessing the Internet.

Configuring access control is the same for each of the services, so we'll describe how to enable and configure only the Web Proxy services. To enable access control for Web Proxy, follow these steps:

1. Open the Internet Information Services MMC snap-in and right-click Web Proxy. Choose Properties from the shortcut menu to open the Web Proxy Service Properties window for that server, shown earlier in Figure 30-11.

2. Click the Permissions tab, shown in Figure 30-27.

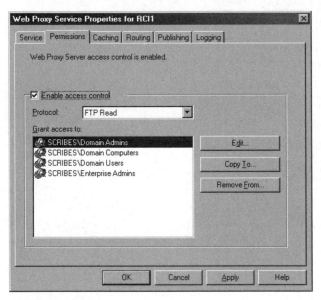

Figure 30-27. *The Permissions tab of the Web Proxy Service Properties window.*

3. Select the Enable Access Control check box.

4. Select the protocol to configure from the Protocol drop-down list. For Web Proxy, you can grant access to FTP (read only), Web (HTTP), Secure (HTTPS), and Gopher protocols individually.

5. To add particular users or groups that you will grant access to the protocol, click the Edit button and select the group or user name.

6. Once you've added all the users and groups to each protocol, click Apply to apply the changes to Web Proxy and continue configuring other settings, or click OK to apply the changes and close the window.

Caution   We strongly advise that you control access to the various proxy protocols using groups. Controlling at the individual user level will make it difficult to manage and troubleshoot problems that arise.

Enabling Domain Filters

You can manage Internet access to particular domains or IP addresses for all users. This allows you to provide strictly limited access to key sites, for example, or to exclude certain sites from your users. However, managing this for a large number of sites could be a major management problem, especially since objectionable sites seem to move far more frequently than desirable sites. Third-party add-ons exist for Proxy Server that better handle this problem and are updated on a regular basis. To enable domain filters, follow these steps:

1. Open the Internet Information Services MMC snap-in and right-click Web Proxy. Choose Properties from the shortcut menu to open the Web Proxy Service Properties window for that server, shown earlier in Figure 30-11.

2. Click the Security button. Choose the Domain Filters tab, shown in Figure 30-28.

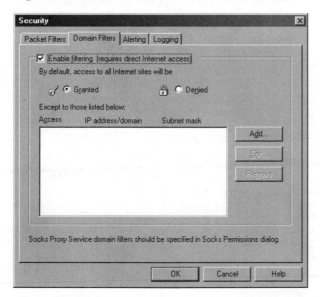

Figure 30-28. *The Domain Filters tab of the Security dialog box.*

3. Select the Enable Filtering check box.

4. To list domains that are denied access, thus preventing access to all other domains, select the Granted option.

5. To deny access to all domains except those explicitly allowed, select the Denied option.

6. To add a domain to the list of excluded or granted domains, click the Add button to open the Deny Access To dialog box (or the Grant Access To dialog box if you're listing domains that users are explicitly allowed access to). You can specify the access by single computer, by group of computers, or by domain name.

7. When you've made your selections, click OK to return to the Domain Filters tab.

8. To add more selections, click Add again. To remove a selection, highlight it and click Remove. To change a previously created selection, click Edit.

9. When you've finished editing the domain filters, click OK to return to the main Web Proxy Service Properties window. Click Accept to accept the settings and continue configuring, or click OK to implement the changes and close the window.

Note Only proxy servers that are directly connected to the Internet can perform domain filtering. Proxy servers that are downstream of another proxy server must leave the domain filtering to the upstream proxy server.

Alerting

When packet filtering is enabled, you can set alerts that warn you of suspicious behavior on the external interface. You can be alerted when packets are rejected, protocol violations occur, or the disk becomes full. And you can have the alert simply added to the event log, or have an SMTP e-mail sent. To configure alerting for Web Proxy, follow these steps:

1. Open the Internet Information Services MMC snap-in and right-click Web Proxy. Choose Properties from the shortcut menu to open the Web Proxy Service Properties window for that server.

2. Click the Security button. Choose the Alerting tab, shown in Figure 30-29.

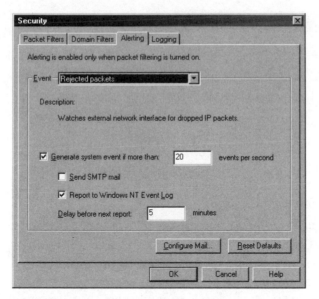

Figure 30-29. *The Alerting tab of the Security dialog box.*

3. Configure the settings for alerts. The settings are set separately for each type of event, allowing you to tune for the area of greatest concern. The settings are as follows:

- **Event**   Rejected packets, protocol errors, or disk full.
- **Generate System Event If More Than**   Allows you to set the threshold of suspicious events that will trigger the alarm.
- **Send SMTP Mail**   Allows you to send mail, including mail to a pager, in the event of an alert.
- **Report To Windows NT Event Log**   Creates an entry in the event log.
- **Delay Before Next Report**   The number of minutes before this type of event will trigger an additional alert.

4. To configure the mail settings, click Configure Mail. The Configure Mail Alerting dialog box appears, as shown in Figure 30-30.

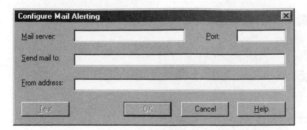

Figure 30-30. *You can configure alerting to send you SMTP mail.*

5. In the Mail Server text box, fill in the SMTP server, the port used, the user or mailbox to send the alert to, and the sending user. You can send a test message by clicking the Test button.

6. When the SMTP alert mail is working correctly, click OK to return to the mail Alerting tab in the Security dialog box.

7. When you've finished editing the alerts, click OK to return to the main Web Proxy Service Properties window. Click Accept to accept the settings and continue configuring, or click OK to implement the changes and close the window.

Logging

By default, Proxy Server logs a variety of information about security events. You can configure the logging to use standard files or to go to a database for more detailed analysis, as well as configuring the level of detail stored. To configure logging for the security events, follow these steps:

1. Open the Internet Information Services MMC snap-in and right-click WinSock Proxy. Choose Properties from the shortcut menu to open the WinSock Proxy Service Properties window for that server.

2. Click the Security button. Choose the Logging tab.

3. Select your configurations and click OK to accept the changes and close the window, or click Apply to simply apply the changes and leave the window open for further configuration changes.

The available settings are as follows:

- **Enable Logging Using**   Regular or verbose format. Controls how much detail is logged.
- **Log To File**   Change the settings for file logging. Options include:
  - **Automatically Open A New File**   Daily, weekly, or monthly.
  - **Limit The Number Of Old Files**   To Set the number of log files to save.
  - **Stop Service If Disk Is Full**   Stop the proxy service if the disk becomes full and you can't continue logging.
  - **Log File Directory**   Location of log files.
- **Log To SQL/ODBC Database**   Allows connection to any SQL or ODBC data source. Options are:
  - **ODBC Data Source Name (DSN)**   The ODBC connection name.
  - **Table**   The table in the data source to store the log information.
  - **User name**   The user name used to connect to the data source.
  - **Password**   The password to use to connect to the data source.

Summary

You can install Proxy Server on a Windows 2000 server using the Microsoft Proxy Server Setup Wizard. When installed, it provides an isolation layer between your internal network and the Internet, and you can configure it to act as secure gatekeeper. While not a full-featured firewall, it does provide many of the benefits of a firewall and, with the addition of third-party products, can act as a secure, full-featured firewall providing robust protection for your network. The next chapter covers two completely new Windows 2000 features: remote access and routing.

Chapter 31
Connection Services

Routing and remote access services have been around in one form or another—under the names Remote Access Service (RAS), Routing and Remote Access Service (RRAS), and Dial-Up Networking—in every version of Microsoft Windows NT. In Microsoft Windows 2000, this service is called Routing and Remote Access, though you may still see the acronym RRAS used.

A computer running Microsoft Windows 2000 Server and Routing and Remote Access acts as a remote access server. This server authenticates users and enables the use of services typically available to a LAN-connected user (file and print sharing, applications, messaging, and so forth). The remote access server can connect remote users to the network using both virtual private network (VPN) and dial-up technology. Windows 2000 also supports Remote Authentication Dial-In User Service (RADIUS), the well-known authentication method used by many Internet service providers (ISPs). The user signs in with a name and password, which is then passed on to a server that authenticates the user and authorizes access.

Routing and Remote Access is a very large subject. This chapter focuses on new models and functionalities in Windows 2000. As in many areas of network administration, the complexities of Routing and Remote Access are more apparent than real. However, it is possible to plunge in and create an amazing amount of confusion if you don't first understand the concepts underlying the options.

How Dial-Up Remote Access Works

Dial-up remote access, also called Dial-Up Networking, allows an off-site computer to tap into an office computer's resources via a modem. Figure 31-1 shows the usual dial-up connections made to a network.

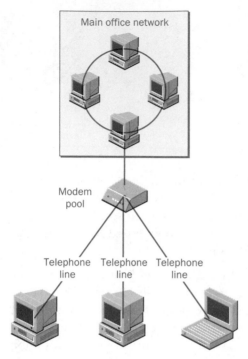

Figure 31-1. *Dial-up connections to a network.*

Remote or mobile users using a dial-up communications link can access network resources as if they were directly connected. Windows 2000 remote access servers can connect to clients running Microsoft Windows 2000, Windows NT, Windows 95/98, Windows for Workgroups, MS-DOS, or Apple Macintosh. Typically the client connects over a standard telephone line or over an ISDN line to a modem, modem pool, or ISDN "modem."

Understanding Virtual Private Networks

A virtual private network is an extension of a private network across a public network such as the Internet. Using a VPN, connections across the public network can transfer data in a form that resembles a private Point-to-Point Tunneling Protocol (PPTP) link. VPNs use the routing infrastructure of the Internet, but to the user it appears as though the data were being sent over a dedicated private link.

The appeal of a VPN is the Internet and its global presence. Communication links can be made quickly, cheaply, and safely across the world. Dedicated private lines aren't required, and security can be configured at very high levels. In 1997, VPNs made up just 0.2 percent of total domestic network connections, according to Infonetics Research, a firm in San Jose, California that specializes in networking. Infonetics predicts that by the end of 2001, more than 27 percent of all U.S. connections will be made via VPNs.

Real World   When a VPN Isn't Appropriate

While VPNs are great methods of connectivity for branch offices and remote users of every stripe, there are conditions under which a VPN isn't appropriate:

- When performance at any price is the primary concern
- When most traffic is synchronous, as in voice and video transmissions
- When using an application with unusual protocols that are not compatible with TCP/IP

In these situations, a dedicated private line is almost always the best choice.

How VPNs Work

In a virtual private network, both ends of the connection make a link to the Internet. (Technically, they can link to any public network, but it's almost always the Internet.) The link can take the usual forms—a regular telephone line, an ISDN line, or a dedicated line of some sort. Instead of sending a packet as the originating node produces it, the VPN, using a tunneling protocol, encapsulates the packet in an additional header. The header provides routing information so that the encapsulated data can traverse the intermediate internetwork. For privacy, the data is encrypted and, if packets are intercepted, they cannot be unencrypted without the encryption keys.

This technology allows a remote user in Connecticut, for example, to establish a dial-up connection with any ISP and, through that connection, make a direct connection to a server on the company network in California. It's quick, it's cheap, and it's easy to set up. Figure 31-2 shows a VPN set up so that traveling employees, telecommuters in home offices, and employees in branch offices can all connect to the main network at a company's headquarters. Each component is connecting to the ISP though a different type of communications channel, but all are part of the same VPN. Figure 31-3 shows a more typical VPN, in which the connection is made from one router to another.

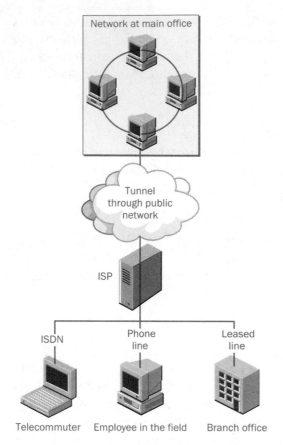

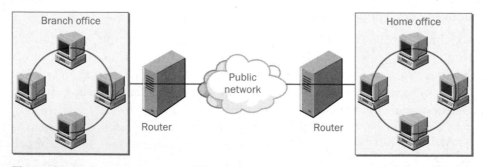

Figure 31-2. *A virtual private network.*

Figure 31-3. *A router-to-router VPN.*

Components of a VPN

A VPN connection in Windows 2000 consists of a VPN server, a VPN client, a VPN connection (the portion of the connection in which the data is encrypted), and the tunnel (the portion of the connection in which the data is encapsulated). The tunneling is done through one of the tunneling protocols included with Windows 2000, both of which are installed with Routing and Remote Access:

- **Point-to-Point Tunneling Protocol (PPTP)** An extension of the point-to-point protocol (PPP) in use for many years, PPTP was first used in Windows NT 4.

- **Layer Two Tunneling Protocol (L2TP)** A combination of PPTP and Layer Two Forwarding (L2F), a tunneling protocol developed by Cisco Systems. L2TP employs Internet Protocol security (IPSec) for encryption, so the VPN client and server must support both L2TP and IPSec.

More Info For more information on the VPN protocols, see RFC 2637, "Point-to-Point Tunneling Protocol," and RFC 2661, "Layer Two Tunneling Protocol." Both can be found at (among other places) *http://www.vpnc.org/rfcs.html* on the Internet.

Installing a Remote Access Server

To allow the connection of multiple, simultaneous dial-up clients, you must have modem-pooling equipment (hereafter referred to as the modem bank) with the appropriate connections to the local telecommunications provider. A typical modem bank for Windows 2000 includes an adapter that installs in the computer running Windows 2000 Server. Make sure that the modem equipment is on the Windows 2000 Hardware Compatibility List (HCL), and that all the protocols needed for the dial-up connections are installed on this server.

Configuring the Connection to Dial-Up Networking Clients

To enable Routing and Remote Access, follow these steps:

1. Choose Routing And Remote Access from the Administrative Tools folder on the Programs menu.

2. By default, the local computer is shown as a server. To enable Routing and Remote Access on the local computer, right-click the computer in the console tree, and choose Configure And Enable Routing And Remote Access from the shortcut menu.

3. The Routing And Remote Access Server Setup Wizard starts. To continue, click Next.

4. In the Common Configurations dialog box, select Remote Access Server and click Next.

5. Verify that the remote client protocols are listed. (If they are not, you will have to cancel this wizard and install them.) Click Next.

6. Select your choice for IP address assignment. Automatic assignment is highly recommended. Click Next.

7. In the Managing Multiple Remote Access Servers dialog box, select the option of not using a RADIUS server. (If you will have multiple remote access servers, see the section "Using RADIUS for Multiple Remote Access Servers," later in this chapter.) Click Next, then click Finish. The Routing and Remote Access service starts and initializes automatically.

Setting Remote Access Policies

In Windows NT 4.0 and 3.51, remote access is granted based solely on whether the user's account has dial-in permission. The permission is configured in User Manager or the Remote Access Administration utility. In Windows 2000, remote access is somewhat more complicated. Authorization is determined by a combination of the dial-in properties for the user account and the remote access policies. With remote access policies, connections can be authorized or denied based on the time of day, the Windows 2000 group to which the user belongs, the type of connection being requested, and many other variables. By default, only one policy is in place when you install Routing and Remote Access: Allow Access If Dial-In Permission Is Enabled. However, this policy operates quite differently, depending on which administration model you use.

Real World **Authorization and Authentication**

The similarity between the words "authorization" and "authentication" can cause some confusion, and it's important to understand the differences. *Authorization* is the process of giving a user access to system objects based on the user's identity. *Authentication* is the process of identifying a user. In remote access connections, this is done when the client sends the user's credentials (user name and password) to the server via an authentication protocol. Authentication ensures that the individual is who he or she claims to be, but says nothing about the access rights of the individual.

Understanding the Default Policy

When you open Routing And Remote Access from the Administrative Tools folder and click Remote Access Policies in the console tree, the details pane lists a single policy (Figure 31-4). This policy is called Allow Access If Dial-In Permission Is Enabled, and it is referred to often in this chapter. Understanding what it does and doesn't do is essential to grasping the administration of remote access.

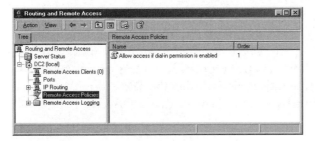

Figure 31-4. *The default remote access policy.*

Right-click the policy in the details pane, and choose Properties from the short-cut menu to open the dialog box shown in Figure 31-5. This policy has a single condition that must be matched by anyone seeking remote access. Click the Edit button to view the condition. As you can see, the condition is Any Day, Any Time. You might not think that access at any day, any time is a condition, but it is. It's just not a restrictive condition, and it makes this policy essentially transparent.

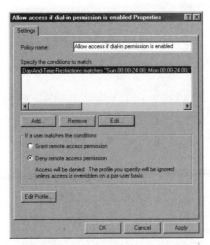

Figure 31-5. *The Properties window for the default remote access policy.*

Close the Time Of Day Constraints dialog box to return to the policy's Properties window. In the area labeled If A User Matches The Conditions are two options: Grant Remote Access Permission and Deny Remote Access Permission. You might think that the default setting of Deny Remote Access Permission would prevent anyone from dialing into this remote server, but you would be mistaken. Whether these options actually allow or prevent a connection depends on the Dial-In setting on the user account.

The confusion arises because people tend to use the terms "permission" and "policy" as if they were interchangeable. Permission is in fact set on the user account, and it is granted by default. The dial-in permission set on the user account overrides the permission option in this Properties window except in the case of the native-mode administration model (described in the next section), in which all user accounts are set to Control Access Through Remote Access Policy.

Read the sections on administrative policies that follow carefully, and study the logic diagrams. The administrative approach you choose should be as simple as possible while still meeting your needs.

Choosing an Administrative Model for Remote Access Policies

In Windows 2000, you can choose from among three models for administering remote access permissions and connection settings:

- Access by user
- Access by policy in a Windows 2000 mixed-mode domain
- Access by policy in a Windows 2000 native-mode domain

An essential part of planning for remote access is determining which models you can use and deciding on an appropriate one. There is enough variation among the models that attempting to mix them is a recipe for confusion. No matter which model you choose, plan on thoroughly testing your chosen access policies to make sure that you're getting the results you intend.

Administering Access by User

In the access-by-user administrative model, remote access permissions are determined by the remote access permissions on the Dial-In tab of the Properties window for the user account. To enable or disable remote access permission for individual users, set Remote Access Permission to either Allow Access or Deny

Access, as in Windows NT Server. This administrative model is by far the simplest, and it works very well when the number of remote users is small and the access uncomplicated.

If remote access permission for the user account is set to either Allow Access or Deny Access, the remote access permission setting on the remote access policy is effectively overridden. Access by user can be administered with multiple policies, but doing so can be complicated because a connection attempt might be rejected even when the remote access permission on the user account is set to Allow Access. If a connection attempt matches the conditions of a policy but does not match the profile settings or does not match any of the remote access policies, the connection attempt is rejected, as shown in Figure 31-6. In the access-by-user administrative model, you can control access in three ways:

- **Explicit allow** The remote access permission for the user account is set to Allow Access, and the connection attempt doesn't conflict with a policy or the settings of the profile and the dial-in properties of the user account.

- **Explicit deny** The remote access permission for the user account is set to Deny Access.

- **Implicit deny** The connection attempt doesn't match the conditions set in any remote access policies.

The access-by-user administrative model can be used on a stand-alone remote access server, a remote access server on a Windows 2000 native-mode domain, a remote access server on a Windows 2000 mixed-mode domain, or a remote access server on a Windows NT 4 domain.

Granting Access by User

The access-by-user model resembles the administrative model of Windows NT 4. Individual user accounts are set to Allow Access or Deny Access. The default policy in Routing and Remote Access, Allow Access If Dial-In Permission Is Enabled, is in place with the following settings:

- The single condition of day and time restrictions is set to allow access at all times on all days.

- The profile is set to the default settings.

- The Deny Remote Access Permission option is selected.

But wait! If Deny Remote Access Permission is selected, isn't remote access permission denied? No; it means basically *nothing* in this scenario. Access is determined solely by the settings in the Properties window for the individual user account. Figure 31-6 shows the progression of a connection under the access-by-user administrative model.

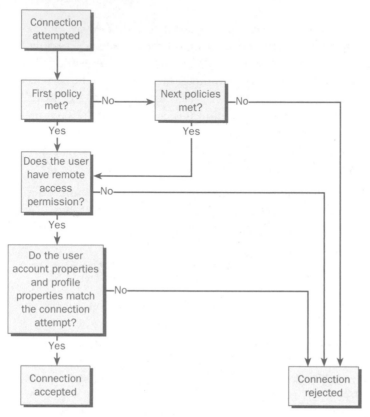

Figure 31-6. *Progression of a connection attempt when administering access by user.*

Administering Access by Policy for a Mixed-Mode Domain

In the access-by-policy administrative model for a Windows 2000 mixed-mode domain, the remote access permission on every user account is set to Allow Access, the default remote access policy is deleted or demoted, and separate remote access policies are created to define the types of connections that are allowed. On a remote access server running Windows 2000 that is a member of a Windows 2000 mixed-mode domain, the Control Access Through Remote Access Policy option is not available for remote access permission on the user account. If a connection attempt corresponds to the conditions of a policy (subject to the profile and user account dial-in settings), the connection is accepted.

> **Tip** The access-by-policy administrative model also applies to a remote access server running Windows 2000 that is a member of a Windows NT 4 domain.

In the access-by-policy administrative model for a Windows 2000 mixed-mode domain, you can control access in three ways:

- **Explicit allow** The connection attempt matches the conditions of a policy, subject to the settings of the profile and the dial-in properties of the user account.

- **Explicit deny** The connection attempt matches the conditions of a policy but not the settings of the profile. You can do an explicit deny in this model by editing the profile and enabling the Restrict Dial-In To This Number Only option on the Dial-In Constraints tab and typing a number that does not correspond to any dial-in number being used by the remote access server.

- **Implicit deny** The connection attempt does not match the conditions of any remote access policies.

If you do not delete the default remote access policy, Allow Access If Dial-In Permission Is Enabled, all users can obtain a remote access connection.

> **Tip** The access-by-policy administrative model for mixed-mode domains can be used with Windows NT servers running Routing and Remote Access if the Windows NT servers are configured as RADIUS clients to a Windows 2000 Internet Authentication Service (IAS) server. A Windows NT server running RAS cannot use access by policy. You must upgrade the server to Windows NT RRAS (or to Windows 2000) to employ the remote access policy authorization.

Granting or Denying Access by Group Membership

To allow connections for users by group membership, all user accounts must have Remote Access Permission on the Dial-In tab set to Allow Access. To set up the access by groups, the administrator makes the following settings:

- In Routing and Remote Access, delete the default policy, Allow Access If Dial-In Permission Is Enabled.
- Create a new policy named Accept If Member Of Selected Groups.
- Add the *Windows-Groups* attribute to the policy.
- Select the group or groups to be granted access.
- On the policy, select the Grant Remote Access Permission option.

In this case, the Grant Remote Access Permission option means what it says. Figure 31-7 shows the progression of a connection attempt when a remote user dials in and access is controlled by group membership.

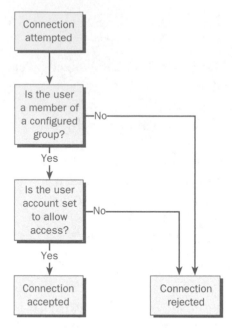

Figure 31-7. *Progression of a connection attempt when administering access by group membership.*

Perhaps it would be easier in your situation to specify who *isn't* allowed access than to specify who is. For example, employees in production might have user accounts on the network but have no need for dial-in access. In this case, you will need to make the following settings:

- Leave the default policy, Allow Access If Dial-In Permission Is Enabled, in place.
- Create a new policy named Reject Production Group.
- Add the *Windows-Groups* attribute to the policy.
- Select the Production group.
- On the policy, select the Deny Remote Access Permission option.
- Click Edit Profile and, on the Dial-In Constraints tab, select Restrict Dial-In To This Number Only and type in a number that is not a dial-in number of the remote access server, as shown in Figure 31-8.
- In the details pane of the Routing and Remote Access snap-in, right-click the new policy and select Move Up so that it is the first to be evaluated.

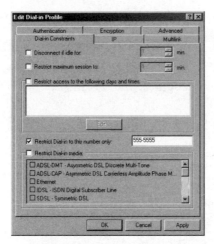

Figure 31-8. *Configuring the dial-in constraints to deny access to a group.*

Figure 31-9 shows the logic of the connection attempt when access is denied by group membership.

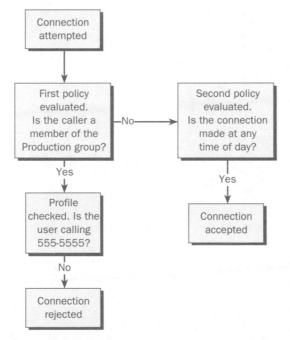

Figure 31-9. *Progression of a connection attempt when the policy is to deny access by group membership.*

Administering Access by Policy for a Native-Mode Domain

In a Windows 2000 native-mode domain, you can use the access-by-policy administrative model, which has the following settings:

- The remote access permission on every user account is set to Control Access Through Remote Access Policy.

- Remote access permissions are determined by the remote access permission setting on the remote access policy.

These settings mean that the Remote Access Permission setting on the remote access policy determines whether remote access permission is allowed or denied. Figure 31-10 shows the progression of a connection attempt in a native-mode domain.

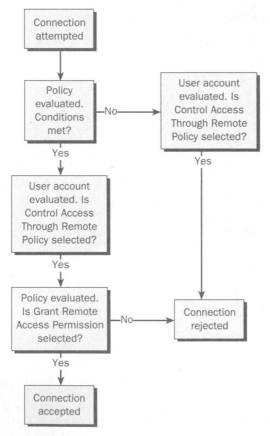

Figure 31-10. *Progression of a connection attempt when administering access by policy in a native-mode domain.*

In the access-by-policy administrative model for a Windows 2000 native-mode domain, you can control access in three ways:

- **Explicit allow**   The remote access permission on the remote access policy is set to Grant Remote Access Permission, and the connection attempt matches the conditions of the policy, subject to the settings of the profile and the dial-in properties of the user account.

- **Explicit deny**   The remote access permission on the remote access policy is set to Deny Remote Access Permission, and the connection attempt matches the conditions of the policy.

- **Implicit deny**   The connection attempt does not match the conditions of any remote access policies.

Note   If you use the access-by-policy administrative model for a native-mode domain, don't add remote access policies, and don't change the default remote access policy (Allow Access If Dial-In Permission Is Enabled), then no users are allowed remote access. By default, the remote access permission on the default remote access policy is set to Deny Remote Access Permission. If you change the setting to Grant Remote Access Permission, all users are allowed remote access.

The access-by-policy administrative model for a Windows 2000 native-mode domain also applies to stand-alone remote access servers that are not members of a domain. You can't use the access-by-policy administrative model for a Windows 2000 native-mode domain if you have Windows NT 4 RAS or RRAS or IAS servers because a native-mode domain by definition has no Windows NT servers.

Tip   If you use the access-by-policy administrative model for a Windows 2000 native-mode domain and you do not use groups to specify which users get access, verify that the Guest account is disabled and that its remote access permission is set to Deny Access.

Granting or Denying Access by Group Membership

In a native-mode domain, setting access by policy requires that all user accounts have the Control Access Through Remote Access Policy option selected on the Dial-In tab of the user account's Properties window. To allow access by specified groups, the administrator must do the following:

- Delete the default policy, Allow Access If Dial-In Permission Is Enabled.
- Create a new policy called Accept If Member Of Selected Groups.

- Add the *Windows-Groups* attribute to the policy.
- Select the group or groups to be granted access.
- On the policy, select the Grant Remote Access Permission option.

Figure 31-11 shows the progression of a connection attempt with this policy setting.

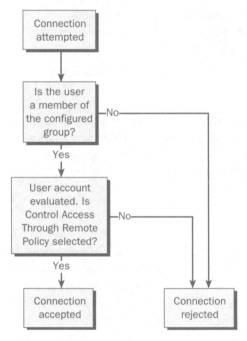

Figure 31-11. *Progression of a connection attempt when the policy is to allow access by group membership in a native-mode domain.*

In a native-mode domain, you can easily reverse the criteria just described and deny access based on group membership. This policy also requires that all user accounts have the Control Access Through Remote Access Policy option selected on the Dial-In tab of the user account's Properties window. As in the mixed-mode domain, two policies are needed, one to reject members of a specified group and another to allow a connection made by anyone else. Follow this procedure to deny access based on group membership:

- Leave in place the default policy, Allow Access If Dial-In Permission Is Enabled. Select the Grant Remote Access Permission option on the default policy.
- Create a new policy named Deny Configured Group.

- Add the *Windows-Groups* attribute to the policy.
- Add the groups that are to be denied remote access.
- On the new policy, select the Deny Remote Access Permission option.
- In the details pane of Remote Access Policies, right-click the new policy and select Move Up so that it is the first to be evaluated.

Figure 31-12 shows the logical progression when a connection attempt is made with these settings in effect.

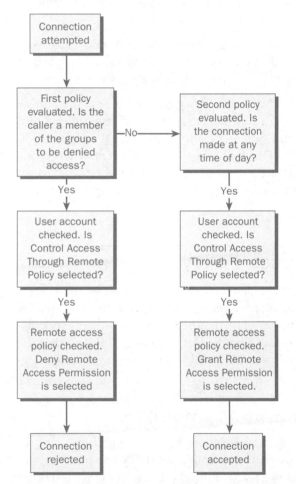

Figure 31-12. *Progression of a connection attempt when access is controlled by groups in a native-mode domain.*

Real World   Windows NT 4 Remote Access in a Windows 2000 Domain

In a Windows 2000 domain, a server running Windows NT 4 and either RAS or RRAS can't authenticate the credentials of domain accounts unless it (the Windows NT server) is also a domain controller. A Windows NT server that is not a domain controller does not have permission to read Active Directory and therefore can validate only local accounts. This same restriction applies when you have a remote access server (running Windows NT *or* Windows 2000) in a Windows NT domain that needs to validate user accounts in a trusted Windows 2000 domain.

The recommended solution in the first case is to upgrade the Windows NT server to a domain controller or to Windows 2000. In the second situation, the best answer is to upgrade the Windows NT domain to Windows 2000.

However, you can loosen the normal Active Directory security so that the remote access server can read the user account properties. Open a command prompt window on a domain controller and type *net localgroup "Pre-Windows 2000 Compatible Access" everyone /add*. This will add the special identity Everyone to the Pre-Windows 2000 Compatible Access group so that the remote access server can use NT LAN Manager security to read the domain user accounts.

Configuring a Remote Access Policy

A remote access policy consists of three elements that make up a rule for analyzing remote connections. These elements are the conditions, the profile, and the remote access permission for the policy. The remote access permission was discussed earlier, in the section "Understanding the Default Policy." Recall that the remote access permission for the policy applies only when an administration-by-policy model is being employed.

Specifying Conditions of Remote Access Policies

When granting or denying access by group membership in the previous sections, you added the *Windows-Groups* attribute as a condition that users making connection attempts had to match (Figure 31-13). Table 31-1 describes this and other attributes that can be included in a remote access policy.

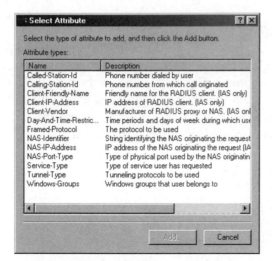

Figure 31-13. *The remote access attributes that can be added to policies.*

Table 31-1.   Attributes for remote access policies

Attribute Name	Description
Called-Station-Id	Phone number of the remote access server. To receive this information, the phone line, hardware, and hardware drivers must support the passing of the information. Otherwise, the called station ID is set manually for each port.
Calling-Station-Id	Phone number used by the caller. If you configure a caller ID number for a user, the phone system, remote server, and all connecting hardware must support the passing of caller ID information. If any link in the connection does not support caller ID, the connection attempt is denied.
Client-Friendly-Name	(IAS server only) Name of the RADIUS client computer that is seeking authentication.
Client-IP-Address	(IAS server only) IP address of the RADIUS client.
Client-Vendor	(IAS server only) Vendor of the network access server that is a RADIUS client. Used to configure different policies for different manufacturers.
Day-And-Time-Restriction	Days and times for connection attempts.
Framed-Protocol	Protocol such as PPP, SLIP, Frame Relay, or X.25 to be used for framing incoming packets.
NAS-Identifier	(IAS server only) String to identify the originating network access server (NAS).
NAS-IP-Address	(IAS server only) IP address of the originating NAS.
NAS-Port-Type	Medium used by the originating caller. Examples are analog telephone and ISDN lines.
Service-Type	Type of service the caller requests. Examples are framed (PPP) and login (Telnet).
Tunnel-Type	Tunneling protocols to be used. Examples are PPTP and L2TP.
Windows-Groups	Groups that the caller is a member of.

Configuring Profiles in Remote Access Policies

The profile in a remote access policy is a set of conditions that apply when a connection is authorized. The profile applies whether the condition has been authorized by permission in the user account or by permission in the policy. To see the profile that applies to a policy, open the policy's Properties window and click the Edit Profile button. The Edit Profile window has six tabs that can be configured (Figure 31-14). Each tab is discussed in the sections that follow.

Figure 31-14. *Settings in the remote access policy profile.*

Specifying Dial-In Constraints

On the Dial-In Constraints tab, you can set the following limitations on the dial-in connection:

- **Disconnect If Idle For** The time after which an idle connection is terminated. By default, no connection is automatically terminated when idle.

- **Restrict Maximum Session To** The time after which a connection is disconnected. By default, there is no time limit on connections.

- **Restrict Access To The Following Days And Times** The days and hours when a connection is allowed. This option is cleared by default. The remote access server will not disconnect a connection that is active at a time when connection attempts aren't allowed.

- **Restrict Dial-In To This Number Only** The specific number that a user must call for a connection to be allowed.

- **Restrict Dial-In Media**   The type of medium the caller must be connecting with, such as ISDN, T1, or ADSL. If the medium specified doesn't match the medium being used, the call will be rejected.

Specifying IP Address Policies

The IP tab defines the IP address policies for the profile:

- **IP Address Assignment Policy**   By default, the server supplies an IP address for the connection, but you can specify that the server must supply an address or that the client can request an IP address.

- **IP Packet Filters**   Specifies the types of packets that are allowed (or not allowed) in the traffic to the client or from the client or both. Packet filtering can be based on such things as the source and destination IP addresses, protocol type, source or destination port, and so forth.

Enabling Multilink and the Bandwidth Allocation Protocol

On the Multilink tab, you can choose settings to enable Multilink and the Bandwidth Allocation Protocol (BAP). The server must have Multilink and BAP enabled for these settings to be enforced in the profile. Enabling Multilink allows clients to combine multiple physical connections into a single logical connection. If you enable Multilink, you should also enable BAP so that links can be dynamically added or dropped as needed. (Multilink has no mechanism for adapting to changing bandwidth needs.)

- **Multilink Settings**   Disables Multilink completely or sets the maximum number of ports that a connection can use. This option defaults to the server's setting.

- **Bandwidth Allocation Protocol Settings**   Causes a Multilink connection to be reduced automatically if the lines fall below a specified capacity for a specified length of time.

Specifying Authentication Methods

On the Authentication tab, you set the authentication methods that are allowed for the connection. The same authentication methods must be enabled on the remote access server for the properties of the profile to be enforced. For more on authentication methods, see the section "Configuring Authentication for a Remote Access Server" in Chapter 18.

Specifying an Encryption Method

The Encryption tab lets you set the encryption properties for this profile. The settings are as follows:

- **No Encryption** Allows a nonencrypted connection. To require encryption, clear this check box.
- **Basic** Uses Microsoft Point-to-Point Encryption (MPPE) with a 40-bit key for dial-up and PPTP connections. For L2TP over an IPSec-based VPN, uses 56-bit Data Encryption Standard (DES) encryption.
- **Strong** Uses MPPE with a 56-bit key for dial-up and PPTP connections. For L2TP over an IPSec-based VPN, uses 56-bit DES encryption.

Setting Advanced Attributes

On the Advanced tab, you can set RADIUS attributes that are sent to the RADIUS client by the IAS server. These attributes are specific to RADIUS authentication and are ignored by the remote access server.

Configuring a Remote Access Server

Some of the profile settings described in the previous section must have corresponding entries on the remote access server. This section covers those settings as well as other specific configurations that can be performed on a server. To make configuration changes to a remote access server, open Routing And Remote Access, right-click the server name in the console tree, and choose Properties from the shortcut menu. The various settings available in the Properties window are as follows:

- **Authentication Settings** To access the authentication settings, click the Security tab in the server's Properties window, and then click the Authentication Methods button. By default, Microsoft's Challenge Handshake Authentication Protocols (MS-CHAP and MS-CHAP v2) are selected.
- **IP Routing And Assignment** The IP tab on the server's Properties window gives access to the IP parameters. By default, the profiles in remote access policies use the server's settings for IP addresses. In turn, the server defaults to allowing IP routing and to assignment of IP addresses using DHCP. If you need to use a static address pool, choose that option and provide a range of addresses to be assigned to connections.

- **Multilink And The BAP**   Click the PPP tab to access the options for enabling Multilink and the BAP. See the section "Enabling Multilink and the Bandwidth Allocation Protocol," earlier in this chapter, for more information.
- **Other Protocols**   On the PPP tab, click Software Compression to enable (or remove) support for the Microsoft Point-to-Point Compression (MPPC) protocol. You can also select the Link Control Protocol (LCP) Extensions to PPP.

More Info   For more information on the MPPC protocol, see RFC 2118, "Microsoft Point-to-Point Compression Protocol." See RFC 1570, "PPP LCP Extensions," for more about the LCP extensions.

Configuring a Virtual Private Network

The uses and types of virtual private networks were described earlier in this chapter and in some detail in Chapter 17. This section outlines the steps involved in configuring and using a VPN for PPTP connections across the Internet.

Configuring the Internet Connection

Your connection to the Internet will be over a dedicated line of some sort— most typically T1, Fractional T1, or Frame Relay. You'll need to be sure that the WAN adapter is on the Windows 2000 HCL. The WAN adapter includes drivers that are installed in the Windows 2000 operating system, allowing the WAN adapter to appear as a network adapter. The WAN adapter will need to be configured with the IP address and subnet mask assigned for your domain or supplied by an ISP, as well as with the default gateway of the ISP router.

Configuring the Remote Access Server as a Router

For the remote access server to forward traffic properly inside your network, you must configure it as a router with either static routes or routing protocols, so that all of the locations of the intranet are reachable from the remote access server.

To configure the server as a router, open Routing And Remote Accesss, right-click the server name, and choose Properties. On the General tab, select the Enable This Computer As A Router option. Then indicate whether you want the router to handle local area network routing only or LAN and demand-dial routing. Click OK to close the Properties window.

Configuring PPTP Ports

You'll need to confirm that you have the number of PPTP ports you need. To verify the number of ports or to add more, follow these steps:

1. Open Routing And Remote Access from the Administrative Tools folder.

2. In the console tree, click the appropriate server, and then right-click Ports and choose Properties from the shortcut menu.

3. In the Ports Properties window (Figure 31-15), highlight WAN Miniport (PPTP), and click the Configure button.

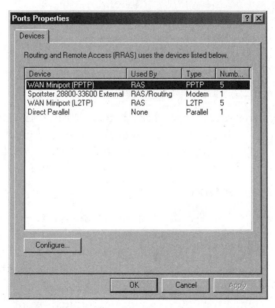

Figure 31-15. *Configuring the PPTP ports.*

4. In the Configure Device dialog box, you can set a maximum number of ports for the device and specify whether the device is to be used for incoming connections only or for both incoming and outgoing connections.

5. Click OK when you're finished.

More Info An excellent overview of routing concepts can be found in *Microsoft TCP/IP Training* (Microsoft Press, 1997).

Configuring PPTP Filters

Most networks need to filter packets based on their incoming or outgoing addresses. To set the PPTP filters, follow these steps:

1. Open Routing and Remote Access from the Administrative Tools folder.
2. In the console tree, expand the appropriate server, then IP Routing, and then General.
3. In the details pane, right-click the interface to be filtered, and choose Properties from the shortcut menu.
4. Click either Input Filters or Output Filters and supply the source, destination, and/or protocol to be filtered. (The last step in configuring a VPN is to set up remote access policies, as described earlier in this chapter.)

Caution   Filtering can be a tricky business, so proceed with caution. It's all too easy to filter too much or too little. Consult the online Help files of Windows 2000 Server for additional information.

Elements of a Router-to-Router VPN Connection

A router-to-router VPN is typically used to connect remote offices over a permanent link such as a dedicated T1 line. However, a router-to-router VPN can also be configured to be available *on demand*, which means that the connection is made only when needed. This section describes the components of a Windows 2000 router-to-router VPN connection.

VPN Clients

The client is the calling router that initiates the VPN connection. For router-to-router connections, you can use computers running Windows 2000 Server, or Windows NT Server 4 with RRAS, as VPN clients.

VPN Servers

The VPN server is the answering router that accepts the connection from the calling router. Computers running Windows 2000 Server and computers running Windows NT Server 4 with RRAS can be set up as VPN servers.

LAN and Remote Access Protocols

LAN protocols such as TCP/IP and IPX are used to transport information. Windows 2000 Server supports the routing of LAN protocol packets by using the PPP remote access protocol in a router-to-router VPN connection.

Tunneling Protocols

Tunneling protocols encapsulate one network protocol inside another. VPN clients and VPN servers use tunneling protocols to manage tunnels and send tunneled data. Windows 2000 includes PPTP and L2TP. Windows NT Server 4 with RRAS includes only PPTP.

Demand-Dial Interfaces

The VPN client (the calling router) must have a demand-dial interface configured for

- The host name or IP address of the interface of the VPN server on the Internet
- A PPTP port (for a PPTP-based VPN connection) or an L2TP port (for an L2TP-based connection)
- The user account credentials (user name, domain, password) for a user account that can be validated by the VPN server

The answering router (the VPN server) must have a demand-dial interface with the same name as the user account being used by the calling router (the VPN client). The interface must be configured for a PPTP port (for a PPTP-based VPN connection) or an L2TP port (for an L2TP-based connection). The section "Adding a Demand-Dial Interface," later in this chapter, describes how to set up a demand-dial interface.

User Accounts

The calling router needs a user account with dial-in permissions either through the user account or through remote access policies.

Static Routes or Routing Protocols

To be able to forward packets across the router-to-router VPN connection, each router has to have the appropriate routes in the routing tables. Routes are added to the routing tables of both routers either as static routes or by enabling a routing protocol to operate across a persistent router-to-router VPN connection. Static routing is best for a small, single-path internetwork. The section "Setting Up Routing Tables or a Static Route," later in this chapter, describes how to add routes to the routing tables.

Security Options

Because a Windows 2000 remote access router validates the router-to-router VPN connection, you can use all of the security features of Windows 2000 remote access, including data encryption, RADIUS, smart cards, and callback. See Chapter 18 for more on security considerations.

Adding a Demand-Dial Interface

To add a demand-dial interface to a router, follow these steps:

1. Open Routing and Remote Access from the Administrative Tools folder.

2. In the console tree, click the appropriate router.

3. Right-click Routing Interface. Choose New Demand-Dial Interface from the shortcut menu to start the Demand Dial Interface Wizard. Click Next.

4. Enter a name for the demand-dial interface (Figure 31-16). Use a name that will help you recall the connection being made, such as the name of the branch office or network to which you're connecting. Click Next.

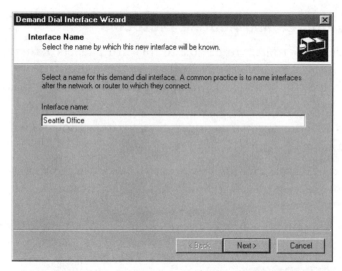

Figure 31-16. *Supplying a name for the demand-dial interface.*

6. Choose a connection type:

   - If you're not using VPN on this interface, select the Connect Using a Modem option, and click Next.

     Enter the phone number to be called. In addition to the primary number, you can click Alternates and specify additional numbers to be tried automatically if the primary number can't be reached.

   - If you select Connect Using Virtual Private Networking (VPN), click Next to open the VPN Type screen. Choose the tunneling protocol appropriate for your needs. Click Next.

     In the Destination Address screen, provide either the host name or the IP address for the remote router. Click Next.

7. Under Protocols And Security, select all of the conditions that apply to the connection. If you select either the Add A User Account So A Remote Router Can Dial In option or the Use Scripting To Complete The Connection With The Remote Router option (this second option is not a valid option for the VPN interface-type) or if you select both options, the wizard will present a screen to configure each of the items.

8. Supply the Dial Out Credentials requested, including the user account name and password.

9. When you're finished, the new interface is added to the routing interfaces in Routing and Remote Access. Right-click the name of the interface and choose Properties to change or add to the configuration.

Setting Up Static Routes and Routing Protocols

As was mentioned earlier, for routers to be able to forward packets across the router-to-router VPN connection, each router has to have the appropriate routes in the routing table. Routes can be added as static routes to the routing tables of both routers. To add a static route to the routing table, follow these steps:

1. Open Routing And Remote Access from the Administrative Tools folder.

2. Click the appropriate router, and then click IP Routing.

3. Right-click Static Routing and choose New Static Route from the shortcut menu. (You can also view the existing IP routing table from this menu.)

4. In the Static Route dialog box, select the interface and supply the IP address for the destination router (Figure 31-17).

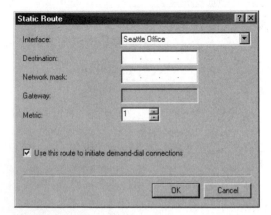

Figure 31-17. *Configuring a static route to be added to the routing table.*

The route must also be configured on the corresponding router at the other end of the VPN. For a persistent connection, you can add a routing protocol instead of a static route. To do so, right-click General under IP Routing and choose New Routing Protocol from the shortcut menu.

Using the Internet Authentication Service

The Internet Authentication Service is the central component in Windows 2000 for authenticating, authorizing, and auditing users who connect to a network through a VPN or via dial-up access. The IAS server is used with a RADIUS server. RADIUS is the authentication protocol most commonly used by ISPs. IAS uses data stored on a domain controller to verify the authentication requests received through the RADIUS protocol.

IAS Authentication

IAS uses the authentication protocols within PPP to authenticate users. These include Challenge Handshake Authentication Protocol (CHAP) and its Windows-specific variant, Microsoft Challenge Handshake Authentication Protocol (MS-CHAP). Other methods of authentication include Extensible Authentication Protocol (EAP) for smart cards, certificates, and one-time passwords. Other methods are also supported, based on the telephone number that the user calls or calls from, although these methods are inherently less secure.

Installing and Configuring IAS

To use IAS for dial-up or VPN connections, you must perform several tasks, including installing IAS, configuring clients and servers, and setting remote access policy. This section describes each of these tasks in turn.

Installing IAS

The first step is to install IAS on the primary and backup remote servers. You may need the Windows 2000 Server or Advanced Server CD-ROM.

1. On the remote server, open Control Panel.
2. Open Add/Remove Programs and click Add/Remove Windows Components.
3. In the Windows Components Wizard, highlight Networking Services and click the Details button.

4. Select Internet Authentication Service. Click OK to close the details window.

5. Click Next, and IAS will be installed. You may be asked for the Windows 2000 CD-ROM during the installation.

Configuring IAS

The default IAS configuration is correct in most cases. If your remote access scenario is very complex, you may need to change the configuration. To check the configuration, follow these steps:

1. Open Internet Authentication Service from the Administrative Tools folder.

2. In the console tree, right-click Internet Authentication Service and choose Properties.

3. On the Service tab, you can change the description or the event logging options.

4. Click the RADIUS tab to view the default UDP ports. If your RADIUS authentication and accounting ports differ, make the changes here.

5. Click the Realms tab to change the realm information. Click OK when you're finished.

More Info A *realm* is a security authentication device used by Kerberos version 5. The uses of realms are spelled out in RFC 1510, "The Kerberos Network Authentication Service (V5)."

Configuring Clients for IAS

The next step is to add the network access servers (NASs) and, if you're using a VPN, the PPTP servers as clients on the primary IAS server. To add clients, follow these steps:

1. Select Internet Authentication Service from the Administrative Tools folder.

2. In the console tree, right-click Clients and choose New Client from the shortcut menu.

3. Supply a friendly name for the client, and click Next.

4. Supply the client address and a shared secret.

5. Click Finish when you're done.

Note   A *shared secret* is a password used between an IAS server and other servers connected to it. The shared secret must be the same on both machines and must follow general password rules—it's case sensitive, can use alpha-numeric and special characters, and can be up to 255 characters long. Because shared secrets are embedded in the software and you don't have to type them in all the time as you do passwords, you can easily make them quite long. Longer shared secrets are more secure than short ones.

Real World   How RADIUS Works

RADIUS authenticates users through a series of communications between the client and the server. Once a user is authenticated, the client provides that user with access to the appropriate network services.

Using a modem, the user dials in to a modem connected to an IAS server. Once the modem connection is completed, the server prompts the user for a name and password. The server creates a data packet—the *authentication request*—from this information. The packet includes information identifying the specific server sending the authentication request, the port that is being used for the modem connection, and the user name and password.

The authentication request is sent over the network from the RADIUS client to the RADIUS server. If the RADIUS server cannot be reached, the RADIUS client can route the request to an alternate server. When an authentication request is received, the authentication server validates the request and then decrypts the data packet to access the user name and password information. This information is passed to the appropriate security system (Kerberos version 5 in Windows 2000).

If the user name and password are correct, the server sends an authentication acknowledgment that includes information regarding the user's network system and service requirements. If at any point in this logon process conditions are not met, the RADIUS server sends an Authentication Reject to the server and the user is denied access to the network.

Using RADIUS for Multiple Remote Access Servers

When you have more than one Windows 2000 remote access server, the administration of their remote access policies can become cumbersome very quickly. Instead, you can configure a single computer running Windows 2000 and IAS as a RADIUS server and configure the remote access servers as RADIUS clients. The IAS server provides centralized remote access authentication, authorization, accounting, and auditing. Assuming that you've already configured the remote access servers to provide access for dial-up or VPN clients, you can accomplish this by performing the procedures listed below. Each of these procedures is described in the sections that follow.

- Configure the remote access servers for RADIUS authentication.
- Configure the remote access servers for RADIUS accounting.
- Configure the IAS server.

Tip To provide redundancy and fault tolerance, configure a primary and a secondary IAS server, and copy the remote access policies from the primary server to the secondary one. Then configure each remote access server with *two* RADIUS servers that correspond to the two IAS servers. If the primary IAS server becomes unavailable, the remote access servers will automatically fail over to the secondary IAS server.

Configuring a Remote Server for RADIUS Authentication

When you configure the properties of a remote access server running Windows 2000, you need to select RADIUS as the authentication provider. To change a server to RADIUS authentication, follow these steps:

1. Right-click the server name in Routing and Remote Access and choose Properties from the shortcut menu.
2. Click the Security tab. Under Authentication Provider, select RADIUS Authentication, and then click the Configure button.
3. Provide the server name—the host name or IP address of the IAS server. If you already have IAS installed, you do not need to change the shared secret. Otherwise, you will need to change it. The remote access server running Windows 2000 and the IAS server share a secret that is used to encrypt messages sent between them. The two servers must share the same secret.
4. Click OK when you're finished.

Note The remote access server sends its authentication requests to the UDP port on which the IAS server listens. The default value of 1812 is based on RFC 2138, "Remote Authentication Dial-in User Service (RADIUS)," and does not need to be changed when you're using an IAS server.

Configuring the Remote Server for RADIUS Accounting

When you configure the properties of a remote access server running Windows 2000, you need to select RADIUS accounting as the accounting provider.

To change a server to RADIUS accounting, follow these steps:

1. Right-click the server name in Routing and Remote Access and choose Properties from the shortcut menu.

2. Click the Security tab. Under Accounting Provider, select RADIUS Accounting, and then click the Configure button.

3. Provide the server name—the host name or IP address of the IAS server.

4. If you already have IAS installed, you do not need to change the shared secret. Otherwise, you will need to change it. Note that the remote access server running Windows 2000 and the IAS server share a secret that is used to encrypt messages sent between them. Both the remote access server and the IAS server must share the same secret. Click OK.

Configuring the IAS Server for RADIUS

You will need to register each of the remote access servers as clients on the IAS server. Once the remote access servers are configured to use RADIUS authentication, only the remote access policies stored on the IAS server are used, so if one of the remote access servers contains the remote access policies that are applied to all of the remote access servers, you need to copy the remote access policies to the IAS server. To copy the policies from a remote server to the IAS server, open a command window and type *netsh aaaa show config <path\file>.txt*. The path can be relative, absolute, or a UNC path. This command creates a text file that includes all of the configuration settings.

Copy the text file to the destination IAS server, and open a command prompt on the destination machine. Type *netsh exec <path\file>.txt*. A message appears telling you whether the update was successful. This procedure will not work unless both the source and destination computers are running the same version of Windows 2000.

Summary

Consistent and reliable remote access is a necessity for many, if not most, organizations today. Windows 2000 includes tools for setting up access ranging from a simple dial-in connection to multiple remote access servers running virtual private networks. In the next chapter, we move on to a new section of the book, which deals with performance tuning, disaster prevention, and disaster recovery.

Part VI

Tuning, Maintenance, and Repair

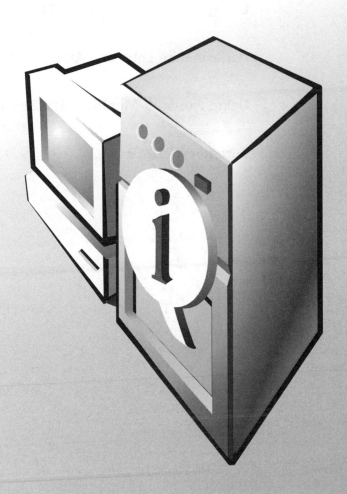

Chapter 32
Performance Monitoring and Tuning

Performance monitoring is the process of identifying bottlenecks that may be slowing down Microsoft Windows 2000 Server or the network on which it is running. To maximize the performance of a Windows 2000 system, you must be able to recognize bottlenecks wherever they may exist and take action to eliminate them. This chapter covers the system and network monitoring tools that Windows 2000 provides, which enable you to detect bottlenecks and tune your system to its optimum performance level. These tools include Event Viewer, System Monitor, and Network Monitor.

More Info   For further information about performance monitoring and tuning, refer to the information at these Microsoft sites: *http://www.microsoft.com/windows/ server/Technical/management/MonitorRel.asp* and *http://www.microsoft.com/ windows2000/en/server/help/*

You can also refer to the following Technet articles, which can be found at *www. microsoft.com/technet*: "Monitoring Network Activity," "Understanding Counter Organization," and "Understanding Memory Usage in Windows 2000."

What Is a Bottleneck?

Simply put, a *bottleneck* is a condition in which one process is preventing another process from functioning at its best. For example, when one application monopolizes the system processor to the exclusion of all other operations, there is a bottleneck at the processor. Bottlenecks can occur in virtually any Windows 2000 subsystem or on any element of the network.

Bottlenecks might occur for any of several reasons:

- Resources are not sharing workloads equally.
- The system does not have sufficient resources.
- Settings are configured incorrectly.
- A resource is malfunctioning.
- A program is monopolizing a particular resource.

Using Event Viewer

Event Viewer is a utility designed to track events recorded in the application, security, and system logs. It enables you to gather information about software, hardware, and system problems and track Windows 2000 security events. When you start Windows 2000, the Event Log service starts automatically. Event Viewer takes the form of a Microsoft Management Console (MMC) snap-in. It is named Eventvwr.msc and can be found in the %SystemRoot%\system32 folder. When you launch Event Viewer from the Administrative Tools folder on the Programs menu, you see the Event Viewer console (Figure 32-1).

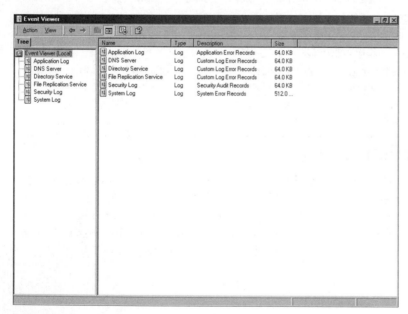

Figure 32-1. *The Event Viewer console.*

Event Log Files

Windows 2000 records events in three kinds of logs:

- **Application log**   Contains events logged by programs or applications. For example, a database program might log a file error in the program log. Application and program developers determine the events that are logged. All users can view this log.

- **Security log**   Records security events such as invalid and valid logon attempts and events related to resource use, such as creating, opening, or deleting files. The security log is turned off by default. The administrator can turn on the security log to record events by setting auditing attributes or events through the Group Policy feature in Windows 2000. For example, if you have enabled auditing for logging on, all attempts to log on to the system are recorded in the security log. An auditing policy can also be set in the registry to cause the system to halt when the security log becomes full. Only administrators can view this log. More information on setting auditing policy can be found in Chapter 10.

- **System log**   Contains events logged by the Windows 2000 system components. For example, the log will record the failure of a system component that is meant to load during startup. The event types logged here are predetermined by Windows 2000. All users can view this log.

By default, each log file has a maximum size of 512 KB and logs are overwritten as necessary, provided that the events are older than seven days. You can change the size of each log file by selecting the log you want to modify and choosing Properties from the Action menu of Event Viewer. In the Maximum Log Size box on the General tab, specify the new log size in kilobytes. The maximum log size can be as large as the capacity of the hard disk and memory. You can also decrease the size of the log file, but you have to clear the log of events first.

Logging will stop if the log file becomes full and cannot overwrite itself because the events in the log are not old enough or because you have the log set to be cleared manually. You can specify the event logging parameters for specific logs with the Event Log Wrapping options on the General tab of the Properties dialog box for each log. Choose Overwrite Events As Needed, Overwrite Events Older Than *x* Days, or Do Not Overwrite Events. (Event Log is also covered as part of day-to-day administration in Chapter 10.)

The Components of an Event

The two key components in the interpretation of an event are the event header and the event description. The event description is the most useful piece of information because it indicates the significance of the event.

The Event Header

Event headers are displayed in columns in the Event Viewer console (Figure 32-2) and are broken down into the following components:

- **Type**   Lists the severity of the event. Events in the application and system logs are classified as Information, Warning, or Error. Events in the security log are classified as Success Audit or Failure Audit. Event Viewer represents these classifications as symbols in its normal list view. These symbols include the following:

  - **Information**   Describes the successful operation of a service, driver, or application. For example, when the Event Log service is started successfully, it is recorded as an Information event.

  - **Warning**   Indicates events that (although not necessarily significant) pose a possible future problem. For example, when the hard disk is at or near capacity, you will be advised to delete some files.

  - **Error**   Indicates that a significant problem has occurred, such as loss of functionality or loss of data. For example, if a service such as Net Logon fails to load, it is logged in Event Viewer as an error.

  - **Failure Audit**   Lists a failed attempt to perform an audited security event. For example, if a user tries to log on and fails, that attempt will be logged as a Failure Audit event.

  - **Success Audit**   Lists a successful attempt to perform an audited security event. For example, when a user logs on successfully, it will be logged as a Success Audit event.

- **Date**   Indicates the date the event occurred.
- **Time**   Indicates the (local) time the event occurred.
- **Source**   Lists the software that logged the event. The software can be either a program name, a component of the system, or a component of a large program, such as a driver name.
- **Category**   Shows the way the event source classifies the event; primarily used in the security log. Security audits are one of the event types that are classified here.

- **Event** Lists a number that identifies the particular event type. The name of the event type is usually contained in the first line of its associated description.

- **User** Indicates the user name of the user for whom the event occurred. If the event was caused by a server process, the user name is the client ID. If impersonation is not taking place, the primary ID is displayed here. Impersonation occurs when one process is permitted to take on the security attributes of another process. The security log entry lists both the primary and the impersonation IDs when applicable.

- **Computer** Specifies the name of the computer on which the event took place.

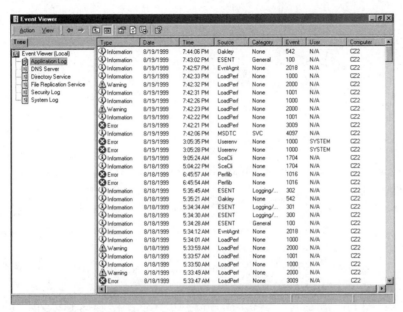

Figure 32-2. *Event headers in the Event Viewer console.*

The Event Description

Double-clicking a specific event in Event Viewer displays a text description in the Event Detail tab of the Properties window (Figure 32-3) that is often helpful in the analysis of the event. Binary data is also generated for some events and can be helpful in interpreting those events because it is generated by the program that originated the event records. If you retain event descriptions, save them as binary data files. Don't save event descriptions in text format or comma-delimited text format, because these formats both discard binary data.

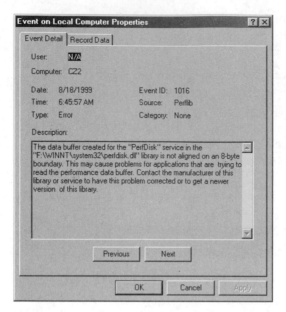

Figure 32-3. *The Event Properties window.*

Archiving an Event Log

You can save an event log to a file by right-clicking the log name in Event Viewer and choosing Save Log File As. You can archive event logs in one of the following three formats:

- **Log format** Allows you to view the log in Event Viewer. Its extension is .EVT.

- **Text format** Lets you use the detail contained in this file in a program such as Microsoft Word. Its extension is .TXT.

- **Comma-delimited text format** Enables you to use the data in a spreadsheet or flat-file database. Its extension is .CSV.

Archived logs save the event description in the following order: date, time, source, type, category, event, user, computer, description. The entire log file is saved, regardless of any filtering options you may have set. The information is saved sequentially, even if you have established a sort order for the events.

You can open an archived log file from the Action menu by pointing to New and then choosing Log View. In the Add Another Log View dialog box, select Saved (Opens A Previously Saved Log), and click the Browse button to search for the log name in the Open dialog box. You can open only an archived log file with the .EVT filename extension in Event Viewer. (Archived log files with the .TXT and .CSV extensions can be opened in any word processing program.) The information displayed in an archived log cannot be updated by refreshing.

Viewing an Event Log on Another Computer

You can connect to another computer to view its event log by right-clicking Event Viewer (Local) at the top of the tree and choosing Connect To Another Computer. In the Select Computer dialog box (Figure 32-4), you can browse for or enter the name of the other computer whose event log you want to view.

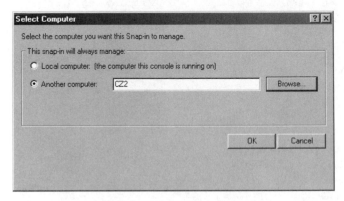

Figure 32-4. *The Select Computer dialog box.*

Event Viewer enables you to view machines running Microsoft Windows NT Workstation or Windows 2000 Professional, a server or domain controller running Windows NT Server or Windows 2000 Server, or a server running LAN Manager 2.x. You can configure a low-speed connection for the remote machine you want to view. To do this, select the log you want to view from the console tree, choose Properties from the Action menu, and then select the Low Speed Connection option.

Using System Monitor

System Monitor is a utility designed to track various processes on a Windows 2000 system in real time, using a graphical display. You can use the data from System Monitor to target processes and components that need to be optimized, monitor the results of tuning and configuration efforts, understand and observe trends in workloads and their effect on resource usage, and assist with tasks such as planning for upgrades. System Monitor takes the form of an MMC snap-in. It is named Perfmon.msc and can be found in the %SystemRoot%\system32\ folder.

Running System Monitor

When you launch System Monitor from the Administrative Tools folder on the Programs menu, you see the main console (Figure 32-5). The console tree in the left pane lists the MMC snap-ins associated with System Monitor, and the details pane is reserved for the graphic view where the counters you want to monitor will be charted.

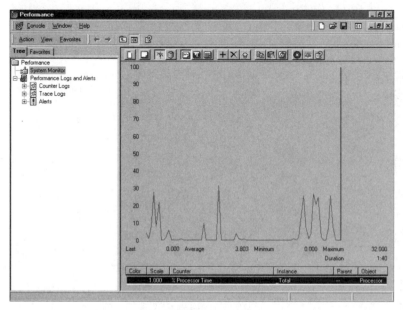

Figure 32-5. *The System Monitor console.*

System Monitor uses three types of items to monitor the system: objects, counters, and instances:

- **Object**   A collection of counters associated with a resource or service that generates data that you can evaluate. Each time an object performs a function, its corresponding counters are updated. A range of objects typically corresponding to major hardware components is built into the operating system. Other components and their corresponding objects are added by programs installed on the machine. The following are the objects you'll use most frequently:

  - **Browser**   Monitors the Browser service for a domain or workgroup.

- **Cache**   Monitors disk cache usage.
- **Memory**   Monitors memory performance for physical and virtual memory.
- **Objects**   Monitors the number of events, mutexes, processes, sections, semaphores, and threads on the computer at the time of data collection.
- **Paging File**   Monitors pagefile usage.
- **Physical Disk**   Monitors hard disks with one or more partitions.
- **Process**   Monitors all processes running on a machine.
- **Processor**   Monitors each processor on the system.
- **Server**   Monitors bytes, sessions, certain system errors, pool nonpaged usage, and pool paged usage.
- **System**   Monitors the counters that affect all of the hardware and software running on the system.
- **Thread**   Monitors all threads running in the system.

- **Counter**   A component within an object that represents data for a specific aspect of the system or service.
- **Instance**   A single occurrence of multiple performance objects of the same type on a machine. If a particular object has multiple instances, you can track the statistics for each instance by adding a counter for each. You can also add a counter to track all instances at once. An instantaneous counter, such as Process\ Thread Count, is an example of an instance. It displays the most recent count of the number of threads for a particular process. An instance can also be an average of the last two values for a process over a period of time between samples.

Adding Counters

By default, System Monitor displays the system's current processor utilization as a line graph. You can add counters by clicking the Add Counters button to display the Add Counters dialog box (Figure 32-6) or by clicking the Data tab in the Properties window. System Monitor will compress the data as necessary to fit the details pane, and you can display dozens of counters at a time, more than you can comfortably view on a single screen.

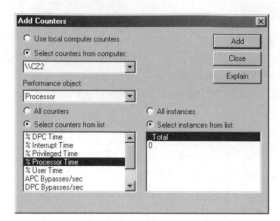

Figure 32-6. *The Add Counters dialog box.*

Selecting Counters

In the Add Counters dialog box, you can select either the Use Local Computer Counters option or the Select Counters From Computer option. If you're monitoring the computer on which the System Monitor is running, you'll want to select Use Local Computer Counters. If you want to monitor a different computer, select the Select Counters From Computer option, and then choose the name of the computer to be monitored from the list box.

In the Performance Object list box, specify an object to monitor. The Processor object is selected by default. For each object, you can choose to monitor all of the available counters or only ones that you specify. To monitor all of the available counters for a particular object, select the All Counters option. To monitor only counters that you specify, select the Select Counters From List option. When you choose to select specific counters, you can obtain a description of any counter by clicking the name of the counter and then clicking the Explain button.

If you select a counter that has multiple instances, choose All Instances to monitor all instances of the selected counter, or choose Select Instances From List to specify the instances you want to monitor. If you monitor multiple instances of the same counter, you should be aware that the instance index number assigned to a particular instance might change over time. This possible change is a result of the instance starting and stopping and in the process being assigned a different instance index number.

Matching Counters to Graph Lines

You can determine which counter matches a line on the graph in two ways. First, a color and bar thickness is assigned to each counter within the legend. If you aren't monitoring many counters, you can easily match the color to the counter. Second, when you double-click a line in the graph, the corresponding counter is selected in the legend located under the graph. If chart lines are close together, try to locate a position in the graph where they diverge; otherwise, System Monitor will have difficulty pinpointing the actual line you're interested in.

Note   You can also highlight a chart line by clicking the counter you want to highlight and then pressing Ctrl+H.

Deleting Counters

When you want to stop monitoring one or more counters, you have two options: you can delete only specific counters or you can delete all counters. To stop monitoring specific counters, open System Monitor, click the name of a counter in the legend on the System Monitor details pane, and click the Delete button on the toolbar. To delete all of the counters currently being monitored, click the New Counter Set button on the toolbar. You would do this if you wanted to start monitoring a new set of counters.

Modifying the Display

You can change the way in which System Monitor displays information by using the System Monitor Properties window (Figure 32-7). To access this window, either click the Properties button on the toolbar or right-click in the details pane and choose Properties from the shortcut menu. On the General tab, you can choose whether to view the data in the form of a graph, a histogram, or a report. (The sections that follow give details on each of these views.) Depending on how you choose to view the data, these options in the Display Elements area may also be available:

- **Legend**   Displays a legend at the bottom of the details pane that shows the data scale used for each counter, the counter name, the instance, the parent object (if applicable), the object the counter belongs to, the computer being monitored, and the color used to draw the line for the

Figure 32-7. *The System Monitor Properties window.*

counter. The legend is available for the graph and histogram views. You need to display the legend in order to see the counter name associated with the data line.

- **Value Bar** Displays a value bar at the bottom of the details pane that provides a way to highlight the values for a specific counter. Clicking a particular value in the legend or clicking directly on a data line will display statistics for the last, average, minimum, and maximum values recorded. The duration time is also displayed here. The values are calculated from the number of samples and time period displayed in the graph. The time period is reflected by the duration value rather than actual time elapsed since monitoring was started. The duration value is based upon the update interval time and is calculated to show the total elapsed time displayed in the graph. This display element is available for the graph and histogram views and is helpful for monitoring a specific value that you want to keep a close watch on.

- **Toolbar** Displays the toolbar functions across the top of the details pane. It's advisable to have this option turned on because it's the only way you can perform certain functions.

Graph View

Graph view presents information in a traditional line graph format. Each of the counters and instances are displayed in a different color and line thickness, as shown in Figure 32-8. This view is the default, and it offers the greatest variety of options. For instance, you can highlight a particular counter by either clicking the counter name in the legend or double-clicking the data line in the graph and then clicking the Highlight button on the toolbar. A black line replaces the colored data line if the background color of the chart is white or a light color; for all other background colors, the line is white. If you would like to highlight another line instead, simply double-click the line. As long as the Highlight button is depressed, any line you click will be highlighted on the screen.

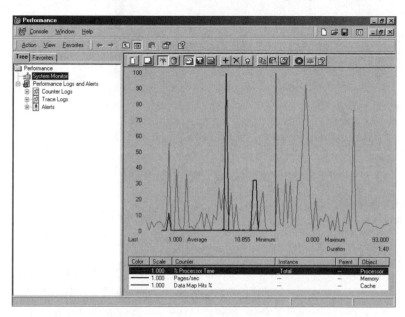

Figure 32-8. *Displaying system information in graph view.*

Although graph view is the most versatile, you are better off using histogram view or report view for tracking a large number of counters because the chart lines become increasingly difficult to view when a large number of counters are being monitored.

Histogram View

Histogram view presents information in a bar graph format, as shown in Figure 32-9. As in graph view, each of the counters and instances are presented in different colors. You can easily track up to 100 counters using this view because System Monitor adjusts the bars to fit the display.

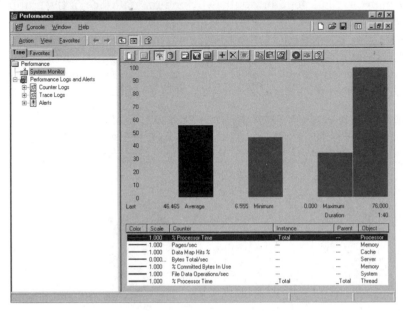

Figure 32-9. *Displaying system information in histogram view.*

Report View

Report view presents the counter data in a report list format, as shown in Figure 32-10. Objects are listed in alphabetical order, as are each of the chosen counters for each object. The data itself is displayed numerically. Each object displays the total percentage of processor time in use for the chosen counters. This view is best if you need to track a large number of counters.

Choosing the Monitoring Time Interval

You can sample data for all three views at a regular periodic interval. To set this option, open the System Monitor Properties window (by clicking the Properties button on the toolbar) and, on the General tab, select the Update Automatically Every *n* Seconds box. The default interval is 1 second, but you might want to change this value to prevent a strain on your machine. Select the update interval that is best for capturing the type of activity you want to view.

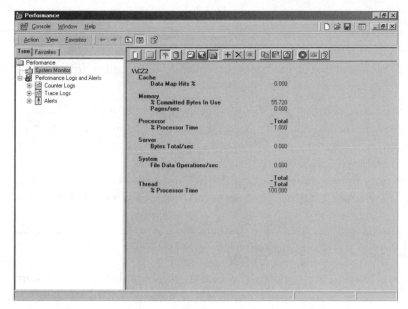

Figure 32-10.   *Viewing system information in report view.*

Selecting Additional Properties

You can add vertical and horizontal grid lines to the graph and histogram views by clicking their respective boxes on the Graph tab of the System Monitor Properties window. These elements are very helpful in quickly determining a counter's associated value.

You can also change the maximum and minimum vertical scale values on the Graph tab; the defaults are 100 for the maximum value and 0 for the minimum value. The highest value that you can specify is 999999999, and the lowest value is 0. Both of these values must be a positive integer. You will need to determine the vertical scale range from the ranges of values for the counters you are monitoring.

You may need to adjust the counter scale settings for a specific counter to improve the visibility of its data within the graph. Counter scale settings for individual counters are adjusted on the Data tab of the System Monitor Properties window. Counter scale values can range exponentially from 0.0000001 to 1000000.0. Adjusting the scale does not affect the statistics displayed in the value bar.

Monitoring a Different Computer

By default, System Monitor displays information about the local system, but you can also configure it to monitor another computer on the network. It is also possible for you to monitor more than one computer at once in System Monitor. To do so, click the Add Counters button, select the Select Counters From Computer option, and then type the name of the computer to be monitored in the text box. You can choose and delete counters and modify the display in the same manner described in the previous sections.

You need administrative permissions on the other computer in order to monitor that computer through System Monitor. If you don't have administrative permissions, an error message is generated. The counter will appear in the display, but no data or graph lines will be associated with it. If a particular counter that you want to monitor does not appear in the counter list, it is likely that the service or feature providing the counter has not been installed or enabled on that computer.

Performance Logs and Alerts

Performance Logs and Alerts expands the monitoring capabilities of System Monitor to include features for logging counter and trace data and for generating performance alerts. Using the capabilities of Performance Logs and Alerts has a number of advantages. Logged counter data information can be exported to spreadsheets or databases for analysis and report generation. The data can be stored in three formats: comma-separated format, tab-separated format, or in a binary log-file format that can be used for logging instances that may have started after the log had already begun collecting data or for circular logging. In circular logging, new data is continuously logged into a single file, with the new data overwriting the old data.

Performance logging runs as a service. As a result, a user doesn't have to be logged on to the monitored computer for data collection to occur. You can manage multiple logging sessions from a single console window and view data as it is collected as well as after collection has stopped. Automatic log generation enables you to define parameters such as filename, file size, and start and stop time. An alert can be set on a counter to cause a specific action to occur, such as starting a specified program, sending a notification message, or starting a log when the value of a selected counter falls below or exceeds a specified setting.

Counter Logs

A counter log collects data at a predefined interval. Counter logs are helpful for recording data about system services activities and hardware usage from the local machine or a remote machine. You can log data manually on demand or schedule logging to start and stop automatically. The system can also perform continuous logging, depending on the file size and duration limits you set. The logged data can be viewed through the System Monitor display or exported to spreadsheets or databases.

You can view the counters configured in the counter log dynamically through System Monitor by saving log settings such as counters as an HTML page. The resulting page hosts the System Monitor control through an ActiveX control that provides the interface for the monitoring user.

Trace Logs

Rather than measure samples at a predefined interval, as counter logs do, a trace log monitors data continuously and waits for specific events, such as page faults, to occur. That data is then recorded into a trace log file. To interpret the trace log output, you need a parsing tool.

Note   A parsing tool is software that reads the raw data and puts it into a form you can understand. Developers can create parsing tools by using the APIs provided at Microsoft's MSDN Online Library site at *http://msdn.microsoft.com/ library/default.htm.*

Creating Counter and Trace Logs

To create a counter log or a trace log, perform the following steps:

1. Open System Monitor, and double-click Performance Logs And Alerts.

2. Choose Counter Logs to create a counter log, or choose Trace Logs to create a trace log.

3. Right-click in a blank area of the details pane and choose New Log Settings. In the Name text box, enter the name of the counter or trace log you are creating and click OK. A Properties window for configuring the counter or trace log you are creating is displayed.

4. Configure the counter or trace log to monitor your local or remote machine by choosing the proper counters for the resources to be monitored, selecting log file properties, and choosing the desired scheduling options. Any logs that already exist will be listed in the details pane. A red icon indicates a log that is not running or that has been stopped; a green icon indicates a log that is running.

The sample data interval for counter logs is set on the General tab of the Properties window for the log. For guidelines on setting time intervals, see "Determining How Often to Monitor" later in this chapter.

Adding Counters to Counter Logs

Counters are added on the General tab of a log's Properties window (Figure 32-11). When you create a counter log file, the Properties window is displayed automatically. If you need to add counters later, you can display the Properties window by right-clicking the name of the log file, choosing Properties from the shortcut menu, clicking the Add button on the General tab, and then choosing the desired counters. The procedure for selecting counters is identical to that described earlier in the section "Selecting Counters."

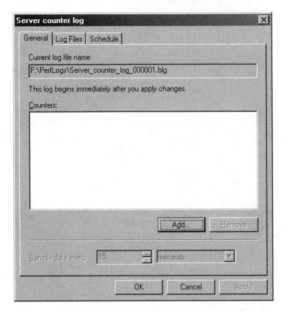

Figure 32-11. *The General tab of a log's Properties window.*

Saving Log and Alert File Settings

To save the settings for a log or an alert file, right-click the name of the log or alert file in the details pane, and then choose Save Settings As from the shortcut menu. Enter the name you want to give to the log or alert file, and save it as an .HTM file. You can use the saved settings for a new log or alert by right-clicking in the details pane, choosing New Log Settings From, and then selecting the .HTM file containing the settings you want to reuse.

Selecting System and Nonsystem Providers for Trace Logs

Events in trace logs are monitored not by counters but by providers. You can choose to log events by system or nonsystem providers. The default system provider, the Windows Kernel Trace Provider, monitors threads, processes, disk input/output, network TCP/IP, page faults, and file details. The system provider uses the most overhead to monitor events. Only one trace log at a time can be run using the system provider. If you attempt to run more than one, you will receive an error message.

System and nonsystem providers are chosen on the General tab of the log's Properties window (Figure 32-12). To see this window, right-click the name of the trace log file and choose Properties from the shortcut menu. On the General tab, either select the Events Logged By System Provider option and then choose the events you want to monitor, or select the Nonsystem Providers option and then add the nonsystem providers of your choice by clicking the Add button.

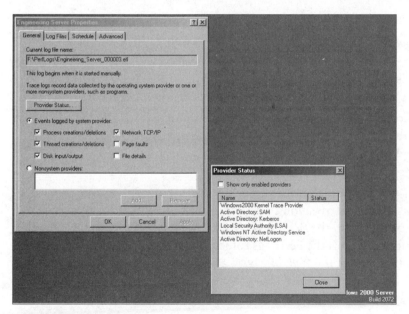

Figure 32-12. *Specifying events logged by the system provider.*

It is important to remember that trace logging of page fault and file details generates a huge amount of data. Microsoft recommends that you limit trace logging using these fault options to a maximum of two hours; otherwise you may run out of disk space on your machine.

Choosing nonsystem providers to monitor the system incurs less overhead. With nonsystem providers, you can select the data providers of your choice. You cannot run concurrent multiple trace logs using the same nonsystem provider, but you can do so using different nonsystem providers. The nonsystem providers available in Windows 2000 are Active Directory: Kerberos, Active Directory: Net Logon, Active Directory: SAM, Local System Authority (LSA), and Windows NT Active Directory Service.

Setting File Parameters for Counter and Trace Logs

To set file parameters for counter and trace logs, follow these steps:

1. Double-click Performance Logs And Alerts in System Monitor.
2. Click Counter Logs to set file parameters for counter logs, or click Trace Logs to set file parameters for trace logs.
3. Double-click the name of the log for which you want to set the file parameters. A window displaying the properties of the log appears.
4. Click the Log Files tab, and set the desired parameters for the log file. (The available parameters are described in the next section.)

Understanding the Log File Parameters

The Log Files tab of the Properties window for a counter or trace log (Figures 32-13 and 32-14) allows you to set a number of file parameters. You can specify a folder other than the default chosen by Windows 2000 in the Location box. The default location is the PerfLogs folder at the root directory. You are also given the option of ending the filename with a set of sequential numbers or a date to keep track of multiple log files. This is helpful for log files that are automatically generated with the same filename.

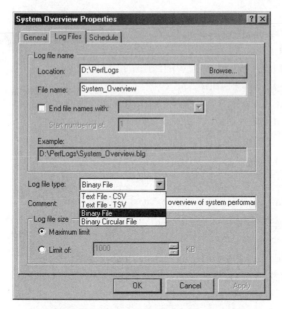

Figure 32-13. *The Log Files tab of a counter log's Properties window.*

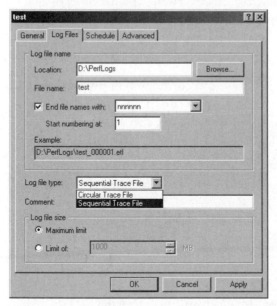

Figure 32-14. *The Log Files tab of a trace log's Properties window.*

A file size option is available with which you can either allow the log file to become as large as disk quotas or the operating system will permit or limit the size to a specific number of kilobytes. Limit the size of a log file if you want to use one of the circular logging options. In conjunction with limiting the size of a log file, you can use the When The Log File Is Full option on the Schedule tab to run a command if you want a particular action to occur when the log file reaches its limit. You can choose from among four file types for a counter log:

- **Text File - CSV** This format is used to export data to a spreadsheet program. The data is stored as a comma-delimited log file that uses the file extension .CSV.

- **Text File - TSV** This format can also be used to export data to a spreadsheet program. The data is stored as a tab-delimited log file that uses the file extension .TSV.

- **Binary File** This format is used for intermittent instances (instances that stop and start after the log has been started). The data is stored as a sequential, binary-format log file that uses the file extension .BLG.

- **Binary Circular File** This format is used to record data continuously to the same log file, where the new records overwrite the previous ones. The data is stored in binary format as a circular file that uses the file extension .BLG.

Trace logs can be either of two file types:

- **Circular Trace File** This format is used to record data continuously to the same log file, where the new records overwrite the previous ones. The data is stored in a circular file that uses the file extension .ETL.

- **Sequential Trace File** This format is used to collect data until a user-defined limit is reached. Once the limit is reached, the current file is closed and a new one is started. The data is stored as a sequential file that uses the file extension .ETL.

The default file type for counter logs is Binary File (with the extension .BLG), and the default file type for trace logs is Sequential Trace File (with the extension .ETL).

Using Alerts

An alert notification is sent to the user by means of the Messenger service when a predefined counter value reaches, falls below, or rises above a defined threshold. The Messenger service must be running for alert notifications to be sent to the user.

Creating an Alert

To create an alert, follow these steps:

1. Open System Monitor, and double-click Performance Logs And Alerts.

2. Click Alerts.

3. Right-click in a blank area of the details pane, and choose New Alert Settings. In the Name text box, enter the name of the alert you are creating, and click the OK button. A Properties window for configuring the alert you are creating appears (Figure 32-15).

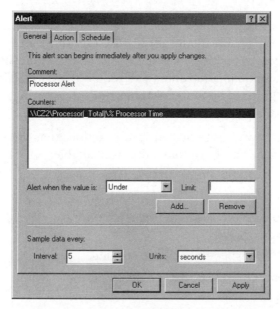

Figure 32-15. *The Properties window for an alert.*

4. Configure the alert by specifying whether to monitor the local machine or a remote machine, choosing one or more counters, setting threshold values for the counters, selecting an action to perform when an alert is triggered, and choosing the desired scheduling options. These settings are described in the next section. Any alerts that already exist will be listed in the details pane. A red icon indicates an alert that is not running or has been stopped; a green icon indicates an alert that is running.

Configuring an Alert

For information on specifying a computer to monitor and on selecting counters for the alert, see the section "Selecting Counters" earlier in this chapter.

You must choose threshold values for each counter on which you set an alert. This is done on the General tab of the Properties window for the alert. When you create an alert, the Properties window is displayed automatically. If you need to add counters at a later date, you can access the Properties window by right-clicking the name of the alert file, choosing Properties from the shortcut menu, and clicking the Add button on the General tab.

You set thresholds to trigger an alert when the value of the counter falls either above or below a certain baseline for your organization. To establish a baseline, you must determine the level of system performance that is acceptable when your system is experiencing a typical workload and running all required services. You do this by reviewing logged data graphed by System Monitor or by exporting the data and generating reports for analysis.

On the Action tab of the Properties window, you can specify actions that should occur when a threshold is exceeded. You have four options available:

- **Log An Entry In The Application Event Log**   Causes the alert to log an entry that is visible to you in Event Viewer.
- **Send A Network Message To**   Triggers the Messenger service to send an alert message to a specified computer.
- **Start Performance Data Log**   Runs an existing counter log.
- **Run This Program**   Specifies a command file and command-line arguments to run when an alert occurs.

Permissions for Counter Logs, Trace Logs, and Alerts

To create or modify a log or alert, you must have Full Control permission for the registry entry KEY_LOCAL_MACHINE\SYSTEM\CurrentControlSet\Services\SysmonLog\LogQueries. Administrators are usually assigned this permission by default, and they can grant this permission to users in Regedt32.exe through the Security menu.

To run the Performance Logs and Alerts service, you must have permissions to configure or start services on the system. Administrators are usually assigned this permission by default, and they can grant this permission to users in the Group Policy snap-in. Furthermore, to log data for a remote computer, the Performance Logs and Alerts service is required to run under an account that has access to that remote system. The service runs in the background once a log or alert is configured and running.

Real World   **Tuning and Testing Strategies**

Before starting System Monitor or Performance Logs and Alerts on the computer you are monitoring, do the following:

- Increase the paging file to the physical memory size plus 100 MB.
- Turn off any screen-saver programs.
- Shut down services that are not relevant or essential to monitoring the system.

Keep the following best practices in mind when preparing to tune your system:

- Set up Performance Logs and Alerts to monitor and report data on counters at a regular interval, such as every 10 to 15 minutes. It's a good practice to retain your logs for an extended period of time. You can store the data in a database and use it for trend analysis, performance assessment, and capacity planning.

- Make only one change at a time. Bottlenecks can be the fault of several components. Don't confuse the issue by making too many changes at once because that can make it impossible to assess the impact each change has on the system.

- Keep a record of each change you make, and repeat the monitoring process after every change. This practice is important because tuning changes can affect other resources and such records will help you to determine the effect of each change and whether additional changes are necessary.

- Do a comparison of programs that run over the network against those that run locally. This will tell you whether network components might be playing a part in performance problems.

- Pay attention to event logs; certain performance problems generate output that you can view in Event Viewer.

- Under certain conditions, the performance tools will increase overhead. If you find that this is a problem, you can reduce it as follows:
  - Be selective in the objects and counters you monitor. The more you choose, the higher the overhead.
  - Don't run System Monitor in graph view. This view incurs the highest overhead.

- Specify sampling intervals of 3 seconds or more; anything less than 3 seconds is too frequent.

- Run Performance Logs and Alerts instead of using a System Monitor graph.

- Reduce the amount of disk space used by log files by extending the update interval and logging to a disk other than the one being monitored. Frequent logging places a greater demand on disk input and output.

- When logging data through Performance Logs and Alerts, you should exclude times that include start-up events. Start-up events tend to skew overall performance results because they show temporarily high values.

- When you save the performance tools settings to a file after you have completed the configuration, save the file under a name other than Perfmon.msc. Otherwise, you are permanently changing the configuration of the performance tools on the computer.

Selecting a Monitoring Method

If you need to observe a system event as it's happening, use a graph in System Monitor. Graphs are helpful for real-time short-term monitoring of a remote or local computer. Choose an update interval that best captures the data for the type of activity you are observing. Performance logs are better suited for long-term monitoring and record keeping. You can export logged data and use it to generate reports, and you can also view the information as graphs or histograms using System Monitor. Logging in this manner is also more practical when you need to monitor several computers at once.

Determining How Often to Monitor

For routine logging of data logs, start out by setting the value in the Sample Data Every box to every 15 minutes. To find this option, display the Properties window of the specific counter log. You can adjust this interval to fit the type of data you are monitoring. If you have a slow memory leak, for example, you will want to use a longer time interval. Another consideration is the overall length of time that you monitor a system. If you are monitoring for less than 4 hours, a 15-minute interval is acceptable. If you are monitoring a system for 8 hours or more, don't set a time interval that is shorter than 5 minutes (300 seconds). Monitoring at a frequent rate will cause the system to generate a lot of data, producing large log files. It will also increase the overhead tremendously.

Monitoring Memory Usage

If you are experiencing performance problems, the first step in examining the problem is usually to monitor memory usage because memory usage is the most important factor in system performance. If you find that your system is paging frequently, you may have a memory shortage on your machine. Some paging is good because it helps to expand memory somewhat, but too much paging is a drain on system performance.

> **Note** Paging is used to free memory for other uses by moving fixed-size blocks of data and code from RAM to your disk in units called pages.

Before you start to monitor memory usage, you should perform a few checks. For example, verify that your system has the recommended amount of memory for running the operating system as well as other applications and services. If you don't know what the memory requirements are for a process, you can discover its working set within System Monitor, shut the process down, and observe the effect on paging activity. The amount of memory that is freed when you terminate a process is the amount of memory the process was using.

> **Note** A *working* set is the portion of physical memory allocated to each program running on the computer.

Excessive paging can result when Windows 2000 Setup configures your system with settings that optimize file sharing. In some cases, this can increase paging significantly because it causes the system to maintain a large system-cache working set. If you are not using the server for file sharing, you can reduce the amount of paging on your server by turning off the file-sharing settings. To do so, follow these steps:

1. On the Start menu, point to Settings and then choose Network And Dial-Up Connections.

2. Right-click Local Area Connection and choose Properties from the shortcut menu.

3. In the Components Checked Are Used By This Connection box, highlight File And Printer Sharing For Microsoft Networks and click the Properties button.

4. In the Server Optimization area, the Maximize Data Throughput For File Sharing option is selected by default. Select Maximize Data Throughput For Network Applications instead (Figure 32-16). This action will reduce paging activity on your system.

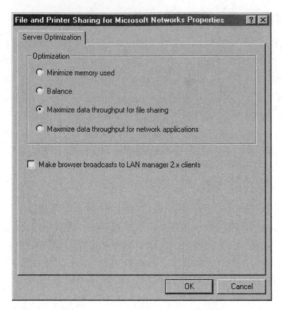

Figure 32-16. *The File And Printer Sharing For Microsoft Networks Properties window.*

Recommended Counters

Monitor memory counters for a low-memory condition. This section lists the minimum recommended counters for monitoring the server's memory component. To check for possible memory leaks or bottlenecks, monitor these counters:

- **Memory\ Pages/Sec**   Displays the number of pages written to or read from disk in order to resolve hard page faults. A *hard page fault* occurs when a process requires code or data that must be retrieved from disk rather than from its working set or elsewhere in physical memory. If this value is above 20, you need to research paging activity and make adjustments as necessary. A high value for this counter may be more indicative of a paging problem than a memory problem.

- **Memory\ Committed Bytes**   Displays the amount of committed bytes of virtual memory on your system and is an instantaneous counter. Monitor this counter, along with Memory\ Available Bytes, over a period of time if you suspect a memory leak.

- **Memory\ Pool Nonpaged Bytes**   Displays the number of bytes allocated to the nonpaged pool for objects that cannot be written to disk but must instead remain in physical memory as long as they are allocated. If this value is high, you will need additional memory on your system. Use this counter in conjunction with Memory\ Pool Nonpaged Allocs if you suspect that a kernel-mode process is the cause of a memory leak.

- **Memory\ Pool Nonpaged Allocs** Shows the number of calls to allocated space in the nonpaged pool. Use this counter in conjunction with Memory\ Pool Nonpaged Bytes to determine whether you have a memory leak.

- **Server\ Bytes Total/Sec** Monitors the number of bytes the machine has received from and sent to the network. The value is indicative of how busy the server is. You will need to add memory if you have a sustained, dramatic increase in this value.

- **Server\ Pool Paged Bytes** Monitors the number of bytes of pageable computer memory currently in use by the system. You can use this information to determine values for the MaxPagedMemoryUsage entry in the Windows 2000 registry.

- **Server\ Pool Nonpaged Bytes** Monitors the number of bytes of nonpageable computer memory in use by the system. You can use this information to determine the values for the MaxNonpagedMemory-Usage entry in the Windows 2000 registry.

To monitor for a low memory condition, use these counters:

- **Memory\ Available Bytes** Windows 2000 uses free bytes to satisfy the memory requirements of programs. When free byes fall into short supply, the shortage is replenished by taking memory from the working sets of less active programs. Subsequently, you will notice an increase in the working set value for one program and a steady decrease in the values of other programs. The result is an increase in paging that causes performance to suffer. To resolve this problem, you will need to add memory to the machine.

- **Memory\ Cache Bytes** Monitors the number of bytes being used by the file system cache. Use this counter in conjunction with Memory\ Available Bytes. If the value for Memory\ Cache Bytes rises above 4 MB, you may need to add more memory to the machine.

- **Physical Disk\ % Disk Time and Physical Disk\ Avg. Disk Queue Length** These counters can indicate a memory shortage when used in conjunction with Memory\ Page Read/Sec. If an increase in queue length is not accompanied by a decrease in the Memory\ Page Read/Sec value, a shortage does exist.

To check for excessive paging, monitor these counters:

- **Paging File\ % Usage (all instances)** Paging files are shared by every process and are used to store pages of memory on your system. If you suspect that paging is to blame for your bottleneck, it is helpful to review this value, along with Memory\ Available Bytes and Memory\ Pages/Sec. The acceptable threshold for this value is 99 percent. Enlarge Pagefile.sys if the value increases to 100 percent.

- **Paging File\ % Usage Peak** If the value for this counter approaches the maximum paging file setting, the size of Pagefile.sys needs to be increased.

- **Physical Disk\ Avg. Disk Sec/Transfer and Memory\ Pages/Sec** The Physical Disk\Avg. Disk Sec/Transfer counter displays the average disk transfer in seconds. The Memory\ Pages/Sec counter displays the number of pages written to or read from the disk when a process requires information that is no longer in its working set and must be retrieved from disk. To help determine whether your system is paging excessively, multiply the values of these two counters. If the result exceeds 0.1, paging is taking up more than 10 percent of disk access time. If this condition persists over a long period of time, you will need additional memory.

Tuning and Upgrading Tips for the Memory Component

If you are experiencing problems with memory, check the following possibilities:

- **Paging file** Make sure that the paging file is the correct size, and create multiple paging files to reduce excessive paging. You can also split the paging file between multiple disks of similar speeds to increase access time.

Caution When the paging file reaches the maximum limit assigned to it, a warning is displayed and your system may halt.

- **Physical memory** Increase the physical memory above the minimum that is required.

- **Memory settings** Verify that memory settings are configured properly.

- **Memory-intensive programs** Run programs that are memory hogs when your system workload is lightest or on your highest-performing computers.

Monitoring Processor Activity

When monitoring processor usage, you need to consider the role of the computer and the work being done on it. High processor values could mean either that your machine is handling the workload in a very efficient manner or that it is struggling to keep up.

When a bottleneck occurs because a process's threads need more processor cycles than are available, long processor queues build up, causing the system response to suffer. The two common causes of processor bottleneck are an excess demand placed on the processor by CPU-bound programs, and excess interrupts generated by drivers or subsystem components, such as disk or network components.

Minimum Recommended Counters

The following list shows the minimum recommended counters you should use to monitor the server's processor component for possible bottlenecks:

- **System\ Processor Queue Length (all instances)**   Two or more items in the queue indicate a bottleneck. Because this is an instantaneous counter, the only way to get an accurate analysis is to observe this value over several intervals.

- **Server Work Queues\ Queue Length**   A queue length of greater than four over a sustained period of time indicates possible processor congestion.

- **Processor\ Interrupts/Sec**   You can use this counter to determine whether interrupt activity is causing a bottleneck. If you find a dramatic increase in this counter value without a corresponding increase in system activity, a hardware problem is likely. To resolve this problem, you need to find the network adapter or other device that is causing the interrupts. Refer to the manufacturer's specifications for the acceptable processor threshold.

- **Processor\ % Interrupt Time**   This counter displays the percentage of time the processor spends receiving and servicing hardware interrupts during the sample interval. This value gives you an indirect indication of the activities of devices that generate interrupts, such as disk drives, network adapters, and other peripheral devices. These devices interrupt the processor when they require attention or complete a task. Look for a dramatic increase in the value without a corresponding increase in system activity.

To monitor possible usage problems, use these counters:

- **Processor\ % Processor Time (all instances)**   Use this counter to discover a process that is using more than 85 percent of processor time. You may need to install an additional processor or upgrade to a faster one.

- **Processor\ % User Time**   Monitors the percentage of nonidle processor time that is spent in user mode. A high rate may indicate a need to upgrade or install additional processors. Use this counter in conjunction with Processor\ % Processor Time (all instances).

- **Processor\ % Privileged Time**   Monitors the percentage of nonidle processor time designated for hardware-manipulating drivers and operating system components. A high rate might be attributed to a large number of interrupts being generated by a device that is failing. Use this counter in conjunction with Process\ % Processor Time (all instances).

Tuning and Upgrading Tips for the Processor Component

You can try the following solutions to resolve problems you are experiencing with the processor:

- **Upgrade the processor**   Upgrade to a faster processor, replace a failing one, or add another processor to the machine, especially if you are running multithreaded programs.

- **Adjust the workload of the system**   Distribute programs more efficiently among servers, or schedule programs to run at off-peak hours.

- **Manage processor affinity on multiprocessor computers**   Managing the processor affinity with respect to interrupts and process threads can improve performance because it reduces the number of processor cache flushes during thread movement from one processor to another.

Note   You set affinity for a particular process or program when you assign it to a single processor in order to improve its performance, at the expense of the other processors. Be forewarned that when you dedicate a process or program to a processor, your other program threads may not be permitted to migrate to the least-busy processor. You can set affinity in Task Manager, and it is available only on multiprocessor systems.

Monitoring Disk Activity

Monitoring disk usage helps you to balance the load of your network servers. When you are monitoring disk performance, log the performance data to another disk or computer to prevent it from skewing the data for the disk you are testing.

> **Note**   The operating system collects the Physical Disk counter data by using the Diskperf -yd command by default. This is not true of the Logical Disk counter data, however. In order to obtain performance counter data for logical drives, you must type *Diskperf -yv* at the command prompt. This command causes the driver used for collecting disk performance data to report data for logical drives. To obtain further information about the Diskperf command, type *diskperf -?* at a command prompt.

Minimum Recommended Counters

The following list shows the minimum recommended counters you should use to monitor the server's disk performance for possible bottlenecks:

- **Physical Disk\ Current Disk Queue Length (all instances)**   Monitors the number of system requests that are waiting for disk access. This number should remain steady at no more than 1.5 to 2 times the number of spindles that make up the physical disk. Most disks have one spindle. The exception is redundant array of independent disks (RAID) devices, which usually have more than one spindle. You will need to observe this value over several intervals because it is an instantaneous counter.

- **Physical Disk\ % Disk Time**   Indicates how busy your server's disk drives are by displaying the percentage of time that a drive is active. If the value of this counter rises to more than 90 percent or if you are using a RAID device, check the Physical Disk\ Current Disk Queue Length counter to see how many disk requests are queued for disk access. RAID devices can cause the Physical Disk\ % Disk Time value to exceed 100 percent and thus give an incorrect reading.

- **Physical Disk\ Avg. Disk Sec\Transfer**   Monitors the amount of time a disk takes to fulfill a request. A high value may indicate that the disk controller is continually trying to access the disk as a result of failures. For most systems, a value of 0.3 seconds or higher indicates a high average disk transfer time.

To monitor possible usage problems, use these counters:

- **Physical Disk\ Avg. Disk Bytes/Transfer**   Monitors the average number of bytes that are transferred from or to a disk during read or write operations. A value less than 20 KB indicates that an application is accessing the disk drive inefficiently.

- **Physical Disk\ Disk Reads/Sec and Disk Writes/Sec**   These counters can help you balance the workload of your network servers. Make sure that the specified transfer rate for your disk doesn't exceed the manufacturer's recommended specifications.

Tuning and Upgrading Tips for Disk Activity

If you are experiencing problems with disk performance, try the following solutions:

- Install the latest driver software for your host adapters to improve the efficiency of disk access.

- Install additional disks, or upgrade your hard disk to a faster disk. Update the bus and the disk controller at the same time.

- On servers, create striped volumes on several physical disks to increase throughput.

- Distribute applications among your servers to help balance the workload.

- Optimize disk space by running Disk Defragmenter.

- Isolate tasks that use disk I/O heavily to separate disk controllers or physical disks in order to help balance the server's workload.

Monitoring Network Activity

Monitoring the network consists of observing the use of server resources and measuring overall network traffic. Although you can do both with Performance Monitor, Network Monitor, discussed later in this chapter, gives you a more in-depth analysis of traffic.

Start monitoring your system by tracking the minimum recommended counters. Observe the resource usage on your system. Use the counters that correspond to the various layers of your network's configuration in order to concentrate on network-related resource usage. Abnormal network counter values are usually an indication of problems with a server's processor, memory, or hard disks. We recommend that you monitor network counters in conjunction with Memory\ Pages/Sec, Processor\ % Processor Time, and Physical Disk\ % Disk Time. For example, if Memory\ Pages/Sec increases dramatically, accompanied by a decrease in Memory\ Bytes Total/Sec handled by the server, the system is most likely running short of physical memory for network operations.

Minimum Recommended Counters

The following list shows the minimum recommended counters you should use to monitor the network's performance for possible bottlenecks:

- **Server\ Pool Paged Peak**   Indicates the amount of physical memory and the maximum paging file size. The acceptable threshold is the amount of physical RAM.

To monitor possible usage problems, use these counters:

- **Server\ Bytes Total/Sec**   Indicates the number of bytes the server has sent to and received from the network. This value is helpful in providing an indication of how busy the server is. It may be necessary for you to segment the network if the sum of the Bytes Total/Sec for all servers is close to equaling the maximum transfer rate of your network.

- **Server\ Work Item Shortages**   Indicates the number of times no work items are available to service incoming requests. Consider tuning InitWorkItems or MaxWorkItems in the registry key HKEY_LOCAL_ MACHINE\SYSTEM\CurrentControlSet\Services\LanmanServer if the value of this counter reaches or exceeds the threshold of 3.

Tuning and Upgrading Tips for Network Activity

Try the following solutions if you are experiencing problems with network performance:

- To significantly increase performance, unbind infrequently used network adapters and upgrade each network adapter to a high-performance one.
- When you configure your network, make sure that the systems shared by the same group of people are on the same subnet.
- Install multiple network adapters to increase file-sharing throughput.
- Set the order in which the workstation and NetBIOS software bind to each protocol when you are using more than one protocol. Average connection time decreases when the protocol that is used most frequently is set to be first in the binding list.

Using Network Monitor

You use Network Monitor to capture and display statistics about the frames that a server receives from the LAN. Network Monitor troubleshoots networking problems and helps you analyze network traffic. You can install Network Monitor only on a server.

Network Monitor consists of two components—Network Monitor itself and the Network Monitor driver—both of which must be installed on the server that is running Network Monitor so that you can capture frames. The Network Monitor driver enables Network Monitor to receive frames from the network adapter. The driver can be installed only on machines running Windows 2000 Server or Windows 2000 Professional.

Note The Systems Management Server (SMS) of Network Monitor 2 puts the network adapter in promiscuous mode, which means that the adapter reads all of the frames (packets) it receives over the network, instead of just the ones addressed to itself.

Network Monitor and the Network Monitor driver can be installed in one of two ways. You can install them both when you install the Windows 2000 Server operating system. Or, to install them at a later time, you can install Network Monitor by opening Add/Remove Programs in Control Panel and selecting Add/ Remove Windows Components. You'll then need to install the Network Monitor driver separately by pointing to Network And Dial-up Connections on the Settings menu and then choosing Local Area Connection Properties.

A *frame* is a portion of information from the network data stream that has been divided into smaller pieces by the networking software and is sent out across the wire. Network Monitor makes it possible to capture frames directly from the network. It enables you to display, filter, save, and print the captured frames to help identify network traffic patterns and network problems. A frame contains the following items:

- The source address of the machine that sent the frame. The source address is a unique hexadecimal number that identifies the sending machine.

- The destination address of the machine that received the frame. The destination address is a unique hexadecimal number that identifies the receiving machine.

- The header information for the protocol that sent the frame.
- The actual data that was sent to the destination computer.

Network Monitor for Windows 2000 stores data captures to a temporary capture file. When you save the capture file, it is given the .CAP extension, and you can view the capture files within Network Monitor.

To isolate a specific subset of frames, you need to design a capture filter. The capture filter behaves like a database query used to isolate specific information. Frames can be filtered on the basis of several options that include protocols, protocol properties, and source and destination addresses. You can also set up a capture to respond to specific conditions by designing a capture trigger that is detected by Network Monitor.

Viewing the Frame Viewer Window

Before you start capturing frames, you must choose the correct network interface. It is important to note that all network interfaces, including modems, are included in the network interface list. To specify the network interface, in the Capture window, choose Networks from the Capture menu.

To capture frames from the Capture window, you have three options: you can click the Start Capture button on the toolbar, choose Start from the Capture menu, or press the F10 function key. To examine the frames, you need to stop the capture of the current session in one of three ways: by selecting Stop And View from the Capture menu, by clicking the Stop Capture button on the toolbar, or by pressing the F11 function key. If you don't select Stop And View, you can view the Frame Viewer window by pressing the F12 function key.

The Frame Viewer window is used to view the contents of the captured frames (Figure 32-17). You can view captured information by choosing Stop And View from the Capture menu during data capture. You can zoom into a specific pane in the Frame Viewer window by selecting the pane and then choosing Zoom Pane from the Windows menu. This action places a check mark next to the Zoom option in the Windows menu. The Frame Viewer window has three panes:

- The summary pane displays general information about the captured frames in the order in which they were captured.
- The detail pane displays the frames' contents, including the protocols used to send them.
- The hex pane displays the ASCII and hexadecimal representation of the data that is captured.

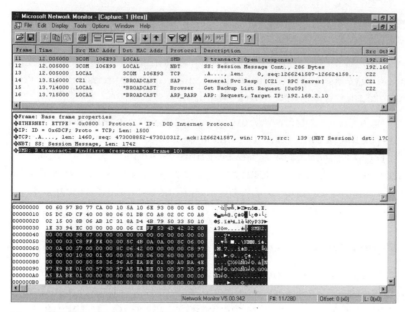

Figure 32-17. *The Frame Viewer window.*

Viewing the Capture Window

The statistics for the captured frames are displayed in the Capture window (Figure 32-18). The Capture window has four panes that display frame statistics:

- The graph pane (the upper left pane in Figure 32-18) graphically displays the total capture statistics of current network activity, such as percentage of available network resources in use by the current capture and the number of frames, bytes, broadcasts, and multicasts that the network transmits every second. This pane is displayed in the upper left corner of the Capture window by default.

- The session statistics pane (the middle left pane in the figure) displays statistics for current individual network sessions. Both participants in a session are identified, and information relating to the amount of information passed between them in either direction is displayed. The session statistics pane includes information such as the first participant's network address, labeled Network Address 1; the second participant's network address, labeled Network Address 2; the number of frames sent from the address listed as Network Address 1 to the address listed

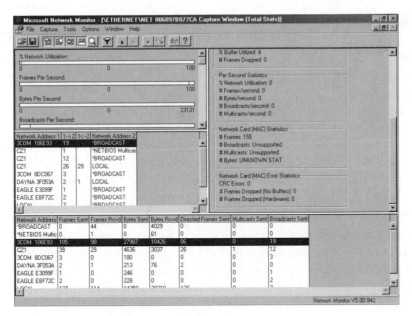

Figure 32-18. *The Capture window.*

as Network Address 2, labeled 1-->2; and the number of frames sent
from the address listed as Network Address 2 to the address listed as
Network Address 1, labeled 1<--2. Only the first 128 unique addresses
are reflected in this pane, so it is best to design a capture filter if you
need to capture statistics on a specific workstation. This pane is displayed in the center left section of the Capture window by default.

- The station statistics pane (the bottom pane in the figure) displays statistics about activities that occur from or to the local machine running
  Network Monitor. This pane is displayed at the bottom of the Capture
  window by default and includes the network address from which the
  frames were captured, the number of frames and bytes sent from the
  network address, the number of frames and bytes received by the network address, and the number of directed frames, multicasts, and
  broadcasts sent from the network address to other computers on the
  network. As with the session statistics pane, only the first 128 unique
  addresses are reflected in this pane.

- The total statistics pane (the right pane in the figure) summarizes statistics about overall network activity detected by Network Monitor from
  the time the current capture process began. Not all network adapter

cards support all of the statistics displayed by this pane. The label for a statistic will be replaced by the word "Unsupported" if the network adapter card doesn't support it. This pane is displayed in the upper right corner of the Capture window by default. The total statistics pane consists of five panels:

- Network Statistics displays statistics about the total amount of traffic that has occurred since the current capture on Network Monitor began. These statistics include the total number of frames dropped and the total number of frames, broadcasts, multicasts, and bytes sent to the network. The network status is also displayed. The status will always be Normal on an Ethernet network and will reflect the status of the ring on a token ring network.

- Captured Statistics displays statistics regarding the current capture that is running. These statistics include the total number of captured frames and bytes, the total number of frames and bytes in the temporary capture file, the percentage of allotted buffer space that is being utilized, the number of frames that were dropped by Network Monitor, and when the allotted buffer space was exceeded.

- Per Second Statistics displays averages of current activity and is constantly updated to reflect per-second activity. All frames, even those excluded by a filter, are included in these statistics. The statistics displayed in this panel include the average percentage of network utilization and the average frames, bytes, broadcast messages, and multicast messages detected per second from the time the current capture process began.

- Network Card (MAC) Statistics reflects the average activity detected by the network adapter from the time the current capture session began. These statistics include the total number of frames, broadcast frames, multicast frames, and bytes detected by the network adapter card.

- Network Card (MAC) Error Statistics displays network adapter card errors that have occurred from the time the current capture session began. These statistics include the number of errors that occurred because the actual bytes received did not match the cyclical redundancy check (CRC) and the number of frames that were detected but dropped by the network adapter card, either because insufficient buffer space was available to Network Monitor or as a result of hardware constraints.

Configuring and Customizing Network Monitor

You must be logged on as a user with administrative rights in order to run Network Monitor. You can customize Network Monitor in a number of ways to meet your needs, as described in this section.

Modifying the Capture Buffer

To adjust the size of the capture buffer in Network Monitor, choose Buffer Settings from the Capture menu. You can adjust the Buffer Size (MB) or Frame Size (Bytes) options in the Capture Buffer Settings dialog box (Figure 32-19). The buffer size or frame size can be reduced if you find that your system becomes low on resources while you are capturing data with Network Monitor. Make sure that your buffer setting does not exceed the amount of physical memory you have available on your system because memory swapping may cause frames to be dropped.

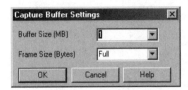

Figure 32-19. *The Capture Buffer Settings dialog box.*

Displaying Address Names

To see address names instead of hexadecimal network addresses in Network Monitor, choose Show Address Names from the Options menu. A check mark appears next to Show Address Names when this option is active. This option is very helpful to the administrator because it causes Network Monitor to replace the hexadecimal network addresses of the computers from which the frames have been captured with their user-designated machine names.

Creating an Address Database

You may often need to capture frames that originated with or were sent to specific computers. To do this, you must know the addresses of the computers on the network. You can find the IP address of a computer in one of two ways: by using the Ping command or by using the mechanism that Network Monitor provides for associating the addresses of the network computers with their user-defined names. If you use the mechanism provided by Network Monitor, you can save the information to an address database once the association is made and later use the database to design display or capture filters.

To create an address database, choose Find All Names from the Display menu in the Frame Viewer window. The system may take a few minutes to process the information from the current frames. To display the addresses, choose Addresses from the Display menu of the Frame Viewer window (Figure 32-20). Save the database to a file if you want to use the addresses to design filters in the future.

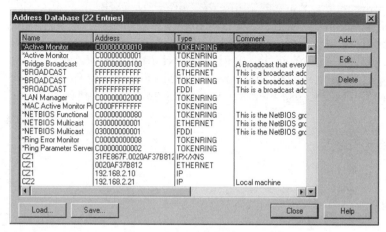

Figure 32-20. *The Address Database dialog box.*

Displaying Adapter Card Vendor Names

To replace the hexadecimal computer addresses with the names of the vendors of the adapter cards on the computers from which frames have been captured, in Network Monitor, choose Show Vendor Names from the Options menu. When this option is active, a check mark appears next to it.

Adding a Protocol Parser

Network Monitor uses programs called protocol parsers to separate protocol information into smaller pieces in order to be able to act on the information. Each parser can parse one protocol or family of protocols. Parser DLLs from Network Monitor 1.2 can be added to Network Monitor 2. To add a protocol parser, take the following steps:

1. While Network Monitor is not running, copy the parser file to the %SystemRoot%\System32\Netmon\Parsers folder. The parser file should have a .DLL extension.

2. In the %SystemRoot%\System32\Netmon folder, find the Parser.ini file and open it. Enter the information about the parser you are adding in this file.

3. Start Network Monitor, close any open Frame Viewer windows, and then choose Default Parsers from the Options menu.

4. A window warning about disabling protocols via this option appears. Click Yes to continue.

5. The currently enabled protocols are listed under Enabled Protocol Parsers in the Protocol Parsers dialog box (Figure 32-21). All of the parsers present in your %SystemRoot%\System32\Netmon\Parsers subfolder are enabled by default.

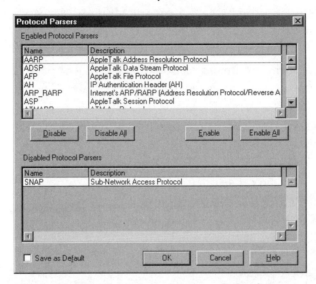

Figure 32-21. *The Protocol Parsers dialog box.*

6. The name of the parser you just added to the %SystemRoot%\System32\Netmon\Parsers folder will appear under Disabled Protocol Parsers. Click on the name, and then click Enable. The name of the protocol should move to the Enabled Protocol Parsers box.

7. If you want the new parser to be included in the default configuration, select the Save As Default option.

It is important to verify that the parser is working correctly. If the parser is handling frames properly, the Protocol column of the summary pane in the Frame Viewer window will list the protocol.

Adding a Comment Frame to a Capture

A comment frame is a very useful tool that you can use to add comments or other information to a capture file within the Network Monitor Frame Viewer. For example, you can use comment frames to mark the beginning and ending points for a group of packets. The Trail protocol is contained in the comment frame and includes such information as the bandwidth and the number of frames consumed.

To add a comment frame, choose Insert Comment Frame from the Tools menu, or right-click the Frame column at the point where you want to insert the comment frame and choose Insert Comment from the shortcut menu. The Insert Comment Frame dialog box appears (Figure 32-22). The options in this dialog box are as follows:

- **Frame Number**   The frame position where Network Monitor places the comment frame within the capture. The default frame number is the current location.

- **Type Of Frame To Insert**   The Comment or Bookmark protocol parser used to process the comment frame after the Trail protocol runs. The default parser is Comment.

- **No Statistics**   Disables statistical generation for the comment frame. This check box is selected by default.

- **Apply Current Filter To Statistics**   Calculates statistics using the current display filter. This check box is selected by default.

- **Enter In A Comment For This New Frame**   Indicates the comment text that you want to attach to the frame by using the protocol parser chosen in Type Of Frame To Insert.

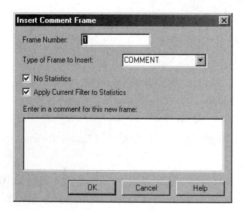

Figure 32-22. *The Insert Comment Frame dialog box.*

Printing Captured Frames

To print captured frames, choose Print from the File menu in the Frame Viewer window. Select the desired output options on the Netmon tab in the Print dialog box (Figure 32-23). The Output Detail area enables you to specify the amount of detail you want to print for each of the frames. The choices presented to you include Print Frame Summary Lines, Print Protocol Details, and Print Hex Data. You can also set filters and add page breaks to the output.

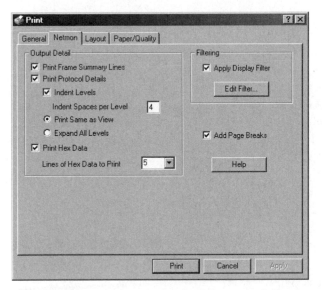

Figure 32-23. *The Netmon tab of the Print dialog box.*

Capturing Network Data

To begin the process of capturing frames, you must open the Capture window of Network Monitor and choose Start from the Capture menu. Network Monitor then begins to capture frames sent from the local machine or sent to the local machine from the network data stream and copies those frames to a temporary capture file. To halt the data capture temporarily, choose Pause from the Capture menu. To stop the capture and display the captured frames, you must choose Stop And View from the Capture menu. This displays the Frame Viewer window so that you can examine the contents of the captured frames. Network Monitor displays the session statistics for only the first 100 unique network sessions. To view information for the next 100 unique network sessions, you must choose Clear Statistics from the Capture menu.

Designing a Capture Filter

A capture filter must be designed when Network Monitor is not running and no frames are being captured. You specify capture criteria to identify frames you want captured on the network. To design a capture filter, choose Filter from the Capture menu of the Capture window. You specify criteria to be used in the design of a capture filter expression through capture filter protocols, address pairs, and data pattern matches.

Specifying Capture Filter Protocols

You use filter protocols when you want to capture frames sent using a specific protocol. To design filter protocols, choose Filter from the Capture menu in the Capture window. Double-click the default line SAP/ETYPE = Any SAP Or Any ETYPE in the decision tree. As you disable protocols, the information in this line will change to reflect those changes. For example, if you disable the AppleTalk Address Resolution Protocol (ARP), the line will change to SAP/ETYPE = Other SAPs Or Other ETYPEs Or NOT AppleTalk ARP. You enable and disable protocols for use in the capture filter in the Capture Filter SAPs And ETYPEs dialog box. The default is to enable all of the protocols.

Specifying Address Pairs

You designate address pairs in order to capture only traffic sent to and from the specified computers or to exclude traffic between the specified computers. You can specify up to three address pairs.

To designate address pairs, choose Filter from the Capture menu in the Capture window. Double-click the AND (Address Pairs) line in the decision tree, and specify address pair properties in the Address Expression dialog box. When an address pair is added, it is displayed under the AND (Address Pairs) line in the decision tree. You can edit or delete an address pair at any time by clicking the address pair name and then choosing Edit or Delete from the Capture Filter dialog box. You specify address pair properties in the following manner:

1. Choose whether to include or exclude capture data that travels between the members of the address pair you want to create.

2. Choose the first address from the Station 1 list box and the second address from the Station 2 list box. Which address becomes the originating address and which becomes the destination address depends upon the arrow you select in the Direction list box.

3. Choose one of the three arrows from the Direction list box to indicate the direction of the traffic between the two addresses.

  • <--> This arrow specifies capturing frames that travel in either direction between the Station 1 and Station 2 computers. This arrow is the default.

  • --> This arrow captures frames that travel from Station 1 to Station 2.

  • <-- This arrow captures frames that travel from Station 2 to Station 1.

4. You can modify the existing address database by clicking the Edit Addresses button and then adding, editing, or deleting information.

Note   Broadcast and Multicast are always destination addresses.

Defining Pattern Matches

Pattern matches enable you to capture frames that consist of a specific pattern at a specified offset. You can define up to four pattern matches.

To specify data pattern matches, choose Filter from the Capture menu in the Capture window. Double-click the AND (Pattern Matches) line in the decision tree, and specify data pattern match properties in the Pattern Match dialog box (Figure 32-24). When you add a pattern match, it is displayed under the AND (Pattern Matches) line in the decision tree. You can edit or delete the pattern matches at any time by clicking the data pattern match name and then choosing Edit or Delete from the Capture Filter dialog box.

To define pattern matches, enter the hexadecimal or ASCII data pattern that you want the captured frames to match. Then, in the Offset box, enter the hexadecimal number that specifies the byte where the pattern begins. Network Monitor interprets the number depending upon whether you specify the From Start Of Frame option or the From End Of Topology Header option. The topology header is the section of the frame that is added by the network topology to identify the network type. Information such as the source and destination address of the frame is included in the topology header. For example, 14 bytes are added to the frame at the Ethernet layer for an Ethernet network. The number of topology header bytes varies in a token ring environment.

Figure 32-24. *The Pattern Match dialog box.*

Setting a Capture Trigger

A capture trigger is used to set conditions that, when met, initiate an action. For example, you can set a trigger to stop data capture and cause a program or command file to execute when certain criteria are met. To set a capture trigger, follow these steps:

1. Open Network Monitor from the Administrative Tools menu and choose the area to monitor.

2. Choose Trigger from the Capture menu to open the Capture Trigger dialog box (Figure 32-25).

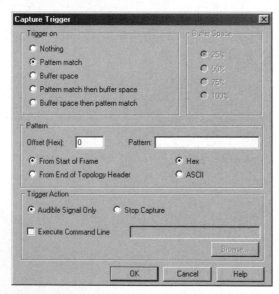

Figure 32-25. *The Capture Trigger dialog box.*

3. Choose from the options in the Trigger On area:

- **Pattern Match**   When a specified hexadecimal or ASCII pattern match occurs, the trigger is engaged.

- **Buffer Space**   When a capture fills a specified percentage of the capture buffer, the trigger is engaged.

- **Pattern Match Then Buffer Space**   Causes Network Monitor to monitor the buffer space after the specified data pattern match occurs and then to engage the trigger function when both of the specified conditions exist.

- **Buffer Space Then Pattern Match**   Causes Network Monitor to detect when a capture has filled the specified percentage of buffer space and then to perform the trigger action when the specified data pattern match is detected.

Note   If you choose the Pattern Match Then Buffer Space option and set Buffer Space to 100 percent, the frame that has the data pattern match will be overwritten by Network Monitor—because Network Monitor doesn't start counting the buffer space until after the pattern match has been found.

4. In the Trigger Action area, choose the action you want to have occur when the trigger criteria are met:

- **Audible Signal Only**   When the trigger condition is met, the computer will beep and will continue to capture frames. This is the default option.

- **Stop Capture**   When the trigger condition is met, the capture process will end.

- **Execute Command Line**   Causes a command line to execute or a file to open when the trigger condition is met. The command can be up to 259 characters.

5. Click OK when you're finished.

Designing a Display Filter

A display filter acts on information that has already been captured and behaves in much the same way as a database query because it is used to specify the types of captured data you want to examine. You can indicate how much of the captured data you want displayed in the Frame Viewer window or what types of displayed data you want to save to a file, such as protocols and computer addresses.

Using the Display Filter Dialog Box

The Display Filter dialog box helps you make changes to the display filter decision tree for the Frame Viewer window. The expression option is added to the display filter decision tree when you click OK. There are two default branches on the decision tree: the Protocol branch, which lists the protocols you want to display, and the Computer Address Pairs branch, which lists the computer address pairs you want to display. The sections that follow describe the various options available in the Display Filter dialog box.

Adding Expression   The Expression option is found in the Add group of the Display Filter dialog box and is used to write or edit an expression to specify the protocols, protocol properties, and computer address pairs you want to display. Only one expression at a time can be added in the Expression dialog box. If you click the Protocol tab or the Property tab before you have saved the specified expression to the decision tree by clicking OK, you will lose the expression. You can specify options for three categories, each of which is represented by a tab:

* **Address tab**   The Address tab, shown in Figure 32-26, is used to specify an address that you want to find or to add or edit an address expression within a display filter decision tree. You can also display this tab by double-clicking the default ANY line in the decision tree. Refer to the "Specifying Address Pairs" section earlier in this chapter for information on how to design address pairs.

Note   Broadcast, Functional, and Multicast should be specified only as destination addresses. You will filter out all frames if Broadcast or Multicast are used in the construction of an expression because they are always destination addresses.

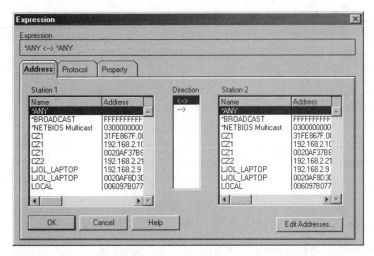

Figure 32-26. *The Address tab of the Expression dialog box.*

- **Protocol tab**   This tab, shown in Figure 32-27, is used to specify protocols you want to display in Frame Viewer or to specify protocols in the display filter decision tree. The Enabled Protocols and Disabled Protocols list boxes display the protocol names. You choose the protocols you want displayed by clicking the Disable, Enable, Disable All, and Enable All buttons. You can also see this tab by double-clicking the default Protocol line in the decision tree. The default is to enable all protocols.

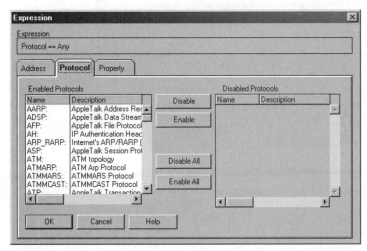

Figure 32-27. *The Protocol tab of the Expression dialog box.*

- **Property tab**   This tab, shown in Figure 32-28, specifies the protocol properties you want to find or allows you to add or edit a protocol property expression within the display filter decision tree. Follow these steps to design protocol properties:

  1. Choose the desired properties from the Protocol:Property box. If a plus sign appears next to a protocol name, you can expand the protocol to choose a property from its list.

  2. Choose a relational operator from the Relation list box. A relational operator is used to specify the connection between the protocol property and its possible values.

  3. Type the value that you want to use as a comparison to the highlighted property into the Value box.

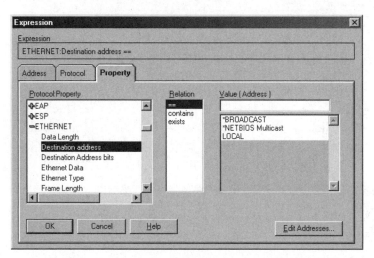

Figure 32-28.   *The Property tab of the Expression dialog box.*

Note   The Hex Offset box will appear for some properties. This box is used to specify the number of hex digits from the beginning of the frame to the point where you want to look for the specified property.

Inserting Operators   The Insert group box defines logical operators for the decision tree. The operators available to you are And, Or, and Not. Using them, you can specify up to 4000 decision tree operators.

Editing Expressions/Changing Operators   Edit Expression is used to edit an operator expression listed in the decision tree. It is not intended to edit address pairs, protocols, or protocol property expressions that are defined with the Add

Expression option. The Edit Expression button will change to read Change Operator if you have an operator selected on the decision tree. This option allows you to toggle through the operator values.

Deleting Criteria   The Delete group box deletes decision criteria from the decision tree. The options available here are to delete a specific line, a specific branch, or the entire decision tree.

Summary

Windows 2000 Server is equipped with tools for monitoring your network, finding problems, and fine-tuning performance. Although some of the processes may appear daunting, they can be approached gradually and adopted as needed. The next chapter discusses how to prepare and implement a plan for recovering from the inevitable failure of hardware.

Chapter 33
Disaster Planning

Smart bicycle riders wear helmets even though they ride carefully and certainly don't plan to perform a headfirst landing. Schools and businesses have fire drills even though the vast majority of buildings *never* burn down. Similarly, system administrators sincerely hope never to need those verified backups and emergency repair disks. Nevertheless, we keep them because there are only two types of networks, those that have experienced disaster and those that haven't yet.

Disaster can take many forms, from the self-inflicted pain of a user or administrator doing something really, really unwise to the uncontrollable, unpreventable results of a natural disaster such as a flood or earthquake. In any case, your competence as a system administrator will be judged by how well you were prepared for the disaster and how well you and your team responded to it and recovered from it.

This chapter covers emergency preparedness. It discusses creating a disaster recovery plan, with standardized procedures to follow in the event of catastrophe. It also describes how to prepare for a disaster, including how to make an emergency repair disk, how to make Microsoft Windows 2000 setup disks, how to make a boot disk, how to install the Recovery Console, how to specify recovery options in Windows 2000, and how to create an external recovery drive.

Planning for Disaster

Some people seem to operate on the assumption that if they don't think about a disaster, one won't happen. This is similar to the idea that if you don't write a will, you'll never die—and just about as realistic. No system administrators should feel comfortable about their network's degree of preparedness without a clear disaster recovery plan that has been thoroughly tested. Even then, it's wise to be always looking for ways to improve the plan.

Planning for disaster or emergencies is not a single step, but an iterative, ongoing process. Systems are not mountains, but rivers, constantly moving and changing, and your disaster recovery plan needs to change as your environment changes. To put together a good disaster recovery plan, one you can bet your business on, you need to

1. Identify the risks
2. Identify the resources
3. Develop the responses
4. Test the responses
5. Iterate

Identify the Risks

The first step in creating a disaster recovery plan is to identify the risks to your business and the costs associated with those risks. The risks vary from the simple deletion of a critical file to the total destruction of your place of business and its computers. To properly prepare for a disaster, you need to do a realistic assessment of the risks, the potential costs and consequences of each disaster scenario, and how likely any given disaster scenario is.

Identifying risks is not a job for only one person. As with all of the tasks associated with a disaster recovery plan, all concerned parties must participate. There are two important reasons for this: you want to make sure that you have commitment and buy-in from the parties concerned, and you also want to make sure you don't miss anything.

No matter how carefully and thoroughly you try to identify the risks, you'll miss at least one. You should always account for that missing risk by including an "unknown risk" item in your list. Treat it just like any other risk: identify the resources available to address it and develop countermeasures to take should it occur. The difference with this risk, of course, is that your resources and countermeasures are somewhat more generic, and you can't really test your response to the risk, since you don't yet know what it is.

Start by trying to list all of the possible ways that your system could fail. If you have a team of people responsible for supporting the network, solicit everyone's help in the process. The more people involved in the brainstorming, the more ideas you'll get and the more prevention and recovery procedures you can develop and practice.

Next, look at all of the ways that some external event could affect your system. The team of people responsible for identifying possible external problems is probably similar to a team looking at internal failures, but with some important differences. In a large industrial plant, for example, when you start to look at external failures and disasters, you'll want to involve the security and facilities groups, since they will need to understand your needs as well as provide input on how well the plant is protected from these disasters.

An important part of this risk assessment phase is to understand and quantify just how likely a particular risk is. If you're located in a flood plain, for example, you're much more likely to think flood insurance is a good investment.

Identify the Resources

Once you've identified the risks to your network, you need to identify what your resources are to address those risks. These resources can be internal or external, people or systems, hardware or software.

When you're identifying the resources available to deal with a specific risk, be as complete as you can, but also be specific. Identifying everyone in the IT group as a resource to solve a crashed server may look good, but realistically only one or two key people are likely to actually rebuild the server. Make sure you identify who those key people are for each risk, as well as what more general secondary resources they have to call on. So, for example, the primary resources available to recover a crashed Exchange server may consist of one or two staff members who can recover the failed hardware and another one or two staff members who can restore the software and database. General secondary resources would include everyone in the IT group as well as the hardware vendor and Microsoft Premier Support.

An important step in identifying resources in your disaster recovery plan is to specify both the first-line responsibility *and* the back-end or supervisory responsibility. Make sure everyone knows who to go to when the problem is more than they can handle or when they need additional resources. Also, clearly define when they should do that. The best disaster recovery plans include clear, unambiguous escalation policies. This takes the burden off the individual to decide when and who to notify and makes it simply part of the procedure.

Develop the Responses

An old but relevant adage comes to mind when discussing disaster recovery scenarios: when you're up to your elbows in alligators, it's difficult to remember that your original objective was to drain the swamp. This is another way of saying that people lose track of what's important when they are overloaded by too many problems that require their immediate attention. To ensure that your swamp is drained and your network gets back online, you need to take those carefully researched risks and resources and develop your disaster recovery plan. There are two important parts of any good disaster recovery plan:

- Standard operating procedures (SOPs)
- Standard escalation procedures (SEPs)

By having these procedures in place and clearly understood by all before a disaster strikes, you'll be in a far better position to recover gracefully and with a minimum of lost productivity and data.

Standard Operating Procedures

Emergencies bring out both the best and worst in people. If you're prepared for the emergency, you can be one of those who come out smelling like a rose, but if you're not prepared and let yourself get flustered or lose track of what you're trying to accomplish, you can make the whole situation worse than it needs to be.

While no one is ever as prepared for a system emergency as they'd like to be, careful planning and preparation can give you an edge in recovering expeditiously and with a minimal loss of data. It is much easier to deal with the situation calmly when you know you've foreseen and prepared for this problem and you've got a well organized and tested standard operating procedure to follow.

Since the very nature of emergencies is that you can't predict exactly which one is going to strike, you need to plan and prepare for as many possibilities as you can. The time to decide how to recover from a disaster is *before* the disaster happens, not in the middle of it when users are screaming and bosses are standing around looking serious and concerned.

Your risk assessment phase involved identifying as many possible disaster scenarios as you could, while in your resource assessment phase you identified the resources that are available and responsible for each of those risks. Now you need to write up SOPs for recovering the system from each of the scenarios. Even the most level-headed system administrator can get flustered when the system has crashed, users are calling every 10 seconds to see what the problem is, the boss is asking every 5 minutes when you'll have it fixed, and your server won't boot.

Reduce your stress and prevent mistakes by planning for disasters before they occur. Practice recovering from each of your disaster scenarios. Write down each of the steps, and work through questionable or unclear areas until you can identify exactly what it takes to recover from the problem. This is like a fire drill, and you should do it for the same reasons—not because a fire is inevitable, but because fires do happen, and the statistics demonstrate irrefutably that those who have prepared for a fire and practiced what to do in a fire are far more likely to survive it.

Your job as a system administrator is to prepare for disasters and practice what to do in those disasters, not because you expect the disaster, but because if you do have one, you want to be the hero, not the goat. After all, it isn't often that the system administrator gets to be a hero, so be ready when your time comes.

The first step in developing any SOP is to outline the overall steps you want to accomplish. Keep it general at this point—you're looking for the big picture here. Again, you want everyone to be involved in the process. What you're really trying to do is make sure you don't forget any critical steps, and that's much easier when you get the overall plan down first. There will be plenty of opportunity later to cover the specific details.

Once you have the broad, high-level outline for a given procedure, the people you identified as the actual resources during the resource assessment phase should start to flesh in the outline. You don't need every detail at this point, but you want to get down to at least a level below the original outline. This will help you identify missing resources that will be important to a timely resolution of the problem. Again, don't get too bogged down in the details at this point. You're not actually writing the SOP, just trying to make sure that you've identified all of its pieces.

When you feel confident that the outline is ready, get the larger group back together again. Go over the procedure and smooth out the rough edges, refining the outline and *listening* to make sure you haven't missed anything critical. Then, when everyone agrees that the outline is complete, you're ready to add the final details to it.

The people who are responsible for each procedure should now work through all of the details of the disaster recovery plan and document the steps thoroughly. They should keep in mind that the people who actually perform the recovery may not be who they expect. It's great to have an SOP for recovering from a failed router, but if the only person who understands the procedure is the network engineer, and she's on vacation in Bora Bora that week, your disaster recovery plan has a big hole in it.

When you create the documentation, write down *everything*. What seems obvious to you now, while you're devising the procedure, will not seem at all obvious in six months or a year when you suddenly have to use it under stress.

Real World   Multiple Copies, Multiple Locations

It's tempting to centralize your SOPs into a single, easily accessible database. And you should do that, making sure everyone understands how to use it. But you'll also want to have alternative locations and formats for your procedures. Not only do you not want to keep them in a single database, you also don't want to have only an electronic version. Always maintain hard copy versions as well. Every good server room should have a large binder, prominently visible and clearly identified, that contains all of the SOPs. Each responsible person should also have one or more copies of at least the procedures he or she is either a resource for or likely to become a resource for. We like to keep copies of all our procedures in several places so that we can get at them no matter what the source of the emergency or where we happen to be when one of our pagers goes off.

Once you have created the SOPs, your job has only begun. You need to keep them up to date and make sure that they don't become stale. It's no good having an SOP to recover your ISDN connection to a branch office when you ripped the ISDN line out a year ago and put in a DSL line with three times the bandwidth at half the cost.

You also need to make sure that all of your copies of an SOP are updated. Electronic ones should probably be stored in a replicated database. However, hard copy documents are notoriously tricky to maintain. One way to do so is to make yet another SOP that details who updates what SOPs and who gets fresh copies whenever a change is made. Then put a version control system into place and make sure everyone understands his or her role in the process.

Standard Escalation Procedures

No matter how carefully you've identified potential risks, and how detailed your procedures to recover from them, you're still likely to have situations you didn't anticipate. An important part of any disaster recovery plan is a standardized escalation procedure. Not only should each individual SOP have its own procedure-specific SEP, but you should also have an overall escalation procedure that covers everything you haven't thought of—because it is certain that you haven't thought of everything.

An escalation procedure has two functions—resource escalation and notification escalation. Both have the same purpose: to make sure that everyone who needs to know about the problem is up to date and involved as appropriate, and to keep the overall noise level down so that the work of resolving the problem can go forward as quickly as possible.

The *resource escalation procedure* details the resources that are available to the people who are trying to recover from the current disaster, so that they don't have to try to guess who (or what) the appropriate resource might be when they run into something they can't handle or something doesn't go as it is supposed to. This helps them stay calm and focused. They know that if they run into a problem, they aren't on their own, and they know exactly who to call when they do need help.

The *notification escalation procedure* details who is to be notified of serious problems. Even more important, it should provide specifics regarding when notification is to be made. If your print server crashes but comes right back up, you may want to send only a general message to the users of that particular server letting them know what happened. However, if your mail server has been down for more than half an hour, a lot of folks are going to be concerned. The SEP for that mail server should detail who needs to be notified if the server is unavailable for longer than some specified time, and it should probably detail what happens and who gets notified when it's still down some significant amount of time after that.

This notification has two purposes: to make sure that the necessary resources are made available as required and to keep everyone informed and aware of the situation. If you let people know that you've had a server hardware failure and that the vendor has been called and will be on site within an hour, you'll cut down the number of phone calls exponentially, freeing you to do whatever you need to do to ensure that you're ready when the vendor arrives.

Test the Responses

A disaster recovery plan is nice to have, but it really isn't worth a whole lot until it has actually been tested. Needless to say, the time to test the plan is at your convenience and under controlled conditions, rather than in the midst of an actual disaster. It's a nuisance to discover that your detailed disaster recovery plan has a fatal flaw in it when you're testing it under controlled conditions. It's a bit more than a nuisance to discover it when every second counts.

You won't be able to test all aspects of all disaster recovery plans. Few organizations have the resources to create fully realistic simulated natural disasters and test their response to each of them under controlled conditions. Nevertheless, there are things you can do to test your response plans. The details of how you test them will depend on your environment, but they should include as realistic a test as feasible and should, as much as possible, cover all aspects of the response plan.

The other reason to test the disaster recovery plan is that it provides a valuable training ground. If you've identified primary and backup resources, as you should, chances are that the people you've identified as backup resources are not as skilled or knowledgeable in a particular area as the primary resource. Testing the procedures gives you a chance to train the backup resources at the same time.

You should also consider using the testing to cross-train people who are not necessarily in the primary response group. Not only will they get valuable training, but you'll also create a knowledgeable pool of people who might not be directly needed when the procedure has to be used for real, but who can act as key communicators with the rest of the community.

Iterate

When you finish a particular disaster recovery plan, you may think your job is done, but in fact your work is just beginning. Standardizing a process is actually just the first step. You also need to improve it.

You should make a regular, scheduled practice of pulling out your disaster recovery plan with your group and making sure it's up to date. Use the occasion to actually look at it and see how you can improve upon it. Take the opportunity to examine your environment. What's changed since you last looked at the plan? What servers have been retired, and what new ones added? What software is different? Are all of the people on your notification and escalation lists still working at the company, in the same roles? Are the phone numbers up to date?

Another way to iterate your disaster recovery plan is to use every disaster as a learning experience. Once the disaster or emergency is over, get everyone together as soon as possible to talk about what happened. Find out what they think worked and what didn't in the plan. Actively solicit suggestions for how the process could be improved. Then make the changes and test them. You'll not only improve your responsiveness to this particular type of disaster, but you'll improve your overall responsiveness by getting people involved in the process and enabling them to be part of the solution.

Preparing for a Disaster

As good old Ben Franklin was known to say, "Failure to prepare is preparing to fail." This is truer than ever with modern operating systems, and while Windows 2000 includes a number of exceptionally useful recovery modes and tools, you still need to prepare for potential problems. Some of these techniques are covered in detail in other chapters and are discussed here only briefly, while others are covered here at length.

Setting Up a Fault-Tolerant System

A fault-tolerant system is one that is prepared to continue operating in the event of key component failures. This technique is very useful for servers running critical applications. Here are a few of the many ways to ensure fault tolerance in a system:

- Use one or more RAID arrays for system and data storage, protecting you from hard disk failure. If a hard disk in the array fails, only that disk needs to be replaced—and no data is lost. See Chapter 14 for information on using Windows 2000 to implement software RAID.

- Use multiple SCSI adapters to provide redundancy if a SCSI controller fails.

- Use an uninterruptible power supply (UPS) to allow the server to shut down gracefully in the event of a power failure.

- Use multiple network cards to provide redundancy in case a network card fails.

- Use multiples of everything that is likely to fail, including power supplies and so on.

Backing Up the System

Back up the system and system state regularly using a good Windows 2000 backup program. If a hard disk fails and must be replaced and you're not using some sort of RAID array, the data and system can be restored from backup. (If you lose the system entirely, you'll need to install Windows 2000 on it before restoring the original system.) See Chapter 34 for details on using the Windows 2000 backup program. Appendix E covers an assortment of third-party backup tools for the enterprise.

Creating Emergency Repair Disks

Windows 2000, like Microsoft Windows NT, can create an emergency repair disk (ERD) to help rescue the system in the event of a disaster. The ERD contains important information that can be used to fix system files, the boot sector, and the startup environment. The ERD is easy to make, and it is *very* useful in the event of a disaster.

> **Tip** In Windows 2000, you may have noticed that you didn't get prompted to create an emergency repair disk during installation, as you do during Windows NT setup. In fact, the entire procedure has changed. Now, to create an emergency repair disk, you run Windows 2000's Backup program.

To make a fresh emergency repair disk, you will need a floppy that you don't mind being formatted. Always use a freshly formatted floppy to create an ERD. It's also a good idea to have a backup of your ERD, so always keep at least one generation back. We also like to keep an original ERD created immediately after the installation process as a kind of ultimate fallback position. To make an ERD, follow these steps:

1. Open the Windows 2000 Backup program from the Start menu by pointing to Programs, Accessories, and System Tools and then choosing Backup.

2. Click the Emergency Repair Disk button, as shown in Figure 33-1.

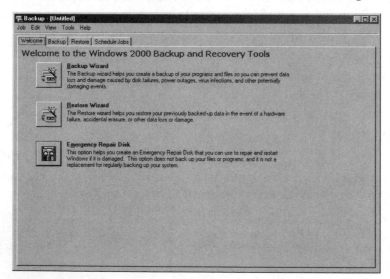

Figure 33-1. *The Windows 2000 Backup window.*

3. Select the check box in the Emergency Repair Diskette dialog box if you want to back up the system registry to the repair folder on the hard disk, for use if the registry becomes corrupt.

4. Insert a blank floppy disk in drive A, and click OK.

Note The emergency repair disk is not bootable; it must be used in conjunction with the Windows 2000 setup disks.

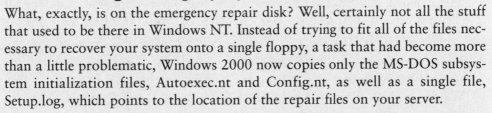

Real World **Using the Emergency Repair Disk Effectively**

What, exactly, is on the emergency repair disk? Well, certainly not all the stuff that used to be there in Windows NT. Instead of trying to fit all of the files necessary to recover your system onto a single floppy, a task that had become more than a little problematic, Windows 2000 now copies only the MS-DOS subsystem initialization files, Autoexec.nt and Config.nt, as well as a single file, Setup.log, which points to the location of the repair files on your server.

Unfortunately, with this change, it's a little more difficult to maintain multiple generations of repair information. Get in the habit of saving a copy of the %windir%\repair directory onto a secondary or even tertiary location before updating the emergency repair disk. This will give you a fallback should you inadvertently update the information before you're sure it's stable. If you need to go back to earlier information, just copy it back into the %WinDir%\repair directory (probably by using the Recovery Console, discussed later in this chapter and in Chapter 37).

Whenever you make a major change to your system, it's a good idea to make a fresh copy of the ERD *before* you make the change. This lets you have a fallback position if something goes wrong. If something doesn't work right, you can quickly restore the previous configuration. Once you've confirmed that the new configuration is stable and working, then and only then should you update your ERD for that server. Before you make a new emergency repair disk, copy the entire %WinDir%\repair directory tree to your failsafe location. At worst, you can recover from that failsafe location.

What constitutes a major change? Adding, removing, or otherwise modifying the hard disks or their partitions, formats, configurations, and so on, for one. Any time you make a change to the hard disk configuration, you'll definitely want to make a fresh ERD just before you make the change. Another major change would be the addition of a new component to the server, such as adding Microsoft Exchange Server or Microsoft SQL Server. Any changes made from Control Panel are candidates for redoing the ERD as well.

Creating Windows 2000 Setup Disks

Windows 2000 includes a set of four disks that can be used to boot the computer if you cannot boot from the hard disk. If the system supports booting from a CD-ROM using the El Torito standard, you can boot from the Windows 2000 CD-ROM. Otherwise, you need these disks to boot the system in the case of an emergency.

If you have lost the original disks or need to create another set, you can do so. You will need four 1.44-MB floppy disks. While it would be really handy to use a single Zip disk instead, booting from a Zip disk is not supported. (OK, if your Zip drive is drive A: you *can* use your Zip drive, but you'll still need four disks—they'll just be mostly empty). Follow these steps to create new setup disks:

1. Insert the Windows 2000 CD-ROM for which you want to create setupdisks. Note that setup disks are specific to each version of Windows 2000—that is, Windows 2000 Professional and Windows 2000 Server use different setup disks.

2. Insert a blank, 1.44-MB floppy disk in drive A: of the computer.

3. At a command prompt or in the Run dialog box, enter the command *d:\bootdisk\makeboot a:*, replacing *d* with the CD-ROM drive letter.

Creating a Boot Disk

We know; you're thinking that you just did this, but there is yet another floppy disk you can create for safety and recovery convenience. It's a plain old boot disk. Although a Windows 2000 boot disk doesn't get you to a command prompt, as a Windows 95 or Windows 98 boot disk does, it does permit you to boot the system under the following circumstances (provided that your actual Windows 2000 installation isn't damaged in any other way):

- Corrupted boot sector
- Corrupted master boot record (MBR)
- Virus infections of the MBR
- Missing or corrupt Ntldr or Ntdetect.com files
- Incorrect Ntbootdd.sys driver

The boot disk can also be used to boot from the shadow drive of a broken mirror set, although you may need to edit the Boot.ini file on the boot disk.

Real World   Why MS-DOS Boot Disks Won't Help

More than one person new to Windows 2000 has accidentally deleted or corrupted a key file required to boot the system and tried to recover by digging out an old MS-DOS boot floppy. Alas, it doesn't work.

The files you need to get your hard drive back to booting condition aren't even on an MS-DOS floppy. When you install Windows 2000, it modifies the system's boot sector to look for and run a file called Ntldr. When you format a floppy under MS-DOS, even when you make it a system disk, this file doesn't get created, since MS-DOS doesn't know anything about Windows 2000.

As such, a boot disk is occasionally useful, and since it's easy to make and floppy disks grow on trees (although these trees are rarely seen outside of the Microsoft campus), you might as well make one. The boot disk is *not* generic for every Windows 2000 machine. However, if you have a standard configuration across several machines, this disk will work for all of the machines that use the same partition and disk controller as their Windows 2000 boot partition. Follow these steps to create a boot disk:

1. Insert the first Windows 2000 setup disk into the floppy drive.

   Tip   If you're currently using a Windows 2000 computer, you can simply format a disk using Windows 2000's Format utility and then proceed to step 6.

2. At a command prompt, enter the command *diskcopy a: a:*.
3. Follow the directions on the screen to make a copy of the first setup disk.
4. Delete all files on the new disk by entering *del *.** at the *a:* command prompt.
5. Copy the Ntdetect.com and Ntldr files from the i386 folder on the Windows 2000 CD-ROM to the floppy disk.
6. Rename Ntldr to Setupldr.bin.
7. Create a Boot.ini file, or copy the file from the boot drive to the floppy disk.
8. If you're using a SCSI system, copy the device driver for the SCSI controller to the floppy disk, and rename it Ntbootdd.sys.

Tip To find out what drive file you're using for the SCSI adapter, open the Computer Management snap-in from the Administrative Tools folder on the Programs menu. Then click Device Manager in the console tree, select the SCSI adapter, and click the Properties toolbar button. Click the Driver tab, and then click the Driver Details button. The driver file is listed in the Driver File Details dialog box.

Real World   ARC Naming Conventions

Understanding how the hard disks and partitions are named on your system is not a trivial task, unfortunately. To provide a uniform naming convention across multiple platforms, Microsoft uses a fairly arcane designation for all of the disks and partitions on your computer. Called ARC—short for Advanced RISC Computing—this is a generic naming convention that can be used in the same way for both Intel-based and RISC-based computers.

The convention describes the adapter type and number, the disk number, the rdisk number, and finally the partition number. The format is as follows:

$<adaptertype>(x)disk(y)rdisk(z)partition(n)$

where *<adaptertype>* can be either scsi, multi, or signature. Use multi for all non-SCSI adapters and for SCSI adapters that use a BIOS—as most adapters used with Intel-based processors do. The *(x)* will be the adapter number, starting at zero. If *<adaptertype>* is signature, *(x)* will be an 8-character drive signature.

The value for *(y)* will be the SCSI ID of the disk for SCSI adapters. For multi this will always be zero. The number for *(z)* will be zero for scsi, and it will be the ordinal number of the disk for multi, starting with zero. Finally, the partition number *(n)* will be the number of the partition on the target disk. Here the partitions start at one, with zero reserved for unused space.

Installing the Recovery Console

One of the most useful new recovery features in Windows 2000 is the Recovery Console. This is basically an enhanced, NTFS-enabled, secure command prompt that can be used to copy files, start and stop services, and perform other recovery actions if you can't boot the system using Windows 2000's new safe mode. The Recovery Console is always available for use via the four Windows 2000 setup disks or the CD-ROM; however, you can also install it as an option on the Boot menu for use in those instances when you can't boot using Windows 2000 safe mode. You'll still need to use the boot disk if you can't get to the Boot menu or if the Recovery Console is damaged. To install the Recovery Console, follow these steps:

1. While in Windows 2000, Windows NT, Windows 95, or Windows 98, insert the Windows 2000 CD-ROM.

2. Close the Autorun dialog box.

3. At a command prompt or in the Run dialog box, enter the command *d:\i386\winnt32\cmdcons,* replacing *d* with the drive letter of the Windows 2000 CD-ROM or network share.

4. Click Yes to install the Recovery Console, as shown in Figure 33-2.

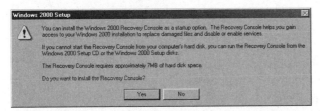

Figure 33-2. *The Windows 2000 Setup window.*

Specifying Recovery Options

You can specify how you want Windows 2000 to deal with system crashes by changing a few options in the System tool in Control Panel. To do so, follow these steps:

1. Open the System tool from Control Panel, and click the Advanced tab.

2. Click the Startup And Recovery button to display the Startup And Recovery dialog box, shown in Figure 33-3.

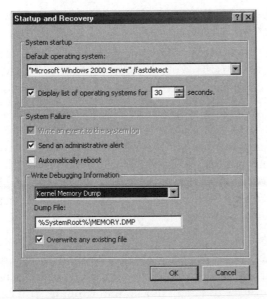

Figure 33-3. *The Startup And Recovery dialog box.*

3. Select the operating system you want to have boot by default from the Default Operating System list box.

4. If you want to boot the default operating system automatically, without waiting, clear the Display List Of Operating Systems check box. Otherwise, specify how long you want to display a list of options in the box provided.

5. Select the Write An Event To The System Log check box, if available, to record an entry in the event log when the system experiences a crash.

6. Select the Send An Administrative Alert check box to send an alert to administrators over the network when the system crashes.

7. Select the Automatically Reboot option to instruct Windows 2000 to reboot the system in the event of a crash. Otherwise the system will remain at a blue screen until an administrator manually reboots it.

8. Select how much debugging information you want to record from the Write Debugging Information list box. Note that if you have a large amount of RAM you will need a lot of disk space if you want to use the Kernel Memory Dump option.

9. Enter the filename for the dump file in the Dump File text box, and select the Overwrite Any Existing File check box to maintain only a single dump file.

Creating and Using a Recovery Drive

An excellent way to recycle an old, small drive that's not good for much else is to use it as an external recovery drive. This drive needs to be only about 700 MB at a minimum. The recovery drive can even be used for several servers if you set it up as a portable device. Using a recovery drive in this way offers a somewhat cheaper alternative to mirroring the drive.

To create the recovery drive, install a minimal Windows 2000 Server on the drive, configuring your swap file to be on that drive. Make sure that the installation includes the tape driver you will be using for tape backup. Create a bootable Windows 2000 floppy disk, following the procedure outlined earlier in the section "Creating a Boot Disk," and edit the Boot.ini file on it to point to the SCSI address of the recovery drive.

When a system failure occurs, simply cable the recovery drive to the server and boot from the boot disk that points to the recovery drive. If the recovery drive has sufficient user accounts and software to keep your system running, you can run off the recovery drive until you can schedule a full-scale repair or replacement of the failed drive. When you are able to take the system down and replace the failed drive, all you need to do is restore your backup tape to it and restart the server. You can even do the restore in the background while you continue to run off the recovery drive if necessary.

Summary

Assume that disaster will eventually occur, and plan accordingly. Create standardized recovery procedures and keep them up to date. When there's a lot of turmoil, as always happens in the case of a major failure, people forget important steps and can make poor decisions. Standardized procedures provide a course of action without the need for on-the-spot decisions. The next chapter describes how to use the Windows 2000 Backup utility.

Chapter 34
Using Backup

Backing up the data on your network is essential, and Microsoft Windows 2000 adds a new wrinkle to an already complicated problem with the need to back up the Active Directory directory service. Fortunately, the operating system includes the Windows 2000 Backup utility licensed from Veritas Software that, while it doesn't include all of the bells and whistles of the third-party network backup products, at least gets the job done in a reasonably efficient manner. You can use Windows 2000 Backup to protect the Windows 2000 system on which it runs and to back up other systems accessible by way of the network. This chapter examines the capabilities and limitations of Windows 2000 Backup and describes some basic strategies you can use to protect your network against data loss related to hardware failure, virus attack, or accidental file deletion.

Selecting a Backup Medium

The first decision you must make when planning a backup strategy is where you intend to store your data. Windows 2000 Backup supports magnetic tape, the traditional backup medium, but it can also archive your data to a backup file that you can store on any device addressable by the Windows 2000 file systems, including cartridge drives (such as Iomega Zip and Jaz drives), floppy disks, and even recordable CD-ROMs. For more extensive archiving, Windows 2000 Backup also supports the use of *media pools*—that is, libraries of disks or tapes that you access through a jukebox or autochanger. The medium you choose should depend on your budget, the amount of data you have to back up, and how much time you have available for creating the backup.

Estimating the cost of a backup storage medium isn't simply a matter of pricing tape drives and disk drives. The cost of the recording medium is also an important consideration. For example, a magneto optical drive like the Jaz that holds 2 GB might seem like a bargain, but the cartridge it uses can cost as much as $200, or 10 cents per megabyte. In contrast, you can find recordable CD-ROM (CD-Rs) for well under $1, at a cost per megabyte of about 15 hundredths of a cent. Tape media prices per megabyte tend to fall somewhere between these two extremes. Remember, too, that a CD-R or cartridge drive solution is useful for other storage besides backups, while a tape drive can be used for nothing else.

Using Removable Storage

When you install a tape, CD-ROM, cartridge drive, or autochanger in Windows 2000 by using the Add New Hardware Wizard, the drive falls under the control of the Removable Storage service. The Windows 2000 Backup utility relies on this service to provide basic media-handling functions. When you mount, dismount, or eject a disk or tape, the Removable Storage service manages the device, not Windows 2000 Backup.

The Removable Storage service has its own user interface, separate from Windows 2000 Backup, in the Computer Management snap-in for the Microsoft Management Console (MMC), as shown in Figure 34-1. You use this tool when you need to send commands directly to a tape drive or other device, such as when you want to eject, format, or retension a tape.

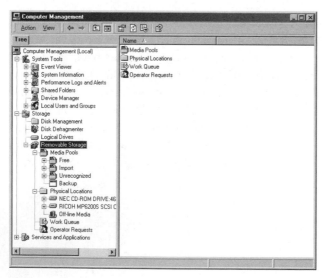

Figure 34-1. *The Removable Storage service on the Computer Management snap-in.*

Backing Up to Files

As an alternative to backing up by using a device registered in the Removable Storage service, you can also back up system data to a file. Windows 2000 Backup can create the file on any writable storage device addressable by using a standard drive letter, such as a hard disk, cartridge, or floppy disk drive. By default, the backup file has a .BKF extension, but you can name the file anything you want and store it on any supported device.

Using CD-ROMs

Because of their extremely low media cost, recordable CD-ROMs can be an excellent storage medium for system backups. Two types of writable CD-ROMs are commonly used: *CD-Rs,* which are WORM (write once, read many) devices, and *CD-RWs,* which you can write to many times. Using CD-Rs for backups might seem wasteful because you can fill them only once, but blank disks are cheap enough to make this feasible. As an added benefit, you get a permanent archive of your system, eliminating the need to develop a media rotation system and keep track of how many times you have used a particular tape or cartridge.

Note   Windows 2000 Backup doesn't provide direct support for WORM devices like recordable CD-ROMs. You must use third-party software to make these devices directly addressable by the Windows 2000 Backup application.

Developing a Backup Strategy

To effectively back up a network, you must plan your approach to this complex task. Network backups are more complicated than simply putting a tape in the drive and starting up the software. Your backup strategy should address all of the following questions:

- How much data do you have to back up?
- How much time do you have to perform backups?
- How often should you back up the data?
- Who is going to be responsible for seeing that backups are completed?
- How many tapes (or other media) do you plan to use?
- How often will you overwrite your tapes?

The Backup Window

The concept of the backup window should determine which devices you purchase for backing up your network and which types of backups you'll perform. The *backup window* is the amount of time you have available to perform backups of your data. You should compare the length of your backup window with the amount of data you have to back up to determine the optimum backup rate for your network. If, for example, your organization works overlapping shifts, leaving only a few hours of network time during which to perform backups, you might have to purchase faster equipment or run several devices in parallel to back up all of your data in the time allotted.

Backup Types

Part of creating a strategy to fit your available backup window involves selecting the type of backups you'll perform. Windows 2000 Backup supports five types of backup jobs that specify how much of your data will be backed up during each job. By selecting the appropriate job type, you can minimize the number of tapes (or other media) and the amount of time required to perform your backups without compromising the safety of your data.

Most of these backup types depend on the archive attribute to determine when the files on a given disk have changed and must be backed up again. The archive attribute in Windows 2000 is the same as that in MS-DOS, no matter which file system you're using. The attribute is a single bit included in the directory entry for each file, which the backup software can set or clear as needed.

Typically, a backup program will clear the archive attributes for all of the files it backs up during a particular job. When you modify a file later, the system automatically sets the attribute as it writes to the disk. This enables the backup software to examine the archive attributes during the next job and back up only the files for which the attribute is set—that is, the files that have changed since the last backup. The backup types described in the following sections are variations on this technique.

Normal Backup

A *normal backup,* in Windows 2000 parlance, is a full backup of all of the files and directories you select in the Windows 2000 Backup software. As part of the job, the program clears the archive attribute on each file. This type of job is the baseline for future jobs that back up only the modified files.

Incremental Backup

During an *incremental backup*, the program examines the archive attributes and backs up only the files that have changed since the last normal or incremental backup. As with a normal backup, this type of job also clears the archive attribute on each file it copies. Incremental backups use the minimum amount of tape and also save time by not copying all of the files that remain unchanged during every job. However, performing a restore is inconvenient.

For example, if you perform a normal backup on Monday and incremental backups on Tuesday through Friday, you must restore from all five of these tapes in the order in which they were written to ensure that you have the most current version of every file. If a particular file is updated daily, Windows 2000 Backup will overwrite it with a newer version during the restoration of each tape. However, if you restore only the Monday and Friday tapes, because they represent the last normal backup and the most recent incremental back up, you will lose the most current versions of files that were modified on Tuesday through Thursday, but not on Friday.

Differential Backup

A *differential backup* is identical to an incremental backup except that the program doesn't clear the archive attributes for the files that it copies to tape. This means that during each differential backup you are copying every file that has changed since the last normal or incremental backup. Thus, after a normal backup on Monday, a differential backup on Tuesday will copy all of the files that have changed (just like an incremental job). However, the differential backups performed on Wednesday through Friday will copy all of the files changed since Monday's normal backup. In other words, some redundancy of data is likely during this kind of job because a file modified only once on Tuesday will be copied during each day's differential backups.

This type of job requires more tape than using incremental jobs, and more time as well, but the advantage is that when you perform a restore, you need only the tapes containing the last normal backup and the most recent differential. Thus, if you have to rebuild a system on Saturday, you need restore only the normal backup from the previous Monday and the most recent differential backup from Friday.

A network backup strategy will typically use incremental or differential backups in addition to normal jobs, but not both. If you're faced with a lot of data to back up and a limited backup window, incrementals are faster and more economical. However, if you have to perform frequent restores, differentials make the process far easier.

Daily Backup

A *daily backup* copies only the files that have changed on the day that the backup job is performed, disregarding the current state of the archive attribute. This type of job also doesn't clear the archive attributes of the files it copies as it runs. Daily jobs are useful when you want to perform an extra backup on a given day without disturbing an established backup strategy by modifying the archive attributes.

Copy Backup

A *copy backup* job is the equivalent of a normal backup, except that the program doesn't clear the archive attributes of the files it writes to the tape or other backup medium. You can use a copy backup job to perform an extra full backup without disturbing the archive attributes used by an established backup strategy.

Media Rotation

A *media rotation scheme* dictates how many tapes (or other media) you will use for your backups. In most cases, you'll want to keep copies of your backups for a while in case you need to perform a restore from them, but eventually, they will become obsolete and you can reuse the tapes. For example, a small network might use a total of five tapes to perform a full backup each weekday and reuse the same tapes each week. In contrast, a large, security-conscious organization might use new tapes for every backup and permanently archive all of the used ones. Most media rotation schemes fall somewhere between these two extremes.

One popular rotation scheme is known as the grandfather-father-son method because it uses three "generations" of tapes representing monthly, weekly, and daily backups, respectively. In this rotation scheme, you perform a full backup every month and retain the tape for a year (preferably off-site); this is the "grandfather." You also perform a full backup every week and retain the tape for a month; this is the "father." The "son" backups are performed daily and retained for a week. The daily jobs can be either full, incremental, or differential backups.

The point of a media rotation scheme is to ensure that you always have a current copy of your data on tape and to reuse the tapes in an even and organized manner. Be sure to label your tapes carefully and store them in a safe place, away from magnetic fields and other adverse environments. We also strongly recommend that you store a copy of your backups off-site, such as in a safety deposit box or other fireproof vault, so that in the event of a true disaster such as a fire, your data is protected.

> **Note**   Some of the third-party network backup products can automatically implement a customizable rotation scheme by tracking the tapes, the number of times they're used, and the names that you should put on the labels. These programs will also tell you which tape to put in the drive each day and let you know which tapes you must use to restore particular files. Unfortunately, Windows 2000 Backup lacks this feature.

Backing Up Data

The Windows 2000 Backup program provides several methods that you can use to create and execute backup jobs. When you launch Windows 2000 Backup for the first time—by clicking Start, pointing to Programs, choosing Accessories, choosing System Tools, and selecting Backup—you see the Welcome tab shown in Figure 34-2, from which you can choose a wizard to help you create a backup or restore job. To bypass the hand-holding provided by the wizard, you can also create a backup job by clicking the Backup tab in this dialog box and accessing the backup interface directly.

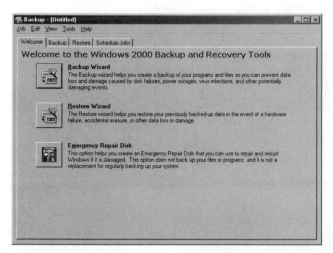

Figure 34-2. *The Welcome tab of Windows 2000 Backup.*

In addition to wizards and the GUI, you can execute Windows 2000 Backup jobs from the command line by running the executable program Ntbackup.exe with the appropriate parameters. See "Executing Jobs from the Command Line" later in this chapter for more information.

The following sections examine the various methods for creating a backup job. Regardless of the particular method you use, creating any backup job involves the following basic steps:

- Select the drives, directories, and files you want to back up.
- Specify the storage medium that will be the destination for the backup.
- Configure backup options like backup type, logging, and file exclusions.
- Specify when the backup is to occur.

Using the Windows 2000 Backup Tab

The Backup tab of the Windows 2000 Backup program (Figure 34-3) is where you select the files and directories to be backed up and choose their destination. You use a Microsoft Windows Explorer–like hierarchical display to browse local and network drives and make selections with the check boxes. You can select entire drives or individual files and directories for backup. The System State item backs up the registry and the Active Directory database on the local machine, as well as other system elements required in a disaster recovery situation. See "Backing Up the System State" later in this chapter for more information on the system state and disaster recovery.

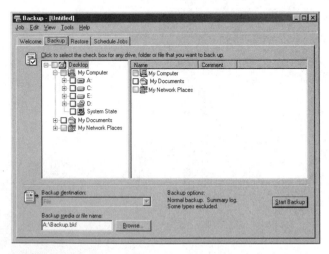

Figure 34-3. *The Backup tab of Windows 2000 Backup.*

Creating Selection Scripts

Once you've selected the files and directories to back up, you can create a selection script that contains the job configuration you created. After choosing Save Selections from the Job menu, you specify a filename with a .BKS extension for the selection script and the directory where the program should create it. You can use selection scripts to create an identical backup job during a subsequent session by loading the selection script from the Job menu. When you do this, the same system elements you selected before creating the script will be selected again. You can then run the job as is or make additional selections. You can also use the script to execute the job from the Ntbackup.exe command line.

Accessing Files and Folders for Backup

To back up any files and folders, the account used to run the job must have the appropriate permissions granting access to those files and folders. A user who is a member of the local Backup Operators group or Administrators group is automatically granted permission to back up any and all files and folders on the local machine. Members of the domain Backup Operators group and Administrators group can back up all files and folders on any computer in the domain, as well as any computer in a domain with which a two-way trust relationship exists.

A user who isn't a member of any of these groups must either be the owner or have the Read, Read and Execute, Modify, or Full Control permission for each of the files and folders to be backed up. Disk quota restrictions can also limit a user's ability to back up systems.

Selecting the Storage Medium

After you specify what you want to back up, you must tell the program where to write the data. By default, Windows 2000 Backup provides the File option only in the Backup Destination field. If you've installed a tape drive or other device so that it is managed by the Removable Storage service, that device is also provided as a destination option. After you make a selection, you use the Backup Media field or the File Name field to specify a tape or disk name or the path and filename the program should use to create a backup file.

When you select a tape or other removable storage drive, the Backup Media field enables you to select it by the name that you've already created with Windows 2000 Backup or to select New Media, which enables you to specify a name for a new blank device.

Configuring Backup Options

At this point, you can click the Start Backup button to trigger the backup job using the parameters specified on the Backup tab of the Backup window, or you can further configure the job by choosing Options from the Tools menu. On the General tab of the Options dialog box, you can specify whether the program should use certain media-handling features and, most importantly, select whether the program should verify the data on the tape after completing the backup job. A verification pass compares the data that has been written to the tape or other medium with the original copy on the hard disks to ensure that the data has been written properly. Although the verification process considerably lengthens the time required to run the job, it's a good precaution to take, especially when you're working with a newly installed drive.

> **Caution** Although verifying the backup data written to any tape is a wise precaution to take, it isn't foolproof. Many times a backup job has seemed to complete successfully and has even been verified, but the data can't be restored for one reason or another. The *only* absolutely reliable method for ensuring that the data you've backed up has actually been written to the tape is to perform test restores.

On the Backup Type tab of the Options dialog box, you select the type of job that you want to run (either normal, incremental, differential, copy, or daily, as described in "Backup Types" earlier in this chapter). The default is to run a normal backup, which might be undesirable if you're in the midst of a backup sequence that relies on the archive attributes to determine which files the program should copy to the tape.

> **Note** You'll be prompted to specify values for the Backup options when you run a backup job by using either the Start Backup button or the Windows 2000 Backup Wizard. The settings that you specify for these options now will be the default values in the prompts generated later.

Logging Backups

On the Backup Log tab of the Options dialog box (Figure 34-4), you can specify whether the program should keep a log of the activities that occur during the job and the level of detail in the log. Since a detailed log lists every file and directory copied during the job, the file can be quite long. If you want to review the job only to see that all of the procedures completed successfully, you can select the Summary option.

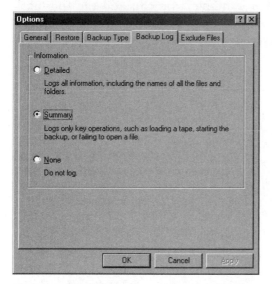

Figure 34-4. *The Backup Log tab of the Options dialog box.*

The backup logs are stored as ASCII files with a .LOG extension in a subfolder named Local Settings\Application Data\Microsoft\Windows NT\NTBackup\Data. This path is located in the Documents And Settings folder named for the user logged on while the backup is performed. You can view the logs with any text editor, but unfortunately, Windows 2000 Backup gives the files incremental names like Backup01.log and Backup02.log, making it difficult to locate the log for a particular job. To view a log by the job name, you choose Report from the Backup program's Tools menu, highlight a particular job, and click the View button or the Print button. This displays or prints the log file using Notepad.

Excluding Files

On the Exclude Files tab (Figure 34-5), you can list specific files and directories that the program should skip during the backup process. By default, the list already contains the files that you never need to back up, like the Windows 2000 memory paging file (Pagefile.sys). You can add other items to the list as needed. The advantage of using the Files Excluded For All Users list instead of simply clearing specific files on the Backup tab is that you can use wildcards to skip files located anywhere in the job. For example, you can add the file mask Backup*.wbk to the list to exclude all of Microsoft Word's automatically created document backup files, wherever they occur in the selected drives and directories.

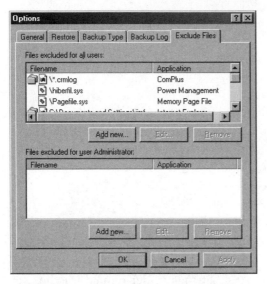

Figure 34-5. *The Exclude Files tab of the Options dialog box.*

The Exclude Files tab contains two lists: one to exclude files owned by all users on the system and one to exclude only files owned by the user currently logged on. With this option, you can add the Backup*.wbk file mask to the current-user-only list and safely skip your Word document backups without disturbing anyone else's.

To add files to either list, you click the appropriate Add New button and either select a registered file type or specify a custom file mask in the Add Excluded Files dialog box (Figure 34-6). You can also specify a particular path in which the files—selected either by file type or by file mask—are to be excluded. By default, the program will exclude the files in the chosen folder and all of its subfolders, but you can limit the exclusion to the selected folder only by clearing the Applies To All Subfolders check box.

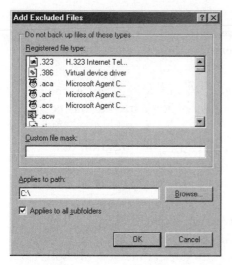

Figure 34-6. *The Add Excluded Files dialog box.*

Running a Job

After you have configured the options for the job, you start it by clicking the Start Backup button on the Backup tab, which displays the Backup Job Information dialog box shown in Figure 34-7. The program prompts you to specify a descriptive name for the backup set and to decide whether the job should be appended to the selected tape (or other medium) or whether to overwrite any existing data. If you intend to overwrite the tape, you must specify a new name for it. If you choose to overwrite the tape, you can also control access to the data written to the tape by selecting a check box that permits only the owner of the job and members of the Administrators group to restore its files.

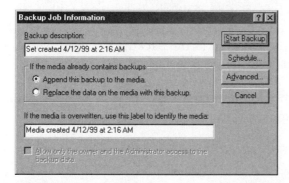

Figure 34-7. *The Backup Job Information dialog box.*

When you click the Advanced button in the Backup Job Information dialog box, the program prompts you for a backup type (with the value selected on the Backup Type tab of the Options dialog box as the default), and you must decide whether to enable the following options:

- **Back Up Data That Is In Remote Storage**   When selected, causes the program to back up the placeholder files referencing data that has been migrated to remote storage.

- **Verify Data After Backup**   When selected, causes the program to compare the data written to the tape with the original data. The default value is taken from the equivalent item on the General tab of the Options dialog box.

- **If Possible, Compress The Backup Data To Save Space**   When selected, activates the data compression capabilities built into the selected tape drive or other device. Windows 2000 Backup doesn't include any software-based compression capabilities; it facilitates only the use of your storage device's hardware-based compression. This option is enabled by default if the selected device has hardware-based compression capabilities and disabled if it doesn't.

- **Automatically Backup System Protected Files With The System State**   This option is enabled only if the System State object has been selected for backup. When this option is selected, all of the system files in the %SysDir% folder and any subfolders are backed up in addition to the files normally backed up for a system state backup.

Scheduling a Job

At this point, you can start the backup job immediately by clicking the Start Backup button in the Backup Job Information dialog box, but to establish an organized backup strategy, you'll want to schedule your jobs to execute at specific intervals. When you click the Schedule button in the Backup Job Information dialog box, if the backup selections have not been saved, you will be instructed to do so before you can schedule a backup. Otherwise, the program prompts you to specify the user name and password for the account that the system should use when running the job. The program then calls for you to specify a name for the job and displays the current date and time for the start date. To execute the job later, click the Properties button to display the Schedule Job dialog box shown in Figure 34-8.

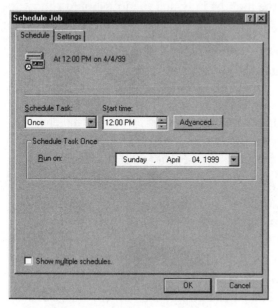

Figure 34-8. *The Schedule Job dialog box.*

Here you can specify whether the job is to be executed once at a certain time or repeated at regular intervals. The options available in the Schedule Task selector are as follows:

- **Once**   Executes the job once at a specific time on a specific date.
- **Daily**   Executes the job at the specified time each day or, if you modify the value of the Schedule Task Daily selector, each specified number of days.
- **Weekly**   Executes the job at the specified time on each of the specified days of the week or, if you modify the value of the Schedule Task Weekly selector, each specified number of weeks.

- **Monthly** Executes the job at the specified time once a month, based on either a selected date (such as the first of every month) or a day of the week (such as the first Monday of every month). By clicking the Select Months button, you can specify the months in which the job should run.

- **At System Startup** Executes the job the next time the system is started.

- **At Logon** Executes the job the next time the job owner logs on.

- **When Idle** Executes the job when the system has been idle for a specified number of minutes.

Note The scheduling capabilities of Windows 2000 Backup are quite comprehensive but not always intuitive. For example, you must select Weekly to run a daily job only on weekdays, and then select all of the days except Saturday and Sunday.

If you select the Show Multiple Schedules box, the heading on the Schedule tab changes to a selector in which you can create and manage separate schedules for the same job. You can, for example, schedule a normal backup job to execute every weekday and create a separate event to execute the same job on the last Sunday of each month, to create an extra copy for off-site storage.

If you select Once, Daily, Weekly, or Monthly from the Schedule Task list, the Advanced button becomes active. Clicking this button opens the Advanced Schedule Options dialog box. In this dialog box, you can specify a date at which a repeating job should no longer be rescheduled and you can also configure a job to repeat continually after a specified interval has elapsed. You can use this feature to copy important and volatile data to a backup file every few minutes, as an extra precaution against data loss.

On the Settings tab of the Schedule Job dialog box, you can specify conditions under which the system is instructed not to run the job, such as when the computer has not been idle for a specified length of time or when it's running on battery power. You can also configure the job to terminate if it doesn't finish within a specified length of time.

Once you've scheduled a job for later execution, you will see an icon representing it in the backup program's Scheduled Jobs tab (Figure 34-9). You can modify the parameters for any scheduled job by clicking its icon to access its Scheduled Job Options dialog box.

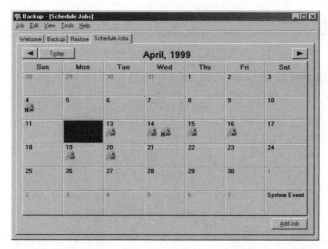

Figure 34-9. *The Scheduled Jobs tab of Windows 2000 Backup.*

Using the Windows 2000 Backup Wizard

Windows 2000 Backup also includes a wizard that walks you through the process of configuring and creating a backup job. You can launch the wizard either from the Windows 2000 Backup program's Welcome tab, by double-clicking a particular calendar date on the Schedule Jobs tab, or by clicking the Add Job button on the Schedule Jobs tab. If you have already selected drives, folders, or files to back up on the Backup tab, the program offers to use those selections in the wizard when you select a date.

The prompts presented by the wizard correspond to the options available in the program's regular GUI dialog boxes, thus reminding users of the program's capabilities and preventing them from inadvertently omitting an important option.

Executing Jobs from the Command Line

In addition to creating backup jobs by using the GUI and the wizard, you can also execute jobs from the command line. In fact, when you schedule a job for later execution by using the GUI or the Backup Wizard, the program actually uses the Windows 2000 Task Scheduler to launch the job with the command-line equivalents to the options you've chosen. When you open the Scheduled Tasks application in Control Panel and then double-click the name of the saved backup job, you can see the command line for your job in the Run field on the dialog box's Task tab (Figure 34-10).

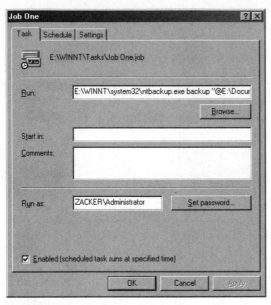

Figure 34-10. *The Task tab of the Job One dialog box.*

The executable file for the Windows 2000 Backup program is still called Ntbackup.exe and is located in the \%SysDir%\System32 folder. The best application for this command-line capability is to execute selection scripts that you've previously created in the backup program's GUI interface from batch files or other scripts. The syntax for running Ntbackup.exe from the command line is as follows:

```
Ntbackup backup [systemstate] bksfilename|foldername /J "jobname"
 [/P "poolname"] [/G "guidname"] [/T "tapename"] [/N "medianame"]
 [/F "backupfilename"] [/D "setdescription"] [/DS "servername"]
 [/IS "servername"] [/A] [/V:{yes|no}] [/R:{yes|no}] [/L:{f|s|n}]
 [/M backuptype] [/RS:{yes|no}] [/HC:{on|off}]
```

- **backup**   Specifies that the program will be performing a backup operation (even though *restore* is not a valid parameter on the command line).

- **systemstate**   Specifies that the program should back up the system state in addition to the files and folders specified on the local computer's command line or in a selection script.

- *bksfilename\foldername*   Specifies the name of a selection script file or the name of a folder that the program will back up (along with its subfolders).
- /J *"jobname"*   Specifies a name for the backup job that the program will use to identify it in the log file.
- /P *"poolname"*   Specifies the name of the media pool from which the program should take the tape (or other medium) to perform the backup. This option must not be used with the /A, /G, /F, or /T switch.
- /G *"guidname"*   Specifies that the program perform the backup to a tape or other medium identified by the *guidname* variable. This option cannot be used with the /P switch.
- /T *"tapename"*   Specifies that the program perform the backup to a tape or other medium identified by the *tapename* variable. This option cannot be used with the /P switch.
- /N *"medianame"*   Specifies the new name for a tape or other medium that is being overwritten by the backup job. This option cannot be used with the /A switch.
- /F *"backupfilename"*   Specifies the name of the .BKF file to which the program should back up the selected files and folders. This option cannot be used with the /P, /G, or /T switch.
- /D *"setdescription"*   Specifies a descriptive label to be assigned to the backup set.
- /DS *"servername"*   Causes the program to back up the directory service file for a specified Microsoft Exchange server.
- /IS *"servername"*   Causes the program to back up the information store file for a specified Microsoft Exchange server.
- /A   Causes the program to append the backup job to the tape or other medium specified by the /G or /T switch. This option cannot be used with the /P switch.
- /V:{yes|no}   Specifies whether or not the program should verify the data after the backup is completed.
- /R:{yes|no}   Specifies whether or not access to data on the tape or other medium should be restricted to the owner of the job and members of the Administrators group.

- **/L:{f|s|n}** Specifies the type of log that the program should keep while executing the backup job, where *f* = full, *s* = summary, and *n* = none.
- **/M *backuptype*** Specifies the type of backup to be performed, where *backuptype* is replaced by one of the following values: *normal, incremental, differential, copy,* or *daily.*
- **/RS:{yes|no}** Specifies whether or not the program should back up the Removable Storage database.
- **/HC:{on|off}** Specifies whether or not the program should activate the hardware compression capabilities of the tape drive.

The default states of the /V, /R, /L, /M, /RS, and /HC switches correspond to the current settings of the corresponding options in the backup program's GUI dialog boxes.

Restoring Data

Of course, backups are useless unless you can restore files from them, and Windows 2000 Backup enables you to select individual files and directories for restoration or simply to restore the entire backup set to its original location. As with the program's backup function, you can create restore jobs by using GUI screens or a wizard.

Selecting Files to Be Restored

When you display the Restore tab in the Windows 2000 Backup program, you see a list of the media in the backup media pool and the backup files you've created. As part of each backup operation, Windows 2000 Backup creates a catalog of the backup set and stores it on the tape or other medium. (If a backup job spans two or more tapes, the backup set catalog is stored on the last tape.) The program accesses this catalog whenever you select a tape from the list for restoration.

After you insert the proper tape into the drive, the program reads the catalog and shows the contents of the tape in a hierarchical display just like that of the Backup tab (Figure 34-11). You can select drives, folders, and files to restore just as you selected them to be backed up.

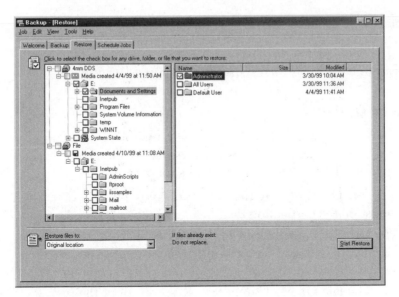

Figure 34-11. *The Restore tab.*

Selecting Destinations for Restored Files

In a disaster recovery situation, you will probably want to restore an entire backup set to its original location, but in most cases, network administrators perform restores to retrieve a copy of a file or folder that a user has accidentally deleted or that has become corrupted somehow. When this is the case, you might not want to restore the files to their original location, and Windows 2000 Backup provides options that enable you to specify another location. The Restore Files To selector on the Restore tab provides the following options:

- **Original Location**   Restores all of the selected files and folders to their original locations on local or network drives, preserving the original directory structure

- **Alternate Location**   Restores all of the selected files and folders to a specified folder, preserving the directory structure of the restored material

- **Single Folder**   Restores all of the selected files to a single specified folder, disregarding the original directory structure

Caution If you elect to use the Single Folder option when performing a restore and you have files with identical names in the selected directories, the program will use the settings from the Restore tab in the Options dialog box to determine whether to overwrite the first files with subsequent, identically named files.

Setting Restore Options

On the Restore tab of the Options dialog box, you specify how the backup program should behave when it encounters existing files with the same names during a restore operation. The available options are as follows:

- **Do Not Replace File On My Computer** Restores only the files that don't already exist on the destination disk

- **Replace The File On Disk Only If The File On Disk Is Older** Compares the dates of the identically named files and overwrites existing files on the destination disk only if the backed-up version is newer

- **Always Replace The File On My Computer** Restores all of the selected files to the destination disk, overwriting any existing files with identical names

When you click the Start Restore button, the Confirm Restore dialog box gives you the opportunity to click the Advanced button to configure the following advanced restore options before beginning the restore process:

- **Restore Security** Specifies whether the program should restore all of the security settings for each file and folder, including ownership, permissions, and audit entries. To restore the security settings, the destination for the restore job must be an NTFS drive (and the files and folders must have been backed up from an NTFS drive).

- **Restore Removable Storage Database** Specifies whether the program should restore the Removable Storage database to the \%SysDir%\ System32\Ntmsdata folder, overwriting any existing Removable Storage database at that location.

- **Restore Junction Points, And Restore File And Folder Data Under Junction Points To The Original Location** Specifies whether the program should restore the junction points created with mounted drives as well as the data that the junction points reference. When this feature is disabled, Windows 2000 Backup restores the junction points themselves but doesn't necessarily restore the referenced data.

- **When Restoring Replicated Data Sets, Mark The Restored Data As The Primary Data For All Replicas**   Specifies whether the program should restore file replication service (FRS) data so that it will be replicated to other servers. When this feature is disabled, Windows 2000 Backup restores the FRS data, but because of its age, it is likely to be overwritten later by data from the replicas on other servers.

Note   Windows 2000 Backup can only execute restore jobs immediately. The program can't schedule restores for execution later.

Planning for Disaster

A catastrophic server hard disk failure is every network administrator's worst nightmare, and many other disasters can result in the destruction of disks or even entire systems. Making sure that you have current backups of your disks is an essential part of any disaster recovery plan, as described in Chapter 33, but other Windows 2000 system elements should also be protected. Windows 2000 Backup includes additional features that enable you to protect the entire system configuration and simplify the process of restoring the computer to its former state.

Backing Up the System State

A separate entry called System State appears with the local drive letters under the My Computer heading on the Backup tab of Windows 2000 Backup. Selecting the System State entry causes the program to back up the components of the local system configuration that aren't directly accessible through the file system. These components include the following:

- Registry (on both servers and workstations)
- Class Registration database (on both servers and workstations)
- System boot files (on both servers and workstations)
- Certificate Services database (on certificate servers only)
- Active Directory (on domain controllers only)
- SYSVOL folder (on domain controllers only)

Backing up these components makes it possible for you to completely restore a system to a new disk, without losing any of the domain and local user accounts or the rights and permissions associated with them. You can back up the system state only for the local machine, meaning that if you have multiple Windows 2000 systems on your network, you will have to run the backup program on each computer to fully protect them. In most cases, however, only Windows 2000 servers will contain system state information that is irreplaceable.

Because of dependencies between the system state elements, you can't back them up or restore them individually; you must treat them as a unified system element. However, you can restore the system state to an alternate location, in which case the program will restore only the registry, SYSVOL, and system boot files.

Tip Even if you can't back up the system state on remote systems, you can back up disks from those systems over the network. You can effectively protect all of your systems by first running a backup job on each Windows 2000 computer; this job saves only the system state to a file on the computer that has the tape drive (or other backup medium). Then, by backing up that entire machine to tape, along with the disks on the remote systems, you'll be protecting all of the disks as well as the system state for each machine.

Handling Backup and Restore Problems

Backing up and restoring data in a network environment is a process that has always been subject to special problems and considerations. Windows 2000 Backup addresses some of these problems, as discussed in the following sections.

Backing Up Exchange Servers

Because they can be constantly in use, mail servers like Microsoft Exchange have particularly difficult backup problems. Windows 2000 Backup includes a feature specifically designed to back up Exchange servers, which is available only when the program detects an Exchange module called Edbbcli.dll on the local system. When this module is present, a Microsoft Exchange item appears in the backup program's Tools menu, enabling you to specify the uniform naming convention (UNC) name of the Exchange server you want the program to access. Also, the expandable display on the Backup tab includes a Microsoft Exchange icon that you select to back up the mail server (Figure 34-12).

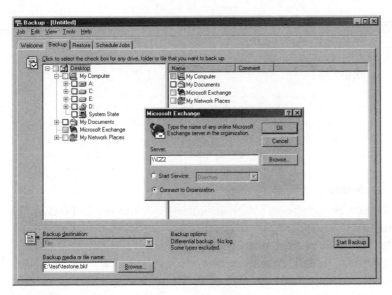

Figure 34-12. *The Backup tab with the Microsoft Exchange dialog box displayed.*

Backing Up Encrypted Files

Encrypted files aren't stored any differently than unencrypted files by the Windows 2000 file systems; only their data format is different. Therefore, backing up encrypted files doesn't in any way compromise their security status. The files are copied to the tape or other medium in their encrypted form and restored the same way. The personnel responsible for backing up the files don't need to have access to the encryption codes, nor does access to the tape itself present a risk.

Restoring the System State

Backing up the system state is as simple as selecting the appropriate box on the Backup tab, but restoring it is a bit trickier. The restoration process must not only overwrite vital system data that is currently in use, such as the registry, but it must also (in the case of a domain controller) restore the Active Directory database. This problem is particularly difficult because in a domain with multiple domain controllers, the replication system can overwrite the newly restored data because of its outdated update sequence numbers.

Therefore, to effectively restore the system state on a domain controller, you must perform two special procedures during the restoration process: start the computer in directory services restore mode and perform an authoritative restore of the Active Directory database.

Note You can restore the system state only on the local system. The Windows 2000 Backup program automatically determines the correct destination for the restored data, based on the location of the system root directory (typically C:\Winnt), and it overwrites the existing system state data on the computer.

Directory Services Restore Mode

To restore Active Directory and the SYSVOL volume on a Windows 2000 domain controller, you must first reboot the system in directory services restore mode, a form of safe mode that ensures that the system is ready to have its Active Directory database overwritten. To do this, restart the system and press the F8 key when you see the Please Select The Operating System To Start message. From the Boot menu, select Directory Services Restore Mode. After checking the system's local drives to ensure their integrity, Windows 2000 loads the operating system in a stand-alone server configuration with a set of generic drivers that permit safe-mode access to the operating system.

Because your domain controller system won't be functioning as a domain controller at this time, you might see error messages stating that Active Directory–dependent services have failed to load. This is to be expected. Because the machine isn't functioning as a domain controller, it isn't using the user and group objects associated with the domain. Instead, the system is using a small set of user and group accounts stored in the registry rather than in Active Directory. At this point, you can run Windows 2000 Backup and restore the system state.

Authoritative Restore

When you restore the system state on a domain controller, the restored Active Directory objects have the same update sequence numbers as when they were backed up. These numbers are necessarily older than those currently in use in Active Directory and, as a result, they will be considered to be outdated and overwritten during the next replication pass. To prevent this from happening, you must perform an authoritative restore of the Active Directory data stored as part of the system state on the backup medium. An authoritative restore is one that flags the restored Active Directory objects as authoritative, meaning that during the next replication event they will overwrite the equivalent objects on the domain controllers containing the replicas.

To perform an authoritative restore, you must run the Windows 2000 Ntdsutil.exe program after you restore the system state and before you reboot the computer. Ntdsutil.exe will modify the update sequence numbers of the restored objects so that they appear to the replicas to contain the newest data available. During the next replication pass, the system will use the restored Active Directory database objects to overwrite the data on the domain's other controllers.

Ntdsutil

The Ntdsutil.exe program is an interactive command-line utility copied to the \%SysDir\System32 folder by default during the operating system installation. You see a prompt labeled *ntdsutil:* when you run the executable file from the command line. The program uses a series of menus to navigate its various functions. Type a question mark (?) or *help* at any prompt to list the available commands and submenus for that prompt. To perform an authoritative restore, you type *authoritative restore* at the ntdsutil prompt and then type *help* to display the available commands, which are as follows:

- **Restore Database**   Modifies the update sequence numbers of all Active Directory objects, making them authoritative for the entire domain

- **Restore Database Verinc %d**   Authoritatively restores the entire database specified by the variable %d and overrides version increase

- **Restore Subtree %s**   Modifies the update sequence numbers of Active Directory objects in the subtree specified by the %s variable, making them authoritative for the entire domain

- **Restore Subtree %s Verinc %d**   Authoritatively restores the subtree specified by the variable %s and overrides version increase

Thus, to use the entire Active Directory database restored with the system state as authoritative information, you use the Restore Database command at the Ntdsutil.exe *authoritative restore:* prompt. The program opens the database and increases the version number of all the Active Directory objects by 100,000. Once the process is completed, you can exit the program by typing *quit* twice and restart the system in normal mode. When the computer is functioning as a domain controller again, it will replicate its Active Directory database to all of the other controllers in the domain, and because the version numbers of its objects will be substantially higher than those of the other replicas, the system will copy the restored data to all of the replicas in the domain.

Preserving NTFS Permissions

File system permissions are an essential element of any network storage policy, and for a backup program to function in a network environment, it must be able to save the permissions along with the files and restore them either to the same or a different location. However, the various file systems supported by Windows 2000 complicate this process considerably. The FAT file systems don't support permissions, and if you restore a backup of an NTFS drive to a FAT drive, those permissions are lost.

The introduction of NTFS 5 in Windows 2000 presents another significant incompatibility, and that is with NTFS drives created in Microsoft Windows NT 4. When you restore a backup of an NTFS 5 drive to a Windows NT 4 NTFS drive, you lose the following file system elements:

- Permissions
- Encrypting file system (EFS) settings
- Disk quota information
- Mounted drive information
- Remote storage information

The loss of these elements can compromise network security and make it impossible to access data that is encrypted or stored on another drive or medium. Restoring NTFS 5 data files to another file system can also cause you to lose data from embedded or linked documents and from alternate data storage formats such as those used by Services for Macintosh, disk image files, and custom file types created by certain non-Microsoft applications. You should always consider the file system used on your destination drive before you perform any NTFS restores.

Third-Party Backup Utilities

The Windows NT backup utilities suffer from serious deficiencies in their tape drive support, scheduling capabilities, and other features. However, Windows 2000 has a backup program that provides all of the essential functions required by a network backup program and a few extras as well. (Of course, there's still room for improvement.)

One of the shortcomings of the Windows 2000 Backup program is that because the backup set catalogs are stored on the backup media themselves, you can't tell whether a particular file is on a tape without loading it so that the program can read the catalog. Some third-party backup products store the catalog information in a database on the local drive, enabling you to search for particular files (and even particular versions of files) to discover which tape you must use to restore them. This procedure can require a lot of extra disk space, but if you perform frequent restores, the sacrifice can be worthwhile.

Most third-party programs also simplify the process of creating a media rotation scheme by enabling you to specify the types of jobs you want to run each day and indicating when to run them. The program takes charge of the tape labeling by telling you which tape to insert each day and assigning it a new name. After overwriting each tape a specified number of times, the program advises you to retire it and add a new tape into the rotation. This also makes restoring to a specified file easier because the program can tell you by name exactly which tape you need to restore from. You'll find more information on third-party backup utilities in Appendix E.

Some network backup solutions also provide additional capabilities such as modules that enable you to back up certain types of files while they're in use or that allow you to back up workstations running non-Windows operating systems. While third-party network backup solutions are no longer necessary, they can provide simplified backup administration and expanded capabilities.

Summary

Once you've developed an adequate backup strategy and have configured the software to implement it, it's up to the administrator to see that it is carried out. Frequently, backups require no more attention than the insertion of a new tape into the drive, and yet even this simple task is often overlooked. Too many administrators learn about the importance of keeping current backups the hard way, through the irretrievable loss of important data. Those who find suitable employment afterward have usually learned their lesson, but it's always better if you can learn painful lessons without the pain. The next chapter focuses on the tools for building a Windows 2000 environment that is both fault-tolerant and available.

Chapter 35
Planning Fault Tolerance and Avoidance

Microsoft Windows 2000 Server, and especially Advanced Server with its clustering support, provides an excellent environment in which to build a truly fault-tolerant system. Of course, avoiding the faults in the first place is even better than handling them once they've happened, but the realistic system administrator knows that a problem will occur sooner or later, and he or she plans for it. Chapter 33 covered disaster planning in depth, so you should refer to that chapter for information on how to prepare for major problems and how to build a full disaster recovery plan to quickly resolve them.

This chapter focuses primarily on the hardware and software tools that will allow you to build a highly available and fault-tolerant Windows 2000 environment. Remember, however, that no matter what hardware and software you deploy, building and deploying for high availability and fault tolerance requires time and discipline. You'll need to make informed decisions about your real requirements as well as determine the resources available to meet those requirements. When planning for a highly available and fault-tolerant deployment, you should consider all points of failure and work to eliminate any single point of failure. Redundant power supplies, dual disk controllers, multiple network interface cards (multihoming), and fault-tolerant disk arrays (RAID) are all strategies that you can and should employ.

Mean Time to Failure and Mean Time to Recover

Two important metrics are most commonly used to measure fault tolerance and avoidance. These are *mean time to failure* (MTTF), the mean time until the device will fail, and *mean time to recover* (MTTR), the mean time it takes to recover once a failure has occurred. Keep in mind that even if you have a finite failure rate, if your MTTR is zero or near zero, this may be indistinguishable from a system that hasn't failed. Downtime is generally measured as MTTR/MTTF, but since it can be prohibitively expensive to increase MTTF beyond a certain point, you should spend both time and resources on managing and reducing the MTTR for your most likely and costly points of failure.

Most modern electronic components have a distinctive "bathtub" curve that represents their failure characteristics, as shown in Figure 35-1. During the early life of the component (referred to as the burn-in phase), it's more likely to fail; once this initial phase is over, a component's overall failure rate remains quite low until it reaches the end of its useful life, when the failure rate increases again.

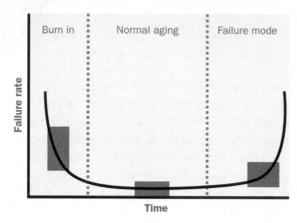

Figure 35-1. *The normal statistical failure rates for mechanical and electronic components: a characteristic "bathtub" curve.*

The typical commodity hard disk of 10 years ago had an MTTF on the order of three years. Today, a typical MTTF for a commodity hard disk is more likely to be 35 to 50 years! But at least part of that difference is a direct result of counting only the portion of the curve in the normal aging section, taking externally caused failure out of the equation. So a hard disk that fails because of a power spike that wasn't properly filtered doesn't count against the MTTF of the disk. This may be nice for the disk manufacturer's statistics, but it doesn't do much for the system administrator whose system has crashed because of a disk failure. Consequently, you can understand the importance of looking at the total picture and carefully evaluating all the factors and failure points on your system. Only by looking at the whole system, including the recovery procedures and methodology, can you build a truly fault-tolerant system.

Protecting the Power Supply

The single biggest failure point for any network is its power supply. If you don't have power, you can't run your computers. Seems pretty obvious, and most of us slap an uninterruptible power supply (UPS) on the order when we're buying a new server or at least make sure that the current UPS can handle the extra load.

However, this barely scratches the surface of what you can do to protect your network from power problems. You need to protect your network from four basic types of power problems:

- **Local power supply failure**   Failure of the internal power supply on a server, router, or other network component
- **Voltage variations**   Spikes, surges, sags, and longer-term brownouts
- **Short-term power outages**   External power failures lasting from fractions of a second to several minutes
- **Long-term power outages**   External power failures lasting from several minutes to several hours or even days

Each type of power problem poses somewhat different risks to your network and will likely require somewhat different protection mechanisms. The possible threat that each one poses to your environment varies depending on the area in which you live, the quality of power available to you, and the potential loss to your business if your computers are down.

Local Power Supply Failure

The weakest links in all networks are the mechanical moving parts, and the mechanical moving parts most likely to fail are the internal power supplies on the servers and network components. All the power conditioning, uninterruptible power supplies, and external generators in the world won't help much if your server's power supply fails. Most higher end servers these days either have a redundant power supply or have the option of including one. Take the option! The extra cost associated with adding a redundant power supply to a server or critical piece of network hardware is usually far less than the cost of downtime should the power supply fail.

If your server or another piece of network hardware doesn't have the option of a redundant power supply, order a spare power supply for it when you order the original hardware. Keep all of your spares in a central, well-known, and identified location, and clearly label the machine or machines the power supply is for.

Finally, practice replacing the power supplies of your critical hardware. Include clear, well-illustrated, detailed instructions on how to replace the power supplies of your critical hardware as part of your disaster recovery standard operating procedures. If you can change the power supply in a very short time, the cost of having it fail diminishes significantly. If you have to wait for your original equipment supplier to get a replacement to you, even if you're on a four-hour response service contract, the cost can be a *lot* higher than the cost of keeping a spare around.

Voltage Variations

Even in areas with exceptionally clean power that is always available, the power that is supplied to your network will inevitably fluctuate. Minor, short-term variations merely stress your electronic components, but major variations can literally fry them. You should never, ever simply plug your computer into an ordinary wall socket without providing some sort of protection against voltage variations. The following sections describe the types of variations and the best way to protect yourself from them.

Spikes

Spikes are large but short-lived increases in voltage. They can occur because of external factors, such as lightning striking a power line, or because of internal factors, such as a large motor starting. The most common causes of severe voltage spikes, however, are external and outside your control. And the effects can be devastating. A nearby lightning strike can easily cause a spike of 1000 volts or more to be sent into equipment designed to run on 110 to 120 volts. Few, if any, electronic components are designed to withstand large voltage spikes of several thousand volts, and almost all will suffer damage if they're not protected from them.

Protection from spikes comes in many forms, from the $19.95 power strip with built-in surge protection that you can buy at your local hardware store to complicated arrays of transformers and specialized sacrificial transistors that are designed to die so that others may live. Unfortunately, those $19.95 power strips just aren't good enough. They *are* better than nothing, but barely. They have a limited ability to withstand really large spikes.

More specialized (and more expensive, of course) surge protectors that are specifically designed to protect computer networks are available from various companies. They differ in their ability to protect against really large spikes and in their cost. There's a fairly direct correlation between the cost of these products and their rated capacity and speed of action within any company's range of products, but the cost for a given level of protection can differ significantly from company to company. As always, if the price sounds too good to be true, it is.

In general, these surge protectors are designed to work by sensing a large increase in voltage and creating an electrical path for that excessive voltage that doesn't allow it to get through to your server. In the most severe spikes, the surge protectors should destroy themselves before allowing the voltage to get through to your server. The effectiveness of these stand-alone surge protectors depends on the speed of response to a large voltage increase and the mechanism of failure when their capacity is exceeded.

Many of the newer UPSs also provide protection from spikes. They have built-in surge protectors, plus isolation circuitry that tends to buffer the effects of spikes. The effectiveness of the spike protection in a UPS is not directly related to its cost, however—the overall cost of the UPS is more a factor of its effectiveness as an alternative power source. Your responsibility is to read the fine print and understand the limitations of the surge protection a given UPS offers. Also remember that just as with simple surge protectors, large voltage spikes can cause the surge protection to self-destruct rather than allow the voltage through to your server. That's the good news; the bad news is that instead of having to replace just a surge protector, you're likely to have to repair or replace the UPS.

Finally, one other spike protection mechanism can be helpful—the constant voltage transformer. You're not likely to see one unless you're in a large industrial setting, but they are often considered to be a sufficient replacement for other forms of surge protection. Unfortunately, they're not really optimal for surge protection. They will filter some excess voltage, but a large spike is likely to find its way through. However, in combination with either a fully protected UPS or a good stand-alone surge protector, a constant voltage transformer can be quite effective. And they provide additional protection against other forms of voltage variation that surge protectors alone can't begin to manage.

Surges

Voltage surges and voltage spikes are often discussed interchangeably, but we'd like to make a distinction here. For our purposes, a *surge* lasts longer than most spikes and isn't nearly as large. Most surges last a few hundred milliseconds and are rarely over 1000 volts. They can be caused by many of the same factors that cause voltage spikes.

Providing protection against surges is somewhat easier than protecting against large spikes. Most of the protection mechanisms just discussed will also adequately handle surges. In addition, most constant voltage transformers are sufficient to handle surges and may even handle them better if the surge is so prolonged that it might threaten to overheat and burn out a simple surge protector.

Sags

Voltage *sags* are short-term reductions in the voltage delivered. They aren't complete voltage failures or power outages and are shorter than a full-scale brownout. Voltage sags can drop the voltage well below 100 volts on a 110- to 120-volt normal line and will cause most servers to reboot if protection isn't provided.

Stand-alone surge protectors provide no defense against sags. You need a UPS or a very good constant voltage transformer to prevent damage from a voltage sag. Severe sags can overcome the rating of all but the best constant voltage transformers, so you generally shouldn't use constant voltage transformers as the sole protection against sags. A UPS, with its battery power supply, is an essential part of your protection from problems caused by voltage sag.

Brownouts

A *brownout* is a planned, deliberate reduction in voltage from your electric utility company. Brownouts most often occur in the heat of the summer and are designed to protect the utility company from overloading. They are *not* designed to protect the consumer, however.

In general, a brownout will reduce the available voltage by 5 to 20 percent from the normal value. A constant voltage transformer or a UPS provides excellent protection against brownouts, within limits. Prolonged brownouts may exceed your UPS's ability to maintain a charge at the same time that it is providing power at the correct voltage to your equipment. Monitor the health of your UPS carefully during a brownout, especially because the risk of a complete power outage will increase if the power company's voltage reduction strategy proves insufficient.

The best protection against extended brownouts is a constant voltage transformer of sufficient rating to fully support your critical network devices and servers. This transformer will take the reduced voltage provided by your power company and increase it to the rated output voltage. A good constant voltage transformer can handle most brownouts for an extended time without problems, but you should still supplement the constant voltage transformer with a quality UPS and surge protection between the transformer and the server or network device. This extra protection is especially important while the power company is attempting to restore power to full voltage because during this period you run a higher risk of experiencing power and voltage fluctuations.

Short-Term Power Outages

Short-term power outages are those that last from a few milliseconds to a few minutes. They can be caused by either internal or external events, but you can rarely plan for them even if they are internal. A server that is unprotected from a short-term power outage will, at the minimum, reboot or, at the worst, fail catastrophically.

You can best protect against a short-term power outage by using a UPS in combination with high-quality spike protection. Be aware that many momentary interruptions of power are accompanied by large spikes when the power is restored. Further, a series of short-term power outages often occur consecutively, causing additional stress to electronic components.

Long-Term Power Outages

Long-term power outages, lasting from an hour or so to several days, are usually accompanied by other, even more serious problems. Long-term power outages can be caused by storms, earthquakes, fires, and the incompetence of electric power utilities, among other causes. As such, long-term power outages should be part of an overall disaster recovery plan. (See Chapter 33 for more on disaster planning.)

Protection against long-term power outages really becomes a decision about how long you will want or need to function if all power is out. If you need to function long enough to be able to gracefully shut down your network, a simple UPS or a collection of them will be sufficient, assuming that you've sized the UPS correctly. However, if you need to be sure that you can maintain the full functionality of your Windows 2000 network during an extended power outage, you're going to need a combination of one or more UPSs and an auxiliary generator.

If your situation requires an auxiliary generator to supplement your UPSs, you should carefully plan your power strategy to ensure that you provide power to all of the equipment that the network will require in the event of a long-term power outage. You should regularly test the effectiveness of your disaster recovery plans and make sure that all key personnel know how to start the auxiliary generator manually in the event it doesn't start automatically. Finally, you should have a regular preventive maintenance program in place that tests the generator and ensures that it is ready and functioning when you need it.

Disk Arrays

The most common hardware malfunction is probably a hard disk failure. Even though hard disks have become more reliable over time, they are still subject to failure, especially during their first month or so of use. They are also subject to both catastrophic and degenerative failures caused by power problems. Fortunately, disk arrays have become the norm for most servers, and good fault-tolerant RAID systems are available in Windows 2000 Server and RAID-specific hardware supported by Windows 2000.

The choice of software or hardware RAID, and the particulars of how you configure your RAID system, can significantly affect the cost of your servers. To make an informed choice for your environment and needs, you must understand the trade-offs and the differences in fault tolerance, speed, configurability, and so on.

Hardware vs. Software

RAID can be implemented at the hardware level, using RAID controllers, or at the software level, either by the operating system or by a third-party add-on. Windows 2000 supports both hardware RAID and its own software RAID.

Hardware RAID implementations require specialized controllers and cost much more than an equal level of software RAID. But for that extra price, you get faster, more flexible, and more fault-tolerant RAID. When compared to the software RAID provided in Windows 2000 Server, a good hardware RAID controller supports more levels of RAID, on-the-fly reconfiguration of the arrays, hot-swap and hot-spare drives (discussed later in this chapter), and dedicated caching of both reads and writes.

The Windows 2000 Server software RAID requires that you convert your disks to dynamic disks. The disks will no longer be available to other operating systems, although this really shouldn't be a problem in a production environment. However, you should consider carefully whether you want to convert your boot disk to a dynamic disk. Dynamic disks can be more difficult to access if a problem occurs, and the Windows 2000 setup and installation program provides only limited support. For maximum fault tolerance, we recommend using hardware mirroring on your boot drive; if you do use software mirroring, make sure that you create the required fault-tolerant boot floppy disk and test it thoroughly before you need it. (See Chapter 33.)

RAID Levels for Fault Tolerance

Except for level 0, RAID is a mechanism for storing sufficient information on a group of hard disks such that even if one hard disk in the group fails, no information is lost. Some RAID arrangements go even further, providing protection in the event of multiple hard disk failures. The more common levels of RAID and their appropriateness in a fault-tolerant environment are shown in Table 35-1.

Table 35-1.   RAID levels and their fault tolerance

Level	Number of Disks*	Speed	Fault Tolerance	Description
0	N	+++	---	Striping alone. Not fault-tolerant, but provides for the fastest read and write performance.
1	2N	+	++	Mirror or duplex. Slightly faster read than single disk, but no gain during write operations. Failure of any single disk causes no loss in data and minimal performance hit.
3	N+1	++	+	Byte-level parity. Data is striped across multiple drives at the byte level with the parity information written to a single dedicated drive. Reads are much faster than with a single disk, but writes operate slightly slower than a single disk since parity information must be generated and written to a single disk. Failure of any single disk causes no loss of data but can cause a significant loss of performance.
4	N+1	++	+	Block-level parity with a dedicated parity disk. Similar to RAID-3 except that data is striped at the block level.
5	N+1	+	++	Interleaved block-level parity. Parity information is distributed across all drives. Reads are much faster than a single disk but writes are significantly slower. Failure of any single disk provides no loss of data but will result in a major reduction in performance.
0+1 (also known as level 10)	2N	+++	++	Striped mirrored disks. Data is striped across multiple mirrored disks. Failure of any one disk causes no data loss and no speed loss. Failure of a second disk could result in data loss. Faster than a single disk for both reads and writes.
Other	Varies	+++	+++	Array of RAID arrays. Different hardware vendors have different proprietary names for this RAID concept. Excellent read and write performance. Failure of any one drive results in no loss of performance and continued redundancy.

*In the Number of Disks column, N refers to the number of hard disks required to hold the original copy of the data. The plus and minus symbols show relative improvement or deterioration compared to a system using no version of RAID. The scale peaks at three symbols.

When choosing the RAID level to use for a given application or server, consider the following factors:

- **Intended use**   Will this application be primarily read-intensive, such as file serving, or will it be predominately write-intensive, such as a transactional database?

- **Fault tolerance**   How critical is this data, and how much can you afford to lose?

- **Availability**   Does this server or application need to be available at all times, or can you afford to be able to reboot it or otherwise take it off-line for brief periods?

- **Performance**   Is this application or server heavily used, with large amounts of data being transferred to and from it, or is this server or application less I/O intensive?

- **Cost**   Are you on a tight budget for this server or application, or is the cost of data loss or unavailability the primary driving factor?

You need to evaluate each of these factors when you decide which type of RAID to use for a server or portion of a server. No one answer fits all cases, but the final answer will require you to carefully weigh each of these factors and balance them against your situation and your needs. The following sections take a closer look at each factor and how it weighs in the overall decision-making process.

Intended Use

The intended use, and the kind of disk access associated with that use, plays an important role in determining the best RAID level for your application. Think about how write-intensive the application is and whether the manner in which the application uses the data is more sequential or random. Is your application a three-square-meals-a-day kind of application, with relatively large chunks of data being read or written at a time, or is it more of a grazer or nibbler, reading and writing little bits of data from all sorts of different places?

If your application is relatively write-intensive, you'll want to avoid software RAID if possible and avoid RAID-5 if other considerations don't force you to it. With RAID-5, any application that requires greater than 50 percent writes to reads is likely to be at least somewhat slower if not much slower than it would be on a single disk. You can mitigate this to some extent by using more but smaller drives in your array and by using a hardware controller with a large cache to off-load the parity processing as much as possible. RAID-1, in either a mirror or duplex configuration, provides a high degree of fault tolerance with no significant penalty during write operations—a good choice for the Windows 2000 system disk.

If your application is primarily read-intensive, and the data is stored and referenced sequentially, RAID-3 or RAID-4 may be a good choice. Because the data is striped across many drives, you have parallel access to it, improving your throughput. And since the parity information is stored on a single drive, rather than dispersed across the array, sequential read operations don't have to skip over the parity information and are therefore faster. However, write operations will be substantially slower, and the single parity drive can become an I/O bottleneck.

If your application is primarily read-intensive and not necessarily sequential, RAID-5 is an obvious choice. It provides a good balance of speed and fault tolerance, and the cost is substantially less than RAID-1. Disk accesses are evenly distributed across multiple drives, and no one drive has the potential to be an I/O bottleneck. However, writes will require calculation of the parity information and the extra write of that parity, slowing write operations down significantly.

If your application provides other mechanisms for data recovery or uses large amounts of temporary storage that doesn't require fault tolerance, a simple RAID-0, with no fault tolerance but fast reads and writes, is a possibility.

Fault Tolerance

Carefully examine the fault tolerance of each of the possible RAID choices for your intended use. All RAID levels except RAID-0 provide some degree of fault tolerance, but the effect of a failure and the ability to recover from subsequent failures can be different.

If a drive in a RAID-1 mirror or duplex array fails, a full, complete, exact copy of the data remains. Access to your data or application is unimpeded, and performance degradation is minimal, although you will lose the benefit gained on read operations of being able to read from either disk. Until the failed disk is replaced, however, you will have no fault tolerance on the remaining disk.

In a RAID-3 or RAID-4 array, if one of the data disks fails, a significant performance degradation will occur since the missing data needs to be reconstructed from the parity information. Also, you'll have no fault tolerance until the failed disk is replaced. If it is the parity disk that fails, you'll have no fault tolerance until it is replaced, but also no performance degradation.

In a RAID-5 array, the loss of any disk will result in a significant performance degradation, and your fault tolerance will be gone until you replace the failed disk. Once you replace the disk, you won't return to fault tolerance until the entire array has a chance to rebuild itself, and performance will be seriously degraded during the rebuild process.

RAID systems that are arrays of arrays can provide for multiple failure tolerance. These arrays provide for multiple levels of redundancy and are appropriate for mission-critical applications that must be able to withstand the failure of more than one drive in an array.

Real World   Multiple Disk Controllers Provide Increased Fault Tolerance

Spending the money for a hardware RAID system will increase your overall fault tolerance, but it can still leave a single point of failure in your disk subsystem: the disk controller itself. While failures of the disk controller are certainly less common, they *do* happen. Many hardware RAID systems are based on a single multiple-channel controller—certainly a better choice than those based on a single-channel controller, but an even better solution is a RAID system based on multiple identical controllers. In these systems, the failure of a single disk controller is not catastrophic but simply an annoyance. In RAID-1 this technique is known as duplexing, but it is also common with many of the proprietary arrays of arrays that are available from server vendors and in the third-party market.

Availability

All levels of RAID, except RAID-0, provide higher availability than a single drive. However, if availability is expanded to also include the overall performance level during failure mode, some RAID levels provide definite advantages over others. Specifically, RAID-1, mirroring/duplexing, provides enhanced availability when compared to RAID levels 3, 4, and 5 during failure mode. There is no performance degradation when compared to a single disk if one half of a mirror fails, while a RAID-5 array will have substantially compromised performance until the failed disk is replaced and the array is rebuilt.

In addition, RAID systems that are based on an array of arrays can provide higher availability than RAID levels 1 through 5. Running on multiple controllers, these arrays are able to tolerate the failure of more than one disk and the failure of one of the controllers, providing protection against the single point of failure inherent in any single-controller arrangement. RAID-1 that uses duplexed disks running on different controllers—as opposed to RAID-1 that uses mirroring on the same controller—also provides this additional protection and improved availability.

Hot-swap drives and hot-spare drives (discussed later in this chapter) can further improve availability in critical environments, especially hot-spare drives. By providing for automatic failover and rebuilding, they can reduce your exposure to catastrophic failure and provide for maximum availability.

Performance

The relative performance of each RAID level depends on the intended use. The best compromise for many situations is arguably RAID-5, but you should be suspicious of that compromise if your application is fairly write-intensive. Especially for relational database data and index files where the database is moderately or highly write-intensive, the performance hit of using RAID-5 can be substantial. A better alternative is to use RAID-0+1 (also known as RAID-10 from some vendors).

Whatever level of RAID you choose for your particular application, it will benefit from using more small disks rather than a few large disks. The more drives contributing to the stripe of the array, the greater the benefit of parallel reading and writing you'll be able to realize—and your array's overall speed will improve.

Cost

The delta in cost between RAID configurations is primarily the cost of drives, potentially including the cost of additional array enclosures because more drives are required for a particular level of RAID. RAID-1, either duplexing or mirroring, is the most expensive of the conventional RAID levels, since it requires at least 33 percent more raw disk space for a given amount of net storage space than other RAID levels.

Another consideration is that RAID levels that include mirroring/duplexing must use drives in pairs. Therefore, it's more difficult (and more expensive) to add on to an array if you need additional space on the array. A net 18-GB RAID-0+1 array, comprising four 9-GB drives, requires four more 9-GB drives to double in size, a somewhat daunting prospect if your array cabinet has bays for only six drives, for example. A net 18-GB RAID-5 array, however, can be doubled in size simply by adding two more 9-GB drives, for a total of five drives.

Hot-Swap and Hot-Spare Disk Systems

Hardware RAID systems can provide for both hot-swap and hot-spare capabilities. A *hot-swap* disk system allows failed hard disks to be removed and a replacement disk inserted into the array without powering down the system or rebooting the server. When the new drive is inserted, it is automatically recognized and either will be automatically configured into the array or can be manually configured into it. Additionally, many hot-swap RAID systems allow you to add hard disks into empty slots dynamically, automatically or manually increasing the size of the RAID volume on the fly without a reboot.

A *hot-spare* RAID configuration uses an additional, preconfigured disk or disks to automatically replace a failed disk. These systems usually don't support hot-swapped hard disks so that the failed disk can't be removed until the system can be powered down, but full fault tolerance is maintained by having the hot spare available.

Distributed File System

The Distributed file system (Dfs) is primarily a method of simplifying the view that users have of the available storage on a network—but it is also, when configured appropriately, a highly fault-tolerant storage mechanism. By configuring your Dfs root on a Windows 2000 domain controller, you can create a fault-tolerant, replicated, distributed file system that will give you great flexibility while presenting your user community with a cohesive and easy-to-navigate network file system.

When you create a fault-tolerant Dfs root on a domain controller and replicate it and the links below it across multiple servers, you create a highly fault-tolerant file system that has the added benefit of distributing the load evenly across the replicated shares, giving you a substantial scalability improvement as well. See Chapter 16 for more on setting up your Dfs and ensuring that replication works correctly.

Clustering

Windows 2000 Advanced Server supports two different kinds of clustering, either of which can greatly improve your fault tolerance:

- For many TCP/IP-based applications, the Network Load Balancing service provides a simple, "shared nothing," fault-tolerant application server.
- Server clusters provide a highly available fault-tolerant environment that can run applications, provide network services, and distribute loads.

Network Load Balancing

The Network Load Balancing service (called Windows Load Balancing Service in Microsoft Windows NT 4) allows TCP/IP-based applications to be spread dynamically across up to 32 servers. If a particular server fails, the load and connections to that server are dynamically balanced to the remaining servers, providing a highly fault-tolerant environment without the need for specialized, shared hardware. Individual servers within the cluster can have different hardware and capabilities, and the overall job of load balancing and failover happens automatically, with each server in the cluster running its own Windows 2000 copy of Wlbs.exe, the Network Load Balancing service.

Server Clusters

Server clusters, unlike network load balancing, depend on a shared resource between nodes of the cluster. This resource, which in the initial shipment of Windows 2000 Advanced Server must be a shared disk resource, is generally a shared SCSI or Fibre Channel–attached disk array. Each server in the cluster is connected to the shared resource, and the common database that manages the clustering is stored on this shared disk resource.

Nodes in the cluster generally have identical hardware and identical capabilities, although it is technically possible to create a server cluster with dissimilar nodes. In the initial release of Windows 2000 Advanced Server, only two node clusters are supported for server clusters, although this restriction and the restriction on the type of shared resource are likely to change with later releases.

Server clusters provide a highly fault-tolerant and configurable environment for mission-critical services and applications. Applications don't need to be specially written to be able to take advantage of the fault tolerance of a server cluster, although if the application is written to be clustering aware, it can take advantage of additional controls and features in a failover and fallback scenario.

Summary

Building a highly available and fault-tolerant system requires you to carefully evaluate both your requirements and your resources to eliminate single points of failure within the system. You should evaluate each of the hardware subsystems within the overall system for fault tolerance, and ensure that recovery procedures are clearly understood and practiced, to reduce recovery time in the event of a failure. Uninterruptible power supplies, RAID systems, distributed file systems, and clustering are all methods for improving fault tolerance. In the next chapter, we discuss the registry: what it is, how it's structured, and how to back it up and restore it.

Chapter 36
Using the Registry

The registry is a source of fear to many system administrators because it's the central repository of system configuration settings. Making mistakes while editing the registry can have undesirable consequences, but it's not so different from using a power saw—or an automobile, for that matter. All powerful tools cause negative consequences if misused. If you know what you're doing and take a few simple safety precautions, you can take advantage of a powerful tool—like the registry—without grief.

Introducing the Registry

The registry is a binary database that organizes all of a system's configuration settings into a hierarchy. Applications, system components, device drivers, and the Microsoft Windows 2000 kernel all use the registry to store their own preferences, read them back again, and obtain information about the system's hardware configuration, the current user's preferences, and the default settings that should be used when no predefined settings exist (such as when a new user logs on to the machine for the first time).

The Origins of the Registry

Back in the days of Microsoft Windows 3.1, applications and Windows stored their configuration information in .INI files. These files were simple to edit, which was both a blessing and a curse—users could easily make changes when needed, but they could also easily make changes when they *weren't* needed. The proliferation of Windows applications soon meant that machines were littered with dozens of .INI files, each with its own combination of settings—not all of which were documented or even understood by anyone other than the application programmers.

Windows NT 3.1 largely eliminated .INI files; it introduced the predecessor to what is now known as the Windows 2000 Registry. The Windows NT 3.1 Registry has some important features that have continued on more or less unchanged to Windows 2000.

- Registry data is organized by category, so settings that pertain to a single user (like your choice of default wallpaper) are kept separate from settings for other users or the system's own internal parameters. Each setting is stored as an independent piece of data.

- Registry data is stored in binary database files on disk; the only way to view or edit these files is to use special-purpose tools that call the registry access routines of the Win32 API.

- Each data item in the registry has a data type, like REG_DWORD (a long integer) or REG_SZ (an ASCII string). The system's registry editors enforce these data types, so you can't put a string where a number belongs. This restriction helps weed out one class of mistakes—well-intentioned but misinformed attempts to put a round peg into a square hole.

- Like every other object in the system, each registry item has an owner, and it can have its own independent set of security access control lists (ACLs) and auditing controls.

- With appropriate permissions, administrators or programs on one computer can connect to, read, and modify the registries of remote computers.

Some of these features made it into Windows 95/98, which shares the organizing principles of the Windows NT registry without its security or remote access features. The two operating system (OS) families use different internal formats for their registry databases even though their registries look similar to registry-editing tools; their files aren't interchangeable or interoperable.

Perhaps the most remarkable aspect of the Windows 2000 registry is how little it has changed from the Windows NT 4 version. The binary structures used to store the data remain the same, as do the structural underpinnings discussed later in this chapter.

What Registry Data Is Used For

Now that you have a general understanding of what the registry's data is used for, it's time to get more specific. Registry data is used in six different areas:

- Registry data is used during setup, installation, configuration, and removal of the OS itself, of OS components like Internet Information Services (IIS) or Certificate Services, and of hardware devices. Any time you see an "Add/Remove Something-or-Other Wizard," you can bet that registry data is being used.

- At boot time the Windows 2000 recognizer (Ntdetect.com) and some associated code in the Windows 2000 kernel search for hardware devices and store their findings in a memory-based portion of the registry.

- The Windows 2000 kernel uses the information gathered at boot time to figure out which device drivers to load and in what order; it also stores information needed by those drivers in the registry.

- Device drivers use the data written by the recognizer and the kernel to configure themselves to work with the physical hardware in the machine.

- System tools and applications like control panels and some MMC snap-ins read and write configuration data in the registry.

- Applications can store their own settings in the registry; in addition, they can read (and possibly write) the data gathered by other software that uses the registry.

Note that during the boot, kernel, and device driver phases, the system can't use the disk—until the device drivers are loaded, the system can't "talk" to the disk. You'll learn how the system works around this seemingly severe limitation in the section "Volatile Keys" later in the chapter.

Real World   Being on Your Best Behavior

Microsoft continually warns us that editing the registry is dangerous—is it really, or are they just covering themselves? The answer is somewhere between the two extremes. Because the registry is used by virtually every part of Windows 2000, and because most programmers are lazy when it comes time to write code to check the validity of values that come from the registry, making an improper or ill-advised registry change can certainly harm your machine. Having said that, however, if you're careful and attentive, you don't need to be afraid of the registry. A few simple rules will keep you out of trouble:

- Don't edit a part of the registry for fun. If you don't know how a certain change will affect your system, don't make it unless you can live with the consequences.

- Be careful about adding new values or keys. Software will pay attention only to keys that have names it understands. Adding a new key or value in the hope that some component will recognize it and change its behavior is like adding a new switch labeled "Jet Boost" to your car's dashboard and expecting it to increase your car's speed. The exception to this rule is that Microsoft often uses code that can recognize hidden (or at least under documented) keys and change its behavior accordingly.

- Maintain a current backup of your system state.

Understanding the Registry's Structure

In a file system, the root objects are disks, which contain folders and files. A single folder can contain an arbitrary number of other folders and files; each folder or file has a name. By combining the names of the folders that enclose a file, we can construct a path that unambiguously names only one file on the disk, so that C:\Windows\Mapi32.dll and C:\Winnt\Mapi32.dll are completely separate files, for example.

The Windows 2000 registry is organized much like a file system, except that the vocabulary needed to describe it is somewhat different. At the root of the registry structure are the *root keys* (likened to a disk in a file system). Each root key contains several *subkeys* (folders); in turn, these subkeys contain other subkeys and *values* (the registry equivalent of files). Like files, each value has a name that must be unique in the subkey or folder that encloses it; each value also has an associated data type that governs what kind of data it can hold.

Any registry value can be identified by specifying its full path, starting at the root. For example, the path HKEY_LOCAL_MACHINE\SOFTWARE\Microsoft\ Exchange\Security\ObscureWireDataFormat specifies a particular value in the Security subkey that belongs to Microsoft Exchange Server. Figure 36-1 shows an annotated section of the Windows 2000 registry so that you can identify the root keys, subkeys, and values in it.

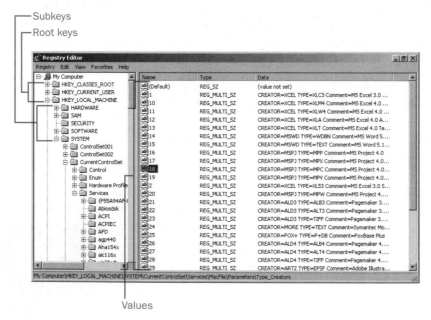

Figure 36-1. *The three separate components of a registry value.*

The Root Keys

When you open the My Computer icon on your desktop, you always see certain items, such as icons that represent the logical disk volumes on your computer. The same is true of the registry. When you open it with a Registry Editor, you'll always see the same set of root keys. Each root key has a distinct purpose:

- HKEY_LOCAL_MACHINE (HKLM) stores all settings that pertain to the local machine. For example, the HARDWARE subkey of HKLM is where the system and its device drivers record and share information about the hardware devices that the system finds at boot time (as well as other Plug-and-Play devices that you can add after the system is booted). Applications are supposed to store data here only if it pertains to everyone who uses a machine; for example, a printer driver might store a set of default print settings here and copy them to each new user's profile when he or she logs on.

- HKEY_USERS (HKU) contains one entry for each user who has previously logged on to your computer. Each user's entry is owned by that user's account, and it contains the profile settings that were in effect for that user. When you use group policies (see Chapter 9), the policy settings you specify are applied to an individual user's profile here.

- HKEY_CURRENT_CONFIG (HKCC) stores information about the system's current boot configuration. In particular, it contains information about the current set of system services and which devices were present at boot time. This root key is actually a pointer to sections inside HKLM.

- HKEY_CURRENT_USER (HKCU) points to the currently logged on user's profile inside HKU. Microsoft requires that Windows 2000 applications store any user-specific preferences in subkeys under HKCU; for example, HKCU\SOFTWARE\Binary Research\GhostSrv\Settings holds a user's personal preferences for Symantec's Ghost product. Another user's settings for the same product would be available in the same key only when that user is logged on.

- HKEY_CLASSES_ROOT (HKCR) ties file extensions and OLE class identifiers together; it actually points to HKLM\SOFTWARE\Classes. System components like Windows Explorer (and Microsoft Internet Explorer, for that matter) use these associations to determine which applications or components to use when opening or creating a particular type of file or data object. Since Windows 2000 relies heavily on the Component Object Model (COM), which in turn relies on the object identifiers stored in HKCR, this key and its subkeys are more important than you might think at first.

Note In the Windows 2000 documentation, Microsoft identifies only two registry root keys: HKLM and HKU. Since HKCU, HKCC, and HKCR are actually pointers to subkeys of HKLM and HKU, this is technically correct, but you might be confused if you're used to the idea of five separate root keys. To avoid that confusion, we'll use the old-style notation.

Real World   HKCR in Windows 2000

One important registry change in Windows 2000 involves HKCR. In Windows NT 4 and earlier, the data in HKCR is the same for all users. In some ways, this was a reasonable design decision for Microsoft to make—all users on the machine have access to the same set of installed OLE components and file mappings.

However, one common complaint from administrators whose users have to share machines is that two users' preferred associations might differ. If one user chooses Netscape Navigator as the preferred Web browser, that modifies HKCR; if another user later sets Internet Explorer as the preferred browser at the same machine, that undermines the original choice. More importantly, the ability for users to change these values reduces system security in two ways: it allows users to change associations for other users (increasing the risk of introducing malicious code), and it forces administrators to remove permissions from HKLM\SOFTWARE\ Classes, since all users need access to it.

In Windows 2000, Microsoft changed this behavior so that HKCR actually contains data from two sources: the user's profile (where user-specific customizations are stored) and HKLM\SOFTWARE\Classes, where systemwide settings live. Users can register and unregister COM components, change file associations, and so on without affecting other users. Administrators can adjust permissions on HKLM\SOFTWARE\Classes so users can't tamper with the systemwide settings you want them to have. Each user's unique settings are stored in the Usrclass.dat file, which is treated like its own registry hive. (See "Where Data Goes on Disk" later in the chapter for more details on hive files.)

Major Subkeys

Within these root keys, several subkeys are noteworthy. Because each root key has so much information under it, you'll usually hear these individual subkeys referred to—after all, HKLM\HARDWARE and HKLM\SOFTWARE don't have much in common except their root key.

HKLM\HARDWARE

The HKLM\HARDWARE subkey stores information about the hardware found in the system. All of the values stored here are held only in RAM, not on disk, because of the device driver ordering problem mentioned earlier. When the hardware recognizer starts, it enumerates every device it can find, both by walking the system buses and by searching for specific classes of devices like parallel ports or keyboards. Three major subkeys live under HKLM\HARDWARE:

- The DESCRIPTION subkey contains descriptions of the CPUs, floating-point processors, and multifunction devices in the system. The information stored here is considerably expanded over what is available in Windows NT 4; for example, the CentralProcessor subkey now tracks a number of settings that aren't present in Windows NT 4. For computers that use multipurpose chipsets like Intel's BX series, one of the multifunction devices listed in this key will reflect the chipset's integrated controllers, with separate entries for disk, keyboard, pointer, parallel, and serial controllers.

- The DEVICEMAP subkey links a specific device to a specific driver. For example, DEVICEMAP\Video has a value named \Device\Video1 that contains the string \REGISTRY\Machine\SYSTEM\ControlSet001\ Services\mnmdd\Device0, which is a pointer to the place where the driver for that video controller stores its parameters.

- The RESOURCEMAP subkey exists in Windows NT 4, but it is completely revamped in Windows 2000. It now contains three primary subkeys: one for the hardware abstraction layer (HAL) to use when keeping track of the devices it finds, one for the Plug-and-Play Manager to record devices it knows how to handle, and one that reflects the amount of system resources (Microsoft-speak for RAM) available on the machine.

Additional subkeys can exist, depending on the configuration of your machine. For example, systems that support the Advanced Configuration Power Interface (ACPI) will have an ACPI subkey that contains information about the specific ACPI subfeatures that the computer supports.

HKLM\SAM

Just because Windows 2000 includes the Active Directory directory service, don't assume that no vestiges of the Security Accounts Manager (SAM) have survived. When you create local accounts or groups on a Windows 2000 machine, they are stored in HKLM\SAM, just as they are in Windows NT. However, you can't normally view or change data in this subkey, and it is mostly useful for compatibility with earlier Windows NT code that expects SAM to exist. The programming routines that access SAM data have all been revamped to use Active Directory data when it exists, or SAM when no Active Directory server is present.

HKLM\SECURITY

HKLM\SECURITY contains a lot of security information, as you might expect. Its format isn't documented, and you can't do anything in the subkey. However, the system caches logon credentials, policy settings, and shared server secrets in this subkey. The SECURITY\SAM subkey contains a copy of most of the data from HKLM\SAM.

Real World   Look, but Don't Touch!

If you're feeling adventurous and want to see what's in HKLM\SAM and HKLM\SECURITY, you can open these keys by running Regedt32 in the Local-System security context. The easiest way to do this is to use the At command to schedule Regedt32 to run in an interactive session. Just schedule it to run a minute or so into the future, like this:

```
at 12:34 /interactive regedt32.exe
```

That command tells the system to schedule Regedt32 to run one minute from now (this being written at 12:33); when it runs, the system scheduler service will launch the application, so it runs in the LocalSystem context instead of the context you're logged on as. While this is an interesting way to see what's in these subkeys, be forewarned of two things. First, you won't be able to make much sense out of the values in these keys, since they're intentionally obfuscated. Second, and more importantly, remember that changing any of these values will provoke unintended and probably undesirable consequences. In other words, look, but don't touch.

HKLM\SOFTWARE

The HKLM\SOFTWARE subkey serves as the root location for applications and system components to store their machine-wide settings. For example, HKLM\SOFTWARE\Microsoft\EnterpriseCertificates contains keys that hold the certificate trust lists (CTLs) and trusted CA certificates for this machine—individual users' CTLs and trusted CAs are stored elsewhere. Individual programs, control panels, and the like can create their own subkeys under HKLM\SOFTWARE; the de facto standard is for each vendor to create its own top-level key (for example, HKLM\SOFTWARE\Intel) and then create subentries beneath that key.

The most interesting parts of this subkey are HKLM\SOFTWARE\Microsoft\ Windows\CurrentVersion (which stores much of the GUI preference data; it's named the same as the corresponding key under Windows 95/98) and HKLM\ SOFTWARE\Microsoft\Windows NT\CurrentVersion. This latter subkey is significantly expanded in Windows 2000; for example, there are new keys for automatic server recovery handling, the Encrypting File System, the Security Configuration Editor, Terminal Services, and other new goodies.

HKLM\SYSTEM\CurrentControlSet

When you boot Windows 2000, the last action in the boot phase is to update the registry to reflect which set of controls and services was last used for a successful boot. CurrentControlSet always points to the set of controls actually in use on the system. If you look under HKLM\SYSTEM, you'll see many ControlSetXXX keys. Each ControlSetXXX subkey represents a control set that existed at one time, whether or not it was successfully used to boot. CurrentControlSet is just a pointer to the most recent successful boot set, but because it isn't easy to determine *which* set that was, the OS and applications use CurrentControlSet instead.

Beneath this set are four keys whose names carry over from earlier versions of Windows NT, although their guts are somewhat different in Windows 2000:

- **Control**   Contains control information for services and system tools. For example, Control\BackupRestore\KeysNotToRestore contains a list of keys that Windows 2000 Backup shouldn't restore (including the contents of the Plug-and-Play subkey) when it restores the registry.

- **Enum**   Contains one entry for every physical device or pseudo-device that the system can find. For example, Enum\USB\Vid_0461&Pid_4d03\Inst_0 contains information about the USB mouse plugged in to someone's laptop. Since it was present at boot time, it is included in the enumeration list.

- **Hardware Profiles**   Contains one entry for each hardware profile defined on a machine. As with HKLM\SYSTEM itself, each profile has a serial number, starting with 0001. HKLM\SYSTEM\Hardware Profiles\ Current always points to the profile that was selected at boot time.

- **Services**   Contains one subkey for each installed service. These subkeys, in turn, hold all the configuration information that the service needs. The exact set of subkeys on two machines will be different if they have different services loaded on them.

HKLM\SYSTEM\MountedDevices

Windows 2000 dynamic disk volumes (discussed in Chapter 14) are a neat technical achievement and a boon to administrators, but they depend on having information about the current configuration of the logical volumes on disk. Applications (and snap-ins, like the Disk Management snap-in) get this information from the Logical Volume Manager service; in turn, this service stores its list of mounted and available devices in the MountedDevices subkey.

How Data Is Stored

Although programs and services that use the registry don't have to understand how registry data is stored, administrators do—that way you'll know where data is stored, how the registry handles different types of data, and which files need to be safeguarded as part of your backups. You don't need to understand the internal format that the registry tools use, but you should understand the basic data types and storage locations.

Each value in the registry (Microsoft calls them *value entries*) has three parts: a name, a data type, and an actual value. For example, if you see a Microsoft Knowledge Base article that talks about some key—REG_SZ: HKLM\SYSTEM\ CurrentControlSet\Services\Replicator\Parameters\GuardTime, for example— you're seeing a complete definition of a value entry (although it's always nice to see a full path for values, so you know where to add or remove them).

Useful Data Types

Seven data types can be used to store data in the registry. Actually, only two of these types are used for most registry data: REG_DWORD and REG_SZ. The seven types are as follows:

- REG_BINARY stores arbitrary binary data in raw form, without any reformatting or parsing. You can view binary data in binary or hex forms by using one of the Windows 2000 registry editors (described later in the chapter).

- REG_DWORD stores an 8-byte long integer (or double word) value. This data type is usually used when a value indicates a count or interval, but it's also common to see REG_DWORD flags—0 means the flag is off, and 1 means it's on.

- REG_SZ is an ordinary Unicode string. These strings can be of any length; this data type is usually used to store paths, human-readable messages or device names, and so on.

- REG_EXPAND_SZ is a REG_SZ with a twist—applications can embed a special token in the string and then expand the token when they read the value from the registry. For example, *Something* is a REG_EXPAND_SZ whose normal value is %SystemRoot%\System32\Something. When Windows 2000 reads the string, it expands %SystemRoot% to the full path where the operating system is installed.

- REG_MULTI_SZ is a collection of an arbitrary number of REG_SZ values. For example, the list of DNS servers you specify in the TCP/IP Properties dialog box is stored in a REG_MULTI_SZ value. Applications must know how to pick apart a single REG_MULTI_SZ into its component parts.

- REG_FULL_RESOURCE_DESCRIPTOR is a rare bird; it is used to encode information about the system resources required by a particular device. We've never seen it appear outside of subkeys of HKLM\HARDWARE.

- REG_NONE is just a placeholder. It is used to indicate that a registry value exists but doesn't contain any actual data. Some components look for the presence or absence of a specified key or value to control their behavior at runtime; it's common for those components to look for an item of type REG_NONE—since this type doesn't hold any data, users can't mess these values up.

In day-to-day administration, what you'll need to know about these data types is mostly restricted to understanding the difference between REG_DWORD and REG_SZ values. A REG_DWORD value whose contents are 0 (the numeric value for zero) is different from a REG_SZ whose contents are "0" (the character "0"). If you need to add a new registry value (perhaps because a Microsoft Knowledge Base article recommends doing so), you'll have to ensure that you get the type right, or you might have problems with the components that use the value.

Volatile Keys

Some registry keys and values are *volatile,* in the original sense of the word—they aren't persistent and can evaporate at any moment. As an example, none of the data in HKLM\HARDWARE exists anywhere on disk; that entire subkey and all its contents reside entirely in memory. Every time you boot a Windows 2000 machine, that subkey is created anew, and when you shut it down, its contents disappear.

Disk-Based Keys

Volatile keys are useful for data that doesn't need to stay around between reboots, but most of the data stored in the registry would be pretty useless if it weren't persistent. Imagine having to reconfigure all your preferences and settings after every reboot of your desktop machine—that would get old fast. The majority of registry keys are disk-based, meaning that their contents are held in structures on disk. When a key's contents are updated, the version on disk is updated too.

Even though disk-based keys are eventually stored on disk, Windows 2000 maps them into the paged memory pool (an area of memory whose contents can be written to the pagefile when not being used) to provide more efficient access. The registry size limit, discussed later in this chapter, regulates how much registry data can be stored in the paged pool.

Where Data Goes on Disk

Microsoft uses the term "hive" to refer to a group of keys and values that belong together. A hive can be a root key, or it can be a subkey; for example, HKCC is a hive (even though it's just a pointer to part of HKLM), and so is HKLM\SAM. The important concept to remember about hives is that a hive is a self-contained unit that can be loaded and unloaded independently of other hives.

Windows 2000 uses six hives: DEFAULT (corresponding to HKU\.DEFAULT), SAM (HKLM\SAM), SECURITY (HKLM\SECURITY), SOFTWARE (HKLM\SOFTWARE), and SYSTEM (HKLM\SYSTEM). The sixth hive, which corresponds to the contents of HKCU, is better known as a user profile—a *user profile* is really just a hive that is loaded into the registry when the user logs on and unloaded at logout.

Each hive exists in its own file on disk (the files have the same names as the hives), along with a separate log file that acts as a journal of all changes made to that hive. Hive files don't have extensions, and the system keeps them open all the time—that's why you have to use a special-purpose backup tool like Windows 2000 Backup or ARCServe to back them up.

So, where do these hive files live? As with so many other Windows 2000–related questions, the answer is a hearty "It depends." In this case, the answer depends on which hives you're talking about. The big five (DEFAULT, SAM, SECURITY, SOFTWARE, and SYSTEM), along with their .LOG files, are stored in the System32\Config subfolder of the Windows 2000 Install folder.

The location of the user profile files (Ntuser.dat and Ntuser.dat.log for the logged-on user, Default and Default.log for the default user) depends on which operating system was on the machine before Windows 2000. Machines that were upgraded from Windows NT 4, or those on which Windows 2000 was cleanly installed, keep these profiles in the Profiles\Username subfolder of the system root folder. (Each user has his or her own subfolder.) For machines that were upgraded from Windows 95 or Windows 98, profiles are stored in a folder named for the user in the system's Documents and Settings folder.

Using the Registry Editors

On those occasions when you need to change values in the registry, you'll have to use some kind of registry editor. Many of the settings that you can change in control panels, Group Policy objects, or MMC snap-ins are actually stored in the registry, so you can think of these utilities as a kind of registry editor. Another kind is the custom-written script that you use to make a specific change, perhaps as part of a logon script or a file you distribute to your users. However, most of the time when you need to make a change directly to the registry, you'll use one of the two tools Microsoft includes with Windows 2000: Regedt32.exe or Regedit.exe.

What You Get

Why are there two registry editors in Windows 2000? Blame it on Windows NT 4. When Windows NT 3.1, 3.5, and 3.51 shipped, they included a registry editor called Regedt32. This tool was written to manipulate Windows NT registry keys and values, and it reflects Microsoft's standards for user interface design at the time it was written—1992 or thereabouts.

When Windows 95 was being developed, Microsoft realized that Regedt32 wasn't a good match for the Windows 95 interface *or* the underlying structural differences between the two systems' registries. Since Windows 95 needed a registry editor also, Microsoft developed a companion tool, Regedit, and shipped it with Windows 95.

To complicate matters, Microsoft includes *both* Regedt32 and Regedit with Windows NT 4. While this might seem unnecessarily redundant, it is actually an advantage, since the two programs have different and complementary abilities. Microsoft continued to ship both programs as part of Windows 2000; except for a few minor cosmetic tweaks and plumbing-related bug fixes, the Windows 2000 versions are identical to their predecessors.

Regedit vs. Regedt32

With two editors to choose from, how do you know which one to use in a given circumstance? Both tools have the same fundamental capabilities. They allow you to

- Browse a graphical structure that represents the registry hierarchy
- See and modify keys, subkeys, values, and value contents, subject to the security privileges you have
- Connect to a remote computer for which you have privileges and inspect, or even change, the contents of its registry

However, some significant differences exist, most of which revolve around features that are in one editor but not the other. Let's start with Regedt32. Since it was engineered specifically for Windows NT, it has some useful features that carry over into Windows 2000:

- Allows you to see and change security ACLs on registry keys
- Allows you to enable auditing on keys so that you can see who has attempted—or who has succeeded—in removing, adding, or editing keys or their contents
- Supports all of the registry data types described earlier in the chapter; in addition, you can edit a value of one type using another type's editor (handy when editing REG_BINARY values)
- Has a read-only mode that lets you inspect the registry without allowing changes
- Can save and load hive files or individual keys
- Uses the old-style multiple-document interface (MDI) paradigm, in which each root key has its own document window

In contrast, Regedit was designed to make full use of the Windows 95–style interface, so it looks quite a bit different from Regedt32. It also has different functionality:

- Searches keys, value names, and value contents for a specified string. This feature is invaluable and is the primary reason to use Regedit.
- Uses the familiar two-pane Windows Explorer interface, making it somewhat easier to compare the location of two keys or values. It also includes other Windows Explorer–like features, such as context menus, in-place editing, and the familiar tree control.

- Imports and exports selected keys (and their subordinate items) in a human-readable text file, instead of importing and exporting registry keys in binary form.

- Includes a Favorites menu (in the Windows 2000 version), to which you can add whatever keys you feel the need to edit repeatedly.

How do you know which tool to use? Most of the time your personal preferences will dictate which one you use. Some people like the way that Regedit works, while others prefer the old-school Regedt32 interface. If you're trying to find which key holds a particular value, you're better off using Regedit; on the other hand, if you need to set security permissions on a key, you'll have to use Regedt32.

A Whirlwind Tour of Regedit

As a user of Windows Explorer (or any version of Windows), you already know about 85 percent of what you need to use Regedit. This familiarity is entirely by design—Microsoft has tried to make it an easy-to-use tool by copying the user interface that you're already familiar with.

Regedit's main window is shown in Figure 36-2. The important parts of the interface are fairly simple to understand. Notice the following features:

- The tree in the left pane of the Registry Editor window shows all of the root keys and subkeys; what you see here depends on which keys and subkeys you've expanded.

- The right pane shows the values associated with the selected key in the left pane. Each value is shown with three items: the value name (the name (Default) is used for the unnamed default value that every key has), the value's type, and the value's contents or data.

- The status bar at the bottom of the window shows the full path to the currently selected key. (Regedit can also copy this key's path to the clipboard for you, thanks to the Copy Key Name command on the Edit menu; this is handy when you're writing a book or otherwise documenting your work.)

Because these interface features are written with the standard Windows controls, all the keyboard navigation and control shortcuts you're accustomed to using with Windows Explorer work here. For example, you can jump to a particular key by clicking anywhere in the left pane and typing the first few letters of the key's name. And you can use the arrow keys to move around in either half of the Regedit window.

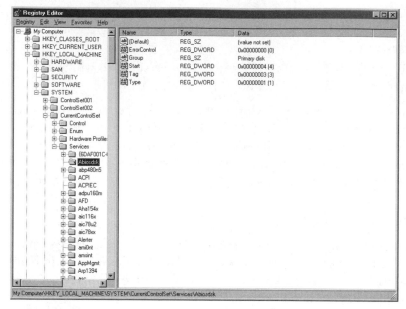

Figure 36-2. *The Regedit user interface.*

Searching for Keys and Values

The Find command on the Edit menu in Regedit is worth its weight in gold when you need to find which key, or value, has a specific name or contents. The interface to this function is uncomplicated—as Figure 36-3 shows. Even with the simple interface, the tool is extremely valuable because it searches the entire registry for a specific value. Here's how to use the Find dialog box to get what you're looking for:

- Type the pattern you're looking for into the Find What box. You can search only for plain ASCII text—no wildcards are allowed. If you're searching for values, Regedit will search only string values (REG_SZ, REG_EXPAND_SZ, and REG_MULTI_SZ) for the pattern you give.

- Use the options in the Look At box to control where Regedit looks for the specified value. By default, it will search for key names (the Keys check box), value names (the Values check box), and value contents (the Data check box), but you can fine-tune it.

- The Match Whole String Only check box tells Regedit to find the entire search string, not just a portion of it. For example, if you search for "Windows" with this check box selected, the search will ignore HKLM\SOFTWARE\Microsoft\Windows NT.

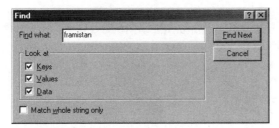

Figure 36-3. *Regedit's Find dialog box.*

When you have made your selections in the Find dialog box, click the Find Next button, and Regedit will begin searching. Eventually, one of two things will happen: either Regedit will hit the end of the registry (in which case it will tell you that it didn't find any matches), or it will find a match. In the latter case, the match will be highlighted; if the match isn't really what you were looking for, the Find Next command on the Edit menu (or F3, its accelerator) will continue the search.

Tip Every time you do a search, Regedit starts at the beginning of HKCR and works its way toward the end of HKCC. You can't change this search order, so you might as well get used to it.

Editing Value Contents

The Modify command on the Edit menu lets you change the contents of the selected value entry. (You can also edit a value by selecting it and pressing Enter.) What you see next depends on the type of value you're editing; separate editor dialog boxes exist for string values, DWORD values, and binary values. Regedit will let you edit data types it doesn't support, such as REG_FULL_RESOURCE_ DESCRIPTOR or REG_MULTI_SZ; for those types, it opens the binary editor dialog box. The editor dialog boxes themselves are straightforward—each presents the current value and lets you edit it. The keyboard shortcuts for the Cut, Copy, and Paste commands work in the editor dialog boxes, too.

Adding and Removing Keys and Values

Regedit also allows you to add and remove keys, subkeys, and individual values. Now is a good time to reiterate Microsoft's frequent warning: making unnecessary changes to the registry will likely damage your computer. Be careful when you add data, and be doubly careful when you remove it. (See "Being on Your Best Behavior," earlier in this chapter, for more details on why this is a good idea.)To add a new key as a child of the selected key, open the Edit menu, point to New, and choose Key. Regedit will create a new key and select its name so you can set it correctly. (It defaults to New Key #1.)

The new key will automatically have an unnamed value attached to it. You can add more values using the three remaining commands on the New submenu: String Value, Binary Value, and DWORD Value. Note that Regedit can't create any other data types, and if you create a binary value, components will interpret it as raw REG_BINARY data. Creating a new value adds it as a child of the selected key and gives it a default name (New Value #1, New Value #2, and so on), which you can immediately change. Once you're done adding and naming the new values, you can use the standard editor dialog boxes to change their contents to the appropriate values.

Removing values and keys is simple. Select the item you want to zap and choose Delete from the Edit menu, or just press the Delete key. Regedit will ask you to confirm your command; once you confirm it, the value or key will be immediately removed.

Importing and Exporting Registry Data

You can import and export registry data from Regedit. The resulting text files are easy to read, and you can safely move them from machine to machine. In fact, the default association for .REG files automatically launches Regedit and loads the contents of the file when you double-click it. The Export Registry File command on the Registry menu lets you save the selected key to a file, and the Import Registry File command does the reverse. Note that importing a registry file from within Regedit happens immediately—a confirmation dialog box appears that tells you whether the import succeeded or not, but you don't get a chance to stop it. (If you launch a .REG file by clicking it, however, you *do* get a confirmation dialog box.)

Real World   Creating Your Own .REG Files

If you need to distribute registry changes to your users, one way to do it is with the policy mechanisms discussed in Chapter 9. However, sometimes using a .REG file makes more sense. For example, sites that don't have direct access to Active Directory resources can't receive group policy updates. You can easily mail out .REG files and have your users double-click them. (Of course, that creates a potential security problem, since anyone can send your users the same kinds of files—make sure to educate them about proper e-mail etiquette.)

The first, and easiest, way to create your own .REG file for distribution is to use Regedit to export the keys and values you want to pass around. As an alternative, you can create your own files using NotePad or any other text editor. Here's an example:

```
Windows Registry Editor Version 5.00

[HKEY_LOCAL_MACHINE\SOFTWARE\Microsoft\Windows NT\CurrentVersion\AeDebug]
"Auto"="1"
"Debugger"="drwtsn32 -p %ld -e %ld -g"
"UserDebuggerHotKey"=dword:00000000
```

The first line tells Regedit that it's looking at a .REG file. (The blank line that follows is required, too.) After that, the format is easy to understand: define a key by putting its full path in square brackets, and then follow it with each value you want to import, one per line. Enclose value names in double quotes, as well as string value contents. REG_DWORD values are specified using the DWORD: prefix; they don't have to be enclosed in quotes. You can bundle multiple keys into the same file, as long as you add a blank line before each key name; each key can contain any number of values.

One tip: while you're becoming proficient with .REG files, you should practice by using a harmless destination path. Create your own key (say, HKLM\ SOFTWARE\Testing123) and import your .REG files under it until you're sure that they make only the changes you want made.

Connecting to a Remote Machine's Registry

If you're logged on with the right permissions, you can use Regedit to connect to another computer's registry and inspect or edit it. To accomplish this voodoo, your account must have administrative privileges on both the machine on which you're running Regedit *and* the other machine whose registry you wish to inspect/edit. In addition, Group Policy settings might prevent you from gaining access.

Assuming that your credentials are in order, you actually connect to the remote machine by choosing Connect Network Registry from the Registry menu. This command lets you browse your network to find the machine you want to connect to; once you've successfully connected, the computer's name appears in the left pane on the same level as My Computer. You can expand its root keys, poke around in the subkeys, search, and modify data to your heart's content. When you're done, choose Disconnect Network Registry from the Registry menu and select the computer to disconnect.

Renaming Keys and Values

You can change the name of a key or a value by choosing Rename from the Edit menu. In most cases, you won't want or need to do this. Since software looks for specific named values in the registry, changing the name of one of them is a bad idea.

However, when you add keys or values based on advice from Microsoft Knowledge Base articles, it's possible to misspell the name (or, worse yet, to type it correctly but find out that the name in the Knowledge Base article is wrong!), and the Rename command is your only alternative to deleting and re-creating the key.

A Whirlwind Tour of Regedt32

Regedt32 is a more sophisticated and powerful tool than Regedit, but it's a little harder to use. Figure 36-4 shows a representative session. Notice that the user interface doesn't look like Windows Explorer. That's because Regedt32 uses the old-style MDI interface, in which each root key has its own child window. This arrangement actually works as an advantage, because it's easy to make icons of the windows you're not using (especially when you connect to a remote machine).

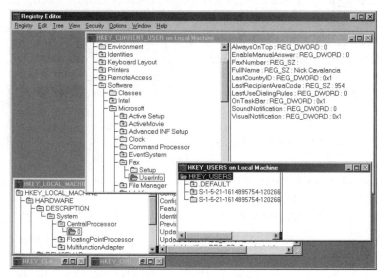

Figure 36-4. *The old-style MDI interface and appearance of Regedt32.*

Editing Value Contents

To edit a value, just double-click it and the appropriate editor dialog box will open. This is easy enough, and the editors themselves are easy to understand—except the editor for REG_FULL_RESOURCE_DESCRIPTOR. But that's OK because you shouldn't be editing items in HKLM\HARDWARE anyway, especially since changes won't be saved.

Regedt32 also allows you to edit an item as though it were of a different type. For example, you can edit a REG_SZ as binary data, or a REG_DWORD as a string. Most of the time this is fairly useless, but sometimes you'll need to take advantage of this facility to do something like editing a bit mask that's stored as a REG_DWORD. Use the bottom four commands on the Edit menu—there's one for each supported data type (Binary, String, DWORD, and Multi String) that you can edit.

When using these data type editors, be aware of these quirks:

- In the Binary Editor, you can see items in either binary or hex. The editor marks offsets in the data by showing you a 32-byte offset count on the left and a 0–31 scale across the top. This makes it easy to locate bytes at specific offsets if you need them.

- The Multi-String Editor expects you to enter one string per line, using the Return or Enter keys to skip to the next line.

- The DWORD Editor lets you enter values in binary, hex, or decimal. The editor dialog box is smart enough to ignore any illegal keystrokes (like 2 when editing a binary value).

As with Regedit, Regedt32 doesn't do any sanity checking on the values you enter, so it's your responsibility to make sure that they're correct.

Adding Keys and Values

To add a key, select the key under which you want the new key to appear. For example, to add a subkey to HKLM\SOFTWARE\Microsoft\Windows NT\ CurrentVersion\ESENT, you would select that key and then choose Add Key from the Edit menu, which opens a dialog box in which you name the new key. Once it's named, the new key will immediately appear.

Unlike Regedit, Regedt32 doesn't automatically add an unnamed value to the new key, so if you need that default value for some reason, you'll have to add it manually. To add a value, you use the Add Value command on the Edit menu. Adding a value requires the following steps:

1. Select the key to which you want to add a value, and then use the Add Value command. The Add Value dialog box shown in Figure 36-5 appears.

2. Type the name of the new value into the Value Name field. (Leave it blank if you want to add the <No Name> default value.)

3. Use the Data Type list box to select the type for the new value. Click the OK button. A type-specific editor dialog box appears; which one you get depends on the type you specified in the Value Name field.

Figure 36-5. *The Regedt32 Add Value dialog box.*

4. Fill in the data you want stored in the value, and then click OK to save the new value or click Cancel to leave the registry untouched.

Removing Keys and Values

Regedt32 allows you to remove a key (and all its subordinate items) or a single value—just select the target item and press the Delete key (or choose Delete from the Edit menu). By default, Regedt32 makes you confirm what you're doing; if you feel daring, you can save yourself an extra step by clearing the Confirm On Delete command on the Options menu (although we strongly recommend that you leave it selected).

Loading, Unloading, and Importing Registry Data

Regedt32 offers you two different ways to move data between your registry and an external disk file. The first way involves loading and saving individual sets of keys with the Registry menu's Save Key and Restore commands, while the second involves loading and unloading entire hive files with the Load Hive and Unload Hive commands (on the Registry menu).

What's the difference? Recall that hive files are self-contained entities that contain a particular set of keys. When you save a key with the Save Key command, you're really creating a new hive that coexists equally with the predefined hives you read about earlier in the chapter. You can then reattach that hive in two ways: by creating a new key inside an existing hive (which is what the Load Hive command does) or by overwriting a key with the contents of the saved hive, as Restore does.

Creating a new hive with a set of saved keys in it is easy: Select the key you want to save, and then choose the Save Key command from the Registry menu. When prompted, give the new hive file a name, and Regedt32 will save it. Notice that you can't save a hive unless you have adequate permission to all subkeys of the selected key; for example, even when you are logged on as administrator, you can't save HKLM\HARDWARE to a hive.

Once you have saved the hive file, you can load it into a new key or load it over the top of an existing key. To load the hive file into a new key, select the HKLM or HKU root keys and then choose Load Hive from the Registry menu. (It will be disabled the rest of the time.) When prompted, choose the hive file you want to load, and then name the new key you want the hive to be loaded under.

To load a hive file over the top of an existing key, select the key you want to overwrite and then choose Load Key from the Registry menu; after you choose the file and confirm that you're ready to eliminate the selected key, Regedt32 will load the hive and replace *all* of the key's existing contents with the hive contents (provided, of course, that you have permission to do so).

For example, let's say you save the contents of HKLM\SOFTWARE\AOL to a hive file. If you select HKLM and use the Load Hive command, you can create a new key (called, perhaps, AOL) and load the original contents into it. If you select the existing copy of HKLM\SOFTWARE\AOL and use the Restore command, then whatever is stored in the key before restoring the hive will be lost.

Connecting to a Remote Machine's Registry

To connect to a remote machine using Regedt32, choose Select Computer from the Registry menu. The familiar Select Computer dialog box will open, in which you can browse your domain or workgroup and pick the machine whose registry you want to administer. You will be connected if you have administrative access to the remote machine; you might also see a dialog box alerting you that the registry keys from the remote machine won't be updated automatically. As soon as you dismiss that confirmation message, two more MDI windows will open: one for HKLM and one for HKU. Each window's title includes the name of the remote machine (for example, HKEY_LOCAL_MACHINE on FALCON) so you can identify which windows contain what information.

Once these windows are open, you can browse and edit just as you would on the local machine (subject, of course, to permissions on the keys you're editing). When you establish a connection to a remote machine, you're actually making a remote procedure call (RPC) connection, which remains open until you use the Close command to close the last window displaying data from that server.

Managing Security on Registry Keys

Regedt32 allows you to set security on registry keys by selecting a key and choosing the Permissions command from the Security menu. Everything you learned about setting permissions on files (see Chapter 9) is still true here, and the basic operations work exactly the same way: you select an object and then grant or deny specific privileges to specific users and groups. Figure 36-6 shows an example. Note that five security principles are shown in the Permissions dialog box: Administrators, Authenticated Users, CREATOR OWNER, Server Operators, and SYSTEM. The exact contents you see on your computer will vary according to the security template you have applied; more restrictive templates might change these permissions significantly.

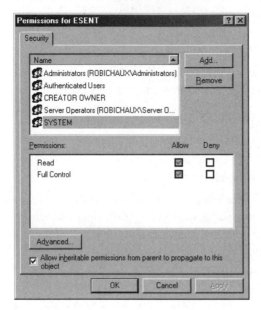

Figure 36-6. *The standard Permissions dialog box for a registry key.*

In the Permissions dialog box, you can grant and deny the Read and Full Control permissions on keys. However, in general, you shouldn't do so on keys owned by the system; that's why Microsoft includes the security templates. You can easily set permissions accidentally that are so restrictive that software that needs registry access can't get it, or you can easily err in the opposite direction and set permissions that are unnecessarily loose.

When you set permissions using the Permissions dialog box, be sure to note whether you select the Allow Inheritable Permissions From Parent To Propagate To This Object check box. By default, this check box is selected, so when you apply new permissions, they will be automatically propagated to all subkeys of the selected key. Depending on the level at which you apply these permissions, inheritance might have unintended consequences—if you loosen permissions on a key, you might accidentally loosen permissions on a subkey that should remain secure. Before you change permissions on any keys, be sure to make a good backup of your registry *and* make a note of the changes you've made so you can reverse them later.

Settings that belong to applications, of course, are another matter altogether. In Windows NT 4, the only way to determine appropriate permissions for most applications' keys is to tighten them down as much as possible, then gradually relax controls until the application starts working properly. Unfortunately, this approach is still required in Windows 2000.

When you click the Advanced button in the Permissions dialog box, you get the three-tabbed Access Control Settings dialog box. Each tab has a special meaning for registry keys:

- The Permissions tab's View/Edit button allows you to assign more granular permissions to individual users. For example, you can fine-tune who can create new values in a key by adjusting the setting for the Set Value permission. Table 36-1 shows the permissions you can grant or deny. Since most registry keys gain their permissions from inheritance, be aware that you might not be able to make changes here without turning inheritance off.

Table 36-1.   What the registry permissions mean

Permission	What Happens When Granted
Query Value	Allows user to query the registry for a specific value by providing the full path to that value
Set Value	Allows user to create new values beneath a key or to overwrite an existing value
Create Subkey	Allows user to create a new subkey beneath the specified key
Enumerate Subkeys	Allows user to get a list of all subkeys of a particular key; similar to directory traversal of an NTFS volume
Notify	Allows user to register a callback function that is triggered when the selected value changes
Create Link	Allows user to create a link to a specified key (just as HKCR links to HKLM\Classes)
Delete	Allows user to delete an individual value or key
Write DAC	Allows user to rewrite access controls on the specified key
Write Owner	Allows user to take ownership of the selected key
Read Control	Allows user to read the discretionary access control list (DACL) for the specified key

- The Auditing tab lets you set auditing permissions for the selected key. First, you specify the users or groups whose actions you want to audit; next, you specify which particular actions you want recorded (Figure 36-7). Note that the actions you can audit are the same as the permissions shown in Table 36-1. You can audit successful or failed attempts to exercise these permissions.

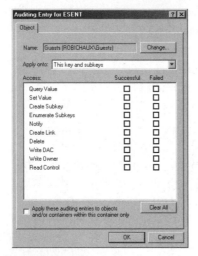

Figure 36-7. *Assigning auditing permissions.*

- The Owner tab lets you reassign ownership of the selected key, either with or without propagating that change to all subitems beneath it. Note that depending on your security settings, a change in ownership might result in an audit trail being generated.

Miscellaneous Useful Tricks

Four useful Regedt32 commands don't really fit elsewhere in this exposition:

- Regedt32 can't search values, but it can look for a key with a specified name. The Find Key command on the View menu lets you search the registry (beginning with the selected key and proceeding either up or down) for a particular key name. Searches can be case sensitive or not, and you can choose to search for the supplied text on its own or when it appears as part of another name.

- You've already briefly worked with the Confirm On Delete command on the Options menu. When selected (as it is by default), Regedt32 will ask you to confirm your intentions when you attempt to remove a key.

- The Read Only Mode command on the Options menu toggles Regedt32 between read-only and normal modes. Read-only mode is a great boon, since you can't mess anything up when it's on. It's a great way to learn by exploring with no risk of accidental damage.

- The Auto Refresh command on the Options menu controls whether Regedt32 will automatically update your root key windows periodically. By default, it is enabled, so Regedt32 will update local windows by itself. On machines where lots of registry changes exist, you might want to disable automatic updates and use the View menu's Refresh All and Refresh Active commands to trigger updates only when you need them.

Backing Up and Restoring the Registry

In Chapter 34 you learned how to use the Windows 2000 Backup application to back up and restore the overall state of your system. This is somewhat different from Windows NT, where you can easily back up the registry by making an emergency repair disk (ERD) or running Ntbackup and selecting the Include Local Registry check box.

The reason for these differences revolves around Active Directory. In Windows NT, a registry backup contains a copy of the SAM database for the local machine (as well as the domain SAM, when you back up a domain controller). In a network using Active Directory, the directory contains most of the information that was formerly in the SAM, which is why you have to perform a two-step recovery process for domain controllers. (See the section "Restoring the System State" in Chapter 34 for more details on how the process works.) First you restore the local machine's SAM registry hive so you can log on, and then you restore the Active Directory store.

Caution   As a side effect of the way these changes are implemented, the emergency repair disk no longer contains registry information—the only backup copy on the computer itself is in the %SystemRoot%\Repair folder. With no ERD to fall back on, it's extra important to make regular and usable backups.

Choosing a Backup Method

Since the registry is more than an ordinary file, it makes sense that you have to give your backup and restore procedures more than the ordinary amount of thought. You can back up and restore your registry in other ways besides making a complete backup of the entire system state. Of course, you should still perform regular backups of your data *and* the system state for each computer you administer. It is still useful to back up the registry by itself, since the registry is where most applications and system components store their preferences and settings.

Windows 2000 Backup

When you use the Windows 2000 Backup utility to back up the system state, it includes a complete copy of that machine's registry. It also includes copies of the system volume (on domain controllers), certificate data, COM+ class registration information, and other information that is unrelated to what is in the registry. On the other hand, Windows 2000 Backup automates the process of backing up the registry, so it's easy to use and understand. In addition, keeping your registry data with the rest of your server data ensures that you'll be able to recover everything without having to hunt for third-party CDs, drivers, and the like.

The Emergency Repair Disk

You can use Windows 2000 Backup's Emergency Repair Disk feature to back up the registry, too; most Windows NT administrators use this as their first line of defense against a failure, since the repair tools included on the Windows NT 4 CD can restore registry data from an ERD. Windows 2000 uses ERDs too, but they don't include registry information. When you use Windows 2000 Backup to create an ERD, you must manually specify that you want registry information backed up, and it doesn't get stored on the ERD floppy disk itself—you have to manually save a copy and then replace registry files during recovery by copying them using the recovery console.

Third-Party Products

Many Windows NT and Windows 2000 sites use third-party backup tools like Computer Associates' ARCServe or St Bernard Software's OpenFile Manager. In general, these tools provide more sophisticated backup capabilities than the tools that Microsoft ships; for example, ARCServe can use tape autoloaders and optical media, and it can back up machines running several operating systems. If you're using a third-party backup product, you might want it to back up your registry too. Be sure that you have everything on hand that you would need to restore data backed up with a third-party tool, and double-check to make sure that your vendor's software is fully compatible with the version of Windows 2000 that you're running.

Do-It-Yourself Backups

Since Regedt32 allows you to load and unload hive files and keys, you might think that you can approximate what Windows 2000 Backup does by manually saving to a hive file the keys you're most interested in, copying the resulting files someplace safe, and reloading them if you need them. This approach works fine, but it's labor-intensive, since there's no way to automate the process of telling Regedt32 which keys to save. (At that point, you might as well use the Win32 registry programming interfaces to write your own backup program!)

Backing Up the Registry

When you're ready to make a backup, you'll be happy to see how simple the process is—it's a great improvement over Windows NT 4.

Using Windows 2000 Backup

Chapter 34 covered the mechanics of backing up and restoring your system state, of which the registry is a small but critical part. If you're comfortable with the process of making and restoring a system state backup with Windows 2000 Backup, you're in good shape. However, a quick review might be in order.

1. Launch the Windows 2000 Backup application; when it appears, click the Backup tab.
2. Specify the backup device or location you want to use with the Backup Destination and Backup Media Or File Name options.
3. If necessary, expand the My Computer icon.
4. Select the System State check box. (Remember, the system state items are interrelated and can't be backed up individually.)
5. Click the Start Backup button. When the system backs up the system state information, the registry files will be included, so you can restore them later.

Saving a Copy of the Registry

When you create an ERD, Windows 2000 Backup offers to save a copy of the registry for you (Figure 36-8). When you select the check box, an extra copy of your registry hive files is stored in the %SystemRoot%\Repair\REGBACK folder. Besides the standard hive files (SECURITY, SAM, SYSTEM, SOFTWARE, DEFAULT, Ntuser.dat, and Usrclass.dat), you'll also see files representing any hives you have manually loaded into your registry.

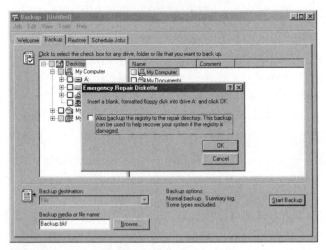

Figure 36-8. *Saving a copy of the registry.*

Once Windows 2000 Backup has finished copying these files, they're all yours—you can move them, copy them, back them up, or do whatever you want to. In particular, you can compress them and store them on a floppy, or you can move them to any kind of removable media that you have on hand.

Tip If you store your backup files in compressed format or on any medium that requires a special device, make sure you will be able to access the files when you're restoring the machine.

Restoring the Registry

The process of restoring the registry from a system state backup is discussed at length in Chapter 34, so we won't go into it here. However, just be aware that if you have a backup of the %SystemRoot%\Repair\REGBACK folder, you can use the system's Recovery Console to restore the backup of the registry. Once you start the Recovery Console, you can copy the registry files you need to restore back to their normal locations on disk, and then restart the machine. Remember that by doing so, you'll wipe out any changes you've made since the time the files were backed up.

Summary

Windows 2000 depends on the registry for storing and retrieving vital configuration data. Knowing what's in it, how and when to edit the registry, and how to back it up and restore it is vital for system administrators. In particular, knowing how Regedit and Regedt32 work and what they can do is a key skill you'll need to keep your Windows 2000 machines healthy. The next chapter addresses troubleshooting relative to isolating and recovering from network troubles of all kinds.

Chapter 37
Troubleshooting and Recovery

No matter how good an operating system is, disasters can occur. Furthermore, they almost always occur unexpectedly, and usually at a very inconvenient time. (Remember, Murphy was an optimist.) This chapter helps you get out of trouble when a disaster does occur, focusing mainly on total disaster scenarios involving a nonbooting system. Other problems are highly variable in their causes and solutions, and we've found that the best source of information in such cases is the Microsoft Knowledge Base. We also highly recommend studying Chapter 33 to learn what you can do to prevent future problems.

Performing a System Recovery

This is everyone's least favorite part of the book, because, of course, if you're reading it you're probably not in a good mood. With that in mind, we'll get right to the point and help you get your system functioning again. Here we focus mainly on getting the system to boot. Later sections also discuss fixing the underlying problem and other situations you might encounter.

A Microsoft Windows 2000 server that won't boot defines "emergency" for most system administrators. Therefore, you'll want to haul out your disaster recovery plan (as described in Chapter 33) and follow the procedures step by step. If you're reading this section for the first time because you're in the middle of a disaster and you don't *have* a disaster recovery plan, there's no need to panic. You can still survive.

The recovery steps outlined in the rest of this chapter proceed from least drastic to most drastic. In any recovery procedure, always adopt a *minimalist* approach. Start with the least invasive steps. If they succeed, you'll have minimized both the loss of information and the impact on the network and your users.

Using Boot Options

It's what we all dread. You reboot the system, and it hangs or crashes. While this is indeed a dire situation, fear not (yet), for Windows 2000 comes with an arsenal of tools that you can use to get the system running again. The first set of tools are the boot options, available from the Boot menu at startup. These options allow you to start the system safely so that you can fix the problem that is causing the system to fail to boot properly (perhaps a faulty driver or service). To use the boot options to get the system running again, follow these steps:

1. Boot the system to the Boot menu, and select the Windows 2000 installation you want to boot into.
2. Press F8 to display the Windows 2000 Advanced Options menu.
3. Choose the option you want to use, and press Enter. Table 37-1 lists the boot options and their purposes.
4. From the Boot menu, select the operating system that is having the problem, and press Enter to boot the system.

If you frequently find yourself using boot options on the computer, you may want to set up the boot options you use frequently in the Boot menu for quick access. To do this, open the Boot.ini file, copy the line pointing to the Windows 2000 installation you want to modify, and add one of the switches listed in Table 37-2 to the end of the new line. A sample SafeBoot.ini file that includes these settings can be found on the CD that accompanies this book.

Table 37-1.   Boot options available in Windows 2000

Boot Option	Explanation
Safe Mode	Starts Windows 2000 with a minimal set of files and drivers (basic mouse support, monitor, keyboard, mass storage, default system services but no network connections, basic VGA driver). Useful for fixing driver problems.
Safe Mode With Networking	Adds networking support to safe mode.
Safe Mode With Command Prompt	Starts Windows 2000 in safe mode with Networking, but launches a command-prompt window instead of displaying the Windows desktop, Start menu, and taskbar (Windows Explorer).
Enable Boot Logging	Creates a log file with all of the drivers and services loaded or failed during the boot process. The file is called Ntbtlog.txt and is stored in the %WinDir% folder. This mode is useful for determining the cause of the system failure. Note that a log file is also automatically created in all safe modes.

Table 37-1.   *continued*

Boot Option	Explanation
Enable VGA Mode	Starts Windows 2000 using the standard VGA driver (640 by 480 with 16 colors). Otherwise, Windows 2000 is started normally. This mode is useful when you've installed a bad display driver or have set the screen resolution to one that is not supported and are having trouble changing it.
Last Known Good Configuration	Starts Windows 2000 using the registry information from the last time Windows was shut down. This mode doesn't solve problems related to missing or corrupted drivers or other system files, and all changes made since the last successful startup are lost.
Directory Service Restore Mode	Starts Windows 2000 in safe mode with networking, and restores the SYSVOL and Active Directory directory service on a domain controller.
Debugging Mode	Starts Windows 2000 while sending debug information to another computer via a serial cable connection.
Recovery Console	Boots to the Recovery Console command line (only if it is installed).

More Info   The password used to log on in directory services restore mode is the directory services restore mode password you set when you promoted the computer to a domain controller. For information on changing the password, see the Microsoft Knowledge Base article Q239803.

Table 37-2.   Boot.ini switches for the various Windows 2000 boot options

Boot Option	Switch to Use in Boot.ini
Safe Mode	/safeboot:minimal /sos /bootlog /noguiboot
Safe Mode With Networking	/safeboot:network /sos /bootlog /noguiboot
Safe Mode With Command Prompt	/safeboot:minimal(alternateshell) /sos /bootlog / noguiboot
Enable Boot Logging	/bootlog
Enable VGA Mode	/basevideo
Directory Service Restore Mode (domain controllers only)	/safeboot:dsrepair /sos
Debugging Mode	/debug

What to Do When You Really Can't Boot

The only thing dreaded more than not being able to boot the system is not being able to boot the system in a safe mode. Fortunately, Windows 2000 still has a few tricks to help you get the system working in this situation. The main tools at your disposal here are the emergency repair disk and the Recovery Console (covered separately later in this chapter), although boot disks also occasionally come in handy. And yes, if these techniques fail, you can always reinstall Windows (discussed later in this chapter). But try the suggestions in this section first.

Using the Emergency Repair Process

If you can't boot using one of the boot options mentioned earlier in this chapter, try the emergency repair process. This method involves booting from either the Windows 2000 CD-ROM or the four setup disks, and then using the Windows 2000 repair process. To do so, follow these steps:

1. Boot from the Windows 2000 setup disks or the Windows 2000 CD-ROM.

2. Type *R* to choose to repair an existing Windows 2000 installation.

3. Type *R* again to use the emergency repair process to fix an existing installation of Windows 2000.

4. Type *F* to use the Fast Repair option to automatically repair registry problems, system files, the boot sector of the boot volume, and problems with the startup environment if you have a dual-boot system.

Caution Fast Repair repairs registry problems by using a backup copy of the system registry that was created when Windows 2000 was installed. Using this option may result in the loss of settings and preferences created since that instalation.

Or type *M* to use the Manual Repair option to manually specify what you want to repair, although the registry cannot be repaired in this way. (You can use the Recovery Console to manually repair individual registry files or to replace the entire registry if you like.)

5. If you chose Manual Repair, select the repair options you want by using the arrow keys and pressing Enter to select or clear each check box. Table 37-3 provides a list of the repair options. When you're done, select the Continue option and press Enter.

6. After you've selected the repair options, insert the emergency repair disk (ERD) and press Enter. (Creating an ERD is discussed in Chapter 33.) If

you don't have an ERD, type *L*. Windows 2000 searches for the installation and displays any that it finds. To repair the found installation, press Enter; otherwise press Esc.

Table 37-3. Manual Repair options

Option	Purpose
Inspect Startup Environment	Examines the files used to boot the computer (Boot.ini, Ntldr, etc.) and fixes any problems it finds.
Verify Windows 2000 System Files	Scans the Windows 2000 system files for changes or corruption and restores changed files from the Windows 2000 CD-ROM.
Inspect Boot Sector	Checks the master boot record (MBR) and fixes any problems that were preventing the Windows 2000 system from booting. Note that this doesn't eradicate MBR viruses.

Using a Boot Disk to Recover the System

You don't need us to tell you how to use a boot disk (insert disk, boot computer). However, you might find it useful to know a little more about what a boot disk does and doesn't do. (For information on creating a Windows 2000 boot disk, see Chapter 33.)

When you boot the system from a Windows 2000 boot disk, you are bypassing the hard disk's master boot record, boot sector, and startup environment and booting straight from the floppy drive into the operating system you choose from the floppy's Boot menu. This can be a great way of accessing Windows 2000 on a system with a corrupted MBR, boot sector, or startup environment, but booting in this way doesn't mean that the problem has been fixed—you will have the same problem the next time you try to boot normally. However, a boot disk allows you to gain access to the Windows 2000 system, which you can then use to re-create the Boot.ini file and to copy missing or corrupted files such as Ntldr or Ntdetect.com. To fix the MBR or boot sector, you may need to run the emergency repair process, but at least you will know what the problem is.

Using the Recovery Console

The Recovery Console is one of the most useful new recovery tools provided with Windows 2000. It allows you to securely access the hard drive of a nonbooting Windows 2000 computer via a special command prompt, which you can then use to copy files, start and stop services, and perform other recovery. For information on installing the Recovery Console, see Chapter 33.

Before you use the Recovery Console, you should know what you can and can't do with it. You can use the Recovery Console to securely log on to a Windows 2000 installation and access any NTFS, FAT, or FAT32 drives you have, although you can use only the root folder of each drive, the %SystemRoot% folder and subfolders, the Cmdcons folder (if present), and any removable media drives attached to the system. You cannot copy files from the hard disk to a floppy disk, although you can copy files from a floppy to the hard disk or from one hard disk to another. You can use the Recovery Console to disable services or devices from starting the next time you boot the system as well as to reenable them. You can also repair the boot sector and MBR, manage and format partitions, and use, copy, rename, replace, and extract new versions of operating system files. To use the Recovery Console, follow these steps:

1. Boot the system with the Windows 2000 CD-ROM or setup disks.

2. Type *R* to choose to repair an existing Windows 2000 installation. Then type *C* to use the Recovery Console.

3. Enter the number corresponding to the Windows 2000 installation you want to log on to and press Enter.

4. Enter the local system administrator password. (This is the password you originally assigned when installing Windows 2000.)

5. Type *help* at the command prompt for a list of available commands, or enter the commands you want to execute. See Appendix D for a list of the commands available and a description of what they do.

Tip The password used to log on to a domain controller is the directory services restore mode password you set when you promoted the computer to a domain controller. For information on changing the password, see the Microsoft Knowledge Base article Q239803.

Booting from Mirrored Boot Partitions

If you're using mirrored boot partitions and your primary boot drive fails, you'll need the boot disk we discussed in Chapter 33 to get into the system. Fortunately, hard disks have gotten much more dependable in recent years. The general rule is that if they last the first couple of months, they should last at least as long as the computer. The problem with this, of course, is that just when you become totally dependent on a system, Murphy comes along and smiles on you. And the whole point of running a mirrored boot drive, of course, is that you really, really don't want to have trouble, and if you do have problems, you want to get back online quickly.

Therefore, if your boot disk crashes, you need to switch over quickly to running off its mirror while you get a replacement for that boot disk. To do this, you'll need to create a boot floppy disk using the procedure outlined in Chapter 33, with one additional step. For an Intel-based processor, you'll need to edit the Boot.ini file on the floppy to change the ARC name of the boot partition to point to the secondary mirror drive, rather than the primary one. So, for example, if you have a pair of Adaptec 2940 adapters and you have duplexed your boot drives, using the SCSI BIOS to boot from the primary partition on the first hard disk, you might have a line like this in your Boot.ini file:

```
multi(0)disk(0)rdisk(0)partition(1)\WINNT="Microsoft Windows 2000
Advanced Server" /fastdetect
```

However, if you need to boot from the secondary mirror pair, you would need to change that line to

```
multi(1)disk(0)rdisk(0)partition(1)\WINNT="Microsoft Windows 2000
Advanced Server" /fastdetect
```

Once you've booted your system and replaced the failed drive, re-create the mirror (as described in Chapter 14).

Restoring a Completely Failed Server

So the worst has happened. You've had a server totally crash. You've replaced the failed hard disk, and you've got a backup tape to restore with, but you have to be able to boot before you can restore the tape.

The first step is to reinstall Windows 2000 Server on the new disk. Use a temporary directory name so it doesn't interfere with the original installation. Once you have the minimal system installed, you can restore the registry and partition information using your emergency repair disk and the backup tape. Run Windows 2000's Backup program and restore the tape and the registry. The tape drive should be locally attached, and you'll want to make sure you select the Restore Local Registry option to recover the rest of your registry information. Restart the server and you're ready to go.

This process can take a significant amount of time. In an environment such as manufacturing or another production operation, where the server *must* be available, you may find that you can't afford the time this process takes. The most efficient solution to this problem is to mirror or, better yet, duplex the system disk, preferably with a hardware RAID controller. But even using Windows 2000 Disk Management to mirror the system disk will save you significant amounts of downtime.

Fixing the Underlying Problem

Once you have the system operating again, you may need to perform some further troubleshooting in order to fix the underlying problem. Booting the computer successfully in safe mode is a relief, but it is of little consolation if you still can't boot normally. Unfortunately, solving the underlying problem can be very complex and, as a result, the recommendations here are only a starting point. If these recommendations don't help you fix the problem, consult the Microsoft Windows 2000 Knowledge Base for further information. The advice dispensed in the next several sections can help you fix the majority of the problems you are likely to experience.

Tip When troubleshooting, act like a scientist running an experiment. Change only one thing at a time to minimize the likelihood of confounding variables. Also, do some deep thinking about the results you get. If you see that the system is hanging on a certain service that is failing, check to make sure that the failing service isn't dependent on some other services that aren't starting. And for your own sanity, start with the least painful steps first. Save reinstalling Windows for last.

Undo Anything You've Changed

It is very unusual for a system to start having trouble by itself. Usually problems are a result of some action that we perform on the system—installing a new driver or program, changing a registry setting, and so on. Therefore, the first thing to do once you get the system booting again is to undo anything that you've done recently. Start by undoing registry changes, and then uninstall recently added drivers, and finally uninstall any suspect programs.

Check Event Viewer

Your first move when trying to track down the source of system problems should be to check Event Viewer, located in the Administrative Tools folder of the Programs menu. Event Viewer (Figure 37-1) will often give you a string of clues as to the cause of the problem and sometimes will even tell you what to do to fix it. For more information on using Event Viewer, see Chapter 10. Carefully scrutinize any errors or warnings you see in the system log and any other logs that are relevant to the problem; also glance at the Information events—they sometimes give clues.

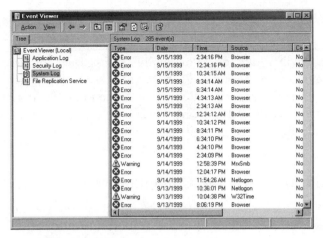

Figure 37-1. *The Event Viewer window.*

Check Device Manager

If a device in the system is causing a resource conflict or some other problem, you should check the Device Manager snap-in, located in the Computer Management snap-in. Examine the system for devices with conflicts or errors, and consider disabling these devices or removing them from the system. (Note that removing them from Device Manager will usually just cause the devices to be redetected the next time the system boots, potentially causing the same problem.) It is standard practice when troubleshooting resource conflicts to disable or remove every device in the system that you can boot without (such as sound cards, network cards, and modems) until the system works normally, and then add the devices back one by one until the problem reappears. Then you can troubleshoot the device in question.

Real World   Setting Resources Manually

Advanced Configuration Power Interface (ACPI) systems automatically configure all PCI devices, preventing you from changing a device's resource settings to resolve a conflict. The only way to deal with resource conflicts in this situation is to remove devices from Device Manager and allow it to rescan them. You can also set the BIOS to reset Extended System Configuration Data (ESCD) settings, reconfiguring the PCI devices, or you can try manually specifying resources in the BIOS for each PCI slot or reinstalling Windows 2000 and disabling ACPI. (Follow the instructions in the "ACPI BIOS Compatibility Problems" sidebar in Chapter 5 to disable ACPI support during installation.) If you have a standard PC (no

ACPI), you can expand the Computer category in Device Manager, select Standard PC, click Properties, click the IRQ Steering tab, and clear the Use IRQ Steering check box. This procedure will allow you to manually set resources for the PCI devices. Keep in mind that while the Standard PC hardware abstraction layer, or HAL (ACPI, standard PCs, and multiprocessor PCs all use different HALs) may allow for more manual control, ACPI in almost all cases does a better job of managing resources and should be used whenever the system supports it.

Use System Information to Check the Configuration

The System Information tool by itself does nothing to help you get the system working properly again. However, it can give you some important information about the system configuration that you can then use to resolve the conflicts or errors. To open the System Information snap-in, launch the Computer Management snap-in from the Administrative Tools folder on the Programs menu, and then double-click the System Information icon in the console tree and select the subfolder of interest to you, as shown in Figure 37-2.

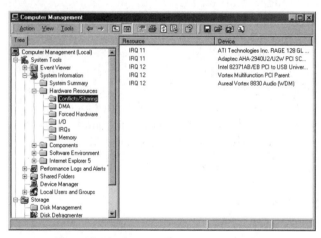

Figure 37-2. *The System Information console in the Computer Management window.*

Check the Services

As with Microsoft Windows NT, checking the services in Windows 2000 can be invaluable in solving a problem. If a key service isn't starting, you're going to have problems. Make sure that the key services are set to start automatically, and consider disabling services that could potentially cause trouble, or at least set them to start manually (although an automatically starting service will start any services it needs—even services set to start manually—unless the services are disabled).

Also, you may want to specify what actions to take if the service fails. To perform some of these actions with the Services snap-in, follow these steps:

1. Launch the Services snap-in from the Administrative Tools folder on the Programs menu.

2. Use the window shown in Figure 37-3 to view the status of the services.

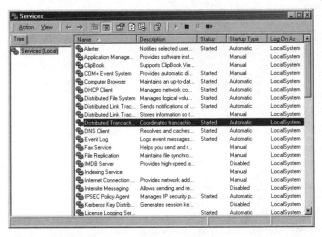

Figure 37-3. *The Services window.*

3. Use the Start Service, Stop Service, Pause Service, and the especially useful Restart Service toolbar buttons to make changes to the state of the services.

4. To change advanced settings for a service, double-click the service to open its Properties window, shown in Figure 37-4.

5. Use the Startup Type list box on the General tab to change how you want the service started.

6. Use the Log On tab to control what account you want the service to log on with. The default is the Local System account, but you can change this to a user account as needed.

7. Click the Recovery tab, and then choose what actions you want to take on the first, second, and subsequent failures of the service, as shown in Figure 37-5.

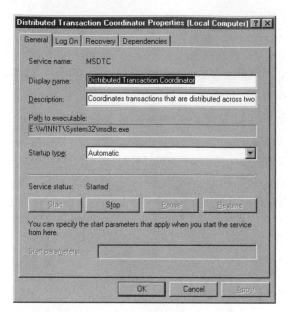

Figure 37-4. *A service's Properties window.*

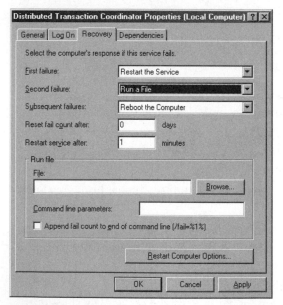

Figure 37-5. *The Recovery tab of a service's Properties dialog box.*

8. In the Reset Fail Count After box, enter the number of days after which you want to start over counting service failures.

9. Click the Dependencies tab to view the services that the specified service is dependent upon.

Use the System File Checker

The System File Checker is a command-line tool that allows you to verify that all of the protected system files are intact. This tool can be handy if you suspect that the system files may be corrupt. If the System File Checker finds that a protected system file has been overwritten, it will retrieve the correct version from the %SystemRoot%\system32\dllcache folder and use it to replace the incorrect version.

To use the System File Checker, log on as an administrator, go to a command prompt, and enter *sfc* followed by the appropriate parameter. See Table 37-4 for a list of parameters and what they do.

> **Tip**   If the %SystemRoot%\system32\dllcache folder becomes corrupted or is deleted, use one of the following commands to repair the folder: *sfc /scannow*, *sfc /scanonce*, or *sfc /scanboot*.

Table 37-4.   System File Checker options

Parameter	Action
/scannow	Immediately scans all protected system files.
/scanonce	Scans all protected files only a single time.
/scanboot	Scans all protected files every time the computer is booted.
/cancel	Cancels all scheduled scans.
/quiet	Scans and replaces incorrect files without prompting the user for action.
/enable	Resets Windows File Protection to its default status. Users will be prompted to restore any files that are overwritten.
/purgecache	Deletes all files in the %SystemRoot%\system32\dllcache folder (the Windows File Protection cache) and immediately scans the protected system files.
/cachesize=*x*	Specifies how large (in megabytes) the %SystemRoot%\system32\dllcache folder (the Windows File Protection file cache) should be.

Restore from a Backup

Once again, you probably don't need us to tell you how to restore from a backup, but if you can get into Windows 2000 and you feel confident that the system was in a good state at the last backup, you might consider restoring from the backup rather than wasting time trying to track down a corrupt file. Remember, however, that any changes you've made since the last backup will most likely be lost, so use this option as one of your last choices.

Reinstall Windows 2000

Reinstalling Windows 2000 is your last resort. It provides a way to thoroughly clean the system, possibly without reinstalling programs. (If you run Setup from within Windows 2000, you can install right over the old installation and preserve the settings.)

If you can get into Windows 2000 to run the 32-bit Winnt32.exe setup program, by all means do so. You can then choose to install over the old version, thus simply fixing any corrupted files. This method is by far the easiest, safest, and least painful way to go—if it fixes the problem. (See Chapter 7 for more information on performing this type of setup.)

Your problems, however, may be so deeply rooted that even this type of reinstall can't fix them. In such cases, the problem usually lies in the settings, which are largely preserved during a reinstall. It then becomes necessary to perform a clean install, either by uninstalling Windows 2000 via the method described in the section "Uninstalling Windows 2000" (or by just formatting the disk) or by performing a parallel installation (after which you probably will want to delete the damaged installation). See Chapter 5 for information on performing a clean installation of Windows 2000.

Miscellaneous Challenges

This section covers some tasks (we like to call them "challenges") that you may need to perform with Windows 2000. If you don't find the task or problem you're looking for here, don't panic; check the Microsoft Windows 2000 Knowledge Base—the definitive source for information on problems with Windows 2000.

Adding a Processor to the System

Occasionally you might find yourself adding a second processor to a dual-processor-capable system. The procedure for doing this is a little different in Windows 2000 than it was in Windows NT 4, so we'll walk you through it. Upgrading from a single-processor Windows 2000 system to a multiprocessor system is actually a fairly major change for Windows 2000, causing Windows 2000 to change its entire hardware abstraction layer (HAL). Thus, it is *very* important that you don't muck around when choosing a HAL. Stick with the one Windows picks, because if you choose an incompatible HAL, the only way to recover is to perform a clean install of Windows 2000. After installing your additional processor, use the following procedure to switch HALs from uniprocessor to multiprocessor:

1. Open the Computer Management snap-in from the Administrative Tools folder on the Programs menu.

2. Click Device Manager in the console tree.

3. In the details pane, expand the Computer branch of the Device Manager tree, as shown in Figure 37-6.

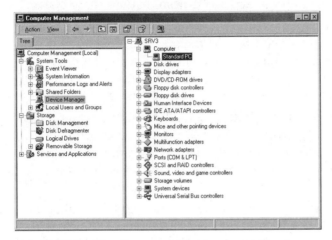

Figure 37-6. *The Computer Management console.*

4. Right-click the computer item (most likely ACPI Uniprocessor PC) and choose Properties from the shortcut menu.

5. Click the Driver tab and then click Update Driver.

6. Use the Update Device Driver Wizard to locate a more suitable HAL for the multiprocessor system. Note that if Windows 2000 doesn't find a different HAL, you should contact the system manufacturer for an updated HAL or system BIOS.

Uninstalling Windows 2000

Yes, there may be times when you want to uninstall Windows 2000. Perhaps you've had a system failure and performed a parallel installation, leaving you with an unwanted Windows 2000 installation. Or maybe you've decided that you'd rather have the raw power of MS-DOS 4 again. (If you have, get help—fast!) Whatever the reason, here's how to remove Windows 2000:

1. Verify the location of Windows 2000 and how the hard disk is partitioned. (The Disk Management snap-in located in the Computer Management console will show the partition information.)

2. Make sure that no valuable files are located in the %SystemRoot% or Program Files folders.

3. Determine what you want to do with the partitions. If you will be using an operating system other than Windows 2000 or Windows NT 4 with Service Pack 4 or later, you'll need to repartition and reformat any NTFS partitions that you want to be able to access from that operating system.

4. To completely remove Windows 2000 from the system, replace the Windows 2000 boot sector with that of the operating system you want to use. (See the operating system's manual. For MS-DOS or Windows 95/98, boot from a floppy and type *sys c:* at the command prompt. Windows NT users can use the emergency recovery process.)

   Alternately, you can leave the Windows 2000 boot sector intact and simply edit the Boot.ini file to remove the Windows 2000 installation you're uninstalling, set the default to the desired operating system, and optionally set the timeout to 0 to boot the default operating system without displaying the Boot menu.

5. Delete the %SystemRoot% folder that the Windows 2000 installation was located in, as well as the Program Files, Documents and Settings (be careful with the data though!), Recycler, and System Volume Information folders, as desired, to free up disk space.

6. Delete the following files in the root directory of the boot partition:
   - Pagefile.sys
   - Ntdetect.com
   - Ntbootdd.sys (if you're using a SCSI system)
   - Cmldr
   - Cdldr
   - Arcldr.exe
   - Arcsetup.exe
   - Boot.ini (Do not delete if you want to keep using Windows 2000's Boot menu.)
   - Ntldr (Do not delete if you want to keep using Windows 2000's Boot menu.)

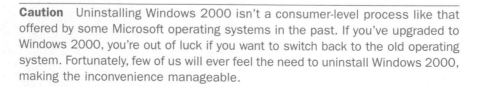

Caution Uninstalling Windows 2000 isn't a consumer-level process like that offered by some Microsoft operating systems in the past. If you've upgraded to Windows 2000, you're out of luck if you want to switch back to the old operating system. Fortunately, few of us will ever feel the need to uninstall Windows 2000, making the inconvenience manageable.

Summary

Windows 2000 provides a great set of tools that you can use to recover from the disasters that inevitably occur, even in relatively stable operating systems like Windows 2000. The most frequently used are the boot options, such as safe mode (à la Windows 95/98) and the Last Known Good Configuration option, which is useful for recovery from registry errors. If you still can't boot the system, you can use Windows 2000's emergency repair process to get the system running again. Windows 2000 also features the new Recovery Console, which allows you to access the drives (including secure access to limited areas of NTFS drives) via a command prompt when all else fails.

Part VII
Appendixes

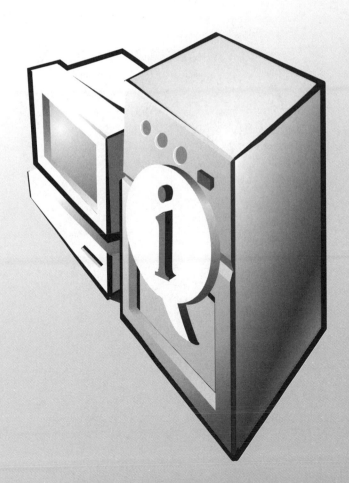

A Quick Guide to Interface Changes

Initially, both the Microsoft Windows 2000 Professional and Server interfaces look much like the Microsoft Windows NT 4 interface, but enough differences exist that you might find yourself periodically stymied by a "missing" function. This appendix lists some of the components that have been renamed, moved, or introduced since the first release of Windows NT 4. These components are listed by their Windows NT name if they have a new name in Windows 2000.

Clipboard Viewer

Clipboard Viewer has been renamed ClipBook Viewer. ClipBook Viewer shows any information you've copied to the clipboard. This information can be stored permanently in your Local ClipBook and shared with other users. The Local ClipBook opens when you start ClipBook Viewer. To open ClipBook Viewer, select Run from the Start menu, type *clipbrd*, and then press Enter.

Compression Agent

Windows 2000 doesn't include Compression Agent. You can compress NTFS drives by following these steps:

1. Open My Computer.
2. Right-click the drive you want to compress. Choose Properties from the shortcut menu.
3. On the General tab, select Compress Drive To Save Disk Space. Click OK.

To compress a single file or folder, follow these steps:

1. Open Microsoft Windows Explorer. Right-click the file or folder to be compressed and choose Properties from the shortcut menu.

2. Click the Advanced button. Select the Compress Contents To Save Disk Space check box. Click OK twice.

3. If you're compressing a folder, you'll be asked whether you want changes to apply to only the folder or to subfolders and files as well. Select the option you want. Click OK again.

The compression option is available only on disks formatted with NTFS. When you add or copy a file into a compressed folder, it is compressed automatically. If you move a file from a *different* NTFS drive into a compressed folder, it is also compressed. However, if you move a file from the *same* NTFS drive into a compressed folder, the file retains its original state, whether it is compressed or uncompressed. Compressed files can't be encrypted.

Computers Near Me

If your Windows 2000 Professional is a member of a workgroup, Computers Near Me will appear inside My Network Places. Computers Near Me shows the computers and other resources that are accessible by members of the workgroup. Computers Near Me won't be created when Windows 2000 is installed on a machine that is a member of a domain.

Devices

Devices has been renamed Device Manager and is located in Computer Management. On a machine running Windows 2000 Server or Windows 2000 Professional, right-click My Computer and choose Properties from the shortcut menu. Click the Hardware tab. Click the Device Manager button. From a machine running Windows 2000 Server, an administrator can view Device Manager on a remote computer by following these steps:

1. Open Active Directory Users And Computers.

2. In the console pane under the appropriate domain, click Computers.

3. In the details pane, right-click the computer name and select Manage.

4. In the new Computer Management window, click System Tools and then Device Manager.

Dial-Up Networking

You can find Dial-Up Networking in Network And Dial-Up Connections in Control Panel. Or right-click My Network Places and choose Properties from the shortcut menu. Unless you're logged on as an administrator or a member of the Administrators group, some features of Network And Dial-Up Connections won't be available.

Disk Administrator

Disk Administrator has been renamed Disk Management. Disk Management is a graphical tool for managing disks and volumes. It supports partitions, logical drives, new dynamic volumes, and remote disk management. To open Disk Management, right-click My Computer and choose Manage from the shortcut menu. In the console pane, click Storage and then click Disk Management.

Find

In Windows 2000, Find has been renamed Search and is located on the Start menu.

MS-DOS Prompt

The MS-DOS prompt has been renamed the Command Prompt and is now located on the Accessories menu. The Command Prompt now comes with a number of functions, including file and folder autocompletion. See Chapter 10 for more information.

You set Command Prompt options such as color and font by right-clicking the Command Prompt title bar and selecting Properties; in the Apply Properties To Shortcut dialog box, select the Modify Shortcut That Modified This Window option. To set these options for a single session, right-click the Command Prompt title bar and choose Properties; in the Apply Properties To Shortcut dialog box, select the Apply Properties To Current Window Only option.

My Briefcase

You can now access My Briefcase, a default presence on the Windows NT 4 desktop, by right-clicking the desktop and selecting New and then Briefcase. A briefcase will be created and placed on the desktop.

My Documents

My Documents is a new folder on every Windows 2000 desktop. It's the default location for saved files. Inside My Documents is the subfolder My Pictures, the default location for graphics files. My Documents is one of the special folders that can be redirected to a location on the network. See Chapter 9 for information on using Group Policy for folder redirection.

Network Neighborhood

Network Neighborhood has been replaced by My Network Places. My Network Places shows the shared computers, files and folders, printers, and other resources on the network to which your computer is connected. Right-click My Network Places and choose Properties to view Network And Dial-Up Connections and Computers Near Me.

Personalized Menus

By default, Windows 2000 uses personalized menus for the Start menu and its offshoots. This means that Windows 2000 keeps track of how often you access items on each menu and places the most frequently used items at the top. Figure A.1 shows a personalized Programs menu. Click the double arrowheads at the bottom of the menu—or just rest the mouse pointer on the double arrowheads for a few seconds—to see the rest of the menu items.

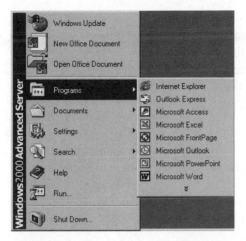

Figure A-1. *A personalized Programs menu.*

To return to menus where all items are shown, right-click the taskbar and choose Properties. Clear the Use Personalized Menus check box, and click OK.

Quick Launch Bar

The Quick Launch bar is a Microsoft Windows 98 feature that has been incorporated into the taskbar in Windows 2000. By default, shortcuts for Microsoft Internet Explorer, Microsoft Outlook Express, and the Desktop are on the Quick Launch bar. You can drag other shortcuts to the Quick Launch bar and drag off any of the default ones. The Desktop icon is particularly handy because it allows you to minimize all open windows with a single click. Click the Desktop icon a second time and the windows you just minimized will all reopen.

Start Menu

The Start menu isn't new, but it has changed somewhat from Windows NT 4. For example, the Logoff command is no longer on the Start menu by default. To add it, follow these steps:

1. Click Start, point to Settings, and then click Taskbar & Start Menu.
2. Click the Advanced tab.
3. In Start Menu Settings, select Display Logoff.

While you're on the Advanced tab, note the other additions you can make to the Start menu. You can still drag and drop shortcuts on the Start button to add items to the menu. Now you can also click and drag those items on the menu to change their order and right-click any of the added items to rename them.

System Information

System Information displays your system configuration data. To see System Information, right-click My Computer and choose Manage from the shortcut menu. In the console pane, click System Tools and then System Information. From a machine running Windows 2000 Server, you can view System Information on a remote computer by following these steps:

1. Open Active Directory Users And Computers.
2. In the console pane under the appropriate domain, click Computers.
3. In the details pane, right-click the computer name and select Manage.
4. In the new Computer Management window, click System Tools and then System Information.

TCP/IP

To install, remove, or configure TCP/IP in Windows 2000, open Network And Dial-Up Connections. Right-click the connection and choose Properties.

User Manager

In Windows 2000, User Manager has been renamed Local Users And Groups and is located in Computer Management. Right-click My Computer and choose Manage from the shortcut menu.

User Manager for Domains

Most of the functions of User Manager For Domains have been replaced by Active Directory Users And Computers. On Windows 2000 Server, Active Directory Users And Computers is on the Administrative Tools menu. Active Directory Domains And Trusts is used for creating and managing trust relationships.

View Options

In Windows 2000, View Options has been renamed Folder Options and is on the Tools menu in many places, including My Computer, My Documents, My Network Places, and Control Panel. Use Folder Options to change the appearance of your desktop and folder content and to specify how folders open. You can also specify whether folders open with a single click or a double click, and you can set how folders display.

Windows NT Explorer

Windows NT Explorer has been renamed Windows Explorer and is located on the Accessories menu.

Appendix B
Optional Components

The Microsoft Windows 2000 Server platforms have a number of optional components that you can install or remove to configure your system the way you want it. Some of these components are available only as part of Windows 2000 Advanced Server and are so indicated.

Adding and Removing Windows Components

To add or remove one of these optional components, click the Add/Remove Windows Components button on the left side of the Add/Remove Programs Control Panel dialog box. The various components are grouped by type, with the currently installed components checked.

To remove a component, clear its check box; to add a component, select its check box. After you've made your selections, click Next. If you've selected Terminal Services, you'll be prompted for the mode to use: Remote Administration Mode or Application Server Mode. For more on what these modes mean, see Chapter 25. Click Next again, and your Windows components will be updated. You might be prompted to insert your Windows 2000 CD-ROM. Once the update completes, click Finish. In some cases, you might be prompted to reboot the server, depending on the changes you're making, so it's best to add or remove components when you can afford to have the server off line for long enough to reboot.

Accessories and Utilities

Within the Accessories And Utilities grouping, there are additional component groups. To see the specifics of any component grouping, highlight the grouping and click the Details button. If the Details button is dimmed, that means you are highlighting an individual component and not a group of components.

Accessibility Wizard

The Accessibility Wizard allows you to configure your system to make it more accessible to those with special vision, hearing, and mobility needs. Installed with the wizard are additional accessibility tools, including Narrator, Magnifier, and On-Screen Keyboard, as well as the Utility Manager to manage the configuration of these utilities.

Accessories

Accessories is a grouping of applications and features each designed for a single use or purpose. These include:

- **Calculator**   A simple on-screen graphical calculator
- **Character Map**   Displays all the characters in any installed font and allows you to insert special characters and symbols into your current document
- **Clipboard Viewer**   Enables you to view and save the contents of the clipboard
- **Desktop Wallpaper**   Provides additional background images and pictures for enhancing your Windows desktop
- **Document Templates**   Allows opening of new documents using your right mouse button
- **Mouse Pointers**   Provides additional mouse pointers, including larger pointers and animated pointers
- **Object Packager**   Allows documents to include embedded or linked objects from another source
- **Paint**   A basic bitmap painting program
- **WordPad**   A simple word processor that can read Microsoft Word documents and handle ASCII text documents

Communications

Communications is a grouping of three simple programs that enhance the Windows 2000 communications abilities. The three programs are:

- **Chat**   Installs a useful chat application but doesn't create an icon for it on your Start menu. To use Chat, open the Start menu, choose Run, and type *Winchat.exe*.

- **HyperTerminal**   Uses a modem (or null modem cable) to connect to other computers or online services that still require terminal emulation.
- **Phone Dialer**   Allows you to dial a phone through your attached modem.

Games

Games is a grouping of four games that are normally installed in Windows 2000 Professional but are optional in Windows 2000 Server and Advanced Server. The four games are:

- **FreeCell**   A difficult solitaire card game
- **Minesweeper**   The familiar strategy game
- **Pinball**   A 3D computer version of an arcade pinball machine
- **Solitaire**   The classic card game

Tip   All of these games except for Pinball have a boss key. Press Esc while playing and the game minimizes to your taskbar—it appears to be a Microsoft Excel spreadsheet called Budget.xls.

Multimedia

Multimedia is a collection of utilities and sounds to take advantage of your server's multimedia capabilities. The group includes:

- **CD Player**   Plays music CDs in your computer's CD-ROM drive
- **Media Player**   Plays a variety of audio and video formats
- **Sample Sounds**   Provides a collection of sound clips
- **Sound Recorder**   Records sounds using your sound card
- **Utopia Sound Scheme**   Provides a collection of sounds that can be attached to various actions on your computer
- **Volume Control**   Lets you adjust the output volume from your sound card

---

Certificate Services

Microsoft Certificate Services includes a certification authority server that can issue public-key security certificates. It also includes support for adding Web pages to your Web server that allow you to submit and issue certificates.

Cluster Service (Advanced Server Only)

The Windows 2000 Cluster Service allows multiple servers to act together to provide highly available and scalable applications. See Chapter 15 for more on clusters.

Indexing Service

The Windows 2000 Indexing Service speeds up full text searching of files. See Chapter 26 for more on the Indexing Service.

Internet Information Services

Internet Information Services (IIS) includes several components you can add to any Windows 2000 server:

- **Common Files**   Required IIS program files used by many of the components
- **Documentation**   Documentation for the various IIS components, including samples
- **File Transfer Protocol (FTP) Server**   Support for uploading and downloading files using the FTP protocol
- **FrontPage 2000 Server Extensions**   Support for additional functionality when running Microsoft FrontPage 2000–created Web pages
- **Internet Information Services Snap-in**   MMC snap-in for managing IIS and its services
- **Internet Services Manager (HTML)**   HTML-based management interface for IIS services
- **NNTP Service**   Support for running a News server
- **SMTP Service**   Support for forwarding and receiving Internet Mail via SMTP
- **Visual InterDev RAD Remote Deployment Support**   Allows you to remotely deploy applications on your Web server
- **World Wide Web Server**   The IIS Web server

Management and Monitoring Tools

Management And Monitoring Tools is a group of three management and monitoring applications or protocols, including:

- **Connection Manager Components** Adds the Phone Book Services and the Connection Manager Administration Kit
- **Network Monitor Tools** Allows you to capture and analyze network traffic at the packet level
- **Simple Network Management Protocol** Provides SNMP support, allowing monitoring and reporting of the activity of a variety of network devices

Message Queuing Services

Installs the Microsoft Message Queuing service to improve network communications from supported applications. See Chapter 26 for more on Message Queuing.

Networking Services

Networking services is a group of optional networking components that you can add. The components in the Networking Services group include:

- **COM Internet Services Proxy** Provides support for DCOM objects to use HTTP and IIS
- **Domain Name System (DNS)** Adds the Microsoft dynamic DNS server
- **Dynamic Host Configuration Protocol (DHCP)** Adds a DHCP server to automatically assign IP addresses and configuration information to network client computers
- **Internet Authentication Service** Adds support for the RADIUS protocol for dial-up and VPN users
- **QoS Admission Control Service** Provides support for specifying network connection quality by individual subnets

- **Simple TCP/IP Services** Provides support for a variety of minor TCP/IP services including Echo and Quote of the Day
- **Site Server ILS Services** Updates directory information by scanning TCP/IP stacks
- **Windows Internet Name Service (WINS)** Adds a WINS server for supporting NetBIOS names in mixed-mode networks

Other Network File and Print Services

A group of three file and print services that provide support for clients on other operating systems:

- **File Services for Macintosh** Support for Macintosh computers to both store files and access files on Windows 2000 servers
- **Print Services for Macintosh** Supports Macintosh computers printing to Windows 2000 printers
- **Print Services for UNIX** Supports UNIX and Linux users printing to Windows 2000 printers using line printer remote (LPR)

Remote Installation Services

Remote Installation Services adds support for remote installation of Windows 2000 Professional onto client computers with appropriate remote boot-enabled network cards.

Remote Storage

Remote Storage provides services and tools to allow you to store less frequently accessed files and data on tape, freeing up hard disk space.

Script Debugger

Script Debugger enables you to more easily debug Web pages, Active Server Pages, and other script files.

Terminal Services

You can use Windows 2000 Terminal Services to switch between Remote Management Mode and Application Server Mode. See Chapter 25 for more on Windows 2000 Terminal Services. Terminal Services also installs the necessary files to create Terminal Services Client setup disks.

Terminal Services Licensing

Terminal Services Licensing provides client access licenses on the network. The Terminal Services license server must run on a domain controller.

Windows Media Services

Windows Media Services provides support for using Windows 2000 Server as a streaming media server. Media Services includes both the actual media server and the administrator program used to manage the service.

Appendix C
The OSI Reference Model

As with any emerging technology, the early days of networking were characterized by strictly proprietary hardware and software. No one agreed on any particular method of building and implementing networks. That meant your choices for suppliers were limited.

You could choose to buy your network from IBM, DEC, Burroughs, or a few others. This decision was momentous because after purchasing components from one manufacturer, you were locked in. No one else's equipment or software would work with yours. You had to buy everything from the original vendor, and if they didn't happen to make a product that you really, truly needed, you were just out of luck.

To cut across this entirely proprietary universe, the International Organization of Standards developed a standard to make possible open systems that could communicate with one another no matter who manufactured them. Today, many proprietary systems still exist, and they don't always communicate with one another as well as we might hope, but they do have the Open Systems Interconnection (OSI) reference model in common. This model provides a framework for depicting the organization of network components and can give you a clearer picture of how these components relate to one another.

The OSI reference model is made up of seven layers. Each layer has its job to do and has to relate only to the layers directly on either side of it. The layers are shown in Figure C-1. From the bottom up, they are:

- Physical
- Data link
- Network
- Transport
- Session
- Presentation
- Application

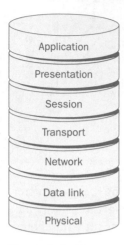

Figure C-1. *Layers of the OSI reference model.*

Each layer in a network communication model assumes that it's speaking to the same layer on another machine and uses a common protocol. The collection of protocols is called a *protocol stack*.

Physical Layer

The physical layer deals with how the data signals are transmitted on the network cable or other transmission medium. The physical layer handles the mechanical and electrical procedures and is oblivious to whether the signal is made up of digital bits or is in analog form. Parts of the physical layer include the type of cabling and the network interface card (NIC).

Data Link Layer

The data link layer is the first layer that handles the packet as such. It groups bits that have been organized into low-level logical units called *frames*. It then waits for acknowledgment that the frames were received and retransmits any frames that are lost, performing a cyclical redundancy check (CRC) on each frame. The data link layer connects the physical aspects of a network with the abstractions of software.

Network Layer

The network layer builds on the connection made by the data link layer. It adds the unit of information called *packets*. The network layer handles routing (the process of delivering packets through an internetwork) and congestion control. It's the highest layer of the OSI model that understands the network's topology—that is, the physical configuration of the machines, the type and length of cabling, and so forth.

Examples of network layer protocols are IPX, IP, and AppleTalk's Datagram Delivery Protocol (DDP).

Transport Layer

The transport layer builds on the error-control mechanisms of the lower layers. This is the last stop for ensuring that corrections are made in the sending and receiving of packets. The transport layer breaks up large pieces of data into smaller pieces and assigns sequence numbers. Examples of transport layer protocols are TCP, User Datagram Protocol (UDP), and the AppleTalk Transaction Protocol (ATP).

Session Layer

The session layer deals with two-way communications between nodes. When a dialog between nodes begins, a session is initiated. A good example of this is when a workstation connects to a Windows 2000 server. Rules are established about how the two will communicate and the protocols to be used. If a system is running multiple network applications, the system layer organizes communications so that incoming data is directed to the correct application. Remote procedure calls (RPCs) and NetBIOS are examples of session layer functionality.

Presentation Layer

The presentation layer handles how data is represented. It handles how data is formatted, how lines of characters are to be shown, whether data is encoded, and so forth. For example, if you're sending encrypted communications over the Internet, it is the function of the presentation layer to encrypt and decrypt the data. SNMP and Unicode are examples of presentation layer protocols supported in Microsoft Windows 2000.

Application Layer

The application layer handles the information transfer between two network applications, including remote file services, message handling for e-mail, and remote database access. Many of the services under this layer are called application programming interfaces (APIs). APIs are programming libraries used to write applications.

Tip The OSI model layers are usually numbered in the order listed in Figure C-1. So if you see a reference to Layer 3 of the OSI model, you'll know it's the network layer being described.

The OSI reference model is useful because every networking protocol stack is based in some way on the OSI structure. None of the protocol stacks you encounter will fit the model exactly, but there's always enough correspondence to help you understand the relationship among the parts—and certainly enough to get you started if you want to delve deeper into the technical core of networking.

The Microsoft TCP/IP Stack

Microsoft's TCP/IP protocols use a four-layer conceptual model, also called the PC model, that combines some of the OSI model layers. Table C-1 compares the two models. The layers are simplified, but the same elements are present in the Microsoft TCP/IP stack as in the traditional OSI model.

Table C-1. Comparing conceptual models

Microsoft Model	OSI Model
Network interface layer	Physical and data link layers
Internet layer	Network layer
Transport layer	Transport layer
Application layer	Session, presentation, and application layers

The OSI Model in Action

Let's say you want to retrieve a spreadsheet file called Budget.xls from a network file server. Here's how the layers would work to accomplish the retrieval.

First the application layer on your computer detects that you're asking for information from a remote server and formulates a request that Budget.xls should be read from the file server's hard disk. The presentation layer then encrypts the request, if necessary, and passes the packet to the session layer. The session layer adds information about which application is requesting the information and which service is being requested from the file server. The packet is then handed off to the transport layer.

The transport layer verifies that a reliable connection exists to the file server and then breaks down the accumulated information into blocks. If more than one frame is necessary, sequence numbers are added. Next, the blocks are passed to the network layer.

The network layer adds the network address for both the system that is the source of the request and the file server. This is added to each chunk of information before it is passed to the data link layer.

The data link layer packages the blocks into frames and adds a frame header and the source and destination MAC addresses. The MAC addresses plus the content of the frame are used to create a CRC trailer. The frames are then handed off to the physical layer. The physical layer knows no more about frames than a highway knows about cars. It is just the road by which the data is moved.

At the file server, the data link layer reads the transmitted frame and identifies the MAC address for the destination system as its own MAC address. The data link layer performs a CRC and if all is well, strips off the header and trailer and passes the frame to the network layer. (If the CRC isn't valid, the data link layer discards the frame and requests a replacement from the source computer.)

The network layer on the file server analyzes the information that was added by the network layer on the source computer, notes the network address of the source computer, and records it in a table. The frames are then passed up to the transport layer.

The transport layer reviews the information in the frame that was supplied by the transport layer on the source system. If sequencing was used, it queues the frames until all are received. The sequencing is used to identify any missing frames, and a request for any missing data is sent to the source computer. If all the data is present, the transport layer passes the request to the session layer.

The session layer verifies that the data is from a valid connection and that all security criteria have been met. The data is then passed to the presentation layer. The presentation layer performs any necessary decryption and passes the data on to the application layer. The application layer passes the request to the process responsible for access to the file system.

Then, incredibly enough, the process reads the requested file and passes the information back to the application layer, and the whole process begins again. That a file request can be processed in less than a day is remarkable—that in reality it takes only a few seconds is quite astounding.

Although when this model is broken down into steps, it appears to be complex (and it is), it's also a good way to ensure flexibility and reliability. Because Ethernet confines its functionality to the data link layer, it can work with any number of protocols such as IP and IPX, which operate in the network layer. You should also bear in mind that the OSI model is a *model* and isn't exactly adhered to anywhere.

Using the Windows 2000 Recovery Console

This appendix is based on article Q229716 from the Microsoft Knowledge Base, and was written shortly before the release of Microsoft Windows 2000. It might not reflect any last minute changes. Check the Knowledge Base on line for modifications (*http://support.microsoft.com/search/*). Be aware that these descriptions of the commands relate to their performance in the Recovery Console; many will have additional functions available when issued from the Windows 2000 command prompt.

Description of the Windows 2000 Recovery Console

This article discusses a Beta release of a Microsoft product. The information in this article is provided as-is and is subject to change without notice. No formal product support is available from Microsoft for this Beta product. For information about obtaining support for a Beta release, please see the documentation included with the Beta product files or check the Web location from which you downloaded the release.

The information in this article applies to

- Microsoft Windows 2000 Professional
- Microsoft Windows 2000 Server
- Microsoft Windows 2000 Advanced Server
- Microsoft Windows 2000 Datacenter Server

Summary

This article describes the functionality and limitations of the Windows 2000 Recovery Console. The Recovery Console is designed to help you recover when your Windows 2000–based computer does not start properly or at all.

More Information

With the Windows 2000 Recovery Console you can obtain limited access to NTFS, FAT, and FAT32 volumes without starting the Windows graphical interface. In the Recovery Console you can:

- Use, copy, rename or replace operating system files and folders.
- Enable or disable services or devices from starting when you next start your computer.
- Repair the file system boot sector or the Master Boot Record (MBR).
- Create and format partitions on drives.

Note that only an administrator can obtain access to the Recovery Console so unauthorized users cannot use any NTFS volume.

Starting the Recovery Console

To start the Recovery Console, use any of the following methods:

- Start your computer with the Windows 2000 Setup floppy disks or with the Windows 2000 CD-ROM. At the "Welcome to Setup" screen press F10, or press R to Repair, and then C to start the Recovery Console.
- Add the Recovery Console to the Windows 2000 Startup folder by using Winnt32.exe with the "/cmdcons" switch. This requires approximately 7 MB of disk space on your system partition to hold the cmdcons directory and files. Note that if you are using software mirroring, please see the following article in the Microsoft Knowledge Base:

  Q229077 *Mirroring prevents pre-installing the Recovery Console*

- Follow the instructions in the following article in the Microsoft Knowledge Base:

  Q222478 *Template to Run Recovery Console Using a Remote Install Server*

Using the Command Console

After you start the Recovery Console, you receive the following message:

```
Windows NT(TM) Recovery Console Command Interpreter.

WARNING:

The Recovery Console provides system repair and recovery functionality.
```

Type 'exit' to quit the recovery console and restart the computer.

1: C:\WINNT

Which Windows 2000 installation would you like to log on to? (To cancel, press ENTER.)

After you enter the number for the appropriate Windows 2000 installation, enter the Administrator account password. Note that if you use an incorrect password 3 times, the Recovery Console quits. Also, if the SAM database is missing or damaged, you will not be able to use the Recovery Console because you cannot be properly authenticated. After you enter your password and the Recovery Console starts, typing "exit" restarts your computer.

Restrictions and Limitations of the Recovery Console

From the Recovery Console you can only use the following folders:

- The root folder.
- The %SystemRoot% folder and the subfolders of the Windows 2000 installation you are currently logged in to.
- The Cmdcons folder.
- Removable media drives such as CD-ROM drives.

Note   If you try to obtain access to other folders, you receive an "Access Denied" error message. Also, while in the Recovery Console you cannot copy a file from the local hard disk to a floppy disk. You can copy a file from a floppy disk or CD-ROM to a hard disk, and from one hard disk to another hard disk.

Available Commands

HELP

HELP lists all of the following supported commands:

ATTRIB	DEL	EXPAND	MAP	RMDIR
BATCH	DELETE	FIXBOOT	MD	SYSTEMROOT
CD	DIR	FIXMBR	MKDIR	TYPE
CHDIR	DISABLE	FORMAT	MORE	
CHKDSK	DISKPART	HELP	RD	
CLS	ENABLE	LISTSVC	REN	
COPY	EXIT	LOGON	RENAME	

ATTRIB

The ATTRIB command with any of the following parameters can change attributes of a file or folder:

-R

+R

-S

+S

-H

+H

-C

+C

\+ Sets an attribute.

\- Resets an attribute.

R Read-Only file attribute.

S System file attribute.

H Hidden file attribute.

C Compressed file attribute.

Note At least one attribute must be set or cleared. To view attributes use the DIR command.

BATCH

BATCH *inputfile* [*outputfile*]

Executes commands specified in a text file.

inputfile Specifies the text file that contains the list of commands to be executed.

outputfile If specified, contains the output of the specified commands. If not specified, the output is displayed on the screen.

CD and CHDIR

CD and CHDIR [*drive:*] [...] [*path*]

The CD and CHDIR commands change the folder. *CD* .. specifies that you want to change to the parent folder. Type *CD drive:* to display the current folder in the specified drive. Type *CD* without parameters to display the current drive and folder. The CD and CHDIR commands treat spaces as delimiters. Because of this, you must enclose a subfolder name that contains a space with quotation marks. For example: CD "\winnt\profiles\username\programs\start menu"

The CHDIR command only operates within the system folders of the current installation of Windows 2000, removable media, the root folder of any hard disk partition, or the local installation sources.

CHKDSK

CHKDSK [*drive:*] [/P] [/R]

Checks, and if needed, repairs or recovers a drive. Also marks bad sectors and recovers readable information.

drive: Specifies the drive to check. The /P switch instructs CHKDSK to do an exhaustive check of the drive even if the drive is not marked with problems and corrects any errors found. The /R switch locates bad sectors and recovers readable information. Note that specifying the /R switch implies the /P switch. CHKDSK may be specified without arguments, in which case the current drive is implied with no switches. Optionally, the listed switches are accepted. The CHKDSK command requires the Autochk.exe file. CHKDSK automatically locates this file in the bootup folder. This would typically be the Cmdcons folder if the Recovery Console was pre-installed. If it cannot be found in the bootup folder, CHKDSK tries to locate the Windows 2000 CD-ROM installation media. If the installation media cannot be found, CHKDSK prompts you to provide the location of the Autochk.exe file.

CLS

Clears the screen.

COPY

COPY [*source*] [*destination*]

Copies a file.

source Specifies the file to be copied. Wildcards or folder copies are not permitted. A compressed file from the Windows 2000 CD-ROM is automatically decompressed as it is copied.

destination Specifies the folder or file name for the new file. If this is not specified, it defaults to the current folder. If the file already exists, you are prompted to overwrite it.

DEL and DELETE

DEL [*drive:*] [*path*] [*filename*]

DELETE [*drive:*] [*path*] [*filename*]

Deletes a file.

drive: path filename specifies the file to delete.

The DELETE command only operates within the system folders of the current Windows 2000 installation, removable media, the root folder of any hard disk partition, or the local installation sources. The DELETE command does not accept wild card (*) characters.

DIR

DIR [*drive:*] [*path*] [*filename*]

Displays a list of files and subfolders in a folder.

drive: path filename Specifies drive, folder, and/or files to list. The DIR command lists all files including hidden and system files. Files may have the following attributes:

```
D - Directory        R - Read-only file
H - Hidden file      A - Files ready for archiving
S - System file      C - Compressed
E - Encrypted        P - Reparse Point
```

The DIR command only operates within the system folders of the current Windows 2000 installation, removable media, the root folder of any hard disk partition, or the local installation sources.

DISABLE

DISABLE *servicename*

The DISABLE command disables a Windows 2000 system service or driver.

servicename The name of the service or driver to be disabled. Use the LISTSVC command to display all eligible services or drivers to disable. DISABLE prints the old start_type of the service before resetting it to SERVICE_DISABLED. Because of this, you should record the old start_type, in case it is necessary to re-enable the service.

The start_type values that the DISABLE command displays:

> SERVICE_DISABLED
> SERVICE_BOOT_START
> SERVICE_SYSTEM_START
> SERVICE_AUTO_START
> SERVICE_DEMAND_START

DISKPART

DISKPART [/*add*] | /*delete*] [*device name* | *drive name* | *partition name*] [*size*]

Use the DISKPART command to manage the partitions on your hard disk volumes.

/*add* Create a new partition.

/delete Delete an existing partition.

device name Device name for creating a new partition. The name can be obtained from the output of the MAP command. For example: \Device\HardDisk0

drive name This is a drive-letter based name for deleting an existing partition. For example, D:

partition name This is a partition-based name for deleting an existing partition and can be used in place of the drive name argument. For example, \Device\ HardDisk0\Partition1

size Size of the new partition in megabytes.

Note   If no arguments are used, a user interface for managing your partitions appears.

ENABLE

ENABLE *servicename* [*start_type*]

You can use the ENABLE command to enable a Windows 2000 system service or driver.

servicename The name of the service or driver to be enabled. Use the LISTSVC command to display all eligible services or drivers to enable. The ENABLE command prints the old start_type of the service before resetting it to the new value. You should note the old value, in case it is necessary to restore the start_type of the service.

start_type Valid start_type values are:

> SERVICE_BOOT_START
> SERVICE_SYSTEM_START
> SERVICE_AUTO_START
> SERVICE_DEMAND_START

Note   If you do not specify a new start_type, ENABLE prints the old start_type for you.

EXIT

You can use the EXIT command to quit the Recovery Console and restart your computer.

EXPAND

EXPAND *source* [*/F:filespec*] [*destination*] [Y]

EXPAND *source* [*/F:filespec*] /D

Expands a compressed file.

source Specifies the file to be expanded; cannot include wildcards.

destination Specifies the folder for the new file. Default is the current folder.

/F:filespec If the source contains more than one file, this parameter is required to identify the specific file(s) to be expanded; can include wildcards.

/Y Do not prompt before overwriting an existing file.

/D Do not expand; only display a folder of the files that are contained in the source.

The destination can be any folder within the system folders of the current Windows 2000 installation, the root of any drive, the local installation sources, or the Cmdcons folder, but not removable media. The destination file cannot be read-only.

FIXBOOT

FIXBOOT *drive*

Writes new Windows 2000 boot sector code on the boot partition. This fixes problems where the Windows 2000 boot sector is corrupted. The Emergency Repair process also fixes the boot sector.

drive Drive letter where the boot sector will be written. This overrides the default of writing to the system boot partition. The FIXBOOT command is only supported on the x86 platform.

FIXMBR

FIXMBR *device name*

Repairs the master boot record (MBR) of the boot partition. This is used in scenarios where a virus has damaged the MBR and Windows 2000 cannot start.

Caution This command has the potential to damage your partition tables if a virus is present or a hardware problem exists. This command may lead to inaccessible partitions. Microsoft suggests running anti-virus software before using this command.

device name Optional device name that specifies the device that needs a new MBR. The name can be obtained from the output of the MAP command. If this is left blank, the boot device's MBR is fixed. For example:

FIXMBR \device\harddisk2

If FIXMBR detects an invalid or non-standard partition table signature, it prompts you for permission before rewriting the MBR. The FIXMBR command is only supported on the x86 platform.

FORMAT

FORMAT [*drive:*] [*IQ*] [*/FS:file-system*]

Formats the specified drive to the specified file system.

drive: Drive letter of the partition to format.

/Q Performs a quick format of the drive.

/FS:file-system Specifies the type of file system to use, FAT, FAT32, or NTFS. If none is specified, then the existing file system format is used, when available.

LISTSVC

The LISTSVC command lists all available services, drivers and their start types for the current Windows 2000 installation. This may be useful when using the DISABLE and ENABLE commands.

Note   These are extracted from the %SystemRoot%\System32\Config\SYSTEM hive. Should the SYSTEM hive become damaged or missing, unpredictable results may occur.

LOGON

LOGON

The LOGON command lists all detected installations of Windows 2000 and Windows NT, and then requests the local administrator password for the copy of Windows you chose to log on to. If more than three attempts to logon do not succeed, the console quits and your computer restarts.

MAP

MAP [*arc*]

The MAP command lists drive letters, file system types, partition sizes and mappings to physical devices.

arc The arc parameter tells MAP to use ARC paths instead of Windows 2000 Device paths.

MD and MKDIR

The MD or MKDIR commands make folders. Wildcard characters are not supported. The MKDIR command only operates within the system folders of the current installation of Windows 2000, removable media, the root folder of any hard disk partition, or the local installation sources.

MORE

MORE *filename*

The MORE command displays a text file to the screen.

RD and RMDIR

The RD and RMDIR commands delete a folder.

The RMDIR and RD commands only operate within the system folders of the current Windows 2000 installation, removable media, the root folder of any hard disk partition, or the local installation sources.

REN and RENAME

The REN and RENAME commands can rename a file. Note that you cannot specify a new drive or path for your destination file. The REN and RENAME commands only operate within the system folders of the current Windows 2000 installation, removable media, the root folder of any hard disk partition, or the local installation sources.

SET

The SET command allows you to display or modify four environment options.

```
AllowWildCards = FALSE
AllowAllPaths = FALSE
AllowRemovableMedia = FALSE
NoCopyPrompt = FALSE
```

SYSTEMROOT

The SYSTEMROOT command sets the current working folder to the %SystemRoot% folder of the Windows 2000 installation you are currently logged into.

TYPE

TYPE *filename*

The TYPE command displays a text file.

Appendix E
Enterprise Backup Solutions

In addition to the Microsoft Windows 2000 Backup utility licensed from Seagate Software, other excellent options are available for enterprise-wide backup that parallel the capabilities of mainframe backup/recovery storage requirements. Going to automated backup with robotic libraries or storage area networks (SAN) requires specialized hardware and software but can provide increased availability and protection when large amounts of data are involved.

Six of the most popular backup applications and some of their individual characteristics are discussed here as alternatives to Windows 2000 Backup. These applications include the following:

- **ARCserve** from Computer Associates (*http://www.cheyenne.com/*)
- **Backup Exec** from Seagate Software (recently purchased by Veritas Software)
- **NetBackup** from Veritas Software (*http://www.veritas.com/*)
- **NetWorker** from Legato Systems (*http://www.legato.com/*)
- **REELbackup** from SCH Technologies (*http://www.sch.com/*)
- **Tivoli Storage Manager** from IBM (recently transferred to the Tivoli group)—formerly Adstar Distributed Storage Manager (ADSM) (*http://www.trivoli.com/*)

This appendix is not a definitive description of backup options but is intended to provide guidance for the enterprise administrator searching for advanced backup solutions.

ARCserve

ARCserve is a Windows 2000 and NetWare backup/restore solution from Computer Associates. Originally from Cheyenne, ARCserve has been used in Microsoft Windows NT and NetWare environments, with support for UNIX clients also available. ARCserve is a product that suits backup/recovery needs typically seen in smaller organizations.

ARCserve uses system resources well while returning excellent performance figures. However, with the ARCserve architecture, only one backup can be written to a single tape at a given time. Therefore, to use more than one drive (for example, DLT7000 tape drives), you must have sufficient processor and memory resources.

Sites that have implemented ARCserve 6.6 on backup/restore servers configured with 512 MB or more of memory have recorded between 6 MBps and 7 MBps sustained throughput to a single DLT7000 drive. Backup and restore times across a switched 100-MB network have also produced 4–5 MBps. This is achievable with ARCserve only when using large amounts of physical memory.

Server Recommendations

When configuring an ARCserve 6.6 backup/restore server in Windows 2000, be sure to configure the amount of physical memory to meet backup performance expectations. Minimum server specifications should be 512 MB of RAM and 300 MHz or faster processors.

Backup Exec

Backup Exec is a Windows 2000 and NetWare backup/restore solution from Veritas. Originally from the Arcada and Seagate Software companies, Backup Exec has been used mostly in Windows NT and NetWare environments, with support for UNIX clients also available. Backup Exec is the most common of the lower-end backup/restore software solutions. A compact version is licensed to Microsoft and incorporated into Windows 2000.

An obvious shortcoming in Backup Exec is that it uses only one processor during the course of the backup. While excellent performance is achieved out of the box, the employment of only a single processor makes it a poor choice for multiprocessor servers.

The minimum hardware configuration for a Backup Exec environment should be 256 MB of RAM (512 MB or more is preferable) and a single fast processor (that is, 450 MHz or faster). Performance can also be improved up to 20 percent by increasing the block size to 64 KB (the default is 32 KB) and by increasing buffer size and count parameters for each tape device. Because data varies, you should experiment with the parameters and examine the results in conjunction with Windows 2000 Performance Monitor.

NetBackup

NetBackup by Veritas provides a high performance backup/restore solution that has the same functionality as its UNIX version. A key part of NetBackup's architecture is its ability to multiplex streams of backup data to a single tape, which results in maximum use of the tape drive. Another advantage of NetBackup is its ability to tune the backup/restore environment and use available system resources efficiently.

When configuring a NetBackup server, you should configure the server not only with ample physical memory, but also with fast and efficient network interface cards (NIC). NetBackup can easily achieve backup speeds of 7–8 MBps through the combination of memory tuning and its multiplexing functionality.

Another feature of NetBackup is its master/slave architecture, which reduces the amount of data being transmitted across the network and cuts backup and restore times. NetBackup can restore as little as a single file, and it can restore to a different directory or node when the original server is down and another is commissioned to replace it.

Server Recommendations

The most obvious requirement of NetBackup is the availability of physical memory. By configuring large blocks of physical memory, you can use NetBackup's functionality to tune memory and increase overall performance. Fast dual processors (300 MHz or faster) are also recommended to shorten database queries and updates.

NetWorker

Legato's NetWorker is the current release for Windows 2000. NetWorker is widely used as an original equipment manufacturer (OEM) product by companies such as Silicon Graphics and Compaq. The product offers high performance over both network-centric and distributed environments, while also supporting a wide range of operating systems.

With NetWorker, you can run multiple backup jobs to a single tape device, maintaining both high performance and throughput. Tests have achieved over 8 MBps (with compression) by using parallelism. However, studies indicate that for this type of architecture, the backup/restore server must be configured with multiple fast processors and sufficient amounts of memory according to the type of activity for the server. As with NetBackup from Veritas, you can accomplish concurrent backups of databases such as Oracle by using additional software from Legato.

Server Recommendations

To take advantage of NetWorker's speed, the backup/restore server must be configured with multiple fast processors and enough memory to match the type of throughput the server is expected to manage.

REELbackup

REELbackup features *multiplexing*, or interleaving data to as many as 10 different backup streams—either from Windows NT, UNIX, or both—to a single or multiple tape drives. The product also supports the use of fast write/read, enabling the storage and retrieval of large volumes of data on a single tape. It has been clocked in the range of 8 MBps on the channel running with a DLT7000. Online database backup support is a feature that enables systems and database administrators to reduce downtime in order to make databases such as Microsoft Exchange Server continually available to users.

While backup and restore to Windows NT clients has been a function of the REELs software suite for some time, the ability to host NetMaster (server version 3) on a Windows NT operating system is relatively new in the marketplace. NetMaster has been available in UNIX environments for several years and is one of the pioneers in the world of backup and recovery. REELbackup accommodates several platforms and flavors of UNIX-based hosts and can exploit the transfer rates of extremely high-performance tape units.

The REELs suite is currently the only complete storage area network architecture in production that performs dynamic switching of tape and library devices. Legato's NetWorker and Veritas's NetBackup products are in the final phases of implementing dynamic switching SAN solutions in the market.

Server Recommendations

REELbackup relies heavily on caching, so be sure to configure it with sufficient memory. The recommended minimum available memory is 128 MB of RAM, but 512 MB or more is preferable. One gigabyte is the recommended starting point for disk space, but the eventual amount you will need depends on how much material you intend to back up.

Tivoli Storage Manager

Tivoli Storage Manager is the new name for Tivoli Adstar Distributed Storage Manager (ADSM). Version 3.7 is an enterprise backup/restore software solution originally from IBM. Tivoli Storage Manager is usually configured to perform one initial full backup and incremental backups thereafter, although you can run full backups any time.

Tivoli Storage Manager can run multiple backup processes concurrently; while individual performance might be slow, overall performance is usually acceptable. The slow individual performance is a consequence of Tivoli Storage Manager's unique "one full, incremental forever" architecture. As Tivoli Storage Manager attempts to back up each file, it must first verify that the file meets the policy that the administrator has specified. Having to check each file before backup degrades the performance somewhat. Tivoli Storage Manager masks this by performing only incremental backups (by default) that require the movement of much less data across the network, and that, theoretically, result in a shorter backup time. This characteristic is evident when performing backups of larger files, as Tivoli Storage Manager can move large files at reasonable speeds.

Another performance indicator is how well the software restores large amounts of data. Because of the architecture, when recovering multiple files, Tivoli Storage Manager restore times are substandard as compared to other products. Before you implement a Tivoli Storage Manager environment, you should investigate other features that are relevant to its performance, such as colocation and reclamation.

Server Recommendations

An important factor when configuring a Tivoli Storage Manager backup/restore server is the inclusion of sufficient disk space for the Tivoli Storage Manager database and recovery logs. With more versions of a file to be kept and longer retention times, Tivoli Storage Manager requires a significant amount of overall disk space. The minimum server specifications should consist of 256 MB of RAM, 200 MHz processors, and sufficient disk space for the database and recovery log files.

> **Tip**   For improved reliability, allocate database and recovery log volumes in an NTFS file system, not a FAT file system. By using NTFS, you can take advantage of the Windows 2000 capability to recover from problems that can occur during I/O to a disk.

Configuring a Backup Server

When configuring a Windows 2000 backup/restore server, be sure to configure physical hardware according to the software and the demands that are to be placed on the server (that is, the number of tape drives). Wherever you can, configure as much physical memory as possible, which allows products such as ARCserve, Backup Exec, NetBackup, NetWorker, and REELbackup to use and further adjust memory as required.

Also keep in mind that performance can vary according to the type of data that is being written or read from tape. For example, a file that is 100 MB can, in most cases, be written to tape faster than 100 files of 1 MB each.

The Windows 2000 default configuration is also limited to a maximum block size of 64 KB when writing data to tape. However, this can be increased to 128-KB blocks using the variable block size technique. Higher block sizes typically aren't allowed because of host bus adapter restrictions.

The Price of Backup and Restore Solutions

Dedicated telecommunications lines—one for voice, one for video, and one for data—are no longer required. Telecommunications transport methodologies and packetized multiplexing methods of data transfer support a variety of signals on the same line. Recent technological advances in data concentrators and multiplexers allow users with different types of data distributed throughout their enterprises, created at different locations, to maximize their investment by sharing common telecommunications lines for various functions, sources, and types of data.

Research indicates that on average costs for T1, T3, and Synchronous Optical Network (SONET) lines are coming down at a rate of 30 percent annually in the U.S. In 1992, line charges were about $80,000 per month for T3 services installed. Today, that equivalent line charge is about $1,000 a month. Table E-1 compares the transfer times for 1 gigabyte of uncompressed data across different channels.

Use of private networks, dark fiber, and SONET are enabling increased communications bandwidth. All these advances are driving increased competition and lower-cost transmission and communication lines.

Table E-1.   Transfer times by topology

Topology	Time to Transfer 1 G (in hours)	Time to Transfer 1 G (in minutes)
56 K Link	41.7711	2506.27
T1 Link	1.5189	91.14
T3 Link	0.0520	3.12
10BaseT	0.3086	18.52
100BaseT	0.0309	1.85
1000BaseFX	0.0033	0.20
FDDI	0.0234	1.40
Token Ring 4Mb	0.5848	35.09
Token Ring 16Mb	0.1462	8.77
ATM OC-3	0.0221	1.32
ATM OC-12	0.0055	0.33

Hardware compression has reached the high end of computing. T3 data compression, impossible until recently, is now enabling twice the effective data rate from 44 Mb to over 88 Mb across a single dedicated line.

Internet- and intranet-based remote data storage and access open a new frontier for business continuity. Secure, off-site, and high-availability data solutions are technologically ripe for the picking.

Automated Tape as a Tool for Enterprise Backup

Tape is the ideal medium for enterprise backup and recovery because it's fast, reliable, and affordable. Until recently, tape backup didn't offer the benefit of data separation from the enterprise server. SCSI distances are limited to 100 feet or less. Thus, tapes still had to be manually carried off-site. New channel extension technology makes direct off-site recording possible. Deemed *remote electronic vaulting,* data extension capabilities allow data transfer across unlimited distances.

Recent developments in automated tape libraries supporting virtually all computing platforms solve the automation problem. Automated libraries of all sizes abound, from the desktop version carrying a dozen or so tapes to huge systems holding thousands of tape cartridges. Automation, combined with remote connections for your tape system, offers the most promising solution. No matter where you locate a robotic tape library, it can be a valuable asset in its role as the backup/recovery repository. Recovery can be accomplished remotely from an alternate site, enabling the rapid routing of data to remote users.

The robot-controlled library and its partner—high-capacity/high-speed tape—can be located away from the prime processing sites and can be logically connected over great distances. The price of these lines is no longer a deterrent to good data protection and storage management practices.

StorageTek (STK), for example, makes robotic libraries that vary from a model that holds 18 tapes and one or more tape drives to the gigantic Powderhorn, which holds up to 6000 tapes and as many as 80 tape drives. These devices are now in their fifth generation and have populated most large-scale mainframe shops since the early 1980s.

Tape transports from StorageTek, IBM, and DLT, or even a mix of assorted transports, can be attached to these robotic libraries. This allows the appropriate high-capacity tape drive to be matched with the robot depending on the specifications. By separating which library is needed and which tape transport is considered necessary, individual requirements can be met efficiently and economically with future growth allowed for. All libraries offer a cartridge access port that allows for manual discards and entries of tapes and a user interface for exercising and controlling the unit. Tape transports are also becoming increasingly more affordable as vendors compete in the areas of cost, performance, capacity, and scalability.

Choosing a Tape Platform

Tape transfer speed, throughput, and reliability are major factors when you consider developing a backup/restore solution. Table E-2 compares three of the leading tape transports.

Specifications such as these can help you judge which drive would suit a particular business's needs. For example, cost per cartridge for StorageTek's 9840 is three times the cost of IBM's 3590, but it has twice the native capacity and it boasts longevity and better wear on the tape cartridge. The Sony DTF-1 features a transfer speed of 12 MBps but because of tape load times, the actual recall time is slower than StorageTek but faster than IBM. Gathering figures such as these and constructing your own tables is the best way to decide which figures are important and which are superfluous.

Table E-2.   Comparing tape transports

Tape Attribute	StorageTek 9840	Sony DTF-1 (GY-2120)	IBM Magstar B11
U.S. list purchase price	$27,400	$12,500	$32,500
Data transfer rate	10 MBps	12 MBps	9 MBps
Access time (sec, load + init)	4 sec	7 sec	27 sec
Average recall time (sec, load + init + search)	11.6 sec	42 sec	62 sec
High speed search (meters/sec)	8–10	Not published	5
High speed search (MBps)	656 MBps	300 MBps	Not published
Throughput 1 GB (average recall time + transfer rate)	111.6 sec	125.3 sec	205.6 sec
Cartridge costs (U.S. $)	20 GB $90	42 GB (GW730L) $120; 12 GB (GW240S) $50	10 GB $30
Maximum drives per silo frame	20	0	4
Interface	Ultra SCSI, Fibre & ESCON	SCSI Fast & Wide	Ultra SCSI & ESCON
Native capacity	20 GB	42 GB and 12 GB	10 GB
Storage capacity	80 GB	108 GB and 31GB	30 GB
Compression	LZ1 (4:1)	ALDC (2.59:1)	LZ1 (3:1)
Media type	½" metal particle	½" metal particle	½" metal particle
Midpoint load	Yes	Yes	Yes
Recording technique	Linear	Helical	Serpentined longitudinal

Data supplied by StorageTek, Inc.

Storage Area Network Technology

One of the newest technologies for server data storage has the potential to greatly improve the backup and recovery process. This technology is called storage area network. A SAN is a high-speed subnetwork of *shared storage devices*—machines that contain only disks for storing data. These devices are connected by an ultra high-speed network (called the *fabric*). This fabric consists of Fibre Channel hubs, bridges, or switches designed to enable many-to-many access between storage and servers. Figure E-1 shows a diagram of a SAN implementation.

A SAN-based storage infrastructure has the potential to provide higher levels of business continuity than were previously possible. Today, many corporations are faced with backup windows that are steadily creeping into operational windows. A Fibre Channel fabric allows access to the higher bandwidth available on SANs (up to 100–200 MBps), translating into shorter backup windows. Fibre Channel also provides greater distances between servers and storage devices, enabling an open path to remote electronic vaulting.

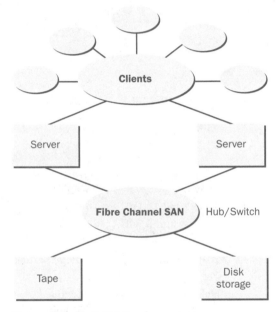

Figure E-1. *A SAN implementation.*

While SANs are attractive for these reasons, they also make storage more complex (and more expensive) and add new categories of storage resources that need to be monitored and managed: bridges, hubs, switches, switched fabrics, and Fibre Channel components. They also present a number of deployment challenges to IT managers, including the following issues:

- How much tape capacity will have to be added to back up the SAN?
- How will the health of the SAN be monitored once deployed?
- How much capacity is needed now? In the future?
- How will you partition the SAN disks?

- Which servers and workstations will have access to which SAN partitions?
- Which RAID systems, tape libraries, and other storage resources need to be included in the SAN?

One hurdle that remains in the deployment of SANs is the lack of industry standards for interoperability and management. Unfortunately, many devices from various SAN vendors don't work with each other.

Interoperability Between Operating Systems

SANs can make fast, reliable storage devices more cost-effective. In the majority of data centers, once the backup is done, the equipment just sits until the next scheduled backup. Each separate system and different platform (Windows 2000, UNIX, and NetWare) requires its own storage subsystem of backup devices and connections. A SAN opens up multiple connections between different servers, allowing a free flow of information to storage—void of device incompatibility problems.

SAN-Ready Solutions

Vendors of SAN-ready hardware include Advanced Digital Information Corp. (ADIC), IBM, EMC, StorageTek, and Storage Computer. All offer tape, optical disk, and disk solutions with SAN compatibility via Fibre Channel or other SAN interfaces. Leading backup software vendors such as SCH, Legato, and Veritas support SAN architectures that simplify the administrative upkeep of backup and recovery as well as mirrored site implementations.

Serverless Backups via SAN

In 1999, several vendors debuted direct disk-to-tape serverless backups via SAN technology. Specialized software drivers and storage managers enable intelligent and direct disk-to-tape data transfer, without server overhead and loss of bandwidth. Offloading the server backup workload encourages more frequent backups. In addition, offloading backup cycles from the CPUs inspires more point-in-time backups, with frequency based on the criticality of the application. This strategy decreases response time and increases productivity in the event of a failure.

As the requirements for speed and availability of data and applications increase and more pressure is placed on networks, emerging technologies such as SANs might allow companies to keep pace.

Appendix F
Windows 2000 Support Tools

Tool	Filename	Format	Description
ACL Diagnostics	Acldiag.exe	Cmd	Diagnoses and troubleshoots permissions problems
Active Directory Administration Tool	Ldp.exe	GUI	Performs Lightweight Directory Access Protocol (LDAP) operations
Active Directory Diagnostic Tool	Dsastat.exe	Cmd	Compares two directory trees within a domain or across different domains
Active Directory Object Manager	Movetree.exe	Cmd	Moves objects (such as users) between domains, leaving all linked group policies intact
Active Directory Search Tool	Search.vbs	Cmd	Script tool used to search an LDAP directory
ADSI Edit	Adsiedit.msc	GUI	Low-level editor for Active Directory; enables adding, moving, and deleting objects within Active Directory
Advanced Power Management Status	Apmstat.exe	Cmd	Provides information on Advanced Power Management features in older laptop computers
Application Compatibility Program	Apcompat.exe	Cmd, GUI	Tests for compatibility with Windows 2000 (and other versions of Windows)
Browser Status	Browstat.exe	Cmd	Determines whether a browser is running in a domain
Clone Principal	Clonepr.dll	Cmd	Creates clones of Windows NT 4 users and groups so they can be migrated to Windows 2000
DcAcls	Dsacls.exe	Cmd	Manages access control lists
Dependency Walker	Depends.exe	GUI	Scans any Win32 module and reports all dependent modules; used to find the minimum set of files needed to load an application and to find what functions a module uses or exports

Tool	Filename	Format	Description
Distributed file system Utility	Dfsutil.exe	Cmd	Queries and troubleshoots Dfs
DNS Troubleshooting Tool	Dnscmd.exe	Cmd	Allows administrators to view and modify DNS servers, zones, and resources
Domain Controller Diagnostic Tool	Dcdiag.exe	Cmd	Analyzes and reports on the state of domain controllers in an enterprise
Dump Check	Dumpchk.exe	Cmd	Reports and analyzes dump files
File and Directory Comparison	Windiff.exe	Cmd, GUI	Compares ASCII text files or folders
FileVer	Filever.exe	Cmd	Reports version information for a file or folder
Global Flags Editor	Gflags.exe	GUI	Edits global registry settings or flags in use by the kernel
Kerberos Keytab Setup	Ktpass.exe	Cmd	Configures a non-Windows 2000 Kerberos service to be a security principle in Windows 2000
Kerberos Setup	Ksetup.exe	Cmd	Configures Windows 2000 clients to use an MIT Kerberos server
Memory Profiling Tool	Memsnap.exe	Cmd	Takes a snapshot of the memory resources being used by all processes and reports the information to a log file
Migration Planning Document	Dommig.doc	GUI	Considers plans for migrating Windows NT domains to Windows 2000
Nltest	Nltest.exe	Cmd	Queries the status of trusts; lists primary domain controllers; forces a shutdown; forces a user database into sync on a Windows NT domain; usable on both Windows NT and Windows 2000
Point-to-Point Tunneling Protocol Ping (PPTP Ping)	Pptpclnt.exe, Pptpsrv.exe	Cmd	Tests functionality of PPTP clients and servers
Poolmon	Poolmon.exe	Cmd	Detects memory leaks
Process Resource Monitor	Pmon.exe	Cmd	Tracks CPU and memory usage to measure process resource usage
Process Viewer	Pviewer.exe	GUI	Changes process priority; allows the killing of processes
Registry Console Tool	Reg.exe	Cmd	Modifies the registry database from the command line; used to query, add, delete, copy, save, and restore entries

Tool	Filename	Format	Description
Remote Command Line	Remote.exe	Cmd	Runs command-line programs on remote computers using named pipes only
Remote Storage Diagnostic Utility	Rsdiag.exe	Cmd	Queries and reports on remote storage databases
Replication Diagnostics Tool	Repadmin.exe	Cmd	Diagnoses replication problems between controllers in Windows 2000
Security Administration Tools	Sidwalk.exe, Showaccs.exe, Sidwalk.msc	Cmd, Cmd, GUI	Manage access control lists
Security Descriptor Check Utility	Sdcheck.exe	Cmd	Displays the effective access controls on an object
SNMP Query Tool	Snmputilg.exe	GUI	Graphical version of Snmputil.exe used to troubleshoot Simple Network Management Protocol
System Information	Msinfo32.exe	Cmd	Reports system configuration information
Task Killing Utility	Kill.exe	Cmd	Ends one or more processes
Task List Viewer	Tlist.exe	Cmd	Displays list of currently running processes
Windows 2000 Error and Event Messages Help	W2000msgs.chm	GUI	Lists error and system-information messages in an HTML document
Windows Installer Cleanup Utility	Msicuu.exe, Msizap.exe	GUI, Cmd	Removes registry entries from a faulty installation
Windows Report Tool	Winrep.exe	GUI	Gathers information about a Windows problem for uploading to a support center or help desk
Winsock Remote Console	Wsremote.exe	Cmd	Allows a connection to a server running a console operation using sockets or named pipes

Glossary

A

Access control entry (ACE) An entry in an access control list (ACL) that defines the level of access for a user or group.

Access control list (ACL) A set of data associated with a file, directory, or other resource that defines the permissions users or groups have for accessing it. In Active Directory, the ACL is a list of access control entries (ACEs) stored with the object it protects. In Microsoft Windows NT, an ACL is stored as a binary value called a security descriptor.

Account lockout A security feature that disables a user account if failed logons exceed a specified number in a specified period of time. Locked accounts can't log on and must be unlocked by an administrator.

Active Directory In Microsoft Windows 2000 Server, Active Directory replaces the Windows NT collection of directory functions with an integrated implementation that includes DNS, DHCP, LDAP, and Kerberos.

Active Server Pages (ASP) A specification for dynamically created Web pages that contain either Microsoft Visual Basic or Microsoft JScript code. When a user requests such a page, the script is executed on a server and the page is transmitted to the user as an HTML document.

ActiveX A loosely defined set of technologies that allows software components to interact with each other in a networked environment.

ActiveX control A software component that adheres to the ActiveX specification and can operate in an ActiveX compliant environment.

Address A precise location where a piece of information is stored in memory or on disk. Also, the unique identifier for a node on a network. On the Internet, the code by which an individual user is identified. The format is username@hostname, where "username" is your user name, logon name, or account number, and "hostname" is the name of the computer or Internet provider you use. The host name might be a few words strung together with periods.

Address Resolution Protocol (ARP) A TCP/IP and AppleTalk protocol that provides IP-address-to-MAC (media access control) address resolution for IP packets.

Advanced Configuration Power Interface (ACPI) An industry specification defining power management on a range of computer devices. ACPI compliance is necessary for devices to use the power management capabilities in Windows 2000.

Allocation unit The smallest unit of managed space on a hard disk or logical volume. Also called a cluster.

Anonymous FTP A way to use the FTP program to log on to another computer to copy files when you don't have an account on that computer. When you log on, enter *anonymous* as the user name and your address as the password. This gives you access to publicly available files. See *File Transfer Protocol (FTP)*.

AppleTalk Local area network architecture built into Macintosh computers to connect them with printers. A network with a Windows 2000 server and Macintosh clients can function as an AppleTalk network with the use of AppleTalk network integration (formerly Services for Macintosh).

Associate To connect files having a particular extension to a specific program. When you double-click a file with the extension, the associated program is launched and the file you clicked is opened. In Windows, associated file extensions are usually called registered file types.

Asynchronous Transfer Mode (ATM) A network technology based on sending data in cells or packets of a fixed size. It is asynchronous in that the transmission of cells containing information from a particular user isn't necessarily periodic.

Attribute A characteristic. In Windows 2000 file management, it is information that shows whether a file is read-only, hidden, compressed, encrypted, ready to be backed up (archived), or should be indexed.

Audit policy Defines the type of security events to be logged. It can be defined on a server or an individual computer.

Authentication Verification of the identity of a user or computer process. In Windows 2000 and Windows NT, authentication involves comparing the user's security identifier (SID) and password to a list of authorized users on a domain controller.

B

Backup domain controller (BDC) In a Windows NT domain, a computer that stores a backup of the database that contains all the security and account information from the primary domain controller (PDC). The database is regularly and automatically synchronized with the copy on the PDC. A BDC also authenticates logons and can be promoted to a PDC when necessary. In a Windows 2000 domain, backup domain controllers aren't required; all domain controllers are peers, and all can perform maintenance on the directory. Windows NT 3.51 and 4 BDCs can participate in a

Windows 2000 domain when it is running in mixed mode.

Backup media pool A logical set of backup storage media used by Windows 2000 Backup.

Bandwidth On a network, the transmission capacity of a communications channel stated in megabits per second (Mbps). For example, Ethernet has a bandwidth of 10 Mbps. Fast Ethernet has a bandwidth of 100 Mbps.

Binding A software connection between a network card and a network transport protocol (such as TCP/IP).

BOOTP Boot Protocol. Used on TCP/IP networks to enable a diskless workstation to learn its own IP address, the location of a BOOTP server on the network, and the location of a file to be loaded into memory to boot the machine. This allows a computer to boot without a hard disk or a floppy disk.

Broadcasting To simultaneously send a message to everyone on a network. See *multicasting*.

Browser service The service that maintains a current list of computers and provides the list to applications when needed. When a user attempts to connect to a resource in the domain, the Browser service is contacted to provide a list of available resources. The lists displayed in My Network Places and Active Directory Users And Computers (among others) are provided by the Browser service. Also called the Computer Browser service.

C

Certificate A credential used to prove the origin, authenticity, and purpose of a public key to the entity that holds the corresponding private key.

Certificate authority (CA) The service that accepts and fulfills certificate requests and revocation requests and that can also manage the policy-directed registration process a user completes to get a certificate.

Certificate revocation list (CRL) A digitally signed list (published by a certificate authority) of certificates that are no longer valid.

Child domain Domains located directly beneath another domain name (parent domain). For example, Engineering.scribes.com is a child domain of scribes.com, the parent domain. Also called a subdomain.

Child object An object inside another object. For example, a file is a child object inside a folder, which is the parent object.

Cluster A set of computers joined together in such a way that they behave as a single system. Clustering is used for load balancing as well as fault tolerance. Members of a cluster are referred to as *nodes*.

Cluster service The collection of software on each node that manages all cluster-specific activity.

Console tree The default left pane in Microsoft Management Console

(MMC) that shows the items contained in a console.

Container An Active Directory object that has attributes and is part of the Active Directory namespace. Unlike other objects, it doesn't usually represent something concrete. It is a package for a group of objects and other containers.

Cross-link trust A transitive trust relationship between two Windows 2000 domains in different domain trees but within the same forest. Cross-link trusts must be explicitly created.

D

Daemon A background program that runs unattended, gathering information or performing other tasks.

Delegation Assigning administrative rights over a portion of the namespace to another user or group.

Directory service Provides the means for storing directory data and making this data available to network users and administrators. For example, Active Directory stores information about user accounts, such as names, passwords, phone numbers, and so on, and enables other authorized users on the same network to access this information.

Disk quota A limitation set by an administrator on the amount of disk space available to a user.

Distinguished name (DN) In the context of Active Directory, "distinguished" means the qualities that make the name distinct. The distinguished name identifies the domain that holds the object as well as the complete path through the container hierarchy used to reach the object.

Distributed file system (Dfs) A file management system in which files can be located on separate computers but are presented to users as a single directory tree.

DNS name servers Servers that contain information about part of the Domain Name System (DNS) database. These servers make computer names available to queries for name resolution across the Internet. Also called domain name servers.

Domain In Windows 2000, a group of computers that share a security policy and a user account database. A Windows 2000 domain is not the same as an Internet domain. See *domain name*.

Domain controller A server in a domain that accepts account logons and initiates their authentication.

Domain local group A local group used on ACLs only in its own domain. A domain local group can contain users and global groups from any domain in the forest, universal groups, and other domain local groups in its own domain.

Domain name In Active Directory, the name given to a collection of networked computers that share a common directory. On the Internet, the unique text name that identifies a specific host. A machine can have more than one domain name, but a given domain name points to only one machine. Domain names are resolved to IP addresses by DNS name servers.

Domain Name System (DNS) A service on TCP/IP networks (the Internet included) that translates domain names into IP addresses. This allows users to employ friendly names like FinanceServer or Ourbusiness.com when querying a remote system, instead of using an IP address such as 198.45.233.59.

Domain naming master The one domain controller assigned to handle the addition or removal of domains in a forest. See *Operations Master*.

Downlevel Term used to describe Microsoft services for clients, servers, and networks prior to Windows 2000, when viewed from Windows 2000.

Dynamic Data Exchange (DDE) Communication between processes implemented in the Windows family of operating systems. When programs that support DDE are running at the same time, they can exchange data by means of conversations. Conversations are two-way connections between two applications that transmit data alternately.

Dynamic Host Configuration Protocol (DHCP) A TCP/IP protocol used to automatically assign IP addresses and configure TCP/IP for network clients.

Dynamic-link library (DLL) A program module that contains executable code and data that can be used by various programs. A program uses the DLL only when the program is active, and the DLL is unloaded when the program closes.

E

Enterprise Term used to encompass all of a business's operation including all remote offices and branches.

Environment variable A string of environment information such as a drive, path, or filename associated with a symbolic name. The System option in Control Panel or the Set command from the command prompt can be used to define environment variables.

Ethernet A local area network protocol developed by Xerox Corporation in 1976. Ethernet supports data transfer rates of 10 Mbps and uses a bus topology and thick or thin coaxial, fiber-optic, or twisted-pair cabling. A newer version of Ethernet called Fast Ethernet supports data transfer rates of 100 Mbps, and an even newer version, Gigabit Ethernet, supports data transfer rates of 1000 Mbps.

Extended partition A nonbootable portion of a hard disk that can be subdivided into logical drives. There can be only a single extended partition per hard disk.

F

File allocation table (FAT) A file system consisting of a table that keeps track of the size and location of files on a hard disk.

File Transfer Protocol (FTP) A method of transferring one or more files from one computer to another over a network or telephone line. Because FTP has been implemented on a variety of systems, it's a simple way to transfer information between usually incongruent systems such as a PC and a minicomputer.

Firewall A protective filter for messages and logons. An organization connected directly to the Internet uses a firewall to prevent unauthorized access to their network. See *proxy server.*

Folder redirection An option in Group Policy to place users' special folders such as My Documents on a network server.

Forest A group of one or more Active Directory trees that trust each other via two-way transitive trusts. All trees in a forest share a common schema, configuration, and Global Catalog (GC). When a forest contains multiple trees, the trees don't form a contiguous namespace. Unlike trees, a forest doesn't need a distinct name.

Fully qualified domain name (FQDN) A domain name that includes the names of all network domains leading back to the root so as to clearly indicate a location in the domain namespace tree. An example of an FQDM is Accts.finance.dataflointl.com or Sales.europe.microsoft.com.

G

Gateway A device used to connect networks using dissimilar protocols so that information can be passed from one to another.

Global Catalog (GC) Contains a full replica of all directory objects in its host domain plus a partial replica of all directory objects in every domain in the forest. A GC contains information about all objects in all domains in the forest, so finding information in the directory doesn't require unnecessary queries across domains. A single query to the GC produces the information about where the object can be found.

Global group A group that can be used in its own domain and in trusting domains. However, it can contain user accounts and other global groups only from its own domain.

Globally unique identifier (GUID) Part of the identifying mechanism generated by Active Directory for each object in the directory. If a user or computer object is renamed or moved to a different name, the security identifier (SID), relative distinguished name (RDN), and distinguished name (DN) will change, but the GUID will remain the same.

Group Policy Setting of rules for computers and users in Windows

2000. Group Policy includes the registry-based policy found in Windows NT Server 4 but is also able to store policies for file deployment, application deployment, logon/logoff scripts, startup/shutdown scripts, domain security, Internet Protocol security (IPSec), and so on.

Group Policy object (GPO) A collection of policies stored in two locations: a Group Policy container (GPC) and a Group Policy template (GPT). The GPC is an Active Directory object that stores version information, status information, and other policy information (for example, application objects). The GPT is used for file-based data and stores software policy, script, and deployment information. The GPT is located in the system volume folder of the domain controller.

H

Hive One of five sections of the registry on a hard disk. Each hive is a discrete body of keys, subkeys, and values that record configuration information for the computer. Each hive is a file and can be moved from one system to another but can be edited only by using the Registry Editor.

Host Any device on the network that uses TCP/IP. A host is also a computer on the Internet you might be able to log on to. You can use FTP to get files from a host computer and use other protocols (such as Telnet) to make use of the host computer.

Hosts file A local ASCII text file that maps host names to IP addresses. Each line represents one host, starting with the IP address, one or more spaces, and then the host's name.

Hypermedia A system that can link text, pictures, sound, video, or all four.

Hypertext A system of writing and displaying text that enables the text to be linked in multiple ways, available at several levels of detail. Hypertext documents can also contain links to related documents, such as those referred to in footnotes.

Hypertext Markup Language (HTML) A system used for writing pages for the World Wide Web. HTML allows text to include codes that define fonts, layout, embedded graphics, and hypertext links.

Hypertext Transfer Protocol (HTTP) The method by which Web pages are transferred over the network.

I

IntelliMirror A suite of technologies that allows a complete operating environment to follow the user to other computers, as well as off-line. Components include the user's profiles, data, and applications.

Internet The vast collection of interconnected networks that all use TCP/IP and that evolved from ARPANET of the late 1960s and early 1970s. The Internet connects roughly 70,000 independent networks into a global network.

Internet Control Message Protocol (ICMP) A protocol used to report problems encountered with the delivery of data, such as unreachable hosts or unavailable ports. ICMP is also used to send a request packet to determine whether a host is available. The receiving host sends back a packet if it is available and functioning. See *ping*.

Internet Explorer Microsoft's Windows-based, WinSock-compliant program for browsing the World Wide Web.

Internet Protocol (IP) The internet work layer protocol used as a basis of the Internet. IP enables information to be routed from one network to another in packets and then reassembled when they reach their destination.

Internet Protocol next generation (IPng) or IP version 6 (IPv6) A new version of Internet Protocol. The official name of IPng is IPv6, where "v6" stands for version 6. The current version of IP is version 4, also known as IPv4. IPng is an evolutionary upgrade and will coexist with v4 for some time.

Internet Relay Chat (IRC) A system that enables Internet users to talk with each other in real time over the Internet.

Internetwork Packet Exchange/ Sequenced Packet Exchange (IPX/ SPX) Transport protocols used in Novell NetWare networks.

IP number or IP address A four-part number separated by periods (for example, 165.113.245.2) that uniquely identifies a machine on the Internet. Every machine on the Internet has a unique IP number; if a machine doesn't have an IP number, it isn't really on the Internet. Most machines also have one or more domain names that are easier for people to remember.

IPSec Internet Protocol Security. An Internet Engineering Task Force (IETF) standard for creating virtual private networks (VPNs).

J

Java An advanced programming language similar to C and C++ used in Web pages to provide animation and other advanced features that make Web pages unique.

K

Kerberos An identity-based security system that authenticates users at logon. It works by assigning a unique key, called a *ticket,* to each user who logs on to the network. The ticket is then embedded in messages to identify the sender of the message. The Kerberos security protocol is the primary authentication mechanism in the Windows 2000 operating system.

Kernel The part of the executive (or operating system) that manages the processor. The kernel performs thread scheduling and dispatching, interrupt and exception handling, and multiprocessor synchronization.

L

Lightweight Directory Access Protocol (LDAP) A protocol used to access a directory service. LDAP is a simplified version of the Directory Access Protocol (DAP), which is used to gain access to X.500 directories. LDAP is the primary access protocol for Active Directory.

LISTSERV A family of programs that manage Internet mailing lists by distributing messages posted to the list, adding and deleting members automatically.

Lmhosts file An ASCII text file like Hosts but used to associate IP addresses to host names inside a network. To remember which is which, remember Lmhosts as LAN Manager Hosts.

Local area network (LAN) A group of connected computers, usually located close to one another (such as in the same building or the same floor of the building) so that data can be passed among them.

Log on The act of entering into a computer system; for example, "Log on to the network and read your e-mail."

Logon The account name used to gain access to a computer system. Unlike a password, the logon name isn't a secret.

Logon script or logoff script Typically a batch file set to run when a user logs on or logs off a system. A logon script is used to configure a user's initial environment. A logoff script is used to return a system to some predetermined condition. Either script can be assigned to multiple users individually or through Group Policy.

M

Media access control (MAC) address A unique 48-bit number assigned to network interface cards by the manufacturer. MAC addresses are used for mapping in TCP/IP network communication.

Member server A computer running Windows 2000 Server or Windows NT Server that is *not* a domain controller. Member servers can be dedicated to managing files or printer services or other functions. A member server doesn't verify logons or maintain a security database.

Mirror 1. Two partitions on two hard disks configured so that each will contain identical data as the other. If one disk fails, the other contains the data and processing can continue. 2. An FTP server that provides copies of the same files as another server. Some FTP servers are so popular that other servers have been set up to mirror them and spread the FTP load to more than one site.

Mixed mode A domain in which domain controllers running both Windows 2000 and earlier versions of Windows NT coexist. In mixed mode, the domain features from previous versions of Windows NT Server are still enabled, while some Windows 2000 features are disabled. Windows 2000 Server domains are installed in mixed mode by default. In mixed mode, the domain might have Windows NT 4 backup domain controllers present. Nested groups aren't supported in mixed mode.

Modem (modulator/demodulator) A device that connects between a computer and a telephone line to allow the computer to talk to other computers through the system. Modems convert the computer's digital signals into analog waves that can be transmitted over standard voice telephone lines. Modem speeds are measured in bits per second (bps)—also sometimes expressed as kilobits (thousands of bits) per second (Kbps). For example, 28.8 Kbps and 28,800 bps are the same measurement—28,800 bits per second.

Multicasting Simultaneously sending a message to more than one destination on a network. Multicasting is distinguished from broadcasting in that multicasting sends to only selected recipients.

Multimaster replication A feature of Active Directory, multimaster replication automatically propagates every object (such as users, groups, computers, domains, organization units,

security policies, and so on) created on any domain controller to each of the other participating domain controllers. All domain controllers contain the same directory data, so the domain doesn't depend on a single source for directory information.

Multitasking Computer legerdemain by which tasks are switched in and out of the processor so quickly that it appears they are all happening at once. The success of a multitasking system depends on how well the various tasks are isolated from one another.

Multithreading The simultaneous processing of several threads inside the same program. Because several threads can be processed in parallel, one thread doesn't have to finish before another one can start. See *thread*.

N

Name resolution The process of mapping a name to its corresponding address.

Namespace A name or group of names defined according to a naming convention; any bounded area in which a given name can be resolved. Active Directory is primarily a namespace, as is any directory service. The Internet uses a hierarchical namespace that partitions names into categories known as top-level domains, such as .com, .edu, and .gov.

Native mode The condition of a domain when all domain controllers have been upgraded to Windows

2000 and the administrator has enabled native mode operation. See *mixed mode*.

NetBIOS Enhanced User Interface (NetBEUI) A small and fast protocol that requires little memory but can't be routed. Remote locations linked by routers can't use NetBEUI to communicate.

Net Logon service Accepts logon requests from any client and provides authentication from the Security Accounts Manager (SAM) database of accounts.

Network Two or more computers connected for the purpose of sharing resources.

Network News Transfer Protocol (NNTP) A protocol defined for distribution, inquiry, retrieval, and posting of news articles on the Internet.

Newsgroup On the Internet, a distributed bulletin board system about a particular topic. USENET News (also known as Netnews) is a system that distributes thousands of newsgroups to all parts of the Internet.

Node A location on a tree structure with links to one or more items below it. On a LAN, a device that can communicate with other devices on the network. In clustering, a computer running Windows 2000 Advanced Server that is a member of a cluster.

NTFS file system The native file system for Windows 2000 and Windows NT. Supports long filenames, a variety of permissions

for sharing files, and a transaction log that allows the completion of any incomplete file-related tasks if the operating system is interrupted.

O

Object An object is a particular set of attributes that represents something concrete, such as a user, a printer, or an application. The attributes hold data describing the thing that is identified by the object. Attributes of a user might include the user's given name, surname, and e-mail address. The classification of the object defines which types of attributes are used. For example, the objects classified as "users" might allow the use of attribute types like "common name," "telephone number," and "e-mail address," while the object class "organization" allows for attribute types like "organization name" and "business category." An attribute can take one or more values, depending on its type.

Object identity Every object in Active Directory has a unique identity. Objects can be moved or renamed, but their identities never change. Objects are known internally by their identity, not their current name. An object's identity is a globally unique identifier (GUID), which is assigned by the Directory System Agent (DSA) when the object is created. The GUID is stored in an attribute, the object GUID, that is part of every object. The object GUID attribute can't be modified or deleted. When storing a reference to an Active Directory object in an external store (for example, a database), you should use the object GUID because, unlike a name, it won't change.

Operations Master Active Directory operations that are single master—that is, operations that are not permitted to occur at different places in the network at the same time. Examples of these operations include the primary domain controller (PDC) emulator, schema modification, domain naming, and the relative identifier (RID) allocator.

Organizational unit (OU) A container object in Active Directory used to separate computers, users, and other resources into logical units. An organizational unit is the smallest entity to which Group Policy can be applied.

P

Packet The basic unit of information sent over a network. Each packet contains the destination address, the sender's address, error-control information, and data. The size and format of a packet depends on the protocol being used.

Page A document, or collection of information, available via the World Wide Web. A page can contain text, graphics, video, and sound files. Also, a portion of memory that the virtual memory manager can swap to and from a hard disk.

Paging A virtual memory operation in which pages are transferred from memory to disk when memory becomes full. When a thread accesses a page that's not in memory, a page fault occurs and the memory manager uses page tables to find the page on disk and then loads the page into memory.

Peer-to-peer A network in which two or more machines can communicate with each other without the need for any intermediary device. On a peer-to-peer network, a computer can be both a client and a server.

Ping A network management tool that checks to see whether another computer is available and functioning. It sends a short message to which the other computer automatically responds. If the other computer doesn't respond to the ping, you usually can't establish communications.

Point of presence (POP) A physical site in a geographic area where a network access provider, such as MCI, has equipment to which users connect. The local telephone company's central office in a particular area is also sometimes referred to as their POP for that area.

Point-to-Point Tunneling Protocol (PPTP) A protocol that provides router-to-router and host-to-network connections over a telephone line (or a network link that acts like a telephone line). See *Serial Line Internet Protocol (SLIP)*.

Post Office Protocol (POP) A protocol by which a mail server on the Internet lets you access your mail and download it to a PC or Macintosh. Most people refer to this protocol with its version number (POP2, POP3, and so on) to avoid confusing it with points of presence (POPs).

Primary domain controller (PDC) In a Windows NT domain, the server that authenticates domain logons and maintains the security policy and master database for a domain. In Windows 2000, running in mixed mode, one of the domain controllers in each domain is identified as the PDC for compatibility with downlevel clients and servers.

Primary partition A portion of the hard disk that's been marked as a potentially bootable logical drive by an operating system. MS-DOS can support only a single primary partition, but Windows NT and Windows 2000 can support multiple ones. Only four primary partitions can live on any hard disk.

Profile Loaded by the system when a user logs on, the profile defines a user's environment, including network settings, printer connections, desktop settings, and program items.

Proxy server A server that receives Web requests from clients, retrieves Web pages, and forwards them to clients. Proxy servers can dramatically improve performance for groups of users by caching retrieved pages. Proxy servers also provide security by shielding the IP addresses of internal clients.

Public-key cryptography A method of secure transmission in which two different keys are used—a public key for encrypting data and a private key for decrypting data.

Q

Quality of Service (QoS) A set of standards for assuring the quality of data transmission on a network.

R

Redundant array of independent disks (RAID) A range of disk management and striping techniques to implement fault tolerance.

Relative distinguished name (RDN) Active Directory uses the concept of a relative distinguished name (RDN), which is the part of the distinguished name that is an attribute of the object itself.

Relative identifier (RID) The part of the security identifier (SID) that is unique to each object.

Remote Access Service (RAS) Allows users to connect from remote locations and access their networks for file and printer sharing and e-mail. The computer initiating the connection is the RAS client; the answering computer is the RAS host.

Remote Authentication Dial-In User Service (RADIUS) A security authentication system used by many Internet service providers (ISPs). A user connects to the ISP and enters a username and password. This information is verified by a RADIUS server, which then authorizes access to the ISP system.

Remote Installation Services (RIS) Allows clients to boot from a network server and use special pre-boot diagnostic tools installed on the server or to automatically install Windows 2000 Professional on the client system.

Replication On network computers, enables the contents of a directory, designated as an export directory, to be copied to other directories, called import directories.

Requests for comments (RFCs) An evolving collection of material that details the functions within the TCP/IP family of protocols. Some RFCs are official documents of the Internet Engineering Task Force (IETF), defining the standards of TCP/IP and the Internet, while others are simply proposals trying to become standards, and others fall somewhere in between. Some are tutorial in nature, while others are quite technical.

Router A special-purpose computer (or software package) that handles the connection between two or more networks. Routers look at the destination addresses of the packets passing through them and decide which route to use to send them.

S

Schema A definition of the object classes and attributes that can be stored in Active Directory. Like other objects in Active Directory, schema objects have an access control list (ACL) to limit alterations to only authorized users.

Schema master The single domain controller assigned to track all updates to a schema within a forest.

Scope In DHCP, the range of IP addresses available to be leased to DHCP clients by the DHCP service. In groups, scope describes where in the network permissions can be assigned to the group.

Security Accounts Manager (SAM) Manager of user account information including group membership. A logon service of both Windows 2000 and Windows NT.

Security Identifier (SID) A unique number assigned to every computer, group, and user account on a Windows 2000 or Windows NT network. Internal processes in the operating system refer to an account's SID rather than a name. A deleted SID is never reused.

Serial Line Internet Protocol (SLIP) A protocol used to run IP over serial lines or telephone lines using modems. Rapidly being replaced by Point-to-Point Tunneling Protocol (PPTP).

Server A computer that provides a service to other computers on a network. A file server, for example, provides files to client machines.

Site In Active Directory, an area of one or more well-connected subnets. When users log on to a site, clients use Active Directory servers in the same site. See *well connected*.

Smart card A credit card–sized device that securely stores user credentials such as passwords, certificates, public and private keys, and other types of personal information.

Snap-in A tool that can be added to a console supported by the Microsoft Management Console (MMC). You can add a snap-in extension to extend the function of a snap-in.

Socket An endpoint to a connection. Two sockets form a complete path for a bidirectional pipe for incoming and outgoing data between networked computers. The Windows Sockets API is a networking API for programmers writing for the Windows family of products.

Subdomain A domain in the DNS namespace that is located directly under another domain. See *child domain*.

Subnet The portion of a TCP/IP network in which all devices share a common prefix. For example, all devices with an IP address that starts with 198 are on the same subnet. IP networks are divided using a subnet mask.

Superscope A collection of scopes grouped into a single administrative whole. Grouping scopes together into a superscope makes it possible to have more than one logical subnet on a physical subnet.

SystemRoot The path and folder where the Windows 2000 system files are located. The value %SystemRoot% can be used in paths to replace the actual location. To identify the SystemRoot folder on a computer, type %SystemRoot% at a command prompt.

T

Telnet The protocol and program used to log on from one Internet site to another. The Telnet protocol/program gets you to the logon prompt of another host.

Terminal A device that allows you to send commands to another computer. At a minimum, this usually means a keyboard, a display screen, and some simple circuitry. You will usually use terminal software in a personal computer—the software pretends to be, or emulates, a physical terminal and allows you to type commands to another computer.

Thread An executable entity that belongs to one (and only one) process. In a multitasking environment, a single program can contain several threads, all running at the same time.

Transitive trust The standard trust between Windows 2000 domains in a domain tree or forest. Transitive trusts are always two way. When a domain joins a domain tree or forest, a transitive trust relationship is established automatically.

Transmission Control Protocol/Internet Protocol (TCP/IP) The protocol that networks use to communicate with each other on the Internet.

Tree A tree in Active Directory is just an extension of the idea of a directory tree. It's a hierarchy of objects and containers that demonstrates how objects are connected, or the path from one object to another. Endpoints on the tree are usually objects.

Trojan horse A destructive program designed to disguise itself as a benign application. Unlike viruses, Trojan horses don't replicate themselves but can be just as dangerous.

Trust relationship A security term meaning that one workstation or server trusts a domain controller to authenticate a user logon on its behalf. It also means a domain controller trusts a domain controller in another domain to authenticate a logon.

U

Uniform Naming Convention (UNC) A PC format for indicating the location of resources on a network. UNC uses the following format: \\Server\Shared_resource_path. So to identify the Example.txt file in the Sample folder on the server named Ample, the UNC would be \\Ample\Sample\Example.txt.

Uniform Resource Locator (URL) The standard way to give the address of any resource on the Internet that is part of the World Wide Web. For example, *http://www.capecod.net/~fcollege/index.htm*. The most common way to use a URL is to enter it into a Web browser program, such as Microsoft Internet Explorer or Netscape Navigator.

Universal group A group that can be used anywhere in a domain tree or forest. Members can come from any domain, and rights and permissions can be assigned at any domain. Universal groups are available only when the domain is in native mode.

UNIX A computer operating system designed to be used by many computer users at the same time (multiuser) with TCP/IP built in. The most common operating system for servers on the Internet.

User account A user's access to a network. Each user account has a unique username and security ID (SID).

User profiles Information about user accounts. See *profile*.

V

Viewer A program used by Gopher, Wide Area Information Server (WAIS), or Web client programs to show files with contents other than text. You use a viewer to display graphics or video files or to play sound files.

Virtual Reality Modeling Language (VRML) A file format for 3-D models and scenes that is used primarily on the World Wide Web. VRML objects and scenes can be viewed and interactively navigated with a VRML browser, and VRML scenes can have embedded hyperlinks, allowing for a type of three-dimensional Web site.

W

Well connected Sufficiently fast and reliable for the needs of Active Directory clients and servers. The definition of "sufficiently fast and reliable" for a particular network depends on the work being done on the specific network.

Wide area network (WAN) Any Internet or network that covers an area larger than a single building or campus.

Windows Internet Name Service (WINS) A name resolution service that converts computer names to IP addresses in a routed environment.

Windows Sockets (WinSock) WinSock is a standard way for Windows-based programs to work with TCP/IP. You can use WinSock if you use SLIP to connect to the Internet.

Workstation In Windows NT, a computer running the Windows NT Workstation operating system. In a wider context, used to describe any powerful computer optimized for graphics or computer-aided design

(CAD) or any of a number of other functions requiring high performance.

World Wide Web (WWW) or Web. A hypermedia-based system for accessing information on the Internet.

X

X.500 A standard for a directory service established by the International Telecommunications Union (ITU). The same standard is also published by the International Standards Organization/International Electrotechnical Commission (ISO/IEC). The X.500 standard defines the information model used in the directory service. All information in the directory is stored in entries, each of which belongs to at least one object class. The actual information in an entry is determined by attributes that are contained in that entry.

Z

Zone A part of the DNS namespace that consists of a single domain or a domain and subdomains managed as a single, separate entity.

Index

Note: page numbers in italics refer to figures or tables.

Charlie Russel and **Sharon Crawford** are coauthors of numerous books on operating systems. Their titles include *Running Microsoft Windows NT Server 4*, *UNIX and Linux Answers*, *NT and UNIX Intranet Secrets*, and *Upgrading to Windows 98*.

Charlie Russel has years of system administration experience with a specialty in combined Windows NT and UNIX networks. In addition to his books with Ms. Crawford, he has also written *ABCs of Windows NT Workstation 4.0* and *SCO OpenServer and Windows Networking*.

Sharon Crawford is a former editor now engaged in writing full time. She is the author of *Windows 98: No Experience Required*, *ABCs of Windows 98* and the coauthor of *Windows 2000 Professional for Dummies* (with Andy Rathbone). Ms. Crawford also writes a regular column on Windows 2000 and Windows 98 for the online bookseller Fatbrain.com (at *http://www.fatbrain.com/hottechnologies.html*).

Jason Gerend has contributed to a number of computer books, including *Outlook 2000 At a Glance*, *FrontPage 2000 At a Glance*, *The Complete Reference to Office 2000*, and *The Microsoft Help Desk for Windows NT Workstation*. He began fooling around with operating systems as far back as MS-DOS 2. Since 1995, Mr. Gerend has been a freelance Webmaster and computer consultant.

The manuscript for this book was prepared and galleyed using Microsoft Word 2000. Pages were composed by Microsoft Press using Adobe PageMaker 6.52 for Windows, with text in Sabon and display type in ITC Franklin Gothic. Composed pages were delivered to the printer as electronic prepress files.

Cover Designer:	Greg Hickman
Interior Graphic Designer:	James D. Kramer
Principal Compositor:	Elizabeth Hansford
Principal Proofreader:	Cheryl Penner
Indexer:	Julie Kawabata

System Requirements

Windows 2000

The compact disc that accompanies this Administrator's Companion book is designed for a system running Microsoft Windows 2000 Server.

To test the samples you must have Windows 2000 installed, but you can read any of the files on the CD with Windows 98 or Windows NT and a Web browser. To use the CD, simply insert the disc into your CD-ROM drive; the start page should appear automatically. If this page does not appear, consult the Readme.txt file.

Electronic Version of the Book

The complete text of the print book, *Microsoft Windows 2000 Server Administrator's Companion,* has been included on the CD as a fully searchable electronic book. To install the electronic book, run Setup.exe in the \Ebook folder and follow the instructions that appear on your screen.

To view the electronic book, you must have Microsoft Internet Explorer 4.01 or later installed on your system. If you do not have Internet Explorer 4.01 or later, the setup wizard will ask you if you would like to have Internet Explorer 5 installed.

Third-Party Software

For the user's convenience, this CD includes third-party software and links to third-party Web sites. Please note that these products and links are not under the control of Microsoft Corporation, and Microsoft is not responsible for their content, nor should their inclusion on this CD be construed as an endorsement of the product or the site.

Additional hardware or software may be required to use these resources.

Microsoft Press Support Information

Every effort has been made to ensure the accuracy of the book and the contents of this companion disc. Microsoft Press provides corrections for books through the World Wide Web at

http://mspress.microsoft.com/support/

If you have comments, questions, or ideas regarding the book or this companion disc, please send them to Microsoft Press via e-mail to

MSPINPUT@MICROSOFT.COM

or via postal mail to

Microsoft Press
Attn: Microsoft Windows 2000 Server Administrator's Companion Editor
One Microsoft Way
Redmond, WA 98052-6399

Please note that product support is not offered through the above addresses.

MICROSOFT LICENSE AGREEMENT

Book Companion CD

user manual, in "online" documentation, and/or in other Microsoft-provided materials. Any supplemental software code provided to you as part of the Support Services shall be considered part of the SOFTWARE PRODUCT and subject to the terms and conditions of this EULA. With respect to technical information you provide to Microsoft as part of the Support Services, Microsoft may use such information for its business purposes, including for product support and development. Microsoft will not utilize such technical information in a form that personally identifies you.

- **Software Transfer.** You may permanently transfer all of your rights under this EULA, provided you retain no copies, you transfer all of the SOFTWARE PRODUCT (including all component parts, the media and printed materials, any upgrades, this EULA, and, if applicable, the Certificate of Authenticity), **and** the recipient agrees to the terms of this EULA.

- **Termination.** Without prejudice to any other rights, Microsoft may terminate this EULA if you fail to comply with the terms and conditions of this EULA. In such event, you must destroy all copies of the SOFTWARE PRODUCT and all of its component parts.

3. **COPYRIGHT.** All title and copyrights in and to the SOFTWARE PRODUCT (including but not limited to any images, photographs, animations, video, audio, music, text, SAMPLE CODE, REDISTRIBUTABLES, and "applets" incorporated into the SOFTWARE PRODUCT) and any copies of the SOFTWARE PRODUCT are owned by Microsoft or its suppliers. The SOFTWARE PRODUCT is protected by copyright laws and international treaty provisions. Therefore, you must treat the SOFTWARE PRODUCT like any other copyrighted material **except** that you may install the SOFTWARE PRODUCT on a single computer provided you keep the original solely for backup or archival purposes. You may not copy the printed materials accompanying the SOFTWARE PRODUCT.

4. **U.S. GOVERNMENT RESTRICTED RIGHTS.** The SOFTWARE PRODUCT and documentation are provided with RESTRICTED RIGHTS. Use, duplication, or disclosure by the Government is subject to restrictions as set forth in subparagraph (c)(1)(ii) of the Rights in Technical Data and Computer Software clause at DFARS 252.227-7013 or subparagraphs (c)(1) and (2) of the Commercial Computer Software—Restricted Rights at 48 CFR 52.227-19, as applicable. Manufacturer is Microsoft Corporation/One Microsoft Way/Redmond, WA 98052-6399.

5. **EXPORT RESTRICTIONS.** You agree that you will not export or re-export the SOFTWARE PRODUCT, any part thereof, or any process or service that is the direct product of the SOFTWARE PRODUCT (the foregoing collectively referred to as the "Restricted Components"), to any country, person, entity, or end user subject to U.S. export restrictions. You specifically agree not to export or re-export any of the Restricted Components (i) to any country to which the U.S. has embargoed or restricted the export of goods or services, which currently include, but are not necessarily limited to, Cuba, Iran, Iraq, Libya, North Korea, Sudan, and Syria, or to any national of any such country, wherever located, who intends to transmit or transport the Restricted Components back to such country; (ii) to any end user who you know or have reason to know will utilize the Restricted Components in the design, development, or production of nuclear, chemical, or biological weapons; or (iii) to any end user who has been prohibited from participating in U.S. export transactions by any federal agency of the U.S. government. You warrant and represent that neither the BXA nor any other U.S. federal agency has suspended, revoked, or denied your export privileges.

DISCLAIMER OF WARRANTY

NO WARRANTIES OR CONDITIONS. MICROSOFT EXPRESSLY DISCLAIMS ANY WARRANTY OR CONDITION FOR THE SOFTWARE PRODUCT. THE SOFTWARE PRODUCT AND ANY RELATED DOCUMENTATION ARE PROVIDED "AS IS" WITHOUT WARRANTY OR CONDITION OF ANY KIND, EITHER EXPRESS OR IMPLIED, INCLUDING, WITHOUT LIMITATION, THE IMPLIED WARRANTIES OF MERCHANTABILITY, FITNESS FOR A PARTICULAR PURPOSE, OR NONINFRINGEMENT. THE ENTIRE RISK ARISING OUT OF USE OR PERFORMANCE OF THE SOFTWARE PRODUCT REMAINS WITH YOU.

LIMITATION OF LIABILITY. TO THE MAXIMUM EXTENT PERMITTED BY APPLICABLE LAW, IN NO EVENT SHALL MICROSOFT OR ITS SUPPLIERS BE LIABLE FOR ANY SPECIAL, INCIDENTAL, INDIRECT, OR CONSEQUENTIAL DAMAGES WHATSOEVER (INCLUDING, WITHOUT LIMITATION, DAMAGES FOR LOSS OF BUSINESS PROFITS, BUSINESS INTERRUPTION, LOSS OF BUSINESS INFORMATION, OR ANY OTHER PECUNIARY LOSS) ARISING OUT OF THE USE OF OR INABILITY TO USE THE SOFTWARE PRODUCT OR THE PROVISION OF OR FAILURE TO PROVIDE SUPPORT SERVICES, EVEN IF MICROSOFT HAS BEEN ADVISED OF THE POSSIBILITY OF SUCH DAMAGES. IN ANY CASE, MICROSOFT'S ENTIRE LIABILITY UNDER ANY PROVISION OF THIS EULA SHALL BE LIMITED TO THE GREATER OF THE AMOUNT ACTUALLY PAID BY YOU FOR THE SOFTWARE PRODUCT OR US$5.00; PROVIDED, HOWEVER, IF YOU HAVE ENTERED INTO A MICROSOFT SUPPORT SERVICES AGREEMENT, MICROSOFT'S ENTIRE LIABILITY REGARDING SUPPORT SERVICES SHALL BE GOVERNED BY THE TERMS OF THAT AGREEMENT. BECAUSE SOME STATES AND JURISDICTIONS DO NOT ALLOW THE EXCLUSION OR LIMITATION OF LIABILITY, THE ABOVE LIMITATION MAY NOT APPLY TO YOU.

MISCELLANEOUS

This EULA is governed by the laws of the State of Washington USA, except and only to the extent that applicable law mandates governing law of a different jurisdiction.

Should you have any questions concerning this EULA, or if you desire to contact Microsoft for any reason, please contact the Microsoft subsidiary serving your country, or write: Microsoft Sales Information Center/One Microsoft Way/Redmond, WA 98052-6399.

For information about Microsoft Press®

products, visit our Web site at

mspress.microsoft.com